Network Troubleshooting

Customer Reviews

"Where has this book been all my life?

At last, a complete & up to date resource for those of us in the trenches. I wish I had this book 5 years ago. Technical, yet comprehensible. A great reference containing the information I need to get the network troubleshooting job done. If you are responsible for resolving problems with 'slow servers' or 'slow networks' this book is an invaluable resource. Get it!"

JEROMME LAWLER,
NETWORK ANALYST, CROSS TIMBERS OIL COMPANY

"Not only did I find this work to be one of the most comprehensive technical references for network analysis and troubleshooting I've ever read, I was also impressed with the structural foundations and financial principles conveyed when analyzing network uptime and error management in a corporate IT enterprise."

DAVID PROUTY,
WIDE AREA NETWORK ENGINEER, INTEGRIS HEALTH

"This book provides a wealth of useful information for a wide scope of users, and at the same time is a very practical help for diagnosing and solving network problems."

JACQUES DEN TOOM,
CHANNEL MARKETING MANAGER, CISCO SYSTEMS

"The troubleshooting sections were excellent. Each section can be read from start to finish, or specific chapters can be used as a reference when working on a particular problem (Token-Ring problem, Ethernet problem, etc.). The use of 'Symptoms and Causes' is great, and the summaries at the end of each chapter listing the most frequent causes of problems provide a good overview of what could be wrong."

GILBERT GARCIA,
NETWORK ENGINEER, GETRONICS INC.

Network
Troubleshooting

by Othmar Kyas

An Agilent Technologies Publication

 Agilent Technologies

Printed in the United States of America

ISBN 0-9703331-0-2

AUTHOR: Othmar Kyas
TECHNICAL CONTRIBUTORS: Bill Message, Gregan Crawford,
Thomas Heim, Luis Hernandez, Raul Sitavi,
Peter Scharpfenecker, Roland Tscheinig,
Christopher Semturs, Hans Juergen Gauch,
Christian Dinten, Duane Lotharius, Sandy McKinsey.
EDITOR: Clelia deMoraes
PAGE LAYOUT: Jörg Nestle
COVER DESIGN: Jörg Nestle, Peter Przybylla
PRODUCT MARKETING MANAGER: Pamela Frankenfield
PROJECT MANAGER: Melissa Ames
CORE PROJECT TEAM: Michelle Gyulai, Pat Huppenthal,
Dan Van Wijk, Tony Crawford, Phil Sexton.
PROGRAM SUPERVISOR: Karen Spahr

Contents

CONTENTS

CONTENTS

Introduction

The challenge to design, deploy and operate communications networks is daunting. The gap between the availability of skilled network operators and the need for them is widening. With the proliferation of new technologies, the expectations for high availability of services and applications, and the demand for interoperability between networks, the knowledge and experience of these people becomes more critical.

How can network operators develop the skills and expertise to be successful in this changing environment? They need to understand how different services and applications affect network design, vendor selection, configuration, commissioning and optimization. As applications become increasingly critical to business, outages and poor performance become intolerable. Network operators need the expertise and experience to deal with a wide range of problems and technologies. Training must not only focus on networking technologies, services and applications, but also on the tools and techniques to deploy, troubleshoot and optimize them.

What tools can help network operators do their jobs more effectively? Tools must be sophisticated in terms of diagnostic capabilities, while being easy to operate. They need convenient connection to the network. They must observe all activity or conditions on the network, while determining which ones are relevant to troubleshooting or optimization. They must address all the technologies used in the network for delivering the offered services or in running the deployed applications. They need to identify the causes of network problems and to recommend how these problems can be resolved.

Even though there are many courses and books on networking technologies, very few cover the practical aspects of troubleshooting and optimizing networks, services and applications. This book endeavors to fulfill this need. It provides information about technologies and techniques that is essential to get networks, services and applications up and keep them running effectively, and it provides a comprehensive and consolidated set of potential causes for different problem symptoms.

There is a critical need to collect and compile this kind of information and make it readily available to network operators to help them isolate, characterize and solve problems more effectively and quickly.

With the help of many contributors, Othmar Kyas has created an indispensable reference book for troubleshooting and optimizing networks, services and applications. If you are interested in contributing to subsequent revisions, please contact Othmar Kyas by email at *othmar_kyas@agilent.com*.

BILL MORTIMER
VICE PRESIDENT AND GENERAL MANAGER
COMMUNICATIONS SERVICES SOLUTIONS
AGILENT TECHNOLOGIES, INC.

Section I
Basic Concepts

Network Availability 1

"Waiting for an alarm is not the ideal form of network management."

BOB BUCHANAN, THE NETWORK JOURNAL

1.1 The Strategic Importance of Information Technology

Growing financial and competitive pressures in the business world mean that companies everywhere must continuously optimize their internal and external structures in order to survive. All business processes and routines must be reviewed regularly for effectiveness ("Are we doing the right things?") and for efficiency ("Are we doing things right?"). Most business processes today consist of physical activities, such as the manufacture of a metal part, combined with information flow: How many parts should be produced? When? In what sizes? Increasingly, key business processes—in insurance companies, travel agencies, banks, and airlines, for example—consist entirely of information flow. Today, of course, the flow of information is largely dependent on information technology— that is, computers, databases and networks. A high-performance, high-availability information technology (IT) system is becoming a prerequisite for successful execution of the business practices that are decisive in maintaining a leadership position in today's competitive markets. The role of the computer in business has changed radically over the past few years, from a tolerated plaything to a cornerstone of corporate infrastructures. This change has taken place so rapidly that in many companies IT still has not taken a central position in managerial circles, even though it has long since become indispensable for day-to-day business functions.

The reliance of enterprises on smoothly functioning IT infrastructures will continue to grow in the coming years. Areas of business that until recently had little to do with computer technology, such as marketing and customer service, are increasingly IT-based. This is largely due to the advent of customer interfaces that allow consumers to perform many transactions electronically, such as placing orders or making reservations. In fact, the proportion of people who work directly or indirectly with IT has grown in recent years to more than 50 percent (see Figure 1.1).

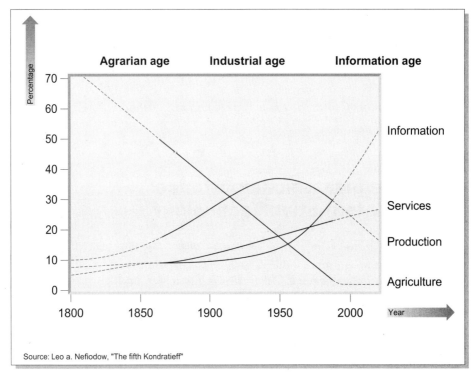

Source: Leo a. Nefiodow, "The fifth Kondratieff"

Figure 1.1 Changes in employment patterns in Western industrial countries since 1800

Industry	Business processes	Downtime costs per hour (US$)
Financial services	Stock trading	6,000,000
Financial services	Credit card/telecash transactions	2,400,000
Media	Pay-per-view	150,000
Retail	Home shopping (TV)	100,000
Retail	Mail order (catalog)	80,000
Travel/tourism	Airline reservation	82,500
Shipping	Parcel service	25,500

Source: AT&T/Gartner Group

Figure 1.2 Costs of network failure

In keeping with these developments, the professional operation and management of computer networks has long since ceased to be a necessary evil. On the
contrary, it has become a decisive strategic necessity for the success of almost
any enterprise. A network failure that lasts only a few hours can cost millions of
dollars. According to a study carried out by AT&T, companies that deal in
financial services, such as investment brokerages or credit card firms, can suffer
losses of 2.5 to 5 million dollars from just 1 hour of network downtime (see
Figure 1.2).

1.2   Intranets and the Internet: Revolutions in Network Technology

The difficulties involved in the professional operation of high-performance data
networks have been further complicated by the Internet revolution, which has
brought about radical changes in network technology and applications. Since
the mid-1990s the Internet has not only developed into a universal communications medium, but has also become a global marketplace for the exchange of
goods and services. As a result, growing numbers of business are faced with the
necessity of providing their employees with Internet access. Special network
infrastructures are now required in order to provide electronic access for
increasing numbers of Internet-based consumers. Once it was sufficient to have
just a few carefully controlled wide-area network (WAN) links in an otherwise
homogenous local-area network (LAN). Today, however, a secure, high-performance LAN-WAN structure is indispensable.

Internet technologies are also being introduced into company networks, leading
to the development of "corporate intranets". This has necessitated further restructuring so that broad areas of internal data processing can be adapted to the
transport mechanisms, protocols and formats used in the Internet. All of these
developments have caused the World Wide Web (WWW) to take on a position of
global importance as a uniform user interface. At the same time, these changes
have placed enormous demands on network managers. In many cases, the skills
and tools available for managing computer systems and networks can barely
keep up with the increasing complexity of data network structures. And to add
to the difficulty of the task, the technology cycles in data communications—the
intervals at which new and more powerful data communication technologies are
introduced—are getting shorter all the time. Whereas the classic 10 Mbit/s
Ethernet topologies shaped computer networking throughout the 1980s, the
1990s have seen the introduction of new technologies almost every year, including LAN switching, 100 Mbit/s Ethernet, Gigabit Ethernet, ATM (Asynchronous

Transfer Mode), IP (Internet Protocol) switching, Packet over Sonet (PoS) and ADSL (Asynchronous Digital Subscriber Mode), to name just a few. Product life cycles in the IT field are often measured in months now rather than years. This rapid pace of technological development puts manufacturers and users alike under tremendous pressure to keep abreast of constant innovation (see Figure 1.3).

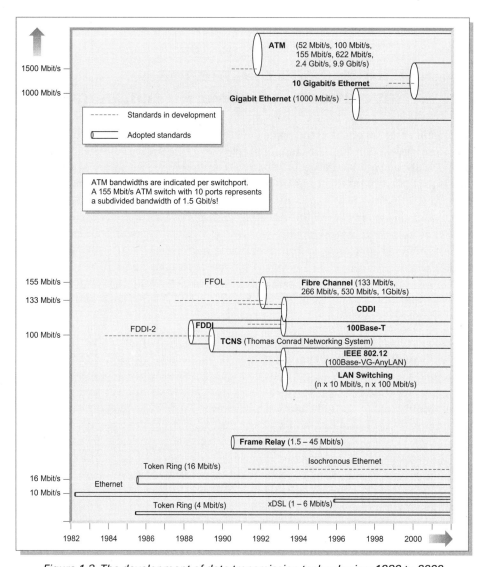

Figure 1.3 The development of data transmission technologies: 1980 to 2000

1.3 The Behavior of Complex Network Systems: Catastrophe Theory

The enormous technological complexity in combination with the large numbers of hardware and software components used in networks makes operation and management a difficult task, to say the least. Communication media, connectors, hubs, switches, repeaters, network interface cards, operating systems, data protocols, driver software, and application software must all function smoothly under widely varying conditions, including network load, number of nodes connected, and size of data packets transmitted. Even when a given system has attained a relatively stable operating state, its stability is constantly put to the test by dynamic variations as well as by operator errors, administrative errors, configuration changes, and hardware and software problems. In general, the more complex a system is and the greater the number of parameters that influence it, the more difficult it is to predict its behavior. Catastrophe theory (see René Thom, 1975) offers an excellent model for describing the behavior of systems as complex as computer networks. This theory can provide at least qualitative descriptions of system behavior, especially for non-linear operating states, such as those that often accompany a network breakdown. Catastrophe theory postulates seven elementary catastrophes, which behave in a given manner according to the *number* rather than the *type* of control parameters influencing the system. The behavior model for catastrophes determined by two parameters, for example, is called a cusp graph. The cusp is a three-dimensional surface whose upper side represents balanced states, while the lower surface represents unstable maxima. Catastrophe theory can be applied to Ethernet networks, for example, to show the effects of two control parameters, slot time and network load, on throughput. Slot time, which is defined as twice the time it takes a signal to travel between the two nodes that are farthest apart in an Ethernet segment, is influenced by the network components that cause signal transmission delay or latency, such as cables, repeaters or hubs. Figure 1.4 shows the behavior pattern for throughput when all other variables, such as network load, average packet size and number of network nodes, are constant.

An increase in traffic in a network with a given slot time a moves the operating state across the upper surface of the cusp. The rise along the x-axis indicates increasing throughput. Starting from the higher slot time b, however, the same increase in traffic drastically reduces network efficiency. All processes take place on the surface of the cusp and are thus linear. If the operating state is a when the network load increases, and subsequently the slot time increases from state c (Figure 1.5), an abrupt departure from the balanced state takes place at point d in order to arrive directly at point e. Point e represents a stable operating state, but one in which throughput is minimal. The abrupt transition from *d* to *e* constitutes a catastrophe.

The model provided by catastrophe theory clearly illustrates how complex and unpredictable a network can be. The symptoms that indicate problems in a network are often caused by a series of errors. One event triggers another, and the resulting state yet another, and so on. Feedback may either amplify or reduce the effects of error events. When the error symptom is finally detected, it may be far removed from its original locus in a completely different form and appear to have been triggered by some trivial event.

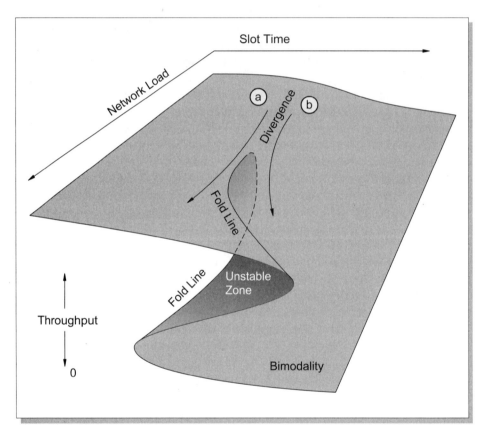

Figure 1.4 Catastrophe with two control parameters: the cusp

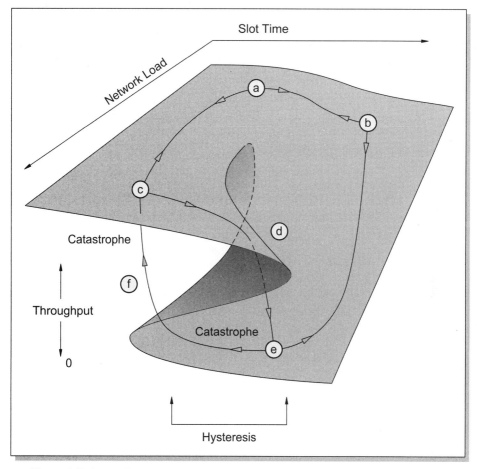

Figure 1.5 A non-linear operating state (network failure) in an Ethernet network

1.4   The Causes of Network Failure

There are five categories of errors that can lead to system failure:

- Operator error
- Mass storage problems
- Computer hardware problems
- Software problems
- Network problems

1.4.1   Operator Error

On the average, operator error is responsible for over 5 percent of all system failures—a large enough proportion to merit a closer look. Operator errors can be classified as intentional or unintentional mistakes, and as errors that do or do not cause consequential damage.

The term "intentional error" does not necessarily indicate that the error itself was the operator's intent, but rather that it resulted from some intentional action, such as trying to take a shortcut. The belief that a given process can be shortened, or that certain quality control or safety guidelines are superfluous, can lead to error situations with or without consequential damage. Less common are the truly intentional errors motivated, for example, by an employee's desire for "revenge" against a superior or the company, by the desire to cause trouble for a colleague (by making mistakes that the colleague will be blamed for), or out of destructiveness brought on by general frustration.

Unintentional errors usually result either from insufficient understanding of a given process or from poor concentration. Other common causes include software and hardware errors (the system does not behave as it should even though it is configured and operating correctly) or installation and configuration errors (errors occur when the system is operating correctly and the software or hardware is functioning according to specification). Sometimes a series of minor errors, which individually go undetected because no harmful effects are noted, are eventually compounded so that serious errors or even system failures result.

1.4.2   Mass Storage Problems

Problems with hard disks are the most common cause of failures in data processing. More than 26 percent of all system failures can be traced to faults in mass storage media. Although high-performance mass storage can attain a mean time between failures (MTBF) of over 10^6 hours, this could still mean replacing hard disks almost every month if the system has a large number of disk drives. There is usually a wide gap between theoretical MTBF and the operational MTBF that can be achieved in practice. The probability that a hard disk drive with a theoretical MTBF of 10^6 hours (almost 114 years) will actually run that long without error is only 30 percent. To calculate the number of hard disks that will have to be replaced within a certain period of time in a given system, multiply the total number of hard disk drives in the system by the period of system service in hours, and then divide this number by the theoretical MTBF. For example, in a system that has 1,000 disk drives, each of which has a theoretical MTBF of 10^6 hours, the number of failures A in the first 5 years (43,800 hours) comes to 44 (see the following equation).

$$A = \frac{1{,}000 \cdot 43{,}800 \; \frac{hours}{disk}}{1{,}000{,}000 \; \frac{hours}{disk}} = 44$$

This is based on the assumption that all of the hard disk systems have the same MTBF and are operated under similar conditions. Tests have shown that mass storage units operating in warm ambient conditions tend to show a lower actual MTBF than those operated in well-cooled environments. Furthermore, frequent disk search operations and changes in location have both been shown to have negative effects on the service life of mass storage media. For this reason, some hard disk manufacturers use another value in addition to the theoretical and operational MTBF to indicate the probable period of error-free operation for their products. This value, called the cumulative distribution function (CDF), indicates the probability that a mass storage medium will fail within a specified time. For example, a CDF of 4 percent over 5 years means that there is a 4 percent chance that the medium in question will break down within the first 5 years of use.

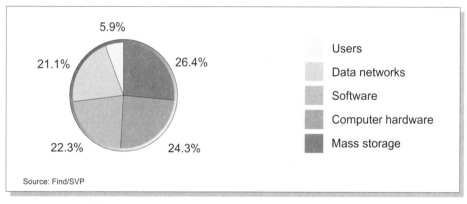

Figure 1.6 Causes of system failures in data processing

1.4.3   Computer Hardware Problems

Roughly one-quarter of all system failures are caused by computer hardware problems. By definition, this includes problems with any computer hardware component, including monitor, keyboard, mouse, CPU, RAM, hard disks and floppy disk drives. The average error-free service life of a system is calculated from the sum of the MTBF values of its components divided by the number of components. The following are some average MTBF values for various computer system components:

- RAM chips: 8,000,000 hours
- Floppy disk drives, mice, CD-ROM drives: 2,000,000 hours
- 10Base-T interface cards: 5,000,000 hours
- FDDI, ATM interface cards: 400,000 hours
- CPUs: 100,000 hours

The MTBF values calculated for today's computer systems average between 10,000 and 50,000 hours. In general, the more complex a system is, the lower the average MTBF. A system with multiple processors and multiple network links, for example, is more error-prone than a comparatively simple server with only one processor.

The Annual Failure Rate (AFR) is a better indicator of reliability than the MTBF. The AFR is the MTBF divided by the number of hours per year that the system is in operation. When a server system with a MTBF of 25,000 hours is in constant operation, the AFR amounts to $25,000/8,760 = 2.8$, or about 3 failures every year. Another important parameter for the availability of computer systems is the mean time to repair (MTTR), which indicates the average length of time it takes to repair the system after a failure. The MTTR is the total repair time divided by the number of system failures. Typical MTTR values lie between 2 and 3 hours when the repair time used in the calculation is the amount of work time actually spent repairing the system.

1.4.4   Software Problems

Software problems cause almost as many failures as hardware problems do. The widespread use of client-server architectures and distributed platforms in enterprise networks have led to such complex combinations of software that it is almost impossible to monitor system behavior under all network loads and in all operating states. In the age of corporate intranets and the Internet, the update schedules for software applications are becoming shorter all the time, so that sufficient time is not allowed for detailed testing before software is released. Automatic testing tools, such as LoadRunner (from Mercury Interactive—*www.loadrunner.com*) or AutoTester (from AutoTester Inc—*www.autotester.com*), which attempt to simulate various extreme operating situations, provide only limited assistance. Problems with new software that can lead to system failure arise not only at the application level, but also as a result of unstable software drivers, faulty installation or backup procedures, or operating system errors.

1.4.5 Network Problems

The fifth major category of IT problems encompasses errors that occur within the network itself. When the software and hardware problems that are directly related to network operation are included in this category—such as problems with network interface cards or with certain components of application software, protocols and card drivers—this group accounts for more than one-third of all IT failures. These network errors can be classified by OSI layer. As shown in Figure 1.7, 30 percent of all LAN errors occur on OSI layers 1 and 2. Typical causes are defective cables, connectors, or interface cards; defective modules in hubs, bridges or routers; collisions (in Ethernet networks); beacon processes

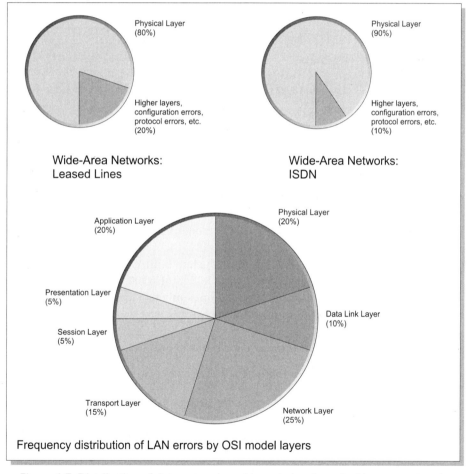

Frequency distribution of LAN errors by OSI model layers

Figure 1.7 Distribution of data network problems in local- and wide-area networks

(in Token-Ring networks); checksum errors, and incorrect packet sizes. The development and implementation of more reliable hardware components, coupled with the continuous improvement of cabling systems, have meant a decrease in the absolute numbers of these types of errors, but developments in software have had similar effects on the higher OSI layers as well. More stable network operating systems and applications as well as mature protocol stacks have also reduced the number of failures per network segment. As a result, the distribution of error sources over the seven OSI layers remains roughly the same over the past years.

In wide-area networks (WANs), the proportion of errors occurring on the physical layer is even higher. Where permanent WAN links (leased lines) are employed, 80 percent of all errors—in the case of ISDN (Integrated Services Digital Network), as many as 90 percent of all errors—can be traced to component failure, defective modems, or cable and connector faults (see Figure 1.7).

1.5   Calculation and Estimation of Costs Incurred Due to Network Failures

It is becoming increasingly important to estimate the costs that are incurred in the event of network failure. These can be difficult to quantify, however. Nonetheless, a fairly clear idea of the financial impact of system failure is essential in order to determine the optimum infrastructure dimensions from the perspective of network management and maintenance. Knowing the costs of system failure enables the enterprise to make informed decisions regarding the level of investment in redundant components or network management and troubleshooting systems. All too often the costs of system failure are grossly underestimated. It may be true that the exorbitant losses of $100,000 per minute and more reported in some superficial studies apply only to a few special cases, such as when system failure affects production control systems, financial services offered by credit card companies, or investment brokerages. Nonetheless, the consequences of a network breakdown even in smaller- or medium-sized companies should not be underrated.

The average availability of a data network today is between 98 and 99 percent. A system that is in operation 10 hours a day, 5 days a week can expect network downtime totaling between 52 and 104 hours per year. If an average of 100 employees are affected by a network failure, this means a maximum loss of productivity between 5,200 and 104,000 hours. This type of oversimplified calculation, however, quickly leads to inflated figures that do not necessarily reflect real situations.

The first step toward a more realistic analysis of network downtime costs is to distinguish between immediate costs incurred within the first 24 hours following the failure and consequential costs that arise after the first 24 hours. Costs in each of these categories are further divided into direct and indirect costs. Direct costs include all expenditures that are directly involved in correcting the network problem, while indirect costs include such factors as lost employee productivity and delayed project completion.

1.5.1   Immediate Costs

(Costs arising within the first 24 hours)

Direct Costs

- Replacement parts (network cards, cable, repeaters, hubs, etc.)
- New components (bridges, routers, servers, etc.)
- Rental or purchase of diagnostic equipment
  (network analyzers, cable testers, etc.)
- Consulting fees charged by network specialists
- Consulting fees charged by software/hardware manufacturers
- Overtime compensation for network support staff

Indirect Costs

- Loss of employee productivity at computer workstations
- Loss of productivity on production lines, in shipping and receiving departments, or in warehouse management; downtime of automated warehousing systems, etc.
- Loss of consumer or customer orders and confidence

Easiest to calculate are the direct immediate costs, such as the purchase of replacement components or consultants' fees, because these are automatically documented by invoices. In mid-sized networks (around 500 nodes) with an availability of 99 percent, the average downtime of 52 hours results from an average of 10 to 20 failures of the network or parts of it, lasting between 1 and 5 hours each. If the direct immediate costs of solving the problem average $1,250 per case, then the direct cost of restoring operation after 10 failures comes to $12,500.

Quantifying the indirect immediate costs is more difficult. In general, only the cumulative loss of employee productivity is calculated. The extent of this loss, however, depends mainly on the degree to which employee productivity is dependent on network availability. Often a number of employee activities can be postponed until the next day, or at least for a few hours, without significant loss of productivity. In mid-sized office environments, therefore, loss of employee productivity is usually estimated at roughly 25 percent of the total network downtime. For example, if an average of 100 employees are affected by the network breakdown, at 52 hours of downtime per year the loss of productivity amounts to $52 \cdot 0.25 \cdot 100 = 1{,}300$ hours. If the average gross salary costs come to $40 per hour, this puts the immediate indirect costs at $52,000.

1.5.2   Consequential Costs

(Costs arising after the first 24 hours)

Direct Costs

- New or adjusted hardware configuration in the network (restructuring of servers, bridges, etc.)
- Testing of other network segments for errors similar to those that caused the failure
- Documentation of the system failure

Indirect Costs

- Delayed project completion (product development, production, etc.)
- Delayed services (tenders, invoices, entering transactions in accounts, etc.)
- Loss of customer loyalty and satisfaction

Consequential indirect costs resulting from network failure are the most difficult to calculate. These costs are also referred to as "company losses" because they cannot be attributed to any one department or cost center. The amount of such costs is proportional to the degree to which the company depends on network-supported processes. Tenders may have to be printed and sent a day later than planned, for example. Incoming orders and payments may be similarly delayed. Incoming deliveries may be blocked if receiving slips cannot be printed or automated warehousing equipment cannot be operated. Urgent shipments sent by special courier result in higher shipping rates. Late charges may be incurred for bills that cannot be processed. Sales may be lost due to unavailable Web-based ordering systems. Customers may grow dissatisfied if they cannot reach a support hotline, which means a loss of future orders. These are just a few examples of company losses as consequential costs of network failures. At a fairly low estimate of $1,000 in consequential indirect costs and $250 in consequential direct costs per failure, the total loss per year in this category, based on the conditions described previously, is $77,000. This means each hour of downtime costs the company $1,480. Or, to look at the case from another perspective, an improvement of a mere 0.1 percent in network availability saves the company $7,700.

Network availability	99%
Annual downtime (hours)	52
Number of employees affected per failure	100
Dependency of employee productivity on network availability	25%
Average annual failures	10
Average direct, immediate costs per year / per failure (replacement parts, etc.)	$ 12,000 ($1,200 per failure)
Average indirect, immediate costs (loss of employee productivity)	$100 \cdot 0.25 \cdot 52 =$ 1300 h $\cdot$ $\$40 = \$52,000$
Average direct, consequential costs per year / per failure (planning, failure documentation, reconfiguration)	$2,500 ($250)
Average indirect, consequential immediate costs per year / per failure (company losses)	$10,000 ($1,000)
Annual network failure costs	**$77,000**
Hourly network failure costs	**$1,481**
Network failure costs per 0.1% downtime	**$7,700**

Figure 1.8 Calculating the costs of network downtime

1.6 High Availability and Fault Tolerance in Networks

High-availability data processing infrastructures have become a basic requirement for smooth business processes in commercial data processing. Barring
special measures taken to maximize network availability, the average availability of today's IT systems is between 98 and 99 percent, which corresponds to a
total annual downtime of 50 to 100 hours. For a growing number of companies,
however, even this is too much downtime. Special systems can be added to boost
network availability to between 99.9 and 99.9999 percent (99.999 percent uptime is equivalent to 6.8 minutes downtime in one year). In this way the average
downtime-per-year can be reduced to a few hours or even, in the extreme case, a
few minutes.

Architecture	Availability	Typical failure duration	Annual downtime
Uninterruptible operation	100%	None	None
Fault tolerance	99.9999%	Ticks	0.5 minutes
Fail-over by cluster	99.999%	Ticks to seconds	Up to 5 minutes
Fault resilience (fail-over)	99.99%	Seconds to minutes	Up to 50 minutes
High availability	99.9%	Minutes	Up to 8 hours
Standard system	99%	Hours	Several days

Source: AT&T/Gartner/TPPC

Figure 1.9 Availability levels and downtime

The costs of availability, however, increase almost exponentially with each additional decimal place. Before planning a high-availability system, it is important to specify exactly what service levels are required. This determines the degree of availability that must be guaranteed. Availability is expressed as a percentage, calculated from the total operating time and the downtime:

$$Availability = \frac{total\ operating\ time - downtime}{total\ operating\ time}$$

Another important factor is the average downtime resulting from system failure, which is called the mean time to repair or MTTR. In most cases, a large number of short service interruptions, lasting only seconds or minutes, is acceptable, while just a few failures that last for several hours each have serious consequences.

The main prerequisite for a high-availability infrastructure is the use of high-quality components. Even without any special equipment or configuration for ultra-high availability, the quality of components is an important factor in the reliability of hardware and software. Component quality is also decisive for the performance of diagnostic tools and system and network management applications, as well as for the level of maintenance and support that can be attained. If no concessions are made in these areas, the availability of the data processing structure is bound to be significantly above average. Availability can only be improved beyond this level by the addition of components and services. These can include:

36

- Redundant components
- Software and hardware switching
- Detailed planning of every scheduled downtime
- Reduction of system administration tasks
- Development of automatic error reaction systems
- Thorough acceptance testing prior to installation of new hardware or software components
- Specifications and practice drills for operator response to system failure
- Replicated databases and application software
- Clustering

Redundant components can reduce the number of single points of failure in the network. When a given network component fails, its redundant counterpart is activated automatically. If the installation of fallback components is combined with software and hardware switching technologies, the redundant components

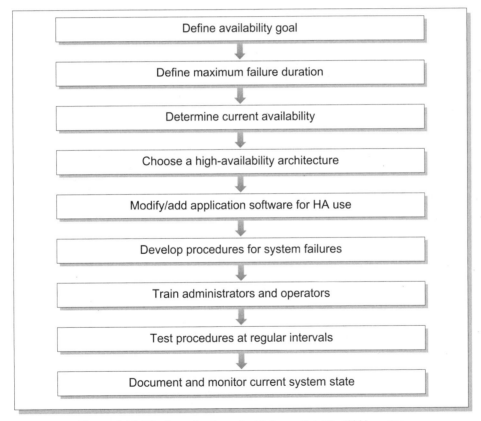

Figure 1.10 The introduction of a high-availability (HA) system

can take over for malfunctioning components within seconds or even fractions of seconds. Reducing the level of interaction between the network and administrator is a useful step in establishing deterministic reactions to different error scenarios—ideally, a given error should consistently trigger a single, defined process. The individual steps involved in introducing a high-availability system are shown in Figure 1.10.

1.7   Summary

Mission-critical systems in today's enterprise networks are growing more dependent every day on smoothly functioning data processing systems. Network managers are thus faced with the enormous challenge of increasing the availability of their data processing infrastructures while these infrastructures grow in both size and complexity. Network management is further complicated by the fact that corporate intranets are increasingly accessible through remote or public networks, such as the Internet, telecommunication service providers, customers' networks, telecommuters' systems and so on. It is no longer possible to have complete, end-to-end control over a company network. This makes it even more important to plan network operation and maintenance systematically, to implement appropriate procedures, and to have experienced network support staff equipped with advanced diagnostic and management tools.

Error Management
in Data Networks

2

"...All those occasions on which a planned sequence of mental or physical activities fails to achieve its intended outcome."

NEVILLE STANTON, DEFINITION OF "ERROR"

It is practically impossible to operate and maintain today's large and complex data networks without carefully structured management systems and adherence to precisely defined procedures. Modern network management is primarily based on service level agreements (SLAs), which specify precise quality characteristics for guaranteed services. The network manager's overriding responsi-

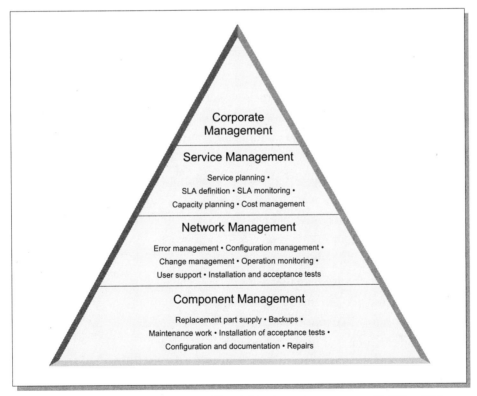

Figure 2.1 Service management: All activities have the purpose of fulfilling SLAs

bility is to ensure that SLAs are fulfilled. This represents a significant change in network management philosophy. Until recently, the individual components of network operation—such as network management, error management, installation, configuration and planning—were largely handled by separate operational entities. The new concept of service management unites all of these tasks under the common goal of fulfilling SLAs. This permits more efficient and purposeful utilization of available resources. Furthermore, keeping track of service level agreements is equivalent to constantly monitoring the data processing infrastructure, which in turn makes capacity planning realistic and documentable, and allows detailed cost management for the entire data processing infrastructure.

As can be seen in Figure 2.1, error management takes place at the network management level. The many aspects of error management, however, are so closely connected with all other areas of data-processing service management that these also have a role to play in strategic error management planning. For example, a given SLA includes a definition of the maximum mean time to repair (MTTR) for the service in question, which in turn has a direct impact on staff and equipment requirements in the network support department. Thus a comprehensive error management strategy must include specifications for the following network management elements:

- Corporate guidelines for data processing utilization
- All the services to be provided in the network
- Documented service level agreements for all services
- Systematic network planning
- Systematic documentation of all network components
- Use of network management tools
- Use of monitoring and diagnostic tools
- Regular network audits
- Use of network simulation tools
- Procedures for change management
- Procedures for problem handling and diagnostics
- Documentation of network problems
- Continuous training of network support staff

2.1 Corporate Guidelines for Data Processing Systems

Every enterprise should have clearly formulated guidelines regarding the use of their data processing systems and networks. Such corporate guidelines provide a framework for the data processing environment and form the best starting point for developing a comprehensive error management strategy. Unfortunately, these guidelines are often imprecisely formulated, leaving room for disagreements between network support staff and other personnel about responsibilities for particular areas of network operation or management. Some departments or business units, for example, assume that they can acquire and install whatever network hardware or software they like because they have always done so. Users generally see only the PC on their own desks, and some believe they are free to configure their "own" machines as they see fit. Obviously such activities make centralized network management impossible. This is why corporate guidelines must provide clear instructions for all personnel. In addition, steps must be taken to ensure that all staff members are aware of, and appropriately trained in, their areas of responsibility.

Corporate guidelines are usually based on a general definition of functions and tasks for the data network and computer system. As a rule, they include descriptions of the services to be provided, as well as the security and network availability requirements. The exact content of such guidelines varies according to the conditions within the organizational unit in question. In any case, it is essential that measures specified in these corporate guidelines be economically and technologically feasible and that the enterprise management guarantee their implementation. The task of formulating the guidelines should be shared between the network support department and enterprise management. Responsibility for interpreting the guidelines must also be defined in individual cases. No matter how detailed the guidelines are, there are always situations that require further interpretation of the guidelines before a decision can be reached.

2.1.1 Corporate Guidelines for Employees

Guidelines for employees should describe the rights and obligations of all network users and user groups, including permanent employees, guests, temporary employees, system administrators, service and maintenance personnel, and external consultants. Guidelines should cover the following topics for all user groups:

- Access to systems and services
- Restrictions on the use of systems and services, including prohibition of such actions as:
  - Breaking into other systems
  - Revealing passwords
  - Manipulating data in other users' files
  - Sharing user accounts
  - Copying copyright-protected software
- Authorization to create user accounts
- Duties of each user:
  - Preserving confidentiality of user passwords
  - Changing user passwords regularly
  - Backing up user data
  - Preserving confidentiality of sensitive data
  - Adhering to guidelines regarding:
    - The use of system resources (data storage, CPU time, etc.)
    - Internet use
    - The use of company data processing services for private purposes
  - Monitoring user accounts for unauthorized use
  - Reporting unusual operating behavior, viruses, etc.

2.1.2   Corporate Guidelines for Network Hardware

Guidelines for hardware in the data processing infrastructure must include:

- Security regulations for individual hardware components (servers, routers, terminals, wiring closets, etc.)
- Security regulations for the company as a whole (concerning fire and flood alarm systems, air conditioning systems, etc.)

All critical components of the data processing infrastructure, including programs, file servers, routers, bridges, root terminals, etc., should be physically shielded and installed in air-conditioned rooms. Access to these rooms should be controlled via personal access codes or ID cards with magnetic strips, for example.

2.1.3   Corporate Guidelines for Network Software

Another important part of a holistic network strategy is the control of software applications used in the company. Users configuring their own computers without supervision from network managers often cause networks errors due to the loss of data, faulty data storage, or system incompatibilities. The unauthorized installation of applications (often unlicensed!) or computer games can result in computer virus infection or Trojan horse infiltration. The network administration staff must have documentation of all computer system configurations as well as all network components. Only authorized personnel should be allowed to make changes in any configuration. Last but not least, a systematic backup strategy should be implemented to provide security for user data, including offsite backups (Disaster Recovery).

2.2 Services and Service Level Agreements

A service level agreement should be defined for each of the main services specified in the corporate guidelines. Each SLA must include a precise description of the service, the funds that can be spent to attain it, its user group, and the date from which the SLA is effective. Furthermore, it should give the number of hours per day and the number of days per week or month during which the service in question shall be available, taking the required maintenance time into account. SLAs must also specify the exact number and location of users, as well as the hardware provided for the services in question. In addition, SLAs must describe procedures for reporting problems and requesting changes, and must define escalation procedures and network management response times for such requests. Finally, SLAs must state the specific goals for such service quality parameters as:

* Average availability
* Minimum availability
* Average response time
* Maximum response time
* Average throughput

Unfortunately, users' obligations to participate in training programs or to adhere to certain procedural guidelines, for example, are often overlooked in SLAs. A user who does not fulfill such obligations may be responsible for a violation of the SLA. Typical services covered by SLAs in many companies include user support, network printing services, e-mail services, Internet access services, server access, and network operation in general. In addition to such services, there should also be SLAs for all mission-critical applications, such as customer ordering systems, databases, and production control systems.

2.3   Network Planning and Documentation

The next step in implementing an error management strategy is to compile comprehensive documentation if such does not already exist. Network management in general, and error management in particular, are impossible without detailed documentation of all hardware and software components in the entire information processing infrastructure. Comprehensive documentation must include the following components:

- Building floor plans that show the cable infrastructure, wall jacks, wiring closets, network components and terminals
- Functional block diagrams
- Configuration database of all network components
- Documentation of equipment test results

The most time-consuming of these tasks is creating a diagram of the cable infrastructure. If possible, a computer-aided cable management system should be used. Usually the building floor plan already exists in electronic form and can be imported into such a system. Most computer-aided cable management systems can store visual representations of each network component as well as details about it, such as cable test results, device specifications or configuration data. If there is no such program available, copies of the original building floor plans must be obtained and every cable end and wall jack in the network clearly marked on it. The cables and connectors should be designated in such a way that users can quickly inform network management personnel of the cables and connections in their own system. Ideally a dedicated label maker should be used to produce clear and professional looking labels. If the pin assignments of a given cable or connector are not standard, the exact pin assignments must also be listed. Once all the data on cable routes, wall jacks and user terminals has been collected, it can be entered on the floor plan or in the cable management software. Wiring closets are usually depicted on separate diagrams that include both structural diagrams of the closet itself and detailed slot lists. If bus topologies (10Base2, 10Base5) are used, care must be taken to ensure that all connectors are included on the cabling diagram. Furthermore, passive components, such as repeaters and hubs, are often overlooked when documenting networks. It is important that these also be documented in detail, however, and included on cabling diagrams.

Another important part of network documentation is the functional block diagram. This diagram depicts all network components and segments, including all terminals, repeaters, hubs, bridges, routers, switches, and media access units (MAUs), along with their functions, connections, port bandwidths and redundancies. The third component of network documentation is a database containing the system configurations and specifications of all network components. The fourth component is a comprehensive record of all test results gathered during network audits and troubleshooting.

Building cabling plan	Wiring closet plan	Wiring closet layout
Cable routes [include manufacturer, dimensions, use (power/data, data rate)]	Location (building, floor, room)	Wiring closet number
Wiring closet locations	Wiring closet number	Make and model
Sockets	Incoming/outgoing cable feeds	Installation position
Terminal equipment	Ground buses	Equipment lists
Date of last modification	Incoming/outgoing cable feeds	Sockets
	Date of last modification	Date of last modification

Figure 2.2 Components of cable documentation

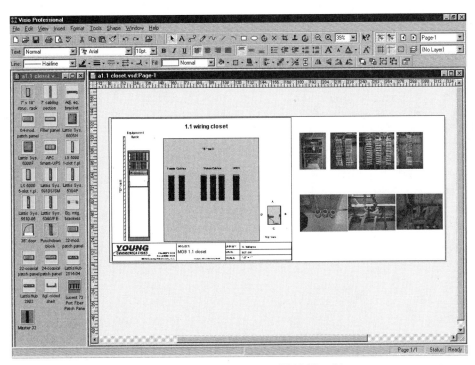

Figure 2.3 Wiring closet documentation with the "IMAP" cable management system

The TIA/EIA 606 specification, "The Administration Standard for the Telecommunications Infrastructure of Commercial Buildings", describes standardized nomenclature for the documentation of data networks. This specification, available from Global Engineering Documents at *http://www.global.ihs.com*, is the "bible" of cable infrastructure management. Every computer-aided cable management system used should be based on TIA/EIA 606.

2.4   Network Management Tools

Network management systems (NMS) are essential for the operation of today's complex data processing infrastructures and, by the same token, are indispensable for any error management system. In networks with more than 1000 users, controlled network operation with careful consideration of expenditures is almost impossible without a network management system. Such systems are software applications that monitor and manage the individual software and hardware components in a network as well as the overall network structure. According to the definition in the ISO/IEC 7498-4 standard ("Information Processing Systems–Open Systems Interconnection–Basic Reference Model–Part 4: Management Framework"), a comprehensive network management system is composed of the following five parts:

- Configuration management
- Performance management
- Security management
- Accounting management
- Error management

Configuration management encompasses the administration of all hardware systems and applications used in the network. This includes system configuration and component management, distribution and licensing of software, and management of client and server system inventories. Furthermore, all network topologies must be surveyed and continuously updated.

Performance management consists of monitoring hardware and software performance by means of dedicated software agents. These agents monitor the relevant objects and report results to a central analytical application. The system may be configured to send an alarm signal to the network manager when defined thresholds are exceeded. In addition to monitoring applications and hardware, performance management has the task of monitoring network efficiency. This involves continuous monitoring of data streams between and within each network segment and recording the characteristics of traffic on each segment, such as packet size distribution, packet error rate, transmission delay, etc.

Security management involves the administration of network addresses, file areas, access rights, and passwords for each user. Additionally, system- and network-critical components, such as servers, routers, gateways, firewalls, etc., must be monitored for unauthorized or unusual activities.

The purpose of accounting management is to register all network use and classify overall usage of system resources by user. Such classification can be performed on the basis of a number of different parameters, such as hard disk storage on file servers, database access time, or the number and length of data packets transmitted over the network. The goal is to achieve a fair distribution of the total costs of data processing so that users are motivated to use the available resources sensibly and economically.

Error management is probably the most widely implemented component of the ISO network management model. Every network requires some kind of error management system, even if only in rudimentary form. According to the ISO definition, error management in the strictest sense means defining and following procedures for detecting symptoms, restricting error domains, solving problems, testing solutions and documenting errors and their solutions. In practice, error management is far more complex, encompassing aspects of practically every area of responsibility in network operation, from documentation to planning.

Aside from the five aspects of network management described in the ISO model, the importance of data storage management has risen dramatically in recent years, and with it the amount of time and money involved. This area has thus developed into a separate network management field. With the sharp increase in storage space requirements and the growing dependence of companies on the availability of stored information, backup systems and their management have become new challenges in the data processing field. The amounts of data to be stored grow larger every day, and backup operations must be performed either outside working hours ("cold backups") or during working hours ("hot backups"). Furthermore, separate procedures must be defined for storing data on local backup media and for transmitting data over the network to central storage media. Storage management tasks also include defining backup cycles, determining how long backups take, and controlling data restoration processes.

Management of all these components and their communication links is based upon software agents that run within the network components being monitored or controlled and on the communication protocols used for transmitting and receiving the corresponding information to and from a central network management station. The protocols available for these management tasks include the

Simple Network Management Protocol (SNMP) and the less widely used Common Management Information Protocol (CMIP). Most modern network components have integrated SNMP agents, which use SNMP to read operating statistics and to load configuration parameters. For network components with proprietary control mechanisms, proxies are used to translate SNMP into the control commands used.

In view of the wide variety of tasks involved in network operation, it is clear that high-performance management tools are required for maximum support. Monitoring and diagnostic systems are also indispensable when problems occur—and beforehand, as well, for preventive action.

2.5   Monitoring and Diagnostic Tools

Special monitoring and diagnostic tools are essential for systematic trouble-shooting and proactive error management in data networks. In very small networks, experienced network managers can solve some network problems without such tools—when the source of an error can be localized from the error symptoms alone, for example, or when problems are prevented before they occur by running routine tests and replacing a component or two "just in case". Unfortunately, this is only possible in a limited number of situations. In some of these cases the symptom may be removed, but the magnitude of the actual problem remains unknown. Another difficulty with this basically reactive method is that it neglects opportunities for proactive prevention of errors. Even in small networks, it is a good idea to use monitoring and diagnostic tools, at least to some extent. In larger networks with 1,000 nodes or more, such tools are indispensable as part of a universal network management system.

Diagnostic tools can be divided into two categories: tactical and strategic. Tactical systems are mobile, and are deployed in the affected network segment only until the problem in question has been solved. Strategic diagnostic tools are used continuously, to monitor a given network segment, for example. Strategic tools can be used to perform long-term studies or trend analyses. They can also be programmed to set off an alarm when defined threshold values are exceeded during network operation. Strategic and tactical diagnostic tools are often used in combination. The operating parameters detected by these diagnostic systems range from characteristics of the cable infrastructure to detailed analyses of communication protocols on the higher OSI layers. The test instruments used include cable testers, multimeters, optical time-domain reflectometers (OTDRs), protocol analyzers, bit error testers, and system probes. Details on the functions and uses of diagnostic tools are discussed in the next chapter.

2.6   Regular Network Audits

Regular network check-ups are an essential part of successful error management. Comprehensive audits of the network, including the cable infrastructure, should be performed at long intervals, such as once a year. Less detailed audits, involving a review of the principal operating parameters, should be performed at weekly or monthly intervals. These audits should be supplemented by continuous measurements of key parameters, such as the network traffic load, data packet sizes, numbers of error packets and service response times. When performed conscientiously, the combination of continuous measurements and regular audits keeps the network manager apprised of characteristic network operating parameters. This makes it possible to detect and correct many types of network problems at a very early stage. Experience has shown that in over 50 percent of serious network problems a comparison of the active operating parameters with those recorded previously on the same weekday at the same time of day can quickly limit the error domain to a very small range. This significantly reduces the mean time to repair. Network audits generally include examinations of the first three OSI layers: the physical, data link and network layers.

2.6.1   Physical Layer Audit

Testing the entire cable infrastructure during a network audit may seem extravagant at first glance, but in practice it has repeatedly proven to be a highly effective preventive measure. Although today's cable and connector systems are far more sturdy and reliable than those manufactured just a few years ago, a fair proportion of those errors that are intermittent or otherwise difficult to localize can be traced to these components. Such errors are often caused by the aging of materials—which is accelerated by the effects of light and humidity or by mechanical wear and tear, poor workmanship or defective materials. In many cases the consequences of these defects become evident only gradually; the proportion of defective data packets with checksum errors increases, service response times grow longer, but communication basically continues and the diminished throughput and mounting error rates often go unnoticed until the system fails completely. Yearly cable audits can reveal wear and tear in copper and fiber-optic cable segments. Replacing all lines that no longer fulfill minimum performance requirements can prevent errors during network operation. Some of the tests performed on cables require that the LAN or WAN connection be shut down. Redundant network structuring is useful in this case because the flow of data can be automatically switched to backup segments when an important connection is broken. In Token-Ring and FDDI networks the data flow is shifted to the secondary ring; when routing and switching are used, network traffic is sent over alternative ports. Disconnecting individual lines for measurements during the annual cable infrastructure audit can also test these mechanisms.

Cable Audits in Local-Area Networks

Cable audits in local-area networks should include testing of the following parameters, as applicable:

Copper Twisted-Pair Cable

- Cable length
- Near-end crosstalk (NEXT)
- Signal-to-noise ratio (SNR)
- Attenuation

Coaxial Cable

- Cable length
- Reflection at connectors
- Number of stations

Fiber-Optic Cable

- Cable length
- Total attenuation
- Attenuation caused by splices

Token Ring, FDDI, Routers with Backup Routes, ATM Switches with PVCs

- Backup test: disconnect line to test backup switching/routing

Cable Audits in Wide-Area Networks

The most important Layer 1 tests in wide-area networks are signal condition and bit-error-rate (BER) measurements. The first step is to use a protocol analyzer to check all packets in network traffic for Cyclic Redundancy Check (CRC) errors. The next step is to check signal levels and signal conditions with an interface tester. The test results may indicate anomalies, such as deviations from the nominal output voltage, distorted signal shape, or jitter. If the line can be disconnected briefly, separate bit-error-rate testing (BERT) should also be performed. In this procedure, a number of different bit patterns are transmitted over the WAN link under test—either framed in 64 Kbit/s channels or unframed, depending on the transmitting port—and then looped back from the receiving end and evaluated by the BER tester upon return. To obtain meaningful BERT results, these tests should be carried out over a period of several hours. The quality of the WAN link under test can be determined from the following BERT results:

- Bit-error rate
- Block-error rate
- Number of error-free seconds
- Number of errored seconds

Audit parameter	Test instruments	Type of test
Local-area networks		
Twisted pair		
Cable length	Cable tester	Out-of-service
Near-end crosstalk (NEXT)	Cable tester	Out-of-service
Signal-to-noise ratio (SNR)	Cable tester	Out-of-service
Attenuation	Cable tester	Out-of-service
Coaxial cable		
Cable length	Cable tester	Out-of-service
Reflections at connectors	Cable tester	Out-of-service
Number of nodes	Protocol analyzer, LAN probes	In-service
Fiber optic		
Cable length	OTDR	Out-of-service
Total attenuation	OTDR	Out-of-service
Splice attenuation	OTDR	Out-of-service
Wide-area networks		
Signal level	Interface tester	In-service
Signal condition	Interface tester	In-service
Bit error parameters		Out-of-service
OSI Layer 1 stress tests (at capacity load)		

Ethernet
    Network load (sent = received)
    FCS errors; Collisions
	Protocol analyzer	In-service

Token Ring
    Token rotation time
    beacon packets
    jitter
	Protocol analyzer	In-service

FDDI beacon packets; jitter	Protocol analyzer	In-service

ATM
    Cell BERT
    SDH frame alarms (AIS; yellow alarm)
	Protocol analyzer	In-service

X.25 CRC error monitoring	Protocol tester	In-service
Frame-Relay CRC error monitoring	Protocol tester	In-service
ISDN CRC error monitoring	Protocol tester	In-service

Figure 2.4 OSI Layer 1 auditing

Stress Tests for the OSI Layer 1 Audit

Many problems that occur on the physical layer are only noticeable once a certain network load level is reached. Problems of this sort include those caused by electromagnetic interference (pulse-dialing telephones, current surges on powering up equipment, etc.), weak signals at hubs, or problems with terminating resistors. The final tests in an OSI Layer 1 audit should be performed under heavy traffic conditions, with special attention paid to the errors that are typical for the topology under test. The table in Figure 2.4 shows the recommended tests and techniques used in OSI Layer 1 audits. Detailed explanations of the values measured and the methods used are found in the following chapters.

All test results should be clearly and systematically documented so that they are available for comparison with later audits.

2.6.2   Data Link Layer Audit

Operating parameters on the data link layer must also be monitored over a long period in order to obtain meaningful results. This period can span 24 hours, a week, or even a month. In central backbones, as well as in main network segments and wide-area links, operating statistics should also be monitored continuously as a standard network management practice. The data link layer parameters relevant for all transmission techniques include capacity use, activity statistics, connection matrices and transmission delay. Capacity use should be recorded over a period of 1 working week, and the maxima and minima marked. The capacity use statistics must include network load (in Kbyte/s and as a percentage of capacity), packet size distribution, and numbers of packets. This data supplies useful information about network operating behavior. Activity statistics provide information about the most active network nodes. As a rule these are server and router systems, which are responsible for a large proportion of all data traffic. A significant change in the distribution of activity in a particular segment may point to a potential source of future problems. Reconfiguration of the device in question may be sufficient to head off trouble. Documenting connection matrices is important for similar reasons. This involves compiling statistics on the most active connections in order to list significant network relationships, such as the heaviest traffic load across a single router into the Internet or across a WAN link between two LANs. In addition to these general data link layer characteristics, many topology-specific Layer 2 parameters should be tested and documented. Figure 2.5 lists the main parameters to be measured for Ethernet, Token Ring, FDDI, ATM and wide-area networks. Details on obtaining and interpreting these measurements are found in subsequent chapters.

Ethernet	Token Ring	FDDI	ATM	WAN
Capacity use	Capacity use	Capacity use	Capacity use	Capacity use
Activity statistics	Activity statistics	Activity statistics	Activity statistics	Activity statistics
Communication matrix	Communication matrix	Communication matrix	Communication matrix	Communication matrix
Collisions	Beacons	Beacons	SDH Parameters (frame loss, line AIS, path AIS, line FEBE, line FERF, path FERF	Connection statistics (number of completed/failed connection setups)
FCS errors	Ring purges	FCS errors	Total cells, idle cells, busy cells	CRC errors
Runts	Claim tokens frames	Claim frames	HEC errors	Transmission delay measurements
Jabbers	Receiver congestion	SMT and void frames	Cell sync loss	
Misalignment errors	FCS errors	Token rotation time	Cell BERT	
Broadcasts	Token rotation time	Number of nodes	Test cell insertion (O.191); measurement of cell loss and cell delay	
Multicasts	Number of nodes			
Number of nodes				

Figure 2.5 OSI Layer 2 auditing

2.6.3   Network Layer Audit

The data collected in the network layer audit is used to analyze the performance and efficiency of user data transport protocols in the various network topologies. The first step is to determine the network layer protocols used with their respective proportions of the overall network load, throughput, and the number of stations using each protocol. The next step is to collect detailed data on each individual protocol. The information to be gathered depends on the architecture of each protocol. For the widely used Internet Protocol, for example, the pertinent statistics include information on IP broadcasts, ICMP redirects, ICMP unreachables, low TTL, ARP packets, routing packets, DNS, low window size and other similar parameters. In the case of ISDN and ATM, the signaling protocol must also be monitored; in ATM, this can be UNI 3.0, 3.1 or 4.0; in ISDN, it is generally DSS1. Information used in analyzing network layer performance includes both the number of connections and the numbers of successful and unsuccessful connection attempts. In X.25 and Frame Relay, network protocol analysis is also performed on the corresponding logical channels (LCNs in X.25, DLCIs in Frame Relay). This involves observing and analyzing each channel as if it were a separate WAN link. As in network auditing on Layers 1 and 2, it is essential to document all results on OSI Layer 3 clearly and systematically. The data gathered can be used to plot trends as a basis for subsequent network planning, for example, and for use as reference values in future error situations.

LAN	ATM	Frame Relay	X.25	ISDN
Protocol distribution in correlation with network load, packet size, distribution and number of nodes	Protocol distribution	List of all active channels (DLCIs)	List of all active channels (LCN)	D channel: Number of completed/failed connection setups
Protocol throughput	Protocol throughput	Distribution of encapsulated protocols (IP, PPP, etc.)	Distribution of encapsulated protocols (IP, PPP, etc.)	B channel: Distribution of encapsulated protocols (IP, PPP, etc.), throughput station lists, activity statistics, communication matrices
Protocol statistics (protocol-specific): window sizes, ICMP packets, broadcasts, ARP packets, low TTL, etc.	Number of completed/failed connection setups	Station lists	Station lists	Release messages with causes
Layer 3 (e.g., IP) response times	Release messages with causes	Activity statistics	Activity statistics	Layer 3 (e.g., IP) response times
Routing analyses	Layer 3 (e.g., IP) response times	Communication matrices	Communication matrices	
		Layer 3 (e.g., IP) response times	Layer 3 (e.g., IP) response times	

Figure 2.6 OSI Layer 3 auditing

2.7 Network Simulation Tools

Network simulation tools are software applications designed to predict the network behavior that follows a given change in the network. These tools use complicated algorithms to extrapolate probable network behavior based on existing topology specifications in combination with operating statistics collected from the network and its management systems. Planned configuration changes, such as the addition of servers, clients or applications, can then be simulated in the software and the resulting predictions used to estimate future service levels, downtimes, application performance levels, and capacity use. Network simulation tools can be used in change management or for designing new networks, and provide valuable assistance in fulfilling SLAs and optimizing network availability, especially in large and complex systems.

2.8 Change Management and Problem Solving

In addition to network monitoring, change management and problem solving are central tasks in network management. These are both extraordinarily complex

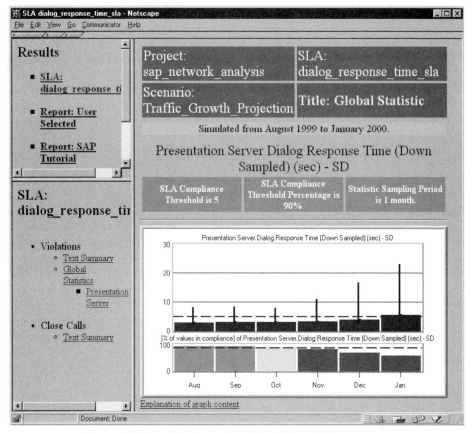

Figure 2.7 User interface of a network simulation program

tasks, and what seems a minor mistake can have unpredictable consequences. Clearly defined and documented procedures for change management and problem solving are essential in order to minimize the likelihood of errors.

Change management encompasses such activities as the installation of software, PCs, workstations, bridges, routers and switches. It also includes administrative tasks, such as training staff for new duties or reconfiguring user access when employees change workstations. IP addresses must be assigned, changes must be made in the wiring closet patch panel, and access rights to servers and gateways must be modified or created. All of these tasks must be carried out in accordance with proven procedures and documented in careful detail. A large proportion of network problems result from poor planning or execution of changes. A detailed record of all recent changes, including the date and time each modification was made, gives network support staff a sizable head start in locating error sources.

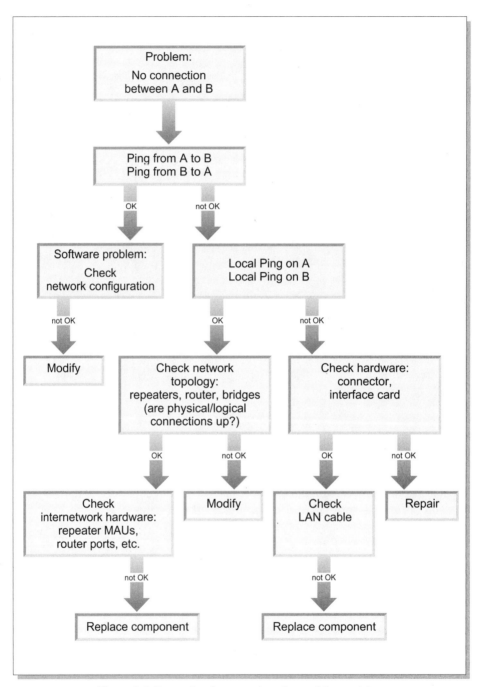

Figure 2.8 Example of a procedure for problem solving

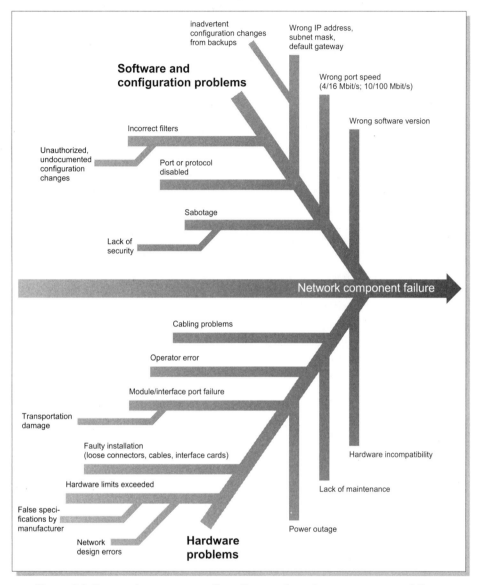

Figure 2.9 Excerpt from a cause-effect diagram based on router system failures

For problem solving and diagnostics, just as for change management, detailed specifications of systematic routines should be provided. Today's networks are far too complicated to proceed on the basis of intuition or a sixth sense. Detailed problem handling routines are especially useful to have available where similar types of error scenarios occur frequently, as is the case with some network printer, file server or WAN link problems.

Cause-and-effect diagrams have proven useful for visualizing mechanisms and relationships in complex structures, such as those encountered in network troubleshooting. In Figure 2.9 , the relationships between error symptoms and their manifold causes are plotted on a fishbone diagram. The error symptom is positioned at one end of the "spine" and each cause is entered at the end of a "bone". More than one cause or category of causes may be entered for a given symptom, each of which can have further subgroups. Figure 2.9 shows a section of a cause-effect diagram based on router system failures.

The influence of a given cause or group of causes on the occurrence of a given error symptom is relative to the frequency with which the cause in question occurs. Taking proactive measures to prevent the most frequent causes can be an efficient way to improve network performance. As shown in Figure 2.10, a correlation diagram provides an overview of the relationships involved. This example shows the relationship between the mean time to repair (MTTR) and the availability of the network. Network availability is determined by three characteristics: the frequency with which failures occur, the length of time that elapses before a failure is recognized, and the time it takes to restore the network to service. If 5 failures occur per month in a given network with an average MTTR of 3.5 hours and it takes an average of 30 minutes before the failure is recognized, the availability of this network is 93 percent. The three values can be entered on a correlation diagram and then each of the values altered, in turn, to estimate the effects of various changes on overall network availability.

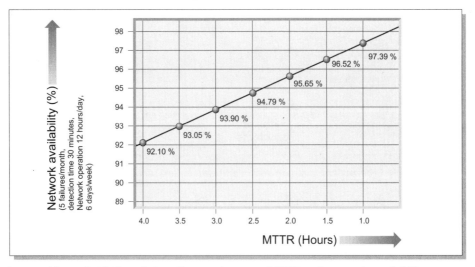

Figure 2.10 Correlation diagram between MTTR and network availability

2.9   Documentation of Network Problems

The importance of documenting network problems and their solutions cannot be stressed enough. In many organizations, such records are incomplete or even non-existent. All too often no clear instructions are defined for response to network problems. Standard procedures for documentation and for methodical troubleshooting provide a structure that allows network staff to record and examine error symptoms calmly, form hypotheses about the possible causes, and plan tests for those hypotheses. In the absence of strict guidelines, responses to network failure may have unexpected results and, worse yet, may be impossible to reconstruct afterwards. For this reason, a special procedural form should be created for technicians to fill in when any network problem occurs. This form should include at least the date and time the symptom was detected, the number and type of systems and applications affected, suggestions as to possible causes, and a description of the measures planned for testing theories and handling the problem. Once the problem has been solved, a brief description of the solution can be added before the form is filed. Conscientious use of these forms should be required, not only to help in establishing systematic, well-planned working methods, but also to provide a valuable source of material for the network problem-solving database (see Figure 2.11).

2.10   Network Support Staff Training

The most valuable capital any enterprise can have is thoroughly trained and highly motivated staff, especially in such a complicated area as network operation and maintenance. Today's computer networks are so complex that it is not possible to let them run "automatically", even when the most powerful management equipment on the market is in use. Even the most expert diagnostics system available is no substitute for the knowledge and skill of an experienced network specialist. This is why ongoing, high-quality staff training programs are just as important for comprehensive error management as adherence to meticulously-defined procedures and the use of appropriate diagnostics tools.

Network Problem Documentation   Case No.: _____

Date: ___. ___. _____
Time: ___:___ am/pm
Network engineer: _____

Urgency: ☐ 1 (<10 min) ☐ 2 (10–30 min) ☐ 4 (1–3 hrs)
☐ 3 (30–60 min) ☐ 5 (3–8 hrs)

Reported symptoms:

Hardware affected: ☐ PC (client) ☐ PC (server)

☐ Printer ☐ Router ☐ Workstation (client) ☐ Workstation (server)

☐ Hub ☐ Switch ☐ Optical coupler ☐ Cabling

Applications affected: ☐ WWW ☐ Mail ☐ FTP

☐ Office ☐ Printing ☐ Database ☐ File server ☐ Directory

Possible causes:

Action planned:

Action: _____ Result: _____
Action: _____ Result: _____
Action: _____ Result: _____

Remedy:

Description: _____

Attachments: Test logs, topological maps, etc.
Date: _____ Time: _____

Figure 2.11 Example of a problem documentation form

Diagnostic Tools

3

"You can't manage what you can't measure."

U<small>NKNOWN</small>

High-performance testing and diagnostic instruments are essential for professional maintenance of high-availability data networks. These tools enable network managers to observe network operating states at all times, and are indispensable for localizing problem domains and performing detailed analyses. These instruments are divided into two basic categories: those for use in analyzing the physical layer (OSI Layer 1), and those used on higher protocol layers (OSI Layers 2 through 7). Among the most important parameters of the physical layer are line characteristics, such as cable length, resistance, attenuation, crosstalk, reflections caused by connectors and terminating resistors, and electromagnetic interference from external sources. The devices for measuring these characteristics include multimeters, cable testers, optical time-domain reflectometers (OTDRs), oscilloscopes, signal level meters and spectrum analyzers. Processes on OSI Layers 2 through 7 are monitored and analyzed using protocol analyzers. There are a variety of protocol analyzers: universal devices with special modules for different tasks, small hand-held devices, and software solutions installed in high-performance network nodes. Application performance is measured using software agents that simulate network use by typical applications to determine throughput and other characteristics.

In addition to the classification of diagnostic tools by OSI layer, a distinction can also be made between tactical and strategic testing systems. Strategic systems are installed permanently to monitor, evaluate and record the vital statistics of a given segment 24 hours a day, 365 days a year, and are usually configured to send alarm messages when certain thresholds are exceeded. Tactical testing devices are mobile systems that are installed when problems occur or during a network audit, and are removed once the problem has been solved or the audit completed. Today, both tactical and strategic testing systems are available for all OSI layers. Strategic systems on the physical layer are used primarily for constant monitoring of a network's main optical links. On the higher OSI layers, strategic monitoring is performed using SNMP-based network management systems, which can be implemented either as distributed test systems using LAN or WAN probes or as distributed software agents.

A combination of both tactical and strategic test instruments is usually the best solution in network management. Strategic systems are used primarily for operations monitoring and planning; tactical devices for direct problem-solving tasks.

3.1   Tactical Test Systems

Tactical test systems can be either mobile hardware systems or temporarily active software applications. They are generally used for preventive analyses, to monitor the network operating state at critical moments (during the installation of components or power supplies, for example), in diagnostics and problem handling.

3.1.1   Tactical Test Systems for Physical Parameters (OSI Layer 1) in Local-Area Networks

Cable testers and multimeters are usually sufficient to measure the physical characteristics of data communication, including cable length, resistance, attenuation, reflections, and crosstalk in copper twisted-pair cabling. In rare cases, an oscilloscope or a spectrum analyzer may be required to determine the signal shape or frequency spectrum.

Multimeters

A multimeter is adequate for measuring physical layer characteristics. More than one network problem has been diagnosed simply by measuring the resistance or voltage on the network. Multimeters are always useful for narrowing down possible error sources. Detailed descriptions of measurement procedures are contained in later chapters.

Cable Testers for Copper

A wide variety of cable testers have been developed for testing copper cable in local-area networks. Which parameters must be measured depends on the exact type of cable under test. Tests can include length, attenuation, resistance, crosstalk, reflections and noise. Some instruments can also be used to locate cables: the cable tester inserts a specific sequence of audio signals into the cable, and a small auxiliary device that functions as an audio amplifier is used to hear the signal at a distance of up to 30 or 40 centimeters from the cable. This method can be used to trace the cable routing under floors or behind partitions. An

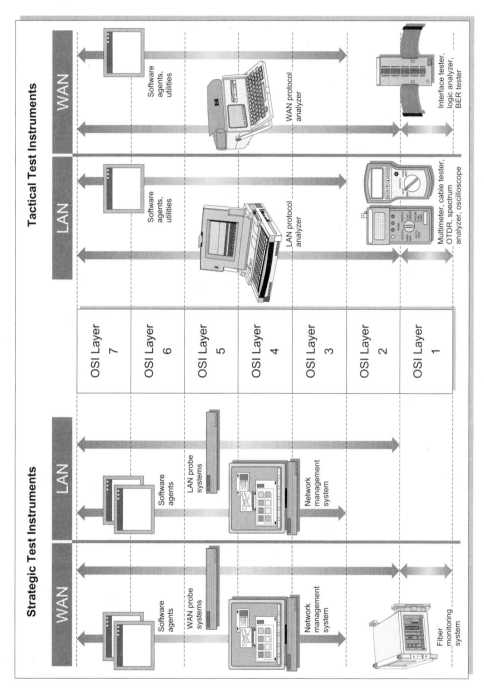

Figure 3.1 Test instruments and their uses in network management

auxiliary signal generator can also be used to test pin assignments and detect wiring faults, such as broken cables, short circuits or reversed pairs.

It is important that the cable tester operates in the required frequency range because certain parameters, such as crosstalk or attenuation, are directly dependent upon signal frequency. For example, a frequency range of 1 to 100 MHz is required to test cables used for high-speed data transmission technologies, such as Fast Ethernet or ATM. The TSB 67 specification (Telecommunications Systems Bulletin 67, Sept. 1995) describes measuring methods and precision requirements for testing data cable. Two levels of precision are defined: Levels I and II. Level II testers are more precise than Level I testers. Any cable tester in the higher price ranges should conform to TSB 67 Level II. For occasional troubleshooting, however, a TSB 67 Level I device is sufficient.

Parameter	Level 1 (100 MHz)	Level 2 (100 MHz)
Residual NEXT	40 dB	55 dB
Random Noise Floor	50 dB	65 dB
Output Signal Balance	27 dB	37 dB
Common Mode Rejection	27 dB	37 dB
Dynamic Accuracy	± 1 dB	± 0.75 dB
Return Loss	15 dB	15 dB

Figure 3.2 Precision requirements in TSB 67 Levels I and II

In addition to twisted pair, testers have also been developed for the coaxial cables used in 10Base2 and 10Base5 Ethernet networks. Because these network topologies are becoming less common, however, coax testers are disappearing from the market. Testing fiber-optic cable requires special testing devices that operate on the principle of optical time-domain reflectometry.

Optical Time-Domain Reflectometers (OTDRs)

Until recently, OTDRs were used primarily in wide-area networks. With the increasingly widespread use of multimode and single-mode fiber-optic cable in local-area networks, however, these instruments are now essential for installation, maintenance and troubleshooting in LANs as well. OTDRs are used to test the transmission characteristics of fiber links. The OTDR inserts defined light pulses into the cable under test and records both the reflected signals and the time elapsed since the outbound signal was transmitted. From the signals received, the OTDR calculates an attenuation profile, the response time and the signal propagation speed in the fiber under test. This profile indicates sources of attenuation (such as splices, connectors, cables) with their exact locations. The

Function	Manufacturer:	Manufacturer:	Manufacturer:
TSB-67 Level 1 or Level 2 conformance			
Serial port for connection to computer			
Auto-test function (automatic sequence of most common tests)			
Memory for test results			
Crosstalk (NEXT)			
Attenuation			
Noise			
Wire map/pin assignment			
Cable length			
Impedance			
Capacitance			
Guarantee, service, hotline			
Cable finder			
Price			

Figure 3.3 Checklist for cable testers

Portable OTDRs: Function	Manufacturer:	Manufacturer:	Manufacturer:
PC interface			
PC analysis software			
1310/1550 nm single-mode sensitivity			
800/1300 nm multimode sensitivity			
Memory for test results			
Connectors (ST, SC, etc.)			
Price			

Figure 3.4 Checklist for portable OTDRs

main criteria to consider when choosing an OTDR include both general operating functions (intuitive user interface, PC interface, analysis software, etc.), and the availability of single-mode and multimode modules to support the appropriate fiber types and light wavelengths. Because cables tend to be considerably shorter in local-area networks than in wide-area networks, the sensitivity of the ODTR is not as important in LAN testing as it is in testing WAN cables.

Oscilloscopes

Oscilloscopes are not often required in troubleshooting data and telecommunication networks, but in certain difficult error situations they can be indispensable. For example, a particularly high bit-error rate (BER) may be caused by any of a number of faults, ranging from a defective output stage in the transmitting station, to noise or jitter that occurs when an electric motor on the same power circuit is turned on, to signals in parallel communication lines. The only way to localize such problems is by analyzing signals with an oscilloscope.

Oscilloscopes detect and display signal voltage timing. This permits the analysis of signal characteristics, such as level, rise time and decay time, as well as frequency, noise and jitter. If the tolerance limits defined in the relevant specifications are exceeded the BER may increase, which in turn can lead to considerable transmission problems. The applicable data communications and telecommunications standards provide pulse masks and eye diagrams to simplify con-

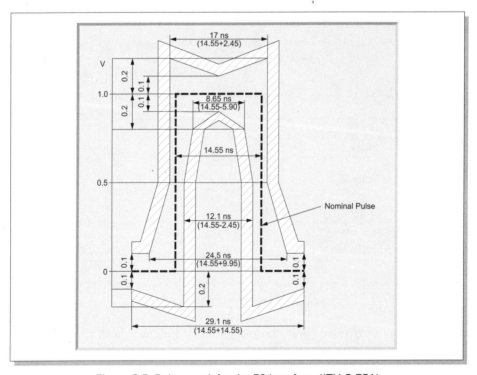

Figure 3.5 Pulse mask for the E3 interface (ITU G.751)

formance testing. The actual signal is compared to the pulse mask using an isolated signal pulse. A pulse is considered isolated if it precedes and follows at least two logical 0 states.

Eye diagrams, by contrast, are compared with the overlapping high and low signal pulses displayed by triggering the oscilloscope continuously at the clock rate of the signal stream. The eye diagram delineates a range of values—the tolerance limits—in the middle of two overlapped pulses. Today's high-performance oscilloscopes come with software libraries of the pulse masks and eye diagrams defined within the principal telecommunications standards. Furthermore, every violation of the threshold values is automatically counted to simplify long-term tests.

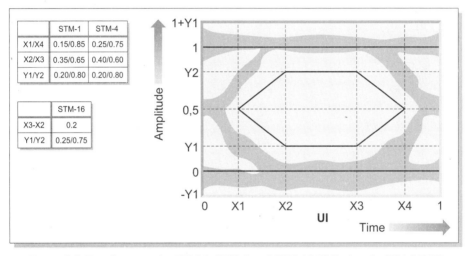

	STM-1	STM-4
X1/X4	0.15/0.85	0.25/0.75
X2/X3	0.35/0.65	0.40/0.60
Y1/Y2	0.20/0.80	0.20/0.80

	STM-16
X3-X2	0.2
Y1/Y2	0.25/0.75

Figure 3.6 Eye diagrams for STM 1, STM 4 and STM 16 SDH signals (ITU G.707)

Many signals encountered in data networks are differential signals and must be converted into signals referenced to ground potential before an oscilloscope can measure them. The adapters used for this purpose must have the same impedance as the transmission medium under test (75Ω, 100Ω, 120Ω, etc.). In order to measure signals on fiber-optic media with an oscilloscope, an opto-electric converter is also required.

When using a digital oscilloscope, it is important to make sure its sampling rate is fast enough for the signal under test. According to Nyquist, if the signal has a frequency f, then a sampling rate of $2f$ is required. For example, a 4 kHz signal must be sampled at a rate of 8,000 per second—in other words, at 8 kHz. Figure 3.7 lists the most common LAN technologies together with their frequencies and the required sample rates. It is important to keep in mind that the transmission frequency measured on the medium is not necessarily equal to the data rate. Depending on the coding, the transmission frequency may be higher than the data rate (as in Manchester coding, for example) or significantly lower (as in CAP64 coding). Furthermore, in low-quality, twisted-pair cable, data is distributed over three or four wire pairs, which means a further reduction in the actual signal frequency on the physical medium.

Communication technology	Data rate	Communication medium	Number of fibers/ wire pairs	Encoding	Transmission frequency	Digital oscilloscope sampling rate
FDDI	100 Mbit/s	fiber optic	2	4B5B	125 MHz	250 Msamples/s
CDDI	100 Mbit/s	twisted pair	4	MLT-3	31.25 MHz	62.5 Msamples/s
100Base-T	100 Mbit/s	twisted pair	4	8B/6T	25 MHz	50 Msamples/s
10Base-T	10 Mbit/s	twisted pair	2	Manchester	20 MHz	40 Msamples/s
ATM	155 Mbit/s	twisted pair	2	CAP-64	25 MHz	50 Msamples/s
ATM	155 Mbit/s	multimode	2	8 B10 B	194.4 MHz	388 Msamples/s
ATM	155 Mbit/s	plastic fiber	2	NRZ	155.520 MHz	311 Msamples/s
ATM	155 Mbit/s fiber	single-mode	2	Scrambled	155.520 MHz	311 Msamples/s
ATM	622 Mbit/s fiber	single-mode	2	Scrambled	622.080 MHz	1.24 Gsamples/s
ATM	2.4 Gbit/s fiber	single-mode	2	Scrambled	2.488320 GHz	4.9 Gsamples/s
ATM	9.9 Gbit/s fiber	single-mode	2	Scrambled	9.953280 GHz	19.9 Gsamples/s

Figure 3.7 Transmission technologies, transmission frequencies and sampling rates in local-area networks

Oscilloscope Function	Manufacturer: _____	Manufacturer: _____	Manufacturer: _____
PC interface			
PC analysis software			
Sampling rate (digital oscilloscopes only)			
Datcom/telecom masks (pulse masks, eye graphs)			
Memory for test results			
Adapters for differential signals and impedances (120, 100, 75)			
Opto-electric converter			
Price			

Figure 3.8 Checklist for oscilloscopes

Spectrum Analyzers

Spectrum analyzers are important for identifying sources of electromagnetic interference (EMI), which can cause significant problems in copper cables. The amount of EMI that a network is exposed to depends in part on the other types of equipment operated in the vicinity. Environments with a high incidence of EMI include production facilities where electric motors, welding facilities or elevators are in use, and hospitals where X-ray devices and intensive-care equipment are operated. If there is no obvious source of EMI nearby, the first step in troubleshooting EMI problems is to determine the frequency spectrum of the interference using a spectrum analyzer. Unlike oscilloscopes, which chart the signal amplitude over time, spectrum analyzers display the distribution of signal amplitudes over a frequency band. Thus a spectrum analyzer can be used to determine the strength and frequency of external EMI. To detect the interference signals that are potentially detrimental at today's high data speeds, a device with a bandwidth of 1 GHz is sufficient.

3.1.2 Tactical Test Systems for Physical Parameters (OSI Layer 1) in Wide-Area Networks

Detailed measurements of physical transmission characteristics are even more important in wide-area networks than in local-area networks because the likelihood of physical problems increases as cable lengths increase. Standard testing devices include interface testers and bit-error-rate testers. Logic analyzers, oscilloscopes or spectrum analyzers are sometimes required as well to obtain information leading to the source of transmission problems. Special line testing instruments are available for WAN links, including OTDRs for fiber-optic links and signal level meters for copper.

Interface Testers (Break-Out Boxes)

Interface testers display the activity on individual signal lines. They are often used to perform quick checks on interface operating states at the first signs of trouble. In addition to red and green LED indicators, most interface testers also have a built-in wiring block that can be used to modify the wiring of individual signal lines. Interface testers have high impedance inputs so that the signal is not influenced by measurement and testing can be performed during network operation.

Figure 3.9 Interface tester

Bit-Error-Rate Testers

In addition to a universal interface tester, a bit-error-rate (BER) tester also forms part of the basic equipment required for maintenance and operation of wide-area networks. Almost all fault testing on the physical layer concerns BER values in one way or another. To determine the bit-error rate, the tester inserts signals into the network that are looped back and evaluated upon return. The test signals are pseudorandom binary sequences (PRS) in cycles of 2^9-1 to $2^{23}-1$ bits, periodically repeating bit sequences, or text blocks. ITU Recommendations G.821 and G.826 (or V.53) define the following characteristics for evaluating the bit-error rate of a given segment. A high-quality BER tester can evaluate and display all of these characteristics:

- Bit-error rate
- Block-error rate
- Error-free seconds (EFS)
- Errored seconds (ES)
- Severely errored seconds (SES)
- Available time
- Unavailable time

The results are usually presented either as numerical values or in the form of bar graphs.

Some higher-layer protocol analyzers also have built-in BER testing functions. Whether it is preferable to have a separate BER tester available depends on how often such testing is required. In any case, it is important to keep in mind that BER testing is performed over long periods of time—days or even weeks—during which no other functions of the test instrument are available.

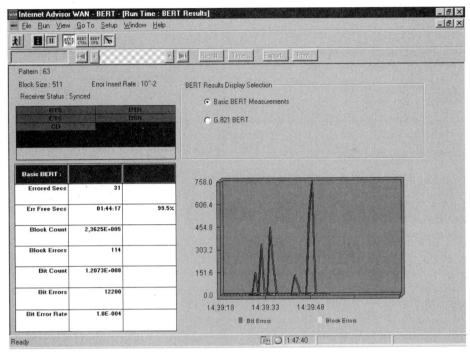

Figure 3.10 Example of bit-error-rate measurement

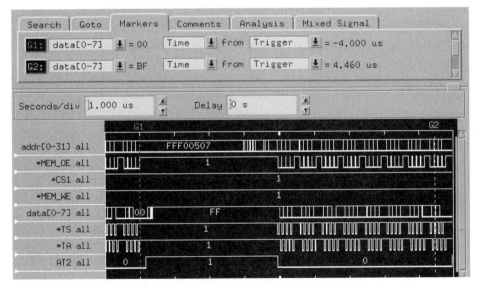

Figure 3.11 Measurements with a logic analyzer

Logic Analyzers

Logic analyzers are used to record signal timing. These devices are similar to oscilloscopes in that they record the signal voltage level over time, but logic analyzers are optimized for testing digital signals. A number of signal lines can be monitored simultaneously and the signal levels recorded in parallel. In this way, the exact timing of signals on different lines can be observed. Furthermore, certain combinations of signal states on the lines under test can trigger the device. This feature is useful for recording specific, one-time events (see Figure 3.11).

Signal Level Meters and Line Testers

Signal level meters are used to investigate communication problems in analog networks. Unlike BER testers, which require the line to be taken out of operation for testing, signal level meters can be used during network operation. These tools are used to monitor the network when it is first put into operation, during routine checks, and in troubleshooting WAN links. The characteristics that can be measured include operational attenuation, insertion loss, attenuation due to reflection, and crosstalk. A distinction is made between broadband and selective signal level meters. Broadband signal level meters determine the effective value of a signal within a broad frequency band without having to match the meter frequency to the signal frequency. These measurements can be performed quickly and easily, but cannot be used to measure signals below a certain strength. Selective signal level meters, by contrast, record only signals that are within the selected bandwidth: 100 Hz, 400 Hz, 1 kHz, 2 kHz, 3.1 kHz, etc. This allows measurement of very low-level signals and interference frequencies that are within or outside a given transmission band.

Many of the transmission parameters that are important in wide-area networks are frequency-dependent. The devices used to measure these parameters must be operated at the appropriate frequencies. These measurements include group delay time and attenuation distortion tests, for example. Measurement over a range of frequencies is called sweeping. Instruments with this capability are known as sweeping line test instruments.

Oscilloscopes and Spectrum Analyzers

In difficult cases, when detailed analysis of signal shapes or signal frequencies is required, oscilloscopes and spectrum analyzers are also used in wide-area networks. The technical considerations and selection criteria are the same as those described previously for Layer 1 LAN test instruments.

Optical Time-Domain Reflectometers(OTDRs)

Today's wide-area networks are increasingly fiber-based, which is why OTDRs are among the most important tools for network maintenance and troubleshooting. Unlike local-area networks, wide-area networks can have fiber-optic cables of up to 100 km and longer that must be tested. Thus it is essential that the ODTR have a wide range of sensitivity (such as 40 dB) to permit measurement of even the weakest reflections. As noted previously for Layer 1 testing in LANs, other important criteria in selecting an ODTR include an intuitive user interface, a PC interface and modules for both single-mode and multimode testing.

3.1.3 Tactical Test Systems for OSI Layers 2–7

Protocol Analyzers

Protocol analyzers are a key component in network troubleshooting. These instruments not only analyze protocol packets, but also produce statistical analyses of data traffic. A protocol analyzer can also be used to generate specific network traffic for test purposes. Furthermore, many protocol analyzers can record defective packets and packet fragments, which point to sources of network errors. Protocol analyzers are available in a variety of models and price classes. The simplest systems consist of software installed in standard PCs that are equipped with the appropriate LAN and/or WAN interfaces. More powerful protocol analyzers combine specialized hardware with high-performance analytical software that is often based on an expert system. The best type of analyzer to use depends on the size, complexity and topology of the network in question.

Software-Based Analyzers

The variety of software-based protocol analyzers on the market ranges from freeware and shareware programs—some of which are surprisingly powerful—to more complex professional software. Software-based protocol analyzers are especially well suited for use in small networks based on traditional topologies, such as 10/100 Mbit/s Ethernet and 4 or 16 Mbit/s Token Ring in local-area networks, and 64 or 256 Kbit/s in WANs. The software is ready to use as soon as it is installed on a network PC or notebook with the required interfaces. In LANs, especially, it is important to use high-performance interface adapters and fast PC systems. Standard LAN adapters are designed to recognize only their own address in data packets, not to receive all packets in the transmission stream. When the number of packets received exceeds a certain limit, the interface begins dropping packets. A fast PC is required because the system CPU must perform the analysis of all data packets, as well as filtering and triggering functions, in real time. When using a software-based protocol analyzer in a network of the newest generation, a network adapter with a PCI bus is required in order to obtain meaningful results. Furthermore, the adapter's receive and transmit buffers should be ample—4 Kbytes for the receive buffer and 2 Kbytes for the transmit buffer, for example. The higher performance of adapters with direct memory access (DMA) makes them preferable to those that use shared memory for communication with the computer. Another prerequisite for the interface card used for protocol analysis is support for "promiscuous mode" so that the card can process not just broadcasts and packets with its own address, but everything that is transmitted over the LAN. Not all network cards support this mode. For a list of the cards that are known to support promiscuous mode, see *www.networktroubleshooting.com*, for example.

If the network adapter in question has an NDIS version 4.0 or later driver, however, even cards that do not support promiscuous mode directly can be used for network analysis. By configuring a filter to deactivate the Local Only bit in the driver, the card will forward all data on the network to the analysis software.

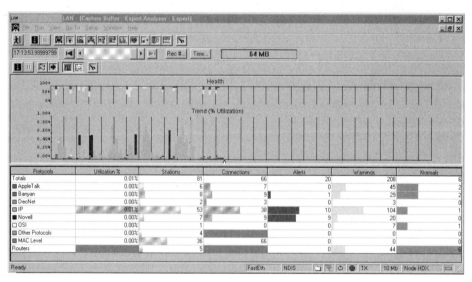

Figure 3.12 Software-based protocol analyzer

Hardware-Based Analyzers

Hardware-based analysis systems are considerably more powerful than software analyzers, but more expensive as well. These systems are based on specially developed hardware platforms, and can analyze and record 100 percent of network traffic with great precision. They can also generate network loads for test purposes, whether in a traditional network topology with relatively low throughput, or in high-speed networks such as 100 Mbit/s Ethernet, Gigabit Ethernet and ATM. Hardware-based filtering ensures the desired filtering conditions regardless of network load, while a high-resolution internal clock provides a time stamp. The receive buffers, which may vary in size from 8 to 64 Mbytes or

Function	Manufacturer: _____	Manufacturer: _____	Manufacturer: _____
Support for the required data interfaces (LAN/WAN): 10/100/1000 Mbit/s Ethernet 4/16 Mbit/s Token Ring FDDI ATM (155 Mbit/s, 622 Mbit/s, 2.4 Gbit/s) WAN V interfaces up to 2 Mbit/s WAN E1/T1 WAN E3/T3 ISDN (S_O, S_{2M})			
High-resolution time base (100 ns)			
Hardware performance – Packet loss at a certain load – Hardware filters – Software filters			
Receive buffer size			
Support for expert systems			
Support for all relevant LAN/WAN protocols			
Complete OSI Layer 2 statistics			
Complete OSI Layer 3 statistics			
Standard equipment (hard disk drive, display, PCMCIA slots, etc.)			
Remote control			
SNMP agent capability for integration in network management systems			
Analysis of RMON-MIBs, SMON-MIBs, Switch Vendor MIBs			

Figure 3.13 Checklist for hardware-based protocol analyzers

more, are constructed using special high-speed memory chips so that data coming in at high rates is recorded reliably, even in the heavy traffic typically carried over enterprise backbones. Most devices today are equipped with both LAN and WAN interfaces, so that the distinction between LAN and WAN analyzers is becoming irrelevant.

A strong trend is the increasing use of software applications based on expert systems. An expert system compares the network problems that occur with information in its knowledge base. If an error scenario is found in the database that matches the situation at hand, the system suggests possible diagnoses and troubleshooting tips. Some systems also support dual port measurements, which permit performance testing on components such as routers and bridges.

Multiprotocol PC

In addition to a protocol analyzer, it is often very useful to have a multiprotocol PC available for network diagnostics. A multiprotocol PC is simply a portable PC with one or more interface adapters, as needed, and all the network operating systems used in the network. For example, it might be equipped with a 10/100 Mbit/s Ethernet adapter and a Token-Ring adapter, along with an assortment of protocol stacks (NetWare, TCP/IP, etc.). A simple LAN monitoring program completes the equipment required for a multiprotocol PC.

Once a mobile PC has been prepared and configured, a model network node is available that is known to be fully functional. This can preclude the necessity of checking software configurations or re-installing programs in workstations "just in case". All of the settings and options in the multiprotocol PC are known in detail. By temporarily installing the multiprotocol PC in place of the station where error symptoms have been discovered, the problem can be immediately attributed either to the station itself or to the network.

3.2   Strategic Test Systems

Unlike tactical systems, strategic testing systems are deployed around the clock to monitor and manage data communications infrastructures. As a rule, these systems consist of distributed hardware and software components that communicate data to a central network management station by means of a defined communication protocol. Two standards, Remote Monitoring Management Information Base (RMON MIB) and the Simple Network Management Protocol (SNMP), have emerged to define both the format in which network data is stored and the communication protocol between the monitoring components and the central management station.

3.2.1 SNMP and Management Information Bases (MIBs)

Since its introduction in 1988, the Simple Network Management Protocol has become the de facto industry standard for network management. SNMP is based on two components, a manager and agents. The SNMP manager functions as a console for monitoring and controlling all of the network components that have SNMP agents installed. SNMP agents integrated in the network devices act as an interface between the components' network functions and the SNMP protocol. In other words, these agents translate SNMP management commands into corresponding actions in the network components. For this purpose, standardized objects are defined for network components. These objects are organized in a virtual database known as the Management Information Base. Both the format and the contents of the MIB are standardized (see RFC 1213 for definitions). In spite of the fact that SNMP-v2 (RFC 1213) split MIB II into several MIB modules (SNMPv2-MIB, IP-MIB, TCP-MIB, UDP-MIB), the MIB-II grouping is still in widespread use:

system:	Information about network nodes (location, service, contact addresses for administration)
interfaces:	Number and types of interfaces
at:	Address translation group. This group has been deleted from the MIB-II specification because every network protocol group must now have two address translation tables
ip:	IP implementation and parameters
icmp:	ICMP implementation and parameters
tcp:	TCP implementation and parameters
udp:	UDP implementation and parameters
egp:	EGP implementation and parameters
transmission:	Designation and parameters of the transmission medium
snmp:	SNMP implementation and parameters

Not every SNMP agent must have all of these MIB groups, however. The SNMP protocol defines four commands for accessing individual MIB objects:

Get	Retrieve management information contained in a specific MIB object
Get Next	Retrieve all management information contained in the entire MIB

Set	Modify MIB variables
Trap	Report an event

A free version of SNMP software that can be compiled for a number of operating system platforms is available from Carnegie Mellon University. The software is available, together with a comprehensive MIB collection, at their Web site location:

http://www.net.cmu.edu/groups/netdev/agentx/

The objects in the MIB I and II specifications serve mainly to control and monitor individual network components, not to monitor or analyze traffic. Other remote-monitoring (RMON) MIB groups, known as RMON1 MIB and RMON2 MIB, have been defined for monitoring overall network operation. RMON 1 (RFC 1757) defines nine MIB groups for OSI Layer 2 analysis in Ethernet networks. A tenth RMON 1 group was added later (RFC 1513) for Token-Ring topologies:

Statistics (1):	List of typical Ethernet statistics (multicasts, fragments, collisions, etc.)
History (2):	Storage of Ethernet statistics over a defined period
Alarm (3):	Definition of alarm thresholds and trigger events
Hosts (4):	Collection of statistics sorted by network host
Host TopN (5):	List of top n hosts, sorted by selected criteria (for example, "Top 5 talkers")
Matrix (6):	Record of communication relationships between network nodes (connection matrix)
Filter (7):	Filtering of data packets by selected criteria
Capture (8):	Recording of data packets for later analysis
Event (9):	Definition of actions that can be triggered by parameters in other MIB groups.
Token Ring (10):	Statistics and trends in MAC layer performance, number and status of active ring stations, etc.

Unlike RMON 1, RMON 2 defines MIB objects for the analysis and evaluation of OSI Layer 3 activities in the network, which means it can monitor all LAN and WAN data communication infrastructures regardless of topology. The following MIB groups are defined for RMON 2 (RFC 2021):

Protocol directory (11):   Directory of the protocols supported

Protocol distribution (12):   Network traffic (packet and byte counts) sorted by protocol

Address mapping (13):   Network addresses mapped to MAC addresses

Network-layer host (14):   Number of packets sent and sorted by host

Network-layer matrix (15):   Connection matrix for network protocols

Application-layer host (16):   Statistics on application protocols (TCP, UDP, FTP, HTTP, etc.) sorted by host

Application-layer matrix (17): Connection matrix for application protocols

User history (18):   Long-term monitoring of RMON 1 group history and alarms

Probe configuration (19):   Standardized configuration parameters for RMON probe systems

RMON conformance (20):   Implementation requirements for RMON conformance

Expanded RMON specifications for switched networks (SMON, RFC 2613), for highly utilized switch ports (Interface TopN Reporting), and for determination of the IP quality of service parameters (Differentiated Services Statistics Collection Monitoring) have been approved or are being worked on by the IETF RMON MIB Working Group (*http://www.ietf.org/html.charters/rmonmib-charter.html*). Some of these still are in draft status, while others are now RFC (Request for Comments).

3.2.2   RMON (Remote Monitoring) Systems

RMON agents for network monitoring can be implemented as standalone systems, called probes, or as optional equipment integrated in network components such as switches and routers. RMON probes are available for use in LAN and WAN topologies. Because a probe has dedicated hardware, it can monitor and record network statistics reliably at much higher traffic loads than software agents installed in existing network components. In addition, most LAN or WAN probes can be used in designing a monitoring infrastructure that is independent of the operating state in the network under observation. This means that an out-of-band connection, such as a modem link, is used as an alternative to the network transmission path between the probe and the management station. This alternative path is automatically activated when the primary communication link is not available.

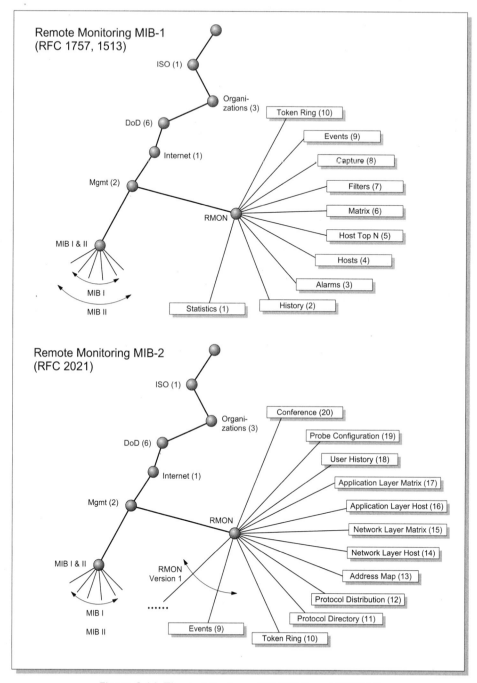

Figure 3.14 The architecture of RMON 1 and RMON 2

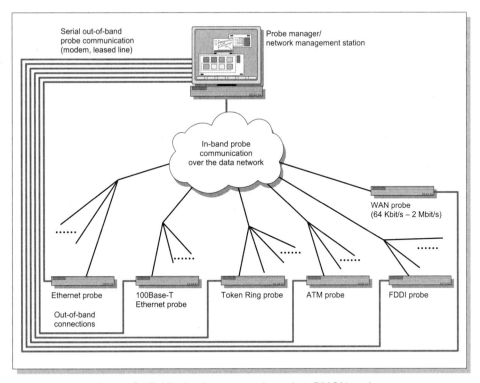

Figure 3.15 Monitoring system based on RMON probes

- Support for all RMON 1 groups
- Support for all RMON 2 groups
- Sufficient local memory (16 – 64 Mbytes)
- Guaranteed packet processing rate in RMON 1 / RMON 2 mode, depending on packet size and number of active filters
- Topology support (Ethernet 10/100, Token Ring, FDDI, ATM, WAN)
- Integration in existing network management system
- Correlation of data from different segments
- Generation of long-term statistics
- Extensive analysis and decoding functions

Figure 3.16 Criteria for selection of a RMON probe system

RMON probes are especially practical in communication infrastructures of critical strategic importance, such as enterprise backbones. Important criteria for selecting a probe system include complete support for both RMON 1 and 2 objects, sufficient local memory (4 to 128 Mbytes, depending on network topology), and the most powerful hardware available, especially in high-speed topologies such as FDDI, 100 Mbit/s Ethernet or ATM. Manufacturers often neglect to mention the threshold beyond which packets can no longer be processed in RMON 1 or 2 mode, and these thresholds vary widely.

When selecting a network management application for the analysis of RMON information it is important to make sure that it presents all RMON parameters in a readable format, and that functions are available for exporting data (in Common Separated Value format, for example). Furthermore, it should be possible to integrate the monitoring program, at least partially, into existing network management systems.

When switches or routers with built-in RMON agents are installed, the switch or router manufacturer should be asked to provide detailed information about the hardware performance and the exact RMON groups implemented. Inadequate hardware may mean that RMON functions are automatically deactivated under certain circumstances, especially during periods of particularly heavy network traffic when network components are operating near the limit of their capabilities. From the point of view of network planning and maintenance, however, it is precisely such high-traffic periods that are most important to monitor. Furthermore, some RMON implementations include only a small subset of the RMON groups, so care must be taken to obtain the most complete RMON 1 and 2 implementation possible.

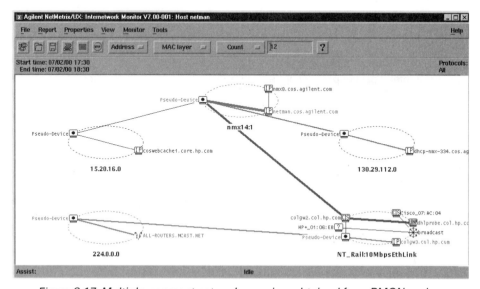

Figure 3.17 Multiple-segment network overview obtained from RMON probes

3.2.3 Strategic Systems Based on Software Agents

In addition to RMON-based systems, there are a number of proprietary software applications for network management. Some of these collect statistics other than those monitored by RMON MIBs. These can include the principal application-specific parameters often specified in service level agreements, such as the response times for accessing databases, Web servers or Internet connections. This monitoring is performed using application test packets exchanged between software agents installed in both the client and server or via agents capable of directly monitoring application transactions. The response time statistics thus gathered can be used to monitor the parameters defined in SLAs (see Figure 3.18).

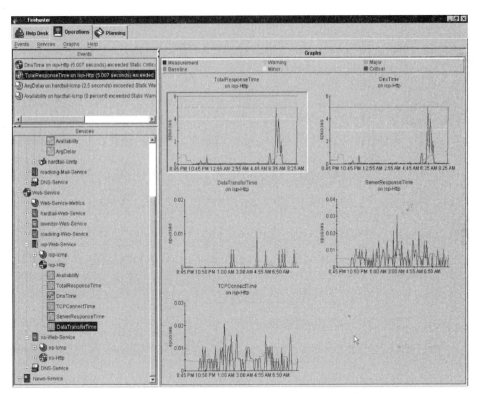

Figure 3.18 Data collected by a software-based SLA monitoring system (Agilent Firehunter)

3.2.4 Network Management Systems

Aside from the specialized troubleshooting and performance management tools described previously, a strategic network management system is part of the basic equipment for network operation. Such a system encompasses all network management activities and furnishes a large volume of data concerning the activities and status of the individual network components. This data provides a foundation for systematic procedures in data network maintenance.

The SNMP communication protocol, SNMP agents and MIBs comprise the basis of most distributed network management systems. These tools allow network managers to monitor the activities and modify the configurations of all network components equipped with SNMP agents. The features in today's network management systems go far beyond these basic functions to support additional integrated features, such as line management, security management, accounting, software management, user management and operations management.

Fundamentals of Testing in Wide-Area Networks

4

"Failure to prepare is preparing to fail."

BENJAMIN FRANKLIN

4.1   Basic Concepts

Before we begin discussing test methods and parameters for data networks, it may be helpful to recall the relationships between data rate, signal encoding and frequency bandwidth, as well as a variety of basic data communications technologies.

Data streams can be transmitted as analog or digital signals. Analog signals transport data using the amplitude modulation, frequency modulation or phase modulation of sine-shaped carrier waves (the broadband principle). Digital signals represent data as a sequence of voltage states or light pulses (the

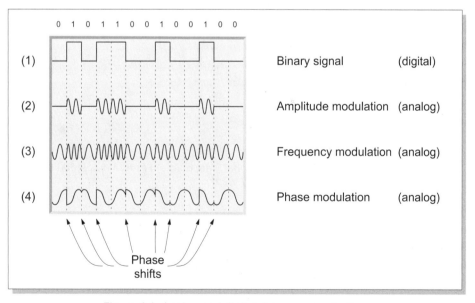

Figure 4.1 Analog and digital data communications

baseband principle). The number of analog or digital signal changes per second is called the baud rate. The number of binary information units transmitted per second is the bit rate.

The distinction between baud rate and bit rate is important because the two values are only equal if every signal change represents exactly 1 bit. If several different signal levels or phase states are used to represent data, then one signal change can represent 2 or more bits of information. For example, if four different potentials are used rather than two, then each change of level (that is, each baud) can represent 2 bits of information. In analog communication, phase modulation can be used instead of amplitude modulation to increase the bit rate per baud. If the system distinguishes among eight different phase states, then each baud can contain 3 bits of information. If every signal change is coded as a combination of phase and amplitude modulation (as in Quadrature Amplitude Modulation or QAM), then the amount of information per baud can be increased still further. Common QAM signals encode 16, 64, 128 or 256 bits per baud.

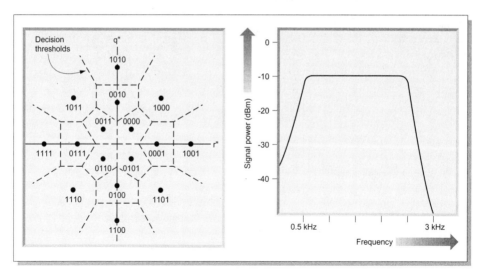

Figure 4.2 Frequency spectrum and signal state diagram for QAM at 9,600 bit/s (ITU V.29)

4.1.1   Capacity of Data Lines

According to Nyquist, the maximum number of changes in signal state per second—that is, the maximum baud rate—that can be transmitted in a limited frequency band is:

$$\textit{theoretical max. baud rate} = 2H \cdot log_2 V$$

where H is the available transmission bandwidth and V is the number of voltage levels or phase states used in the signal encoding. If the signal is coded into just two different voltage levels (corresponding to 0 and 1), then $\log_2 2$ yields 1, so that the maximum baud rate is found to be twice the transmission bandwidth. This means that a frequency band of 3 kHz can carry a maximum of 6 kbaud. More efficient encoding schemes can be used, however, to attain a bit rate significantly higher than the maximum baud rate. Still, the laws of physics set certain limits. The noise level present on any electrical data line requires a certain minimum interval between two adjacent signal levels in order for each of them to be distinguishable. The actual maximum data rate over a given line is limited by the signal-to-noise ratio (SNR), which is expressed in decibels as follows:

$$SNR = 10 \cdot \log_{10} S/N$$

Shannon calculates the maximum bit rate of a noisy channel, regardless of the encoding, as:

$$maximum\ data\ rate\ in\ bit/s = H \cdot \log_2(1+SNR)$$

where H once again is the bandwidth in Hz and SNR is the signal-to-noise ratio. Thus a typical telephone line with a bandwidth limited to H = 3,000 Hz and a signal-to-noise ratio of 30 dB can never carry more than 30,000 bit/s.

4.1.2　Analog Data Communications (Broadband Systems)

In analog communication, data is coded onto a carrier frequency by modems using amplitude, frequency or phase modulation, or a combination of these techniques. Systems that work on this principle are known as broadband systems. Unlike baseband systems, which transmit digital signals directly without a carrier, broadband systems are able to transmit data streams over long distances (30 km or more). Furthermore, they are often designed to provide several channels in several frequency bands. The disadvantage is that broadband systems require expensive transmitter and receiver components and are substantially more difficult to maintain than baseband systems.

When data streams are transmitted over analog public telephone networks, as they have been for decades, a distinction is made between the transmission of low bit rates over the narrow-band voice telephony channel, in the frequency band from 300 Hz to 3,400 Hz, and the transmission of higher bit rates over broadband analog channels with a bandwidth of 48 kHz. Strictly speaking, only the latter are broadband systems because the ITU defines "broadband" as

ITU modem standard	Modulation type	Carrier frequency	Line type	Baud rate	Bit rate	Synchronous/ Asynchronous
V.21	Frequency modulation	Upper channel 1080 Hz Lower channel 1750 Hz	Two-wire line, full duplex	300	50 bit/s – 300 bit/s	both
V.22	(Phase modulation) DPSK	Upper channel 1200 Hz Lower channel 2400 Hz	Two-wire line, full duplex	600	1,200 bit/s	both
V.23	Frequency modulation	Upper channel 1300 Hz Lower channel 1700 Hz	Two-wire line, half duplex	600	600 bit/s	both
V.23	Frequency modulation	Upper channel 1300 Hz Lower channel 2100 Hz	Two-wire line, half duplex	1200	1,200 bit/s	both
V.26	(Phase modulation) DPSK	1800 Hz	Four-wire line, full duplex	1200	2,400 bit/s	synchronous
V.26 bis	(Phase modulation) DPSK (2, 4 stage)	1800 Hz	Four-wire line, full duplex	1200	2,400 bit/s 1,200 bit/s	synchronous
V.26 ter	(Phase modulation) DPSK (2, 4 stage)	1800 Hz	Four-wire line, full duplex	1200	2,400 bit/s 1,200 bit/s	both
V.27	(Phase modulation) DPSK (8 stage)	1800 Hz	Four-wire line, full duplex	1600	4,800 bit/s	synchronous
V.27 bis	(Phase modulation) DPSK (4, 8 stage)	1800 Hz	Four-wire line, full duplex	1200/1600	2,400 bit/s 4,800 bit/s	synchronous
V.27 ter	(Phase modulation) DPSK (4, 8 stage)	1800 Hz	Two-wire line, half-duplex	1200/1600	2,400 bit/s 4,800 bit/s	synchronous
V.29	QAM (4, 16 stage)	1700 Hz	Four-wire line, full duplex	2400	9,600 bit/s	synchronous
V.29	(Phase modulation) (4, 8 stage)	1700 Hz	Four-wire line, full duplex	2400	4,800 bit/s 7,200 bit/s	synchronous
V.32	QAM (4, 16, 32 stage with trellis coding)	1800 Hz	Two-wire line, full duplex	2400	4,800 bit/s 9,600 bit/s	synchronous
V.32 bis	QAM (64, 128 stage with trellis coding)	1800 Hz	Two-wire line, full duplex	2400	12,000 bit/s 14,400 bit/s	synchronous
V.33	QAM (64, 128 stage with trellis coding)	1800 Hz	Four-wire line, full duplex	2400	4,800/7,200/9,600/ 12,000/14,400 bit/s	synchronous
V.34	QAM (1664, 4D trellis coding)	1959 Hz	Two-wire line	3429	33,600 bit/s	synchronous
V.90	Upstream: V.34 QAM Downstream: digital transmission (PCM)	Upstream: 1959 Hz Downstream: N/A	Two-wire line, digital telephone network required	3429	56,000 bit/s	synchronous

Figure 4.3 Data communications by modem over analog telephone networks

ITU modem standard	Modulation type	Carrier frequency	Signal bandwidth	Bit rate
V.35	Partial-response encoding	100 kHz	24/28 kHz	48/56 Kbit/s
V.36	Partial-response encoding	100 kHz	24/28/32/36 kHz	48/56/64/72 Kbit/s
V.37	Partial-response encoding	100 kHz	24/28/32/36/42 kHz	48/56/64/72/80 Kbit/s

ITU broadband analog data communication standards

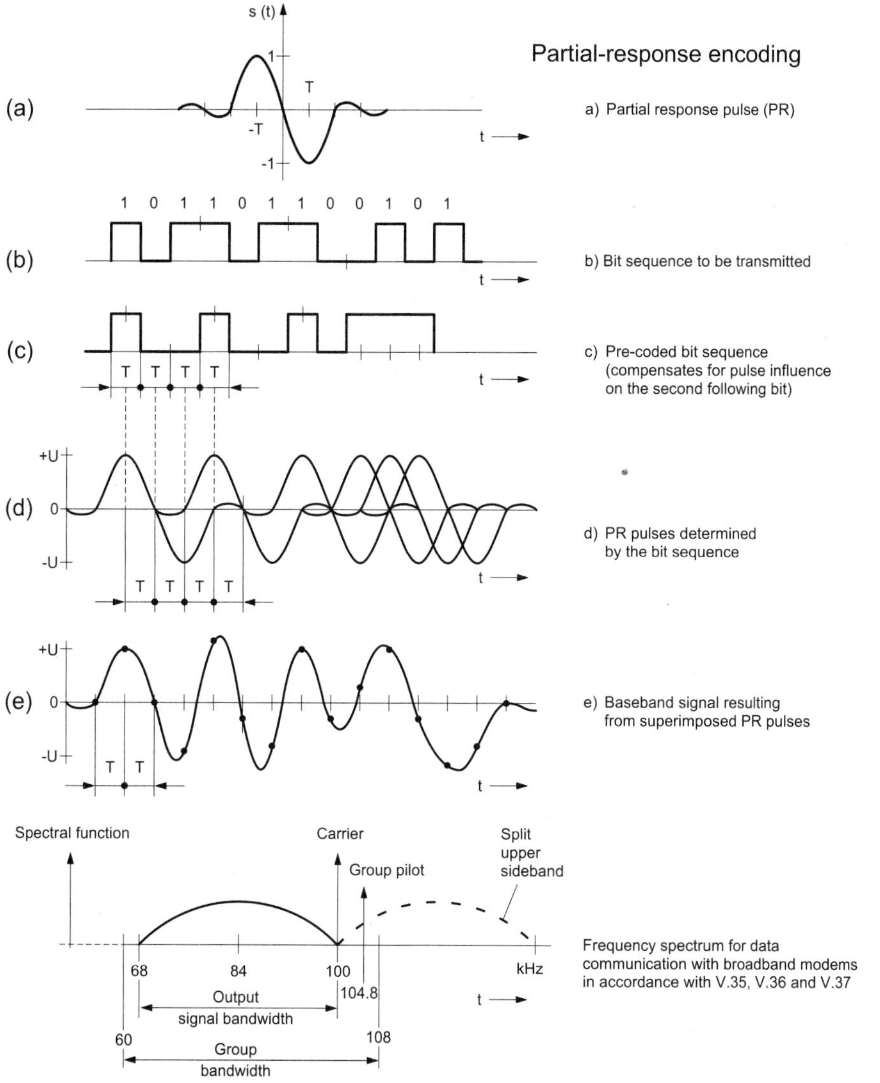

Partial-response encoding
s (t)
1
-1
T
-T
t
(a)
a) Partial response pulse (PR)
1 0 1 1 0 1 1 0 0 1 0 1
(b)
b) Bit sequence to be transmitted
(c)
c) Pre-coded bit sequence (compensates for pulse influence on the second following bit)
(d)
+U
0
-U
d) PR pulses determined by the bit sequence
(e)
e) Baseband signal resulting from superimposed PR pulses
Spectral function
Carrier
Group pilot
Split upper sideband
68
84
100
104.8
kHz
Output signal bandwidth
60
108
Group bandwidth
Frequency spectrum for data communication with broadband modems in accordance with V.35, V.36 and V.37

Figure 4.4 Broadband analog data communication

referring to greater bandwidth than the 4 kHz telephony band. The principle of modulating a higher-frequency carrier signal to encode a digital signal stream is common to both types of analog communication, however. Originally, the 48 kHz frequency band was only used to transmit 12 analog telephony channels using frequency multiplexing; its use for data is a more recent development. The various modulation techniques and the corresponding bit rates for data communication over telephone networks (in the 4 and 48 kHz bands) are defined in the V series of ITU recommendations. Figures 4.3 and 4.4 list the bit rates, carrier frequencies and modulation techniques of the ITU V series standards.

The 56 Kbit/s defined in the V.90 standard represents the maximum bit rate that can be transmitted over the analog telephone network's 4 kHz voice band. In fact, even the 56 Kbit/s data rate cannot be attained in a classical, purely analog telephone network. A 56 Kbit/s data rate is only reached if the remote system (such as an Internet router) has a digital connection to the network, so that only the local loop (the "last mile") of the data connection is an analog telephone line, and even then the system can only receive at 56 Kbit/s. (In the transmitting direction, the QAM technique of V.34 is used, with a maximum data rate of 33,600 bit/s.) In V.90, the analog "last mile" is treated as a digital link: the data stream is pulse-encoded onto a carrier frequency with no analog modulation. Because most modern telephone lines can carry bandwidths of up to 1 MHz, however, the fact that V.90 uses far more than the 4 kHz voice band is not a problem.

Before digital data lines for telecommunication subscribers, other, wider frequency bands were made available to carry higher data rates than modems could transmit over the 4 kHz voice telephony band. Telecommunications operators used a frequency range based on a 100 kHz carrier signal with a signaling bandwidth of 48 kHz. A filter split off the upper side band of the resulting frequency spectrum so that the main frequency of the line signal was 84 kHz. Special broadband modems were used to modulate the data stream onto the 100 kHz carrier using Partial Response Encoding. This technique attained data rates between 48 and 144 Kbit/s. The ITU recommendations for broadband analog transmission of digital data streams are V.35, V.36 and V.37. Due to the widespread availability of various digital data communication methods (ISDN, xDSL, PDH, SDH) which permit significantly higher data rates, broadband analog communication is no longer a major issue.

4.1.3   Digital Data Communications (Baseband Systems)

Systems that feed the data stream into the transport medium directly, with no carrier signal, are known as baseband systems. The distances that can be

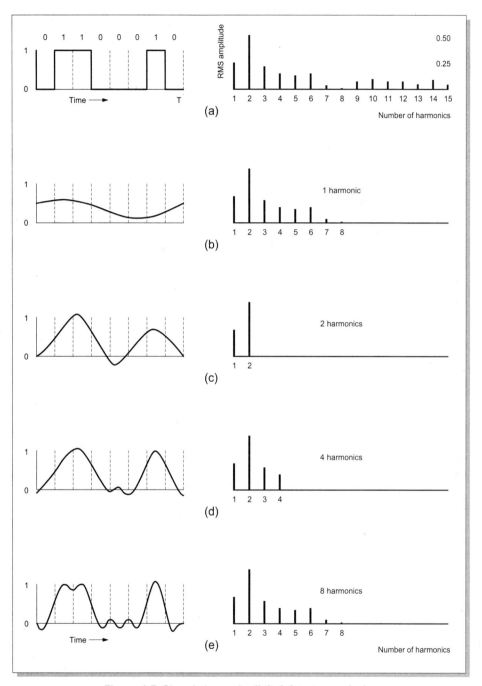

Figure 4.5 Signal shapes in digital data transmission

spanned in this way are shorter, and the line carries only a single data channel. The key advantage, however, is that the technology required is substantially simpler and cheaper than broadband. Another advantage is that digitized voice, image and audio signals can be transmitted as well as data, so that separate communications infrastructures are no longer required for different services. Due to the rapid development of digitizing technology and the declining costs of the necessary components, digital data communication has become the norm in wide-area networking. Even the classic analog telephone network is now largely transported over digital lines.

Signal Shapes in Digital Data Communications

When digital data streams are transmitted directly in the form of approximately right-angled voltage level changes, the actual signal is a frequency spectrum that consists of a theoretically infinite number of superimposed sine waves with the frequencies f (the fundamental frequency), 2f, 3f, ... nf (the nth harmonic frequency).

In order to be completely transmissible, digital signals with ideal, square wave-forms require an infinite frequency spectrum—even though the energy level of the nth harmonic approaches zero. The physical properties of the transmission media and the characteristics of transmitters and receivers limit the available bandwidth, so that in practice the frequency band for the digital signal stream is not unlimited. Yet a sufficient number of harmonics must be transmitted for the receiver to obtain a signal form that is an adequate approximation of the square waveform that the transmitter sent out (see Figure 4.5).

Line Encoding of Digital Data Streams

The efficiency of both analog and digital data transmission can be increased by means of error-correcting codes, such as polynomial encoding, Reed-Solomon encoding, etc. Unlike analog communication, however, digital data communica-tion requires the use of another type of code, called line encoding. The purpose of line encoding is to prevent a net DC current on the line by ensuring an even distribution of 0 and 1 states in the data stream and to keep the power density low in the lowest frequency spectra. The transmission equipment used in tele-communications networks is usually impervious to DC components. Further-more, clock synchronization with DC-unbalanced signal sequences, such as sequences of three or more successive 1 states, for example, is difficult. The most widely used line coding methods are:

Unipolar codes: either all signals are greater than 0 volts or all signals are less than 0 volts. Example: +1 volt = logical 0, +3 volts = logical 1.

Polar codes: signals are greater than and less than 0 volts. Example: +3 V = logical 1; –3 V = logical 0.

Bipolar codes: signals alternate among three levels.

Alternate Mark Inversion (AMI) codes: A change in polarity represents a logical 1.

Figure 4.6 shows the most commonly used types of line encoding techniques, along with the resulting frequency band shifts.

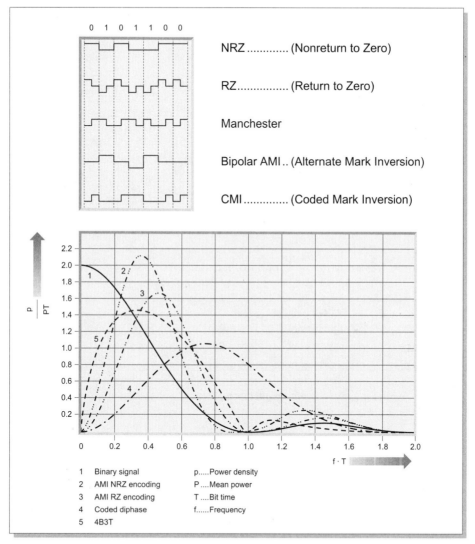

Figure 4.6 Line codes and their frequency shifts

Digital Data Communications Standards:
ITU-T X Series Recommendations, ISDN, PDH, SDH and xDSL

The ITU Recommendations for the digital transmission of data streams at rates of 50 bit/s to 64 Kbit/s are defined in the X series of recommendations. The specifications adopted in 1984 for the Integrated Services Digital Network (ISDN) with data rates of up to 2 Mbit/s are found in the ITU series I recommendations (I.120–I.451).

ITU modem standard	Communication technique	User class	Bits per second
X.20, X.20 bis	asynchronous	1	300
X.20, X.20 bis	asynchronous	2	50 – 200
X.21	synchronous	3	600
X.21	synchronous	4	2,400
X.21	synchronous	5	4,800
X.21	synchronous	6	9,600
X.21	synchronous	7	48,000
X.21	synchronous	19	64,000
X.21, X.32	synchronous	8	2,400
X.21, X.32	synchronous	9	4,800
X.21, X.32	synchronous	10	9,600
X.21, X.32	synchronous	11	48,000
X.21, X.32	synchronous	12	1,200
X.21, X.32	synchronous	8	2,400
X.28	asynchronous	20	50 – 300
X.28	asynchronous	20	50 – 300

Figure 4.7 ITU X series digital interfaces for public data networks

Both the X series interfaces and ISDN were originally conceived as digital interfaces for end subscribers. In 1972, a set of interfaces called the Plesiochronous Digital Hierarchy (PDH) was specified for multiplexed transmission of digital 64 Kbit/s user data streams over telecom operators' backbone networks. These standards permit efficient transmission of time-multiplexed data streams in a hierarchy of throughput rates from 1.5 to 140 Mbit/s. The bit rates are defined in ITU Recommendation G.702, and the physical and electrical properties of the interfaces in G.703. The bit rates in the various hierarchical levels are calculated as follows:

$$T(i+1) = m(Ti + x)$$

Hierarchical level	North America	Europe	Japan	Transatlantic
0	64	64	64	64
1	1,544	2,048	1,544	2,048
2	6,312	8,048	6,312	6,312
3	44,736	34,368	32,064	44,736
4	139,264	139,264	97,728	139,264

Figure 4.8 Bit rates in the Plesiochronous Digital Hierarchy (PDH)

where m and x are defined for each hierarchical level. Due to the continuously increasing demand for bandwidth in recent years, PDH interfaces are no longer limited to network operator backbones, but are also being used as subscriber interfaces (see Figure 4.8).

Multiplex element	Bit rate in Kbit/s	1,544	2,048	6,312	8,448	34,368	44,736	139,264	C-11	C-12	C-21	C-22	C-31	C-32	C-4	TU-11	TU-12	TU-21	TU-22	TUG-21	TUG-22	TU-31	TU-32	AU-31	AU-32	AU-4	STM-1
		Digital signals G.702							Multiplex element																		
C-11	1,600	x																									
C-12	2,176		x																								
C-21	6,784			x																							
C-22	9,088				x																						
C-31	36,864					x														x	x						
C-32	48,384						x													x							
C-4	149,760							x												x	x	x	x				
TU-11	1,728								x																		
TU-12	2,304									x																	
TU-21	6,912										x																
TU-22	9,216											x															
TUG-21	6,912															x	x	x									
TUG-22	9,216															x	x		x								
TU-31	37,440												x														
TU-32	49,152													x													
AU-31	37,440												x														
AU-32	50,304													x													
AU-4	150,912														x												
STM-1	155,520																							x	x	x	
STM-4	622,080																										x
STM-16	2,488,320																										x
STM-64	9,953,280																										x

Figure 4.9 SDH bit rates and multiplex elements

Although PDH networks have continued to evolve over the past thirty years, certain features are no longer ideally suited to today's data communication requirements. For example, to obtain a given primary-rate channel of 139,264 Mbit/s out of a PDH top-level bit stream, all the intermediate levels of the hierarchy have to be demultiplexed. If the given channel needs to be transported further in a different 139,264 Mbit/s stream, then that stream must be re-multiplexed through all the intermediate hierarchical levels as well. This makes the system inflexible and expensive. Furthermore, the various PDH high-speed links are connected by manual cross-connects that only permit limited monitoring and control of the old PDH frame structure. To overcome these problems, a new, international standard for digital data transmission was adopted in 1988: the Synchronous Digital Hierarchy (ITU G.707) or SDH (SONET in North America). The main advantage of SONET/SDH over the older PDH structures lies in its use of a transparent multiplexing method. This means that a 64 Kbit/s channel can be directly read out of or inserted into the highest SONET/SDH multiplex level (currently 9.95 Gbit/s). This capability is also called single-stage multiplexing. Moreover, the SONET/SDH frame overhead supports modern, highly automatic switching and network management systems (see Figure 4.9).

In order to achieve adequate digital data rates for today's application requirements over the existing telephone cabling infrastructure, a number of standards were developed in the 1990s that are known collectively as xDSL (Digital Subscriber Line). Until then, modem data communications over telephone lines

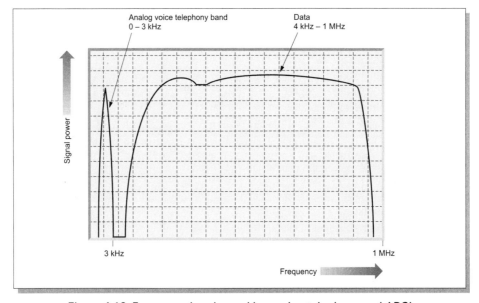

Figure 4.10 Frequency bands used by analog telephony and ADSL

used only the 3 kHz analog telephony band although most of the telephone lines in place today are able to carry frequencies of up to 1 MHz. The xDSL technologies take advantage of this fact and obtain throughput of up to 50 Mbit/s (see Figure 4.10).

DSL technology originated after ISDN had first produced digital data communication over the analog telephone network's cable plant. The 160 Kbit/s data rates obtained by two B channels and one D channel are no longer sufficient today to transport modern multimedia applications. Five new communications standards have been developed for different application scenarios: ADSL, HDSL, RADSL and VDSL.

ADSL (Asymmetric Digital Subscriber Line) provides an interface with unequal transmitting and receiving bandwidths. The uplink bandwidth can be from 64 to 384 Kbit/s, and the downlink bandwidth from 1.544 to 6 Mbit/s. ADSL is mainly used for high-speed access to the Internet because WWW surfing calls for high downlink but low uplink bandwidth.

HDSL (High-Speed Digital Subscriber Line) is a symmetrical interface with throughput of 128 Kbit/s to 1.544 Mbit/s in both directions. Potential applications include video-conferencing or Web server connections.

RADSL (Rate-Adaptive Digital Subscriber Line) is a variation on ADSL that is able to vary the available bandwidth depending on the line quality. The uplink rates are up to 1.544 Mbit/s, downlink bandwidth can be as high as 6.1 Mbit/s.

SDSL (Symmetrical Digital Subscriber Line) is a single-pair version of HDSL.

VDSL (Very High-Speed Digital Subscriber Line) provides uplink rates from 1.6 to 2.3 Mbit/s and downlink rates of up to 51 Mbit/s.

	ADSL	HDSL	RDSL	VDSL	SDSL	ISDN (S_0)
Download bit rate	1.544 Mbit/s – 6 Mbit/s	128 Kbit/s – 1.544 Mbit/s	up to 6.1 Mbit/s	up to 51 Mbit/s	128 Kbit/s – 1.544 Mbit/s	160 Kbit/s
Upload bit rate	64 Kbit/s – 384 Kbit/s	128 Kbit/s – 1.544 Mbit/s	up to 1.544 Mbit/s	1.6 Mbit/s – 2.3 Mbit/s	128 Kbit/s – 1.544 Mbit/s	160 Kbit/s
Encoding	CAP, DMT	CAP, 2B1Q	DMT	CAP	CAP	2B1Q
Standard	ANSI T1.413					ITU I.120 – I.451

Figure 4.11 xDSL technologies and standards

The xDSL technologies achieve their high data rates by using the full physical transmission bandwidth of 1 MHz in conjunction with efficient encoding schemes, such as CAP and DMT. ISDN, an older standard, uses the simpler multilevel code 2B1Q (two binary, one quaternary), in which each pair of bits is encoded as one of the four signal levels −3, −1, +1, +3. By contrast, xDSL uses the two encoding techniques that come closest to the theoretical maximum line capacity determined by the Shannon limit: Carrierless Amplitude/Phase (CAP) modulation and Discrete Multi-Tone (DMT) modulation. CAP is based on the same principle as QAM, but generates the phase/amplitude modulated signals not by means of mixed sine and cosine carriers, but by using two digital band pass filters whose frequency response differs by pp/2. DMT, however, divides the available frequency band into n subcarriers, and transmits bits over each channel in the form of phase/amplitude modulated signal tones. In this way it works as n parallel QAM systems, with each QAM system using the carrier frequency of one of the DMT subchannels (see Figure 4.12).

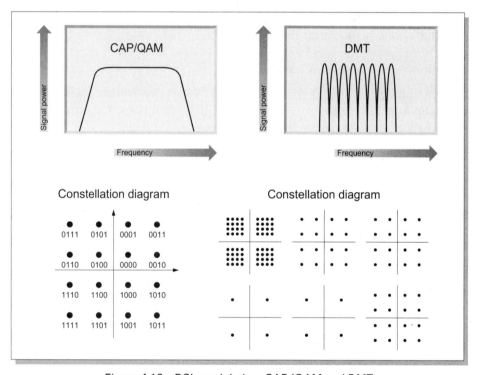

Figure 4.12 xDSL modulation: CAP/QAM and DMT

4.1.4   Data Communications over Fiber-Optic Links

In backbone links of both local- and wide-area networks, fiber-optic media have almost entirely replaced copper cable due to their greater throughput capacity.

Data is transmitted over optical fiber using optical signals with wavelengths just above those of visible light (visible light: 400–800 nm; fiber-optic signals: 850–1,550 nm). A pulse of light represents a logical 1; no light represents a logical 0. The entire band of wavelengths that can potentially be used for optical data communications ranges from ultraviolet to infrared, a bandwidth of 250 THz (terahertz). This is an indication of the enormous potential of fiber-optic media. It is expected that systems with bandwidths of up to 25 THz will be developed in the years to come.

Two basic techniques are conceivable for increasing throughput over fiber. One is the use of ever shorter light pulses. Commercially available systems today attain data rates of up to 9.9 Gbit/s in this way. By combining light pulses of different wavelengths, several parallel pulse streams can be sent over a single fiber. This technique, called wavelength division multiplexing (WDM), permits even higher throughput. Today, WDM systems are already able to transmit up to 64 light pulse streams at 2.4 Gbit/s each, for a total data rate of 153 Gbit/s per fiber.

Frequency Bands for Optical Data Communications

Data transmission over optical fiber uses three bands of light wavelengths, which are determined by the attenuation characteristics of the medium. These wavelengths are 850, 1,300 and 1,550 nm. The attenuation coefficients of both multimode and single-mode fiber-optic media have minima at exactly these wavelengths (Figure 4.13).

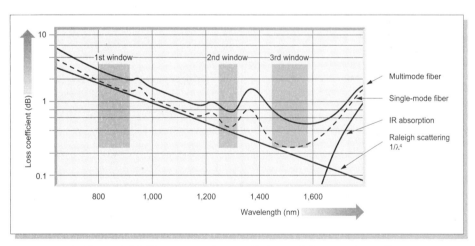

Figure 4.13 The attenuation coefficients of fiber-optic media

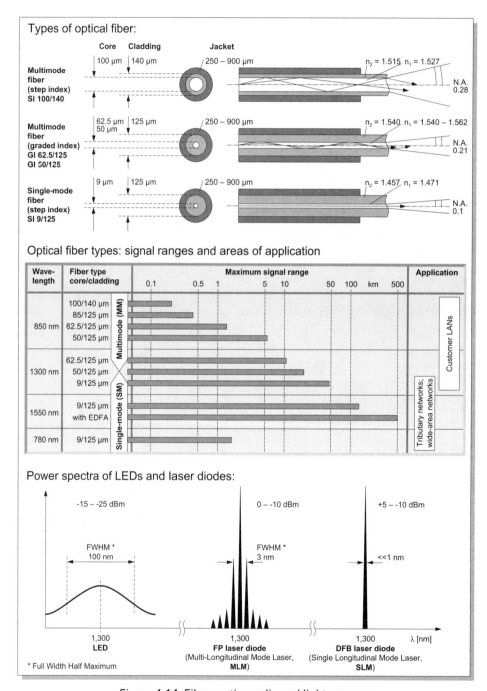

Figure 4.14 Fiber-optic media and light sources

Multimode and Single-Mode Fiber Optics

Each fiber-optic cable consists of an inner fiber, called the core, and an outer layer, called the cladding. Both of these are made of transparent glass or plastic, but have different refraction indices. (The refraction index of an optical medium is the ratio of the speed of light in a vacuum to the speed at which it travels in the given medium.) Step-index multimode fiber, for example, has an abrupt change in the index of refraction at the transition from core to cladding. Light rays in the core strike the cladding at different angles and are reflected at different angles. This increases the modal dispersion of the light signal with increasing distance so that a signal can only travel 200 m before regeneration. In multimode cables with a finely graded transition in the angle of refraction, the modal dispersion effect is reduced: signals can travel up to 10 km. Single-mode cables use an extremely small fiber diameter (7–9 mm) and a cladding with a precisely specified refraction index: only one wavelength can travel along the fiber with no reflection at all. Single-mode fiber requires expensive laser diode transmitters while multimode fibers can be operated using more economical LEDs. The narrower the bandwidth of the light source, the higher the ratio of bandwidth-to-bit rate that can be attained over a fiber-optic link. LEDs, for example, have a spectral bandwidth of some 100 nm, while Distributed Feed Back (DFB) laser diodes have a bandwidth of less than 1 nm.

4.1.5 Synchronous and Asynchronous Data Communications

In order for a data stream to be sent successfully from one point to another, the transmitter and the receiver must be synchronized with one another during the transmission. In asynchronous data communication, synchronization is achieved by means of start and stop bits before and after each symbol is transmitted. This principle is only suitable for low data rates, however, and is rarely used in wide-area communications today. The start and stop bit technique is typically used with data rates of 50 to 300 bits/s in applications such as teletype machines or telemetry exchange systems in public utilities. The advantage of the asynchronous principle is that synchronization must be maintained only for one symbol at a time. Clock rate tolerances are therefore greater than in modern synchronous communication. The drawback is that some 20 percent of the transmission time is taken up with start and stop bits that carry no user data. Today, asynchronous data communication is used primarily in computer peripheral interfaces such as printer connections.

In synchronous communication, entire streams of symbols are transmitted. Clock and symbol synchronization must therefore be carried out so that the receiver can distinguish first the individual bits and then the individual symbols. Clock synchronization is achieved either by the use of special data stream encoding (scrambling, coded diphase encoding, NRZ, etc.), which allows the receiver to derive clock information from the data stream itself, or by sending clock information over dedicated channels. Symbol synchronization is achieved in character-oriented control systems by sending a SYN character. In bit-oriented control techniques, bit sequences are used as starting and ending flags.

4.1.6   The Decibel

A number of testing and specification parameters in telecommunications are expressed in decibels. The decibel is especially well suited to express the relationship between two values that are on different orders of magnitude, as in measurements of signal attenuation, noise or reflection. Named after the inventor of the telephone, Alexander Graham Bell, the decibel—to put it in general terms—expresses a proportion between two electrical quantities and not an absolute value. These quantities may refer to power, current or potential. The proportion it expresses is not a linear ratio, but a logarithm. This makes it possible to use smaller numbers when comparing absolute values whose difference is great.

A decibel is defined as 10 times the base 10 logarithm of the ratio of input power to output power. The logarithm of a number is the exponent to which the base (10 in this case) must be raised to yield that number. For example, the logarithm to the base 10 of 2, or $\log_{10} 2$, is 0.301 because $10^{0.301} = 2$.

$$dB = 10 \log_{10} (P_1/P_2)$$

By this definition, a power drop of 3 dB indicates that the ratio of P_1 to P_2 is 2 to 1. (The inverse logarithm of 0.3 is 2.)

Because power $P = U \cdot I = U^2/R$ (substituting U/R for I), the ratio P_1/P_2 is equal to the square of the voltage ratio: $P_1/P_2 = U_1^2/U_2^2$.

Accordingly, 1 dB can also be defined as:

$$dB = 10 \log_{10} (U_1^2/U_2^2)$$

or

$$dB = 20 \log_{10} (U_1/U_2)$$

When a voltage ratio is expressed in decibels, a drop of 3 dB represents a ratio of input to output voltage of 1.41 to 1. (A 3 dB *power* loss, by contrast, corresponds to a 2:1 ratio of input power to output power). For this reason, the decibel value is meaningless unless the corresponding electrical quantity—power, voltage, current, etc.—is specified.

Decibels (dB)	Power Ratio
0	1:1
3	2:1
6	4:1
9	8:1
10	10:1
13	20:1
16	40:1
19	80:1
20	100:1
23	200:1
26	400:1
29	800:1
30	1,000:1
33	2,000:1
36	4,000:1
39	8,000:1
40	10,000:1

Figure 4.15 Power measurements in decibels

Another frequently used measurement parameter derived from the decibel is the absolute power level in dBm (read "decibels referenced to 1 milliwatt"), which is the decibel value of a power ratio where the reference power (P_2 in the previous definition) is 1 milliwatt. A power level of 1 watt can thus be expressed as 30 dBm:

Power level:	dBm:
1 W	30 dBm
10 mW	10 dBm
1 mW	0 dBm
1 μW	−30 dBm

4.2   In-Service Testing in Wide-Area Networks

In testing wide-area networks, a distinction is made between tests performed during network operation—in-service testing—and tests that require that the communication link be taken out of operation. Tests that can be performed without interrupting normal operation include: signal condition measurements, switching delay measurements, signal level and reflection measurements, protocol analysis and various statistical measurements. Which measurements need to be performed in detail depends on the type of data communication interface (analog or digital) and on the transport medium (twisted pair, coaxial, fiber optic). The test instruments may be connected in parallel with the data stream or inserted in series in the data stream by feeding the signals from the testing device's output port back into the network. When measurements are performed on electrical interfaces, a parallel connection is generally made using an Y adapter inserted in the link being tested. This requires interrupting the data line for a few seconds. To avoid data loss, the Y adapter should be inserted when little or no data traffic is expected. For measurements that are repeated at regular intervals, the Y adapter should be left in the line. The same applies when a test instrument is inserted in the line itself. The entire data stream then travels from the sending node to the test instrument's input port. The instrument evaluates and regenerates the signal, and forwards it to the receiving node.

Many wide-area components are equipped with special test ports and can be configured by system management to copy the data stream from any of their communication ports to the test port. This eliminates the need to interrupt the line, at least for simple protocol analysis. Signal level and shape measurements must be performed on the actual communication line, however.

When coaxial cables are tested, a bridging amplifier can be used to decouple the signal. A simple T connector must not be used because it would affect the impedance of the cable.

For data analysis on fiber-optic links, power splitters are used rather than Y cables. A power splitter is a passive component inserted into the link under test to create a branch output by splitting off a certain percentage of the signal power, depending upon the splitter type. This fraction of the signal is sufficient for decoding and analysis of the data stream. Here once again, though, the data link must be interrupted for a moment in order to insert the power splitter. An alternative is to use a clamp-on probe to detect the signal in the fiber without disconnecting it. To measure physical signal parameters, however, such as attenuation, the test instrument must be inserted directly in the line (see Figure 4.16).

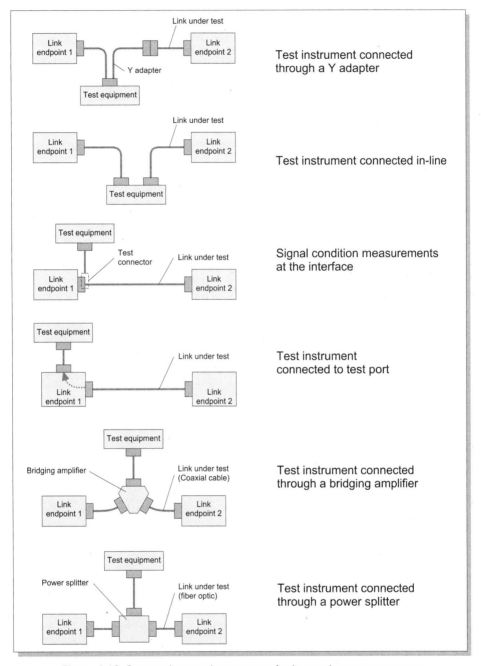

*Figure 4.16 Connecting test instruments for in-service measurements
on wide-area links*

4.2.1   Signal Condition Measurements

Signal condition tests are performed by measuring the signal shapes on the data and clock lines of the interface under test and comparing them with the parameters recommended in the relevant standards. Typical causes of diminished throughput can be identified in this way, such as insufficient voltage levels, sloping pulse flanks, signal jitter or bad timing on the control signals. These may be caused by electromagnetic interference, excessive cable attenuation, or faulty line termination. If electrical communication lines are not terminated with the correct impedance, reflections occur that deform subsequent signals.

Signal condition measurements require special interface testing devices with high-impedance inputs that are connected to the communication line by means of Y cable adapters. LEDs indicate voltage levels and signal conditions on the data lines. To determine the exact shape of the signal, an oscilloscope must be used.

4.2.2   Switching Delay Measurements

The correct timing of control signals is a prerequisite for error-free data communication. If certain signals, such as Request to Send (RTS) or Clear to Send (CTS), are not received within the specified time window, processes malfunction. Data analyzers can be used to quickly test the major signaling processes on various kinds of interfaces. Similar tests can be performed using logic analyzers, which provide more precise results but are more expensive to purchase and require more time to use.

4.2.3   Protocol Analysis and
Statistical Measurements

Many communication problems have their causes not in the physical layer, but in higher OSI layers. Higher-layer problems are diagnosed using protocol analyzers. These instruments can monitor, record and analyze data packet formats and protocol processes. Defective data packets (such as oversized packets, undersized packets, Cyclic Redundancy Check (CRC) errors, etc.) and protocol procedures (timeouts, incorrect window sizes, frequent retransmissions, etc.) are automatically tagged so that the error domain can be narrowed down quickly. Modern communication systems, such as SDH or ATM, also incorporate special protocols to carry information about the current operating status and errors (for example, OAM protocols, SDH overhead bytes, etc.). This information can also be evaluated using protocol analyzers. The protocol analyzer may be inserted in the data line or may be connected to the network by a passive, high-impedance input and a Y adapter.

In addition to decoding and analyzing data packets and protocol processes, one of the most valuable capabilities of a protocol analyzer is the generation of communication statistics. Often the analysis of various statistics yields enough information to identify the cause of a problem without a painstaking analysis of individual packets. Statistical parameters observed over a longer period in order to analyze problems typically include the "hit list" of the most active transmitting and receiving nodes; packet length distributions; link capacity use as a percentage and in kilobits per second; protocol distribution (such as the proportion of FTP, SMTP, HTTP, signaling packets, etc.); bad packet counts; retransmission counts; and response times.

4.3 Out-of-Service Testing in Wide-Area Networks

Tests that require shutting down a wide-area link include bit-error-rate measurements, distortion measurements, transport path measurements, conformance tests, and load tests. Tests of this sort are usually conducted as part of the final inspection of newly installed communication links, but sometimes operational links also have to be temporarily shut down for maintenance work. In this case the data has to be routed over an alternative path. In some cases, an out-of-service measurement can be made on an unused, reserve wire pair or fiber in the same cable with the line under test. In fiber-optic cables, for example, such indirect measurements actually can detect nearly 90 percent of the errors that occur.

4.3.1 Bit-Error-Rate Measurement

One of the most important tests in wide-area data networks is the measurement of the proportion of bits that are transmitted incorrectly: the bit-error rate (BER). Important clues to the cause of a malfunction are found not only in the absolute numbers of bit errors, but also in their distribution over time—whether sporadic, periodic, or bundled. The bit-error rate is calculated as the number of bits transmitted incorrectly divided by the total number of bits:

$$BER = \frac{f_B}{n_B} = \frac{f}{t_v}$$

f_B = *number of bits incorrectly transmitted*
n_B = *number of bits transmitted*
t = *measurement time*
  = *throughput*

Other conditions being constant, the measured bit-error rate approaches the bit-error probability as the measurement time increases:

$$BER = P_B \text{ for } t =$$

A distinction is made between short-term bit-error measurements (over a minute to an hour) and long-term measurements (over hours to several days). Short-term measurements make it possible to draw conclusions about the error structure, while long-term measurements can indicate correlations between the occurrence of bit errors and certain operational processes or environmental factors. ITU Recommendation V.53 lists tolerance limits for bit-error rates at different throughput levels in data communication over analog telephone networks. For BER tolerances in digital data communications, see G.821 and G.826.

To identify the characteristics of the occurrence of bit errors, the block-error rate (F_{BL}) is calculated. The block-error rate is important because it reflects the actual effects of bit errors on the operation of the communication link. For example, bit errors that occur in "bursts" may cause a high bit-error rate, while leaving the number of defective blocks and thus the number of data packet retransmissions relatively low. Conversely, fewer but widely distributed bit errors can cause a high block-error rate. The block-error rate is calculated using test blocks of different lengths (511–2,047 bits), depending on throughput (ITU V.52). The block-error rate is defined as the number of defective blocks divided by the total number of blocks:

$$F_{BL} = \frac{f_{BL}}{n_{BL}}$$

f_{BL} = *number of defective blocks*
n_{BL} = *number of blocks transmitted*

Another description for the communication quality of a line is the number of intervals without bit errors, called error-free intervals (EFI). The recommended measurement interval is 1 second for data rates up to 64 Kbit/s, and 0.1 or 0.01 seconds for higher throughput. If a bit error occurs in a given time interval, the interval is considered "errored". The probability of an Errored Second (ES) can be calculated as:

$$P_{ES} = P_B n_{BS}$$

Consequently, the probability that a 1 second interval is error-free is given by:

$$P_{EFS} = 1 - P_B n_{BS}$$

As an approximation, it is assumed that the mean time between bit errors is much larger than the interval of 1 second.

ITU Recommendations G.821 and G.826 describe guidelines for determining the quality of digital data communication links. G.821 deals with data rates up to 64 Kbit/s; higher rates are treated in G.826. These recommendations define the following error events: Errored Second (ES) and Severely Errored Second (SES), from which the corresponding test parameters Errored Second Ratio (ESR) and Severely Errored Second Ratio (SESR) are derived.

Errored Second (ES): a second during which one or more bit errors occur

Severely Errored Second (SRS): a second during which the bit-error rate exceeds 10^{-3}

$$ESR = \frac{ES}{t(s)}$$

$$SESR = \frac{SES}{t(s)}$$

The tolerance levels for the ESR and SESR in international ISDN lines and in local, metropolitan and wide-area data communication links, according to G.821 and G.826, are shown in Figure 4.17:

Line type (64 Kbit/s)		ESR	SESR
International ISDN lines		< 0.08	< 0.002
Local grade, (local grade + medium grade < 1,250 km)		< 0.012	< 0.00015
Medium grade, (local grade + medium grade < 1,250 km)		< 0.012	< 0.00015
Long grade, < 25,000 km		< 0.032	< 0.0004

The following tolerances for higher data rates are listed in G.826:

Line type (1.5 – 155 Mbit/s)		ESR	SESR
High grade, < 25,000 km	1.5 – 5 Mbits	< 0.024	< 0.0012
High grade, < 25,000 km	5 – 15 Mbits	< 0.03	< 0.0012
High grade, < 25,000 km	15 – 55 Mbits	< 0.045	< 0.0012
High grade, < 25,000 km	55 – 150 Mbits	< 0.096	< 0.0012

Figure 4.17 Tolerances for bit-error rates in digital data communication links (ITU G.821, G.826)

ITU Recommendation G.821 also defines the parameters:

- available time, and
- unavailable time

A period of unavailability begins when 10 severely errored seconds (with a bit-error rate of more than 10^{-3}) occur consecutively. A line is considered to be available again when the measured bit-error rate is better than 10^{-3} for 10 consecutive seconds.

As mentioned previously, the accuracy of bit-error-rate measurements depends on the duration or number of bit errors measured. For randomly distributed bit errors, the table in Figure 4.18 shows the confidence ranges for 70, 90 and 95 percent accuracy in bit-error-rate measurements. The likelihood that the actual bit-error probability is outside the range:

$$k_0 f_B > P_B > k_u f_B$$

is 70, 90 or 95 percent, as shown.

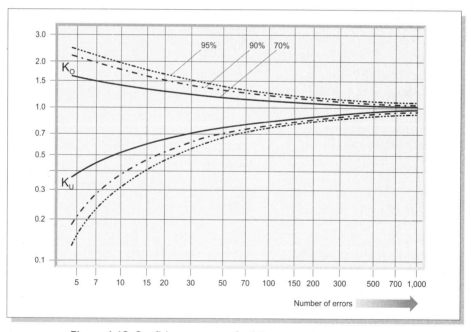

Figure 4.18 Confidence ranges for bit-error rate measurements

The bit sequences used to test bit-error rates are defined in the ITU Recommendations V.52, O.152, and O.151. These specifications distinguish between pseudorandom binary sequences (PRS), periodically repeating bit sequences and text blocks. The period of cyclical pseudorandom sequences depends on the throughput of the link under test. The corresponding ITU recommendations are listed in Table 4.19.

PRS	$2^9 - 1$	$2^{11} - 1$	$2^{15} - 1$	$2^{15} - 1$	$2^{23} - 1$	$2^{23} - 1$
Cycle length	511 bits	2,047 bits	32,767 bits		8,388,607 bits	
Data rate	9.6 Kbit/s	9.6 Kbit/s	2 Mbit/s	8.4 Mbit/s	34 Mbit/s	140 Mbit/s
f_T	9.6 kHz	64 kHz	2 MHz	8.4 MHz	34 MHz	140 MHz
T_z	53.2 ms	32 ms	16 ms	3.9 ms	244 ms	60 ms
ITU Recommendation	V.52	O.152	O.151		O.151	

Figure 4.19 ITU recommendations for PRS cycles

Repetitive bit sequences are used to detect systematic, pattern-dependent bit errors. In asynchronous data communication links, simple text blocks are used. The "quick brown fox" test is a common one, which consists of repeatedly sending the sequence:

THE QUICK BROWN FOX JUMPS OVER THE LAZY DOG 1234657890

and checking for errors in transmission.

Test Setup for Bit-Error-Rate Measurements

Bit-error rates can be measured using two different basic test setups. In the non-looping test setup, the bit-error tester consists of separate transmitter and receiver modules connected to the two ends of the communication link under test. Once the transmitter has begun sending the test sequences, the receiver performs its clock and pattern synchronization based on the incoming bit stream, and then the bit-error-rate test begins. In the loopback test setup, the transmitter and receiver modules are both at the same end of the link under test. At the far end, the transmission and reception lines are connected together, so that the test sequences immediately return through the loop to the receiver. Testing different loops can successively eliminate possible error sources. Loopback connections for bit-error rate measurements in telephone networks are listed in ITU Recommendation V.54, and for public data networks in X.150. Figure 4.20 shows a diagram of the test setup for bit-error rate measurements.

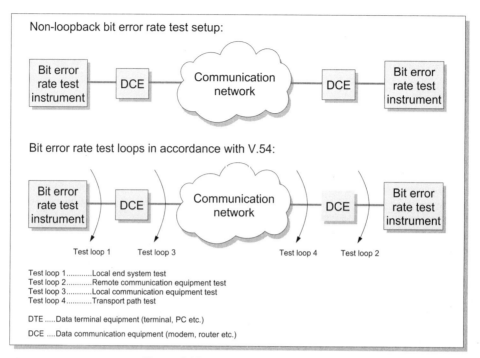

Figure 4.20 Bit-error-rate test setup

4.3.2   Signal Distortion Measurement

Signal distortion refers to a deviation from the nominal timing of a transition from one signal state to the next. Distinctions are made among various types of signal distortion; bias distortion, individual distortion, peak distortion and start-stop distortion. These parameters need to be measured only in analog data communication (see also ITU V.52, V.53 and V.57). As described previously, analog communication encodes the data stream by modulating a carrier frequency. Asymmetry in modulation or demodulation and interference over the communication link can cause the kinds of signal distortion listed. In baseband communication, however, the clock pulse can be regenerated from the line encoding so that no distortion occurs in the receiver.

In bias distortion, a signal state is consistently lengthened or shortened, while the opposite signal state is conversely shortened or lengthened. In the case of a 101010 sequence, for example, where T_1 is the duration of the logical 1 state and T_0 the duration of the logical 0 state, bias distortion is defined as:

$$\delta_e = \frac{T_1 - T_0}{T_1 + T_0} \cdot 100\%$$

Individual distortion, by contrast, is defined as the temporal deviation t from the nominal time, T_N:

$$\delta_{ind} = \frac{\Delta t}{T_N} \cdot 100\%$$

A sequence of alternating 0 and 1 bits is used as a test signal to measure both types of distortion. The difference between the greatest and least deviation from the nominal time T_N (individual distortion) is called the peak distortion $_P$:

$$\delta_P = \frac{\Delta t_{max} - \Delta t_{min}}{T_N} \cdot 100\%$$

In asynchronous communication systems, start-stop distortion is also measured. This refers to the maximum signal shift that occurs within a start bit–stop bit sequence:

$$\delta_{ST} = \frac{\Delta t_{max}}{T_N} \cdot 100\%$$

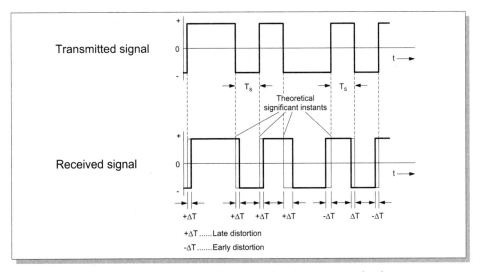

Figure 4.21 Signal distortion in analog data communication

4.3.3   Testing Electrical Communication Lines

In both analog and digital data communication the properties of the physical medium can deform signals during transmission. This deformation is composed of attenuation and phase shift. Ideally, the attenuation over a communication link is constant and the phase shift is proportional to the frequency. This is called distortion-free signal transmission. In reality, however, attenuation varies along the signal path, and phase shifts occur without relation to the signal frequency, distorting the signal shape. The quality of a communication path can thus be described in terms of the deviation of attenuation and phase shift from the ideal.

Line Testing in the Analog Telephone Network

In telephone networks, the overall loss and the related attenuation distortion of a communication link are specified for a frequency of 1,020 Hz. The tolerance for attenuation distortion in data connections over telephone networks is ±4 dB for long-term variance (ITU M.1020, M.1025).

Phase distortion in telephone networks corresponds to the variation in group delay (group delay distortion). This is not a major concern in subscriber lines, however.

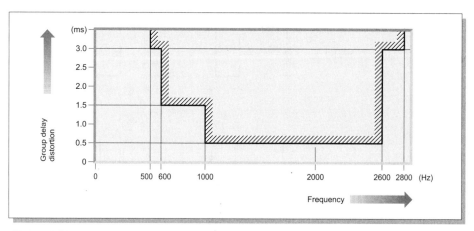

Figure 4.22 Tolerances for group delay distortion in the analog telephone network (ITU M.1020)

Line Testing in the Digital Data Network

In digital data communication the bandwidth of the signal data stream is significantly greater than in analog transmission over the telephone network. For this reason, line attenuation and not attenuation distortion is the decisive criterion for the transmission quality of a line. The line attenuation, and thus the maximum range of the data link, is dependent on the wire diameter of copper cable (0.4, 0.6, or 0.8 mm). The maximum range at a data rate of 64 Kbit/s is about 4 km for 0.4 mm copper cable and 10 km for 0.8 mm wire.

Due to the high bandwidth used by digitally transmitted data streams, the group delay distortion in baseband data systems is more critical than in telephone networks. High group delay distortion can lead to an overlap of adjacent signals, resulting in increased bit-error rates.

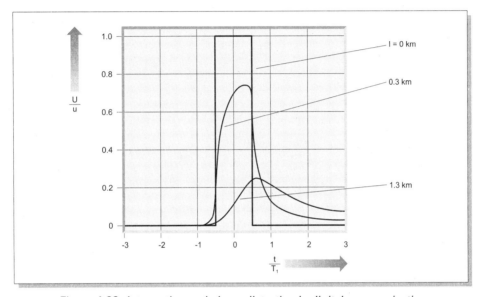

Figure 4.23 Attenuation and phase distortion in digital communication

Signal Reflection

In addition to attenuation and phase distortion, undesirable signal reflections due to inadequate line impedance can also cause communication errors. The reflected signal is superimposed on the user signal, causing increased bit-error rates. Impedance measurements can give an indication of the part played by reflection in the diminished communication quality of a data link.

4.3.4   Interference Measurements for Electrical Communication Lines

In addition to the physical properties of the signal path, external interference can also lead to malfunctions in the communication link. For electrical communication lines such interference may include:

- Crosstalk
- Noise
- Non-linear distortion
- Phase jitter
- Frequency shifts
- Line interruptions
- Pulse interference
- Phase jumps

Crosstalk

Crosstalk is one of the most common forms of external interference in electrical communication media. In parallel communication cables, the signals in one wire pair produce a capacitive and inductive coupling in an adjacent pair. As frequency increases, capacitive and inductive characteristics also increase so that the effects of crosstalk are greater at higher data speeds. If the induced signal is a locally produced signal with relatively high amplitude, it is called near-end crosstalk or NEXT. Signals sent by the system at the far end of the cable that appear as interference with relatively low amplitude are known as Far-End Crosstalk (FECT). To test for crosstalk, a test signal is sent over one wire pair while the signal induced in the other parallel conductors is measured. The magnitudes of NEXT and FECT are given in decibels.

Noise

The term "noise" refers to non-linear interference that has been induced in the communication path. Noise often consists of several components. The most important of these are thermal noise, intermodulation noise, crosstalk and quantizing noise. Thermal noise is mainly generated by the various active and passive components along the communication path. Crosstalk and intermodulation noise are the result of the non-linear transmission characteristics of modulators and amplifiers; quantizing noise arises through the quantization of the analog signals into discrete values when pulse-code modulation is used.

Non-Linear Distortion

Non-linear distortion, such as that generated by modulators and broadband amplifiers, is measured in terms of harmonic distortion. ITU M.1020 recommends tolerances of under 25 dB.

Phase Jitter

Phase jitter is characterized by constant phase variations in the data signal. Phase jitter alone seldom causes bit errors, but it can trigger errors in combination with other types of interference. ITU Recommendation M.1020 prescribes a maximum tolerance of 15 degrees in peak-to-peak phase shift for a 1,020 Hz test signal, with the permissible jitter frequency between 20 Hz and 300 Hz.

Frequency Shifts

When different carrier frequencies are used in modulating and in demodulating data streams, this is referred to as a frequency shift, and also results in deformation of the transmitted signal.

Interruptions

According to ITU M.1060, no line interruption with a duration between 3 ms and 1 minute may occur during a measurement period of 15 minutes. A line interruption is any sudden drop in the signal level of 10 dB or more. If such an interruption is measured, the test period is increased to 1 hour, during which no more than two interruptions are allowed. Typical causes of line interruptions include cold solder joints, short circuits, intermittent contact, and power outages.

Pulse Interference

Pulse interference is a relatively common phenomenon in data networks. Interference pulses can occur as isolated events or in bursts, and in sufficient amplitude they cause bit errors. Typical causes of pulse interference include electrical storms, rotary telephone dialing and electromechanical equipment (elevators, rail vehicles, etc.). The characteristics of an interference pulse are its amplitude and its duration. In ITU Recommendation M.1020, pulse interference is defined as beginning at –21 dBm. Such pulses must not occur more than 18 times in a 15 minute test period.

Phase Jumps

Phase jumps are sudden changes in the phase of a data signal. Causes of phase jumps include carrier frequency changes in radio links. According to ITU M.1060, no more than 10 phase jumps of over 15 degrees may be tolerated within a 15 minute period.

4.3.5   Measurements and Interference in Fiber-Optic Links

Signal transmission over fiber-optic media is much more reliable than over conventional copper cables. There are fewer potential malfunctions with fewer possible causes. Because interference cannot be introduced by inductive or capacitive coupling, errors arise only due to the following conditions in the fiber medium or the transmitter and receiver modules:

* Loss (attenuation) along the fiber
* Loss at splices
* Loss at connectors; impurities
* Aging
* Light power problems
* Line interruptions

Thus only three measurements are needed to determine the quality of a fiber-optic link: the signal power at the transmitter and receiver, the loss of signal amplitude in transmission, and reflections along the signal path. The signal power is measured using an optical power meter; attenuation and reflections are measured by means of an optical time-domain reflectometer.

4.3.6   Conformance and Interoperability Testing

A special topic of no small importance in data communications is conformance testing. Special systems are used to test terminal devices and network components for correct behavior in operation. Such testing is the only way to ensure that systems made by different manufacturers are compatible in actual practice, or "interoperable". Especially in public wide-area networks, conformance to national and international standards is extremely important. This is why legislation is passed to require testing and certification. In wide-area networks, conformance testing has become far more important than in local networks.

Abstract Test Suite (ATS), PICS and PIXIT

Conformance testing usually takes place as follows; the testing equipment first places the system being tested—the "implementation under test" or IUT—in a specific initial state. Then the testing equipment initiates a certain protocol event and evaluates the IUT's reaction. The result of each test case is logged and classified as:

* passed,
* failed, or
* inconclusive

The latter case can occur when the protocol processes being tested are complex and the conformance testing system cannot evaluate the IUT's response unambiguously. The test equipment operator must then evaluate the procedure manually. The set of all test cases for a given system is called a test suite. Abstract test suites (ATS) specify which events are initiated from which initial state for each test case. An ATS consists of a number of "test purposes" or procedures, which are generally specified in tree and tabular combined notation (TTCN). The implementation of an abstract test suite in a program that can be executed by a conformance testing system is called an executable test suite (ETS). Because the various protocol implementations often incorporate only a subset of the many functions included in a protocol specification, the appropriate test purposes for the IUT must be selected from the full test suite before the beginning of a test run. Configuring all parameters specific to a given protocol does this. The protocol parameters are defined in two specifications, called Protocol Implementation Conformance Statement (PICS) and Protocol Implementation Extra Information for Testing (PIXIT). The PICS describes the IUT's capabilities with respect to the protocol. The PIXIT contains parameter values necessary for communication between the tester and the IUT. In practice, the PICS, PIXIT and the entire test suite are implemented in the form of an executable program in the conformance testing system. The PICS and PIXIT values can be specified in input dialogs, and the program automatically selects and performs the corresponding test cases.

Interoperability Tests

Interoperability tests are performed to ensure that two or more systems are able to work together. Unlike conformance testing, interoperability testing focuses not on an abstract standard but on operation with respect to another actual implementation. Interoperability tests are thus relative tests, and do not necessarily test the entire scope of an implementation's capabilities, but only those functions that are necessary for interoperability. Because such tests require a great deal of expensive hardware, they are often performed at trade fairs or special test workshops organized by independent testing laboratories or universities. Interoperability test software is also available for a number of protocols. Such software packages generally consist of conformance tests with specific interoperability tests added. Two network components that pass such a test program are very likely to be interoperable.

Functional Tests

In private data networks it is often impossible to perform involved conformance and interoperability tests before deploying a component. Nonetheless, a short functional test of network components can be performed using protocol analyzers that are able to simulate the communication protocols in question. The protocol analyzer sets up connections to the component under test, monitors the connection setup processes, and analyzes the protocol processes if necessary. Then the test is performed in the opposite direction. The protocol analyzer emulates the appropriate communication protocol, behaving as either a network node or an end system.

4.3.7   Load Tests

Performance tests are especially important on network components that are to be used on the most exposed wide-area links. Because different products show widely varying performance capacities, it is a good idea to analyze the product's operating specifications before making a purchase. Not only are the individual technical specifications often inaccurate or imprecise, or not published at all, but manufacturers often list parameters that make their products appear in a favorable light, but which are not found in any comparable products. For these reasons, the IETF Benchmarking Working Group (IETF-BMWG)

http://www.ietf.org/html.charters/bmwg-charter.html

has drafted documents to establish a uniform terminology for measuring the performance of networking components, and thus to permit comparable performance measurements. These are:

- Terminology for Frame Relay Benchmarking (RFC Draft)
- Benchmarking Methodology for LAN Switching Devices (RFC 2889)
- Benchmarking Terminology for LAN Switching Devices (RFC 2285)
- Methodology for IP Multicast Benchmarking (RFC Draft)
- Terminology for IP Multicast Benchmarking (RFC 2432)
- Methodology for ATM Benchmarking (RFC Draft)
- Terminology for ATM ABR Benchmarking (RFC Draft)
- Terminology for ATM Benchmarking (RFC 2761)
- ATM Forum Performance Testing Specification (af-test-tm-0131.000.pdf)
- Benchmarking Terminology for Network Interconnection Devices (RFC 1242)
- Benchmarking Methodology for Network Interconnect Devices (RFC 2544)
- Benchmarking Terminology for Firewall Performance (RFC 2647)

The performance parameters explained and defined in these documents describe significant functions of wide-area network components. Before a product is put into operation, these parameters should be known and, if possible, verified by in-house tests.

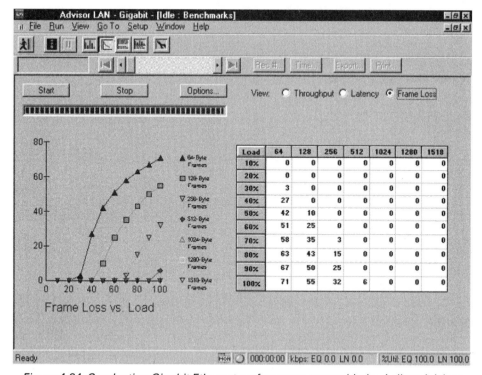

Figure 4.24 Conducting Gigabit Ethernet performance tests with the Agilent Advisor

Fundamentals of Testing in Local-Area Networks

5

"I don't have a solution, but I certainly admire the problem."

ASHLEIGH BRILLIANT

5.1   Basic Concepts

Local-area networks (LANs) operate over much shorter distances than those covered by wide-area networks. This is why only baseband systems are used in LANs. As discussed in the previous chapter, baseband data communication involves the digital transmission of data as sequences of voltage states or light pulses that represent logical 1s and 0s (see Figure 4.1). As in wide-area networks, the digital data streams are encoded before transmission to optimize data rates and minimize transmission errors. The line encoding schemes used in the various LAN technologies include the following:

- Simple Manchester encoding (10Base-T)
- Differential Manchester encoding (Token Ring)
- 4B5B encoding (FDDI, 100Base-TX, 100Base-FX)
- 8B6T encoding (100Base-T4), 8B10B (Gigabit Ethernet)
- CAP-4, CAP-64 encoding (ATM over UTP3)
- NRZ encoding (ATM over UTP5, STP)

Data rates can be optimized even in lower-quality cables, such as UTP3 (Category 3 unshielded twisted-pair copper cable), by using more than two data lines for transmission. For example, in a Fast Ethernet LAN with UTP3 cabling (100Base-T4), three wire pairs are used to transfer user data, while a fourth pair is used for collision detection. The 8B6T encoding technique reduces the transfer rate of the 100 Mbit/s data stream to 75 Mbit/s by encoding every 8 data bits in 6 tri-state symbols, which are then distributed over three wire pairs at 25 Mbit/s per pair. The resulting bandwidth is barely higher than that of 10 Mbit/s Ethernet, which uses the simple Manchester scheme to encode 10 Mbit/s data streams in 20 Mbit/s signals.

5.1.1 Local-Area Network Topologies: Bus, Ring, Switch

Significant developments in LAN communication techniques and data speeds have taken place in recent years. In the 1980s, the classic 10 Mbit/s Ethernet bus topology led the field, joined later by Token Ring and FDDI ring topologies. The principle of network switching, originally implemented for wide-area networks, became established in the 1990s as a LAN technology.

At the beginning of the 1990s, more than 90 percent of LANs were still using technologies developed the decade before: 10 Mbit/s Ethernet (IEEE 802.3, 1982) and 4 or 16 Mbit/s Token Ring (IEEE 802.5, 1985). As microprocessors became ever faster, opening the door to increased use of multimedia and distributed applications, the number of stations per network had to be reduced because the relevant standard did not provide for a corresponding increase in data speeds. Just a few years ago, it was not unusual to have more than 300 nodes in a 10 Mbit/s Ethernet/802.3 network. Today, the typical number of stations in a similarly equipped network segment is generally between 10 and 20, and the trend is toward even fewer.

A new LAN specification was developed at the end of the 1980s, called Fiber Distributed Digital Interface (FDDI). FDDI is a fiber-optic ring topology with a throughput of 100 Mbit/s. Although this technology made it possible to implement the first high-performance backbone structures, market acceptance was sluggish due to the expensive hardware components required, such as lasers in the network interface cards and fiber-optic cable infrastructures. Furthermore, it soon became evident that even a bandwidth of 100 Mbit/s, when shared among all network nodes, would not be sufficient for the emerging multimedia applications. This meant that FDDI was a medium-term solution at best. Still, for lack of a better alternative, a large number of backbones were re-structured to use FDDI technology in the years following its introduction. This trend changed, however, as LAN switching, 100/1,000 Mbit/s Ethernet and ATM entered the market in the mid-nineties.

Data Communications Using the Broadcast Principle

The LAN technologies developed in the 1980s, such as Ethernet, Token Ring and FDDI, are based on the "broadcast" principle: every station in the network receives every data packet transmitted. Each station must analyze the destination address information in every packet to determine whether the packet should be accepted, ignored or forwarded. The more nodes in a given network, the higher the network load and the more time each node spends evaluating addresses in packets that are for other nodes. In the first few years following the introduction of local-area networks, this was not seen as a problem because the

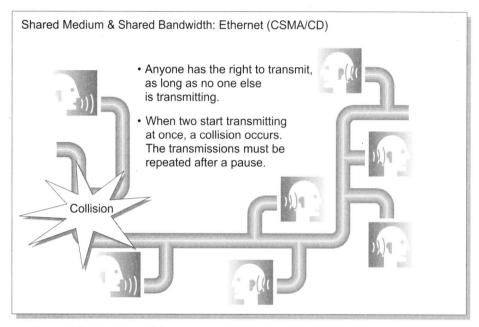

Figure 5.1 Principles of data communication in local-area networks in the 1980s: CSMA/CD and Ethernet

amount of bandwidth available in the network nodes was huge compared to the transmission capacity of any single station. More than a hundred network nodes could communicate over a single transport medium without difficulty. With the advances in computer system performance, however, bottlenecks soon developed (see Figures 5.1 and 5.2). This is why networks today are divided into segments, which are interconnected by selective devices such as bridges and routers. With this new technology, local data remains on the local segment, and neighboring segments are not unnecessarily burdened with foreign traffic.

Structure and Operation of Switching Systems

Wide-area networks have a different structure from local-area networks due to the simple fact that WANs cover distances up to hundreds of kilometers while LANs usually span no more than several hundred meters. The need for technologies that could transfer data over long distances led to the development of large network switching systems. WAN switches forward incoming packets directly to the switch output port that leads to the packet's destination segment. Outgoing packets are multiplexed with other connections' data and transmitted over high-speed lines.

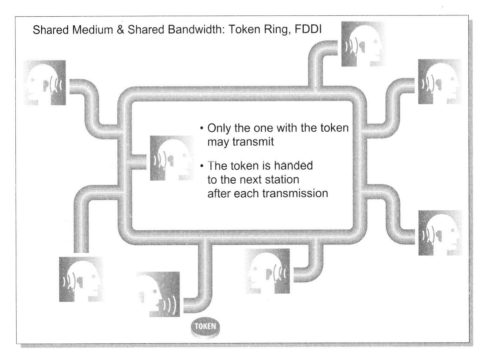

Figure 5.2 Principles of data communication in local-area networks in the 1980s: Token Ring and FDDI

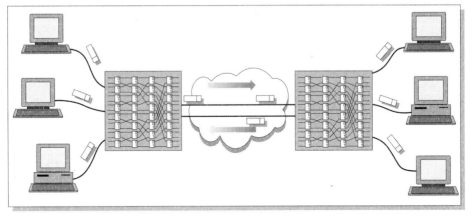

Figure 5.3 Switching and multiplexing in wide-area data communication

The development of economical, high-performance microprocessors and chipsets in the early 1990s paved the way for the development of complex switching and multiplexing technologies for data communication in local-area networks. Since then, the use of switching equipment in LANs has increased steadily.

The central component of switched networks is the switch, which forwards incoming packets to the appropriate output port as quickly as possible with minimum collisions. Switching technologies can be classified by distinguishing between cell switching and frame switching, as well as between single-frame and multi-frame switching.

Cell Switching and Frame Switching

In cell switching networks, all data packets or "cells" have the same length. This allows cell-switching systems to achieve faster throughput than frame-switching systems, in which data packets can have varying lengths. Because the cells arriving synchronously on all input ports are all the same size, they can all be forwarded simultaneously to their output ports in one working cycle of the switch.

This regular processing pace cannot be achieved in frame-based systems because frames can differ in length by as much as several hundred percent. Ethernet packets, for example, are from 64 to 1,518 bytes long, while packet lengths in Token Ring and FDDI have even broader ranges (see Figure 5.4).

Network type	Minimum packet length	Maximum packet length	Ratio
Ethernet	64 bytes	1,518 bytes	1 : 23
Token Ring	13 bytes	4,500 bytes (4 Mbit/s), 17,800 bytes (16 Mbit/s)	1 : 346 1 : 1,369
FDDI	12 bytes	4,500 bytes	1 : 375
ATM	53 bytes	53 bytes	1 : 1

Figure 5.4 Variations in packet length: Ethernet, Token Ring, FDDI, ATM

In Figure 5.5, a short packet can be switched from input port A to output port B in a fraction of the time it takes to transfer a longer packet from input C to output D. This increases the likelihood that packets will be blocked when two or more compete for the same output port. In the time it takes an Ethernet packet of maximum length to be sent over port D, up to 23 minimum-length packets of 64 bytes may be blocked while trying to reach the same output port (assuming the switch in question has two input ports and two output ports). The blocked packets are either stored in a buffer or discarded. In a comparable cell-based system, a given cell cannot block more than one other cell. Thus a frame-switching system cannot attain the processing efficiency of a cell-switching system.

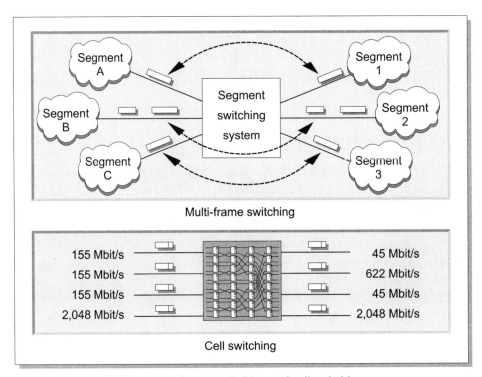

Figure 5.5 Frame switching and cell switching

Segment Switching (LAN Switching)

Segment switching is a special implementation of the switching principle, and is used to link traditional LAN topologies (Ethernet, Token Ring and FDDI) in a high-performance network. LAN segments are connected by switches, which forward incoming packets to their destination segments. Like bridges, LAN switches stop packets whose destination is on the source segment from being sent to the other connected segments. This allows multiple simultaneous communication connections between segments. The ability to process communications in parallel is the primary advantage of LAN switching. A LAN switch deployed in place of a bridge for inter-segment communication increases the available bandwidth several times over (see Figure 5.6).

A six-port LAN switch, for example, can create up to three parallel data communication paths. If station A accesses Server 1, station B accesses Server 2 and station C accesses Server 3 all at the same time over 100 Mbit/s media (see Figure 5.6), the LAN switch provides three parallel 100 Mbit/s connections for a total bandwidth of 300 Mbit/s. Data packets are transferred within the switching systems at extremely high speeds by means of application-specific inte-

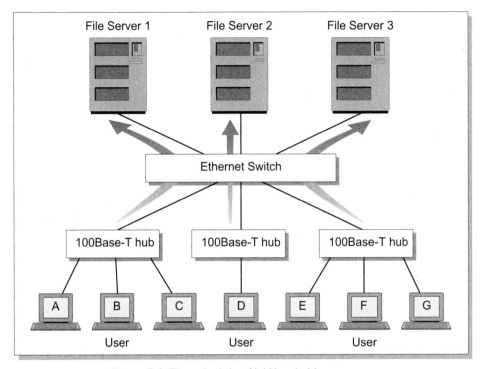

Figure 5.6 The principle of LAN switching systems

grated circuits (ASICs). Packets are buffered only until the complete destination address is received. Once the address is complete, it is analyzed and the packet is forwarded immediately.

In the previous example, the cumulative inter-segment bandwidth reaches 300 Mbit/s only because three independent communication paths are involved. If stations A, B and C all attempt to access Server 1, the available bandwidth remains 100 Mbit/s even though a switch is used. Server 1 cannot use more than the 100 Mbit/s bandwidth theoretically available in its Ethernet segment.

LAN switching systems are available for all the established LAN topologies: 10/100/1,000 Mbit/s Ethernet, Token Ring and FDDI.

Full-Duplex Connections

By definition, all three of the traditional LAN types—Ethernet, Token Ring and FDDI—are half-duplex technologies. This means that a given station can either receive or transmit data, but not both simultaneously. Many switching systems, however, provide both half- and full-duplex modes, especially for connecting server systems to LAN switches, and for increased throughput in connections between individual LAN switches. The full-duplex mode allows simultaneous transmission and reception of data, which effectively doubles the available bandwidth of the link. Full-duplex techniques can only be used in point-to-point topologies, in which media access no longer needs to be regulated by CSMA/CD (in Ethernet) or token passing (in Token Ring and FDDI). This means that where full-duplex components are used, the network is no longer connected through passive hubs or concentrators, but only through full-duplex Ethernet, Token Ring or FDDI switches. Otherwise, only two network nodes (such as two servers, for example) can be connected using full-duplex technology. The full-duplex operating mode increases the theoretical bandwidth from 100 to 200 Mbit/s in Ethernet networks, from 4 (or 16) Mbit/s to 8 (or 32) Mbit/s in Token Ring, and from 100 to 200 Mbit/s in FDDI. In addition to the traditional LAN technologies, the newer high-speed networks can also be operated in full-duplex mode so that Gigabit Ethernet can provide not 16 bit/s but 2 Gbit/s, and STM-1 ATM not 155 but 310 Mbit/s.

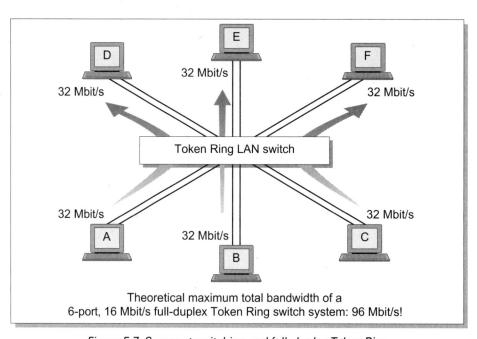

Figure 5.7 Segment switching and full-duplex Token Ring

5.1.2 Standards for Local-Area Data Networks

Unlike the specifications for wide-area networks, most of which are defined by ITU working groups, the Institute of Electrical and Electronics Engineers (IEEE) and various industry forums define standards for LAN technologies. Table 5.8 shows an overview of the various LAN standards along with their communication characteristics.

Technology	Standard	Application	Architecture
ATM	ITU I Series recommendations / ATM Forum standards	Data, voice, multimedia	Multi-cell switching
100Base-VG	IEEE 802.12	Data, multimedia	Single-frame switching DP protocol, half-duplex
100Base-T	IEEE 802.30	Data	Shared media, half-duplex, CSMA/CD
Gigabit Ethernet	IEEE 802.3z	Data, limited multimedia	Shared media, half-duplex, CSMA/CD
1000Base-T	IEEE 802.3ab ANSI X3T9.5	Data, limited multimedia	Shared media, half-duplex, CSMA/CD
FDDI	ISO 9314	Data, limited multimedia	Shared media, half-duplex, token passing
Fibre Channel	ANSI X3T9.3	Data	Multi-frame switching
Isochronous Ethernet	IEEE 802.9	Data, voice, limited multimedia	Shared media CSMA/CD combined with ISDN.
Full-duplex Ethernet 10/100/1,000	IEEE 802.3x	Data, multimedia	Shared media, full-duplex point-to-point
Full-duplex Token Ring	No standard, IEEE 802.5 data format	Data, multimedia	Shared media, full-duplex point-to-point
Full-duplex FDDI	No standard, ANSI X3T9.5 data format	Data, multimedia	Shared media, full-duplex point-to-point
Switched 10Base-T	No standard, IEEE 802.3 compatible	Data, limited multimedia	Multi-frame switching
Switched Token Ring	No standard, IEEE 802.3 compatible	Data, limited multimedia	Multi-frame switching
Switched FDDI	No standard, ANSI X3T9.5 compatible	Data, limited multimedia	Multi-frame switching
Switched 100Base-T	No standard, IEEE 802.3 compatible	Data, limited multimedia	Multi-frame switching
Switched 100Base-VG	No standard, IEEE 802.12 compatible	Data, multimedia	Multi-frame switching

Figure 5.8 Standards and characteristics of various LAN technologies

5.2   In-Service Testing
in Local-Area Networks

As in wide-area networks, a distinction is made between tests performed during LAN operation—in-service testing—and tests for which the communication link must be taken out of operation. Tests that can be performed without interrupting normal operation include signal condition measurements, protocol analysis, and various statistical measurements. Tests that require the segment or component under test to be taken out of operation include cable tests, load tests, bit-error-rate tests and conformance tests.

5.2.1   Signal Condition Measurements

Signal condition measurements involve using an oscilloscope to determine physical signal shapes. The signals can be measured either directly at a connector (on a coaxial or twisted-pair cable, for example) at transceivers; or at the interfaces of active network components, such as repeaters, bridges or routers. Information about the quality of the cable infrastructure, media access unit or interface under test can be determined from the signal shapes displayed on the oscilloscope. Signal condition measurements are not as significant in LANs as they are in WANs, however, because the signals travel relatively short distances and deterioration is relatively minor. In troubleshooting, however, and especially in diagnosing faulty interfaces in network nodes, repeaters or bridges, or when dealing with problems in the cable infrastructure, signal condition measurements are very useful for narrowing down the range of possible causes.

5.2.2   Protocol Analysis
and Statistical Measurements

A protocol analyzer records and interprets data packets transmitted over the network. This makes it a useful tool for monitoring packet types and protocol processes, as well as for collecting statistical data and identifying trends. The protocol analyzer is attached like any other network node to the LAN segment under test. In broadcast LAN topologies, that is, 10/100/1,000 Mbit/s Ethernet, 4/16 Mbit/s Token Ring, and FDDI, the analyzer can monitor and analyze all communication on the segment.

The protocol analyzer can monitor only the segment in which it is installed. Traffic that is beyond a bridge or router cannot be tested because the router or bridge limits local traffic to its segment of origin. In order to analyze traffic in two segments simultaneously—to observe inter-segment traffic as it crosses a

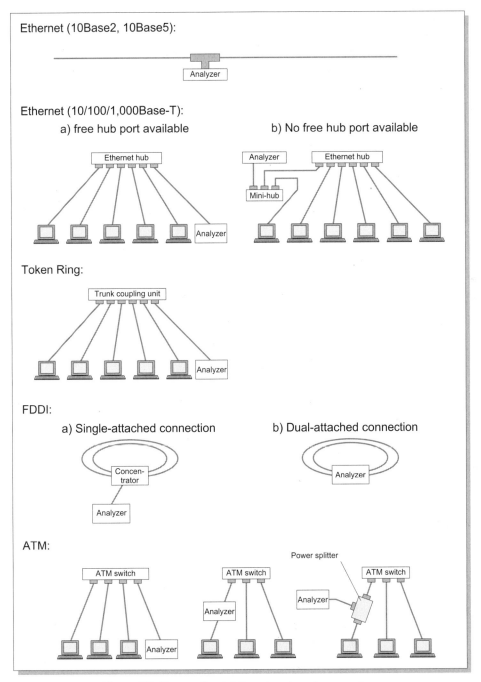

Figure 5.9 Connecting LAN protocol analyzer systems

particular router or bridge, for example—a protocol analysis system with two ports is required. It is not possible to monitor several segments at once with a single-port device for the simple reason that the device cannot be connected in two places at one time. Network-wide monitoring is performed by a system of measurement probes or software agents, installed in all LAN segments. These agents collect pertinent data and time-stamp it, then transmit it using the

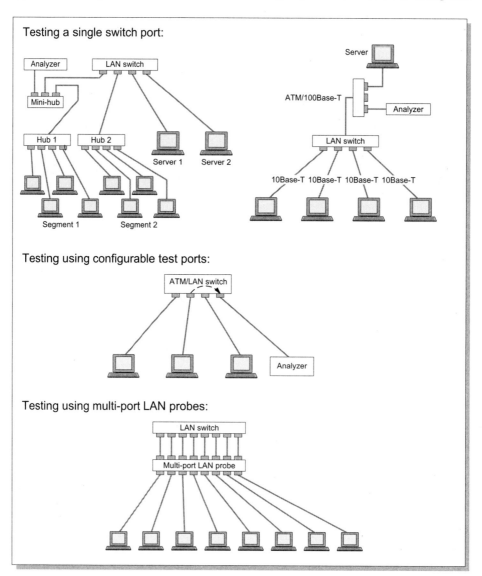

Figure 5.10 Connection options for protocol analyzer systems in switched LANs

Simple Network Management Protocol (SNMP) to a central network monitoring station, where it is correlated and analyzed.

It is more difficult to perform network analyses in topologies based on the switching principle, such as switched LANs or ATM networks. Unlike Ethernet hub or ring concentrator ports, each port on a LAN or ATM switch transmits only those packets that are addressed to the connected segment or node. If a given LAN or ATM switch port is connected only to a single station, then each protocol analyzer port can monitor only one connection. To monitor all switch ports simultaneously, a multiport analyzer system is required. This has led to the development of multiport LAN probes for use in switched-LAN environments. These have 4, 8, 12 or more ports and can be used to monitor the corresponding number of switch ports. Alternatively, many switches offer the option of defining unused ports as test ports, and can be configured to copy data packets from the active ports to these designated test ports (mirror ports). This allows a single analyzer port to monitor data from a number of active switch ports. When the switch is operating at peak loads, however, the capacity of individual test ports is not sufficient to monitor all or even a few ports reliably because the test port usually has the same total capacity as any one of the ports being monitored. Thus data packets that exceed the test port capacity are discarded at random.

5.3   Out-of-Service Measurements in Local-Area Networks

5.3.1   Cable Testing

Cable measurements are the most common testing procedures that require shutting down entire LAN segments. Which characteristics are measured depend on whether the cable under test is coaxial, twisted pair or optical fiber.

Testing Twisted-Pair Cables

Characteristics to be measured in twisted-pair cable infrastructures include cable length, attenuation, crosstalk, pin assignments, noise, impedance and capacitance. The pin assignments of the cable connectors should be checked first, before the quality indicators are tested. Faulty pin assignments can be the result of incorrect manual wiring, but may also be due to the use of different color-coding systems. The specifications TIA/EIA 568A and TIA/EIA 568B, for example, define different systems of color-coding for twisted-pair wiring. Pin assignments are tested by connecting the wall jack to different resistances and performing measurements at the patch panel on each wire pair with each resistance. Some wiring faults, however, such as split pairs cannot be detected using this method. This type of fault can only be detected indirectly by near-end crosstalk (NEXT) testing, which yields particularly poor results on split pairs.

Attenuation

Attenuation measurements test the loss of signal amplitude in transmissions over a given network segment. Attenuation is indicated in decibels. The total attenuation of a given transmission path must not exceed the specified limits. The maximum permitted attenuation is called the loss budget. In addition to the characteristics of the cable, the connectors used in adding segment extensions can also add substantially to the total attenuation.

Crosstalk and Near-End Crosstalk (NEXT)

Crosstalk is the most significant source of noise over twisted-pair cable in local-area networks. Crosstalk occurs when signals in one wire pair produce a capacitive and inductive coupling in an adjacent pair. The magnitude of crosstalk is measured as the ratio of the amplitude (in volts) of the actual signal to that of the coupled signal. When these are both measured at the same end of the transmission path, the effect is referred to as near-end crosstalk, or NEXT, and is expressed in dB. The higher the NEXT value, the lower the crosstalk on the line, and the better the quality of the transmission path. Because crosstalk is influenced by the frequency of the data signal, it is important that measurements be taken at different frequencies on every possible combination of wire pairs. Thus when testing for crosstalk in a twisted-pair cable with four wire pairs, for example, at least 12 measurements must be taken. The TSB67 specification prescribes NEXT measurements in the range from 1 to 31.25 MHz at 150 kHz intervals, and from 31.25 MHz to 100 MHz at 250 kHz intervals. The need to minimize crosstalk is the reason why wires in twisted-pair cables are twisted. This is also why the cables used in LANs (TIA/EIA Category 3, 4 or 5) have more tightly twisted-wire pairs than those used in telephone cables (TIA/EIA Category 1).

Attenuation-to-Crosstalk Ratio (ACR)

To estimate the effect of attenuation and crosstalk on the bit-error rate of a transmission path, the next characteristic to test in twisted-pair infrastructures is the attenuation-to-crosstalk ratio (ACR). The ACR can be calculated by subtracting the measured NEXT (in dB) from the attenuation (also in dB). As the ACR value approaches zero dB, the probability of communication errors increases.

Signal-to-Noise Ratio (SNR)

The relationship of signal amplitude to noise amplitude, called the signal-to-noise ratio (SNR), is almost identical to ACR. The only difference is that the SNR value reflects not only NEXT, but also all other noise. Usually, however, the total noise caused by other interference sources is low in comparison to that caused by NEXT.

Reflections (Return Loss)

Reflections are caused by impedance anomalies at cable connectors. The resulting signal overlap can cause jitter. Jitter is measured by comparing the actual signal shape to eye diagrams supplied in the relevant standards. Reflection is measured in decibels and, like NEXT, must be measured at various frequencies.

Impedance

Impedance is a complex characteristic of LAN cable segments. Its magnitude is determined by the cable's capacitance, inductance and resistance. Error-free data communication requires that the impedance remain as constant as possible throughout the entire segment and all connector elements. Abrupt transitions in impedance cause signal reflections, which can lead to jitter and bit errors. The faster the data rate, the more sensitive the signal stream is to impedance anomalies. The length of any untwisted cable sections must be kept to a strict minimum, not exceeding 13 mm. Furthermore, cable segments with different impedances may not be coupled under any circumstances. Impedance measurements are also useful in identifying split wire pairs.

Resistance

Resistance measurements can indicate faulty connections, short circuits or broken cables. The resistance of twisted-pair cable should be between 9Ω and 12Ω per 100 meters in UTP and between 6Ω and 7Ω per 100 meters in STP.

Cable Length

The length of a cable segment is measured by time-domain reflectometry. A time-domain reflectometer (TDR) inserts signal pulses into the segment under test and measures the time in nanoseconds that elapses before it receives the signal's reflection from the far end of the cable. The length is calculated from this value and the known values for signal propagation speed in a given type of cable. Because reflections occur not only at the end of a cable segment, but also at every connection point along the path under test, the number and location of faults in the cable are also detected and displayed.

Testing Coaxial LAN Cables

The most important characteristics to measure in coaxial cable infrastructures are the segment length, attenuation and terminating resistance. Typical coaxial cable problems, such as kinks, short circuits, loose BNC connections, faulty or missing terminating resistors, or excessive segment length, can be detected quickly. It is important when performing voltage and TDR tests on coaxial cable that all network nodes are switched on but none are transmitting. Any repeaters in the segment under test should be deactivated before taking measurements. This is because many repeaters have an automatic segmenting function that deactivates the entire segment when malfunctions are detected, then transmits test signals at regular intervals to determine whether the malfunction persists. These test signals skew the results of voltage and TDR measurements.

To measure resistance, all nodes on the segment must be completely powered down or disconnected from the LAN cable. When disconnecting a station from the LAN, it is important to keep in mind that the station and the LAN cable may be grounded to different potentials. To avoid hazardous electrical discharge, do not touch the Medium Access Unit (MAU) cable and the LAN cable at the same time. Transceivers and MAUs usually operate at 12 volts. If there is a short

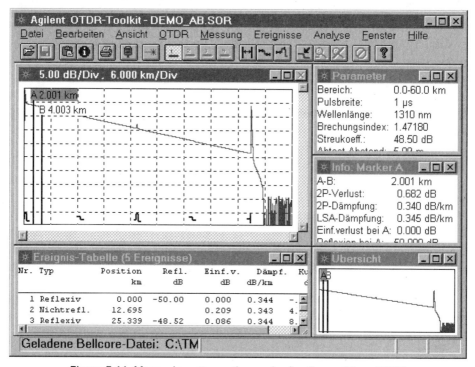

Figure 5.11 Measuring attenuation and reflections with an OTDR

circuit in any MAU, this potential may also be on the network cable. If the LAN cable is not properly grounded, the potential on it may be even higher. Because there may be 12 volts or more on the LAN cable, it is a good idea to avoid touching the cable contacts.

Testing Fiber-Optic Lines

The procedures for testing fiber-optic links in LANs are similar to those used in testing wide-area networks. Here again tests are performed for attenuation and reflections along the transmission path, as well as for signal power at transmitters and receivers. Typical problems that can be identified by such tests include:

- Loss (attenuation) along the fiber
- Loss at splices
- Loss at connectors; contamination
- Aging
- Light power problems
- Line interruptions

Signal power is measured using an optical power meter, while attenuation and reflections are measured using an optical time-domain reflectometer (OTDR) (see Figure 5.11).

5.3.2 Detecting External Interference

In environments with high levels of electromagnetic interference (EMI), serious transmission problems can result from induced noise in copper cabling. If there is no obvious source of EMI in the vicinity, frequency measurements can help to identify possible causes of EMI. These measurements are performed using a spectrum analyzer, which can display all signals within a given frequency band on the transport medium. The most common sources of EMI are:

Potential source of interference	Operating frequency
FM radio and TV signals	1-100 MHz
GSM telephones	800 MHz
Pagers	500 MHz
PCs	100-400 MHz
Fluorescent tubes, electric motors	10-150 kHz

The most reliable way to prevent EMI problems is to use fiber-optic cables, which are not subject to electrical induction.

5.3.3   Conformance and Interoperability Testing

Testing for conformance to standards is not as critical in LANs as it is in wide-area networks. This is because LAN technologies are used primarily in private data networks, so that adherence to the national and international standards defined for network devices is not prescribed by law. Due to the growing complexity of LAN technologies and the importance of interoperability among network elements, however, a number of test suites (standard test protocols) have been developed by various industry forums, such as the Fast Ethernet Consortium, the Gigabit Ethernet Alliance and the ATM Forum. These suites are used by manufacturers to test their LAN components for conformance to standards and interoperability. The InterOperability Lab of the University of New Hampshire (IOL), which can be found in the World Wide Web at *http://www.iol.unh.edu/*, is the leading LAN test laboratory worldwide. IOL has developed test suites for all major LAN technologies, including 10/100/1,000 Mbit/s Ethernet, Token Ring, FDDI, and ATM. For Fast Ethernet alone, there are five test suites available:

- Fast Ethernet Repeater Test Suite
- 100Base-TX MAC and PCS Test Suite
- 100Base-TX TP PMD Test Suite
- 100Base-X Interoperability Test Suite
- Auto Negotiation Test Suite

5.3.4   Load Tests

Load testing is at least as important in local-area networks as it is in wide-area networks. While today's network components for traditional LAN technologies such as 10 Mbit/s Ethernet, Token Ring or FDDI, can generally operate at maximum load without difficulty, the same is not true of high-speed LANs based on 100/1,000 Mbit/s Ethernet or ATM. In these data speed ranges, the capabilities of network components vary widely between different manufacturers. In some cases the manufacturer's specifications for the components may not be correct, or may be knowingly based on a different interpretation of performance characteristics than might be expected. For example, when a manufacturer of ATM switches declares that its product can process a certain number of connections per second, this claim may be based on test conditions that define a connection as the signaling sequence:

> Setup
< Call Proceeding
> Connect
< Connect Acknowledge

over a constant combination of input and output ports. Under realistic load conditions, however, traffic flows through a number of different ports, and a connection consists of the complete signaling sequence for setting up and clearing down a connection, that is:

> Setup
< Call Proceeding
> Connect
< Connect Acknowledge
> Release
< Release Complete

When the same ATM switch is tested under these conditions, the actual signaling performance of the system is likely to be a fraction of that claimed by the manufacturer. For example, the manufacturer might claim that the switch processes 2,000 calls/s, while the realistic performance is closer to 500 calls/s.

The IETF Benchmarking Working Group
    (IETF-BMWG *http://www.ietf.org/html.charters/bmwg-charter.html*) and the ATM Forum have drafted documents intended to establish a uniform terminology for measuring the performance of networking components in order to permit comparable performance specifications. These are:

* Benchmarking Methodology for LAN Switching Devices (RFC 2889)
* Benchmarking Terminology for LAN Switching Devices (RFC 2285)
* Methodology for IP Multicast Benchmarking (RFC Draft)
* Terminology for IP Multicast Benchmarking (RFC 2432)
* Methodology for ATM Benchmarking (RFC Draft)
* Terminology for ATM ABR Benchmarking (RFC Draft)
* Terminology for ATM Benchmarking (RFC 2761)
* ATM Forum Performance Testing Specification (af-test-tm-0131.000.pdf)
* Benchmarking Terminology for Network Interconnection Devices (RFC 1242)
* Benchmarking Methodology for Network Interconnect Devices (RFC 2544)
* Benchmarking Terminology for Firewall Performance (RFC 2647)

The performance parameters defined and explained in these documents describe significant functions of wide-area network components, including:

* Packet throughput
* Packet delay
* Transmission fairness
* Packet loss rate
* Packet burst size

Before a product is put into operation, its specifications should be known in accordance with RFC 2544and, if possible, verified by in-house tests.

Section II
Troubleshooting
Local-Area Networks

Cable Infrastructures in Local-Area Networks

6

"Always expect the worst and you will never be disappointed."

PETER WASTHOLM

The main prerequisite for trouble-free operation of a local-area network is the use of a high-quality cable infrastructure with specified data transmission parameters. Estimating the overall transmission characteristics of network cable infrastructures is an extremely complicated task. In practice, the only way to design a physical foundation for reliable data communications is through strict adherence to accepted standards for the cabling. The ISO/IEC IS 11801 specification, from which the European standard EN 50173 is derived, is an internationally recognized standard that describes customer premises cabling. The corresponding North American standard is the EIA/TIA 568A Commercial Building Telecommunications and Wiring Standard.

The ISO/IEC IS 11801 specification distinguishes between three types of cable by range: campus backbone, for use over distances of up to 1,500 meters; vertical backbone, for up to 500 meters; and horizontal cabling, for connecting components on the same floor over distances of up to 90 meters. ISO/IEC IS 11801 also

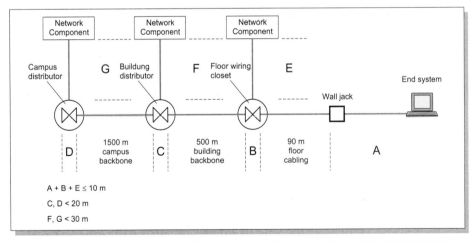

Figure 6.1 Campus, vertical and horizontal cabling according to ISO/IEC IS 11801

defines the maximum permissible lengths for cabling systems, as well as the upper limits for work area and device cabling (see Figure 6.1).

The transmission media described in the cable performance categories are twisted copper wire and single-mode and multimode fiber-optic cabling. Coaxial cable, or coax, is used in 10Base2 and 10Base5 networks, but is not suitable for structured cabling and thus not in the specifications mentioned previously. The only standard that defines coaxial cabling is EIA/TIA 568, which describes 50 coax as an option for horizontal cabling.

The different types of twisted-pair data cable available are divided into seven performance categories, numbered 1 through 7. Twisted-pair cabling can be used over various distances in any of the six ISO/IEC application classes (A through F) defined for copper cabling, depending on the transmission characteristics of each category. A seventh application class has been defined for the use of optical transmission media. Bandwidth ranges and typical applications are also defined for each class. Class A applications, for example, require bandwidths of up to 100 kHz; this class includes such applications as X.21/V.11 and ISDN S_0. Class F applications can require up to 600 MHz bandwidth, and include Gigabit Ethernet and 622 Mbit/s ATM (see Figure 6.2).

Application classes per ISO/IEC IS 11801	Definition
Class A	Applications up to 100 kHz (analog telephony, X.21, ISDN S_0, etc.)
Class B	Applications with bandwidths of up to 1 MHz (X.21, ISDN S_0)
Class C	Applications with bandwidths of up to 16 MHz (ISDN S_{2M}, 10Base-T, 4/16 Mbit/s Token Ring)
Class D	Applications with bandwidths of up to 100 MHz (100Base-TX, ATM 155 Mbit/s, Gigabit Ethernet)
Class E	Applications with bandwidths of up to 200 MHz (ATM 155 Mbit/s, Gigabit Ethernet)
Class F	Applications with bandwidths of up to 600 MHz (ATM 155 Mbit/s, Gigabit Ethernet)
Optical data transmission	Data communications over multimode and single-mode optical fiber

Figure 6.2 Application classes for structured cabling per ISO/IEC IS 11801

6.1 Coaxial Cable

6.1.1 Coaxial Cable:
Specification and Implementation

Coaxial cable has a copper inner conductor at the center and an outer conductor that acts as shielding. Between the two conductors is an insulator, and the whole is encased in a plastic jacket. Called "coax" (two syllables) for short, coaxial cable can provide data speeds of several gigabits per second and is used for both digital data and television signals.

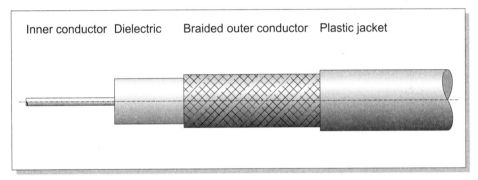

Inner conductor Dielectric   Braided outer conductor   Plastic jacket

Figure 6.3 Structure of coaxial cable

The types of coax most commonly used for data communications, besides the traditional 50   cable of 10Base2 and 10Base5 Ethernet networks, are RG-62 coaxial cable, which has an impedance of 93   (used to connect IBM 3270 terminals), RG-6 and RG-11 coax, with 75   impedance, and twin-axial cable, with an impedance of 105   (AS/400, IBM /36 /38 series). Detailed specifications for the various types of cable are found in the MIL-C-17G standard (see Figure 6.4).

There are two ways to connect network components to coaxial cable in bus-based Ethernet networks (10Base2, 10Base5). The first method consists of cutting the cable and inserting a T-connector. The second method involves drilling a hole in the coaxial cable until the inner conductor is just reached, and then inserting a special connector known as a tap or vampire tap. This method is used with 10Base5 cabling ("yellow cable" or "thick Ethernet"), while T-connectors are commonly used in 10Base2 networks ("thin Ethernet" or "cheapernet").

The advantage of vampire taps is that new components can be installed without interrupting network operation. This can be an important factor, especially in

Cable designation	RG-58 10Base2 cable, thin Ethernet, Cheapernet	RG-8A/U 10Base5 cable, thick Ethernet, yellow cable
Use	10Base2	10Base5
Impedance (Ω)	50	50 ± 2
Attenuation (dB/100 m)	4.6 at 10 MHz	1.7 at 10 MHz
Velocity factor	0.77	0.83 – 0.86
Inner conductor (mm)	0.94	2.7
Insulation (mm)	2.52	6.15
PVC outer jacket (mm)	4.62	10.3
Bending radius (cm)	5	25

*Figure 6.4 Specifications for RG-58 and RG-8A/U coaxial cable
(10Base2 and 10Base5)*

production networks. Care must be taken in using this method, however, as the cable may break if the hole is drilled too deep. If the hole is not deep enough, the connection will be unstable. In either case, serious network problems can result.

10Base5 cable is usually equipped with N-type connectors; 10Base2 cable with BNC connectors. To prevent reflections, each cable end must be connected to a 50 terminating resistor. It is essential that one of the terminating resistors be grounded, and equally important that the second one *not* be grounded. If neither terminating resistor is grounded this could result in an electrical charge through-out the entire network. If both are grounded and the two grounds have different electrical potentials, considerable current on the line may result.

In addition to observing segment length limitations (185 meters for 10Base2; 500 meters for 10Base5), it is especially important to respect the minimum bending radius for coaxial cable (5 cm for 10Base2; 25 cm for 10Base5) and to install pressure relief fixtures over the cables where necessary to prevent damage caused by equipment housings, other objects resting on the cables or other mechanical stress.

	10Base2	10Base5
Maximum segment length	185 m	500 m
Maximum bending radius	5 cm	25 cm
Maximum number of nodes per segment	30	100
Maximum attenuation per segment	8.5 dB	8.5 dB
Maximum transmission delay per segment	950 ns	2,165 ns

Figure 6.5 Design guidelines for 10Base2 and 10Base5 networks (IEEE 802.3)

6.1.2 Troubleshooting Coaxial Cable (10Base2, 10Base5)

The first steps in tracking down the source of a problem in coaxial cable include checking the voltage, resistance, terminating resistors, noise, cable lengths, reflections and attenuation. When these tests are performed conscientiously, they often lead directly to the cause of the problem.

Measuring the Voltage in Network Cabling

The easiest way to measure the voltage in a segment of network cabling is to use a voltmeter on an unused T-connector or vampire tap. If the voltage is less than ±100 mV (±200 mV at one end of the cable), then there is probably nothing wrong in this area. If the voltage exceeds 100 mV–especially if the reading is several volts–then it is likely that the supply voltage of a media access unit (MAU) or other component on the cable segment is leaking into the network cable. In this case, disconnect the MAUs one at a time and repeat the voltage measurements after each unit is removed. Because more than one MAU may be defective, do not re-connect the deactivated units to the network until the source of the problem has been isolated. If the voltage is still too high even after all components have been disconnected, the cable is probably grounded in more than one place, with different electrical potentials at each ground. Remove all grounds except one. Sometimes a second ground is created by a defective network component that

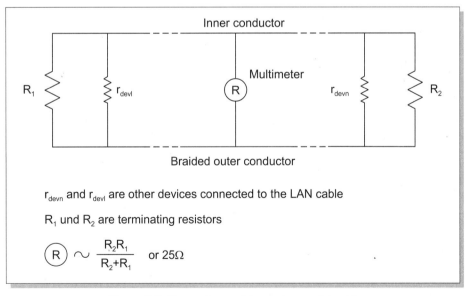

r_{devn} and r_{devl} are other devices connected to the LAN cable

R_1 und R_2 are terminating resistors

$(R) \sim \dfrac{R_2 R_1}{R_2 + R_1}$ or 25Ω

Figure 6.6 Measuring resistance in coaxial cable

does not electrically isolate network components from the data transport medium. If this is the case, a simple network interface card may be the cause of the voltage problem.

Measuring the Cable Resistance

All network components must be switched off before performing resistance measurements. Measure resistance at a T-connector or vampire tap (see Figure 6.6, 6.7).

If the values measured are between 24.0 and 26.6   for 10Base5 or between 24.4 and 26.6   for 10Base2, then the level of resistance in the cable is not the root of the problem.

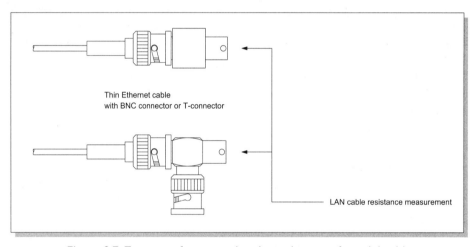

Figure 6.7 Test setup for measuring the resistance of coaxial cable

If the resistance is high, the cable is broken somewhere along its length. In this case, isolate the defective cable segment by repeating the resistance measurements on neighboring T-connectors or vampire taps until you detect normal values.

If the resistance is very low, the cable is short-circuited. You can quickly pinpoint the location of the short using a time-domain reflectometer (TDR).

Testing the Terminating Resistor

If you suspect that you have a defective terminating resistor, make sure you test the T-connector and the terminating resistor simultaneously. It is possible that the terminating resistor is in perfect condition, but connected to a defective T-connector (see Figure 6.9).

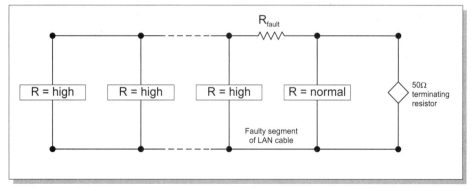

Figure 6.8 Systematic search for defects in coaxial cable

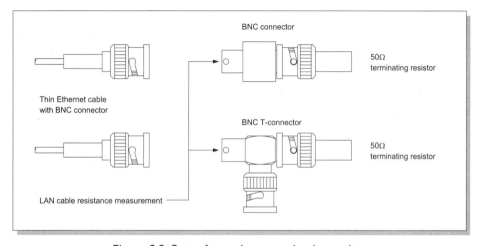

Figure 6.9 Setup for testing a terminating resistor

Measuring Electromagnetic Interference

When line noise is measured using a cable scanner or a spectrum analyzer, the frequency of electromagnetic interference in the line can be identified. Noise is measured between the shielding (outer conductor) and the core (inner conductor). If the noise exceeds permissible levels, check the area around the affected cable route for possible sources of interference, including production environments, elevators, photocopiers, fluorescent tubes, arc welding equipment and X-ray devices. If a spectrum analyzer is available you may try to determine the frequency spectrum of the interfering equipment. Typical interference frequency ranges are listed:

Potential source of interference	Operating frequency
FM radio and TV signals	1-100 MHz
GSM telephones	800 MHz
Pagers	500 MHz
PCs	100-400 MHz
Fluorescent tubes, electric motors	10-150 kHz

Measuring Cable Lengths, Reflections and Short Circuits

Cable length, reflections and short circuits can be measured using a time-domain reflectometer or TDR. The TDR transmits a signal and then measures the time that elapses until the signal's reflection is received. Any irregularity in a given cable segment will cause reflections of greater or lesser intensity, depending on the magnitude of the irregularity. The TDR can be set to wait either for the largest reflection that occurs or to measure smaller reflections, such as those that amount to only 30 percent of the original signal. The latter method allows you to determine the distance to impedance anomalies along the cable. To determine the overall cable length, remove the far terminating resistor and set the TDR to measure the greatest reflected signal. If the cable is broken at any point along its length, however, the reflection will come from the break, not from the far end. As is the case with most cable measurement procedures, the cable segment to be tested must be taken out of operation completely before performing TDR measurements.

6.1.3   Symptoms and Causes: Coaxial Cable

Symptom: Intermittent Loss of Connection

Cause (1):   Poor or no physical connection to the network cable due to a loose BNC connector or a vampire tap that does not reach the inner conductor.

Cause (2):   Terminating resistors exceed tolerance limits.

Symptom: Complete Failure of a Segment

Cause (1):   Short circuit in the cable (outer conductor touching inner conductor) due to kinks, defective cable, or vampire tap drilled too deep.

Cause (2):   Voltage on the network exceeds permissible levels due to defective MAU or lack of grounding.

Symptom: Unusually High Number of Collisions

Cause (1): Strong reflections in the cable, resulting in collisions.
Check to see if terminating resistor is missing, defective or out of tolerance.

Cause (2): Segment may have too many MAUs.

Cause (3): Segment grounded in more than one place.

Cause (4): Maximum cable length exceeded.

Symptom: Intermittent or Frequent Collisions and Fragments

Cause: Electromagnetic interference.
Check whether photocopiers, pagers, elevators or x-ray devices are being used near the cabling.

Symptom: No Connection or Intermittent Loss of Connection After New Installation

Cause (1): High attenuation in newly installed cables; variations in impedance between connectors or in patch panels.

Cause (2): Impedance of new cable is outside tolerance limits; wrong cable type installed.
Check tolerances and specifications of all new components.

Gathering Information; Common Errors

Most problems in cabling infrastructures arise in conjunction with external alterations. Such changes may have been made intentionally or even inadvertently, as can happen during the course of other activities. Specific information about the context of the problem can provide clues to its exact location and possible causes. Questions to ask at this stage include:

- Has anyone connected or disconnected a PC (laptop or desktop) or any other component to or from the network?

- Has anyone installed an interface card in a computer?

- Has anyone stepped on a cable?

- Has any maintenance work been performed in the building recently (by a telephone company or building maintenance personnel, for example)?

- Has anyone (including cleaning personnel) moved any equipment or furniture?

Figure 6.10 lists the most common causes of problems in coaxial cabling infrastructures:

- Cable continuity is interrupted at a T-connector.
- Continuity fault in a connector.
- Connector has a short circuit.
- Cable insulation is damaged (shielding is visible).
- Cable is kinked or bent too tightly.
- Cable is too long.
- Cable is not grounded.
- Cable is grounded in two places.
- Cable segments look similar, but have different impedances.
- Electromagnetic interference (elevators, electric machinery) or mechanical stress (doors, furniture) exists along cable route.
- Impedance in new cabling exceeds tolerance limits, or the wrong cable type has been installed.
- A MAU is defective.
- Newly installed vampire taps act as mini-antennae and induce signals.
- Network voltage exceeds allowable levels due to a defective MAU or lack of grounding.
- New cables with high attenuation have been installed; variations in impedance between connectors or in patch panels.
- Physical connection to the network cable is poor or does not exist due to loose BNC connectors or to vampire taps that do not reach the inner conductor.
- The segment is grounded in more than one place.
- Short circuit in the cable. This can be caused by any of the following: kinks, cable defects, vampire tap drilled too deep, outer conductor touching copper core.
- Terminating resistor is missing or defective.
- Terminating resistors exceed tolerance limits.
- Terminating resistor is missing, defective or not to specification.
- Too many MAUs exist on the segment.
- Voltage induced by electromagnetic interference. Check whether photocopiers, pagers, elevators or x-ray devices are in use near the affected cable route.

Figure 6.10 The most common causes of problems in coaxial cabling infrastructures

6.2 Twisted-Pair Cable

6.2.1 Twisted-Pair Cable: Specification and Implementation

Whereas coaxial cabling is unbalanced because the outer conductor is always at ground potential, twisted pair is balanced cabling because the signals on each wire of a pair have opposite potentials. Twisted-pair cable can have two or four wire pairs, which are twisted together with 6 to 26 rotations per meter of cable. Twisting the conductors together improves the cable's immunity to electromagnetic interference (EMI). Cable with four wires twisted together is also referred to as twisted quad. A distinction is made between shielded twisted pair (STP) and unshielded twisted pair (UTP). STP has braided shielding, metal foil, or a combination of the two wrapped around each wire pair. In addition to blocking external EMI, this shielding also significantly reduces interference emitted by the wire pairs themselves. Metal foil is more effective than braided shielding against high-frequency EMI, while braided shielding is more effective in absorbing low-frequency radiation. In high-performance Category 7 cabling, for example, which is specified to 600 MHz, each pair of wires is wrapped in metal foil. Cable with this type of shielding is also referred to as pairs in metal foil (PIMF). Another cable type, known as screened STP (S/STP), has shielding around each wire pair plus an additional wrapping of braided shielding around all pairs.

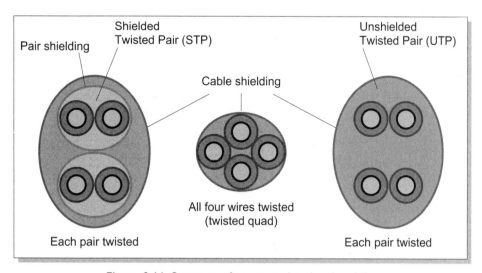

Figure 6.11 Structure of copper twisted-pair cabling

The ISO/IEC IS 11801 standard, divides twisted-pair cabling into seven categories according to frequency ratings. Twisted-pair cabling is specified for frequencies of up to 600 MHz. Figure 6.12 shows the different categories with the
maximum distances that they can span.

Cable type	Class A (100 kHz)	Class B (1 MHz)	Class C (16 MHz)	Class D (100 MHz)	Class E (200 MHz)	Class F (600 MHz)	Optical links
Category 3 (symmetrical copper cable)	2 km	500 m	100 m	—	—	—	—
Category 4 (symmetrical copper cable)	3 km	600 m	150 m	—	—	—	—
Category 5 (symmetrical copper cable)	3 km	700 m	160 m	100 m	—	—	—
150Ω (symmetrical copper cable)	3 km	1 km	250 m	150 m	—	—	—
Category 6 (symmetrical copper cable)	—	—	—	—	100 m	—	—
Category 7 (symmetrical copper cable)	—	—	—	—	—	100 m	—
Multimode fiber	—	—	—	—	—	—	2 km
Single-mode fiber	—	—	—	—	—	—	3 km

Figure 6.12 Performance categories for structured cabling
according to ISO/IEC IS 11801

The key operating parameters of twisted-pair cabling are the signal propagation
speed, attenuation, near-end crosstalk (NEXT) and the attenuation-to-crosstalk
ratio (ACR) (see Figure 6.13).

Essential factors for trouble-free network operation include not only the use of
high-quality cable of the appropriate category, but also connectors of the right
category. When components of different categories are used in the same network, the lowest-performance component on a given transmission path determines the overall transmission characteristics of that path. As with coaxial
cable, it is also important to make sure the minimum bending radius allowed for

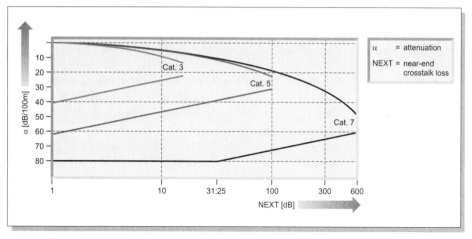

Figure 6.13 Specifications concerning attenuation and NEXT for cabling of Categories 3, 5 and 7

Cable type	Minimum bending radius during installation under tension	Minimum bending radius in installed state	Minimum one-time bending radius
100 Ω, 120 Ω twisted pair	8 times the cable's outside diameter	6 times the cable's outside diameter (in backbones) 4 times the cable's outside diameter (workgroup areas)	N/A
150 Ω twisted pair	N/A	7.5 cm	2 cm

Figure 6.14 Minimum bending radii for twisted-pair cabling (ISO/IEC IS 11801)

the cable is low enough for your installation requirements, and to install protective fixtures where necessary to prevent undue mechanical stress on the cables.

Grounding Twisted-Pair Cable Infrastructures

Proper grounding of the cabling infrastructure is absolutely essential. Cable shielding must be grounded both in the patch panel, which should have a ground bus connected to the building ground, and in the wall jack. Connecting cables and patch cables must be grounded in both the wall jack and the end device. It is important that the potential in the wall jack ground is the same as that in the patch panel and terminal device. A simple measurement with a multimeter is sufficient to determine whether there is a difference in potential between the wall jack shielding and the patch cable shielding. If a noticeable voltage level is detected, the grounding of the individual components must be reviewed so that they all end at the same grounding block. Fiber-optic cabling is used to connect floor wiring closets to the building distributor. This prevents current due to varying ground potentials. This is even more important in connecting building distributors to the campus backbone cable because there can be significant differences in ground potentials from one building to another.

Electromagnetic Interference

It is important to make sure that the cable is installed at a sufficient distance from potential sources of electromagnetic interference, especially when using unshielded twisted-pair cables. The North American specification EIA 569 describes the following guidelines for determining appropriate distances:

Source of electromagnetic interference	Minimum distance at line power < 2 kVA	Minimum distance at line power 2 to 5 kVA	Minimum distance at line power > 5 kVA
Unshielded power lines or electrical equipment near open or non-metallic cable ducts	5 in	1 ft	2 ft
Unshielded power lines or electrical equipment near metallic, grounded cable ducts	3 in	6 in	1 ft
Power lines or electrical equipment in grounded metallic shielding near metallic, grounded cable ducts	—	6 in	1 ft
Transformers, electric motors	—	—	3 ft
Flourescent tubes	—	—	1 ft

Figure 6.15 Guidelines for minimum distances between cabling and potential sources of electromagnetic interference (EIA 569)

6.2.2   Troubleshooting Twisted-Pair Cable

The main task in troubleshooting twisted-pair cabling infrastructures is the measurement of key operating parameters, such as cable length, attenuation, NEXT, ACR, and signal-to-noise ratio (SNR). To eliminate the possibility of incorrect pin assignments right at the outset, however, it is a good idea to begin by comparing the pin assignments in the patch panel with those in the corresponding wall jacks. This type of wiring fault can result from incorrect manual wiring, but may also be due to the use of different color-coding systems. The specifications TIA/EIA 568A and TIA/EIA 568B, for example, define different systems of color-coding for twisted-pair wiring. Figure 6.16 points out typical wiring errors, as well as the color-coding systems used in TIA 568A and in TIA 568B.

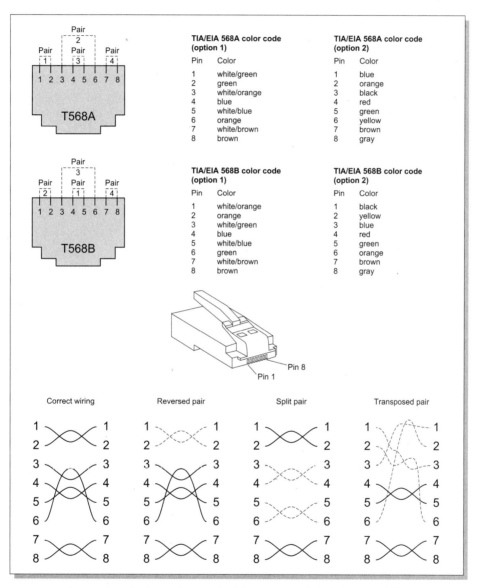

Figure 6.16 Color coding and wiring errors in twisted-pair cabling

To test for faulty pin assignments in the cable, connect the wall plug to a number of different terminating resistors in turn, and test the wire pairs coming from the patch panel with each of the resistors. Reversed pairs are the most common wiring errors and are caused by a simple reversal of the wires, usually at the patch panel. Some wiring errors, such as split pairs, cannot be detected using this procedure. Split pairs can only be detected indirectly, when NEXT tests produce unusually poor results. Split pairs are usually the result of incorrect installation by technicians unfamiliar with twisted pair. Transposed pairs usually result from counting pins from the wrong side of the jack.

Special testing equipment can perform most measurements on twisted-pair cables. Cables are directly connected to a tester using an RJ-45 connector. In some cases, it is also necessary to perform TDR measurements to create a detailed impedance profile for a given length of cable. This requires an oscilloscope, which can easily be connected to a wire pair by means of an RJ-45 breakout box. The pulse for the TDR test can be produced by most cable testing devices. Figure 6.17 shows typical TDR measurement results. Each deviation in

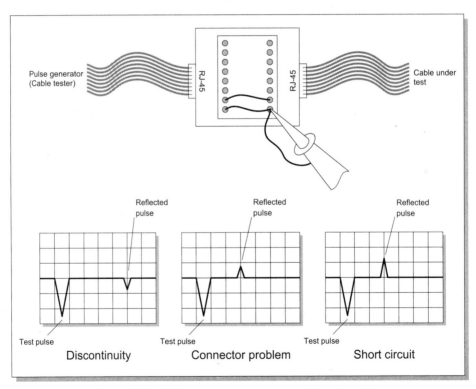

Figure 6.17 TDR measurements on twisted-pair cables

impedance along the cable under test (interruptions, connector problems, short circuits, etc.) causes a reflection of the test pulse. The oscilloscope display shows the type and location of the impedance deviation. Often a number of minor impedance anomalies are detected, none of which would cause a problem on its own, but which are compounded with other errors to cause serious malfunctions.

6.2.3   Symptoms and Causes: Twisted-Pair Cable

**Symptoms: Diminished Network Performance, Collisions,
Frame Check Sequence (FCS)Errors**

Cause (1):   Crosstalk due to split pairs, untwisted cable segments in patch panels or Token-Ring concentrators.

Cause (2):   Crosstalk due to insufficient cable quality for the data speeds used.

Cause (3):   Crosstalk and reflections due to unsuitable connector systems (connectors, wall jacks, etc.) for high data speeds.

Cause (4):   Electromagnetic interference: cables near photocopiers, power lines, x-ray systems, pagers, production environments or other source of EMI.

Cause (5):   Cable and wall plug shielding not grounded or grounded to different potentials.

Symptom: Unusually High Number of Collisions and Fragments

Cause (1):   Cable impedance exceeds tolerance limits.
This can be caused by the poor quality of the cable itself or by poor installation (cabling bundled too tightly or bent).

Cause (2):   Faulty wiring in patch panel; faulty or loose connectors.

**Symptom: Intermittent Loss of Connection or No Connection After New
Installation**

Cause (1):   Excessive attenuation in newly installed cables; variations in impedance between connectors and cables or in patch panels; inadequate wiring through several patch panels.

Cause (2):   Wiring faults (reversed pairs, split pairs, transposed pairs).

Cause (3):   Patch faults at patch panel.

Symptom: Complete Failure of a Station

Cause (1):   Faulty cable; bent cable.

Cause (2):   Faulty connection between cable and connector due to defective or low-quality crimp components.

Twisted-pair cable can have either solid or stranded wire. If RJ-45 plugs designed for stranded wire cables (primarily used as patch cables) are used for solid wire, the crimp contacts just touch the surface of the wire and lose contact over time (see Figure 6.18).

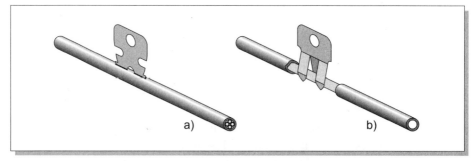

Figure 6.18 Crimping solid and stranded wire cables

Cause (3):   Short circuit in the cable due to kinks, excessive bending, defective material, or a nail inadvertently driven through the cable.

Gathering Information; Common Errors

As with coaxial cable, comprehensive information about the context of a problem with twisted-pair cable provides a detailed description of the symptoms and clues to possible causes. Questions to ask at this stage include:

- Has anyone connected or disconnected a PC (laptop or desktop) or any other component to or from the network?
- Has anyone installed an interface card in a computer?
- Has a telephone or fax machine been installed?
- Has anyone stepped on a cable?
- Has any maintenance work been performed in the building recently (by a telephone company or building maintenance personnel, for example)?
- Has anyone (including cleaning personnel) moved any equipment or furniture?

Figure 6.19 lists the most common causes of problems in twisted-pair cabling infrastructures:

- Wiring errors in patch panels
- Wiring errors in connectors
- Crosstalk due to split pairs
- Near-end crosstalk due to inferior cable unsuitable for high-speed data
- Continuity faults due to poor crimp connections in connectors
- Continuity faults due to bends, kinks, loose connectors
- Short circuits due to mechanical stress or material defects
- Near-end crosstalk due to faulty installation of patch panels or cable routing
- Near-end crosstalk due to untwisted patching (in patch panels or TCUs)
- Impedance anomalies due to cramped cable bundles
- Excessive attenuation because cables are too long
- Electromagnetic interference (elevators, electric machinery) or mechanical stress (doors, furniture)

Figure 6.19 The most common causes of problems in twisted-pair cabling infrastructures

6.3 Fiber-Optic Cable

6.3.1 Fiber-Optic Cable: Specification and Implementation

In recent years fiber-optic cabling has proven to be a sturdy, high-performance transmission medium for use in both primary (campus) and secondary (building or vertical) cabling. The fiber-optic cables most commonly used are multimode cables with wavelengths of 850 nm or 1,300 nm. At power levels of -10 dBm to -20 dBm, signals can travel distances of some 5 kilometers. The dynamic range of such segments is between 15 dB and 20 dB. With the trend toward data speeds of 622 Mbit/s and 2.4 Gbit/s, however, even LAN infrastructures are increasingly coming to rely on single-mode, fiber-optic cabling with a wavelength of 1,550 nm.

Two types of connectors are used in fiber-optic LANs: those that make contact between one fiber and the next fiber (mated connections), and those that leave an air gap between the fiber end and the connector (unmated connections). Unmated connections are easier to work with because they are not as easily contaminated as mated connections, but they have a higher insertion loss.

Figure 6.20 lists the types of fiber-optic cabling and connection systems used in various LAN topologies.

LAN topologies:	Ethernet FOIRL	10Base-F	Token Bus	Token Ring	FDDI (multimode)	FDDI (single-mode)	Fibre Channel	Gigabit Ethernet
Wavelength (nm)	850 (790 – 910)	850 800 – 910 (active) 820 – 910 (passive)	850 800 – 910	850 800 – 910	1300 (1270 – 1380)	1300 (1270 - 1340, Cat. 1) (1290 - 1330, Cat. 2)	1300	850 (multimode) 13,000 (single-mode)
Signal power (dBm)	-12 to -15	-12 to -20 (active) -11 to -15 (passive)	-7 to -11	-13 to -22	-14 to -20	-14 to -20 (Cat. 1) -15 to -37 (Cat. 2)		
Receiver sensitivity (dBm)	- 9 to -27	-12 to -32.5 (active) - 27 to -41 (passive)	-31/41 to -11/-21	-12 to -30	-14 to -31	-14 to -31 (Cat. 1) -15 to -37 (Cat. 2)		
Maximum network length (km)	4.5	4.5	4.5	4.5	200	200		
Maximum segment length (km)	1	2	1	2	2	2	1 (200 Mbit/s) >10 (800 Mbit/s)	0.55 (multimode 5 single-mode)
Connector types	F-SMA, ST	ST, F-SMA	MIC; ST; Biconic, F-SMA, Mini-BNC	MIC; ST; Biconic, F-SMA, Mini-BNC	MIC, ST	SM-MIC	SC	SC

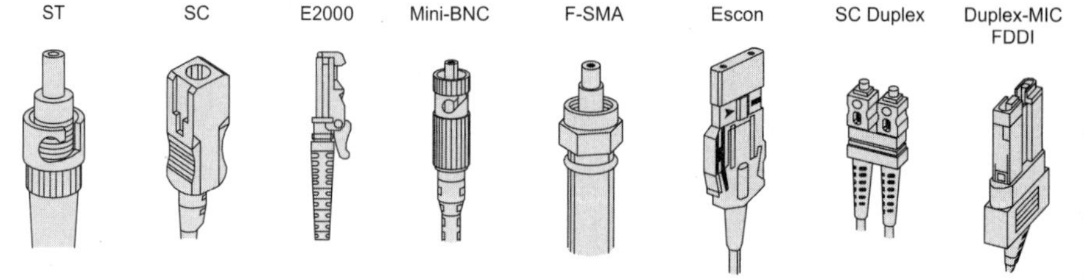

Figure 6.20 Fiber-optic cabling and connectors in local-area networks

The permissible length for a fiber-optic cable is derived from the available attenuation budget, which in turn depends on the performance of the transmitting device and the sensitivity of the receiver. Each splice in a cable increases the attenuation by about 0.1 dB; each connector by up to 0.5 dB.

6.3.2   Troubleshooting Fiber-Optic Cable

The most important tasks in diagnosing problems with fiber-optic cable involve checking the power and attenuation, and taking measurements with an optical time-domain reflectometer (OTDR).

Attenuation is measured in order to determine whether or not the total attenuation of a cable segment exceeds the attenuation budget. The first step is to set up the testing conditions in accordance with IEC 874-1, Method 6. This involves inserting a reference cable in place of the cable segment to be tested, between the transmitter and receiver of the measuring instrument. A reference measurement is taken from this cable and compared with the results measured on the actual network cable. The reference values serve to offset the influence of the test location and the test connector. Once the reference values have been recorded, the same measurements are performed on the cable to be tested (see Figure 6.21).

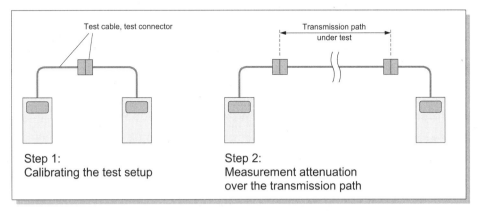

Figure 6.21 Attenuation measurement with test setup calibration
in accordance with IEC 874-1

OTDR measurements are used to detect individual components of the overall attenuation along a segment of fiber-optic cable, and to precisely locate each component. When performing OTDR measurements, keep in mind that most OTDR devices have a "dead zone" at close range. The dead zone is the range that cannot be reliably evaluated due to reflections in the device connector and an overdriven OTDR. The sensitivity of the OTDR determines the maximum amplitude difference that the testing device can detect between the signal pulse and the reflected signal. Over longer cable segments, a higher dynamic means the ability to measure greater distances. With the relatively short distances found in LANs, high dynamics are also an advantage because they allow the use of shorter pulses, resulting in higher resolution. The shorter the signal pulse, the easier it is to detect separate reflections that arrive in rapid succession.

Regular maintenance of fiber-optic cables is also important. Cable maintenance tasks include regular measurements of the signal strengths of all active components, as well as checking the connector contacts for crossed fibers and contamination.

6.3.3   Symptoms and Causes: Fiber-Optic Cable

Symptom: No Connection

Cause: Line break due to external shock or extreme bending in the cable
The bending radius of the cable must not be less than 20 times the cable diameter. Thus for internal fiber-optic cables with a diameter of 3 mm, for example, the minimum bending radius allowed is 6 cm. Check all bend radii; if necessary, switch to an intact pair for the connection in question.

Use an OTDR to check for breaks in the cable. If no suitable test device is available, the "lighter test" can be used for cable segments of up to several hundred meters: hold a lighter to the cross section of the fiber at one end and verify that light is visible with the naked eye at other end.

Symptom: No Connection or Intermittent Connection Problems

Cause (1):   Attenuation too high due to poor workmanship on splices or too many splices.
Check the signal strength using an optical source and power meter.

Cause (2):   Contamination of connectors (dust, fingerprints, humidity, etc.)

Cause (3):   Transmitter signal strength too low.
Increase light power or replace the LED/laser module.

Symptom: No Connection After New Installation

Cause (1):   Faulty connection in wiring closet.

Cause (2):   Poor splice; attenuation too high.

Cause (3):   Dirty connectors (dust, fingerprints, humidity, etc.).

Gathering Information; Common Errors

As with copper cables, comprehensive information about the context of a problem with fiber-optic cable provides a detailed description of the symptoms and clues to possible causes. Questions to ask at this stage include:

• Has anyone connected or disconnected a PC (laptop or desktop) or any other component to or from the network?

• Has anyone installed an interface card in a computer?

• Has anyone stepped on a cable?

• Has any maintenance work been performed in the building recently (by a telephone company or building maintenance personnel, for example)?

• Has anyone (including cleaning personnel) moved any equipment or furniture?

The most common causes of problems in fiber-optic cabling infrastructures are listed here:

- Excessive loss due to faulty splices or connectors; too many splices or connectors
- Fiber break due to mechanical stress or insufficient bending radius
- Wrong fiber connected in splice tray or at patch panel
- Insufficient transmitter power
- Excessive loss due to contaminated connector
- Excessive loss due to excessive cable length

Figure 6.22 The most common causes of problems in fiber-optic cabling infrastructures

10/100/1,000 Mbit/s Ethernet

7

"Hofstadter's Law: It always takes longer than you expect, even when you take Hofstadter's Law into account."

D0UG HOFSTADTER

7.1   10/100/1,000 Mbit/s Ethernet: Specification and Implementation

Ethernet, the classic LAN topology, is still the most popular in local-area networks. Originally designed for data speeds of only 10 Mbit/s, Ethernet exists today in three widely used versions: the original 10 Mbit/s Ethernet (IEEE 802.3), Fast Ethernet transmitting at 100 Mbit/s (IEEE 802.3u), and Gigabit Ethernet, with a throughput of 1,000 Mbit/s (IEEE 802.3z).

Ethernet's half-duplex transmission technique uses the non-deterministic Carrier-Sense Multiple Access/Collision Detection (CSMA/CD) algorithm to control access to the LAN medium. In half-duplex transmission technologies, it is not possible to transmit and receive data at the same time. When one network node is transmitting, all other nodes in the segment must be in 'receive' mode. If two Ethernet stations transmit simultaneously, their data packets collide and are destroyed. After a collision, the nodes involved must pause for a random delay period before starting the next transmission attempt. The probability of collisions increases with the number of active nodes in a segment. Another important factor determining the likelihood of collisions is the length of the network segment: the greater the distance between two nodes in a network segment, the greater the so-called "slot time", which is the critical parameter of the CSMA/CD algorithm. Slot time is defined as twice the time it takes a signal to travel between the two nodes that are farthest apart in an Ethernet segment, and is therefore the longest time it can take for a transmitting node to detect the occurrence of a collision (see Figure 7.1).

TROUBLESHOOTING LOCAL-AREA NETWORKS

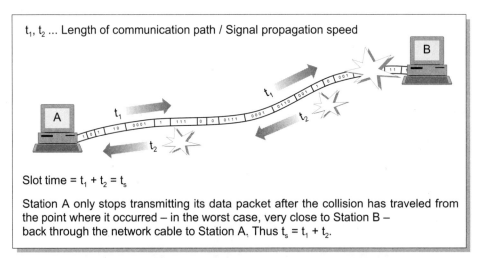

$t_1, t_2 \ldots$ Length of communication path / Signal propagation speed

B

A

Slot time $= t_1 + t_2 = t_s$

Station A only stops transmitting its data packet after the collision has traveled from the point where it occurred – in the worst case, very close to Station B – back through the network cable to Station A. Thus $t_s = t_1 + t_2$.

Figure 7.1 The CSMA/CD algorithm in Ethernet

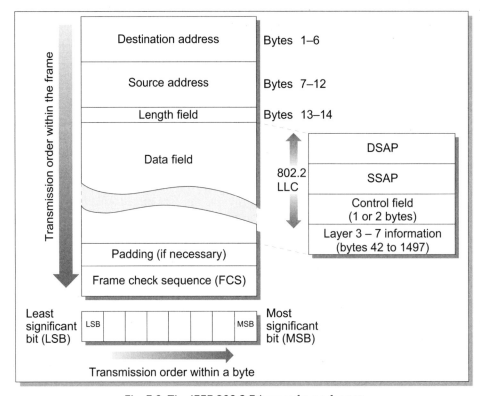

Transmission order within the frame

Destination address	Bytes 1–6
Source address	Bytes 7–12
Length field	Bytes 13–14
Data field	
Padding (if necessary)	
Frame check sequence (FCS)	

802.2 LLC

DSAP

SSAP

Control field (1 or 2 bytes)

Layer 3 – 7 information (bytes 42 to 1497)

Least significant bit (LSB)   LSB   MSB   Most significant bit (MSB)

Transmission order within a byte

Fig. 7.2 The IEEE 802.3 Ethernet frame format

7.1.1   The Ethernet Frame Format

Ethernet data packets, called "frames", are between 64 and 1,518 bytes long and consist of the following six fields: the preamble (7 bytes), the starting frame delimiter (1byte), source and destination address fields (6 bytes each), the length field or "type field" in Ethernet 2.0 (2 bytes), and the data field. At the end of each frame, a 4-byte frame check sequence (FCS), calculated from the two address fields, the length/type field and the data field, is used by the receiver to detect whether the frame was received without errors. A minimum interval of 9.6 µs (92 bits at 10 Mbit/s) is required between frames. This is called the inter-frame spacing gap.

The minimum packet size is equal to the number of bits that can be transmitted in the maximum allowed slot time of 51.2 µs. (51.2 µs corresponds to 512 bit times, or 64 bytes in 10 Mbit/s networks). Any packet shorter than 64 bytes is considered a collision fragment and discarded. All packets longer than 1,518 bytes, called jabbers, are also discarded as invalid.

The Preamble

The preamble is used by the receiving hardware of an Ethernet node to synchronize with the transmitting node's clock. It consists of 56 alternating 0 and 1 bits.

The Starting Frame Delimiter

The 8-bit starting frame delimiter field immediately follows the last preamble bit and marks the beginning of the actual Ethernet frame. The bit sequence of the starting frame delimiter is: 10101011.

The MAC Address Fields

Every Ethernet frame contains two MAC address fields, one containing the destination address and the other the source address. Each address field consists of 48 bits (6 bytes). The first bit (the least significant bit or LSB) distinguishes between single node and group addresses (LSB=1 for a group address, LSB=0 for an individual address). In the source address field, the first bit is reserved; the default value is 0. The second bit distinguishes between locally and globally administered addresses (bit 2=0: global address; bit 2=1: local address). If a packet is broadcast to all stations, all bits of the destination field are set to 1, so that the address in hexadecimal is FF-FF-FF-FF-FF-FF.

The Length Field (Type Field)

The 2-byte length field indicates the number of logical link control (LLC) data bytes—excluding any padding—contained in the data field. This was designated as the type field in the older Ethernet 2.0 specification because it indicated the type of network layer protocol carried in the data field. ("Ethernet 2.0" refers to the original Digital/Intel/Xerox Ethernet specification, "The Ethernet Version 2.0", dated November, 1982.)

The Data Field

The data field contains between 46 and 1,500 bytes of data. If the data in this field amounts to less than the minimum field length, padding bits are added to make up the difference.

Frame Check Sequence (FCS)

The FCS field contains a 4-byte cyclical redundancy check (CRC) value calculated from the MAC address fields, the type/length field and the data field. The receiving station performs the same checksum calculation on the type/length and data fields of every Ethernet frame received and compares the result with the contents of the FCS field received to detect transmission errors.

7.1.2   Ethernet Network Topologies

In 10 Mbit/s Ethernet networks, a choice must be made between linear bus topologies using coaxial cables and star-shaped topologies using twisted-pair cabling with multiport repeaters (also known as hubs). In the Fast Ethernet and Gigabit Ethernet variants, however, linear bus topologies are no longer an option. High-speed Ethernet networks require star topologies of high-performance, twisted-pair or fiber cabling. To further increase the efficiency of Ethernet networks, segments that carry high data loads are increasingly designed using LAN switches instead of hubs. These Ethernet switches route all incoming packets directly to their destination ports, rather than broadcasting them to all ports as passive hubs do. This means that adjacent segments are not unnecessarily burdened with traffic addressed to stations not present. Aside from the frame format, however, this method of packet transmission has little in common with the original Ethernet transmission mechanisms. Both the broadcast and the CSMA/CD transmission algorithms have been abandoned in favor of the more efficient switching method.

The third variant, alongside hub and switch-based Ethernet topologies, is full-duplex Ethernet. It is specifically designed for high-speed, point-to-point server connections. Each full-duplex node is equipped with a full-duplex Ethernet interface so that transmission and reception can take place at the same time. This doubles the effective transmission bandwidth to 20 Mbit/s, 200 Mbit/s or 2 Gbit/s. When full-duplex nodes are connected by full-duplex switches, complete full-duplex Ethernet segments can be built.

7.1.3 Design Guidelines for 10 Mbit/s Ethernet Networks

10Base2, 10Base5

The minimum segment length in 10Base2 networks is 0.5 meters; the maximum is 185 meters. The maximum number of nodes on a single segment is 30 and the minimum distance between two nodes is 0.5 meters. For 10Base5 networks, the segment length must be between 2.5 and 500 meters, and the maximum number of stations per segment is 100. Up to four repeaters can be used to extend the segment length. The maximum transmission path between two nodes thus consists of five segments, four repeaters, two media access units (MAUs) and two attachment universal interface (AUI) cables. However, the overall network length must not exceed 2.5 kilometers, with a maximum propagation delay per segment of 2,165 ns in 10Base5 and 950 ns in 10Base2 networks (see Figure 7.3).

Distant Ethernet segments can be connected either by intermediate segments or by inter-repeater links (IRLs). IRLs using optical fiber, called fiber-optic, inter-repeater links (FOIRLs), can extend the maximum segment range to as much as 4.5 kilometers. Each end of the FOIRL counts as a full repeater, however, which

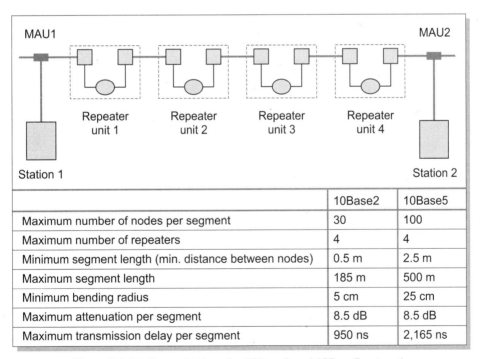

	10Base2	10Base5
Maximum number of nodes per segment	30	100
Maximum number of repeaters	4	4
Minimum segment length (min. distance between nodes)	0.5 m	2.5 m
Maximum segment length	185 m	500 m
Minimum bending radius	5 cm	25 cm
Maximum attenuation per segment	8.5 dB	8.5 dB
Maximum transmission delay per segment	950 ns	2,165 ns

Figure 7.3 Design guidelines for 10Base2 and 10Base5 networks

means no more than two FOIRL links are allowed in each segment. Furthermore, the bit-error rate of each FOIRL must be less than 1 error in 10^{10} transmitted bits.

If possible, the entire segment should be built from a single, homogeneous cable. If a segment consists of several cable sections, all cables should be obtained from the same manufacturer. When connecting a number of long cable segments, make sure the reflections that occur at either end are out of phase with one another. This can be achieved by using cable segments with lengths that are equal to an odd multiple of one-half wavelength in the cable at 5 MHz. Standard cable lengths of 23.4, 70.2, and 117 meters can be combined for every section, up to a total of 500 meters, to eliminate reflection interference.

10Base-T

In 10Base-T networks the maximum distance between hub and wall jack is 90 meters, with another 10 meters allowed for the work area cable between the wall jack and the MAU. The total distance between hub and node must be less than 100 meters. The attenuation of the transmission medium (at 10 MHz) must not exceed 11.5 dB; the NEXT value must be over 30.5 dB. The maximum transmission delay allowed for the entire segment is 1,000 ns. Figure 7.4 lists the critical parameters for 10Base-T as well as for the fiber-based 10 Mbit/s variants 10Base-FB and 10Base-FL (FB stands for Fiber Backbone; FL stands for Fiber Link: IEEE 802.3j).

10Base-T parameter	Limit
Maximum segment length	100 m
Maximum attenuation	< 11.5 dB
Interference voltage (40 Hz - 150 kHz)	< 50 mV
Interference voltage (150 kHz - 16 MHz)	< 50 mV
Interference voltage (16 MHz - 100 MHz)	< 300 mV
Maximum transmission delay per segment	1,000 ns
NEXT (4 MHz - 15 MHz)	> 30.5 dB

	Maximum segment length	Maximum attenuation	Propagation speed	Maximum signal delay
FOIRL	1 km	9 dB	0.66 c	5,000 ns
10Base-FB	2 km	12.5 dB	0.66 c	1,000 ns
10Base-FL	2 km	12.5 dB	0.66 c	1,000 ns

Figure 7.4 Network design guidelines for 10Base-T, 10Base-FB, 10Base-FL and FOIRL

Calculation of the Propagation Delay in 10 Mbit/s Ethernet Networks

The 10Base-F specification was the first to describe an accurate method for calculation of the propagation delay Path Delay Value (PDV) in Ethernet networks, and lists maximum values for the various 10 Mbit/s topologies. In 10Base-F, the PDV is equal to the product of a cable-specific coefficient and the segment length (meters), plus a topology-specific base value. The default value for the drop cables in this calculation is 2 meters; if you use longer drop cables, the calculation must be adjusted accordingly. The total PDV must not exceed 575 bit times:

Segment type	Base for first segment	Base for intermediate segment	Base for last segment	Coefficient (bit times)	Maximum length (m)
10Base5	11.75	46.5	169.5	0.0866	500
10Base2	11.75	46.5	169.5	0.1026	185
10Base-T	15.25	42	165	0.113	100
10Base-FP	11.25	61	183.5	0.1	1,000
10Base-FB		24		0.1	2,000
10Base-FL	12.25	33.5	156.5	0.1	2,000
AUI (-2m)				0.1026	48
FOIRL	7.75	29	152	0.1	1,000

Figure 7.5 Path delay components in 10 Mbit/s Ethernet networks

Another important factor in the evaluation of Ethernet network design is the inter-packet gap shrinkage, expressed by the Path Variability Value (PVV). The PVV measured across the longest transmission path in a network must not exceed 49 bit times. Figure 7.6 lists the inter-packet gap shrinkage in bit times for individual Ethernet segments.

Segment type	Transmission segment (bit times)	Intermediate segment (bit times)
Coaxial cable	16	11
10Base-FB	–	2
10Base-FP	11	8
All other	10.5	8

Figure 7.6 Inter-packet shrinkage per segment in 10 Mbit/s Ethernet networks

7.1.4   Design Guidelines for 100 Mbit/s Ethernet Networks

The main differences in network design between 10 Mbit/s and 100 Mbit/s Ethernet networks are the maximum segment lengths and the number of repeaters allowed in a transmission path at 100 Mbit/s. This is because the CSMA/CD algorithm only functions efficiently up to a certain segment length. Increasing the distance between two Ethernet nodes also increases the propagation delay of the frames and, therefore, the size of the collision window, that is, the time during which a station can transmit before recognizing that a collision has occurred. Because the propagation delay of the signals is the same in 10Base-T and 100Base-T networks (about 0.6 c), the change in collision behavior due to the higher transmission speed must be compensated for by shortening the maximum segment length. Leaving the distance limit unchanged could result in collision fragments of up to 640 rather than 64 bytes because the transmission rate is ten times faster. Packets shorter than 640 bytes might be lost in collisions without the transmitting station noticing—the collision signal would arrive at the transmitting station only after the transmission process had been completed. The station would not associate the collision event with the successfully transmitted packet, and thus would not repeat the transmission. The entire CSMA/CD algorithm would, therefore, no longer function for a significant portion of network traffic.

Calculation of the Propagation Delay in 100 Mbit/s Ethernet Networks

As with the 10Base-F specification, a method has been defined for calculating the maximum propagation delay in 100Base-T networks. This method uses the following equation:

$$PDV = \Sigma\ LSDV + S\ repeater\ delays + \Sigma\ MII\ cable\ delays + \Sigma\ node\ delays$$
$$\leq 511\ bit\ times$$

where

$$LSDV = 2\ x\ segment\ length\ x\ cable\ delay.$$

Figure 7.7 lists values for the various delay components in 100Base-T networks.

Network topology	Delay in bit times per meter	Maximum signal delay in bit times
Two nodes	—	100
Cat. 3 UTP	0.57	114
Cat. 4 UTP	0.57	114
Cat. 5 UTP	0.556	111.2
STP	0.556	111.2
Fiber optic	0.501	408
Class 1 repeater	—	168
Class 2 repeater	—	92
MII	1	—

Figure 7.7 Delay components in 100Base-T networks

100Base-T Full-Duplex Connections

The maximum distance between two 100Base-T nodes connected in full-duplex mode is 100 meters with twisted-pair cabling; 400 meters with multimode fiber in half-duplex mode; 2 kilometers with multimode fiber in full-duplex mode; and up to 15 kilometers with single-mode media in full-duplex operation. Most network element vendors support the usage of high-speed interconnections (ISLs) to increase the inter-switch or inter-router capacity. Multiple ISLs are called trunks.

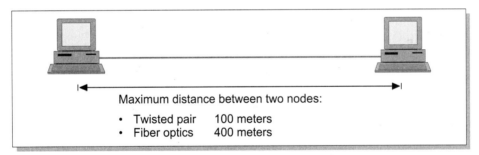

Maximum distance between two nodes:

- Twisted pair   100 meters
- Fiber optics   400 meters

Figure 7.8 Connecting network nodes in 100Base-T full-duplex mode

Cable Length Restrictions and Number of Repeaters (Hubs) in 100Base-T Networks

A maximum of two Class 2 repeaters or one Class 1 repeater is allowed within a single collision domain. Class 1 repeaters can be used to connect several different 100Base-T media (such as 100Base-TX, 100Base-T4 and 100Base-FX), whereas Class 2 repeaters can be used only for 100Base-TX or 100Base-T4 in combination with 100Base-FX. Class 1 repeaters are therefore more flexible, but they are also slower so that no more than one repeater of this type may be used per transmission path. When Class 1 repeaters are used, the maximum network diameter is 200 meters for two twisted-pair segments, 240 meters for two fiber-optic segments, and 230 meters for a mixed twisted-pair/fiber-optic segment.

Class 2 repeaters can only connect 100Base-T segments of the same medium. Up to two Class 2 repeaters can be cascaded. The limits for segments with one Class 2 repeater are 200 meters for Cat. 3 UTP cable, 318 meters for fiber optic,

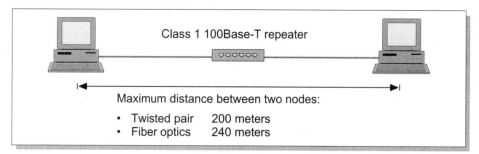

Figure 7.9 Design guidelines for 100Base-T networks with Class 1 repeaters

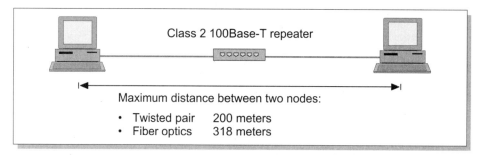

Figure 7.10 Design guidelines for 100Base-T networks with one Class 2 repeater

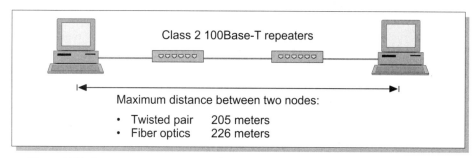

Figure 7.11 Design guidelines for 100Base-T networks with two Class 2 repeaters

and 285 meters for fiber optic and twisted pair. When two Class 2 repeaters are used, the network diameter can be up to 205 meters for Cat. 5 UTP cable, 226 meters for fiber optic, or 212 meters for fiber optic and twisted pair.

100Base-T Uplinks

Uplinks to LAN switches must not exceed 100 meters of twisted-pair cabling or 163 meters when using fiber and Class 1 repeaters. If fiber and Class 2 repeaters are used, the maximum uplink distance can be extended to 189 meters.

100Base-T Switch Links

Connections between 100Base-T switches are limited in length to 100 meters of twisted-pair cable, and to 400 meters when fiber-optic cabling is used. Thus two 100Base-T segments can be connected by two fiber-linked 100Base-T switches over a distance of 778 meters (2 x 189 m fiber uplink + 400 m switch interconnection). The price for this range, however, is that two additional switching systems must be used.

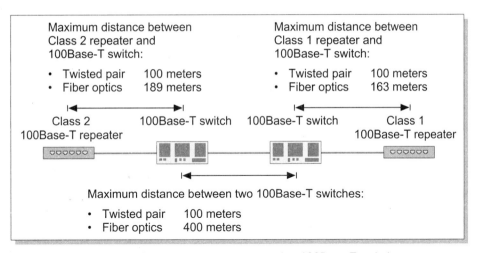

Figure 7.12 Connecting workgroups using 100Base-T switches

7.1.5 Design Guidelines for 1,000 Mbit/s Ethernet Networks

Gigabit Ethernet (IEEE 802.3z) increases data speed to 1,000 Mbit/s and, in full-duplex mode, reaches a throughput of up to 2 Gbit/s. Gigabit Ethernet uses the same frame format as 10 and 100 Mbit/s Ethernet and, like the slower variants, can be operated in either half- or full-duplex mode. In half-duplex mode, however, frames which are between 64 and 511 bytes long are artificially extended to 512 bytes in order to expand the diameter of a collision domain to 200 meters. This process is called "Carrier Extension". However, the Frame Check Sequence (FCS) is calculated only on the original frame. When a station has several packets to transmit, "Packet Bursting" can be used. In this case packets are transmitted back to back separated only by the Inter-frame gap until a burst timer expires. Bursting increases the throughput substantially. In full-duplex transmission mode no collisions can occur. Therefore there is no need for carrier extension on frame bursting in Gigabit Ethernet full-duplex operation. In full-duplex mode, the CSMA/CD access mechanism, and consequently this frame extension, is not required; the minimum packet size remains 64 bytes.

The Gigabit Ethernet standard specifies multimode and monomode fiber or Cat. 5 UTP cable as the transmission media. The following table lists the distance limitations of Gigabit Ethernet.

Standard	Communication medium (MM = multimode fiber, SM = single-mode fiber, UTP = unshielded twisted pair)	Fiber diameter/ wavelength	Bandwidth (MHz · km)	Minimum and maximum link length (m)	Connector
1,000Base-SX	MM	62.5/830nm	160	2 – 220	Duplex SC
1,000Base-SX	MM	62.5	200	2 – 275	Duplex SC
1,000Base-SX	MM	50	400	2 – 500	Duplex SC
1,000Base-SX	MM	50	500	2 – 550	Duplex SC
1,000Base-LX	MM	62.5	500	2 – 550	Duplex SC
1,000Base-LX	MM	50	400	2 – 550	Duplex SC
1,000Base-LX	MM	50	500	2 – 550	Duplex SC
1,000Base-LX	SM	9	—	2 – 5,000	Duplex SC
1,000Base-CX	Coax	—	—	25	STP (DB9); IEC6 1076
1,000Base-T	UTP-5 (four pairs)	—	—	100	RJ-45

Figure 7.13 Distance limitations for IEEE 802.3z Gigabit Ethernet

7.1.6   Ethernet Standards

IEEE Std 802.3, Carrier Sense Multiple Access with Collision Detection (CSMA/CD) Access Method and Physical Layer Specifications.

IEEE Std 802.3a-1988, 10 Mb/s MAU 10BASE2 (Clause 10).

IEEE Std 802.3b-1985, Broadband Medium Attachment Unit and Broadband Medium Specifications, Type 10BROAD36 (Clause 11).

IEEE Std 802.3c-1985, Repeater Unit for 10 Mb/s Baseband Networks (Subclauses 9.1-9.8).

IEEE Std 802.3d-1987, Medium Attachment Unit and Baseband Medium Specification for a Vendor Independent Fiber Optic Inter Repeater Link (Section 9.9).

IEEE Std 802.3e-1987, Physical Signaling, Medium Attachment, and Baseband Medium Specifications, Type 1BASE5 (Clause 12).

IEEE Std 802.3h-1990, Layer Management (Clause 5).

IEEE Std 802.3i-1990, System Considerations for Multisegment 10 Mb/s Baseband Networks (Clause 13) and Twisted-Pair Medium Attachment Unit (MAU) and Baseband Medium, Type 10BASE-T (Section 14).

IEEE Std 802.3j-1993, Fiber Optic Active and Passive Star-Based Segments, Type 10BASE-F (Clauses 15-18).

IEEE Std 802.3k-1992, Layer Management for 10 Mb/s Baseband Repeaters (Clause 19).

IEEE Std 802.3l-1992, Type 10BASE-T Medium Attachment Unit (MAU) Protocol Implementation Conformance Statement (PICS) Proforma (Subclause 14.10).

IEEE Std 802.3m-1995, Second Maintenance Ballot.

IEEE Std 802.3n-1995, Third Maintenance Ballot. IEEE Std 802.3p-1993, Layer Management for 10 Mb/s Baseband Medium Attachment Units (MAUs) (Clause 20).

IEEE Std 802.3q-1993, Guidelines for the Development of Managed Objects (GDMO) (ISO 10165-4) Format for Layer-Managed Objects (Clause 5).

IEEE Std 802.3r-1997, Type 10BASE5 Medium Attachment Unit PICS Proforma.

IEEE Std 802.3s-1995, Fourth Maintenance Ballot.

IEEE Std 802.3t-1995, Informative Annex for Support of 120 Ohm Cables in 10BASE-T Simplex Link Segment (Annex D.5).

IEEE Std 802.3u-1995, Type 100BASE-T MAC Parameters, Physical Layer, MAUs, and Repeater for 100 Mb/s Operation.

IEEE Std 802.3v-1995, Informative Annex for Support of 150 Ohm Cables in 10 BASE-T Link Segment (Annex D.6).

IEEE Std 802.3x&y-1997, Specification for 802.3 Full-Duplex Operation and Physical Layer Specification for 100 Mb/s Operation on Two Pairs of Category 3 or Better Balanced Twisted Pair Cable (100BASE-T2).

IEEE Std 802.3z-1998, Physical Layers, Repeater, and Management Parameters for 1000 Mb/s Operation.

IEEE Std 802.3aa-1998, Maintenance Revision #5 (Revisions to 100BASE-T).

IEEE 802.3.ab, Physical Layer Parameters and Specifications for 1000 Mb/s Operation Over 4-Pair Category 5 Balanced Copper Cabling, Type 1000BASE-T.

IEEE Std 802.3ac-1998, Supplement to IEEE Std 802.3, 1998 Edition, Carrier Sense Multiple Access with Collision Detection (CSMA/CD)—Frame Extensions for Virtual Bridged Local Area Network (VLAN) Tagging on 802.3 Networks.

IEEE 802.3w, Standard for Enhanced Media Access Control Algorithm.

IEEE 1802.3 d-1993, Supplement to IEEE Std 1802.3-1991, Local and Metropolitan Area Networks: Conformance Test Methodology: Carrier Sense Multiple Access with Collision Detection (CSMA/CD) Access Method and Physical Layer Specifications:

RFC 1271 Remote Network Monitoring Management Information Base.

RFC 2074 Remote Network Monitoring MIB Protocol Identifiers.

The IEEE 802.3 Working Group can be reached through the Internet at

http://grouper.ieee.org/groups/802/3/index.html

7.2 Troubleshooting in 10/100/1,000 Mbit/s Ethernet

7.2.1 Gathering Information on Symptoms and Recent Changes

The first step in any troubleshooting process is to gather information. The more information you have about the symptoms and characteristics of a problem—including *when* it first occurred—the better your chances of solving the problem quickly and efficiently. Typical questions you might ask at this stage include:

* Do the symptoms occur regularly or intermittently?
* Are the symptoms related to certain applications (running simultaneously with), or do they affect all network operations?
* Are similar applications malfunctioning?
* How many users are involved?
* Do the symptoms correlate to other activities in the network?
* When was the first occurrence of the symptom?
* Was there any change in any hardware or software network component?
* Has anyone connected or disconnected a PC (laptop or desktop) or any other component to or from the network?
* Has anyone installed an interface card in a computer?
* Has anyone stepped on a cable?
* Has any maintenance work been performed in the building recently (by a telephone company or building maintenance personnel, for example)?
* Has anyone (including cleaning personnel) moved any equipment or furniture?

In general, it is advised to restart a device immediately after a change has been made to it. Otherwise a problem resulting from a change may come into effect at a later time, when another user starts the device.

7.2.2 Starting the Troubleshooting Procedure

Troubleshooting in Ethernet LANs is primarily performed using protocol analyzers, network management software, and cable testers. If the network is still up and running, the first step in the troubleshooting procedure involves using a protocol analyzer to determine the main operating statistics of the network. These statistics include capacity use in bytes and as a percentage, packet throughput per second, the collision rate, the packet length distribution, FCS errors, the proportions of broadcast and multicast packets, the numbers of runts and jabbers and the number of transmitting stations.

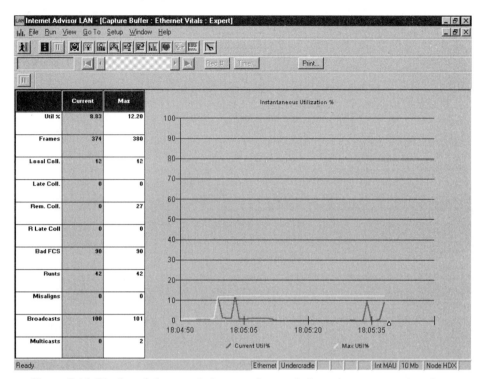

Figure 7.14 Display of characteristic operating statistics using a protocol analyzer

In many cases, the analysis of operating statistics leads directly to the source of the problem. However, because Ethernet networks use a bus topology, many problem symptoms that are detected in one segment can originate in an adjacent segment or in more remote parts of the network. If the problem cannot be localized, longer-term measurements are necessary. Characteristic operating statistics are recorded systematically over time and analyzed for correlated parameters. For example, if a correlation is observed between the number of active stations, the number of collisions and the network capacity use, it is highly likely that performance problems are related to the active components (network nodes, repeaters, etc.) in the network. If there is no such correlation, it is more likely that the source of the problem lies in the cabling infrastructure.

In many cases, such measurements must be taken in several network segments concurrently (using LAN probes, for example). When the results are displayed in a graph, an analysis of any temporal correlations can indicate whether events in a given segment caused symptoms in others or vice versa. This measurement and analysis procedure is repeated until the range of possible problem sources can be limited to a small area.

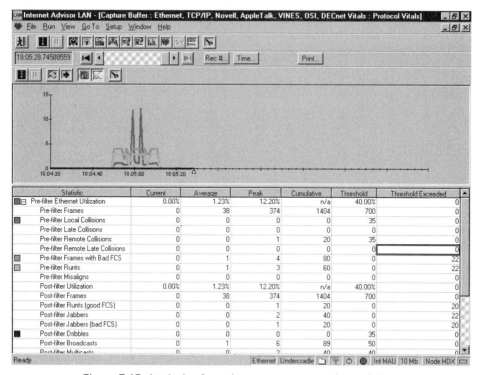

	Statistic	Current	Average	Peak	Cumulative	Threshold	Threshold Exceeded	
▣⊟	Pre-filter Ethernet Utilization	0.00%	1.23%	12.20%	n/a	40.00%	0	
	Pre-filter Frames	0	38	374	1404	700	0	
■	Pre-filter Local Collisions	0	0	0	0	35	0	
	Pre-filter Late Collisions	0	0	0	0	0	0	
	Pre-filter Remote Collisions	0	0	1	20	35	0	
	Pre-filter Remote Late Collisions	0	0	0	0	0	0	
▣	Pre-filter Frames with Bad FCS	0	1	4	80	0	22	
▢	Pre-filter Runts	0	1	3	60	0	22	
	Pre-filter Misaligns	0	0	0	0	0	0	
	Post-filter Utilization	0.00%	1.23%	12.20%	n/a	40.00%	0	
	Post-filter Frames	0	38	374	1404	700	0	
	Post-filter Runts (good FCS)	0	0	1	20	0	20	
	Post-filter Jabbers	0	0	2	40	0	22	
	Post-filter Jabbers (bad FCS)	0	0	1	20	0	20	
■	Post-filter Dribbles	0	0	0	0	35	0	
	Post-filter Broadcasts	0	1	6	89	50	0	
	Post-filter Multicasts	0	0	2	40	40	0	

Figure 7.15 Analysis of trend measurements and correlations

What steps to take after a protocol analyzer performs the basic measurements depends on the nature of the symptoms. If the symptoms can be localized or occur periodically, or can at least be reproduced, then the troubleshooting process continues with the network component nearest the problem. If the problem source cannot be detected there, the range of analysis is successively expanded. For example, if the problems are found to be related to a single network node, the next step is to analyze the station's software and hardware components. If no fault is found, the examination progresses to the station's MAU and AUI cable, its power cable connector, the wall jack, the cable to the hub, the hub itself, the cable to the server, and so on. If the problem cannot be localized at all, or if problems that were thought to have been localized cannot be pinpointed, the only way to find the source of the problem is through systematic segmentation of the network. The first thing to do is to refer to the network documentation to identify how many hubs, switches or wire centers are in-volved. If a small number of hubs are involved, it makes sense to isolate one at a time to see if the problem disappears. If the segment comprises a large number of (cascaded) hubs, the network needs to be cut off physically into two (or more) parts and monitored. The portion of the network found to produce the problem is then segmented again, until the segment containing the source of the trouble is found. Theoretically, this procedure can lead to the source of the problem very quickly—but only with some luck in the selection of segmentation points. In practice, this drastic method causes considerable disruption in network opera-

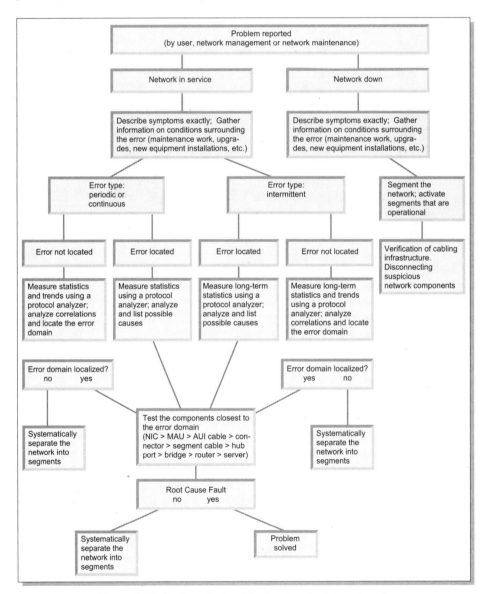

Figure 7.16 Systematic troubleshooting in data networks

tion, and is therefore only applied as a last resort when the problem itself severely impairs normal network operation.

If the symptoms occur intermittently, long-term measurements are necessary. These must be performed continuously until the basic network operating statistics have been measured during the occurrence of the fault. This information usually provides the first clue to the source of the error. You can also try defining filters and alarms for Ethernet frame errors: if you configure your protocol analyzer accordingly, you may be able to capture the Ethernet packets that are transmitted in the error situation. Furthermore, it is essential to log the exact time of each error event. Later this information can be used to find correlations with other events in the network or on a given node, such as backups, the start of specific applications, connections through routers, access to the Internet, working hours of neighboring departments (for example, an error might occur only when employees in the neighboring department boot their network nodes between 7:45 and 8:00 a.m.), etc. If this does not help to track down the error, you may have to resort to the segmentation method. Depending on which causes the least inconvenience to users, you can either systematically disable network functions and applications, or physically separate the segments. These methods usually leads to the error source.

Another simple, but sometimes effective troubleshooting method if nothing else is working, is the compare and analyze method. The principle idea is to compare the network element in question to similar or identical network elements that are working. However, in many cases this method has limited use because in today's networks routers and servers are rarely truly identical.

7.2.3   Error Symptoms in Ethernet

Many of the problem symptoms in Ethernet networks occur in normal network operation and are not necessarily due to errors. These conditions include high traffic loads, high collision rates due to large numbers of active stations per segment, or a high proportion of broadcasts due to the use of certain protocols, such as Windows NT resource sharing. However, the occurrence of certain types of defective packets can point directly to problems that have nothing to do with normal operating conditions. These defective packets are divided into the following categories: fragments from local, remote, or late collisions; undersized packets; jabbers (oversized packets); FCS errors; alignment errors; noise errors; and length errors.

Collisions

Collisions result when two stations on the same segment begin transmitting Ethernet frames at the same time. In Ethernet LANs operating in half-duplex mode, the occurrence of collisions is perfectly normal. If the distance limitations are respected, it takes 25.51 μs in the worst case for the first bit of a 10 Mbit/s Ethernet packet to travel to the furthest node and collide with the frame that node is beginning to send. In the collision, the voltages of the two signals are added together and the resulting collision signal takes a maximum of 25.51 μs to return to the original sender. Thus the longest time it can take a station to recognize the occurrence of a collision and stop transmission is 51.2 μs or 512 bit times, which is equal to 64 bytes. In other words, normal collision fragments do not exceed a length of 64 bytes. Another characteristic of collision fragments is that the frame contents are completely destroyed so that no checksum is detectable.

Remote and Local Collisions

Collisions that occur in a local segment are called local collisions. These collisions happen within a cable section without a repeater unit in 10Base2 networks, or between hub and node in 10Base-T networks. These collision fragments are less than 64 bytes long, have a signal voltage higher than that of a normal signal, and carry an invalid FCS.

Remote collisions are collision fragments that are exported to other segments by repeaters or hubs. Their signal voltages are not higher than normal because they are corrected by the repeater hardware. In most cases, this type of collision ends with a sequence of jam bits. As soon as a collision is detected on one port, repeaters and hubs emit jam bits on all ports in order to prevent further collisions by stopping transmission in the connected segments.

Late Collisions

Late collision fragments are longer than 64 bytes. They can be recognized as collision fragments by the increased signal voltage (in local late collisions) or by the lack of a checksum and the presence of jam bits (in remote late collisions). Late collisions can be caused by defective interface hardware or by cable segments that exceed distance limitations. Because the transmitting station does not detect the collision (the packet had already been emitted in its entirety before the collision occurred), the consequences of this type of collision can be doubly harmful: retransmission is requested only by the higher-layer protocols, which can have adverse effects on application performance.

Short Packets

A short packet is less than 64 bytes long, but carries a valid FCS. Faulty packets most often are the cause. In rare cases, active network components such as bridges may use such short packets to exchange data. Short packets are also referred to as runts with valid FCSs.

Runts

'Runt' is not an officially defined term, but is a widely-used expression for a short, invalid packet. The term generally refers to any frame that is shorter than 64 bytes, and thus may indicate a local or remote collision fragment or a short frame with or without a valid FCS.

Jabbers

According to IEEE 802.3, a jabber is any frame longer than 1,518 bytes, whether its FCS is valid or not. The most common causes of jabber frames include faulty interface cards, defective cabling, and grounding problems.

Long Packets

Long packets are longer than 1,518 bytes, but carry a valid FCS. Long packets can be caused by faulty interface card drivers or by software problems in bridges or routers.

FCS Errors

Frames that contain invalid frame check sequences usually indicate a faulty network interface card. In most cases the headers of these frames are readable, so that the station that transmitted them can be identified by capturing and decoding the packets with a protocol analyzer. FCS errors can also be caused by defective hub ports or by induction voltage in the cabling.

Alignment Errors

Ethernet frames that do not end on an octet boundary (the number of bits in such a packet is not an integer multiple of 8) are called alignment error frames. This type of error is typically caused by defective software drivers or by collision fragments on the segment.

Noise Errors

Noise errors are caused by voltage induced in the network cables by external sources, leading other nodes in the network to assume that the network medium is busy transmitting data. Repeaters and hubs sometimes even exacerbate the symptoms. Symptoms of noise errors (also known as "ghosts") are low capacity use combined with extremely low network performance. Typical causes of noise errors are ground loops, a MAU power supply leaking voltage into the cabling, or other wiring problems.

Length Errors

A length error means that the length field of a given Ethernet frame does not match the actual length of its data field.

7.2.4   Cabling Problems

Problems with cabling are still very common in Ethernet networks. Typical causes include defective or low-quality cables, incorrect characteristic impedance, defective terminating resistors, wiring mistakes or electromagnetic interference (noise). These types of problems are discussed in detail in the section on cabling.

7.2.5   Problems with Ethernet Interface Cards

Two types of Network Interface Cards (NICs) are used in Ethernet networks: cards with integrated MAUs (transceivers), which are connected directly to the communication medium by BNC, RJ-45 or fiber-optic subscriber connectors (SC); and cards with external MAUs. In the latter case, a MAU is chosen to fit the medium (coaxial cable, twisted pair, or fiber) and connected to the network interface card by an AUI cable. The interface card is configured using the manufacturer's software or by means of hardware switches on the card. A number of symptoms, such as invalid FCSs, jabber packets or late collisions, are often caused by faulty interface cards.

The first step in localizing a faulty interface card is to identify suspicious nodes on the network. Begin by making a list of all network nodes that transmit defective packets. Most protocol analyzers provide this information using fully automatic test programs. If the source addresses of the defective packets are invalid and cannot be decoded, try the correlation method: begin by simultaneously charting the activity of the suspicious nodes and the number of defective packets on the segment. If you observe a correlation between the activity of a certain node and the number of defective packets, then you have probably found the faulty interface card. If this strategy also fails, the only alternative is to employ the segmentation method described previously, systematically disconnecting network segments (hubs) until the error ceases to occur.

Once suspicious nodes have been isolated, they are tested individually. Interface cards with AUI connectors are tested using an adapter installed between the AUI connector and the transceiver. The test adapter indicates the status of the AUI signal lines, the signal quality error (SQE) signal and the transceiver power voltage. If the packets sent do not activate the corresponding LED on the AUI test adapter, then the interface card is not configured correctly or is defective. The next step is to check all software settings and hardware switches. If the configuration is correct, the card must be replaced. If the card has an integrated MAU, test the interface card in mini-networks connected to the interface card, rather than use your actual network. In 10Base2 Ethernet, a mini-network consists of no more than a T-connector with two 50Ω terminating resistors. In

10/100/1,000Base-T, the minimum network is the computer with its NIC and a mini-hub. Transmit simple loopback packets (IP loopback to address 127.0.0.1, Ethernet Configuration Test Packets (CTPs), IEEE 802.2 LLC Test Packet, 802.2 LLC XID Test Packet) while monitoring the activity on the mini-network with a protocol analyzer. If the analyzer detects no defective packets, then the card is probably defective.

Symptoms and Causes of Faulty Ethernet Interface Cards

Characteristic symptoms of faulty Ethernet interface cards include high collision rates, jabber packets, packets with invalid FCSs, and intermittent connection problems in individual network nodes. The most common problem sources are faulty MAUs, blown fuses on network interface cards, incorrectly configured card settings or card failures due to defective components.

Carrier Sense Failures

Jabber packets and high collision rates are most often caused by faulty MAUs. If the MAU is defective, then the card's carrier sense function does not work, and the station transmits packets regardless of traffic sent by other stations on the segment.

Configuration Errors

If the station cannot transmit or receive packets at all, the first thing to check is the card configuration. Common configuration errors are:

- The wrong port on the card is activated (the RJ-45 connector instead of the AUI connector, or vice versa).
- The interrupt level configured on the card is already in use by another device.

MAU (Transceiver) Has No Power

If a card is connected to the network by an external transceiver, use an AUI test connector to check for correct interaction between card and transceiver. If the card does not provide proper voltage to the transceiver, check whether the card's fuse (if it has one) has blown. If the fuse is intact, the card must be replaced.

Illegal Coaxial Cable Connection

In small 10Base2 networks, inexperienced operators sometimes attach an interconnection cable between the Ethernet bus T-connector and the station, rather than connecting the station's network card directly to the T-connector. This does not work. The interface card must be connected directly to the Ethernet bus cable. The maximum length of the connection between the T-connector and the interface card, according to the IEEE standard, is 4 cm.

7.2.6   Problems with Media Access Units (MAUs)

External MAUs allow more freedom of location when connecting nodes to the network, for example, when the Ethernet cable is several meters away from the station. The 15-pin AUI interface connector on the interface card is always the same, no matter what type of cabling is used (optical fiber, twisted pair, thin coaxial, thick coaxial). Multiport transceivers can be used to connect more than one node to the network at a single physical access point. Because MAUs (transceivers) and AUI cables provide the actual connection between the network node and the network, it is essential that they function correctly. Today's MAUs and AUI cables are suitable for both Ethernet v2.0 and 10/100 Mbit/s IEEE 802.3 networks. They have LEDs to indicate collisions, data transmission and signal quality error (SQE) signals. The SQE is sent by the MAU to the interface card when non-standard signals, such as collisions, are received. However, not all interface cards use the SQE in accordance with the standard. Older Ethernet 2.0 cards, for example, require an SQE signal (heartbeat) after every "read" or "write" operation. MAUs that are connected to such interface cards must be operated in the heartbeat mode. There is usually a switch located on the housing of the MAU to change its operating mode.

Connecting and Removing AUI Cables and MAUs

When a MAU is connected to a live network node, the computer's power supply may cause voltage spikes. This can cause loss of data on the hard disk or damage to the hardware itself. For this reason it is important to switch off network nodes before connecting or removing MAUs.

Equipment for Troubleshooting

The following equipment is required to test MAUs and AUI cabling:

- A mini-network of the appropriate topology (a terminated T-connector for 10Base2 and 10Base5; mini-hubs for 10/100/1,000Base-T)
- A fully functional MAU
- An AUI test connector with LEDs
- A functional AUI cable
- A multimeter

Symptoms and Causes of Faulty MAUs

A faulty MAU usually results in the complete breakdown of a network node's connection to the rest of the network, or in a significantly increased collision rate accompanied by jabber frames. The most likely causes are described here.

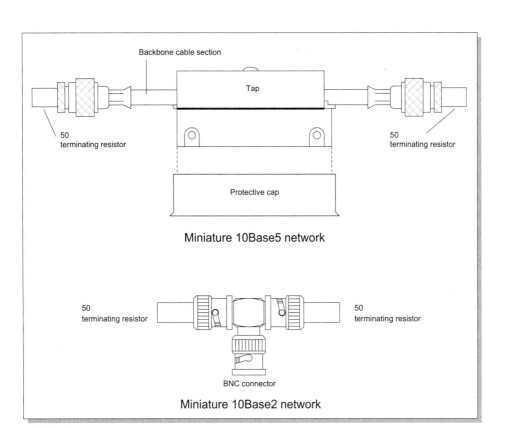

Figure 7.17 Mini-networks for 10Base2 and 10Base5 networks

IEEE 802.3 Instead of Ethernet v2.0 AUI Cabling

Using IEEE 802.3-compliant AUI cabling together with Ethernet 2.0-compliant MAUs and interface cards can cause severe problems. According to the IEEE 802.3 standard, pin 4 of the AUI interface is grounded and pin 1 is assigned to the signal-in line. In Ethernet 2.0, these assignments are reversed: pin 4 is defined as signal-in and pin 1 is grounded (see Figure 7.18).

Signal Quality Error Problems

As discussed earlier, MAUs can be operated in either heartbeat or SQE mode. If a MAU in heartbeat mode is connected to an IEEE 802.3-compliant interface card, it acknowledges every "read" and "write" operation with an SQE signal. The card interprets this as a collision, however, and attempts to retransmit data packets.

Loose Connections

Loose connectors often cause intermittent problems. Checking connectors, however, as simple as it may sound, can be difficult or even impossible in some cases. If the AUI cable is not accessible (if it is located under flooring or above ceiling panels, for instance) you may not be able to test the plug connection directly. In this case, proceed directly to loopback tests. In 10Base2 and 10Base5 networks, you should check the MAU's connection as well as the terminating resistor and its grounding. It is not altogether unusual to find that a MAU has been mistakenly connected to the end of the cable in place of a terminating resistor. In 10/100/1,000Base-T networks, you should also inspect the grounding of the cable shielding and of the wall jacks.

If the problem persists after you have checked all plug connections, you can systematically localize the error source by disconnecting the MAU from the live

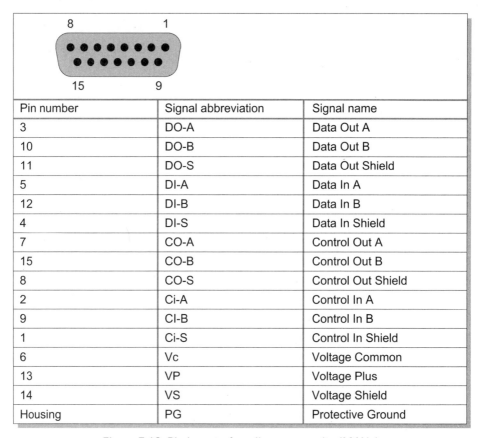

Pin number	Signal abbreviation	Signal name
3	DO-A	Data Out A
10	DO-B	Data Out B
11	DO-S	Data Out Shield
5	DI-A	Data In A
12	DI-B	Data In B
4	DI-S	Data In Shield
7	CO-A	Control Out A
15	CO-B	Control Out B
8	CO-S	Control Out Shield
2	Ci-A	Control In A
9	CI-B	Control In B
1	Ci-S	Control In Shield
6	Vc	Voltage Common
13	VP	Voltage Plus
14	VS	Voltage Shield
Housing	PG	Protective Ground

Figure 7.18 Pin layout of media access units (MAUs)

network and connecting it to a mini-network. If loopback packets can now be sent without problems, then the network node, the AUI cable and the MAU are not defective and the problem source must be in the live network. If the loopback test fails, replace the MAU, the AUI cable, and the interface card successively until the error is eliminated. To determine whether the MAU or the interface card is the defective device, you can measure the voltage the card supplies to the MAU between pins 13 and 6. It should be between 11.28 and 15.75 volts. Some cards have built-in fuses to prevent hardware damage due to voltage spikes. If this fuse blows, the power supply to the MAU fails and the node loses its connection to the network.

7.2.7 Problems with Repeaters and Hubs

Repeaters are used to connect Ethernet segments and to overcome distance limitations within segments. Repeaters that connect 10/100/1,000Base-T nodes in star topology are called hubs or multiport repeaters; their basic functions, however, are identical to those of repeaters as defined in IEEE 802.3. Today's repeaters are modular and capable of connecting segments of different transmission media (coaxial, twisted pair, and fiber optic). The maximum number of repeaters within the transmission path of a segment is limited : the transmission delay increases with each additional repeater and each additional cable segment, which increases the slot time. Longer signal transmission times also mean a higher probability of collisions and thus have a negative effect on network efficiency.

Repeater Functions

Repeaters that conform to the IEEE 802.3 standard fulfill the following functions:

- Regeneration of signal amplitude and removal of phase jitter in the pulse flanks
- Temporary storage of frames so that signals can be forwarded with correct timing
- Carrier sensing (checking for transmission media activity before transmitting signals)
- Replacement of missing bits in the preamble. Each Ethernet frame starts with a 62-bit preamble made up of a sequence of 0s and 1s (1010 1010 1010 1010), which is required by the receiving nodes to synchronize on the data stream. Because today's receiver chips need approximately 30 bit times to synchronize, and some bits get lost in the transmitter electronics on the NIC or on the medium, each repeater needs to replace missing bits in the pre-

amble. Otherwise the preamble would disappear by the time it passed through the second repeater.

- Extending collision fragments with jam bits to a length of 96 bits. This ensures clean collision detection in the connected segments.
- Collision detection and generation of jam bits. Once a repeater detects a collision it must transmit jam bits to all other repeater ports to prevent additional transmissions in the remaining segments. The jam signal must have a minimum length of 62 bits and consist of a 101010 sequence, of which the first bit must be a 1. The transmission of the jam signal must occur within 5 bit times after the end of the collision.
- Automatic partitioning. If high error rates occur in one segment, modern repeaters interrupt transmission and deactivate the corresponding port. The trigger for auto-partitioning of a port is 30 successive collisions or abnormally long collisions. After receiving 500 collision-free bits, the repeater reactivates the port.

The transmission delay introduced by 10 Mbit/s Ethernet repeater ports must not exceed the values listed in Figure 7.19.

Ethernet type	Input + output delay	Total delay in bit times
10Base5	6.5 + 3.5	14
10Base2	6.5 + 3.5	14
FOIRL	3.5 + 3.5	11
10Base-T	8 + 5	17
10Base-FP	3 + 4	11
10Base-FB	2 + 2	4
10Base-FL	5 + 5	11

Figure 7.19 The maximum latency for valid signals on repeater ports

Repeaters cannot detect MAC-layer errors such as invalid FCSs or illegal frame sizes.

Diagnosing Repeater Problems

Localizing Collision Domains

Once a repeater detects a collision, it starts transmitting jam bits to all ports. A collision that occurs in one segment is visible as a jammed fragment or a remote collision in all other segments connected to the repeater. Remote collision packets are thus nothing but local collision packets exported by the repeater or hub of the segment.

If concurrent measurements in all segments show that the occurrence of remote collisions correlates with local collisions in another segment, then the source of the remote collisions is easily found. However, this strategy is only practical in 10Base2 and 10Base5 segments because in 10Base-T networks every node has a segment to itself. In 10/100/1,000Base-T networks, collision sources must be identified by correlating the network load due to the most active stations with collision rates. If the collision history seems to correlate with the packet output of a certain station, then that node could be the source of the collision problem.

MAU Jabber Lockup Due to No Auto-Partitioning

The MAU jabber lockup mechanism provides another important symptom of repeater problems. If no segment is connected to an open repeater port, the repeater transmits 5 ms of jam bits, alternating with 0.01 ms transmission gaps. The gaps are necessary to avoid activating the jabber lockup function of the interface cards. If the receiving electronics of an interface card detect jabbering that lasts longer than 5 ms, the card starts transmitting jam bits itself in order to stop the "jabber station". If jabber packets occur with a length of 6,250 bytes (equal to a 5 ms frame in 10 Mbit/s Ethernet) and a 10 μs gap (equal to 100 bits in 10 Mbit/s Ethernet), the cause is likely to be an open repeater port or a segment without a proper terminating resistor. In these cases, modern repeaters activate auto-partitioning and disable the port.

Phantom Addresses

Quite frequently the analysis of Ethernet frames using a protocol analyzer shows source and destination addresses with the following content:

55555555 or

AAAAAAAA

Defective packets often contain these types of addresses. They appear at first glance to indicate a mysterious transmission error, but on closer examination of the binary representation of the hex format they are seen to be nothing but jam bits:

5555 5555 is equivalent to

1010 1010 1010 1010 1010 1010 1010 1010   in binary format and

AAAA AAAA is equal to

0101 0101 0101 0101 0101 0101 0101 0101.

These are the jam sequences sent by a repeater to all connected segments once a collision is detected on one of the ports. (Remember that a jam signal consists of alternating 0s and 1s.)

Hub (Repeater) Problems: Symptoms and Causes

Typical symptoms of hub problems are low network performance, intermittent connection losses, high collision rates or the occurrence of jabber frames. The most likely causes are described here.

Packets Missing Due to a Short Inter-Frame Gap

If an interface card does not maintain the required minimum inter-frame spacing (9.6 µs in 10 Mbit/s, 0,96 Mbit/s Ethernet) between successive frames, slow repeaters cannot forward the frames fast enough and packets are lost. The data loss is detected in the higher-layer protocols, causing retransmission requests. This can result in significantly lower application performance for connections across one or more routers.

The inter-frame gap may be too short for any of several reasons. Some interfaces will transmit a data packet very soon after the occurrence of a collision, but otherwise perform in conformity with the 9.6 µs rule. Others stick very close to or drop below the 9.6 µs spacing. Packet fragments also can cause problems. Each hub has to extend fragments to the minimum length of 96 bits (including preamble). If a 64-bit fragment is received, the hub extends it to 96 bits by adding 32 jam bits, while at the same time reducing the gap between it and the following frame by 32 bit times or 3.2 µs. This can make the inter-frame gaps too short. However, modern hubs should be able to maintain constant inter-frame gaps by the use of buffers, whether a given packet needs to be extended or not. The symptoms of such hub problems are often only recognized at the application level. Typical cases are file transfers that take significantly longer between two stations that communicate through hubs than between stations located in the same segment. If all TCP packets are present with the correct sequence numbers before a repeater, for example, but sequence numbers are missing after the hub, then the hub is the cause of the problem. The file transfer throughput may then be only a few hundred Kbit/s instead of Mbit/s because the lost packets have to be retransmitted.

10Base2 Repeater Grounding Problems

Segments of 10Base2 or 10Base5 networks must be grounded only at one point. If a grounded repeater and a grounded terminating resistor form a current loop with the network cable, and if the two grounds have different electrical potentials, current will flow along the segment cable, resulting in severe interference, high collision rates and often a complete breakdown of network operation.

Problems Due to an Excessive Number of Repeaters in the Transmission Path

If a frame has to travel not only long distances but also across several repeaters, the maximum transmission delay (25.6 µs) may be exceeded because every repeater adds latency. However, the higher the delay in an Ethernet network, the less efficient the CSMA/CD algorithm becomes. Collisions result, often in the form of late collisions, as well as reduced network performance and intermittent connection losses. As mentioned previously, the maximum number of repeaters per segment is limited to four.

Installation and Configuration Errors

Among the leading causes of problems with hubs are faulty installations or configurations of the equipment. Incorrectly configured ports (port not enabled; wrong operating mode, for example, 10 Mbit/s instead of 100 Mbit/s), loose connections (loose cables, connectors, or plug-in modules), and wiring defects on the back plane or in the wiring cabinet are the most common error sources.

Hardware Problems

To locate or rule out hardware problems, check the power supply and connectors and run the hub's self-test function.

Diagnosing Problems with Optical Components in Ethernet Networks

Optical fiber is increasingly the medium of choice for long-distance connections in Ethernet networks. Fiber-optic links are set up using either active hub modules or simple passive star couplers.

Passive Stars

Passive star couplers have no active components and thus do not require a power supply. Their only purpose is to connect optical fiber in a star topology with minimum attenuation. To optimize the use of passive optical stars, the IEEE 802.3 10Base-FP standard defines a modified preamble for frames transported over 10Base-FP segments.

Active Optical Stars

Optical repeater components must be able to perform all functions defined for repeaters in the IEEE 802.3 specification. These include signal regeneration, fragment extension, collision detection, inter-frame gap verification and generation of jam bits.

Optical Power Problems

The optical power of some optical repeater modules can be adjusted. A power level that is too low can cause transmission problems, especially when a packet travels over a number of fiber lines. In this case, you need to measure the loss over the various fiber lines as well as the optical power that is emitted from the router port. Symptoms of low optical power or high fiber-line attenuation are generally low network performance between specific nodes and an increased incidence of short packets (runts).

Problems with Non-Standardized Optical Repeater Components

Simple electrical-to-optical converters are sometimes used instead of optical repeater ports that fulfill all the functions specified in the IEEE 802.3 standard. When these converters are deployed in high numbers, problems may occur. Typical symptoms include:

- Runts
- Insufficient inter-frame gaps
- Noise (especially when using converters without retiming boards because these neither regenerate amplitude nor remove phase jitter)

Hardware Problems

As with simple repeaters, if you suspect that there is a problem with the hardware, check the power supply and the connectors, and run the self-test function.

7.2.8   Problems with Bridges

Bridges are inter-network elements that connect network segments on OSI Layer 2 (the MAC layer). Independent of higher-layer protocols, bridges store and filter the Ethernet frames they receive from connected segments and transmit them to their destination segments. The main function of a MAC-layer bridge is to prevent the spreading of local traffic to neighboring segments and to overcome such limitations of the particular network topology as the maximum number of nodes per segment, the transmission delay or the distance limits. Packet filtering is based on an address table. This table is also called the "forwarding table", and can either be generated by the bridge in the learning mode (see the following) or manually defined by the operator. In the learning mode, the bridge acts as a repeater, except that the source address of each packet arriving at a bridge port is stored in the forwarding table together with the corresponding port number. This operating mode is also called "transparent bridging", and must be implemented in every bridge according to the IEEE 802.1 specification. After a short time the bridge knows which node is located in which segment and can begin operating in bridge mode. From that point on, frames are forwarded selectively. Each frame is forwarded only to the segment in which its destination node is located. To limit the size of the forwarding table and take changes in the network topology into account, all address entries are maintained according to an aging process. If no activity is detected for a given address entry for a certain period of time, the entry is automatically deleted.

Another important bridge function is checking Ethernet frames. Unlike repeaters, bridges discard defective packets, such as those with an illegal length, an invalid FCS or incorrect alignment.

While local bridges are used to connect neighboring segments, wide-area bridges consist of two separate components connected over a wide-area network. WAN bridges can link networks that are located at different sites. A unified standard for bridges, published in 1990, is part of IEEE 802.1. This document has been updated by the ISO standard IS 10038.

Features and Functions of Bridges

Bridge Networks with the Spanning Tree Algorithm

If two subnetworks can be reached through more than one path, a mechanism is needed that selects the optimum route in each case. Furthermore, the creation of loops must be avoided. The spanning tree algorithm (STA) is designed to prevent loops in Ethernet networks. If a network that contains loops uses bridges that do not support STA, this can lead to "sputniks", or packets that circulate continuously in network loops and reproduce themselves. One copy of such a frame may reach its destination while one or more copies remain in the loop, unnecessarily increasing the network load.

The spanning tree algorithm recognizes one bridge as a root bridge for the network. On each remaining bridge, one port that leads to the root bridge is defined as the root port. The bridges are configured with the bridging protocol, which uses special frames (bridge protocol data units or BPDUs) to select the root bridge and the root ports. Initially, all bridges are defined by default as root bridges and begin broadcasting packets to all connected segments every two seconds. Each broadcast contains the sender's 8-byte identification together with notification of its status as a root bridge. The bridge with the lowest identification value is then selected as the root bridge, and each of the other bridges defines the root port it will use to connect to the root bridge. In each network that is not directly connected to the root bridge, the bridges inform each other of the identification of their root bridges and the corresponding transmission capacities. The transmission capacity is expressed as the reciprocal of the communication speed, or the sum of all transmission delays. We recommend using the expression 1,000/(data speed in Mbit/s). This yields transmission coefficients of 2,000 for a 512 Kbit/s line, 250 for 4 Mbit/s Token Ring, 100 for 10 Mbit/s Ethernet, 62 for 16 Mbit/s Token Ring, 10 for FDDI and 100 Mbit/s Ethernet, and 1 for Gigabit Ethernet. If there is more than one connection between a subnetwork and the root bridge, the path with the best transmission characteristics can be selected. The remaining ports for this path are then deactivated. Configuration requires both configuration BPDUs and topology BPDUs. Bridges periodically distribute the configuration BPDUs within the network. The starting age of packets sent out by the root bridge is defined as zero, and each bridge increases the age counter of forwarded packets by one. Packets age as the distance increases; the age value, however, must never exceed 20. If it does, the information from the last configuration BPDU is discarded and a new reconfiguration of the root port is initiated. The bridge informs the remaining network of the change by transmitting a topology-change BPDU. The root bridge acknowledges the reconfiguration with a configuration BPDU in which a topology-change bit is set.

Protocol ID = 0			
Protocol version ID = 0		BPDU type = 0	
TCA	Flags	TC	
Root ID			
Transport cost to root bridge			
Bridge ID			
Port ID			
Message age			
Maximum age			
Hello timer			
Forwarding delay			

TCA (Topology Change Acknowledgment):	The bridge acknowledges receipt of a topology change BPDU
TC (Topology Change):	The root bridge notifies the other bridges of a topology change
Bridge ID	Priority of the bridge (0 = highest; 65535 = lowest; default=32768)
Port ID	Throughput capacity to root bridge (1= highest; 65535 = lowest)
Message age	Delay between receipt of previous and current configuration BPDUs
Maximum age	Maximum message age (6 - 40 seconds; recommended value: 20 seconds)
Hello timer	Maximum interval between root bridge configuration BPDUs
Forwarding delay	Delay between learning and forwarding phases (4 - 30 seconds; recommended value: 15 seconds)

Format of a configuration BPDU

Protocol ID = 0	
Protocol version ID = 0	BPDU type = 0

Format of a topology change BPDU

Figure 7.20 Configuration and topology change BPDUs

Other important parameters for bridge operation are the maximum bridge latency, the BPDU transmission delay and the minimum time between configuration changes (hold time):

Bridge latency: 1 second recommended; 4 seconds maximum
BPDU transmission delay: 1 second recommended; 4 seconds maximum
Hold Time (minimum time between two BPDUs): 1 second

Bridge Filters

For most bridges, manually-defined filters can also be created in addition to the forwarding table generated in the transparent bridging mode. These filters can be based on various criteria, including source or destination address, type field, or other bit masks. Logical operators (AND, OR, NOT) can also link the filters. Bridge filters can be a powerful tool for actively avoiding error situations and restricting network traffic. Their usefulness is limited, however, by the fact that they are static; higher-layer protocols that select port addresses dynamically, such as FTP or Telnet, cannot be filtered properly.

MAC Switching Bridges

The latest generation of bridges combines bridge functions with MAC-layer switching. These bridges are able to make forwarding decisions and carry them out for several packets concurrently. Replacing hubs by MAC-layer switching bridges has the advantage that each frame is routed directly to its destination segment without blocking the other stations on the same network. This can significantly increase the communication bandwidth available in the network. The principles of segment switching are discussed in more detail in Chapter 11.

Remote Bridges

Remote bridges usually consist of one LAN port and several serial ports, over which the LAN can be connected to remote locations using WAN links. The serial ports can be V series interfaces (such as V.24 or V.35), ISDN lines or PDH interfaces (E1/T1, E3/T3). The protocols used for transporting the bridged data over the wide-area links are usually Point-to-Point Protocol (PPP) or proprietary variants of the High-level Data Link Control Protocol (HDLC).

Load Balancing

Network traffic can be distributed over several parallel transmission paths using the non-standard load-balancing protocol (distributed load sharing or DLS). When used in conjunction with WAN bridges, the load-balancing protocol calculates the transmission cost for each transmission path based on the available bandwidth. The traffic is then distributed to minimize the total cost. Because the data packets of a single communication process may be distributed over various lines, the packet sequence may change. Thus protocols or applications that rely on unchanged packet sequences should not be operated over links that use load balancing.

Connecting Different LAN Topologies

If bridges are used to connect different LAN topologies (for example, Ethernet, Token Ring, FDDI, ATM), a number of special functions are required in order to overcome the differences in data speed, packet format and media access technique. Because not only the packet lengths but also the entire frame formats are different for each of these topologies, each packet must be translated before transmission, which requires additional CPU performance. The difference in data speeds can also present difficulties. For example, if a long sequence of frames is being transmitted from a 16 Mbit/s Token Ring to a 10 Mbit/s Ethernet network, the bridge cannot forward the traffic at the same speed at which it arrives. Therefore, packets must be stored in the bridge buffer, which can overflow if the transmission sequence is too long. Timers in the higher-layer protocols present another significant problem, and one that is often overlooked. If a Layer 3 timeout occurs before a given packet has arrived at a destination in a slower LAN, the transmitting station may start retransmissions too soon. After several unsuccessful attempts, the sender gives up any further attempt on the assumption that the connection has been interrupted.

Another special bridge function is necessitated by the differences in packet lengths. While the maximum packet size in IEEE 802.3 Ethernet is 1,518 bytes, Token Ring packets can have up to 4,500 bytes (in 4 Mbit/s Token Ring) or 17,800 bytes (in 16 Mbit/s Token Ring); FDDI also allows 4,500 bytes. Because there is no OSI Layer 2 mechanism defined that would allow packets to be divided into several parts and then reassembled, packets that are too long for their destination LAN topology must be discarded by the bridge. Due to the problems involved in translating between two completely different transmission methods (translation bridging), encapsulation bridging was defined as an alternative in IEEE 801.2H. In encapsulation bridging, a backbone such as a FDDI ring transports Ethernet frames as a simple payload from one ring node to another, paying no attention to the frame headers. Analogously, RFC 1483 defines the encapsulation of LAN packets (Ethernet, Token Ring, FDDI) for transport in ATM cells without regard to network packet headers.

All in all, there are many difficulties and restrictions involved when bridges are used to couple different network topologies, which is one reason why most networks now use routers for this purpose.

Diagnosing Bridge Problems

The challenge when analyzing bridge problems is to correlate the occurrence of symptoms in several different network segments. Using probe-based monitoring systems to provide concurrent measurements in several segments can be very helpful. Performance measurements of bridges by expensive, specialized multiport systems are less important: most modern bridges are capable of forwarding packets at line speed anyway, so performance measurements in most cases just confirm the manufacturer's technical data. It is more efficient to request system specifications from the manufacturer based on standardized test methods, as specified in RFC 1242 and RFC 2544.

Most problems that affect bridges can best be located by a process of elimination that involves the correlation of specific measurements and an analysis of the network topology. Symptoms of bridge problems can include poor network performance in particular segments, intermittent or permanent loss of connection for particular stations, or the failure of certain protocols and services. The first step of the troubleshooting process is, as always, a review of all configuration changes that were made in the network before the error occurred and, of course, general information gathering. If the symptoms correlate to particular connections, you can begin by checking all bridges located along the corresponding transmission path. Otherwise, the next step is to prepare a list of all the stations, connections, protocols and services affected by the problems observed. To do this, measure the current parameters in the various network segments and compare the results with statistics gathered during normal operation. This involves recording and analyzing throughput and performance parameters of network nodes, protocols, and services as well as reviewing the log files that contain operating statistics on all bridges in the network. The log files provide bridge parameters such as CPU capacity use, port capacity use, buffer capacity use and error statistics. To measure the response times of connections across bridges, transmit loop-back packets—Ethernet configuration test packets (CTP), IEEE 802.2 LLC test packets, 802.2 LLC XID test packets, IP pings—from different network segments across the bridges. Automatic long-term response time measurements can be made using dedicated response time agents distributed throughout the network. This type of long-term measurement can be especially useful in the case of intermittent problems. Based on the results of such measurements, the range of potential sources of the error in question can usually be narrowed down to specific components.

Symptoms and Causes of Bridge Problems

This section summarizes typical symptoms of bridge problems and their most frequent causes.

Throughput Capacity Problems

The throughput capacity of bridges is expressed in frames per second. The nominal value usually refers to the shortest possible frame length for the network topology in question. However, when throughput is given in bytes per second, the figures usually refer to an average or even the maximum possible frame length. Throughput capacity and the actual throughput rate should thus be checked, especially when dealing with older bridge models. State-of-the-art bridges have throughput capacities well in excess of the frame rates that occur in practice, so that bottlenecks caused by limited throughput capacity are becoming increasingly rare.

Loss of Frames

In addition to the loss of packets due to capacity problems, a correctly function-ing bridge discards damaged frames (runts, jabbers, collisions, collision frag-ments) as well as frames that have exceeded their lifespan. Although a bridge does not examine the time stamp on a frame (this is left to higher-layer proto-cols), it can place a limit on the time a packet is buffered in the bridge. If this latency limit (maximum 4 seconds) is exceeded, the packet is discarded. A latency limit that is too short could cause problems in a network with heavy traffic.

Problems with Bridge Filters

The following are potential sources of problems when filters are used:

- Overly complex filter structures, whose effects cannot be foreseen in every operational situation, may result in unwanted filtering under certain oper-ating conditions.
- When multiport bridges are used in redundant areas of the network, keep in mind that data that normally has another transmission path may also be transmitted over the backup port in certain situations. Filters must there-fore be checked to ensure that they do not block packet streams in backup mode.
- Depending on their architecture, some bridges show a significant perfor-mance reduction once a given number of filters are active. Check with the manufacturer for information on how active filters may affect the operating performance of the bridge.

Buffer Overflow

To handle short-term peak traffic, bridges store incoming packets in a buffer until the CPU is ready to forward them to their final destination. If the buffer is full, the bridge has to start discarding packets.

Excessive Data Packet Length

Often, when bridges translate between different network topologies (between Ethernet and FDDI, for example), the packets to be forwarded exceed the maximum packet length allowed in the destination network. These packets must be discarded because OSI Layer 2 does not define a fragmentation mechanism for bridges. The maximum packet length to be transmitted by the bridge can also be set manually. However, setting the value too low can lead to performance problems, especially when using time-critical protocols such as Local Area Transport Protocol (LAT).

Changes in Packet Sequence

Bridges usually forward packets in the same order in which they are received. However, if the bridge is using a distributed load-sharing (DLS) mechanism, packets are sent over a number of redundant links or bridge ports and do not arrive in exactly the same order as they are sent (non-FIFO load sharing). In this case, only those protocols that can tolerate changes in the packet sequence (TCP/IP, XNS, IPX, etc.) will be able to communicate successfully across the bridge. The User Datagram Protocol (UDP), for example, requires packets to be in the correct sequence. Any irregularity in the transfer sequence would have to be corrected by the application that uses UDP as a transport protocol, but this is often not done. For this reason, UDP applications sometimes function properly within a local segment, but have major problems when working across bridges or routers.

Problems Related to the Address Table (Forwarding Table)

As discussed previously, each entry in the address table of a bridge is coupled with an "aging" algorithm. Entries that reach a certain age without being used are deleted from the address table. The maximum age of an entry can be configured manually, and usually has a value between 10 and 1,000,000 seconds. In addition to such dynamic address tables, most bridges also have static address tables. These must be set up manually and often contain special addresses, such as broadcast or group addresses. When the operation of a bridge is based entirely on the use of static address tables, the bridge is said to be operating in "protected mode". In this mode, addresses of new stations (stations just beginning network activity) are not automatically added to the address table, and are therefore unable to communicate across the bridge. Manually creating or editing such static tables often leads to errors. Together with incorrectly configured bridge filters, address tables account for the majority of bridge problems. The first step in your troubleshooting process should be to check the address and filter tables.

Wrong Operating Mode

Bridge ports operating in Ethernet v2.0 mode instead of IEEE 802.3 mode sometimes cause problems with various older network interface cards. However, state-of-the-art NICs are able to adjust to either operating mode automatically. Another common configuration error is setting a port for 10 Mbit/s Ethernet instead of 100 Mbit/s Ethernet or vice versa. Again, most of today's network components identify and adjust to the required Ethernet frame type automatically.

Remote Bridge Problems

The wide-area lines used to connect remote bridge ports are often too slow or of poor quality. In these cases, timeouts and lost packets result in retransmissions at peak loads. This problem may be solved by using data compression or by upgrading the wide-area line to a higher bandwidth. Frequent checks of the line's capacity use and quality by means of a protocol analyzer are recommended in order to avoid the sudden occurrence of serious communication problems.

Problems with Bridges Connecting Different Network Topologies

Bridges that connect different network topologies are faced with a number of basic problems due to differences in line speed and access mechanisms:

Token Ring to Ethernet Connection: The A and C bits in the frame status byte of IEEE 802.5 frames inform the transmitting station whether the destination node was able to receive the packet and copy it into its receive buffer. The bridge can be configured to set these bits to "packet received" and "frame copied" by default, but this will obviously create problems in the event that the receiving station is not ready to receive: the transmitting station will assume its packet was delivered successfully even if the destination station was not active and never received the frames in question.

FDDI to Ethernet Connection: As with Token Ring, the A and C bits in the frame status bytes inform the sender whether its packet was delivered successfully. Again, a default setting for these bits in the bridge is only useful as long as the packet really is delivered; otherwise the transmitting FDDI station may receive the message that its packet arrived even though the Ethernet station was not active.

Installation and Configuration Errors

Among the leading causes of bridge problems are errors due to faulty installation or configuration of the equipment. Incorrectly configured ports (port not active; wrong operating mode, for example, 10 Mbit/s instead of 100 Mbit/s); faulty connections (loose cables, connectors, or plug-in modules); and wiring errors on the back plane or in the wiring cabinet are the most common error sources.

Hardware Problems

To locate or rule out hardware problems, check the power supply and connectors and run the bridge's self-test function.

7.2.9   Problems with Routers

Routers are inter-networking components that connect network segments on OSI Layer 3. Because they operate on this level, routers can link networks regardless of their topologies. The router extracts and analyzes the network layer contents (IP packets for example) from the OSI Layer 2 frames it receives (Ethernet, Token Ring, FDDI, ATM, X.25, Frame Relay, ISDN), and forwards them encapsulated in the Layer 2 packet format of the destination network. Analysis of the Layer 2 packets is, therefore, of no use in diagnosing routers because no data transport takes place at this layer. Only the Layer 3 protocols involved (IP, IPX, NS, IDP, OSI, and others) are of interest here. Most of today's routers are multiprotocol routers, which are able to process several protocol stacks in parallel. Single-protocol routers specialize in forwarding just one Layer 3 protocol. Because some Layer 3 protocols are poorly—or not at all—suited for routing, modern systems support both routing and bridging. The system then decides whether to route or bridge each packet. Such systems are sometimes referred to as brouter (bridge + router) systems. Special routing protocols have been defined to ensure efficient route selection for packets forwarded through routers.

Router Protocols

The most widely used routing protocols are:

- RIP (routing information protocol), OSPF (open shortest path first) for TCP/IP
- RIP, NLSP (NetWare link services protocol) for NetWare/IPX
- DRP (digital routing protocol) for DECNet
- IS–IS (intermediate system—intermediate system) for OSI/CLNS
- RTMP (routing-table maintenance protocol) for AppleTalk
- IGRP (inter-gateway routing protocol)
- BGP (border gateway protocol)

Basically, there are two different methods for selecting routes within a network: static routing and dynamic routing. Static routing is used for static connections with fixed transmission characteristics (bandwidth, availability, bit-error rate). Static routes are rarely used unless called for by a very stringent security policy or if the connections between the routers are established over wide-area, packet-switched networks, such as ATM or X.25. Apart from these cases, dynamic routing methods are used, especially in local-area networks. Today's dynamic routing protocols are based either on the vector distance (Bellman-Ford) routing algorithm or the "shortest path first" (link-state) algorithm (SPF).

Vector Distance (Bellman-Ford) Routing

In vector distance routing the distance between the routers is given in hops, where each section of the overall link between two routers is one hop. Each router maintains a table that contains all possible routes to the various destinations and the distance in hops along each route. This table is sent periodically to all adjacent routers, which also broadcast their tables. The disadvantages of the vector distance routing algorithm are that route changes are distributed relatively slowly over the network, and that the size of the routing tables is proportional to the size of the network. The algorithm considers only the number of hops for its routing decisions, not the transport capacity of the links. The updates are time-based and are not based on available routes.

Shortest Path First (SPF) Routing

In SPF routing, each router has two tasks: the first is to test the status of the links to adjacent routers, and the second is to broadcast this routing table to all routers in the network. In this algorithm, the size of the routing update packets is independent of the size of the network because only the status of the adjacent neighbors is transmitted. However, each router in the network has the latest routing table, valid for the entire network, available at all times. The local router calculates the most efficient route and is not dependent on routing calculations made by other routers. The routing table updates are link-state-change based and not time-based, as is the case in vector distance routing.

Routing Internet Protocol (RIP)

In IP networks, the two most popular routing protocols are RIP and OSPF. Due to its simplicity, RIP (RFC 1058) is used in the majority of IP networks. It uses routing tables that are generated by the individual routers and contain the subnet addresses (not the host addresses) for all subnetworks. The size of the routing table is proportional to the number of segments, not to the number of hosts. Based on the routing tables it receives, each router can calculate the distance to the destination network and select the best route. This technique allows for no more than 14 routers between the transmitter and the receiver. An address that is 15 or more hops away is considered unreachable.

Alternatively, the routing table can be made smaller by including only the directly accessible subnets and designating a default route for all other subnets. All packets that cannot be forwarded directly to their destination subnet are then transmitted to the default gateway. In general RIP is primarily used for smaller networks due to its hop count limitation and due to its relatively bandwidth-intensive update mechanisms.

Open Shortest Path First (OSPF)

The second most popular routing protocol in IP networks is OSPF (RFC 1247). OSPF differs from RIP primarily in that it has a hierarchical structure, can bridge more than 14 hops and uses the link-state algorithm SPF. The main strength of OSPF is its ability to pool several networks in so-called "areas". Each router receives a topology database (link-state database) for each area, which is identical for all routers in the area. Each router broadcasts the state of its own links (bandwidth, throughput, transmission delay) to all other routers within its area. Based on this topology database, each router calculates a tree structure locally, with itself as the trunk and the shortest routes to the various destinations as branches. OSPF provides fast network convergence because the routing table updates are not time-based, however, in large networks with frequent link-state changes it can consume bandwidth. Bandwidths of communication links are being taken into consideration for routing decisions.

Inter-Gateway Routing Protocol (IGRP)

IGRP is based on the distance vector algorithm with the addition of various enhancements that enable it to provide faster route selection while generating less overhead. Each router transmits routing table updates to all neighboring routers every 90 seconds. The neighboring routers interpret the updates but do not distribute them further. To evaluate the performance of the various links, the parameters describing response time, bandwidth, link length and availability are combined in the following formula:

Link cost = {(K1·B)+(K2·B)/(256–L) + (K3·Dc)}·{K5/(r+K4)}

where

K1   = bandwidth weighting

K2   = capacity use weighting

K3   = delay weighting

K4, K5 = reliability weighting

B   = bandwidth

L   = capacity use (0 ... 255; 255 = 100% capacity use)

Dc   = composite delay in units of 10 µs

r   = number of frames sent / number of frames successfully transmitted (reliability)

The IGRP default values are K1=1, K2=0, K3=1, K4=0 and K5=0.

Diagnosing Router Problems

Unless the errors are caused by hardware or installation problems, trouble-shooting router problems begins by focusing on the protocols being used and routed. The first step is to gather protocol performance statistics using a protocol analyzer in order to get an idea of the current operating status of the network. In an IP network, for example, this would include statistics such as

- IP broadcasts
- ICMP redirects
- Low TTL messages
- Routing packets
- The proportion of IP traffic in the total network load
  (in percentages and kilobytes)
- Fragmented IP packets
- ICMP unreachable messages
- Other ICMP messages

In addition, the log files that contain the operating statistics of all active routers should be analyzed. There are a variety of router commands for retrieving data, such as CPU capacity use, memory capacity use, port capacity use, number of packets transmitted and received per protocol, timeouts, fragmentations, and numbers of connections and broadcasts (for Cisco routers, for example, these commands would include the following: show interfaces, show controllers, show buffers, show memory, show processes, show stacks).

If the symptoms can be related to a particular connection, you can begin by checking all routers located along its transmission path. Be sure to check the following items:

- Address tables (Are the address entries for the affected nodes correct?)
- Mapping tables (Is the mapping between network address and host name correct?)
- Routing tables (Is a route to the destination network available?)
- Filter entries
- Protocols (Are all protocols active?)
- Default gateways (Does the configuration define a default gateway or default route? This is represented by the destination network 0.0.0.0 and is used when a packet has a destination that is not contained in the routing table)
- Timer values (Are correct values configured for the active timers, such as the Hello timer or Dead timer in OSPF?)
- Static routes (Are static routes active? If so, are the links working?)
- WAN ports (Are all WAN links up and running?)

A check of the router's event log can provide additional clues to the cause of the problem.

Symptoms and Causes of Router Problems

The following summarizes the typical symptoms of router problems and their most frequent causes.

Throughput Capacity Problems

Due to the trend towards high-speed network technologies, bottlenecks often occur during peak traffic even in state-of-the-art routers based on modern RISC processor technology. If the router manufacturer has provided detailed operating characteristics based on standardized test methods (RFC 1242, RFC 2544), you can compare this data with the actual peak loads that occur in your network. Based on the results of this comparison, you can make a rough estimate as to whether the traffic through the router might cause throughput problems or not. In addition, reviewing the operating statistics log may help you determine whether there are performance problems in your router.

Address Table Problems

Many router problems are caused by address tables that have not been updated or are otherwise incorrect. This type of error is often the result of configuration changes in the network that were not implemented on the routers. The problem symptoms are not seen until the next time the affected service is used, often hours or even days after the configuration changes. This can make it difficult or impossible to detect a correlation between the altered network configuration and the failure of a particular service, such as database or Internet access. Localizing such problems can be very time consuming, especially if the network configuration changes have not been documented, as is often the case.

Faulty Subnet Masks

Faulty subnet masks are another common cause of router problems. Unique host addresses, for example, can become subnet broadcasts due to a faulty subnet mask on the router. The only way to solve this type of problem is by systematic checking and documentation of all subnet masks.

No Default Gateway

A typical cause of partial connection losses—that is, when connections are possible between some nodes or subnets but not others—is the lack of a default gateway configuration on the router. In this case, connections to subnets that are directly linked to the router function properly, but connections through more distant routers do not because there is no default gateway available for the router to forward packets to.

Faulty Timer Configuration

Great care must be taken when setting protocol timer values on routers. Incorrect timer settings can lead to delayed distribution of routing information within the network (caused by incorrect setting of the OSPF Hello or Dead timer or the IGRP Active timer) as well as to early timeouts of particular connections. When combining routers from different manufacturers it is especially important to check the timer settings and adjust them if necessary.

WAN Problems

The second most common sources of router errors, after faulty address tables, are problems with WAN links. These may be problems in the public telecommunications network (link failures, high bit-error rates, long delays) or basic problems such as insufficient bandwidth in WAN links, or incorrect protocol settings (such as timers or window size).

Routing Protocol Problems

Another class of error sources involves problems in router-to-router communication. Analyzing the activity and content of the routing protocols with the help of a protocol analyzer may help you track down these faults.

Installation and Configuration Errors

As with hubs and bridges, the leading causes of router problems are errors due to faulty installation or configuration of the equipment. Incorrectly configured ports (port not active; protocol not active; wrong operating mode, for example, 10 Mbit/s instead of 100 Mbit/s), faulty connections (loose cables, connectors, or plug-in modules), and wiring errors on the back plane or in the wiring cabinet are the most common error sources.

Hardware Problems

To locate or rule out hardware problems, check the power supply and connectors and run the router's self-test function.

7.2.10 Symptoms and Causes: 10/100/1,000 MBit/s Ethernet

Symptom: Diminished Network Performance in Conjunction with FCS Errors

Invalid checksums (FCS errors) are a side effect of collisions, which in limited numbers are a normal consequence of the CSMA/CD algorithm. If FCS errors occur together with collisions, and if their number is within reasonable limits, there is no reason to worry. Use a protocol analyzer to measure the number of collisions and the number of FCS errors over a period of time and compare the resulting curves. If there is no correlation between the collision and the FCS error curves, you might have one of the following problems:

Cause (1): Noise and interference on the network.

Noise results when the network is not grounded or if the grounding is faulty. Use a cable scanner or multimeter to check the noise level on your network. A 10Base2/10Base5 network segment must have no more than one ground connection. If there is a second ground connection, due to a faulty network interface card or a bad cable connection, for example, a voltage difference between the two grounds may cause current leak in the network cable.

Cause (2): Electromagnetic interference along the cable path.

Electromagnetic interference from devices such as photocopiers, mobile telephones, elevators or pagers can also cause FCS errors. Use a multimeter to check for interference and a cable tester to check for noise. If you detect interference, check whether the cable routes lead along elevator shafts, electric machinery, transformers, lighting bays, computer systems with high clock rates or X-ray equipment.

Cause (3): Faulty network interface card.

To determine whether a faulty NIC is the source of FCS errors, generate statistics of all defective packets sorted by network node (this is a standard report generated automatically by most protocol analyzers). If you find a suspicious station, measure its activity (for example, in packets/second) and the number of FCS errors occurring on the segment. If the two numbers seem to correlate, there is a good chance you have found the cause of your problems. Keep in mind that many faults on network interface cards occur only intermittently, for example, only after the card has reached a certain temperature. For this reason it may be necessary to take measurements over longer periods of time before you can obtain exact and repeatable results.

Cause (4): Defective or loose connectors (on NICs, wall jacks, MAUs, repeaters, hubs).

Check all connections in the network path.

Symptom: **Diminished Network Performance in Conjunction with Late Collisions**

An increase in the number of collisions is often caused by cable problems (cable segments too long), defective network interface cards, excessive repeater cascading, or defective or missing terminating resistors. Determining whether the collisions are "late" or normal collisions can help to narrow down the possible causes. Possible causes for late collisions include:

Cause (1): Cables longer than the specified maximum segment length for the given topology.

Measure length using a cable scanner.

Cause (2): Too many cascaded repeaters in network.

Replace one of the repeaters with a bridge, or change the network configuration.

Cause (3): Defective network interface card or MAU.

Use a protocol analyzer to collect statistics on the stations that send the most defective packets. Also gather statistics on numbers of collisions and active nodes, and look for correlations. If this does not help to localize the problem, the network segmentation method must be used.

Symptom: **Diminished Network Performance in Conjunction with Early Collisions**

Cause (1): Terminating resistor defective or not installed.

$10Base2$ and $10Base5$ networks must be terminated by 50Ω resistors. Make sure all required terminating resistors are installed and use a multimeter to check the resistance ($48 \ \Omega < R < 52 \ \Omega$).

Cause (2): Loose or defective T-connector.

Check all connections in the network path.

Cause (3): Too many nodes in one segment.

Check the number of MAUs per segment; the number must not exceed 100 in a $10Base5$ segment or 30 in a $10Base2$ segment.

Cause (4): Kink in a cable.

Use a cable scanner to try to locate the damage and replace the affected cable.

Cause (5): Cable does not conform to IEEE 802.3.

IEEE 802.3 $10Base5$ cables are marked with a color code every 2.5 meters. In order to minimize the interference due to reflections at connection points, connectors should be inserted only at these markings. In addition, keep in mind that not all cables with BNC connectors are 50Ω cables. Although Ethernet works even on

75Ω cables over tens of meters, increasing network length will lead to problems sooner or later. Always check the specification of the cables you are using.

Symptom: Slow Network, High Response Time (No Excessive Collisions or FCS Errors)

Cause (1): Buffer overflow in a bridge or router in the transmission path. Check router and bridge statistics (CPU capacity use, port capacity use). Use a protocol analyzer to try to determine which nodes create the most traffic across the bridge or router. Do timeouts occur? Use pings to perform systematic measurements of response times across the bridge/router to check whether the interconnection devices are part of the problem. If this is the case, reconfigure the network (by moving a server or client to another segment, for example) to reduce the traffic over heavily-loaded interconnection devices.

Cause (2): Transmission problems over optical-fiber connections. Fiber links bridging great distances can sometimes lead to performance problems without showing FCS errors if the line attenuation is too high or the light power emitted is too low. Use pings to check the response times of connections over the fiber connection in question. Check the settings of the fiber-optic couplers and the line attenuation.

Cause (3): Local segment routing. Local routing is a common cause of slow networks. Local routing typically occurs for connections between two nodes with different subnet addresses connected to the same LAN switch, which is connected to a router (also called one-armed routing). In order to reach its destination a packet has to be switched to the router, then routed within the router before being transferred through the same switch again to the destination node.

Symptom: Intermittent Problems with Connections and Network Performance, Alignment Errors

Cause (1): Network interface card transmits a few extra bits after each FCS. Use a protocol analyzer to capture the frames that have extra bits following the FCS (known as dribble frames or alignment-error frames). The source address of the captured packets identifies the faulty network interface card.

Cause (2):   Maximum length of the transmission path exceeds that defined in the Ethernet specification.

Whether the signal arrives at its destination depends on the transmitting and receiving stations. Stations that are closer together (within the specified distance limits) can communicate without problems, while stations that have to communicate over a longer distance, but are still located in the same segment, have connection problems. Try to find a pattern in the connection problems to determine whether only certain nodes are affected. Use a cable tester to check the length and quality of the transmission path. Insert a bridge or router in the transmission path if necessary (see the section entitled "Network Design Guidelines" for details).

Cause (3):   Too many bridges or routers are cascaded, resulting in long signal transmission delays and protocol timeouts (such as TCP timeouts). Use pings or response time agents to check response times. Review the network design with regard to the maximum allowable cascading of bridges and routers (see the section entitled "Network Design Guidelines" for details).

Symptom: Intermittent Connection Problems in Conjunction with Short Packets

Cause: Faulty network interface card.

Use a protocol analyzer to try to capture the short packets and identify the emitting node by the source address. If the source address is corrupt, try to track down the defective card by evaluating correlation measurements (see the section titled "Troubleshooting in 10/100/1,000 Mbit/s Ethernet" for details).

Symptom: Intermittent Connection Problems in Conjunction with Jabber Packets

Cause (1):   Double grounding in 10Base2 and 10Base5 networks, resulting in DC currents in the network cable.

Check the network grounding; use a cable tester to check for DC current.

Cause (2):   Defective network interface card.

Defective interface cards sometimes generate jabber frames (excessively long frames), which lead to connection problems in the affected segment. Capture the jabber frames using a protocol analyzer and identify the faulty network interface card by analyzing the source addresses.

Symptom: **Intermittent Connection Problems in Conjunction with Short Inter-Frame Spacing**

Cause: Packet loss due to insufficient inter-frame spacing.

If a station does not maintain the required minimum inter-frame spacing gap (9.6 µs in 10 Mbit/s, 0.96 µs in 100 Mbit/s networks) some hubs will be unable to repeat the frames correctly. In such cases, packets sometimes mutate into jabber packets. Use a protocol analyzer to check the inter-frame gaps (calculated from the packet time stamps in the analyzer trace). The faulty network interface can then be identified by analyzing the source addresses.

Symptom: **Intermittent Connection Problems in Paths Across Bridges**

Cause: Change in packet sequence due to load-sharing mechanisms in the bridge.

Check the bridge configuration and deactivate load sharing if necessary.

Symptom: **Intermittent Connection Problems in Routes Across Routers**

Cause: Router connected to overloaded or low-quality WAN lines. Use a protocol analyzer to check capacity use, FCS rate and bit-error rates in the WAN link; analyze router port logs.

Symptom: **Loss of a Single Node's Connection**

Cause (1):   Loose or faulty connection from the MAU to the network cable or from the NIC to the network.

A sudden complete failure of a single network node is often caused by one of the following:

- MAU plug not firmly connected
- Break, short circuit or noise in connecting cable
- Faulty network interface card

Check the cable and connector and the network interface card; replace if necessary. Replace the faulty node with a system known to be functioning correctly (such as a notebook). If the replacement node functions, the problem is inside the disconnected node; if not, the problem is on the network side.

Cause (2):   Incorrectly configured network interface card: wrong connector activated (for example, AUI instead of twisted pair), or the selected interrupt is already assigned.

Send loopback pings (ping 127.0.0.0) to check whether the card is working and whether packets are being transmitted and received. Has anyone installed any hardware or software on the node recently? As described for Cause (1), replace the faulty node with a system known to be functioning correctly (such as a notebook) to determine whether the problem is inside the node or on the network side.

Cause (3):   Defective network card, blown fuse.
Check whether the power supply to the MAU is intact (when using an external MAU). Send loopback pings (ping 127.0.0.0) to check whether the card is working and whether packets are being transmitted and received.

Cause (4):   The MAU sends heartbeat signals (when working with an external MAU) but the interface card, in conformance with the standard, reads them as signal quality errors and aborts transmission.
Monitor the LEDs on the MAU. If the SQE LED lights up every time transmission is attempted, deactivate the heartbeat mode in the MAU (change it from Ethernet 2.0 mode to IEEE 802.3 mode).

Cause (5):   Learning mode of a bridge not active because the bridge is operating in protected mode, and its aging function has deleted the address entry of the problem node.
Check the bridge address tables and the operating mode. (Is the learning mode on?)

Cause (6):   Incorrectly configured bridge or router filters.
Check the filter settings and compare them with the address of the problem station. In particular, check the packet streams that occur when the bridge activates a backup path or load sharing.

Cause (7):   MAC-IP address mapping problem, caused by change of static IP address or simultanous configuration with static IP address and Dynamic Host Configuration Protocol (DHCP).

Symptom: An Entire Segment Has No Bridge Connection to the Rest of the Network

Cause (1):   Incorrectly configured bridge port (port not active; wrong operating mode, for example, 10 Mbit/s instead of 100 Mbit/s); faulty connections (loose cables, connectors, or plug-in modules); wiring errors on the back plane.
Check installation and configuration of the bridge.

Cause (2):   Learning mode of a bridge is not active (that is, the bridge is operating in protected mode), and its aging function has deleted the address entry of the problem node.
Check the bridge address tables and the operating mode. (Is the learning mode on?)

Cause (3):   Incorrectly configured bridge or router filters.
Check the filter settings; check wild card entries in particular.

Symptom: **An Entire Segment Has No Router Connection to the Rest of the Network**

Cause (1): Incorrectly configured router port (port not active; wrong operating mode, for example, 10 Mbit/s instead of 100 Mbit/s); protocol not active; faulty connections (loose cables, connectors, or plug-in modules); wiring errors on the back plane.
Check installation and configuration of the router.

Cause (2): Incorrectly configured address tables, mapping tables, routing tables.
Check router configuration.

Cause (3): Incorrectly configured router filters.
Check the filter settings. In particular, check wild card settings and filters that might block backup or load-sharing routes.

Cause (4): Failure of the wide-area connection on the router's WAN port.
Check whether the WAN line is up and running.

Cause (5): No default gateway setting.
Check whether a default gateway is set in the router configuration.

Cause (6): Incorrectly configured subnet mask.
Systematically check all subnet masks in the network.

Cause (7): Incorrectly configured timer settings.
Check the set timer values for the various protocols. Compare the default values, especially when using routers from different manufacturers.

Symptom: **Intermittent Connection Problems Between Client and Network**

Client connects, but loses connection periodically. Pings are returned, however, packet losses occur.

Cause (1): NIC or switch/router port misconfigured.
Both sides are not configured for the same operation mode. Check NIC, port settings.

Cause (2): NIC or switch/router port misconfigured (one side set to manual, one side set to auto negotiation).
Check NIC, port settings. Avoid using the auto-negotiate feature.

Cause (3): Host busy or overloaded, server experiencing problems.
Analyse server operating statistics and server response time.

Common Errors

The most frequent sources of problems in Ethernet networks are listed in figure 7.21 in alphabetical order:

- AUI cable defective
- Bridge address list incorrectly configured; bridge in protected mode
- Bridge filter incorrectly configured
- Bridge overloaded
- Bridge's aging function deletes address entry
- Bridges or repeaters: too many are cascaded, resulting in timeouts and long response times
- Cable length exceeds specification
- Connectors, loose or defective: interface cards, wall jacks, MAUs, hubs, bridges, or routers
- Electromagnetic interference
- External MAU defective
- Faulty installation of physical router, bridge or hub (cable, connectors, plug-ins are loose; cable connections on the backplane are wrong)
- Grounding problems
- Inter-frame spacing gap too short
- Network grounded in more than one location
- NIC incorrectly configured
- Packets out of sequence due to bridge's load sharing function
- Signal power problems in optical components (optical hub ports)
- Router filters incorrectly configured
- Router incorrectly configured (port not active, protocol not active, wrong operating mode)
- Router overloaded
- Router protocol entries incorrectly configured (address tables, mapping tables, subnet masks, default gateways, routing tables, timer)
- Routing protocol problems (OSPF Hello timer, Dead timer, IGRP Active timer setting wrong)
- Terminating resistor defective or missing (10Base2, 10Base5)
- WAN connections down, overloaded, or of poor quality (high Bit-Error Rate (BER))

Figure 7.21 The most frequent sources of problems in Ethernet networks

Token Ring

8

"If the odds are a million to one against something occurring, the chances are 50-50 that it will."

U<small>NKNOWN</small>

8.1   Token Ring: Specification and Implementation

Unlike Ethernet, Token-Ring networks are based on deterministic data transmission techniques. Each station in the ring is periodically given an opportunity to transmit data, and no two stations can transmit simultaneously. Token-Ring technologies offer data speeds of 4 and 16 Mbit/s. Special frames, known as "tokens", control access to the LAN medium. A token is a sequence of bits that

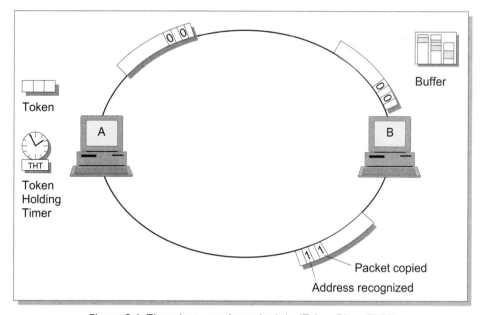

Figure 8.1 The token-passing principle (Token Ring, FDDI)

circulates continuously through the ring. When a station receives a token it can transmit data. The token must be released after a specified period called the token holding time, at which point it becomes available to the next station. When no data needs to be transmitted, the token circulates unused through the ring. If a station that receives the token has data waiting for transmission, it immediately begins transmitting its own data rather than passing the token to the next station.

When a station recognizes its own address as the destination for a data packet, it copies the packet to its receive buffer, sets the address recognized and frame copied bits in the frame header to 1, and returns the modified frame to the source station. When the station that originally sent the data receives the modified frames, it evaluates the information in the frame status field (address recognized, frame copied) and removes the frame from the ring. Stations not participating in a given data exchange act as repeaters, simply forwarding frames downstream to the next station in the direction of ring traffic (Figure 8.1).

Data packets cannot collide in Token-Ring networks because only the station that has the token can transmit data. Consequently, theoretical total bandwidth is used more efficiently in Token Ring than in Ethernet networks. Only when capacity use rises above 80 percent, the time a station must wait for the token doubles, and a decrease in network performance becomes noticeable.

8.1.1   The Physical Layer in Token-Ring Networks

Token Ring distinguishes between four types of signal on the physical layer:

0   binary 0

1   binary 1

J   non-data J

K   non-data K

Signals are transmitted in Differential Manchester encoding (as opposed to the simple Manchester encoding used in Ethernet). In this process, voltage transitions can occur at the beginning and in the middle of each bit time. A logical 1 is identified by the fact that there is no voltage transition at the beginning of the bit; for a logical 0 there is a transition at the beginning. A voltage transition always occurs in the middle of the bit interval. This ensures that the resulting signal is DC-balanced and can be inductively or capacitively coupled. Only the J and K symbols deviate from the rule described for splitting signals. A J signal begins with the same polarity as the signal that preceded it, and a K signal begins with the opposite polarity of its preceding signal. To avoid a residual DC component in the ring, J and K symbols are transmitted in pairs. One disadvantage of Differential Manchester coding is that, as in Ethernet, the effective bit rate of 4 or 16 Mbit/s is only half the actual baud rate of 8 or 32 MHz.

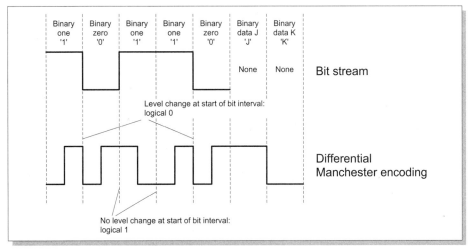

Figure 8.2 Differential Manchester encoding

Physical and Logical Ring Lengths

From the physical point of view, a Token-Ring network consists of stations daisy-chained together in a circle. Each station has a one-bit buffer into which each bit that is received is copied before being passed on along the ring. While this bit is in the buffer it can be analyzed and changed if necessary. Each station increases the ring length by exactly one bit time. At a typical signal propagation speed of 200 m/μs (approximately 0.7 c), each bit in a 4 Mbit/s Token-Ring network travels some 50 meters (or 12.5 meters in a 16 Mbit/s ring). Consequently, each additional station increases the apparent ring length by some 50 meters (or 12 meters in the case of a 16 Mbit/s ring). Furthermore, by this calculation, a ring that is 1,000 meters long can only hold 20 bits at a time! Yet a Token Ring must be capable of carrying at least 24 bits at a time, which is the length of a token. This is why the active monitor, the station charged with monitoring the ring, operates a delay buffer to guarantee a logical ring length of at least 24 bits at a time.

Synchronization and Pulse

The physical layer of each station regenerates the clock information and minimizes phase jitter in the signal received. During normal operation, a Token Ring has one active monitor that sets the ring clock rate to its own local oscillator. All other stations are synchronized with the frequency and phase of this clock by a phase-locked loop with the following minimum precision requirements:

- The maximum dynamic jitter permitted in a station is 3 sigma (= 10 degrees).
- When a station enters the ring or has lost synchronization, it must be able to resynchronize in phase with the active monitor within 1.5 ms.
- The timing of the implementation must be precise enough to permit at least 250 active stations on the ring at one time.

Jitter and synchronization problems are among the most common sources of malfunctions in Token-Ring networks. If the signal deviates too far from the clock rate during data transmission, the ring's stations may get out of sync with the data stream. Technologically advanced Token-Ring components can stabilize themselves without the help of the active monitor using their own local oscillators.

Phase Jitter Compensation

A slight variation in data speeds in the ring can result from signal jitter. With 250 stations in a ring, this can lead to differences in data speed of up to ±3 bits. If the round trip time is decreased, bits are lost. To prevent this, a dynamic buffer of up to 6 bits (corresponding to 12 signal elements or 12 voltage transitions) is added to the 24-bit circulation buffer in the active monitor. The total buffer is initialized with a capacity of 27 bits. If the speed of the data received by the active monitor is slightly higher than that of the master oscillator, the buffer capacity can be expanded to 28, 29 or 30 bits as required. If the data speed is lower, buffering can be reduced to 24 bits.

Connecting Ring Stations

Each station is connected to the Token-Ring network by means of a concentrator, also called a trunk coupling unit (TCU) or multi-station access unit (MSAU). The cable that connects the station to the concentrator, called the lobe cable, consists of shielded, four-lead copper cable with an impedance of $150 \pm 15 \, \Omega$. The connector at the concentrator end (medium interface connector or MIC) specified for Token Ring is an IBM Type 1 connector. When a station is inserted in the ring, two DC voltages are applied to the concentrator (one over each wire pair), and the two DC circuits are inductively coupled with both the station's and concentrator's actual transmit and receive leads. In this way the AC signals, or data streams, are transported through the inductive coupling, while the DC current in the two wire pairs can be monitored to detect open or short circuits. The DC voltage also controls the relay in the concentrator, which creates the actual mechanical connection between the station and the ring. When the

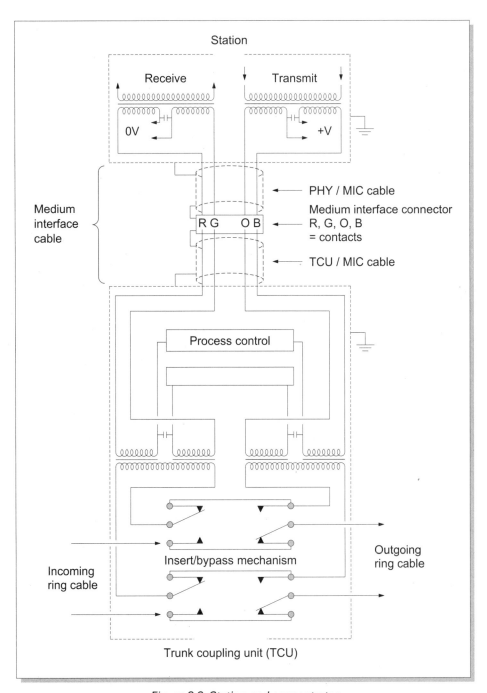

Station

Receive   Transmit

0V   +V

Medium
interface
cable

PHY / MIC cable

R G   O B

Medium interface connector
R, G, O, B
= contacts

TCU / MIC cable

Process control

Insert/bypass mechanism

Incoming
ring cable

Outgoing
ring cable

Trunk coupling unit (TCU)

Figure 8.3 Station and concentrator

station is included in the ring, 4.1 to 7.0 volts are applied across points B and O (Figure 8.3), resulting in a current of 0.65 to 2.0 mA between points G and R. In the bypass state, that is when the station is not participating in the ring, the voltage is below 1 volt.

8.1.2   The Token-Ring Data Format

There are two types of frames in Token-Ring networks: tokens and data packets. A token is 3 bytes long and consists of a starting delimiter, an access control

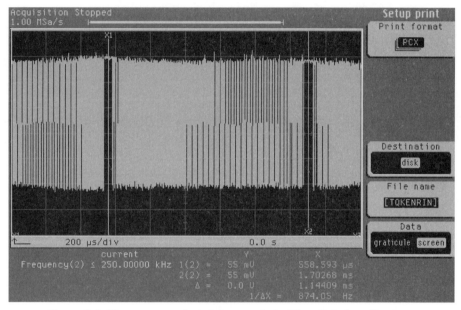

Figure 8.4 Bit sequence of a token recorded with a digital oscilloscope

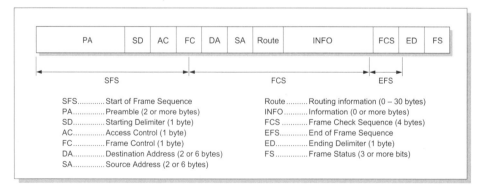

Figure 8.5 Data packet format in Token Ring

field, and an ending delimiter. Figure 8.4 shows a token sequence recorded with a digital oscilloscope, circulating in an empty ring at a frequency of 250 kHz.

All other data packets can have lengths from 13 to 4,500 bytes in a 4 Mbit/s ring, or 13 to 17,800 bytes in a 16 Mbit/s ring, and consist of the following fields: start of frame sequence, preamble, starting delimiter, access control, frame control, destination address, source address, information, frame check sequence, end of frame sequence, ending delimiter and frame status.

Token and Data Packet Fields

Starting Delimiter (SD)

Every frame, including tokens, begins with this field. Any sequence of bits that does not begin with this field is discarded.

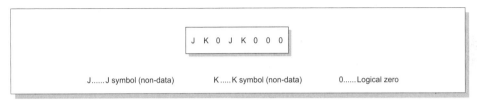

Figure 8.6 The starting delimiter field in Token Ring

Access Control (AC)

The access control field is responsible for controlling access to the network medium in Token Ring. The priority bits (PPP) specify the priority level of the token. There are eight levels of priority, increasing from 000 to 111 (for example, priority 110 is higher than 011). In a token, the token bit T is set to 1; in all other frames it is set to 0. When a station receives a token with a priority level equal to or lower than that of the data packet in its send queue, the station can transform the token into a start of frame sequence and transmit its data. The monitor bit M prevents data packets and tokens with a priority greater than 0 from circulating continuously in the ring. The default value for this bit in all frames, including tokens, is 0. The active monitor, the station acting as ring manager, sets this bit to 1 before forwarding any frame. Whenever a frame has the monitor bit set to 1,

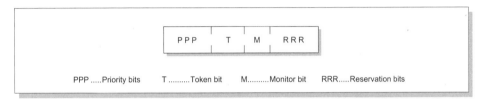

Figure 8.7 The access control field in Token Ring

this indicates that the frame has passed through the active monitor since its generation.

By setting the reservation bits RRR, stations can request a token with a specific priority level. This may be necessary when a station has data packets that need to be sent urgently and cannot wait for a normal token.

Frame Control (FC)

The frame control field identifies the frame type. It is used to distinguish between MAC frames and LLC frames. MAC frames are used for ring management, while LLC frames contain user data. The information about the frame type is contained in the two format bits (FF):

00   MAC frame
01   LLC frame
1X   Undefined

How stations react to a MAC frame is determined by the control bits the frame contains. In an LLC frame, the first three control bits ZZZ are set to 0, and the data packet's priority is indicated in the remaining three bits.

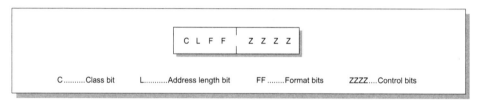

Figure 8.8 The frame control field in Token Ring

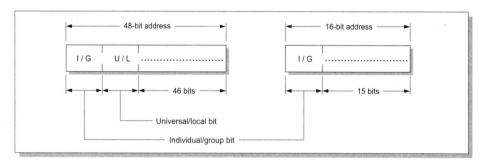

Figure 8.9 The destination address field in Token Ring

Destination Address (DA)

The destination address identifies the station that is the intended recipient of a given data packet. The first bit indicates whether the destination is an individual address (bit 1=0) or a group address (bit 1=1); the second bit (only in 48-bit addresses) shows whether the address is locally administered (bit 2=1) or universally administered (bit 2=0). If the destination address field contains all 1s, then the destination is a broadcast address, which means the packet is intended for all stations on the ring. An address consisting entirely of 0s is called a "zero address"; packets with this address are not intended for any station.

Source Address (SA)

The source address identifies the station from which a data packet originates. The length and format are the same as in the destination address field, but the first bit is always a 0.

Routing Information

The routing information field, with a length of up to 30 bytes, is required only when source routing is implemented to determine transmission paths in the network. When this field is present, it consists of a 2-byte routing control field and a variable number of route designator fields.

Information (INFO)

The information or data field can contain zero, one or more bytes, which may be addressed to the MAC layer, the LLC layer, or to network management functions—the total packet length must not exceed 4,500 bytes (4 Mbit/s)/17,800 bytes (16 Mbit/s). If the information field is part of a MAC frame it is directly processed by the Token-Ring protocol. In an LLC frame, the information field contains user data, which is passed to the higher protocol layers at the destination node. Each byte in the information field is transmitted starting with the most significant bit. The information field of an LLC frame begins with the following three fields: destination service access point (DSAP, 1 byte), source service access point (SSAP, 1 byte) and the LLC control field (1 or 2 bytes). The DSAP and SSAP designate the protocol in the subsequent information fields. These fields can specify any of 128 different protocols. The Sub-Network Access Protocol (SNAP), which is designated by the values DSAP=AA, SSAP=AA and LLC Control=03, is a kind of meta-protocol: it suspends the limit of 128 protocols by adding another field to allow manufacturers practically unlimited use of proprietary protocols.

Frame Check Sequence (FCS)

The FCS field contains a 32-bit checksum calculated from the FC, DA, SA and INFO fields. This field allows the receiving node to detect bit errors in transmission.

Ending Delimiter (ED)

A receiving station considers the ending delimiter to be valid if the first six symbols, JK1JK1, are received correctly. The intermediate frame bit indicates whether other frames follow in the sequence. If the value of the 1 bit is 0, the frame is the last in its sequence. The error detection bit of a data packet, token, or abort sequence is always set to 0 by the transmitting node. If any station detects an error (FCS error, non-data signal, etc.) when forwarding a frame, it sets the error detection bit to logical 1. Otherwise, the frame is passed along with the error detection bit unchanged.

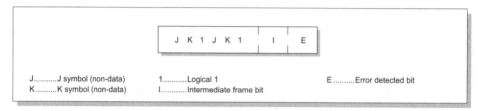

Figure 8.10 Ending delimiter

Frame Status

The destination node uses the frame status field to provide the source node with confirmation that the frame was received. When a frame is first sent, the transmitting node sets the A (address recognized) and C (frame copied) bits to 0. When a receiving station identifies the destination address of the data packet as its own, it sets the address recognized bit to 1. If the receiving station is able to copy the data packet to its receive buffer, the frame copied bit is also set to 1. This allows the transmitting node to distinguish between three cases upon receiving the returning frame:

- The destination node does not exist in the ring or is inactive,
- The station exists but the data packet was not received, or
- The data packet was copied into the receive buffer of the destination node.

The A and C bits are used regardless of the status of the error detection bit as long as the frame is found to be valid.

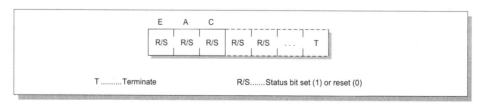

Figure 8.11 The frame status field

Abort Sequence

An abort sequence consists of a starting delimiter and an ending delimiter. This sequence can be transmitted anywhere in the bit stream without regard to byte alignment and stops all transmission.

Figure 8.12 The abort sequence

MAC Layer Token-Ring Frames

MAC layer Token-Ring frames are used by the Token-Ring control protocol to conduct ring management operations, including error handling, in various operating states. The value in the control field of a MAC frame indicates one of three priority levels, which determine whether the packet is copied into the buffer of a receiving station. If this value is 00, the packet is copied into the receive buffer only if sufficient memory is available. Packets with 01 in the control field are always copied into the receive buffer, even if this means discarding existing data. All other MAC frames with a control field value greater than 01 are addressed to all stations, but are only copied into a station's receive buffer if enough memory is available. There are five different types of MAC frames.

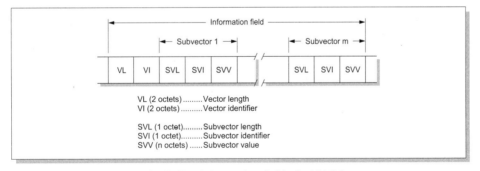

Figure 8.13 The information field of a MAC frame

Claim Token

If a station recognizes that there is no active monitor because the Timer Standby Monitor (TSM) has run out, it initiates a monitor contention process to select a new active monitor by sending a claim token frame. When a new active monitor has been selected, the selected station will return the ring to operational status by issuing a new token.

The station initiating the process begins transmitting claim token frames while noting the source address of any claim token frame it receives. Other stations can choose whether or not to take part in the monitor contention process. A station that does not take part in this process simply repeats the claim token frames and starts its own claim token timer. Stations that actively participate in the claim token process compare the source address of each claim token frame received with their own address. If the value of the source address in the claim token frame is greater than that of the station's own address, the station withdraws from the process. If the station's address is higher, it replaces the source address of the claim token frame with its own address before passing the frame on. Once a station receives a claim token frame with its own address as the source, it becomes the active monitor. It clears all data circulating in the ring (that is, performs a ring purge) and issues a new token.

Priority	0	
Frame Control field	0000 0011	Claim token
Destination address	1111 1111 1111 1111	Broadcast
Info field VI	0003 hex	Claim token
Info field SVI-1	02 hex	Received upstream neighbor address
Info field SVV-1	XXXX ...	(The upstream neighbor's address)

Figure 8.14 The fields in a claim token MAC frame

Duplicate Address Test (DAT)

When a new station enters the ring it transmits a DAT frame. The new station sends a frame with its own address as the destination. If the address recognized bit is set to 1 when the frame returns, then another station already exists with the same address. In this case, the new station removes itself from the ring.

Priority	0	
Frame Control field	0000 0000	
Destination address		(= sender's address)
Info field VI	0007 hex	Duplicate address test

Figure 8.15 The fields in a duplicate address test frame

Active Monitor Present (AMP)

An AMP frame is transmitted by the active monitor after a ring purge, or when the Timer Active Monitor (TAM) times out, to inform the standby monitor stations of its presence. Each station that receives an AMP frame resets its TSM to 0.

Priority	7	
Frame Control field	0000 0101	
Destination address		Broadcast
Info field VI	0005 hex	Active monitor present
Info field SVI-1	02 hex	Received upstream neighbor address
Info field SVV-1	XXXX ...	(The upstream neighbor's address)

Figure 8.16 The fields in an active monitor present frame

Standby Monitor Present (SMP)

Standby monitors transmit SMP frames to announce their presence. (A standby monitor is any station in the ring that is not currently serving as active monitor.) When a station receives an SMP or AMP frame from its upstream neighbor with the A and C bits set to 0, it saves the source address as its current next active upstream neighbor (NAUN) and sets the A and C bits to 1. The station also starts its Timer Queue PDU (TQP) and transmits its own SMP frame when the timer expires. The TQP ensures that the process of circulating SMP and AMP frames— the neighbor notification or "ring poll" process—does not take up more than 1 percent of the ring's bandwidth.

Priority	0	
Frame Control field	0000 0110	
Destination address		Broadcast
Info field VI	0006 hex	Standby monitor present
Info field SVI-1	02 hex	Received upstream neighbor address
Info field SVV-1		(The upstream neighbor's address)

Figure 8.17 The fields in a standby monitor present frame

Beacon (BCN)

A BCN frame is transmitted when there is a problem in the ring that the Token-Ring protocol cannot solve otherwise. Such a problem may involve the cabling, a

network interface card (NIC), or a concentrator. The failure domain begins with
the station directly upstream from the one transmitting the beacon frame. Its
address is placed in the SVV-1 information field of the beacon frame.

Priority	0	
Frame Control field	0000 0010	
Destination address		Broadcast
Info field VI	0002 hex	Beacon
Info field SVI-1	02 hex	Received upstream neighbor address
Info field SVV-1		(The upstream neighbor's address)
Info field SVI-2	01 hex	(Reserved for future use)
Info field SVV-2	0002 hex	Continuous non-data J waveform; see physical layer
	0003 hex	TNT (Timer No Token) expired and no claim token frame detected
	0004 hex	TNT (Timer No Token) expired during claim token process

Figure 8.18 The fields in a beacon frame

```
┌──┐                      Token-Ring Detailed Decode
└──┘
Control  Config  Actions  Format  Other displays  Help
   Frame: 2            Time: Sep 22@16:17:48.6817660  Length: 36
Field                          Value                    Description
Access Control:
   Frame Priority              000.-....               Non-Priority
   Token Bit                   ...1-....               Frame
   Monitor Bit                 ....-0...               Not Passed Monitor
   Reservation                 ....-.011               Reserved
Frame Control:
   Frame Type                  00..-....               MAC Frame
   Reserved                    ..00-....               Reserved
   Control                     ....-0100               Express Buffered
MAC Destination Address        Broadcast               Broadcast
MAC Source Address             4000F602661A            No source routing
Destination Class              0000-....               Ring Station
Source Class                   ....-0000               Ring Station
MAC Frame Type                 04                      Ring Purge
   Subvector Type              00000000                Physical Location
   Subvector Type              IBM---26E062            NAUN
Frame check sequence           6B-C4-D4-C7
> Intermediate bit             ....-..0.               Single Frame
> Error bit                    ....-...0               No Errors Detected
> AC bits                                              Recognized and Copied
> Data size                    0
```

Figure 8.19 Ring purge recorded with a protocol analyzer

Purge (PRG)

A PRG frame initializes the ring, deleting all data in it. A PRG frame is transmitted in the following situations:

* After a token claiming process, but before the new token is transmitted
* After the Timer, Valid Transmission (TVX) expires
* Following the appearance of a monitor bit set to 1 in an access control field

Priority	0	
Frame Control field	0000 0100	
Destination address		Broadcast
Info field VI	0004 hex	Purge
Info field SVI-1	02 hex	Received upstream neighbor address
Info field SVV-1		(The upstream neighbor's address)

Figure 8.20 The fields in a purge frame

Timers in Token Ring

All processes in the Token-Ring protocol are time-controlled. Analysis of timer activity can yield valuable information about the state of a ring. The main timers are described here.

Timer Return to Repeat (TRR)

Every station has a TRR. This timer ensures that the station returns from transmission to repeat state within a defined period. The timer setting must be higher than the transmission delay in the ring plus the sum of the delay times of all stations. The default setting for the TRR is 2.5 ms.

Timer Holding Token (THT)

The THT limits the time during which a station can transmit once it has received a token. The default setting is 10 ms.

Timer Queue PDU (TQP)

The TQP defines how long a station waits after receiving the upstream neighbor's AMP or SMP frame before it transmits its own SMP frame. This limits the overhead traffic on the ring due to the AMP/SMP process to less than 1 percent. The default value is 10 ms.

Timer Valid Transmission (TVX)

Every station has a TVX. A token error occurs when the active monitor does not receive a valid signal before its TVX expires. The setting for this timer is the sum of the settings for the THT and TRR. The default setting is 12.5 ms.

Timer No Token (TNT)

The TNT allows the ring to recover from a variety of token errors. The value for this timer is $n \cdot$ THT + TRR, where n equals the number of ring stations. The default setting for the TNT is 1 second.

Timer Active Monitor (TAM)

Every station has a TAM. When the active monitor's TAM expires, it transmits an AMP frame. The default setting is 3 seconds.

Timer Standby Monitor (TSM)

Every station has a TSM. This timer ensures that there is always an active monitor in the ring (see the previous description of the claim token frame). The default setting for this timer is 7 seconds.

8.1.3   Process Control in Token-Ring Networks

As described at the beginning of this chapter, access to the transmission medium in Token Ring is controlled by a token: a station must receive a token before it can transmit data over the ring. The data to be transmitted must also have a priority level that is equal to or higher than that of the token. If the token cannot be used, or has a higher priority level than the data packets to be transmitted by a given station, the station can request a lower priority token by entering the corresponding priority level in the token's RRR bit in the access control field. Once a suitable token is received, this token is transformed into a start of frame sequence by setting the token bit. The station then begins transmitting its own outgoing data rather than repeating received data.

Beaconing and Neighbor Notification

When persistent problems occur in the ring, the Token-Ring protocol is often able to recover or at least indicate the failure domain by means of the beacon and neighbor notification processes. Neighbor notification, or ring polling, is an essential process for automatic recovery because it ensures that all active stations and their relative positions are known at all times. The active monitor initiates neighbor notification at regular intervals by broadcasting an AMP frame. The nearest downstream neighbor reacts as follows when it receives this frame:

- It resets its TSM.
- It copies the AMP broadcast frame into its receive buffer and saves the NAUN address (or UNA).
- It sets the A and C bits of the AMP frame to 1 and forwards it.
- It transmits an SMP frame.

One after another, each station receives an SMP frame with the A and C bits set to 0, which indicates that the frame was sent by the NAUN. At the conclusion of the neighbor notification process, each station knows the address of its NAUN.

The beacon process allows the ring to recover after a failure. The station downstream from the location of the failure is the first to notice a ring error because it no longer receives valid signals. This node's first reaction to the absence of valid signals is to start a claim token (or monitor contention) process. If this does not succeed before the station's claim token timer expires, it enters the beacon state and begins broadcasting beacon frames. Beacon frames contain both the address of the station that generated them and that of its NAUN. No new station can enter the ring while beaconing is occurring. If the NAUN of the station that initiated the beacon process receives eight beacon frames that contain its address in the NAUN field, it assumes that it is the cause of the error, removes itself from the ring and performs a self-test. If no error is found, it re-enters the ring. After a defined period (usually 26 seconds), the station that initiated beaconing also removes itself from the ring, assuming that it might be the cause of the error, and performs a self-test. If this does not pinpoint the source of the error, the ring goes into the "streaming beacon" state. At this point, the ring can no longer recover automatically.

There are four types of beacon frames: Type 1 beacon frames are only used by stations that implement the Dual Ring protocol (IEEE 802.5c). Type 2 beacon frames indicate a complete loss of valid signals. Type 3 beacon frames indicate bit-streaming (the NAUN is transmitting a continuous stream of padding bits) and Type 4 beacon frames indicate "claim streaming" (the NAUN is continuously transmitting claim token frames).

Optional Token-Ring Services

In addition to the functions described previously, Token Ring can include a number of other functional elements to optimize management: these include the ring parameter server, ring error monitor, configuration report server and LAN bridge server. Ring stations report the required data to these services regardless of whether the corresponding components are present in the ring. In practice, this data is analyzed by special Token-Ring management software packages or monitored using a protocol analyzer. The ring parameter server saves all ring operating data, such as timer settings, active monitor stations and standby monitor stations. The ring error monitor keeps track of any errors that occur. The configuration report server informs network management services on the configuration of individual ring stations. And the LAN bridge server can be used to analyze the performance of bridges in the network.

8.1.4   Design Guidelines for Token-Ring Networks

The most important guidelines for designing Token-Ring networks are those governing the maximum number of stations (250) and the maximum distance between adjacent nodes on the ring. In 4 Mbit/s rings, this distance must not exceed 240 meters when using IBM type 1 cabling, or 100 meters when using Cat. 3 UTP cabling. The corresponding limitations for 16 Mbit/s rings are 100 meters for IBM type 1 and 45 meters for Cat. 3 UTP cabling.

Verifying Your Token-Ring Design

You can check your Token-Ring network against the tables 8.21 through 8.24 to make sure it conforms to the design guidelines. All you need to ascertain is the number of concentrators (MAUs), the number of wiring closets that contain the concentrators, and the cable lengths between the wiring closets. Begin by using these numbers to calculate the adjusted ring length (ARL): add the length of the cables between wiring closets and subtract the length of the shortest cable connecting two wiring closets. Tables 8.21 through 8.24 contain the values for

Token Ring (4 Mbit/s) over Type 1 and Type 2 cabling: Maximum ARL (in meters)
(When Type 6 or Type 9 cabling is used, divide values by 1.33.
For Type 8 cabling, divide by 2.)

Concen-trators	Number of wiring closets										
	2	3	4	5	6	7	8	9	10	11	12
2	363										
3	354	350									
4	346	341	336								
5	337	332	328	323							
6	329	324	319	316	310						
7	320	315	311	306	301	297					
8	311	306	302	297	293	288	283				
9	302	298	293	289	284	279	274	270			
10	294	289	284	280	275	271	266	262	257		
11	285	280	276	271	266	262	257	253	248	244	
12	276	272	267	262	258	253	249	244	240	235	230
13	268	263	258	254	249	244	240	235	231	226	222
14	259	254	250	245	240	236	231	227	222	217	213
15	250	246	241	236	232	227	223	218	213	209	204

Figure 8.21 Token-Ring design table: 4 Mbit/s, Type 1, Type 2 cabling

Token Ring (16 Mbit/s) over Type 1 and Type 2 cabling: Maximum ARL (in meters)
(When Type 6 or Type 9 cabling is used, divide values by 1.33.
For Type 8 cabling, divide by 2.)

Concen-trators	Number of wiring closets								
	2	3	4	5	6	7	8	9	10
2	162								
3	155	150							
4	148	144	138						
5	142	137	132	127					
6	135	130	125	120	115				
7	129	123	19	113	109	103			
8	122	350	112	197	105	97	92		
9	115	110	105	100	95	90	85	80	
10	108	104	98	93.6	88	84	79	73	69
11	102	97	92	87	82	77	72	67	62
12	95	90	85	80	75	70	65	60	55
13	247	77	72	67	62	57	52	47	42
14	69	64	59	54	49	44	39	34	29
15	56	51	139	41	36	31	26	21	16

Figure 8.22 Token-Ring design table: 16 Mbit/s, Type 1, Type 2 cabling

Token Ring (4 Mbit/s) over UTP cabling				
Concentrators	Number of wiring closets			
	1	2	3	4
1	223			
2	217	206		
3	211	201	196	
4	205	195	190	185
5	199	189	184	179
6	194	183	178	173
7	188	178	173	167
8	182	172	167	162
9	176	166	161	156
10	170	160	160	150

Figure 8.23 Token-Ring design table: 4 Mbit/s, UTP cabling

the stations' maximum drive distances when using passive concentrators, which equal the maximum ARL plus the maximum lobe cable length. If active concentrators are used, the table values correspond directly to the maximum ARL.

Token Ring (16 Mbit/s) over UTP cabling				
Concentrators	Number of wiring closets			
	1	2	3	
1	55			
2	45	39		
3	35	29	23	
4	26	20		
5	16			

Figure 8.24 Token-Ring design table: 16 Mbit/s, UTP cabling

If a 16 Mbit/s Token Ring is made up of the three wiring closets A, B and C, of which A and B contain one concentrator each and C houses two concentrators, and the distances between them are AB = 34 meters, BC = 56 meters and CA = 64 meters, then the ARL calculation yields:

ARL = 34 + 56 + 64 - 34 = 120 meters

The corresponding field in table 8.22 (four concentrators, three wiring closets) provides the value for the maximum allowable ARL, which is 144 meters. If passive concentrators are used, the maximum allowable length of lobe cables is 144 - 120 = 24 meters. If the lobe cables do not exceed this length, the ring design is suitable for use with passive or active concentrators. If the lobe cables are longer, active concentrators must be used.

8.1.5   Token-Ring Standards

IEEE Std 802.5c-1991, Supplement to IEEE Std 802.5-1989, Local and Metropolitan Area Networks: Recommended Practice for Dual Ring Operation with Wrapback Reconfiguration.

IEEE 802.5e, Token Ring Station Management Entity Specifications.

IEEE Std 802.5j-1997, Supplement to Information Technology—Telecommunications and Information Exchange Between Systems—Local and Metropolitan Area Networks—Specific Requirements—Part 5: Token Ring Access Method and Physical Layer Specifications—Fiber Optic Media Requirements.

IEEE Std 802.5r-1997, Standard for Information Technology—Telecommunications and Information Exchange Between Systems—Local and Metropolitan Area Networks—Specific Requirements—Part 5: Token Ring Access Method and Physical Layer Specifications—Dedicated Token Ring Operation.

IEEE 802.5t, Supplement to ISO/IEC 8802-5: 1995 Specific Requirements—Part 5: Token Ring Access Method and Physical Layer Specifications—100 Mbit/s Dedicated Token Ring Operation Over 2-Pair Cabling.

IEEE 802.5u, Supplement to ISO/IEC 8802-5: 1995 Specific Requirements—Part 5: Token Ring Access Method and Physical Layer Specifications—100 Mbit/s Dedicated Token Ring Operation Over Multi-mode Fiber.

IEEE 802.5v, Supplement to ISO/IEC 8802-5: 1995, Specific Requirements—Part 5: Token Ring Access Method and Physical Layer Specifications. Media Access Control Parameters, Physical Layers, and Management Parameters for 1000 Mbit/s Operation or Above.

RFC 1231 IEEE 802.5 Token Ring MIB.

The IEEE 802.5 Working Group can be reached on the Internet at

http://www.8025.org/802.5/documents/

8.2 Troubleshooting in Token-Ring Networks

8.2.1 Gathering Information on Symptoms and Recent Changes

The first step in any troubleshooting process is to gather information. The more information you have about the symptoms and characteristics of a problem—including *when* it first occurred—the better your chances of solving the problem quickly and efficiently. Typical questions you might ask at this stage include:

- Do the symptoms occur regularly or intermittently?
- Are the symptoms related to certain applications, or do they affect all network operations?
- Do the symptoms correlate to other activities in the network?
- When was the first occurrence of the symptom?
- Was there any change in any hardware or software network component?
- Has anyone connected or disconnected a PC (laptop or desktop) or any other component to or from the network?
- Has anyone installed an interface card in a computer?
- Has anyone stepped on a cable?

- Has any maintenance work been performed in the building recently (by a telephone company or building maintenance personnel, for example)?
- Has anyone (including cleaning personnel) moved any equipment or furniture?

8.2.2 Starting the Troubleshooting Procedure

Troubleshooting in Token-Ring LANs is primarily performed using protocol analyzers, network management software and cable testers, and special Token-Ring management software that tracks and displays Token-Ring operating messages. Unlike Ethernet, Token Ring is second-generation network technology and has a number of self-diagnosis functions that enable it to resolve certain critical operation states on its own. Key requirements for successful troubleshooting in Token-Ring networks include a detailed understanding of its operational processes and the availability of a protocol analyzer and specialized Token-Ring management software to monitor these processes.

The first step in the troubleshooting procedure involves using a protocol analyzer to determine the main operating statistics of the network. These statistics

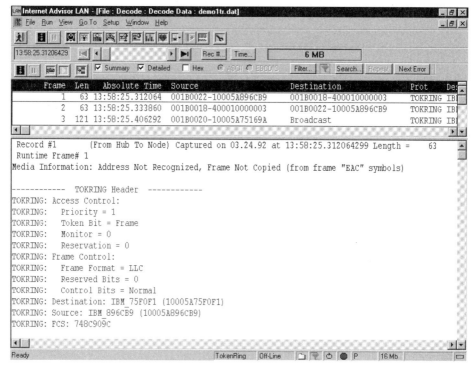

Figure 8.25 Display of characteristic Token-Ring operating data on the Agilent Advisor

include ring capacity use as a percentage; throughput in frames per second; the number of receiver congestion messages, burst errors, line errors, beacons, monitor contentions and ring purges; and the number of transmitting stations. The analysis of these statistics often points to possible causes of the problem. Unlike the defective frames found in Ethernet, the various Token-Ring MAC frames that report and handle errors generally give a fairly precise indication of how the errors came about. If the problem cannot be located in this way, however, additional trend measurements are necessary. This involves recording the main operating parameters over a period of hours, or even days, and analyzing the results for correlations. By charting the network load together with the number of active nodes and the number of ring purges, for example, you can tell at a glance whether there is a correlation between the occurrence of ring purges and stations entering or leaving the ring. If this is the case, these ring purges are probably normal operating behavior. Otherwise, defective NICs or concentrator ports may be the cause. Measurement results from different network segments connected by bridges can be similarly correlated. In this way, possible causes can be systematically eliminated until the source of the problem is limited to a small area.

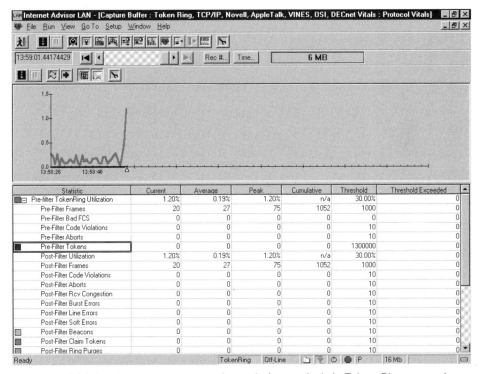

Figure 8.26 Trend measurements and correlation analysis in Token-Ring networks

The steps to take after a protocol analyzer performed the basic measurements depend on the nature of the symptoms. If the symptoms can be localized, occur periodically, or can at least be reproduced, then the troubleshooting process continues with the network component nearest to the problem. If the problem source cannot be detected there, the range of analysis is successively expanded. For example, if the problems are found to be related to a single network node, the next step is to analyze the station's software and hardware components. If no fault is found, the examination progresses to the lobe cable, the connector, the wall jack, the cable to the concentrator, the concentrator itself, the cable to the server, and so on.

If the problem cannot be localized at all, or if problems that were thought to have been localized cannot be pinpointed, the only way to find the source of the problem is through systematic segmentation of the network. To do this, check each of the concentrators in turn and replace any defective units found. If the error persists, physically remove each concentrator in turn until the source of the problem becomes apparent. This method causes considerable disruption in network operation, and is therefore applied only as a last resort, when the problem itself severely impairs normal network operation.

If the symptoms occur intermittently, long-term measurements are necessary. These must be performed continuously until the basic network operating statistics have been measured during the occurrence of the fault. This information usually provides the first clue to the error source. Furthermore, it is essential to log the exact time of intermittent error events. Later this information can be used to find temporal correlations with other events in the network or on a given node, such as backups, the start of specific applications, connections through routers, access to the Internet, users' working hours, or other possible factors. If this does not help to track down the error, you may have to resort to the segmentation method. Depending on which causes the least inconvenience to users, you can either systematically disable network functions and applications, or physically separate concentrators. These methods usually lead to the error source.

8.2.3   Error Symptoms in Token Ring

The Token-Ring protocol has built-in operation management functions that generate highly specific messages in most cases of error. Errors in Token Ring can be divided into two categories: isolating errors, which can be traced to a specific node, and non-isolating errors. Error messages that report isolating errors contain both the address of the station reporting the error and the address of its upstream neighbor; this information points to the probable failure domain. Non-isolating errors, by contrast, such as token errors or lost frames, do not provide information about the location of the failure. The following error types are reported by the Token-Ring protocol.

Error Types

Abort Error (Isolating)

Token-Ring nodes transmit abort error messages if they have recovered from an internal operating error, if recovery from an internal error failed, or after having received a corrupt token.

A/C Error (Isolating)

An A/C error is reported if a station receives more than one AMP frame, or if it receives an SMP frame without having received an AMP frame to initiate a neighbor notification process. This is often caused by problems in the upstream neighbor or by errors involving bridges or routers.

Beacon Error (Token-Ring Protocol)

Beacons are transmitted if a station is no longer able to receive frames of any type, and its attempt to initiate a claim token process has failed. Common causes are defective concentrators, interface cards or cabling.

Burst Error (Isolating)

Burst errors are reported if a station does not receive a valid signal for more than five half-bit times between a starting delimiter and an ending delimiter.

Claim Token (Token-Ring Protocol)

Claim token frames are circulated in the monitor contention process to select a new active monitor. There are a number of reasons why such a frame may be transmitted, including the following:

* A standby monitor is not receiving valid signals
* A standby monitor is not receiving tokens
* A standby monitor has noticed the lack of a neighbor notification process
* The active monitor is unable to perform a ring purge
* A new station is inserted into the ring
* A station detects a clock error
* A beaconing station receives its own beacon frame
* A station receives a given frame a second time
* A station receives beacon frames for an extended period

If the monitor contention process cannot be completed successfully, the ring goes into a beaconing state.

Frame Copy Error (Non-Isolating)

If a station receives a frame in which its own address is given as the destination but the address recognized bit is already set, that station reports a frame copy error. This error is often caused by a duplicate Token-Ring address in the ring.

Frequency Error (Non-Isolating)

A frequency error is reported if the clock rate of the signal received exceeds the frequency tolerance limits.

Internal Error (Isolating)

A Token-Ring node reports internal errors after recovering from an internal operating error.

Line Error (Isolating)

A line error is reported if a station detects frames that contain invalid checksums or coding errors.

Lost Frame (Non-Isolating)

If a station's transmitted frame does not return to it, the station reports a lost frame error.

Purge (Token-Ring Protocol)

An active monitor transmits a purge frame if it does not receive a valid token before its TNT expires. If the purge frame returns to the active monitor successfully, the ring is considered operational and a new token is released.

Receiver Congestion Error (Non-Isolating)

If a destination node is not able to copy a frame into its receive buffer due to memory overflow, it reports a receive congestion error. So long as such errors do not originate from bridges or routers, they are of minor importance and have little impact on ring performance.

Token Error (Non-Isolating)

A token error is reported if a token is detected with a monitor bit set to 1, if a corrupt token is received, or if a TNT timeout occurs.

Principle Error Conditions During Normal Ring Operation

As in Ethernet, there are error conditions in Token Ring that occur during normal operation and do not present a problem so long as they do not exceed certain levels. The following events trigger the error messages listed:

Station insertion:

Active monitor:	Ring purge
Inserted station:	2 Duplicate Address tests, 1 Report NAUN frame
Downstream neighbor:	1 Report NAUN frame
Inserted station:	2-4 Request Initialization frames
Active monitor:	Report Soft Error frame (1-4 lost tokens)
Downstream neighbor:	Report Soft Error frame (2-4 burst errors)
Other stations:	Report Soft Error frame (1 lost frame)

Station removal:

Active monitor:	Ring purge
Downstream neighbor:	1 Report NAUN frame
Active monitor:	1 Report Soft Error frame (1-4 lost tokens)
Downstream neighbor:	2-4 Burst errors
Other stations:	Report Soft Error frame (approximately 1 lost frame)

Station shutdown:

Downstream neighbor:	4 Claim Token frames
New active monitor:	Ring purge
Downstream neighbor:	Report Soft Error frame (reports loss of the old active monitor; 1-4 burst errors)
New active monitor:	Report New Monitor frame
Downstream neighbor of the former active monitor:	Report NAUN frame

Critical Error States Requiring Investigation

Operational states that indicate possible problems on the ring may be indicated by:

* Ring purges that are not related to station insertion or removal
* Incomplete neighbor notification processes
* Report active monitor errors
* Change of active monitor
* Beaconing or streaming beaconing

8.2.4   Cabling Problems

As in other networks, cabling problems are among the most common causes of errors in Token-Ring networks. Typical causes include defective or low-quality cables; incorrect characteristic impedance; and wiring mistakes or electromagnetic interference (noise) caused by air conditioning systems, photocopiers, pagers, elevators or production environments. These problems are discussed in detail in the chapter on cabling. One factor that must be mentioned with specific reference to Token Ring, however, is the limit on the distance between two active ring stations (see the section on design guidelines). If this limit is not observed, switching off ring stations may temporarily result in node distances that exceed these limits. Consequently, the Token-Ring signals may no longer be transported reliably between two nodes; this can lead to extraordinarily high error rates or even a complete failure of the ring. Another common source of problems is upgrading 4 Mbit/s rings to 16 Mbit/s. If you do not take into account the fact that the maximum distance allowed between two nodes on 16 Mbit/s rings is significantly less than that specified for 4 Mbit/s rings, the distance limitations may be exceeded.

8.2.5   Problems with Token-Ring Interface Cards

The first step in localizing a defective NIC is to identify suspicious nodes on the network. Begin by making a list of all network nodes that transmit defective frames. Most protocol analyzers provide this information with fully automatic test programs. If the source addresses of the defective frames are invalid and cannot be decoded, try the correlation method: begin by simultaneously charting the activity of the suspicious nodes and the error rate in the network. If you observe a correlation between the activity of a certain node and the error frequency, then you have probably found the defective interface card. Monitoring the states of the ring stations (active monitor, standby monitor) in correlation with error frames can provide additional information about the source of the problem. For example, if ring errors frequently occur when one particular station is the active monitor, there is a good chance that the station's NIC is defective.

Symptoms of Defective Token-Ring Interface Cards

Characteristic symptoms of defective Token-Ring interface cards include the occurrence of claim token frames in the absence of any ring activity, beacon frames, or receiver congestion errors. Common causes are station configuration errors, problems with power to the interface card, or a hardware failure on the interface card.

Defective Interface Card Hardware

If a defective interface card causes the concentrator relay to remain in the closed position, the ring goes into a beaconing state and cannot recover on its own.

Duplicate Token-Ring Addresses

When a new station is inserted into the ring, it may detect that it has the same address as another active node. In this case, the new station cancels the insertion process and removes itself from the ring. Duplicate addresses can result from typing errors during station configuration, from copying configuration files between stations, or from cloning a station (that is, copying a one-to-one disk drive image from one node to another).

Incorrect Ring Speed

An interface card or a bridge or router port configured for the wrong ring speed (for example, 4 Mbit/s instead of 16 Mbit/s) also cause beaconing.

8.2.6 Problems with Concentrators (MAUs/TCUs)

The nodes are connected to the ring by concentrators. Smooth functioning of the concentrators is, therefore, a key requirement for error-free ring operation. One defective concentrator can often cause complete failure of the entire ring. The following equipment is required for troubleshooting in concentrators:

- A backup concentrator known to be in working order
- A lobe cable in working order
- A MAU port reset connector (for resetting stuck concentrator ports)
- A Token-Ring mini-network (see Figure 8.27)

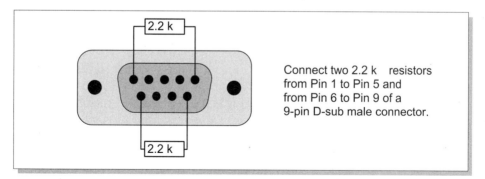

Figure 8.27 Mini-network for Token-Ring simulation

Symptoms of Defective Concentrators

The most common symptom of trunk concentrator unit (TCU) problems is the sporadic or continuous occurrence of beacon frames. This symptom is often caused by stuck TCU ports, defective lobe cables, loose or defective connectors, or general TCU hardware problems. To locate the source of the problem, use a protocol analyzer to capture and analyze the beacon frames. The addresses in the beacon frames, those of the beacon sender and its upstream neighbor, provide the information needed to locate the failure domain. The exact error source can be determined by systematically replacing the components in the failure domain with components known to be in working order (lobe cable, connector, interface card, TCU) and by testing components in the Token-Ring mini-network.

8.2.7   Problems with Bridges

Bridges are inter-network elements that connect network segments on OSI Layer 2 (the MAC layer). Bridges buffer and filter the frames they receive from connected segments and transmit them to their destination segments without regard to higher-layer protocols. The main functions of a MAC-layer bridge are preventing the spread of local traffic to neighboring segments and overcoming such limitations of the particular network topology as the maximum number of nodes per segment, the transmission delay or the distance limits.

Token-Ring Bridges

The basic functions of bridges are described in detail in the chapter on Ethernet networks; the following discussion deals only with the source-routing bridges developed specifically for Token-Ring topologies.

Source-Routing Bridges

Unlike the spanning-tree algorithm used by Ethernet bridges, the source-routing algorithm used to select routes in Token-Ring topologies lets the transmitting node rather than bridges determine the transmission path. The actual route information is contained in the optional routing information field of Token-Ring frames where route control information and route designators describe the exact route. Before actual communication occurs between two nodes in separate rings linked by one or more source-routing bridges, an explorer frame is sent to determine the optimum route. The explorer frame is duplicated by each bridge and copied into all linked rings until one of the explorers reaches the destination. Each crossed bridge writes its identification into the explorer's route designator field so that the entire transmission path is stored in the explorer frame on arrival. If more than one explorer frame reaches the destination, the one that contains the shortest route is selected. The maximum allowable hop count is seven. The destination node then copies the route information from the explorer frame and returns it to the sender, which then starts the actual data transmission. The source-routing protocol is defined in the source-routing annex of IEEE 802.1 and is not part of the IEEE 802.5 standard. Today there are bridges available, known as source-routing transparent (SRT) bridges, that can link both source-routing and spanning-tree networks to one another.

Linking Token-Ring Networks to Other LAN Topologies

When linking Token-Ring networks to other network topologies, such as Ethernet or FDDI, the differences in data speeds, frame formats and access mechanisms can present a number of difficulties that necessitate certain special capabilities in the bridges used. These problems are discussed in detail in the section on Ethernet bridges.

Diagnosing Bridge Problems

The challenge when analyzing bridge problems is to correlate the occurrence of symptoms in several different network segments. Concurrent measurements in several segments—using probe-based monitoring systems, for example—can be very helpful. Less important are performance measurements of bridges by means of expensive, specialized multiport test systems. Most modern bridges are capable of forwarding frames at line speed anyway so that performance measurements in most cases just confirm the manufacturer's technical data. It is more efficient to request system specifications from the manufacturer based on standardized test methods, as specified in RFC 1242 and RFC 2544.

Most problems that affect bridges can best be located by a process of elimination that involves the correlation of specific measurements and an analysis of the network topology. Symptoms of bridge problems can include poor network performance in particular segments, intermittent or permanent loss of connection to particular stations, or the failure of certain protocols and services. The first phase of the troubleshooting process is, as always, a review of all configuration changes that were made in the network before the error occurred as well as the general information-gathering steps described previously. If the symptoms correlate to particular connections, begin by checking all bridges located along the corresponding transmission path. Otherwise, the next step is to prepare a list of all the stations, connections, protocols and services affected by the problems observed. To do this, measure the current parameters in the various network segments and compare the results with statistics gathered during normal operation. This involves recording and analyzing throughput and performance parameters of network nodes, protocols and services, as well as reviewing log files that contain the operating statistics on all bridges in the network.

The log files provide bridge statistics such as CPU capacity use, port capacity use, buffer capacity use and error rates. To measure the response times of connections across bridges, send loopback packets across the bridges from different network segments. Long-term response time measurement statistics can be gathered using dedicated response-time agents distributed throughout the network. This type of long-term measurement can be especially useful in diagnosing intermittent problems. Based on the results of these measurements, the potential sources of error can usually be narrowed down to specific components.

Symptoms and Causes of Bridge Problems

The symptoms for most bridge problems in Token-Ring networks differ only slightly from those in Ethernet or FDDI networks. As described in the section on Ethernet bridges, the most common difficulties are throughput problems, incorrectly configured filter settings, bridge buffer overflow, and faulty address tables. Problem characteristics of Token-Ring networks include incorrect ring speed settings, bridge ports configured with duplicate Token-Ring addresses, and incorrect frame length settings.

Incorrect Ring Speed

If the ring speed setting on the bridge port does not match the actual speed on the ring (4 Mbit/s versus 16 Mbit/s), beaconing begins and communication on the ring breaks down.

Bridge Port Configured with Duplicate Token-Ring Address

Because Token-Ring addresses are configured by software, the occurrence of duplicate Token-Ring addresses due to incorrect configuration (typing errors, copied configuration files) is not uncommon.

Inefficient Maximum Frame Length

Incorrectly configured bridge ports that restrict the maximum frame size can have a negative effect on performance. The throughput in 4 Mbit/s rings, for example, decreases significantly when the maximum frame size is under 256 bytes.

Installation and Configuration Errors

Among the leading causes of problems with bridges are incorrect installation or configuration of the equipment. Incorrectly configured ports (port not enabled; wrong operating mode, for example, 4 Mbit/s instead of 16 Mbit/s), bad connections (loose cables, connectors, or plug-in modules), and faulty connections to the back plane or the MAU are the most common error sources.

Hardware Problems

If you suspect hardware problems, check the power supply and connectors and run the bridge's self-test function.

8.2.8   Problems with Routers

Routers are internetworking components that connect network segments on OSI Layer 3. Because they operate on this layer, routers can link networks of any topology. Refer to the section on router problems in Chapter 7 for a detailed description of procedures for troubleshooting and diagnosing router errors.

8.2.9   Symptoms and Causes: Token Ring

Symptom: Active Monitor Error or Active Monitor Change

Cause (1):   Active monitor detects a claim token frame, quits active monitor status, and sends a report active monitor frame.
This generally occurs when a standby monitor does not detect an active monitor in the ring. (Any station in the ring that is not the active monitor is a standby monitor.)

Cause (2):   Active monitor detects an AMP frame that it did not generate
When this happens, the active monitor transmits a report active monitor frame with subvector 2 (duplicate monitor).

Cause (3):   Station participating in the monitor contention process detects a claim token frame with its own address as the source but a NAUN address that does not match the NAUN address in its memory.
This station then transmits a report monitor error frame with subvector 3 (duplicate address during monitor contention).

Symptom: Address Recognized Error

Cause: Station detects more than one AMP frame or an SMP frame not preceded by an AMP frame.

Symptom: Burst Errors

Cause: Hardware problem such as a defective cable, NIC, MAU or concentrator.
A burst error frame is sent if no signal is received for five half-bit times between the starting and ending delimiters of a frame. Decode Token-Ring messages to locate the fault: determine which station reported the error and what stations are upstream from it (refer to the list of active stations). Analyze correlations between station activity and errors in the failure domain. Check the con-

centrator (run its self-test function). Check cables using a cable scanner.

Symptom: Beaconing, Streaming

Cause (1):   Defective concentrator or NIC.

Cause (2):   Loose or defective connectors (interface cards, wall jacks, concentrators, bridges, routers).

Analyze the beacon frames and trace the failure domain from the addresses for the sending station and its NAUN. The failure domain consists of the station transmitting the beacon frame and its incoming line, the sending station's NAUN and its outgoing line, and the concentrator between the two stations. All components within this domain (NICs, concentrators, cables, connectors, wall jacks) need to be inspected.

Symptom: Failed Insertion

Cause (1):   Duplicate address.

During the duplicate address check (part of the station insertion process), the new station detects another station already in the ring with the same address.

Cause (2):   Station unable to participate successfully in the neighbor notification process.

Cause (3):   Station parameters not initialized correctly.

Symptom: Frame Copied Error

Cause: Station receives frame addressed to it, but detects that the address recognized/frame copied bits are not 0.

One likely reason for this is a duplicate MAC address in the ring. To locate another station with the same address, use a protocol analyzer and check for a failed insertion frame. Once you have identified the node with the duplicate MAC address, reconfigure it.

Symptom: Lost Frame Error

Cause: Failure to receive a transmitted frame.

This can happen when other stations enter or leave the ring.

This error is non-isolating and can't be assigned to any particular station.

Symptom: Frequency Error

Cause (1):   Ring clock rate and NIC's internal clock rate differ significantly.

Cause (2):   Poor cabling.

Cause (3):   Defective NIC.

Frequency errors are non-isolating and can't be assigned to any particular station. Typical causes of frequency errors are poor-quality cabling, cabling that exceeds distance limitations, or defective NICs.

Symptom: Intermittent Errors and Connection Failures

Cause (1):   Cabling exceeds the distance limitations between two ring stations.

If a station is removed from the ring, the distance between two ring nodes can become so great that the signals can no longer be transmitted reliably and serious connection problems can occur (non-isolating errors, token errors, etc.). Check the maximum allowable distance between two stations on the ring and redesign the ring if necessary.

Cause (2):   Phase jitter, frequency errors, timeouts in Token-Ring protocol timers, or intermittent beaconing (see Figure 8.28).

Verify whether the maximum number of stations allowed in the ring has been exceeded (see the section "Network Design Guidelines for Token-Ring Networks" for details).

Cable type	Maximum number of nodes at 4 Mbit/s	Maximum number of nodes at 16 Mbit/s
IBM Type 1	260	140
Cat. 3 UTP	72	72
Cat. 5 UTP	132	132

Fig. 8.28 Maximum number of stations in a Token-Ring network

Symptom: Internal Error

Cause: Station detects an internal error and recovers on its own.

Internal errors are isolating errors and can be traced to the station where they originate. Capture and decode the internal error frame using a protocol analyzer and observe the node identified.

Symptom: No Connection to Server

Cause (1):   Cable from the node to the concentrator is loose or disconnected, broken, short-circuited, or exposed to electromagnetic interference.

Cause (2):   Defective network interface card.

Check cable, connectors and interface card and replace if necessary.

Cause (3):   Address table of a bridge in the transmission path to the server missing the node's MAC address.

Addresses that are not used over a certain period are deleted by the bridge's aging function. If the bridge is in protected mode (that is, learning is deactivated), the transmitting node's address cannot be automatically added to the bridge table. Check the address tables and operating modes of the bridges in the transmission path to the server.

Cause (4):   Bridge port deactivated or defective.

Check bridge ports, send ping packets to nodes beyond the bridge, and analyze the bridge logs.

Cause (5):   Incorrectly configured bridge filter.

Examine the filter settings in bridges along the transmission path to the server.

Symptom: Intermittent Connection Failures

Cause: Duplicate MAC address.

If a station attempts to enter the ring with an address that is already in use, it is refused entry and receives a request to remove frame. To locate the other station with the same address, use a protocol analyzer to capture request to remove frames. When you have identified the node with the duplicate MAC address, reconfigure it.

Symptom: High Network Load

Cause: Overloaded or incorrectly configured router(s) and/or bridge(s).

Use a protocol analyzer to identify the most active stations in the ring and search for routing or bridging problems. If timeouts occur, measuring response times can provide clues to the source of the problem. Check the statistics on the routers and bridges involved. How many frames are discarded? Check the bridges' forwarding tables and filter settings. Deactivate optional bridge functions, such as the ring parameter monitor or configuration port server if they are not in use.

Symptom: Network Slow, Stations Locking Up

Cause: Line errors, burst errors, FCS errors, and superfluous ring purges.

Burst and line errors are usually caused by defective station cables or hardware defects in the concentrator or the interface card. Check the network for line errors and burst errors. Then check the concentrators, cabling and connectors upstream from the station reporting the error.

Symptom: **Neighbor Notification Error**

Cause (1): Insertion or removal of a node.

Cause (2): Intermittent hardware problems in a NIC.

Symptom: **Report Neighbor Notification Incomplete**

Cause: Active monitor sends process incomplete frame to the ring error monitor and initiates a new AMP frame.

The neighbor notification process is initiated every 7 seconds, when the active monitor sends an AMP frame. When a station detects an AMP frame, it compares the address recognized bits and the frame copied bits in the AMP frame. If the frame has not yet been copied by any other station, the receiving station compares the source address of the AMP frame with its own NAUN address. If the addresses are different, the source address of the AMP frame is stored as the new NAUN address, and a report NAUN change frame is sent to the configuration report server. If the AMP frame is not returned to the active monitor before the neighbor notification timer expires, the active monitor sends a process incomplete frame to the ring error monitor and initiates a new AMP frame.

Use a protocol analyzer to check for request to remove frames and try to identify the stations with duplicate MAC addresses.

Symptom: **Network Slow Despite Low Traffic**

Cause (1): Poor configuration, inefficient protocols, or insufficient NIC memory.

Cause (2): Router or bridge port settings restrict the maximum allowable frame size.

The network load (as a percentage of its capacity) is not the only factor determining network performance. Other important factors include the size and type of frames being transported. LLC frames, for example, carry no user data but serve to set up and maintain connections. A high proportion of short LLC and MAC frames indicates an inefficient protocol. In the NetBIOS/SMB protocol, for example, the ratio of LLC frames to user data packets is about 1:1. The reason for this exceptionally poor ratio is that NetBIOS/SMB uses a connection-oriented protocol at the LLC level. NetWare IPXuses, a connectionless service, transfers user data without waiting for acknowledgement of receipt. LLC frames are rare in IPX, whereas connection-oriented protocols usually generate a huge number of management frames.

Small frame sizes can also have other causes, however. The data packet size that can be handled by a NIC depends on the card's memory. In a 4 Mbit/s ring the maximum frame size is 4,500 bytes, and in a 16 Mbit/s ring 17,800 bytes. Older NICs with 8 Kbytes of RAM can only process data packets of up to 1,000 bytes. State-of-the-art cards, however, usually support the maximum frame lengths of 4,500 and 17,800 bytes. Furthermore, certain network operating systems can restrict the maximum frame size. NetWare 3.11, for example, supports frames only up to 4,000 bytes.

Symptom: Ring Purges

Cause (1):   Short-circuited cable.
Cause (2):   Noise or crosstalk.
Cause (3):   Token rotation time too long.
Cause (4):   Defective NIC.
            Ring purges are initiated by the active monitor to delete all signals on the ring in preparation for the release of a new token. They frequently occur when a station enters or leaves the ring. If ring purges occur when no station has been inserted or removed, this indicates hardware problems on the ring.

Symptom: Ring Resetting

Cause: Several consecutive claim token frames transmitted; ring recovers after beaconing.
            See the previous section on beaconing as an error symptom.

Symptom: Receiver Congested

Cause: Insufficient buffer space to copy a frame.
            If this error occurs frequently, you must replace or upgrade the interface cards of the affected nodes to increase card memory.

Symptom: Token Error

Cause (1): Station entering or leaving the ring.
Cause (2): Noise.
Cause (3): Defective NIC or cable.
Cause (4): Extremely high number of broadcasts.
A Token Error frame is transmitted in any of the following situations:
- A token with a priority greater than 0 and a monitor count of 1 is detected beyond the active monitor (indicating that the token is already on its second round).
- No token or frame is encountered before the Good Token timer expires (10 ms).
- Illegal coding is detected.
- Token errors are non-isolating and can't be assigned to any particular station.

Symptom: Request Station Removed

Cause: Duplicate Token-Ring MAC address.
Use a protocol analyzer to capture request to remove MAC frames and examine their source addresses.

Symptom: Token Direction Change

Cause (1): Insertion or removal of stations.
Cause (2): Problems with hardware or software components in the ring.
To determine the direction of rotation, use a protocol analyzer to analyze frames transmitted by the station that is the direct (physical) neighbor of the analyzer, making sure that neither the protocol analyzer nor the neighboring node is the active monitor at the time. If the monitor bit of these frames is set to 1, then the frames are moving from the analyzer to the selected neighbor node. If the value is 0, the frames are moving in the other direction. If the direction of token rotation changes, this indicates that at least one ring purge has occurred. This can be caused by normal operating events, such as the insertion or removal of stations, or by problems with hardware or software components in the ring.

Common Errors

The following list summarizes the most frequent sources of problems in Token-Ring networks (in alphabetical order):

- Bridge address list incorrectly configured; bridge in protected mode
- Bridge filter incorrectly configured
- Bridge overloaded
- Bridge's aging function deletes address entry
- Cable length between neighboring nodes exceeds specifications
- Connectors, loose or defective: interface cards, wall jacks, concentrators, bridges, routers
- Defective Trunk Concentrator Unit (TCU)
- Defective lobe cable
- Defective network interface card
- Duplicate MAC addresses
- Electromagnetic interference
- Faulty physical installation of router, bridge or concentrator (cable, connectors, plug-ins are loose; cable connections on the backplane are wrong)
- Frame length restrictions on router/bridge ports
- Frequency and jitter problems due to cabling, noise, too many stations
- Maximum frame length not supported by interface cards due to insufficient card memory
- NIC incorrectly configured
- Protocol inefficient, not well adapted to Token Ring (NetBIOS/SMB)
- Receive buffer on interface card insufficient
- Ring speed incorrectly set on bridge/router port: for example, 4 Mbit/s vs. 16 Mbit/s
- Router filter incorrectly configured
- Router overloaded
- Router protocol entries incorrectly configured (address tables, mapping tables, subnet masks, default gateways, routing tables, timers)
- Router settings incorrectly configured: port not active, protocol not active
- Short circuit in cable
- Source-routing problems
- Stations: too many on the ring
- WAN connections overloaded or of poor quality (high BER)

Figure 8.29 The most frequent sources of problems in Token-Ring networks

FDDI

9

"Any time you think things seem to be going better, you have overlooked something."

ANONYMOUS

9.1   FDDI: Specification and Implementation

Like Token Ring, the Fiber Distributed Data Interface (FDDI) is based on a token-passing principle. With this technique, access to the LAN medium is controlled primarily by means of a specific sequence of bits called a token. Unlike Token Ring, however, FDDI uses a dual ring architecture for increased

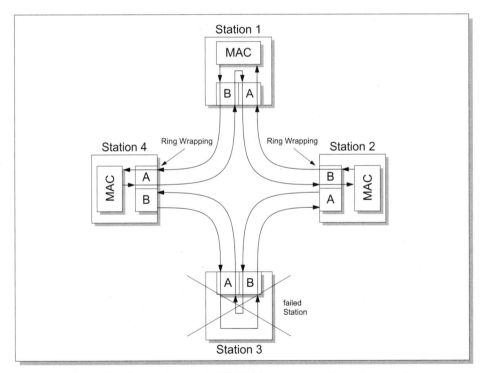

Figure 9.1 Fault tolerance in FDDI: Ring recovery through wrapping

reliability, and its greater bandwidth allows a data speed of 100 Mbit/s. The dual ring architecture enables FDDI to tolerate the complete failure of one of its nodes with no significant effect on network performance. This fault-tolerant feature is called "ring wrapping": if a station fails, the ring doubles back on itself on either side of the failed station, thus forming a single ring, isolating the source of error and providing continuous data transmission (see Figure 9.1).

Two types of nodes are defined in FDDI: dual-attachment stations (DAS) and single-attachment stations (SAS). An SAS is attached to the primary ring through a concentrator, similar to the concentrators used in Token Ring. An SAS requires only a single FDDI port and can be inserted into or removed from the ring without affecting network operation. Dual-attachment stations require two ports attached to both the primary and secondary rings. Connecting or disconnecting a DAS disrupts ring operation.

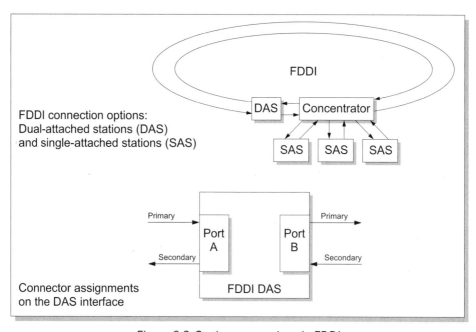

Figure 9.2 Station connections in FDDI

Dual homing is another fault-tolerant feature of FDDI for connection of critical devices, such as servers and routers. With dual homing, the component is attached to two concentrators. The second concentrator link remains passive unless the primary link fails.

FDDI protocols can be implemented over two pairs of single-mode or multimode optical fibers, or over four pairs of shielded or unshielded twisted-pair copper wires (STP, UTP). FDDI over copper wire is called Copper Distributed Data Interface (CDDI).

9.1.1 The Physical Layer in FDDI Networks

The FDDI physical layer is defined for single- and multimode optical fiber, as well as for shielded and unshielded twisted-pair copper wire (CDDI). Transmission is limited to defined symbols in 4B/5B encoding. When an optical data medium is used, 4B/5B-encoded data streams are transmitted directly in the form of light pulses. With twisted-pair wiring, the Multi-Level Transition–Three-Level Technique (MLT-3) is used. MLT-3 alternates between three voltage levels, reducing the frequency of the transmitted signal to 31.25 MHz. FDDI and CDDI also have different idle signals: in FDDI, a bit stream consisting of binary 1s indicates an idle line station, whereas in CDDI the idle signal is a random series of 1s and 0s because a continuous sequence of 1s would distort the frequency spectrum and increase electromagnetic interference.

The FDDI protocol uses three types of symbols:

- Line-state symbols, indicating one of the following:
  - Quiet Line State (QLS)
  - Master Line State (MLS)
  - Halt Line State (HLS)
  - Idle Line State (ILS)
  - Active Line State (ALS)
  - Noise Line State (NLS);
- Control symbols, including the starting delimiter, ending delimiter, and control indicators
- Data symbols

Line-state symbols are sent as padding bits during pauses in transmission and indicate the operating state of the FDDI ring. Halt symbols, for example, either announce control sequences or report the removal of invalid symbols, while at the same time minimizing any DC imbalance in signals on a CDDI ring. Quiet symbols report an absence of voltage transition, which means there is no signal in the line. Idle symbols indicate a normal operating state between transmissions. These consist of continuous padding bits, which provide clock information for synchronization.

The starting delimiter (SD) and ending delimiter (ED) control symbols mark the beginning and end of a transmitted data sequence. The ending delimiter, however, is not necessarily the last symbol in a transmission; it may be followed by a set (S) or reset (R) control indicator. If no control indicators are sent, then the

FDDI Symbol Coding			
Decimal Binary		Symbol	Description
Line state symbols			
00 ·00000		Q	Quiet
31 11111		I	Idle
04 00100		H	Halt
Starting delimiter			
24 11000		J	First symbol of the SC pair
17 10001		K	Second symbol of the SD pair
Data symbols			
			Hexadecimal Binary
30 11110		0	0 0000
09 01001		1	1 0001
20 10100		2	2 0010
21 10101		3	3 0011
10 01010		4	4 0100
11 01011		5	5 0101
14 01110		6	6 0110
15 01111		7	7 0111
18 10010		8	8 1000
19 10011		9	9 1001
22 10110		A	A 1010
23 10111		B	B 1011
26 11010		C	C 1100
27 11011		D	D 1101
28 11100		E	E 1110
29 11101		F	F 1111
Ending delimiter			
13 01101		T	Marks the end of the data stream
Control markers			
07 001111		R	Logical 0 (reset)
25 11001		S	Logical 1 (set)
Invalid codes			
01 00001		V or H	These symbols violate the conditions
02 00010		V or H	for zero bits in the code stream or
03 00011		V	the mandatory sequence, and should
05 00101		V	not be transmitted.
06 00110		V	If received, codes 1, 2, 8 and 16
08 01000		V or H	should always be interpreted as Halt.
12 01100		V	
16 10000		V or H	
12345		Transmission order of code symbol bits	

Figure 9.3 4B/5B symbol encoding in FDDI

transmission ends with two ending delimiters. If there is an even number of control indicators, an additional ED follows the last control indicator.

Valid data symbols are the 16 hexadecimal values from 0 to F, transmitted in any order. Invalid symbols are any symbols that do not fulfill this definition. A node may receive invalid symbols due to an error situation or during synchronization with the ring clock rate (see Figure 9.3).

FDDI Line States

The line state is the fundamental indication of the operational status of the FDDI ring. It is monitored continuously by each node's station management (SMT) entity. The various line states are signaled as described here:

Quiet Line State (QLS)

When a physical connection is first set up, a steady stream of quiet (Q) symbols is transmitted. QLS is also entered any time the signal is lost, or after 16 or 17 consecutive Q symbols are received. QLS ends when any symbol other than a Q is received.

Master Line State (MLS)

MLS is indicated by a continuous stream of alternating halt (H) and quiet (Q) symbols, and is also used to set up a new physical connection. This state is entered whenever eight or nine consecutive HQ or QH symbol pairs are received, and ends as soon as any other symbol pair is received.

Halt Line State (HLS)

HLS is entered when H symbols are transmitted continuously while a connection is being set up. This state is detected as soon as 16 or 17 H symbols are received, and exited when any other symbol is received or when the signal is lost.

Idle Line State (ILS)

The ILS, characterized by a continuous stream of I symbols, is entered while a connection is being set up and during the transmission pauses between data packets. The state is recognized when four or five consecutive I symbols are received. The elasticity buffer (see the following) may increase this value by up to 11 bits. ILS is exited when any other symbol is received or when the signal is lost.

Active Line State (ALS)

ALS indicates that the incoming bit stream consists of valid FDDI frames, meaning that the nearest upstream neighbor has an active connection to the ring. This state is entered once a starting delimiter is received. ALS is exited upon receipt of any symbol other than I, n, R, S or T (n=any data symbol), upon loss of a valid signal, or on entering ILS.

Noise Line State (NLS)

This line state indicates that the incoming signals are distorted by noise and that the physical connection is faulty. This state is entered upon receipt of 16 or 17 consecutive invalid symbols. The following events are interpreted as noise:

- Invalid signals
- Elasticity buffer errors while receiving
- A mixed symbol pair (such as a control indicator paired with a data symbol)
- An n, R, S or T symbol (or a symbol pair containing at least one of these symbols) received while the line state is not ILS or ALS
- Reception of an I, n, R, S or T symbol while the clock detect function (a mechanism that monitors clock synchronization) reports a synchronization error

The Elasticity Buffer

Differences are bound to occur between a receiving node's internal oscillator and the clock rate of the incoming bit stream due to the transmission medium and to tolerance limits in network components. If the transmission rate of a given station is significantly lower than the incoming data rate, data could be lost. To prevent this, each station has an elasticity buffer to compensate for differences of up to 4.5 bits, or 0.01 percent. The frequency of the local oscillator must meet the following specifications:

Nominal frequency:	125 MHz ± 0.005% (50 ppm)
Phase jitter at 20 kHz:	< 8 degrees
Harmonic content at 125.02 MHz:	< 20 dB
Nominal code bit time:	8.0 ns
Nominal symbol time:	40.0 ns

Smoothing

The smoothing function ensures that the preamble of an FDDI frame is not lost in the process of passing through a number of elasticity buffers. This function removes surplus symbols from oversized preambles and adds them to undersized preambles. The smoothing function can increase the length of a 0 to 13 symbol preamble to 14 symbols, and reduce a preamble of 15 symbols or more to a length of 14 symbols. Frames with preambles shorter than 12 symbols are usually not forwarded on the FDDI layer, and frames with a preamble of less than 2 symbols are ignored altogether.

Repeat Filter

If a station in the ring is acting as a repeater but the FDDI protocol stack does not check incoming signals, the repeat filter prevents the propagation of code violations and invalid line states.

Ring Delay

To ensure trouble-free operation of the ring, every station with an FDDI MAC layer must have a minimum delay of 3 bytes, while stations without an FDDI MAC layer must guarantee a delay of 2 bytes. The resulting maximum ring delay is the sum of the delay caused by all stations and the signal delay inherent in the medium. Both the MAC layer and the SMT have timers that take this figure for maximum ring delay into account. The following parameters are used in calculating the overall delay:

SD_Min: The minimum latency of a starting delimiter sequence in a station (default: 74 bits, or 592 ns).

SD_Max: The maximum latency of a starting delimiter sequence in a station. The maximum extension due to the smoothing function is 2 symbols, or 10 bits; the elasticity buffer may add a similar delay:
$\pm$ 4.5 bits = maximum addition of 9 bits
Sampling and timing errors are estimated at a maximum of 4 bits.
Consequently, SD_Max $\leq$ 592 ns + 4 + 80 + 80 = 756 ns

P_Max: The number of physical FDDI interfaces in the ring. The default value is 1,000, which corresponds to 500 dual-attachment stations.

D_Max: The maximum transmission delay of a starting delimiter sequence when no noise is present.

Thus a combination of 1,000 FDDI interfaces, a ring length of 100 km and a signal propagation speed of 5,085 ns/km yields:

D_Max £ (P_Max x SD_Max) + (2 x 100 x 5085) = 1.773 ms.

The default value for D_Max should be less than 1.773 ms; the specification calls for 1.617 ms.

9.1.2   The FDDI Data Format

There are two types of frames in FDDI networks: tokens and data packets. A token is 3 bytes long and consists of a starting delimiter, a frame control field, and an ending delimiter. A token is a special frame that is passed from station to station and controls access to the LAN medium. If a given station receives a valid token, but cannot forward it for some reason (such as a ring timing error), then the station issues a new token.

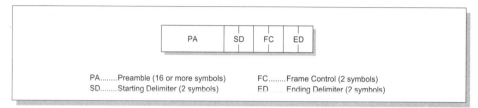

Figure 9.4 Structure of an FDDI token

All other data packets can have lengths of 12 to 4,500 bytes and consist of the following fields: preamble, starting delimiter, frame control, destination address, source address, information, frame check sequence, end of frame sequence, ending delimiter, and frame status.

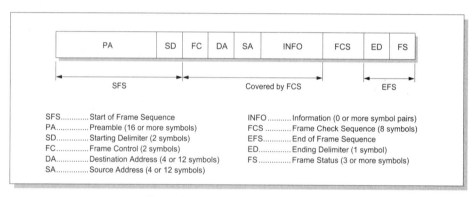

Figure 9.5 Format of an FDDI frame

Token and Data Packet Fields

Preamble (PA)

A preamble consists of at least 16 idle symbols, although the length can vary during circulation through the ring due to differences in nominal frequency and to smoothing and elasticity buffering. Frames with a preamble of fewer than 12 symbols are not copied into the destination station's receive buffer.

Starting Delimiter (SD)

Every frame, including tokens, begins with this field, which consists of the symbol sequence JK.

Frame Control (FC)

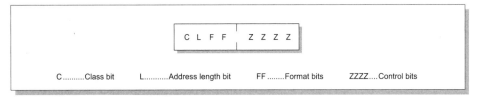

Figure 9.6 The frame control field in FDDI

The frame control field identifies the frame type. It consists of frame class bits, address length bits, format bits, and control bits.

Frame Class bit C=0: The frame is asynchronous
Frame Class bit C=1: The frame is synchronous
Address Length bit L=0: 16-bit MAC addresses
Address Length bit L=1: 48-bit MAC addresses

The frame format bits (FF), together with the C, L and ZZZZ bits, indicate the frame type as follows:

CLFF bits	ZZZZ bits	
0X00	0000	Void Frame (content is ignored)
1000	0000	Unlimited token
1100	0000	Limited token
0L00	0001 – 1111	Station Management frame
1L00	0001 – 1111	MAC frame
1L00	0010	MAC beacon frame
1L00	0011	MAC claim token frame
CL01	r000 – r111	LLC frame
0L01	RPPP	Asynchronous transmission with priority (LLC)
1L01	Rrrr	Synchronous transmission (LLC)
0L00	0001 – 1111	SMT frame
0L00	1111	Next Station Addressing SMT frame
CL10	r000 – r111	Reserved for implementation
CL11	Rrrr	For future standardization

X Any value
r Reserved and set to 0
L Length
C Class

The control bits, in conjunction with the corresponding CLFF bits, have the following meanings:

MAC Beacon Frames (1L00 0010)

MAC beacon frames are transmitted when the ring is unable to recover from an error situation, usually a hardware fault that results in signal failure, jabber frames, or frequency differences.

MAC Claim Token Frames (1L00 0011)

These frames are usually transmitted when a token is lost. When a station receives a claim token frame containing its own address as the source, it reinitializes the ring and issues a new token.

SMT Next Station Addressing Frame (0L00 1111)

This frame is used for station management functions.

LLC Frame (0L01 rPPP)

This LLC frame is used for asynchronous transmission. The last three bits, PPP, indicate the priority. The highest priority is 111 and 000 is the lowest.

LLC Frame (1L01 rrrr)

This LLC frame is used for synchronous transmission.

Address Fields

The address fields in FDDI can be either 16 or 48 bits in length. Stations with 16-bit addresses, however, must be able to function in rings with 48-bit addresses. This means they must be able to repeat 48-bit addresses and to react correctly on receiving claim token and broadcast frames with 48-bit addresses. Stations with 48-bit addresses must have also a fully functional 16-bit address and be able to recognize other 16-bit addresses.

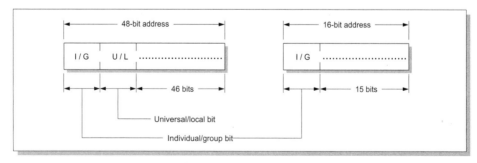

Figure 9.7 The address field in FDDI

The first bit of a destination address indicates whether the destination is an individual address (bit 1 = 0) or a group address (Bit 1 = 1). (bit 1 of the source address is always set to 0, however.) A group address consisting entirely of 1s is a broadcast address used to send a frame to every station in the ring. An address consisting entirely of 0s is called a "zero address": frames with this address are not intended for any station. The second bit in a destination address shows whether the address is locally administered (bit 2 = 1) or universally administered (bit 2 = 0). Figure 9.8 shows a FDDI data packet that has been decoded using a protocol analyzer. Occasionally FDDI addresses are shown in both the MSB (Most Significant Bit First) format and the canonical format used in Ethernet and other network protocols. To convert between the canonical bit order and MSB format, the nibbles (half-bytes) are switched and the bit order in each half reversed. Thus a hexadecimal 43 becomes 34 or, in binary, 0011 0100. Reversing the bit order of each nibble yields 1100 0010 or, in hexadecimal, C2. The canonical address 01-80-C2-00-01-10 corresponds to an MSB address of 80-01-43-00-80-08.

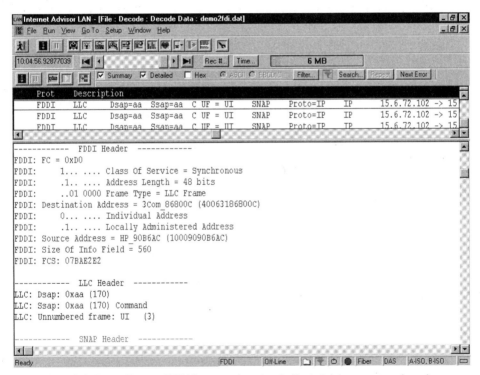

Figure 9.8 Decoding an FDDI frame using the Agilent Advisor protocol analyzer

Information Field

The information or data field contains user data—the payload of the FDDI frame. The data type is described in the frame control field and evaluated accordingly by the receiving node's MAC, LLC or SMT module. The length of the data field is variable, but the length of the entire frame must not exceed 9,000 symbols or 4,500 bytes.

Frame Check Sequence (FCS)

This is a 32-bit checksum calculated from the content of the frame control, source address, destination address, and data fields. Each receiving station evaluates the checksum.

Ending Delimiter (ED)

The ending delimiter marks the end of a token or data packet. This field consists of two consecutive T symbols in a token or one T in a data packet.

Frame Status (FS)

The frame status field consists of control indicators that follow the ending delimiter. The first three control indicators—E (error detected), A (address recognized) and C (frame copied)—are required, and are set to R (reset) by the source station on transmission. Other control indicators are optional.

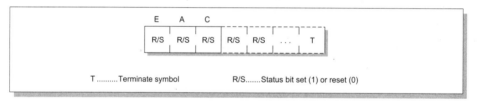

Figure 9.9 The frame status field in FDDI

Error Detected (E)

If a ring node detects an error in the frame, it sets the value in the E field to S.

Address Recognized (A)

When a node recognizes the destination address of a frame as its own, it sets the value in the A field to S.

Frame Copied (C)

When the receiving node copies the frame into its receive buffer, it sets the value in the C field to S.

Timers and Counters

Every FDDI node has three timers for controlling ring activities. The values set for these timers are calculated using the following parameters:

D_Max = maximum ring delay (default: 1.617 ms)

M_Max = 1,000 (maximum number of FDDI interfaces in the ring)

I_Max = 25.0 ms (maximum station insertion time)

A_Max = 1.0 ms (maximum signal access time)

Token_Time = 0.00088 ms (the time it takes to transmit a token (6 symbols) with preamble (16 symbols))

L_Max = 0.0035 ms (maximum time between receipt of token and start of transmission)

F_Max = 0.361 ms (maximum time for transmitting a data packet; equals the transmission time for 9,000 symbols plus 16 preamble symbols)

Claim_FR = 0.00256 ms (time required for transmission of a claim token frame)

S_Min = 0.3545 ms (the time it takes for the ring to recover from the effects of noise: S_Min (F_Max + L_Max))

Token Holding Timer (THT)

The THT controls the amount of time during which a station may transmit data packets. Once the station has obtained a token, it may transmit until this timer expires and the Token Rotation Timer (TRT) remains below the node's priority level, T_Pri. When a node receives a token, it resets its THT with the value remaining in the TRT; (see the following).

Timer Valid Transmission (TVX)

The TVX allows a node to recover from an error situation:

TVX > max (D_Max, F_Max) + Token_Time + F_Max + S_Min, and TVX > 2.35 ms

The default value of TVX is at least 62,500 symbol times or 2.50 ms.

Token Rotation Timer (TRT)

The TRT controls the ring timing during normal operation. When this timer runs out, or when an early token is received (a token that arrives at a node before the TRT runs out), the TRT is initialized with the value currently valid for the operative Token Rotation Timer, the T_Opr. In the former case, the Late counter, Late_Ct, is also increased by one. T_Opr is between the T_Min and T_Max values for the ring, and is set upon completion of a claim token process (see the following). Due to the nature of the token-passing protocol, it may take up to a whole T_Opr period for a station to receive a token. If a station offers a guaranteed T_Resp, then T_Opr should be set to 0.5 T_Resp.

If a station's T_Min value is higher than T_Opr, the station cannot participate in normal ring traffic.

T_Min = 4.0 ms (default)

T_Max = $4 \cdot$ T_Init > 165 ms,
where T_Init is the time the ring has operated without noise:

T_Init = T_React + T_Resp < 40.58 ms,
where

T_React < I_Max + D_Max + A_Max + TVX,
and T_React < 30.24 ms

T_Resp < $((3 \cdot$ D_Max$) + (2 \cdot$ M_Max $\cdot$ Claim_FR$)$ + S_Min$)$,
and T_Resp < 10.34 ms

Late_Ct is set to 1 when the node is initialized or reset, and is incremented every time the TRT runs out without a token having been received. Once a token is received, the Late_Ct is reset to 0.

To simplify troubleshooting and the isolation of failure domains in the ring, every FDDI station has counters that count every data packet, whether defective or not. However, the frames are counted only if they end in an ending delimiter (T symbol). Data packets that end with idle or invalid symbols are not counted.

Frame_Ct

Counts all frames received.

Error_Ct

The number of frames identified by this node as defective: in other words, those frames whose error detected (E) field is R on arrival at this node, but S on retransmission. Frames received with E already set to S are not counted.

Lost_Ct

The number of frames, including tokens, that are in the process of being received by a station when an error occurs. The lost counter is incremented and the rest of the frame is replaced with idle symbols. The next node does not count this frame because it ends with idle symbols.

9.1.3   Process Control in FDDI Networks

Access to the medium in FDDI networks is controlled by a token; timers and counters control various related processes. A station with data to send must wait for a free token. When the token is received, transmission can begin. Unlike Token Ring, in which a transmitting node waits for its frame to return before releasing the token, FDDI nodes release the token as soon as transmission is completed. Each node is responsible for removing the frames that it transmitted from the ring. When a node detects a frame containing its own address as the source, it replaces the data field of the frame with idle symbols. This results in frame fragments consisting of the PA, SD, FC, DA and SA fields followed by idle symbols. These "remnants" do not negatively affect ring performance, however, because they have recognizable defects, such as the lack of an ending delimiter, they are deleted by the next station that detects them while in the transmitting state. Stations that are not in the transmitting state simply repeat and amplify the incoming bit stream.

A FDDI ring supports two types of communication: synchronous, in which each node is granted a defined portion of the available bandwidth, and asynchronous with dynamic bandwidth sharing. If a token is received by a node before the node's TRT has reached the TTRT (this is known as an early token), the token can be used for synchronous or asynchronous transmission. If the token is late, however, Late_Ct is increased by one, the TRT is initialized with the value for T_Opr, and the node may only transmit synchronously. The Late_Ct is reset to 0 and asynchronous transmission is allowed only after a token has been received within the TTRT. This ensures an average synchronous response time $\leq$ TTRT and a maximum synchronous response time of 2 TTRT.

Synchronous Transmission

In synchronous transmission, every station is assigned a certain bandwidth, expressed as a percentage of the TTRT. This bandwidth allocation is 0 when a node is initialized; a higher value is then negotiated by the SMT. The sum of all allocated bandwidths must not exceed the maximum usable synchronous bandwidth, Bsyn_Max:

Bsyn_Max = TTRT − (D_Max + F_Max + Token_Time)

Asynchronous Transmission

There are two types of tokens for asynchronous transmission: nonrestricted tokens, which are available to all ring nodes, and restricted tokens, which are reserved for certain nodes. When the ring is (re)initialized, a nonrestricted token is issued. At this point, priority levels can be distinguished by assigning

T_Pri values. A node can capture a nonrestricted token only if the node's T_Pri is higher than the TRT. Thus heavy ring traffic can be relieved to a certain extent by defining low T_Pri values. As soon as a node captures a token, its THT is initialized with the value remaining in the TRT. The TRT itself is initialized with the current value of TTRT, so that the time of the next token rotation is measured relative to the target time.

If a node has a large amount of data to transmit in a short time, it initiates the restricted token state. With this technique, the node first captures a nonrestricted token and begins its data transmission. When the THT runs out, the node issues a restricted token, which is simply forwarded by all other nodes until it is returned to its source node. The restricted token state lasts until completion of the transmission for which it was started, usually a period of several TRTs. While the ring is in this state, all other asynchronous transmission is stopped. Synchronous transmission, however, which uses both types of token, is not affected. The maximum duration of the restricted token state is negotiated by the SMT.

Claim Token Process

All nodes monitor the ring for errors that necessitate reinitialization of the ring, such as inactivity (when the TVX runs out) or signal errors (if TRT runs out and Late_Ct is already set, for example). When a node detects such an error, it sets the ring operational variable to 0 and transmits a claim token frame indicating its desired TTRT. It begins checking the TTRT values of all claim token frames it receives. The lower the TTRT value, the higher the sender's priority. If the TTRTs of two frames are equal, the one with the higher source value has higher priority. When a node detects claim token frames with a higher priority level than its own, it stops issuing claim token frames. Eventually, the ring contains only claim token frames from the node with the lowest TTRT. This node initializes the ring, resets T_Opr to its own TTRT, starts the TRT and issues a nonrestricted token. If a station's TRT expires before another higher-priority node initializes the ring, then this station begins sending claim token frames again rather than sending beacon frames. This prevents sporadic beacon frames in the ring. The token cannot be captured by any station during its first rotation because the ring operational variable is cleared when the claim token process starts. Once the first rotation has been completed, both Ring_Operational and Late_Ct are set to 1 and TRT is initialized. Synchronous transmission can begin in the second token rotation; asynchronous transmission in the third.

Beacon Process

If a node's TRT runs out while a node is in the claim token state, the node considers the claim token process to have failed and starts the beacon process.

As a rule this only happens when the ring is physically interrupted and must be globally reconfigured—when one logical ring is broken into two, for example. After entering the beacon state, the node resets its TRT and transmits beacon frames continuously. A node that is not in the beacon state repeats any beacon frames it receives. When a node receives its own beacon frames, it assumes that the ring has recovered and begins the claim token process again.

The FDDI Station Management Specification (SMT)

SMT in FDDI is a special functional module integrated in the FDDI protocol stack that provides increased security and automatic fault recovery mechanisms. SMT includes the following functions:

- Inserting the node in the ring and removing it
- Reconfiguring the paths in the node (when a link fails, for example)
- Checking the physical connection before inserting the node
- Controlling node behavior during the beacon process
- Reporting the current node configuration
- Transmitting status report frames to isolate possible error sources

SMT is composed of four modules: Entity Coordination Management (ECM), Physical Connection Management (PCM), Configuration Element Management (CEM) and Ring Management (RMT).

Entity Coordination Management (ECM)

ECM controls the optical bypass system as well as all other SMT functions. As soon as an FDDI node becomes active, ECM deactivates the optical bypass and starts all other SMT functions. Similarly, when the node leaves the ring, ECM first stops all other SMT functions and then reactivates the optical bypass. In the context of these processes, ECM also performs a number of tests on the physical layer:

- Checks all internal data paths in the node
- Performs loopback tests
- Checks the parameters passed to the FDDI layer (TTRT, etc.)
- Tests the FDDI recovery processes (beacon, claim token, etc.)

Physical Connection Management (PCM)

PCM controls station output and the redundant fiber-optic line to the neighboring node. Together with the PCM of the neighboring node, it tests the connection between the two nodes and checks the BER to determine whether a connection can be set up or not. Each of the station's ports has its own PCM. The 10 bits used in this bit signaling between nodes are explained in the following:

Bit 0   Always set to 0 (reserved for future applications)

Bits 1, 2 Indicates the station's own interface type:
           00 = A, 01 = B, 10 = S, 11 = M

Bit 3   Compatibility of the output ports:
           If Bit 3 = 0 for both ports, the connection is not set up.

Bits 4, 5 Link Confidence Test (LCT) : This function tests the reliability of the
           connection. How long the test takes depends on the previous BER:

           00 = short (50 ms)
           01 = medium (500 ms)
           10 = long (5 s)
           11 = extended (50 s)

Bit 6   Indicates whether the MAC layer is used during the LCT

Bit 7   Indicates whether the BER was low enough to pass the LCT

Bit 8   Indicates whether a MAC loopback test should be performed

Bit 9   Indicates whether there is a MAC layer at the station output port

Once the PCM has reached the active state, the station begins transmitting either QLS signals or data. The PCM also starts the link error monitor (LEM), which checks the BER in the FDDI port and deactivates the port if the BER is too high. When the BER reaches 10^{-8}, a warning is sent; if it goes up to 10^{-7}, the connection is shut down.

Configuration Element Management (CEM)

CEM configures the station's internal data paths, including the primary, second-ary and local paths. For this purpose, each port has a logical module called the configuration control element (CCE), which distributes incoming data among these internal paths. When the CEM changes the status of a CCE, it also deletes all data in the ring by transmitting ILS signals. This causes the ring nodes to begin transmitting claim token frames.

Ring Management (RMT)

RMT controls the FDDI protocol stack. It is not active until a physical connection exists and the input and output ports have been assigned to internal data paths. The RMT has six main tasks:

- It initializes the MAC layer once a physical connection has been set up.
- When the MAC layer is not active, it checks for duplicate addresses by monitoring claim token and beacon processes. To do this, the station's RMT

evaluates all claim token and beacon frames: if a node receives its own claim token or beacon frame after more than 2 D_Max, another station has the same address (D_Max is the maximum length of time a frame can take to travel around the entire ring). Furthermore, the station assumes the existence of a duplicate address if it receives a claim token frame with its own address as the source but a TTRT that differs from its own.

- When the MAC layer is active, the RMT checks for duplicate addresses by verifying the A bit in neighbor information frames. If it detects a duplicate address, the RMT reacts in one of three ways: it closes down the connection, removes the station from the ring, or changes the FDDI MAC address.
- The RMT also detects and responds to beacon states.
- It controls and initiates Halt Line States.
- It supports and monitors restricted tokens. When a station receives a restricted token, the RMT starts a timer to monitor the duration of the restricted-access dialog. If the timer expires, a claim token or beacon process is triggered.

SMT Agents

In addition to the four functional modules described previously, every SMT also has an SMT agent that checks all incoming FDDI frames and acts on them if necessary. The SMT agents use a number of special FDDI ring management frames in performing their tasks:

Neighbor Information Frame (NIF)

NIFs are used to determine the identities of neighboring nodes. Each node broadcasts a NIF approximately every 30 seconds. The first station to receive an NIF—with the A bit (address recognized) cleared—is the nearest downstream neighbor of the node that sent that frame; this neighbor transmits an answer.

Status Information Frame (SIF)

SIFs provide information about the status of a node. There are two types of SIF:

- SIF configuration frames describe the station's current configuration, including the number of input and output ports, the number of interfaces, and information on neighboring nodes.
- SIF operation frames describe the current operating state of a node, including MAC parameters, LEM status of the ports, and frame counters.

SIFs can be transmitted as request or response frames. An SIF configuration response frame can contain up to 10 parameters, including time stamp, station descriptor, SMT versions supported, station state, station policy, added transmission delay, neighboring nodes, path descriptors and parameter change count.

SIF operations response frames can contain the following: time stamp, MAC status, port LEM status, MAC frame counter, MAC frame not-copied counter, MAC priority values, elasticity buffer status, vendor code, user field and parameter change count.

Echo Frame (ECF)

When an ECF is received, the SMT copies the data field and returns it as an echo response frame.

Request Denied Frame (RDF)

When the SMT receives a data packet with an unknown format or with an SMT version it does not support, it transmits an RDF. Other causes for denial of a request may be oversized frames or the lack of reception authorization.

Status Report Frame (SRF)

These frames report changes in the station's status, including any of the following events:

• Change in configuration
• Unwanted connection attempts
• MAC: neighbor change
• MAC: Frame error condition
• MAC: Path change condition
• Port: Path change event
• Port: Link-error-rate condition
• Port: Wrapping in a neighboring station
• MAC: Frame not copied
• MAC: Duplicate address
• Port: Elasticity buffer error
• Vendor-specific events

The hold-off and back-off timers ensure that the station is not flooded with SRFs. The hold-off timer prevents transmission of status change reports more than once every 2 seconds, while the back-off timer controls the interval between change report transmissions. Because no acknowledgement is sent in response to these frames, the SMT repeats SRFs at ever-increasing intervals (2, 4, 8, 16, 32 seconds).

Parameter Management Frame (PMF)

Network management devices can use these frames to read or change certain SMT variables. The parameter management process corresponds to the structure of network management protocols, such as SNMP or CMIP. There are two types of PMF:

- PMF Get
- PMF Set

Extended Service Frame (ESF)

The ESF format can be used to define custom SMT frames.

Resource Allocation Frame (RAF)

RAFs are used to allocate synchronous bandwidth.

9.1.4   Design Guidelines for FDDI Networks

The guidelines for designing FDDI networks include specifications for the various cable types as well as limits on the maximum distances between neighboring nodes and the maximum number of nodes per ring.

The maximum distance between two adjacent nodes is 2 km on multimode fiber rings, 40 km on single-mode fiber rings, and 500 meters in low-cost fiber (LCF) rings. It is important to keep in mind that when a ring wraps due to node failure, the ring length doubles. The wavelength used in all fiber optic rings is 1,300 nm. The specifications for diameter and signal power are as follows:

Multimode:

Diameter: 62.5/125 mm, 50/125 mm, 85/125 mm, 100/140 mm
Signal power: -14 dBm to -20 dBm

Single mode:

Diameter: 9/125 mm
Signal power: -14 dBm to -20 dBm (Category 1)
                      -15 dBm to -37 dBm (Category 2)

When shielded (STP-1) or unshielded (UTP-5) twisted-pair cabling is used, the maximum distance between two nodes is 100 meters. There are no values defined for minimum distances between nodes in either FDDI or CDDI.

Connection Rules for SAS and DAS Nodes

When connecting a dual-attachment station (DAS), port A of one DAS must be connected to port B of the neighboring node. For single-attachment stations

(SAS), the S port of the node must be connected to the M port of the concentrator:

	A	B	M	S
A	–	+	+	–
B	+	–	+	–
M	+	+	x	+
S	–	–	+	–

+   recommended connection

–   connection could lead to problems; may be deactivated in the manufacturer's default configuration

x   connection not permitted

9.1.5   FDDI Standards

ANSI X3.139-1987, ISO 9314-2:1989, Media Access Control (MAC)

ANSI X3.148-1988, ISO 9314-1:1989, Physical Layer Protocol (PHY)

ANSI X3.166-1990, ISO 9314-3:1990, Physical Layer, Medium Dependent (PMD)

ANSI X3.229-1994, ISO 9314-6, Station Management (SMT)

ANSI X3.184-1993, ISO 9314-4, Single-Mode Fiber PMD (SMF-PMD)

ANSI X3.237-1995, ISO 9314-9, Low-Cost Fiber PMD (LCF-PMD)

ANSI X3.263-1995, ISO 9314-10, Twisted Pair PMD (TP-PMD)

ANSI X3.278, Physical Layer Repeater (PHY-REP)

ANSI X3.262 ISO 9314-13, Conformance Test PICS Proforma for FDDI (CT-PICS)

ANSI X3.245-199x, ISO 9314-26, Abstract Test Suite for MAC (MAC-ATS)

ANSI X3.248-199x, ISO 9314-21, Abstract Test Suite for PHY (PHY-ATS)

ANSI X3.255-199x, ISO 9314-20, Abstract Test Suite for PMD (PMD-ATS)

ANSI X3T9.5/92-102, Rev 1.4, Abstract Test Suite for SMT (SMT-ATS)

RFC 1285, FDDI-MIB

9.2   Troubleshooting FDDI Networks

9.2.1   Gathering Information on Symptoms and Recent Changes

The first step in any troubleshooting process is to gather information. The more information you have about the symptoms and characteristics of a problem—including *when* it first occurred—the better your chances of solving the problem quickly and efficiently. Typical questions you might ask at this stage include:

- Do the symptoms occur regularly or intermittently?
- Are the symptoms related to certain applications, or do they affect all network operations?
- Do the symptoms correlate to other activities in the network?
- When was the first occurrence of the symptom?
- Was there any change in any hardware or software network component?
- Has anyone connected or disconnected a PC (laptop or desktop) or any other component to or from the network?
- Has anyone installed an interface card in a computer?
- Has anyone stepped on a cable?
- Has any maintenance work been performed in the building recently (by a telephone company or building maintenance personnel, for example)?
- Has anyone (including cleaning personnel) moved any equipment or furniture?

9.2.2   Starting the Troubleshooting Procedure

Troubleshooting in FDDI LANs is primarily performed using cable testers for optical fiber and twisted-pair copper wire, protocol analyzers, and special FDDI ring management software to track and display SMT functions. FDDI has several self-diagnosis functions that enable it to recover from a number of critical states on its own. Key requirements for successful troubleshooting in an FDDI network include a detailed understanding of its operational processes and of the SMT functions.

If the ring is still functional, the first step in the troubleshooting procedure involves using a protocol analyzer to determine the main operating statistics of the network. These statistics include ring load as a percentage of capacity, throughput in frames per second, token rotation time, the numbers of stripped and void frames, the numbers of claim and beacon frames, the number of frames with undersized preambles, and the number of frames with invalid checksums.

The analysis of these statistics often points to possible causes of the problem. Furthermore, all SMT frames should be recorded and analyzed, including SRF and RDF, which can point to the failure domain. Furthermore, you can use the SHOW INTERFACES FDDI command (exact command depends on the equipment type) to check the statistics of the interface cards of ring nodes The following is a sample result of a SHOW INTERFACES FDDI command entered on a DAS:

Fddi 0 is up, line protocol is up

Hardware is cBus Fddi, address is 0000.0b14.32e2 (bia 0000.0b14.32e2)

Internet address is 18.187.1.29, subnet mask is 255.255.254.0

MTU 4470 bytes, BW 100000 Kbit, DLY 100 usec, rely 255/255, load 1/255

Encapsulation SNAP, loopback not set, keepalive not set

ARP type: SNAP, ARP Timeout 3:00:00

Phy-A state is active, neighbor is B, cmt signal bits 008/20C, status ILS

Phy-B state is active, neighbor is A, cmt signal bits 20C/008, status ILS

CFM is thru A, token rotation 5000 usec, ring operational 2:13:46

Upstream neighbor 0000.7640.0e50, downstream neighbor 0000.0a02.5bf2

Last input 0:00:00, output 0:00:00, output hang never

Last clearing of "show interface" counters 1w3d

Output queue 0/40, 0 drops; input queue 0/75, 132 drops

Five minute input rate 264000 bits/sec, 81 frames/sec

Five minute output rate 267000 bits/sec, 88 frames/sec

33457636 frames input, 2146812161 bytes, 8 no buffer

Received 2456722 broadcasts, 0 runts, 0 giants

15256 input errors, 11561 CRC, 176 frame, 0 overrun, 53676 ignored, 0 abort

124789478 frames output, 4146709113 bytes, 379 underruns

0 output errors, 0 collisions, 0 interface resets, 0 restarts

5460 transitions, 0 traces, 2405 claims, 4 beacon

If the problem cannot be isolated using the information described previously, additional trend measurements are necessary. This involves recording the main operating parameters over a period of hours, or even days, and analyzing the results for correlations. In this way, possible causes can be systematically eliminated until the source of the problem is limited to a small area.

The steps to take after the basic measurements have been performed using a protocol analyzer depend on the nature of the symptoms. If the symptoms can be

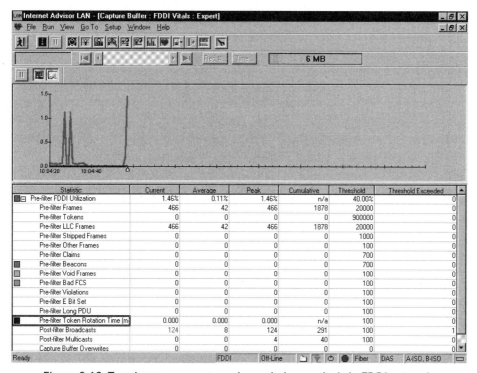

Figure 9.10 Trend measurements and correlation analysis in FDDI networks using the Agilent Advisor protocol analyzer

localized, occur periodically, or can at least be reproduced, then the trouble-shooting process continues with the network component nearest to the problem. If the problem source cannot be detected there, the range of analysis is succes-sively expanded. For example, if the problems are found to be related to a single network node, the next step is to analyze the station's software and hardware components. If no fault is found, the examination progresses to the patch cables, the connectors, the wall jack, the concentrator, and the cabling.

If the problem cannot be localized at all, or if problems that were thought to have been isolated cannot be pinpointed, then the only way to find the source of the problem is through systematic segmentation of the network. To do this, divide the ring physically into two rings, determine which of these still shows the error condition, divide that ring into two, and so on until the error is localized. This method causes considerable disruption in network operation and is therefore applied only as a last resort, when the problem itself severely impairs normal network operation.

If the symptoms occur intermittently, long-term measurements are necessary. These must be performed continuously until the basic network operating statistics have been measured during the occurrence of the fault. This information usually provides the first clue to the error source. Furthermore, it is essential to log the exact time of intermittent error events. Later this information can be used to find temporal correlations with other events in the network or on a given node, such as backups, the start of specific applications, connections through routers, access to the Internet, users' working hours, or other possible factors. If this does not help to track down the error, you may have to resort to the segmentation method. Depending on which causes the least inconvenience to users, you can either systematically disable network functions and applications or physically separate concentrators. These methods usually lead to the error source.

9.2.3   Error Symptoms in FDDI

The most common symptoms of problems in FDDI networks are ring wrapping, a large number of claim or beacon frames, frequent reinitialization of the ring (ring state transitions), and large numbers of lost token errors accompanied by increasing numbers of claim and beacon frames.

A physical break in the cabling or a power outage in a station or concentrator usually triggers ring wrapping. You can usually identify the node at which the wrap occurred by analyzing status information frames with a protocol analyzer, or by querying the status of interfaces, such as bridge or router ports. Then you can test all the components (connector, cable, concentrator, interface cards, bridge/router ports) that were cut out of the ring when it wrapped.

Large numbers of claim and beacon frames in the ring in conjunction with frequent transitions may indicate problems either in the cabling (kinks, contaminated connectors) or in the transmit and receive ports of an interface card. In such cases, trend measurements of the relevant parameters (concurrent tracking of active stations and error rate) and an analysis of status information frames can be useful in tracing the fault.

Principal Error Conditions During Normal Ring Operation; Claim Initiator Identification

State transitions in an FDDI network do not necessarily constitute a sign of trouble in the ring. Ring reinitialization is usually triggered by a node's LEM function when the error rate in its interface exceeds a certain threshold. In this case, the ring is temporarily deactivated while the LEM tests the link in question. The ring is also reinitialized any time a node's TVX expires, indicating that the node has not received a token or other valid data packet in the last 2.5 ms. The reinitialization procedure takes only a few milliseconds, so the higher-layer protocols, with timer values on the order of whole seconds, are not affected. If an error that triggers reinitialization occurs as part of normal operation—when a node is connected or disconnected, a router or bridge is rebooted, etc.—then the reinitialization process does not indicate a problem. If transitions happen several times a minute, however, then the higher-layer protocols are affected. If you can localize the station that started the claim process, you should be able to isolate the failure domain and solve the problem. To determine which station initiated a claim process, assign a different TTRT value to each station in the ring. To illustrate this method, consider a ring with three nodes. Node A has TTRT=10, Node B has TTRT = 15, and Node C has TTRT = 5. Analyze the claim counters (Claim_Ct) in each station. In this example, assume Node B starts the claim process. Node A repeats the frame transmitted by Node B, because $TTRT_A$ > $TTRT_B$. Node C, however, replaces B's frame with its own claim frame because $TTRT_C$ < $TTRT_B$). The claim counters of the three stations contain the following values at this point: B=1, C=1, A=0. In this way the combination of TTRT and claim counter values can be used to trace the node that initiated the claim process.

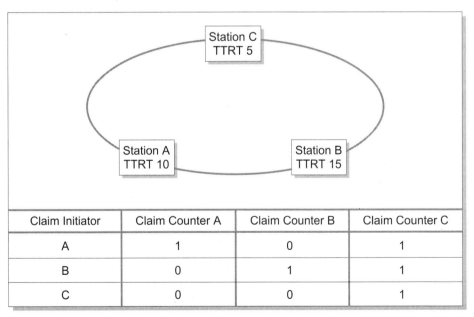

Claim Initiator	Claim Counter A	Claim Counter B	Claim Counter C
A	1	0	1
B	0	1	1
C	0	0	1

Figure 9.11 Identifying the node that initiated a claim process in an FDDI network

Void Frames

A void frame is one with the value 0X00 0000 in its frame control field, where X stands for the address length bit and has a value of either 1 (indicating a 48-bit address) or 0 (indicating a 16-bit address). Void frames are not actually data packets and are usually ignored by all ring nodes. Some manufacturers use void frames for special purposes, however, such as deleting frame fragments or stripped frames. Thus the occurrence of void frames does not necessarily indicate an error condition. Contact the manufacturer of the components in question for further details.

9.2.4   Cabling Problems

As in other networks, cabling problems are frequent causes of errors in FDDI networks. Typical causes include defective or low-quality cables; cable lengths exceeding the specified maximum; defective or low-quality connectors or, in a CDDI network, incorrect impedance; or electromagnetic interference (noise) caused by air conditioning systems, photocopiers, pagers, elevators or production environments. These problems are discussed in detail in the chapter on cabling.

Two factors that must be mentioned with specific reference to FDDI, however, are the maximum bit-error-rate (BER) permitted between two FDDI stations and the optical bypass function.

The BER due to signal repetition must not exceed 2.5×10^{-10}. (If the signal power exceeds the minimum requirement by 2 dB, then the BER must not exceed 1×10^{-12}). At the receive port, a signal power of –31 dBm or more must be recognized as valid within 100 µs.

Another possible source of errors is the optical bypass function in ring nodes. This function isolates a node upon failure so that the double-ring architecture of the network is maintained. Without the bypass function, failure of a node causes the ring to wrap, which means it doubles back on itself and is reconfigured as a single ring. The following specifications are defined for bypass functions used in FDDI:

	Min	Max	Units
Attenuation (input – output)	0.0	2.5	dB
Optical switching time	–	15	ms
Station switching time	–	25	ms

The optical switching time is the time during which the primary and secondary optical signal is interrupted during the switching process (measured from the time the signal drops more than 1.5 dB below the original signal level S1 to the time the signal recovers above S1-1.5 dB). The station switching time is the duration of the insertion or removal process from beginning to end (completion is defined as 1.5 dB below the final signal level). Other problems in the physical layer that are not specific to FDDI, and their remedies, are discussed in detail in Chapter 5.

9.2.5   Problems with FDDI Interface Cards

Typical symptoms of defective interface cards in FDDI rings are high numbers of claim and beacon frames in conjunction with frequent transitions. The first step in localizing a defective FDDI NIC is to identify suspicious nodes on the network. Begin by making a list of all network nodes that transmit defective frames. Most protocol analyzers provide this information with fully automatic test programs. You can also use the method described in Section 9.2.3 to determine which node initiates the claim process. If this does not pinpoint the problem, or if the symptoms are intermittent, try the correlation method: begin by simultaneously charting the activity of the suspicious nodes and the error rate in the network. If there is a correlation between the activity of a certain node and the error rate, then you have probably found the defective interface card.

9.2.6   Problems with Bridges

Bridges are components that connect network segments on OSI Layer 2 (the MAC layer). Bridges buffer and filter the frames they receive from connected segments and transmit them to their destination segments without regard to higher-layer protocols. The basic functions of bridges are described in detail in the chapter on Ethernet networks; the following discussion deals only with bridge problems specific to FDDI.

Diagnosing Bridge Problems

The challenge in analyzing bridge problems is to correlate the occurrence of symptoms in several different network segments. It is not as important to measure network performance in several LAN segments simultaneously. Performance measurements would only be required to determine throughput or transmission delay. It is more efficient to request system specifications from the manufacturer based on standardized test methods as specified in RFC 1242 and RFC 1944.

Most problems that affect bridges can best be located by a process of elimination that involves the correlation of specific measurements and an analysis of the network topology. Symptoms of bridge problems can include poor network performance in particular segments, intermittent or permanent loss of connections to particular nodes, or the failure of certain protocols and services. The first phase of the troubleshooting process is, as always, a review of all configuration changes that were made in the network before the error occurred, as well as the general information-gathering steps described previously. If the symptoms correlate to particular connections, begin by checking all bridges located along the corresponding transmission path. Otherwise, the next step is to prepare a list of all the stations, connections, protocols and services affected by the problems observed. To do this, measure the current parameters in the various network segments and compare the results with statistics gathered during normal operation. This involves recording and analyzing throughput and performance parameters of network nodes, protocols and applications, as well as reviewing log files that contain the operating statistics on all bridges in the network. The log files provide bridge statistics such as CPU capacity use, port capacity use, buffer capacity use, and error rates. To measure the response times of connections across bridges, send echo frames across the bridges from different network segments. Long-term response time measurement statistics can be especially useful in diagnosing intermittent problems. Based on the results of the measurements, the range of potential sources of error can usually be narrowed down to specific components.

Symptoms and Causes of Bridge Problems

The symptoms for most bridge problems in FDDI networks differ only slightly from those in Ethernet or Token Ring networks. As described in the section on Ethernet bridges, the most common difficulties are throughput problems, incorrectly configured filter settings, bridge buffer overflow, and faulty address tables. Problem characteristics of FDDI networks include bridge ports configured with duplicate FDDI addresses and incorrect frame length settings.

Bridge Port Configured with Duplicate FDDI Address

Because FDDI addresses are configured by software, the occurrence of duplicate addresses due to incorrect configuration (typing errors, copied configuration files) is not uncommon.

Inefficient Maximum Frame Length

Incorrectly configured bridge ports that restrict the maximum frame size can have a negative effect on performance.

Installation and Configuration Errors

Among the leading causes of problems with bridges are incorrect installation or configuration of the equipment, especially in the use of increasingly complex modular bridges. Incorrectly configured ports (FDDI interface not activated), bad connections (loose cables, connectors, or plug-in modules) and faulty connections to the back plane or the wiring cabinet are the most common error sources.

Hardware Problems

If you suspect hardware problems, check the power supply and connectors and run the bridge's self-test function.

9.2.7   Problems with Routers

Routers are internetworking components that connect network segments on OSI Layer 3. Because they operate on this layer, routers can link networks of any topology. Refer to the section on router problems in Chapter 7 for a detailed description of procedures for troubleshooting and diagnosing router errors.

9.2.8   Symptoms and Causes: FDDI

Symptom: Frequent Ring Reinitialization, High Bit-Error-Rate (Detected by LEM)

Frequent ring initializations and high bit-error-rates are often symptoms that the signal power of a NIC or concentrator is too weak. To determine whether this is the case, measure the power at a node's receiving port when a constant stream of Halt symbols is transmitted. The average must be at least –20 dBm.

Cause (1):   Loose connectors; dust or fingerprints on optical fiber or connector.

Cause (2):   DAS deactivated.

If a dual-attachment station or concentrator fails or is deactivated, the distance between two stations may exceed the maximum specifications. In a network with high redundancy, the ring should be designed so that no two neighboring nodes are more than 400 meters apart. Then the ring can remain operational even if up to four contiguous stations fail.

Cause (3):   Active optical bypass switch.

Optical bypass switches are activated when a node fails, and can increase attenuation caused by the ring by up to 2 dB. If several bypasses are active, the resulting loss can lead to high bit-error-rates and consequent increases in claim and beacon frames.

Cause (4):   Defective interface card.

Cause (5):   Defective port in a router, bridge, or concentrator.

Symptom: Large Number of Status Report Frames

Cause (1):   New MAC neighbor.

Cause (2):   Change in port's operating status.

FDDI stations transmit SRFs to inform other components of changes in their configuration. The presence of a large number of status report frames may indicate problems in the FDDI ring. Use a protocol analyzer or the ring management system to collect and analyze the SRFs. If they do not indicate any unusual conditions, transmit SIFs to poll stations on their status. Keep in mind that the error counters maintained by each node count only frames that end with a valid ending delimiter. Frames that end in Idle symbols or invalid characters can only be detected using a protocol analyzer.

Symptom: High Numbers of Claim Frames

Cause: Expired TVX or TRT.

The station has not received a valid token or data packet for over 2.5 ms. This may be due to a high BER, which may in turn result from cable or connector problems, defective FDDI ports, or problems with optical bypass switches.

Symptom: High Checksum Error Rates (FCS Errors)

Cause: Defective cable; defective FDDI interface card; dust, dirt or fingerprints on the MIC connector.

Symptom: FDDI Frames with the Error Bit Set

Cause: Defective cable, defective FDDI interface card.

The error domain is directly upstream from the station that sets the E bit in the frames. Check all the components in the upstream transmission path, including concentrators, cables, connectors, and the interface card in the neighboring station, until you locate the source of the error.

Symptom: Oversized Data Packets (Length Error Bit Set)

Cause: Problems with the interface card or driver software.

An oversized frame is any frame of more than 4,500 bytes. Its LE bit is set to 1.

Symptom: Token Rotation Time is Too Long

Cause: Problems with station configuration or cabling.

Similar to statistics on capacity use, the TRT is also an indicator of ring performance. It should lie below the TTRT negotiated during the claim process. If the TRT regularly goes over the negotiated TTRT, this could be an indication of incorrect station configuration or of problems in cables or connectors.

Symptom: Invalid Frames (Violation Frames)

Cause: Station detects invalid symbols.

When a station detects invalid symbols, it reports this in the next valid frame it transmits. The frame with the error message is not the frame that contains the coding violation or error. The error domain is upstream from the station that reports the violation. Check all the components in the upstream transmission path, including concentrators, cables, connectors, and the interface card in the neighboring station, until you locate the source of the error.

Symptom: Interface Overflow (Wedged Interface)

Cause: Bursts of small packets that overflow the queue.

Wedged interface ports are a common problem. In these cases the input/output queue exceeds the maximum value supported by the router port. The solution is either to increase the queue size or to reload the router.

Common Errors

The following list summarizes the most frequent sources of problems in FDDI networks (in alphabetical order):

- Bridge address list incorrectly configured; bridge in protected mode
- Bridge filter incorrectly configured
- Bridge overloaded
- Bridge's aging function deletes address entry
- Cable length between neighboring nodes exceeds specifications (especially after a DAS node failure or ring wrapping)
- CDDI only: electromagnetic interference
- Connectors, loose or defective: interface cards, wall jacks, concentrators, bridges, routers
- Defective patch cable
- Defective concentrator
- Duplicate FDDI ring addresses
- Faulty physical installation of router, bridge or concentrator (loose cable, connectors, plug-in modules; incorrect cable connections on the backplane)
- Fiber only: dust or fingerprints on the connector
- Frame length restrictions on router/bridge ports
- Frequency and jitter problems due to cabling, noise, too many stations
- Network interface card defective
- Network interface cards incorrectly configured (TTRT, driver, interrupt)
- Receive buffer on interface card insufficient
- Router filter incorrectly configured
- Router overloaded
- Router protocol entries incorrectly configured (address tables, mapping tables, subnet masks, default gateways, routing tables, timers)
- Router settings incorrectly configured: port not active, protocol not active
- Signal loss due to active optical bypass switch
- Stations: too many on the ring
- WAN connections down, overloaded or of poor quality (high BER)

Figure 9.12 The most common causes of errors in FDDI networks

ATM

10

"To err is human, but to really foul things up requires a computer."

ANONYMOUS

10.1 ATM: Specification and Implementation

Since the early 1980s, data communications have been divided into two separate areas with little in common: local-area and wide-area networking. For technical reasons, data transport methods have been fundamentally different in these two areas. In wide-area networks, data communication has been connection-oriented: before the first bit of user data is transmitted, a signaling process takes place in which a dedicated connection to a given remote station is set up. Local-area networks, by contrast, have used "connectionless" broadcast transmissions: every data packet is sent out over a medium shared among all stations without waiting for acknowledgment. It is the receiver's job to detect packets in the data stream that have its address as the destination and process them.

Asynchronous Transfer Mode (ATM) was originally conceived for wide-area data communication, but was soon adapted for local-area networks. ATM creates a unified system that does away with the historical distinction between local- and wide-area data communication techniques. In both ATM LANs and WANs, data is transported by means of switches according to principles that had been customary only in wide-area communications, such as telephony. Every ATM end system is connected to a dedicated switch port. Every data packet, or "cell", that is addressed to a given station is delivered by an ATM switch to a corresponding switch port. Consequently, all data packets no longer travel over the same shared broadcast medium. Pick-up and delivery of cells (data packets) is managed entirely by an ATM switch. The key advantage of this technique is that every station connected to an ATM switch is guaranteed a certain bandwidth on its port regardless of how many other nodes are connected. This is possible because the switch's internal data throughput is many times higher than the bandwidth of any switch port. In conventional LANs, the average bandwidth available to any node is inversely proportional to the total number of active nodes. Furthermore, the switching principle is combined in ATM networks with connection-oriented data transmission. The traffic parameters necessary for a given service can be negotiated during the signaling or provisioning procedure required for every connection. For example, an end system may request a transmission path to a destination with a certain bandwidth and a certain maximum transmission delay. If the switches along the transmission route have the capacity necessary to grant the requested connection, then these communication parameters are guaranteed for the duration of the connection and appropriate network resources are reserved.

10.1.1   ATM in Homogeneous Private Networks

If a network is built using only ATM components, then data communication can take place using classic ATM transmission techniques. Because ATM is connection-oriented, the data virtual channel used to transport actual user data must be defined before the data transmission by means of a signaling or provisioned connection. With signaling, special communication protocols govern the negotiation of the user data connection parameters (bandwidth, delay, routing, etc.). Data transmission takes place until the connection is terminated by an appropriate command on the signaling virtual channel. Different signaling protocols are used at the interface between the end system and the ATM switch (the user-to-network interface, or UNI) and at the interfaces between ATM switches (network-to-network interfaces, or NNI).

In a private network, NNIs (that is, interfaces between two ATM switches) use the Private Network to Network Interface (PNNI) protocol. It makes no difference whether the private network is a LAN or a WAN. In public ATM WANs, however, the NNI protocol commonly used is the Broadband ISDN User Part (B-ISUP) protocol. The reason for the use of different protocols in the private and public spheres is that the ITU standardization body has left the internal operating aspects of public data networks in the control of national telecommunications companies. For example, B-ISUP does not specify how routing information is propagated or how topology detection mechanisms should be implemented. In private networks, however, it is desirable for all data communication mechanisms to be precisely defined so that communication works automatically without custom additions. For this reason, PNNI also specifies appropriate routing mechanisms in addition to the signaling processes. Because PNNI has the basic capabilities necessary for use in public WANs, and because many ATM system manufacturers provide an implementation of PNNI, but not B-ISUP, PNNI is sometimes also used in public networks, especially in North America. In Europe and Asia, however, almost all public networks use B-ISUP.

At the interface between an ATM switch and an ATM end system, that is, the UNI, connection setup is governed by the ITU-T Recommendation Q.2931 (and Q.2971 for point-to-multi-point connections), or by one of the ATM Forum's UNI signaling protocols, UNI 3.0, 3.1 or 4.0.

When an ATM end system is installed or becomes active, it must first register with its assigned ATM switch. Information exchanged in this process includes the network address of the switch, the user address of the ATM end system, and the service characteristics of the ATM end system. All of this information is stored in the ATM switch in a defined format as the Management Information Base (MIB). In order for this registration to be carried out automatically, a separate protocol for the exchange of MIB parameters was created, called the Integrated Local Management Interface (ILMI).

Because most network applications today build on the Internet Protocol (IP), and few native ATM applications are available to date, ATM is also able to serve as a fully transparent transport layer for IP. However, the Internet Protocol was originally designed for connectionless Ethernet networks, and therefore uses the broadcast principle for a number of functions. In the Classical IP over ATM protocol defined for ATM networks, broadcasts cannot easily be translated to connection-oriented ATM; this is possible only with the LAN Emulation (LANE) protocol. Nonetheless, IP can still be transported transparently over pure ATM networks. Address resolution is performed by specially defined ATM Address Resolution Protocol (ATMARP) and Inverse ATM Address Resolution Protocol (InATMARP) functions; other broadcast types, however, are not supported.

10.1.2   ATM in Heterogeneous LAN Environments

ATM is used not only in new networks planned exclusively on the basis of ATM, but often in combination with evolved existing network structures. In order to integrate ATM smoothly in such heterogeneous networks, the protocols LANE and Multiprotocol over ATM (MPOA) have been defined for ATM. These protocols permit complete, transparent interoperability between ATM networks and end systems, on the one hand, and conventional LAN topologies such as Ethernet and Token Ring, on the other. When the LANE protocol is used in an ATM network segment, every ATM end system in this network can communicate directly with every other Ethernet or Token-Ring station connected through an ATM router. Furthermore, selected stations in the LAN can be assigned to an ATM LANE workgroup. That is, end systems can be grouped regardless of their location or network interface into "virtual LANs" (VLANs). MPOA provides transparent interconnection of several ATM LANE segments.

Note that, because LANE is a Layer 2 (link layer) protocol, emulated LANs (ELANs) are either Ethernet or Token-Ring based, not a mixture of both. Layer 3 (network layer) routing is necessary to provide communication between Ethernet and Token-Ring based ELANs via, for example, the MPOA protocol.

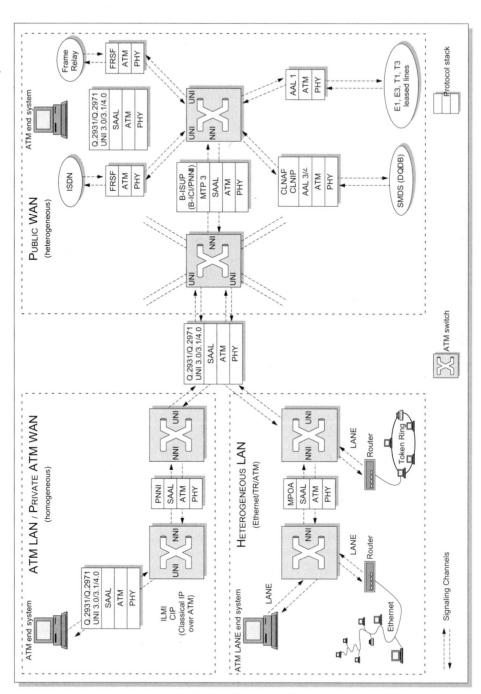

Figure 10.1 ATM in LAN and WAN: General view

10.1.3   ATM in Public Wide-Area Networks

When used for data communication in public wide-area networks, ATM can be transparently connected with Frame Relay and Switched Multimegabit Data Services (SMDS) networks, the latter being obsolescent. Transparent connection in this context means that not only user data but also protocol information is extracted from the foreign network topology and interpreted. In the case of Frame Relay, for example, the ATM network interprets and understands the Frame Relay Forward Explicit Congestion Notification (FECN) bit and the Discard Eligible (DE) bit, and represents them using the corresponding ATM protocol parameters (EFCI and CLP). In connection with Frame Relay networks, ATM emulates the Frame Relay UNI by means of the Frame Relay Service Function (FRSF). Because Frame Relay is also connection-oriented, it can be emulated relatively easily in ATM. Connecting SMDS networks to ATM is some-what more complicated, because these networks, like conventional LANs, are based on the principle of connectionless communication. As in the case of LAN emulation, the connectionless transmission principle of SMDS must be trans-lated to ATM's connection-oriented structure. This is done by means of the two protocols: Connectionless Network Interface Protocol (CLNIP) and Connectionless Network Access Protocol (CLNAP).

Another way to transport data over an ATM Network is to use the ATM Circuit Emulation Service (CES). With CES, the ATM network becomes a conduit for circuits such as E1, T1, E3, T3, etc., so any service that can be transported over these circuits is, by default also transported over ATM. Permanent virtual circuits are frequently used for CES and special interface equipment is needed to implement CES. More details are given later in the section dealing with the ATM Adaptation Layer (10.1.8).

As mentioned previously, the B-ISUP communications protocol developed by the ITU-T is used at the NNI between two ATM switches in a public network. The Broadband Inter-Carrier Interface (B-ICI) is an enhanced network-to-network interface protocol developed by the ATM Forum for connecting the networks of different carriers (communications service providers), and is used mainly in North America. A number of telecommunications providers use PNNI between their public ATM switches, however, for the sake of greater simplicity in opera-tion.

10.1.4   Asynchronous Transfer Mode: ATM

ATM is defined as a packet-switched, connection-oriented data communication technique based on asynchronous time-division multiplexing and data packets of a fixed length. ATM data packets are called cells because of their constant

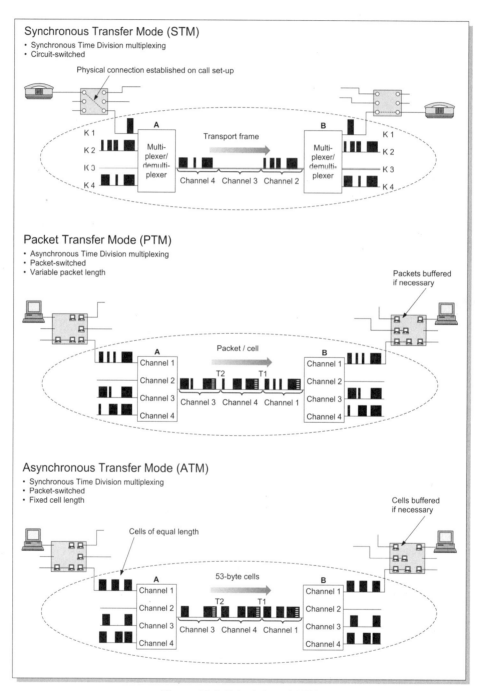

Figure 10.2 Principles of ATM

length of 53 bytes. Five of the 53 bytes form the cell header, which contains the Virtual Channel Identifier (VCI) and the Virtual Path Identifier (VPI). Note that ATM is "asynchronous" because cells are sent asynchronously, not because the octets (bytes) are asynchronous, as in RS-232C. All network nodes are connected by one or more ATM switches that forward the cells toward their destination point. The fixed cell size makes it possible for the ATM switches to forward multiple cells simultaneously with high efficiency, so that a very high throughput is attained in comparison to conventional routers. The network nodes do not share a communication medium as LAN nodes do, but simply give up their cells to the local ATM switch, without having to deal with media access algorithms. Before an actual data transmission begins, however, the transmission path for the user data cells is defined and set up by a signaling or provisioning procedure. A "traffic contract" guarantees that the traffic parameters granted, such as the maximum transfer delay, bandwidth or cell loss ratio, will be provided for the duration of the connection. This feature makes it possible to transmit many high-quality multimedia communication services over ATM networks. If the requested traffic parameters cannot be met by the network at call setup time, the call is rejected by the network so that the quality of service of other network users is not compromised.

The fixed cell length of 53 bytes results from a necessary compromise between the requirements of analog voice (low bandwidth, delay sensitive) and digital data communication (often higher bandwidth and almost always delay insensitive). A cell length of 53 bytes is short enough to be well suited to the transmission of delay sensitive low bandwidth digital signals in ATM's higher megabit/s and gigabit/s throughput ranges. The small cell size also permits quick and exact bandwidth allocations as well as parallel cell processing at high speed in ATM switches.

10.1.5   The ATM Layer Model

The transmission procedure commonly referred to as the ATM protocol actually consists of a number of protocol layers that build on one another, and map the various network services to ATM cells. Taken as a whole, this set of protocol layers is called the B-ISDN protocol reference model. This name is a reminder of the origins of the ATM specification, which has its roots in the ITU-T's Broadband-ISDN project for a universal wide-area network. Since ATM technology in the data communications field has spread beyond the boundaries of conventional telecommunications, ATM has become accepted as the universal name for the B-ISDN layers as a whole, although in a strict sense ATM refers only to cell-based data transport, that is, the ATM layer within the B-ISDN model.

The logical B-ISDN network architecture was designed for four independent levels of communication, after the ISO OSI reference model (ITU-T Recommendation X.200). Whereas the OSI model provides for seven layers, however, the B-ISDN protocol reference model defines the Physical Layer, the ATM Layer, the ATM Adaptation Layer (AAL) and the application layer designated in the model as "Higher Layer Protocols".

The physical layer consists of two "sublayers", the Transmission Convergence (TC) sublayer and the Physical Medium Dependent (PMD) sublayer. The TC sublayer embeds the ATM layer cells in the transmission framework of the given transport medium. If ATM cells are transported over a 34 Mbit/s E3 link, for example, they must be fitted into the user data field of E3 frames. The transport medium could also be a Synchronous Digital Hierarchy/Synchronous Optical NETwork (SDH/SONET) or a Plesiochronous Digital Hierarchy (PDH) frame such as DS1, E1, E3, DS3 or E4. In the case of direct cell transfer over the physical medium with no intermediate transport frame ("cell-based physical layer"), this sublayer is not necessary (that is, it is "null").

The functions of the ATM layer are completely independent of the underlying physical layer. Their chief purpose is to bring the data received from the higher-order AAL to its destination. The 53-byte cells comprise the information units of the ATM layer. Each cell has an identification number in its header that assigns it to a certain connection. The cells belonging to various connections are multiplexed into a cell stream in each direction, unused bandwidth being filled with unassigned or idle cells. These cell streams are hierarchically structured in virtual channels (VC) and virtual paths (VP), which correspond to one or more virtual connections. A physical transport medium (such as an optical fiber) can transport a number of virtual connections. Each cell on the medium can be unambiguously attributed to a certain connection by the VPI and VCI in its header, comprising the identification number referred to earlier.

The AAL disassembles the higher-layer data streams into 48-byte information segments for transport in ATM cells (five of the cell's 53 bytes are used for header information, so that 48 bytes of user data are transported in each cell). At the receiving end, the original data streams must be reassembled from the individual ATM cells. The functions of the AAL are thus dependent to a great degree on the characteristics of the higher-order applications. For this reason, the AAL functions are performed by two sublayers, the Convergence Sublayer (CS) and the Segmentation and Reassembly (SAR) sublayer. To limit the number of different AAL implementations, four AAL types have been defined: AAL1, AAL2, AAL3/4 and AAL5. Each of these AAL types is defined for a certain class of applications. By far the most widely used AAL variant today is the simplest one to implement, AAL5.

The actual network services are transported on the basis of the appropriate AALs. The most common applications are:

- Ethernet, Token Ring (using LAN emulation)
- Classical IP over ATM
- MPEG Video (Moving Pictures Experts Group)
- Frame Relay
- Leased-Line Data Links
- Voice (Telephony)

10.1.6   The ATM Physical Layer

Three methods can be used to transport ATM cells: cell adaptation to the frame structure of the transport medium (such as PDH, SDH/SONET or DXI); transport in PLCP frames, or cell-based physical layer.

In order to continue using existing data communications infrastructures, techniques have been developed to transport ATM cells in the container frames of the most common communications interfaces. Cell transport in SDH containers or SONET Synchronous Payload Envelopes (SPEs) is the most widely used transport method for ATM cells today. Adaptation methods have also been developed to transport ATM cells in wide-area networks over the older but still widely used E1, E3, E4, T1 and T3 PDH interfaces. In this technique the cells are inserted directly into the user data field of the given transport frame, and the cell rate is adapted to the throughput capacity of PDH by inserting fillers, called "idle" cells. In North America, "unassigned" cells are often used (for most purposes idle and unassigned cells can be considered identical). Adaptation to the existing PDH frame is defined in ITU-T Recommendation G.804 for the following transfer rates: 1.544 Mbit/s, 2.048 Mbit/s, 6.312 Mbit/s, 34.360 Mbit/s, 97.728 Mbit/s and 139.264 Mbit/s. Cell transport over the T3 line type (44.736 Mbit/s), common in North America, was once defined only using the T3-PLCP frame format (Bellcore TR-TSV-000772, TR-TSV-000773), originally developed for metropolitan area networks. However a more efficient, direct mapping was introduced a few years ago and is now the preferred mapping, even though the PLCP mapping is still very common in older equipment.

In the cell-based physical layer, the cells are not inserted in an additional transport frame, but simply converted bit-for-bit into the given communication medium's electrical or optical signals and transmitted. A different scrambling arrangement is performed from that used in other interfaces in order to provide sufficient clock transitions so that the clock timing can be recovered from the incoming bit stream; this "distributed sample scrambler" (DSS) uses a 31st order polynomial $(x^{31} + x^{28} + 1)$ and is described in I.432.1. One advantage of a cell-based physical layer is the efficient utilization of bandwidth. Because the ATM cell is not inserted in another frame structure with its own overhead, the ratio of total overhead to user data is maintained at about 1:9 (5 bytes of header, 48 bytes of data). The disadvantage is that existing transport infrastructures can no longer be used. Another problem with direct cell transfer in wide-area networks is the need to transport monitoring and management information. In both classical PDH and modern SDH/SONET networks, the frames or containers in which data are transported also contain the monitoring and error handling information required by the switching equipment. For this reason, special operation control cells have been defined for the physical layer, called Physical Layer Operation and Maintenance (PL-OAM) cells. These cells transport information required for the monitoring and management of the cell stream.

Many of the existing infrastructures in wide-area networking are unable to support ATM cell-based physical layers, however. The use of this technique is therefore limited to local-area networks. In practice, transportation of ATM cells in SDH/SONET frames has also become accepted in LANs even though, as ATM

Transport frame	Communication medium	Data rates (Mbit/s)
SDH/SONET	Single-mode fiber	155, 622, 2460, 9960
SDH/SONET	Multimode fiber	155, 622
SDH/SONET	POF, HPCF	155
SDH	75Ω coaxial cable	155
SDH/SONET	UTP3, UTP5, 150Ω STP	12.96, 25.92, 51.84, 155
PDH	75Ω coaxial cable	2.048, 34.36, 44.73, 139.26
PDH	100Ω TP	1.544, 2.048
DXI (not cell, but AAL-5 or AAL-3/4 based)	V.35, EIA/TIA 449, HSSI	up to 52
Cell stream	Single-mode fiber	155, 622
Cell stream	Multimode fiber	155, 622
Cell stream	V.35, EIA/TIA 449, HSSI	up to 52
Cell stream	UTP3, 120Ω Cat.4, 150Ω STP	25.6
Cell stream	FDDI multimode/ single-mode (TAXI)(obsolete)	100

Figure 10.3 ATM transmission interfaces

transport containers, these frames with their relatively simple structures (no multiplexing hierarchies or spatial limitations) are actually superfluous. Cell-based physical layers are therefore currently only used in a few applications developed especially for this transport method, such as video.

ATM Data Rates

At present, a large number of transmission interfaces are defined both for LAN and WAN use, spanning a wide range of bandwidths and transport media. Data rates range from 1.544 Mbit/s to 9.9 Gbit/s or even higher. The differences between the LAN and WAN specifications are primarily associated with the transport medium. Whereas single-mode fiber optic and coaxial cable are the primary media for WAN interfaces, multimode fiber, plastic optical fiber (POF) and copper twisted pair are becoming increasingly common in local-area networking. Figure 10.3 lists the currently available transmission interfaces.

ATM in PDH Networks

ATM over DS1: 1.544 Mbit/s

The mapping of ATM cells to DS1 line framing is specified in ITU-T Recommendation G.804. Under this standard, ATM cells can be transported in a 24-frame multiframe (Extended Superframe, or ESF) with the cells occupying bits 2 to 193. The individual ATM cells are byte-aligned with the DS1 frame, but not frame-aligned. This means that an ATM cell can be split across two DS1 frames.

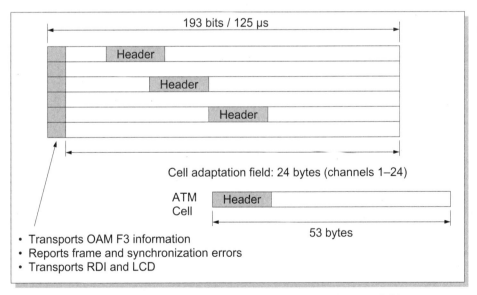

Figure 10.4 Direct cell adaptation to the DS1 frame format (G.804)

By inserting idle or unassigned cells when no valid ATM user data cells are available, the cell transfer rate is adapted to the user data bandwidth of DS1. Scrambling of the ATM cell's data field is optional, in contrast to the E1 ATM mapping. The self-synchronizing scrambling method is used with the generator polynomial $x^{43}+1$.

ATM over E1: 2.048 Mbit/s

Like DS1 mapping, the mapping of ATM cells to E1 frames is also described in ITU-T Recommendation G.804. The ATM cells can be transported in bits 9–128 and 137–256, which correspond to timeslots 1 through 15 and 17 through 31. The cell rate is adapted to the E1 frame payload bandwidth of 1.920 Mbit/s by means of idle cells when no ATM cells are queued for insertion. Once again, the ATM cells are byte-aligned with the E1 frame, but not frame-aligned.

The 48 data bytes of each ATM cell are scrambled before transport using self-synchronizing scrambling (SSS) with the generator polynomial $x^{43}+1$. This permits fast cell delineation, allowing the receiving station to recover quickly from a loss of cell delineation due to physical layer bit errors, for example.

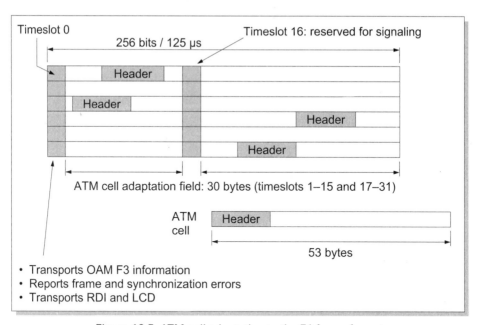

Figure 10.5 ATM cell adaptation to the E1 frame format

ATM over E3: 34.368 Mbit/s

The mapping of cells to the E3 frame format is described in ITU-T Recommendation G.804. The E3 frame format used is not the E3 frame format described in

G.751, however, but a modified frame format described in G.832. The mapping of ATM cells to the older G.751 frame structure is difficult to accomplish: the cells would have to be "nibble-aligned" because each G.751 subframe is an integer multiple of 4 rather than 8 bits. The newer G.832 frame consists of 537 bytes, of which 7 bytes are used for overhead information (see Figure 10.6). The remaining 530 user data bytes correspond exactly to the length of ten ATM cells, so that these can be byte- and frame-aligned (though the latter is not required). The ATM cell rate is adapted to the E3 user data rate by the insertion of idle cells when no ATM cells are queued for transport; in North America, unassigned cells are often used for this purpose—both idle and unassigned cells are discarded at the input to switches, etc. The 48-byte data field of the ATM cell (including idle/unassigned cells) is scrambled using self-synchronizing scrambling with the generator polynomial $x^{43}+1$.

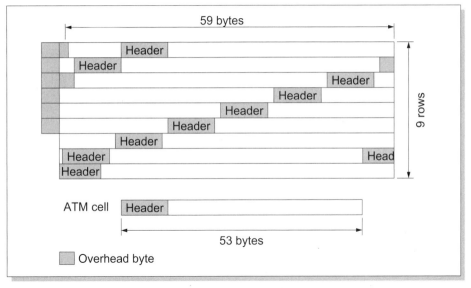

Figure 10.6 Cell adaptation to the E3 frame format

ATM over DS3: 44.736 Mbit/s

ATM cells can be transported over DS3 links using either the Physical Layer Convergence Protocol (PLCP) mapping found in older equipment or the direct cell mapping to the DS3 frame format preferred today. A DS3 PLCP frame consists of twelve rows of 57 bytes each. The last row contains an additional trailer of twelve or thirteen nibbles (half-bytes) to fill out the user data field of a DS3 multiframe. The DS3 PLCP frame has a transmission time of 125 μs, corresponding to a rate of 44.21 Mbit/s, and thus fits exactly in the user data field of a DS3 multiframe (Figure 10.7).

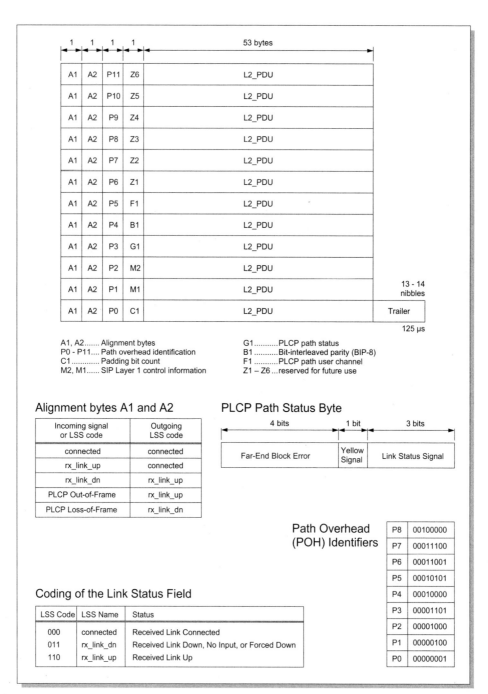

Figure 10.7 The DS3 PLCP frame

The PLCP frame mapping of ATM cells is thus a two stage process that is complicated and also inefficient, because there is additional overhead associated with the PLCP frame structure; the cell payloads are not normally scrambled. The more efficient direct mapping of cells to the DS3 frame, sometimes referred to as "HEC" mapping, makes use of the same cell delineation process used for DS1, E1 and E3 mapping; cell payload scrambling again uses the self-synchronizing scrambling with the generator polynomial $x^{43}+1$.

ATM over E4: 139.264 Mbit/s

Similar to E3, ATM cell transport in the E4 transmission frame (ITU-T Recommendation G.804) does not use the E4 frame format described in G.751, but a modified frame described in G.832. The ATM cells are inserted byte-aligned in the E4 frame payload field of the 2,160 byte G.832-E4 frame. All other processing, such as the scrambling of the ATM cell payload and the cell rate adaptation, is performed as in the mapping of ATM cells to the E3 format.

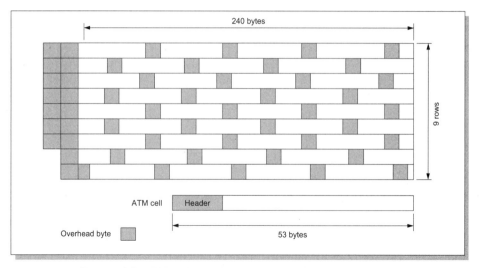

Figure 10.8 ATM cell adaptation to the G.832 E4 frame format

ATM over 6.312 Mbit/s and 97.728 Mbit/s

For the sake of thoroughness, we may mention at this point that ATM cell transport is also specified for the PDH bit rates 6.312 and 97.728 Mbit/s. These interfaces are only of regional importance, however, because they are almost never used outside Japan.

Bytes 1 - 5	ATM cell header: GFC=0, VPI=0, VCI=0, PTI=101, CLP=1, HEC
Byte 6	IMA label for compatibility with UNI 3.1 OAM cell format (OAM type field)
Byte 7	Cell ID: Bit 7: IMA OAM Cell Types (0: idle cell, 1: ICP cell) Link ID: Bits 6–5: not used; set to 0 Bits 4–0: logical ID for lines 0 to 31
Byte 8	IMA frame sequence number: 0–255, cyclical
Byte 9	ICP cell offset range (0 to M–1): indicates ICP cell position in the IMA frame

Byte 10	Link stuff indication:
	Bits 7–3: not used; set to 0
	Bits 2–0: 111 = No imminent stuff event
	                100 = Stuff event in 4 ICP cell locations (optional)
	                011 = Stuff event in 3 ICP cell locations (optional)
	                010 = Stuff event in 2 ICP cell locations (optional)
	                001 = Stuff event at the next ICP cell location (mandatory)
	                000 = this is one of the two ICP cells compromising the stuff event (mandatory)

Byte 11	Status and control change indication: Bits 7–0: Status change indication: 0 to 255
Byte 12	IMA ID

Byte 13	Group status and control
	Bits 7–4: Group state
	                0000 = Group is active and ready to add further links
	                0001 = Group is inactive and not ready to add further links
	                0010 = Group start-up
	                0011 = Failure, protocol error
	                0100 = Failure, insufficient links
	                0101 = Failure, unsupported value of M
	                0110 = Failure, incompatible group symmetry
	                0111 = Failure, symmetry not supported
	Bits 3–2: Group symmetry mode
	                00 = Symmetrical configuration and operation
	                01 = Symmetrical configuration and asymmetrical operation (optional)
	                10 = Asymmetrical configuration and operation (optional)
	                11 = Reserved
	Bits 1–0: IMA Frame length (00: M=32, 01: M=64, 10: M=128, 11: M=256)

Byte 14	Transmit timing information
	                Bits 7–6: not used; set to 0
	                Bit 5: Transmit clock mode (0: ITC mode; 1: CTC mode)
	                Bits 4–0: Tx LID of the timing reference (0 to 31)

Byte 15	Tx test control Bits 7–6: not used; set to 0
	                              Bit 5: Test link command (0: inactive; 1: active)
	                              Bits 4–0: Tx LID of test link (0 to 31)

Byte 16	Tx test pattern Bits 7–0: Tx test pattern (values 0–255)
Byte 17	Rx test pattern Bits 7–0: Rx test pattern (values 0–255)

Byte 18	Link 0 information Bits 7–5: Tx status
	                              Bits 4–2: Rx status
	                              Bits 1–0: Remote Defect Indicator

Bytes 19–49	Link 1–31 info status
Byte 50	not used; set to 6A hex (ITU I.432)
Byte 51	End-to-end channel (proprietary channel set to 0 if not used)
Bytes 52–53	CRC-10 (ITU I.432)

Figure 10.9 ICP cell format

Inverse Multiplexing for ATM (IMA)

ATM inverse multiplexing is the process of dividing an ATM cell stream into several component streams for transport, which are then reassembled into the original stream at the receiving end. This makes it possible to transport high bandwidths over several bundled data links of lower capacity. For example, bandwidths of 4 to 34 Mbit/s can be realized by bundling the appropriate number of E1 links, though it becomes uneconomical to consider bundles or "link groups" with more than about 6 - 8 links. The ATM cells are transported one at a time over each of the available lines in turn. For every M cell, a special IMA Control Protocol (ICP) cell is inserted. The ICP cell, together with the corresponding ATM user data cells, comprise an "IMA frame". Each ICP cell contains a Link Identifier (LID) indicating the individual line, an IMA frame sequence number, and various information fields used to monitor and synchronize the transmission (Figure 10.9).

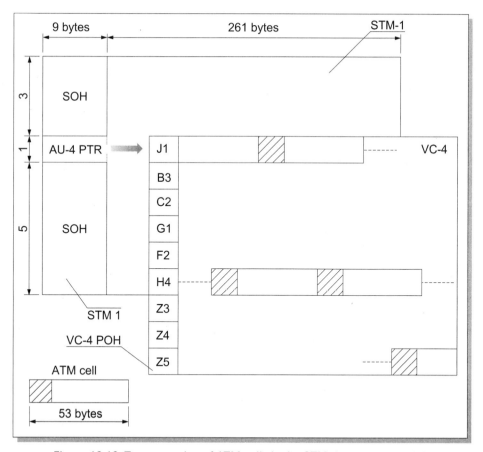

Figure 10.10 Transportation of ATM cells in the STM-1 transport module

ATM in SDH and SONET Networks

The transportation of ATM cells over SDH and SONET networks (ATM mapping) is specified in ITU-T Recommendation G.707 and ANSI T1.105 respectively; SONET is the North American equivalent of SDH and can be considered to be identical in most respects for equivalent interface rates. The cell stream is encapsulated with byte alignment in VC-x or in concatenated VC-xc containers (synchronous payload envelopes or SPEs in SONET). Because the container/ SPE payload is not an integer multiple of 53 bytes, a cell can be split across two containers/SPEs. Before the ATM cells are inserted in the containers/SPEs for transport, the user data field of the cell is scrambled in order to facilitate delineation of the individual cell at the receiving station. The scrambling method used is self-synchronizing scrambling (SSS) with the generator polynomial $x^{43}+1$. If the cell transfer rate is different from the user data bandwidth of the

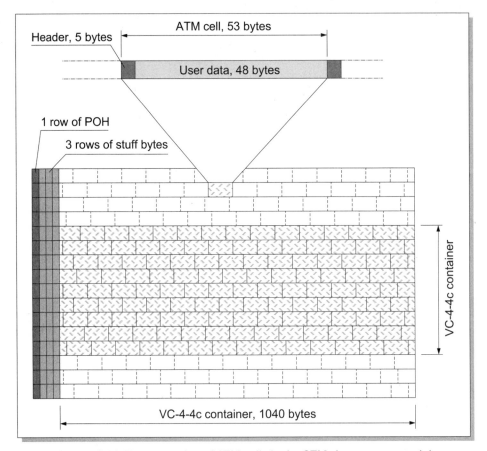

Figure 10.11 Transportation of ATM cells in the STM-4c transport module

SDH/SONET containers/SPEs, empty (idle/unassigned) cells are inserted. ATM cells that exceed the available bandwidth are discarded, with low priority cells being discarded preferentially. The resulting bit rate of the ATM cell stream is synchronous with that of the SDH container or SONET SPE. Note that, while Figure 10.10 shows cell mapping to an SDH STM-1 transport module, cell mapping to a SONET STS-3c transport system is essentially identical. Similarly, the mapping of cells to a SONET STS-12c transport system is identical to the mapping of cells to the SDH STM-4c transport module shown in Figure 10.11.

Byte	Function	Coding[1]
STM-1/STS-3c Section Transport Overhead		
A1, A2	Frame alignment	
C1	STM-1 identifier	
B1	Regenerator section error monitoring[2]	BIP-8
B2	Multiplexer section error monitoring	BIP-24
H1, H2	AU-4 pointer, path AIS[4]	A11 1s
H3	Action pointer	
K2 (bits 6–8)	Multiplexer section AIS / section FERF	111/110
Z2 (bits 18–24)	Multiplexer section error reporting (FEBE)[5]	B2 error count
VC-4 Path overhead		
J1	Path ID/verification	BIP-8
B3	Path error monitoring	ATM cell[3]
C2	Path signal level	B3 error count
G1 (bits 1–4)	Path error reporting (REI)	1
G1 (bits 5)	Path RDI	
FFS	Cell delineation supervision	FFS
FFS	Header error performance monitoring	FFS

1. Only the codes that are relevant for the monitoring function are listed.
2. The use of B1 for regenerator section error monitoring is optional.
3. The code for ATM cells is: C2 = 13hex
4. The use of H1 and H2 for path AIS is provisional.
5. The use of Z2 for multiplexer section error monitoring is provisional.

Figure 10.12 SDH/SONET overhead bytes in ATM cell transport

Alarm and Monitoring Signals

Two types of monitoring signal are defined for ATM cell transport over SDH/SONET networks: the Alarm Indication Signal (AIS) and the Remote Defect Indicator (RDI, formerly known as FERF for Far End Receive Failure) signal. An AIS is sent downstream to report an error. An RDI signal is sent upstream to report a receiving or transmission error. Both kinds of monitoring signal can be implemented using the Section/Transport Overhead (SOH/TOH) bytes of the STM-1/STS-3c frame, or with the Path Overhead (POH) of the VC4 container/SPE. Figure 10.12 shows the use of the corresponding SDH overhead bytes for ATM cell transport (the equivalent SONET overhead bytes are similar).

ATM over Single-Mode Fiber

ITU-T Recommendation G.957 defines six different single-mode fiber optic types that can be used to transport SDH/SONET in three different communication scenarios: in-house links, medium-range WAN links and long-range WAN links.

In-house links can attain a maximum range of 2 km. The optical transmitters may consist of light emitting diodes (LEDs) or multilongitudinal mode (MLM) lasers with a wavelength of 1,310 nm. The permissible loss is between 0 and 7 dB.

Medium-range WAN links span distances of up to 15 km. The optical transmitters may be either single longitudinal mode (SLM) or multilongitudinal mode (MLM) lasers with wavelengths of 1,310 or 1,550 nm. Permissible loss is between 0 and 12 dB.

For long-range WAN links of up to 40 km, lasers with a wavelength of 1,310 nm can be used. If high-power SLM (500 µW or –3 dBm) or MLM lasers are used at wavelengths of 1,550 nm, the range can be up to 80 km. Permissible loss is between 10 and 24 dB.

Parameter	Medium-range WAN links (15 km)	In-house links (2 km)	Units
Transmission characteristics			
Wavelength	1293 – 1334	1261 – 1360	nm
Spectral width: Max. RMS width	4	14.5 (MLM Laser35 (LEDs))	nm
Mean signal power	-15 to -8	-15 to -8	dBm
Minimum extinction rate	8.2	8.2	dB
Eye diagram	See T1.646	See T1.646	
Reception characteristics			
Minimum sensitivity	-28	-23	dBm
Minimum overload	-8	-8	dBm
Optical path power penalty	1	1	dB

Figure 10.13 Single-mode fiber-optic parameters for 622.08 Mbit/s interfaces (ITU-T Recommendation G.957)

Using single-mode fiber, the attainable ATM data rates are 155 Mbit/s with STM-1/OC-3, 622 Mbit/s with STM-4/OC-12, 2.4 Gbit/s with STM-16/OC-48, and 9.9 Gbit/s with STM-64/OC-192. In practice, ATM is transported over single-mode fiber optic links primarily in wide-area networks. Due to the steadily growing demands for range and capacity in local-area networks, however, these

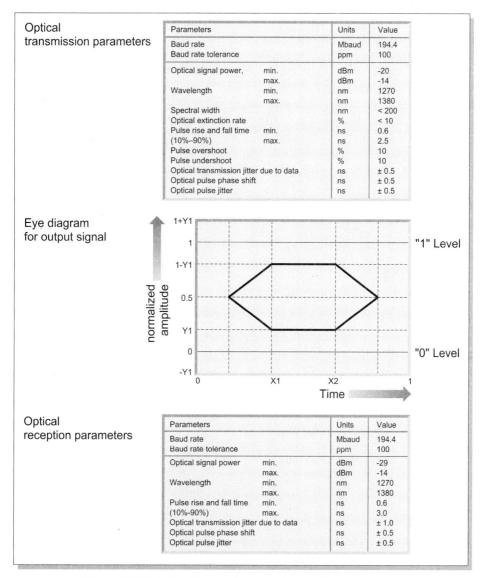

Optical transmission parameters

Parameters		Units	Value
Baud rate		Mbaud	194.4
Baud rate tolerance		ppm	100
Optical signal power,	min.	dBm	-20
	max.	dBm	-14
Wavelength	min.	nm	1270
	max.	nm	1380
Spectral width		nm	< 200
Optical extinction rate		%	< 10
Pulse rise and fall time	min.	ns	0.6
(10%–90%)	max.	ns	2.5
Pulse overshoot		%	10
Pulse undershoot		%	10
Optical transmission jitter due to data		ns	± 0.5
Optical pulse phase shift		ns	± 0.5
Optical pulse jitter		ns	± 0.5

Eye diagram for output signal

Optical reception parameters

Parameters		Units	Value
Baud rate		Mbaud	194.4
Baud rate tolerance		ppm	100
Optical signal power	min.	dBm	-29
	max.	dBm	-14
Wavelength	min.	nm	1270
	max.	nm	1380
Pulse rise and fall time	min.	ns	0.6
(10%-90%)	max.	ns	3.0
Optical transmission jitter due to data		ns	± 1.0
Optical pulse phase shift		ns	± 0.5
Optical pulse jitter		ns	± 0.5

*Figure 10.14 Optical transmission and reception parameters
for the 155 Mbit/s ATM multimode fiber-optic interface*

media are found increasingly often in LANs as well. Figure 10.13 lists the single-mode fiber optic parameters as specified in ITU-T Recommendation G.957 for 622.08 Mbit/s interfaces.

ATM over Multimode Fiber

For the transmission of ATM cells in SDH/SONET frames in the LANs at data rates of 155 Mbit/s and 622 Mbit/s, the ATM Forum has also specified multimode fiber in place of the single-mode fiber prescribed in the ITU-T recommendations. The maximum range of 2 km is lower than the range for single-mode fiber, but this is seldom a problem in the LAN field, especially in indoor cabling structures with typical segment lengths of 100 to 1,000 m. The cost of the communication infrastructure can be significantly lowered, however, by avoiding expensive single-mode fiber and the high-quality laser sources it requires. In addition to ATM cell transmission over single-mode SDH/SONET WAN interfaces, multimode fiber also makes it possible to implement the STM-4c/OC-12 (622 Mbit/s), STM-1/OC-3 (155 Mbit/s) and STM-0/STS-1 (51.84 Mbit/s) interfaces in LANs.

The STM-1/OC-3 multimode fiber optic interface uses a wavelength of 1,300 nm over a 62.5/125 µm multimode fiber with a modal bandwidth of 500 MHz/km. 50/125 µm is also permissible. The data stream is 8B/10B-encoded for transmission, so that the physical medium's 194.4 Mbaud yields an effective data rate of 155.52 Mbit/s. Either SC or BFOC/2.5 (IEC 86B) connectors may be used. This specification, originally defined for UNI 3.0, has been rarely implemented, and is described here for the sake of completeness because it is still contained in the UNI 3.1 specification. Figure 10.14 lists the parameters for the multimode fiber optic interface.

The multimode fiber (MMF) interfaces are specified for 622 Mbit/s interfaces using LEDs or short-wave (SW) lasers. Both types of MMF interfaces support the following multimode fiber types:

- 62.5/125 µm IEC 793-2 Type A1b
- 50/125 µm IEC 793-2 Type A1a

The data stream is NRZ-encoded. LED-based MMFs can be used for segments of 300 to 500 m; SW MMFs have a range of about 300 m. Figure 10.15 lists the transmission and reception parameters for both MMF types at 622 Mbit/s.

ATM over Plastic Optical Fiber

As an alternative to both single-mode and multimode fiber optic media, the ATM Forum has also specified plastic optical fiber as a transport medium for ATM networks. For STM-1/OC-3 interfaces (155 Mbit/s) and segments of up to 100 m, Plastic Optical Fiber (POF) can be used, and segments of up to 100 m can use Hard Polymer Clad Fiber (HPCF). The POF medium is 1,000 µm multimode

LED-based MMF parameters			
Transmitter characteristics	62.5 μm MMF	50 μm MMF	Units
Wavelength	1270 to 1380	1270 to 1380	nm
Maximum spectral width	200	200	nm
Mean optical power	-20 to -14	-24 to -14	dBm
Minimum extinction rate	10	10	dB
Maximum rise and fall time (10% – 90%)	1.25	1.25	ns
Maximum systematic interface peak-to-peak jitter	0.4	0.4	ns
Maximum random interface peak-to-peak jitter	0.15	0.15	ns
Maximum overshoot	25	25	%
Receive characteristics			
Minimum sensitivity	-26	-26	dBm
Minimum overload	-14	-14	dBm
Maximum rise and fall time (10% – 90%)	1.6	1.6	ns
Maximum systematic interface peak-to-peak jitter	0.5	0.5	ns
Maximum random interface peak-to-peak jitter	0.15	0.15	ns
Minimum eye diagram aperture at receiver	0.31	0.31	ns
Software-based MMF parameters			
Transmission characteristics	62.5 μm MMF	50 μm MMF	Units
Wavelength	770 to 860	770 to 860	nm
Maximum spectral width	9	9	nm
Mean optical power	-10 to -4	-10 to -4	dBm
Minimum extinction rate	9	9	dB
Maximum rise and fall time (10% – 90%)	0.75	0.75	ns
Maximum systematic interface peak-to-peak jitter	0.35	0.35	ns
Maximum overshoot	25	25	%
Receiver characteristics			
Minimum sensitivity	-16	-16	dBm
Minimum overload	0	0	dBm
Maximum rise and fall time (10% – 90%)	1.2	1.2	ns
Maximum interface peak-to-peak jitter	0.55	0.55	ns
Minimum eye diagram aperture at receiver	0.31	0.31	ns

Figure 10.15 Optical transmission and reception parameters for the two 622 Mbit/s ATM multimode fiber-optic interfaces

plastic fiber (IEC 793-2 Section 4 A4d), and for HPCF, 225 μm multimode polymer fiber is used (IEC 793-2 Section 3 A3d). The maximum loss is 9.1 dB for POF media and 1.8 dB for HPCF. The minimum modal bandwidth for both fiber types must be at least 10 MHz/km at a wavelength of 650 nm. The data stream is NRZ encoded; the PN and F07 connectors used must conform to IEC 1753-BB (FFS). Figure 10.16 lists the transmission and reception parameters for POF and HPCF interfaces.

ATM over 75 Coaxial Cable

SDH-based ATM transmission at 155 Mbit/s over 75 Ohm coaxial cable is used almost exclusively in European wide-area networks; this interface is rarely used in North America, where it is called "EC-3" (EC stands for "Electrical Carrier").

Transmission parameters for ATM plastic fiber interfaces	POF	HPCF	Units
Maximum spectral width (FWHM)	40	40	nm
Numerical aperture (transmitter)	0.2 to 0.3	0.2 to 0.3	
Mean optical power	-8 to -2	-20 to -14	dBm
Wavelength	640 to 660	640 to 660	nm
Minimum extinction rate	10	10	dB
Maximum rise and fall time (10% – 90%)	4.5	4.5	ns
Maximum overshoot	25	25	%
Maximum systematic jitter	1.6	1.6	ns
Maximum random interface jitter	0.6	0.6	ns
Reception parameters for ATM plastic fiber interfaces	**POF**	**HPCF**	**Units**
Minimum sensitivity	-25	-26.5	dBm
Minimum overload	-2	-14	dBm
Maximum rise and fall time (10% – 90%)	5.0	6.0	ns
Maximum systematic jitter	2.0	2.0	ns
Minimum eye diagram aperture (time interval reserved for clock regeneration after electrical/optical conversion)	1.23	1.23	ns
Maximum random interface jitter	0.6	0.6	ns

*Figure 10.16 Optical transmission and reception parameters for
POF and HPCF interfaces ATM over 75 Ohm Coaxial Cable*

The physical medium and the encoding technique are the same as those specified in ITU-T Recommendation G.703 for the 140 Mbit/s E4 interface. Two 75
coaxial cables are used: one for transmission and one for reception. The signals
are coded using Coded Mark Inversion (CMI) at a voltage level of ± 0.5 volts.

ATM over 100   Copper Cable (Cat. 3 Unshielded Twisted Pair)

Using a special coding technique called CAP-64, which obtains high data rates at
low frequency bandwidths, ATM in SDH/SONET framing can be transported at a
speed of 155 Mbit/s even over low-quality UTP-3 data cable, which is very
common in North America. The maximum segment length is 100 m. In addition
to the STM-1/OC-3 rate of 155 Mbit/s, the ATM Forum has also specified
slower rates for this cable type, 51.84 Mbit/s, 25.92 Mbit/s and 12.96 Mbit/s. The
coding of the corresponding bit stream is CAP-16 for 51.84 Mbit/s, CAP-4 for
25.92 Mbit/s, and CAP-2 for 12.96 Mbit/s. CAP stands for Carrierless Amplitude
Modulation/Phase Modulation, and is an extremely efficient method for achiev-
ing high data rates in spite of low available frequency bandwidth. The encoding
process divides the symbol stream to be transmitted into n data paths (where n
is the symbol period). Of the resulting symbol streams, one is sent through an in-
phase filter, and the others through phase-shift filters. The output signal of the
in-phase filter is added to the inverted output signal of the phase-shift filter and
then sent to the twisted pair through a low pass filter. In this way the informa-

tion is coded in the form of phase shifts. Each phase now contains not just one data bit, but an entire bit sequence. In the case of CAP-16, a given signal level can represent any of 16 different values, depending on its phase. The information contained in a single signal amplitude thus corresponds to 4 bits. If each amplitude/phase state is to represent 6 bits, a total of 64 different phase states are necessary.

The ATM cells are framed in STM-1/STS-3c containers/SPEs in accordance with ITU-T Recommendation G.707/ANSI T1.646 (Section 7.4). At transfer rates of 51.84 Mbit/s, the ATM cells are transported in the payload field of the STM-0/STS-1 frame. The entire payload field of the STM-0/STS-1 frame is filled with cells, with the exception of columns 30 and 59, for a net bandwidth of 48.384 Mbit/s. The 25.92 Mbit/s and 12.96 Mbit/s data rates are obtained by reducing the STS-1 frame rate.

- 51.84 Mbit/s: frame period of 125 μs
- 25.92 Mbit/s: frame period of 250 μs
- 12.96 Mbit/s: frame period of 500 μs

As in the case of 155 Mbit/s network, the maximum length of network segments at 51.84 Mbit/s is 90 m, plus 10 m of flexible patch cable. If higher-quality Cat. 5 cable is used rather than Cat. 3, up to 160 m can be spanned at 51.84 Mbit/s. The lower rates, 25.92 Mbit/s and 12.96 Mbit/s, permit segment lengths of 320 and 400 m with Cat. 5 copper cabling. UTP-3 cabling is used with 8-pin RJ-45 connectors (IEC 603-7) that conform to the electrical specification ANSI/TIA/EIA-568-A.

ATM over 100   Copper Cable (Cat. 5 Unshielded Twisted Pair)

When Category 5 UTP cabling is used to transmit data at up to 155 Mbit/s, the segment length must not exceed 150 m. As for Cat. 3 wiring, the standard connector is the 8-pin RJ-45 plug. With higher-quality receivers, segments can be up to 350 m long. The electrical signal is NRZ-encoded.

ATM over 150   Shielded Twisted Pair (STP)

The use of 150   shielded twisted pair also permits segment lengths of up to 350 m at 155 Mbit/s. Nine-pin D-sub connectors or IBM MIC connectors, as used in Token Ring networks, are recommended. Here too the bit stream is NRZ-encoded.

Cell-Based Physical Layer

When ATM cells are transmitted over data lines as a plain bit stream, using neither PDH nor SDH/SONET framing, this is called cell-based physical layer. Interface specifications exist for cell-based physical layer at 51.84 Mbit/s (with optional partial transfer rates of 25.92 Mbit/s and 12.96 Mbit/s), 155 Mbit/s and

622 Mbit/s. The cells are transmitted in a continuous stream of ordinary ATM data cells, OAM cells and idle/unassigned cells. Every 27th cell at most may be a physical layer cell, which is either an idle cell inserted when no ATM user data cells are queued for transmission, or a PL-OAM cell. The latter type is used to carry out the operation monitoring functions that are otherwise accomplished by SDH/SONET headers. At least one PL-OAM cell is required for every 513 cells.

ATM Cell Streams over V.35, EIA/TIA 449/530, HSSI, and E1

The ATM Forum has specified a cell-based transmission convergence sublayer based on ITU-T Recommendation I.432 for "clear channel" interfaces. This term designates all interfaces that are capable of transporting any data stream without imposing bit stream encoding and framing restrictions. Examples include V.35, EIA/TIA 449/530, EIA/TIA 612/613 (High Speed Serial Interface or HSSI) and unframed E1. Any other clear channel interface can also be used, however. The cells are transferred in a continuous stream (of ordinary ATM cells, OAM cells, and idle/unassigned cells). No F1 or F2 OAM functions are specified for monitoring the network. F3 OAM functions can be optionally implemented using special physical layer OAM cells to monitor processes at the level of transmission paths. In this case, the following parameters can be analyzed:

- The number of included cells (NIC) per OAM cell: 128
- The number of cells for which transmission error values are calculated (Monitoring Block Size or MBS): 16
- The number of blocks monitored per OAM cell: 8
- The number of monitored blocks received by the remote station: 8

The cell rate is decoupled from an interface's data rate by inserting idle/unassigned cells. The remote station is synchronized with the individual ATM cells using the Header Error Control (HEC) mechanism described in the next section. Cells may be transmitted either in scrambled or in unscrambled form.

ATM Cell Streams over FDDI Infrastructures (TAXI)

TAXI is a special variant of cell-based ATM transmission is TAXI. The TAXI interface was defined to support the use of existing FDDI infrastructures to transport ATM cells. In this way FDDI rings can be converted into ATM networks while conserving most of the existing FDDI hardware. The name TAXI originated with the first commercially available chipset for FDDI-based ATM. The fiber optic media and signal characteristics specified for TAXI communication are exactly the same as those defined in the FDDI standard ISO 9314-3. The ATM cells are 4B/5B-encoded and transmitted without any additional framing. In 4B/5B encoding, 4 bits of data are transmitted as symbols of 5 bits. This is due to the requirement that no more than three '1' bits occur in a row. The bit sequence 1111 is coded as 11101, for example. Of the 32 possible 5-bit symbols, only 16 are used to transmit data (a byte is represented by a symbol pair). Some of the remaining 16 symbols are used as line state or control symbols in FDDI and some others are unusable as they have long runs of 1s or 0s. The symbol pair sequence JK, for example, announces the beginning of an FDDI frame; the I or Idle symbol is used as a continuous padding-bit stream for clock synchronization. The beginning of an ATM cell is marked by the control symbol pair sequence TT. In TAXI, the JK sequence is used as an idle symbol and is sent when there are no assigned cells to send (unassigned and idle cells are not used in the TAXI interface – this is a truly "asynchronous" interface). In case of noise, interfaces resynchronize only when the next idle signal is received. If higher cell losses are tolerable, fewer idle symbols may be required, but not less than one every 0.5 seconds. The MIC connector described in ISO 9314-3, customary in FDDI networks, is also used in TAXI. The TAXI interface is now obsolete, as STM-1/OC-3 interfaces have become commonplace in the local area, offering a higher bandwidth.

ATM Cell Streams at 25.6 Mbit/s

Originally developed to allow the economical connection of workstation computers to ATM networks but more recently associated with ATM over ADSL modem interfaces, a further specification for a 25.6 Mbit/s ATM interface was developed independently of the cell-based physical layer interfaces described previously. The ATM Forum specification calls for Cat. 3 100   UTP (unshielded twisted pair), 120   Cat. 4 (ISO/IEC11801) or 150   STP (shielded twisted pair). As for the TAXI interface, the bit stream is 4B/5B-encoded (the actual coding is different from TAXI) and transmitted asynchronously without further framing. The transfer rate of 25.6 Mbit/s with 4B/5B encoding implies a line rate of 32 Mbaud. This interface is closely based on an original specification developed by IBM and is derived from Token-Ring technology.

The specified maximum segment length for all three cable types is 100 m (90 m plus 10 m for patch cables). The cables must also conform to the values specified in EIA/TIA-568-A or ISO/IEC 11801 for attenuation and near-end crosstalk (NEXT). The connectors are RJ-45 for Cat. 3 UTP or STP-MIC for shielded twisted pair.

ATM and DXI Interfaces

The Data Exchange Interface (DXI) is a simple transmission protocol developed for interfaces such as V.35, EIA/TIA 449/530 or EIA/TIA 612/613 (HSSI). Originally, DXI was conceived as a data tributary protocol for metropolitan area networks (SMDS-DXI, SMDS Interest Group Technical Specification SIG-TS-005/1993). For lack of an ATM-specific DXI to connect their systems to ATM networks, many manufacturers began by implementing the simpler SMDS-DXI as an interface protocol. The ATM Forum subsequently drafted a DXI variant tailored to the requirements of ATM (af-dxi-0014).

The functions of ATM DXI are divided into user-end processes (Data Terminal Equipment or DTE, Modes 1a and 1b) and network-end processes (Data Communications Equipment or DCE, Mode 2). In Mode 1a, user interfaces support up to 1,023 virtual connections with AAL5 Protocol Data Units or PDUs and data packets (Service Data Units or SDUs) of up to 9,232 bytes. The DTE SDUs, which correspond to AAL5 PDUs, are encapsulated in DXI frames for transmission. Mode 1b also supports AAL3/4 with a maximum SDU length of 9,224 bytes. The

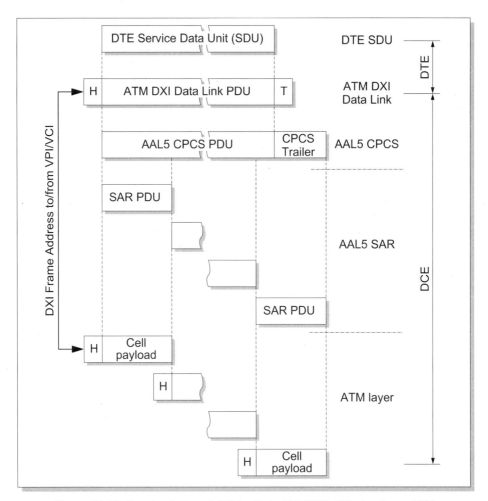

Figure 10.17 Encapsulation of ATM cells in DXI PDUs (Modes 1a and 1b)

AAL3/4 PDUs are encapsulated by the DTE, but all segmentation and reassembly (AAL3/4 SAR) must be performed by the DCE (Figure 10.17).

In Mode 2, network interfaces support up to 16,777,215 virtual connections for AAL5 and AAL3/4. SDUs can be up to 65,535 bytes long.

The DXI frame address (DFA) is carried in the DXI header. It is used to convey the VPI and VCI information between DTEs (Data Terminal Equipment) and DCEs (Data Communication Equipment). The DFA is 10 bits long in Modes 1a and 1b, and 24 bits long in Mode 2 (Figure 10.18). Note that no ATM cells are involved at this interface, only AAL frames.

Flag	DXI header	DTE SDU	DXI FCS	Flag
1	2	$0 < N \leq 9232$	2	1
		(Bytes)		

Figure 10.18 DXI data packet for Modes 1a and 1b (DTE, AAL5)

ATM Physical Layer Operations and Maintenance (OAM F1 – F3)

A total of five information flows are defined for operations and maintenance of ATM networks, called the OAM flows. Each of these flows, numbered F1 to F5, is responsible for the monitoring of a certain part of a connection. Flows F1 to F3 are concerned with the physical layer of the B-ISDN protocol model; F4 and F5 with virtual paths (VP) and virtual channels (VC) in the ATM layer. The OAM parameters are determined by different mechanisms depending on the network topology used for ATM cell transport (SDH/SONET, PDH, cell-based physical layer). A transmission path is defined as the path between two network components that insert the user data into the transport medium and extract it again from the medium. Examples of transmission paths include the link between a B-NT2 and a switch (VP cross-connect), or between a B-NT2 and the connection end point. A transmission path is composed of several digital sections, each of which may lead through one or more regenerator sections.

OAM F1 – F3 for SDH/SONET-Based ATM Systems

In SDH/SONET-based ATM networks, the OAM flows F1 and F2 are transported in the SOH/TOH of the transport frames, and F3 in the POH of the given virtual container /SPE. Part of the F3 information can also be transported in specially indicated physical layer OAM cells (PL-OAM).

OAM F1 – F3 for PDH-Based ATM Systems

In PDH networks, F1 and F3 information can be transported in the PDH header. The frame alignment byte of the header is analyzed for F1 functions, while F3 parameters are taken from the remaining header bytes. There is no provision for an F2 flow.

OAM F1 – F3 for Cell-Based Physical Layer

In cell-based physical layer networks, the OAM information flows are transmitted by means of special physical layer OAM cells (PL-OAM cells). As described in I.432.2, evaluation of OAM-F1 and OAM-F3 is provided for, but there is no provision for an F2 flow. The corresponding parameters are communicated as part of F3. PL-OAM cells may be inserted in the cell stream no more than once every 27 data cells, and no less than once in 513 cells. The F1 cell contains OAM parameters for the regenerator section; F3 cells are used to monitor the trans-

OAM flow	Byte 1	Byte 2	Byte 3	Byte 4	Byte 5
F1	0000000	0000000	0000000	0000011	Valid HEC = 0101110
F3	0000000	0000000	0000000	0001001	Valid HEC = 0110101

Because the PL OAM cells are not passed to the ATM layer, the field values are of no significance as ATM cells.

Figure 10.19 PL-OAM cell headers

Byte		Byte		Byte		
1	R	17	R	33	EB4	EB3
2	AIS	18	R	34	EB6	EB5
3	PSN	19	R	35	EB8	EB7
4	NIC	20	R	36	R	
5		21	R	37	R	
6	MBS	22	R	38	R	
7	NMB-EDC	23	R	39	R	
8	EDC-B1	24	R	40	R	
9	EDC-B2	25	R	41	R	
10	EDC-B3	26	R	42	R	
11	EDC-B4	27	R	43	R	
12	EDC-B5	28	R	44	R	
13	EDC-B6	29	R	45	R	
14	EDC-B7	30	RDI (1)	46	STET	
15	EDC-B8	31	NMB-EB	47	CEC (10)	
16	R	32	EB2 EB1	48		

Figure 10.20 PL-OAM cell format for F1 and F3 cells

mission path. OAM cells have a special header that makes them easily reco-gnizable (Figure 10.19). Note that the lower limit of 27 exists to allow easier interworking between cell-based interfaces running at 155 Mbit/s and 622 Mbit/s and the corresponding SDH/SONET interfaces (STM-1/OC-3 and STM-4c/OC-12) because the overhead in SDH/SONET (SOH/TOH + POH) occu-pies exactly 1/27 of the bandwidth (that is, 9+1 columns out of 270).

Figure 10.20 illustrates the structure of PL-OAM F1 and F3 cells. The following fields are reserved for the F1 and F3 flows:

OAM-F1 Cell Fields

PSN	PL-OAM Sequential Number (8 bits, modulo 256)
NIC	Number of Included Cells (maximum value: 512)
MBS	Monitoring Block Size (maximum value: 64)
NMB-EDC	Number of Monitored Blocks (recommended value: 8)
EDC	Error Detection Code (BIP 8 value calculated from the cells of the MBS)
NMB-EB	Number of Monitored Blocks at the Far End (recommended value: 8)
REI	Remote Error Indication (number of bit parity errors in each block)
AIS	Alarm Indication Signal (an AIS sent downstream to report an upstream error) (AIS-L for SONET)
RDI	Remote Defect Indicator (sent upstream to report a reception failure downstream. This occurs when frame synchronization or the data signal is lost, for example.)
CRC	CRC-10 Checksum
R	Reserved (set to 01101010)

OAM-F3 Cell Fields

PSN	PL-OAM Sequential Number (8 bits, modulo 256)
NIC	Number of Included Cells (maximum value: 512)
MBS	Monitoring Block Size (maximum value: 64)
NMB-EDC	Number of Monitored Blocks (EDC octets) (recommended value: 8)
EDC	Error Detection Code (BIP 8 - Bit Interleaved Parity - value calculated from the cells of the MBS)

NMB-EB   Number of Monitored Blocks at the Far End
          (recommended value: 8)

REI   Remote Error Indication
          (number of bit parity errors in each block) (REI-P for SONET)

AIS   Alarm Indication Signal (AIS-P for SONET)

TP-RDI   Transmission Remote Defect Indicator
          (formerly TP-FERF) (RDI-P for SONET)

CRC   CRC-10 Checksum

R   Reserved (set to 01101010)

10.1.7   The ATM Layer

The actual transport of ATM cells takes place at the ATM layer. In order to provide for the varying connection quality requirements of different applications, Quality-of-Service (QoS) parameters are first negotiated in the signaling process or provisioned by the network operator. After a successful connection setup transmission begins with the ATM cells of virtual channel connections (VCCs) and virtual path connections (VPCs) multiplexed in a continuous cell stream. During the connection, monitoring and control mechanisms operate to ensure that the connection parameters agreed upon in the ATM switching negotiation are maintained.

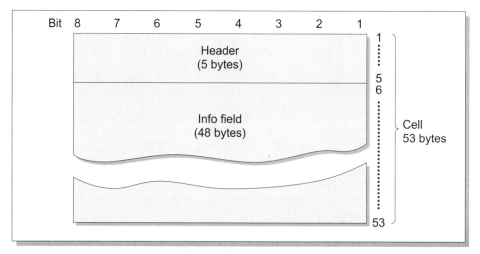

Figure 10.21 ATM cell

An ATM cell consists of a 5-byte header and a 48-byte information or user data field. There are two basic types of cells, UNI cells and NNI cells. UNI cells are transferred at user–network interfaces, NNI cells at network–node interfaces. The two cell types differ only in 4 header bits, which are specified for flow control in UNI cells (though, in reality not used for this) and to extend the virtual path identification (VPI) field to 12 bits in NNI cells.

Bit 8 is the most significant bit in all fields. The bits within each byte are therefore transmitted beginning with bit 8. The bytes in turn are transmitted in ascending order, that is, beginning with byte 1. Figure 10.22 illustrates the header structure of UNI cells. The header consists of the six fields GFC (4 bits), VPI (8 bits), VCI (16 bits), PT (3 bits), CLP (1 bit) and HEC (8 bits).

Byte \ Bit	8	7	6	5	4	3	2	1
1	Generic Flow Control (GFC)				Virtual Path ID (VPI)			
2	Virtual Path ID (VPI)				Virtual Channel ID (VCI)			
3	Virtual Channel ID (VCI)							
4	Virtual Channel ID (VCI)				Payload Type (PT)			CLP
5	Header Error Control (HEC)							

CLP: Cell Loss Priority

Figure 10.22 UNI cell header

The Generic Flow Control Field (GFC)

The generic flow control field, which consists of 4 bits, is used to control local functions and to manage access and transmission rights in ATM networks. Its contents are not forwarded beyond the range of the local ATM switch because this field is replaced with VPI data at the NNI. Its significance is thus limited to the local ATM network segment. In practice, although specified by the ITU-T in Recommendation I.361, generic flow control has seldom, if ever, been implemented, and the ATM Forum in particular does not support this function.

The ATM Routing Label Field (VPI-VCI)

The UNI header contains a total of 24 bits for ATM layer routing purposes: 8 bits for the Virtual Path Identifier (VPI) and 16 bits for the Virtual Channel Identifier

(VCI). The VPI-VCI value is a label that has only local significance, that is, between two ATM interfaces in a single transmission link. This label has no end-to-end significance, which is why the VPI-VCI field is referred to as a label, not an address. There is such a thing as an ATM Address that is used in connection with signaling (see the section on *Connection Setup at the Caller's End*), and some publications do refer, incorrectly, to the VPI-VCI as an address. The value of the VPI-VCI field changes as cells of a given virtual connection pass through ATM switches. The "translation" of the VPI-VCI label value is determined by the contents of a "translation table" whose contents are determined by the signaling process, in the case of switched virtual connections (SVCs); network management provisioning, in the case of (semi-) permanent virtual connections (PVCs); or a label distribution protocol, in the case of multiprotocol label switching (MPLS).

An ATM virtual channel (VC) refers to a two-way transmission link for ATM cells, although both directions may not always be used. All cells in a given virtual channel have the same VCI value in a given link. Several ATM virtual channels may be carried within an ATM virtual path (VP). As with the virtual channel, all cells transported by a given ATM virtual path are identified by a particular VPI. Rather than the physical channels and paths familiar from older telecommunications techniques, the ATM concept of virtual paths permits substantially more efficient use of available bandwidth.

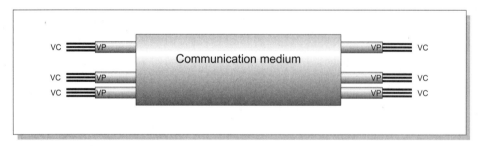

Figure 10.23 Virtual channels (VCI) and virtual paths (VPI)

The Payload Type Field (PT)

Three bits of the ATM header are used to identify the type of data the cell payload contains. This makes it possible to distinguish between ordinary user data and various special types, such as traffic or network management information, for example. The default value of the PT field is 000.

Cell Loss Priority (CLP)

The cell loss priority bit can be used to assign cells a relative priority. If the CLP bit is set to 1, the cell has low priority; 0 indicates normal (higher) priority. If the capacity of a connection is exceeded, or if other transmission problems arise, cells with low priority are discarded first.

Header Error Control (HEC)

Before an ATM cell is transmitted, a cyclic redundancy check (CRC) of the entire cell header is calculated and placed in the 8-bit header error control field. At the receiving end of each link, the header is checked to see if the HEC value is correct; it would normally only be correct if there were no bit errors anywhere in the header. If a single bit error has occurred somewhere in the header, including the HEC itself (because of physical layer bit errors, for example), there is sufficient redundancy in the HEC to allow that bit error to be corrected. Similarly, two bit errors will always be detectable. However, the detection of three or more bit errors in the header may not be detectable. For example, multiple bit errors may change the header such that it becomes a header with a different (corrupt) VPI-VCI value and for which the (corrupt) HEC is "correct". If the new VPI-VCI value happened to be a "legal" value, that is, one belonging to an existing virtual connection, the cell with the corrupt header would be misinserted into this other virtual connection (and, of course, lost from the

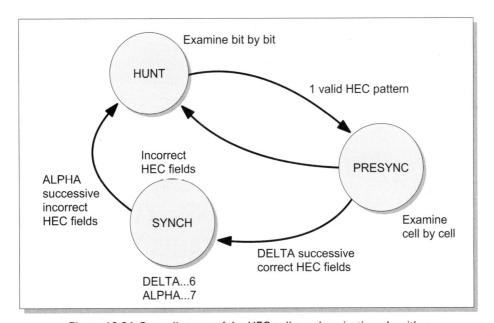

Figure 10.24 State diagram of the HEC cell synchronization algorithm

connection to which it really belongs). However, if the new VPI-VCI value was not supported, the switch would not forward it but would discard it because no translation table entry for it would exist. Note that some interfaces restrict the use of the HEC to detecting errors but not correcting them; this is because certain types of physical layer scrambling can give rise to error multiplication, making reliable correction impossible.

In addition to bit-error detection (and correction), the HEC field also allows receiving stations to synchronize with the beginning of the cell. This process is called "cell delineation".

The following algorithm is applied in order to detect the beginning of an ATM cell in a bit stream:

- In the HUNT state, the incoming signal is analyzed bit-by-bit to determine whether it could be part of an HEC pattern. As soon as a potential HEC pattern has been found, the receiver changes to the PRESYNC state.

- Under the assumption that a cell has been detected, the PRESYNC state examines subsequent "candidate cells". If the HEC fields of the next DELTA candidate cells are also possible checksums, then the receiver assumes that it has synchronized with the cell stream, and switches to the SYNC state and cell synchronization or "delineation" is declared. If less than DELTA consecutive cells meet the HEC test, the receiving station reverts to the HUNT state.

- If ALPHA consecutive cells fail the HEC test, the receiver in SYNC state assumes it has lost its cell delineation and switches to HUNT state. Loss of Cell Delineation (LCD) is then declared.

- For SDH/SONET physical layers the value of ALPHA and DELTA are 7 and 6 respectively; for cell-based physical layers these values are 7 and 8 respectively (see ITU-T Recommendation I.432.1).

Data Field Scrambling

The data field (payload) of the ATM cells is scrambled in order to optimize cell delineation by HEC patterns. In the HUNT state, potential HEC sequences are easier to detect when the data is scrambled. In the PRESYNC and SYNC states, an unscrambling function is activated for the 48 user data bytes of the cell, but is not applied to the cell headers. In all framing types except cell-based physical layer, the scrambling of the data field is always based on the self-synchronizing scrambler (SSS) $x^{43}+1$; scrambling is optional in some interface types. Due to the relatively poor overall communication characteristics of the SSS process, cell-based physical layer uses Distributed Sample Scrambling (DSS) with the generator polynomial $x^{31}+x^{28}+1$. Note that, because the scrambling takes place within the transmission convergence sublayer of the physical layer for non cell-based interfaces, all cells at the interface are scrambled using the SSS process, independent of the header routing label value (VPI-VCI) and including any idle/ unassigned and OAM cells, etc.

Reserved Header Values

Certain header values are reserved for cells with special operation, management or signaling functions in the ATM network. Such cells include broadcasts, meta-signaling, resource management cells and, in cell-based physical layer, PL-OAM cells. All special cells have a VCI value in the range 0 through 31; the ITU-T reserves to itself all values of VCI below 16 and makes available all values between 16 and 31 for proprietary purposes; the ATM Forum has used several values in this range for its purposes (for example, VCI = 16 is used for ILMI, VCI = 17 is used for LANE, VCI = 18 is used for PNNI). With the exception of these defined values, all values (VCI = 32 and above) can be used for user traffic by the ATM layer. Figure 10.25 lists the reserved header byte values (ITU-T Recommendation I.361). Furthermore, the ITU-T recommendations and ATM Forum specifications define certain UNI cell header values as reserved. These are listed in Figure 10.26.

Reserved Header Bytes in UNI ATM cells (ITU I.361, I.432)				
	Byte 1	Byte 2	Byte 3	Byte 4
Reserved for physical layer [1, 2]	PPPP 0000	0000 0000	0000 0000	0000 PPP1
Physical layer F1 OAM cell	0000 0000	0000 0000	0000 0000	0000 0011
Physical layer F3 OAM cell	0000 0000	0000 0000	0000 0000	0000 1001
IMA ICP cell	0000 0000	0000 0000	0000 0000	0000 1011
Idle cells	0000 0000	0000 0000	0000 0000	0000 0001
Unassigned cells	AAAA 0000	0000 0000	0000 0000	0000 AAA0

A ...... Bit available for use by the ATM layer
P ...... Bit available for use by the physical layer
[1] .... In cells with the VPI-VCI value equal to 0-0, the four bits normally used to represent the PT and CLP fields are reinterpreted to distinguish between different types of unassigned and physical layer cells.
[2] .... Cells identified by header information as physical layer cells are not passed to the ATM layer.

Reserved VPI and VCI Values in UNI ATM cells (ITU I.361)

	VPI	VCI
Meta-signaling channel	0000 0000	0000 0000 0000 0001
Broadcast signaling channel	0000 0000	0000 0000 0000 0010

Figure 10.25 Reserved header bytes and VPI/VCI values

Use	Value[1,2,3,4]			
	Octet 1	Octet 2	Octet 3	Octet 4
Unassigned cell indication	00000000	00000000	00000000	0000xxx0
Meta-signalling (default) [5,7]	00000000	00000000	00000000	00010a0c
Meta-signalling [6,7]	0000yyyy	yyyy0000	00000000	00010a0c
General Broadcast signalling (default) [5]	00000000	00000000	00000000	00100aac
General Broadcast signalling [6]	0000yyyy	yyyy0000	00000000	00100aac
Point-to-point signalling (default) [5]	00000000	00000000	00000000	01010aac
Point-to-point signalling [6]	0000yyyy	yyyy0000	00000000	01010aac
Invalid Pattern	xxxx0000	00000000	00000000	0000xxx1
Segment OAM F4 flow cell [7]	0000aaaa	aaaa0000	00000000	00110a0a
End-to-End OAM F4 flow cell [7]	0000aaaa	aaaa0000	00000000	01000a0a

[1] ..... "a" indicates that the bit is available for use by the appropriate ATM layer function.
[2] ..... "x" indicates "don't care" bits.
[3] ..... "y" indicates any VPI value other than 00000000.
[4] ..... "c" indicates that the originating signalling entity shall set the CLP bit to 0. The network may change the value of the CLP bit.
[5] ..... Reserved for user signalling with the local exchange.
[6] ..... Reserved for signalling with other signalling entities (e.g. other users or remote networks).
[7] ..... The transmitting ATM entity shall set bit 2 of octet 4 to zero. The receiving ATM entity shall ignore bit 2 of octet 4.

Figure 10.26 Header bytes reserved by the ATM Forum

The NNI Header

Unlike the UNI header, the NNI header provides 28 bits for addressing: 12 bits for the VPI and 16 bits for the VCI. This permits the definition of a greater number of virtual paths at the network-node interface. The payload type field, the priority bit and the HEC field correspond with the same fields in the UNI cell header. Figure 10.27 lists the reserved byte values in the NNI header:

	Byte 1	Byte 2	Byte 3	Byte 4
Reserved for physical layer [1,2]	0000 0000	0000 0000	0000 0000	0000 PPP1
Physical layer OAM cell	0000 0000	0000 0000	0000 0000	0000 1001
Idle cells	0000 0000	0000 0000	0000 0000	0000 0001
IMA ICP	0000 0000	0000 0000	0000 0000	0000 1011
Unassigned cells	AAAA 0000	0000 0000	0000 0000	0000 AAA0

A ...... Bit available for use by the ATM layer
P ...... Bit available for use by the physical layer
[1] .... In cells with the VPI-VCI value equal to 0-0, the four bits normally used to represent the PT and CLP fields are reinterpreted to distinguish between different types of unassigned and physical layer cells.
[2] .... Cells identified by header information as physical layer cells are not passed to the ATM layer.

Figure 10.27 Reserved header bytes in the NNI ATM cell

ATM Cell Types

In addition to user ATM cells (cells whose VCI > 31), there are several types of cells that are used not to transport user data, but to perform certain operational functions. These include idle cells, unassigned cells, PL-OAM cells, ICP cells, RM cells and VP/VC-OAM cells. Note that in cells having a VPI-VCI = 0-0, the least 4 bits in the 4th byte normally used to convey the PT and CLP fields are re-assigned for other purposes (see Figure 10.27).

Idle Cells

Idle cells are physical layer cells and carry no useful information. They are used to adapt the cell rate to the bandwidth of the transmission medium. If there are not enough ordinary cells to fill the allocated bandwidth, idle cells are inserted by the transmission convergence Sublayer. This permits alignment of the ATM cell stream with the throughput of the physical medium (such as an SDH-VC4 container/SONET SPE). Unlike unassigned cells, idle cells are not passed to the ATM layer. The ATM Forum, following the Bellcore definition, calls the idle cell header pattern an "invalid header", revealing some confusion in the minds of Bellcore (and hence ATM Forum) specifiers (see *Unassigned Cells* for more on this). See Figure 10.27.

Unassigned Cells

Unassigned cells (VPI-VCI = 0-0) are ATM layer cells and carry no useful payload information. They are used when no assigned cells are available to send from the ATM layer. At the receiver, they are treated similarly to idle cells and discarded. In North America (and implementations elsewhere based on certain ATM Forum specifications), unassigned cells are used where the ITU-T would specify idle cells; in particular, they are specified for rate adaption by the ATM Forum, adopting Bellcore usage which, strictly, conflicts with ITU-T usage. Despite this confusion, idle and unassigned cells can normally be considered equivalent. See Figure 10.27.

Physical Layer OAM Cells

In the cell-based physical layer, special cells can be inserted up to once in every 27 cells to transmit operation and maintenance information concerning the physical layer. These are called PL-OAM cells. When received, these cells are used by the physical layer and not passed along to the ATM layer. Their purpose is to convey some of the information (such as alarms) normally carried by the overhead of frame-based physical layers, such as SONET.

IMA Control Protocol (ICP) Cells

These are special control cells used with implementations of the ATM Forum's Inverse Multiplexing for ATM specification.

VP-OAM and VC-OAM Cells

VP-OAM and VC-OAM cells are used to transport the F4 and F5 maintenance flows respectively. This information allows the network to monitor and test the capacities and availability of ATM virtual paths and virtual channels. VP-OAM cells use reserved values of VCI = 3 and 4 for each VPI value for segment and end-to-end F4 OAM flows respectively; VC-OAM cells use a reserved value of PT field = 100 (binary 4) and 101 (binary 5) for each value of VPI-VCI for segment and end-to-end F5 OAM flows.

VP/VC-RM Cells

These are resource management cells used, so far, for implementations of the available bit rate (ABR) traffic type. VP-RM cells have a reserved value of VCI = 6, VC-RM cells have a reserved PT field value of 110 (binary 6).

VP/VC Cells

VP/VC cells are common cells used for communication within ATM virtual channels (VCs) and virtual paths (VPs). VP/VC cells can be of the following five types:

- User data transport cells (any VPI, VCI > 31)
- Metasignaling cells (VPI = 0, VCI = 1)
- Broadcast signaling cells (VCI = 2)
- Point-to-point signaling cells (VCI = 5)
- ILMI cells for ATM network management (VPI-VCI = 0-16)

User data are assigned to a specific connection by their VPI/VCI values and transport data for higher-layer services in the 48-byte payload field. Meta-signaling cells were originally conceived to select and define signaling virtual channels. Because meta-signaling is not used in present-day networks, however, these cells do not occur in actual practice. Broadcast signaling cells are used to send signaling information to all network stations. Network nodes that do not support broadcast signaling simply ignore all cells in the broadcast virtual channel, VCI 2. VCI 5 cells are used for point-to-point signaling. For this reason the virtual channel VCI 5 is also called the signaling virtual channel. Finally, ILMI cells are used for ATM network local management tasks at the UNI, which include registration of new active stations with the ATM switch, querying ATM MIBs or configuring network components.

ATM Connections

In order to manage the wide variety of communication situations in ATM networks, the ATM layer provides for different connection types with different characteristics. Both virtual channel and virtual path connections can be structured as point-to-point or point-to-multipoint. The bandwidth allocated to a connection can also be asymmetric: that is, the bandwidth for transmission can be lower than for reception, or vice versa. Furthermore, a number of Quality-of-Service (QoS) parameters can be negotiated for each connection.

Virtual Channel Connections (VCCs)

ATM virtual channels represent the lowest level in the structural hierarchy of ATM data streams. All virtual channel connections have the following four properties:

- The ATM switch assigns each virtual channel connection QoS parameters, that define properties such as cell loss ratio or cell delay.

- Virtual channel connections can be either dynamically switched (SVC) or (semi-) permanent (PVC).

- The sequential order of cells in a virtual channel is preserved during transportation through the ATM network (the virtual channel is "connection-oriented").

- For each virtual channel connection, traffic parameters, such as the maximum bandwidth available for the connection; the result is the "traffic contract". Cells sent to the network by the user are monitored to ensure conformance with the traffic contract.

A VCC can be set up by using four different signaling methods:

- No signaling (for example, a (semi-) permanent connection is set up through network management)

- Meta-signaling

- User-to-network signaling

- Network-to-network signaling

Setting up permanent or semi-permanent VCCs is a good idea especially when a relatively low number of network nodes need to be interconnected over statically defined connections, or when dynamic signaling processes are undesired for security reasons. In ATM networks with a large number of nodes, connections are set up dynamically over individual transmission sections using signaling protocols:

UNI<>NNI   Signaling from an end system into an ATM network that consists of several networked switches (user-to-network)

NNI<>NNI   Signaling within an ATM network that consists of several networked switches (network-to-network)

Meta-signaling is not used in practice because the use of the reserved signaling virtual channel, VCI 5, has been found to be sufficient even in large ATM networks.

Virtual Path Connections (VPCs)

Virtual path connections are a hierarchical level above virtual channel connections. In other words, a virtual path can contain several virtual channels (note, however, that in terms of the layered model, the VC is above the VP in the stack). VPCs have the same properties as VCCs. Path connections can likewise be set up manually as permanent virtual paths, or on request by means of signaling processes or network management functions. One aspect of VPC worth noting is that, while the VPI of a VPC changes at every switching node in the network, the VCI values of all VCs within the VP are preserved end-to-end.

Quality-of-Service (QoS) Parameters

In ATM networks, services with widely differing communication requirements are transported concurrently. Real-time applications with varying bit rates are much more exacting with regard to average cell delay, for example, than simple data transfers at a constant bit rate. For this reason, the ATM layer assigns each connection QoS parameters that specify certain characteristics of the connection when the connection is set up. ITU-T Recommendation I.356 defines seven cell transfer performance parameters:

- Cell Error Ratio
- Severely Errored Cell Block Ratio
- Cell Loss Ratio
- Cell Misinsertion Rate
  (the proportion of cells with a valid but incorrect header)
- Cell Transfer Delay
- Mean Cell Transfer Delay
- Cell Delay Variation

On connection setup, any user can request a "traffic contract" that specifies a particular QoS class for each direction of communication. Once the traffic contract has been negotiated, the ATM network, or rather the ATM switches along the transfer path, guarantee the QoS parameters granted for as long as the user respects the traffic contract. A distinction is made between service classes with defined QoS parameters and service classes without performance parameters. QoS classes with performance parameters must specify at least two such parameters. If a QoS class contains two parameters for cell loss ratio, then one value applies to cells with a cell loss priority (CLP) of 1, and the other to cells with CLP=0. Performance parameters that can be specified in a QoS class include:

- Maximum Cell Transfer Delay
- Cell Delay Variation
- Cell Loss Ratio for cells with CLP = 0
- Cell Loss Ratio for cells with CLP = 1

Quality-of-service classes and traffic parameters are defined for each of the six service classes defined in the ATM Forum's Traffic Management specification:

- CBR   Constant Bit Rate
- rt-VBR   Real-Time Variable Bit Rate
- nrt-VBR Non-Real-Time Variable Bit Rate
- UBR   Unspecified Bit Rate
- ABR   Available Bit Rate
- GFR   Guaranteed Frame Rate

A service class can be requested without QoS parameters, such as in a request for a connection with the "best possible network service", for example. Such a request, in which no QoS parameters are specified, may be made when no explicit network performance guarantee is required. The load level and error frequency in ATM networks have a direct influence on the QoS parameters.

ATM Payload Types (PT)

Ordinary user data cells can be distinguished from special-purpose, non-user cells by means of the payload type field. The PT values 0, 1, 2 and 3 identify user data cells; 4, 5 and 6 indicate virtual channel segment OAM, end-to-end OAM, and resource management (RM) cells respectively. Figure 10.28 lists the possible values of the payload type field.

Payload type field	Meaning
000	User data cell, no congestion detected SDU type = 0
001	User data cell, no congestion detected SDU type = 1
010	User data cell, congestion detected SDU type = 0
011	User data cell, congestion detected SDU type = 1
100	Segment OAM F5 cell
101	End-to-end OAM F5 cell
110	VC resource management
111	Reserved for future use

Figure 10.28 Payload type field

Cell Loss Priority and Selective Discarding of Cells

To protect the network from users who produce unauthorized traffic loads or otherwise violate their traffic contract, each station's data stream is monitored by the Usage Parameter Control (UPC). This entity analyzes and regulates the cell stream on each virtual path and virtual channel connection. The UPC can act in three ways at the cell level to regulate the data stream: each cell can be passed along, tagged or discarded. Cell passing is the normal transfer of all cells that conform to the traffic contract. Cell tagging is performed on traffic that does not conform to the sustainable cell rate for one particular traffic contract type (VBR.3/SBR3). When such cells are tagged, their CLP value is changed by the UPC from 0 (normal priority) to 1 (low priority). In case of network congestion, these cells will then be among the first to be discarded. If cell tagging is not supported, then cells that do not conform to the traffic contract are discarded immediately.

Traffic Shaping

The traffic contract negotiated during the connection setup includes a Connection Traffic Descriptor that defines the parameters for permissible traffic, including peak cell rate, duration of the peak cell rate (maximum burst size, MBS), etc. A transmitting station can then force its communication to conform to the negotiated traffic contract by means of the optional traffic shaping function. Another user strategy would be to send all queued cells as they occur, and simply tolerate tagging of high-priority cells (if supported) and discarding of low-priority cells.

340

Monitoring in ATM Networks (OAM Flows)

Of the five ATM network operations and maintenance information flows F1 through F5, F4 and F5 are situated in the ATM layer. All F4 and F5 OAM information is gathered and transmitted by means of special OAM cells. The F4 information flow is used for segment or end-to-end management at the virtual path level. A segment refers to one section of a connection, such as the link between two ATM switches (more than one switch may exist within a section); end-to-end refers to the entire communication path between the two endpoints for the complete virtual path. The information flow F5 is used for segment or end-to-end management at the virtual channel level; in this case, end-to-end refers to the entire communication channel between the two endpoints for the complete virtual channel, which may be longer than the virtual path. The purpose of F4 and F5 OAM cells is to provide the measurement data necessary to monitor the availability and performance of a given virtual channel or virtual path. Figure 10.29 lists the individual OAM functions of the ATM layer.

OAM function	Use
AIS (Alarm Indication Signal)	Error reports in the direction of transmission
RDI (Remote Defect Indication)	Error reports from the receiving system
Continuity check	Continuous monitoring of cell transport
Loopback	• Monitoring connections as needed • Localizing errors • Testing connections before making a link available
Forward performance monitoring	Estimating performance in the direction of transmission
Backward reporting	Returning results of forward performance monitoring
Activation/Deactivation	Activating or deactivating performance monitoring and continuity checking
System management	Managing by the given end systems
APS	ATM protection switching

Figure 10.29 ATM layer OAM functions

OAM Cell Format

The F4 OAM cells that transport management and monitoring information for virtual path connections have the same VPI value as the user cells on the virtual path being monitored. They are identified as F4 cells by the reserved VCI value 3 for F4 segment cells or 4 for F4 end-to-end cells. F5 OAM cells have the same VPI and VCI values as the user cells of the virtual channel connection to which they are related. They are identified by the payload type field (PT). The PT value 100 (decimal 4) denotes F5 segment OAM cells; 101 (decimal 5) indicates an F5 end-to-end OAM cell. End-to-end OAM cells must pass unchanged through all network nodes between the two connection endpoints. Only the endpoints may remove them from the cell stream. Segment OAM cells must be removed from the stream at the end of the given segment. There are five types of ATM-layer OAM cell: fault management, APS coordination protocol, performance management, activation/deactivation cells and system management. The OAM cell type is indicated by the first (4 bit) field in the OAM cell payload.

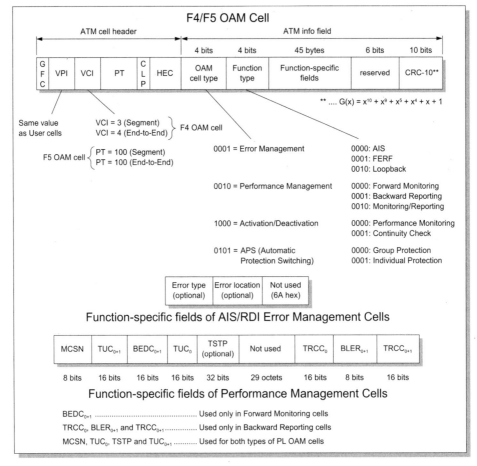

Figure 10.30 F4 and F5 OAM cell format

Fault management OAM cells are used to detect and localize communication faults and report them to the stations concerned. Performance management OAM cells detect parameters such as the cell block ratio, cell loss ratio, or the cell misinsertion rate, and thus provide information about the performance of a connection. APS coordination protocol OAM cells are used to manage ATM protection switching. Activation/deactivation cells are used to start and stop OAM functions such as error or performance management. The fourth OAM cell type, system management cells, has no defined purpose in the specifications: its usage is left to individual manufacturers' implementations.

OAM Fault Management (AIS/RDI)

In analogy to *SDH/SONET*, fault management in the ATM layer involves two kinds of alarm signals, Alarm Indication Signal (AIS) and Remote Defect Indication (RDI). The VP-AIS or VC-AIS is sent by the virtual path or virtual channel node that detects the fault downstream to all network nodes directly affected. The VP/VC-AIS OAM cell is transmitted periodically (approximately 2 second intervals) until the fault is eliminated. Immediately after the AIS has been sent, a VP-RDI or VC-AIS OAM cell is sent upstream to the endpoint of the virtual path or virtual channel connection concerned. This OAM cell is likewise repeated periodically as long as the AIS condition persists. VP-AIS and VP-RDI messages are always transmitted by means of cells with VCI = 4, while VC-AIS and VC-RDI messages are transported in cells with PT = 101.

A fault at the virtual path level inevitably affects the virtual channels contained within that virtual path. This faulty virtual path may terminate at a switch before the endpoint of these virtual channels, which will continue in one or more new virtual paths determined by switching. It is therefore necessary that the virtual channels affected continue to be notified of the fault condition. This is not done by propagating AIS or RDI on the F4 flows of the new virtual paths, which would be misleading because the new virtual paths probably are not themselves faulty. Instead, the fault management system causes the fault condition to propagate upwards to the F5 (virtual channel) flow level at the endpoints of the faulty virtual path and VC-OAM cells now carry RDI or AIS fault signals over all virtual channels that were contained in the original faulty virtual path. This can obviously result in an explosion of fault indications, of course, but this is inevitable if full fault management is to be achieved.

Fault management uses two mechanisms to detect fault conditions: continuity checks (CC) and loopback tests. Continuity check cells can be inserted in the user data stream at regular intervals to provide continuous verification of the availability of a connection. The ATM network nodes along the connection path can then monitor the presence of these cells. If expected CC cells are not received, loss of continuity (LOC) is signaled by AIS OAM cells. The insertion of

CC cells is useful where user traffic is intermittent because the absence of user traffic does not necessarily mean that the virtual connection has been terminated. Without CC cells, there would be no cells at all belonging to that virtual connection for perhaps long periods so, if a fault had occurred during this period, there would be no other mechanism to recognize this.

Loopback Cells

Loopback cells are used to verify connections to specific sections of the ATM network. There are five distinct kinds of loopback tests: end-to-end, access-line, inter-domain, network-to-endpoint, and intra-domain.

End-to-end loopback cells sent to one endpoint of a VP or VC connection are sent back to the originating endpoint. The connection may cross several subnetworks or "operator domains". In this way the entire connection is tested from end system to end system. By contrast, access line loopback cells are returned by the first ATM network node that receives them. This tests exactly one connection section or segment. Inter-domain loopback cells are reflected by the first network node of a neighboring operator domain. This makes it possible to test the connection to the neighboring network. Network-to-endpoint loopback cells can be used by a network operator to test the connection out of the network to an endpoint in an adjacent network. Finally, intra-domain loopback cells can be sent from a segment node to any other node in another segment within the same operator domain. This tests the data flow across a certain sequence of segments within a domain.

Loopback cells are F4 or F5 OAM cells that contain the value 0100 in the function type field (see Figure 10.30). The function-specific fields are the Loopback Indication, the Correlation Tag, the Loopback Location ID and the Source ID. All loopback cells other than end system to end system loopback cells are segment cells; the point at which they loop back is determined by the Loopback Location ID field. If a station receives a loopback OAM cell with a value other than 0 in the Loopback Indication field, it must return the cell within one second. Stations that transmit loopback cells must do so at such an interval that the management cell traffic is less than one percent of the capacity of each virtual channel or virtual path involved in the connection. It should be obvious from the above that only the loopback OAM cells are looped; related user cells are unaffected, so loopback test can be performed safely at any time.

OAM Performance Management

In addition to faults, the performance of the individual VPs and VCs can also be monitored by the periodical insertion of special performance management OAM cells in the user cell stream. Analysis of the special measurement data contained in these cells (cell sequence number, total user cell count, time stamp, cell loss count) yields direct information about the operating condition of the given ATM connection. OAM performance management involves two distinct functions known as forward performance monitoring and backward reporting. If both functions are activated, then information is transmitted in both directions when OAM performance information about a given cell block is determined. The individual fields of performance management cells are the following:

- Monitoring cell sequence number (MCSN, 8 bits).
- Total user cell count for the CLP_{0+1} user cell flow (TUC_{0+1}, 16 bits). This is the number of cells transmitted with cell loss priority of 0 or 1 up to the time of OAM cell insertion.
- Total user cell number for the CLP_0 user cell flow (TUC_0, 16 bits). Identical to TUC_{0+1}, but counting only cells with $CLP = 0$.
- Block error detection code for the CLP_{0+1} user cell flow ($BEDC_{0+1}$, 16 bits). This field is used only in forward monitoring cells. It contains a BIP-16 checksum of the information fields of the cells transmitted since the last forward monitoring cell.
- Time Stamp (TSTP, 32 bits). This is the time at which the OAM cell was inserted in the cell stream. Currently the time stamp is optional; its use has yet to be fully defined.
- Total received cell count for the CLP_{0+1} user cell flow ($TRCC_{0+1}$, 16 bits). This field is used only in backward reporting OAM cells. It contains the number of cells received before the corresponding forward monitoring cell.
- Total received cell count for the CLP_0 user cell flow ($TRCC_0$, 16 bits). This field is used only in backward reporting OAM cells. It contains the number of cells with $CLP = 0$ received before the corresponding forward monitoring cell.
- Block error result (BLER, 8 bits). This field is used only in backward reporting OAM cells. It contains the number of incorrect parity bits determined on the basis of the BIP-16 code in the corresponding forward monitoring cell.

Performance monitoring is done over blocks of cells, the size of the blocks N being related to the peak cell rate of the virtual connection being monitored. A forward performance monitoring OAM cell is sent after each N user cell providing information about the cell block. At the receiving end, the same calculation is performed on the cells of the block and the results compared with the information in the forward performance monitoring OAM cell. The results are reported to network management and, optionally, via a backward reporting OAM cell to the originating end.

The reason for having both forward performance monitoring and backward reporting cells is that the endpoints of the monitored virtual path or virtual channel may lie in the domains of different network operators. Normally, one

service provider does not have access to the information in the network management system of another network operator, so the backward reporting cell provides the means to transfer the results back across the domain boundary/
boundaries between the relevant network operators. When no domain boundaries are crossed, backward reporting cells need not be sent because network
management can access all nodes in their networks.

Activation and Deactivation of OAM Functions

The performance monitoring and continuity check functions are started and
stopped by means of special activation and deactivation cells. Figure 10.31
shows the format of these cells.

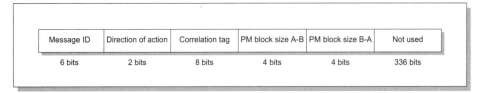

Message ID	Direction of action	Correlation tag	PM block size A-B	PM block size B-A	Not used
6 bits	2 bits	8 bits	4 bits	4 bits	336 bits

Figure 10.31 Function-specific fields of activation/deactivation cells

The message-ID field contains the various commands of the OAM activation/
deactivation cell:

Activate   000001
Activation confirmed   000010
Activation request denied   000011
Deactivate   000101
Deactivation confirmed   000110
Deactivation request denied   000111

The correlation tag serves to correlate commands with the corresponding responses. The direction-of-action field specifies the direction of transmission of
the activated OAM cells. A–B indicates the direction away from the activator or
deactivator; B–A indicates transmission toward the activator. The fields PM
block size A–B and PM block size B–A specify the cell block length to be used for
a performance measurement.

10.1.8   The ATM Adaptation Layer (AAL)

The AAL maps data structures of higher application layers to the cell structure
of the ATM layer and provides appropriate control and management functions.
In order to meet the different requirements of various services, four AAL types
were originally defined: AAL Type 1 the real-time sensitive services with con-

stant bit rates; AAL Type 2 for real-time sensitive services with variable bit rates; AAL Types 3 and 4 for connection-oriented and non-connection-oriented transmission of non-real-time sensitive data. Later, AAL Type 5 was defined by the ATM Forum as a simplified version of AAL3 and was quickly adopted by the ITU-T. Early on, the distinction between connection-oriented and non-connection-oriented data communication in the AAL was found to be unnecessary, and AAL Types 3 and 4 were accordingly merged into AAL Type 3/4. Note that AAL types are never mixed within a single virtual channel for reasons that will become obvious.

Service Parameter	Class A	Class B	Class C	Class D
Time Compensation	required		not required	
Bit rate	constant	variable		
Communication mode	connection-oriented			connectionless
Example	circuit emulation	wireless voice communication	connection-oriented data communication	connectionless data communication
AAL type	AAL1	AAL2	AAL3, AAL5	AAL4

Figure 10.32 Service classes and AAL types

AAL Type 0

The AAL Type 0 indicates the absence of any AAL capability. The application data is inserted directly in the payload fields of the ATM cells and transmitted. Strictly speaking, AAL0 is thus not an AAL type at all; the communication mechanisms are already cell-based and the adaptation layer functions don't exist.

AAL Type 1

The Type 1 ATM Adaptation Layer (ITU-T Recommendation I.363.1) serves to transport data streams with constant bit rates (these include all the interfaces in the PDH hierarchy: T1, E1, T3, etc.), and provide them to the destination node in synchronization with the original transmission clock. This requires that the

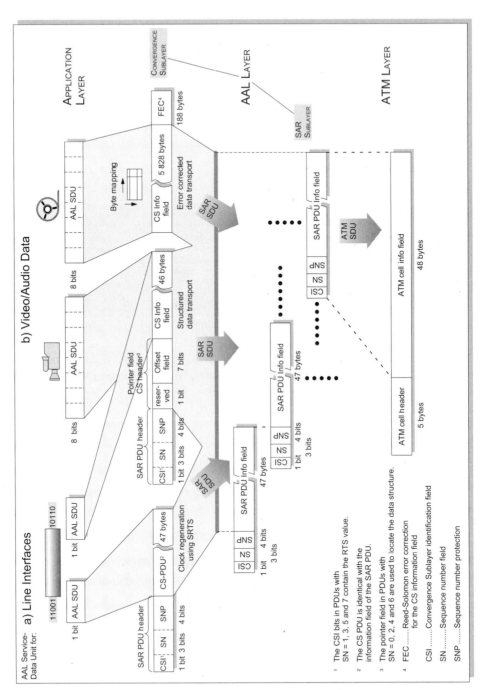

Figure 10.33 Structure of AAL Type 1

ATM network transport not only the data, but also the clock information. For this reason the AAL1 protocol is capable of transporting both continuous bit streams and byte-structured data, such as data based on an 8-kHz sampling interval. Lost or erroneous data is not repeated or corrected. Events such as cell loss or the transmission of incorrect service data units (SDUs), loss of synchronization or clock signal, buffer overflow or the occurrence of invalid AAL header information (AAL Protocol Control Information, or AAL-PCI) are passed from the user layer to the management layer. The AAL1 is composed of two sublayers, the Segmentation and Reassembly Sublayer (SAR) and the Convergence Sublayer (CS). The data to be transported is first broken into 47-byte data blocks (CS PDUs). Each such data block is given a one-byte header that contains a 3 bit sequence count and CRC-3 protection with parity plus a bit (the CSI bit) that is used to carry a multi-cell "synchronous residual time stamp" (SRTS). The 48-byte SAR PDU is then transported in the data field of an ATM cell. At the receiving station, the original data rate of the transmitting station can be synchronously regenerated using the clock information in the CS PDU header. In simple terms, the SRTS process compares the clock rate of the encapsulated service (that is the constant bit rate service carried over AAL1) with the physical layer clock (for example, the SDH/SONET clock) at the source and derives the SRTS, which is transported to the receiver. The physical layer clock and the SRTS are then processed to recover the service clock. An assumption is that there is a fixed relationship between physical layer clocks at both ends of the virtual channel carrying the AAL1 service, normally the case within national networks at least.

AAL Type 2

The Type 2 ATM Adaptation Layer (ITU-T Recommendation I.363.2) is used for efficient transportation of delay-sensitive, narrow-band applications with variable bandwidth (such as telephony). The network must guarantee certain QoS parameters, such as maximum cell delay or cell loss ratio, for each connection while making varying bandwidth available. AAL2 guarantees the QoS parameters for each connection using the QoS mechanisms of the underlying ATM layer. AAL2 itself only specifies the format of the short AAL2 SDUs (or "mini-cells") optimized for real-time applications, and their transport within ATM cells. The bi-directional AAL2 connections can be set up either as PVCs or as SVCs, but provide only non-guaranteed transport services. Corrupt or lost CPS SDUs are neither corrected nor repeated. The data to be transported is first filled into Common Part Sublayer (CPS) packets, which consist of 3 header bytes and 1 to 45 or 64 bytes of user data. AAL2 connection setup, the assignment of Channel IDentifiers (CIDs) and the negotiation of CPS service parameters takes place on AAL2 channel 1 using the ANP protocol (AAL2 Negotiation Procedure).

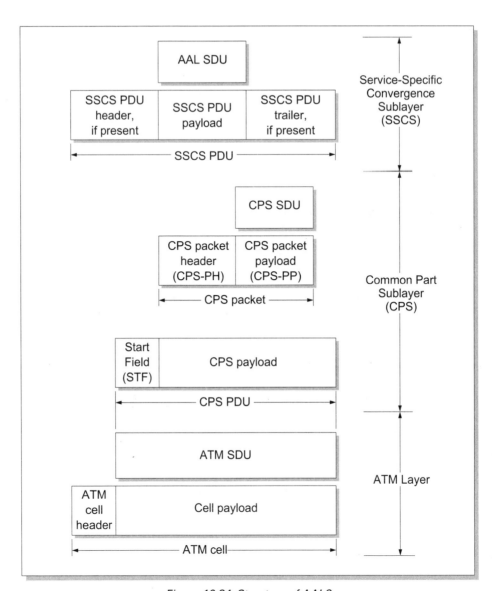

Figure 10.34 Structure of AAL2

The CPS packets (mini-cells) are then inserted in CPS PDUs, which consist of 1 header byte and 47 payload bytes. The CPS PDUs in turn are transported in the payload fields of ATM cells. The start field (STF) comprises an offset value pointing to the start of the next CPS packet to aid CPS packet delineation recovery in the event that an ATM cell has been lost. Figure 10.34 shows a diagram of the structure of AAL2.

AAL2 Error Messages

The following error messages in Figure 10.35 are passed to the layer management in case of transmission errors in AAL2:

Error number	Description
0	The start field in the CPS PDU indicates a parity error. The entire PDU is discarded.
1	The sequence number in the start field is invalid. If the offset is 0, the entire PDU is discarded. Otherwise, processing continues at the byte indicated by the offset.
2	The number of bytes of an overlapping CPS packet does not match the parameters in the start field. If the offset is less than 47, processing continues at the byte indicated by the offset.
3	The offset value is greater than 47. The entire PDU is discarded.
4	The HEC checksum of a CPS packet indicates a transmission error in the header. The corresponding part of the CPS PDU is discarded.
5	The padding bits extend into the following CPS PDU. This extension is ignored and not processed.
6	A CPS packet fragment was received and had to be discarded before it could be reassembled.
7	The HEC checksum of a CPS packet that extends across a CPS PDU boundary indicates a transmission error in the header. If the offset is less than 47, processing continues at the byte indicated by the offset.

Figure 10.35 AAL2 error messages to the layer management

The history of AAL2 is complex. It was originally proposed by the ITU-T in the late 1980s as the adaptation layer to handle Class B services (variable bit-rate, connection-oriented services, specifically video), then withdrawn. It returned through the initially separate then later joint efforts of the ATM Forum and the ITU-T in the latter half of the 1990s to solve the problems inherent in AAL1 for low (and sometimes variable) bandwidth delay sensitive services, such as (compressed) voice, and the inefficiency of AAL5 for handling very short data packets. It was at one point nearly called AAL6 by the ATM Forum before it was concluded that it really did fulfill the original requirements for AAL2 defined a decade earlier. At the time of this writing, therefore, two service types have been defined for AAL2: trunking and SAR. ITU-T Recommendation I.366.2 describes the "AAL type 2 Service Specific Convergence Sublayer for Trunking"–the circuit emulation service used for the transportation of narrow-band, delay-sensitive traffic. AAL2 also provides the means to handle

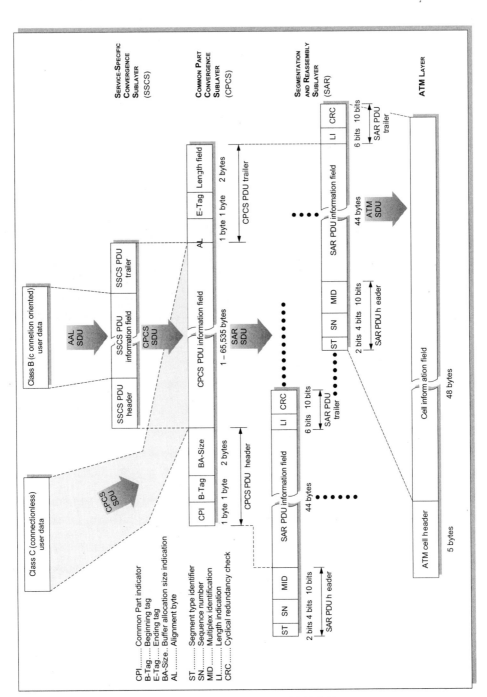

Figure 10.36 Structure of AAL3/4

very short data packets more efficiently, reducing the "cell tax" (inefficient use of ATM cell payloads) inherent in AAL3/4 and AAL5. ITU-T Recommendation I.366.1 describes the "Segmentation and Reassembly Service Specific Convergence Sublayer for AAL type 2". This allows the encapsulation of higher layer variable-length data packets (1 to 65,535 bytes) over AAL2 "mini-cells" in almost exactly the same way that the SAR function of AAL5 allows the encapsulation of data packets over ATM cells (see AAL type 5 in the following discussion). Even the AAL2 SSTED-PDU trailer structure is similar to that of the AAL5 CPCS PDU trailer: it is 8 bytes long and provides a length field and CRC-32 field in the same positions, thus allowing the re-use of hardware designs for processing the SAR function. Third generation wireless services make use of this AAL2 SAR process for carrying data services.

AAL Type 3/4

AAL Type 3/4 (ITU-T Recommendation I.363.3) specifies connection-oriented and non-connection-oriented transportation of data packets in ATM networks. Both point-to-point and point-to-multipoint connections can be set up. The AAL3/4 protocol is thus suitable for transportation of non-connection-oriented communications services, such as SMDS/CBDS (Switched Multi Megabit Data Service / Connectionless Broadband Data Service) metropolitan area networks or Frame Relay. Like AAL Type 1, the AAL3/4 protocol consists of two sublayers, the Segmentation and Reassembly (SAR) sublayer and the Convergence Sublayer (CS), although the CS includes both a Common Part Convergence Sublayer (CPCS) and a Service Specific Convergence Sublayer (SSCS). The variable-length data packets (1 to 65,535 bytes) of the application building on AAL3/4 are first padded to an integer multiple of 32 bits to permit an efficient, hardware-based implementation of the AAL processes, and a header and trailer are added. The resulting CS PDU is then split into 44-byte fragments, each of which receives another header and trailer, and is then passed to the ATM layer as a 48-byte SAR PDU. In reality this AAL is now only used for legacy SMDS services, which are themselves obsolescent. AAL5 has overtaken AAL3/4 for interworking with Frame Relay and for the support of almost all other services because it is so much more efficient.

AAL Type 5

AAL Type 5 was invented by the ATM Forum in the beginning of the 1990s to simplify the handling of data over ATM. The ITU-T later adopted it and it is now defined in ITU-T Recommendation I.363.5. AAL5 corresponds to a highly simplified implementation of AAL Type 3/4. Like AAL3/4, it is suitable for connection-oriented and non-connection-oriented data communications. And like AAL3/4, AAL5 also consists of a Segmentation and Reassembly (SAR) sublayer and a Convergence Sublayer (CS), with the CS subdivided into a Common Part

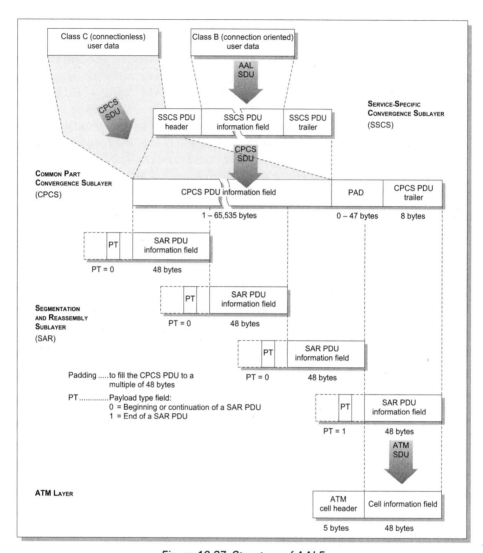

Figure 10.37 Structure of AAL5

Convergence Sublayer (CPCS) and a Service Specific Convergence Sublayer (SSCS).

The processes within the AAL Type 5 sublayers are significantly simpler than in AAL3/4. There is no mechanism for cell multiplexing, for example. All cells that belong to an AAL5 CS PDU are transmitted in one sequential cell stream. The variable-length data packets (1 to 65,535 bytes) of the application building on AAL5 are first padded to an integer multiple of 48 bytes (this ensures that no partially filled cells are transmitted after segmentation) and a trailer is added (no header). The resulting CS PDU is then broken into 48-byte segments that fit directly into the data field of ATM cells. The PT field of the ATM header is used to identify whether further segments follow, or whether the data field contains the end of the CS PDU. Trailer-based PDUs are efficient to process because the large amounts of data often involved can be further processed without having to move them in memory-based implementations. The next section will describe the SAAL, which is also a trailer-based PDU building on AAL5; processing of the higher sublayers of the SAAL is thus simplified. Additionally, AAL5 allows processing on 32-bit boundaries – hence the 8-byte length of the trailer (2 x 32 bits); there is really no need for more than 7 bytes in the trailer, the CPCS-UU and CPI fields (8 bits each) are rarely used and could have shared a single byte.

The Signaling ATM Adaptation Layer (SAAL)

As in narrow-band ISDN, B-ISDN signaling is also handled in signaling virtual channels that are separate from the user connections. The Signaling AAL, ITU-T Recommendations Q.2100 – Q.2144 (SAAL) is the AAL used for all ITU-T signaling protocols and ATM Forum UNI signaling protocols versions 3.1 and 4.0, (Version 3.0 used a prenormative version of the SAAL; UNI 3.0 was published about a year before the ITU-T had completed Recommendation Q.2931; UNI 3.0 is now obsolete.). Figure 10.38 shows the protocol layer model for ITU-T UNI and NNI signaling in ATM networks, with the position of the SAAL in the protocol model.

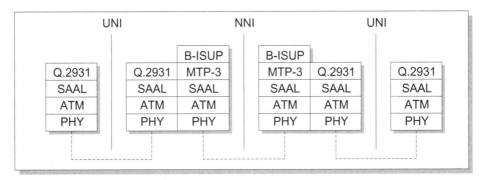

Figure 10.38 Protocol layer model for UNI and NNI signaling

The SAALs for UNI and NNI signaling have several features in common, but the NNI-SAAL has a more complex structure due to the greater number of mechanisms that need to be provided for MTP-3 and B-ISUP. The purpose of the SAAL is to provide the actual signaling layers situated above it in the protocol hierarchy (Q.2931; MTP-3 and B-ISUP) with a reliable transportation service, because these signaling protocols have no error compensation mechanisms themselves. Fault tolerance is provided by SAAL's SSCS sublayer using the Service-Specific

Connection-Oriented Protocol (SSCOP), which builds on the CPCS and SAR sublayers of AAL3/4 or AAL5. Because the CPCS sublayer of AAL3/4 and AAL5 is only able to perform unassured information transfer, a substantial part of the SSCOP protocol is concerned with procedures to guarantee transmission of the SSCOP information field contents. This is analogous to the function of the TCP layer used with IP for guaranteeing reliable transport of data across IP networks. The given signaling layer's requests are translated to SSCOP by an appropriate Service-Specific Coordination Function (SSCF). Although specified as an option for use, in practice AAL3/4 is not used for signaling.

The SSCOP protocol defines 15 distinct PDUs that are used to implement different functions. The PDUs Begin (BGN) and Begin Acknowledge (BGAK) are used to set up the SSCOP connection between two stations and reset the send and receive buffers of the receiving station. Assured data communication can then take place in two ways: the data packets can be sequentially numbered (SD PDUs), and each data packet may contain an individual request for confirmation of receipt (SDP PDUs). Such confirmation is sent by the receiver in a STAT PDU. After the receiver has analyzed the sequential numbers of the PDUs received, it can send USTAT PDUs if necessary to report lost PDUs, indicating the number range missing. Data can also be sent in an unassured mode using Unnumbered

Function	Description	PDU Name	Value
Establishment	Request initialization	BGN	0001
	Request acknowledgement	BGAK	0010
Release	Disconnect command	END	0011
	Disconnect acknowledgement	ENDAK	0100
Resynchronization	Resynchronization command	RS	0101
	Resynchronization acknowledgement	RSAK	0110
Reject	Connection reject	BGREJ	0111
Recovery	Recovery command	ER	1001
	Recovery acknowledgement	ERAK	1111
Assured data transfer	Sequenced connection mode data	SD	1000
	Transmitter state information with request for receiver state information	POLL	1010
	Solicited receiver state information	STAT	1011
	Unsolicited receiver state information	USTAT	1100
Unacknowledged data transfer	Unnumbered user data	UD	1101
Management data transfer	Unnumbered management data	MD	1110

Figure 10.39 SSCOP PDUs and their functions

Data (UD) PDUs. Figure 10.39 lists the 15 types of SSCOP PDUs and their functions.

The SSCOP Timers

The SSCOP protocol defines four timers that control the protocol process. These are the POLL, KEEP-ALIVE, NO-RESPONSE and CONNECTION CONTROL (CC) timers.

The POLL timer monitors the maximum time interval between the transmissions of successive POLL PDUs while SD or SDP PDUs are being transmitted.

Error Type	Error Code	PDU or event that triggered the error
Receipt of unsolicited or inappropriate PDU	A	SD PDU
	B	BGN PDU
	C	BGAK PDU
	D	BGREJ PDU
	E	END PDU
	F	ENDAK PDU
	G	POLL PDU
	H	STAT PDU
	I	USTAT PDU
	J	RS
	K	RSAK PDU
	L	ER
	M	ERAK
Unsuccessful retransmission	O	$VT(CC) \geq MaxCC$
	P	Timer_NO_RESPONSE expired
Other list elements error type	Q	SD or POLL, N(S) error
	R	STAT N(PS) error
	S	STAT N(R) or list elements error
	T	USTAT N(R) or list elements error
	U	PDU length violation
SD loss	V	SD PDUs must be retransmitted
Credit condition	W	Lack of credit
	X	Credit obtained

Figure 10.40 SSCOP error codes

When no SD or SDP PDUs are being transmitted, the KEEP-ALIVE Timer controls the interval between successive POLL PDUs. The NO-RESPONSE timer specifies the maximum delay between two PDUs of the type POLL or STAT. The value of the NO-RESPONSE timer must be greater than both that of the KEEP-ALIVE timer and that of the POLL timer. Furthermore, the value of the NO-RESPONSE timer must be more than twice the signal delay over the connection concerned.

The CONNECTION CONTROL timer determines the maximum delay between the transmission of two BGN, END or RS PDUs if no answering PDU is received. The CC timer must also have a value greater than twice the signal delay over the connection concerned.

SSCOP Error Messages to the Management Layer

Error codes are used to forward SSCOP error events to the management layer. The table in Figure 10.40 lists the various SSCOP error types.

SAAL Connection Setup

The connection setup between two SAAL system components is triggered by an AA-ESTABLISH message from the SSCF sublayer. This command contains the parameters SSCOP User to User Parameter (SSCOP-UU) and Buffer Release (BR), which are used in generating the SSCOP sublayer's BGN message. The receiver decodes the BGN message and passes an AA-ESTABLISH.ind to the receiving SSCF. This sublayer responds with an AA-ESTABLISH.res command, which likewise contains the parameters SSCOP-UU and BR. The resulting BGAK message is sent back to the originating SSCOP, which passes an AA-ESTABLISH.conf to the initiating SSCF (see Figure 10.41).

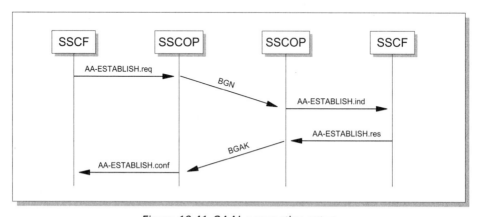

Figure 10.41 SAAL connection setup

10.1.9   ATM Signaling

Signaling in ATM refers to all processes necessary to set up a connection between two or more stations. In contrast to conventional signaling mechanisms, signaling in ATM networks is an extremely complex procedure. All kinds of traffic parameters—such as the AAL type, streaming or message mode, assured or unassured transfer, cell rates (peak cell rate and sustainable cell rate), cell loss ratio, cell delay, cell delay variation tolerance and maximum burst size—must be negotiated and guaranteed over all segments of the connection path. Moreover, novel connection-oriented topologies, such as point-to-multipoint or broadcast connections, must also be handled. For this reason the existing UNI and NNI signaling protocols, Q.931 and Q.933 or ISUP, on which B-ISDN signaling is based and which were originally developed for narrow-band ISDN, have undergone major extension for ATM networks to produce Q.2931 or B-ISUP. Signaling at the user interface takes place either based on ITU-T Recommendation Q.2931 (B-DSS2) or by means of one of the ATM Forum specifications, UNI 3.0, 3.1 or 4.0. At the network interface, public networks use B-ISUP (ITU-T Recommendation Q.2761 – Q.2764) or the corresponding ATM Forum protocols, B-ICI or PNNI.

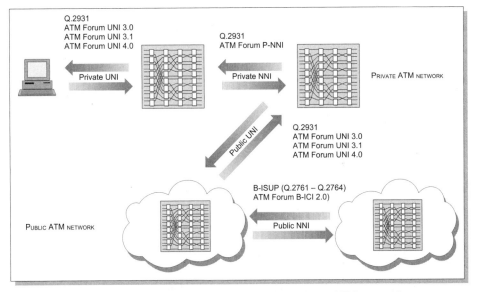

Figure 10.42 ATM signaling in public and private ATM networks

Connection setup can take place either on the reserved signaling virtual channel, VPI-VCI = 0-5, or over VCs selected by means of meta-signaling. Any signaling VCs can be set up without an existing AAL connection, because the simple meta-signaling commands can be transferred in one cell. Once the signaling virtual channel has been determined, the AAL for the signaling virtual channel (SAAL) is established. At this point the signaling protocol becomes active. In practice, however, the signaling virtual channel VPI-VCI = 0-5 is generally used, and meta-signaling is not necessary.

The Q.2931 Message Format

Q.2931 defines a total of 15 UNI signaling messages, which can be classified in groups for connection setup, connection clear-down and other messages. For all ordinary signaling processes, the following ten message types are available:

Connection Setup:

- ALERTING
- CALL PROCEEDING
- CONNECT
- CONNECT ACKNOWLEDGE
- SETUP

Connection Clear-Down:

- RELEASE
- RELEASE COMPLETE

Other:

- NOTIFY
- STATUS
- STATUS ENQUIRY

For interoperability with narrow-band ISDN, three more messages have been defined in addition to those listed previously:

Connection Setup (Additional Messages for N-ISDN Interworking):

- SETUP ACKNOWLEDGE
- PROGRESSING

Other (Additional Messages for N-ISDN Interworking):

- INFORMATION

Furthermore, the messages RESTART and RESTART ACKNOWLEDGE are defined for the purpose of requesting a new connection setup attempt (in the event that a connection enters an undefined state, for example). These messages may be used only with the global call reference 0. Every signaling message consists of the following five sections, called information elements:

- Protocol discriminator
- Call reference
- Message type
- Message length
- Message-specific information elements

The first four information elements are mandatory and must be present in every Q.2931 message. The usage of other information elements is dependent on the message type. The diagram in Figure 10.43 illustrates the structure of a UNI signaling message.

Bit	8	7	6	5	4	3	2	1	Byte
	Protocol Discriminator								1
	0 0 0 0				Call Reference Length				2
	Flag	Call Reference							3
	Call Reference								4
									5
	Message Type								6
									7
	Message Length								8
									9
	Information Elements								...n

Figure 10.43 Q.2931 message format

Protocol Discriminator

The protocol discriminator is the first element in every Q.2931 message. It identifies the protocol used and is coded as 00001001 (decimal 9) for Q.2931. The ATM Forum signaling variants (UNI 3.x, 4.0) share the same protocol discriminator value.

Bit	8	7	6	5	4	3	2	1
	0	0	0	0	1	0	0	1

Protocol discriminator value for Q.2931 messages

Bit 8765 4321	
0000 0000 to 0000 0111	Reserved
0000 1000	Q.931/ I.415 user network call control
0000 1001	Q.2931 user network call/connection control
0001 0000 to 0011 1111	Other Layer 3 protocols (X.25 etc.)
0100 0000 to 0100 1111	National use
0101 0000 to 1111 1110	Other Layer 3 protocols (X.25 etc.)

Figure 10.44 The protocol discriminator field

Call Reference

The call reference serves to associate Q.2931 messages with a given connection. When a new connection is established, all messages concerning that connection have the same call reference value. When the connection has been cleared down, the call reference is released and can be used again. The same call reference can be used by two connections within an ATM virtual channel only if the respective connection setups take place in opposite directions. The length of the call reference field is measured in bytes; the default length is 3 bytes. The call reference flag identifies the sending and receiving stations. The station that indicates the connection always sets this flag to 0 in its messages, while messages originating from the receiving station have the flag set to 1. The call reference value 0 is known as the global call reference and refers to all connections within a signaling virtual channel.

Message Type

This field indicates the message type. All message types except SETUP ACKNOWLEDGE and INFORMATION are also supported by the corresponding ATM Forum specification UNI 4.0 (see Figure 10.46).

Call Reference Format

Bit	8	7	6	5	4	3	2	1	Byte
	0	0	0	0	Length of the Call Reference field in bytes				1
	Flag								2
	Call Reference								3
									4

Flag: 1 Message sent by the station called
0 Message sent by the calling station

The Global Call Reference

Bit	8	7	6	5	4	3	2	1	Byte
	0	0	0	0	0	0	1	1	1
	0/1 Flag	0	0	0	0	0	0	0	2
	0	0	0	0	0	0	0	0	3
	0	0	0	0	0	0	0	0	4

Figure 10.45 Call reference and global call reference

The Message Length Field

The message length field indicates the length of the signaling message in bytes, not counting the protocol discriminator, call reference, message type, and message length fields. The length field itself can be 1 or 2 bytes long. In the first byte, only the first 7 bits can be used. Bit 8 indicates whether the length field includes a second byte. If bit 8 is set to 0, the length field is continued in the following byte; otherwise the length field is a single byte. If the message contains no other information elements after the length field, the message length is coded as all 0s.

UNI Information Elements

After the four mandatory information elements, the various message types use specific information elements of varying lengths to fulfill their respective func-

Bit	8	7	6	5	4	3	2	1	Byte
	Message Type								1
	1 Ext.	0	0	Flag	0	1	Message Action Indicator		2

Bits 8765 4321	Q.2931 Message
0000 0000	Escape sequence for national message types
Connection set-up	
0000 0001	ALERTING
0000 0111	CONNECT
0000 1111	CONNECT ACKNOWLEDGE
0000 0010	CALL PROCEEDING
0000 0011	PROGRESS
0000 0101	SETUP
0000 1101	SETUP ACKNOWLEDGE
Connection clear-down	
0100 1110	RESTART ACKNOWLEDGE
0100 0110	RESTART
0101 1010	RELEASE COMPLETE
0100 1101	RELEASE
Other Messages	
0110 1110	NOTIFY
0111 1011	INFORMATION
0111 0101	STATUS ENQUIRY
0111 1101	STATUS

Figure 10.46 Q.2931 (B-DSS2) signaling messages

tions. Each of these information elements consists of an information element identifier, a length field, a compatibility indicator, and the actual information element contents. Figure 10.47 illustrates the general format of information elements and lists the specific information elements defined.

Connection Setup at the Caller's End (UNI)

The caller initiates the connection setup by transmitting a SETUP message containing the desired ATM virtual path, the ATM virtual channel, and quality-of-service and traffic parameters. If the network is able to provide the service requested, and if the specified ATM virtual path and virtual channel are available, the network answers with a CALL PROCEEDING message and forwards

Bit	8	7	6	5	4	3	2	1	Byte
	Information Element Identifier								1
	1 Ext.	Coding Standard	IE Instruction Field						2
			Flag	Res	Action Indicator				
	Information Element Length								3
									4
	Information Element Contents								5

Information Element Identifiers	
Bits 8 7 6 5 4 3 2 1	
0 1 1 1 0 0 0 0	Called Party Number
0 1 1 1 0 0 0 1	Called Party Sub-Address
0 1 1 1 1 0 0 0	Transit Network Selection
0 1 1 1 1 0 0 1	Restart Indicator
0 1 1 1 1 1 0 0	Narrow-Band Low Layer Compatibility
0 1 1 1 1 1 0 1	Narrow-Band High Layer Compatibility
0 1 1 0 0 0 0 0	Broadband Locking Shift
0 1 1 0 0 0 0 1	Broadband Non-Locking Shift
0 1 1 0 0 0 1 0	Broadband Sending Complete
0 1 1 0 0 0 1 1	Broadband Repeat Indicator
0 1 1 0 1 1 0 0	Calling Party Number
0 1 1 0 1 1 0 1	Calling Party Sub-Address
0 1 0 1 1 0 0 0	ATM Adaption Layer Parameters
0 1 0 1 1 0 0 1	ATM Traffic Descriptor
0 1 0 1 1 0 1 0	Connection Identifier
0 1 0 1 1 0 1 1	OAM Traffic Descriptor
0 1 0 1 1 1 0 0	Quality of Service Parameter
0 1 0 1 1 1 1 0	Broadband Bearer Capability
0 1 0 1 1 1 1 1	Broadband Low Layer Information (B-LLI)
0 1 0 1 1 1 0 1	Broadband High Layer Information (B-HLI)
0 1 0 0 0 0 1 0	End-to-End-Transit Delay
0 0 1 0 0 1 1 1	Notification Indicator
0 0 0 1 0 1 0 0	Call State
0 0 0 1 1 1 1 0	Progress Indicator
0 0 0 0 0 1 0 0	Narrowband Bearer Capability
0 0 0 0 1 0 0 0	Cause

Figure 10.47a Format and coding of information elements

Information Field Coding: Byte 2 Compatibility Indicator	
Extension indicator, bit 8	Set to 1; reserved for future use
Coding standard, bits 7 6 0 0 0 1 1 0 1 1	 ITU-T coding ISO/IEC standard National standard Network-specific standard (private, public)
Flag bit 5 0 1	 Ignore instruction indicator Obey instruction indicator
Reserved field, bit 4	Set to 0; reserved for future use
Action indicator, bits 3 2 1 0 0 0 0 0 1 0 1 0 1 0 1 1 1 0	 Clear Call Discard info element and proceed Discard info element, proceed and report status Discard info element and ignore Discard info element and report status

Figure 10.47b Format and coding of information elements

the setup request to the receiving station. If the station called is able to receive the request, the network sends the caller an ALERTING message. If the station called accepts the call, the network sends the caller a CONNECT message. The caller may optionally respond with a CONNECT ACKNOWLEDGE. This completes the connection setup, and the call is then in the active state.

Connection Setup at the Station Called (UNI)

After the receiving station has been notified of an incoming call by a SETUP message from the network, it performs a compatibility check. This test compares the address information, the QoS parameters, and the traffic parameters of the SETUP request with the local services available. If the SETUP parameters requested are not locally available, the receiving station responds with a RELEASE-COMPLETE message and Cause 88, "Incompatible Destination". If the SETUP parameters are compatible, the receiving station can respond with a CALL PROCEEDING, ALERTING, or CONNECT message, depending on the type of end system. The network confirms a CONNECT message with a CONNECT ACKNOWLEDGE and the connection enters the active state.

Numbers

The SETUP message identifies the station called by its number in the information elements "Called Party Subaddress" and "Called Party Number". The net-

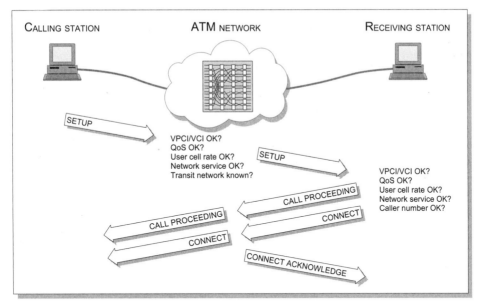

Figure 10.48 UNI connection setup

work verifies that this is a valid number. If not, the network sends a RELEASE COMPLETE with one of the following messages:

\#   1 Unassigned (unallocated) number
\#   2 No route to destination
\#   3 Number changed
\# 28 Invalid number format (incomplete number)

ATM Addressing

Six types of ATM addresses are specified in Q.2931:

- Unknown
- International number
- National number
- Network-specific number
- Subscriber number
- Abbreviated number

The format of the address types "abbreviated number" and "network-specific number" is different from case to case, depending on the network. "Network-specific numbers" can be used for administrative services (such as operator numbers). "Abbreviated number" addresses contain a shortened form of a complete ATM address, and may be defined by the network operator according to the internal structure of the network. All other address types use one of the following address formats:

- Unknown
- ISDN Telephony Numbering Plan (E.164)
- ISO NSAP Addressing (ISO 8348/AD2)
- Private Numbering Plan

The address format "unknown" is used when the user or network does not know any address format. The use of the ISO NSAP address format is optional and takes the ATM address type "unknown".

Connection Clear-Down

Before describing the processes involved in clearing down a connection, we must define the three states "Connected", "Disconnected", and "Released". An ATM virtual channel is in the "Connected" state when it forms part of an active B-ISDN connection. The virtual channel is in the "Disconnected" state when it is not part of such a connection, but is not available for any other connection. When an ATM virtual channel is in the "Released" state, then it is not part of an existing B-ISDN connection and is available for use.

Connection clear-down is normally initiated by a "RELEASE" command, except in the following three cases:

a) If a SETUP message is received without a mandatory information element, the receiver may refuse the connection setup by sending a RELEASE COMPLETE and Cause 96, "Mandatory information element is missing".

b) If a SETUP message is received with an incorrect mandatory information element, the receiver may refuse the connection setup by sending a RELEASE COMPLETE and message #100, "Invalid information element contents".

c) After VPI/VCI negotiation has failed, the system that initiated the call may terminate the connection setup with a RELEASE COMPLETE.

Connection Clear-Down by the User

In all cases except the three mentioned previously, sending a RELEASE command begins the connection clear-down. If the user initiates the connection clear-down, the user's timer T308 is started when the RELEASE message is sent. The first time T308 expires, the user repeats the RELEASE command and starts T308 again. If no RELEASE COMPLETE is received from the network in answer to the second connection clear-down attempt, the user considers the virtual channel concerned as out of order and enters the null state. If the user receives a RELEASE COMPLETE from the network before T308 expires, it clears down the virtual channel, releases the call reference, and enters the null state.

Connection Clear-Down by the Network

The network can initiate a connection clear-down by sending a RELEASE command and starting its timer T308. The user responds with a RELEASE COMPLETE, whereupon the network stops T308, clears down the virtual channels and releases the call reference. The connection clear-down is then complete. If timer T308 expires before a RELEASE-COMPLETE is received from the user, the RELEASE command is repeated and T308 restarted. If T308 expires a second time before a RELEASE COMPLETE is received, the network marks the ATM virtual channel as out of order and clears the call reference.

ATM Forum UNI Signaling: UNI 3.0, 3.1, 4.0

In order to allow for manufacturers to develop ATM components before the definitive adoption of international standards by the ITU-T, the ATM Forum also developed specifications for ATM signaling in its UNI 3.0 document. The signaling specifications in UNI 3.0 were published a year before ITU-T Recommendation Q.2931, and are largely incompatible with it because of the use of a different SSCOP layer, as mentioned earlier. UNI 3.1, however, drafted after work on Q.2931 had been completed, corrected this by specifying the ITU-T Q.2110 SSCOP (the higher layer signaling messages were largely unchanged) and represented a significant step toward harmonization. Next, the ITU-T introduced Q.2971, which added route-initiated join point to multi-point signaling. Finally, the ATM forum introduced UNI 4.0 which, in most respects, is a superset of both Q.2931 and Q.2971 but additionally contains specifications for leaf-initially join point to multi-point signaling; the only signaling messages not contained in UNI 4.0 from the ITU-T recommendations concern interworking with narrow-band ISDN services. The following sections are more detailed but are limited to a description of the major differences that remain between the signaling mechanism described in UNI 3.0, UNI 3.1 and UNI 4.0 on one hand and in Q.2931 and Q.2971 on the other.

Signaling: ATM Forum UNI 3.1 Versus ITU-T Recommendation Q.2931

The AAL for signaling (SAAL) specified in UNI 3.1 is based only on AAL5. The AAL sublayer definitions for this SAAL, CP-AAL and SSCS with the Service-Specific Coordination Function (SSCF) and the Service-Specific Connection-Oriented Peer-to-Peer Protocol (SSCOP), are identical with those in the corresponding ITU-T Recommendation. While the use of VPCIs is supported for identification of the ATM virtual path used for data transmission, these VPCIs are limited to a length of 8 bits (as opposed to 16 bits in Q.2931) in order to be identical with the VPI. Furthermore, no negotiation is possible between user and network regarding the VPCI/VCI values to be used. UNI 3.1 addressing also differs from the Q.2931 specification in that it uses only two number types

Timer Number	Default Value	Start	Stop	On First Expiration	On Second Expiration	Implementation
T301 (Q.2931 only)	≥ 3 min	ALERT received	CONNECT received	Clear call	—	M (if symmetrical connections supported)
T302 (Q.2931 only)	10 – 15 s	SETUP ACK sent	SENDING COMPLETE indication	if information in-complete, clear call Otherwise, CALL PROCEEDING	—	M (if overlap sending and receiving supported)
T303	4 s	SETUP sent	CONNECT, CALL PROCEEDING, ALERT RELEASE COMPLETE received	Repeat SETUP restart T303	Abort call set-up	M
T304 (Q.2931 only)	30 s	SETUP ACK received; restart when INFO received	CALL PROCEEDING; ALERT; CONNECT received	Clear call	—	M
T308	30 s	RELEASE sent	RELEASE COMPLETE or RELEASE received	Repeat RELEASE, restart T308	—	
T309	10 s	SAAL aborted	SAAL active again	Clear call; delete VCIs and call references	—	M
T310	30 – 120 s	CALL PROCEEDING received	ALERT, CONNECT or RELEASE received	send RELEASE	—	M
T313	4 s	CONNECT sent	CONNECT ACK received	send RELEASE	—	M
T316	2 min	RESTART sent	RESTART ACK received	Repeat RESTART several times	Repeat RESTART several times	M
T317	Implemen-tation specific, but < T316	RESTART received	All call references deleted	Report error	—	M
T322	4 s	STATUS ENQUIRY sent	STATUS, RELEASE or RELEASE COMPLETE received	Repeat STATUS ENQUIRY	Repeat STATUS ENQUIRY	M
T398 (ATM Forum only)	4 s	DROP PARTY sent	DROP PARTY ACK or RELEASE received	Send DROP PARTY ACK or RELEASE COMPLETE	Timer is not restarted	M
T399 (ATM Forum only)	14 s (UNI 3.0/3.1) 34 – 124 s (UNI 4.0)	ADD PARTY sent	ADD PARTY ACK, ADD PARTY REJECT, or RELEASE received	Delete party	Timer is not restarted	M
T331 (ATM Forum 4.0 only)	60 s	LEAF SETUP REQUEST sent	SETUP, ADD PARTY, or LEAF SETUP FAILURE received	Repeat LEAF SETUP REQUEST and restart T331	Delete connection	M

Figure 10.49 Timers for UNI signaling processes: Q.2931 and ATM Forum (user system)

Timer Number	Default Value	Start	Stop	On First Expiration	On Second Expiration	Implementation
T301 (Q.2931 only)	≥ 3 min	ALERT received	CONNECT received	Clear call	—	M (if symmetrical connections supported)
T302 (Q.2931 only)	10 – 15 s	SETUP ACK sent; restart when INFO sent	SENDING COMPLETE indication	if information in-complete, clear call Otherwise, CALL PROCEEDING	—	M (if overlap sending and receiving supported)
T303	4 s	SETUP sent	CONNECT, CALL PROCEEDING, ALERT SETUP ACK, RELEASE COMPLETE received	Repeat SETUP restart T 303	Abort call set-up	M
T304 (Q.2931 only)	20 s	SETUP ACK received	INFO sent or CALL PROCEEDING, ALERT, CONNECT received	Clear call	—	M
T306 (Q.2931 only)	20 s	RELEASE with Progress Indicator 8 sent	RELEASE COMPLETE received	Stop ringing	—	M (if inband alarms supported)
T308	30 s	RELEASE sent	RELEASE COMPLETE or RELEASE received	Repeat RELEASE, restart T308	Set VC to maintenance state	M
T309	10 s	SAAL aborted	SAAL active again	Clear call; delete VCIs and call references	—	O
T310	10 s	CALL PROCEEDING received	ALERT, CONNECT or RELEASE received	Clear call	—	M
T316	2 min	RESTART sent	RESTART ACK received	Repeat RESTART several times	Repeat RESTART several times	M
T317	Implemen-tation specific, but < T316	RESTART received	All call references deleted	Report error	—	M
T322	4 s	STATUS ENQUIRY sent	STATUS, RELEASE or RELEASE COMPLETE received	Repeat STATUS ENQUIRY	Repeat STATUS ENQUIRY	M
T398 (ATM Forum only)	4 s	DROP PARTY sent	DROP PARTY ACK or RELEASE received	Send DROP PARTY ACK or RELEASE	Timer is not restarted	M
T399 (ATM Forum only)	14 s	ADD PARTY sent	ADD PARTY ACK, ADD PARTY REJECT, or RELEASE received	Delete party	Timer is not restarted	M

Figure 10.50 Timers for UNI signaling processes: Q.2931 and ATM Forum (network system)

("Unknown" and "International number") and the numbering plans E.164 (the ISDN numbering system) and ISO NSAP. When E.164 numbers are used, the number type is "International number". ISO NSAP numbers are designated as "Unknown".

UNI 3.1 does not support the following Q.2931 signaling messages:

- ALERTING
- PROGRESS
- SETUP ACKNOWLEDGE
- INFORMATION
- NOTIFY

Due to the lack of support for the NOTIFY message, the information element "Notification Indicator" is also not supported. This information element is used in the Q.2931 NOTIFY message to obtain information about the connection state, or more specifically the messages CALL PROCEEDING, CONNECT ACKNOWL-EDGE, RELEASE, and SETUP. For point-to-multipoint signaling, UNI 3.1 provides following message types not defined in Q.2931:

- ADD PARTY
- ADD PARTY ACKNOWLEDGE
- ADD PARTY REJECT
- DROP PARTY ACKNOWLEDGE

UNI 3.1 supports only the standard code set 0, while Q.2931 also supports code sets 5, 6, and 7. Furthermore, the definitions of certain UNI 3.1 information elements are slightly modified. The maximum length of the "Traffic Descriptor" information element in the SETUP message, for example, is increased to 30 bytes (as opposed to 20 in Q.2931); the length of the "Transit Network Selection" element is limited to 8 bytes. A complete list of the differences between UNI 3.1 and Q.2931 signaling is found in Appendix E of the ATM Forum UNI specification.

The timers defined in UNI 3.1 for B-ISDN signaling are the same as those in Q.2931 with the exception of T301, T302, and T304, which are not supported by UNI 3.1. The ATM Forum defines additional timers for point-to-multipoint processes: T398 and T399 (UNI 3.1), and T331 (UNI 4.0). Figures 10.49 and 10.50 list the UNI protocol timers.

ATM Forum Signaling: UNI 3.0

The most important difference between the signaling specifications in UNI 3.0 and 3.1 is that the adaptation layer for signaling (SAAL) in UNI 3.1 is compatible with the corresponding definition in Q.2931. This is not true of UNI 3.0, which uses the older SAAL specifications Q.SAAL1 and Q.SAAL2. Furthermore, UNI 3.0 signaling supports neither meta-signaling nor broadcast signaling.

ATM Forum Signaling: UNI 4.0

The current ATM Forum signaling specification UNI 4.0 closely approximates ITU-T Recommendation Q.2931 with Q.2971 (point-to-multipoint signaling extensions). With the exception of the messages SETUP ACKNOWLEDGE and INFORMATION, which in any case are only required in the case of transitions between narrow-band and broadband ISDN networks, UNI 4.0 supports all the Q.2931 and Q.2971 signaling messages. In addition to the messages specific to ATM Forum UNI 3.1, 4.0 also provides the messages PARTY ALERTING and LEAF SETUP REQUEST, as well as the corresponding protocol states. It is worth noting that UNI 4.0 was based primarily upon Q.2931 and Q.2971, rather than UNI 3.1. Furthermore, as in much standardization work, many of the same signaling experts were involved in the development of both ITU-T recommendations and ATM Forum specifications. Consequently, with the exception of the SETUP ACKNOWLEDGE and INFORMATION messages previously mentioned, UNI 4.0 can be considered to be a superset of ITU-T UNI recommendations; equipment conforming to the ATM Forum's UNI 4.0 signaling protocols generally are compatible with equipment based on ITU-T recommendations.

NNI Signaling

For connection setup between two NNIs, the ITU-T developed the broadband protocol B-ISUP (ITU-T Recommendations Q.2761-Q.2764), modeled after the narrow-band ISDN protocol ISUP. B-ISUP contains many of the mechanisms and functions of the proven ISUP. Only the characteristic parameters and processes of broadband networks with their virtual connections are added. By the same token, ISUP functions that are only practical in conventional connection-oriented networks are omitted. While B-ISUP is used for NNI signaling in wide-area networks, NNIs in private local ATM networks use the ATM Forum PNNI protocol. Unlike B-ISUP, PNNI is able to select routes for the desired connections, a function that has to be implemented completely independently by manufacturers of B-ISUP switching systems. In local ATM networks, the ATM network can be made operational immediately based on PNNI, whereas large, public ATM WAN networks with B-ISUP signaling first require the definition and implementation of route selection and bandwidth monitoring functions. Although designed for private networks, PNNI is also being used in some large public networks, particularly in the United States.

B-ISUP Signaling

The B-ISUP protocol is the NNI counterpart to the UNI protocol in ITU-T Recommendation Q.2931 (or ATM Forum UNI 4.0) and extends virtual UNI connections across the ATM network to the end system called. There the NNI connection is translated back into a UNI connection. However, B-ISUP is unable to fulfill functions such as:

- Bandwidth management
- Route selection
- Routing table maintenance
- OAM process control for existing virtual connections

The implementation of these functions is left to the component manufacturers or the operators of B-ISDN networks. The B-ISUP protocol builds on Message Transfer Protocol Version 3 (MTP-3) specified especially for ATM, whose data packets are transported in turn by means of the NNI SAAL layer.

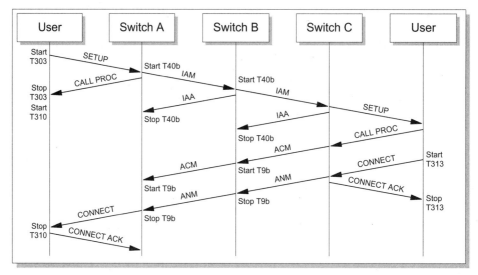

Figure 10.51 Connection setup and tear-down in the UNI/NNI network

PNNI Signaling

PNNI (Private Network to Network Interface) signaling consists of two protocols: a topology protocol, which distributes information about the network topology to the individual network stations, and a signaling protocol, which is necessary for connection setup between PNNI nodes. The signaling protocol is mainly based on the ITU-T Q.2931 signaling recommendation. In addition to the signaling mechanisms drawn from Q.2931, however, PNNI also contains a number of completely new functions. These include searching for alternative routes, which can involve "crankback" (back-tracking) when an attempt to move forward fails for various reasons, maintenance of connection matrices for ascertaining routes, and the operation of a dedicated routing control virtual channel, used only to distribute routing information. Furthermore, all PNNI nodes save updated topology state information at regular intervals. These "topology state parameters" provide information about the availability of connections to adjacent nodes, and are continuously updated by means of a special "hello" procedure carried out between all PNNI nodes.

10.1.10 ATM Interworking

LAN-ATM: LLC Encapsulation (RFC 1483)

The first specifications available for connecting LANs with ATM networks were the two Requests for Comments (RFCs) RFC 1483 (superceded in 1999 by RFC 2684) and RFC 1577 (superceded in 1998 by RFC 2225), published in 1993 by the IETF (Internet Engineering Task Force). RFC 2684 specifies two methods for the encapsulation of LAN data packets in ATM:

- LLC encapsulation
- VC-based multiplexing

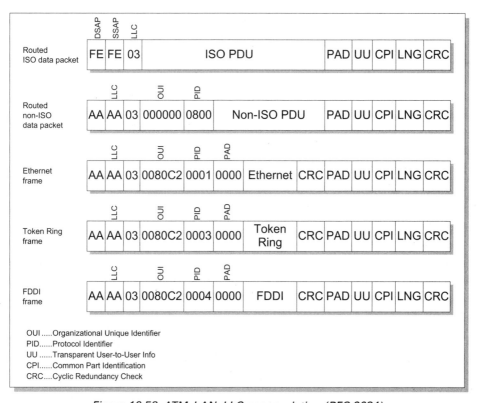

Figure 10.52 ATM-LAN: LLC encapsulation (RFC 2684)

The first method transports all LAN protocols by encapsulating the Logical Link Control (LLC) data packets in AAL5 CPCS PDUs. The entire data stream is transmitted within one VC. All protocols based on Ethernet, Token Ring, FDDI, or Distributed Queue Dual Bus (DQDB) (IEEE 802.6 MAN) can be transported over ATM networks in this way (see Figure 10.52).

LLC encapsulation is used mainly in networks that only support PVCs, and which are unable to manage constantly changing VCs in use. In networks using SVCs, which typically have no trouble dynamically managing a large number of VCs, VC-based multiplexing can be used. This method avoids transporting the LLC header by setting up a separate virtual channel for each protocol. This makes transportation significantly more efficient overall, which is why this method is preferable to LLC encapsulation wherever possible (Figure 10.53).

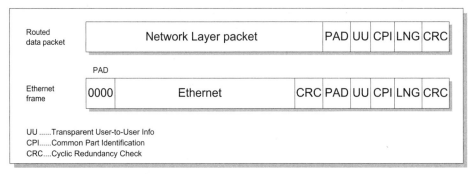

Figure 10.53 VC-based multiplexing (RFC 2684)

LAN-ATM: Classical IP and ARP over ATM (RFC 2225)

Classical IP and Address Resolution Protocol (ARP) over ATM go beyond the RFC 2684encapsulation technique to provide a complete implementation of the Internet protocol for ATM. IP address resolution, which is realized in Ethernet by ARP and Reverse Address Resolution Protocol (RARP), is handled by ATMARP and InATMARP functions. The mapping tables for the ATMARP and InATMARP functions are stored in an ATMARP server, which must be present in each logical IP subnet (LIS). The ARP client itself is responsible for registering its own IP/ATM address information with the ATMARP server, and for obtaining the IP/ATM address of the desired destination system from the ARP server. Entries in clients' and servers' ATMARP are subject to an aging process. Client ATMARP entries are valid for a maximum of 15 minutes, server ATMARP entries for at least 20 minutes. ATMARP PDUs, like the IP data packets themselves, are transported in AAL5 CPCS PDUs according to the rules of LLC encapsulation (see Figure 10.54).

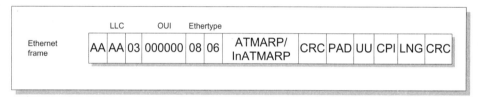

Figure 10.54 ATMARP and InATMARP (RFC 2225)

The following rules govern the design and operation of Classical IP subnetworks (LISs):

- All IP nodes of an LIS must be directly connected to the ATM network.
- All IP nodes of an LIS must have the same IP network or subnet work address.
- Network nodes outside the LIS must be accessible only through routers.
- All IP nodes in an LIS must be able to resolve addresses by ATMARP.
- Every IP node in an LIS must be able to communicate with all other IP nodes.
- Address resolution must function both for PVCs and for SVCs.

The default packet size in CIPs is 9,180 bytes. Adding the 8-byte LLC/SNAP header yields a default AAL5 PDU size of 9,188 bytes in CIP networks. The differences between RFC 2225 and its predecessor RFC 1577 lie mainly in the in the progress made in signaling procedures during the intervening 5 years.

LAN Emulation (LANE)

The most universal method of efficiently integrating ATM networks in existing, conventional LAN structures involves a complete emulation of the LAN MAC layer, which allows all existing LAN applications to be extended across ATM networks without modification. From the point of view of traditional local-area networking, the LAN emulation service behaves the same as a conventional MAC LAN driver. The ATM Forum's LAN Emulation (Version 2) is defined in the two documents LANE-LUNI and LANE-LNNI, and is based on five ATM service modules that build on AAL5:

- LAN Emulation Client (LE Client or LEC)
- LAN Emulation Server (LE Server or LES)
- LAN Emulation Configuration Server (LE Configuration Server or LECS)
- Broadcast and Unknown Server (BUS)
- Selected Multicast Server (SMS)

LUNI describes the processes at the interface to the LE Client, while LNNI specifies the protocols for networking LE Client, LE Server, BUS and SMS components. The use of LNNI components permits the coordination of several LE Servers, LE Configuration Servers and BUS systems so that redundant LANE structures can be built. LE Clients can also be grouped in subnetworks regardless of their location or the LE Server or BUS used, which makes it possible to build virtual Emulated LANs (ELANs).

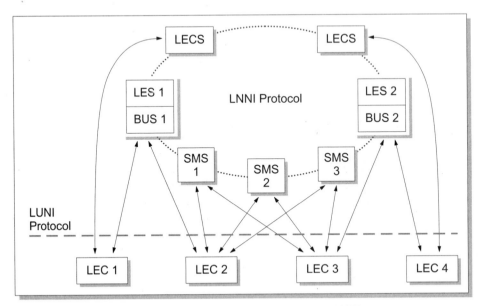

Figure 10.55 LAN emulation: LUNI and LNNI

With regard to the protocol stacks of end systems, LANE emulates the most widely used protocol driver specifications: Network Driver Interface Specification (NDIS), Open Data Link Interface (ODI) and Data Link Provider Interface (DLPI). The LAN data packets themselves (IEEE 802.3 Ethernet or IEEE 803.5 Token Ring) are transported over AAL5 in "LAN emulation frames". No special LANE frame type is defined for FDDI: either Ethernet or Token-Ring frames can be used. Using the Token-Ring frame format yields better results because the MAC address format is the same as in FDDI. LANE also provides quality-of-service functions for communication between LANE stations connected by ATM.

The LE Client software performs all the necessary control functions as well as the actual data communication over the ATM interface, providing a standard LAN MAC interface (NDIS, ODI or DLPI) to higher-layer applications. LE Clients consist of the following components:

- System hardware (PC, workstation, router, etc.)
- Standard LAN software (MAC address, protocol stack, drivers, etc.)
- LE Client software
- ATM interface with ATM address

The LE Server module controls the emulated LAN (ELAN). It includes functions such as registration of LE Clients and MAC-to-ATM address resolution for all registered stations. Every LE Client participating in an ELAN reports its LAN MAC address, the corresponding ATM address, and any necessary route information to the LE Server. When a LAN data packet needs to be sent, the ATM address of the destination is first sought in the address table of the LE Server. If it is not found there, address resolution must be performed by BUS broadcasts.

The LE Configuration Server manages the assignments of LE Clients to various ELANs by maintaining the configuration information of the ELANs in a configuration database. An LE Client can belong to several ELANs simultaneously.

The BUS module retransmits all the LE Clients' broadcast and multicast data packets. These include:

- All data packets with broadcast or multicast addresses
- Data packets sent to a MAC address for which the LE Client does not know the corresponding ATM address and which could not be resolved by the LE Server
- The source routing mechanism's explorer data packets used to determine optimum routes

Data packets received by the BUS are retransmitted in sequence to the appropriate group of destination LE Clients. This is necessary in order to avoid overlapping of AAL5 data packets from different senders.

Functional Processes in LAN Emulation

Process control between the individual LE Servers takes place by means of control VCCs and data VCCs. Control virtual channels are used to connect LE Clients with LE Servers and with LE Configuration Servers. Communication between LE Clients, as well as between BUSs and LE Clients, takes place over data virtual channels (data VCCs). In contrast to LANE Specification 1.0, LANE v2 also supports LCC Multiplexing. This means that the data streams of several ELANs, and of several different protocols, can be transported over a single VCC.

When a new LE Client is added to an ELAN, the LE Client first sets up a Configuration Direct VCC to the LE Configuration Server in order to register as a member of a particular ELAN. At the same time it may optionally use the LE configuration protocol to negotiate a variety of parameters (addresses, name of the ELAN, maximum frame size).

Next, the Control Direct VCC to the LE Server is set up. At this point the LE Client should be in possession of all information necessary for participation in the LAN emulation service, including the LE Client Identifier (LECID), the LAN type (802.3 Ethernet, 802.5 Token Ring), etc. If necessary, the LE Server may also set up a one-way, point-to-multipoint Control Distribute VCC to several LE Clients. (Point-to-multipoint connections are supported in LANE Version 2.0, but not in LANE 1.0). Finally, communication with the BUS is opened over a Data Direct VCC. The LE Client is then ready for operation under the LAN emulation service (see Figure 10.56). The various connections are set up and cleared down by means of the ATM Forum UNI signaling protocols (UNI 3.0, UNI 3.1, UNI 4.0).

In LAN emulation, data flows either between the LE Client and the BUS, or between one LE Client and another. If an LE Client needs to send a packet to a station whose ATM address is unknown, it first sends an LE-ARP message to the LE Server. The LE Server either forwards the LE-ARP request directly to the desired station, or provides the sender with the desired ATM address in the form of an LE-ARP response. Several data VCCs may be set up between two LE Clients, if both of them support this. The application layer may specify QoS parameters for the connections, such as ATM Traffic Descriptor, Alternative ATM Traffic Descriptor (only in UNI 4.0), Minimum Acceptable Traffic Descrip-

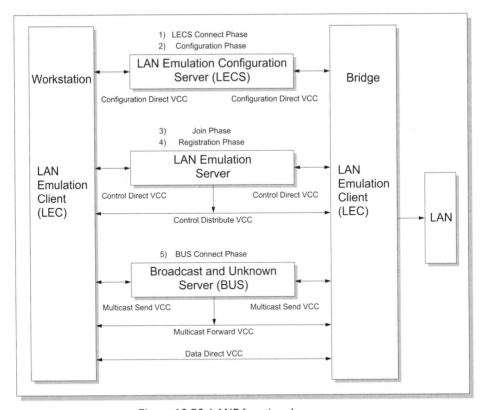

Figure 10.56 LANE functional processes

tor (only in UNI 4.0), Broadband Bearer Capability, QoS parameters, End-to-End Transmit Delay (only in UNI 4.0) etc. If no specific QoS parameters are requested, the default QoS parameters for LANE data VCCs must be used (UBR or ABR, QoS class 0).

Because LE Clients can send data packets to the same destination by different paths—via the BUS or over different data VCCs, for example—the Flush Message protocol is used to preserve the order of the LAN data packets during transmission over the ELAN. The Flush Message protocol in effect "deletes" the old transmission path when communication is moved to a new path. The LE Client sends an LE Flush message over the given VCC to ensure that all data packets sent over that virtual channel have arrived at the receiving station, and that no more packets are forthcoming in the opposite direction. On receiving the Flush response, the LE Client knows that no more data will be sent to it over the given VCC, and can begin using the new VCC.

All LANE components must support one of the following maximum sizes for AAL5 SDUs: 1,516; 1,580; 4,544; 9,234; or 18,190 bytes for non-multiplexed data packets, and 1,528; 1,592; 4,556; 9,246 or 18,202 bytes for multiplex LLC data.

The SDU length of 1,516 is due to the fact that LANE data packets contain the 2-byte LAN emulation header (LEH), but not the 4-byte checksum. For Token Ring, maximum packet sizes of 4,450 bytes (for 4 Mbit/s) and 18,200 bytes (for

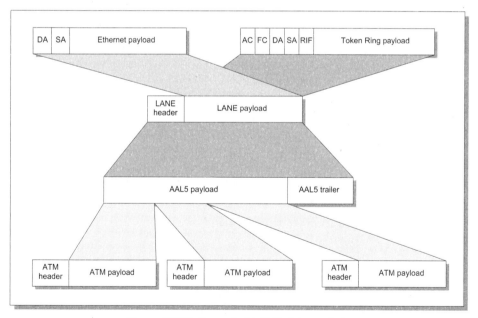

Figure 10.57 Format of LANE data packets

16 Mbit/s) are calculated based on a Token Holding Timer value of 9.1 ms. However, LANE data packets contain no SD, FCS, ED, or FS fields and no interframe spacing gap, so that the resulting lengths are 4,544 and 18,190 bytes.

Multiprotocol over ATM (MPOA)

ATM networks can use LAN Emulation to emulate Ethernet and Token Ring topologies. Such emulated ELANs can then form the basis of subnetworks (virtual LANs) that include network nodes of all three network topologies: Ethernet, Token Ring and ATM. Any ATM network can contain several ELANs, but LAN Emulation alone does not make it possible to connect ELANs to one another, except through the use of conventional routers. The MPOA specification does away with this restriction. MPOA, or Multiprotocol over ATM, integrates LANE v2 with the Next Hop Resolution Protocol (NHRP) and the Multicast Address Resolution Protocol (MARS), and permits inter-ELAN communication without the use of additional routers. By separating the route selection and data forwarding functions, MPOA is able to provide efficient routing even in large, complex networks.

Every MPOA network consists of MPOA servers (MPS) and MPOA clients (MPC). MPOA servers are responsible for route selection, while MPOA clients perform the actual forwarding of data from their LE Client interfaces, requesting the appropriate routes from the MPS as necessary.

Prerequisites for the use of MPOA in the LAN include support for:

- ATM UNI signaling (UNI 3.0, 3.1, 4.0)
- LANE v2
- Next Hop Resolution Protocol

Basic MPOA Processes

As in LANE, all MPOA processes are managed through control virtual channels, while the actual data transport takes place through separate data virtual channels. All control and data flows are transported over VCCs with LLC encapsulation (RFC 1483). Channels are set up and cleared down in accordance with one of the UNI signaling specifications, UNI 3.0, 3.1, or 4.0. Four kinds of control virtual channels are defined:

- MPS - MPC configuration virtual channels
- MPC–MPS control virtual channels
- MPS–MPS control virtual channels
- MPC–MPC control virtual channels

MPOA components obtain configuration information from the LE Configuration Server. The MPOA clients obtain route information from the MPOA server over the MPC–MPS control virtual channel. The MPS–MPS control virtual channels are used by standard routing protocols and NHRP to exchange route information. MPCs exchange control information with one another only if one MPC receives misrouted data packets from another. In this case, the sender MPC is notified so that it can delete the incorrect routing information from its cache. MPOA networks are characterized by the following five basic operating processes:

- Configuration
- Discovery
- Target resolution
- Connection management
- Data communication

MPOA obtains all its configuration information from the ELANs' LE Configuration Servers. Additionally, MPOA components can also be directly configured by means of the MPOA MIB. All MPCs and MPSs automatically detect each other's existence by using an extended LE-ARP protocol. This protocol transports not only the ATM addresses of the individual stations, but also information about the MPOA type (MPC or MPS). The target resolution process determines the route to the destination, and is carried out using modified NHRP Resolution Request messages. The connection management process is responsible for setting up and operating the virtual control and data connections, and the data transport process consists of transmitting the user data over the selected routes. The various MPOA processes are controlled by means of eight MPOA and two NHRP control messages:

- MPOA Resolution Request
- MPOA Resolution Reply
- MPOA Cache Imposition Request
- MPOA Cache Imposition Reply
- MPOA Egress Cache Purge Request
- MPOA Egress Cache Purge Reply
- MPOA Keep Alive
- MPOA Trigger
- NHRP Purge Request
- NHRP Purge Reply

Route Selection in MPOA Networks

In selecting routes for data packet transport, MPOA makes a distinction between default routes and shortcuts. Data packets initially enter the MPOA network through an MPC. Because the MPC generally does not know the ATM address that corresponds to the Layer 3 destination address of the packet, it does not attempt to set up a direct VC to the destination. By default, the data is first encapsulated in a LANE frame and forwarded to the default MPS router by the MPC's LE Client unit. This router forwards the data to the destination MPC according to the information available in its routing tables. Then the MPC attempts to resolve the network address of the packets by sending an MPOA Resolution Request message to the MPS. The MPS obtains the corresponding ATM address, along with the information whether a direct connection (shortcut) is available for the given connection, from its assigned Next Hop Server (NHS). If a shortcut is available, the MPS sends an Imposition Request message to the destination MPC to ask whether it is able to accept the shortcut connection. The destination MPC responds with an Imposition Reply message, which the MPS forwards to the originating MPC in the form of an MPOA Resolution Reply. The originating MPC can then set up the shortcut connection. The shortcut route information is entered in the MPC's routing cache, and all data packets for the given destination address are then sent directly over the shortcut. Figure 10.58 shows a schematic illustration of the MPOA route selection process. The default

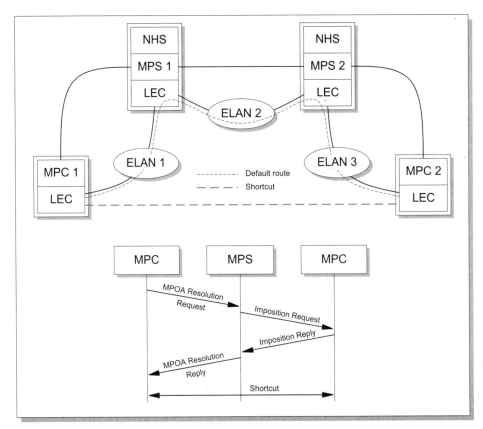

Figure 10.58 Route selection and shortcuts in MPOA networks

route between the MPOA clients MPC1 and MPC2 leads first to the LE Client interfaces of the three MPOA components connected to one another over the three ELANs. Once the shortcut has been obtained from the Next Hop Server, a direct connection can be set up between the LE Client interfaces of the two MPOA clients.

The Next Hop Resolution Protocol (NHRP)

Route optimization in MPOA networks is performed by means of the Non-Broadcast Multiple Access (NBMA) and NHRP because broadcast-based address resolution mechanisms are completely unsuitable for ATM networks. The purpose of NHRP is to find the ATM address that corresponds to a given network address (such as an IP address) so that a direct connection (shortcut) can be set up between two communicating stations. NHRP is based on a client-server model in which Next Hop Clients (NHC) send address resolution requests to a NHS. In MPOA, the MPOA servers play the part of NHCs and initiate Next Hop Resolution requests to the NHS as required by MPCs. Every NHR request contains the following information:

- Network address (for example, IP address) of the destination
- Network address of the sender
- ATM address of the sender

The NHS analyzes the incoming address resolution request and verifies whether it is itself competent to resolve the given destination. If not, it forwards the request to another NHS. Next Hop Servers may forward address resolution requests only to other NHSs that are not more than one hop away—thus the name "next hop" server. If the NHS is competent for the destination indicated in the request, it resolves the address and sends a reply packet containing the Next Hop Network address and the ATM address of the destination to the MPS, which forwards the information to the MPC. The MPC can then set up a direct VCC, or shortcut, to the destination.

10.1.11 Design Rules for ATM Networks

The design of ATM networks is subject to far fewer restrictions than classical LAN technologies such as Ethernet, FDDI or Token Ring. This is due to the wide range of possible transmission media, and to the fact that ATM was originally designed for use in wide-area networks. Distance limitations are therefore not a fundamental issue. So long as the specifications for the various segments of an ATM network are respected, distances of several thousand km can be bridged. The transmission delay can be calculated using a value of 6 µs per km and 2 µs per switch. The transmission delay for a path of 1,000 km and five switches is 6.01 ms.

The following tables list the limits for the maximum distances that can be spanned using various transmission media as defined in the appropriate ATM standards:

SDH/SONET-based ATM over twisted-pair cabling

Cable type	Transmission speed	Maximum distance
UTP-5	12.96 Mbit/s	400 m
UTP-5	25.92 Mbit/s	320 m
UTP-5	51.85 Mbit/s	160 m
UTP-5	155 Mbit/s	150 m
UTP-3	155 Mbit/s	100 m

Cell-based ATM over twisted-pair cabling

Cable type	Transmission speed	Maximum distance
UTP-3 (100W)	25 Mbit/s	100 m
UTP-4 (120W)	25 Mbit/s	100 m
STP (150W)	25 Mbit/s	100 m

SDH/SONET-based ATM over plastic fiber

Cable type	Transmission speed	Maximum distance
Plastic Optical Fiber (POF)	155 Mbit/s	50 m
Hard Polymer Clad Fiber (HPCF)	155 Mbit/s	100 m

SDH/SONET-based ATM over single-mode fiber

Fiber type	Wavelength	Transmission speed	Laser type	Maximum attenuation	Maximum distance
SM	1,310 nm	- 9.9 Gbit/s	SLM, MLM	0-7 dB	2 km
SM	1,310, 1,550 nm	- 9.9 Gbit/s	SLM, MLM	0-12 dB	15 km
SM	1,310, 1,550 nm	- 9.9 Gbit/s	SLM, MLM	10-14 dB	40 km

SDH/SONET-based ATM over multimode fiber

Fiber type	Wavelength	Transmission speed	Laser type	Maximum distance
MM	1,300 nm	155 Mbit/s	SW, LED-MMF	2 km
MM	1,300 nm	622 Mbit/s	LED-MMF	500 m
MM	1,300 nm	622 Mbit/s	SW-MMF	300 m

10.1.12 ATM Standards

All the important standards for ATM technology are developed by the ITU-T, the ATM Forum and the IETF. A selection of the most important ITU-T, ATM Forum and IETF Recommendations is listed here. A complete list of ITU-T and ATM Forum standards can be found in the Appendix or at the web sites listed below:

ATM Forum Standards

Technical Working Group	Approved Specifications	Specification	Approved Date
B-ICI	B-ICI 2.0 (integrated specification)	af-bici-0013.003	Dec, 1995
Control Signaling	PNNI Version 1.0 Security Signaling Addendum	af-cs-0116.000	May, 1999
	UNI Signaling 4.0 Security Addendum	af-cs-0117.000	May, 1999
Data Exchange Interface	Data Exchange Interface version 1.0	af-dxi-0014.000	Aug, 1993
Frame-Based ATM	Frame Based ATM over Sonet/SDH	af-fbatm-0151.000	July, 2000
LAN Emulation/ MPOA	LANE Servers Management Spec v1.0	af-lane-0057.000	Mar, 1996
	LANE v2.0 LUNI Interface	af-lane-0084.000	July, 1997
	LAN Emulation Client Management Specification Version 2.0	af-lane-0093.000	Oct, 1998
	LAN Emulation over ATM Version 2 - LNNI Specification	af-lane-0112.000	Feb. 1999
	Multi-Protocol Over ATM Specification v1.0	af-mpoa-0087.000	July, 1997
	Multi-Protocol Over ATM Version 1.0 MIB	af-mpoa-0092.000	July, 1998
	Multi-Protocol Over ATM Specification, Version 1.1	af-mpoa-0114.000	May, 1999
	Multi-Protocol Over ATM Version 1.0 MIB	af-mpoa-0092.000	July, 1998

Technical Working Group	Approved Specifications	Specification	Approved Date
Physical Layer	Utopia	af-phy-0017.000	Mar, 1994
	Mid-Range Physical Layer Specification for Category 3 UTP	af-phy-0018.000	Sep, 1994
	E3 UNI	af-phy-0034.000	Aug, 1995
	Physical Interface Specification for 25.6 Mb/s over Twisted Pair	af-phy-0040.000	Nov, 1995
	A Cell-Based Transmission Convergence Sublayer for Clear Channel Interfaces	af-phy-0043.000	Jan, 1996
	622.08 Mbps Physical Layer	af-phy-0046.000	Jan, 1996
	155.52 Mbps Physical Layer Specification for Category 3 UTP (See also UNI 3.1, af-uni-0010.002)	af-phy-0047.000	Nov, 1995
	120 Ohm Addendum to ATM PMD Interface Spec for 155 Mbps over TP	af-phy-0053.000	Jan, 1996
	DS3 Physical Layer Interface Spec	af-phy-0054.000	Mar, 1996
	155 Mbps over MMF Short Wave Length Lasers, Addendum to UNI 3.1	af-phy-0062.000	July, 1996
	WIRE (PMD to TC layers)	af-phy-0063.000	July, 1996
	E-1 Physical Layer Interface Specification	af-phy-0064.000	Sep, 1996
	155 Mbps over Plastic Optical Fiber (POF) Version 1.0	af-phy-0079.000	May, 1997
	155 Mb/s Plastic Optical Fiber and Hard Polymer Clad Fiber PMD Specification Version 1.1	af-phy-0079.001	Jan, 1999
	Inverse ATM Mux Version 1.0	af-phy-0086.000	July, 1997
	Inverse Multiplexing for ATM (IMA) Specification Version 1.1	af-phy-0086.001	Mar, 1999
	Physical Layer High Density Glass Optical Fiber Annex	af-phy-0110.000	Feb, 1999
	622 and 2488 Mbit/s Cell-Based Physical Layer	af-phy-0128.000	July, 1999
	ATM on Fractional E1/T1	af-phy-0130.000	Oct, 1999
	2.4 Gbps Physical Layer Specification	af-phy-0133.000	Oct, 1999
	Physical Layer Control	af-phy-0134.000	Oct, 1999
	Utopia 3 Physical Layer Interface	af-phy-0136.000	Nov, 1999
	Multiplexed Status Mode (MSM3)	af-phy-0142.000	Mar, 2000

Technical Working Group	Approved Specifications	Specification	Approved Date
	Frame-Based ATM Interface (Level 3)	af-phy-0143.000	Mar, 2000
	UTOPIA Level 4	af-phy-0144.001	Mar, 2000
PNNI	PNNI ABR Addendum	af-pnni-0075.000	Jan, 1997
	PNNI v1.0 Errata and PICs	af-pnni-0081.000	July, 1997
	PNNI 1.0 Addendum (soft PVC MIB)	af-pnni-0066.000	Sep, 1996
Service Aspects ...... and Applications	Audio/Visual Multimedia Services: Video on Demand v1.0	af-saa-0049.000	Jan, 1996
	Audio/Visual Multimedia Services: Video on Demand v1.1	af-saa-0049.001	Mar, 1997
	ATM Names Service	af-saa-0069.000	Nov, 1996
	FUNI 2.0	af-saa-0088.000	July, 1997
	Native ATM Services DLPI Addendum Version 1.0	af-saa-api-dlpi-0091.000	Feb, 1998
	H.323 Media Transport over ATM	af-saa-0124.000	July, 1999
Traffic .... Management	Traffic Management 4.1	af-tm-0121.000	Mar, 1999
Voice & Teleph- .... ony over ATM	(DBCES) Dynamic Bandwidth Utilization in 64 KBPS Time Slot Trunking Over ATM - Using CES	af-vtoa-0085.000	July, 1997
	ATM Trunking Using AAL1 for Narrow Band Services v1.0	af-vtoa-0089.000	July, 1997
	ATM Trunking Using AAL2 for Narrowband Services	af-vtoa-0113.000	Feb, 1999
	Low Speed Circuit Emulation Service	af-vtoa-0119.000	May, 1999
	ICS for ATM Trunking Using AAL2 for Narrowband Services	af-vtoa-0120.000	May, 1999
	Low Speed Circuit Emulation Service (LSCES) Implementation Conformance Statement Performance	af-vtoa-0132.000	Oct, 1999

ITU-T ATM Standards

I.113	Vocabulary of terms for broadband aspects of ISDN
I.121	Broadband Aspects of ISDN
I.150	B-ISDN ATM Functional Characteristics
I.211	B-ISDN: Service Aspects
I.311	B-ISDN: General Network Aspects
I.321	B-ISDN Protocol Reference Model and Its Application
I.327	B-ISDN Functional Architecture
I.361	B-ISDN ATM Layer Specification
I.363.1	B-ISDN ATM Adaptation Layer Specification: Type 1 AAL
I.363.2	B-ISDN ATM Adaptation Layer Specification: Type 2 AAL
I.363.3	B-ISDN ATM Adaptation Layer Specification: Type 3/4 AAL
I.363.5	B-ISDN ATM Adaptation Layer Specification: Type 5 AALI.432.1 B-ISDN User-Network Interface – Physical Layer (General) Specification
I.610	B-ISDN Operation and Maintenance Principles and Functions
I.356	B-ISDN ATM Layer Cell Transfer Performance (formerly I.35B)
I.371	Traffic Control and Congestion Control in B-ISDN
I.350	General Aspects of Quality of Service and Network Performance in Digital Networks, Including ISDNs
I.555	Frame Relaying Bearer Service Interworking
I.365.1	B-ISDN ATM Adaptation Layer Sublayers: Frame Relaying Service Specific Convergence Sublayer (FR-SSCS)
I.370	Congestion Management for the ISDN Frame Relaying Bearer Service
I.372	Frame Relaying Bearer Service Network-to-Network Interface Requirements
I.233.1	ISDN Frame Mode Bearer Services: ISDN Frame Relaying Bearer Service
F.811	Broadband Connection-Oriented Bearer Service

Q.2931   Broadband Integrated Services Digital Network (B-ISDN) – Digital Subscriber Signaling System No. 2 (DSS 2) – User-Network Interface (UNI) - Layer 3 Specification for Basic Call/Connection Control

Q.2951.1 Stage 3 Description for Number Identification Supplementary Services Using B-ISDN Digital Subscriber Signaling System No. 2 (DSS 2) – Basic Call [Clauses 1–6 and 8; DDI, MSN, CLIP, CLIR, COLP, COLR, SUB]

Q.2957.1 Stage 3 Description for Additional Information Transfer Supplementary Services Using B-ISDN Digital Subscriber Signaling System No. 2 (DSS 2) – Basic Call: Clause 1 – User-to-User Signaling (UUS)

Q.2971   Broadband Integrated Services Digital Network B-ISDN - DSS 2 - Digital Subscriber Signaling System No. 2 - User-Network Interface Layer 3 Specification for Point-to-Multipoint Call/Connection Control

IETF ATM Standards

RFC2379 RSVP over ATM Implementation Guidelines, L. Berger, August, 1998

RFC2225 Classical IP and ARP over ATM, M. Laubach, J. Halpern, April, 1998 (Obsoletes RFC1626, RFC1577)

RFC2226 IP Broadcast over ATM Networks T. Smith, G. Armitage, October, 1997

RFC2320 Definitions of Managed Objects for Classical IP and ARP Over ATM Using SMIv2 (IPOA-MIB), M. Greene, J. Luciani, K. White, T. Kuo, April, 1998

RFC2331 ATM Signaling Support for IP over ATM - UNI Signaling 4.0 Update, M. Maher, April, 1998

RFC2380 RSVP over ATM Implementation Requirements, L. Berger, August, 1998

RFC2381 Interoperation of Controlled-Load Service and Guaranteed Service with ATM, M. Garrett, M. Borden, August, 1998

RFC2382 A Framework for Integrated Services and RSVP over ATM, E. Crawley, L. Berger, S. Berson, F. Baker, M. Borden, J. Krawczyk, August, 1998

RFC2383 ST2+ over ATM Protocol Specification - UNI 3.1 Version, M. Suzuki, August, 1998

RFC2417 Definitions of Managed Objects for Multicast over UNI 3.0/3.1 based ATM Networks, C. Chung, M. Greene, September, 1998 (Obsoletes RFC2366)

RFC2492 IPv6 over ATM Networks, G. Armitage, P. Schulter, M. Jork, January, 1999

RFC2512 Accounting Information for ATM Networks, K. McCloghrie, J. Heinanen, W. Greene, A. Prasad, February, 1999

RFC2515 Definitions of Managed Objects for ATM Management, K. Tesink, Ed, February, 1999 (Obsoletes RFC1695)

RFC2601 ILMI-Based Server Discovery for ATMARP, M. Davison, June, 1999, ASCII

RFC2684 Multiprotocol Encapsulation over ATM Adaptation Layer 5, D. Grossman, J. Heinanen, September, 1999, ASCII (Obsoletes RFC1483)

RFC2761 Terminology for ATM Benchmarking, J. Dunn, C. Martin, February, 2000

RFC2823 PPP over Simple Data Link (SDL) using SONET/SDH with ATM-like framing, J. Carlson, P. Langner, E. Hernandez-Valencia, J. Manchester, May, 2000, ASCII

RFC2844 OSPF over ATM and Proxy-PAR, T. Przygienda, P. Droz, R. Haas, May, 2000

RFC2955 Definitions of Managed Objects for Monitoring and Controlling the Frame Relay/ATM PVC Service Interworking Function, K. Rehbehn, O. Nicklass, G. Mouradian, October, 2000

ITU-T Recommendations:
http://www.itu.int/itudoc/itu-t/rec/

ATM Forum Specifications:
http://www.atmforum.com/atmforum/specs

The IETF RFCs :
http://www.ietf.org/rfc.html

10.2 Troubleshooting ATM

In addition to protocol analyzers and cable testers for twisted pair and fiber optics, troubleshooting in ATM networks involves the use of ATM switch and node management software that is able to track and display the various ATM Operations and Maintenance (OAM) information flows.

ATM contains a number of powerful OAM functions. Because ATM is based on a switched architecture, these integrated monitoring functions are very important; it is no longer possible to monitor the entire activity in a network from a single point, as in traditional network technologies such as Ethernet, Token Ring or FDDI. Monitoring of a single ATM connection only yields information about the traffic between the two connection endpoints (such as a computer system and an ATM switch port). The first step in diagnosing problems in an ATM network is to monitor and analyze data obtained from operation logs and OAM statistics of the various ATM network nodes. Although many of today's ATM components only support, interpret, or display a small proportion of the ATM diagnostics functions, a protocol analyzer can be used to analyze all five OAM flows (F1–F5) and determine whether they report a problem or not.

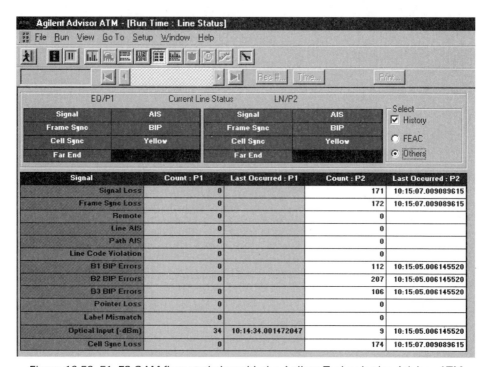

Figure 10.59 F1–F3 OAM flow statistics with the Agilent Technologies Advisor ATM

Analysis of the integrated network diagnostic functions and the OAM flows is usually sufficient to isolate the systems that are affected by the problem. The troubleshooting process then entails basic functional tests of these components, including loopback tests on the ATM interfaces, firmware tests (is the firmware active?) and hardware self-tests. Cabling and connectors are checked by running bit-error ratio tests and performing OTDR and LED/laser power spectrum measurements. (OTDRs, or optical time domain reflectometers, are physical-layer test instruments for fiber connections. They send defined light pulses over the fiber and measure amplitude and response time of the reflected return signal. The test results include the fiber length and all attenuation components—splices, connectors, fiber loss—along the segment.) If the components pass the basic functional tests, OAM flows F1–F3 in the SDH/SONET layer are examined. If no fault is found here, the ATM layer and the application protocols above it must be analyzed. This begins with checking whether the required PVCs and SVCs are active and working, and whether the ATM addresses are correct. To determine whether the traffic contract parameters for the connections or applications in question are being met, characteristic ATM-layer traffic parameters are measured, including

- User cell rate
- Cell loss
- Cell delay
- Number of cell-sync losses
- Number of cells with corrected headers
- ATM payload bit-error ratio

Finally, if the ATM layer seems to work correctly, the application layer protocols, such as Classical IP over ATM, IP encapsulation, LAN emulation, or PNNI, must be examined.

Each step in the ATM troubleshooting process outlined previously is discussed in detail in the following sections.

10.2.1   Troubleshooting the Physical Layer

Once the error domain has been located, the troubleshooting process can start. If connections are interrupted or network nodes are down, the first step usually consists of basic functional tests of the component systems. Do the activity LEDs of the interface in the problem domain indicate normal working order? Most ATM interfaces indicate normal sending and receiving by a green LED, SDH/SONET-level problems by a yellow LED, and complete signal loss by a red LED. The ATM interface can also be tested using a fiber loop or a UTP loopback connector. If the loopback connection is in order but the loopback test fails, the firmware may not be loaded correctly or may not detect the hardware. If the loopback test is successful, the ATM interface and the firmware are in order. In this case, you must test whether the physical layer connection exists between the network interfaces in the problem domain. This can be done by inserting a protocol analyzer in pass-through mode into the connection between the two nodes. The analyzer may be inserted directly into the ATM connection (active monitoring), or may be connected in passive mode by means of optical power

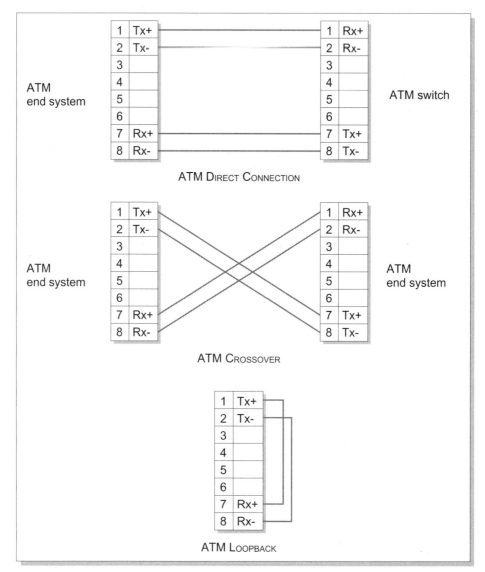

Figure 10.60 UTP Cat. 5 pin assignments for ATM direct connection, crossover, and loopback cables

splitters. Note that the transmitter ports of many analyzers are equipped with single-mode lasers. When actively monitoring multimode fiber components, the transmitters must be fitted with 10 dB attenuators in order to avoid overdriving the receiver electronics. This does not result in damage to the multimode receivers, however. Because lasers still emit a small amount of light when "off" (that is, when sending a "0"): sensitive multimode receivers misinterpret this as a "1" and never see the difference between "0" and "1". Attenuators can correct this.

Analyzing Physical Layer OAM Information Flows

ATM's integrated error detection mechanisms are contained in the OAM information flows F1 to F5. Flows F1–F3 yield information about the operating state of the SDH/SONET transport structure, while F4 and F5 contain the corresponding ATM layer data. F4 concerns ATM virtual path connections (VPCs), F5 the virtual channel connections (VCCs). The error management function in ATM is based on two types of alarms: Alarm Indication Signal (AIS) and Remote Defect Indicator (RDI). The AIS is sent by the VC or VP node, which recognizes the error condition to all upstream nodes so long as the error condition persists. Immediately after the AIS, an RDI signal is sent upstream to the end nodes of the connections affected. These signals are also sent periodically until the error condition is resolved. VP-AIS and VP-RDI messages are always sent in cells with VCI = 4, while VC-AIS and VC-RDI messages are sent in cells with PT = 101.

Two mechanisms are available to detect error conditions: continuity checks (CC) and loopback tests. Continuity checks continuously monitor the availability of a connection. To this end, CC cells are periodically inserted into the user cell stream. ATM network nodes along the connection path can then check for the presence of these CC cells. When no more cells are received, an AIS alarm for loss of continuity (LOC) is triggered.

If the ATM network components support OAM cell processing, they can often locate the failure domain by analyzing the contents of the OAM flows. If not, the OAM flows must be captured and analyzed using a protocol analyzer.

Verifying ATM Cell Transmission on the Physical Layer

The analysis of ATM cell transmission parameters with the help of a protocol analyzer can also provide information about problems in the physical layer. The traffic parameters to examine include corrected header ratio, discarded cell ratio, loss of cell delineation rate, and the demux error ratio.

Corrected Header Ratio

The corrected header ratio is the number of cells with errored but correctable headers divided by the total number of cells received. This parameter is mainly influenced by the bit-error ratio of the transmission path. There is a small probability that cells with errored headers may appear as valid cells, and thus lead to incorrect transmissions (misinserted cells). The probability of such an event can be calculated from the number of errored headers containing more than two incorrect bits—the HEC checksum of such a header no longer indicates

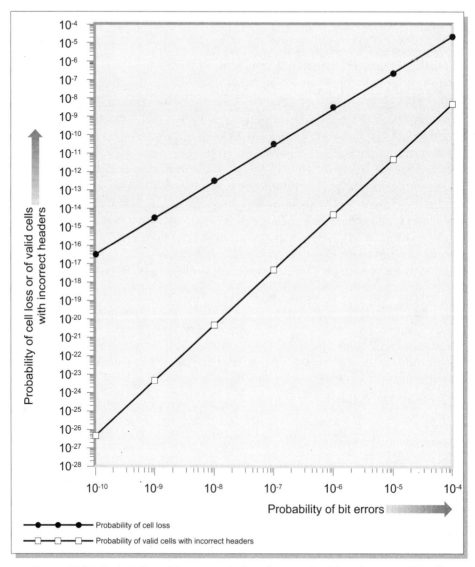

Figure 10.61 Probability of the transmission of errored cell headers as valid cells in relation to the bit-error ratio

whether it is corrupt—and the ratio of valid header values to the number of all possible header values. Figure 10.61 shows the probability of the transmission of errored cell headers as valid cells in relation to the bit-error ratio.

Discarded Cell Ratio

The discarded cell ratio equals the number of cells received with errored headers that cannot be corrected and which are therefore discarded, divided by the total number of cells received (valid or not). This quantity is also influenced by the bit-error ratio of the transmission path.

Loss of Cell Delineation Rate

The loss of cell delineation rate is the number of cell synchronization losses over a certain time interval.

Mean Loss of Delineation Duration

The mean loss of delineation duration is defined as the number of missing Cell Received Events (CRE_2) due to cell synchronization loss within a given time interval divided by the total number of expected CRE_2 events in this time interval (see Figure 10.66).

Demux Error Ratio

The demux (demultiplex) error ratio is the number of all correctly transmitted cells containing an invalid VPI value divided by the total number of correctly transmitted cells.

Causes of Problems in the Physical Layer

Physical layer problems in ATM networks may have a variety of causes. Many problems occur on the connections to ATM switches, where a change of the physical transmission media is required (connectors, fiber, switch port). Transmission errors can arise due to aging, humidity, dust, or material flaws. Furthermore, the signal quality of the cabling determines the bit-error ratio in the transmission framework (SDH/SONET, E3, T3, etc.) and consequently the performance of the ATM network.

10.2.2   Troubleshooting the ATM Layer

If no faults can be detected in the physical layer, the ATM layer must be examined. This involves checking whether the required PVCs and SVCs are working, and whether the ATM addresses are correct. The OAM PM cell streams are then monitored using protocol analyzers to determine whether the ATM layer traffic conforms to the traffic contract parameters for the connections or applications in question. Parameters to examine include:

- User cell rate
- Cell loss ratio (CLR)
- Cell transfer delay (CTD)
- Cell delay variation (CDV)
- Number of cell-sync losses
- Number of cells with corrected headers
- Number of cells that violate the traffic contract (non-conforming cells or NCC)

Verifying PVCs, SVCs and Addressing

The first step in troubleshooting the ATM layer is to verify whether the ATM connections are working at all. Configuring one ATM node to send a constant stream of pings to another can do this. If the ping does not get through to its destination, use the activity LEDs on the ATM interfaces or a protocol analyzer to determine whether the cells leave the initiating system, reach and leave the switch, and arrive at the interface of the destination node. If no ping packets

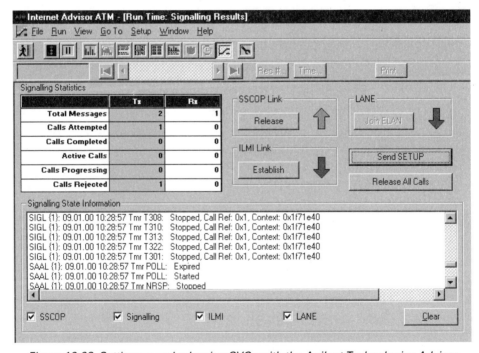

Figure 10.62 Setting up and releasing SVCs with the Agilent Technologies Advisor

arrive, check on the switch whether the PVC is set up at all, the VCI values are correctly configured, and the internal path between the two switch ports is functional.

If you use SVCs you must make sure the signaling process that sets up your connections is working. If pings do not go through between two SVC nodes, the first step once again is to check the configuration of the switch and the end systems. In the case of Classical IP over ATM, are the systems registered on the ATMARP server with their ATM and IP addresses? Is the correct address of the ARP server registered on the clients? If so, at least the SVC setup between the clients and the ARP server should succeed. If the clients are still unable to communicate with one another, make sure the ILMI stack is active on the switch and on the clients. If the problem still persists, you must monitor and analyze the signaling process with a protocol analyzer. Finally, the switch ports and the switch configuration should be examined in detail.

Verifying ATM Performance Parameters

If the connections are set up successfully, but problems persist on the application layer and during data transfers, the next step is to examine the ATM performance parameters. Oftentimes functional tests of ATM connections (such as sending pings between two nodes, setting up and clearing down SVCs, etc.) seem to show that everything is working fine, but once application data is transmitted at higher traffic loads problems arise. Reasons for this type of behavior can be excessive cell loss or cell delay values, traffic contracts that provide insufficient bandwidth and therefore cause cells to be discarded, or simply an overloaded switch. Measurements that determine these types of ATM performance parameters can be made either in-service or out-of-service. Out-of-service measurements are performed using special out-of-service test cells defined in ITU-T Recommendation O.191.

5 bytes	4 bytes	4 bytes	37 bytes	1 byte	2 bytes
ATM header	sequence number	time stamp	not used	TCPT	(CRC10)

TCPT ....Test Cell Payload Type field

Figure 10.63 Format of the O.191 test cell

Out-of-service test cells have standard ATM cell headers and can be sent using any VPI/VCI label value (VCI > 31). In the payload they carry a 32-bit sequence number to permit detection of cell loss and cell misinsertion errors, and a 32-bit time stamp to measure cell delay and cell delay variation. This allows CDV and 2-

point CDV measurements up to transmission speeds of 2.4 Gbit/s. The least significant bit of the time stamp has a granularity of 10 ns, though for physical links slower than 2.4 Gbit/s the time stamp is normally incremented from a higher order bit. In the simplest case, a protocol analyzer with one transmit and one receive port is sufficient to perform these out-of-service measurements. Care must be taken with using loopbacks, however, because the traffic contracts of virtual circuits may be asymmetrically specified for the different directions.

A very useful extension to the use of ITU-T Recommendation O.191 test cells is available if the test cells can be shaped to simulate traffic that only just meets the traffic contract in terms of peak cell rate (PCR), cell delay variation tolerance (CDVT), sustainable cell rate (SCR), and maximum burst size (MBS). Shaped test cell traffic can be injected into a network at the UNI and on the far side UNI, and measurements can be made of the delivered QoS in terms of cell loss, CDV, etc. With a pair of analyzers capable of simultaneously sending shaped traffic and analyzing received traffic, bi-directional measurements can be made simultaneously. Asymmetrical traffic contracts can be tested without difficulty in this configuration because each analyzer can independently shape traffic according to the traffic contract for that direction. The fact that it may be impossible to synchronize the clocks of the analyzers with respect to phase as well as frequency need not invalidate the most useful measurements because often the absolute delay is less important than CDV and cell loss.

For in-service measurements, however, more sophisticated test equipment with at least two independent but time-correlated receivers and transmitters is required. Such a tester can be inserted into the lines of transmit and receive ports of the ATM element under test, as shown in Figure 10.64.

If supported by the network components, in-service tests can also be carried out with the help of special performance management OAM cells. These cells are periodically inserted in the user cell streams of the connections to be monitored. The measurement parameters contained in the payload of these cells (sequence number, user cell count, time stamp, cell loss counter) provide information about the operational condition state of the ATM connection.

The ATM layer performance parameters are defined in the following sections.

Cell Error Ratio

The cell error ratio is the number of invalid cells divided by the sum of the number of successfully transmitted cells and the number of invalid cells. Successfully transferred cells, tagged cells, and errored cells contained in severely errored cell blocks are excluded from the calculation of cell error ratio.

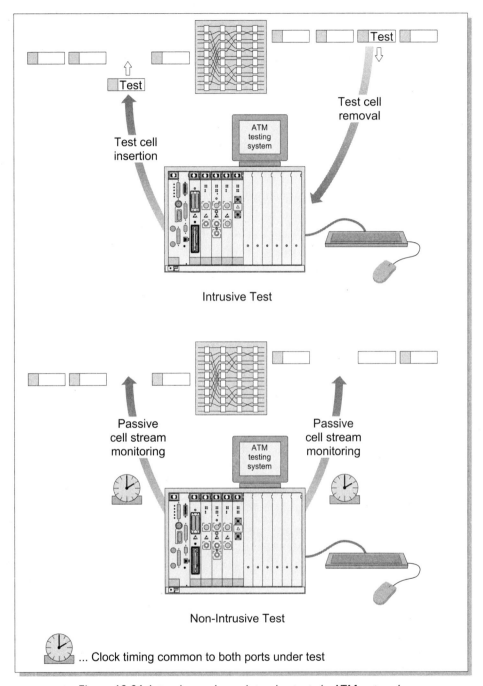

Test cell
removal

ATM
testing
system

Test cell
insertion

Intrusive Test

Passive
cell stream
monitoring

Passive
cell stream
monitoring

ATM
testing
system

Non-Intrusive Test

... Clock timing common to both ports under test

Figure 10.64 Intrusive and non-intrusive tests in ATM networks

Cell Loss Ratio

The cell loss ratio is the number of cells lost divided by the total number of cells transmitted. Lost cells and transmitted cells in severely errored cell blocks are excluded from the calculation of cell loss ratio. There are three different cell loss ratio measurements:

a) Cell loss ratio for cells with high priority (cell loss priority bit = 0): CLR_0
   If $N_t(0)$ is the number of cells with CLP = 0 and $N_l(0)$ is the number of lost cells plus the number of tagged cells, then CLR_0 is defined as $N_l(0) / N_t(0)$.

b) Cell loss ratio for the entire cell stream: CLR_{0+1}
   If $N_t(0 + 1)$ is the number of all cells transmitted and $N_l(0 + 1)$ is the number of lost cells, CLR_{0+1} is defined as $N_l(0 + 1) / N_t(0 + 1)$.

c) Cell loss ratio for cells with low priority: CLR_1
   If $N_t(1)$ is the number of cells with CLP = 1 and $N_l(1)$ the number of lost cells, CLR_1 is defined as $N_l(1) / N_t(1)$.

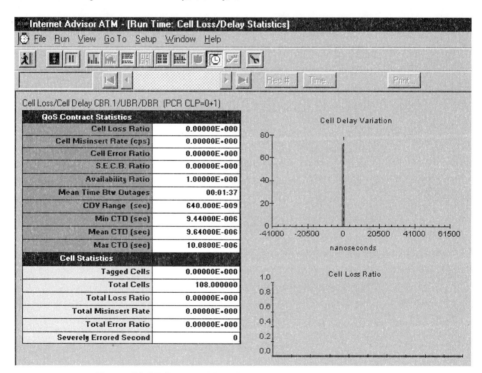

Figure 10.65 Determining CDV using a protocol analyzer

Cell Misinsertion Rate

The cell misinsertion rate is defined as the number of defective cells (cells containing a wrong VPI/VCI due to non-corrected header errors) transmitted within a time interval divided by this interval.

Cell Transfer Delay (CTD)

The cell transfer delay is defined as the time t_2-t_1 between two corresponding cell transmission/reception events CRE_1 (t_1) and CRE_2 (t_2) (where $t_2 > t_1$).

Cell Delay Variation (CDV)

Two types of variations in the cell transfer delay are defined: one-point cell delay variation, which examines cells arriving at one measurement point, and two-point cell delay variation, which examines cell delay variation at measurement point two relative to measurement point one.

One-Point Cell Delay Variation

The one-point cell delay variation (y_k) for cell k at measurement point MP is defined as the difference between the reference arrival time (c_k) of the cell and

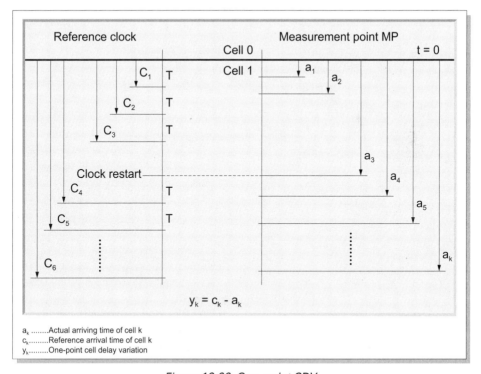

Figure 10.66 One-point CDV

the actual arrival time (a_k), that is, $y_k = c_k - a_k$, where the reference arrival time is defined as follows:

$$c_0 = a_0 = 0$$

$$c_{k+1} = c_k + T \qquad if \ c_k > a_k$$

$$c_{k+1} = a_k + T \qquad in \ all \ other \ cases$$

Two-Point Cell Delay Variation

The two-point cell delay variation (v_k) for cell k between MP1 and MP2 is defined as the difference between the actual cell delay (x_k) and the reference delay $(d_{1,2})$ between the two measurements points $v_k = x_k - d_{1,2}$. The actual cell delay (x_k) is defined as the difference between the actual cell arrival time at MP2 $(a2_k)$ and the actual arrival time at MP1 $(a1_k)$: that is, $x_k = a2_k - a1_k$. The reference cell delay $(d_{1,2})$ between MP1 and MP2 equals the actual cell delay of cell 0 between the two measurement points.

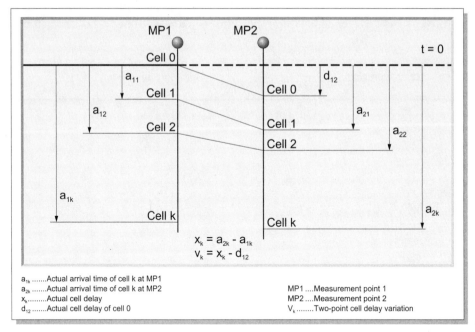

Figure 10.67 Two-point CDV

Figure 10.68 shows an overview of the ATM layer performance parameters for the various QoS classes, that can be attained in ATM wide-area networks with the reference diameter of 27,500 km.

			QoS Class			
	Limit	Default	Stringent	Tolerant	Bi-level	U
CTD	Maximum average CTD	none	400 ms	U	U	U
2-point CDV	Maximum difference between upper and lower 10^{-8} range of CTD	none	3 ms	U	U	U
CLR_{0+1}	Maximum cell loss probability	none	$3 \cdot 10^{-7}$	10^{-5}	U	U
CLR_0	Maximum cell loss probability	none	none	none	10^{-5}	U
CER	Maximum cell error probability	$4 \cdot 10^{-6}$	default	default	default	U
CMR	Maximum cell misinsertion rate	1/day	default	default	default	U
SECBR	Maximum SECB probability	10^{-4}	default	default	default	U
U....unspecified or unlimited						

Figure 10.68 ATM layer performance parameters

Symptoms and Causes

The most frequent causes of cell loss are buffer overflows or faults in the physical layer that lead to non-correctable errors. Cell misinsertion is caused by multiple bit transmission errors in the header, which can no longer be corrected as a result of physical layer problems or malfunctions in the switching fabric. Cell errors usually indicate the occurrence of bit errors in the payload field (bit errors in the header are reflected in cell loss figures). In most cases these bit errors are caused by a higher degree of signal jitter than the ATM interface can tolerate. Cell transfer delay is caused by ordinary electronic switching and signal propagation delays. The cause of cell delay variations usually lies in the varying states of buffers that the cells must pass through on their way to the destination, and in the effects of cell encapsulation in the physical layer transmission framing. Thus two cells within a single SDH container (SONET SPE) will have a smaller CDV relative to one another than two cells transported in different containers /SPEs.

Figure 10.69 lists the typical causes of problems in the ATM layer, grouped by symptoms: Cell Error Rate (CER), Cell Loss Ratio (CLR), Cell Misinsertion Rate (CMR), Mean Cell Transfer Delay (MCTD), Cell Delay Variation (CDV).

Sources of error	CER	CLR	CMR	MCTD	CDV
Signal propagation delay				X	
Fault in communication medium	X	X	X		
Switch architecture		X		X	X
Buffer capacity		X		X	X
Number of nodes along a given VPC/ VCC connection	X	X	X	X	X
Network load		X	X	X	X
Error		X			
Bandwidth allocation to a given VPC/ VCC		X		X	X

Figure 10.69 Symptoms and causes of problems in ATM networks

10.2.3   Troubleshooting Higher Layers

If the ATM layer is working and the problem persists, the higher layer protocols in use must be analyzed. Two of the most common higher layer protocols— besides UNI signaling—are LAN Emulation (LANE) and the Private Network to Network Interface (PNNI).

LAN Emulation

If problems occur in LAN emulation environments, the first step is to make sure that the connected traditional LANs (10/100/1,000 Mbit/s Ethernet, FDDI, etc.) and the LAN interfaces of the LAN/ATM interworking devices are functioning correctly. This includes verifying the various LAN configuration settings and measuring basic network statistics with a protocol analyzer. Examination of the LAN emulation components begins only after the LAN part has been proven to be working properly. The first step in LANE troubleshooting is to send pings between two LE Clients and check whether a connection can be set up at all. If the ping does not go through, check the IP interfaces of the LE Clients. Examine whether the IP interfaces are active at all, and whether the IP addresses and subnet masks are correct and in the same subnet. Then determine whether the LANE software on the clients is active, and whether both LE Clients belong to the same ELAN. If no error is found, the following configuration parameters must be systematically checked through the system management interface of the ATM components:

- Are both LE Clients registered on the same LE Server and Broadcast-Unknown Server (BUS)?
- Is the ATM address of the primary (and secondary, if configured) LE Server correct, and are the Configuration Direct VCCs set up?
- Is the ATM address of the primary (and secondary) BUS correct, and are the Multicast Send VCCs set up?

If it is still impossible to set up data VCCs between the LE Clients, the last error cause to check for is a restricted VC capacity on one of the systems due to traffic contracts. This is done by verifying the compatibility of the traffic contracts for the LE Client interfaces. If a protocol analyzer is available, a trace of the unsuccessful connection setups is the fastest way to find the cause of the problem.

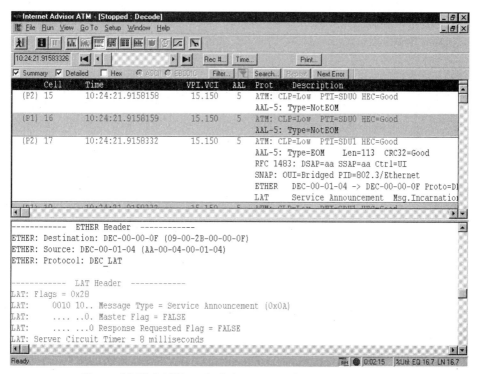

Figure 10.70 LANE analysis by means of a protocol analyzer

UNI Signaling

The first steps in troubleshooting ATM UNI signaling problems are the following basic checks:

- Are the interfaces of the affected systems active?
- Are the affected systems using compatible signaling variants (for example, UNI 3.1, 4.0)?
- Are ILMI (if supported) and the SSCOP layer active?

If no error is detected, the next step is to try to set up an SVC connection while using the debug mode of the ATM nodes or a protocol analyzer to trace the signaling process. Such an analysis of the signaling process usually leads to the cause of the problem. Typical causes are invalid called party or calling party addresses; invalid, unknown or disordered mandatory information elements; invalid call reference numbers; or rejection of the connection setup by a RE-LEASE message from the destination station.

The most important error states in UNI 3.1/4.0/Q.2931 signaling that can occur during the connection setup and clear-down processes are described in the following sections:

Invalid protocol discriminator

Messages with an invalid protocol discriminator are discarded.

Short messages

Messages that are too short to contain a complete information element are discarded.

Invalid call reference format

If bytes 1 and 5 through 8 of the call reference information element are not set to the value 0, or if the call reference length field contains a value other than 3, the message is discarded.

Invalid call reference

a) Whenever any message except SETUP, RELEASE, RELEASE COMPLETE, STATUS ENQUIRY, or STATUS is received with a call reference that does not refer to an active call or to a call in progress, the receiver shall initiate clearing by sending a RELEASE COMPLETE message with cause No. 81, "Invalid call reference value", specifying the call reference of the message received, and shall remain in the null state.

b) When a RELEASE COMPLETE message is received with a call reference that does not refer to an active call or to a call in progress, no action should be taken.

c) When a SETUP message is received with a call reference that does not refer to an active call or to a call in progress, and with a call reference flag incorrectly set to "1", the message shall be ignored.

d) When a SETUP message is received with a call reference that *does* refer to an active call or to a call in progress, the SETUP message shall be ignored.

e) When any message except RESTART, RESTART ACKNOWLEDGE, or STATUS is received with the global call reference, no action should be taken on this message, but a STATUS message shall be returned using the global call reference with a call state indicating the current state associated with the global call reference and cause No. 81, "Invalid call reference".

f) When a STATUS message is received specifying a call reference that is not recognized as relating to an active call or to a call in progress, it shall be cleared with cause 101 "Message not compatible with call state". Alternatively, any other action specific to the implementation that attempts to recover from this mismatch can be taken.

g) If a STATUS or a STATUS-ENQUIRY message is received with a call reference that does not refer to an active call or to a call in progress, a STATUS ENQUIRY message shall be sent to check the correctness of the call state.

h) When a RESTART message is received specifying the global call reference with a call reference flag incorrectly set to "1", or when a RESTART AC-KNOWLEDGE message is received specifying the global call reference with a call reference flag incorrectly set to "0", no action should be taken on this message, but a STATUS message shall be returned with a call state indicating the current state associated with the global call reference and cause No. 81, "Invalid call reference".

Message type or message sequence errors

Whenever an unexpected message is received, except RELEASE, RELEASE COMPLETE, or when an unrecognized message is received, no state change shall occur and a STATUS message shall be returned with one of the following causes:

a) No. 97, Message type non-existent or not implemented
b) No. 101, Message not compatible with call state

Two exceptions to this procedure exist, however. The first is when the network or the user receives an unexpected RELEASE message in response to a SETUP message. In this case, a no STATUS or STATUS ENQUIRY message is sent. Whenever the network receives an unexpected RELEASE message, the network shall release the virtual channel, clear the network connection and the call to the remote user indicating the cause received in the RELEASE message sent by the user or, if no cause was included, cause No. 31, "Normal, unspecified". Furthermore, the network shall return a RELEASE COMPLETE message to the user, release the call reference, stop all timers, and enter the null state. Whenever the user receives an unexpected RELEASE message, the user shall release the virtual channel, return a RELEASE COMPLETE message to the network, release the call reference, stop all timers, and enter the null state.

The second exception is when the network or the user receives an unexpected RELEASE COMPLETE message. Whenever the network receives an unexpected RELEASE COMPLETE message, the network shall disconnect and release the virtual channel, clear the network connection and the call to the remote user indicating the cause given by the user or, if no cause was included, cause No. 111, "Protocol error, unspecified". Furthermore, the network shall release the call reference, stop all timers, and enter the null state. Whenever the user receives an unexpected RELEASE COMPLETE message, the user shall disconnect and release the virtual channel, release the call reference, stop all timers, and enter the null state.

Information Element Sequence

Information elements must be sent in the following order:

- Protocol discriminator
- Call reference
- Message type
- Message length
- Other information elements

Information elements of variable length can be sent in any order.

Duplicate Information Elements

If an information element is repeated in a message in which repetition of the information element is not permitted, only the contents of the information element appearing first shall be handled. All subsequent repetitions of the information element are ignored.

Mandatory Information Element Missing

When a message other than SETUP, RELEASE, or RELEASE COMPLETE is received that lacks one or more mandatory information elements, no action shall be taken on the message and no state change should occur. A STATUS message is then returned with cause No. 96, "Mandatory information element is missing".

When a SETUP message is received that lacks one or more mandatory information elements, a RELEASE COMPLETE message is returned with cause No. 96, "Mandatory information element is missing".

Mandatory Information Element Content Error

When a message other than SETUP, RELEASE, or RELEASE COMPLETE is received in which one or more mandatory information elements have invalid contents, no state change occurs. A STATUS message is returned with cause No. 100, "Invalid information element contents". When a SETUP message is received in which one or more mandatory information elements has invalid contents, a RELEASE COMPLETE message is returned with cause No. 100, "Invalid information element contents".

Unrecognized Information Element

If a message is received that contains one or more unknown information elements, action is taken on the message and those information elements that are recognized and have valid contents. If the received message is not a RELEASE or RELEASE COMPLETE, a STATUS message is returned containing one cause information element. The information element contains cause No. 99, "Information element non-existent or not implemented", and the diagnostic field, if present, contains the information element identifier of each unrecognized information element.

When a RELEASE message is received that has one or more unrecognized information elements, a RELEASE COMPLETE message with cause No. 99, "Information element non-existent or not implemented" is returned. The cause information element diagnostic field, if present, contains the information element identifier of each unrecognized information element. A RELEASE COMPLETE message with unknown information elements is ignored completely.

If a message contains one or more information elements with contents that are in part invalid, then action is taken on those information elements that appear correctly. A STATUS message is also sent with cause No. 100, "Invalid information element contents", and the information element identifier of each invalid information element in the diagnostic field. If address information fields are also corrupt, then cause 43, "Access information discarded", is sent in place of cause 100. If an information element is recognized but should not be present in the given message, it is treated as an unrecognized information element.

AAL Signaling Error

If an AAL signaling error occurs, all connections not yet started are initialized and a T309 timer is started for each active connection. Then a restart of the AAL signaling layer is initiated. If a connection's T309 expires before the signaling layer can be restarted, that connection is deactivated with cause 27, "Destination out of order", and its call reference is deleted.

Status Enquiry

A STATUS ENQUIRY message can be sent to check the call state at a peer entity. Furthermore, whenever the SAAL indicates that a disruption has occurred at the data link layer, a STATUS ENQUIRY message is sent to check for a correct call state at the peer entity. When the STATUS ENQUIRY message is sent, timer T322 is started in anticipation of an incoming STATUS message. Only one unanswered STATUS ENQUIRY may be outstanding at any given time. The receiver of a STATUS ENQUIRY message responds with a STATUS message indicating cause 30, "Response to STATUS ENQUIRY", and reporting the current call state.

If no STATUS response is received before T322 expires, the STATUS ENQUIRY can be repeated one or more times, depending on the implementation. If the timer expires after the last attempt, the connection is cleared down with cause 41, "Temporary failure".

Procedure on Receipt of a STATUS Message

When a STATUS message is received that indicates that the peer station is in an incompatible state for call handling, the connection can be cleared down with cause 101, "Message not compatible with call state", or–if so implemented–an attempt may be made to correct the fault. The decision as to whether the two stations' call states are incompatible with one another is left to the given implementation, except in the following three cases:

a) If a STATUS message is received signaling that the peer station is in a state other than null, and the station receiving the STATUS message is in the null state itself, then the receiver responds with a RELEASE message and cause 101, "Message not compatible with call state".

b) If a STATUS message is received signaling that the peer station is in a state other than null, and the station receiving the STATUS message is in the "Release Request" state, the receiver shall not respond.

c) If a STATUS message is received signaling that the peer station is in the null state, and the station receiving the STATUS message is not in the null state, then the receiver of the STATUS message shall change to the null state.

If a STATUS message is received that signals a compatible call state but contains cause 96, 97, 99, 100 or 101, the response is left to the given implementation. If no particular reaction is specified, the connection in question should be cleared down with the cause indicated in the STATUS message received.

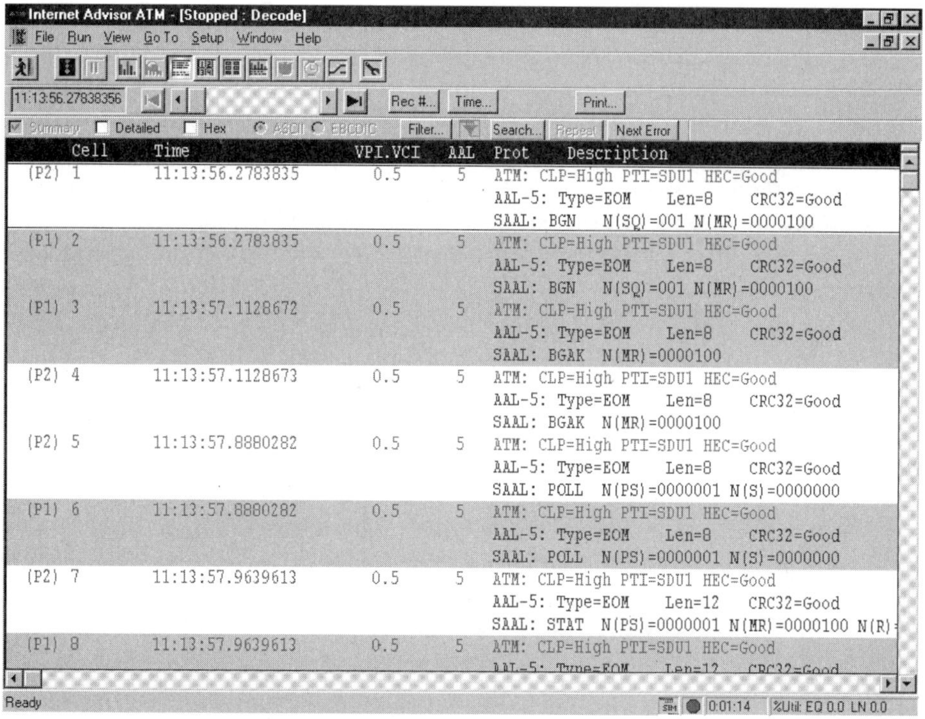

Figure 10.71 UNI signaling decoded by a protocol analyzer for LANE analysis

PNNI Signaling

PNNI is the signaling protocol used to set up SVC connections between two NNIs (that is, switch-to-switch signaling). It actually consists of two protocols: the topology protocol, which distributes information about the network topology to the network nodes, and the signaling protocol, which is basically an extension of the ITU-T Recommendation Q.2931 UNI protocol.

Diagnosis of PNNI problems begins with an examination of the UNI signaling functions at the end systems in the problem domain:

- Are the interfaces of the ATM nodes and switches active?
- Are the signaling versions of all systems compatible (UNI 3.1, 4.0)?
- Are ILMI and the SSCOP layer active?

If the end systems begin signaling processes that cannot be finished successfully, the next step is to analyze the PNNI SVC routing. First, read out the PNNI routes determined by the UNI send port of the switch to the destination node. Then check whether an active route to the destination was found. This is done using the vendor's system management interface to read out the PNNI operations log and examine the PNNI routes calculated by the sending node. If the route leads to a wrong node, a wrong ATM address is probably involved. If the switch cannot find a route to the destination at all, its topology information may be incorrect. If the topology information does not contain the destination node, this may be due either to physical problems in the network, or to the switch's inability to update its topology database. If the sending node does have an uninterrupted route to the destination system, but the connectivity problem remains, the trouble may be caused by traffic parameters that cannot be provided by one of the ATM switches.

If the topology information is wrong or incomplete, the first troubleshooting step is to list all peer neighbors that can be reached directly from the UNI port and their PNNI operation states (up, down, changing, loading). Then the topology information (PNNI Topology State Elements or PTSE) of the peer nodes at the lowest hierarchical level are analyzed to determine whether they reach the peer group leader. Conversely, the PTSEs of the peer group leaders must also be examined to verify that they reach the peer nodes at the lowest level. If all the PTSEs are in order and no configuration errors can be detected (peer group

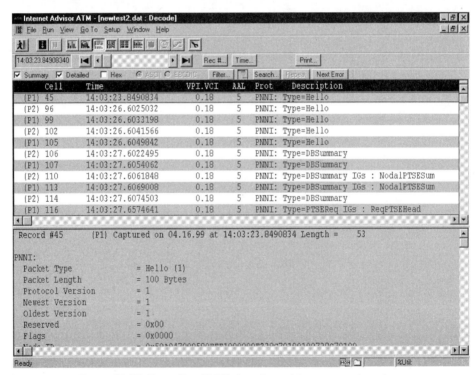

Figure 10.72 Decoding PNNI signaling with a protocol analyzer

leader status is active; parent logical group node (LGN) is configured), then the following checks can be performed successively:

- Is the Hello protocol active on the PNNI?
- Is the PNNI Routing Control Channel (SVCC-RCC) active?
- Are the PNNI port parameters set correctly (cell rate, cell delay, cell rate)?
- Are the peer group uplinks configured and active?
- Are the PNNI addresses (prefixes) and the PNNI short form addresses (summary addresses) correct?

Once again, the fastest way to diagnose the problem is to monitor the PNNI messages during connection setup with a protocol analyzer.

10.2.4   Cabling Problems

Cabling problems are also very common in ATM networks. Typical causes include bad splices, low quality cables, wiring faults, excessive segment length and, for UTP, incorrect characteristic impedances or noise due to electromagnetic interference caused by air condition systems, photocopiers, pagers, elevators or production environments. These types of problems are discussed in detail in Chapter 6.

10.2.5   Problems with ATM Interface Cards

The typical symptoms of defective interface cards in ATM networks are high rates of cell errors or complete loss of cell synchronization. Because of ATM's connection-oriented architecture, it is easy to determine whether the problem is caused by a network interface card. Starting in the middle of the affected connection, the number of cells received is compared with the number of cells transmitted at each ATM interface. If the numbers do not match, the QoS parameters of the given interface must be examined. If no restrictions can be detected, a loopback test shows whether or not cells are being lost due to NIC problems. When changing ATM interface cards, care must be taken due to the high temperatures at which these cards normally operate. Either wait until the card cools, or avoid touching the chips on the card.

10.2.6   Problems with Routers

Routers are internetwork components that connect network segments at OSI Layer 3, and are therefore able to link networks of different topologies. For this reason, there are no troubleshooting issues for routers that apply specifically to ATM networks. Please refer to the troubleshooting section on routers in Chapter 7.

10.2.7   Symptoms and Causes: ATM

Symptom: No Connection over a PVC

Cause (1):   Problems with ATM interface card or driver.
Cause (2):   No PVC set, selected VCI is incorrect.
Cause (3):   Hardware or software problems on the switch.
Cause (4):   Misconfigured ATM port (bit rate, scrambling, interface type, frame type (PLCP, SDH/SONET, SONET)).

Symptom: No Connection over SVC (UNI Signaling Problems)

Cause (1):   Problems with ATM interface card or driver.
Cause (2):   ATMARP server misconfigured; clients are not set up with their correct ATM and IP address on the ATMARP server.
Cause (3):   The address of the ATMARP server is not configured correctly on the client system.
Cause (4):   ILMI is not active on the client or the server.
Cause (5):   The ILMI software versions on client and server are incompatible.
Cause (6):   SSCOP layer not established.
Cause (7):   Incompatible UNI signaling variants (UNI 3.0, 3.1, 4.0).
Cause (8):   Wrong Called Party or Calling Party number.
Cause (9):   Unknown or invalid information elements, or mandatory information elements in wrong order.
Cause (10): Incorrect call reference numbers.
Cause (11): Called party is not ready to accept call, call setup attempt is rejected with RELEASE message.
Cause (12): Misconfigured ATM port (bit rate, scrambling, interface type, frame type (PLCP, G.804, SDH, SONET)).
Cause (13): Hardware or software problems on the switch.

Symptom: High Cell Error Rate (CER)

Cause (1):   Problems on the physical layer (cabling, connectors, ATM port).
Cause (2):   Too many nodes along the transmission path of a VP or VC connection.

Symptom: High Cell Loss Ratio (CLR)

Cause (1):   Problems on the physical layer (cabling, connectors, ATM port).
Cause (2):   Too many nodes along the transmission path of a VP or VC connection.
Cause (3):   ATM switch overloaded.
Cause (4):   Insufficient buffering in the switch.
Cause (5):   High network load.
Cause (6):   Limits of traffic contract are exceeded.

Symptom: High Cell Misinsertion Rate (CMR)

Cause (1):   Problems on the physical layer (cabling, connectors, jitter, ATM port)

Cause (2):   Too many nodes along the transmission path of a VP or VC connection

Cause (3):   High network load

Cause (4):   ATM switch malfunction

Symptom: High Mean Cell Transfer Delay (MCTD)

Cause (1):   High signal delay due to long transmission path

Cause (2):   Too many nodes along the transmission path of a VP or VC connection

Cause (3):   ATM switch overloaded

Cause (4):   Insufficient buffering in the switch

Cause (5):   High network load

Cause (6):   Limits of traffic contract are exceeded

Symptom: High Cell Delay Variation (CDV)

Cause (1):   Too many nodes along the transmission path of a VP or VC connection

Cause (2):   ATM switch overloaded

Cause (3):   Insufficient buffering in the switch

Cause (4):   High network load

Cause (5):   Limits of traffic contract are exceeded

Symptom: No Connection over Emulated LAN (ELAN)

Cause (1):   Problems with the connected traditional LANs (Ethernet, FDDI, Token Ring)

Cause (2):   IP interfaces on the LAN emulation clients are not active or not functioning

Cause (3):   IP addresses and subnet masks are incorrect; interfaces belong to different subnets

Cause (4):   LANE software on the client is not active

Cause (5):   The LE Clients trying to communicate do not belong to the same ELAN

Cause (6):   The LE Clients are not registered on the same LE Server/BUS

Cause (7):   The VCC and ATM address of the LANE server (LE Server) are incorrect

Cause (8):   The VCC and ATM address of the BUS are incorrect

Cause (9):   LANE-ARP entries are incorrect (MAC-ATM address resolution is not working)

Cause (10): The traffic contracts of the LE Clients are incompatible

Cause (11): The primary LANE service failed and the backup LANE service was not activated

Symptom: No Connection over PNNI Network

Cause (1): Signaling problems (SVC) between the end systems involved
Cause (2): Wrong route selection due to incorrect ATM addressing of the end systems
Cause (3): Topology information on the switch port is incomplete or out-dated
Cause (4): Misconfigured peer group leader (PGL not active or no designated parent LGN)
Cause (5): Hello protocol is not active on the PNNI
Cause (6): The PNNI Routing Control Channel (SVCC-RCC) is inactive
Cause (7): Misconfigured PNNI port parameters (cell rate, cell transfer delay, bit rate)
Cause (8): Uplinks to neighboring peer groups are inactive or not defined
Cause (9): PNNI addresses, prefixes or summary addresses are incorrect

Symptom: Loss of ATM Connections

Cause (1): Violation of the traffic contract; traffic shaping activated
Cause (2): Cell streams with different priorities are transmitted at high load, and cells with low priority are discarded
Cause (3): Clocking and synchronization problems due to configuration errors on the ATM port
Cause (4): Problems on the physical layer (cabling, connectors, ATM port)

Gathering Information; Common Errors

The first step in any troubleshooting process is to gather information. In diagnosing ATM problems, comprehensive information about the context of the problem provides a detailed description of the symptoms and clues to possible causes. Questions to ask at this stage include:

- Do the symptoms occur regularly or intermittently?
- Are the symptoms related to certain applications, or do they affect all network operations?
- Do the symptoms correlate to other activities in the network?
- When was the first occurrence of the symptom?
- Was there any change in any hardware or software network component?
- Has anyone connected or disconnected a PC (laptop or desktop) or any other component to or from the network?
- Has anyone installed an interface card in a computer?
- Has anyone stepped on a cable?

- Has any maintenance work been performed in the building recently (by a telephone company or building maintenance personnel, for example)?
- Has anyone (including cleaning personnel) moved any equipment or furniture?

The following table lists the most common causes of problems in ATM networks:

- ATM interface card defective
- ATM interface card incorrectly configured (interrupt, driver, timers)
- Cell streams with different priorities are being transmitted at high load, and cells with low priority are discarded
- Classical IP: ATM ARP server address not configured on the client systems
- Classical IP: Misconfigured ATM ARP server: clients are not registered at all or registered under a wrong address
- Faulty cable infrastructure: see Chapter 6
- Electromagnetic interference (ATM over UTP)
- Hardware or software problems on the switch
- High signal transit delay due to long transmission path
- ILMI not active on the client or on the ATM switch
- Incompatible ILMI software versions on client and server
- Incorrect port configuration: bit rate, scrambling, interface type, frame type (PLCP, G.804, SDH, SONET)
- Incorrect router configuration (port inactive, wrong operating mode, protocol not active)
- Incorrect router filters
- Insufficient buffering in the switch
- LANE: IP addresses and subnet masks are incorrect; interfaces belong to different subnets
- LANE: IP interfaces on the LE clients are not active or not functioning
- LANE: LANE software on the client or switch is not active
- LANE: LANE-ARP entries are incorrect (MAC-ATM address resolution is not working)
- LANE: LE Clients are not registered on the same LE Server/BUS
- LANE: LE Clients trying to communicate do not belong to the same ELAN
- LANE: The primary LANE service failed and the backup LANE service was not activated
- LANE: The traffic contracts of the LE Clients are incompatible

---

Figure 10.73a The most frequent causes of trouble in ATM networks

- LANE: The LE server (LES) VCC is inactive or the ATM address of the LES is incorrect
- LANE: The BUS VCC is inactive or the ATM address of the BUS is incorrect
- Loose or defective connectors on interface cards, wall jacks, MAUs, hubs, bridges, routers
- Misconfigured ATM interface card (interrupts, drivers, timers)
- Misconfigured routing protocol entries (address tables, mapping tables, subnet masks, default gateways, routing tables, timers)
- PNNI: Hello protocol on the PNNI interface is not active
- PNNI: Misconfigured peer group leader
  (PGL is not active or no designated parent LGN)
- PNNI: Misconfigured PNNI port parameters
  (cell rate, cell transfer delay, bit rate)
- PNNI: PNNI addresses, prefixes or summary addresses are incorrect
- PNNI: The PNNI Routing Control Channel (SVCC-RCC) is inactive
- PNNI: Topology information on the switch port is incomplete or outdated
- PNNI: Uplinks to neighboring peer groups are inactive or not defined
- PNNI: Wrong route selection due to incorrect ATM addresses
  for the destination node
- PVC not set up; invalid VCI
- Faulty physical router or switch installation (cables, connectors, plug-in modules are loose, backplane connections are miswired)
- Problems on the physical layer (cabling, connectors, ATM port)
- Switch is overloaded
- Too many nodes along the transmission path of a VPI/VCI connection
- Traffic contract is exceeded, cells are being discarded

Figure 10.73b The most frequent causes of trouble in ATM networks

Switched LANs

11

"You can observe a lot by watching."

YOGI BERRA

11.1 Switched LANs: Specification and Implementation

LAN switches connect network segments or nodes and use a direct forwarding technique for data transmission. The LAN switch forwards each incoming frame directly to the switch port that is connected to the destination device. Multiple ports on a given LAN switch can operate simultaneously (As long as the transmission paths involved do not overlap), which can help ease congestion in network traffic. The high-performance forwarding hardware that makes this multiple parallel forwarding possible is the main difference between a LAN switch and a router or multiport bridge. The way in which frames are forwarded by the LAN switch is configured for each switch port. Thus, any port on a given LAN switch can act as a repeater, a bridge, or a router (see Figure 11.1).

LAN switches can be deployed in all traditional LAN topologies, including 10/100/1,000 Mbit/s Ethernet, 4/16 Mbit/s Token Ring, and FDDI. LAN switches generally use one of two techniques for forwarding data packets: "cut-through" or "store-and-forward". When the cut-through technique is employed, the switch makes the forwarding decision for each incoming frame as soon as it has received the first 6 bytes (which contain the destination address). The benefit of this technique is that the switch can forward frames at a high rate; latency is reduced to around 40 µs. The drawback is that the switch begins forwarding the data packet before it can determine whether there are errors in the frame, which could result in the propagation of defective frames.

By contrast, with the store-and-forward technique, which is increasingly used in state-of-the-art switches, the switch does not make the forwarding decision until it has received the entire frame. This has the advantage of not propagating defective frames. The drawback, however, is greater latency that is dependent on the frame size. The latency of a 1,000-byte data packet in a 10Base-T network introduced by a store-and-forward switch, for example, is over 800 µs. If the transmission path leads through multiple store-and-forward switch ports, the transmission delays could be significant and higher-layer timers might run out. The search for a solution to this problem has led to the development of "fragment-free" cut-through forwarding. In this method, the forwarding decision is not made until the first 64 bytes of a packet have been received. This eliminates the majority of defective packets because the most common errors (for example, including Ethernet runt packets) can be detected within the first 64 bytes. At the same time, the latency involved is not as long as in store-and-forward switching. Many of the LAN switches available today also offer an "adaptive forwarding" feature, which enables each switch port to change between the store-and-forward and cut-through techniques based primarily on the numbers of runts and defective packets received at that port.

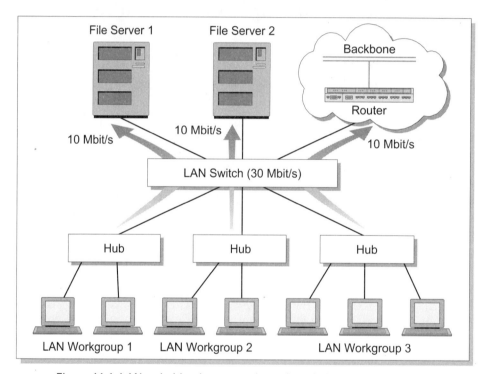

Figure 11.1 LAN switching increases throughput in inter-segment traffic

Another important difference between LAN switches is whether each switch port supports only a single MAC address or multiple MAC addresses. "Single-MAC" switches, also called desktop switches, are usually very economically priced and are primarily designed for direct connection to end devices. "Multi-MAC" or workgroup switches are used to connect multiple LAN segments. Workgroup switches support multiple hardware addresses for each port.

11.2 Design Guidelines for Switched LANs

To gain the full benefit of the high throughput capacity available with LAN switches, several basic guidelines must be followed when installing LAN switching components. It is essential to begin with an analysis of the network traffic, including the types of packets transmitted between the stations or segments to be linked by switches. A LAN switch cannot alleviate problems caused by broadcasts, for example, because switches distribute broadcasts over all ports just as bridges do, unless a Layer 3 switch capable of routing is used.

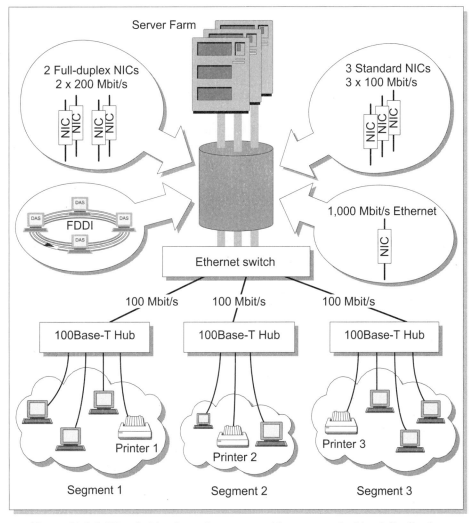

Figure 11.2 LAN switching in environments with asymmetrical load distribution

LAN Switching in Topologies with Symmetrical Load Distribution

If the network traffic is primarily symmetrical, you can distribute the nodes that share a given set of global resources (such as applications or servers) in one segment and connect this segment to the LAN switch. This allows the nodes in that segment, or workgroup, to access their main server while the nodes in another workgroup access another main server, without the two workgroups competing for bandwidth (see Figure 11.1).

LAN Switching in Topologies with Asymmetrical Load Distribution

If the load distribution in the LAN is strongly asymmetrical, as is the case between a server farm and several LAN workgroups, this must be taken into consideration when installing LAN switches. The nodes and segments that handle the majority of the intersegment load must be connected to LAN switches with high-bandwidth interfaces. This can be implemented by means of multiple interface cards in each node (n x 100 Mbit/s Ethernet, n x 16 Mbit/s Token Ring), full-duplex connections, or high-speed technologies such as ATM or Gigabit Ethernet. Most network element vendors support the usage of multiple ISLs (Inter Switch Links) to increase the inter-switch capacity. These bundles of ISLs are called trunks (see Figure 11.2).

11.3   Troubleshooting in Switched LANs

11.3.1   Gathering Information on Symptoms and Recent Changes

The first step in any troubleshooting process is to gather information. The more information you have about the symptoms and characteristics of a problem— including *when* it first occurred—the better your chances of solving the problem quickly and efficiently. Typical questions you might ask at this stage include:

- Was there any change in any hardware or software network component?
- Do the symptoms occur regularly or intermittently?
- When was the first occurrence of the symptom?
- Are the symptoms related to certain applications or limited to certain connections?
- Have any components or PCs been added or removed to or from the network?
- Have any new interface cards been added?
- Has anyone stepped on a cable?

- Has any maintenance work been performed in the building recently (by a telephone company or building maintenance personnel, for example)?
- Has anyone (including cleaning personnel) moved any equipment or furniture?

11.3.2   Starting the Troubleshooting Procedure

The errors that occur in switched networks are the same as those that lead to problems in LAN topologies. The difficulties in troubleshooting switched environments lie not so much in finding individual error sources as in actually noticing the errors. Because a LAN switch forwards every data packet directly from the port it arrives at to the port that is connected to the destination node, you cannot monitor the data that flows through a switch by simply connecting a protocol analyzer to a switch port. In a switched network, a variety of measurement methods must be used to obtain the same information that is readily available in a shared-medium environment. These methods include evaluating switch management information, connecting a hub as an access point for a network analyzer, port tapping, circuit tapping and switch tapping.

The network management information in LAN switches is carried by Simple Network Management Protocol (SNMP) agents, which store information about switch operating states in the form of standard Monitoring Information Bases (MIBs), such as MIB I, MIB II, Remote Monitoring (RMON) MIB, and proprietary MIBs. The data about a given switch that can be obtained from the switch MIBs include the following:

- Traffic load on each port
- Error rates at each port
- Numbers of broadcasts and multicasts
- Number of discarded packets

In practice these monitoring functions are often implemented only in a very rudimentary fashion; and at peak network loads—just when the information is needed most—they either malfunction or are deactivated. Thus, in addition to evaluating the switch MIBs it is often necessary to use dedicated measurement systems, such as protocol analyzers or LAN probes. There are a number of methods for doing this. Some switches include a monitor port, which allows you to analyze network communications through port tapping, circuit tapping, or switch tapping. In port tapping, the LAN switch is configured to copy all traffic from a given port to the monitor port, where it can be monitored using a protocol analyzer. Theoretically, traffic from several ports can be copied to a monitor port. If the ports being monitored have the same bandwidth as the monitor port, however, there is a danger of losing data packets when traffic is heavy. The circuit tapping technique is basically the same as port tapping, except that traffic is monitored between two ports rather than on a given port. With switch tapping, the traffic from all ports is copied to the monitoring port. If no monitor port is available on the LAN switch, a mini-hub can be inserted to connect the test instrument to the switch port you wish to monitor (see Figure 11.3).

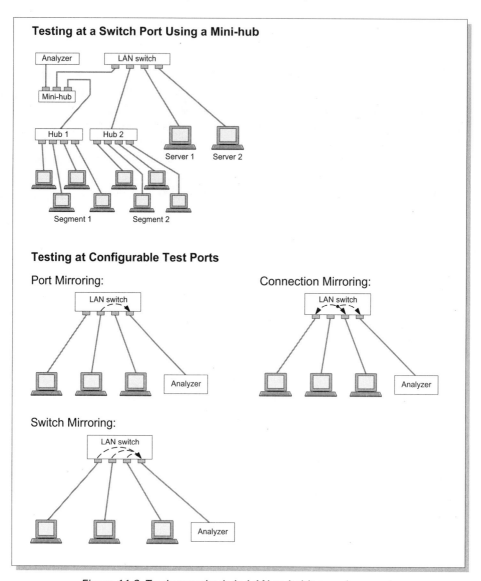

Figure 11.3 Testing methods in LAN switching environments

The first step in troubleshooting a switched LAN is to determine such parameters as network load and packet types (numbers of broadcasts and multicasts, packet lengths, error rates) at the switch ports, or call up this data from the integrated switch management software. The next step is to check the forwarding tables and port configurations in the switch. In many cases this information will narrow down the source of the problem to a particular segment or node. From this point, the troubleshooting procedure continues as described in one of the earlier chapters for the topology in question.

11.3.3 Error Symptoms in Switched Networks

Symptoms that indicate a fault involving a LAN switch include: interrupted connections between segments that are linked by LAN switches, broadcast storms, and throughput problems.

When connections over LAN switches break down, the most common causes are defective cabling, problems with the power supply, and faulty switch hardware. When Ethernet switches are used and extreme peaks occur in the number of broadcasts, bridge loops usually cause the problem. These loops result when the spanning tree protocol or algorithm is not supported or is deactivated. Broadcasts from one segment are then forwarded by a switch to a neighboring segment, and from there by another switch back to the original segment, and so on around the loop (see Figure 11.4).

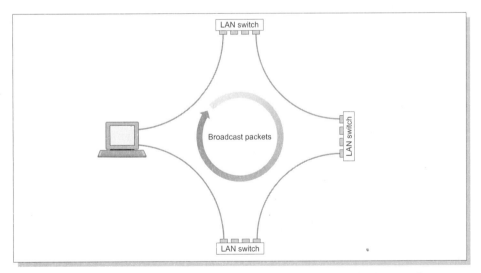

Figure 11.4 Broadcast storms due to bridge loops in switched networks

Bottlenecks at switch ports are usually caused either by design errors in networks with asymmetrical data loads, or by configuration errors at switch ports. For example, in Ethernet switches, ports mistakenly configured as full-duplex lead to frame check sequence (FCS) and alignment errors, while ports mistakenly configured as half-duplex lead to late collisions. In Token-Ring switches, errors commonly result when source routing is not activated or the ring speed configured at the port is incorrect.

11.3.4   Symptoms and Causes: LAN Switching

Symptom: No Connection Between Segments Linked by a LAN Switch

Cause (1): Defective cabling.
Cause (2): Switch power supply failure.
Cause (3): Faulty switch hardware.
Cause (4): Incorrectly configured switch: for example, wrong ring speed (Token Ring), 10 Mbit/s rather than 100 Mbit/s Ethernet, half-duplex rather than full-duplex Ethernet, etc.
Cause (5): Incorrect IP address, subnet mask, or default gateway setting in the switch.
Cause (6): Incorrect VLAN configuration; one of the nodes that cannot communicate is located in a different VLAN.
Cause (7): Source routing deactivated (Token Ring).
Cause (8): Duplicate FDDI address configured for an FDDI switch port.
Cause (9): Duplicate Token-Ring address configured for a Token-Ring switch port.
Cause (10): Defective interface card in the node that cannot communicate.

Symptom: Broadcast Storms

Cause (1): Transmission paths form a loop because the spanning tree algorithm is not activated or not supported.

Symptom: Low Throughput

Cause (1): Poor network design; asymmetrical loads on symmetrical bandwidth at the switch ports.
Cause (2): Incorrectly configured switch ports (10 Mbit/s rather than 100 Mbit/s Ethernet; half-duplex rather than full-duplex Ethernet, etc.).
Cause (3): High number of defective frames generated by a defective switch port.
Cause (4): Cable length exceeds specifications.

The following list summarizes the most frequent sources of problems in LAN-switched networks (in alphabetical order):

- Broadcast storms due to loops through several switches; spanning tree algorithm not activated
- Defective switch hardware
- Duplicate FDDI address configured for an FDDI switch port
- Duplicate Token-Ring address configured for a Token-Ring switch port
- Faulty cable infrastructure; excessive cable lengths (see Chapter 6)
- Faulty network design, asymmetrical traffic over switch ports with symmetrical bandwidth
- Faulty physical switch installation (loose cable, connectors or plug-ins; faulty wiring on the backplane)
- Incorrect Layer 3 switch settings: IP address, subnet mask, or default gateway
- Incorrect router or bridge settings for switch ports operating in router/bridge mode
- Incorrect VLAN configuration; nodes that cannot communicate are located in different VLANs
- Source routing deactivated (Token Ring)
- Switch overloaded
- Switch power supply failure
- Switch settings incorrectly configured: port not activated; wrong ring speed (Token Ring); wrong Ethernet speed; half-duplex instead of full-duplex Ethernet or vice versa

Figure 11.5 The most common causes of problems in LAN switched networks

Section III
Troubleshooting
Wide-Area Networks

ISDN

12

12.1   ISDN: Specification and Implementation

Integrated Services Digital Network, or ISDN, was the first communications infrastructure designed for transmission of both voice and data. The transmission technique is based on 64-Kbit/s bearer channels (B channels) and out-of-band signaling channels (D channels). There are two distinct types of network access in ISDN, each with different bandwidth capacities: basic rate access provides an access rate of up to 128 Kbit/s over two B channels and unused bandwidth in the D channel of up to 16 Kbit/s; primary rate access provides access rates of up to 1,536 Kbit/s in North America (23 B channels and one D channel) or up to 1,984 Kbit/s in Europe (30 B channels and one D channel).

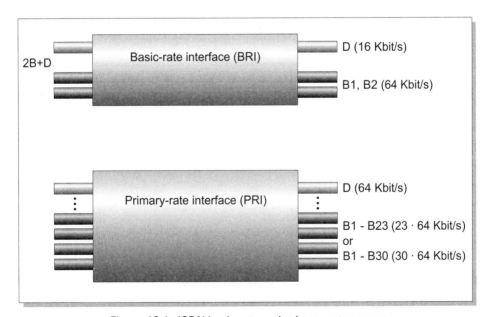

Figure 12.1: ISDN basic rate and primary rate access

From today's standpoint, the major drawbacks of ISDN are the limitation of the data speed to a maximum of 1,536 or 1,984 Kbit/s, which cannot be incrementally expanded, and the synchronous structure of the transmission channels, which does not permit dynamic allocation of bandwidth within the network. The latter characteristic was one of the reasons for the development of Frame Relay, a dedicated data transmission service that dynamically adjusts the bandwidth in use for more efficient data transfer. However, ISDN has the advantage of being an established international standard, providing a uniform digital interface for voice and data transmission worldwide.

12.1.1   ISDN Interface Reference Model

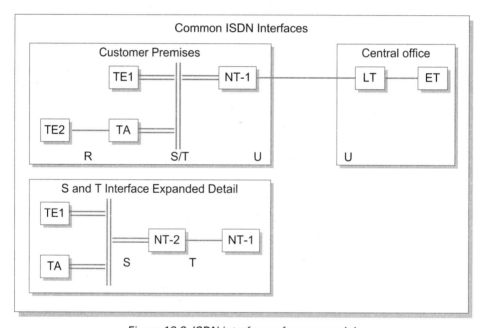

Figure 12.2 ISDN interface reference model

- Exchange termination (ET) and line termination (LT) comprise the Central Office interface, called the V-Interface.
- In North America, the U reference point is the standard interface and demarcation line between the network and the customer premises equipment (CPE). Outside North America the send (S)/transmit (T) reference point represents the border line between the CPE and the network. For the basic rate access the U-Interface is a 2-wire 2B1Q-coded line from the Central Office, for primary rate access the U-Interface consists of a 4-wire T1 (Digi-

tal Speech Interpolation or DSI) in North America or an E1 outside North America. In Germany the U-Interface for primary rate is often referred to as a S_{2M} interface.

- NT-1 is a network termination unit that converts the 2-wire 2B1Q line code into a 4-wire code used on the S and T interfaces. Most equipment used in North America will not have an S or T interface connector.
- NT-2 is a network termination unit that is ISDN-capable at both sides of the unit. A good example is an ISDN PBX or ISDN concentrator.
- S and T interface terms are largely interchangeable. They are both 4-wire interfaces. In Germany the terminology S_0 is used for the S-bus interface of basic access.
- TE1 is ISDN-capable terminal equipment.
- TE2 is non-ISDN capable terminal equipment (for example, a standard telephone set, etc.).
- TA is a terminal adapter and is responsible for interfacing non-ISDN equipment to the ISDN line.

The following interfaces are most commonly found at the reference point (R) a/b for connecting analog terminal equipment, such as telephones, telefax machines, and modems.

V.24:   Connects data terminals with V.24 interfaces

X.21:   Connects terminals with X.21 interfaces using bit-rate adaptation as defined in ITU Recommendations X.30 and X.31

X.25:   Connects terminals with X.25 interfaces as defined in ITU X.31 Case B

12.1.2 The ISDN Protocol

In an ISDN network, the circuit-switched transmission plane is separate from the signaling plane. End-to-end connections in the transmission plane must be set up and a user channel allocated before user data (including digitized voice data) can be transmitted over ISDN. A signaling protocol on a separate D channel, using out-of-band signaling, provides connection setup for user data transmitted over B channels. The communication protocol on OSI Layer 2 (the data link layer) uses the Link Access Procedure D (LAP-D), which is an option of the high-level data-link control (HDLC) protocol defined in ITU Recommendations Q.920 and Q.921. Worldwide there are many different manifestations of the network layer protocols, however, all of them are based on the Digital Subscriber Signaling System No. 1 (DSS1) described in ITU Recommendations Q.930 and Q.931. OSI Layer 1, the bit-transmission layer, is identical on B and D channels and is defined in ITU Recommendations I.430 and I.431. A completely indepen-

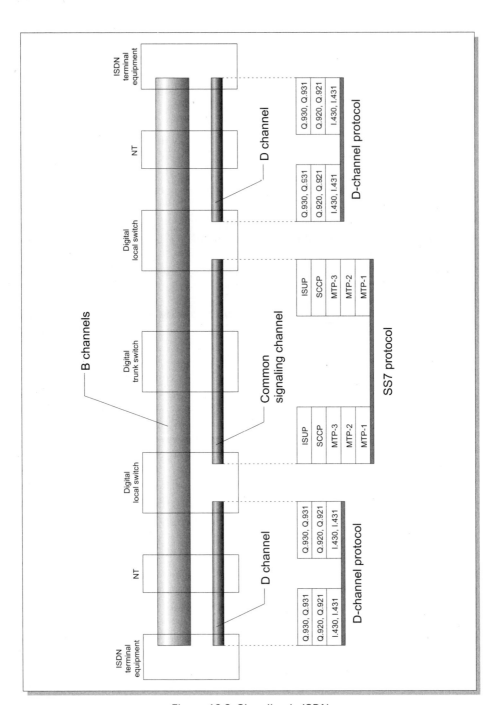

Figure 12.3 Signaling in ISDN

dent data network is available for the signaling plane using the Signaling System No. 7 (SS7), the discussion of which is outside the scope of this book. The Message Transfer Part (MTP), the transport mechanism, is divided into three levels that correspond to the first three OSI layers. The higher SS7 layers correspond only loosely to the OSI model, and include the following application protocols or user parts (UPs):

ISUP (ISDN User Part)   defines ISDN B-channel switching

TUP (Telephone User Part)   governs telephone channels

DUP (Data User Part)   governs data channels

Separate SS7 application protocols are defined for every self-switching service. For example, a Mobile Application Part (MAP) is defined for mobile telephony, and Broadband ISDN User Part (B-ISUP) for ATM. The combination of a large number of protocols with the necessity for interoperability among the various services can make the operation of an SS7 network an exceptionally complex task.

ISDN Layer 1: Bit Transmission Layer

Basic Rate Access

The S/T reference point

The total bit rate of the ISDN basic rate interface (BRI) at the S/T reference point, also referred to as the S-bus, is 192 Kbit/s. The D channel and the two B channels require 144 Kbit/s; the other 48 Kbit/s of bandwidth is reserved for synchronization, interface control, and other overhead. Data is transferred in

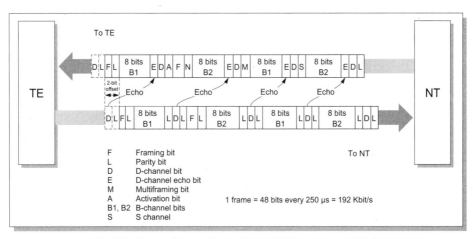

Figure 12.4 The frame format in the ISDN S/T interface (BRI; ITU I.430)

48-bit frames, which carry the D-channel and B-channel data bits as well as the following control and status bits: A (device activation), F (frame start for synchronization), L (parity), S1 and S2 (padding bits), E (echo channel for contention resolution on the passive bus), F_A (additional framing bit), M (multiple frame), and N (this bit is always set to 1). The L parity bit ensures that there is no DC imbalance in the resulting bit stream. The BRI uses Alternate Space Inversion (ASI) or Modified Alternate Mark Inversion (MAMI) line encoding (see Figure 12.4).

After power up of the NT and TE equipment, the framing on the S/T interface is established by exchanging predefined bit patterns between TE and NT. This procedure is called activation and is achieved by means of a finite state machine with five states. The bit patterns used for the transition from "NO SIGNAL" (S-bus deactivated), which is called INFO 0, are as follows:

INFO 1   A continuous signal consisting of a positive pulse, a negative pulse, and a 6-byte interval with no pulse, is transmitted repeatedly at 192 Kbit/s.

INFO 2   Layer 1 frames with binary 0s on channels D, B, E, and A provide the activation request from the NT to the TE, or the NT's response to an activation request from a TE.

INFO 3   Synchronized frames carry user data on the D and B channels (TE > NT).

INFO 4   Frames carry user data on the D, B, and E channels. The A bit is set to 1, both sides continuously exchange frames, and the S-bus is considered activated.

In some jurisdictions, the NT will activate the S-bus (only the NT is allowed to deactivate the S-bus interface) during idle times when no signaling or data message exchange is required. The NT initiates deactivation by sending INFO 0. In North America the S/T interface always remains activated because of the line audit procedure, which is periodically checking the TEs connected to the network.

To prevent blocking or contention on the TE to NT line, terminal devices on the S-bus must make sure the D channel is not in use by another TE before starting with data transmission of its own. For this purpose, the echo channel transmitted in an E bit from the NT to the TE always carries a copy of the D channel bits received by the NT from the TEs. The D channel is considered available for transmission when the TE detects a certain number of consecutive idle bits (binary 1) on the echo channel (E bits); for low priority terminals this number is 9, while higher priority terminals can begin transmission once they detect

8 such bits. Subsequent to a successful transmission, the low priority class TEs have to count 11 consecutive idle bits (high priority TEs count to 10) before transmission of the next frame can commence. After that, the TEs count to 9 or 8 consecutive idle bits again. The connector for the BRI S/T interface is the modular registered phone jack RJ-45 with 8 pin positions defined in the ISO 8877 specification (see Figure 12.5)

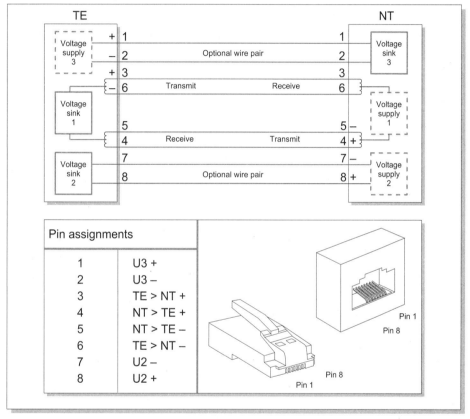

Figure 12.5 Connector and pin assignments in the ISDN basic rate S/T interface: RJ-45 (ISO 8877)

The U Reference Point

The total bit rate of the ISDN BRI at the U reference point is 160 Kbit/s. The D channel and the two B channels require 144 Kbit/s; the other 16 Kbit/s of bandwidth are used for synchronization and framing.

The frame structure depends on the line encoding and modulation scheme. Today the dominant line-encoding scheme is 2B1Q coding, where 2 bits are combined to form a quaternary (4) line voltage state. Outside North America a second coding scheme, the 4B3T (4 bits form 3 ternary states) has been used. Echo cancellation transmission techniques make the use of a single copper pair possible. In the past, so called ping-pong techniques have been used (in Germany also referred to as the U_{p0} interface).

On 2B1Q lines one octet of each B channel and 2 bits from the C channel (18 bits) are passed through a scrambler and then concatenated into a frame consisting of 12 times the 18 bit scrambled frames, forming a data field of 216 bits. Together with 18 synchronization bits and 6 maintenance bits, a data frame of 240 bits is created. Eight of these 240 bit frames form a superframe.

On 4B3T lines, a frame is composed of 120 ternary symbols (108 scrambled data symbols, 11 symbols for synchronization, and 1 symbol for maintenance purposes). Different constructions are used for frames from LT to NT1 and NT1 to LT (synchronization symbols are in different bit positions, that is, offset by 60 symbols).

The connector for the BRI U-Interface is the RJ-45 modular phone jack with 8 pin positions, defined in the ISO 8877 specification (see Figure 12.6), although sometimes different mechanical connector build outs are used.

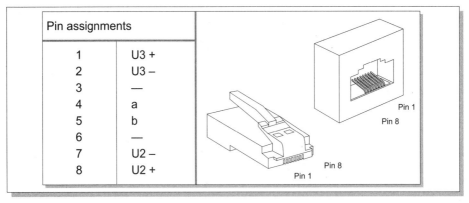

Pin assignments	
1	U3 +
2	U3 −
3	—
4	a
5	b
6	—
7	U2 −
8	U2 +

Figure 12.6 Connector and pin assignments in the ISDN basic rate U-Interface: RJ-45 (ISO 8877)

Primary Rate Access

For ISDN primary rate access, only the U reference point is defined as the demarcation between network equipment and customer premises equipment. Four-wire, full-duplex physical interfaces with Alternate Mark Inversion (AMI) or Bipolar with Eight-Zero Substitution (B8ZS) line encoding are used for North

American T1 lines (1.544 Mbit/s) or High Density Bipolar 3 (HDB3) line encoding on E1 interfaces (2.048 Mbit/s) outside North America, described in ITU Recommendations G.703 and G.704. Each B channel has 64 Kbit/s of available bandwidth. The ISDN specification also defines a 384 Kbit/s H_0 channel, as well as two H_1 channels with 1,536 Kbit/s (H_{11}) and 1,920 Kbit/s (H_{12}). These channels are rarely used, however.

Unlike the S_0 interface, the primary rate interface (PRI) supports only continuous point-to-point connections between two terminals. Thus some of the functions available with basic rate access, such as Layer 1 activation and deactivation of terminal equipment or collision detection, are unnecessary here. The transmission frame and its control fields, which include the alarm indication signal (AIS), cyclical redundancy check (CRC), and remote alarm indication (RAI), correspond exactly to the E1 or T1 Plesiosynchronous Digital Hierarchy (PDH) frame (DS1; see also Chapter 14). The 1,544 Mbit/s T1 interface uses 193-bit frames, each consisting of one F bit followed by 24 time slots. Time slot 24 is reserved for the D channel (if used), while any other slot can be assigned to a B channel. H_0 channels can be assigned to any group of 6 (not necessarily consecutive) time slots, while an H_{11} channel takes up all 24-time slots. The E1 interface uses a 256-bit frame divided into 32 time slots, numbered 0 through 31. Time slot 16 is reserved for the D channel. H_0 channels can again be assigned to any group of six (not necessarily consecutive) time slots, while an H_{12} channel takes up time slots 1–15 and 17–31, and an H_{11} channel occupies time slots 1–15 and 17–25. The type of connectors used for primary rate access depends on the line impedance of various national standards. The two pairs of a T1 line are always operated in balanced mode with 100-Ω impedance, whereas the two pairs of E1 lines could be operated in balanced mode at 120-Ω impedance as well as unbalanced mode with 75-Ω impedance. The most common connector for primary rate is the modular phone jack RJ-48 for T1 lines and E1 lines with balanced pairs. On rare occasions a DB9 connector is used for E1 lines in balanced mode. For E1 lines using unbalanced pairs, a BNC (Bayonet Neil-Concelman, or sometimes British Naval Connector) connector is most often used (see Figure 12.7).

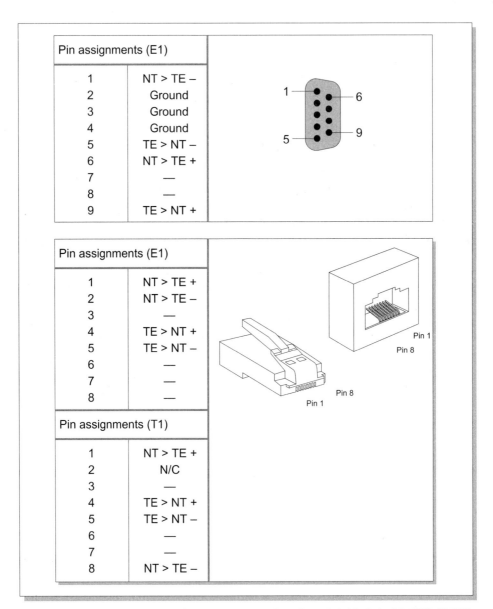

Pin assignments (E1)	
1	NT > TE −
2	Ground
3	Ground
4	Ground
5	TE > NT −
6	NT > TE +
7	—
8	—
9	TE > NT +

Pin assignments (E1)	
1	NT > TE +
2	NT > TE −
3	—
4	TE > NT +
5	TE > NT −
6	—
7	—
8	—

Pin assignments (T1)	
1	NT > TE +
2	N/C
3	—
4	TE > NT +
5	TE > NT −
6	—
7	—
8	NT > TE −

Figure 12.7 Pin assignments, ISDN primary rate interface: RJ-48, Sub-D9 (ISO 10173)

ISDN Layer 2: LAP-D

Link Access Procedure D, or LAP-D, is the Layer 2 (data link layer) protocol for the D channel. LAP-D is responsible for the secure transport of ISDN Layer 3 data, including the following functions:

* Multiplexing of several logical channels over one D channel
* Detection of transmission and format errors at the interface
* Re-transmission of corrupted frames
* Data flow control

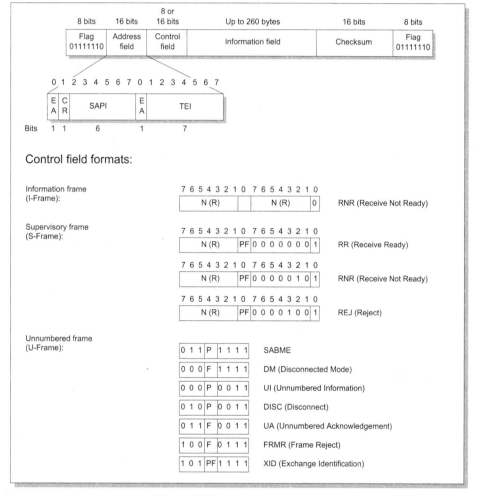

Figure 12.8 LAP-D frame format

Each LAP-D frame consists of a beginning and end flag, address field, control field, an optional information field, and a frame check sequence (FCS) field (see Figure 12.8).

The address field contains the Service Access Point Identifier (SAPI), which defines the network service to be provided on Layer 3 for a given connection, and the Terminal Endpoint Identifier (TEI), which identifies the destination terminal(s).

The following three services are identified by the SAPI:

SAPI 63   Management services (such as TEI administration)
SAPI 0:   Call control (signaling)
SAPI 16:   Data transmission over the D channel (X.25)

Other SAPI values are reserved for national uses.

The TEI values that identify the terminals can be assigned either automatically by the TEI management entity or manually at the terminal itself. TEI values 0 to 63 are reserved for manual assignment; the ISDN switch automatically assigns values 64 through 126. TEI assignment information is transmitted in U frames (see the following) with the address values SAPI=63 and TEI=127. The TEI value reserved for broadcasts, the automatic TEI assignment procedure, and the TEI verification procedure (also known at the link audit) is 127.

The control field of the LAP-D frame indicates one of the following three frame types:

- Information frames (I frames)
- Supervisory frames (S frames)
- Unnumbered frames (U frames)

U frames are used to establish and release Layer 2 logical links, to exchange parameters for negotiation, and report irrecoverable error situations; I frames transport sequenced Layer 3 data; and S frames are used for Layer 3 information acknowledgements and flow control procedures. Frames are numbered to ensure complete transmission. Each I frame has its own transmit number $N_{(S)}$ and receive number $N_{(R)}$. The receive number represents the number of frames that have been correctly received and acknowledged by the peer entity. The transmitting station increments the transmit number by one every time a frame is transmitted. Received I frames must be in sequence without transmission and format errors before they can be acknowledged by means of an appropriate supervisory frame or I frame transmitted to the peer entity. The maximum number of frames that may be sent without acknowledgment of receipt is called the window size. The maximum permissible window size depends on the modulo of the sequence number counters and is 7 for modulo 8 counters (3 bit for the $N_{(S)}$

and $N_{(R)}$) and can be up to 127 for modulo 128 counters (extended sequencing, established with Set Asynchronous Balanced Mode Extended (SABME) as opposed to SABM). Since 1988 equipment using the modulo 8 sequencing has been obsolete, extended sequencing is now mandatory. The default window size for transmission and reception is 7. Larger window sizes require more buffers.

All frames have a bit identified as either P (poll; in commands) or F (final; in responses). A poll bit indicates that an immediate response is expected; in other words, after a command frame with P=1 has been transmitted, only received response frames with the final bit F=1 are considered a valid response. Received response frames with the final bit F=0 under these circumstances are considered unsolicited responses. Most of the frame types are defined as either a command or a response type frame; however, some supervisory frames can be either a command or a response. The type of frame is determined by the knowledge of the data source (NT or TE) and the content (value) of the C/R bit in the first octet of the address field. NTs and TEs have to set this bit differently for commands and responses. The first step in setting up a LAP-D connection is the transmission of a Set Asynchronous Balanced Mode Extended (SABME) command with the P bit set. The receiving side transmits an unnumbered acknowledge (UA) frame with the F bit set to 1 in order to confirm this command. Once this procedure has been completed, I frames can be transmitted.

The T202 timer (2s) monitors the TEI assignment procedure, and the T200 timer (1s) monitors the response to a SABME command. If no response to the SABME

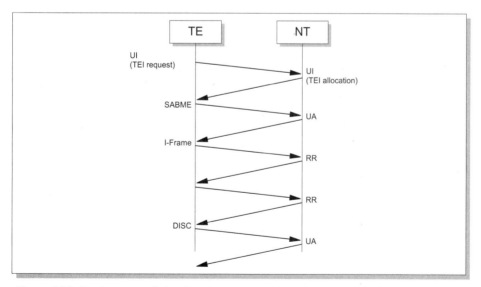

Figure 12.9 Setting up and clearing down Layer 2 connections in ISDN: LAPD protocol

is received within 1 second, the SABME command is repeated. If answers are received from multiple terminal devices while T202 is running, this indicates that a given TEI has been assigned to more than one terminal. Check the terminals to determine which devices have identical TEIs.

ISDN Layer 3: DSS1

The DSS1 protocol, detailed in ITU Recommendation Q.931, is used for Layer 3 transmission of such information as the subscriber numbers, service type (voice or data transmission), and desired channel (B1, B2, etc.). DSS1 recognizes 25 signaling messages, which are divided into the following categories: Call Establishment, Connection Information Phase, Call Clearing, and Miscellaneous. The following types of messages are available for standard signaling procedures:

Call Establishment:

- ALERTING
- CALL PROCEEDING
- CONNECT
- CONNECT ACKNOWLEDGE
- PROGRESS
- SETUP
- SETUP ACKNOWLEDGE

Call Information Phase:

- RESUME
- RESUME ACKNOWLEDGE
- RESUME REJECT
- SUSPEND
- SUSPEND ACKNOWLEDGE
- SUSPEND REJECT
- USER INFORMATION

Call Clearing:

- DISCONNECT
- RELEASE
- RELEASE COMPLETE
- RESTART
- RESTART ACKNOWLEDGE

Miscellaneous:

- INFORMATION
- CONGESTION CONTROL

- NOTIFY
- SEGMENT
- STATUS
- STATUS ENQUIRY

Each signaling message is made up of a number of sections called information elements. The first three information elements, listed here and described later in detail, are mandatory (Mandatory Information Elements):

- Protocol discriminator
- Call reference
- Message type

The inclusion of additional elements depends on the message type. Figure 12.10 shows the schematic structure of these user-to-network interface (UNI) signaling messages.

Bit	8	7	6	5	4	3	2	1	Byte
	Protocol Discriminator								1
	0	0	0	0	Call Reference Length				2
	Flag		Call Reference						3
	Call Reference (continued)								4
									5
	Message Type								6
									7
	Information Elements								8
									9
	Information Elements								...n

Figure 12.10 Q.931 message format

Protocol Discriminator

The protocol discriminator is the first element in each Q.931 message. It is usually set to 8 (decimal) or 00001000 (binary), which indicates the Q.931 protocol. The values 00010000 through 00111111 and 01010000 through

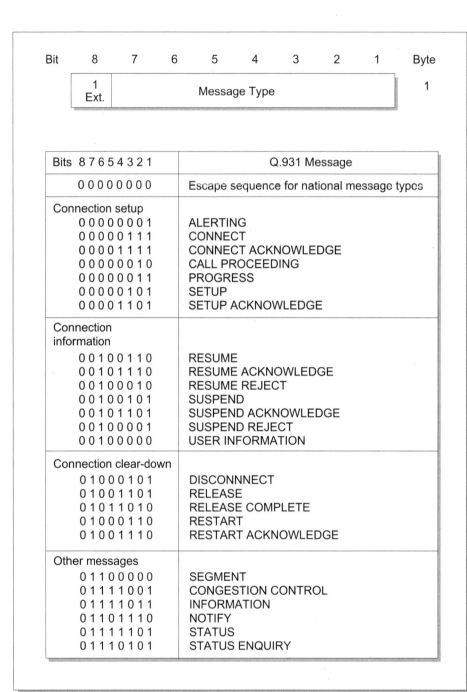

Bit	8	7	6	5	4	3	2	1	Byte
	1 Ext.			Message Type					1

Bits 8 7 6 5 4 3 2 1	Q.931 Message
0 0 0 0 0 0 0 0	Escape sequence for national message types
Connection setup	
0 0 0 0 0 0 0 1	ALERTING
0 0 0 0 0 1 1 1	CONNECT
0 0 0 0 1 1 1 1	CONNECT ACKNOWLEDGE
0 0 0 0 0 0 1 0	CALL PROCEEDING
0 0 0 0 0 0 1 1	PROGRESS
0 0 0 0 0 1 0 1	SETUP
0 0 0 0 1 1 0 1	SETUP ACKNOWLEDGE
Connection information	
0 0 1 0 0 1 1 0	RESUME
0 0 1 0 1 1 1 0	RESUME ACKNOWLEDGE
0 0 1 0 0 0 1 0	RESUME REJECT
0 0 1 0 0 1 0 1	SUSPEND
0 0 1 0 1 1 0 1	SUSPEND ACKNOWLEDGE
0 0 1 0 0 0 0 1	SUSPEND REJECT
0 0 1 0 0 0 0 0	USER INFORMATION
Connection clear-down	
0 1 0 0 0 1 0 1	DISCONNNECT
0 1 0 0 1 1 0 1	RELEASE
0 1 0 1 1 0 1 0	RELEASE COMPLETE
0 1 0 0 0 1 1 0	RESTART
0 1 0 0 1 1 1 0	RESTART ACKNOWLEDGE
Other messages	
0 1 1 0 0 0 0 0	SEGMENT
0 1 1 1 1 0 0 1	CONGESTION CONTROL
0 1 1 1 1 0 1 1	INFORMATION
0 1 1 0 1 1 1 0	NOTIFY
0 1 1 1 1 1 0 1	STATUS
0 1 1 1 0 1 0 1	STATUS ENQUIRY

Figure 12.11 Q.931 (DSS1) signaling messages

11111110 identify other protocols, such as X.25; the range from 01000000 to 01001111 is reserved for national use.

Call Reference

The call reference identifies a call to which particular signaling messages apply. All messages specific to a given connection contain the same call reference. The call reference consists of three fields:

- The first octet of the call reference is the length field, which contains the number of octets to follow. For basic rate access the length is 1, for primary rate 2, if the length field is 0 the call reference is called a "Dummy call reference" or "Null call reference". Dummy call references are used for messages not pertaining to a particular call, such as service profile (SPID) exchanges in North American ISDN applications.

- The most significant bit in the second octet contains the call reference flag; this flag is necessary to distinguish between call references of the same value for different calls because the NT and TE may allocate the call reference numbers independently of one another. Whichever side allocates the call reference number sets the value of the call reference flag to 0.

- Bits 0 to 7 in the second octet and all bits in subsequent octets (depending on the call reference length field) contain the actual call reference value. A value of 0 is called the global call reference, which is used for generic messages pertaining to all active calls on a TE/NT interface.

The global call reference is used only for RESTART, RESTART ACKNOWLEDGE, and STATUS messages.

Message Type

The message type is a one or two octet field and identifies the function of the message (see Figure 12.11). Two octet message types are used for network

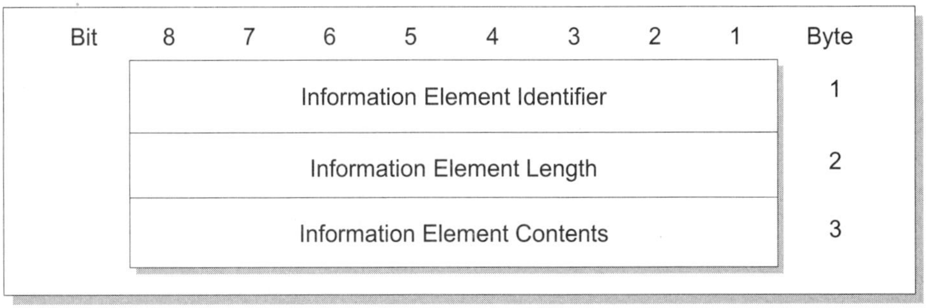

Bit	8	7	6	5	4	3	2	1	Byte
	Information Element Identifier								1
	Information Element Length								2
	Information Element Contents								3

Figure 12.12a Format and coding of information elements (Q.931)

Information Element Identifiers	
Bits 8 7 6 5 4 3 2 1	
1 0 0 0 _ _ _ _	Reserved
1 0 0 1 _ _ _ _	Shift
1 0 1 0 0 0 0 0	More data
1 0 1 0 0 0 0 1	Sending complete
1 0 1 1 _ _ _ _	Congestion level
1 1 0 1 _ _ _ _	Repeat indicator
0 0 0 0 0 0 0 0	Segmented message
0 0 0 0 0 1 0 0	Bearer capability
0 0 0 0 1 0 0 0	Cause
0 0 0 1 0 0 0 0	Call identity
0 0 0 1 1 0 0 0	Call state
0 0 0 1 1 1 1 0	Channel identification
0 0 1 0 0 0 0 0	Progress indicator
0 0 1 0 0 1 1 1	Network specific facilities
0 0 1 0 1 0 0 0	Notification indicator
0 0 1 0 1 0 0 0	Display
0 0 1 0 1 0 0 1	Date/time
0 0 1 0 1 1 0 0	Keypad facility
0 0 1 1 0 1 0 0	Signal
0 1 0 0 0 0 0 0	Information rate
0 1 0 0 0 0 1 0	End-to-end-transit delay
0 1 0 0 0 0 1 1	Transit delay selection and indication
0 1 0 0 0 1 0 0	Packet layer binary parameters
0 1 0 0 0 1 0 1	Packet layer window size
0 1 0 0 0 1 1 0	Packet size
0 1 0 0 0 1 1 1	Closed user group
0 1 0 0 1 0 1 0	Reverse charge indication
0 1 1 0 1 1 0 0	Calling party number
0 1 1 0 1 1 0 1	Calling party subaddress
0 1 1 1 0 0 0 0	Called party number
0 1 1 1 0 0 0 1	Called party subaddress
0 1 1 1 0 1 0 0	Redirecting number
0 1 1 1 1 0 0 0	Transit network selection
0 1 1 1 1 0 0 1	Restart indication
0 1 1 1 1 1 0 0	Low layer compatibility
0 1 1 1 1 1 0 1	High layer compatibility
0 1 1 1 1 1 1 0	User-user
1 1 1 1 1 1 1 1	Escape for extension

Figure 12.12b Format and coding of information elements (Q.931)

specific messages and the first octet has to be coded 00000000 (binary) with all bits set to 0.

ISDN Information Elements

Some messages include other information elements in addition to the mandatory elements described previously. These elements may vary in length. Each information element contains an information element identifier, a length field, and the actual contents of the information element. A single message can contain zero, one, or multiple information elements. Figure 12.12 shows the general structure of information elements and the different element types that are defined.

Codeset Extensions (Message Sets)

The entire set of all information elements valid in a given operating mode is called a codeset (or message set). The information elements described in ITU Recommendation Q.931 comprise codeset 0, which is the default codeset. Defining additional codesets, numbered 1 through 7, expands the number of available information elements. Transitions from one codeset to another, performed using the locking or non-locking shift procedure described in Q.931, may only be made to a codeset with a higher numerical value than one currently used.

Codesets 1 – 3: Reserved for future use by ITU

Codeset 4:   Reserved for future use by ISO/IEC

Codeset 5:   Reserved for national use

Codeset 6:   Reserved for information elements specific to the local network

Codeset 7:   Reserved for user-specific information elements

A locking shift information element switches the codeset permanently. For example, if codeset 0 (the default codeset) is active, a locking-shift element that specifies codeset 5 will cause codeset 5 to become active; all information elements from that point onward are interpreted according to codeset 5. Following a non-locking shift element, the higher-numbered codeset is active only for one subsequent information element. Additional information elements are considered to belong to the previously used codeset. A variety of codesets were used in Europe up to the early 1990s. Since then, the European Telecommunications Standards Institute (ETSI) codeset has become the standard for European ISDN. The table in Figure 12.13 gives an overview of the most common codesets in use today.

ETSI 102 Euro-ISDN	ETS 300-102-1
1TR6 German National ISDN	FTZ 1TR 6
TPH 1962	Telecom Australia TPH_1962 (Basic rate)
TPH 1856	Telecom Australia TPH_1856 (Primary rate)
NT S208	Northern Telecom NIS S208-5 (Basic rate)
NT A211	Northern Telecom NIS A211 (Primary rate)
ATT 41449	AT&T TR41449 (Primary rate)
ATT 5E6	AT&T 5D5 900 321 (Basic rate)
NIU 301 (USA)	North American ISDN Users Forum 301 (Basic rate)
NI1 1953 (USA)	Bellcore National ISDN 1 SR-NWT-001953 (Basic rate)
NI2 (USA)	Bellcore National ISDN 2
Televerkets (Scandinavia)	
VN3, VN4 (France)	CNET VN3/VN4
JT-Q.931 (Japan)	
CCITT 1988	Q.931, Q.932 (1988)
ITU 1993	Q.931, Q.932 (1993)

Figure 12.13 ISDN codesets

ISDN Connection Setup

To initiate an ISDN connection, the TE sends a SETUP command containing information, such as the subscriber numbers, the type of service (voice or data communication), the B channel designation, and the capabilities of the terminal device. The ISDN network responds, depending on the message content, with either a SETUP_ACK or a CALL PROCEEDING command to acknowledge the SETUP command, and forwards the call to the receiving station. When the call is successfully delivered at the destination, the network sends an ALERTING message to the calling station. Once the call is accepted by the called station, the network reports this fact to the calling station in a CONNECT message. The calling station has the option of sending a CONNECT ACKNOWLEDGE message to confirm receipt of the CONNECT message. This concludes the connection setup: the call is now in the active state.

Clearing Down the Connection

Once the connection has been ended by one subscriber (by a person hanging up a telephone receiver, for example) the clearing terminal device transmits a DISCONNECT message to the ISDN network. The network forwards this mes-

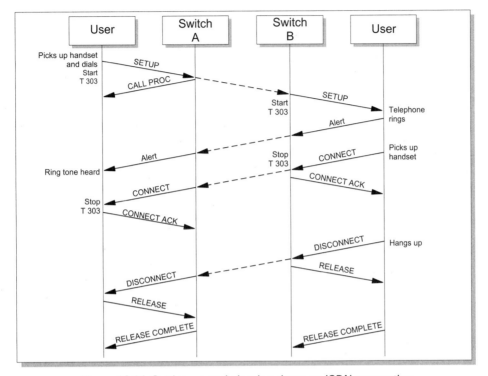

Figure 12.14 Setting up and clearing down an ISDN connection

sage to the other subscriber and sends a RELEASE message to the subscriber that ended the connection. The clear-down procedure is finished once a RELEASE COMPLETE message has been transmitted.

In North American ISDN networks with NI-1 capability, terminals are uniquely identified by a SPID, which usually consists of a directory number (DN) (phone number) plus a two digit terminal identifier (TID). At least one SPID for every Layer 2 link (TEI value) is required. The SPID has to be entered and stored in the terminal by an operator. After power up and establishment of the supported Layer 2 links, the network requests the SPID from the terminal for every Layer 2 link. If this procedure fails, the network will not recognize the terminal, that is, outgoing calls will not proceed because the network does not respond to Layer 3 call control messages. After completion of the SPID request procedure, call control messages for a particular DN must be transmitted over the Layer 2 link matched with a registered SPID or otherwise the messages will be ignored by the network.

12.2   Design Guidelines for ISDN

12.2.1   Basic Rate Interface

An ISDN basic rate line is carried over a 2-wire telephone line from the public telecommunications network's local switch to the subscriber's premises, where a NT provides the interface to the ISDN subscriber's communication equipment. In North America the NT is considered customer premises equipment and has to be provided by the subscriber. Most ISDN equipment is equipped with a built-in NT (collapsed NT) and can be connected directly to the 2-wire pair from the service provider (U-Interface). Whereas if a NT is installed, the 4-wire ISDN S_0/T interface is used to connect the NT to a maximum of 12 ISDN wall jacks, which allows up to eight ISDN terminal devices (such as terminal adapters, telephones, faxes, routers or PC cards) to be connected at any given time. The maximum length of the S_0 bus is 200 meters. The cable connecting the NT to the first ISDN jack must not exceed a length of 10 meters. Because there are no active elements on the bus except the NT, this part of the ISDN network is also called a passive S_0-bus. A S_0-bus must be terminated at each end by two 100-Ohm resistors, one connected across the transmit wire pair and one across the receive pair. The terminating resistors may be either integrated in the last ISDN TE on the bus, where they can be activated by a switch, or installed in the last wall jack on the bus. The NT supplies power to the passive ISDN telephones. Because the NT can only power a maximum of four telephones, no more than four phones may be connected to an S_0-bus unless a line voltage adapter powers the equipment. To ensure that telephone service is still available in the event of a power failure, the local switch can power one ISDN telephone. The NT itself can be installed at any point on the S_0-bus. If only one ISDN terminal device is connected to the bus, the maximum distance between the NT and the ISDN jack is 1,000 meters. If up to four terminals are connected to the bus within 50 meters, the distance from NT to the farthest terminal device may be up to 500 meters.

12.2.2   Primary Rate Interface (PRI)

The primary rate ISDN line (sometimes called the S_{2M} interface or primary rate access) requires a 4-wire E1 or T1 line to the local switch. In contrast to the BRI NT, the NT at the PRI subscriber line can only be connected to a single ISDN terminal device (this is called point-to-point configuration). The TE in this case is usually either a PBX or a router port. The TE is connected to the NT by a 2-pair copper cable no more than 250 meters in length. Regenerators are required if the ISDN connection is to span greater distances.

456

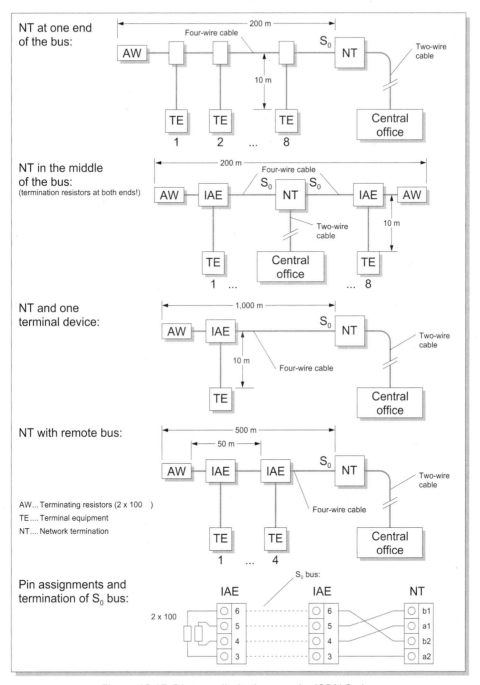

NT at one end of the bus:

NT in the middle of the bus:
(termination resistors at both ends!)

NT and one terminal device:

NT with remote bus:

AW... Terminating resistors (2 x 100)
TE.... Terminal equipment
NT.... Network termination

Pin assignments and termination of S₀ bus:

Figure 12.15 Distance limitations on the ISDN S₀-bus

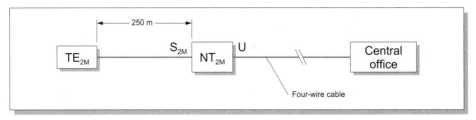

Figure 12.16 Distance limitations of the ISDN primary rate interface

12.3   ISDN Standards

All standards for ISDN were developed by the International Telecommunication Union (ITU, formerly CCITT). The various national codesets have been defined on the basis of the ITU Recommendations by national and international organizations. The most important standards related to ISDN are:

I.430   Basic User-Network Interface–Layer 1 Specification

I.431   Primary Rate User-Network Interface–Layer 1 Specification

Q.920   ISDN User-Network Interface Data Link Layer–General Aspects

Q.921   ISDN User-Network Interface–Data Link Layer Specification

Q.930   ISDN User-Network Interface Layer 3 – General Aspects

Q.931   ISDN User-Network Interface Layer 3 Specification
          for Basic Call Control

See "ATM Standards" in Chapter 10, *ATM Networks*, for a more complete list of I- and Q-series specifications.

The ITU can be reached on the Internet at
http://www.itu.int/

Other important addresses related to ISDN include:

North American ISDN Users Forum
http://www.niuf.nist.gov/

National ISDN Council
http://www.nationalisdncouncil.com/index.html

European ISDN Users Forum
http://www2.echo.lu/eiuf/en/eiuf.html

12.4   Troubleshooting ISDN

12.4.1   Gathering Information on Symptoms and Recent Changes

The first step in any troubleshooting process is to gather information. The more information you have about the symptoms and characteristics of a problem— including *when* it first occurred—the better your chances of solving the problem quickly and efficiently. Typical questions you might ask at this stage include:

- Was there any change in any hardware or software network component?
- Do the symptoms occur regularly or intermittently?
- Is it possible to reproduce or recreate the symptoms?
- When was the first occurrence of the symptom?
- Are the symptoms related to certain applications or connections, for example, outgoing or incoming calls only, or do they affect all network operations?
- Has anyone connected or disconnected equipment to/from the network?
- Has anyone replaced or installed an interface card in a computer?
- Has anyone stepped on a cable?
- Has any maintenance work been performed in the building recently (by a telephone company or building maintenance personnel, for example)?
- Has anyone (including cleaning personnel) moved any equipment or furniture?
- Has there been severe weather (thunderstorms, tornados) in the vicinity (North America, rural areas)?
- Is the network up and running?
- Does a service provider (Internet Service provider) experience general problems in your area?

As with any network topology, troubleshooting ISDN is greatly facilitated if records of the main operating statistics have been maintained prior to the occurrence of the error in question. In an ISDN network, it is also important to have detailed descriptions and user guides/manuals of all ISDN network components (such as bridges, ISDN routers, computer systems with ISDN cards, PBXs, and ISDN telephones), including configuration data and details about physical BRI/PRI interfaces, as well as the protocols and applications that are operated over ISDN lines. Statistics such as capacity use of B channels (peak and average values), sorted by service or by distribution of packet size (in the case of data transmission), can be compared with the corresponding data collected in the error situation: this often points directly to the source of the problem. Troubleshooting tools include an ISDN terminal device known to be in working order, an NT known to be in working order, and an ISDN analyzer—ideally an analyzer that can be used to simulate NT and TE interfaces, both BRI and PRI, as well as to monitor ISDN lines. In most cases a telephone connected to a different service, for example, a cell phone, can be used for testing outgoing and incoming connections.

The first step in diagnosis is to obtain a clear picture of the error symptoms. Is it possible to establish any connection at all on the ISDN line? Are existing connections cut off? Have response times in the ISDN line grown longer; has throughput diminished? What happens when the malfunctioning station is called from a telephone in another service, for example, a pay phone or cell phone?

Because most problems in networks occur in the physical layer, ISDN is no exception; the troubleshooting procedure should start with basic checks. This includes checking the physical interfaces and monitoring ISDN Layer 1 functions. If the symptoms seem to indicate a particular network component (an ISDN card, an ISDN telephone, or an NT), the next step is to replace the

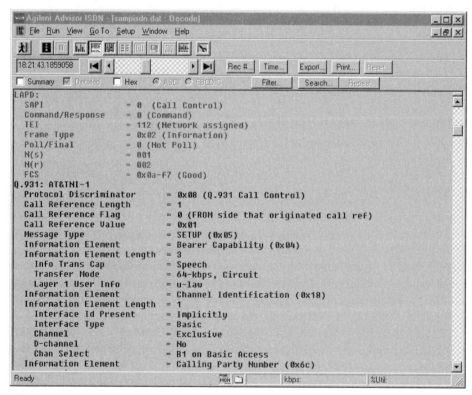

Figure 12.17 Using a protocol analyzer to decode ISDN Q.931 signals: SETUP message

component in question with one that is known to be in working order. If this does not resolve the problem, the next step is to check log data gathered by components in the affected network, such as routers and ISDN cards, for any error indication and to check the configuration of these components. If the source of the error still cannot be found, the use of an ISDN tester to check ISDN Layer 1, as well as the signaling and bearer channel protocols, is suggested. On a BRI line, Layer 1 should reach the Info 3 or 4 state automatically. On a PRI line, test the voltage level, the Layer 1 alarm states (AIS, RAI, CRC), the power supply to the NT (green LED on), and the PRI and U_{k2} (red LEDs off).

If the collected data corroborates that the physical layer connection can be established, then the LAP-D protocol should be analyzed. If no errors are detected there, the next step is to examine signaling procedures on the D channel. Figure 12.17 shows an ISDN SETUP message decoded by a protocol analyzer.

If problems persist despite the fact that ISDN connections can be set up successfully, the user data on the B channels must be analyzed. Factors to be checked include the bit-error rate (BER), capacity use, and the transport protocols used (such as IP or X.25).

12.4.2 Error Symptoms in ISDN

The three most common error symptoms in ISDN networks are a) problems establishing connections, b) interruptions of active connections, and c) significant losses of network performance accompanied by long response times in ISDN applications.

By far the most frequent symptom is the failure to establish a connection when a call is placed from an ISDN telephone or from a computer system with an ISDN card. This type of problem is usually the result of errors in the physical layer (OSI Layer 1); the cause is seldom found in higher layers. Typical causes include faulty power supplies, line breaks, miswired connectors, lack of terminating resistors (BRI), faulty network components (ISDN router ports, ISDN switches, ISDN PC cards, ISDN telephones), or noise on the line. Additional causes in PRI lines can include faulty grounding or faulty shielding in the cables between NT and TE. T1/E1 lines are usually terminated at digital cross connects or patch panels, which may introduce additional reasons for faulty connections, starting with using the wrong type of patch cords or termination resistors, ambiguous labeling of the patch panels, or simply patch cords plugged into the wrong connectors. Incorrect configuration of ISDN interfaces is another common source of errors. A terminal device on a BRI line operated in point-to-point mode rather than in bus mode, for example, results in frame collisions that make it impossible to establish a connection on the physical layer. TE equipment for primary rate interfaces generally require the correct settings of the framing format, line encoding, and the selection of the correct time slot assigned for the signaling channel. In the North American T carrier systems, it is also essential to know the T1 line service type. Due to some legacy services, T1 lines with Zero Code Substitution (ZCS) or Digital Data System (DDS) services cannot transmit unrestricted digital data at 64 Kbit/s. Certain local exchange carriers still offer a maximum data rate of 56 Kbit/s only. The TE equipment must be configured accordingly. The most common errors in Layer 2 occur in the TEI assignment procedure. If the ISDN components involved do not agree on the mode of TEI assignment (manual or automatic), then no communication is possible on the LAP-D protocol level and connection setup fails. Another error associated with TEI assignment is the duplicate assignment of a single TEI value: this also makes it impossible to establish a connection. For the evaluation of Layer 2 TEI assignment problems, it is essential to know how many Layer 2 links are required and configured (TEI values), which links are configured for fixed TEI values, and which ones are for automatic TEI assignment. In North American networks with at least NI-1 capabilities, the SPID values have to be entered into the terminal equipment's memory, therefore the user must be familiar with the configuration procedure for a particular terminal equipment.

Problems on ISDN Layer 3 can have any of a number of causes. Typical examples include incompatibility of Q.931 variants (national ISDN versus Euro-ISDN, for example), incompatibility or unavailability of ISDN services, incorrect implementation of ISDN protocols, and incorrect input of the subscriber number for the call destination.

When established connections are cut off, this is most likely due to the absence of keep-alive frames, such as Receive Ready frames (Layer 2) or Status Enquiry frames (Layer 3). This type of error is usually caused by a high bit-error rate or by terminals that are too slow in responding to polling frames. In North American networks the failure to respond to the periodic line audit (that is, identity check request messages over the broadcast link SAPI 63, TEI 127) will result in a TEI removal procedure by the network.

Long response times in applications operated over ISDN links may also be part of normal operating behavior if B-channel bandwidth is restricted, for example, or if a system that is accessed over ISDN necessitates a call setup for each transaction. If the ISDN router is configured to clear down connections automatically after a short period of line inactivity (to minimize connection costs), the necessity of re-establishing the connection means a few seconds' delay every time the application is accessed. If connections can be established only through the dial-back mode—that is, the calling party is called back by the remote station so that two call setup procedures take place for each call—this can slow network performance considerably. Another reason for long response times, however, might be incorrect configuration of the B-channel transport protocol. If this is the case, timers may expire too often or the window size may be too small. Other causes include problems in activating B channels, which is often the case when using multilink Point-toPoint protocol (PPP). If the threshold configured in the router for activation of the second B channel (of a BRI) is too high, then the second channel may be activated too late, deactivated too early, or not activated at all. As a result, the ISDN line appears to be overloaded even though the theoretical total bandwidth is not being used.

It is important to keep in mind the difference between the Point-to-Point and Point-to-Multipoint (that is, bus) ISDN line configurations. As described previously, the PRI can be operated only inPoint-to-Point mode, while BRI lines can be configured in either mode. If a large PBX is operated over multiple S_0 lines, for example, these generally should be configured for Point-to-Point operation because all connections go through the PBX, not between other devices on the same S_0 bus. If the line is configured for the wrong operating mode, TEI assignment cannot be performed correctly and network operation is impaired.

12.4.3   Symptoms and Causes: ISDN

Symptom: No Connection

Cause (1):   Faulty cabling or connectors.
Cause (2):   Power supply failure.
Cause (3):   Crossed wires (in BRI).
Cause (4):   Wrong number.
Cause (5):   Faulty network components (ISDN router port,
              terminal adapter (TA), PBX, interface card, telephone).
Cause (6):   Incorrect configuration of the ISDN interface
              (ISDN card, router port, or PBX).
Cause (7):   Noise; high BER.
Cause (8):   Problems in TEI assignment (manual vs. automatic mode).
Cause (9):   Duplicate TEIs.
Cause (10):   Incompatible Q.931 variants (national ISDN vs. Euro-ISDN).
Cause (11):   Incompatible ISDN services.
Cause (12):   Q.931 implementation errors.
Cause (13):   Wiring faults on the S_0 bus.
Cause (14):   Lack of terminating resistors on the S_0 bus.
Cause (15):   Faulty grounding (PRI).
Cause (16):   Non-shielded cabling between NT and TE (PRI).
Cause (17):   Signaling messages are sent with wrong TEI value in the case of
              multiple signaling links (BRI North America).

Symptom: Frequent Connection Loss

Cause (1):   High BER.

Cause (2):   Slow terminal equipment.
              (Receive Ready (RR) or Status Enquiry responses too slow).

Cause (3):   Application does not respond.

Symptom: Long Application Response Times over ISDN

Cause (1):   Additional call setup time due to automatic connection clear-
              down (during idle times) by the ISDN router.

Cause (2):   Router does not activate additional B channels at high traffic load.

Cause (3):   Small window size of the application protocol (such as IP)
              used over the B channel.

Cause (4):   Timers expire in B channel application protocols.

Cause (5):   Application is busy.

Cause (6):   Rate adaptation handshake fails due to wrong terminal applica-
              tion settings.

Cause (7):   Calling/called station is a mobile station.

Cause (8):   Call not end-to-end ISDN.

The following list summarizes the most frequent sources of problems with ISDN
(in alphabetical order):

- Call forwarding is active; no incoming calls
- Crossed wires (in BRI)
- Duplicate TEI assignment
- Electromagnetic interference
- Incorrect filter settings in the router
- High bit-error rates
- Incorrect input of multiple subscriber number (MSN)
- Incorrect physical installation of router or switch: loose cabling, connector, plug-in module, or card; faulty wiring on the back plane
- ISDN interface card defective
- ISDN interface incorrectly configured
  (ISDN interface card, router port, PBX, ISDN telephone)
- ISDN line blocked or not enabled by service provider

Figure 12.18a The most common causes of ISDN problems

- ISDN network interface card incorrectly configured (wrong interrupt, driver, or timer configuration, etc.)
- ISDN router port defective
- Incompatible ISDN services; services not available (not ordered from ISDN provider)
- ISDN telephone defective
- Line breaks (in plug or cabling)
- Long response times due to automatic connection clear-down settings in the router
- Loose or defective connectors on network interface cards, in wall jacks, or patch panels
- No grounding (PRI)
- No terminating resistors on the S_0 bus
- NT defective
- PBX defective
- Power supply defective
- Protocol configuration in the router incorrect (address tables, mapping tables, subnet masks, default gateways, routing tables, timers)
- Q.931 implementation incorrect
- Q.931 variant incompatible (national ISDN vs. Euro-ISDN)
- Router does not activate the second (or nth, in PRI) B channel (configuration error)
- Router settings incorrectly configured: port not active, wrong operating mode, protocol not active
- Slow terminal devices (RR or Status Enquiry responses too slow)
- TEI assignment problems (manual vs. automatic mode)
- Terminal adapter defective
- Timers expire in B channel application protocols
- Unshielded cabling between NT and TE (PRI)
- Window size too small in the application protocol (such as IP) on the B channel
- Wrong number called

Figure 12.18b The most common causes of ISDN problems

Frame Relay

13

13.1 Frame Relay: Specification and Implementation

Frame Relay, a data communication technique for wide-area links, was originally developed in the early 1980s as a tributary for ISDN; it was only in the early 1990s that Frame Relay became popular. Frame Relay multiplexes data frames with various source and destination addresses over WAN lines, allocating bandwidth statistically to active logical channels. Plesiochronous Digital Hierarchy (PDH) (E1/T1, E3/T3) or SDH/SONET networks may be used as the underlying transmission infrastructure. As in X.25 or ISDN, the communication is connection-oriented, meaning that a virtual channel must be defined for each data transfer. When Frame Relay is used to create permanent virtual circuits (PVCs), no signaling process is necessary for connection setup. Only a keep alive signaling protocol is carried out within the data channel itself to verify the integrity of the link. To set up and clear down Frame Relay connections dynamically as switched virtual circuits (SVCs), a procedure very similar to ISDN signaling is used called Frame Relay SVC signaling.

An essential difference between Frame Relay and the older X.25 lies in the protocol's error correction mechanisms. X.25 was developed more than 30 years ago for data transmission over analog telephone lines of inherently poor quality. For this reason, extensive error correction mechanisms and algorithms for retransmission of lost data packets had to be implemented. This is no longer necessary with the low error rates of today's digital wide-area links. Consequently Frame Relay has no need for retransmitting lost or corrupt data frames; correction of transmission errors is left to the higher-layer application protocols. The only checks performed are for address validity and bit errors. As a result, the protocol overhead is significantly lower. Frame Relay links can therefore carry up to 30 percent more user data than X.25 connections with the same line bandwidth.

Statistical multiplexing is the second major advantage of Frame Relay over X.25. Every connection channel is guaranteed a minimum communication bandwidth by the Committed Information Rate (CIR) parameter. Actual transmission may significantly exceed this rate, however, if more bandwidth is available. In contrast to time multiplexing, statistical multiplexing dynamically allocates bandwidth to the individual channels based on the volume of data to be transmitted. This permits much more efficient transport, particularly for traffic profiles with

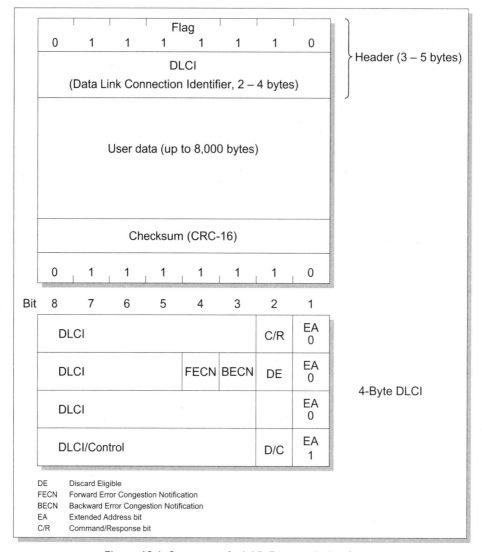

Figure 13.1 Structure of a LAP-F transmission frame

varying peak loads, and is the main reason Frame Relay was able to establish itself so rapidly as the preferred communication protocol in wide-area networks.

Frame Relay, different than X.25 or ISDN, uses only the Layer 2 protocol LAP-F. Unlike the corresponding ISDN or X.25 Layer 2 protocols, LAP-D and LAP-B, however—which include functions for flow control, packet receipt acknowledgment, and retransmission requests for lost packets—LAP-F is limited to channel multiplexing, data framing, and error detection functions. Accordingly, the structure of a Frame Relay data packet is simple. Between the beginning and ending flags of the frame are a 2- to 4-byte header field, which includes the Data Link Connection Identifier; the Information Field, which contains user data; and the Frame Check Sequence, a checksum to permit bit-error detection. The information field may contain up to 8 Kbytes of higher-layer protocol data (see Figure 13.1).

A given user channel can be identified by the Data Link Connection Identifier (DLCI), a unique numerical value assigned to each virtual channel. The DLCI value is only locally significant, however: it is replaced by each Frame Relay node as the frame is forwarded along the transmission path. The DLCI value 0 denotes in-band signaling messages; the range 1 to 15 is reserved; values from 16 to 1007 can be used to identify Frame Relay connections. DLCIs 1008 to 1022 are also reserved. DLCI 1023 is used to transmit Local Management Interface (LMI) frames.

The DLCI field can be 2, 3, or 4 bytes long. The Extension bit (EA) at the end of each header byte is zero if the header continues in the next byte; only the last byte of the header has the EA bit set to one. When DLCIs of 3 or 4 bytes are used, the maximum number of Frame Relay connections increases accordingly (see Figure 13.2).

Two-byte DLCI	Three-byte DLCI	Four-byte DLCI	DLCI Value
0	0	0	In-channel signaling
1 – 15	1 – 1023	1 – 131071	Reserved
16 – 1007	1024 – 64511	131072 – 8257535	Frame Relay connections
1008 – 1022	64512 – 65534	8257536 – 8388606	Reserved
1023	65535	8388607	Local Management Interface (LMI)

Figure 13.2 Values for 2, 3, and 4 byte DLCI fields

The Forward Explicit Congestion Notification (FECN) and Backward Explicit Congestion Notification (BECN) bits in the second Frame Relay header byte are used to transmit overload messages. When a Frame Relay node is overloaded, it sends frames with BECN = 1 upstream and frames with FECN = 1 downstream. When the transmitting station receives a BECN frame, it can reduce its output rate. The Discard Eligibility (DE) bit is set to one to tag frames sent in excess of the guaranteed minimum bandwidth. When a Frame Relay node is overloaded, it may discard these frames.

Operation and Monitoring (In-Channel Signaling, LMI)

Operational states in Frame Relay networks are monitored by means of signaling messages, which are analogous to ISDN Q.931 messages. Frame Relay signaling messages are transported in LAP-F frames. These messages were originally designated as Local Management Interface (LMI), but current standards describe them and the corresponding processes as "in-channel signaling" (ANSI T1.617 Annex D, T1.618, ITU Q.933 Annex A). In-channel signaling entails processes for defining and clearing down PVCs, requesting status reports on certain DLCIs, and testing the availability and error rates of connections. Operational monitoring is based on the periodic transmission of STATUS ENQUIRY messages, which are answered by the destination system in STATUS messages. It is important to note that some of the different in-channel signaling standards use different DLCIs (DLCI 0 or 1023), or the same DLCI 0 but different bit setups or extra bytes (Codeshift set, for example), which makes them mutually incompatible. Thus the in-channel signaling or LMI defined in ANSI T1.617 Annex D and ITU-T Q.933 Annex A uses DLCI 0, for example, whereas the original LMI (OLMI) defined by the four original collaborating companies (also known as "the gang of four") in T1S1 messages is sent using DLCI 1023.

The availability of a Frame Relay connection is measured by the Link Integrity Verification (LIV) procedure. In this procedure, one station sends STATUS ENQUIRY messages at regular intervals containing a polling sequence number and the value of the last polling sequence number received. Within a few seconds, the Frame Relay node being queried must send a response containing the polling sequence number received as well as a new polling sequence number of its own. The default value for the interval between such STATUS ENQUIRY messages is ten seconds. The format of the messages is exactly the same as that of ISDN D-channel messages (ITU Q.931) and consists of a header followed by information elements. The protocol discriminator identifies whether the message is an ANSI or ITU-T in-channel signaling message (PD = 08h) or an original LMI message (PD = 09h).

Committed Information Rate (CIR)

CIR is the minimum bandwidth that the provider guarantees under any circumstances upon establishing a Frame Relay connection. If additional bandwidth is available, data can be transmitted in excess of the CIR, up to a maximum bandwidth that is also negotiated called the Access Rate. The CIR is specified in ANSI T1.606a and is calculated from the Committed Burst Size (B_C) and the Committed Rate Measurement Interval (T_C), as shown in Figure 13.3.

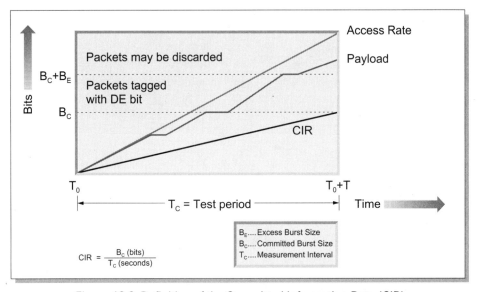

Figure 13.3 Definition of the Committed Information Rate (CIR)

Frame Relay SVCs

In a large communication infrastructure with full mesh connectivity over permanent Frame Relay connections (PVCs), the number and cost of these connections increases rapidly and the establishment of virtual connections on demand becomes more economical. The mechanism for establishing connections on demand is possible with the switched virtual connection (SVC) procedure. Frame Relay connections can be established and released as needed using X.121 or E.164 dial-up numbers to avoid having to set up permanent connections.

The signaling protocol used is a simplified version of ISDN D-channel signaling. As in the case of in-channel signaling, the message format corresponds exactly to that of ISDN D-channel messages (ITU Q.931) and consists of a header followed by information elements. Sixteen different signaling messages are defined, but not all of them are actually used (see Figure 13.5). The signaling

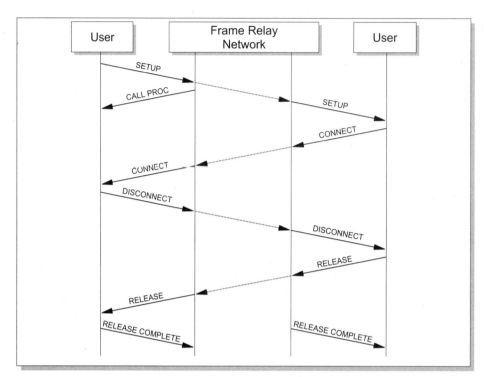

Figure 13.4 Frame Relay SVC connection setup

messages are transmitted with the reserved DLCI value zero. Connection setup begins with the transmission of a SETUP message containing parameters for the connection characteristics and the number of the node called. The Frame Relay network responds with a CALL PROCEEDING message, in which it supplies the DLCI for the requested connection, and forwards the SETUP message to the destination node. If the station called accepts the call, a CONNECT message is sent to the caller. Once the connection has been established, both end systems can send user data. When the transfer is finished, either side may clear down the connection by sending a DISCONNECT message.

Bit	8	7	6	5	4	3	2	1	Byte
	Protocol Discriminator								1
	0	0	0	0	Call Reference Length				2
	Flag		Call Reference						3
	Call Reference (continued)								4
									5
	Message Type								6
									7
	Information Elements								8
									9
	Information Elements								...n

Message Type Bits 8 7 6 5 4 3 2 1	ANSI T1.607 Messages
0 0 0 0 0 0 0 0	Escape sequence for national message types
Connection set-up	
0 0 0 0 0 0 0 1	ALERTING
0 0 0 0 0 1 1 1	CONNECT
0 0 0 0 1 1 1 1	CONNECT ACKNOWLEDGE
0 0 0 0 0 0 1 0	CALL PROCEEDING
0 0 0 0 0 0 1 1	PROGRESS
0 0 0 0 0 1 0 1	SETUP
0 0 0 0 1 1 0 1	SETUP ACKNOWLEDGE
Connection clear-down	
0 1 0 0 0 1 0 1	DISCONNNECT
0 1 0 0 1 1 0 1	RELEASE
0 1 0 1 1 0 1 0	RELEASE COMPLETE
0 1 0 0 0 1 1 0	RESTART
0 1 0 0 1 1 1 0	RESTART ACKNOWLEDGE
Other messages	
0 1 1 1 1 0 1 1	INFORMATION
0 1 1 0 1 1 1 0	NOTIFY
0 1 1 1 1 1 0 1	STATUS
0 1 1 1 0 1 0 1	STATUS ENQUIRY

Figure 13.5 Message format for Frame Relay SVCs and in-channel signaling (LMI)

Bit	8	7	6	5	4	3	2	1	Byte
	Information Element Identifier								1
	Information Element Length								2
	Information Element Contents								3

Information Element Identifiers (ANSI T1.607)	
Bits 8 7 6 5 4 3 2 1	
1 0 0 0 _ _ _ _	Reserved
1 0 0 1 _ _ _ _	Shift
1 1 0 1 _ _ _ _	Repeat indicator
0 0 0 0 0 0 0 0	Segmented message
0 0 0 0 0 1 0 0	Bearer capability
0 0 0 0 1 0 0 0	PVC status
0 0 0 1 0 0 0 0	Cause
0 0 0 1 0 1 0 0	Call state
0 0 0 1 1 0 0 0	Channel identification
0 0 0 1 1 0 0 1	Data link connection identifier
0 0 1 0 0 1 1 1	Link integrity verification
0 0 0 1 1 1 1 0	Progress indicator
0 0 1 0 0 0 0 0	Network specific facilities
0 0 1 0 1 0 0 0	Display
0 1 0 0 0 0 1 0	End-to-end-transit delay
0 1 0 0 0 1 0 0	Packet layer binary parameters
0 1 0 0 1 0 0 0	Link layer core parameters
0 1 0 0 1 0 0 1	Link layer protocol parameters
0 1 0 0 1 1 0 0	Connected number
0 1 0 0 1 1 0 1	Connected subaddress
0 1 1 0 1 1 0 0	Calling party number
0 1 1 0 1 1 0 1	Calling party subaddress
0 1 1 1 0 0 0 0	Called party number
0 1 1 1 0 0 0 1	Called party subaddress
0 1 1 1 1 0 0 0	Transit network selection
0 1 1 1 1 1 0 0	Low layer compatibility
0 1 1 1 1 1 0 1	High layer compatibility
0 1 1 1 1 1 1 0	User – user
1 1 1 1 1 1 1 1	Escape for extension

Figure 13.6 Format and coding of Frame Relay information elements (ANSI T1.607)

Frame Relay Multiprotocol Encapsulation

Because Frame Relay end systems and switches can receive data with several different DLCIs, the information transported must be identified on the Frame

Relay level in order to forward it quickly to bridge or router modules. Four additional fields for Frame Relay frames have therefore been defined in RFC 2427 (RFC 1490 is obsolete), ITU-T Q.922, and FRF-3.1. The first of these, the Q.922 control field (also called the unnumbered information), is padded to two full bytes and contains the value 03h. Next, the Network Layer Protocol ID field (NLPID) indicates the encapsulation or protocol being transported in the frame. The various protocol IDs used are listed in the ISO/IEC recommendation TR9577.

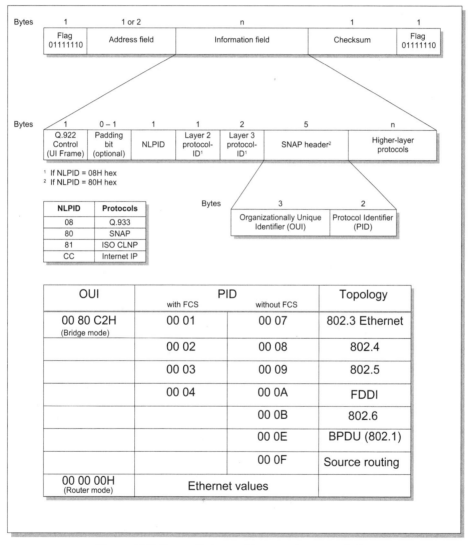

Figure 13.7 Frame Relay multiprotocol encapsulation

The protocol frame itself is transported in the third field. If the required protocol is not one of those listed in ISO/IEC TR9577, there are two other possible ways of transporting it. Either the NLPID is set to 08h (Q.933) and followed by a 2-byte identification number for the Layer 2 and 3 protocols, or NLPID is set to 80h and the Subnetwork Access Protocol (SNAP) address is used as the protocol ID. SNAP is a kind of meta-protocol that allows vendors practically unrestricted use of proprietary protocols. It is also used to identify proprietary protocols in Token Ring frames. The SNAP field consists of the 3-byte Organizationally Unique Identifier (OUI) and the Protocol Identifier (PID). The OUI indicates the standardization body that issued the protocol used, while the PID indicates the specific protocol itself. For data packets of routed protocols (such as Internet Protocol), the OUI is set to 00 00 00h and the PID contains the Ethernet type field value (or "EtherType") for the given protocol. (The Ethernet type field values for the various network protocols are listed in RFC 1700.) LAN data packets such as Ethernet or FDDI frames, which are not routable but can be bridged on OSI Layer 2, have an OUI of 00 80 C2h. The PID indicates the LAN topology (Ethernet, FDDI, etc.) (see Figure 13.7).

In a few cases when a protocol has an assigned NLPID, such as in the case of the Internet Protocol IP, instead of padding the second byte it can be used to directly identify those protocols. For example, IP has the defined value CCh.

13.2 Frame Relay Standards

Frame Relay standards are developed mainly by the ITU and the ANSI. The Frame Relay Forum is an active body working on implementation agreements. The most important Frame Relay standards and implementation agreements are listed below:

ITU:

I.122   Framework for Frame Mode Bearer Services

I.233   Frame Mode Bearer Services: ISDN Frame Relaying Bearer Service

Q.921   ISDN User-Network Interface—Data Link Layer Specification

Q.922   ISDN Data Link Layer Specification for Frame Mode Bearer Services

Q.933   Signaling Specifications for Frame Mode Switched and Permanent Virtual Connection Control and Status Monitoring

The ITU's Web server can be reached at

http://www.itu.ch/.

ANSI:

T1.602   Telecommunications–ISDN–Data-Link Layer Signaling Specification for Application at the User-Network Interface

T1.606   Telecommunications–ISDN–Architectural Framework and Service Description for Frame-Relaying Bearer Service

T1.606a Telecommunications–ISDN–Architectural Framework and Service Description for Frame-Relaying Bearer Service. Supplement to ANSI T1.606.

T1.617   Integrated Services Digital Network (ISDN) Signaling Specification for Frame Relay Bearer Service for Digital Subscriber Signaling System Number 1 (DSS1)

T1.618   Telecommunications–ISDN–Core Aspects of Frame Protocol for Use with Frame Relay Bearer Service

The ANSI Web server can be found at

http://www.ansi.org/.

Frame Relay Forum:

FRF.1.1   User-to-Network (UNI) Implementation Agreement–January 1996

FRF.2.1   Frame Relay Network-to-Network (NNI) Implementation Agreement–July 1995

FRF.3.1   Multiprotocol Encapsulation Implementation Agreement (MEI)–June 1995

FRF.4.1   Switched Virtual Circuit Implementation Agreement (SVC)–January 2000

FRF.5   Frame Relay/ATM Network Interworking Implementation–December 1994

FRF.6   Frame Relay Service Customer Network Management Implementation Agreement (MIB)–March 1994

FRF.7   Frame Relay PVC Multicast Service and Protocol Description–October 1994

FRF.8.1   Frame Relay/ATM PVC Service Interworking Implementation Agreement–February 2000

FRF.9   Data Compression Over Frame Relay Implementation Agreement–January 1996

FRF.10   Frame Relay Network-to-Network SVC Implementation Agreement–September 1996

FRF.11   Voice over Frame Relay Implementation Agreement—May 1997—
Annex J added March 1999

FRF.12   Frame Relay Fragmentation Implementation Agreement—
December 1997

FRF.13   Service Level Definitions Implementation Agreement–August 1998

FRF.14   Physical Layer Interface Implementation Agreement—December 1998

FRF.15   End-to-End Multilink Frame Relay Implementation Agreement—
August 1999

FRF.16   Multilink Frame Relay UNI/NNI Implementation Agreement—
August 1999

FRF.17   Frame Relay Privacy Implementation Agreement–January 2000

The Frame Relay Forum's Web server can be reached at

http://www.frforum.com/.

13.3   Troubleshooting Frame Relay

13.3.1   Gathering Information on Symptoms and Recent Changes

The first step in any troubleshooting process is to gather information. The more information you have about the symptoms and characteristics of a problem—including *when* it first occurred—the better your chances of solving the problem quickly and efficiently. Typical questions you might ask at this stage include:

- Has there been a change in any hardware or software network component?
- Do the symptoms occur regularly or intermittently?
- Is it possible to reproduce or recreate the symptoms?
- When was the first occurrence of the symptom?
- Are the symptoms related to certain applications or connections, or do they affect all network operations?
- Has anyone connected or disconnected a PC (laptop or desktop) or any other component to or from the network?
- Has anyone installed an interface card in a computer?
- Has anyone stepped on a cable?
- Has any maintenance work been performed in the building recently (by a telephone company or building maintenance personnel, for example)?
- Has anyone (including cleaning personnel) moved any equipment or furniture?

13.3.2   Starting the Troubleshooting Procedure

As part of normal maintenance of data communication networks, topology information and the network's key operating statistics should be monitored and archived on a regular basis. In the case of Frame Relay networks, this includes a description of all components (routers, bridges, switches) with their configuration and physical interface description, and a description of the protocols and applications that are operated over the network. In addition, recent statistical data should always be available, such as peak and average capacity use broken down by applications, packet length distribution, and the typical bandwidth use of the various DLCIs. Comparing this data with the corresponding data measured when problems occur usually provides some first clues to the source of the problem.

For the actual troubleshooting procedure a protocol analyzer is required, which should be able to monitor and simulate Data Terminal Equipment (DTE) and Data Communication Equipment (DCE) interfaces at all line rates in use.

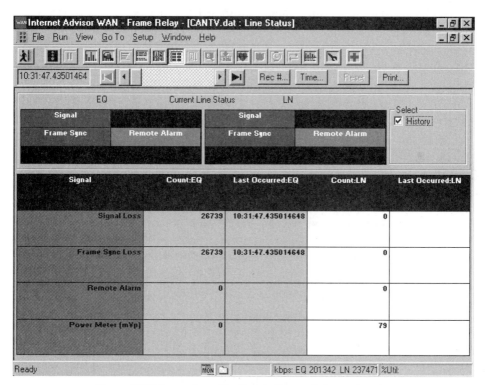

Figure 13.8 Layer 1 verification in Frame Relay networks
using the Agilent Advisor protocol analyzer

Before troubleshooting begins, the exact problem symptoms must be identified. Is it still possible to set up incoming and outgoing connections? Are active connections being interrupted? Has the response time over the Frame Relay link increased or has throughput decreased?

Since many problems in Frame Relay environments are rooted in the physical layer, the first phase of troubleshooting focuses on the physical line interfaces involved and the Layer 1 connection. Examine the operational logs of the affected network nodes (routers, interface cards) and check the configurations of all components involved. An inactive port may indicate a bad cable, a bad connector, or a bad port. If no faults can be detected, Layer 1 of the Frame Relay interfaces must be tested using an appropriate instrument. Complete testing includes verification of the signal levels, the line encoding, clock rates, bit-error rates, and possible Layer 1 alarms (AIS, RAI, CRC).

If no problems are detected on Layer 1, the next step is to analyze the LAP-F protocol. All active DLCI values are examined for frequent protocol errors. If no problems are found at this point, the in-channel signaling (LMI) is analyzed. It is important to verify that the numbers of STATUS ENQUIRY and STATUS messages are equal, indicating error-free connections. Minor differences that occur under heavy traffic can be tolerated, but the continual ocurrence of significant discrepancies between the numbers of enquiries and responses is a strong indicator of problems with the Frame Relay connection. Problems can also be caused by the use of different LMI versions on two systems that are expected to communicate with one another.

The link integrity verification procedure (LIV) must also be examine. Are STATUS ENQUIRY messages being sent every ten seconds (the T391 polling interval)? Is a full STATUS ENQUIRY message (N391 polling) sent every sixth T391 polling cycle? The contents of the full STATUS messages provide detailed information about the operational status of the various PVC connections (present, new, active, inactive, deleted, not deleted). If all PVCs are active, the next step is to verify the functioning of the connection by sending pings. If problems persist even though all Frame Relay links are active and able to transport data, then the configuration of all DLCIs must be checked. Configurations that do not provide maximum throughput must be changed accordingly.

FECN and BECN packets can be analyzed to obtain information on the frequency and duration of overload periods in the Frame Relay network. Even if overload periods last for only seconds or fractions of seconds, their frequent occurrence can significantly diminish network performance. Because the protocol analyzer records a time stamp with every frame, the beginning and the end of each overload period can be determined simply by subtracting the time stamp of the first FECN or BECN frame from that of the last FECN or BECN frame packet at the end of the overload period.

Another indication of an overloaded Frame Relay network is the occurrence of frames with the Discard Eligible bit set to 1. These frames indicate that a user is exceeding the CIR and the frames may be discarded if bandwidth becomes scarce.

Long-term measurements should also be conducted to verify that the service provider reliably supplies the guaranteed minimum bandwidth (that is, the CIR) over longer periods. Configuring a loop at one end of the Frame Relay line, then generating a traffic load equal to the CIR at the other end with a protocol analyzer can do this. All frames should be looped back without errors.

Finally, all router settings should be verified to make sure that no undesired local network traffic is transmitted over the Frame Relay lines.

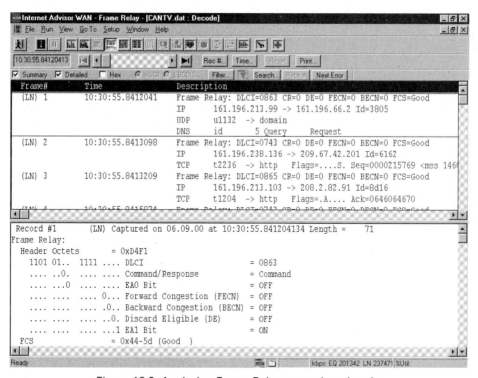

Figure 13.9 Analyzing Frame Relay networks using the
Agilent Advisor protocol analyzer

13.3.3   Error Symptoms in Frame Relay Networks

The two most common symptoms in Frame Relay environments are total connection breakdown and significantly impaired performance due to high response times. Connection interruptions are usually caused by Layer 1 problems,
such as faulty power supplies, line breaks, defective network components (router
ports, bridge ports, Frame Relay nodes), or noise on the line. If the signal clock
is present and the data frame alignment is correct, then the problem probably
lies within the in-channel signaling (LMI). If the remote station is not responding to LMI polling, the cause is usually a misconfigured Frame Relay access
device (FRAD)–generally a router, or a modem, or a Frame Relay switch (FRS).
A common problem is the setting of the T391 in the user equipment. The timeout
value of T391 should be lower than the equivalent timer in the peer equipment
(T392). Due to deviations in the time bases, the STATUS ENQUIRIES may be
received at the network equipment just a fraction after the T392 has expired.
The same is true if a PVC cannot be activated due to a failure at the far end
station, or if activated PVCs are unable to transport data. Once again, the
problem can often be solved by verifying the configuration of all the components
involved, as well as a routine telephone call to the equipment operator at the far
end. The most common causes of long response times over Frame Relay links are
traffic loads that exceed the available bandwidth and insufficient CIR values.
Occasional congestion in Frame Relay network nodes can also increase response
times because the increasing number of overload messages reduces throughput
to the end systems.

13.3.4   Symptoms and Causes: Frame Relay

Symptom: No Connection

Cause (1):   Defective cables or connectors.
Cause (2):   Defective power supply (in router or Frame Relay switch).
Cause (3):   Configuration error in router or Frame Relay switch
              (line rate, clocking, channelization).
Cause (4):   Noise; high bit-error rate.
Cause (5):   Incompatible in-channel signaling (LMI) versions.
Cause (6):   Wrong number called (for Frame Relay SVCs).
Cause (7):   Low signal levels.
Cause (8):   Peer node or peer network inactive or down.

Symptom: High Response Time

Cause (1):   CIR too low for data load.
Cause (2):   Poor DLCI configuration.

Cause (3): Window size too small for the application protocol transported over Frame Relay (for example, TCP/IP).

Cause (4): Frequent retransmission by application level protocols due to timeouts or high bit-error rates.

Cause (5): Maximum packet size too small; frequent fragmentation necessary.

Cause (6): Telecom operator is not providing the guaranteed bandwidth; bit-error rate too high.

Cause (7): Hidden, unintended traffic misrouted over the Frame Relay link.

Cause (8): Frame Relay network nodes congested (FECN, BECN messages occur).

The following list summarizes the most frequent sources of problems in Frame Relay networks (in alphabetical order):

- Cabling or connectors defective or loose at interfaces, wall jacks, patch panels
- CIR (Committed Information Rate) too low for traffic load; excessive peak loads
- Configuration error in router or FR switch
- Congested Frame Relay network node (FECN, BECN messages)
- DLCIs poorly configured
- Electromagnetic interference
- Error in basic router configuration (port not active, protocol not active, wrong operating mode)
- Faulty physical installation of router, bridge or hub (loose cables, connectors or plug-ins; bad backplane connections)
- Frequent retransmissions of application level protocols due to timeouts or high bit-error rates
- Hidden, unintended traffic misrouted over the Frame Relay link
- Incompatible in-channel signaling (LMI) versions
- Maximum packet size too small; frequent fragmentation
- Noise; high bit-error rate
- Power supply defective (in router or FR switch)
- Router or Frame Relay switch defective
- Telecom operator is not providing the guaranteed bandwidth and/or bit error rate
- Window size too small for the application protocol transported over Frame Relay (for example, IP)
- Wrong number called (for FR SVCs)

Figure 13.10 The most common causes of trouble in Frame Relay environments

SDH, SONET and PDH   **14**

"Most problems are either unimportant or impossible to solve."

VICTOR GALAZ

14.1   SDH, SONET and PDH: Specification and Implementation

Back in the late 70s, Bellcore (now Telecordia) saw the need to replace the Plesiochronous (near synchronous) Digital Hierarchy (PDH) in the North American Bell System (as it was then known) with a new synchronous network. It started work on what we now know as SONET, the Synchronous Optical NETwork. PDH networks had evolved in a rather ad hoc manner and it was time to improve on this. A transmission standard was needed that allowed higher rate transmission, properly planned network management facilities and, most importantly, a means to time lock the digital channels being carried so that individual lower rate channels could be accessed directly without the need to break down the PDH signal by hierarchy level, taking into account the justification (stuffing) that had occurred at each level during signal construction. SONET would be able to provide all this.

Initially, SONET was focused on handling PDH rates used in North America only, for example, T1 (1.5 Mbit/s) and T3 (45 Mbit/s), and was thus based on a frame structure of nine subframes of 60 octets (bytes). It turned out, this precluded the more international rates of E1 (2 Mbit/s), E3 (34 Mbit/s), etc. The ITU-T (then called the CCITT) also saw the need for a new synchronous network standard and worked with Bellcore to modify the SONET system to allow a more general standard, based on a frame structure of nine subframes of 90 octets (usually represented diagrammatically as a two dimensional drawing of nine rows by 90 columns) that would be compatible with North American *and* international PDH rates–after all, a new standard had to interwork with what was already in existence. The Synchronous Digital Hierarchy (SDH) was thus defined by the ITU-T in 1988 as an international recommendation (standard) for wide-area data communications and is almost identical to SONET. The main differences are as follows: first, the basic rate of SONET is 51.84 Mbit/s whereas SDH has a basic rate of 155.52 Mbit/s (three times 51.84 Mbit/s). Second, SONET defines the optical layer while SDH defines the signal protocol structure above the optical layer, other ITU-T recommendations focus on the optical layer. And third, different terminology is used with each standard, a source of constant confusion and irritation. There are also some minor interoperability issues that will be mentioned later.

SDH/SONET frames are universal transport containers for all types of digitized data, including data streams, such as ATM, IP ("Packet over SONET"), Frame Relay, and leased lines, as well as the entire range of digital and analog telephony. Even in telecommunication systems that supply subscribers with analog service, voice signals have long been transmitted in digitized form over wide-area backbones and re-converted to analog signals at the destination switch. Today SDH or SONET is used by all major telecom service providers to implement high-speed backbones in wide-area networks.

When ATM was chosen as the transfer mechanism for the ITU-T's Broadband ISDN project, SDH/SONET frames became the transmission vehicles of choice for ATM cell streams. This coupling of ATM and SDH/SONET was still widespread when, some years later, ATM began to be used in local-area networks. This is how SDH/SONET, originally developed for wide-area networks, also came to be used in LANs as well.

As already mentioned, the main advantage of SDH/SONET over the older PDH structures lies in its use of a transparent multiplexing method that allows individual channels to be accessed directly. This means that a 64 Kbit/s channel, for example, can be directly read out of, or inserted into, the highest SDH/SONET multiplex level (currently 39.81 Gbit/s). This capability is also called single-stage multiplexing. This is not possible in PDH networks, where all hierarchical layers must be demultiplexed in succession, taking stuffing into account, in order to make a single channel accessible, and then multiplexed again in order to be forwarded further. A given 64 Kbit/s channel that is multiplexed through two or three hierarchical levels, to the 140 Mbit/s level for example, cannot be directly located in the PDH data stream. SDH/SONET is therefore less expensive to use than PDH because it does not require a large number of expensive multiplexing/demultiplexing systems, and allows far greater flexibility in network design.

Another advantage of SDH/SONET is its overhead structure, which is designed to support modern, highly automatic switching and network management systems. When communication errors occur, the problem domain can be quickly identified by evaluating overhead bytes. This is why the conversion of data transmission structures to SONET or SDH has been increasing steadily over the past few years. All PDH multiplex hierarchies can also be transmitted over the SDH/SONET network, so that the transition from PDH to SDH/SONET is smooth.

14.1.1   The Plesiochronous Digital Hierarchy (PDH)

The Plesiochronous Digital Hierarchy (PDH), specified in 1972 by the ITU-T for North America, Europe and Japan, based on earlier national standards, is also a hierarchy of data structures at different bit rates (see Figure 14.1). These rates are defined in ITU-T Recommendation G.702, and the physical and electrical properties of the interfaces are specified in G.703. The bit rates in the various hierarchical levels are calculated as follows:

$$T_{i+1} = m_i \, (T_i + x_i)$$

Hierarchical level	North America	Europe	Japan	Transatlantic
0	64	64	64	64
1	1544	2048	1544	2048
2	6312	8048	6312	6312
3	44,736	34,368	32,064	44,736
4	139,264	139,264	97,728	139,264

Figure 14.1 Bit rates in the Plesiochronous Digital Hierarchy

where m_i and x_i are specified for each hierarchical level individually. ITU-T Recommendation G.702 defines a time-multiplex structure based on 64 Kbit/s channels for the basic bit rates of 2.048 Mbit/s in E1 and 1.544 Mbit/s in T1. The 64 Kbit/s specification dates back to the early days of digital voice signal transmission, when the conversion of voice signals into digital code was always performed at a sampling rate of 8 kHz. The analog signal is sampled at intervals of 125 µs, which according to Nyquist is sufficient to digitize all the information contained in a 4 kHz voice channel. Because every measured value is coded in 8 bits, the voice channel is transmitted at 64 Kbit/s.

The T1 Interface (Carrying DS1 Signals)

The North American standard defines a primary rate of 1.544 Mbit/s called T1. This provides for the transmission of 24 channels at 64 Kbit/s per channel or for payloads like ATM. Note that "T1" (Transmission level 1) describes the electrical signal, independent of the frame structure. "DS1" (Digital Signal level 1) defines the frame structure carried within T1. In practice, the terms tend to be used interchangeably, although strictly speaking the physical interface should be called "T1". DS1 signals from T1 interfaces can be multiplexed to higher rate signals (DS2, DS3, etc.), whereas it would be wrong, strictly speaking, to talk about DS3 as being a multiplex of T1 signals.

Each DS1 frame is 192 bits long (24 x 8 bits). The addition of 1 bit for frame alignment yields a total of 1.544 Mbit/s (193 bits x 8 kHz). The pattern for frame alignment consists of 6 bits (101010), which are spread out over six frames because each frame carries only one alignment bit. The alignment bit is also used to identify the frames containing signaling bits, by means of another 6-bit pattern (001110). The alignment bit changes between framing and signal framing, so that each of the two patterns is completed once in every 12 frames. A multiframe sequence of 2,316 bits (12 frames of 193 bits) containing both complete alignment patterns is also referred to as a superframe.

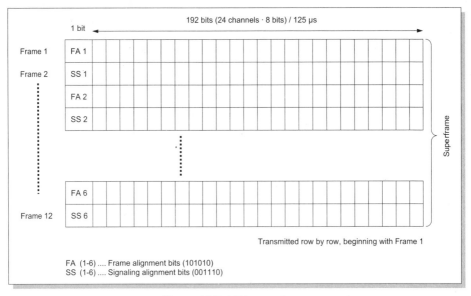

Figure 14.2 DS1 superframe

Signaling in DS1 is comparable to the function of Timeslot 16 in the E1 interface, and is transported in the least significant bit (LSB) of every sixth sampling value for each channel. This method is also called "robbed bit" signaling. The decrease in transmission quality due to this "misuse" of the LSB in every sixth byte per channel is negligible. For data transmission in North America, the least significant bit in a 64 Kbit/s channel is avoided because it is easier to do this than identify which of the one bit in six has been "robbed" from the full 64 Kbit/s signal; this results in a net throughput of 56 Kbit/s (7 bits x 8 kHz).

Because networks have grown increasingly complex over the years, it has become necessary to include more monitoring information in data transmission frames. This has led to a new definition of Channel 0 in the European E1 interface (see the following), and to the introduction of the 24-frame Extended Superframe (ESF) in the North American DS1. The alignment pattern in the ESF consists of six frame alignment bits alternating with six CRC bits forming a CRC-6 checksum of the preceding ESF, and 12 signaling and monitoring bits. The transportation of 12 management bits per 24 frames yields a 4 Kbit/s channel for signaling and error management (Figure 14.3).

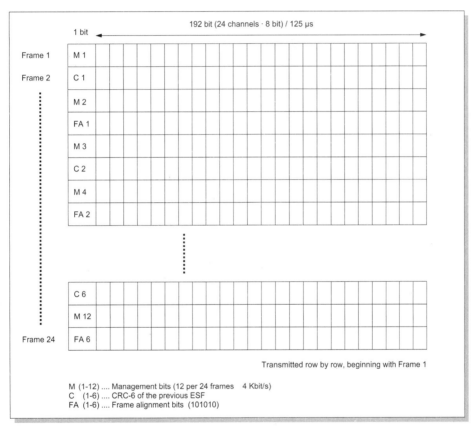

Figure 14.3 DS1 extended superframe (ESF)

At a data rate of 1.544 Mbit/s, the payload bandwidth in DS1 frames is 1.536 Mbit/s, corresponding to a capacity use of 99.5 percent. T1 bit streams are AMI or B8ZS-encoded. The specified transport medium is 100 Ω twisted-pair cable.

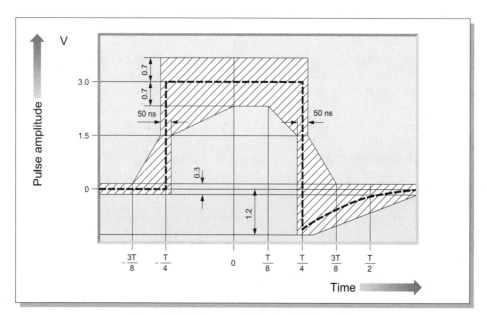

Figure 14.4 Pulse mask for the DS1 interface

The E1 Interface

The E1 system is based on a frame structure of 32 x 8 bit "timeslots" (that is, a total of 256 bits); the timeslots are numbered 0 to 31. Like the DS1 frame, the E1 frame repeats every 125 µs; this creates a signal of 2.048 Mbit/s (256 bits x 8 kHz). Because each 8-bit timeslot is repeated at a rate of 8 kHz, it is able to carry a 64 Kbit/s channel.

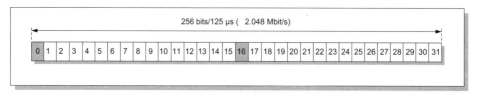

Figure 14.5 E1 frame

Timeslot 0 alternates a frame alignment signal (FAS), containing an alignment bit pattern, with a "Not Frame Alignment" signal (NFAS), containing error management information. Timeslot 16 was originally designed to carry signaling information, such as telephone numbers dialed. This leaves 30 payload timeslots (1 to 15, 17 to 31) available in the so-called PCM-30 system. In a PCM-30 system, Timeslot 16 of each frame carries signaling information for two payload channels (4 bits each). Sixteen consecutive frames (that is, a 16-frame multiframe) are thus required to transmit a signaling command for all E1 payload channels. This method of signaling is known as Channel Associated Signaling (CAS). However, CAS wastes bandwidth because, for any given payload channel, the signaling bits in Timeslot 16 are active only at the beginning of a call to set up the connection and at the end of the call to tear it down. For the duration of the call, or when no call is present on the associated channel, these bits are idle. Consequently a newer, more efficient, signaling method was invented called Common Channel Signaling (CCS) that provides for a reserved 64 Kbit/s channel carrying a messaging protocol that can handle the signaling for many channels from one or more E1 (or DS1) systems. Because the CCS channel is outwardly like any other payload channel, it can be carried in any payload timeslot position. Also, because Timeslot 16 is no longer required for carrying CAS, it can be made available for carrying a payload channel. This gives rise to the PCM-31 system; for example, one CCS channel might handle signaling for four PCM-31 systems so that three additional user payload channels are gained over the equivalent CAS PCM-30 systems. The payload bandwidth in the E1 interface is thus 1,920 Mbit/s in PCM-30 systems and 1,984 Mbit/s in PCM-31 systems.

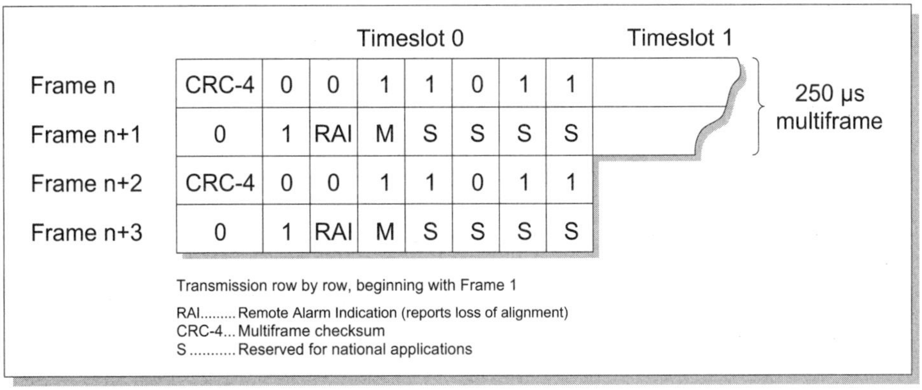

	Timeslot 0								Timeslot 1	
Frame n	CRC-4	0	0	1	1	0	1	1		250 μs multiframe
Frame n+1	0	1	RAI	M	S	S	S	S		
Frame n+2	CRC-4	0	0	1	1	0	1	1		
Frame n+3	0	1	RAI	M	S	S	S	S		

Transmission row by row, beginning with Frame 1

RAI......... Remote Alarm Indication (reports loss of alignment)
CRC-4... Multiframe checksum
S .... Reserved for national applications

Figure 14.6 E1 Timeslot 0

When carrying ATM cells over an E1 interface, the bytes of the cells are spread over Timeslots 1 to 15 and 17 to 31 in order to avoid Timeslots 0 and 16. More details of ATM mappings are available in Chapter 10.

The E1 bit stream is encoded using the High Density Bipolar (HDB3) technique. The specified transport medium is 75 Ω coaxial cable or 120 Ω twisted pair. The voltage level is ± 2.37 V.

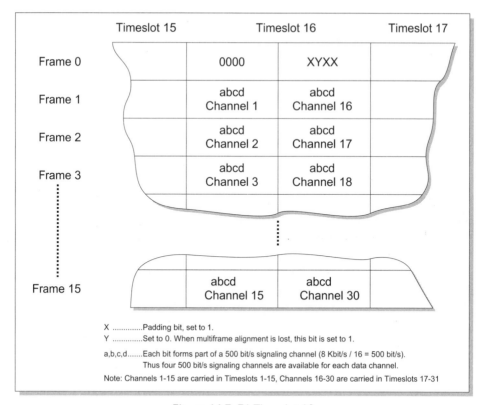

	Timeslot 15	Timeslot 16	Timeslot 17
Frame 0		0000	XYXX	
Frame 1		abcd Channel 1	abcd Channel 16	
Frame 2		abcd Channel 2	abcd Channel 17	
Frame 3		abcd Channel 3	abcd Channel 18	
Frame 15		abcd Channel 15	abcd Channel 30	

X ....Padding bit, set to 1.
Y ....Set to 0. When multiframe alignment is lost, this bit is set to 1.

a,b,c,d.......Each bit forms part of a 500 bit/s signaling channel (8 Kbit/s / 16 = 500 bit/s).
Thus four 500 bit/s signaling channels are available for each data channel.

Note: Channels 1-15 are carried in Timeslots 1-15, Channels 16-30 are carried in Timeslots 17-31

Figure 14.7 E1 Timeslot 16

The E3 Interface

In order to keep costs for primary-rate lines to a minimum, they are multiplexed and transported over higher bandwidth lines. Unfortunately, however, this cannot be accomplished by simply alternating transmission of bytes from the different primary rate signals, which would require global synchronization of all the signals being multiplexed. Global synchronisation is not possible because every primary rate interface in PDH systems can derive its timing from a local clock. The differences in frequency between individual signals must be compensated by the insertion of justification ("stuffing") bits before multiplexing. When the signals are demultiplexed, removal of the justification bit restores the original signal frequency. Four multiplexed E1 signals form an 8.448 Mbit/s E2 channel that can thus carry 120 or 124 basic rate 64 Kbit/s channels (depending on whether PCM-30 or PCM-31 is in use). Four E2 signals yield a 34.368 Mbit/s E3 signal (480 or 496 basic rate 64 Kbit/s channels). Note that these days the E2 rate is not used for transmission purposes, but merely as an intermediate step to E3.

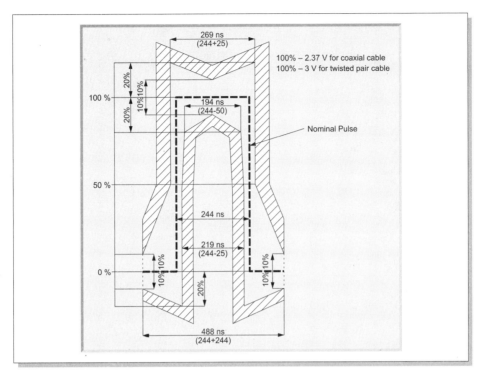

Figure 14.8 Pulse mask for the E1 interface

According to ITU-T G.751, an E3 frame is 1,536 bits long and consists of four 384-bit lines, or subframes. The first 10 bits in the first subframe are reserved for frame alignment, bit 11 is used for remote alarm indication (RAI), and bit 12 is reserved for national use. In the second, third and fourth subframes, the first 4 bits control the frequency adaptation process, or "justification", between the E2 and the E3 carrier frequencies. The first 3 bits in the first column (C1, C2 and C3) are set to the value 111 to indicate justification: in this case the first stuff bit, ST, is empty. If the first 3 bit values are 000, no justification is performed, in which case the stuff bit carries user data. The second, third and fourth C-bit columns are used in the same way as the first. The sum of the bandwidths in the four E2 signals must always be lower than the bandwidth of the E3 signal because stuffing only permits upward adjustment, or "positive justification". The bit stream is encoded using HDB3. The specified transport medium is one 75 Ω coaxial cable for each direction; the voltage level is 1.0 V.

34.36 Mbit/s – E3 Transport Frame in accordance with G.751

1	1	1	1	0	1	0	0	0	0	RAI	Res		Bits 13 ... 384
C1	C1	C1	C1										Bits 5 ... 384
C2	C2	C2	C2										Bits 5 ... 384
C3	C3	C3	C3	St	St	St	St						Bits 9 ... 384

- Frame length: 1,536 bits (4 x 8,448 Kbit/s)
- Frame alignment sequence: 1111 0100 00
- RAI: Remote Alarm Indication
- Res: Reserved
- Cn: Justification control bits
- St: Stuff bits

Figure 14.9 E3 frame

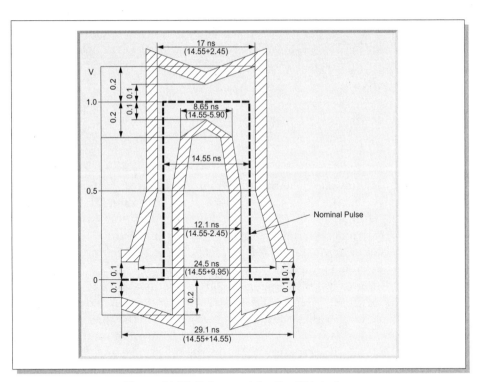

Figure 14.10 Pulse mask for the E3 interface

The G.832 E3 Frame Format

In addition to the E3 frame format described in G.751, a modified E3 frame format is defined in G.832 for transporting ATM cells. Use of this format is almost universal. It is recommended by the ATM Forum (af-phy-0034.000) for E3 ATM links. This is because it is more difficult to adapt ATM to the older G.751 frame format: the cells would have to be nibble-aligned because each G.751 subframe is an integer multiple of 4 bits rather than 8. The newer G.832 frame consists of 537 bytes, 7 of which are used for various types of overhead information (see Figure 14.11). The remaining 530 user data bytes correspond exactly to the length of 10 ATM cells, so that these can be both byte- and cell-aligned, although cell alignment is not required.

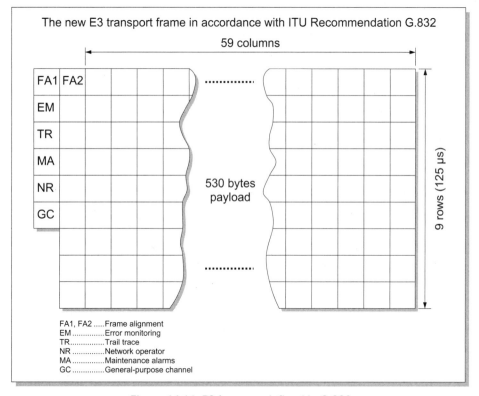

Figure 14.11 E3 frame as defined in G.832

The T3 Interface (Carrying DS3 Signals)

DS3 is the third multiplex level in the North American PDH hierarchy. Four 1.544 Mbit/s DS1 signals are transported in one 6.312 Mbit/s DS2 signal; seven multiplexed DS2 signals yield a 44.736 Mbit/s DS3 signal.

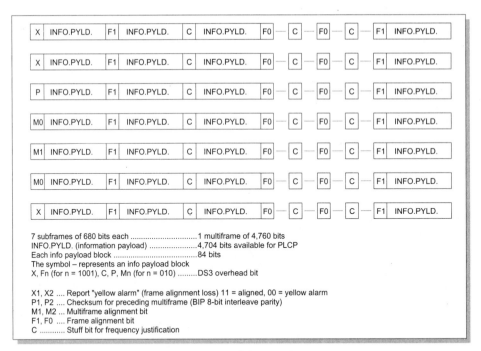

7 subframes of 680 bits each ....1 multiframe of 4,760 bits
INFO.PYLD. (information payload) ....4,704 bits available for PLCP
Each info payload block ....84 bits
The symbol – represents an info payload block
X, Fn (for n = 1001), C, P, Mn (for n = 010) ....DS3 overhead bit

X1, X2 .... Report "yellow alarm" (frame alignment loss) 11 = aligned, 00 = yellow alarm
P1, P2 .... Checksum for preceding multiframe (BIP 8-bit interleave parity)
M1, M2 ... Multiframe alignment bit
F1, F0 .... Frame alignment bit
C .... Stuff bit for frequency justification

Figure 14.12 DS3 frame format

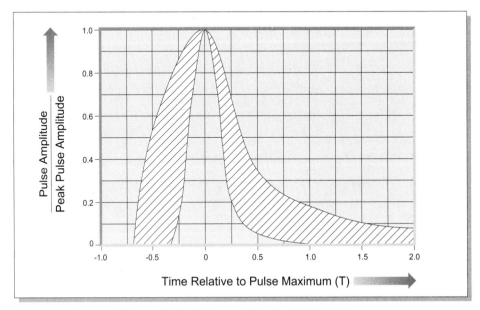

Figure 14.13 Pulse mask for the DS3 interface

A 4,760-bit DS3 multiframe consists of seven 680-bit frames. Each frame contains eight 84-bit payload blocks, separated by a single bit; these single bits are used for framing, stuffing and for management purposes (for example, alarms). Thus there are 4,704 bits of user data in each DS3 multiframe, for a throughput of 44.21 Mbit/s. This corresponds to a bandwidth capacity use of 98.8 percent. The bit stream is B3ZS-encoded. The specified transport medium is one 75 Ω coaxial cable for each direction, and the voltage level is 1.0 V.

The E4 Interface

E4 is the fourth multiplex level in the European PDH interface hierarchy. Four E3 channels are multiplexed to form a single E4 channel. The E4 frame structure is also described in ITU-T G.751. Each G.751 E4 frame is 2,928 bits long and consists of six 488-bit subframes; otherwise the structure is similar to G.751 E3 frames.

139.264 Mbit/s – E4 Transport Frame in accordance with G.751

1	1	1	1	0	1	0	0	0	0	RAI	Res	Res	Res	Bits 17 ... 488
C1	C1	C1	C1											Bits 5 ... 488
C2	C2	C2	C2											Bits 5 ... 488
C3	C3	C3	C3											Bits 5 ... 488
C4	C4	C4	C4											Bits 5 ... 488
C5	C5	C5	C5	St	St	St	St							Bits 9 ... 488

- Frame length: 2,928 bits (4 x 34,368 Kbit/s)
- Frame alignment sequence: 1111 1010 0000
- RAI: Remote Alarm Indication
- Res: Reserved
- Cn: Justification control bits
- St: Stuff bits

Figure 14.14 E4 frame

The bit stream is encoded using Coded Mark Inversion (CMI); the same coding method is used for the 155 Mbit/s SDH STM-1 electrical interface (see the following). The specified transport medium is one 75 Ω coaxial cable for each direction. The voltage level is ±± 0.5 V (see Figure 14.15).

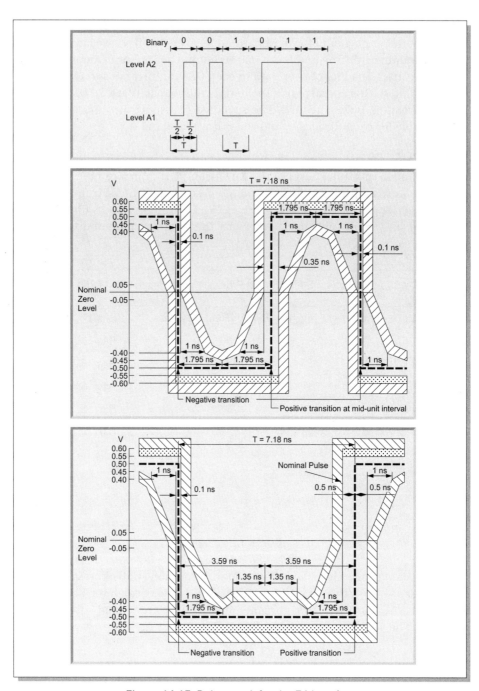

Figure 14.15 Pulse mask for the E4 interface

14.1.2 The Synchronous Digital Hierarchy (SDH) and SONET

The nodes of an SDH/SONET network are connected by different types of transport section. The type of a given section is determined by the types of node at its ends. A section between two signal regenerators (repeaters), for example, is called a Regenerator Section in SDH (just "Section" in SONET), and a section between two multiplexers is a Multiplexer Section in SDH ("Line" in SONET).

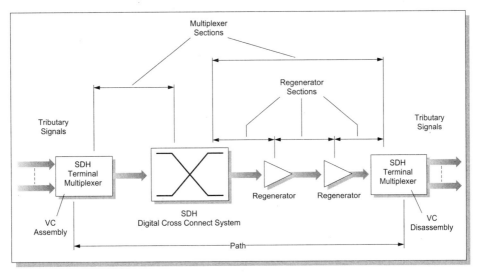

Figure 14.16a Topology of SDH networks

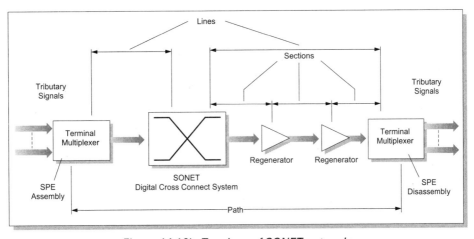

Figure 14.16b Topology of SONET networks

The end-to-end connection through the SDH/SONET network from the point at which a service (tributary signal) enters the network to the point from which it leaves the network is called a "Path" in both SDH and SONET.

In the following sections, different SONET and SDH interfaces are considered. Because SDH and SONET are so closely related, the general principals of operation for both are very similar, so a more detailed explanation of the lowest level (STS-1/OC-1) is given but can, to some extent, be generalized for higher order systems in both standards. Note that, while the original first level of the ITU-T SDH system is at 155 Mbit/s, an SDH system corresponding to STS-1 does now exist, known as STM-0.

The SONET OC-1 Interface

The first hierarchical level in SONET is the Synchronous Transport Signal 1 (STS-1). This is an 810-byte frame that is transmitted at 51.84 Mbit/s and, when transmitted over an optical interface, the resulting signal is known as Optical Carrier 1 (OC-1). STS-1 can also exist as an electrical interface, which is called Electrical Carrier 1 (EC-1), although this term is rarely used. The transmission time of a STS-1 frame corresponds to the 125 μs pulse code modulation (PCM) sampling interval; each byte in the SONET signal thus represents a bandwidth of 64 Kbit/s. The frame is divided into nine subframes of 90 bytes each. The first

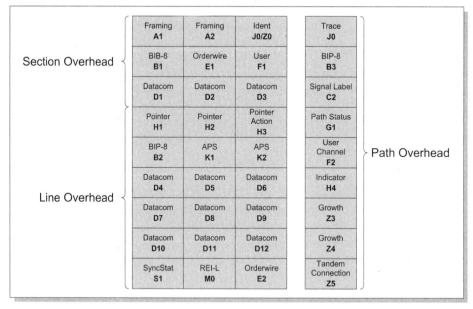

Figure 14.17 STS-1 Transport Overhead (TOH) and Path Overhead (POH)

3 bytes of each subframe comprise 3 bytes of the 27 (that is, 9 x 3) byte Transport Overhead (TOH). The remaining 87 bytes of each subframe are occupied by 87 bytes of the 783 (that is, 9 x 87) byte Synchronous Payload Envelope (SPE). As mentioned previously, it is conventional to show SONET (and SDH) frames as a nine row by N column two dimensional diagram, each row corresponding to a subframe. Consequently the TOH of the STS-1 frame occupies the first three columns of the frame and the STS-1 frame payload or "Envelope Capacity" occupies 87 columns. The 27 TOH bytes control the transport of user data between neighboring network nodes, and contain information required for the transport section in question. The TOH is divided into two parts, the Section Overhead and the Line Overhead. The TOH bytes A1, A2, J0/Z0, B1, E1, F1 and D1 through D3 comprise the Section Overhead, and bytes H1, H2, H3, B2, K1, K2, D4 through D12, S1/Z1, M0, E2 form the Line Overhead.

The SPE, also a structure of 783 bytes, is located in the 9 x 87 byte Envelope Capacity (frame payload area). The first column of this is occupied by the POH and a further two columns (30 and 59) are reserved for "fixed stuff". This leaves 84 columns of "Payload Capacity" for carrying user traffic.

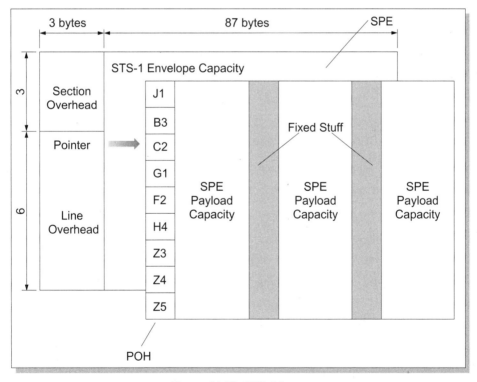

Figure 14.18 STS-1 frame

The relationship between the SPE and the SONET frame is not permanently fixed–the SPE "floats" in the Envelope Capacity and the beginning of the SPE is located via a pointer residing in the TOH (10 bits of the H1 and H2 bytes). Because of this, a SPE typically starts in one frame and finishes in the next. The reason for this arrangement is to allow multiple SONET frames to be aligned so that they can be multiplexed into higher order structures (for example, 3 x STS-1 frames can be multiplexed to become one STS-3 frame). In effect the SPE stays fixed and the frame structure rotates to achieve alignment. Minor frequency differences between the lower order SONET frames can also be accommodated. A SPE can only drift within the SONET frame's Envelope Capacity one byte at a time and the SONET standard limits how frequently this can happen. As the SPE moves within the Envelope Capacity, the H1/H2 pointer value changes and, depending upon which way the drift is occurring, a byte has to be added or removed from the Envelope Capacity. This is a stuffing process comparable to what occurs in PDH multiplexing described earlier. If an additional byte is required because the tributary lower-order SONET frame rate, and hence the SPE, is running at a slightly faster rate to that of the higher-order SONET frame, the H3 byte becomes part of the Envelope Capacity for one frame and is occupied by a byte of the SPE. In other words, the fourth row of the SONET frame payload area grows from 87 to 88 bytes, and the H1/H2 pointer value is decreased by one. By contrast, if one less byte is occasionally required because the lower-order SONET frame is running slightly slower, the first byte in the fourth row of the Envelope Capacity (that is, the byte after the H3 byte) is skipped so that this row shrinks from 87 to 86 bytes for one frame and the H1/H2 pointer value is increased by one. This process is performed at all levels of the SDH/SONET hierarchy as multiplexing occurs. SDH and SONET networks are generally locked to accurate frequency standards but certain effects, such as "wander" (very low frequency variation often caused by the effects of 24 hour temperature cycles on long haul transmission line delay) cannot be avoided, so pointer movements do occur.

The SONET OC-3 and SDH STM-1 Interfaces

The second level of the SONET hierarchy, STS-3, is a byte by byte (or octet by octet, to use telecommunications terminology) interleaving (multiplexing) of three STS-1 frames. Consequently the Transport Overhead now occupies nine columns and the Envelope Capacity (payload area) occupies 261 columns. The whole frame is therefore 270 columns by nine rows (nine subframes of 270 bytes, that is, 2,430 bytes in all); it also has a 125 ms frame rate, the PCM sampling interval. The ITU-T based its first level structure on the STS-3 structure and called it the Synchronous Transport Module (STM-1). Note that, because STM-1 is the first hierarchical level of SDH, the payload is not a multiplex of three lower level frames, unlike STS-3, but can be treated as a single entity, particularly for carrying broadband services, such as ATM or "Packet over SONET". A special variant of the STS-3 structure exists in which the payload, normally comprising bytes from three unrelated payloads from the lower multiplex level STS-1, is instead concatenated into a single entity, renamed STS-3c, where the "c" indicates concatenation. OC-3 (note, no "c") is again the optical carrier. For most purposes, STS-3c can be considered to be identical to STM-1. There is one important distinction, and this lies in the "SS" field (bits 5 and 6) of overhead byte H2: these bits are transmitted with the value 00 in SONET and the value 10 in SDH; for interoperability, receivers for either standard should ignore the value in this field. Figure 14.19 shows the frame structure for STS-3c/STM-1.

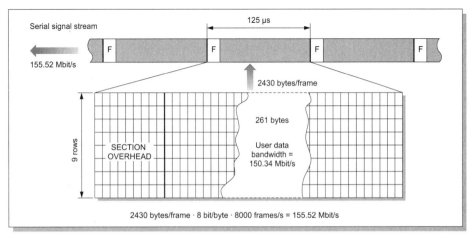

Figure 14.19 STS-3c/STM-1 frame

For the SDH standard, payload data is transported in STM-1 frame component structures called containers. These containers, designated C11, C12, C2, C3, C4, C4-4c, etc., are the multiplex elements of SDH, and are defined for a variety of payload capacities. A container together with its path overhead is called a virtual container, or VC. Path overhead information, or POH, is used to monitor alarm states and transmission quality. The POH accompanies the container from the source path-terminating equipment (PTE) to the destination PTE. A distinction is made between higher-order virtual containers (HVC) and lower-order virtual containers (LVC), which have different transmission capacities. HVCs are the containers VC-4-256c, VC-4-64c, VC-4-16c, VC-4-4c, VC-4 and VC-3; LVCs are the containers VC-3, VC-2, VC-12 and VC-11. Note that VC-3 can be HVC or LVC. A similar distinction is made between the higher-order path overhead (HO POH) and the lower-order path overhead (LO POH).

Multiplex Element (Container)	Transport Capacity (Kbit/s)
C-11	1,600
C-12	2,176
C-21	6,784
C-22	9,088
C-31	36,864
C-32	48,384
C-4	149,760
C-4-4c	599,040
C-4-16c	2,396,160
C-4-64c	9,584,640
C-4-256c	38,338,560

Figure 14.20 SDH container elements

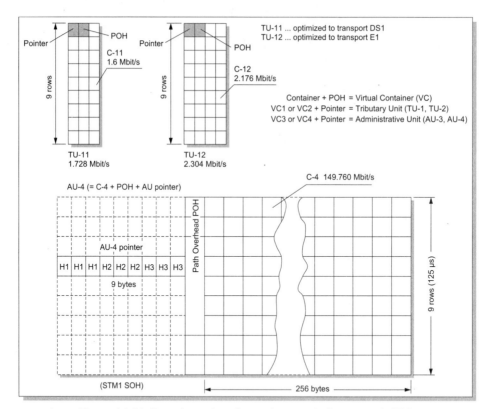

Figure 14.21 Container, virtual container, and tributary unit (TU)

Like the SPE in SONET frames, the containers themselves are usually shown aligned with the SDH transport frames. In practice, however, phase shifts occur due to alignment for multiplexing, latency, clock regeneration errors, etc. In contrast to PDH, however, the location of every virtual container in SDH, or equivalent in SONET, is indicated by a pointer contained in the next higher multiplex layer. Phase shifts between adjacent layers are corrected by adjusting the pointer value, which means the container can be located using the pointer at all times. This is why any container can be accessed individually, at any hierarchical multiplexing level, without demultiplexing the entire signal stream, by moving through the pointers. The combination of a virtual container and its pointer on the next higher hierarchical level (the tributary unit pointer) is called a tributary unit, designated TU-11, TU-12, TU-1, TU-2, etc. Several TU-1s or a single TU-2 can also be called a tributary unit group (TUG). Similarly, a tributary unit combined with its pointer on the next higher hierarchical level is called an administrative unit (AU), and the pointer is called an AU pointer.

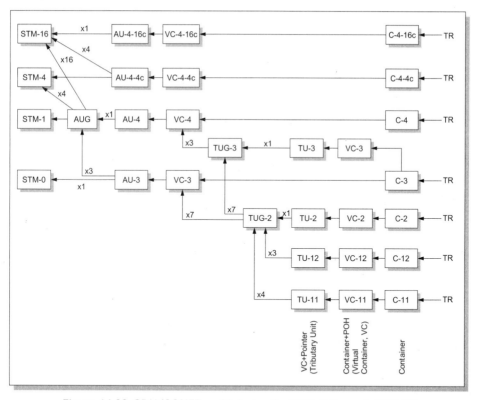

Figure 14.22 SDH/SONET multiplexing for STM-0 through STM-16

The table in Figure 14.23 lists the various bit rates with their multiplex elements.

Multiplex element	Bit rate (Kbit/s)	1,544	2,048	6,312	8,448	34,368	44,736	139,264	C-11	C-12	C-21	C-22	C-31	C-32	C-4	TU-11	TU-12	TU-21	TU-22	TUG-21	TUG-22	TU-31	TU-32	AU-31	AU-32	AU-4	STM-1
		\<Transport / Digital signals G.702\>							\<Multiplex element\>																		
C-11	1,600	x																									
C-12	2,176		x																								
C-21	6,784			x																							
C-22	9,088				x																						
C-31	36,864					x														x	x						
C-32	48,384						x														x							
C-4	149,760							x												x	x	x	x				
TU-11	1,728								x																		
TU-12	2,304									x																	
TU-21	6,912										x																
TU-22	9,216											x															
TUG-21	6,912															x	x	x									
TUG-22	9,216															x	x		x								
TU-31	37,440												x														
TU-32	49,152													x													
AU-31	37,440												x														
AU-32	50,304													x													
AU-4	150,912														x												
STM-1	155,520																								x	x	x	
STM-4	622,080																											x
STM-16	2,488,320																											x
STM-64	9,953,280																											x
STM-256	39,813,120																											x

Figure 14.23 SDH/SONET bit rates and multiplex elements

Three VC-3 containers, for example, can be transported in one VC-4 container, which in turn is transported in a STM-1 frame. The AU-4 pointer indicates the exact position of the VC-4, in which the four TU-3 pointers locate the three VC-3 containers (see Figures 14.23 and 14.24).

In addition to the first SONET hierarchical level STS-1 and the first SDH hierarchical level/second SONET level, STM-1/STS-3, the multiplex streams STM-4/STS-12, STM-16/STS-48, STM-64/STS-192 and STM-256/STS-768 have also been defined with data rates of 622.08 Mbit/s, 2,488.32 Mbit/s, 9.95328 Gbit/s and 39.81312 Gbit/s, respectively. The general formulas for SDH/SONET bit rates are (with the exception of STS-1/STM-0):

$$STM\text{-}n/STS\text{-}3n = n \cdot 155.52 \ Mbit/s$$

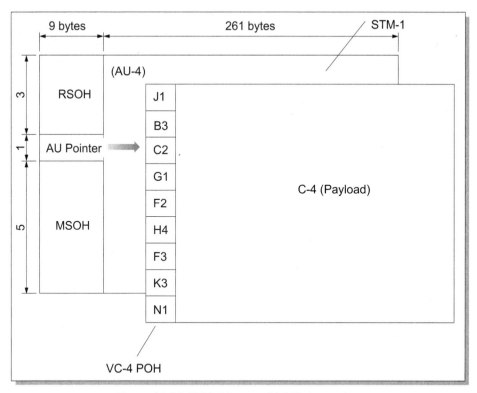

Figure 14.24 STM-1 frame with VC-4 container

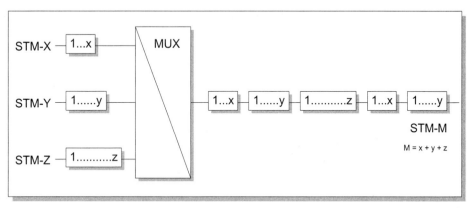

Figure 14.25 Multiplex formation of SDH transport modules

The bit rates of the higher order SDH Synchronous Transport Modules, unlike those of the plesiochronous hierarchy, are integer multiples of the basic 155.52 Mbit/s module. Higher-order SDH/SONET signals are formed from lower-order signals through byte interleaving.

Concatenation of VC-4 Containers

Similar to concatenation in SONET to create STS-3c, etc., for transmitting tributary signals in SDH with higher bit rates than the 149.76 Mbit/s available in a VC-4 in a single multiplex layer, a concatenated container, VC-4-4c, has been defined on the basis of the STM-4 transport module (the small "c" again stands for concatenation). This STM-4c transport module has the same size and SOH structure as an ordinary STM-4 transport frame (the SONET equivalent is STS-12c carried in OC-12). The VC-4-4c container is considered a unit, however, and is multiplexed and routed as such. The transport capacity of a STM-4c transport module is 599.04 Mbit/s. Analogous VC-4-16c, VC-4-64c and VC-4-256c containers are also defined, with nominal capacities of 2.39616, 9.58464, and 38.33856 Gbit/s respectively.

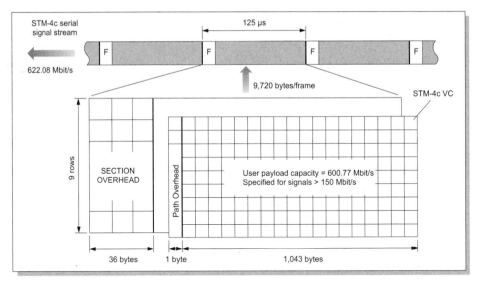

Figure 14.26 STM-4c transport module

14.1.3   Comparing SDH and SONET

The main difference between SDH and SONET is that SONET generally uses the VC-3 virtual container for data transmission, while SDH transports user data for the most part in VC-4 containers. This is because the existing North American PDH hierarchy, especially the third hierarchical layer, DS3 (44.736 Mbit/s), is better suited for transport in a VC-3 than in a VC-4. Furthermore, SONET has the extra STS-1 level with a bit rate of 51.84 Mbit/s that can transport exactly one VC-3 and is thus ideal for transporting DS3 streams.

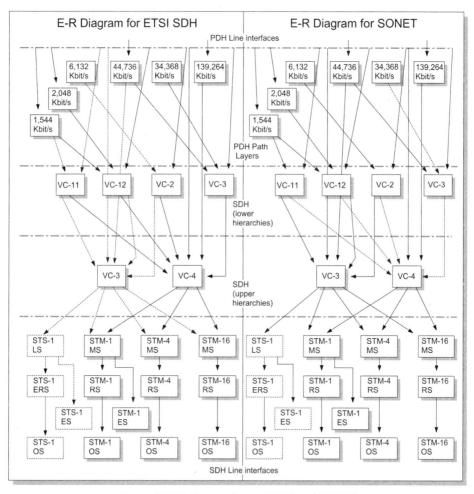

Figure 14.27 Comparison of SDH and SONET

14.1.4 Section Overhead, Transport Overhead and Path Overhead

As mentioned previously, the Section Overhead (SOH) of an STM-1 transport module is divided into multiplex section and regenerator section overhead bytes. These bytes are roughly equivalent to the Section and Line Overheads that make up the Transport Overhead (TOH) of SONET, except that in SDH the fourth row containing the H1, H2, and H3 bytes is not included in the multiplex section overhead, while in SONET these bytes are part of the Line Overhead. The following describes the SDH structure–the SONET structure is similar except for some terminology but, to save repetition and confusion, we will stick to SDH terminology here.

A multiplex section in a SDH network is a physical connection between two multiplexers, while a regenerator section is the physical connection between two regenerators. Multiplexer sections are capable of independent action in the event of transmission errors. For example, if a network component becomes overloaded or even fails completely, the virtual container affected can be re-routed to an alternative physical connection: this procedure is called automatic protection switching (APS). A regenerator section, however, comprises only the physical connections and systems located between a network node and a regenerator, or between two regenerators. Regenerator sections do not have back-up physical connection. Unlike the MSOH and RSOH, path overhead (POH) information accompanies the payload over the entire link from source node to destination node.

Section Overhead Bytes

The multiplexer and regenerator section overheads contain the following SOH bytes:

Multiplexer Section Overhead (MSOH)

B2:   The three B2 bytes contain the bit-interleaved parity (BIP) code calculated from all bits of the previous STM-1 frame plus its MSOH bytes, but without its regenerator overhead bytes. Together these B2 bytes are referred to as BIP-24.

K1, K2:   Bytes K1 and K2 control back-up switching functions in case of system failure, based on automatic protection switching (APS) messages. A distinction is made between linear APS messages (ITU-T G.783, Characteristics of Synchronous Digital Hierarchy (SDH/SONET) Equipment Functional Blocks) and Ring APS messages (ITU-T G.841, Types and Characteristics of SDH/SONET Network Protection Architectures).

D4 – D12:   Bytes D4 through D12 provide a 576 Kbit/s data communication channel (DCC) between multiplex systems for the exchange of network administration and monitoring information. These bytes are defined only for the first STM-1 frame in a STM-n multiplex hierarchy.

S1:   Byte S1 reports the synchronization status.

M1:   Byte M1 indicates the number of B2 errors detected downstream (MS-REI: Multiplex Section Remote Error Indication).

E2:   Byte E2 provides a 64 Kbit/s voice channel between multiplex systems. This too is defined only for the first STM-1 frame in an STM-n multiplex hierarchy.

H1 – H3:   The H bytes implement the pointer functions. H1 and H2 contain the pointer information; byte H3 is the Pointer Action byte and can contain user data in the event of negative justification.

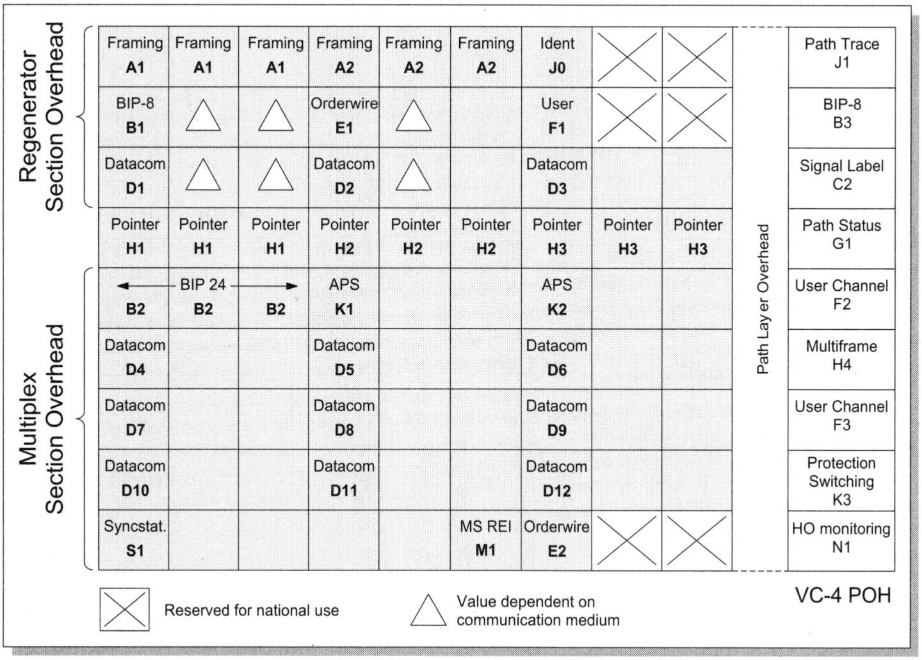

Framing A1	Framing A1	Framing A1	Framing A2	Framing A2	Framing A2	Ident J0				Path Trace J1
BIP-8 B1	△	△	Orderwire E1	△		User F1				BIP-8 B3
Datacom D1	△	△	Datacom D2	△		Datacom D3				Signal Label C2
Pointer H1	Pointer H1	Pointer H1	Pointer H2	Pointer H2	Pointer H2	Pointer H3	Pointer H3	Pointer H3		Path Status G1
◄— BIP 24 —► B2	B2	B2	APS K1			APS K2				User Channel F2
Datacom D4			Datacom D5			Datacom D6				Multiframe H4
Datacom D7			Datacom D8			Datacom D9				User Channel F3
Datacom D10			Datacom D11			Datacom D12				Protection Switching K3
Syncstat. S1						MS REI M1	Orderwire E2			HO monitoring N1

Regenerator Section Overhead / Multiplex Section Overhead / Path Layer Overhead

⊠ Reserved for national use   △ Value dependent on communication medium

VC-4 POH

Figure14.28 The STM-1 SOH and POH bytes

Regenerator Section Overhead (RSOH)

A1, A2:   Bytes A1 and A2 are used for frame alignment
           (A1= 1111 0110; A2= 0010 1000).

J0:   Byte J0 is used to verify transmission between the sending and
           receiving ends of every regenerator section.
           It consists of a 16-byte frame plus a CRC-7 checksum.

B1:   Byte B1 is used to check for transmission errors in the regenerator
           section. It is calculated from all bits in the previous STM-n frame
           before scrambling.

E1:   Byte E1 provides a 64 Kbit/s voice channel between regenerator
           systems.

F1:   Byte F1 is reserved for network operator purposes. It is defined
           only for the first STM-1 frame in a STM-n multiplex hierarchy.

D1 – D3:   Bytes D1 through D3 provide a 192 Kbit/s data channel for admin-
           istrative, service, alarm and other functions between regenerators.

Path Overhead Bytes

A container together with its path overhead is called a virtual container. A path
in SDH/SONET designates the logical connection between the point at which the
tributary signal is interleaved in a virtual container and the point at which the
signal is removed from the container. The HO-POH (higher order path overhead)
header is used for the container overhead in VC-4-16c, VC-4-4c, VC-4 and VC-3
virtual containers. The simpler LO-POH (lower order path overhead) is used for
VC-2, VC-12 and VC-11 containers.

Higher-Order Path Overhead (HO POH)

J1:   Byte J1 repetitively carries a 64-byte or 16-byte data word. This serves to
       test the line between the transmitting and receiving stations,
       and permits detection of misrouted connections in cross-connect systems
       or multiplexers.

B3:   Byte B3 transmits a checksum (BIP-8) calculated from all bits in the
       previous VC-4 frame before scrambling.

C2:   Byte C2 specifies the mapping type in the virtual container. Different
       values (256) are defined for this purpose, known as higher-order path
       signal labels.

G1:   Byte G1 is used to transmit status and monitoring information from
       receiver to sender. This byte, called the higher-order path status byte,
       indicates the number of errors detected.

F2:   Byte F2 is for network operator communication between two pieces of SDH/SONET path termination equipment (PTE).

H4:   Byte H4 indicates whether the payload in the VC-4s consists of several TUs.

F3:   Byte F3, like F2, is used for network operator communication between two PTEs.

K3:   Byte K3 is used in switching back-up paths (higher-order APS).

N1:   Byte N1 is for monitoring and managing interfaces between two SDH/SONET network operators (higher-order tandem connection monitoring).

Lower-Order Path Overhead (LO POH)

V5:   Byte V5 contains a BIP-2 checksum, the signal label and path status information.

J2:   Byte J2 contains 16-byte frames, including a CRC-7 checksum, and performs end-to-end connection monitoring on the lower-order (LO) path.

N2:   Byte N2 is for monitoring and managing cross-connect interfaces between two SDH/SONET network operators (lower-order tandem connection monitoring).

K4:   Byte K4 is used for switching back-up paths (lower-order path APS).

14.1.5   Pointers in SDH/SONET

Pointers are used to align lower-order SDH/SONET tributary signals for frame multiplexing and to allow the toleration of differences between the multiplexed

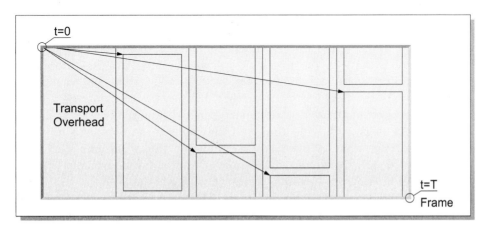

Figure 14.29 SDH/SONET pointers

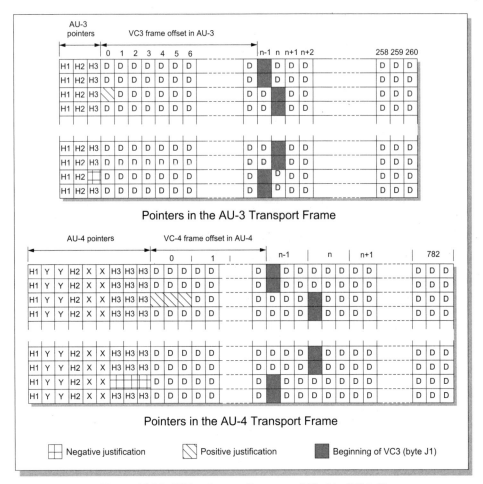

Figure 14.30 AU4 pointer adjustment (VC-4 in STM-1)

SDH/SONET bit rates and the bit rates of tributary SDH/SONET signals, as described for SONET in the previous section covering the OC-1 interface. A pointer indicates the beginning of the frame in each virtual container/envelope capacity of the next lower hierarchical level. If the container/SPE has a different bit rate from that of its transport frame, the container/SPE is shifted by positive or negative justification, and the value of the pointer is adjusted accordingly. If the tributary signal is slower than the transport frame, stuff bytes are inserted to shift the container toward the later end of its transport frame. This process is known as positive justification. Justification occurs in increments of 3 bytes for AU-4 (that is, VC-4 in STM-1), or 1 byte for AU-3 (VC-3 in STM-1).

Bytes H1 through H3 are used for pointer justification of VC-4 containers in STM-1 frames. H1 and H2 contain the actual pointer information—the coordinates at which the VC-4 container begins. The H3 byte is used as the "pointer action byte": if the tributary signal is faster than the transport frame transmission rate, this is compensated by putting VC-4 user data into the H3 byte, so that the virtual container moves forward in its transport frame (see Figure 14.28). This is called negative justification.

Analogous to the procedure described previously for VC-4 and STM-1, the transport of several small containers in one large container also involves data rate justification using pointers. The first byte of a tributary unit is the pointer. Because three or four TUs are combined in a group, a TUG provides three or four pointer bytes for three or four TUs. Similar to bytes H1 through H3 in the STM-1 SOH frame, these pointer bytes are used for positive or negative justification (see Figure 14.31).

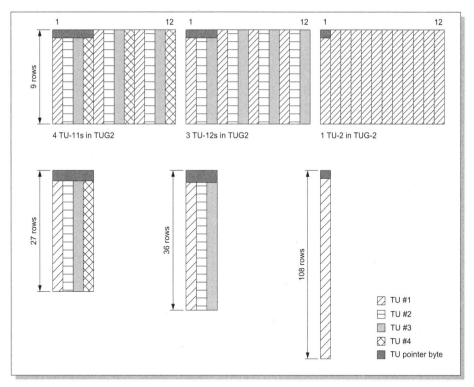

Figure 14.31 TU pointer adjustment (VC-11, VC-12, TU-2 in TUG-2)

14.2   SDH/SONET/PDH Standards

All of the main standards for SDH and PDH technology are developed by the ITU-T. SONET standards are developed by ANSI. The most important standards for these technologies are listed here.

ITU-T

G.702   Digital Hierarchy Bit Rates

G.703   Physical/Electrical Characteristics of Hierarchical Digital Interfaces

G.704   Synchronous Frame Structures Used at 1,544; 6,312; 2,048; 8,488 and 44,736 Kbit/s Hierarchical Levels

G.706   Frame Alignment and Cyclic Redundancy Check (CRC) Procedures Relating to Basic Frame Structures Defined in Recommendation G.704

G.707   Network Node Interface for the Synchronous Digital Hierarchy (SDH)

G.772   Protected Monitoring Points Provided on Digital Transmission Systems

G.810   Definitions and Terminology for Synchronization Networks

G.811   Timing Characteristics of Primary Reference Clocks

G.812   Timing Requirements of Slave Clocks Suitable for Use as Node Clocks in Synchronization Networks

G.813   Timing Characteristics of SDH Equipment Slave Clocks (SEC)

G.821   Error Performance of an International Digital Connection Operating at a Bit Rate Below the Primary Rate and Forming Part of an Integrated Services Digital Network

G.822   Controlled Slip Rate Objectives on an International Digital Connection

G.823   The Control of Jitter and Wander in Digital Networks that are Based on the 2,048 Kbit/s Hierarchy

G.824   The Control of Jitter and Wander in Digital Networks that are Based on the 1,544 Kbit/s Hierarchy

G.825   The Control of Jitter and Wander in Digital Networks that are Based on the Synchronous Digital Hierarchy (SDH)

G.826   Error Performance Parameters and Objectives for International; Constant Bit Rate Digital Paths at or Above the Primary Rate

G.827   Availability Parameters and Objectives for Path Components of International Constant Bit Rate Digital Paths at or Above the Primary Rate

G.832   Transport of SDH Elements on PDH Networks–Frame and Multiplex-
         ing Structures

G.841   Types and Characteristics of SDH Network Protection Architectures

G.957   Optical Interfaces for Equipment and Systems Relating to the Syn-
         chronous Digital Hierarchy

G.958   Digital Line Systems Based on the Synchronous Digital Hierarchy for
         Use on Optical Fiber Cables

M.2100   Performance Limits for Bringing-into-Service and Maintenance of
         International PDH Paths; Sections and Transmission Systems

M.2101.1 Performance Limits for Bringing-into-Service and Maintenance of
         International SDH Paths and Multiplex Sections

M.2110   Bringing-into-Service of International PDH Paths; Sections and
         Transmission Systems and SDH Paths and Multiplex Sections

M.2120   PDH Path; Section and Transmission System and SDH Path and
         Multiplex Section Fault Detection and Localization Procedures

M.2130   Operational Procedures in Locating and Clearing Transmission
         Faults

O.150   General Requirements for Instrumentation for Performance Mea-
         surements on Digital Transmission Equipment

O.151   Error Performance Measuring Equipment Operating at the Primary
         Rate and Above

O.152   Error Performance Measuring Equipment for Bit Rates of 64 Kbit/s
         and N x 64 Kbit/s

O.162   Equipment to Perform In-Service Monitoring on 2,048; 8,448; 34,368;
         and 139,264 Kbit/s Signals

O.163   Equipment to Perform In-Service Monitoring on 1,544 Kbit/s Signals

O.171   Timing Jitter and Wander Measuring Equipment for Digital Systems
         that are Based on the Plesiochronous Digital Hierarchy (PDH)

O.181   Equipment to Assess Error Performance on STM-N Interfaces

The ITU can be found in the World Wide Web at:

http://www.itu.int/

ANSI

ANSI T1.105 1995	Telecommunications–Synchronous Optical Network (SONET)–Basic Description Including Multiplex Structures; Rates; and Formats
ANSI T1.105.01 1995	Telecommunications–Synchronous Optical Network (SONET)–Automatic Protection Switching
ANSI T1.105.02 1995	Telecommunications–Synchronous Optical Network (SONET)–Payload Mappings
ANSI T1.105.03 1994	Telecommunications–Synchronous Optical Network (SONET)–Jitter at Network Interfaces
ANSI T1.105.03a 1995	Telecommunications–Synchronous Optical Network (SONET)–Jitter at Network Interfaces–DS1 Supplement
ANSI T1.105.03b 1997	Telecommunications–Synchronous Optical Network (SONET)–Jitter at Network Interfaces–DS3 Wander Supplement
ANSI T1.105.04 1995	Telecommunications–Synchronous Optical Network (SONET)–Data Communication Channel Protocols and Architectures
ANSI T1.105.05 1994	Telecommunications–Synchronous Optical Network (SONET)–Tandem Connection Maintenance
ANSI T1.105.06 1996	Telecommunications–Synchronous Optical Network (SONET)–Physical Layer Specifications
ANSI T1.105.07 1996	Telecommunications–Synchronous Optical Network (SONET)–Sub STS 1 Interface Rates and Formats Specification
ANSI T1.105.07a 1997	Telecommunications–Synchronous Optical Network (SONET)–Sub STS 1 Interface Rates and Formats Specification (Inclusion of N X VT Group Interfaces)
ANSI T1.105.09 1996	Telecommunications–Synchronous Optical Network (SONET)–Network Element Timing and Synchronization
ANSI T1.119 1994	Telecommunications–Synchronous Optical Network (SONET)–Operations; Administration; Maintenance; and Provisioning (OAM&P) Communications

ANSI T1.119.01 1995   Telecommunications–Synchronous Optical Network (SONET)–Operations; Administration; Maintenance; and Provisioning (OAM&P) Communications–Protection Switching Fragment

ANSI T1.245 1997   Telecommunications–Directory Service for Telecommunications Management Network (TMN) and Synchronous Optical Network (SONET)

ANSI T1.514 1995   Telecommunications–Network Performance Parameters and Objectives for Dedicated Digital Services–SONET Bit Rates

ANSI can be found in the World Wide Web at:

http://www.ansi.org/

14.3 Troubleshooting in PDH Networks

14.3.1 Gathering Information on Symptoms and Recent Changes

The first step in any troubleshooting process is to gather information. The more information you have about the symptoms and characteristics of a problem— including *when* it first occurred—the better your chances of solving the problem quickly and efficiently. Typical questions to ask at this stage include:

- Do the symptoms occur regularly or intermittently?
- Are the symptoms related to certain applications, or do they affect all network operations?
- Do the symptoms correlate to other activities in the network?
- When was the first occurrence of the symptom?
- Has any hardware or software network component been modified?
- Has anyone connected or disconnected a PC (laptop or desktop) or any other component to or from the network?
- Has anyone installed an interface card in a computer?
- Has anyone stepped on a cable?
- Has any maintenance work been performed in the building recently (by a telephone company or building maintenance personnel, for example)?
- Has anyone (including cleaning personnel) moved any equipment or furniture?

14.3.2   Starting the Troubleshooting Procedure

Information about the main network operating parameters recorded during normal operation, that is, before the trouble began, provides invaluable assistance in troubleshooting. This information should include complete descriptions of all components in the network with details on their configuration and physical interfaces, as well as statistics on data traffic and applications, including capacity use and response times.

The first step in diagnosing problems involves checking log data on network components such as routers, interface cards and PDH nodes, as well as checking the configurations in these components. If no information is found that indicates the source of the problem, the next step is to search PDH frame headers for Layer 1 alarms using a PDH tester equipped with the necessary interfaces. Layer 1 alarms can be checksum errors or Remote Alarm Indications (RAI, or "yellow alarms"). The latter usually indicate loss of frame alignment. If no Layer 1 alarms are detected, all other characteristics of the PDH line must be checked. These include:

- Signal levels: compare to pulse mask (peak-to-peak voltage for copper cabling, peak-to-peak power in dB for fiber optic lines)
- Line code errors
- Clock rates (minimum and maximum receiver clock rate)
- Jitter
- Wander
- Framing errors
- Bit-error rate

14.3.3   Error Symptoms in PDH

Typical symptoms of problems in PDH networks are loss of connection and PDH alarm messages during data communication. The source of the problem is most often found on the physical layer of the transmission path. Loss of connection can result from construction work, grounding problems or failure of PDH network components. If the physical transmission path is operational but no connection can be made, the problem most likely lies in the incorrect configuration of one or more network components.

If the connections are not interrupted, but alarm signals occur during transmission, this probably indicates adverse conditions on the physical transmission layer. These may be due to diminished transmitter power or receiver sensitivity at PDH interfaces, faulty connectors on hardware components, electrostatic discharge, grounding errors, or loss of frame alignment due to jitter or wander.

14.3.4   Symptoms and Causes: PDH

Symptom: No Connection

Cause (1):   Cabling fault (broken fiber, loose connector).
Cause (2):   Power failure in a network component.
Cause (3):   Faulty module in a network component.
Cause (4):   Incorrect configuration of a network component.
Cause (5):   Problems involving the operating software of a network component.
Cause (6):   Electrostatic discharge (due to the electrostatic charge on a technician's body or to lightning).
Cause (7):   Faulty solder joints or short circuits (due to dust, humidity or aging).
Cause (8):   Diminished laser power (due to dust, humidity or aging).

Symptom: PDH Alarms

Cause (1):   Insufficient transmitting power at network component interface.
Cause (2):   Optical reflections due to poor splices.
Cause (3):   Overloaded network component.
Cause (4):   Loss of frame alignment.
Cause (5):   Voltage peaks caused by high-voltage switching.
Cause (6):   High bit-error rate.
Cause (7):   Grounding problems.

The following list summarizes the most frequent sources of problems in PDH networks (in alphabetical order):

- Bit-error rate high.
- Cabling fault (broken fiber, loose connector).
- Connector pins corroded.
- Electrostatic discharges (for example, due to electrostatic charge carried by personnel or to lightning).
- Frame alignment error.
- Grounding problems.
- Light power diminished (due to dust, humidity or aging).
- Module in network component faulty.
- Network component configuration incorrect.
- Network component overloaded.
- Optical reflections due to poor splices.
- Power failure in a network component.
- Short circuit (due to dust, humidity, aging).
- Software problems in a network component.

- Solder joints faulty.
- Transmitter power in network component interface insufficient.
- Voltage peaks due to high-voltage switching.

- Failure of a module in a network component
- Power supply failure in a network component
- Static discharge (lightning, static electricity on technician's body)
- Ground faults; wiring closet not grounded
- Configuration error in a network component
- Bad solder joints, short circuits (aging, fatigue, dust, grease, moisture)
- High bit-error rates
- Jitter, wander
- Line breaks
- Voltage surges due to high-voltage switching
- Loose connectors
- Corroded contacts
- Background noise
- Loss of frame synchronization
- Insufficient output signal power/receiver sensitivity at the PDH interface

---

Figure 14.32 The most common causes of errors in PDH networks

14.4 · Troubleshooting in SDH and SONET Networks

See also the "Gathering information on symptoms and recent changes" at the beginning of Section 14.3, "Troubleshooting in PDH Networks".

SDH/SONET networks are operated using powerful systems for centralized configuration, performance and error management of the individual network components. The operating data collected by the network management system represents a major tool in localizing problems in SDH/SONET networks. In many cases, however, the network management system either does not provide data on all network components, or does not provide all the data necessary for optimum troubleshooting. For example, errors on lower hierarchical levels, such as the VC-12 2 Mbit/s level, are not identified by error detection mechanisms that operate on higher hierarchical levels. These problems can be localized only if the data paths in question can be measured directly within the high-speed transport portion of the SDH/SONET network. Low-order path routing errors are a case in point: a network component capable of monitoring J1 bytes (the SDH/SONET header field for recognition of link routes) can detect misrouting and report it to the network management system, but it cannot associate the error with the router or multiplexer that caused the problem. Such difficulties are further compounded if the SDH/SONET network is not managed by a unified network management system, and are even more complicated if the network is not managed by a single operator. In the latter case, the network components at the beginning or end of a transmission path—those components in which data paths are multiplexed into higher SDH/SONET hierarchical levels—are not accessible. For this reason it is important to have portable SDH/SONET testers for each interface type in use, in addition to network management systems. These portable devices provide access to each path in the entire multiplex hierarchy, at any point in the SDH/SONET network, and allow the cause of the error to be localized quickly. Moreover, the POH and SOH/TOH frame overheads can be evaluated fully automatically and any errors displayed directly.

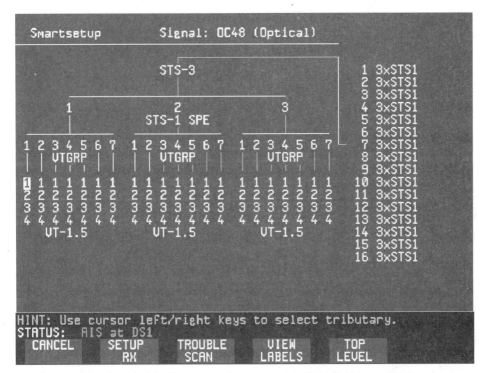

Figure 14.33 SDH/SONET testing using a portable SDH/SONET analysis system

Unlike the older PDH systems, most functions in SDH/SONET network nodes are implemented in software. The correct configuration of the network node is a decisive factor in the node's ability to report errors. This means that in addition to the basic configuration settings for operating a SDH/SONET network component, such as path routes, clock synchronization hierarchies with primary and secondary reference clocks, and backup-path switching, the definition of alarm thresholds for communication errors is also important. These include trigger thresholds and alarm conditions for the following:

- Error rate thresholds (B1, B2 and B3 bytes) for every path or regenerator section that ends in a network component
- Misrouting alarms (called Trace Identifier Mismatch Alarms) for all paths terminated by a network component
- Payload-type detection, with alarms that warn of unexpected payload types (called Signal Label Mismatch Alarms)

The testing and analysis methods that provide detailed insight into SDH/SONET operations can be divided into four categories: transport, pointer, overhead, and interface. These are described in detail in the following section.

14.4.1   SDH/SONET Transport Tests

SDH/SONET transport tests verify whether network components can transport tributary signals (at 2, 34 or 140 Mbit/s) to their destination without error and without loss of quality. This is done by measuring the bit-error rates in the various transport paths and checking for errors in multiplexing (or mapping) and demultiplexing (or demapping) of payload transported to and from the SDH/SONET transport bit stream.

To test bit-error rates, the transmitter port of the SDH/SONET tester is connected to a receiver port on an SDH/SONET switch, and the receiver port of the tester to the transmitter port of the switch. The tester injects a pseudo random binary sequence (PRS) as user data into the tributary signal (TR) to fill the entire bandwidth of a VC. The SDH/SONET network component multiplexes this PRS tributary into a SDH/SONET transport stream and sends it to the transmitter port that is connected to the SDH/SONET tester. The SDH/SONET tester then extracts the test VC from the SDH/SONET transport signal and checks the PRS pattern for bit errors. This test verifies the network component's ability to process tributary signals, even under heavy traffic loads, without loss of quality to the data in the virtual containers during mapping and multiplexing.

To test mapping in the network component, the SDH/SONET tester injects a PRS tributary signal with an intentionally offset bit rate. This tests the SDH/SONET component's alignment capabilities and the robustness of its mapping process.

The SDH/SONET tester is connected to the output port of the network component to extract the test VC from the SDH/SONET transport signal and check it for bit errors.

In the mapping test, demapping is performed by the SDH/SONET tester. To test the SDH/SONET component's demapping, the SDH/SONET tester maps internal or external tributaries in the SDH/SONET structure and injects the resulting SDH/SONET frames into the network component for demapping. The bit-error rate is then checked in the extracted tributary signals at the output port. If the injected tributary signals differ from the defined bit rate, this is compensated for during the mapping process by byte stuffing. The stuff bytes must be removed during demapping. An intentional bit rate offset in the tributary triggers the justification process in the SDH/SONET tester. This makes it possible to test whether the stuff bytes are removed correctly, which tests the robustness of the network component's demultiplexing circuit.

14.4.2   SDH/SONET Pointer Tests

An important part of SDH/SONET testing involves pointer operations. Virtual containers in non-synchronized tributaries must be justified through pointer shifts so that processing is synchronous with the network component's clock. These tests are performed using a SDH/SONET tester that can be operated with independent transmitter and receiver port synchronization. The SDH/SONET tester fills a test VC with a pseudo random sequence and feeds it into the network component under test out of synch with the component's clock. An SDH/SONET tester at the receiving end, synchronized with the network component, checks the bit-error rate in the test VC to determine whether it was correctly synchronized by pointer justification.

Because SDH/SONET pointers perform corrections in 8-bit or 24-bit increments, some amount of quantization in frequency correction is unavoidable. As an example, suppose a given VC-4 is injected into a network component at an input frequency of 150,336.015 kHz, and should exit the component at a frequency of 150,336 kHz. Pointers must compensate for the difference of 15 Hz, or 15 bit/s. The network component's buffer receives 15 more bits per second of the VC than it transmits. To compensate for this difference, a 24-bit negative pointer adjustment must be made every 1.6 seconds (24 bits / 1.6 = 15 bits). Because the output frequency of the signal is corrected every 1.6 seconds, the signal shape is jagged, like a staircase. This jitter in the output frequency is unavoidable, but must be kept within defined limits. To test this capability, the SDH/SONET tester creates transport streams with moving VCs. The VC movements are controlled by deliberate pointer movements. The network component under test must extract these shifting VCs from the data stream. The extracted test VC is inspected for bit errors and jitter by the SDH/SONET tester, and the results compared with SDH/SONET specifications.

14.4.3   SDH/SONET Overhead Tests

SDH/SONET overhead testing is performed to verify the network components' alarm and monitoring functions. Alarm functions are tested by using an SDH/SONET test system to generate Loss of Signal (LOS), Loss of Frame (LOF) and Loss of Pointer (LOP) alarms. The network component should react by transmitting alarm indication signals (AIS) to its downstream neighbors. The SDH/SONET test system monitors the transmission of these alarm indicators. Other alarms, such as Remote Defect Indication (RDI)/Far End Receive Failure (FERF), must be transmitted upstream to warn of downstream error conditions. The procedure for testing this function is parallel to that used in AIS testing.

Monitoring functions in network components are checked by injecting bit errors into the bit-interleaved parity (BIP) byte in the SDH/SONET overhead. State-of-the-art SDH/SONET test systems can generate various bit-error rates while Monitor functions the corresponding Remote Error Indication (REI)/Far End Block Errors (FEBE) messages of the network component. This procedure is used to test whether the network component reports the correct number of errors.

Another test involves checking the data communication channels (DCCs) provided for network management and monitoring in the RSOH/Section and MSOH/Line. A SDH/SONET test device is used to induce alarm messages or parity errors while the data packets transmitted over the DCCs are recorded and analyzed.

All alarm messages that occur in the regenerator section, multiplexer section, higher-order path and lower-order path are listed here.

Regenerator Section/Section Alarms

LOS	Loss of signal
OOF	Out of frame
LOF	Loss of frame alignment
B1	Regenerator section BIP error
RS TIM	Regenerator section trace identifier mismatch

Multiplexer Section/Line Alarms

B2	Multiplexer section BIP error
MS AIS	Multiplexer section AIS
MS RDI	Multiplexer section remote defect indication

MS REI   Multiplexer section remote error indication

Higher-Order Path Alarms

AU LOP   Loss of AU pointer

AU NDF   AU pointer–New data flag

AU AIS   AU alarm indication signal

B3   HP (higher-order path) BIP error

HP UNEQ HP unequipped

HP RDI   HP remote defect indication

HP REI   HP remote error indication

HP TIM   HP trace identifier mismatch

HP PLM   HP payload label mismatch

Lower-Order Path Alarms

TU LOP   Loss of TU pointer

TU NDF   TU pointer–New data flag

TU AIS   TU alarm indication signal

TU LOM   TU loss of multiframe alignment

BIP 2/B3 LP (lower-order path) BIP error

LP UNEQ LP unequipped

LP RDI   LP remote defect indication

LP REI   LP remote error indication

LP RFI   LP remote failure indication

LP TIM   LP trace identifier mismatch

LP PLM   LP payload label mismatch

14.4.4   SDH/SONET Interface Tests

Interfaces in SDH/SONET network components are tested using an oscilloscope and a spectrum analyzer to check whether electrical and optical parameters are within the defined tolerance limits at the transmitting and receiving ports. Electrical interfaces are checked against pulse masks and eye diagrams. Optical interfaces are tested for frequency spectrum, mean signal strength, eye diagram conformance and signal-to-noise ratio.

14.4.5   Error Symptoms in SDH/SONET

The two most common symptoms of problems in SDH/SONET networks are interrupted connections and impaired communication performance. As in PDH, the source of the problem is most often found on the physical layer of the transmission path. Loss of connection can result from construction work, grounding problems or failure of network components.

If the physical transmission path is operational, but no connection can be made, the problem is most likely due to one or more incorrectly configured network components. If several network management systems access a single network component, for example, this can result in incorrect configuration of forwarding routes, which in turn leads to path switching errors. Other sources of error include defects in configuration software or incompatible software versions in network components.

If the connections are not interrupted, but alarm signals occur during transmission, this probably indicates faults in the physical layer. Such errors may be due to diminished receiver sensitivity in one or more network components, faulty connectors at a SDH/SONET interface, electrostatic discharge, grounding problems, loss of frame alignment due to signal jitter or wander, or optical reflections due to poor splices.

14.4.6   Symptoms and Causes: SDH/SONET

Symptom: No Connection

Cause (1):   Cabling fault (broken fiber, loose connector).
Cause (2):   Power supply failure in a network component.
Cause (3):   Faulty module in a network component.
Cause (4):   Incorrect configuration of a network component (such as incorrect path routing configuration).
Cause (5):   Problems with the operating software of a network component.
Cause (6):   Electrostatic discharge (due to the electrostatic charge on a technician's body or to lightning).
Cause (7):   Faulty solder joints or short circuits (due to aging, wear, contamination, humidity).
Cause (8):   Poor laser power (due to aging, wear, contamination, humidity).

Symptom: SDH/SONET Alarms

Cause (1):   Insufficient signal power at network component interfaces.
Cause (2):   Optical reflections due to poor splices.
Cause (3):   Pointer jitter.
Cause (4):   Overloaded network component.

Cause (5):   Invalid pointers; loss of pointer (LOP).
Cause (6):   Loss of frame alignment (LOF).
Cause (7):   Voltage peaks caused by high-voltage switching.
Cause (8):   High bit-error rate.
Cause (9):   Grounding problems.

The following list summarizes the most frequent sources of problems in SDH/SONET networks (in alphabetical order):

- Cabling fault (broken fiber, loose connector).
- Connector pins corroded.
- Electrostatic discharges
  (electrostatic charge carried on the body or lightning).
- Excessive bit-error rate.
- Frame alignment error (LOF).
- Grounding problems.
- Jitter.
- Light power diminished (due to dust, humidity, aging).
- Module failure in network component.
- Network component configuration incorrect.
- Network component overloaded.
- Optical reflections due to poor splices.
- Pointer jitter.
- Pointer lost or invalid (LOP).
- Power supply failure in a network component.
- Short circuit (due to dust, humidity, aging).
- Software problems in a network component.
- Solder joints faulty.
- Thermal noise.
- Insufficient transmitter power or receiver sensitivity
  in network component interface.
- Voltage peaks due to high-voltage switching.
- Wander.

- Voltage surges due to high-voltage switching
- Loose connectors
- Corroded connector contacts
- Network component overloaded
- Loss of pointer
- Loss of frame alignment
- Insufficient output power in a network component module; laser aging

---

Figure 14.34 The most common causes of errors in SDH/SONET networks

V and X Series Interfaces

15

"People only see what they are prepared to see."

RALPH WALDO EMERSON

Standardized interfaces are essential for creating physical and electrical connections between data communication devices from different manufacturers. Such interfaces are used to connect data terminal equipment (DTE), such as computers, routers or bridges, to data communication equipment (DCE), such as modems or X.21 adapters. In practice, these interfaces also represent an important reference point for testing and analyzing data streams. At the same time, however, they can be cause faults that lead to impairments or even total breakdowns of data communication.

Interfaces between DTEs and DCEs in telephone networks—mainly between computers and modems—are defined in the V Series of ITU Recommendations, notably V.24, V.10, V.11, V.35, and V.36. Interfaces between DTEs and DCEs in asynchronous and synchronous public circuit-switched and packet-switched data networks are defined in the X Series of ITU Recommendations: the most important of these are the following:

- X.20 User – Network interface for asynchronous (start-stop) circuit-switched public data networks (CSPDN)

- X.70 Network – Network interface for asynchronous (start-stop) circuit-switched public data networks (CSPDN)

- X.21 User – Network interface for synchronous circuit-switched public data networks (CSPDN)

- X.71 Network – Network interface for asynchronous (start-stop) circuit-switched public data networks (CSPDN)

- X.25 User – Network interface for (synchronous) packet-switched public data networks (PSPDN)

- X.75 Network – Network interface for (synchronous) packet-switched public data networks (PSPDN)

For telephone networks, modem standards such as V.32, V.33, V.34, or V.90 define the interfaces on the network side. The corresponding specifications for data networks differ according to the network type. In synchronous circuit-switched data networks, for example, where a transmission path is physically switched for each logical connection, communication takes place through multi-plexed data streams, such as those specified in X.51.

15.1   Data Communications Interfaces for Telephone Networks

15.1.1   ITU V.24 /EIA/TIA RS-232C

The ITU V.24 interface, which in combination with V.28 is equivalent to the EIA/TIA RS-232C interface in the US, is found in many data communication devices. It has long been the most common data interface in personal computers and modems, and has become a practically universal interface for connecting data terminals, printers, and test instruments. Figure 15.1 shows the pin assignments and signals defined in V.24 and RS-232C.

	ITU V.24	EIA RS232	Pin Assignments	Description
Ground	101	AA	1	Protective ground (GND)
	102	AB	7	
Data	103	BA	2	Transmitted data (TXD)
	104	BB	3	Received data (RXD)
Control signals	105	CA	4	Request to send (RTS)
	106	CB	5	Clear to send (CTS)
	107	CC	6	Data set ready (DSR)
	108.1	CD	20	Connect data set to line
	108.2	CE	20	Data terminal ready (DTR)
	125	CF	22	Ring indicator (RI)
	109	CG	8	Received line signal detector
	110	CH	21	Signal quality detector
	111	CI	23	Data signal rate selector (DTE)
	112	CK	23	Data signal rate selector (DCE)
	126		11	Select transmit frequency
Clocks	113	DA	24	Transmitter signal element timing (DTE)
	114	DB	15	Transmitter signal element timing (DCE)
	115	DD	17	Receiver element timing (DCE)
Auxiliary channel	118	SBA	14	Secondary transmitted data
	119	SBB	16	Secondary received data
	120	SCA	19	Secondary request to send
	121	SCB	13	Secondary clear to send
	122	SCF	12	Secondary carrier detector

Figure 15.1 Signals and pin assignments defined in ITU V.24/V.28 (Europe) and EIA/TIA RS-232C (US)

The V.24 standard defines only the logical signals and signaling sequences for data communication. The electrical and physical characteristics of the interface are described in V.28, which states that a voltage level less than -3 V is a logical 0 and greater than 4 V is a logical 1. The maximum voltage allowed is ± 15 V. The lines are unbalanced, that is, all signals are referenced to signal ground.

When the computer or other data terminal equipment is switched on, the Data Terminal Ready signal (DTR, pin 20) is ON or set to 1. The modem confirms its readiness for operation by activating the Data Set Ready signal (DSR, pin 6). If the modem detects a carrier signal, it activates the Carrier Detect line (CD, pin 8). In order for the data terminal to send data it sets the Request To Send signal high (RTS, pin 4). If the modem is ready to accept data, it sets Clear To Send (CTS, pin 5). The actual data is transmitted over the Transmit (pin 2) and Receive (pin 3) lines. The other conductors are used to determine the data

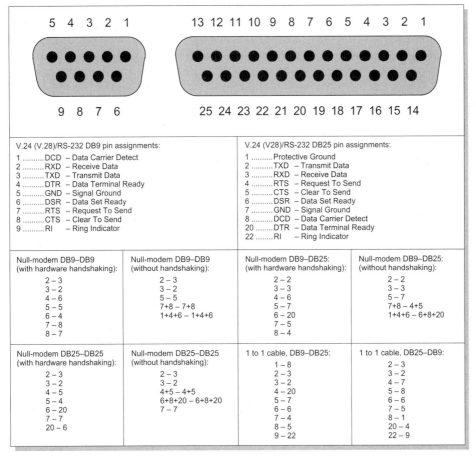

Figure 15.2 Signals and pin assignments defined in ITU V.24 and EIA/TIA RS-232C

speed, test the modem, or synchronize the data. In short, the following nine signals (listed here with their pin numbers) are used in virtually every exchange: Ground (1), Transmit (2), Receive (3), Request To Send (4), Clear To Send (5), Data Set Ready (6), Common Return (7), Carrier Detect (8) and Data Terminal Ready (20). The other signals are used less frequently, and often the corresponding pins are not connected.

The 25-pin connector defined in the ISO 2110 standard is specified for the V.24 interface. This connector has a fixed width of 47.04 ± 0.13 mm, measured between the centers of its two fastening screws. The pins in the upper row are numbered 1 through 13 from left to right, and the lower pins are similarly numbered from 14 to 25. A smaller 9-pin connector (DB9) has also come into widespread use over the past few years. Figure 15.2 shows the pin assignments for both of these V.24 variants, as well as those for the corresponding null-modem combinations. Null modem cables, also called crossover cables or modem eliminators, simply cross the pinouts from one end to the other, so that two DTEs or two DCEs can communicate with one another. Null modem cables are often used to connect two PCs, for example, or to connect a laptop to a router or bridge for use as a configuration terminal.

The maximum data speed defined for V.24 is 20 Kbit/s, and the maximum cable length is 15 meters. In practice, however, considerably higher data speeds are used over shorter distances.

15.1.2   ITU V.35/V.36/V.37

The interfaces defined in ITU Recommendations V.35, V.36, and V.37 are designed for higher data speeds than those provided for in the V.24 specification. V.35 defines data speeds of up to 48 Kbit/s, V.36 up to 72 Kbit/s, and V.37 up to 144 Kbit/s. In contrast to V.24, the data and clock signals in these specifications are balanced, which means they require paired wires, while the control and signaling lines are unbalanced. Because they need no common reference potential, the balanced lines permit significantly higher data speeds. The electrical characteristics of unbalanced signals are defined in ITU V.10 and EIA/TIA RS-423A, while those for balanced signals are specified in ITU V.11 and RS-422A.

Because ITU V.35 was one of the first specifications defined for standardized interfaces, the electrical specifications for balanced lines differ from those in ITU Recommendation V.11 for balanced transmission lines. The voltages specified for data and clock signals are as follows:

1:   −0.55V ±20%
0:   +0.55V ±20%

Thus active interface adaptation is required if V.35 is to be connected to other V.11-compatible interfaces. Both V.36 and V.37, however, are compatible with

V.11. The function descriptions of the interface lines for V.35, V.36, and V.37 are analogous to the corresponding sections of the V.24 Recommendation. Figure 15.3 shows the connector shape and pin assignments for the V.35 interface; Figure 15.4 illustrates the same for V.36.

	ITU V.35	Pin Assignments	Description
Ground		A	Protective ground (PG)
	102	B	Signal ground (SG)
Data	103A	P	Transmitted data (TD)
	104A	R	Received data (RD)
	103B	S	Transmitted data (TD)
	104B	T	Received data (RD)
Control signals	105	C	Request to send (RTS)
	106	D	Clear to send (CTS)
	107	E	Data set ready (DSR)
	108	H	Data terminal ready (DTR)
	125	J	Ring indicator (RI)
	—	K	Reserved
	14	L	Local loopback
	—	M	Reserved
	140	N	Loopback maintenance test
Clocks	113A	U	Transmitter signal element timing DTE
	115A	V	Receiver signal element timing DCE
	113B	W	Transmitter signal element timing DTE
	115B	X	Receiver signal element timing DCE
	114A	Y	Transmitter signal element timing DCE
	—	Z	Reserved
	114B	AA	Transmitter signal element timing DCE
	—	BB	Reserved
	—	CC	Reserved
	—	DD	Reserved
	—	EE	Reserved
	—	FF	Reserved
	—	HH	Reserved
	—	JJ	Reserved
	—	KK	Reserved
	—	LL	Reserved
	—	MM	Reserved
	142	NN	Test indicator

Figure 15.3 Signals and pin assignments defined in V.35

15.1.3   ITU V.10/V.11/RS-449

ITU Recommendations V.10 and V.11 and EIA/TIA RS-449 define balanced and unbalanced interfaces. These specifications permit higher data speeds and greater cable lengths than those specified for the V.24/RS-232C interface (20 Kbit/s, 15 meters) while allowing compatibility with older transmission interfaces. RS-449 is composed of RS-423A for unbalanced transmission and RS-422A for balanced transmission. RS-423A corresponds to ITU Recommendations V.10 and X.26, while RS-422A is equivalent to ITU V.11 and X.27. These specifications allow data speeds of up to 100 Kbit/s for balanced transmission (V.10/RS-422A) and up to 10 Mbit/s for unbalanced transmission (V.11/RS-423A). The specified connectors are a 15-pin connector (defined in ISO 4903) for interfaces in data networks (except RS-449), and a 37-pin connector (ISO 4902) for telephone networks. The 25-pin connectors of the V.24/RS-232C standards are no longer sufficient because balanced transmission requires a pair of wires for each signal, and because signals have been added for local and remote modem testing. Figure 15.4 shows signals, pin assignments, and distance limitations for V.10 and V.11 (Europe) and RS-449 (US).

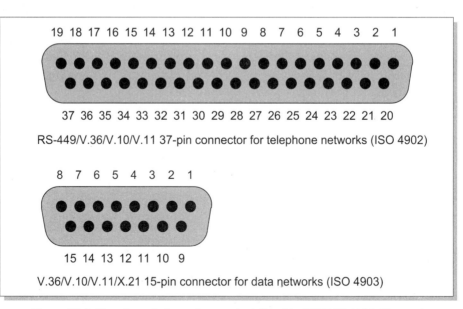

Figure 15.4 Signals and pin assignments defined in ITU V.10, V.11 (Europe) and RS-449 (RS-422A, RS-423A; US)

15.2 Data Communications Interfaces for Data Networks

The use of X Series interfaces, which were originally defined for baseband data communication in public data networks at data speeds of 300 bit/s to several Kbit/s, has become less widespread over the past few years. Circuit-switched networks that use X.20 and X.21 techniques to set up and clear down connections are used only in a few countries. In most regions, these techniques are being replaced by Integrated Services Digital Network (ISDN) and Plesiochronous Digital Hierarchy (PDH), or by Synchronous Digital Hierarchy (SDH) and Asynchronous Transfer Mode (ATM) technologies.

15.2.1 X.20

ITU X.20 describes an unbalanced DTE–DCE interface for asynchronous transmission devices in circuit-switched data networks. The station that initiates the call sets up and clears down the connection, while the station receiving the call responds to the signals received. With regard to data speeds, ITU X.1 distinguishes between User Class 1, with a speed of 300 bit/s and 11 bits per character (7 data bits, 1 parity bit, 1 start bit, 1 stop bit) and User Class 2, at 50 to 200 bit/s with 7.5 to 11 bits per character (5 data bits, 1 start bit, 1.5 stop bits). This interface requires only one transmit (T) and one receive (R) line, as well as DTE and DCE lines and a common ground conductor (G_a, G_b, G). The electrical specifications correspond to those of the V.10 standard. The specified 15-pin connector, shown in Figure 15.4, has the following pin assignments:

Pin 2: T
Pin 4: R
Pin 8: G
Pin 9: G_a
Pin 11: G_b

15.2.2 X.21

ITU X.21 describes a balanced DTE–DCE interface for synchronous data communication equipment in circuit-switched data networks. The X.21 interface is also found in X.25 packet-switched networks, following the leased lines state machine only.

In addition to wire pairs for data transmission (Ta, Tb) and receiving (Ra, Rb), X.21 also requires pairs for control (Ca, Cb), indication (Ia, Ib), and signal element timing (Sa, Sb). Some central offices for circuit-switched synchronous data networks also require the observation of the B (B_a, B_b) circuit, which acts as a strobe signal in order to align individual data bytes with the 8 + 2 envelope interface. The electrical specifications correspond to those of the V.11 standard. The connector specified is a 15-pin connector with the pin assignments shown in Figure 15.4.

The signaling procedure for setting up a circuit-switched X.21 connection is as follows:

A. Ready: T =1, C=OFF

B. Call request: T = 0, C=ON

C. Proceed to select: DCE transmits two or more SYN characters (16 hex) followed by a continuous string of '+' characters (2B hex)

D. Selection signal sequence: DTE transmits two or more SYN characters over T followed by the selection signal sequence (in International Alphabet No. 5)

E. DTE waiting: T=1, C=ON

F. DCE waiting: DCE transmits SYN characters over R line

G. Incoming call: Destination switch transmits two or more SYN characters followed by a string of BEL characters (07 hex) to destination DTE

H. Call accepted: Destination DTE sets C=ON

I. Source and destination switches exchange call information (connection charges, etc.)

H. Connection in progress: R=1, I=OFF

J. Ready for data: Source and destination switches send I=ON to their local DTEs

K. Data transmission begins

This description does not include information on the required timing of the procedures, which is also specified in the X.21 standard. Once the connection has been set up, a transparent transport channel is available so that data can be transmitted in any format. Transmission from an X.21 DCE to the circuit-switched data network is defined in ITU Recommendation X.51. Data is packed in a simple frame (or "envelope") containing a status bit and an alignment bit, is AMI encoded, and transmitted using the baseband technique. As mentioned earlier, however, this transmission technique is rarely used today. X.21 is more often used as a physical connection interface for connecting computer systems or routers to DCEs. DCEs for PDH lines, for example, can be connected to a DTE either directly through a G.703/G.704 interface or through an X.21 interface. As an interim solution for older terminals that have an X.21 interface, an X.21 ISDN terminal adapter can be used for circuit-switched data communication. At the terminal side, connections can be set up and cleared down using X.21 signaling, while the actual transmission takes place over dial-up ISDN lines.

15.2.3 X.25

The X.25 interface is specified for public packet-switched networks. This specification describes connection setup, data transport, and connection clear-down. The X.21 interface creates the physical connection, but X.25 communication does not use the signaling procedure described previously for circuit-switched networks. High-level Data Link Control (HDLC) provides the Layer 2 communication format, while the X.25 protocol defines connection setup and clear-down on Layer 3. Internally, the telecommunications network itself routes and switches the data in accordance with the X.75 protocol. Because bandwidth is limited to 64 Kbit/s, however, X.25 is rarely used today in public telephone networks. ISDN connections, Frame Relay, and ATM networks with user-dialed connections carried over switched virtual circuits are gradually replacing this technology.

15.3   Troubleshooting X and V Series Interfaces

15.3.1   Gathering Information on Symptoms and Recent Changes

The first step in any troubleshooting process is to gather information. The more information you have about the symptoms and characteristics of a problem—including *when* it first occurred—the better your chances of solving the problem quickly and efficiently. Typical questions to ask at this stage include:

- Do the symptoms occur regularly or intermittently?
- Are the symptoms related to certain applications, or do they affect all network operations?
- Do the symptoms correlate to other activities in the network?
- When was the first occurrence of the symptom?
- Has any hardware or software network component been modified?
- Has anyone connected or disconnected a PC (laptop or desktop) or any other component to or from the network?
- Has anyone installed an interface card in a computer?
- Has anyone stepped on a cable?
- Has any maintenance work been performed in the building recently (by a telephone company or building maintenance personnel, for example)?
- Has anyone (including cleaning personnel) moved any equipment or furniture?

Starting the Troubleshooting Procedure

Because problems with V and X Series interfaces involve relatively few components—one DTE, one DCE, and the connecting cables at receiving and transmitting ends—the error domain can usually be located quickly. The first step is to use an interface tester to examine signal levels, first between the DTE (computer or router) and its connecting cable, then between the DCE (X.20/X.21 network interface or modem) and its connecting cable. If the problem is in the DTE, the configuration and status of the DTE communication port must be verified. This involves answering the following questions:

- Has the interface port been activated?
- Does the application use the correct interface port at the right data speed?
- Is the interface hardware defective?

If the problem seems to be in the cabling, the first step is to check cables for visible defects:

- Is the cable kinked or pinched at any point along its length?
- Are any of the pins in the cable connector bent or broken?
- Is the connector dirty or wet?

If no visible sign of trouble is discovered, the next step is to check whether the cable exceeds the maximum length and whether pin assignments are correct. Using a multimeter to systematically test transmitting and receiving pins checks pin assignments. If no faults are found, the DCE must be checked. Any mechanical switches on the device, such as switches to select tone or pulse dialing or to change from standard to loopback operating mode, must be inspected for correct settings. Next, the power supply and the connection to the data or telephone line must be checked. If the problem still cannot be localized, the remote connection must be simulated locally using a second DCE with a second end system connected. If this test connection succeeds, the cause of the problem must be in the communication link or at the remote end of the connection.

15.3.2   Diagnosing Problems in X and V Series Interfaces

The two most common trouble symptoms in X and V Series interfaces are complete loss of connection and drastically impaired communication performance. Loss of connection can usually be traced to a problem on the physical layer. Common causes include loss of power, disconnection of the cable between the DTE and DCE or between the DCE and the communications network, and faulty DCE or DTE components (router ports, computer interfaces, modems). Sometimes defects result from mistakes made during maintenance or reconfiguration work on network components, such as when a null modem cable or a reduced pinout cable without request to send (RTS)/clear to send (CTS) signals is inadvertently used in extending the connection between a DTE and a DCE, for example. Another common mistake of this type is the failure to remove a test loop that was connected to a DCE to measure bit-error rate (BER) or throughput.

In the case of X.21 interfaces, communication problems are often caused by transmission delay, especially if the DTE–DCE cable is long. This is because the X.21 technique synchronizes outgoing signals with the clock rate of incoming signals on the S conductor of the DCE. These signals must travel from the DCE to the DTE, where they are used as the reference clock for outgoing data on the T pins. The outgoing signals must then travel back to the DCE before they are transmitted over the X.21 network. If transmission path between DTE and DCE is too long, phase shifts may prevent the X.21 DCE from sampling the data bits from the DTE correctly. Some X.21 DCEs have optional settings to enable compensation for such phase shifts. Otherwise, using shorter DCE cables may solve the problem. Figure 15.5 lists critical cable lengths for data rates up to 2 Mbit/s based on a signal propagation speed of 0.66c.

Data rate (Kbit/s)	Critical cable length (m)	Data rate (Kbit/s)	Critical cable length (m)
64	781	1,088	46
128	391	1,152	43
192	260	1,216	41
256	195	1,280	39
320	156	1,344	37
384	130	1,408	36
448	112	1,472	34
512	98	1,536	33
576	87	1,600	31
640	78	1,664	30
704	71	1,728	29
768	65	1,792	28
832	60	1,856	27
896	56	1,920	26
960	52	1,984	25
1,024	49	2,048	24

Figure 15.5 Critical cable lengths for X.21 connections

For X.20 as well as X.21 interfaces with in-band call procedures, the timing of the events in state transitions is very critical; for example, the transition from "ready" to "call request" requires that the transmitter (T lead) transmit contiguous logical 0s (T lead transits from MARK to SPACE) and for the C lead to be turned on. These two lead changes have to occur within a limited number of signal element times (clock pulses). Very few, if any, protocol analyzers on the market will report these events properly. The use of a logic analyzer is highly recommended for troubleshooting this kind of interface technology. Poor quality networks, poor quality cables, and electromagnetic interference (EMI) along the transmission path are the most common causes of poor communication performance over X and V interfaces.

15.3.3   Symptoms and Causes: X and V Series Interfaces

Symptom: No Connection

Cause (1):   Incorrect pin assignments (null modem cable used in place of a straight-through modem cable, for example).

Cause (2):   Defective cable (kinked or pinched).

Cause (3):   Defective connector (corroded, broken, or bent connector pin).

Cause (4):   Cable too long.

Cause (5):   Interface on DTE inactive or faulty.

Cause (6):   No power supply to DCE.

Cause (7):   DCE not connected to network.

Cause (8):   Incorrectly configured DCE (pulse rather than tone dialing; active modem loop).

Cause (9):   Line busy (another system is transmitting).

Cause (10): X.21 protocol error (C or I signal not set to ON)

Cause (11): X.21 protocol error (transitions on C/T or I/R not within timing limitations) caused by invalid state transitions (lead signal changes).

Symptom: Diminished Throughput; Long Response Times

Cause (1):   Poor line quality.

Cause (2):   High BER due to excessive cable length between DTE and DCE.

Cause (3):   X.21: DTE–DCE cable of critical length, causing timing problems (critical length at 64 Kbit/s is 781 meters, at 2,048 Kbit/s is 24 meters. See "Diagnosing Problems in X and V Series Interfaces" for details.).

Cause (4):   High BER due to electromagnetic interference along the DTE–DCE connection.

The following list summarizes the most frequent sources of problems in V and X Series DTE–DCE interfaces in telephone networks (serial PC ports, modems) in alphabetical order:

Errors at DTEs and DCEs, telephone networks:

- BER high due to electromagnetic interference in serial port modem connection
- BER high due to excessive cable length between serial port and modem
- Cable fault between serial port and modem (kink or sharp bend in cable)
- Connector fault (corroded, broken, or bent connector pin)
- Connector pin assignments incorrect
  (null modem cable as opposed to straight-through modem cable)
- Interface at DTE (PC serial port, router port) inactive or defective
- Line busy (another system is transmitting)
- Modem connection to telephone line interrupted (no carrier)
- Modem incorrectly configured (pulse instead of tone dialing; wrong number dialed)
- Modem locked: the modem's redialing lock was activated after several
  unsuccessful dialing attempts (no carrier, wrong baud rate, destination busy)
- Modem not connected to network
- Modem not connected to power
- Outside line accessible only through PABX (no carrier without outside dialing
  prefix)
- Poor line quality

Errors at DTEs and DCEs, circuit-switched data networks (X.20, X.21):

- BER high due to electromagnetic interference in DTE-DCE cable
- BER high due to excessive DTE-DCE cable length
- DTE-DCE cable is of critical length (in X.21), causing timing problems
  (critical length at 64 Kbit/s is 781 m; at 2048 Kbit/s 24 m.
  See, "Diagnosing Problems in X and V Series Interfaces", for details)
- Cable defective (kinked or pinched)
- Connector defective (corroded, broken, or bent pin)
- Connector pin assignments incorrect (null modem cable in place of
  straight-through modem cable)
- DCE not connected to network
- DCE not connected to power
- Interface in DTE is inactive or defective
- Line busy (another system is transmitting)
- Modem loop activated inadvertently (by cleaning personnel, for example)
- Modem loop not deactivated after testing
- X.21 protocol error (C or I signal not set to ON)
- Poor line quality

Figure 15.6 The most common causes of errors in X and V Series interfaces

Section IV
Troubleshooting
Higher-Layer Protocols

Internet Protocols

"The important thing is not to stop questioning."

ALBERT EINSTEIN

The most important transport protocol in data communications today is the Internet Protocol (IP). Together with the family of service and application protocols that build on it, IP is used to transport all kinds of communications, including data, voice, and multimedia. The major components of the Internet protocol suite are:

OSI Layer 3 (Network Layer)

IP:	Internet Protocol
ARP:	Address Resolution Protocol
RARP:	Reverse Address Resolution Protocol
IARP:	Inverse Address Resolution Protocol
SLARP:	Serial Line Address Resolution Protocol (Cisco)
ICMP:	Internet Control Message Protocol
OSPF:	Open Shortest Path First
IGRP:	Cisco Interior Gateway Routing Protocol
EIGRP:	Cisco Enhanced IGRP
GGP:	Gateway-to-Gateway Protocol
EGP:	Exterior Gateway Protocol
BGP:	Border Gateway Protocol
RIP:	Routing Information Protocol
RIPng:	Routing Information Protocol–Next Generation
NHRP:	Next Hop Routing Protocol

OSI Layer 4 (Transport Layer)

TCP:	Transport Control Protocol
TCP Compressed:	Van Jacobson compressed TCP
UDP:	User Datagram Protocol
NetBIOS DGM:	TCP/IP Datagram Protocol
DVRMP:	Distance Vector Multicast Routing Protocol

IGMP: Internet Group Management Protocol

RSVP: Resource Resolution Protocol

OSI Layer 5 (Session Layer)

LDAP: Lightweight Directory Access Protocol

DNS: Domain Name Server

NetBIOS NS: TCP/IP Name Server

NetBIOS SSN: TCP/IP Session Protocol

OSI Layer 6 (Presentation Layer)

LPP: Lightweight Presentation Protocol

IMAP4:   Internet Message Access Protocol

OSI Layer 7 (Application Layer)

X Windows   X Windows Protocol

HTTP: Hypertext Transfer Protocol

FTP: File Transfer Protocol

TELNET: Remote Terminal Protocol

SMTP: Simple Mail Transfer Protocol

GDP: Cisco Gateway Discovery Protocol

TACACS: Terminal Access Controller Access Control System

TACACS+:   Terminal Access Controller Access Control System Plus

CMOT: CMIP over TCP

SNMPv1, v2:   Simple Network Management Protocol

TFTP: Trivial File Transfer Protocol

NTP: Network Time Protocol

DHCP: Dynamic Host Configuration Protocol

BOOTP: Bootstrap Protocol

RPRINT: UNIX Remote Print

RSHELL: UNIX Remote Shell

RLOGIN: UNIX Remote Login

REXEC: UNIX Remote Exec

RWHO: UNIX Remote WHO Protocol

RADIUS: Remote Authentication Dial-in User Service

Figure 16.1 lists the individual protocols with their interrelations and their positions in relation to the OSI model.

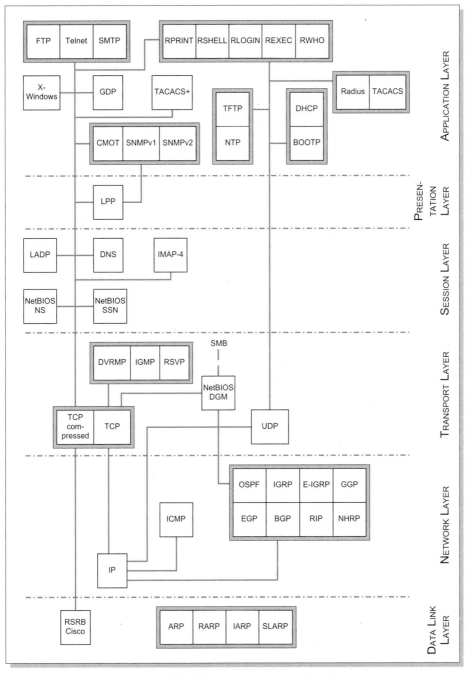

Figure 16.1 The Internet protocol family

The IP itself is the central component of the Internet protocol family. The application protocols build on the IP addressing service to establish connections using the Transmission Control Protocol (TCP) or send connectionless data using the User Datagram Protocol (UDP). UDP is simpler than TCP, but does not offer reliable data communications and often entails sensitive security considerations. For example, if packets arrive at the destination in a different order from that in which they were transmitted, TCP can restore the original sequence, but UDP cannot because it does not provide for sequence numbers. Furthermore, UDP contains no mechanism for acknowledging received packets or requesting retransmission of lost data. Both of these functions are integral parts of TCP.

The Internet protocols are carried over a multitude of network topologies, from Ethernet, Token Ring, and FDDI LANs to wide-area networks such as ATM, X.25, Frame Relay, ISDN, or modems connected to the telephone network.

16.1   The Internet Protocol (IP)

The IP is a basic network protocol. The communication service it provides is described as packet-oriented, connectionless, and non-guaranteed. Packet-oriented means that the stream of data to be transmitted is cut up into discrete packets. Transportation of the packets is connectionless, which means that every packet is treated as an independent entity, without regard to preceding or

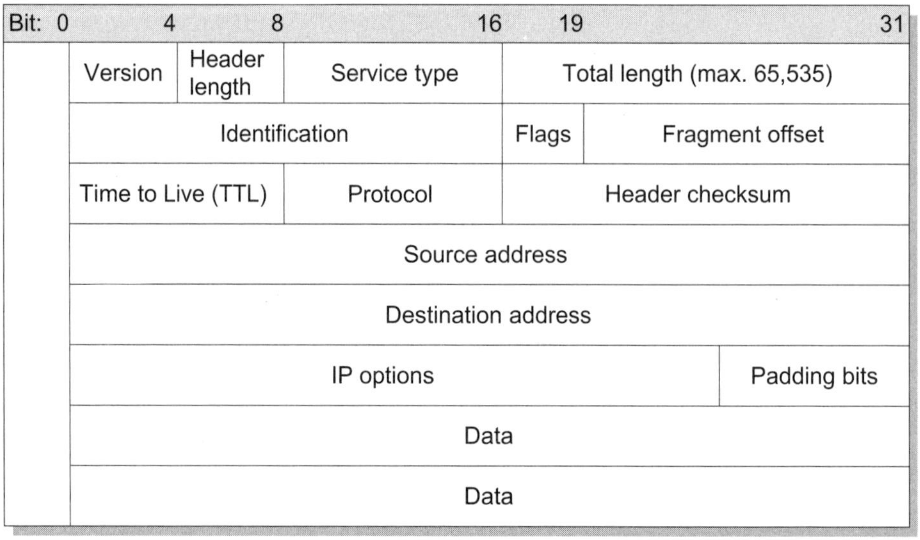

Bit: 0	4	8		16	19	31
Version	Header length	Service type		Total length (max. 65,535)		
Identification				Flags	Fragment offset	
Time to Live (TTL)		Protocol		Header checksum		
Source address						
Destination address						
IP options					Padding bits	
Data						
Data						

Figure 16.2 Format of an IP data packet

subsequent packets. (IP is able to defragment packets correctly, even if the fragments arrive out of sequence). Non-guaranteed service means that no mechanism is provided for repeating lost packets. Figure 16.2 illustrates the format of an IP data packet.

The maximum length of an IP data packet is 65,535 bytes. It may be necessary to fragment packets–to break them up into smaller packets–in order to comply with the restrictions of the network infrastructure over which IP is carried. In Ethernet LANs, for example, the maximum payload per frame is only 1,480 bytes. Some gateways also are unable to forward packets with a maximum length of 65,535 bytes. The IP specification requires that inter-segment components (that is, routers) be able to process packets with a minimum length of at least 566 bytes. When an IP packet is fragmented, each of the resulting fragments also conforms to the IP packet format. The Identification, Flag, and Fragment Offset fields are filled in with appropriate values to permit reassembly of the original IP data packet at the destination (see Figure 16.3). Fragmentation can also be suppressed by setting the first flag bit–the "Do Not Fragment" bit–to one. In this case, however, the packet will be discarded by any component that is unable to forward it without fragmentation.

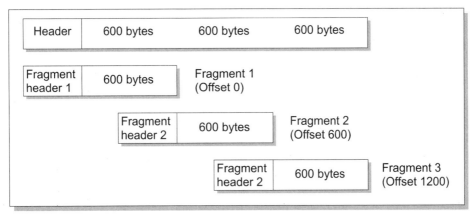

Figure 16.3 Fragmentation of IP data packets

Another important field is the Time to Live (TTL) byte. This limits the time that the IP packet may remain in the data network. As the packet travels toward its destination, each forwarding node decrements the TTL field. If the TTL reaches zero before the packet reaches its destination, the packet is discarded. The checksum field ensures error-free transmission of the packet header, and is followed by the 2 times 32-bit Internet addresses of the source and destination nodes and the payload.

16.2 The Transmission Control Protocol (TCP)

The main Internet transport protocol is called the Transmission Control Protocol or TCP. IP is referred to as a network protocol (OSI Layer 3–network layer); TCP as a transport protocol (OSI Layer 4–transport layer). TCP supplements IP's capabilities with mechanisms to verify whether a data packet has actually been received by the destination system. If a packet is lost, a repeat transmission is requested.

TCP first divides the data stream to be transmitted into segments. The computer systems that want to communicate negotiate a maximum segment size depending on their buffer capacities. The default segment size is 536 bytes, which corresponds to the default IP packet size of 576 bytes minus the 20-byte IP header.

In order to be able to recover from transmit sequences where data is damaged, lost, duplicated, or delivered out of order by the network, the TCP protocol assigns a sequence number to each transmitted octet. If the acknowledgement for having received the octet is not returned within a timeout interval, the data is retransmitted. At the receiver, the sequence numbers are used to correctly order segments that may be received out of order and to eliminate duplicates. Damage is handled by adding a checksum to each segment transmitted, checking it at the receiver, and discarding damaged segments.

To control the amount of data sent by the sending station, the TCP protocol provides a flow control mechanism that is based on the so-called window size. With every acknowledgement the receiver sends a window size parameter that indicates the acceptable range of octets (sequence numbers) the sender may transmit before receiving further permission.

If the window size is n, the transmitting station may send n octets without waiting for acknowledgment from the receiving station. The receiving station determines whether or not an incoming octet sequence is complete by means of the sequence number field. If a sequence is incomplete, all octets that have not yet been acknowledged must be retransmitted. Thus one must not assume that if a TCP packet retransmission occurs, only one octet has to be resent. Typical recovery times for TCP retransmissions caused by a dropped octet are between a half second and a second.

The most common reasons for packet retransmissions are:

1) A sent TCP packet or a returning acknowledgment packet is lost by a overloaded switch or router.
2) A packet is corrupted during the transmission and contains a CRC error.
3) TCP data are corrupted and show a TCP checksum error.
4) A fragment of a fragmented TCP packet is lost or corrupted.
5) There is a buffer overflow at the receiver.
6) The acknowledgment for a TCP packet sequence is too slow.

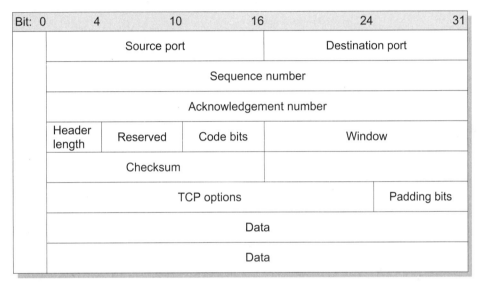

Figure 16.4 Format of a TCP segment

Figure 16.4 shows the format of a TCP segment. The standard TCP header size is 20 bytes. If the TCP implementation supports additional options, such as the maximum segment size (MSS), the header can be longer than 20 bytes. The optimal MSS equals, in most cases, the IP maximum transfer unit (MTU) of the transmission path between client and server minus the protocol overhead. Thus a good MSS for Ethernet would be 1,460 bytes, and for IEEE 802.3 1,452 bytes. Analyzing the window size at SYN time can, in most cases, determine the maximum window size. However, TCP implementations can alter the window size dynamically during a TCP connection. In Windows 95/98/2000/NT the window size uses a default value of 8,760 bytes for Ethernet.

The window size depends on the maximum memory and bandwidth available for a particular virtual connection. It is important to understand that it is a dynamic parameter that is never constant. Once the amount of data that fits into one window is sent, the connection has to wait for the acknowledgment message to arrive. Each time an acknowledgement message is received, the window size is doubled. If a packet loss occurs, the sender cuts the window size back to half. In case of an end-to-end connection collapse (TCP time out occurs), the sender resumes the connection with a small window size. Figure 16.5 shows the changing connection throughput, which is proportional to the window size changes, over time as it occurs in a typical TCP connection.

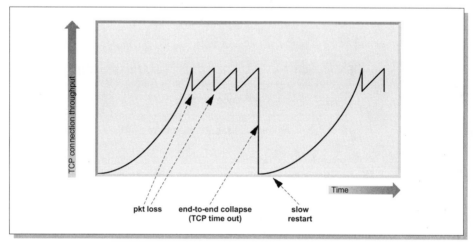

Figure 16.5 The dynamics of the TCP window size

TCP supplements IP addressing by using source and destination ports to provide an additional addressing level. TCP ports are software addresses associated with specific application programs running on a given computer. To communicate with a certain TCP service on another computer, the port number of the service must be known in addition to the computer's address. Once the connection to the specified port number has been set up, payload data is delivered directly to the corresponding service.

Multitasking computer systems are capable of running several communication processes offering different services simultaneously. In this case, each service is assigned a different port number. Theoretically, any TCP service could be assigned any port number, but publicly available services, such as Web or FTP servers, use reserved port numbers that are standard throughout the Internet (for example, 80 for WWW, 21 for FTP, etc.). Otherwise users would not be able to connect to such servers without knowing the specific port number they use (see Figure 16.6).

Port number	Protocol	Name	Description
1	TCP	tcpmux	TCP port multiplexer
7	UDP/TCP	echo	Echo server
13	UDP/TCP	daytime	Time of day service
20	TCP	ftp-data	FTP data channel
21	TCP	ftp	FTP control channel

Figure 16.6 Some of the most commonly used reserved TCP port numbers

16.3   The User Datagram Protocol (UDP)

UDP can be considered a simplified version of TCP. Like TCP it builds on IP, but its additional capability is limited to application addressing by port numbers. UDP cannot guarantee packet transmission or sequencing. UDP applications must be prepared to compensate for events such as packet loss, transmission delay, or packets received out of order.

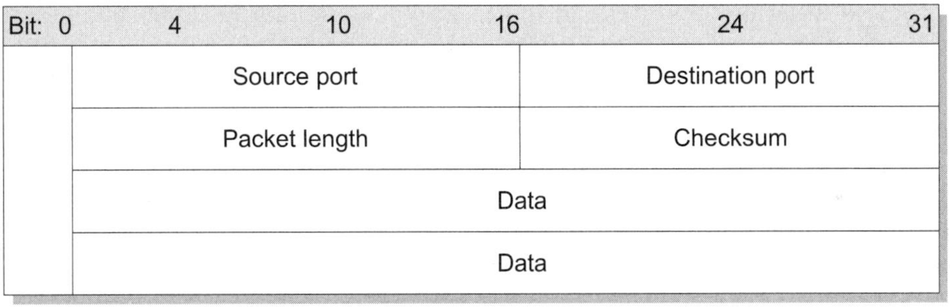

Bit: 0   4   10   16   24   31
Source port	Destination port
Packet length	Checksum
Data
Data

Figure 16.7 The UDP packet format

16.4   IP Encapsulation: SLIP, PPP

16.4.1   Serial Line Internet Protocol (SLIP)

SLIP was developed in 1984 by Rick Adams for Berkeley UNIX Version 4.2 to facilitate the transport of IP data packets over telephone lines. The algorithm used could hardly be simpler. SLIP requires only two control codes, namely the END character (octal 300, decimal 192) and the ESC character (octal 333, decimal 219–not to be confused with the ASCII Escape character, decimal 27!)

Transmission of an IP packet in SLIP requires no additional preamble or header. The packet is simply sent starting with the first IP header byte. At the end of each packet an END character is transmitted (see Figure 16.8). If the END character happens to occur within the IP packet itself, then two ESC characters followed by the bit sequence for decimal 220 are inserted before it. Some SLIP implementations also send an END character before the data packet in order to flush any error or noise bytes. If the data contains the bit sequence of the ESC character, then two ESC characters followed by the bit sequence for decimal 221 are inserted before it.

Figure 16.8 The SLIP protocol

Because SLIP is not an official standard, there is no universal maximum packet length. However, the SLIP implementation for Berkeley UNIX, which is generally regarded as a guideline, has a maximum packet length of 1,006 bytes (not counting END and ESC characters).

Due to its simplicity, SLIP is very easy to implement and very widely used. It does have some functional limitations, however. For example, no addressing information can be exchanged over SLIP—the two systems must know each other's IP addresses before beginning to communicate. Furthermore, SLIP does not have a Protocol Type field, and so can only be used to transport one protocol at a time. It is not suitable for connecting two multiprotocol systems.

Finally, SLIP includes no error correction mechanisms whatsoever. This capability can be provided by TCP over the SLIP, but several packets—depending on the TCP window size—must be transmitted before error correction can take effect. On lines with high bit-error rates this leads to drastic reductions in throughput, and it would be more efficient to have simple error correction on the lowest communication layer.

16.4.2   The Point-to-Point Protocol (PPP)

PPP (RFC 1331) is much more complex than SLIP and can be used to encapsulate multiple protocols over the same connection. It also offers a multitude of functions, such as error correction and dynamic network address assignment.

PPP consists of three components: the encapsulation of data packets, the Link Control Protocol to establish the data connection, and various network control protocols to negotiate the parameters for the individual network protocols (IP, IPX, DECnet, etc.).

PPP Encapsulation

PPP encapsulates the data packets to be transmitted in High-level Data Link Control (HDLC) format, ISO 3309, 1979. Figure 16.9 shows the resulting structure of a PPP data packet. (For asynchronous transmission, HDLC also inserts a

Flag	Address	Control	Protocol	Information	FCS	Flag
0111 1110	1111 1111	0000 0011	16 bits		16 Bits	0111 1110

Protocol field codes:

0001	Padding Protocol	0231	Luxcom
0003	Reserved	0233	Sigma Network Systems
to 001f	(transparency inefficient)	8021	Internet Protocol
0021	Internet Protocol		Control Protocol
0023	OSI Network Layer	8023	OSI Network Layer
0025	Xerox NS IDP		Control Protocol
0027	DECnet Phase IV	8025	Xerox NS IDP Control Protocol
0029	AppleTalk	8027	DECnet Phase IV
002b	Novell IPX		Control Protocol
002d	Van Jakobson	8029	AppleTalk Control Protocol
	Compressed TCP/IP	802b	Novell IPX Control Protocol
002f	Van Jakobson	802d	Reserved
	Uncompressed TCP/IP	802f	Reserved
0031	Bridging PDU	8031	Bridging NCP
0033	Stream Protocol (ST-II)	8033	Stream Protocol Control Protocol
0035	Banyan Vines	8035	Banyan Vines Control Protocol
0037	Unused	8037	Unused
0039	AppleTalk EDDP	8039	Reserved
003b	AppleTalk SmartBuffered	803b	Reserved
003d	Multi-Link	803d	Multi-Link Control Protocol
005d	Reserved	80fd	Compression Control Protocol
	(compression inefficient)	80ff	Reserved
00cf	Reserved (PPP NLPID)	c021	Link Control Protocol
00fd	1st choice compression	c023	Password Authentication Protocol
00ff	Reserved	c025	Link Quality Report
	(compression inefficient)	c223	Challenge Handshake
0201	802.1d Hello Packets		Authentication Protocol
0203	IBM Source Routing BPDU		

Figure 16.9 Structure of a PPP data packet

start bit before and a stop bit after each byte. These start and stop bits are not shown in Figure 16.9.)

The flag field with the value 0111 1110 indicates the beginning or end of a data packet in HDLC. In PPP the address field always has the value 1111 1111, corresponding to "All Stations" in HDLC. The Control field contains 0000 0011, the HDLC value for Unnumbered Information (UI). The 2-byte Protocol field indicates the type of protocol encapsulated in the packet. The Information field can be from 0 to 1,500 bytes in length. The data packet ends with a 2-byte Frame Check Sequence (FCS) and the ending flag 0111 1110.

The PPP Link Control Protocol (LCP)

The LCP sets up and maintains the serial point-to-point connection, invokes the network control protocols, and clears down the connection after the data communication is finished. PPP packets that carry LCP data are identified by the value C021h in the Protocol Type field. After the LCP negotiation has been completed and the remote system receives the "Configure Ack" message the data link is opened. Optionally, LCP Echo Request and LCP Echo Reply packets can be sent to test the line quality. After this test phase, the Link Control Protocol starts the desired Network Control Protocol (NCP) program.

The PPP Network Control Protocol for IP

For every protocol that can be encapsulated by PPP there is a Network Control Protocol. The Network Control Protocol implementation for the Internet Protocol is called the IP Control Protocol or IPCP. The purpose of IPCP is to activate and deactivate the IP modules on the two computers that are to communicate. IPCP is transported in PPP packets with the Protocol Type 8021h. Once IPCP has opened the network layer connection, the IP packets themselves can be transported.

16.5   Addressing in IP Networks

The addressing structure for IP was created to maximize the efficiency of routing across several subnetworks. For this reason, Internet address information not only identifies the desired network user, but also determines the user's location and the routes to it.

Each IP network node is identified by a 32-bit (4-byte) address, which is unique in the entire IP network. In the customary notation for Internet addresses, called "dotted decimal" notation, the 4 bytes of the address are represented by decimal numbers from 0 to 255 and separated from one another by periods, as in

193.174.4.13, for example. Every address consists of two parts: the network address and the host address. Every IP subnetwork is assigned a network address, and host addresses are assigned to the individual nodes in each network. The lengths of these two parts vary, depending on the address class. Internet addresses are divided into Classes A, B, and C, with different lengths for the network and host address fields. There is also a D Class of multicast addresses, which can be used to send data packets to groups of recipients. Certain multicast addresses are officially assigned and others are freely available for temporary use. A fifth address class, Class E, is reserved for future use.

Address class		Length of network address	Length of host address	Number of networks (theoretical maximum)	Number of hosts per network
	A	7 bits	24 bits	128	16,777,214
	B	14 bits	16 bits	16,384	65,534
	C	21 bits	8 bits	2,097,152	254

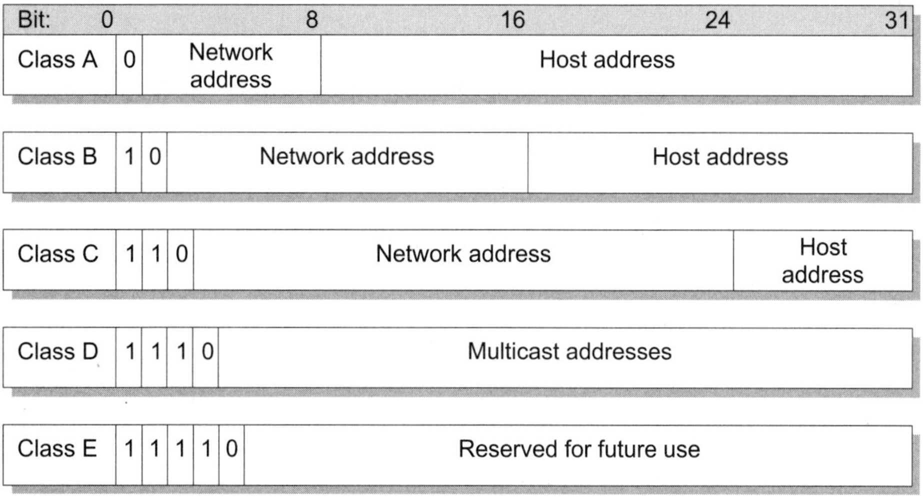

Bit:	0		8	16	24	31
Class A	0	Network address		Host address		

| Class B | 1 | 0 | Network address | | Host address | |

| Class C | 1 | 1 | 0 | Network address | | Host address |

| Class D | 1 | 1 | 1 | 0 | Multicast addresses | |

| Class E | 1 | 1 | 1 | 1 | 0 | Reserved for future use |

Figure 16.10 The five classes of Internet addresses

The network address consists of 7 bits in Class A addresses, 14 bits in Class B addresses, and 21 bits in Class C addresses. This means that the address space for the public Internet can contain: 126 Class A networks (because two addresses are reserved; 0 for the local net, 127 for loopback), each with $2^{24} - 2 = 16,777,214$ host addresses (0.0.0 and 255.255.255 are reserved); 16,384 Class B networks, each with $2^{16} - 2 = 65,534$ host addresses, (0.0 and 255.255 are reserved); and 2,097,152 Class C networks with 254 host addresses (0 and 255 are reserved). The number of public 32-bit Internet addresses is thus limited. To accommodate the growth of the Internet, an improved addressing scheme has been developed called IPv6 (or IPng: the "next generation" of IP). IPv6 will eventually supersede the currently widespread IPv4 protocol. (IP Version 5, also called the Streaming Protocol, is not widespread, but only used in a few routers). IPv6 uses 128-bit addresses for an address space of 2^{128} or $3 \cdot 10^{38}$ addresses, so that the problem of address shortage is solved for the foreseeable future.

16.5.1   The IP Address Space

Until IPv6 is widely deployed, the scarce 32-bit Internet addresses must be used economically and not wasted on nodes in internal company networks that never communicate with the public Internet. In 1994, an IP address space for private corporate networks (intranets) was defined in RFC 1597:

10.0.0.0	to	10.255.255.255
172.16.0.0	to	172.31.255.255
192.168.0.0	to	192.168.255.255

This private address space consists of one Class A network address, 16 consecutive Class B addresses, and 255 consecutive Class C addresses. Any organization may use these addresses for private IP network nodes without registering them with the Internet Assigned Numbers Authority (IANA), the body responsible for assigning Internet addresses. Before assigning IP addresses in an enterprise network, the network nodes (hosts) should be classified into the following three groups:

- Hosts that never need to access hosts in other enterprise networks or in the Internet at large
- Hosts that need access to outside services (such as e-mail, FTP, news, WWW), which can be handled by mediating gateways (for example, application layer gateways). For many hosts in this category an unrestricted external access (provided via IP connectivity) may be unnecessary and even undesirable for privacy/security reasons. Just like hosts within the first category, these hosts may use IP addresses that are unambiguous within an enterprise, but may be ambiguous between enterprises.
- Hosts that need network layer (IP) access outside the enterprise. Hosts in this category require IP addresses that are globally unambiguous.

Hosts in the first category, called private hosts, may use IP addresses that are unique only within the local intranet. The same applies to hosts in the second category. When these computers communicate with hosts outside the enterprise network, they do so through an Internet gateway. The gateway system then establishes the actual Internet connection to the desired host using its own public IP address, while acting as a proxy for the private host. Only hosts in the third category need to have IP addresses that are unique throughout the world.

All private hosts should be assigned IP addresses from the private IP address space defined in RFC 1597. Address assignment should be planned as follows: first, the addressing of the internal, private part of the network should be planned using the RFC 1597 address space. Then subnetworks should be defined for public hosts. If a host later needs to be changed from private to public, its Internet address must be changed. If the network infrastructure supports the use of subnet masks, the Class A network address with 24-bit host addresses (10.255.255.255) should be used. Subnet masks can be used to define a sufficient number of subnetworks for efficient internal packet routing. If the network components do not support subnet masks, then the 254 Class C private addresses can be used to configure up to 254 Intranet clients per network without requiring subnet masks.

16.5.2   Special Internet Addresses

Certain network addresses are reserved for special functions. These include broadcast and loopback addresses.

Broadcast Addresses

A broadcast address is used to send a data packet to all nodes in a network. It must only be used as a destination address; otherwise major network problems can occur. In a broadcast address, all bits in the host address part of the address are set to one. Thus the broadcast address for the network prefix 121, for example, is 121.255.255.255 (a binary numeral of eight ones equals decimal 255).

The broadcast address 255.255.255.255 is a network-wide broadcast to any node in the network and should not appear in the network under normal circumstances. However, due to errors in network devices this address occasionally appears, causing network problems.

0111 1001	1111 1111	1111 1111	1111 1111
121	255	255	255

Figure 16.11 The broadcast address 121.255.255.255

The Loopback Address 127

The Class A address 127 is reserved for the loopback interface. Packets with the destination address 127.0.0.1 return to the sending host immediately without entering the network. This address can be used to test higher-layer functions.

Zero in Network and Host Addresses

The network address 0 is automatically interpreted as the local network. By the same token, the host address 0 refers to the local network node. This address as well must only be used as a destination address, otherwise major network problems can occur.

Internet address		Destination
Network address	Host address	
000 ... 000	000 ... 000	The local node
000 ... 000	host	Another host in the local network
111 ... 111	111 ... 111	Local broadcast: all nodes in the local network
network	111 ... 111	Broadcast into a specific network
0111 1111 (127)	000 ... 000	Loopback

Figure 16.12 Special Internet addresses

16.5.3   Subnetwork Address Masks

Large data networks consist of several thousand hosts and many hundreds of subnetworks. If Internet addresses were assigned randomly to every network node in such a network, then all routers in the network would have to possess a list of all network nodes with their addresses and the router ports through which they can be reached. In large networks, these routing tables would be huge. Under high traffic loads, the finite CPU performance of routers would result in noticeable delays in packet forwarding. By assigning addresses systematically using the principle of subnet masks, routing efficiency in IP networks can be significantly improved. In this scheme, a part of the available host address is used to subdivide the network into several subnetworks. For example, a network with a Class B address 184.69 can be divided into subnetworks X and Y, so that subnet X uses only the address range from 184.69.1.1 to 184.69.1.254, while subnet Y uses only the range from 184.69.2.1 to 184.69.2.254. Then the routers between the two subnetworks can apply a subnetwork address mask—usually called simply the "subnet mask"–to the destination address of any packet and identify quickly whether the packet is local or needs to be forwarded to the other subnetwork or to another IP network. For the network in our example, the subnet mask would be 255.255.255.0. The subnet mask is simply a bit mask formed of zeroes for all the bits used to form local host addresses in each subnet, and ones for all other bits. The routers in this example would analyze only the first 24 bits of a packet's destination address, which is sufficient to identify the subnetwork the packet must be routed to (Figure 16.13). The advantage for the router is great because its routing tables no longer need to list all network nodes, just the subnet addresses. The number of subnetworks is of course much smaller than the number of network nodes, so the router software

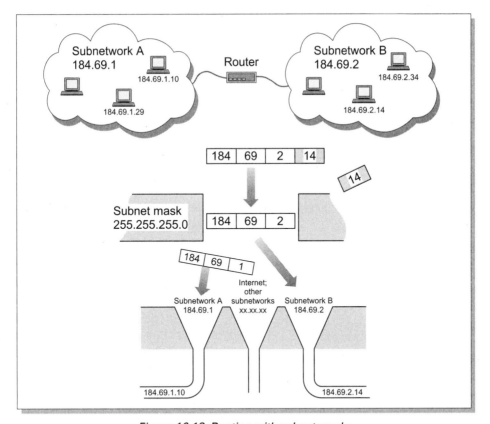

Figure 16.13 Routing with subnet masks

can make routing decisions much faster. The same principle is used not only in private networks, but also in Internet backbones. The definition of subnet masks for all connected Internet provider networks permits efficient routing throughout the Internet.

Incorrect subnetwork address masks can also cause communication problems. In the previous example, if the subnet mask were set to 255.255.0.0 by mistake, then packets with destination addresses matching 184.69.xxx.xxx would no longer be forwarded. The router would only analyze the first 16 rather than the first 24 bits. Because the first 16 bits match both subnet addresses, the router would decide that every packet is already in its destination network! All communication between neighboring networks would be prevented.

16.5.4   The Internet Domain Name System (DNS)

Numerical Internet addresses can have distinctive names associated with them so that users can work with them more easily. Until 1986, it was customary to choose any name desired and enter it with the associated IP number in a central list of host names. As the Internet grew to include over 3,000 host names, however, it became harder to think up new names that were not already in use. For this reason, the hierarchically structured Domain Name System (DNS) was developed. Like numerical IP addresses, fully qualified host names include a part that identifies the host (the "host name" in the strictest sense) and a part that identifies the network (the "domain name"). Each domain name consists of a top-level domain and one or more hierarchically subordinate subdomains. The nesting depth of subdomains is not limited, but the total length of the domain name must not exceed 24 characters. As an example, suppose the name of the computer with the IP address 15.12.144.111 is help.gs1.hp.com. Although this name, like the IP address, is structured in parts separated by periods, these parts bear no relation to the bytes of the IP address! (see Figure 16.14).

Host and subdomain names need not be unique in the Internet, but must be unique in the next higher domain. Thus the network *gs1.network.com* may contain only one host with the name *help*, and the domain *network.com* may contain only one subdomain with the name *gs1*. There is no reason why the domain *system.com* cannot also contain a subdomain named *gs1*, however. Likewise, *gs1.system.com* could also contain a host named *help*.

16.5.5   The Host Command and the DNS Protocol

IP data packets cannot be routed by domain names. Routers need to use numerical Internet addresses and the corresponding subnet masks. For this reason a way to translate domain names into the corresponding numerical IP addresses is required. This is done by means of DNS protocols. If no DNS server is available to translate host names into IP numbers, then a user must indicate the desired numerical address in order to establish a connection. The UNIX commands

host <domain name>

and

host <Internet address>

return the numerical Internet address that corresponds to a domain name and the host and domain names that correspond to a given IP address. The host command obtains this information from domain name servers, which are queried using the DNS protocol. DNS servers maintain tables of numerical addresses and the corresponding domain names. Every intranet must contain at least one such server. In the Internet at large, numerous publicly accessible name server systems are distributed throughout the world. Like the domain name system itself, DNS servers are organized hierarchically. To resolve an unknown name, a "root server" selects the authoritative name server for the top-level domain. This server then determines the appropriate name server for names within the highest subdomain, and so on. Each name server maintains four "zone databases":

- Forward zone
- Reverse zone
- Localhost
- Reverse localhost

The forward zone database maps domain names to the corresponding numerical Internet addresses. The reverse zone database is used to determine domain names on the basis of a known IP address. A special Internet address domain, in-addr.arpa, has been defined for this purpose. The domain name that corresponds to a given IP address aaa.bbb.ccc.ddd can be found by the DNS request:

ddd.ccc.bbb.aaa.in-addr.arpa

This application allows diskless systems in particular to determine their own domain names on the basis of an IP number, which can be obtained from the hardware (MAC) address using the Reverse Address Resolution Protocol (RARP). Applications such as the remote UNIX services rlogin and rsh also use the reverse DNS tables for user authentication. Finally, the localhost zone files are used to support the loopback interface with the network address 127.0.0.0.

To ensure worldwide support for the domain name system, every enterprise connected to the Internet must operate two publicly accessible DNS servers on independent computer systems, with mapping tables for its publicly accessible domains and their subdomains. For security reasons, organizations normally also maintain a separate, internal name server for their own address resolution needs. This internal DNS server forwards name resolution requests for hosts in the Internet at large to the public DNS, then returns the results to the internal client system, which can send data to the IP address.

In order to avoid referring to other domain name servers before every connection—which would aggravate traffic loads with many DNS queries—every DNS server stores the information it has received in a local cache. In its cache it "remembers" the domain names that have already been asked about by local clients and the corresponding Internet addresses received from DNS. After a while the server can answer most queries from its local cache.

The "secondary DNS server"—usually the Internet provider's DNS—can respond to queries when the local, primary server is overloaded and also serves as a backup server in case of problems. The local DNS server's zone files are copied to the secondary server at regular intervals in a "bulk zone transfer".

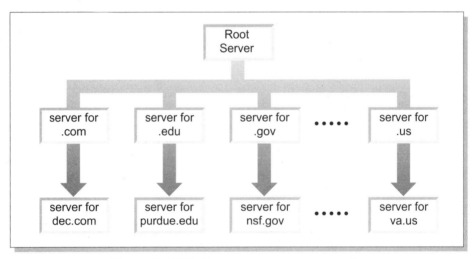

Figure 16.14 The Internet name server hierarchy

16.6   Internet Protocol – The Next Generation (IPv6)

At the beginning of the 1990s, due to the rapid growth of the Internet and a multitude of new multimedia and security-sensitive applications, it became clear that the Internet Protocol needed to be substantially revised. Since 1992, many IETF working groups have been dealing with suggested improvements, drafting 25 requests for comments (RFCs) on this subject. Finally in 1994, the new version of the Internet protocols called IPv6 (or IPng, for "the next generation") was adopted. The main changes in IPv6 as compared with its predecessor, IPv4, include:

- Internet addresses with a length of 128 bits (rather than 32 bits)
- A simplified header format (fields such as Time to Live and Type of Service are eliminated)
- Optional authentication and encryption
- Traffic flow components for improved multimedia capability
- Compatibility with the existing IP version to ensure smooth migration

One of the most fundamental and most urgently needed changes was the expansion of the IP address space. The move from 32-bit to 128-bit addresses increases the number of possible addresses to 2^{128} (or three times 10^{38}), and will solve the problem of address scarcity for the foreseeable future.

The number of 128-bit Internet addresses is large enough to provide every Internet host with a subaddress space that is as big as the entire IPv4 address space used in the public Internet before the adoption of IPv6.

The 128-bit IPv6 addresses are written as decimal byte values separated by colons rather than periods. For example:

145:23:45:62:47:234:567:234:678:5:2:123:23:33:4:128

16.6.1   The IPv6 Address Format

IPv6 uses three distinct types of addresses: unicast, anycast, and multicast. Anycast addresses designate a group of hosts, but packets addressed to an anycast only need to be delivered to the nearest member of the group. Multicast packets must be delivered to each of the addressees. Unicast addresses refer to individual hosts and are assigned with the following formats according to a hierarchical structure:

- Provider-based addresses
- Geographic-based addresses
- (ISO) NSAP (Network Service Access Point) addresses
- Hierarchical IPX addresses
- Local-use addresses
- IPv4-capable host addresses

The introduction of provider addresses allows companies to switch from one Internet provider to another without changing the complete addresses of their computers. The first 3 bits (010) indicate the provider-based address type, and are followed by the registry ID and the provider ID. The subscriber ID and intra-subscriber address are appended to these. When a company changes its Internet provider, the subnetwork and host addresses can remain unchanged. Only the new provider's ID and a new subscriber ID need to be inserted. This principle also benefits networks that are first created with no connection to the Internet, but later want Internet access without completely reconfiguring the network. If the private network uses local addresses, which contain only the subscriber ID and intra-subscriber address, companies have the option of converting these to public Internet addresses simply by adding the appropriate registry ID and provider ID (see Figure 16.15).

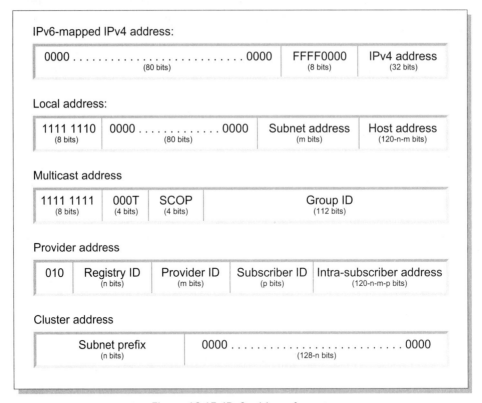

Figure 16.15 IPv6 address formats

In order to provide for the coexistence of IPv4 and IPv6 in a transitional phase, a way to integrate IPv4 addresses in the IPv6 address format also has been defined. IPv4 addressing is indicated by zeroes in the first 80 bits of an IPv6 address, followed by 16 bits with the value 0000 (or FFFF if the IPv4 host is not IPv6-capable). The original IPv4 address is then contained in the remaining 32 bits.

16.6.2   The IPv6 Data Packet Format

The format of IP data packets has also been improved in IPv6. Although IPv6 uses addresses that are four times as long, the IPv6 header is only half as long as in Version 4. Optional extension headers can follow the IPv6 header. Most of the routers that forward the IPv6 data packet on its way to its destination address will only need to analyze the IPv6 header so that routing is faster than with IPv4 headers. The IPv6 header contains the following fields:

- Version number (4 bits)
- Flow label (20 bits; used to support real-time sensitive multimedia applications)
- Payload length (16 bits)
- Next header (8 bits; indicates the type of the extension header immediately following the IPv6 header)
- Hop limit (8 bits; decremented each time the packet is forwarded. The packet is discarded when this counter reaches zero.)
- Source address (128 bits)
- Destination address (128 bits)

Other header extensions for special functions can be inserted between the IPv6 addresses and the transport layer header of the data packet. The length of these options can be any integer multiple of 8 bytes, so that even complex functions, such as encryption or authentication mechanisms, can be implemented. The following optional header fields are defined:

- Hop-by-hop
- Routing
- Fragment
- Destination
- Authentication
- Encapsulating security payload

Routing protocols, such as OSPF, RIP, and IGRP, can be used with IPv6 in the same way as with IPv4. The source station also has the option of specifying an explicit address sequence as a route, which can be used in reverse order by the recipient for replies. This mechanism is intended mainly to support the connection of mobile computer systems to IP networks.

16.6.3   Authentication and Encryption in IPv6

Authentication and security encapsulation options permit authentication of communicating systems and privacy of data contents at the IP level. The optional authentication header can be used to guarantee IPv6 data packets against corruption. The sender applies a special hash function to the data packet (MD5, Message Digest 5, is recommended) and inserts the resulting value in the authentication header. Hash functions are characterized by the fact that the corresponding inverse function is very difficult to perform. On the average, 2^{64} attempts are necessary to find a second input value that results in the same output value of a hash function. Hash functions for use as "message digests" are specified in RFCs 1319, 1320, and 1321 (MD2, MD4, and MD5).

The authentication header offers protection against manipulation of data packets, but does not guarantee the privacy of the data sent. This is the purpose of the Encapsulation Security header. It can be used to transport parts of the data packet or the entire payload in encrypted form.

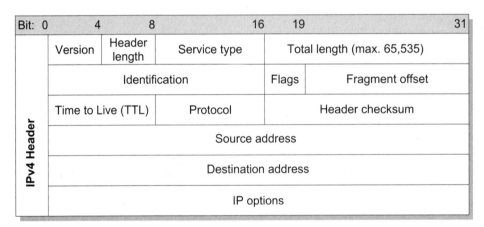

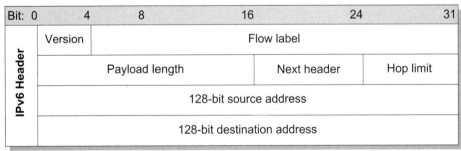

Figure 16.16 The IPv6 and IPv4 data packet format

16.7   The NetBIOS Protocol

The NetBIOS protocol, as the name implies, was originally implemented as BIOS code on a ROM chip for the IBM PC Network Broadband LAN. Today there are three variants of NetBIOS in use as session layer protocols, building on the LLC protocol (NetBEUI), the Novell IPX protocol, and TCP/IP. NetBIOS is described in RFC 1001 (Protocol Standard for a NetBIOS Service on a TCP/UDP Transport: Concepts and Methods) and RFC 1002 (Protocol Standard for a NetBIOS Service on a TCP/UDP Transport: Detailed Specifications).

The most significant difference between NetBIOS for IPX and UDP/TCP, on the one hand, and NetBEUI for the LLC protocol, on the other, is that the latter has no network layer and therefore cannot be routed. The NetBIOS protocol is

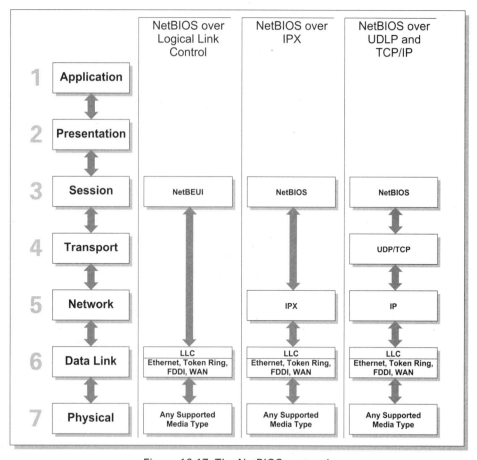

Figure 16.17 The NetBIOS protocols

primarily used for the location of resources in the network (similar to DNS) and the establishment of session layer connections.

16.7.1   NetBEUI (NetBIOS over LLC)

The NetBIOS variant known as NetBIOS Extended User Interface (NetBEUI) is mainly used in Microsoft Windows environments. It is used to register new stations in the network and to log clients into server systems. NetBEUI is initialized using MAC multicast frames (MAC frame ID 030000000001 in Ethernet networks, C000000000080 in Token-Ring networks). Services implemented over NetBEUI include peer-to-peer file sharing in Windows 95/98 or server connections. A local session number (LSN) and a remote session number (RSN) identify every NetBIOS session over IPX.

In "Windows for Workgroups" environments that use NetBIOS over IPX as the session layer protocol, NetBIOS is mainly used for name services. The main differences from NetBEUI are the use of ordinary MAC broadcasts (FFFFFFFFFFFF) rather than NetBEUI's multicasts for initialization and the fact that the protocol is routable. Microsoft's extended implementation of NetBIOS over IPX is called Microsoft Name Management Protocol (NMPI).

16.7.2   NetBIOS over TCP/IP

NetBIOS over TCP/IP uses both TCP (ports 137–139) and UDP (ports 137–139). UDP is used for connectionless services, such as sending and receiving data

Unique (U):	The name may have only one IP address assigned to it. On a network device, multiple occurrences of a single name may appear to be registered. The suffix may be the only unique character in the name.
Group (G):	A normal group; the single name may exist with many IP addresses. The NetBIOS name server (WINS) responds to a name query on a group name with the limited broadcast address (255.255.255.255). Because routers block the transmission of these addresses, the Internet Group was designed to service communications between subnets.
Multihomed (M):	The name is unique, but due to multiple network interfaces on the same computer this configuration is necessary to permit the registration. The maximum number of addresses is 25.
Internet Group (I):	This is a special configuration of the group name used to manage Windows NT domain names.
Domain Name (D):	New in Windows NT 4.0.

Figure 16.18a NetBIOS name suffixes

Name	Number (h)	Type	Usage
<computername>	00	U	Workstation Service
<computername>	01	U	Messenger Service
<\\—__MSBROWSE__>	01	G	Master Browser
<computername>	03	U	Messenger Service
<computername>	06	U	RAS Server Service
<computername>	1F	U	NetDDE Service
<computername>	20	U	File Server Service
<computername>	21	U	RAS Client Service
<computername>	22	U	Microsoft Exchange
<computername>	23	U	Microsoft Exchange Store
<computername>	24	U	Microsoft Exchange
<computername>	30	U	Modem Sharing Server
<computername>	31	U	Modem Sharing Client
<computername>	43	U	SMS Clients Remote
<computername>	44	U	SMS Administrators
<computername>	45	U	SMS Clients Remote Chat
<computername>	46	U	SMS Clients Remote
<computername>	4C	U	DEC Pathworks TCPIP Service on Windows NT
<computername>	52	U	DEC Pathworks TCPIP
<computername>	87	U	Microsoft Exchange MTA
<computername>	6A	U	Microsoft Exchange IMC
<computername>	BE	U	Network Monitor Agent
<computername>	BF	U	Network Monitor
<username>	03	U	Messenger Service
<domain>	00	G	Domain Name
<domain>	1B	U	Domain Master Browser
<domain>	1C	G	Domain Controllers
<domain>	1D	U	Master Browser
<domain>	1E	G	Browser Service
<INet~Services>	1C	G	IIS
<IS~computer name>	00	U	IIS
<computername>	[2B]	U	Lotus Notes Server
IRISMULTICAST	[2F]	G	Lotus Notes
IRISNAMESERVER	[33]	G	Lotus Notes
Forte_$ND800ZA	[20]	U	DCA IrmaLan Gateway

Figure 16.18b NetBIOS name suffixes

573

packets, and for name services when no WINS (NetBIOS name server) is present. TCP is used to communicate with the NetBIOS name server and to set up session connections.

Microsoft restricts the length of NetBIOS names to a maximum of 15 characters, using a sixteenth character as a node type suffix (see Figure 16.18).

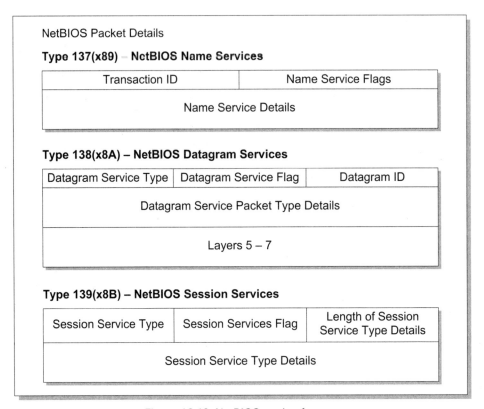

Figure 16.19 NetBIOS packet formats

16.8 The Dynamic Host Control Protocol (DHCP)

DHCP, RFC 2131, is used for dynamic assignment of IP addresses and subnet masks to new clients logging into the network. The key advantage over static, permanently assigned addresses and subnet masks is that the client can connect to any segment of an IP network without requiring manual configuration changes. DHCP automatically assigns the client an IP address and subnet mask, which are valid for the local subnetwork. This is especially advantageous for diskless workstations and mobile clients (notebooks), as well as in the case of changes in network design. As recently as a few years ago, diskless workstations used the Reverse Address Resolution Protocol (RARP) to obtain an IP address. As with ARP, the main disadvantage of RARP is that it uses MAC layer broadcasts, which are not forwarded by routers. The use of RARP therefore requires a RARP server in every network segment. Moreover, RARP servers only hand out IP addresses, not subnet masks. In order to overcome the limitations of RARP, the Bootstrap Protocol (BOOTP) was developed. BOOTP distributes both IP addresses and subnet masks. However, BOOTP requires a static network environment in which a client with a given MAC address is always assigned the same IP address and subnet mask. DHCP, by contrast, permits true dynamic IP address and subnet mask assignments, and also provides a significantly larger vendor options field (312 bytes, compared with 64 bytes under BOOTP). The DHCP packet format is practically identical to the BOOTP format and is illustrated in Figure 16.20. UDP is used as the transport protocol with the reserved ports 67 (DHCP server) and 68 (DHCP client). A protocol analyzer can thus help in troubleshooting DHCP problems by filtering for UDP ports 67 and 68.

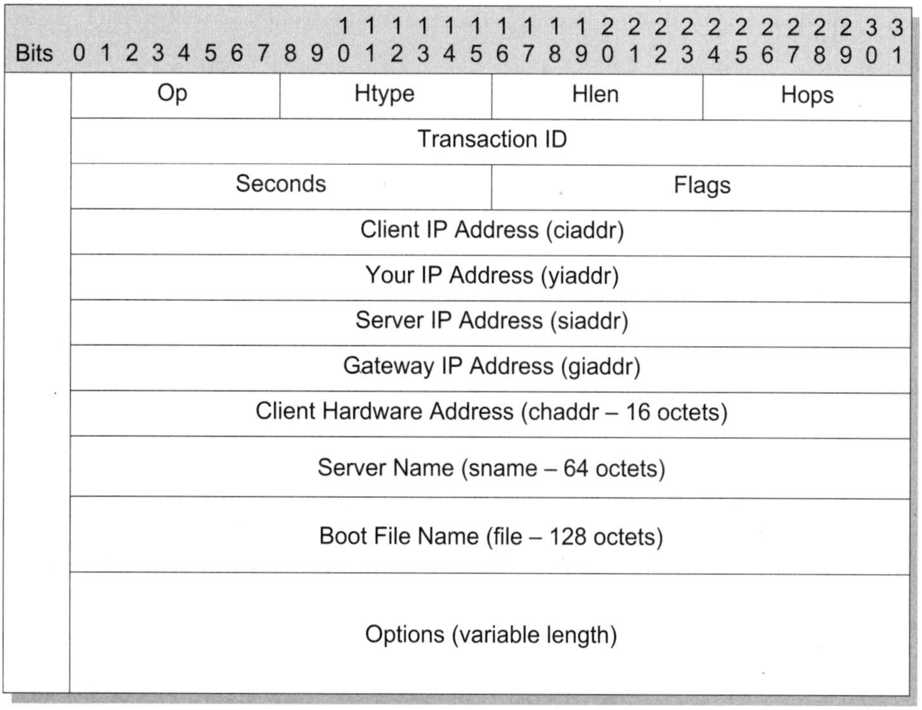

Bits	Op	Htype	Hlen	Hops
0 1 2 3 4 5 6 7	8 9 0 1 2 3 4 5	6 7 8 9 0 1 2 3	4 5 6 7 8 9 0 1	
	Transaction ID			
	Seconds		Flags	
	Client IP Address (ciaddr)			
	Your IP Address (yiaddr)			
	Server IP Address (siaddr)			
	Gateway IP Address (giaddr)			
	Client Hardware Address (chaddr – 16 octets)			
	Server Name (sname – 64 octets)			
	Boot File Name (file – 128 octets)			
	Options (variable length)			

Figure 16.20 The DHCP packet format

16.8.1   Diagnosing DHCP Errors

The most common problems with DHCP arise through the mixture of dynamic and fixed IP addresses. For this reason it is extremely important that no fixed IP addresses be released to the DHCP server for distribution. Another type of problem occurs when DHCP servers are used to manage fixed addresses—that is, when a given IP address is always assigned to the same MAC address: if a station (a MAC address) is moved to a different segment, the DHCP server may assign it its old IP address even though the address is not valid in the new subnet.

16.9   Internet Protocols: Standards

The working groups of the Internet Engineering Task Force (IETF) develop the specifications for the Internet protocol family. The standardization documents, known as Requests for Comments (RFCs), are available from several repositories, including the InterNIC documentation archive at:

http://www.internic.net/.

The most important Internet standards are listed here:

IPoA MIB:	Classical IP and ARP Over ATM MIB, RFC 2320 (Proposed standard)
NETBIOS:	Protocol Standard for a NetBIOS Service on a TCP/UDP Transport, RFC 1001, 1002 (STD 19)
DNS:	Domain Names—Concepts and Facilities [port 53], RFC 1034 (STD 13)
DNS:	Domain Names—Implementation and Specification, RFC 1035 (STD 13)
IP-IEEE:	Transmission of IP over IEEE 802 Networks, RFC 1042 (STD 43)
RPC:	Remote Procedure Call Protocol Version 2 (Sun), RFC 1057
SLIP:	Transmission of IP over Serial Lines, RFC 1055 (STD 47)
RIP:	Routing Information Protocol, RFC 1058 (STD 34)
IP-DVMRP:	Distance Vector Multicast Routing Protocol, RFC 1075
IP-NETBIOS:	Transmission of IP over NetBIOS, RFC 1088 (STD 48)
NFS:	Network File System Protocol (Sun), RFC 1094

IGMP	(Internet Group Multicast Protocol): Host Extensions for IP Multicasting, RFC 1112 (STD 5)
IP-IPX:	Transmission of 802.2 Packets over IPX, RFC 1132 (STD 49)
IP-CMPRS:	Compressing TCP/IP Headers, RFC 1144
SNMP:	Simple Network Management Protocol [port: 161], RFC 1157 (STD 15)
BGP:	Border Gateway Protocol [port 179], RFC 1163
IP–X.121:	IP to X.121 Address Mapping for DDN, RFC 1236
ICMP-ROUT:	ICMP Router Discovery Messages, RFC 1256
TFTP:	Trivial File Transfer Protocol, RFC 1350
IP-X.25:	Multiprotocol Interconnect on X.25 and ISDN in the Packet Mode, RFC 1356
IP-FDDI:	Transmission of IP and ARP over FDDI Networks, RFC 1390
SNMPv2:	Version 2 of the Internet-standard Network Management Framework, RFC 1441ff.
IRCP:	Internet Relay Chat Protocol, RFC 1459
IP-TR-MC:	IP Multicast over Token Ring LANs, RFC 1469 (Proposed standard)
DHCP-BOOTP:	Interoperation Between DHCP and BOOTP, RFC 1534 (Draft standard)
PPP:	The Point-to-Point Protocol (PPP), RFC 1661 (STD 51)
RIP2-APP:	RIP Version 2 Protocol Applicability Statement, RFC 1722 (STD 57)
IPNG:	The Recommendation for the IP Next Generation Protocol, RFC 1752
RMON MIB:	Remote Network Monitoring Management Information Base, RFC 1757, 2021, 2074
ICMP-DM:	ICMP Domain Name Messages, RFC 1788
NFSV3:	NFS Version 3 Protocol Specification, RFC 1813
IPV6-AH:	IP Authentication Header, RFC 1826, 2402
RPC:	Remote Procedure Call Protocol Specification v2, RFC 1831

WHOIS++:   Architecture of the WHOIS++ Service, RFC 1835

IPV6:   Internet Protocol, Version 6 Specification, RFC 1883, 2460

IPV6-Addr: IPv6 Addressing Architecture, RFC 1884

DNS-IPV6:   DNS Extensions to Support IP Version 6, RFC 1886

RTP: A Transport Protocol for Real Time Applications, RFC 1889

POP3:   Post Office Protocol—Version 3 [port: 110], RFC 1939

IITTP-1.0:   Hypertcxt Transfer Protocol—HTTP/1.0, RFC 1945

IPV6-ETHER: Transmission of IPv6 Packets Over Ethernet, RFC 1972, 2464

IPIP: IP Encapsulation within IP, RFC 2003

IPV6-FDDI: Transmission of IPv6 Packets Over FDDI, RFC 2019

IPV6-PPP: IP Version 6 over PPP, RFC 2023, 2472

IMAPV4:   Internet Message Access Protocol—Version 4rev1, RFC 2060

DNS-SEC: Domain Name System Security Extensions, RFC 2065

IP-HIPPI: IP over HIPPI, RFC 2067

HTTP-1.1:   Hypertext Transfer Protocol—HTTP/1.1, RFC 2068

DHCP: DHCP Options and BOOTP Vendor Extensions, RFC 2132

RADIUS: Remote Authentication Dial In User Service [port: 1812], RFC 2138

RSVP: Resource ReSerVation Protocol—Version 1, RFC 2205

IP-ATM: Classical IP and ARP over ATM, RFC 2225

FTP-SECEXT: FTP Security Extensions, RFC 2228

LDAP3:   Lightweight Directory Access Protocol (v3), RFC 2251

OSPF2:   Open Shortest Path First Version 2, RFC 2328 (STD 54)

NHRP: NBMA Next Hop Resolution Protocol, RFC 2332

IARP: Inverse Address Resolution Protocol, RFC 2390

IP-FR: Multiprotocol Interconnect over Frame Relay, RFC 2427

IPV6-FDDI: Transmission of IPv6 Packets Over FDDI, RFC 2467

UDP: User Datagram Protocol, RFC 768 (STD 6)

IP: Internet Protocol, RFC 791 (STD 5)

ICMP:	Internet Control Message Protocol, RFC 792 (STD 5)
TCP:	Transmission Control Protocol, RFC 793 (STD 7)
SMTP:	Simple Mail Transfer Protocol [port: 25], RFC 821 (STD 10)
ARP:	Ethernet Address Resolution Protocol, RFC 826 (STD 37)
TELNET:	Telnet Protocol Specification, RFC 854 (STD 8)
ECHO:	Echo Protocol [port 7], RFC 862 (STD 20)
DAYTIME:	Daytime Protocol [port 13], RFC 867 (STD 25)
TIME:	Time Server Protocol, RFC 868 (STD 26)
ICMPv6:	Internet Control Message Protocol for IPv6, RFC 1885
BOOTP:	Bootstrap Protocol, RFC 951
FTP:	File Transfer Protocol [port 21], RFC 959 (STD 9)
NNTP:	Network News Transfer Protocol [port: 119], RFC 977

16.10 Troubleshooting Internet Protocols

16.10.1 Gathering Information on Symptoms and Recent Changes

The first step in any troubleshooting process is to gather information. The more information you have about the symptoms and characteristics of a problem— including *when* it first occurred—the better your chances of solving the problem quickly and efficiently. Typical questions to ask at this stage include:

- Has any hardware or software network component been modified?
- Do the symptoms occur regularly or intermittently?
- When was the first occurrence of the symptom?
- Are the symptoms related to certain applications or connections, or do they affect all network operations?
- Has anyone connected or disconnected a PC (laptop or desktop) or any other component to or from the network?
- Has application software been installed or updated?
- Have system files been cloned from one network node to another?
- Has anyone installed an adapter card in a computer?
- Has any maintenance work been performed in the building recently (by a telephone company or building maintenance personnel, for example)?
- Has anyone (including cleaning personnel) moved any equipment or furniture?

16.10.2 Error Symptoms in IP Networks

As in every networking process, significant operating data for IP networks should be recorded before trouble arises. Such information includes a description of all IP network components (network stations, routers, switches) with their configurations, IP addresses, host and domain names, physical interfaces, and the protocols and applications that communicate through them. Furthermore, vital statistics such as capacity use (average and peak loads) should also be available. When errors arise, a comparison between current test data and the data recorded during normal operation often provides a first indication of the cause of trouble. If an unusually high number of ICMP packets, broadcasts, rerouting packets, or TCP timeouts is observed this can be considered a clue as to the source of problems. Modern protocol analyzers generate such protocol performance statistics automatically, thus simplifying diagnostic work significantly (see Figure 16.21).

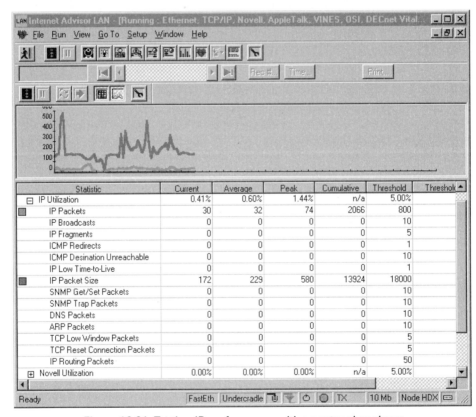

Figure 16.21 Testing IP performance with a protocol analyzer

The first step in diagnosing a problem is to determine the symptoms as exactly as possible. Is it still possible to initiate or accept connections? Do existing connections get interrupted? Are the response times higher or throughput lower for certain services or for all services?

If no connection can be established to one or more hosts in the network—even though standard hardware checks show that the station is connected to the network and its network adapter is correctly configured and operational—then the first step is to determine the extent of the error domain by sending pings. The ping command uses ICMP Echo Request and Echo Reply packets to test the availability and status of IP hosts. Sending pings in the following order can narrow down the error domain:

1) Ping the problem host's loopback address, 127.0.0.1.
2) Ping the problem host from another host in the same subnetwork.
3) Ping another host in the same subnetwork from the problem host.
4) Ping the default router from the problem host.
5) Ping another host in a different subnetwork from the problem host.
6) Ping the problem host by name.
7) Ping another host in the same subnetwork by name.
8) Ping another host in a different subnetwork by name.
9) Telnet to the problem host; telnet to the port number of the problem application on the problem host.

If the ping to the loopback address yields no response, then either the network adapter is defective or the TCP/IP driver is not correctly installed. Note, however, that in certain operating systems, such as UNIX, the loopback interface may function even when the physical interface to the network is defective! If the problem host does not answer a ping from another station in the same subnetwork, the sending host itself must first be tested for a functioning network connection. Then the IP address of the problem host should be verified.

If communication is successful within the subnetwork, the next step is to test the host's availability across a router. Begin by sending a ping from the problem host to the router. If the router does not answer, then the IP address and subnet mask of the problem host must be verified and the router's IP address and configuration must be checked. In order to forward an IP packet, the router must be aware of the destination network (Telnet to the router and retrieve IP route). If no specific route is configured for the network in question, then at least a default route (also called "default gateway") must be configured that leads to the destination network. Note: the router may also be configured to ignore pings (ICMP Type 0 or Echo Request packets) in order to prevent extra traffic due to such tests. If this is the case, the ping will yield no response even if the router is operational and its routing tables are correct.

If the ping test is successful between the problem host and the router, the next step is to test the connection from the problem host to hosts in neighboring networks that are connected through the router. Test destinations are systematically chosen in successively more remote networks until a network or router is identified to which a connection is no longer possible. The traceroute command (tracert in Windows 95 or NT) can be used to trace the packet's path and identify where the route breaks down. The traceroute program uses the ICMP Echo command to send a packet to the destination and back again. In addition to the response time, this command also counts the number of intermediate stations (hops) through which the packet is routed. Each "hop" reduces the packet's Time to Live (TTL) counter by one. Traceroute starts with sending an ICMP echo command using a TTL value of 1. Because the TTL is decremented by every router along the transmission path, this packet only reaches the first router, which decrements the TTL to zero, discards the packet, and sends back the ICMP message "Timeout Exceeded". The traceroute program notes the source address of this message and the delay time, then sends another packet, this time with a TTL of two. The first router reduces the TTL to one as it forwards the packet, and this time the second router sets the TTL to zero and returns a Timeout Exceeded message. This process continues, allowing the traceroute program to record a list of all routers along the path to the packet's destination address. Finally, when a packet with a sufficient TTL reaches the destination, the host responds with an "Unreachable Port" message, and the traceroute procedure is finished. Note, however, that there are routers that do not respond in this way to traceroute packets! In rare cases traceroute may display only a partial path. In addition, depending on the route the ICMP Echo commands are taking, results may differ. Because the traceroute function cannot detect route changes, the traceroute command should be used at least three times in a row to obtain reliable results.

If the traceroute test is successful, then the address resolution must be tested by sending a ping to the problem host using its host and domain name rather than its numeric IP address. If the host does not respond, its configuration and the DNS server's entries must be inspected for correct name/IP address mapping. (A ping to the name server itself indicates whether it is running and connected to the network.) Then a ping by name can be performed in the opposite direction, from the problem host to other hosts within the local subnetwork and in other subnets.

If the description of the symptoms indicates intermittent or periodical interruptions in availability, then the cause is often found in an overloaded network or destination host. Here again the traceroute command can be used to determine whether the destination itself is unavailable or whether the data packets are being lost in an overloaded transit network. Another frequent cause of intermittent availability is another station using the same IP address as the destination host. So long as the other station is active, no IP connection to the actual owner of the IP address can be established. Such duplicate IP addresses can be quickly identified using a protocol analyzer, which sends ARP (Address Resolution Protocol) messages and monitors the resulting ARP responses. If an ARP request evokes two ARP reply packets with different hardware addresses, then the two stations with these addresses are using the same IP address. Finally, if the intermittent connection problems are observed in conjunction with frequent TCP connection timeouts, this may indicate a defective network component such as a bridge or router. In normal operation, less than one percent of network connections should be lost due to TCP timeouts. A protocol analyzer can be used to generate exact statistics on the number of TCP connection timeouts. If an IP connection between two hosts is possible, but certain applications are still unable to communicate over it, then the cause can usually be found in the router access tables. These are lists in which the network administrator specifies the permitted services (by port number). TCP and UDP packets addressed to other ports are blocked. Thus Telnet sessions may be possible while all other network services are blocked between two hosts. For this reason, the next troubleshooting step, if no problems are found at the IP level, is to test the TCP layer connection and the availability of the port addresses that correspond to the desired applications. The simplest way to determine whether a TCP connection can be established is to attempt a Telnet session with the problem host. Even if the Telnet program reports an error such as:

telnet: Unable to connect to remote host

telnet: Connection refused

this is sufficient indication that the TCP/IP stack is working. If a Telnet connection is possible, then at least the corresponding TCP port on the host is available. This is a more reliable indication than the ping command because ping packets can be filtered out along the path between the hosts, and in any case do not indicate the availability of specific applications.

Another common problem in IP networks is "local routing". This phenomenon occurs when a switch is connected to a router. In order to reach a segment that is connected to the same switch, a packet first has to be switched to the router, is routed within the router, and then transferred through the same switch again to the destination segment. Obviously this process doubles the number of packets passed through the switch and consumes buffer and CPU resources in the router. If a protocol analyzer is placed between the switch and the router, the local routing phenomenon can easily be detected by filtering on a station pair and looking for packets with identical TCP sequence numbers. If one of those packets contains the router address as destination address and the second one the router address as source address, and if the TTL value of packet two is decremented by one, a local routed communication path is found.

Another scenario that can cause local routing is when a local segment has two different active subnets at the same time. In this case the router will forward the frames to the same segment, again causing unnecessary resource consumption within the router.

16.10.3 Symptoms and Causes: Internet Protocols

This section lists the typical causes of trouble in IP networks, grouped by the symptoms observed.

Symptom: Ping from Problem Host to Loopback Address 127.0.0.1 Fails

Cause (1):   TCP/IP driver or interface card software is not installed properly.
Cause (2):   Faulty network interface.

Symptom: Ping to Problem Host from a Node in the Same Subnet Fails

Cause (1):   Problem host not connected to the network.
Cause (2):   Incorrectly configured interface card.
Cause (3):   Wrong IP address; incorrect subnet mask.

Symptom: Ping from Problem Host to a Host in the Same Subnet Fails

Cause (1):   Problem host not connected to the network.
Cause (2):   Destination node not active.
Cause (3):   Incorrect IP destination address used in the ping command.

Symptom: Ping from Problem Host to Default Router Fails

Cause (1):   Problem host not connected to the network.
Cause (2):   IP address or subnet mask of the problem host is incorrect.
Cause (3):   Incorrect IP address of the router used in the ping command.
Cause (4):   Incorrectly configured default route.
Cause (5):   Inactive router port.
Cause (6):   DHCP problem. DHCP server used to manage fixed addresses (a given IP address is always assigned to the same MAC address) and station moved to a different segment. The DHCP server assigns old IP address even though the address is not valid in the new subnet.

**Symptom: Ping from Problem Host to Host
Outside the Local Subnet Fails**

Cause (1):   Incorrectly configured default gateway on the router.
Cause (2):   No default gateway configured on the router.
Cause (3):   Remote host inactive.
Cause (4):   Router port to destination subnet inactive.
Cause (5):   Router access list incomplete; does not reflect route updates.
Cause (6):   Incorrecmt router filter activated.

Symptom: Ping to Problem Host by Name Fails

Cause (1):   Problem host not connected to the network.
Cause (2):   The host name ↔ IP address mapping at the problem host
is incorrect.
Cause (3):   The IP address of the DNS server is incorrectly configured.
Cause (4):   DNS server is inactive.
Cause (5):   The table of the host sending the ping contains incorrect
host name ↔ IP address mapping.

**Symptom: Ping by Name from Problem Host to Host
in the Same Subnet Fails**

Cause (1):   Incorrect host/domain name entered in the ping command.
Cause (2):   Remote host not active.
Cause (3):   IP address of the DNS server incorrectly configured
on the problem host.
Cause (4):   DNS server inactive.
Cause (5):   The table of the problem host contains incorrect
host name ↔ IP address mapping for the host sending the ping.

**Symptom: Ping by Name to a Host Outside the Local Subnet
from the Problem Host Fails**

Cause (1):   Incorrect host name entered in the ping command.
Cause (2):   Remote host not active.
Cause (3):   IP address of the DNS server incorrectly configured
on the problem host.
Cause (4):   DNS server inactive.
Cause (5):   The table of the problem host contains incorrect
host name ↔ IP address mapping for the remote host.
Cause (6):   Incorrect IP address of default route in the router table.

Symptom: Intermittent Loss of Connection

Cause (1):   Overloaded destination network or host.

Cause (2):   Duplicate IP address: another node is using the destination's
IP address.

Cause (3):   TCP connections timing out (due to bridge or router problems,
for example).

Cause (4):   Mixture of dynamic (DHCP based) and static assigned IP addresses.

Symptom: IP Connection Working but Application not Available

Cause (1):   Router access list configured to block the application port.

Cause (2):   Application not active.

Symptom: Diskless Stations Unable to Boot

Cause (1):   Router blocking UDP broadcast forwarding: BOOTP broadcasts
not transmitted.

Cause (2):   Incorrectly configured router filter blocking BOOTP packets.

Symptom: Generally Low TCP/IP Performance

Cause (1):   Poorly configured DNS client: client waits until the first DNS
request times out before trying a second DNS server.

Cause (2):   DNS server not configured for reverse lookup; reverse lookup
requests not being handled.

Cause (3):   DNS table incomplete: does not contain IP address <> name
mappings for all hosts.

Cause (4):   Local routing. A switch is connected to a router. In order to reach
a segment that is connected to the same switch, a packet first has
to be switched to the router, is routed within the router, and then
transferred through the same switch again to the destination
segment. The number of packets that are being passed through the
switch are doubled and additional buffer and CPU resources in
the router are consumed.

Cause (5):   Overloaded networks in the path the TCP connection is using.

Symptom: Excessive TCP Retransmissions

Cause (1):   Sent TCP packet or a returning acknowledgement packet lost by
an overloaded switch or router.

Cause (2):   Packet corrupted during the transmission contains a CRC error.

Cause (3):   TCP data corrupted, shows a TCP checksum error.

Cause (4):   Fragment of a fragmented TCP packet lost or corrupted.

Cause (5):   Buffer overflow at the receiver.

Cause (6):   Acknowledgement for a TCP packet sequence is too slow and
sender retransmits.

Symptom: TCP Window Size too Small

Cause (1): Default IP MTU (Maximum Transfer Unit) changed by user.
Cause (2): IP MTU and receive TCP buffer size changed by Internet optimizing application.

Symptom: TCP Window Size Drops Below Maximum

Cause: Application not loading data off the TCP stack fast enough. Likely causes are performance problems on the server or the client. (If the node is a printer, however, this is a normal scenario.)

Symptom: TCP Window Size Constant, Slow Acknowledgement Packets

Cause (1): Overloaded network, routers, or switches.
Cause (2): Dial-up or WAN connection overloaded.

Symptom: TCP Window Size too Large

Cause: In some cases a large TCP window size in combination with a small amount of available interface memory and a slow hard drive can cause performance problems. Communication then has to stop until the TCP segment (for example, a large 64 Kbyte TCP segment) is stored and the data transfer process can resume.

Symptom: OSPF Routing Problems

Cause (1): The Hello and Dead timers of the various routers in the network not coordinated.
Cause (2): IGRP or RIP route distribution incorrectly configured in OSPF.
Cause (3): Incorrectly configured virtual link.
Cause (4): No router port assigned an IP address (OSPF uses IP address as ID).

Symptom: RIP Problems

Cause (1): Incorrect routing tables because of routing information retrieved from wrong interface or protocol.
Cause (2): Incorrect router filter configuration.
Cause (3): Subnet masks of router and host do not match.

The following listing summarizes the most frequent error sources for problems in TCP/IP environments (in alphabetical order):

- Application is not active
- Destination host is not active
- DNS server is not active
- DNS server not configured for reverse lookup. Reverse lookup request cannot be handled
- DNS table incomplete, does not contain IP   domain name mappings for all hosts
- Duplicate IP address: a second node is using the destination host's IP address
- Faulty network interface
- Host name or IP address configuration of problem host is incorrect
- Inactive router port
- Incorrect destination IP address in the ping command
- Incorrect IP address or subnet address mask on problem host
- Incorrect router filter activated
- Incorrect routing tables due to routing information retrieved from wrong interface or protocol
- Incorrect terminal settings
- Incorrect user ID or password
- Incorrectly configured default gateway on the router
- Incorrectly configured interface card
- Incorrectly configured router filter blocking BOOTP frames
- Incorrectly configured virtual links
- IP address of the default route in the router table is incorrect
- IP address of the DNS server is incorrectly configured on the problem host
- IP address or subnet mask of the problem host is incorrect
- No default gateway configured on the router
- No router port has an IP address assigned (OSPF uses IP address as ID)
- Overloaded destination network or host
- Poorly configured DNS client: client waits until the first DNS request times out before trying a second DNS server
- Problem host not connected to the network
- Remote host not reachable via network
- Route distribution of IGRP or RIP is incorrectly configured in OSPF

Figure 16.22a The most common error causes in IP networks

- Router is blocking UDP broadcast forwarding: BOOTP broadcasts cannot be transmitted .
- Router port to destination subnet inactive
- Subnet masks of router and host do not match
- TCP connections timing out (due to bridge or router problems, for example)
- TCP/IP software or interface card driver is not installed properly
- The Hello and Dead timers of the various routers in the network are not coordinated
- The hosts table on the host sending the ping contains an incorrect entry for the problem host (incorrect host name   IP address mapping)
- The hosts table on the problem host contains an incorrect entry for the host sending the ping (incorrect host name   IP address mapping)
- Router access list incomplete: does not contain route updates
- Router access list is configured to block the application port

Figure 16.22b The most common error causes in IP networks

Network Services and Applications

17

"Become a student of change. It is the only thing that will remain constant."

ANTHONY J. D'ANGELO

17.1   E-Mail

E-mail systems, like most network services, are based on a client–server principle. Mail servers—properly known as Message Transfer Agents or MTAs—spool, manage, and transport the messages. E-mail clients, called Mail User Agents or MUAs, provide the interface to the user. MUAs exchange incoming and outgoing messages with the nearest MTA. A number of transport protocols are used for mail communication between e-mail servers and clients, and between one mail server and another. Usually MTAs transfer mail to one another using the classic Simple Mail Transfer Protocol (SMTP, RFC 821). This protocol has been in use since its adoption in 1982, and has gained widespread popularity due to its simplicity and robustness.

Naturally SMTP has limitations, and these have become more apparent as the use of the protocol has increased. For example, because SMTP was developed to transport text messages, it is unable to process any data format except 7-bit ASCII text. The growing demand not just for text messaging, but for asynchronous transfer of all kinds of data makes SMTP an unsatisfactory solution. Another problem is the increasing popularity of X.400 messaging systems. X.400 includes mechanisms to transport non-text messages, so it is difficult if not impossible to interconnect X.400 and SMTP networks. X.400 messages with non-text contents therefore have been rejected at SMTP/X.400 gateways.

In the early nineties it became clear that these major limitations of SMTP would have to be overcome. For this reason, an extension was adopted in 1993, called Multipurpose Internet Mail Extensions (MIME), RFC 1522. MIME defined extensions to the SMTP header—a "content type" header—that managed the problems mentioned previously without creating incompatibilities with existing RFC 821 SMTP implementations. MIME mechanisms are now widely used and have also been incorporated in the Hypertext Transfer Protocol (HTTP) on which the

WWW service is based. Furthermore, in the Secure MIME (S/MIME) specification two additional MIME content types were defined to support the transport of encrypted and digitally signed e-mail messages. With these extensions, SMTP forms the base for a powerful, universal messaging service.

Other protocols besides SMTP are used to transfer messages between mail servers and mail clients. The choice of protocol depends in part on the type of network connection between the client and the server. With dial-up network access (that is, a client dials up a connection to the server, exchanges mail messages, and clears down the connection) the most common protocol is currently Version 3 of the Post Office Protocol (POP3, RFC 1939). For on-line mail access, in which the mail client is connected with the server during the entire mail session and all messages are stored on the server's storage media, POP3 is not ideal and is increasingly being supplanted by the more modern Internet Message Access Protocol (IMAP-4), RFC 1730. As an alternative to dedicated mail protocols, LAN-based intranets often implement messaging services over LAN file system protocols—such as NFS (UNIX) or SMF (Novell) with the corresponding user interface programs (such as MAPI, VIM, AOCE), or with a WWW-based front end over the HTTP protocol (or S-HTTP or SSL). Mailbox information is usually managed and structured by means of the Lightweight Directory Access Protocol (LDAP), a simplified variant of the more complex X.500 protocol.

17.1.1   Simple Mail Transfer Protocol (SMTP, RFC 821)

As the name implies, SMTP is a simplified version of an earlier mail transport scheme, the Mail Transfer Protocol (MTP). As a matter of fact, the SMTP mechanism is surprisingly simple. Messages are transferred in three steps. The sender initiates the process by transmitting a MAIL command with the sender's address:

MAIL FROM:<othmar_kyas@agilent.com> <CRLF>

(where <CRLF> stands for a new line character: Carriage Return and Line Feed). This message informs the receiver that a mail transfer is ready to begin and the input buffer can be cleared. If the receiver is ready, it responds to the MAIL command with:

250 OK <CRLF>

In the second step, the sender provides the name of the intended recipient:

RCPT TO:<michael_meier@hp.com> <CRLF>

If the destination address is known, the receiving MTA acknowledges this command with:

220 OK <CRLF>

Otherwise, if the recipient is not known on the receiving server, it answers:

550 Failure reply <CRLF>

This RCPT TO exchange may be repeated several times if the message is to be delivered to more than one recipient. In the third step, the sender announces the actual message by means of the DATA command:

DATA <CRLF>

The response is:

354 Intermediate reply <CRLF>

after which all characters received are treated as the message (including both the header and the body of the message). A line containing only a period indicates the end of the data stream:

<CRLF>.<CRLF>

The receiving SMTP server acknowledges this by replying:

250 OK <CLRF>

Two further commands are used to open and close communication channels between two SMTP hosts:

HELO <domain name><CLRF>

and :

QUIT <CLRF>

The SMTP server responds to the HELO command with its own domain name:

250 <domain name> <CLRF>

The following example shows a complete SMTP session:

HELO mail.agilent.com
250 mail.agilent.com

MAIL FROM:<Smith@agilent.com>
250 OK

RCPT TO:<Jones@hp.com>
250 OK

RCPT TO:<Green@hp.com>
550 No such user here

RCPT TO:<Brown@hp.com>
250 OK

DATA
354 Start mail input; end with <CRLF>.<CRLF>

Test message – Test message – Test message. <CRLF>.<CRLF>
250 OK

QUIT
221 mail.agilent.com Service closing transmission channel

Figure 17.1 lists all the SMTP commands; Figure 17.2 the response codes.

HELLO (HELO) Identification of the sender-SMTP to the receiver-SMTP	VERIFY (VRFY) This command asks the receiver to confirm that the argument identifies a user.
MAIL (MAIL) Initiation of a mail transaction	EXPAND (EXPN) This command asks the receiver to confirm that the argument identifies a mailing list, and if so, to return the membership of that list.
RECIPIENT (RCPT) Identification of the recipient of the mail data	
DATA (DATA) Following this command mail data is being transmitted	HELP (HELP) This command causes the receiver to send helpful information to the sender of the HELP command
SEND (SEND) Initiation of mail transaction to terminal	NOOP (NOOP) Receiver to reply with OK
SEND OR MAIL (SOML) Initiation of mail transaction to terminal or mailbox	QUIT (QUIT) Receiver to reply with OK and to close the transmission channel.
SEND AND MAIL (SAML) Initiation of mail transaction to terminal and mailbox	
RESET (RSET) Abortion of current mail transaction	TURN (TURN) Receiver to either send an OK reply and then take on the role of the sender-SMTP, or to send a refusal reply and retain the role of the receiver-SMTP.

Figure 17.1 SMTP commands (RFC 821)

211	System status, or system help reply
214	Help message
220	<domain> Service ready
221	<domain> Service closing transmission channel
250	Requested mail action okay, completed
251	User not local; will forward to <forward-path>
354	Start mail input; end with <CRLF>.<CRLF>
421	<domain> Service not available, closing transmission channel
450	Requested mail action not taken: mailbox unavailable
451	Requested action aborted: local error in processing
452	Requested action not taken: insufficient system storage
500	Syntax error, command unrecognized
501	Syntax error in parameters or arguments
502	Command not implemented
503	Bad sequence of commands
504	Command parameter not implemented
550	Requested action not taken: mailbox unavailable
551	User not local; please try <forward-path>
552	Requested mail action aborted: exceeded storage allocation
553	Requested action not taken: mailbox name not allowed
554	Transaction failed

Figure 17.2 SMTP response codes (RFC 821)

The most commonly used software for implementing an SMTP MTA is the UNIX application *sendmail*. This program runs on the mail server as a continually active SMTP daemon "smtpd", receiving and sending e-mail.

From the point of view of communication security, one drawback of SMTP is that the entire communication session takes place in plain 7-bit ASCII text. Another is that no mechanism is provided for verification of the sender's identification: thus any SMTP client can introduce itself with a fraudulent or non-existent address (MAIL FROM:<fake@nobrain.cracker.com>, for example). Reliable identification of e-mail messages is only provided by encryption and digital signature techniques, such as used in Privacy Enhanced Mail (PEM) or S-MIME.

17.1.2   Multipurpose Internet Mail Extensions (MIME, RFC 1521)

The MIME extensions overcome SMTP's restriction to plain 7-bit ASCII text by introducing special MIME headers to supplement the standard mail headers. In addition to the MIME version header, a "content-type" header field is defined with seven possible values:

- Text   for text information in various character sets
- Multipart   for combining several message parts, which may be of different content types, into a single message
- Application   for any kind of binary data
- Message   for encapsulating other mail messages
- Image   for transmitting still pictures
- Audio   for audio or voice data
- Video   for video data

Another special header field, the Content-Transfer-Encoding field, can contain specialized information about the way in which the data has been encoded for SMTP transfer. Finally, the Content-ID and Content-Description header fields can be used to identify more specifically the contents of the message body.

The specific values that are defined for the Content-Type header field are listed in a global document that is maintained centrally by IANA, the Internet Assigned Numbers Authority (ftp://ftp.isi.edu/in-notes/iana/assignments/media-types/media-types). Every new type or subtype must be submitted through a defined registration procedure (RFC 2048) in order to be added to this worldwide register.

The MIME-Version Header Field

Every MIME-compatible message must contain a MIME-version header field that indicates the version of MIME implemented by the sender:

MIME-version: 1.0

The Content-Type Header Field

The Content-Type header field informs the receiving software of the type of information contained in the message so that it can be presented with an appropriate application, for example. The specified content type is divided into a general type, such as text, image, or audio; and a subtype, such as plain or html in the case of text, or jpeg or gif for an image. The header line:

Content-Type: image/xyz

allows a MIME-compatible e-mail client to determine that the data received represents an image file, whether or not it recognizes the "xyz" format. This information can be used to decide whether it is worthwhile to display the raw data on the screen even if the data format is not supported. For example, it may be a good idea to display unknown subtypes of "text", but not of the "image" or "audio" content types. Private content subtypes not registered with IANA may be used provided they begin with "x-", as in "Content-Type: application/x-pkcs10".

Content-Type: Text

The text content type is used to indicate text that can be displayed without specialized software. Certain formatted text documents may be included for which special application software may offer an improved display, but is not strictly necessary in order for the contents to be understood.

Content-Type: Multipart

Multipart messages consist of several concatenated message body parts. A mandatory parameter in the Content-Type: Multipart header field defines the boundary marker that separates the individual parts. The parts may be of the same type or of different types. The following four subtypes are defined for the multipart type:

- Mixed   for message body parts of different types
- Alternative   for alternative representations of the same content (such as plain and HTML-formatted text, for example)
- Parallel   for message body parts to be presented simultaneously
- Digest   for multipart messages in which each part consists of a mail message

Content-Type: Message

The "message" content type is itself an e-mail message. The subtype "partial" can be used to permit fragmented encapsulation of messages in order to overcome the length restrictions of certain gateways.

Content-Type: Image

Image data require special software and/or hardware for presentation (graphic display adapter, printer, fax machine). Originally, two subtypes were defined:

jpeg and gif. Now many other popular image formats have been added including x-windowdump, tiff, x-rgb, etc.

Content-Type: Audio

Data of the content type "audio" (subtypes: x-aiff, x-wav, etc.) require an audio player device for presentation, such as a loudspeaker or telephone.

Content-Type: Video

Video messages also require special software and/or hardware for presentation of the moving-picture content. Common subtypes include quicktime, mpeg, and x-msvideo.

Content-Type: Application

The application content type includes all kinds of binary data that are not covered by any of the content types listed here. If the data cannot be described in more detail, the primary subtype "octet-stream" is used. Today a great number of subtypes are defined, including msword, postscript, zip, and tar.

If no content type is indicated, the default type:

Content-Type: text/plain; charset=us-ascii

is assumed.

Encoding of Data Other Than 7-Bit ASCII

Because the SMTP specification (RFC 821) is limited to 7-bit US-ASCII messages with a maximum line length of 1,000 characters, MIME defines not only other data types but also an encoding scheme to convert all kinds of binary data into an SMTP-compatible format. The data to be encoded can be roughly divided into two kinds:

- Text-based data that does not fall within the 7-bit US-ASCII character set
- Binary data

Two encoding mechanisms have been chosen: quoted-printable and base64. The type of encoding used in a given message is indicated in the Content-Transfer-Encoding header field:

Content-Transfer-Encoding: quoted-printable
                                      base64
                                      8bit
                                      7bit
                                      binary

The values *8bit*, *7bit*, and *binary* indicate that no encoding was performed on the data. At the present time, 8-bit and binary data cannot be sent over SMTP systems without other encoding. These field values have nonetheless been defined for use by future mail systems.

17.1.3 S/MIME – Secure Multipurpose Internet Mail Extensions

An extension to the MIME specification, S/MIME defines two new content types designed to allow the use of digital signatures and encryption mechanisms in MIME messages. The cryptography technique is described in PKCS #7. The contents of MIME-compatible messages can be digitally signed, encrypted, or both. S/MIME is undergoing development by an IETF working group; PKCS #7 is a specification of RSA Security, Inc.

17.1.4 Privacy Enhanced Mail (PEM)

PEM is a proposed Internet standard for the encryption of SMTP messages (RFCs 1421 through 1424). Both RSA (public key encryption implementation by Rivest, Shamir, Adleman) public key encryption and symmetrical Data Encryption Standard (DES) are specified as encryption techniques. Data is first encrypted using the DES algorithm and a randomly generated DES key. The key is then encrypted using the RSA algorithm and the addressee's public key, and sent together with the DES-encrypted data. The advantage of this method is that only a small part of the message, namely the DES key, needs to be encrypted using the CPU-intensive RSA algorithm. The DES algorithm used to encrypt the actual message contents is quicker. Before the encrypted data can be sent by SMTP, it must be converted to 7-bit ASCII by a MIME content transfer encoding method.

17.1.5 E-Mail Standards

RFC 821	Simple Mail Transfer Protocol
RFC 822	Internet Mail Header Format
RFC 1123	Internet Host Requirements
RFC 1869	SMTP Service Extensions
RFC 1891	SMTP Delivery Status Notifications
RFC 1892	Multipart/Report
RFC 1893	Mail System Status Codes
RFC 1894	Delivery Status Notification

RFC 1985	SMTP Service Extension for Remote Message Queue Starting
RFC 2034	SMTP Service Extension for Returning Enhanced Error Codes
RFC 2045	MIME
RFC 2476	Message Submission
RFC 2554	SMTP Service Extension for Authentication
RFC 1421 – 1424	Privacy Enhanced Mail (PEM)
RFC 1939	Post Office Protocol 3 (POP3)
RFC 1730	Internet Message Access Protocol (IMAP-4)
RFC 1777	Lightweight Directory Access Protocol (LDAP)

17.1.6   Troubleshooting E-Mail

The first step in diagnosing e-mail problems is to test the connection to the mail server. The best way to do this is to establish a telnet connection to port 25 on the mail server (a ping may be used to test the host's IP address, but cannot determine whether an MTA is active on port 25):

telnet 15.70.23.112 25

Once the connection to port 25 has been successfully established, a SMTP session can be performed:

SMTP Commands	Expected Response	Description
HELO	250 OK	Initiates the conversation
MAIL FROM: *<user@domain.tld>*	250 OK	Identifies the sender
RCPT TO: *<user@domain.tld>*	250 OK	Identifies the recipient of the mail message
DATA	354 Send Data	Announces message data
[a single period]	250 OK	Marks the end of the message data
QUIT	221	Closes the session

Telnet can also be used in the same way to test the POP3 and IMAP protocols by connecting to the corresponding port addresses:

Protocol	Port
SMTP	25
HTTP	80
NNTP	119
LDAP	389
POP3	110
IMAP4	143

POP3 Commands	Expected Response	Description
USER *Account name*	+OK	Initiates the authentication process
PASS *Password*	+OK	Specifies the password for the POP3 account
LIST	+OK	Lists the messages in the user's mailbox
RETR *Message No.*	*The message text*	Retrieves the text of the specified message
DELE *Message No.*	+OK	Deletes the specified message
QUIT	+OK	Closes the session

All commands issued to an IMAP4 server must be prefixed with a command identifier. This identifier can be used by the client to keep track of command and response pairs. For example, when the IMAP client sends:

local SELECT inbox

the server responds with:

local OK

IMAP4 Commands	Expected Response	Description
LOGIN *Accountname Password*	OK LOGIN	Logs on to the mailbox
SELECT *folder*	*Folder mode* & OK SELECT	Selects a folder to view
FETCH *Message No.*	*Message text* & OK FETCH	Retrieves the specified message
STORE *Message Flags* *flag*	OK STORE	Marks a message for deletion or as read/unread
EXPUNGE	OK	Deletes all marked messages
LOGOUT	OK	Closes the session

Problems can usually be quickly traced by recording and decoding these communication processes with a protocol analyzer. The causes are usually to be found at the TCP/IP level in the configuration or availability of the server, or in the client configuration.

17.2   Internet News

The Internet service "news" consists of a multitude of discussion forums, comparable to mailing lists, which are hierarchically organized by topic. The distribution and function of news differs significantly from e-mail and mailing lists. Internet news articles, posted by users, are not automatically delivered to other users, but are stored on central news servers. To read news, users must have access to such a server. The format in which the articles are stored is specially adapted to the requirements of discussion forums, and for a long time required the use of special presentation programs called news readers. Today, complete news reader capabilities are standard equipment in Web browsers. News servers exchange new articles posted by users at regular intervals. This exchange takes place using the Network News Transfer Protocol (NNTP), with the reserved TCP port 119. A few sites, such as former Usenet nodes, still use the UUCP protocol to exchange news.

17.2.1 The Network News Transfer Protocol (NNTP, RFC 977)

The NNTP protocol defines the organization of the news service, both for server–server and for client–server communication. Client–server news communication involves the following functions:

- Retrieval: sending requested news articles to clients
- Posting: accepting new articles from clients

Furthermore, NNTP also governs replication, that is, the distribution of new articles to all other servers, and provides a reliable, interactive communication mechanism for this purpose. Other server tasks are indexing and linking related articles, monitoring their age, and deleting them when obsolete.

Every NNTP session includes the following seven steps:

- CONNECTION
- GREETING
- CAPABILITIES DISCOVERY
- AUTHENTICATION
- NEWS TRANSFER
- CONCLUSION
- DISCONNECTION

The NNTP server listens on TCP port 119 and responds to client requests with the following three-digit response codes. The first digit indicates whether the operation was successful or not, or whether the preceding command was carried out:

1xx Informative message
2xx Command OK
3xx Command OK, awaiting further commands
4xx Command was correct but could not be executed
5xx Command incorrect, unavailable, or not implemented

The second digit of the response code indicates which function the code refers to:

x0x   Connection, setup, and miscellaneous messages

x1x   Newsgroup selection

x2x   Article selection

x3x   Distribution functions

x4x   Posting

x8x   Nonstandard (private implementation) extensions

Greeting

On requesting the connection to the server's TCP port 119, the client does not need to send any command, but simply waits for the server's first response code, the greeting. This code indicates how the client may proceed. The NNTP server greets the client with code 200 if the client is authorized to post new articles using the POST command, or with 201 if posting is not allowed. The response code 205 indicates that further authentication is required before any other action, and code 502 (service unavailable) indicates that the client is not authorized to interact with the server at all. In all other cases, the server responds with code 400 (service temporarily unavailable). Figure 17.3 lists the NNTP greetings:

200	Hello, you can post
201	Hello, you can't post
205	Authentication required
400	Service temporarily unavailable
502	Service unavailable

Figure 17.3 Response codes during the NNTP greeting phase

Optionally, the client may use the command MODE READER to inform the server that it only wants access to read existing news. The server again responds with the appropriate code. During the greeting phase the client can also issue the command LIST EXTENSIONS. This is a request to the server to list its implemented extensions to the NNTP protocol. If no extensions are supported, the server returns code 503 (program error, function not performed). Otherwise it can respond with 205 (authentication required) and a list of extensions consisting of keywords and the associated parameters.

Authentication

If the server has requested authentication from the client, the client must answer with the command AUTHINFO SIMPLE. If the server accepts this, it responds with code 350 (continue with authorization sequence). The client must send its user name and password, to which the server responds with code 250 (authorization accepted). Then the client can continue with whatever command was interrupted by the authentication request (see Figure 17.4).

250	Authorization accepted
350	Continue with authorization sequence
450	Authorization required for this command
452	Authorization rejected
501	Command not supported or Command syntax error
502	Program error, function not performed

Figure 17.4 Response codes during the authentication phase

Retrieval of News Articles

The news articles stored on news servers can be identified by two parameters: the message ID and the article number. The message ID is an identification string that is unique in the entire network. The article number is formed locally on the news server from the newsgroup name and the number of the article within the newsgroup. The article number is unique on the local news server, but need not be unique in the network. Because one message may be posted to several newsgroups, it is possible for several article numbers from different newsgroups to point to the same article. In order to retrieve an article, the client must first set the "article pointer" to the desired article. Then the pointer can be used to retrieve the article.

17.2.2 NNTP Standards

RFC 977   NNTP protocol
RFC 1036   News article format

17.2.3 Troubleshooting News

The first step in diagnosing problems with the news service is to test the TCP connection to the news server. The easiest way to do so is by using Telnet to connect to port 119 of the corresponding host:

telnet 15.70.23.112 119

If the news server responds on port 119, a NNTP session can be carried out step by step. There are two modes of NNTP access: authenticated and anonymous. Authentication requires the first two commands listed below:

NNTP Commands	Expected Response	Description
AUTHINFO USER *Username*	381 More Info Needed	Supplies authentication information
AUTHINFO PASS *Password*	281 Accepted	Supplies password for authentication
LIST	*List of groups*	Lists all available groups
GROUP *Group*	*Group specifications*	Sets the current group
ARTICLE *Article No.*	*Article text*	Retrieves the specified article in the current group
QUIT	205	Closes the session

17.3   The File Transfer Protocol (FTP)

FTP is one of the oldest network service protocols. It is used to transfer data of any kind—text, image, sound, video, executable programs, etc. The FTP client, the system initiating a connection, controls the complete procedure. The client must have access authorization to the FTP server, however, which is established by checking user ID and password information during the FTP connection setup. FTP is based on the TCP transport protocol and uses two simultaneous TCP connections to transfer files (see Figure 17.5). The client begins by establishing a control connection from any TCP port to the server's port 21. The actual file transfer takes place over a second connection initiated by the server. This data connection is opened from the server's TCP port 20, the standard FTP data port, to a port specified by the client using the PORT command. The data requested by the client flows over this connection in the format used by the Telnet protocol, described in the Network Virtual Terminal (NVT) specification.

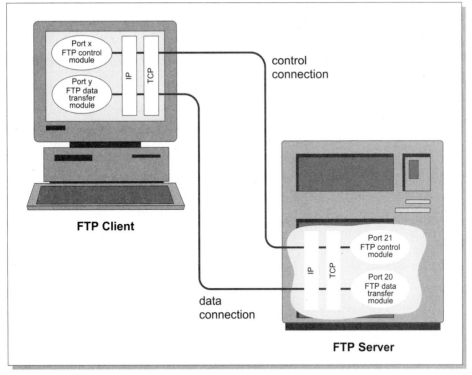

Figure 17.5 The FTP protocol: control and data connections

For each file transfer another data connection is opened. Due to a peculiarity of the TCP protocol, a different client port address is used each time.

dir / ls	display directory / display listing
cd / pwd	change directory / print working directory
bin / ascii	binary / ascii transfer mode
hash	display transfer process using the # sign
get <file>	retrieve file

Figure 17.6 The most important FTP commands

The IETF "FTPEXT" working group is currently coordinating proposed extensions to FTP.

17.3.1   FTP Standards

RFC 959   File Transfer Protocol (FTP). The basic FTP definition (from 1985). All FTP software must comply with this document. Other requests for comments (RFCs) may extend or clarify this document.

RFC 1123   Requirements for Internet Hosts—Application and Support. This RFC defines and discusses the requirements for Internet host software. It covers the application and support protocols; its companion, RFC-1122, covers the communication protocol layers: link layer, IP layer, and transport layer.

RFC 1639   FTP Operation Over Big Address Records (FOOBAR). Description of the convention for specifying address families other than the default Internet address family in FTP commands and replies.

RFC 2228   FTP Security Extensions

RFC 2389   Feature Negotiation Mechanism for the File Transfer Protocol. Amendment of the File Transfer Protocol (FTP). Two new commands (FEAT, OPTS).

RFC 2428   FTP Extensions for IPv6 and NATs

RFC 2577   FTP Security Considerations. Provides a proxy mechanism to decrease traffic load on the network.

RFC 2640   Internationalization of the File Transfer Protocol. Support for multiple character sets.

17.3.2   Troubleshooting FTP

The most frequent sources of problems with FTP are user errors from logging in and connection timeouts. Typical login errors are incorrect (or mistyped) user names, IP addresses or passwords, non-existent or deleted accounts, and missing or modified access privileges. After a successful login, connection timeouts can occur when TCP idle timers expire due to system overload (on the server or client end) or high network loads. Large server directories with thousands of entries may lead to timeouts after a LIST command. The most common symptoms and their causes are listed in Section 17.11.

17.4   Trivial File Transfer Protocol (TFTP)

TFTP is a simplified version of FTP with no authentication mechanisms. It is used for diskless workstations, local software updates, or applications that do not require the full capabilities offered by FTP. Because TFTP does not claim to offer reliable service, it uses UDP as the transport protocol rather than TCP. The resulting program code for TFTP implementations is thus much smaller than for FTP.

17.5   Telnet

Telnet is an application that originated in the UNIX world to allow interactive use of remote computers across data networks: the Telnet client application on the local computer functions as a remote terminal for the server host. Its remote control capabilities are limited to programs with a text-based user interface, however, because the Telnet protocol only transmits ASCII characters. In the Internet this restriction is usually unimportant because the available bandwidth is generally not sufficient for graphical user interface based remote control (such as X Window sessions). Telnet programs are available for practically all computer platforms and operating systems, and are often incorporated in the capabilities of Web browsers.

When the Telnet application has been started and the Internet address of the desired remote system entered, the Telnet program begins a TCP connection to the remote host and invokes its login routine. When the user name and password have been approved, the Telnet session is open. (The remote system that pro- vides a service, such as remote access, is generally called the server; the computer

```
telnet> ?
Commands may be abbreviated.  Commands are:
close      close current connection
display    display operating parameters
mode       try to enter line-by-line or character-at-a-time mode
open       connect to a site
quit       exit telnet
send       transmit special characters ('send ?' for more)
set        set operating parameters ('set ?' for more)
status     print status information
toggle     toggle operating parameters ('toggle ?' for more)
z          suspend telnet
?          print help information
```

Figure 17.7 Telnet commands

that requests the service is the client or user). From this point on, all keyboard input is transmitted to the server, and all the server's output is transmitted to the client. Because all Telnet applications use a standardized interface to the network, called the Network Virtual Terminal (NVT), two systems can still communicate via Telnet even if their internal architectures use completely different data formats. The NVT data format is based on the standard 7-bit US ASCII character set in an 8-bit field, with the higher 8-bit values used as control codes. Thus the entire Telnet session consists of plain text transmission and can be easily recorded by third parties with access to the intermediate systems.

17.5.1   Troubleshooting Telnet

As with FTP, the most common causes of trouble with Telnet are user errors in logging in and connection timeouts. Here once again, entering incorrect user names, IP addresses, or passwords (due to mistyping or to an unfamiliar keyboard layout), nonexistent or deleted accounts, and missing or modified access privileges are typical causes of login errors. Connection timeouts can occur due to system overload (on the server or client end) or high network loads. The most common symptoms and their causes are listed in Section 17.11.

17.6   Hypertext Transfer Protocol (HTTP)

HTTP is the transport protocol on which the Internet service World Wide Web is based. The original 1990 version 0.9 of HTTP only specified the transfer of data identified by Uniform Resource Identifiers (URIs), which combine a Uniform Resource Locator (URL) and a resource name. In HTTP 1.0 (RFC 1945), these capabilities were extended through the definition of MIME elements that could be included in the protocol header to convey information about the type of information transferred. Nonetheless, HTTP 1.0 soon showed limitations in the face of rapidly growing demands in the Internet and in intranets. Most of all, the effects of cascaded proxies (necessitated by firewall schemes) and caching mechanisms led to long response times and high network traffic with a relatively low proportion of user data. Finally, however, the HTTP 1.1 standard that has been adopted represents a significant improvement in protocol performance.

17.6.1   The Basic Mechanisms of HTTP

The HTTP protocol is s single-state, send-and-receive protocol. The HTTP client sends the HTTP server a request containing the following elements:

- Request method
- URI
- Protocol version
- MIME information elements
- Information about the HTTP client
- Message contents (optional)

The server responds with a message containing the following:

- Status information
- Protocol version
- Success/failure rate
- MIME information elements
- Entity information (Meta-information about the content to be transferred)
- The message itself

In the simplest case, the client–server communication consists of a single connection between client and server (see Figure 17.8).

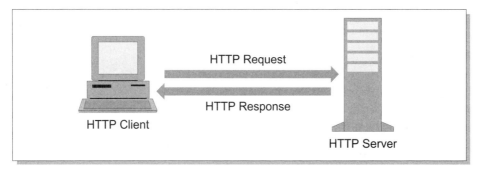

Figure 17.8 The principle of a direct HTTP connection

The situation is somewhat more complex if the communication path is not direct, but leads through several stations. Three kinds of indirect HTTP communication can be distinguished:

- Proxy connections
- Gateway connections
- Tunneling connections

Proxy connections are used mainly in connections with firewalls. Proxy servers HTTP requests from certain clients—usually those in a protected LAN—and set up the connection to the entity addressed by the URL in the client's request, then forward the resulting information received from the actual HTTP server to the requesting client. The purpose of the proxy server is to avoid a through connection from the client to the actual server. The advantage is that the client does not need a public IP address and can be protected against a number of potential attacks from the Internet.

Gateways are systems that can interpret between two different protocols. HTTP messages can be received by gateways and translated into the desired destination protocol.

Tunneling refers to a transport-layer capability that does not affect the contents of the data transported. HTTP messages can be transported between the HTTP client and server by any tunneling transport protocol (Frame Relay, PPP, SLIP, etc.). Figure 17.9 illustrates an indirect connection across three intermediate stations.

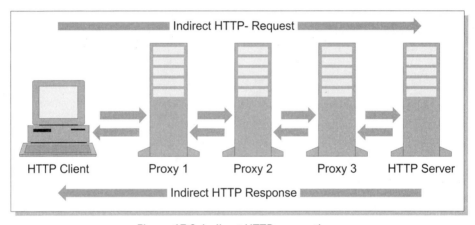

Figure 17.9 Indirect HTTP connections

In this illustration every HTTP request and every HTTP response must travel across the four individual links shown in order to reach their destinations. This is important to remember because certain HTTP options affect only the nearest non-tunneling neighbor, the endpoints of the overall connection, or all links along the connection path. Remember, furthermore, that every node along the path is generally involved in a number of connections simultaneously.

Every communication node that is not a tunnel can also maintain an internal cache from which it can answer requests. The purpose of a cache is to shorten the response times in the case where a requested document has been transferred once before. Besides reducing response time, the caching principle is also important for reducing the total data traffic in the network. For this reason, HTTP 1.1 incorporates special management functions to optimize the use of caches (see Figure 17.10).

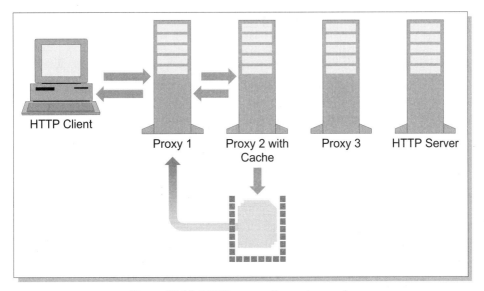

Figure 17.10 HTTP connection using cache

17.6.2 Differences Between HTTP 1.1 and HTTP 1.0

The main difference between the HTTP versions 1.0 and 1.1 is that HTTP 1.0 requires a separate TCP/IP connection to the HTTP server for every request by the client. Once the server has answered the request, it clears down the TCP/IP connection again. Because only one URI element is transferred for each request, five, ten or more TCP connections may have to be set up and cleared down to transfer a single Web page, which can consist of a great many URIs. Because setting up a TCP connection involves a three-step handshake procedure (>request, <response, >response-acknowledge), the network overhead traffic generated is considerable. Furthermore, the server must save information about the connection for a certain period after it has been cleared down (in the TIME-WAIT state, with a default timer value of 240 seconds!) in case a late packet arrives for the connection. This could lead to thousands of connection control blocks being maintained on the server.

The window size for TCP also reduces the performance of HTTP 1.0 over TCP/IP. Under HTTP 1.0 the many TCP connections are generally too brief to attain large window sizes so that the proportion of acknowledgment packets remains extraordinarily high and the thoughput is low.

HTTP 1.1 makes it possible to send several HTTP requests over the connection and to maintain the connection while waiting for the responses. Furthermore, HTTP requests can be "pipelined". This means that a client can send several

HTTP requests in immediate succession, rather than waiting for the response to one request before sending the next. In conjunction with optimized support for cache mechanisms, these TCP features yield substantially improved performance. Tests in the laboratories of the World Wide Web Consortium (W3C) showed significant reductions in response time and network loads.

17.6.3 HTTP Messages

HTTP defines two types of messages:

- HTTP requests
- HTTP responses

The header of an HTTP data packet consists of General-Header, Request-Header, Response-Header, and Entity-Header fields. Every header field consists of the field name followed by a colon and the field value, if any. The actual data payload is called the message body, and its length is indicated in the Content-Length header field.

HTTP Requests

Every request from a client to a server begins with the Request-Line, which contains information about the method to be performed on the requested object, the URI that identifies the object on which to perform the method, and the protocol version used. Example:

GET http://www.lycos.com/graphics/backdrop.gif HTTP/1.1

This request asks the server to perform the method "GET" on the file identified by "http://www.lycos.com/graphics/backdrop.gif". In addition to "GET", the following methods are defined:

- HEAD
- POST
- PUT
- DELETE
- TRACE
- OPTIONS

The methods GET and HEAD must be supported by every server; all other methods are optional. The URI—"http://www.lycos.com/graphics/backdrop.gif", in our example—can take one of three forms. It may be an asterisk (*), indicating that the request applies to the server in general and not to a particular resource. This may be the case, for example, when a client requests the options supported by the server software:

*OPTIONS * HTTP/1.1*

If the request is being sent to a proxy, then the request URI must take the form of an absolute URI with scheme, colon, double slash, host, and absolute path. This is because the proxy needs to know what host to connect to before it can send the message to an actual HTTP server. If the request is being sent not to a proxy or gateway, but to the actual server on which the resource is located—that is, if the destination of the request message is the next network node in the HTTP connection chain—then a relative URI is sufficient, consisting of just the path name of the resource. (In any case, the host addressed is indicated in the second line of the request.) When an HTTP request with an absolute URI is sent through a number of cascaded proxies, the last proxy sends only the path name in its request to the server's HTTP port:

GET /graphics/backdrop.gif HTTP/1.1

Host: www.lycos.com

17.6.4   Connection Types

One of the most important innovations in HTTP 1.1 is its use of persistent TCP connections, which are maintained while several HTTP messages are exchanged between server and client. Under HTTP 1.0, a separate TCP connection had to be set up and cleared down for every URI transferred, so that a number of connections were required for one Web page containing in-line images, for example. Every HTTP 1.1 server assumes that an HTTP 1.1 client will attempt to carry out its communication over persistent TCP connections, unless the client request header contains the token "close" in a connection header.

Pipelining

Clients that support persistent TCP connections can also send several requests in immediate succession over an existing TCP connection without waiting for the server's responses. This mode is called pipelining and is a significant factor in the improved performance of 1.1 implementations over HTTP 1.0. It is particularly important, however, that the principles of persistent connections and pipelining be correctly implemented in proxies. The TCP timeout must be set higher for persistent TCP connections on proxy servers than on HTTP servers because it must be assumed that the client uses the proxy as a communication link for a longer period. Furthermore, when persistent connections are used the client should not open more than two connections simultaneously to prevent excessive loads on the network. (HTTP 1.0 clients used the technique of opening up to eight connections in order to accelerate the transfer of Web pages consisting of multiple URIs. This method is unnecessary due to the pipelining capabilities of HTTP 1.1.)

17.7 The Server Message Block (SMB) Protocol

The Server Message Block Protocol (formerly an Open Group standard "Protocols for X/Open PC Interworking: SMB, Version 2", since withdrawn; see *http://www.opengroup.org/*) provides printing, redirection and server functions to the application layer in OS2, Windows for Workgroups, and Windows 95/98/NT/2000 environments. The redirection function converts local application commands into SMB commands to the appropriate server. SMB is also supported by some UNIX systems. The most popular implementation of SMB for UNIX is Samba. Microsoft is currently trying to establish SMB as an Internet standard under the name CIFS ("Common Internet File System"; see *http://www.cifs.com/*). The SMB packet format is illustrated in Figure 17.11.

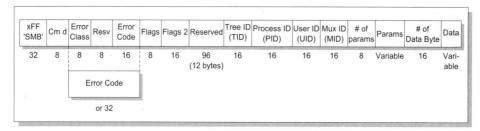

Figure 17.11 The SMB packet format

The protocol process for logging into a Windows NT server is as follows:

a) Request an IP address by DHCP.

b) Register the NetBIOS name with the WINS server (if present).

c) Broadcast SMB NETLOGON Requests to obtain the server name.

d) Request the server address from the WINS server, or by broadcast if no WINS server is present.

e) Start a TCP connection to the server, then a NetBIOS session.

f) Open an SMB session.

Figure 17.12 lists the SMB commands in the latest version of SMB (CIFS). Figures 17.13 through 17.16 list the error classes and error codes. ERRDOS messages generally refer to problems on the client; ERRSRV to server configuration problems; and ERRHRD to server hardware problems:

SMB_COM_CREATE_DIRECTORY	0x00	SMB_COM_IOCTL_SECONDARY	0x28
SMB_COM_DELETE_DIRECTORY	0x01	SMB_COM_COPY	0x29
SMB_COM_OPEN	0x02	SMB_COM_MOVE	0x2A
SMB_COM_CREATE	0x03	SMB_COM_ECHO	0x2B
SMB_COM_CLOSE	0x04	SMB_COM_WRITE_AND_CLOSE	0x2C
SMB_COM_FLUSH	0x05	SMB_COM_OPEN_ANDX	0x2D
SMB_COM_DELETE	0x06	SMB_COM_READ_ANDX	0x2E
SMB_COM_RENAME	0x07	SMB_COM_WRITE_ANDX	0x2F
SMB_COM_QUERY_INFORMATION	0x08	SMB_COM_CLOSE_AND_TREE_DISC	0x31
SMB_COM_SET_INFORMATION	0x09	SMB_COM_TRANSACTION2	0x32
SMB_COM_READ	0x0A	SMB_COM_TRANSACTION2_SECONDARY	0x33
SMB_COM_WRITE	0x0B	SMB_COM_FIND_CLOSE2	0x34
SMB_COM_LOCK_BYTE_RANGE	0x0C	SMB_COM_FIND_NOTIFY_CLOSE	0x35
SMB_COM_UNLOCK_BYTE_RANGE	0x0D	SMB_COM_TREE_CONNECT	0x70
SMB_COM_CREATE_TEMPORARY	0x0E	SMB_COM_TREE_DISCONNECT	0x71
SMB_COM_CREATE_NEW	0x0F	SMB_COM_SESSION_SETUP_ANDX	0x73
SMB_COM_CHECK_DIRECTORY	0x10	SMB_COM_LOGOFF_ANDX	0x74
SMB_COM_PROCESS_EXIT	0x11	SMB_COM_TREE_CONNECT_ANDX	0x75
SMB_COM_SEEK	0x12	SMB_COM_QUERY_INFORMATION_DISK	0x80
SMB_COM_LOCK_AND_READ	0x13	SMB_COM_SEARCH	0x81
SMB_COM_WRITE_AND_UNLOCK	0x14	SMB_COM_FIND	0x82
SMB_COM_READ_RAW	0x1A	SMB_COM_FIND_UNIQUE	0x83
SMB_COM_READ_MPX	0x1B	SMB_COM_NT_TRANSACT	0xA0
SMB_COM_READ_MPX_SECONDARY	0x1C	SMB_COM_NT_TRANSACT_SECONDARY	0xA1
SMB_COM_WRITE_RAW	0x1D	SMB_COM_NT_CREATE_ANDX	0xA2
SMB_COM_WRITE_MPX	0x1E	SMB_COM_NT_CANCEL	0xA4
SMB_COM_WRITE_COMPLETE	0x20	SMB_COM_OPEN_PRINT_FILE	0xC0
SMB_COM_SET_INFORMATION2	0x22	SMB_COM_WRITE_PRINT_FILE	0xC1
SMB_COM_QUERY_INFORMATION2	0x23	SMB_COM_CLOSE_PRINT_FILE	0xC2
SMB_COM_LOCKING_ANDX	0x24	SMB_COM_GET_PRINT_QUEUE	0xC3
SMB_COM_TRANSACTION	0x25	SMB_COM_READ_BULK	0xD8
SMB_COM_TRANSACTION_SECONDARY	0x26	SMB_COM_WRITE_BULK	0xD9
SMB_COM_IOCTL	0x27	SMB_COM_WRITE_BULK_DATA	0xDA

Figure 17.12 SMB commands

Class	Code	Comment
SUCCESS	0x00	The request was successful
ERRDOS	0x01	Error is from the core DOS operating system set
ERRSRV	0x02	Error is generated by the server network file manager
ERRHRD	0x03	Error is a hardware error
ERRCMD	0xFF	Command was not in the "SMB" format

Figure 17.13 SMB error codes and classes

Error	Code	Description
ERRbadfunc	1	Invalid function The server did not recognize or could not perform a system call generated by the server, for example, set the DIRECTORY attribute on a data file, invalid seek mode
ERRbadfile	2	File not found The last component of a file's pathname could not be found
ERRbadpath	3	Directory invalid A directory component in a pathname could not be found
ERRnofids	4	Too many open files The server has no file handles available
ERRnoaccess	5	Access denied The client's context does not permit the requested function. This includes the following conditions: • invalid rename command • write to FID (Format Identifier) open for read only • read on FID (Format Identifier) open for write only • attempt to delete a non-empty directory
ERRbadfid	6	Invalid file handle The file handle specified was not recognized by the server
ERRbadmcb	7	Memory control blocks destroyed
ERRnomem	8	Insufficient server memory to perform the requested function
ERRbadmem	9	Invalid memory block address
ERRbadenv	10	Invalid environment
ERRbadformat	11	Invalid format
ERRbadaccess	12	Invalid open mode
ERRbaddata	13	Invalid data (generated only by IOCTL calls in the server)
ERRbaddrive	15	Invalid drive specified
ERRremcd	16	A Delete Directory request attempted to remove the server's current directory
ERRdiffdevice	17	Not same device (for example, a cross volume rename was attempted)
ERRnofiles	18	A File Search command can find no more files matching the specified criteria
ERRbadshare	32	The sharing mode specified for an Open conflicts with existing FIDs on the file
ERRlock	33	A Lock request conflicted with an existing lock or specified an invalid mode, or an Unlock request attempted to remove a lock held by another process
ERRfilexists	80	The file named in the request already exists

Figure 17.14 SMB ERRDOS return codes

Error	Code	Description
ERRerror	1	Non-specific error code Returned under the following conditions: • Resource other than disk space exhausted • First SMB command was not negotiated • Multiple negotiations attempted • Internal server error
ERRbadpw	2	Bad password The name/password pair in a Tree Connect or Session setup are invalid
ERRaccess	4	The client does not have the necessary access rights in the specified context for the requested function
ERRinvnid	5	The TID specified in a command was invalid
ERRinvnetname	6	Invalid network name in tree connect
ERRinvdevice	7	Invalid device Printer request made to non-printer connection or non-printer request made to printer connection
ERRqfull	49	Print queue full (files) Returned by open print file
ERRqtoobig	50	Print queue full-no space
ERRqeof	51	EOF on print queue dump
ERRinvpfid	52	Invalid print file FID
ERRsmbcmd	64	The server did not recognize the command received
ERRsrverror	65	The server encountered an internal error, for example, system file unavailable
ERRfilespecs	67	The FID and path name parameters contained an invalid combination of values
ERRbadpermits	69	The access permissions specified for a file or directory are not a valid combination The server cannot set the requested attribute
ERRsetattrmode	71	The attribute mode in the Set File Attribute request is invalid
ERRpaused	81	Server is paused (Reserved for messaging)
ERRmsgoff	82	Not receiving messages (Reserved for messaging)
ERRnoroom	83	No room to buffer message (Reserved for messaging)

Figure 17.15 SMB ERRSRV return codes

Error	Code	Description
ERRrmuns	87	Too many remote user names (Reserved for messaging)
ERRtimeout	88	Operation timed out
ERRnoresource	89	No resources currently available for request
ERRtoomanyuids	90	Too many UIDs active on this session
ERRbaduid	91	The UID is not known as a valid user identifier on this session
ERRusempx	250	Temporarily unable to support Raw, use MPX mode
ERRusestd	251	Temporarily unable to support Raw, use standard read/write
ERRcontmpx	252	Continue in MPX mode
ERRnosupport	255	Function not supported

Figure 17.15 SMB ERRSRV return codes

Error	Code	Description
ERRnowrite	19	Attempt to write on write-protected medium
ERRbadunit	20	Unknown unit
ERRnotready	21	Drive not ready
ERRbadcmd	22	Unknown command
ERRdata	23	Data error (CRC)
ERRbadreq	24	Bad request structure length
ERRseek	25	Seek error
ERRbadmedia	26	Unknown media type
ERRbadsector	27	Sector not found
ERRnopaper	28	Printer out of paper
ERRwrite	29	Write fault
ERRread	30	Read fault
ERRgeneral	31	General failure
ERRbadshare	32	An Open conflicts with an existing Open
ERRlock	33	A Lock request conflicts with an existing lock or specifies an invalid mode, or an Unlock request refers to a lock held by another process.
ERRwrongdisk	34	The wrong disk is found in a drive
ERRFCBUnavail	35	No FCBs are available to process request
ERRsharebufexc	36	A sharing buffer has been exceeded

Figure 17.16 SMB ERRHRD return codes

From NT LAN Manager Version 0.12 on, the server may send a 32-bit error code instead of the 8-bit error class and the 16-bit error code (see the SMB packet format in Figure 17.11).

17.7.1 Troubleshooting SMB

SMB errors may have many causes, as the variety of SMB error codes indicates. SMB retransmissions that are necessary when routers or switches drop packets due to overloads are a common cause of excessive response times. This is especially critical when NetBIOS is transported over LLC and the retransmissions must be performed on the SMB layer. Other error sources include server configuration faults, server performance problems, or problems with server applications being accessed by means of SMB.

17.8 The Microsoft Browsing Protocol

In addition to SMB, Microsoft networking environments often use the Microsoft browsing protocol. This protocol maintains the "browse list", that is, the list of computers that are visible when a Windows user browses the "Network Neighborhood" in the Windows Explorer application. Each node in the Microsoft network takes one of the following roles in this protocol:

Non-Browse Servers	Computers that cannot function as browse servers announce themselves every 12 minutes to the Master Browse Server, but do not maintain browse lists.
Potential Browse Servers	Computers that are not currently acting as Browse Servers, but can do so if necessary.
Backup Browse Servers	Computers that keep a list of known servers and domains for retrieval by the Master Browse Server.
Master Browse Server	(Also called the "Master Browser" or "Browse Master".) Computers in each network that respond to clients requesting the current browse list and that send lists of available servers to Backup Browse Servers.

In every domain or workgroup, at least one Master Browse Server exists for every 32 workstations. In TCP/IP networks, there is a Master Browse Server in each IP subnet. If no Master Browse Server can be found, an election takes place to select a new Master Browse Server. The NetBIOS name suffix 1E hex is used in this selection process (see Section 16.7.2). If an excessive number of such election processes are observed, the causes may be a restarting NT server (NT servers are preferred Master Browse Servers) or intermittent problems of the current Master Browse Server.

17.9   Troubleshooting Application Protocols

The first step in diagnosing problems with application protocols such as FTP, Telnet, or HTTP is to analyze the server's message logs. If the logs do not contain any clue as to the cause of the error, then a connection attempt can be monitored using a protocol analyzer. The protocol trace usually permits prompt identification of the reason for the connection failure. If a ping to the server station is successful, but a login fails, this may be because the server application is not running, or because the router's access table disabled the corresponding TCP port. Other typical causes of trouble are defective client configurations (such as an incorrect FTP transfer mode, that is, ASCII rather than binary, or an incorrect Telnet terminal emulation, etc.), or incorrect user ID and password settings.

A common application-related problem is looping: this refers to an application sending the same command over and over again. In order to distinguish application looping from TCP retransmissions, it is important to conduct measurements on both the server and client segments to make sure that the repeated application requests are not caused by TCP responses not reaching their destination. Typical causes of application looping include bugs in the application software, poor bus performance on the server, memory allocation problems on the network interface, or problems with the network interface driver.

Another frequent source of application performance problems is simply inefficient software design. A number of applications are not designed to use the network infrastructure efficiently. They perform small, incremental file reads, or issue overlapping read commands, causing large amounts of data to be transported over the network repetitively.

17.10 Symptoms and Causes: Network Services and Applications in General

Symptom: Application Looping

Cause (1):   Application software problem
Cause (2):   Insufficient server bus performance
Cause (3):   Memory allocation problems on the network interface card
Cause (4):   Problems with the network interface driver

Symptom: Application Slow

Cause (1): Congested network
Cause (2): Overloaded server
Cause (3): Application performs small, incremental file reads
Cause (4): Application performs overlapping read commands
(for example, every read command reads 20% or 30%, sometimes
100% of the data just read in the previous read operation)
Cause (5): Application performs overlapping write commands

Symptom: Connection Timeouts

Cause (1): System overloaded (memory, CPU load at server, client)
Cause (2): Network overloaded (a switch or router is dropping packets)

17.11 Symptoms and Causes: FTP and Telnet

Symptom: No Connection to FTP, Telnet Server

Cause (1): Incorrect user name (typing error, wrong keyboard driver,
US/non-US keyboard layout)
Cause (2): Incorrect password (typing error, wrong keyboard driver,
US/non-US keyboard layout)
Cause (3): User name, password changed
Cause (4): User account does not exist, no permission to log in
Cause (5): User account deleted
Cause (6): Mistyped or wrong IP address
Cause (7): TCP/IP driver misconfiguration
Cause (8): Domain name server incorrectly configured or not working
(try to contact host by IP address)
Cause (9): Firewall blocks FTP or Telnet applications
Cause (10): FTP or Telnet client incorrectly configured for use across firewall
(no proxy configured; wrong FTP proxy configuration)
Cause (11): FTP or Telnet server down (does it respond to ping?)
Cause (12): No route available to FTP or Telnet server segment
(traceroute to server)

Symptom: FTP/Telnet Connection Timeouts

Cause (1): System overload (memory, CPU load at server or client)
Cause (2): Network overload (switch, router dropping packets)

17.12 Symptoms and Causes: Mail

Symptom: Problems Sending and Receiving Mail

Cause (1):   No TCP connection to mail server
Cause (2):   Mail server down
Cause (3):   Server is running, but not listening on port 25
Cause (4):   Incorrectly configured server software
Cause (5):   Incorrectly configured mail client
Cause (6):   Proxy Server Port is not on port 25

Symptom: Slow Mail Exchange

Cause (1):   Large attachments
Cause (2):   Communication via X.400 gateway
Cause (3):   Slow connection to mail server
Cause (4):   Proxy Server has a low performance

Testing
Network Performance

18

"It is a capital mistake to theorize before one has data."

SIR ARTHUR CONAN DOYLE

Unsatisfactory network performance is a major problem that occurs continually in data networks. Because the causes of this condition can vary widely, it is very important to supplement such terms as "a slow network", "a slow server", or "long response times" with objective measurements. The two crucial parameters to be determined are data throughput and response time.

The first step in determining the network performance is to analyze the structure of the applications in use. Application architectures can be divided into three main categories:

- Peer-to-peer (Level 1)
- Client-server (Level 2)
- Client to primary application server and secondary data/application servers (Level 3)

While no dedicated server is involved in peer-to-peer communication (for example, file transfer between two network nodes), a Level 3 application architecture involves not only the client and a primary application server, but also other servers that may function as database or application servers to the primary server. Typical Level 3 application architectures include application or Web servers with back-end connections to database servers.

Response Time Measurements

Once the application architecture and the network topology have been analyzed, the first step in determining and evaluating response times should be to calculate the theoretical communication delay. This figure can then be used to estimate the expected response times.

Typical values for one-way transmission delays over WAN links are best obtained from the service provider or tested using a protocol analyzer. Typical values for Frame Relay links are between 30 and 60 ms. For ATM (STM-1), values of 6 μs/km and 2 ms/switch can be assumed. For a line length of 1,000 km with five ATM switches, this yields a transmission delay of 6.01 ms.

Type of medium	Max. delay per segment (according to standards)	Type of medium	Max. delay per segment (according to standards)
Ethernet 10Base5	2.165 ms	Ethernet 100Base-TX	0.556 ms
Ethernet 10Base2	0.950 ms	Ethernet 100Base-FX	2.040 ms
Ethernet 10Broad36	14 ms	Ethernet AUI	0.257 ms
Ethernet 10Base-FP	5 ms	Ethernet MII	0.0025 ms Typical delay
Ethernet FOIRL	5 ms		
Ethernet 1Base5	4 ms	FDDI	10 – 300 ms
Ethernet 10Base-T	1 ms	Switched 10 Mbit/s Ethernet	0.030 ms
Ethernet 10Base-FB	10 ms	Switched Token Ring	0.030 ms
Ethernet 10Base-FI	10 ms	Switched FDDI	0.010 ms
Ethernet 10Base-T4	0.570 ms	Switched 100Base-T	0.010 ms
		Router	5 – 10 ms

Figure 18.1 Transmission delays in LAN topologies

The actual response time measurements are made, in the simplest case, using Internet Control Message Protocol (ICMP) ping packets. Ping uses the ICMP Echo command to send a packet to the destination and back again. In addition to the response time, the ping command also counts the number of intermediate stations (hops) through which the packet is routed. Each "hop" reduces the packet's Time to Live (TTL) counter by one. If the initial TTL value is known, subtracting the final TTL yields the number of hops along the path. Initial TTL values are:

Windows 3.x/95	32
Windows 98/2000/NT 4.0	128
Routers	255
UNIX	64 or 255

```
C:\WINDOWS>ping 16.70.66.14

Pinging 16.70.66.14 with 32 bytes of data:

Reply from 16.70.66.14: bytes=32 time=54 ms TTL=120
Reply from 16.70.66.14: bytes=32 time=51 ms TTL=120
Reply from 16.70.66.14: bytes=32 time=53 ms TTL=120
Reply from 16.70.66.14: bytes=32 time=54 ms TTL=120

Ping statistics for 16.70.66.14:

Packets: Sent = 4, Received = 4, Lost = 0 (0% loss),
Approximate round trip times in milli-seconds:
Minimum = 51 ms, Maximum = 54 ms, Average = 53 ms
```

Figure 18.2 Results of a response time test using the ping command

Figure 18.2 shows the results of such a response time test. The measured response time varies within a relatively narrow range, from 51 to 54 ms. This means that the communication links involved in this example are not under excessive loads and are able to provide consistent response times. High variations in response time indicates that at least one network segment is under a heavy load.

To determine the delay values for individual segments of the network connection, the tracert command (in UNIX: traceroute) can be used. The traceroute command performs a series of ICMP Echo requests, beginning with a TTL value of 1. Each request is repeated three times, then the TTL value is increased by one, and so on until the TTL is sufficient for the packet to reach its destination. The output of the traceroute command displays the response time for each of the three echo packets with each TTL value (see Figure 18.3).

1	<10 ms	<10 ms	10 ms	center1-west-wien.chello.at [10.34.14.1]
2	10 ms	10 ms	<10 ms	rt113.chello.at [212.17.99.113]
3	<10 ms	10 ms	10 ms	vienna-bgp1-fe-2-0-0.aorta.com [212.17.99.117]
4	40 ms	10 ms	10 ms	tk-uni-eb3-pos-9-0-0.aorta.com [212.17.99.41]
5	50 ms	60 ms	60 ms	atvie202-ta.Ebone.NETWORK [192.121.159.105]
6	60 ms	50 ms	61 ms	demun701-tb-p0-3.ebone.network [195.158.226.153]
7	50 ms	60 ms	60 ms	frpar601-tb-p0-2.ebone.network [195.158.226.150]
8	50 ms	60 ms	60 ms	frpar205-tc-p9-0.ebone.network [195.158.228.157]
9	60 ms	80 ms	80 ms	gblon303-tc-p1-0.ebone.network [195.158.228.150]
10	60 ms	70 ms	60 ms	gblon304-tb-p2-0.ebone.network [195.158.225.30]
11	140 ms	140 ms	150 ms	usnyk106-tc-p0-2.ebone.network [195.158.229.13]
12	151 ms	140 ms	140 ms	uspen201-tb-p1-3.ebone.network [195.158.224.81]
13	—	150 ms	150 ms	icm-bb11-pen-3-0.icp.network [198.67.133.137]
14	—	140 ms	—	icm-bb10-pen-9-0.icp.network [198.67.133.33]
15	140 ms	141 ms	—	icm-bb4-pen-0-0-0.icp.network [198.67.133.62]
16	140 ms	161 ms	140 ms	sprint-nap.cerf.network [192.157.69.5]
17	140 ms	141 ms	180 ms	pos6-2-155M.phl-bb2.cerf.network [134.24.46.113]
18	170 ms	161 ms	170 ms	ser3-5-45M.chi-bb3.cerf.network [134.24.33.193]
19	201 ms	—	—	pos0-0-622M.sfo-bb4.cerf.network [134.24.46.58]
20	210 ms	210 ms	200 ms	pos7-0-622M.sfo-bb3.cerf.network [134.24.32.78]
21	—	220 ms	230 ms	pos1-0-622M.sea-bb2.cerf.network [134.24.46.186]
22	—	220 ms	221 ms	pos11-0-0-155M.sea-bb1.cerf.network [134.24.32.114]
23	220 ms	231 ms	220 ms	boeing-gw.sea-bb1.cerf.network [134.24.108.78]
24	231 ms	220 ms	220 ms	144.116.14.1
25	231 ms	230 ms	—	www1.boeing.com [12.13.226.23]
26	—	230 ms	230 ms	www1.boeing.com [12.13.226.23]

Figure 18.3 Results of a response time test using the TRACERT command

The drawback of response time testing by the ping and traceroute methods is that the server's processing time is reflected along with the network transmission delay. The transmission delay caused by the network alone can be measured using two protocol analyzers or network probes.

Response Time Measurements Using Two Protocol Analyzers

Place one analyzer on either side of the network or network component to be measured. Then send a ping across the network (or component) under test. When the ping passes analyzer A, the analyzer records the arrival time A_1. When it passes analyzer B, this analyzer records arrival time B_1. When the echo response packet returns, it first passes analyzer B, which records arrival time B_2, then analyzer A, which records arrival time A_2. The latency of the device can now be calculated as $((A_2 - A_1) - (B_2 - B_1))/2$.

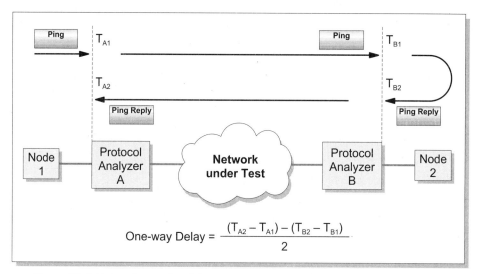

Figure 18.4 Network transfer delay measurements using two protocol analyzers

Throughput Measurements

Like response time measurements, throughput tests should also be preceded by a calculation of the theoretical maximum frame rate and throughput. Note that the throughput over a connection path can never be higher than the throughput over the link with the lowest capacity.

Actual throughput is best measured by means of an File Transfer Protocol (FTP) or Server Message Block Protocol (SMB) file transfer between two stations whose data traffic is being traced with a protocol analyzer. The packets transfered should be close to the maximum size of the transport network, called the

Maximum Transfer Unit or MTU. The average throughput of forty or fifty successive packets can be measured to yield a distribution of the connection's throughput capacity over time.

An important factor in analyzing throughput is the client system. Often the client's performance has a significant influence on the measured throughput. Use a protocol analyzer to measure the time between the server's last response packet and the client's next request packet to obtain an indication of the client's speed in processing the server's responses, which has an effect on throughput as well as response time. Figures 18.5a and 18.5b show the calculation of the theoretical maximum frame rate and throughput for the various Ethernet topologies.

Topology	Theoretical maximum frame rate / throughput
10 Mbit/s Ethernet	Frame rate = B / (F+I+P) B = transmission bandwidth F = frame size in bits P = length of preamble I = inter-frame gap **Maximum frame rate:** 10 Mbit/s / (512 + 96 + 64) = **14,880 frames/s** **Maximum throughput with minimum frame size:** 14,880 frames · 512 bits = **7.62 Mbit/s** With a frame size of 1,518 bytes the maximum frame rate is 812, which equals 98.7% utilization or a throughput of 9.8 Mbit/s. Ethernet is able to achieve this value if only two nodes are active.
100 Mbit/s Ethernet Half Duplex (shared network)	Frame rate = B / (F+I+P)B = transmission bandwidth **Maximum frame rate:** 100 Mbit/s / (512 + 96 + 64) = **148,809 frames/s** **Maximum throughput with minimum frame size:** 148,809 frames/s · 512 bits = **76.19 Mbit/s** With a frame size of 1,518 bytes the maximum frame rate is 8,127, which equals 98.7% utilization or a throughput of 98.69 Mbit/s. Ethernet is able to achieve this value if only two nodes are active.
100 Mbit/s Ethernet Full Duplex (point-to-point)	**Maximum throughput with minimum frame size:** 148,809 frames/s · 512 bits = **76.19 Mbit/s** **for each direction (send and receive)** **Full-duplex link throughput with minimum frame size = 152.19 Mbit/s** With a frame size of 1,518 bytes the maximum frame rate for each direction is 8,127, which equals 98.7% utilization and a throughput of 98.69 Mbit/s. The maximum full-duplex link throughput with maximum frame size equals 197.38 Mbit/s.

Figure 18.5a Theoretical throughput rates for Ethernet network topologies

TROUBLESHOOTING HIGHER-LAYER PROTOCOLS

Topology	Theoretical maximum frame rate / throughput
Gigabit Ethernet	Frame rate (without frame bursting) = B / (max (S,F) + I + P) Utilization with bursting: u=(n+1)F/(max.(S,F)+n(F+I+P)) B = transmission bandwidth F = frame size in bits S = slot time P = length of preamble I = inter-frame gap n = number of consecutive frames transmitted in burst after first frame **Maximum frame rate (without bursting):** 1,000 Mbit/s / (4,096 + 96 + 64) = **234,962 frames/s** **Maximum throughput using minimum frame size (without bursting):** 234,962 frames/s · 512 bits = **120.3 Mbit/s = 12% utilization** **Utilization with bursting (during burst)** **using minimum frame size:** n = (65,536 - 4,096)/(512 + 64 + 96) = 92 (number of frames during burst using minimum frame size) u = 93 · 512/(4,096 + 92 · 672) = **72.2% (during 92 frame burst)** **Maximum frame rate with bursting during 92 frame burst:** 1,000 Mbit/s · 0.722 / 512 = **1,410,156 frames/s**
Gigabit Ethernet Full Duplex (point-to-point)	**Maximum frame rate per direction with minimum frame size:** 1,000 Mbit/s / (512 + 96 + 64) = **1,488,095 frames/s** **Maximum throughput per direction with minimum frame size:** 1,488,095 frames/s x 512 bits = **761.9 Mbit/s** **Full-duplex link throughput with minimum frame size** **= 1,523.8 Mbit/s** With a frame size of 1,518 bytes the maximum frame rate for each direction is 81,274, which equals 98.7% utilization and a throughput of 986.9 Mbit/s. The maximum full-duplex link throughput with maximum frame size equals 1,973.9 Mbit/s.

Figure 18.5b Theoretical throughput rates for Ethernet network topologies

Section V
Appendix

Error Symptoms and Root Causes

A.1 Symptoms & Causes: 10/100/1,000 Mbit/s Ethernet

A.1.1 Symptom: Diminished Network Performance in Conjunction with FCS Errors

Invalid checksums (FCS errors) are a side effect of collisions, which in limited numbers are a normal consequence of the CSMA/CD algorithm. If FCS errors occur together with collisions, and if their number is within reasonable limits, there is no reason to worry. Use a protocol analyzer to measure the number of collisions and the number of FCS errors over a period of time and compare the resulting curves. If there is no correlation between the collisions and the FCS error curves, you might have one of the following problems:

Cause (1):   Noise and interference on the network.
Noise results when the network is not grounded or if the grounding is faulty. Use a cable scanner or multimeter to check the noise level on your network. A 10Base2/10Base5 network segment must have no more than one ground connection. If there is a second ground connection, due to a faulty network interface card or a bad cable connection, for example, a voltage difference between the two grounds may cause current leak in the network cable.

Cause (2):   Electromagnetic interference along the cable path.
Electromagnetic interference from devices such as photocopiers, mobile telephones, elevators or pagers can also cause FCS errors. Use a multimeter to check for interference and a cable tester to check for noise. If you detect interference, check whether the cable routes lead along elevator shafts, electric machinery, transformers, lighting bays, computer systems with high clock rates or x-ray equipment.

Cause (3):   Faulty network interface card.
To determine whether a faulty Network Interface Card (NIC) is the source of FCS errors, generate statistics of all defective packets sorted by network node (this is a standard report generated automatically by most protocol analyzers). If you find a suspicious station, measure its activity (for example, in packets/second) and

the number of FCS errors occurring on the segment. If the two numbers seem to correlate, there is a good chance you have found the cause of your problems. Keep in mind that many faults on network interface cards occur only intermittently, for example, only after the card has reached a certain temperature. For this reason it may be necessary to take measurements over longer periods of time before you can obtain exact and repeatable results.

Cause (4):	Defective or loose connectors (on NICs, wall jacks, MAUs, repeaters, hubs).
	Check all connections in the network path.

A.1.2   Symptom: Diminished Network Performance in Conjunction with Late Collisions

An increase in the number of collisions is often caused by cable problems (cable segments too long), defective network interface cards, excessive repeater cascading, or defective or missing terminating resistors. Determining whether the collisions are "late" or normal collisions can help to narrow down the possible causes. Possible causes for late collisions include:

Cause (1):	Cables longer than the specified maximum segment length for the given topology.
	Measure length using a cable scanner.
Cause (2):	Too many cascaded repeaters in network (longest possible communication path must include no more than four repeaters).
	Replace one of the repeaters with a bridge, or change the network configuration.
Cause (3):	Defective network interface card or MAU.
	Use a protocol analyzer to collect statistics on the stations that send the most defective packets. Also gather statistics on numbers of collisions and active nodes, and look for correlations. If this does not help to localize the problem, the network segmentation method must be used.

A.1.3   Symptom: Diminished Network Performance in Conjunction with Early Collisions

Cause (1):	Terminating resistor defective or not installed.
	10Base2 and 10Base5 networks must be terminated by 50-ohm resistors. Make sure all required terminating resistors are installed

and use a multimeter to check the resistance (48 ohms < R < 52 ohms).

Cause (2): Loose or defective T-connector.

Check all connections in the network path.

Cause (3): Too many nodes in one segment.

Check the number of MAUs per segment; the number must not exceed 100 in a 10Base5 segment or 30 in a 10Base2 segment.

Cause (4): Kink in a cable.

Use a cable scanner to try to locate the damage and replace the affected cable.

Cause (5): Cable does not conform to IEEE 802.3.

IEEE 802.3 10Base5 cables are marked with a color code every 2.5 meters. In order to minimize the interference due to reflections at connection points, connectors should be inserted only at these markings. In addition, keep in mind that not all cables with BNC connectors are 50-ohm cables. Although Ethernet works even on 75-ohm cables over tens of meters, increasing network length will lead to problems sooner or later. Always check the specification of the cables you are using.

A.1.4 Symptom: Slow Network, High Response Time (No Excessive Collisions or FCS Errors)

Cause (1): Buffer overflow in a bridge or router in the transmission path.

Check router and bridge statistics (CPU capacity use, port capacity use). Use a protocol analyzer to try to determine which nodes create the most traffic across the bridge or router. Do timeouts occur? Use pings to perform systematic measurements of response times across the bridge/router to check whether the interconnection devices are part of the problem. If this is the case, reconfigure the network (by moving a server or client to another segment, for example) to reduce the traffic over heavily-loaded interconnection devices.

Cause (2): Transmission problems over optical-fiber connections.

Fiber links bridging great distances can sometimes lead to performance problems without showing FCS errors if the line attenuation is too high or the light power emitted is too low. Use pings to check the response times of connections over the fiber connection in question. Check the settings of the fiber-optic couplers and the line attenuation.

Cause (3):   Local segment routing.

Local routing is a common cause of slow networks. Local routing typically occurs for connections between two nodes with different subnet addresses connected to the same LAN switch, which is connected to a router (also called one-armed routing). In order to reach its destination a packet has to be switched to the router, then routed within the router before being transferred through the same switch again to the destination node.

A.1.5   Symptom: Intermittent Problems with Connections and Network Performance, Alignment Errors

Cause (1):   Network interface card transmits a few extra bits after each FCS.

Use a protocol analyzer to capture the frames that have extra bits following the FCS (known as dribble frames or alignment-error frames). The source address of the captured packets identifies the faulty network interface card.

Cause (2):   Maximum length of the transmission path exceeds that defined in the Ethernet specification.

Whether the signal arrives at its destination depends on the transmitting and receiving stations. Stations that are closer together (within the specified distance limits) can communicate without problems, while stations that have to communicate over a longer distance, but are still located in the same segment, have connection problems. Try to find a pattern in the connection problems to determine whether only certain nodes are affected. Use a cable tester to check the length and quality of the transmission path. Insert a bridge or router in the transmission path if necessary. (See the section entitled "Network Design Guidelines" in Chapter 7 for details.)

Cause (3):   Too many bridges or routers are cascaded, resulting in long signal transmission delays and protocol timeouts (such as TCP timeouts). Use pings or response time agents to check response times. Review the network design with regard to the maximum allowable cascading of bridges and routers. (See the section entitled "Network Design Guidelines" in Chapter 7 for details.)

A.1.6 Symptom: Intermittent Connection Problems in Conjunction with Short Packets

Cause:　　Faulty network interface card.

Use a protocol analyzer to try to capture the short packets and identify the emitting node by the source address. If the source address is corrupt, try to track down the defective card by evaluating correlation measurements. (See the section titled "Troubleshooting in 10/100/1,000 Mbit/s Ethernet" for details.)

A.1.7 Symptom: Intermittent Connection Problems in Conjunction with Jabber Packets

Cause (1):　Double grounding in 10Base2 and 10Base5 networks, resulting in DC currents in the network cable.

Check the network grounding; use a cable tester to check for DC current.

Cause (2):　Defective network interface card.

Defective interface cards sometimes generate jabber frames (excessively long frames), which lead to connection problems in the affected segment. Capture the jabber frames using a protocol analyzer and identify the faulty network interface card by analyzing the source addresses.

A.1.8 Symptom: Intermittent Connection Problems in Conjunction with Short Inter-Frame Spacing

Cause:　　Packet loss due to insufficient inter-frame spacing.

If a station does not maintain the required minimum inter-frame spacing gap (9.6 µs in 10 Mbit/s, 0.96 µs in 100 Mbit/s networks) some hubs will be unable to repeat the frames correctly. In such cases, packets sometimes mutate into jabber packets. Use a protocol analyzer to check the inter-frame gaps (calculated from the packet time stamps in the analyzer trace). The faulty network interface can then be identified by analyzing the source addresses.

A.1.9 Symptom: Intermittent Connection Problems in Paths Across Bridges

Cause: Change in packet sequence due to load-sharing mechanisms in the bridge.

Check the bridge configuration and deactivate load sharing if necessary.

A.1.10 Symptom: Intermittent Connection Problems in Routes Across Routers

Cause: Router connected to overloaded or low-quality WAN lines.

Use a protocol analyzer to check capacity use, FCS rate and bit-error rates in the WAN link; analyze router port logs.

A.1.11 Symptom: Loss of a Single Node's Connection

Cause (1): Loose or faulty connection from the MAU to the network cable or from the NIC to the network.

A sudden complete failure of a single network node is often caused by one of the following:

- MAU plug not firmly connected
- Break, short circuit or noise in connecting cable
- Faulty network interface card.

Check the cable and connector and the network interface card; replace if necessary. Replace the faulty node with a system known to be functioning correctly (such as a notebook). If the replacement node functions, the problem is inside the disconnected node, if not, the problem is on the network side.

Cause (2): Incorrectly configured network interface card: wrong connector activated (for example, AUI instead of twisted pair), or the selected interrupt is already assigned.

Send loopback pings (ping 127.0.0.0) to check whether the card is working and whether packets are being transmitted and received. Has anyone installed any hardware or software on the node recently? As described for Cause (1), replace the faulty node with a system known to be functioning correctly (such as a notebook) to determine whether the problem is inside the node or on the network side.

Cause (3): Defective network card, blown fuse.

Check whether the power supply to the MAU is intact (when using an external MAU). Send loopback pings (ping 127.0.0.0) to check whether the card is working and whether packets are being transmitted and received.

Cause (4): The MAU sends heartbeat signals (when working with an external MAU) but the interface card, in conformance with the standard, reads them as Signal Quality Errors (SQE) and aborts transmission.

Monitor the LEDs on the MAU. If the SQE LED lights up every time transmission is attempted, deactivate the heartbeat mode in the MAU (change it from Ethernet 2.0 mode to IEEE 802.3 mode).

Cause (5): Learning mode of a bridge not active because the bridge is operating in protected mode, and its aging function has deleted the address entry of the problem node.

Check the bridge address tables and the operating mode. (Is the learning mode on?)

Cause (6): Incorrectly configured bridge or router filters.

Check the filter settings and compare them with the address of the problem station. In particular, check the packet streams that occur when the bridge activates a backup path or load sharing.

Cause (7): MAC - IP address mapping problem, caused by change of static IP address or simultanous configuration with static IP address and Dynamic Host Configuration Protocol (DCHP)

A.1.12 Symptom: An Entire Segment has no Bridge Connection to the Rest of the Network

Cause (1): Incorrectly configured bridge port (port not active; wrong operating mode, for example, 10 Mbit/s instead of 100 Mbit/s); faulty connections (loose cables, connectors, or plug-in modules); wiring errors on the back plane.

Check installation and configuration of the bridge.

Cause (2): Learning mode of a bridge is not active (that is, the bridge is operating in protected mode), and its aging function has deleted the address entry of the problem node.

Check the bridge address tables and the operating mode. (Is the learning mode on?)

Cause (3): Incorrectly configured bridge or router filters.

Check the filter settings; check wild card entries in particular.

A.1.13   Symptom: An Entire Segment has no Router Connection to the Rest of the Network

Cause (1):   Incorrectly configured router port (port not active; wrong operating mode, for example, 10 Mbit/s instead of 100 Mbit/s); protocol not active; faulty connections (loose cables, connectors, or plug-in modules); wiring errors on the back plane.
Check installation and configuration of the router.

Cause (2):   Incorrectly configured address tables, mapping tables, routing tables.
Check router configuration.

Cause (3):   Incorrectly configured router filters.
Check the filter settings. In particular, check wild card settings and filters that might block backup or load-sharing routes.

Cause (4):   Failure of the wide-area connection on the router's WAN port.
Check whether the WAN line is up and running.

Cause (5):   No default gateway setting.
Check whether a default gateway is set in the router configuration.

Cause (6):   Incorrectly configured subnet mask.
Systematically check all subnet masks in the network.

Cause (7):   Incorrectly configured timer settings.
Check the set timer values for the various protocols. Compare the default values, especially when using routers from different manufacturers.

A.1.14   Symptom: Intermittent Connection Problems Between Client and Network

Client connects, but loses connection periodically. Pings are returned, however packet losses occur.

Cause (1):   NIC or switch/router port misconfigured.
Both sides are not configured for the same operation mode. Check NIC, port settings.

Cause (2):   NIC or switch/router port misconfigured (one side set to manual, one side set to auto negotiation).
Check NIC, port settings. Avoid using the auto-negotiate feature.

Cause (3):   Host busy or overloaded, server experiencing problems.
Analyze server operating statistics and server response time.

A.2 Common Errors in Ethernet Networks

The most frequent sources of problems in Ethernet networks are listed in figure A.1 in alphabetical order:

- AUI cable defective
- Bridge address list incorrectly configured; bridge in protected mode
- Bridge filter incorrectly configured
- Bridge overloaded
- Bridge's aging function deletes address entry
- Bridges or repeaters: too many are cascaded, resulting in timeouts and long response times
- Cable length exceeds specification
- Connectors, loose or defective: interface cards, wall jacks, MAUs, hubs, bridges, or routers
- Electromagnetic interference
- External MAU defective
- Faulty installation of physical router, bridge or hub (cable, connectors, plug-ins are loose; cable connections on the backplane are wrong)
- Grounding problems
- Inter-frame spacing gap too short
- Network grounded in more than one location
- NIC incorrectly configured
- Packets out of sequence due to bridge's load sharing function
- Signal power problems in optical components (optical hub ports)
- Router filters incorrectly configured
- Router incorrectly configured (port not active, protocol not active, wrong operating mode)
- Router overloaded
- Router protocol entries incorrectly configured (address tables, mapping tables, subnet masks, default gateways, routing tables, timer)
- Routing protocol problems (OSPF Hello timer, Dead timer, IGRP Active timer setting wrong)
- Terminating resistor defective or missing (10Base2, 10Base5)
- WAN connections down, overloaded, or of poor quality (high Bit-Error Rate (BER))

Figure A.1 The most frequent sources of problems in Ethernet networks

A.3   Symptoms and Causes: Token Ring

A.3.1   Symptom: Active Monitor Error or Active Monitor Change

Cause (1):   Active monitor detects a claim token frame, quits active monitor status, and sends a report active monitor frame.

This generally occurs when a standby monitor does not detect an active monitor in the ring. (Any station in the ring that is not the active monitor is a standby monitor.)

Cause (2):   Active monitor detects an Active Monitor Present (AMP) frame that it did not generate.

When this happens, the active monitor transmits a report active monitor frame with subvector 2 (duplicate monitor).

Cause (3):   Station participating in the monitor contention process detects a claim token frame with its own address as the source but a Next Available Upstream Neighbor (NAUN) address that does not match the NAUN address in its memory.

This station then transmits a report monitor error frame with subvector 3 (duplicate address during monitor contention).

A.3.2   Symptom: Address Recognized Error

Cause: Station detects more than one AMP frame or an Standby Monitor Present (SMP) frame not preceded by an AMP frame

A.3.3   Symptom: Burst Errors

Cause: Hardware problem such as a defective cable, NIC, MSAU or concentrator

A burst error frame is sent if no signal is received for 5 half-bit times between the starting and ending delimiters of a frame. Decode Token-Ring messages to locate the fault: determine which station reported the error and what stations are upstream from it (refer to the list of active stations). Analyze correlations between station activity and errors in the failure domain. Check the concentrator (run its self-test function). Check cables using a cable scanner.

A.3.4   Symptom: Beaconing, Streaming

Cause (1):   Defective concentrator or NIC

Cause (2):   Loose or defective connectors (interface cards, wall jacks, concentrators, bridges, routers).

Analyze the beacon frames and trace the failure domain from the addresses for the sending station and its NAUN. The failure domain consists of the station transmitting the beacon frame and its incoming line, the sending station's NAUN and its outgoing line, and the concentrator between the two stations. All components within this domain (NICs, concentrators, cables, connectors, wall jacks) need to be inspected.

A.3.5   Symptom: Failed Insertion

Cause (1):   Duplicate address.

During the duplicate address check (part of the station insertion process), the new station detects another station already in the ring with the same address.

Cause (2):   Station unable to participate successfully in the neighbor notification process

Cause (3):   Station parameters not initialized correctly.

A.3.6   Symptom: Frame Copied Error

Cause: Station receives frame addressed to it, but detects that the address recognized/frame copied bits are not 0.

One likely reason for this is a duplicate MAC address in the ring. To locate another station with the same address, use a protocol analyzer and check for a failed insertion frame. Once you have identified the node with the duplicate MAC address, reconfigure it.

A.3.7   Symptom: Lost Frame Error

Cause: Failure to receive a transmitted frame.

This can happen when other stations enter or leave the ring. This error is non-isolating and can't be assigned to any particular station.

A.3.8   Symptom: Frequency Error

Cause (1):   Ring clock rate and NIC's internal clock rate differ significantly.

Cause (2):   Poor cabling.

Cause (3):   Defective NIC.

Frequency errors are non-isolating and can't be assigned to any particular station. Typical causes of frequency errors are poor-quality cabling, cabling that exceeds distance limitations, or defective NICs.

A.3.9   Symptom: Intermittent Errors and Connection Failures

Cause (1):   Cabling exceeds the distance limitations between two ring stations.

If a station is removed from the ring, the distance between two ring nodes can become so great that the signals can no longer be transmitted reliably and serious connection problems can occur (non-isolating errors, token errors, etc.). Check the maximum allowable distance between two stations on the ring and redesign the ring if necessary.

Cause (2):   Phase jitter, frequency errors, timeouts in Token-Ring protocol timers, or intermittent beaconing (Fig. A.2).

Verify whether the maximum number of stations allowed in the ring has been exceeded (see the section on "Network Design Guidelines for Token-Ring Networks" for details).

Cable type	Maximum number of nodes at 4 Mbit/s	Maximum number of nodes at 16 Mbit/s
IBM Type 1	260	140
Cat. 3 UTP	72	72
Cat. 5 UTP	132	132

Figure A.2 Maximum number of stations in a Token-Ring network

A.3.10   Symptom: Internal Error

Cause: Station detects an internal error and recovers on its own.

Internal errors are isolating errors and can be traced to the station where they originate. Capture and decode the internal error frame using a protocol analyzer and observe the node identified.

A.3.11 Symptom: No Connection to Server

Cause (1):   Cable from the node to the concentrator is loose or disconnected, broken, short-circuited, or exposed to electromagnetic interference

Cause (2):   Defective network interface card.
Check cable, connectors and interface card and replace if necessary.

Cause (3):   Address table of a bridge in the transmission path to the server missing the node's MAC address.
Addresses that are not used over a certain period are deleted by the bridge's aging function. If the bridge is in protected mode (that is, learning is deactivated), the transmitting node's address cannot be automatically added to the bridge table. Check the address tables and operating modes of the bridges in the transmission path to the server.

Cause (4):   Bridge port deactivated or defective.
Check bridge ports, send ping packets to nodes beyond the bridge, and analyze the bridge logs.

Cause (5):   Incorrectly configured bridge filter.
Examine the filter settings in bridges along the transmission path to the server.

A.3.12 Symptom: Intermittent Connection Failures

Cause: Duplicate MAC address.
If a station attempts to enter the ring with an address that is already in use, it is refused entry and receives a request to remove frame. To locate the other station with the same address, use a protocol analyzer to capture request to remove frames. When you have identified the node with the duplicate MAC address, reconfigure it.

A.3.13   Symptom: High Network Load

Cause: Overloaded or incorrectly configured router(s) and/or bridge(s). Use a protocol analyzer to identify the most active stations in the ring and search for routing or bridging problems. If timeouts occur, measuring response times can provide clues to the source of the problem. Check the statistics on the routers and bridges involved. How many frames are discarded? Check the bridges' forwarding tables and filter settings. Deactivate optional bridge functions, such as the ring parameter monitor or configuration port server if they are not in use.

A.3.14   Symptom: Network Slow, Stations Locking Up

Cause: Line errors, burst errors, FCS errors, and superfluous ring purges. Burst and line errors are usually caused by defective station cables or hardware defects in the concentrator or the interface card. Check the network for line errors and burst errors. Then check the concentrators, cabling and connectors upstream from the station reporting the error.

A.3.15   Symptom: Neighbor Notification Error

Cause (1):   Insertion or removal of a node.
Cause (2):   Intermittent hardware problems in a NIC.

A.3.16   Symptom: Report Neighbor Notification Incomplete

Cause: Active monitor sends process incomplete frame to the ring error monitor and initiates a new AMP frame.
The neighbor notification process is initiated every 7 seconds, when the active monitor sends an AMP frame. When a station detects an AMP frame, it compares the address recognized bits and the frame copied bits in the AMP frame. If the frame has not yet been copied by any other station, the receiving station compares the source address of the AMP frame with its own NAUN address. If the addresses are different, the source address of the AMP frame is stored as the new NAUN address, and a report NAUN change frame is sent to the configuration report server. If

the AMP frame is not returned to the active monitor before the neighbor notification timer expires, the active monitor sends a process incomplete frame to the ring error monitor and initiates a new AMP frame.

Use a protocol analyzer to check for request to remove frames and try to identify the stations with duplicate MAC addresses.

A.3.17 Symptom: Network Slow Despite Low Traffic

Cause (1): Poor configuration, inefficient protocols, or insufficient NIC memory.

Cause (2): Router or bridge port settings restrict the maximum allowable frame size.

The network load (as a percentage of its capacity) is not the only factor determining network performance. Other important factors include the size and type of frames being transported. LLC frames, for example, carry no user data but serve to set up and maintain connections. A high proportion of short LLC and MAC frames indicates an inefficient protocol. In the NetBIOS/SMB protocol, for example, the ratio of LLC frames to user data packets is about 1:1. The reason for this exceptionally poor ratio is that NetBIOS/ SMB uses a connection-oriented protocol at the LLC level. NetWare IPX uses, a connectionless service, transfers user data without waiting for acknowledgement of receipt. LLC frames are rare in IPX, whereas connection-oriented protocols usually generate a huge number of management frames.

Small frame sizes can also have other causes, however. The data packet size that can be handled by a NIC depends on the card's memory. In a 4 Mbit/s ring the maximum frame size is 4,500 bytes, and in a 16 Mbit/s ring 17,800 bytes. NICs with 8 Kbytes of RAM can only process data packets of up to 1,000 bytes. Older cards with 1 Kbyte of RAM can handle frames up to 2,000 bytes long. State-of-the-art cards, however, usually support the maximum frame lengths of 4,500 and 17,800 bytes. Furthermore, certain network operating systems can restrict the maximum frame size. NetWare 3.11, for example, supports frames only up to 4,000 bytes.

A.3.18 Symptom: Ring Purges

Cause (1):   Short-circuited cable.
Cause (2):   Noise or crosstalk.
Cause (3):   Token rotation time too long.
Cause (4):   Defective NIC.
Ring purges are initiated by the active monitor to delete all signals on the ring in preparation for the release of a new token. They frequently occur when a station enters or leaves the ring. If ring purges occur when no station has been inserted or removed, this indicates hardware problems on the ring.

A.3.19 Symptom: Ring Resetting

Cause: Several consecutive claim token frames transmitted; ring recovers after beaconing.
See the previous section on beaconing as an error symptom.

A.3.20 Symptom: Receiver Congested

Cause: Insufficient buffer space to copy a frame.
If this error occurs frequently you must replace or upgrade the interface cards of the affected nodes to increase card memory.

A.3.21 Symptom: Token Error

Cause (1):   Station entering or leaving the ring.
Cause (2):   Noise.
Cause (3):   Defective NIC or cable.
Cause (4):   Extremely high number of broadcasts.
A Token Error frame is transmitted in any of the following situations:

- A token with a priority greater than zero and a monitor count of 1 is detected beyond the active monitor (indicating that the token is already on its second round).
- No token or frame is encountered before the Good Token timer expires (10 ms).
- Illegal coding is detected.

Token errors are non-isolating and can't be assigned to any particular station.

A.3.22 Symptom: Request Station Removed

Cause: Duplicate Token-Ring MAC address.
                Use a protocol analyzer to capture request to remove MAC frames and examine their source addresses.

A.3.23 Symptom: Token Direction Change

Cause(1):   Insertion or removal of stations.
Cause (2):   Problems with hardware or software components in the ring.
                To determine the direction of rotation, use a protocol analyzer to analyze frames transmitted by the station that is the direct (physical) neighbor of the analyzer, making sure that neither the protocol analyzer nor the neighboring node is the active monitor at the time. If the monitor bit of these frames is set to one, then the frames are moving from the analyzer to the selected neighbor node. If the value is zero, the frames are moving in the other direction. If the direction of token rotation changes, then at least one ring purge has occurred. This can be caused by normal operating events, such as the insertion or removal of stations, or by problems with hardware or software components in the ring.

A.4   Common Errors in Token-Ring Networks

The following list summarizes the most frequent sources of problems in Token-Ring networks (in alphabetical order):

- Bridge address list incorrectly configured; bridge in protected mode
- Bridge filter incorrectly configured
- Bridge overloaded
- Bridge's aging function deletes address entry
- Cable length between neighboring nodes exceeds specifications
- Connectors, loose or defective: interface cards, wall jacks, concentrators, bridges, routers
- Defective Trunk Concentrator Unit (TCU)
- Defective lobe cable
- Defective network interface card
- Duplicate MAC addresses
- Electromagnetic interference
- Faulty physical installation of router, bridge or concentrator (cable, connectors, plug-ins are loose; cable connections on the backplane are wrong)
- Frame length restrictions on router/bridge ports
- Frequency and jitter problems due to cabling, noise, too many stations
- Maximum frame length not supported by interface cards due to insufficient card memory
- NIC incorrectly configured
- Protocol inefficient, not well adapted to Token Ring (NetBIOS/SMB)
- Receive buffer on interface card insufficient
- Ring speed incorrectly set on bridge/router port: for example, 4 Mbit/s vs. 16 Mbit/s
- Router filter incorrectly configured
- Router overloaded
- Router protocol entries incorrectly configured (address tables, mapping tables, subnet masks, default gateways, routing tables, timers)
- Router settings incorrectly configured: port not active, protocol not active
- Short circuit in cable
- Source-routing problems
- Stations: too many on the ring
- WAN connections overloaded or of poor quality (high BER)

Figure A.3 The most frequent sources of problems in Token-Ring networks

A.5 Symptoms and Causes: FDDI

A.5.1 Symptom: Frequent Ring Re-initialization, High Bit-Error-Rate (Detected by LEM)

Frequent ring initializations and high bit-error rates are often symptoms that the signal power of a NIC or concentrator is too weak. To determine whether this is the case, measure the power at a node's receiving port when a constant stream of Halt symbols is transmitted. The average must be at least -20 dBm.

Cause (1): Loose connectors; dust or fingerprints on optical fiber or connector.

Cause (2): Dual Attachment Station (DAS) deactivated.
If a dual-attachment station or concentrator fails or is deactivated, the distance between two stations may exceed the maximum specifications. In a network with high redundancy, the ring should be designed so that no two neighboring nodes are more than 400 meters apart. Then the ring can remain operational even if up to four contiguous stations fail.

Cause (3): Active optical bypass switch.
Optical bypass switches are activated when a node fails, and can increase attenuation caused by the ring by up to 2 dB. If several bypasses are active, the resulting loss can lead to high bit-error-rates and consequent increases in claim and beacon frames.

Cause (4): Defective interface card.

Cause (5): Defective port in a router, bridge, or concentrator.

A.5.2 Large Number of Status Report Frames

Cause (1): New MAC neighbor.

Cause (2): Change in port's operating status.
FDDI stations transmit Status Report Frames (SRFs) to inform other components of changes in their configuration. The presence of a large number of status report frames may indicate problems in the FDDI ring. Use a protocol analyzer or the ring management system to collect and analyze the SRFs. If they do not indicate any unusual conditions, transmit Status Information Frames (SIFs) to poll stations on their status. Keep in mind that the error counters maintained by each node count only frames that end with a valid ending delimiter. Frames that end in Idle symbols or invalid characters can only be detected using a protocol analyzer.

A.5.3   High Numbers of Claim Frames

Cause: Expired Timer Valid Transmission (TVX) or
Token Rotations Timer (TRT).
The station has not received a valid token or data packet for over
2.5 ms. This may be due to a high BER, which may in turn result
from cable or connector problems, defective FDDI ports, or problems with optical bypass switches.

A.5.4   High Checksum Error Rates (FCS Errors)

Cause: Defective cable; defective FDDI interface card; dust, dirt or fingerprints on the MIC connector.

A.5.5   FDDI Frames with the Error Bit Set

Cause: Defective cable, defective FDDI interface card.
The error domain is directly upstream from the station that sets
the E bit in the frames. Check all the components in the upstream
transmission path, including concentrators, cables, connectors,
and the interface card in the neighboring station, until you locate
the source of the error.

A.5.6   Oversized Data Packets
(Length Error Bit Set)

Cause: Problems with the interface card or driver software.
An oversized frame is any frame of more than 4,500 bytes. Its LE
bit is set to 1.

A.5.7   Token Rotation Time is too Long

Cause: Problems with station configuration or cabling.
Similar to statistics on capacity use, the TRT is also an indicator
of ring performance. It should lie below the Target Token Rotation
Time (TTRT) negotiated during the claim process. If the TRT regularly goes over the negotiated TTRT, this could be an indication of
incorrect station configuration or of problems in cables or connectors.

A.5.8   Invalid Frames (Violation Frames)

Cause: Station detects invalid symbols.

When a station detects invalid symbols, it reports this in the next valid frame it transmits. The frame with the error message is not the frame that contains the coding violation or error. The error domain is upstream from the station that reports the violation. Check all the components in the upstream transmission path, including concentrators, cables, connectors, and the interface card in the neighboring station, until you locate the source of the error.

A.5.9 Interface Overflow (Wedged Interface)

Cause: Bursts of small packets that overflow the queue.

Wedged interface ports are a common problem. In these cases the input/output queue exceeds the maximum value supported by the router. The resolution is either to increase the queue size or to reload the router.

A.6   Common Errors in FDDI Networks

The following list summarizes the most frequent sources of problems in FDDI networks (in alphabetical order):

- Bridge address list incorrectly configured; bridge in protected mode
- Bridge filter incorrectly configured
- Bridge overloaded
- Bridge's aging function deletes address entry
- Cable length between neighboring nodes exceeds specifications (especially after a DAS node failure or ring wrapping)
- CDDI only: electromagnetic interference
- Connectors, loose or defective: interface cards, wall jacks, concentrators, bridges, routers
- Defective patch cable
- Defective concentrator
- Duplicate FDDI ring addresses
- Faulty physical installation of router, bridge or concentrator (loose cable, connectors, plug-in modules; incorrect cable connections on the backplane)
- Fiber only: dust or fingerprints on the connector
- Frame length restrictions on router/bridge ports
- Frequency and jitter problems due to cabling, noise, too many stations
- Network interface card defective
- Network interface cards incorrectly configured (TTRT, driver, interrupt)
- Receive buffer on interface card insufficient
- Router filter incorrectly configured
- Router overloaded
- Router protocol entries incorrectly configured (address tables, mapping tables, subnet masks, default gateways, routing tables, timers)
- Router settings incorrectly configured: port not active, protocol not active
- Signal loss due to active optical bypass switch
- Stations: too many on the ring
- WAN connections down, overloaded or of poor quality (high BER)

Figure A.4 The most common causes of errors in FDDI networks

A.7 Symptoms and Causes: ATM

A.7.1 Symptom: No Connection over a PVC

Cause (1): Problems with ATM interface card or driver.
Cause (2): No PVC set, selected VCI is incorrect.
Cause (3): Hardware or software problems on the switch.
Cause (4): Misconfigured ATM port (bit rate, scrambling, interface type, frame type (PLCP, SDH/SONET, SONET)).

A.7.2 Symptom: No Connection over SVC (UNI Signaling Problems)

Cause (1): Problems with ATM interface card or driver.
Cause (2): ATMARP server misconfigured; clients are not set up with their correct ATM and IP address on the ATMARP server.
Cause (3): The address of the ATMARP server is not configured correctly on the client system.
Cause (4): ILMI is not active on the client or the server.
Cause (5): The ILMI software versions on client and server are incompatible.
Cause (6): SSCOP layer not established.
Cause (7): Incompatible UNI signaling variants (UNI 3.0, 3.1, 4.0).
Cause (8): Wrong Called Party or Calling Party number.
Cause (9): Unknown or invalid information elements, or mandatory information elements in wrong order.
Cause (10): Incorrect call reference numbers.
Cause (11): Called party is not ready to accept call; call setup attempt is rejected with RELEASE message.
Cause (12): Misconfigured ATM port (bit rate, scrambling, interface type, frame type (PLCP, G.804, SDH, SONET)).
Cause (13): Hardware or software problems on the switch.

A.7.3 Symptom: High Cell Error Rate (CER)

Cause (1): Problems on the physical layer (cabling, connectors, ATM port).
Cause (2): Too many nodes along the transmission path of a Virtual Path (VP) or Virtual Circuit (VC) connection.

A.7.4 Symptom: High Cell Loss Ratio (CLR)

Cause (1): Problems on the physical layer (cabling, connectors, ATM port).
Cause (2): Too many nodes along the transmission path of a Virtual Path (VP) or Virtual Circuit (VC) connection.

Cause (3):   ATM switch overloaded.
Cause (4):   Insufficient buffering in the switch.
Cause (5):   High network load.
Cause (6):   Limits of traffic contract are exceeded.

A.7.5   Symptom: High Cell Misinsertion Rate (CMR)

Cause (1):   Problems on the physical layer (cabling, connectors, jitter, ATM port).
Cause (2):   Too many nodes along the transmission path of a VP or VC connection.
Cause (3):   High network load.
Cause (4):   ATM switch malfunction.

A.7.6   Symptom: High Mean Cell Transfer Delay (MCTD)

Cause (1):   High signal delay due to long transmission path.
Cause (2):   Too many nodes along the transmission path of a VP or VC connection.
Cause (3):   ATM switch overloaded.
Cause (4):   Insufficient buffering in the switch.
Cause (5):   High network load.
Cause (6):   Limits of traffic contract are exceeded.

A.7.7   Symptom: High Cell Delay Variation (CDV)

Cause (1):   Too many nodes along the transmission path of a VP or VC connection.
Cause (2):   ATM switch overloaded.
Cause (3):   Insufficient buffering in the switch.
Cause (4):   High network load.
Cause (5):   Limits of traffic contract are exceeded.

A.7.8   Symptom: No Connection over Emulated LAN (ELAN)

Cause (1):   Problems with the connected traditional LANs (Ethernet, FDDI, Token Ring).

Cause (2):   IP interfaces on the LAN emulation clients are not active or not functioning.

Cause (3):   IP addresses and subnet masks are incorrect; interfaces belong to different subnets.

Cause (4):   LANE software on the client is not active.

Cause (5):   The LECs trying to communicate do not belong to the same ELAN

Cause (6):   The LECs are not registered on the same LES/BUS.

Cause (7):   The VCC and ATM address of the LANE server (LES) are incorrect

Cause (8):   The VCC and ATM address of the BUS are incorrect.

Cause (9):   LANE-ARP entries are incorrect (MAC-ATM address resolution is not working).

Cause (10): The traffic contracts of the LECs are incompatible.

Cause (11): The primary LANE service failed and the backup LANE service was not activated.

A.7.9   Symptom: No Connection over PNNI Network

Cause (1):   Signaling problems (SVC) between the end systems involved.

Cause (2):   Wrong route selection due to incorrect ATM addressing of the end systems.

Cause (3):   Topology information on the switch port is incomplete or outdated.

Cause (4):   Misconfigured peer group leader (PGL not active or no designated parent LGN).

Cause (5):   Hello protocol is not active on the PNNI.

Cause (6):   The PNNI Routing Control Channel (SVCC-RCC) is inactive.

Cause (7):   Misconfigured PNNI port parameters (cell rate, cell transfer delay, bit rate).

Cause (8):   Uplinks to neighboring peer groups are inactive or not defined.

Cause (9):   PNNI addresses, prefixes or summary addresses are incorrect.

A.7.10   Symptom: Loss of ATM Connections

Cause (1):   Violation of the traffic contract; traffic shaping activated.

Cause (2):   Cell streams with different priorities are transmitted at high load, and cells with low priority are discarded.

Cause (3):   Clocking and synchronization problems due to configuration errors on the ATM port.

Cause (4):   Problems on the physical layer (cabling, connectors, ATM port).

A.8   Common Errors in ATM Networks

The following table lists the most common causes of problems in ATM networks:

- ATM interface card defective
- ATM interface card incorrectly configured (interrupt, driver, timers)
- Cell streams with different priorities are being transmitted at high load, and cells with low priority are discarded
- Classical IP: ATM ARP server address not configured on the client systems
- Classical IP: Misconfigured ATM ARP server: clients are not registered at all or registered under a wrong address
- Faulty cable infrastructure: see Chapter 6
- Electromagnetic interference (ATM over UTP)
- Hardware or software problems on the switch
- High signal transit delay due to long transmission path
- ILMI not active on the client or on the ATM switch
- Incompatible ILMI software versions on client and server
- Incorrect port configuration: bit rate, scrambling, interface type, frame type (PLCP, G.804, SDH, SONET)
- Incorrect router configuration (port inactive, wrong operating mode, protocol not active)
- Incorrect router filters
- Insufficient buffering in the switch
- LANE: IP addresses and subnet masks are incorrect; interfaces belong to different subnets
- LANE: IP interfaces on the LE clients are not active or not functioning
- LANE: LANE software on the client or switch is not active
- LANE: LANE-ARP entries are incorrect (MAC-ATM address resolution is not working)
- LANE: LE Clients are not registered on the same LE Server/BUS
- LANE: LE Clients trying to communicate do not belong to the same ELAN
- LANE: The primary LANE service failed and the backup LANE service was not activated
- LANE: The traffic contracts of the LE Clients are incompatible
- LANE: The LE server (LES) VCC is inactive or the ATM address of the LES is incorrect
- LANE: The BUS VCC is inactive or the ATM address of the BUS is incorrect

Figure A.5a The most frequent causes of trouble in ATM networks

- Loose or defective connectors on interface cards, wall jacks, MAUs, hubs, bridges, routers
- Misconfigured ATM interface card (interrupts, drivers, timers)
- Misconfigured routing protocol entries (address tables, mapping tables, subnet masks, default gateways, routing tables, timers)
- PNNI: Hello protocol on the PNNI interface is not active
- PNNI: Misconfigured peer group leader
  (PGL is not active or no designated parent LGN)
- PNNI: Misconfigured PNNI port parameters
  (cell rate, cell transfer delay, bit rate)
- PNNI: PNNI addresses, prefixes or summary addresses are incorrect
- PNNI: The PNNI Routing Control Channel (SVCC-RCC) is inactive
- PNNI: Topology information on the switch port is incomplete or outdated
- PNNI: Uplinks to neighboring peer groups are inactive or not defined
- PNNI: Wrong route selection due to incorrect ATM addresses
  for the destination node
- PVC not set up; invalid VCI
- Faulty physical router or switch installation (cables, connectors, plug-in modules are loose, backplane connections are miswired)
- Problems on the physical layer (cabling, connectors, ATM port)
- Switch is overloaded
- Too many nodes along the transmission path of a VPI/VCI connection
- Traffic contract is exceeded, cells are being discarded

Figure A.5b The most frequent causes of trouble in ATM networks

A.9   Symptoms and Causes: LAN Switching

A.9.1   Symptom: No Connection Between Segments Linked by a LAN Switch

Cause (1):   Defective cabling.

Cause (2):   Switch power supply failure.

Cause (3):   Faulty switch hardware.

Cause (4):   Incorrectly configured switch: for example, wrong ring speed (Token Ring), 10 Mbit/s rather than 100 Mbit/s Ethernet, half-duplex rather than full-duplex Ethernet, etc.

Cause (5):   Incorrect IP address, subnet mask, or default gateway setting in the switch.

Cause (6):   Incorrect VLAN configuration; one of the nodes that cannot com-
             municate is located in a different VLAN.
Cause (7):   Source routing deactivated (Token Ring).
Cause (8):   Duplicate FDDI address configured for an FDDI switch port.
Cause (9):   Duplicate Token-Ring address configured for a Token-Ring switch
             port.
Cause (10): Defective interface card in the node that cannot communicate.

A.9.2   Symptom: Broadcast Storms

Cause: Transmission paths form a loop because the spanning tree algo-
             rithm is not activated or not supported.

A.9.3   Symptom: Low Throughput

Cause (1):   Poor network design; asymmetrical loads on symmetrical band-
             width at the switch ports.
Cause (2):   Incorrectly configured switch ports (10 Mbit/s rather than
             100 Mbit/s Ethernet; half-duplex rather than full-duplex Ethernet,
             etc.).
Cause (3):   High number of defective frames generated by a defective
             switch port.
Cause (4):   Cable length exceeds specifications.

A.10 Common Errors in LAN Switched Networks

The following listing summarizes the most frequent sources of problems in LAN-switched networks (in alphabetical order):

- Broadcast storms due to loops through several switches; spanning tree algorithm not activated
- Defective switch hardware
- Duplicate FDDI address configured for an FDDI switch port
- Duplicate Token-Ring address configured for a Token-Ring switch port
- Faulty cable infrastructure; excessive cable lengths (see Chapter 6)
- Faulty network design, asymmetrical traffic over switch ports with symmetrical bandwidth
- Faulty physical switch installation (loose cable, connectors or plug-ins; faulty wiring on the backplane)
- Incorrect Layer 3 switch settings: IP address, subnet mask, or default gateway
- Incorrect router or bridge settings for switch ports operating in router/bridge mode
- Incorrect VLAN configuration; nodes that cannot communicate are located in different VLANs
- Source routing deactivated (Token Ring)
- Switch overloaded
- Switch power supply failure
- Switch settings incorrectly configured: port not activated; wrong ring speed (Token Ring); wrong Ethernet speed; half-duplex instead of full-duplex Ethernet or vice versa

Figure A.6 The most common causes of problems in LAN switched networks

A.11 Symptoms and Causes: ISDN

A.11.1 Symptom: No Connection

Cause (1): Faulty cabling or connectors.
Cause (2): Power supply failure.
Cause (3): Crossed wires (in BRI).
Cause (4): Wrong number.

Cause (5):   Faulty network components (ISDN router port, terminal adapter (TA), PBX, interface card, telephone).

Cause (6):   Incorrect configuration of the ISDN interface (ISDN card, router port, or PBX).

Cause (7):   Noise; high BER.

Cause (8):   Problems in TEI assignment (manual vs. automatic mode).

Cause (9):   Duplicate TEIs.

Cause (10): Incompatible Q.931 variants (national ISDN vs. Euro-ISDN).

Cause (11): Incompatible ISDN services.

Cause (12): Q.931 implementation errors.

Cause (13): Wiring faults on the S_0 bus.

Cause (14): Lack of terminating resistors on the S_0 bus.

Cause (15): Faulty grounding (PRI).

Cause (16): Non-shielded cabling between NT and TE (PRI).

Cause (17): Signaling messages are sent with wrong TEI value in the case of multiple signaling links (BRI North America).

A.11.2 Symptom: Frequent Connection Loss

Cause (1):   High BER.

Cause (2):   Slow terminal equipment (Receive Ready (RR) or Status Enquiry responses too slow).

Cause (3):   Application does not respond.

A.11.3 Symptom: Long Application Response Times over ISDN

Cause (1):   Additional call setup time due to automatic connection clear-down (during idle times) by the ISDN router.

Cause (2):   Router does not activate additional B channels at high traffic load.

Cause (3):   Small window size of the application protocol (such as IP) used over the B channel.

Cause (4):   Timers expire in B channel application protocols.

Cause (5):   Application is busy.

Cause (6):   Rate adaptation handshake fails due to wrong terminal application settings.

Cause (7):   Calling/called station is a mobile station.

Cause (8):   Call not end-to-end ISDN.

A.12 Common Errors in ISDN Networks

The following list summarizes the most frequent sources of problems with ISDN (in alphabetical order):

- Call forwarding is active; no incoming calls
- Crossed wires (in BRI)
- Duplicate TEI assignment
- Electromagnetic interference
- Incorrect filter settings in the router
- High bit-error rates
- Incorrect input of multiple subscriber number (MSN)
- Incorrect physical installation of router or switch: loose cabling, connector, plug-in module, or card; faulty wiring on the back plane
- ISDN interface card defective
- ISDN interface incorrectly configured (ISDN interface card, router port, PBX, ISDN telephone)
- ISDN line blocked or not enabled by service provider
- ISDN network interface card incorrectly configured (wrong interrupt, driver, or timer configuration, etc.)
- ISDN router port defective
- Incompatible ISDN services; services not available (not ordered from ISDN provider)
- ISDN telephone defective
- Line breaks (in plug or cabling)
- Long response times due to automatic connection clear-down settings in the router
- Loose or defective connectors on network interface cards, in wall jacks, or patch panels
- No grounding (PRI)
- No terminating resistors on the S_0 bus
- NT defective
- PBX defective
- Power supply defective
- Protocol configuration in the router incorrect (address tables, mapping tables, subnet masks, default gateways, routing tables, timers)

Figure A.7a The most common causes of ISDN problems

- Q.931 implementation incorrect
- Q.931 variant incompatible (national ISDN vs. Euro-ISDN)
- Router does not activate the second (or nth, in PRI) B channel (configuration error)
- Router settings incorrectly configured: port not active, wrong operating mode, protocol not active
- Slow terminal devices (RR or Status Enquiry responses too slow)
- TEI assignment problems (manual vs. automatic mode)
- Terminal adapter defective
- Timers expire in B channel application protocols
- Unshielded cabling between NT and TE (PRI)
- Window size too small in the application protocol (such as IP) on the B channel
- Wrong number called

Figure A.7b The most common causes of ISDN problems

A.13   Symptoms and Causes: Frame Relay

A.13.1   Symptom: No Connection

Cause (1):   Defective cables or connectors.
Cause (2):   Defective power supply (in router or Frame Relay switch).
Cause (3):   Configuration error in router or Frame Relay switch (line rate, clocking, channelization).
Cause (4):   Noise; high bit-error rate.
Cause (5):   Incompatible in-channel signaling (LMI) versions.
Cause (6):   Wrong number called (for Frame Relay SVCs).
Cause (7):   Low signal levels.
Cause (8):   Peer node or peer network inactive or down.

A.13.2   Symptom: High Response Time

Cause (1):   CIR too low for data load.
Cause (2):   Poor DLCI configuration.
Cause (3):   Window size too small for the application protocol transported over Frame Relay (for example, TCP/IP).
Cause (4):   Frequent retransmission by application level protocols due to timeouts or high bit-error rates.

Cause (5): Maximum packet size too small; frequent fragmentation necessary.

Cause (6): Telecom operator is not providing the guaranteed bandwidth; bit-error rate too high.

Cause (7): Hidden, unintended traffic misrouted over the Frame Relay link.

Cause (8): Frame Relay network nodes congested (FECN, BECN messages occur).

A.14 Common Errors in Frame Relay Networks

The following list summarizes the most frequent sources of problems in Frame Relay networks (in alphabetical order):

- Cabling or connectors defective or loose at interfaces, wall jacks, patch panels
- CIR (Committed Information Rate) too low for traffic load; excessive peak loads
- Configuration error in router or FR switch
- Congested Frame Relay network node (FECN, BECN messages)
- DLCIs poorly configured
- Electromagnetic interference
- Error in basic router configuration (port not active, protocol not active, wrong operating mode)
- Faulty physical installation of router, bridge or hub (loose cables, connectors or plug-ins; bad backplane connections)
- Frequent retransmissions of application level protocols due to timeouts or high bit-error rates
- Hidden, unintended traffic misrouted over the Frame Relay link
- Incompatible in-channel signaling (LMI) versions
- Maximum packet size too small; frequent fragmentation
- Noise; high bit-error rate
- Power supply defective (in router or FR switch)
- Router or Frame Relay switch defective
- Telecom operator is not providing the guaranteed bandwidth and/or bit error rate
- Window size too small for the application protocol transported over Frame Relay (for example, IP)
- Wrong number called (for FR SVCs)

Figure A.8 The most common causes of trouble in Frame Relay environments

A.15 Symptoms and Causes: PDH

A.15.1 Symptom: No Connection

Cause (1):   Cabling fault (broken fiber, loose connector).
Cause (2):   Power failure in a network component.
Cause (3):   Faulty module in a network component.
Cause (4):   Incorrect configuration of a network component.
Cause (5):   Problems involving the operating software of a network component.
Cause (6):   Electrostatic discharge (due to the electrostatic charge on a technician's body, or to lightning).
Cause (7):   Faulty solder joints or short circuits (due to dust, humidity or aging).
Cause (8):   Diminished laser power (due to dust, humidity or aging).

A.15.2 Symptom: PDH Alarms

Cause (1):   Insufficient transmitting power at network component interface.
Cause (2):   Optical reflections due to poor splices.
Cause (3):   Overloaded network component.
Cause (4):   Loss of frame alignment.
Cause (5):   Voltage peaks caused by high-voltage switching.
Cause (6):   High bit-error rate.
Cause (7):   Grounding problems.

A.16 Common Errors in PDH Networks

The following list summarizes the most frequent sources of problems in PDH networks (in alphabetical order):

- Failure of a module in a network component
- Power supply failure in a network component
- Static discharge (lightning, static electricity on technician's body)
- Ground faults; wiring closet not grounded
- Configuration error in a network component
- Bad solder joints, short circuits (aging, fatigue, dust, grease, moisture)
- High bit-error rates
- Jitter, wander
- Line breaks
- Voltage surges due to high-voltage switching
- Loose connectors
- Corroded contacts
- Background noise
- Loss of frame synchronization
- Insufficient output signal power/receiver sensitivity at the PDH interface

Figure A.9 The most common causes of errors in PDH networks

A.17 Symptom and Causes: SDH

A.17.1 Symptom: No Connection

Cause (1): Cabling fault (broken fiber, loose connector).
Cause (2): Power supply failure in a network component.
Cause (3): Faulty module in a network component.
Cause (4): Incorrect configuration of a network component such as incorrect path routing configuration).
Cause (5): Problems with the operating software of a network component.
Cause (6): Electrostatic discharge (due to the electrostatic charge on a technician's body, or to lightning).
Cause (7): Faulty solder joints or short circuits (due to aging, wear, contamination, humidity).
Cause (8): Poor laser power (due to aging, wear, contamination, humidity).

A.17.2   Symptom: SDH Alarms

Cause (1):   Insufficient signal power at network component interfaces.
Cause (2):   Optical reflections due to poor splices.
Cause (3):   Pointer jitter.
Cause (4):   Overloaded network component.
Cause (5):   Invalid pointers; loss of pointer (LOP).
Cause (6):   Loss of frame alignment (LOF).
Cause (7):   Voltage peaks caused by high voltage switching.
Cause (8):   High-bit-error rate.
Cause (9):   Grounding problems.

A.18   Common Errors in SDH Networks

The following list summarizes the most frequent sources of problems in SDH networks (in alphabetical order):

- Voltage surges due to high-voltage switching
- Loose connectors
- Corroded connector contacts
- Network component overloaded
- Loss of pointer
- Loss of frame alignment
- Insufficient output power in a network component module; laser aging

Figure A.10 The most common causes of errors in SDH networks

A.19   Symptoms and Causes:
X and V Series Interfaces

A.19.1   Symptom: No Connection

Cause (1):   Incorrect pin assignments (null modem cable used in place of a straight-through modem cable, for example).
Cause (2):   Defective cable (kinked or pinched).
Cause (3):   Defective connector (corroded, broken, or bent connector pin).
Cause (4):   Cable too long.

Cause (5):   Interface on DTE inactive or faulty.
Cause (6):   No power supply to DCE.
Cause (7):   DCE not connected to network.
Cause (8):   Incorrectly configured DCE
              (pulse rather than tone dialing; active modem loop).
Cause (9):   Line busy (another system is transmitting).
Cause (10):   X.21 protocol error (C or I signal not set to ON).
Cause (11):   X.21 protocol error
              (transitions on C/T or I/R not within timing limitations) caused
              by invalid state transitions (lead signal changes).

A.19.2 Symptom: Diminished Throughput; Long Response Times

Cause (1):   Poor line quality.
Cause (2):   High BER due to excessive cable length between DTE and DCE.
Cause (3):   X.21: DTE–DCE cable of critical length, causing timing problems
              (critical length at 64 Kbit/s is 781 meters, at 2,048 Kbit/s is
              24 meters. See "Diagnosing Problems in X and V Series Interfaces"
              for details.).
Cause (4):   High BER due to electromagnetic interference along the
              DTE–DCE connection.

A.20 Common Errors in X/V Series Connections

The following list summarizes the most frequent sources of problems in V and X
Series DTE–DCE interfaces in telephone networks (serial PC ports, modems) in
alphabetical order:

Errors at DTEs and DCEs, telephone networks:
- BER high due to electromagnetic interference in serial port modem connection
- BER high due to excessive cable length between serial port and modem
- Cable fault between serial port and modem (kink or sharp bend in cable)
- Connector fault (corroded, broken, or bent connector pin)
- Connector pin assignments incorrect
  (null modem cable as opposed to straight-through modem cable)
- Interface at DTE (PC serial port, router port) inactive or defective
- Line busy (another system is transmitting)
- Modem connection to telephone line interrupted (no carrier)
- Modem incorrectly configured (pulse instead of tone dialing; wrong number dialed)
- Modem locked: the modem's redialing lock was activated after several
  unsuccessful dialing attempts (no carrier, wrong baud rate, destination busy)
- Modem not connected to network
- Modem not connected to power
- Outside line accessible only through PABX (no carrier without outside dialing
  prefix)
- Poor line quality

Errors at DTEs and DCEs, circuit-switched data networks (X.20, X.21):
- BER high due to electromagnetic interference in DTE-DCE cable
- BER high due to excessive DTE-DCE cable length
- DTE-DCE cable is of critical length (in X.21), causing timing problems
  (critical length at 64 Kbit/s is 781 m; at 2048 Kbit/s 24 m.
  See, "Diagnosing Problems in X and V Series Interfaces", for details)
- Cable defective (kinked or pinched)
- Connector defective (corroded, broken, or bent pin)
- Connector pin assignments incorrect (null modem cable in place of
  straight-through modem cable)
- DCE not connected to network
- DCE not connected to power
- Interface in DTE is inactive or defective
- Line busy (another system is transmitting)
- Modem loop activated inadvertently (by cleaning personnel, for example)
- Modem loop not deactivated after testing
- X.21 protocol error (C or I signal not set to ON)
- Poor line quality

Figure A.11 The most common causes of errors in X and V Series interfaces

A.21   Symptoms and Causes: Internet Protocols

This section lists the typical causes of trouble in IP networks, grouped by the symptoms observed.

A.21.1   Symptom: Ping from Problem Host to Loopback Address 127.0.0.1 Fails

Cause (1):   TCP/IP driver or interface card software is not installed properly.
Cause (2):   Faulty network interface.

A.21.2   Symptom: Ping to Problem Host from a Node in the Same Subnet Fails

Cause (1):   Problem host not connected to the network.
Cause (2):   Incorrectly configured interface card.
Cause (3):   Wrong IP address; incorrect subnet mask.

A.21.3   Symptom: Ping from Problem Host to a Host in the Same Subnet Fails

Cause (1):   Problem host not connected to the network.
Cause (2):   Destination node not active.
Cause (3):   Incorrect IP destination address used in the ping command.

A.21.4   Symptom: Ping from Problem Host to Default Router Fails

Cause (1):   Problem host not connected to the network.
Cause (2):   IP address or subnet mask of the problem host is incorrect.
Cause (3):   Incorrect IP address of the router used in the ping command.
Cause (4):   Incorrectly configured default route.
Cause (5):   Inactive router port.
Cause (6):   DHCP problem. DHCP server used to manage fixed addresses (a given IP address is always assigned to the same MAC address) and station moved to a different segment. The DHCP server assigns old IP address even though the address is not valid in the new subnet.

A.21.5 Symptom: Ping from Problem Host to Host Outside the Local Subnet Fails

Cause (1):   Incorrectly configured default gateway on the router.
Cause (2):   No default gateway configured on the router.
Cause (3):   Remote host inactive.
Cause (4):   Router port to destination subnet inactive.
Cause (5):   Router access list incomplete; does not reflect route updates.
Cause (6):   Incorrect router filter activated.

A.21.6 Symptom: Ping to Problem Host by Name Fails

Cause (1):   Problem host not connected to the network.
Cause (2):   The host name ↔ IP address mapping at the problem host is incorrect.
Cause (3):   The IP address of the DNS server is incorrectly configured.
Cause (4):   DNS server is inactive.
Cause (5):   The table of the host sending the ping contains incorrect host name <> IP address mapping.

A.21.7 Symptom: Ping by Name from Problem Host to Host in the Same Subnet Fails

Cause (1):   Incorrect host/domain name entered in the ping command.
Cause (2):   Remote host not active.
Cause (3):   IP address of the DNS server incorrectly configured on the problem host.
Cause (4):   DNS server inactive.
Cause (5):   The table of the problem host contains incorrect host name ↔ IP address mapping for the host sending the ping.

A.21.8 Symptom: Ping by Name to a Host Outside the Local Subnet from the Problem Host Fails

Cause (1):   Incorrect host name entered in the ping command.
Cause (2):   Remote host not active.
Cause (3):   IP address of the DNS server incorrectly configured on the problem host.
Cause (4):   DNS server inactive.

Cause (5):   The table of the problem host contains incorrect host name ↔ IP address mapping for the remote host.

Cause (6):   Incorrect IP address of default route in the router table.

A.21.9 Symptom: Intermittent Loss of Connection

Cause (1):   Overloaded destination network or host.

Cause (2):   Duplicate IP address: another node is using the destination's IP address.

Cause (3):   TCP connections timing out
(due to bridge or router problems, for example).

Cause (4):   Mixture of dynamic (DHCP based) and static assigned IP addresses.

A.21.10 Symptom: IP Connection Working but Application not Available

Cause (1):   Router access list configured to block the application port.

Cause (2):   Application not active.

A.21.11 Symptom: Diskless Stations Unable to Boot

Cause (1):   Router blocking UDP broadcast forwarding: BOOTP broadcasts not transmitted.

Cause (2):   Incorrectly configured router filter blocking BOOTP packets.

A.21.12 Symptom: Generally Low TCP/IP Performance

Cause (1):   Poorly configured DNS client: client waits until the first DNS request times out before trying a second DNS server.

Cause (2):   DNS server not configured for reverse lookup; reverse lookup requests not being handled.

Cause (3):   DNS table incomplete: does not contain IP address ↔ name mappings for all hosts.

Cause (4):   Local Routing. A switch is connected to a router. In order to reach a segment that is connected to the same switch, a packet first has to be switched to the router, is routed within the router, and then transferred through the same switch again to the destination segment. The number of packets that are being passed through the switch are doubled and additional buffer and CPU resources in the router are consumed.

Cause (5):   Overloaded networks in the path the TCP connection is using.

A.21.13 Symptom: Excessive TCP Retransmissions

Cause (1):   Sent TCP packet or a returning acknowledgement packet lost by an overloaded switch or router.

Cause (2):   Packet corrupted during the transmission, contains a CRC error.

Cause (3):   TCP data corrupted, shows a TCP checksum error.

Cause (4):   Fragment of a fragmented TCP packet lost or corrupted.

Cause (5):   Buffer overflow at the receiver.

Cause (6):   Acknowledgement for a TCP packet sequence is too slow and sender retransmits.

A.21.14 Symptom: TCP Window Size too Small

Cause (1):   Default IP MTU changed by user.

Cause (2):   IP MTU and receive TCP buffer size changed by Internet optimizing application.

A.21.15 Symptom: TCP Window Size Drops Below Maximum

Cause: Application not loading data off the TCP stack fast enough.
Likely causes are performance problems on the server or the client. (If the node is a printer, however, this is a normal scenario).

A.21.16 Symptom: TCP Window Size Constant, Slow Acknowledgement Packets

Cause (1):   Overloaded network, routers, or switches.

Cause (2):   Dial-up or WAN connection overloaded.

A.21.17 Symptom: TCP Window Size too Large

Cause: In some cases a large TCP window size in combination with a small amount of available interface memory and a slow hard drive can cause performance problems. Communication then has to stop until the TCP segment (for example, a large 64 Kbyte TCP segment) is stored and the data transfer process can resume.

A.21.18 Symptom: FTP Service Unavailable or Not Working

Cause (1):   FTP server host down.
Cause (2):   FTP server application inactive.
Cause (3):   Incorrect FTP transfer mode (ASCII / binary).
Cause (4):   Firewall or router blocking FTP packets.
Cause (5):   Incorrect user ID or password for FTP server.
Cause (6):   FTP user has no access privileges to server directories.

A.21.19 Symptom: Telnet Service not Available

Cause (1):   Telnet daemon on remote host inactive.
Cause (2):   Remote host not reachable over the network.
Cause (3):   Incorrect user ID or password.
Cause (4):   Incorrect terminal settings.
Cause (5):   Router or firewall blocking the Telnet port.

A.21.20 Symptom: OSPF Routing Problems

Cause (1):   The Hello and Dead timers of the various routers in the network not coordinated.
Cause (2):   IGRP or RIP route distribution incorrectly configured in OSPF.
Cause (3):   Incorrectly configured virtual link.
Cause (4):   No router port assigned an IP address (OSPF uses IP address as ID).

A.21.21 Symptom: RIP Problems

Cause (1):   Incorrect routing tables because of routing information retrieved from wrong interface or protocol.
Cause (2):   Incorrect router filter configuration.
Cause (3):   Subnet masks of router and host do not match.

A.22   Common Errors in IP Networks

The following listing summarizes the most frequent error sources for problems in TCP/IP environments (in alphabetical order):

- Application is not active
- Destination host is not active
- DNS server is not active
- DNS server not configured for reverse lookup. Reverse lookup request cannot be handled
- DNS table incomplete, does not contain IP   domain name mappings for all hosts
- Duplicate IP address: a second node is using the destination host's IP address
- Faulty network interface
- Host name or IP address configuration of problem host is incorrect
- Inactive router port
- Incorrect destination IP address in the ping command
- Incorrect IP address or subnet address mask on problem host
- Incorrect router filter activated
- Incorrect routing tables due to routing information retrieved from wrong interface or protocol
- Incorrect terminal settings
- Incorrect user ID or password
- Incorrectly configured default gateway on the router
- Incorrectly configured interface card
- Incorrectly configured router filter blocking BOOTP frames
- Incorrectly configured virtual links
- IP address of the default route in the router table is incorrect
- IP address of the DNS server is incorrectly configured on the problem host
- IP address or subnet mask of the problem host is incorrect
- No default gateway configured on the router
- No router port has an IP address assigned (OSPF uses IP address as ID)
- Overloaded destination network or host
- Poorly configured DNS client: client waits until the first DNS request times out before trying a second DNS server
- Problem host not connected to the network

Figure A.12a The most common error causes in IP networks

- Remote host not reachable via network
- Route distribution of IGRP or RIP is incorrectly configured in OSPF
- Router is blocking UDP broadcast forwarding: BOOTP broadcasts cannot be transmitted
- Router port to destination subnet inactive
- Subnet masks of router and host do not match
- TCP connections timing out (due to bridge or router problems, for example)
- TCP/IP software or interface card driver is not installed properly
- The Hello and Dead timers of the various routers in the network are not coordinated
- The hosts table on the host sending the ping contains an incorrect entry for the problem host (incorrect host name   IP address mapping)
- The hosts table on the problem host contains an incorrect entry for the host sending the ping (incorrect host name   IP address mapping)
- Router access list incomplete: does not contain route updates
- Router access list is configured to block the application port

Figure A.12b The most common error causes in IP networks

A.23 Symptoms and Causes: Network Services and Applications in General

A.23.1 Symptom: Application Looping

Cause (1):   Application software problem.
Cause (2):   Insufficient server bus performance.
Cause (3):   Memory allocation problems on the network interface card.
Cause (4):   Problems with the network interface driver.

A.23.2 Symptom: Application Slow

Cause (1):   Congested network.
Cause (2):   Overloaded server.
Cause (3):   Application performs small, incremental file reads.
Cause (4):   Application performs overlapping read commands (for example, every read command reads 20% or 30%, sometimes 100% of the data just read in the previous read operation).
Cause (5):   Application performs overlapping write commands.

A.23.3 Symptom: Connection Timeouts

Cause (1):   System overloaded (memory, CPU load at server, client).
Cause (2):   Network overloaded (a switch or router is dropping packets).

A.24 Symptoms and Causes: FTP and Telnet

A.24.1 Symptom: No Connection to FTP, Telnet Server

Cause (1):   Incorrect user name (typing error, wrong keyboard driver, US/non-US keyboard layout).
Cause (2):   Incorrect password (typing error, wrong keyboard driver, US/non-US keyboard layout).
Cause (3):   User name, password changed.
Cause (4):   User account does not exist, no permission to log in.
Cause (5):   User account deleted.
Cause (6):   Mistyped or wrong IP address.
Cause (7):   TCP/IP driver misconfiguration.

Cause (8):   Domain name server incorrectly configured or not working (try to contact host by IP address).

Cause (9):   Firewall blocks FTP or Telnet applications.

Cause (10): FTP or Telnet client incorrectly configured for use across firewall (no proxy configured; wrong FTP proxy configuration).

Cause (11): FTP or Telnet server down (does it respond to ping?).

Cause (12): No route available to FTP or Telnet server segment (traceroute to server).

A.24.2 Symptom: FTP/Telnet Connection Timeouts

Cause (1):   System overload (memory, CPU load at server or client).

Cause (2):   Network overload (switch, router dropping packets).

A.25 Symptoms and Causes: Mail

A.25.1 Symptom: Problems Sending and Receiving Mail

Cause (1):   No TCP connection to mail server.

Cause (2):   Mail server down.

Cause (3):   Server is running, but not listening on port 25.

Cause (4):   Incorrectly configured server software.

Cause (5):   Incorrectly configured mail client.

Cause (6):   Proxy Server Port is not on port 25.

A.25.2 Symptom: Slow Mail Exchange

Cause (1):   Large attachments.

Cause (2):   Communication via X.400 gateway.

Cause (3):   Slow connection to mail server.

Cause (4):   Proxy Server has a low performance.

Connector Pin Layouts B

B.1   10/100/1,000 MBit/s Ethernet:

Pin number	Signal abbreviation	Signal name
3	DO-A	Data Out A
10	DO-B	Data Out B
11	DO-S	Data Out Shield
5	DI-A	Data In A
12	DI-B	Data In B
4	DI-S	Data In Shield
7	CO-A	Control Out A
15	CO-B	Control Out B
8	CO-S	Control Out Shield
2	Ci-A	Control In A
9	CI-B	Control In B
1	Ci-S	Control In Shield
6	Vc	Voltage Common
13	VP	Voltage Plus
14	VS	Voltage Shield
Housing	PG	Protective Ground

Figure B.1 Pin layout of Ethernet media access units (MAUs)

B.2   Token Ring

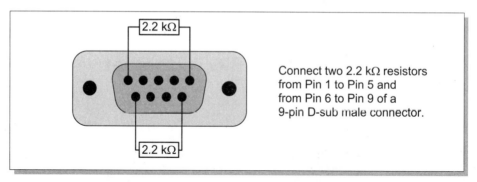

Connect two 2.2 kΩ resistors
from Pin 1 to Pin 5 and
from Pin 6 to Pin 9 of a
9-pin D-sub male connector.

Figure B.2 Mini-network for Token-Ring simulation

B.3   FDDI

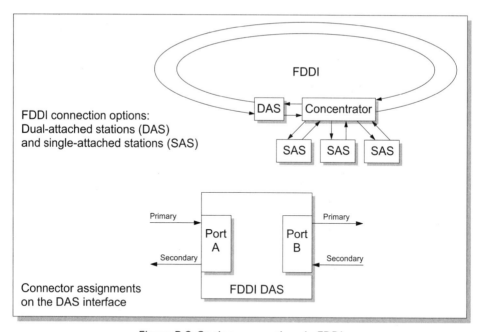

FDDI connection options:
Dual-attached stations (DAS)
and single-attached stations (SAS)

Connector assignments
on the DAS interface

Figure B.3 Station connections in FDDI

B.4 ATM

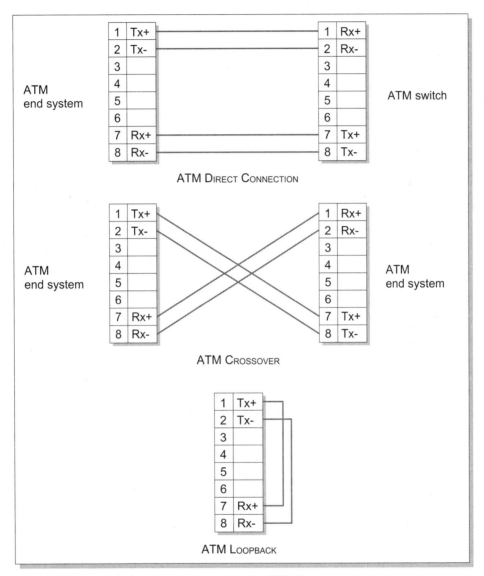

Figure B.4 UTP Cat. 5 pin assignments for ATM direct connection, crossover, and loopback cables

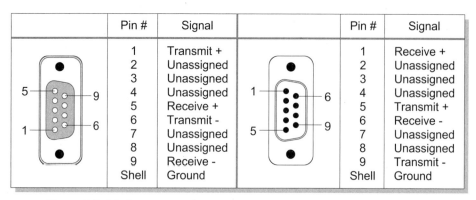

	Pin #	Signal		Pin #	Signal
	1	Transmit +		1	Receive +
	2	Unassigned		2	Unassigned
	3	Unassigned		3	Unassigned
	4	Unassigned		4	Unassigned
	5	Receive +		5	Transmit +
	6	Transmit -		6	Receive -
	7	Unassigned		7	Unassigned
	8	Unassigned		8	Unassigned
	9	Receive -		9	Transmit -
	Shell	Ground		Shell	Ground

Figure B.5 DB-9 connector for 155 Mbit/s ATM over 150 Ohm STP media

B.5   ISDN

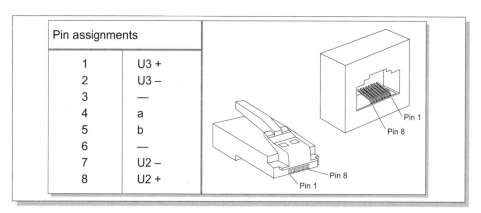

Pin assignments	
1	U3 +
2	U3 –
3	—
4	a
5	b
6	—
7	U2 –
8	U2 +

Figure B.6 Connector and pin assignments in the ISDN basic rate U-Interface:
RJ-45 (ISO 8877)

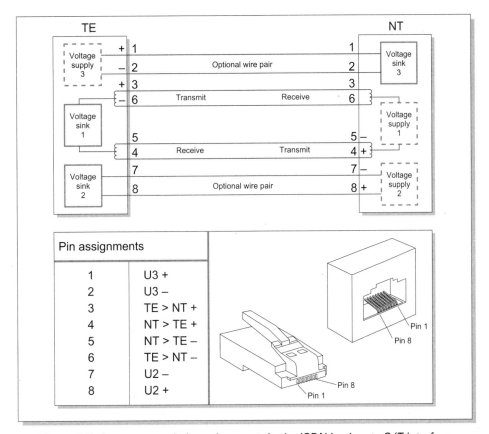

Figure B.7 Connector and pin assignments in the ISDN basic rate S/T interface: RJ-45 (ISO 8877)

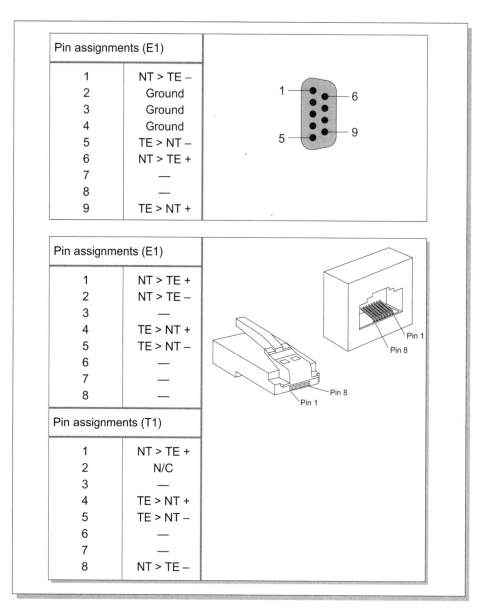

Pin assignments (E1)	
1	NT > TE −
2	Ground
3	Ground
4	Ground
5	TE > NT −
6	NT > TE +
7	—
8	—
9	TE > NT +

Pin assignments (E1)	
1	NT > TE +
2	NT > TE −
3	—
4	TE > NT +
5	TE > NT −
6	—
7	—
8	—

Pin assignments (T1)	
1	NT > TE +
2	N/C
3	—
4	TE > NT +
5	TE > NT −
6	—
7	—
8	NT > TE −

Figure B.8 Pin assignments, ISDN primary rate interface: RJ-48, Sub-D9 (ISO 10173)

B.6   V and X Series Interfaces

	ITU V.24	EIA RS232	Pin Assignments	Description
Ground	101	AA	1	Protective ground (GND)
	102	AB	7	
Data	103	BA	2	Transmitted data (TXD)
	104	BB	3	Received data (RXD)
Control signals	105	CA	4	Request to send (RTS)
	106	CB	5	Clear to send (CTS)
	107	CC	6	Data set ready (DSR)
	108.1	CD	20	Connect data set to line
	108.2	CE	20	Data terminal ready (DTR)
	125	CF	22	Ring indicator (RI)
	109	CG	8	Received line signal detector
	110	CH	21	Signal quality detector
	111	CI	23	Data signal rate selector (DTE)
	112	CK	23	Data signal rate selector (DCE)
	126		11	Select transmit frequency
Clocks	113	DA	24	Transmitter signal element timing (DTE)
	114	DB	15	Transmitter signal element timing (DCE)
	115	DD	17	Receiver element timing (DCE)
Auxiliary channel	118	SBA	14	Secondary transmitted data
	119	SBB	16	Secondary received data
	120	SCA	19	Secondary request to send
	121	SCB	13	Secondary clear to send
	122	SCF	12	Secondary carrier detector

Figure B.9 Signals and pin assignments defined in ITU V.24/V.28 (Europe) and EIA/TIA RS-232C (US)

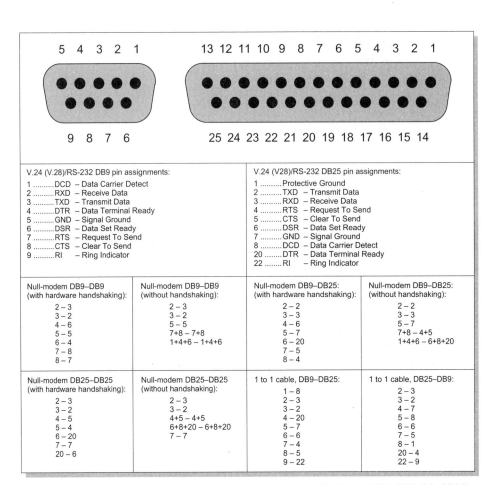

Figure B.10 Signals and pin assignments defined in ITU V.24 and EIA/TIA RS-232C

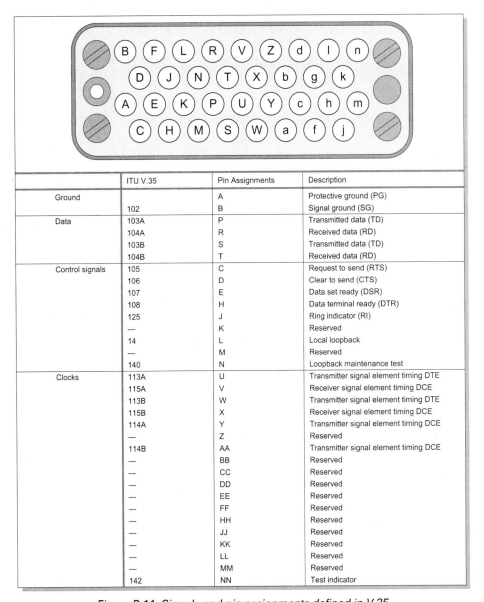

	ITU V.35	Pin Assignments	Description
Ground		A	Protective ground (PG)
	102	B	Signal ground (SG)
Data	103A	P	Transmitted data (TD)
	104A	R	Received data (RD)
	103B	S	Transmitted data (TD)
	104B	T	Received data (RD)
Control signals	105	C	Request to send (RTS)
	106	D	Clear to send (CTS)
	107	E	Data set ready (DSR)
	108	H	Data terminal ready (DTR)
	125	J	Ring indicator (RI)
	—	K	Reserved
	14	L	Local loopback
	—	M	Reserved
	140	N	Loopback maintenance test
Clocks	113A	U	Transmitter signal element timing DTE
	115A	V	Receiver signal element timing DCE
	113B	W	Transmitter signal element timing DTE
	115B	X	Receiver signal element timing DCE
	114A	Y	Transmitter signal element timing DCE
	—	Z	Reserved
	114B	AA	Transmitter signal element timing DCE
	—	BB	Reserved
	—	CC	Reserved
	—	DD	Reserved
	—	EE	Reserved
	—	FF	Reserved
	—	HH	Reserved
	—	JJ	Reserved
	—	KK	Reserved
	—	LL	Reserved
	—	MM	Reserved
	142	NN	Test indicator

Figure B.11 Signals and pin assignments defined in V.35

19 18 17 16 15 14 13 12 11 10 9 8 7 6 5 4 3 2 1

37 36 35 34 33 32 31 30 29 28 27 26 25 24 23 22 21 20

RS-449/V.36/V.10/V.11 37-pin connector for telephone networks (ISO 4902)

8 7 6 5 4 3 2 1

15 14 13 12 11 10 9

V.36/V.10/V.11/X.21 15-pin connector for data networks (ISO 4903)

*Figure B.12 Signals and pin assignments defined in ITU V.10, V.11 (Europe)
and RS-449 (RS-422A, RS-423A; US)*

Tables for Network Design and Operation

C.1 Transmission Delays in LANs

Type of medium	Max. delay per segment (according to standards)	Type of medium	Max. delay per segment (according to standards)
Ethernet 10Base5	2.165 ms	Ethernet 100Base-TX	0.556 ms
Ethernet 10Base2	0.950 ms	Ethernet 100Base-FX	2.040 ms
Ethernet 10Broad36	14 ms	Ethernet AUI	0.257 ms
Ethernet 10Base-FP	5 ms	Ethernet MII	0.0025 ms Typical delay
Ethernet FOIRL	5 ms		
Ethernet 1Base5	4 ms	FDDI	10 – 300 ms
Ethernet 10Base-T	1 ms	Switched 10 Mbit/s Ethernet	0.030 ms
Ethernet 10Base-FB	10 ms	Switched Token Ring	0.030 ms
Ethernet 10Base-FL	10 ms	Switched FDDI	0.010 ms
Ethernet 10Base-T4	0.570 ms	Switched 100Base-T	0.010 ms
		Router	5 – 10 ms

Figure C.1 Transmission delays in LAN topologies

C.2   Ethernet

Topology	Theoretical maximum frame rate / throughput
10 Mbit/s Ethernet	Frame rate = B / (F+I+P) B = transmission bandwidth F = frame size in bits P = length of preamble I = inter-frame gap **Maximum frame rate:** 10 Mbit/s / (512 + 96 + 64) = **14,880 frames/s** **Maximum throughput with minimum frame size:** 14,880 frames · 512 bits = **7.62 Mbit/s** With a frame size of 1,518 bytes the maximum frame rate is 812, which equals 98.7% utilization or a throughput of 9.8 Mbit/s. Ethernet is able to achieve this value if only two nodes are active.
100 Mbit/s Ethernet Half Duplex (shared network)	Frame rate = B / (F+I+P)B = transmission bandwidth **Maximum frame rate:** 100 Mbit/s / (512 + 96 + 64) = **148,809 frames/s** **Maximum throughput with minimum frame size:** 148,809 frames/s · 512 bits = **76.19 Mbit/s** With a frame size of 1,518 bytes the maximum frame rate is 8,127, which equals 98.7% utilization or a throughput of 98.69 Mbit/s. Ethernet is able to achieve this value if only two nodes are active.
100 Mbit/s Ethernet Full Duplex (point-to-point)	**Maximum throughput with minimum frame size:** 148,809 frames/s · 512 bits = **76.19 Mbit/s** **for each direction (send and receive)** **Full-duplex link throughput with minimum frame size** **= 152.19 Mbit/s** With a frame size of 1,518 bytes the maximum frame rate for each direction is 8,127, which equals 98.7% utilization and a throughput of 98.69 Mbit/s. The maximum full-duplex link throughput with maximum frame size equals 197.38 Mbit/s.

Figure C.2 Theoretical throughput rates for Ethernet network topologies

Topology	Theoretical maximum frame rate / throughput
Gigabit Ethernet	Frame rate (without frame bursting) = B / (max (S,F) + I + P) Utilization with bursting: u=(n+1)F/(max.(S,F)+n(F+I+P)) B = transmission bandwidth F = frame size in bits S = slot time P = length of preamble I = inter-frame gap n = number of consecutive frames transmitted in burst after first frame **Maximum frame rate (without bursting):** 1,000 Mbit/s / (4,096 + 96 + 64) = **234,962 frames/s** **Maximum throughput using minimum frame size (without bursting):** 234,962 frames/s · 512 bits = **120.3 Mbit/s = 12% utilization** **Utilization with bursting (during burst)** **using minimum frame size:** n = (65,536 - 4,096)/(512 + 64 + 96) = 92 (number of frames during burst using minimum frame size) u = 93 · 512/(4,096 + 92 · 672) = **72.2% (during 92 frame burst)** **Maximum frame rate with bursting during 92 frame burst:** 1,000 Mbit/s · 0.722 / 512 = **1,410,156 frames/s**
Gigabit Ethernet Full Duplex (point-to-point)	**Maximum frame rate per direction with minimum frame size:** 1,000 Mbit/s / (512 + 96 + 64) = **1,488,095 frames/s** **Maximum throughput per direction with minimum frame size:** 1,488,095 frames/s x 512 bits = **761.9 Mbit/s** **Full-duplex link throughput with minimum frame size** **= 1,523.8 Mbit/s** With a frame size of 1,518 bytes the maximum frame rate for each direction is 81,274, which equals 98.7% utilization and a throughput of 986.9 Mbit/s. The maximum full-duplex link throughput with maximum frame size equals 1,973.9 Mbit/s.

Figure C.3 Theoretical throughput rates for Ethernet network topologies (cont.)

C.2.1   Parameters for 10 Mbit/s Ethernet Operation

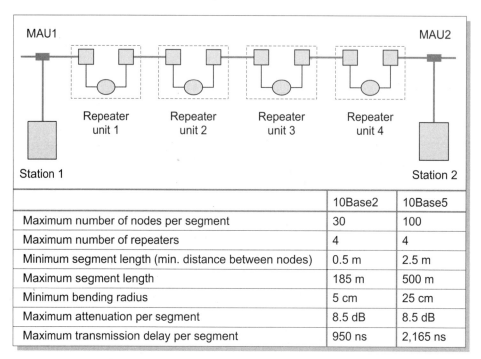

	10Base2	10Base5
Maximum number of nodes per segment	30	100
Maximum number of repeaters	4	4
Minimum segment length (min. distance between nodes)	0.5 m	2.5 m
Maximum segment length	185 m	500 m
Minimum bending radius	5 cm	25 cm
Maximum attenuation per segment	8.5 dB	8.5 dB
Maximum transmission delay per segment	950 ns	2,165 ns

Figure C.4 Design guidelines for 10Base2 and 10Base5 networks

Segment type	Transmission segment (bit times)	Intermediate segment (bit times)
Coaxial cable	16	11
10Base-FB	–	2
10Base-FP	11	8
All other	10.5	8

Figure C.5 Inter-packet shrinkage per segment in 10 Mbit/s Ethernet networks

Segment type	Base for first segment	Base for intermediate segment	Base for last segment	Coefficient (bit times)	Maximum length (m)
10Base5	11.75	46.5	169.5	0.0866	500
10Base2	11.75	46.5	169.5	0.1026	185
10Base-T	15.25	42	165	0.113	100
10Base-FP	11.25	61	183.5	0.1	1,000
10Base-FB		24		0.1	2,000
10Base-FL	12.25	33.5	156.5	0.1	2,000
AUI (-2m)				0.1026	48
FOIRL	7.75	29	152	0.1	1,000

Figure C.6 Path delay components in 10 Mbit/s Ethernet networks

C.2.2   Parameters for 100 Mbit/s Ethernet Operation

10Base-T parameter	Limit
Maximum segment length	100 m
Maximum attenuation	< 11.5 dB
Interference voltage (40 Hz - 150 kHz)	< 50 mV
Interference voltage (150 kHz - 16 MHz)	< 50 mV
Interference voltage (16 MHz - 100 MHz)	< 300 mV
Maximum transmission delay per segment	1,000 ns
NEXT (4 MHz - 15 MHz)	> 30.5 dB

	Maximum segment length	Maximum attenuation	Propagation speed	Maximum signal delay
FOIRL	1 km	9 dB	0.66 c	5,000 ns
10Base-FB	2 km	12.5 dB	0.66 c	1,000 ns
10Base-FL	2 km	12.5 dB	0.66 c	1,000 ns

Figure C.7 Network design guidelines for 10Base-T, 10Base-FB, 10Base-FL and FOIRL

Segment type	Transmission segment (bit times)	Intermediate segment (bit times)
Coaxial cable	16	11
10Base-FB	–	2
10Base-FP	11	8
All other	10.5	8

Figure C.8 Connecting network nodes in 100Base-T full-duplex mode

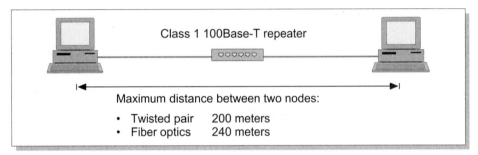

Figure C.9 Design guidelines for 100Base-T networks with Class 1 repeaters

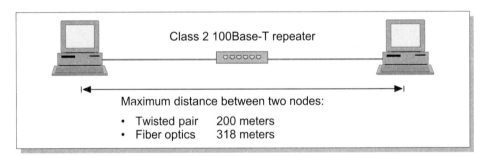

Figure C.10 Design guidelines for 100Base-T networks with one Class 2 repeater

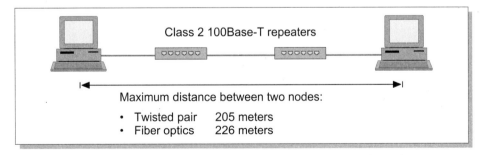

Figure C.11 Design guidelines for 100Base-T networks with two Class 2 repeaters

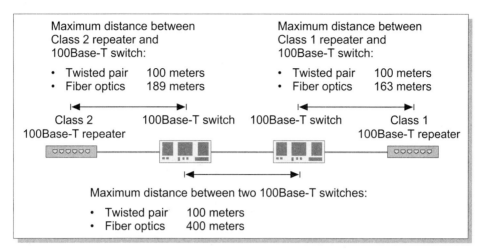

Figure C.12 Connecting workgroups using 100Base-T switches

Network topology	Delay in bit times per meter	Maximum signal delay in bit times
Two nodes	—	100
Cat. 3 UTP	0.57	114
Cat. 4 UTP	0.57	114
Cat. 5 UTP	0.556	111.2
STP	0.556	111.2
Fiber optic	0.501	408
Class 1 repeater	—	168
Class 2 repeater	—	92
MII	1	—

Figure C.13 Delay components in 100Base-T networks

C.2.3   Parameters for Gigabit Ethernet Operation

Standard	Communication medium (MM = multimode fiber, SM = single-mode fiber, UTP = unshielded twisted pair)	Fiber diameter/ wavelength	Bandwidth (MHz · km)	Minimum and maxi- mum link length (m)	Connector
1,000Base-SX	MM	62.5/830nm	160	2 – 220	Duplex SC
1,000Base-SX	MM	62.5	200	2 – 275	Duplex SC
1,000Base-SX	MM	50	400	2 – 500	Duplex SC
1,000Base-SX	MM	50	500	2 – 550	Duplex SC
1,000Base-LX	MM	62.5	500	2 – 550	Duplex SC
1,000Base-LX	MM	50	400	2 – 550	Duplex SC
1,000Base-LX	MM	50	500	2 – 550	Duplex SC
1,000Base-LX	SM	9	—	2 – 5,000	Duplex SC
1,000Base-CX	Coax	—	—	25	STP (DB9); IEC6 1076
1,000Base-T	UTP-5 (four pairs)	—	—	100	RJ-45

Figure C.14 Distance limitations for IEEE 802.3z Gigabit Ethernet

Parameters	Values for Half-duplex	Values for Full-duplex
slotTime	4,096 bit times (4.096 ms)	—
inter-framegap	96 bits times (0.096 ms)	96 bits times (0.096 ms)
attemptLimit	16	—
backoffLimit	10	—
jamsize	32 bits	—
maxFramesize	12,144 bits (1,518 bytes)	12,144 bits (1,518 bytes)
minFramesize	512 bits (64 bytes)	512 bits (64 bytes)
burstLimit	65,536 bits (8,192 bytes)	—
extendsize	3,584 bits (448 bytes)	—

Figure C.15 Characteristics of Gigabit Ethernet Operation

C.3   Token Ring

Token Ring (4 Mbit/s) over Type 1 and Type 2 cabling: Maximum ARL (in meters)
(When Type 6 or Type 9 cabling is used, divide values by 1.33.
 For Type 8 cabling, divide by 2.)

Concen-trators	Number of wiring closets										
	2	3	4	5	6	7	8	9	10	11	12
2	363										
3	354	350									
4	346	341	336								
5	337	332	328	323							
6	329	324	319	316	310						
7	320	315	311	306	301	297					
8	311	306	302	297	293	288	283				
9	302	298	293	289	284	279	274	270			
10	294	289	284	280	275	271	266	262	257		
11	285	280	276	271	266	262	257	253	248	244	
12	276	272	267	262	258	253	249	244	240	235	230
13	268	263	258	254	249	244	240	235	231	226	222
14	259	254	250	245	240	236	231	227	222	217	213
15	250	246	241	236	232	227	223	218	213	209	204

Figure C.16 Token-Ring design table: 4 Mbit/s, Type 1, Type 2 cabling

Token Ring (16 Mbit/s) over Type 1 and Type 2 cabling: Maximum ARL (in meters)
(When Type 6 or Type 9 cabling is used, divide values by 1.33.
For Type 8 cabling, divide by 2.)

Concen-trators	Number of wiring closets								
	2	3	4	5	6	7	8	9	10
2	162								
3	155	150							
4	148	144	138						
5	142	137	132	127					
6	135	130	125	120	115				
7	129	123	19	113	109	103			
8	122	350	112	197	105	97	92		
9	115	110	105	100	95	90	85	80	
10	108	104	98	93.6	88	84	79	73	69
11	102	97	92	87	82	77	72	67	62
12	95	90	85	80	75	70	65	60	55
13	247	77	72	67	62	57	52	47	42
14	69	64	59	54	49	44	39	34	29
15	56	51	139	41	36	31	26	21	16

Figure C.17 Token-Ring design table: 16 Mbit/s, Type 1, Type 2 cabling

Token Ring (4 Mbit/s) over UTP cabling

Concentrators	Number of wiring closets			
	1	2	3	4
1	223			
2	217	206		
3	211	201	196	
4	205	195	190	185
5	199	189	184	179
6	194	183	178	173
7	188	178	173	167
8	182	172	167	162
9	176	166	161	156
10	170	160	160	150

Figure C.18 Token-Ring design table: 4 Mbit/s, UTP cabling

700

Token Ring (16 Mbit/s) over UTP cabling				
Concentrators	Number of wiring closets			
	1	2	3	
1	55			
2	45	39		
3	35	29	23	
4	26	20		
5	16			

Figure C.19 Token-Ring design table: 16 Mbit/s, UTP cabling

If a 16 Mbit/s Token Ring is made up of the three wiring closets A, B and C, of which A and B contain one concentrator each and C houses two concentrators, and the distances between them are AB = 34 meters, BC = 56 meters and CA = 64 meters, then the ARL calculation yields:

$$ARL = 34 + 56 + 64 - 34 = 120 \text{ meters}$$

The corresponding field in the table for 16 Mbit/s Type 1 and Type 2 cabling (four concentrators, three wiring closets) provides the value for the maximum allowable ARL, which is 144 meters. If passive concentrators are used, the maximum allowable length of lobe cables is 144 - 120 = 24 meters. If the lobe cables do not exceed this length, the ring design is suitable for use with passive or active concentrators. If the lobe cables are longer, active concentrators must be used.

C.4   FDDI

The guidelines for designing FDDI networks include specifications for the various cable types as well as limits on the maximum distances between neighboring nodes and the maximum number of nodes per ring.

The maximum distance between two adjacent nodes is 2 km on multimode fiber rings, 40 km on single-mode fiber rings, and 500 meters in low-cost fiber (LCF) rings. It is important to keep in mind that when a ring wraps due to node failure, the ring length doubles. The wavelength used in all fiber optic rings is 1,300 nm. The specifications for diameter and signal power are as follows:

Multimode:

Diameter: 62.5/125 mm, 50/125 mm, 85/125 mm, 100/140 mm
Signal power: -14 dBm to -20 dBm

Single mode:

Diameter: 9/125 mm
Signal power: -14 dBm to -20 dBm (Category 1)
                    -15 dBm to -37 dBm (Category 2)

When shielded (STP-1) or unshielded (UTP-5) twisted-pair cabling is used, the maximum distance between two nodes is 100 meters. There are no values defined for minimum distances between nodes in either FDDI or CDDI.

Connection Rules for SAS and DAS Nodes

When connecting a dual-attachment station (DAS), port A of one DAS must be connected to port B of the neighboring node. For single-attachment stations (SAS), the S port of the node must be connected to the M port of the concentrator:

	A	B	M	S
A	–	+	+	–
B	+	–	+	–
M	+	+	x	+
S	–	–	+	–

+   recommended connection

–   connection could lead to problems; may be deactivated in the manufacturer's default configuration

x   connection not permitted

C.5   ATM

The following tables list the limits for the maximum distances that can be spanned using various transmission media as defined in the appropriate ATM standards:

SDH/SONET-based ATM over twisted-pair cabling

Cable type	Transmission speed	Maximum distance
UTP-5	12.96 Mbit/s	400 m
UTP-5	25.92 Mbit/s	320 m
UTP-5	51.85 Mbit/s	160 m
UTP-5	155 Mbit/s	150 m
UTP-3	155 Mbit/s	100 m

Cell-based ATM over twisted-pair cabling

Cable type	Transmission speed	Maximum distance
UTP-3 (100W)	25 Mbit/s	100 m
UTP-4 (120W)	25 Mbit/s	100 m
STP (150W)	25 Mbit/s	100 m

SDH/SONET-based ATM over plastic fiber

Cable type	Transmission speed	Maximum distance
Plastic Optical Fiber (POF)	155 Mbit/s	50 m
Hard Polymer Clad Fiber (HPCF)	155 Mbit/s	100 m

SDH/SONET-based ATM over single-mode fiber

Fiber type	Wavelength	Transmission speed	Laser type	Maximum attenuation	Maximum distance
SM	1,310 nm	up to 9.9 Gbit/s	SLM, MLM	0-7 dB	2 km
SM	1,310, 1,550 nm	up to 9.9 Gbit/s	SLM, MLM	0-12 dB	15 km
SM	1,310, 1,550 nm	up to 9.9 Gbit/s	SLM, MLM	10-14 dB	40 km

SDH/SONET-based ATM over multimode fiber

Fiber type	Wavelength	Transmission speed	Laser type	Maximum distance
MM	1,300 nm	155 Mbit/s	SW, LED-MMF	2 km
MM	1,300 nm	622 Mbit/s	LED-MMF	500 m
MM	1,300 nm	622 Mbit/s	SW-MMF	300 m

C.5.1   ATM Transmission Delays

The transmission delay can be calculated using a value of 6 µs per km and 2 µs per switch. The transmission delay for a path of 1,000 km and five switches is 6.01 ms.

C.6 ISDN

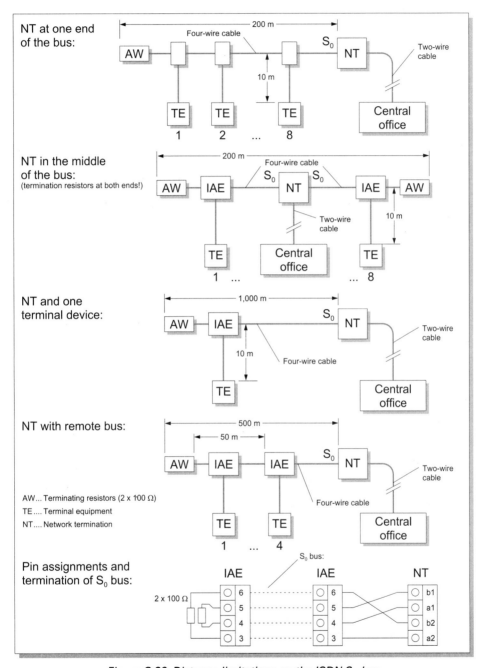

Figure C.20 Distance limitations on the ISDN S_0-bus

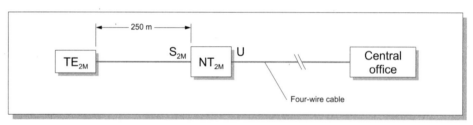

Figure C.21 Distance limitations of the ISDN primary rate interface

LAN Cable Installation Tables

D.1 Connection Categories (ISO/IEC DIS 11801):

Cable Type	Class A	Class B	Class C	Class D	Optical Connection
Category 3	2 km	500 m	100 m	—	—
Category 4	3 km	600 m	150 m	—	—
Category 5	3 km	700 m	160 m	100 m	—
150 Ohm	3 km	1 km	250 m	150 m	—
Multimode Fiber	—	—	—	—	2 km
Monomode Fiber	—	—	—	—	3 km

Class A:	Voice and low frequency applications up to 100 kHz (corresponds to TIA/EIA category 1 cabling)
Class B:	Medium bit-rate applications up to 1 MHz (corresponds to TIA/EIA category 2 cabling)
Class C:	High bit-rate applications up to 16 MHz. (corresponds to TIA/EIA category 3 cabling)
Class D:	Very high bit-rate applications up to 100 MHz. (corresponds to TIA/EIA category 5 cabling)

D.2 Specifications for Backbone Media (TIA/EIA-568)

Media	Application	Distance
100-Ω UTP	Data	90 meters (295 feet)
100-Ω UTP	Voice	800 meters (2,625 feet)
150-Ω STP-A	Data	90 meters (295 feet)
Single-mode 8.3/125 micron optical fiber	Data	3,000 meters (9,840 feet)
Multimode 62.5/125 micron optical fiber	Data	2,000 meters (6,650 feet)

D.3   Copper Cable Parameters

D.3.1   Basic Link Parameters (TIA TSB-67)

	Category 3	Category 5	Category 5e	Category 6
Length including tester cables (meters)	< 94	< 94	< 94	< 94
Attenuation (dB)				
1 MHz	3.2	2.1	2.1	2.1
10 MHz	10.0	6.3	6.3	6.2
100 MHz	—	21.6	21.6	20.7
200 MHz	—	—	—	30.4
NEXT (dB)				
1 MHz	40.1	60.0	64	73.5
10 MHz	24.3	45.5	49	57.8
100 MHz	—	29.3	32.3	41.9
200 MHz	—	—	—	36.9
PS-NEXT (dB)				
1 MHz	—	—	60	71.2
10 MHz	—	—	45.5	55.5
100 MHz	—	—	29.3	39.3
200 MHz	—	—	—	34.3
ELFNEXT (dB)				
1 MHz	—	57	61	65.2
10 MHz	—	37	41	45.2
100 MHz	—	17	21	25.2
200 MHz	—	—	—	19.2
PS-ELFNEXT (dB)				
1 MHz	—	54.4	58	62.2
10 MHz	—	34.4	38	42.2
100 MHz	—	14.4	18	22.2
200 MHz	—	—	—	16.2
Return loss (dB)	—	8	10	12
Propagation delay	—	< 548 ns	< 548 ns	< 548 ns
Delay skew	—	< 45 ns	< 45 ns	< 45 ns

Basic Link	permanently installed cable connection from wall plate to patch panel
Channel Link	end-to-end cable including basic link, patch cables and patch panel jack
NEXT	Near End Cross Talk
PS-NEXT	Power Sum Near End Cross Talk
ELFNEXT	Equal Level Far End Cross Talk
PS-ELFNEXT	Power Sum Equal Level Far End Cross Talk

D.3.2   Channel Link Parameters (TIA TSB-67)

	Category 3	Category 5	Category 5e	Category 6
Length including tester cables (meters)	< 100	< 100	< 100	< 100
Attenuation (dB)				
1 MHz	4.2	2.5	2.1	2.2
10 MHz	11.5	7.0	6.3	6.4
100 MHz	—	24.0	24.0	21.6
200 MHz	—	—	—	31.8
NEXT (dB)				
1 MHz	39.1	60.3	63.0	72.7
10 MHz	22.7	44.0	47.0	56.6
100 MHz	—	27.1	30.1	39.9
200 MHz	—	—	—	34.8
PS-NEXT (dB)				
1 MHz	—	—	60.0	71.2
10 MHz	—	—	44.0	54.0
100 MHz	—	—	27.1	37.1
200 MHz	—	—	—	31.9
ELFNEXT (dB)				
1 MHz	—	57.0	59.0	63.2
10 MHz	—	37.0	39.0	43.2
100 MHz	—	17.0	17.4	23.2
200 MHz	—	—	—	17.2
PS-ELFNEXT (dB)				
1 MHz	—	54.4	56	60.2
10 MHz	—	34.4	36	40.2
100 MHz	—	14.4	14.4	20.2
200 MHz	—	—	—	14.2
Return loss (dB)	—	8	10	12
Propagation delay	—	< 548 ns	< 548 ns	< 548 ns
Delay skew	—	< 45 ns	< 45 ns	< 45 ns

NEXT	Near End Cross Talk
PS-NEXT	Power Sum Near End Cross Talk
ELFNEXT	Equal Level Far End Cross Talk
PS-ELFNEXT	Power Sum Equal Level Far End Cross Talk

Cable designation	RG-58 10Base2 cable, thin Ethernet, Cheapernet	RG-8A/U 10Base5 cable, thick Ethernet, yellow cable
Use	10Base2	10Base5
Impedance (Ω)	50	50 ± 2
Attenuation (dB/100 m)	4.6 at 10 MHz	1.7 at 10 MHz
Velocity factor	0.77	0.83 – 0.86
Inner conductor (mm)	0.94	2.7
Insulation (mm)	2.52	6.15
PVC outer jacket (mm)	4.62	10.3
Bending radius (cm)	5	25

Figure D.1 Specifications for RG-58 and RG-8A/U coaxial cable
(10Base2 and 10Base5)

Cable type	Minimum bending radius during installation under tension	Minimum bending radius in installed state	Minimum one-time bending radius
100 Ω, 120 Ω twisted pair	8 times the cable's outside diameter	6 times the cable's outside diameter (in backbones) 4 times the cable's outside diameter (workgroup areas)	N/A
150 Ω twisted pair	N/A	7.5 cm	2 cm

Figure D.2 Minimum bending radii for twisted-pair cabling (ISO/IEC IS 11801)

Source of electromagnetic interference	Minimum distance at line power < 2 kVA	Minimum distance at line power 2 to 5 kVA	Minimum distance at line power > 5 kVA
Unshielded power lines or electrical equipment near open or non-metallic cable ducts	5 in	1 ft	2 ft
Unshielded power lines or electrical equipment near metallic, grounded cable ducts	3 in	6 in	1 ft
Power lines or electrical equipment in grounded metallic shielding near metallic, grounded cable ducts	—	6 in	1 ft
Transformers, electric motors	—	—	3 ft
Flourescent tubes	—	—	1 ft

Figure D.3 Guidelines for minimum distances between cabling and potential sources of electromagnetic interference (EIA 569)

D.4   Fiber Optic Parameters

Frequency	Multimode Fiber	Single-mode fiber
850 nm	3 - 3.75 dB/km	—
1,300 nm	1 - 1.5 dB/km	0.4 dB/km
1,550 nm	—	up to 0.3 dB/km

Optical Loss Budget =
(number of connectors · 0.5) + (number of splices · 0.2) + (cable length · 3.0 dB/km)

D.5   Decibel Tables

A number of testing and specification parameters in telecommunications are expressed in decibels. The decibel is especially well suited to express the relationship between two values that are on different orders of magnitude, as in measurements of signal attenuation, noise or reflection. Named after the inventor of the telephone, Alexander Graham Bell, the decibel—to put it in general terms—expresses a proportion between two electrical quantities and not an absolute value. These quantities may refer to power, current or potential. The proportion it expresses is not a linear ratio, but a logarithm. This makes it possible to use smaller numbers when comparing absolute values whose difference is great.

A decibel is defined as 10 times the base 10 logarithm of the ratio of input power to output power. The logarithm of a number is the exponent to which the base (10 in this case) must be raised to yield that number. For example, the logarithm to the base 10 of 2, or $\log_{10} 2$, is 0.301 because $10^{0.301} = 2$.

$$dB = 10 \log_{10} (P_1/P_2)$$

By this definition, a power drop of 3 dB indicates that the ratio of P_1 to P_2 is 2 to 1. (The inverse logarithm of 0.3 is 2.)

Because power $P = U \cdot I = U^2/R$ (substituting U/R for I), the ratio P_1/P_2 is equal to the square of the voltage ratio: $P_1/P_2 = U_1^2/U_2^2$.

Accordingly, 1 dB can also be defined as:

$$dB = 10 \log_{10} (U_1^2/U_2^2)$$

or

$$dB = 20 \log_{10} (U_1/U_2)$$

When a voltage ratio is expressed in decibels, a drop of 3 dB represents a ratio of input to output voltage of 1.41 to 1. (A 3 dB *power* loss, by contrast, corresponds to a 2:1 ratio of input power to output power). For this reason, the decibel value is meaningless unless the corresponding electrical quantity—power, voltage, current, etc.—is specified.

Another frequently used measurement parameter derived from the decibel is the absolute power level in dBm (read "decibels referenced to 1 milliwatt"), which is the decibel value of a power ratio where the reference power (P_2 in the previous definition) is 1 milliwatt. A power level of 1 watt can thus be expressed as 30 dBm:

Power level:	dBm:
1 W	30 dBm
10 mW	10 dBm
1 mW	0 dBm
1 µW	−30 dBm

The following tables show the logarithmic progression and decrease of decibels as seen in power and voltage measurements.

Decibel Value (dB)	Actual Power Ratio (output : input)
0	1:1
3	2:1
6	4:1
9	8:1
10	10:1
13	20:1
16	40:1
19	80:1
20	100:1
23	200:1
26	400:1
29	800:1
30	1,000:1
33	2,000:1
36	4,000:1
39	8,000:1
40	10,000:1
50	100,000:1
60	1,000,000:1

The next table displays the various decibel levels and the corresponding voltage and power ratios.

Decibel (dB)	Voltage Ratio	Power Ratio
1	1	1
-1	0.891	0.794
-2	0.794	0.631
-3	0.707	0.500
-4	0.631	0.398
-5	0.562	0.316
-6	0.500	0.250
-7	0.447	0.224
-8	0.398	0.158
-9	0.355	0.125
-10	0.316	0.100
-12	0.250	0.063
-15	0.178	0.031
-20	0.100	0.010
-25	0.056	0.003
-30	0.032	0.001
-40	0.010	0.000
-50	0.003	0.000

D.6   Cabling Newsgroup

One of the most comprehensive resources for information on cabling is the Internet newsgroup comp.dcom.cabling. The Frequently Asked Questions (FAQ) list of this discussion forum can be retrieved from any of the many newsgroup FAQ archives (for example: *www.dejanews.com*)

Other useful Internet resources for cabling related topics are

www.wiring.com

www.cable-design.com

www.tiaonline.com

Ethernet Tables

E.1 Ethernet IEEE 802.3 Ethertype Field Coding

The most recent listing of IEEE 802.3 Ethertype field codes is available under

http://standards.ieee.org/regauth/ethertype/type-pub.html

Ethertype value (Hex)	Description	Ethertype value (Hex)	Description
0000-05DC	IEEE802.3 Length Field	8019	Apollo Computers Chelmsford, MA
0101-01FF	Xerox (Experimental) Webster, NY	802E	Tymshare Cupertino, CA
0200	XEROX PUP Webster, NY	802F	Tigan, Inc. Palo Alto, CA
0201	Xerox PUP Addr Trans Webster, NY	8035	Stanford University Stanford, CA
0400	Nixdorf Paderborn West Germany	8036	Aeonic Systems Billerica, MA
0600	XEROX NS IDP Webster, NY	8044	Planning Research Corp
0660 - 0661	DLOG Olching Germany	8046 - 8047	AT & T Naperville, IL
0800 - 0803	Xerox Webster, NY	8049	ExperData Boulogne, France
0804	Symbolics Research Cambridge, MA	805B - 805C	Stanford University Stanford, CA
0805	Xerox Webster, NY	805D	Evans & Sutherland Salt Lake City, UT
0806	Symbolics, Inc. Cambridge, MA	8060	Little Machines San Diego, CA
0807	Xerox Webster, NY	8062	Counterpoint Computers San Jose, CA
0808	Xerox (Frame Relay ARP) Webster,NY	8065 - 8066	University of Mass. at Amherst Amherst, MA
0844	Planning Research Corp. Bellevue, NE	8067	Veeco Integrated Automation Dallas, TX
0888 - 088A	Xyplex Concord, MA	8068	General Dynamics Fort Worth, TX
0A00	Xerox IEEE802.3 PUP Webster, NY	8069	AT & T Naperville, IL
0A01	Xerox Webster, NY	806A	Autophon Solothurn Switzerland
1000 - 10FF	Xerox Webster, NY	806C	ComDesign Goleta, CA
2000 - 207F	LRW Systems Stamford, CT	806D	Compugraphic Corporation Wilmington, MA
6010 - 6014	3Com Corporation Santa Clara, CA	806E - 8077	Landmark Graphics Corporation Houston, TX
7020 - 7029	LRT Reading, Berks, England	807A	Matra Paris France
8006	Nestar	807B	Dansk Data Elektronik A/S Herlev Denmark
8008	AT & T Naperville, IL	807C	University of Michigan Ann Arbor, MI
8013 - 8016	Silicon Graphics Mountain View, CA	807D - 8080	Vitalink Communications Mountain View, CA

Ethertype value (Hex)	Description	Ethertype value (Hex)	Description
8081 - 8083	Counterpoint Computers San Jose, CA	8150	Rational Corp. Santa Clara, CA
809B	Kinetics Walnut Creek, CA	8151 - 8153	Qualcomm, Inc. San Diego, CA
809C - 809E	Datability New York, NY	815C - 815E	Computer Protocol Pty Ltd. Bentley Western Australia
809F	Spider Systems Ltd. Edinburgh, Scotland	8164 - 8166	Charles River Data Systems, Inc. Framingham, MA
80A3	Nixdorf Computers Paderborn, West Germany	8167 - 816C	Keithley Instruments, Inc. Cleveland, OH
80A4 - 80B3	Siemens Gammasonics, Inc. Des Plaines, IL	817D - 818C	Protocol Engines Inc. Santa Barbara, CA
80C0 - 80C3	Digital Comm. Assoc. Inc. Alpharetta, GA	818D	Motorola Computer X Schaumburg, IL
80C4 - 80C5	Banyan Systems, Inc. Westboro, MA	819A - 81A3	Qualcomm, Inc. San Diego, CA
80C6	Pacer Software La Jolla, CA	81A4	ARAI Bunkichi Yokohama Japan
80C7	Applitek Corporation Wakefield, MA	81A5 - 81AE	RAD Network Devices Torrance, CA
80C8 - 80CC	Intergraph Corporation Huntsville, AL	81B7 - 81B9	Xyplex Boxborough MA
80CD - 80CE	Harris Corporation Fort Lauderdale, FL	81CC - 81D5	Apricot Computers Birmingham England
80CF - 80D2	Taylor Instrument Rochester, NY	81D6 - 81DD	Artisoft, Inc. Tucson AZ
80D3 - 80D4	Rosemount Corporation La Habra, CA	81DE - 81E0	Hewlett Packard Palo Alto, CA
80DD	Varian Associates Palo Alto, CA	81E6 - 81EF	Polygon, Inc. St. Louis, MO
80DE - 80DF	Integrated Solutions San Jose, CA	81F0 - 81F2	Comsat Laboratories Clarksburg, MD
80E0 - 80E3	Allen-Bradley Ann Arbor, MI	81F3 - 81F5	Science Applications International Corp. SAIC Oak Ridge, TN
80E4 - 80F0	Datability New York, NY	81F6 - 81F8	VG Analytical Ltd. Manchester England
80F2	Retix Santa Monica, CA	8203 - 8205	Quantum Software Systems, Ltd. Ontario Canada
80F3 - 80F5	Kinetics Walnut Creek, CA	8221 - 8222	Ascom Banking Systems Ltd. Solothurn Switzerland
80F7	Apollo Computer Chelmsford, MA	823E - 8240	Advanced Encryption Systems, Inc. Santa Clara, CA
80FF - 8103	Wellfleet Communications Bedford, MA	8263 - 826A	Charles River Data Systems Framingham, MA
8130	Hayes Microcomputer Products Ltd. Ontario Canada (formerly Waterloo Microsystems Inc)	827F - 8282	Athena Programming, Inc. Hillsboro, OR
8131	VG Laboratory Systems Cheshire England	829A - 829B	Institute for Industrial Information Tech. Ltd. Swansea, England
8132 - 8136	Bridge Communications, Inc. Mountain View, CA	829C - 82AB	Taurus Controls, Inc. Tualatin, OR
8137 - 8138	Novell, Inc. Provo, UT	82AC - 838F	Walker Richer & Quinn, Inc. Seattle, WA
8139 - 813D	KTI San Jose, CA	8390	LANSoft, Inc. Provo, UT
8148	Logicraft, Inc. Nashua, NH	8391 - 8693	Walker Richer & Quinn, Inc. Seattle, WA
8149	Network Computing Devices Palo Alto, CA	8694 - 869D	Idea Courier Tempe, AZ
814A	Alpha Micro Santa Ana, CA	869E - 86A1	Computer Network Technology Corp. Maple Grove, MN
814B	Keithley Instruments, Inc. Cleveland, OH	86A3 - 86AC	Gateway Communications, Inc. Irvine, CA
814D - 814E	BIIN Hillsboro, OR	86DB	SECTRA - Secure Transmission AB Linkoping Sweden
814F	Technically Elite Concepts, Inc. Torrance, CA		

Ethertype value (Hex)	Description	Ethertype value (Hex)	Description
86DE	Delta Controls, Inc. British Columbia Canada	8866	Lucent Technologies Naperville, IL
86DF	USC-ISI Marina del Rey, CA	8867	Lucent Technologies Naperville, IL
86E0 - 86EF	Landis & Gyr Powers, Inc. Buffalo Grove, IL	8868	NBX Corporation Andover, MA
8700 - 8710	Motorola, Inc. Schaumburg, IL	8869	Broadband Access Systems Marlborough, MA
8711 - 8720	Cray Communications Annapolis Jct, MD	886a	Electronic Theatre Controls,Inc. Middleton, WI
8725 - 8728	Phoenix Microsystems Huntsville, AL	886b	Bay Networks Santa Clara, CA
8739 - 873C	Control Technology, Inc. Knoxville, TN	886c	Epigram, Inc. Sunnyvale, CA
8755 - 8759	LANSoft Inc. Provo, UT	886d	Intel Corporation Hillsboro, OR
875A - 875C	Norand Cedar Rapids, IA	886e	Intel Corporation Hillsboro, OR
875D - 8766	Univ. of Utah Dept./Computer Science Salt Lake City, UT	886f	Microsoft Corporation Redmond, WA
8780 - 8785	Symbol Technologies, Inc. San Jose, CA	8870	Alteon Networks, Inc. San Jose, CA
8804 - 8806	Marathon Technologies Corp. Boxborough, MA	8871	Nippon Telegraph & Telephone Corp. Tokyo, Japan
880F - 8812	Hypercom Network Systems Phoenix, AZ	8872	UUNET Technologies Purchase, NY
8813	Japan Computer Industry Inc. Osaka Japan	8873	Crescent Networks, Inc. Chelmsford, MA
8856	Axis Communications AB Scheelevagen Sweden	8874	Broadcom Corp. San Jose, CA
8A96 - 8A97	Invisible Software Foster City, CA	8875	Adaptive Broadband Corp. Sunnyvale, CA
9000	Xerox Webster, NY	8876	Emware Salt Lake City, UT
FF00 - FF0F	ISC-Bunker Ramo Spokane, WA	8877	Lucent Technologies Atlanta, GA
884C	The ATM Forum Mountainview, CA	8878	Lucent Technologies Atlanta, GA
885a	Foundry Networks Sunnyvale, CA	8879	Expand Networks Tel Aviv, Israel
885b	Hewlett-Packard GmbH Boeblingen, Germany	887e	Space CyberLink, Inc. Seoul, Korea
885c	Hewlett-Packard GmbH Boeblingen, Germany	887f	ESI Plano, TX
885d	Endocardial Solutions, Inc. St. Paul, MN	8880	Exbit Technology Herlev, Denmark
885e	Quantum Corporation Milpitas, CA	8881	TIA Arlington, VA
885f	Digidesign Palo Alto, CA	8882	Comtrol Europe Launton Oxfordhire U.K.
8860	AGCS Phoenix, AZ	8883	2Wire, Inc. San Jose, CA 95131
8861	Intel Hillsboro, OR	8884	The ATM Forum Mountainview, CA
8862	Intel Hillsboro, OR	8885	NETSEC (Network Security Technologies, Inc.) Herdon, VA 20171
8863	UUNET Technologies, Inc. Fairfax, VA	8886	Big Band Networks, Ltd. Tel Aviv, Israel
8864	UUNET Technologies, Inc. Fairfax, VA	8887	Alloptic, Inc. Pleasanton, CA
8865	Visual Networks Rockville, MD	8888	Santera Systems Plano, TX

E.2   Service Access Points (SAPs)

Address (Hex)	Description
00	Null LSAP
02	Individual LLC Sublayer Management Function
03	Group LLC Sublayer Management Function
04	IBM SNA Path Control (individual)
05	IBM SNA Path Control (group)
06	ARPANET Internet Protocol (IP)
07	IP DOD
08	SNA
09	SNA
0C	SNA
0D	SNA
0E	PROWAY (IEC955) Network Management & Initialization
10	IPX Novell
18	Texas Instruments
20	CLNP ISO
34	CLNP ISO
42	IEEE 802.1 Bridge Spanning Tree Protocol
4E	EIA RS-511 Manufacturing Message Service ISO 9506
7E	ISO 8208 (X.25 over IEEE 802.2 Type 2 LLC)
80	Xerox Network Systems (XNS)
81	Xerox Network Systems (XNS)
86	LLC Nestar

Address (Hex)	Description
87	LLC
8E	PROWAY (IEC 955) Active Station List Maintenance
98	ARPANET Address Resolution Protocol (ARP)
AA	SubNetwork Access Protocol (SNAP)
AB	SubNetwork Access Protocol (SNAP) DOD
BC	Banyan VINES
BD	Banyan VINES
E0	Novell NetWare
E1	XNS
EC	CLNP (ISO)
F0	IBM NetBIOS
F1	NetBIOS
F4	LNM IBM LAN Management (individual)
F5	LNM IBM LAN Management (group)
F8	RPL IBM Remote Program Load
F9	RPL
FA	Ungermann-Bass
FB	Ungermann-Bass
FC	RPL
FD	RPL
FE	ISO Network Layer Protocol (NLP)
FF	Global LSAP (IEEE)

E.3   Ethernet Multicast and Broadcast Address Tables

Multicast Addresses

00-00-69-02-XX-XX	Concord Communications DTQNA
01-00-0C-CC-CC-CC	CDP (Cisco Discovery Protocol), VTP (Virtual Trunking Protocol)
01-00-0C-DD-DD-DD	CGMP (Cisco Group Management Protocol)
01-00-10-00-00-20	Hughes Lan Systems Terminal Server S/W download
01-00-10-FF-FF-20	Hughes Lan Systems Terminal Server S/W request
01-00-1D-00-00-00	Cabletron PC-OV PC discover (on demand)
01-00-1D-42-00-00	Cabletron PC-OV Bridge discover (on demand)
01-00-1D-52-00-00	Cabletron PC-OV MMAC discover (on demand)
01-00-3C-xx-xx-xx	Auspex Systems (ServerGuard)
01-00-5E-00-00-00	DoD Internet Multicast Reserved (RFC-1112)
01-00-5E-00-00-01	DoD Internet Multicast All Systems (RFC-1112)
01-00-5E-00-00-02	DoD Internet Multicast All Routers (RFC-1112)
01-00-5E-00-00-03	DoD Internet Multicast Unassigned (RFC-1112)
01-00-5E-00-00-04	DoD Internet Multicast DVMRP Router (RFC-1112)

Multicast Addresses

01-00-5E-00-00-05	OSPFIGP All Routers (RFC 2328)
01-00-5E-00-00-06	OSPFIGP Designated Routers (FRC 2328)
01-00-5E-00-00-07	ST Routers (FRC 1190)
01-00-5E-00-00-08	ST Hosts (RFC 1190)
01-00-5E-00-00-09	RIP2 Router (RFC 1723)
01-00-5E-00-00-0A	Cisco Systems All PIM Routers
01-00-5E-00-00-0B	U. Michigan Mobile Agents
01-00-5E-00-00-0C	DHCP Server Relay Agent (RFC 184)
01-00-5E-00-00-0D	Cisco Systems IGMP
01-00-5E-00-00-0E	ISI RSVP Encapsuation
01-00-5E-00-00-0F	cs.ucl.ac.uk-all-cbt-routers
01-00-5E-00-00-10	Cisco Systems designated sbm
01-00-5E-00-00-11	Cisco Systems all sbms
01-00-5E-00-00-12	Ipsilon VRRP
01-00-5E-00-00-13	Siara IP All L1 ISs
01-00-5E-00-00-14	Siara IP All L2 ISs
01-00-5E-00-00-15	Siara IP All Intermediate Systems
01-00-5E-00-00-16	Cisco Systems IGMP
01-00-5E-00-00-17 through 01-00-5E-00-00-FF	Unassigned

Multicast Addresses

01-00-5E-00-01-00	VMTP Managers Group (RFC 1045)
01-00-5E-00-01-01	NTP Network Time Protocol (RFC 1119)
01-00-5E-00-01-02	SGI (Silicon Graphics)
01-00-5E-00-01-03	Xerox Parc Rwhod
01-00-5E-00-01-04	Standford University VNP
01-00-5E-00-01-05	Artificial Horizons Aviator
01-00-5E-00-01-06	Xerox Parc NSS Name Service Server
01-00-5E-00-01-07	Chalmers AUDIONEWS Audio News Multicast
01-00-5E-00-01-08	SUN NIS Information Service
01-00-5E-00-01-09	Xerox MTP Multicast Transport Protcol
01-00-5E-00-01-0A	Precept IETF 1 LOW AUDIO
01-00-5E-00-01-0B	Precept IETF 1 AUDIO
01-00-5E-00-01-0C	Precept IETF 1 VIDEO
01-00-5E-00-01-0D	Precept IETF 2 LOW AUDIO
01-00-5E-00-01-0E	Precept IETF 2 AUDIO
01-00-5E-00-01-0F	Precept IETF 2 VIDEO
01-00-5E-00-01-10	Guido van Rossum MUSIC SERVICE
01-00-5E-00-01-11	SEANET TELEMETRY
01-00-5E-00-01-12	SEANET IMAGE
01-00-5E-00-01-13	ISI MILOADD
01-00-5E-00-01-14	ISI any private experiment
01-00-5E-00-01-15	Casc DVMRP on MOSPF
01-00-5E-00-01-16	TGV SVRLOC
01-00-5E-00-01-17	Xingte XINGTV
01-00-5E-00-01-18	Microsoft ds
01-00-5E-00-01-19	birch.crd.ge.com-nbc-pro
01-00-5E-00-01-1A	birch.crd.ge.com-nbc-pfn
01-00-5E-00-01-1B	Lockheed Imsc calren 1
01-00-5E-00-01-1C	Lockheed Imsc calren 2
01-00-5E-00-01-1D	Lockheed Imsc calren 3
01-00-5E-00-01-1E	Lockheed Imsc calren 4
01-00-5E-00-01-1F	ampr info
01-00-5E-00-01-20	ISI mtrace
01 00 5E 80 00 00 trough	
01 00 5E FF FF FF	DoD Internet reserved by IANA
01-00-81-00-00-00	Synoptics Network Management
01-00-81-00-00-02	Synoptics Network Management
01-00-81-00-01-00	(snap type 01A2) (Synoptics) autodiscovery
01-00-81-00-01-01	(snap type 01A1) (Synoptics) autodiscovery
01-20-25-00-00-00 through 01-20-25-7F-FF-FF	Control Technology Inc's Industrial Ctrl Proto.
01-80-C2-00-00-00	IEEE 802.1d Spanning tree Bridge Group Address
01-80-C2-00-00-01 through 01-80-C2-00-00-0F	IEEE 802.1d alternate Spanning tree multicast
01-80-C2-00-00-10	IEEE 802.1d Spanning tree (for bridges)
01-80-C2-00-00-01 through 01-80-C2-00-00-0F	802.1 alternate Spanning multicast
01-80-C2-00-00-10	IEEE 802.1d Bridge Management
01-80-C2-00-00-11	IEEE 802.1d Load Server Group Address

Multicast Addresses

01-80-C2-00-00-12	IEEE 802.1d Loadable Device
01-80-C2-00-00-14	OSI ISISDP Route level 1 (within area) IS hello?
01-80-C2-00-00-15	OSI ISISDP Route level 2 (between area) IS hello?
01-80-C2-00-00-16	ISO 10030 All CONS End Systems
01-80-C2-00-00-17	ISO 10030 All CONS SNAREs
01-80-C2-00-01-00	FDDI RMT Directed Beacon
01-80-C2-00-01-10	FDDI Status Report Frame
01-80-C2-00-01-20	FDDI SMT All Root Concentrator MAC
01-80-24-00-00-00	Kalpana Etherswitch every 60 seconds
01-DD-00-FF-FF-FF	Ungermann-Bass boot-me requests
01-DD-01-00-00-00	Ungermann-Bass Spanning Tree
03-00-00-00-00-01	NetBEUI
3-0-0-0-0-40	OS/2 1.3 EE + Communications Manager
3-0-0-0-0-41	OS/2 1.3 EE + Communications Manager
08-00-2B-0X-XX-XX through 08-00-2B-1X-XX-XX	DEC 23 365A1 00 PROM
08-00-2B-20-XX-XX	DEC 23 00XEC 00 Multi-Address ROM
08-00-2B-22-00-00	DEC Bridge Management
08-00-2B-23-XX-XX	DEC 23 365A1 00 PROM
08-00-2B-23-XX-XX through 08-00-2B-3X-XX-XX	DEC PROM 23 365A1 00
08-00-2B-4X-XX-XX	DEC 23 365A1 00 Shadow PROM
08-00-2B-5X-XX-XX through 08-00-2B-7X-XX-XX	DEC 23 365A1 00 Shadow PROM
08-00-2B-E0-XX-XX	DEC VAX 3000 Fault Tolerant LAN
08-00-2B-F0-XX-XX	DEC VAXft 3000 Fault Tolerant LAN
08-00-7C-XX-XX-XX	Vitalink Bridges
09-00-02-04-00-01	Vitalink Printer Messages
09-00-02-04-00-02	Vitalink Bridge Management
09-00-07-00-00-00 through 09-00-07-00-00-FC	AppleTalk Zone multicast addresses
09-00-07-FF-FF-FF	AppleTalk broadcast address
09-00-09-00-00-01	HP Probe
09-00-09-00-00-01	HP Probe
09-00-09-00-00-04	HP DTC
09-00-0D-XX-XX-XX	ICL Oslan Multicast
09-00-0D-02-00-00	ICL Oslan Service discover only on boot
09-00-0D-02-0A-38	ICL Oslan Service discover only on boot
09-00-0D-02-0A-39	ICL Oslan Service discover only on boot
09-00-0D-02-0A-3C	ICL Oslan Service discover only on boot
09-00-0D-02-FF-FF	ICL Oslan Service discover only on boot
09-00-0D-09-00-00	ICL Oslan Service discover as required
09-00-1E-00-00-00	Apollo DOMAIN
09-00-26-01-00-01	Vitalink TransLAN bridge management
09-00-2B-00-00-00	DEC MUMPS
09-00-2B-00-00-01	DEC DSM/DDP
09-00-2B-00-00-02	DEC VAXELN

Multicast Addresses

09-00-2B-00-00-03	DEC Lanbridge Traffic Monitor (LTM)
09-00-2B-00-00-04	DEC MAP End System Hello
09-00-2B-00-00-05	DEC MAP Intermediate System Hello
09-00-2B-00-00-06	DEC CSMA/CD Encryption
09-00-2B-00-00-07	DEC NetBios Emulator
09-00-2B-00-00-0F	DEC Local Area Transport (LAT)
09-00-2B-00-00-1x	DEC Experimental
09-00-2B-01-00-00	DEC LanBridge Copy packets (All bridges)
09-00-2B-01-00-01	DEC LanBridge Hello packets (All local bridges) 1 packet per second, sent by the designated LanBridge
09-00-2B-02-00-00	DEC DNA Level 2 Routing Layer routers
09-00-2B-02-01-00	DEC DNA Naming Service Advertisement
09-00-2B-02-01-01	DEC DNA Naming Service Solicitation
09-00-2B-02-01-09	DEC Availability Manager for Distributed Systems DECamds
09-00-2B-02-01-02	DEC Distributed Time Service
09-00-2B-03-xx-xx	DEC default filtering by bridges
09-00-2B-04-00-00	DEC Local Area System Transport (LAST)
09-00-2B-23-00-00	DEC Argonaut Console
09-00-39-00-70-00	Spider Systems Bridge Hello packet
09-00-4C-00-00-00	BICC 802.1 management
09-00-4C-00-00-02	BICC 802.1 management
09-00-4C-00-00-06	BICC Local bridge STA 802.1(D) Rev6
09-00-4C-00-00-0C	BICC Remote bridge STA 802.1(D) Rev8
09-00-4C-00-00-0F	BICC Remote bridge ADAPTIVE ROUTING (e.g. to Retix)
09-00-4E-00-00-02	Novell IPX (BICC)
09-00-56-00-00-00 through 09-00-56-FE-FF-FF	Stanford reserved
09-00-56-FF-00-00 through 09-00-56-FF-FF-FF	Stanford V Kernel, version 6.0
09-00-6A-00-01-00	TOP NetBIOS
09-00-77-00-00-00	Retix Bridge Local Management System
09-00-77-00-00-01	Retix spanning tree bridges
09-00-77-00-00-02	Retix Bridge Adaptive routing
09-00-7C-01-00-01	Vitalink DLS Multicast
09-00-7C-01-00-03	Vitalink DLS Inlink
09-00-7C-01-00-04	Vitalink DLS and non-DLS Multicast
09-00-7C-02-00-05	Vitalink diagnostics
09-00-7C-05-00-01	Vitalink gateway
09-00-7C-05-00-02	Vitalink Network Validation Message
09-00-87-80-FF-FF	Xyplex Terminal Servers
09-00-87-90-FF-FF	Xyplex Terminal Servers

Multicast Addresses

0D-1E-15-BA-DD-06	HP
33-33-00-00-00-00 through 33-33-FF-FF-FF-FF	IPv6 Neighbor Discovery
AB-00-00-01-00-00	DEC Maintenance Operation Protocol (MOP) Dump/Load Assistance
AB-00-00-02-00-00	DEC Maintenance Operation Protocol (MOP) Remote Console 1 System ID packet every 8-10 minutes, by every: DEC LanBridge, DEC DEUNA interface, DEC DELUA interface, DEC DEQNA interface (in a certain mode)
AB-00-00-03-00-00	DECNET Phase IV end node Hello packets 1 packet every 15 seconds, sent by each DECNET host
AB-00-00-04-00-00	DECNET Phase IV Router Hello packets 1 packet every 15 seconds, sent by the DECNET router
AB-00-00-05-00-00 through AB-00-03-FF-FF-FF	Reserved DEC
AB-00-03-00-00-00	DEC Local Area Transport (LAT) - old
AB-00-04-00-xx-xx	Reserved DEC customer private use
AB-00-04-01-xx-yy	DEC Local Area VAX Cluster groups System Communication Architecture (SCA)
C0-00-00-00-00-01	IEEE 802.5 Active Monitor
C0-00-00-00-00-02	IEEE 802.5 Ring Parameter Server
C0-00-00-00-00-04	IEEE 802.5 Network Server Heartbeat
C0-00-00-00-00-08	IEEE 802.5 Ring Error Monitor
C0-00-00-00-00-10	IEEE 802.5 Configuration Report Server
C0-00-00-00-00-20	IEEE 802.5 Synchronous Bandwidth Manager
C0-00-00-00-00-40	IEEE 802.5 Locate Directory Server
C0-00-00-00-00-80	IEEE 802.5 NETBIOS
C0-00-00-00-01-00	IEEE 802.5 Bridge
C0-00-00-00-02-00	IEEE 802.5 IMPL Server
C0-00-00-00-04-00	IEEE 802.5 Ring Authorization Server
C0-00-00-00-08-00	IEEE 802.5 LAN Gateway
C0-00-00-00-10-80	IEEE 802.5 Ring Wiring Concentrator
C0-00-00-00-20-80	IEEE 802.5 LAN Manager
C0-00-08-00-00-00	IEEE 802.5 Novell Netware
C0-00-FF-FF-FF-FF	IEEE 802.5 Broadcast
CF-00-00-00-00-00	Ethernet Configuration Test protocol (Loopback)
FF-FF-00-60-00-04	Lantastic
FF-FF-00-40-00-01	Lantastic
FF-FF-01-E0-00-04	Lantastic

Broadcast Addresses

FF-FF-FF-FF-FF-FF	0600	XNS packets, Hello or gateway search 6 packets every 15 seconds, per XNS station
FF-FF-FF-FF-FF-FF	0800	IP (e.g. RWHOD via UDP) as needed
FF-FF-FF-FF-FF-FF	0804	CHAOS
FF-FF-FF-FF-FF-FF	0806	ARP (for IP and CHAOS) as needed
FF-FF-FF-FF-FF-FF	0BAD	Banyan
FF-FF-FF-FF-FF-FF	1600	VALID packets, Hello or gateway search? 1 packet every 30 seconds, per VALID station
FF-FF-FF-FF-FF-FF	8035	Reverse ARP
FF-FF-FF-FF-FF-FF	807C	Merit Internodal (INP)
FF-FF-FF-FF-FF-FF	809B	EtherTalk
FF-FF-FF-FF-FF-FF	9001	3Com (ex Bridge) Name Service
FF-FF-FF-FF-FF-FF	9002	3Com PCS/TCP Hello, Approx. 1 per minute per w/s

E.4   Organizationally Unique Identifier (OUI)

The first 48 bits of each Ethernet address are called Organizationally Unique Identifier (OUI). The OUI consists of two parts, each 24 bits long. The first part represents the vendor identification, which is assigned to each vendor of IEEE Ethernet components. The second part contains the adressing within such a vendor domain. The most recent listing of OUI codes is available under

http://standards.ieee.org/regauth/oui/oui.txt

E.4.1   OUI Codes Sorted by Address

company_id	Organization Address	company_id	Organization Address
00-00-00 (hex)	XEROX CORPORATION	000008 (base 16)	XEROX CORPORATION OFFICE SYSTEMS DIVISION M/S/ 105-50C 800 PHILLIPS ROAD WEBSTER NY 14580
000000 (base 16)	XEROX CORPORATION M/S 105-50C 800 PHILLIPS ROAD WEBSTER NY 14580		
00-00-01 (hex)	XEROX CORPORATION	00-00-09 (hex)	XEROX CORPORATION
000001 (base 16)	XEROX CORPORATION ZEROX SYSTEMS INSTITUTE M/S 105-50C 800 PHILLIPS ROAD WEBSTER NY 14580	000009 (base 16)	XEROX CORPORATION 1350 JEFFERSON ROAD ROCHESTER NY 14623
00-00-02 (hex)	XEROX CORPORATION	00-00-0A (hex)	OMRON TATEISI ELECTRONICS CO.
000002 (base 16)	XEROX CORPORATION XEROX SYSTEMS INSTITUTE M/S 105-50C 800 PHILLIPS ROAD WEBSTER NY 14580	00000A (base 16)	OMRON TATEISI ELECTRONICS CO. SECTION NFF, SYSTEM R&D LABS. RESEARCH & TECH. ASSESSMNT DIV SHIMOKAIINJI, NAGAOKAKYO-CITY KYOTO, 617 JAPAN
00-00-03 (hex)	XEROX CORPORATION	00-00-0B (hex)	MATRIX CORPORATION
000003 (base 16)	XEROX CORPORATION ZEROX SYSTEMS INSTITUTE M/S 105-50CEW AVENUE 800 PHILLIPS ROAD WEBSTER NY 14580	00000B (base 16)	MATRIX CORPORATION 1203 NEW HOPE ROAD RALEIGH, NORTH CAROLINA 27610
00-00-04 (hex)	XEROX CORPORATION	00-00-0C (hex)	CISCO SYSTEMS, INC.
000004 (base 16)	XEROX CORPORATION OFFICE SYSTEMS DIVISION M/S 105-50C 800 PHILLIPS ROAD WEBSTER NY 14580	00000C (base 16)	CISCO SYSTEMS, INC. 170 WEST TASMAN DRIVE SAN JOSE CA 95134-1706
00-00-05 (hex)	XEROX CORPORATION	00-00-0D (hex)	FIBRONICS LTD.
000005 (base 16)	XEROX CORPORATION OFFICE SYSTEMS DIVISION M/S 105-50C 800 PHILLIPS ROAD WEBSTER NY 14580	00000D (base 16)	FIBRONICS LTD. MATAM TECHNOLOGY CENTER HAIFA 31905 ISRAEL
00-00-06 (hex)	XEROX CORPORATION	00-00-0E (hex)	FUJITSU LIMITED
000006 (base 16)	XEROX CORPORATION OFFICE SYSTEMS DIVISION M/S 105-50C 800 PHILLIPS ROAD WEBSTER NY 14580	00000E (base 16)	FUJITSU LIMITED COMPUTER SYS. ARCHITECTURE DEP MAIN FRAME DIV. 1015 KAMIKODANAKA, NAKAHARA-KU KAWASAKI 211, JAPAN
00-00-07 (hex)	XEROX CORPORATION	00-00-0F (hex)	NEXT, INC.
000007 (base 16)	XEROX CORPORATION OFFICE SYSTEMS DIVISION M/S 105-50C 800 PHILLIPS ROAD WEBSTER NY 14580	00000F (base 16)	NEXT, INC. 3475 DEER CREEK ROAD PALO ALTO, CA 94304
00-00-08 (hex)	XEROX CORPORATION	00-00-10 (hex)	SYTEK INC.
		000010 (base 16)	SYTEK INC. 1225 CHARLESTON ROAD MOUNTAIN VIEW CA 94043
		00-00-11 (hex)	NORMEREL SYSTEMES
		000011 (base 16)	NORMEREL SYSTEMES 58 RUE POTTIER 78150 LE CHESNAY FRANCE
		00-00-12 (hex)	INFORMATION TECHNOLOGY LIMITED

company_id	Organization Address	company_id	Organization Address
000012 (base 16)	INFORMATION TECHNOLOGY LIMITED MAYLANDS AVE. HEMEL HEMPSTEAD HERTS ENGLAND	000021 (base 16)	SUREMAN COMP. & COMMUN. CORP. 10F-5 NO. 7, SEC. 3 HSIN SHENG N. RD., TAIPEI, TAIWAN, R.O.C.
00-00-13 (hex)	CAMEX	00-00-22 (hex)	VISUAL TECHNOLOGY INC.
000013 (base 16)	CAMEX 75 KNEELAND STREET BOSTON, MA 02111	000022 (base 16)	VISUAL TECHNOLOGY INC. 1703 MIDDLESEX STREET LOWELL, MA 01851
00-00-14 (hex)	NETRONIX	00-00-23 (hex)	ABB INDUSTRIAL SYSTEMS AB
000014 (base 16)	NETRONIX 1372 MCDOWELL BLVD. PETULAMA, CA 94952	000023 (base 16)	ABB INDUSTRIAL SYSTEMS AB DEPT. SEISY/LKSB S-721 67 VASTERAS SWEDEN
00-00-15 (hex)	DATAPOINT CORPORATION	00-00-24 (hex)	CONNECT AS
000015 (base 16)	DATAPOINT CORPORATION 9725 DATAPOINT DRIVE MS S-37 SAN ANTONIO TX 78284	000024 (base 16)	CONNECT AS HOERKAER 7-9 DK 2730 HERLEV DENMARK
00-00-16 (hex)	DU PONT PIXEL SYSTEMS .	00-00-25 (hex)	RAMTEK CORP.
000016 (base 16)	DU PONT PIXEL SYSTEMS . MEADLAKE PLACE THORPE LEA ROAD EGHAM, SURREY TW20 8HE ENGLAND	000025 (base 16)	RAMTEK CORP. 810 W. MAUDE AVENUE SUNNYVALE, CA 94086
00-00-17 (hex)	TEKELEC	00-00-26 (hex)	SHA-KEN CO., LTD.
000017 (base 16)	TEKELEC 26540 AGOURA ROAD CALABASAS CA 91302	000026 (base 16)	SHA-KEN CO., LTD. MINAMI-OTSUKA 2-26-13, TOSHIMA-KU TOKYO JAPAN
00-00-18 (hex)	WEBSTER COMPUTER CORPORATION	00-00-27 (hex)	JAPAN RADIO COMPANY
000018 (base 16)	WEBSTER COMPUTER CORPORATION 16040 REDWOOD LODGE ROAD LOS GATOS CA 95033-9260	000027 (base 16)	JAPAN RADIO COMPANY LABORATORY 5-1-1 SHIMORENJAKU MITAKA-SHI, TOKYO JAPAN
00-00-19 (hex)	APPLIED DYNAMICS INTERNATIONAL	00-00-28 (hex)	PRODIGY SYSTEMS CORPORATION
000019 (base 16)	APPLIED DYNAMICS INTERNATIONAL 3800 STONE SCHOOL ROAD ANN ARBOR, MI 48104-2499	000028 (base 16)	PRODIGY SYSTEMS CORPORATION 2601 CASEY DRIVE MOUNTAIN VIEW CA 94043
00-00-1A (hex)	ADVANCED MICRO DEVICES	00-00-29 (hex)	IMC NETWORKS CORP.
00001A (base 16)	ADVANCED MICRO DEVICES P.O. BOX 3453 M/S 26 SUNNYVALE CA 94088	000029 (base 16)	IMC NETWORKS CORP. 16931 MILLIKEN AVE. IRVINE CA 92714-5013
00-00-1B (hex)	NOVELL INC.	00-00-2A (hex)	TRW - SEDD/INP
00001B (base 16)	NOVELL INC. 122 EAST 1700 SOUTH M/S: E-12-1 PROVO UT 84606	00002A (base 16)	TRW - SEDD/INP 1800 GLENN CURTISS STREET M/S DH6/2826 CARSON CA 90746
00-00-1C (hex)	BELL TECHNOLOGIES	00-00-2B (hex)	CRISP AUTOMATION, INC
00001C (base 16)	BELL TECHNOLOGIES 330 WARREN AVENUE FREMONT, CA 94539	00002B (base 16)	CRISP AUTOMATION, INC 5160 BLAZER PARKWAY DUBLIN, OH 43017
00-00-1D (hex)	CABLETRON SYSTEMS, INC.	00-00-2C (hex)	AUTOTOTE LIMITED
00001D (base 16)	CABLETRON SYSTEMS, INC. 35 INDUSTRIAL WAY P.O. BOX 5005 ROCHESTER NH 03867	00002C (base 16)	AUTOTOTE LIMITED 100 BELLEVUE ROAD NEWARK DELAWARE 19714
00-00-1E (hex)	TELSIST INDUSTRIA ELECTRONICA	00-00-2D (hex)	CHROMATICS INC
00001E (base 16)	TELSIST INDUSTRIA ELECTRONICA RUA VILHENA DE MORAES, 380 BARRA DA TIJUCA RIO DE JANEIRO, RJ CEP 22793 BRAZIL	00002D (base 16)	CHROMATICS INC 2558 MOUNTAIN INDUSTRIAL BLVD TUCKER GA 30084
00-00-1F (hex)	Telco Systems, Inc.	00-00-2E (hex)	SOCIETE EVIRA
00001F (base 16)	Telco Systems, Inc. 63 Nathan Street Norwood, MA 02072	00002E (base 16)	SOCIETE EVIRA ZONE PORTUAIRE DE BREGAILLON 83500 LA SEYNE SUR MER FRANCE
00-00-20 (hex)	DATAINDUSTRIER DIAB AB	00-00-2F (hex)	TIMEPLEX INC.
000020 (base 16)	DATAINDUSTRIER DIAB AB BOX 2029 S-183 02 TABY SWEDEN	00002F (base 16)	TIMEPLEX INC. 530 CHESTNUT RIDGE ROAD WOODCLIFF LAKE NJ 07675
00-00-21 (hex)	SUREMAN COMP. & COMMUN. CORP.	00-00-30 (hex)	VG LABORATORY SYSTEMS LTD

company_id	Organization Address
000030 (base 16)	VG LABORATORY SYSTEMS LTD TRIBUNE AVENUE ALTRINCHAM, MANCHESTER, WA14 5TP ENGLAND
00-00-31 (hex)	QPSX COMMUNICATIONS PTY LTD
000031 (base 16)	QPSX COMMUNICATIONS PTY LTD 33 RICHARDSON STREET WEST PERTH 6005 WESTERN AUSTRALIA
00-00-32 (hex)	Marconi plc
000032 (base 16)	Marconi plc 28 ELSTREE WAY, BOREHAMWOOD HERTFORDSHIRE WD6 1RX UNITED KINGDOM
00-00-33 (hex)	EGAN MACHINERY COMPANY
000033 (base 16)	EGAN MACHINERY COMPANY SOUTH ADAMSVILLE ROAD SOMMERVILLE NJ 08876
00-00-34 (hex)	NETWORK RESOURCES CORPORATION
000034 (base 16)	NETWORK RESOURCES CORPORATION 61 EAST DAGGETT DRIVE SAN JOSE, CA 95134
00-00-35 (hex)	SPECTRAGRAPHICS CORPORATION
000035 (base 16)	SPECTRAGRAPHICS CORPORATION OR LAN MANUFACTURING ENGINEER 9707 WAPLES STREET SAN DIEGO CA 92121
00-00-36 (hex)	ATARI CORPORATION
000036 (base 16)	ATARI CORPORATION 1196 BORREGAS AVENUE SUNNYVALE, CA 94086
00-00-37 (hex)	OXFORD METRICS LIMITED
000037 (base 16)	OXFORD METRICS LIMITED UNIT 8, 7 WEST WAY, BOTLEY,OXFORD, OX2 OJB UNITED KINGDOM
00-00-38 (hex)	CSS LABS
000038 (base 16)	CSS LABS 2134 SOUTH RIPCHEY SANTA ANA CA 92705
00-00-39 (hex)	TOSHIBA CORPORATION
000039 (base 16)	TOSHIBA CORPORATION COMPUTER DIVISION 1-1-1 SHIBAURA, MINATO-KU TOKYO, 105 JAPAN
00-00-3A (hex)	CHYRON CORPORATION
00003A (base 16)	CHYRON CORPORATION 265 SPAGNOLI ROAD MELVILLE NY 11747
00-00-3B (hex)	i Controls, Inc.
00003B (base 16)	i Controls, Inc. 12F Doonsan building, 105-7 Nonhyun-dong, Gangnam-gu Seoul KOREA 135-714
00-00-3C (hex)	AUSPEX SYSTEMS INC.
00003C (base 16)	AUSPEX SYSTEMS INC. 5200 GREAT AMERICA PKWY SANTA CLARA CA 95054
00-00-3D (hex)	UNISYS
00003D (base 16)	UNISYS MS8-010 P.O. BOX 6685 SAN JOSE CA 95150-6685
00-00-3E (hex)	SIMPACT
00003E (base 16)	SIMPACT 9210 SKY PARK COURT SAN DIEGO, CA 92123

company_id	Organization Address
00-00-3F (hex)	SYNTREX, INC.
00003F (base 16)	SYNTREX, INC. 246 INDUSTRIAL WAY WEST EATONTOWN NJ 07724
00-00-40 (hex)	APPLICON, INC.
000040 (base 16)	APPLICON, INC. 4251 PLYMOUTH RD 48015 PO BOX 986 ANN ARBOR MI 48106-0986
00-00-41 (hex)	ICE CORPORATION
000041 (base 16)	ICE CORPORATION 17945 SKYPARK CIRCLE SUITE E IRVINE, CA 92714
00-00-42 (hex)	METIER MANAGEMENT SYSTEMS LTD.
000042 (base 16)	METIER MANAGEMENT SYSTEMS LTD. 3 FOUNDATION STREET IPSWICH SUFFOLK IP4 1BG ENGLAND
00-00-43 (hex)	MICRO TECHNOLOGY
000043 (base 16)	MICRO TECHNOLOGY 4905 EAST LAPALMA ANAHEIM, CA 92807
00-00-44 (hex)	CASTELLE CORPORATION
000044 (base 16)	CASTELLE CORPORATION 3255-3 SCOTT BOULEVARD SANTA CLARA CA 95054
00-00-45 (hex)	FORD AEROSPACE & COMM. CORP.
000045 (base 16)	FORD AEROSPACE & COMM. CORP. COLORADO SPRINGS OPERATION 10440 STATE HIGHWAY 83 COLORADO SPRINGS CO 80908
00-00-46 (hex)	OLIVETTI NORTH AMERICA
000046 (base 16)	OLIVETTI NORTH AMERICA E 22425 APPLEWAY LIBERTY LAKE WA 99019
00-00-47 (hex)	NICOLET INSTRUMENTS CORP.
000047 (base 16)	NICOLET INSTRUMENTS CORP. 5225 VERONA ROAD MADISON, WI 53711
00-00-48 (hex)	SEIKO EPSON CORPORATION
000048 (base 16)	SEIKO EPSON CORPORATION 80 HIROOKA SHIOJIRI-CITY NAGANO-KEN JAPAN 399-07
00-00-49 (hex)	APRICOT COMPUTERS, LTD
000049 (base 16)	APRICOT COMPUTERS, LTD 90 VINCENT DRIVE EDGBASTON, BIRMINGHAM B152SP ENGLAND
00-00-4A (hex)	ADC CODENOLL TECHNOLOGY CORP.
00004A (base 16)	ADC CODENOLL TECHNOLOGY CORP. 200 CORPORATE BLVD. SO. YONKERS NY 10701
00-00-4B (hex)	ICL DATA OY
00004B (base 16)	ICL DATA OY KUTOMOTIE 16-18 00380 HELSINKI P.O. BOX 458 SF-00101 HELSINKI FINLAND
00-00-4C (hex)	NEC CORPORATION
00004C (base 16)	NEC CORPORATION 7-1 SHIBA 5-CHOME MINATO-KU TOKYO 108-01 JAPAN
00-00-4D (hex)	DCI CORPORATION

company_id	Organization Address
00004D (base 16)	DCI CORPORATION 64J PRINCETON-HIGHTSTOWN RD #121 PRINCETON JUNCTION NJ 08550
00-00-4E (hex)	AMPEX CORPORATION
00004E (base 16)	AMPEX CORPORATION 581 CONFERENCE PLACE GOLDEN, CO 80401
00-00-4F (hex)	LOGICRAFT, INC.
00004F (base 16)	LOGICRAFT, INC. 22 COTTON ROAD NASHUA, NH 03063
00-00-50 (hex)	RADISYS CORPORATION
000050 (base 16)	RADISYS CORPORATION 15025 S.W. KOLL PARKWAY BEAVERTON, OR 97006-6056
00-00-51 (hex)	HOB ELECTRONIC GMBH & CO. KG
000051 (base 16)	HOB ELECTRONIC GMBH & CO. KG BRANDSSTATTER-STR.2-10 D-8502 ZIRNDORF GERMANY
00-00-52 (hex)	Intrusion.com, Inc.
000052 (base 16)	Intrusion.com, Inc. 1101 E. ARAPAHO ROAD RICHARDSON TX 75081
00-00-53 (hex)	COMPUCORP
000053 (base 16)	COMPUCORP 2211 MICHIGAN AVENUE SANTA MONICA CA 90404
00-00-54 (hex)	MODICON, INC.
000054 (base 16)	MODICON, INC. ONE HIGH STREET NORTH ANDOVER MA 01845-2699
00-00-55 (hex)	COMMISSARIAT A L'ENERGIE ATOM.
000055 (base 16)	COMMISSARIAT A L'ENERGIE ATOM. 31, RUE DE LA FEDERATION PARIS 75015 FRANCE
00-00-56 (hex)	DR. B. STRUCK
000056 (base 16)	DR. B. STRUCK POB 1147 BAECKERBARG 6 D-2000 TANGSTEDT/HAMBURG W-GERMANY
00-00-57 (hex)	SCITEX CORPORATION LTD.
000057 (base 16)	SCITEX CORPORATION LTD. P.O. BOX 330 46103 HERZLIA B ISRAEL
00-00-58 (hex)	RACORE COMPUTER PRODUCTS INC.
000058 (base 16)	RACORE COMPUTER PRODUCTS INC. 2355 SOUTH 1070 WEST SALT LAKE CITY UT 84119
00-00-59 (hex)	HELLIGE GMBH
000059 (base 16)	HELLIGE GMBH E-SW HEINRICH-VON-STEFAN-STR.4 D-7800 FREIBURG WEST GERMANY
00-00-5A (hex)	SYSKONNECT–A BUSINESS UNIT OF SCHNEIDER & KOCH CO. GMBH
00005A (base 16)	SYSKONNECT–A BUSINESS UNIT OF SCHNEIDER & KOCH CO. GMBH SIEMENSSTRASSE 23 76275 ETTLINGEN GERMANY
00-00-5B (hex)	ELTEC ELEKTRONIK AG
00005B (base 16)	ELTEC ELEKTRONIK AG Galileo-Galilei-Strasse 11 POB 42 13 63 D-55071 MAINZ GERMANY

company_id	Organization Address
00-00-5C (hex)	TELEMATICS INTERNATIONAL INC.
00005C (base 16)	TELEMATICS INTERNATIONAL INC. 1201 CYPRESS CREEK RD FT. LAUDERDALE FL 33309
00-00-5D (hex)	CS TELECOM
00005D (base 16)	CS TELECOM 4-16 AVENUE DU GENERAL LECLERC BP 74 - 92263 FONTENAY AUX ROSES FRANCE
00-00-5E (hex)	USC INFORMATION SCIENCES INST
00005E (base 16)	USC INFORMATION SCIENCES INST INTERNET ASS'NED NOS.AUTHORITY 4676 ADMIRALTY WAY MARINA DEL REY CA 90292-6695
00-00-5F (hex)	SUMITOMO ELECTRIC IND., LTD.
00005F (base 16)	SUMITOMO ELECTRIC IND., LTD. 1-1-3, SHIMAYA KONOHANA-KU OSAKA 554 JAPAN
00-00-60 (hex)	KONTRON ELEKTRONIK GMBH
000060 (base 16)	KONTRON ELEKTRONIK GMBH OSKAR-VON-MILLER-STR. 1 D-85385 ECHING GERMANY
00-00-61 (hex)	GATEWAY COMMUNICATIONS
000061 (base 16)	GATEWAY COMMUNICATIONS 2941 ALTON AVENUE IRVINE CA 92714
00-00-62 (hex)	BULL HN INFORMATION SYSTEMS
000062 (base 16)	BULL HN INFORMATION SYSTEMS 300 CONCORD ROAD M/S 864A BILLERICA MA 01821
00-00-63 (hex)	DR.ING.SEUFERT GMBH
000063 (base 16)	DR.ING.SEUFERT GMBH UWE LINSTROMBERG, DEPT SUPPORT AN DER ROBWEID 5 D-7500 KARLSRUHE 41 WEST GERMANY
00-00-64 (hex)	YOKOGAWA DIGITAL COMPUTER CORP
000064 (base 16)	YOKOGAWA DIGITAL COMPUTER CORP SI HEADQUARTERS DIVISION NO. 25 KOWA BLDG 8-7 SANBANCHO CHIYODA-KU TOKYO 102 JAPAN
00-00-65 (hex)	NETWORK ASSOCIATES, INC.
000065 (base 16)	NETWORK ASSOCIATES, INC. 3965 FREEDOM CIRCLE SANTA CLARA CA 95054
00-00-66 (hex)	TALARIS SYSTEMS, INC.
000066 (base 16)	TALARIS SYSTEMS, INC. 11339 SORRENTO VALLEY ROAD SAN DIEGO CA 92121
00-00-67 (hex)	SOFT * RITE, INC.
000067 (base 16)	SOFT * RITE, INC. 15392 ASSEMBLY LANE, UNIT A HUNTINGTON BEACH, CA 92649
00-00-68 (hex)	ROSEMOUNT CONTROLS
000068 (base 16)	ROSEMOUNT CONTROLS 1300 E. LAMBERT ROAD LA HABRA CA 90632
00-00-69 (hex)	CONCORD COMMUNICATIONS INC
000069 (base 16)	CONCORD COMMUNICATIONS INC 753 FOREST STREET MARLBOROUGH MA 01752
00-00-6A (hex)	COMPUTER CONSOLES INC.

company_id	Organization Address
00006A (base 16)	COMPUTER CONSOLES INC. COMPUTER PRODUCTS DIVISION 9801 MUIRLANDS BLVD. IRVINE CA 92718
00-00-6B (hex)	SILICON GRAPHICS INC./MIPS
00006B (base 16)	SILICON GRAPHICS INC./MIPS 2011 NORTH SHORELINE BLVD. P.O. BOX 7311 - BLDG. #10 MOUNTAIN VIEW CA 94039-7311
00-00-6D (hex)	CRAY COMMUNICATIONS, LTD.
00006D (base 16)	CRAY COMMUNICATIONS, LTD. P.O. BOX 254, CAXTON WAY WATFORD BUSINESS PARK WATFORD HERTS WD1 8XH UNITED KINGDOM
00-00-6E (hex)	ARTISOFT, INC.
00006E (base 16)	ARTISOFT, INC. 691 EAST RIVER ROAD TUCSON AZ 85704
00-00-6F (hex)	MADGE NETWORKS LTD.
00006F (base 16)	MADGE NETWORKS LTD. WEXHAM SPRINGS, FRAMEWOOD RD WEXHAM, SLOUGH SL3 6PJ ENGLAND
00-00-70 (hex)	HCL LIMITED
000070 (base 16)	HCL LIMITED RESEARCH & DEVELOPMENT UNIT 72, LUZ CHURCH ROAD MADRSA-600 004 INDIA
00-00-71 (hex)	ADRA SYSTEMS INC.
000071 (base 16)	ADRA SYSTEMS INC. 59 TECHNOLOGY DRIVE LOWELL MA 01851
00-00-72 (hex)	MINIWARE TECHNOLOGY
000072 (base 16)	MINIWARE TECHNOLOGY BEEMDENSTRAAT 38 5004 CT WEERT (L) THE NETHERLANDS
00-00-73 (hex)	SIECOR CORPORATION
000073 (base 16)	SIECOR CORPORATION P.O. BOX 13625 RESEARCH TRIANGLE PK NC 27709
00-00-74 (hex)	RICOH COMPANY LTD.
000074 (base 16)	RICOH COMPANY LTD. 2446 TODA, ATSUGI CITY KANAGAWA PREF., 243 JAPAN
00-00-75 (hex)	NORTEL NETWORKS
000075 (base 16)	NORTEL NETWORKS GLOBAL OPERATIONS ENGINEERING DEP 6800 PROGRAM MANAGER 8200 DIXIE ROAD, SUITE 100 BRAMPTON, ON L6T 5P6 CANADA
00-00-76 (hex)	ABEKAS VIDEO SYSTEM
000076 (base 16)	ABEKAS VIDEO SYSTEM 101 GALVESTON DRIVE REDWOOD CITY CA 94063
00-00-77 (hex)	INTERPHASE CORPORATION
000077 (base 16)	INTERPHASE CORPORATION 13800 SENLAC DALLAS TX 75234
00-00-78 (hex)	LABTAM LIMITED
000078 (base 16)	LABTAM LIMITED 43 MALCOLM ROAD P.O. BOX 297 BRAESIDE, VICTORIA 3195 AUSTRALIA
00-00-79 (hex)	NETWORTH INCORPORATED

company_id	Organization Address
000079 (base 16)	NETWORTH INCORPORATED 8404 ESTERS BOULEVARD IRVING TX 75063
00-00-7A (hex)	DANA COMPUTER INC.
00007A (base 16)	DANA COMPUTER INC. 550 DEL REY AVENUE SUNNYVALE CA 94086
00-00-7B (hex)	RESEARCH MACHINES
00007B (base 16)	RESEARCH MACHINES P.O. BOX 75 MILL STREET OXFORD OX2 0BW ENGLAND
00-00-7C (hex)	AMPERE INCORPORATED
00007C (base 16)	AMPERE INCORPORATED SHINJUKU ASAHI BLDG. 5-20 7-CHOME NISHI-SHINJUKU SHINJUKU-KU TOKYO JAPAN
00-00-7D (hex)	SUN MICROSYSTEMS, INC.
00007D (base 16)	SUN MICROSYSTEMS, INC. 9480 CARROLL PARK DRIVE SAN DIEGO CA 92121
00-00-7E (hex)	CLUSTRIX CORPORATION
00007E (base 16)	CLUSTRIX CORPORATION 960 HAMLIN COURT SUNNYVALE, CA 94089
00-00-7F (hex)	LINOTYPE-HELL AG
00007F (base 16)	LINOTYPE-HELL AG POSTFACH 56 60 MERGENTHALER ALLEE 55-75 6236 ESCHBORN BEI FRANKFURT GERMANY
00-00-80 (hex)	CRAY COMMUNICATIONS A/S
000080 (base 16)	CRAY COMMUNICATIONS A/S SMEDEHOLM 12-14 2730 HERLEV DENMARK
00-00-81 (hex)	BAY NETWORKS
000081 (base 16)	BAY NETWORKS 4401 GREAT AMERICAN PARKWAY PO BOX 58185 M/S SC01-05 SANTA CLARA CA 95052-8185
00-00-82 (hex)	LECTRA SYSTEMES SA
000082 (base 16)	LECTRA SYSTEMES SA CHEMIN DE MARTICOT RESEARCH DEPARTMENT 33610 CESTAS FRANCE
00-00-83 (hex)	TADPOLE TECHNOLOGY PLC
000083 (base 16)	TADPOLE TECHNOLOGY PLC 137 DITTON WALK CAMBRIDGE CB5 8FN ENGLAND
00-00-84 (hex)	SUPERNET
000084 (base 16)	SUPERNET 846 DEL REY AVENUE SUNNYVALE, CA 94086
00-00-85 (hex)	CANON INC.
000085 (base 16)	CANON INC. DVTECH. DEV. CENTER DEPT.12 3-30-2, SHIMOMARUKO, OHTA-KU TOKYO 146 JAPAN
00-00-86 (hex)	MEGAHERTZ CORPORATION
000086 (base 16)	MEGAHERTZ CORPORATION 605 NORTH–5600 WEST SALT LAKE CITY UT 84116-3738
00-00-87 (hex)	HITACHI, LTD.

company_id	Organization Address
000087 (base 16)	HITACHI, LTD. NETWORK ENGINEERING DIV. HITACHI OMORI 2ND BLDG., 27-18 MINAMI OI 6 CHOME,SHINAGAWA-KU TOKYO 140, JAPAN
00-00-88 (hex)	COMPUTER NETWORK TECH. CORP.
000088 (base 16)	COMPUTER NETWORK TECH. CORP. 6500 WEDGEWOOD DRIVE MAPLE GROVE, MN 55311
00-00-89 (hex)	CAYMAN SYSTEMS INC.
000089 (base 16)	CAYMAN SYSTEMS INC. 26 LANSDOWNE STREET CAMBRIDGE, MA 02139
00-00-8A (hex)	DATAHOUSE INFORMATION SYSTEMS
00008A (base 16)	DATAHOUSE INFORMATION SYSTEMS DIRECTOR OF OPERATIONS MEON HOUSE, EAST TISTED NR. ALTON, HAMPSHIRE GU34 3QW ENGLAND
00-00-8B (hex)	INFOTRON
00008B (base 16)	INFOTRON 9 NORTH OLNEY CHERRY HILL NJ 08003
00-00-8C (hex)	ALLOY COMPUTER PRODUCTS, INC.
00008C (base 16)	ALLOY COMPUTER PRODUCTS, INC. 25 PORTER ROAD LITTLETON MA 01460-1410
00-00-8D (hex)	VERDIX CORPORATION
00008D (base 16)	VERDIX CORPORATION 205 VAN BUREN STREET -4TH FL. HERNDON VA 22070-5336
00-00-8E (hex)	SOLBOURNE COMPUTER, INC.
00008E (base 16)	SOLBOURNE COMPUTER, INC. 1900 PIKE ROAD LONGMONT, COLORADO 80501
00-00-8F (hex)	RAYTHEON COMPANY
00008F (base 16)	RAYTHEON COMPANY 1001 BOSTON POST RD. MAIL STOP 1-1-1475 MARLBOROUGH MA 01752
00-00-90 (hex)	MICROCOM
000090 (base 16)	MICROCOM 500 RIVER RIDGE DRIVE NORWOOD MA 02062-5028
00-00-91 (hex)	ANRITSU CORPORATION
000091 (base 16)	ANRITSU CORPORATION 1800, ONNA ATUGI-SHI KANAGAWA-KEN 243 JAPAN
00-00-92 (hex)	COGENT DATA TECHNOLOGIES
000092 (base 16)	COGENT DATA TECHNOLOGIES 640 MULLIS STREET FRIDAY HARBOR WA 98250
00-00-93 (hex)	PROTEON INC.
000093 (base 16)	PROTEON INC. 4 TECH CIRCLE NATICK MA 01760
00-00-94 (hex)	ASANTE TECHNOLOGIES
000094 (base 16)	ASANTE TECHNOLOGIES 821 FOX LANE SAN JOSE CA 95131
00-00-95 (hex)	SONY TEKTRONIX CORP.
000095 (base 16)	SONY TEKTRONIX CORP. P.O. BOX 5209 TOKYO INT'L TOKYO 100-31 JAPAN
00-00-96 (hex)	MARCONI ELECTRONICS LTD.

company_id	Organization Address
000096 (base 16)	MARCONI ELECTRONICS LTD. BROWNS LANE, THE AIRPORT PORTSMOUTH – HAMPSHIRE P03 5PH UNITED KINGDOM
00-00-97 (hex)	EPOCH SYSTEMS
000097 (base 16)	EPOCH SYSTEMS 313 BOSTON POST ROAD WEST MARLBOROUGH, MA 01752
00-00-98 (hex)	CROSSCOMM CORPORATION
000098 (base 16)	CROSSCOMM CORPORATION 450 DONALD LYNCH BOULEVARD MARLBOROUGH, MA 01752
00-00-99 (hex)	MTX, INC.
000099 (base 16)	MTX, INC. 3301 TERMINAL DRIVE RALEIGH NC 27604
00-00-9A (hex)	RC COMPUTER A/S
00009A (base 16)	RC COMPUTER A/S LAUTRUPBJERG 1 DK-2750 BALLERUP DENMARK
00-00-9B (hex)	INFORMATION INTERNATIONAL, INC
00009B (base 16)	INFORMATION INTERNATIONAL, INC 5F., THE 7TH INDUSTRY BLDG. 1-20-14 JINNAN SHIBUYA-KU TOKYO JAPAN 150
00-00-9C (hex)	ROLM MIL-SPEC COMPUTERS
00009C (base 16)	ROLM MIL-SPEC COMPUTERS 3151 ZANKER ROAD SAN JOSE CA 95148
00-00-9D (hex)	LOCUS COMPUTING CORPORATION
00009D (base 16)	LOCUS COMPUTING CORPORATION 9800 LA CIENEGA INGLEWOOD, CA 90301
00-00-9E (hex)	MARLI S.A.
00009E (base 16)	MARLI S.A. CHEMIN TAVERNEY 3 1218 GENEVA SWITZERLAND
00-00-9F (hex)	AMERISTAR TECHNOLOGIES INC.
00009F (base 16)	AMERISTAR TECHNOLOGIES INC. 47 WHITTIER AVE. MEDFORD NY 11763
00-00-A0 (hex)	TOKYO SANYO ELECTRIC CO. LTD.
0000A0 (base 16)	TOKYO SANYO ELECTRIC CO. LTD. 180 SAKATA OIZUMI-MACHI ORA-GUN GUNMA JAPAN 370-05
00-00-A1 (hex)	MARQUETTE ELECTRIC CO.
0000A1 (base 16)	MARQUETTE ELECTRIC CO. 8200 WEST TOWER AVENUE MILWAUKEE, WI 53223
00-00-A2 (hex)	BAY NETWORKS
0000A2 (base 16)	BAY NETWORKS 4401 GREAT AMERICAN PKWY M/S:SC01-05 SANTA CLARA CA 95052-8185
00-00-A3 (hex)	NETWORK APPLICATION TECHNOLOGY
0000A3 (base 16)	NETWORK APPLICATION TECHNOLOGY 1686 DELL AVENUE CAMPBELL CA 95008
00-00-A4 (hex)	ACORN COMPUTERS LIMITED
0000A4 (base 16)	ACORN COMPUTERS LIMITED FULBOURN ROAD, CHERRY HINTON CAMBRIDGE CB1 4JN, ENGLAND
00-00-A5 (hex)	COMPATIBLE SYSTEMS CORP.

company_id	Organization Address
0000A5 (base 16)	COMPATIBLE SYSTEMS CORP. P.O. BOX 17220 BOULDER, CO 80308-7220
00-00-A6 (hex)	NETWORK GENERAL CORPORATION
0000A6 (base 16)	NETWORK GENERAL CORPORATION 1296 B LAWRENCE STATION ROAD SUNNYVALE CA 94089
00-00-A7 (hex)	NETWORK COMPUTING DEVICES INC.
0000A7 (base 16)	NETWORK COMPUTING DEVICES INC. 350 NORTH BERNARDO MOUNTAIN VIEW CA 94043
00-00-A8 (hex)	STRATUS COMPUTER INC.
0000A8 (base 16)	STRATUS COMPUTER INC. M/S M32-0SG 55 FAIRBANKS BLVD MARLBORO MA 01752
00-00-A9 (hex)	NETWORK SYSTEMS CORP.
0000A9 (base 16)	NETWORK SYSTEMS CORP. 7600 BOONE AVENUE NORTH MINNEAPOLIS MN 55428-1099
00-00-AA (hex)	XEROX CORPORATION
0000AA (base 16)	XEROX CORPORATION OFFICE SYSTEMS DIVISION M/S 105-50C 800 PHILLIPS ROAD WEBSTER NY 14580
00-00-AB (hex)	LOGIC MODELING CORPORATION
0000AB (base 16)	LOGIC MODELING CORPORATION 1520 MCCANDLESS DRIVE MILPITAS, CA 95035
00-00-AC (hex)	CONWARE COMPUTER CONSULTING
0000AC (base 16)	CONWARE COMPUTER CONSULTING KILLISFELDSTRASSE 64 76227 KARLSRUHE GERMANY
00-00-AD (hex)	BRUKER INSTRUMENTS INC.
0000AD (base 16)	BRUKER INSTRUMENTS INC. MANNING PARK BILLERICA MA 01821
00-00-AE (hex)	DASSAULT ELECTRONIQUE
0000AE (base 16)	DASSAULT ELECTRONIQUE 55, QUAI MARCEL DASSAULT 92214 ST CLOUD FRANCE
00-00-AF (hex)	NUCLEAR DATA INSTRUMENTATION
0000AF (base 16)	NUCLEAR DATA INSTRUMENTATION GOLF & MEACHAM ROADS SCHAUMBERG IL 60196
00-00-B0 (hex)	RND-RAD NETWORK DEVICES
0000B0 (base 16)	RND-RAD NETWORK DEVICES ATIDIM TECHNOL'CL BLDG. 1 TEL AVIV 61131 ISRAEL
00-00-B1 (hex)	ALPHA MICROSYSTEMS INC.
0000B1 (base 16)	ALPHA MICROSYSTEMS INC. 3501 SUNFLOWER SANTA ANA CA 92704
00-00-B2 (hex)	TELEVIDEO SYSTEMS, INC.
0000B2 (base 16)	TELEVIDEO SYSTEMS, INC. 550 E. BROKAW ROAD SAN JOSE, CA 95161-9048
00-00-B3 (hex)	CIMLINC INCORPORATED
0000B3 (base 16)	CIMLINC INCORPORATED 1957 CROOKS ROAD TROY MI 48084
00-00-B4 (hex)	EDIMAX COMPUTER COMPANY
0000B4 (base 16)	EDIMAX COMPUTER COMPANY 3F, 50, WU-CHUN 7 RD. TAIPEI TAIWAN

company_id	Organization Address
00-00-B5 (hex)	DATABILITY SOFTWARE SYS. INC.
0000B5 (base 16)	DATABILITY SOFTWARE SYS. INC. ONE PALMER TERRACE CARLSTADT NJ 07072
00-00-B6 (hex)	MICRO-MATIC RESEARCH
0000B6 (base 16)	MICRO-MATIC RESEARCH AMBACHTENLAAN 21 B5 B - 3030 HEVERLEE BELGIUM
00-00-B7 (hex)	DOVE COMPUTER CORPORATION
0000B7 (base 16)	DOVE COMPUTER CORPORATION 1200 NORTH 23RD STREET WILMINGTON, NC 28405
00-00-B8 (hex)	SEIKOSHA CO., LTD.
0000B8 (base 16)	SEIKOSHA CO., LTD. SYSTEM EQUIPMENT DIVISION 4-1-1 TAIHEI SUMIDA-KU TOKYO 130 JAPAN
00-00-B9 (hex)	MCDONNELL DOUGLAS COMPUTER SYS
0000B9 (base 16)	MCDONNELL DOUGLAS COMPUTER SYS DIV MCDONNELL DOUGLAS INF SYS BOUNDARY WAY HEMEL HEMPSTEAD HERTS ENGLAND
00-00-BA (hex)	SIIG, INC.
0000BA (base 16)	SIIG, INC. 6078 STEWART AVENUE FREMONT, CA 94538
00-00-BB (hex)	TRI-DATA
0000BB (base 16)	TRI-DATA 505 EAST MIDDLEFIELD ROAD MOUNTAIN VIEW, CA 94043-4082
00-00-BC (hex)	ALLEN-BRADLEY CO. INC.
0000BC (base 16)	ALLEN-BRADLEY CO. INC. 1 ALLEN-BRADLEY DRIVE MAYFIELD HEIGHT OH 44124-6118
00-00-BD (hex)	MITSUBISHI CABLE COMPANY
0000BD (base 16)	MITSUBISHI CABLE COMPANY 520 MADISON AVENUE NEW YORK, NY 10022
00-00-BE (hex)	THE NTI GROUP
0000BE (base 16)	THE NTI GROUP 4701 PATRICK HENRY DRIVE SUITE 24 SANTA CLARA, CA 95054
00-00-BF (hex)	SYMMETRIC COMPUTER SYSTEMS
0000BF (base 16)	SYMMETRIC COMPUTER SYSTEMS 1620 OAKLAND ROAD SUITE D-200 SAN JOSE CA 95131
00-00-C0 (hex)	WESTERN DIGITAL CORPORATION
0000C0 (base 16)	WESTERN DIGITAL CORPORATION 8105 IRVINE CENTER DRIVE IRVINE CA 92718
00-00-C1 (hex)	Madge Networks Ltd.
0000C1 (base 16)	Madge Networks Ltd. Wexham Springs, Framewood Road, Wexham Slough Sl3 6PJ UNITED KINGDOM
00-00-C2 (hex)	INFORMATION PRESENTATION TECH.
0000C2 (base 16)	INFORMATION PRESENTATION TECH. 23801 CALABASAS ROAD SUITE 2011 CALABASAS, CA 91302
00-00-C3 (hex)	HARRIS CORP COMPUTER SYS DIV

company_id	Organization Address	company_id	Organization Address
0000C3 (base 16)	HARRIS CORP COMPUTER SYS DIV M/S 75 1025 W. NASA BLVD.L 33309 MELBOURNE FL 32919	0000D2 (base 16)	SBE, INC. 4550 NORTH CANYON ROAD SAN RAMON CA 94583
00-00-C4 (hex)	WATERS DIV. OF MILLIPORE	00-00-D3 (hex)	WANG LABORATORIES INC.
0000C4 (base 16)	WATERS DIV. OF MILLIPORE 34 MAPLE STREET MILFORD MA 01757	0000D3 (base 16)	WANG LABORATORIES INC. LOWELL MA 01851
00-00-C5 (hex)	FARALLON COMPUTING/NETOPIA	00-00-D4 (hex)	PURE DATA LTD.
0000C5 (base 16)	FARALLON COMPUTING/NETOPIA 2470 MARINER SQUARE LOOP ALAMEDA, CA 94501	0000D4 (base 16)	PURE DATA LTD. 200 WEST BEAVER CREEK ROAD RICHMOND HILL ONTARIO L4B 1B4 CANADA
00-00-C6 (hex)	EON SYSTEMS	00-00-D5 (hex)	MICROGNOSIS INTERNATIONAL
0000C6 (base 16)	EON SYSTEMS 10601 SOUTH DEANZA BLVD. SUITE 303 CUPERTINO CA 95014	0000D5 (base 16)	MICROGNOSIS INTERNATIONAL 63 QUEEN VICTORIA STREET LONDON EC4N 4UD UNITED KINGDOM
00-00-C7 (hex)	ARIX CORPORATION	00-00-D6 (hex)	PUNCH LINE HOLDING
0000C7 (base 16)	ARIX CORPORATION ENGINEERING MAIL STOP 1152 MORSE AVENUE SUNNYVALE, CA 94089	0000D6 (base 16)	PUNCH LINE HOLDING P.O. BOX 391708 BRAMLEY 2018 SOUTH AFRICA
00-00-C8 (hex)	ALTOS COMPUTER SYSTEMS	00-00-D7 (hex)	DARTMOUTH COLLEGE
0000C8 (base 16)	ALTOS COMPUTER SYSTEMS 2641 ORCHARD PARKWAY SAN JOSE CA 95134	0000D7 (base 16)	DARTMOUTH COLLEGE KIEWIT COMPUTER CENTER HANOVER, NH 03755
00-00-C9 (hex)	EMULEX CORPORATION	00-00-D8 (hex)	NOVELL, INC.
0000C9 (base 16)	EMULEX CORPORATION 3535 HARBOR BOULEVARD COSTA MESA CA 92626	0000D8 (base 16)	NOVELL, INC. 122 EAST 1700 SOUTH M/S:E-12-1 P.O. BOX 5900 PROVO UT 84601
00-00-CA (hex)	APPLITEK	00-00-D9 (hex)	NIPPON TELEGRAPH & TELEPHONE
0000CA (base 16)	APPLITEK 107 AUDOBON ROAD WAKEFIELD MA 01880	0000D9 (base 16)	NIPPON TELEGRAPH & TELEPHONE CORPORATION (NTT) TEISHIN BLDG. 3-1 OOTEMACHI 2 CHOME, CHIYODA-KU TOKYO 100-8116 JAPAN
00-00-CB (hex)	COMPU-SHACK ELECTRONIC GMBH	00-00-DA (hex)	ATEX
0000CB (base 16)	COMPU-SHACK ELECTRONIC GMBH RINGSTR. 56 - 58, 5450 NEUWIED WEST GERMANY	0000DA (base 16)	ATEX 15 CROSBY DRIVE BEDFORD, MA 01730
00-00-CC (hex)	DENSAN CO., LTD.	00-00-DB (hex)	BRITISH TELECOMMUNICATIONS PLC
0000CC (base 16)	DENSAN CO., LTD. 1-23-11, KAMITAKAIDO SUGINAMI-KU, TOKYO 168 JAPAN	0000DB (base 16)	BRITISH TELECOMMUNICATIONS PLC 81 NEWGATE STREET LONDON, EC1A 7AJ ENGLAND
00-00-CD (hex)	Centrecom Systems, Ltd.	00-00-DC (hex)	HAYES MICROCOMPUTER PRODUCTS
0000CD (base 16)	Centrecom Systems, Ltd. Unit 2, 242 Ferry Road PO Box 10 290 CHRISTCHURCH 8030 NEW ZEALAND	0000DC (base 16)	HAYES MICROCOMPUTER PRODUCTS P.O. BOX 105203 ATLANTA, GA 30348
00-00-CE (hex)	MEGADATA CORP.	00-00-DD (hex)	TCL INCORPORATED
0000CE (base 16)	MEGADATA CORP. 35 ORVILLE DRIVE BOHEMIA, NY 11716	0000DD (base 16)	TCL INCORPORATED 41829 ALBRAE STREET FREMONT, CA 94538
00-00-CF (hex)	HAYES MICROCOMPUTER PRODUCTS	00-00-DE (hex)	CETIA
0000CF (base 16)	HAYES MICROCOMPUTER PRODUCTS (CANADA) LTD. 295 PHILLIP STREET WATERLOO, ONTARIO N2L 3W8 CANADA	0000DE (base 16)	CETIA 150 RUE BERTHELOT ZI TOULON EST 83088 TOULON CEDEX FRANCE
00-00-D0 (hex)	DEVELCON ELECTRONICS LTD.	00-00-DF (hex)	BELL & HOWELL PUB SYS DIV
0000D0 (base 16)	DEVELCON ELECTRONICS LTD. 856-51ST STREET EAST SASKATOON SASKATCHEWAN S7K 5C7 CANADA	0000DF (base 16)	BELL & HOWELL PUB SYS DIV OLD MANSFIELD ROAD WOOSTER OH 44691-9050
00-00-D1 (hex)	ADAPTEC INCORPORATED	00-00-E0 (hex)	QUADRAM CORP.
0000D1 (base 16)	ADAPTEC INCORPORATED M/S 180 691 SOUTH MILPITAS BLVD. MILPITAS CA 95035	0000E0 (base 16)	QUADRAM CORP. ONE QUAD WAY NORCROSS, GA 30093
00-00-D2 (hex)	SBE, INC.	00-00-E1 (hex)	GRID SYSTEMS

company_id	Organization Address
0000E1 (base 16)	GRID SYSTEMS 47211 LAKEVIEW BOULEVARD P.O. BOX 5003 FREMONT, CA 94537-5003
00-00-E2 (hex)	ACER TECHNOLOGIES CORP.
0000E2 (base 16)	ACER TECHNOLOGIES CORP. 401 CHARCOT AVE. SAN JOSE, CA 95131
00-00-E3 (hex)	INTEGRATED MICRO PRODUCTS LTD
0000E3 (base 16)	INTEGRATED MICRO PRODUCTS LTD IMP, NO. 1 INDUSTRIAL ESTATE CONSETT, CO DUKHAM ENGLAND, DH86TJ
00-00-E4 (hex)	IN2 GROUPE INTERTECHNIQUE
0000E4 (base 16)	IN2 GROUPE INTERTECHNIQUE IN2 - B.P.63 78373 PLAISIR CEDEX FRANCE
00-00-E5 (hex)	SIGMEX LTD.
0000E5 (base 16)	SIGMEX LTD. SIGMA HOUSE NORTH HEATH LANE HORSHAM, WEST SUSSEX RH12 4UZ ENGLAND
00-00-E6 (hex)	APTOR PRODUITS DE COMM INDUST
0000E6 (base 16)	APTOR PRODUITS DE COMM INDUST 61, CHEMIN DU VIEUX-CHENE ZIRST-BP 177 38244 MEYLAN CEDEX FRANCE
00-00-E7 (hex)	STAR GATE TECHNOLOGIES
0000E7 (base 16)	STAR GATE TECHNOLOGIES 29300 AURORA ROAD SOLON OH 44139
00-00-E8 (hex)	ACCTON TECHNOLOGY CORP.
0000E8 (base 16)	ACCTON TECHNOLOGY CORP. 46750 FREMONT BLVD. #104 FREMONT CA 94538
00-00-E9 (hex)	ISICAD, INC.
0000E9 (base 16)	ISICAD, INC. 1920 WEST CORPORATE WAY ANAHEIM CA 92803-6122
00-00-EA (hex)	UPNOD AB
0000EA (base 16)	UPNOD AB BOX 23051 S-750 23 UPPSALA SWEDEN
00-00-EB (hex)	MATSUSHITA COMM. IND. CO. LTD.
0000EB (base 16)	MATSUSHITA COMM. IND. CO. LTD. 3-1 4-CHOME TSUNASHIMA-HIGASHI KOHOKU-KU YOKOHAMA JAPAN
00-00-EC (hex)	MICROPROCESS
0000EC (base 16)	MICROPROCESS 97 BIS, RUE DE COLOMBES B.P. 87 92400 COURBEVOIE FRANCE
00-00-ED (hex)	APRIL
0000ED (base 16)	APRIL 60, RUE DE CARTALE BP 38 38170 SEYSSINET-PARISET FRANCE
00-00-EE (hex)	NETWORK DESIGNERS, LTD.
0000EE (base 16)	NETWORK DESIGNERS, LTD. UNIT 1A, HORNBEAM PARK HOOKSTONE ROAD HARROGATE, NORTH YORKSHIRE, UNITED KINGDOM, HG2 8QT

company_id	Organization Address
00-00-EF (hex)	KTI
0000EF (base 16)	KTI 2157 O'TOOLE AVENUE SUITE H SAN JOSE, CA 95131
00-00-F0 (hex)	SAMSUNG ELECTRONICS CO., LTD.
0000F0 (base 16)	SAMSUNG ELECTRONICS CO., LTD. 416, MAETAN-3DONG, PALDAL-GU SUWON CITY, KYUNGKI-DO KOREA 442-742
00-00-F1 (hex)	MAGNA COMPUTER CORPORATION
0000F1 (base 16)	MAGNA COMPUTER CORPORATION 22 KEEWAYDIN DRIVE 3ALEM NH 03079
00-00-F2 (hex)	SPIDER COMMUNICATIONS
0000F2 (base 16)	SPIDER COMMUNICATIONS 7491 BRIAR ROAD MONTREAL, QUEBEC H4W 1K4 CANADA
00-00-F3 (hex)	GANDALF DATA LIMITED
0000F3 (base 16)	GANDALF DATA LIMITED 130 COLONNADE ROAD SOUTH NEPEAN ONTARIO K2E 7M4 CANADA
00-00-F4 (hex)	ALLIED TELESYN INTERNATIONAL
0000F4 (base 16)	ALLIED TELESYN INTERNATIONAL CORPORATION 950 KIFER ROAD SUNNYVALE CA 94086
00-00-F5 (hex)	DIAMOND SALES LIMITED
0000F5 (base 16)	DIAMOND SALES LIMITED 17, CHARTERHOUSE STREET LONDON, ECIN 6RA UNITED KINGDOM
00-00-F6 (hex)	APPLIED MICROSYSTEMS CORP.
0000F6 (base 16)	APPLIED MICROSYSTEMS CORP. 5020 148 AVENUE, N.E. P.O. BOX 97002 REDMOND WA 98073-9702
00-00-F7 (hex)	YOUTH KEEP ENTERPRISE CO LTD
0000F7 (base 16)	YOUTH KEEP ENTERPRISE CO LTD 3/F NO. 712 MINTSU E. ROAD TAIPEI, TAIWAN ROC
00-00-F8 (hex)	DIGITAL EQUIPMENT CORPORATION
0000F8 (base 16)	DIGITAL EQUIPMENT CORPORATION LKG 1-2/A19 550 KING STREET LITTLETON MA 01460-1289 01460
00-00-F9 (hex)	QUOTRON SYSTEMS INC.
0000F9 (base 16)	QUOTRON SYSTEMS INC. 5454 BEETHOVEN ST. LOS ANGELES CA 90066
00-00-FA (hex)	MICROSAGE COMPUTER SYSTEMS INC
0000FA (base 16)	MICROSAGE COMPUTER SYSTEMS INC 680 SOUTH ROCK BLVD RENO, NE 89502
00-00-FB (hex)	RECHNER ZUR KOMMUNIKATION
0000FB (base 16)	RECHNER ZUR KOMMUNIKATION BITZENSTR. 11 F-5464 ASBACH GERMANY
00-00-FC (hex)	MEIKO
0000FC (base 16)	MEIKO 650 AZTEC WEST BRISTOL BS12 4SD UNITED KINGDOM
00-00-FD (hex)	HIGH LEVEL HARDWARE

company_id	Organization Address
0000FD (base 16)	HIGH LEVEL HARDWARE PO BOX 170 WINDMILL ROAD HEADINGTON OXFORD OX3 7BN ENGLAND
00-00-FE (hex)	ANNAPOLIS MICRO SYSTEMS
0000FE (base 16)	ANNAPOLIS MICRO SYSTEMS 190 ADMIRAL COCHRANE DRIVE SUITE 130 ANNAPOLIS, MD 21401
00-00-FF (hex)	CAMTEC ELECTRONICS LTD.
0000FF (base 16)	CAMTEC ELECTRONICS LTD. 101 VAUGHAN WAY LEICESTER LE1 4SA ENGLAND
00-01-00 (hex)	EQUIP'TRANS
000100 (base 16)	EQUIP'TRANS 47 Rue du Trou Grillon 91280 - ST PIERRE DU PERRAY FRANCE
00-01-02 (hex)	3COM CORPORATION
000102 (base 16)	3COM CORPORATION 5400 Bayfront Plaza - MS: 4220 Santa Clara CA 95052
00-01-03 (hex)	3COM CORPORATION
000103 (base 16)	3COM CORPORATION 5400 Bayfront Plaza - MS: 4220 Santa Clara CA 95052
00-01-04 (hex)	DVICO Co., Ltd.
000104 (base 16)	DVICO Co., Ltd. Kookmin Card B/D 6F 267-2 Seohyun-Dong Boondange-Gu Sungnam-City Kyungki-Do KOREA (SOUTH) 463-050
00-01-05 (hex)	BECKHOFF GmbH
000105 (base 16)	BECKHOFF GmbH Eiserstr. 5 D-33415 Vere GERMANY
00-01-06 (hex)	Tews Datentechnik GmbH
000106 (base 16)	Tews Datentechnik GmbH Am Bahnhof 7 25469 Halstenbek GERMANY
00-01-07 (hex)	Leiser GmbH
000107 (base 16)	Leiser GmbH Ilmstr. 7 85579 Neubiberg GERMANY
00-01-08 (hex)	AVLAB Technology, Inc.
000108 (base 16)	AVLAB Technology, Inc. 3F-1, No. 134, Sec. 3 Chung Shin Road, Hsin Tien Taipei TAIWAN, R.O.C.
00-01-09 (hex)	Nagano Japan Radio Co., Ltd.
000109 (base 16)	Nagano Japan Radio Co., Ltd. Shimohigano 1163, Inasato-machi Nagano 381-2288 JAPAN
00-01-0A (hex)	CIS TECHNOLOGY INC.
00010A (base 16)	CIS TECHNOLOGY INC. 16F, No. 75 Hsin Tai Wu Road Sec. 1, Hsi Chih, Taipei Hsien TAIWAN 221
00-01-0B (hex)	Space CyberLink, Inc.
00010B (base 16)	Space CyberLink, Inc. 5th Fl. Guppyung Town B 203 Nonhnyun-Dong, Kangham-Gu Seoul KOREA (ROK)

company_id	Organization Address
00-01-0C (hex)	System Talks Inc.
00010C (base 16)	System Talks Inc. 4F, Prime Nihonbashi Bld. 3-35-6, Nihonbashi Hama-cho Chuo-ku Tokyo (03-005) JAPAN
00-01-0D (hex)	CORECO, INC.
00010D (base 16)	CORECO, INC. 6969 Route Transcanadianne Ville St-LAURENT, Qc H4T 1V8 CANADA
00-01-0E (hex)	Bri-Link Technologies Co., Ltd
00010E (base 16)	Bri-Link Technologies Co., Ltd 2F, No. 63, Chow-Tze Street Taipei 114 TAIWAN, R.O.C.
00-01-0F (hex)	Nishan Systems, Inc.
00010F (base 16)	Nishan Systems, Inc. 3850 North First Street BLDG R2 San Jose CA 95134-1702
00-01-10 (hex)	Gotham Networks
000110 (base 16)	Gotham Networks 15 Discovery Way Acton, MA 01720
00-01-11 (hex)	iDigm Inc.
000111 (base 16)	iDigm Inc. 7FL Sindo B/D 1604-22 Seocho-Dong Seocho-Gu Seoul KOREA 137-070
00-01-12 (hex)	Shark Multimedia Inc.
000112 (base 16)	Shark Multimedia Inc. 48890 Milmont Drive #101-D Fremont CA 94538
00-01-13 (hex)	OLYMPUS OPTICAL CO., LTD.
000113 (base 16)	OLYMPUS OPTICAL CO., LTD. 2-3 Kuboyama-cho, Hachioji-shi Tokyo 192-8512 JAPAN
00-01-14 (hex)	KANDA TSUSHIN KOGYO CO., LTD.
000114 (base 16)	KANDA TSUSHIN KOGYO CO., LTD. 23-2, Nishi-Gotanda 2-chome, Shinagawa-ku Tokyo 141-8533 JAPAN
00-01-15 (hex)	EXTRATECH CORPORATION
000115 (base 16)	EXTRATECH CORPORATION 760 Thornton St., Unit 2 Post Falls ID 83854
00-01-16 (hex)	Netspect Technologies, Inc.
000116 (base 16)	Netspect Technologies, Inc. 3945 Freedom Circle - Ste. #360 Santa Clara CA 95054
00-01-17 (hex)	CANAL +
000117 (base 16)	CANAL + 23 Rue LeBlanc Le Ponant C 75906 Paris Cedex 15 FRANCE
00-01-18 (hex)	EZ Digital Co., Ltd.
000118 (base 16)	EZ Digital Co., Ltd. Bitville Bldg. Room 703 #1327 Seocho-Dong Seocho-Gu Seoul KOREA
00-01-19 (hex)	Action Controls Pty. Ltd.

company_id	Organization Address
000119 (base 16)	Action Controls Pty. Ltd. 16/104 Ferntree Gully Road Oakleigh 3166 AUSTRALIA
00-01-1A (hex)	EEH DataLink GmbH
00011A (base 16)	EEH DataLink GmbH Niederberger Str. 75 D-53909 Zuelpich GERMANY
00-01-1B (hex)	Unizone Technologies, Inc.
00011B (base 16)	Unizone Technologies, Inc. 5 Floor HaeSung Bldg. 67-2-YangJae-Dong SeoCho-Ku Seoul KOREA
00-01-1C (hex)	Universal Talkware Corporation
00011C (base 16)	Universal Talkware Corporation 10 Second St. NE Suite #400 Minneapolis MN 55413
00-01-1D (hex)	Centillium Communications
00011D (base 16)	Centillium Communications 47211 Lakeview Blvd. Fremont CA 94538
00-01-1E (hex)	Precidia Technologies, Inc.
00011E (base 16)	Precidia Technologies, Inc. 240 Terence Matthews Cres.- Ste #102 Kanata, Ontario CANADA, K2M-2C4
00-01-1F (hex)	RC Networks, Inc.
00011F (base 16)	RC Networks, Inc. 6727 Flanders Drive - Ste. #212 San Diego CA 92121
00-01-20 (hex)	OSCILLOQUARTZ S.A.
000120 (base 16)	OSCILLOQUARTZ S.A. Rue Des Brevards 16 2002 Neuchatel SWITZERLAND
00-01-21 (hex)	RapidStream Inc.
000121 (base 16)	RapidStream Inc. 1841 Zanker Road San Jose CA 95112
00-01-22 (hex)	Trend Communications, Ltd.
000122 (base 16)	Trend Communications, Ltd. Knaves Beech Estate Loudwter, High Wycombe Bucks, HP10 9QZ ENGLAND
00-01-23 (hex)	DIGITAL ELECTRONICS CORP.
000123 (base 16)	DIGITAL ELECTRONICS CORP. 8-2-52 Nanko Higashi, Suminoe-ku Osaka, 559-0031 JAPAN
00-01-24 (hex)	Acer Incorporated
000124 (base 16)	Acer Incorporated 21F, 88, Sec.1 Hsin Tai Wu Road, Hsichih Taipei Hsien 221 TAIWAN, R.O.C.
00-01-25 (hex)	YAESU MUSEN CO., LTD.
000125 (base 16)	YAESU MUSEN CO., LTD. 4-8-8, Nakameguro Meguro-ku Tokyo 153-8644, JAPAN
00-01-26 (hex)	PAC Labs
000126 (base 16)	PAC Labs 3079 Kilgore Road Rancho Cordova CA 95670
00-01-27 (hex)	The OPEN Group Limited

company_id	Organization Address
000127 (base 16)	The OPEN Group Limited P.O. Box 11-741 Wellington NEW ZEALNAD
00-01-28 (hex)	EnjoyWeb, Inc.
000128 (base 16)	EnjoyWeb, Inc. 3000 Scott Blvd. #107 Santa Clara CA 95054
00-01-29 (hex)	DFI Inc.
000129 (base 16)	DFI Inc. 100, Huan-Ho Street Hsi-Chih City, Taipei Hsien TAIWAN, R.O.C.
00 01 2A (hex)	Telematica Sistems Inteligente
00012A (base 16)	Telematica Sistems Inteligente Rua Miguel Casagrande, 200 Sao Paulo - SP- BRAZIL CEP: 02714-000
00-01-2B (hex)	TELENET Co., Ltd.
00012B (base 16)	TELENET Co., Ltd. KOREA
00-01-2C (hex)	Aravox Technologies, Inc.
00012C (base 16)	Aravox Technologies, Inc. 16725 40th Place North Plymouth MN 55446
00-01-2D (hex)	Komodo Technology
00012D (base 16)	Komodo Technology 170 Knowles Drive Los Gatos CA 95032
00-01-2E (hex)	PC Partner Ltd.
00012E (base 16)	PC Partner Ltd. Rm 1901-1908, 19/F, Shatin Galleria 18-24 Shan Mei Street, Fo Tan Shatin, Hong Kong CHINA
00-01-2F (hex)	Twinhead International Corp
00012F (base 16)	Twinhead International Corp 2FL, 2, Lane 235, Bao-Chiao Road Hsin-Tien TAIWAN, R.O.C.
00-01-30 (hex)	Extreme Networks
000130 (base 16)	Extreme Networks 3585 Monroe Street Santa Clara CA 95051
00-01-31 (hex)	Detection Systems, Inc.
000131 (base 16)	Detection Systems, Inc. 130 Perinton Parkway Fairport NY 14450
00-01-32 (hex)	Dranetz - BMI
000132 (base 16)	Dranetz - BMI 1000 New Durham Road Edison NJ 08818
00-01-33 (hex)	KYOWA Electronic Instruments C
000133 (base 16)	KYOWA Electronic Instruments C 3-5-1, Cyofugaoka Cyofu, Tokyo JAPAN
00-01-34 (hex)	SIG Positec Systems AG
000134 (base 16)	SIG Positec Systems AG Bernstreasse 70 CH-3250 Lyss SWITZERLAND
00-01-35 (hex)	KDC Corp.
000135 (base 16)	KDC Corp. 200-11 AnYang 7 dong ManAn-Gu AnYane-Si Kyunggi-do KOREA
00-01-36 (hex)	CyberTAN Technology, Inc.

company_id	Organization Address
000136 (base 16)	CyberTAN Technology, Inc. 626, Bldg.53, 195-56 Sec.4 Chung Hsing Rd Chutung, Hsinchu TAIWAN R.O.C.
00-01-37 (hex)	IT Farm Corporation
000137 (base 16)	IT Farm Corporation Asashiseimei Fuchu Bldg. 11F 1-14-1 Fuchu-cho, Fuchu-shi Tokyo 183-0055 JAPAN
00-01-38 (hex)	XAVi Technologies Corp.
000138 (base 16)	XAVi Technologies Corp. 9F, No. 129, Hsing Te Rd, Sanchung City Taipei Hsien 241 TAIWAN, R.O.C.
00-01-39 (hex)	Point Multimedia Systems
000139 (base 16)	Point Multimedia Systems 4Ra 507, Shihwa Industrial Complex 669-8 Sungkog-Dong, Ansan-City, Kyunggi-Do Korea 425-110
00-01-3A (hex)	SHELCAD COMMUNICATIONS, LTD.
00013A (base 16)	SHELCAD COMMUNICATIONS, LTD. P.O. Box 8513 New Industrial Zone Netanya 42504 ISRAEL
00-01-3B (hex)	BNA SYSTEMS
00013B (base 16)	BNA SYSTEMS 1637 S. Main Street Milpitas CA 95035
00-01-3C (hex)	TIW SYSTEMS
00013C (base 16)	TIW SYSTEMS 2211 Lawson Lane Santa Clara CA 95054
00-01-3D (hex)	RiscStation Ltd.
00013D (base 16)	RiscStation Ltd. 168 Elliott Street Tyldesley M29 805 UNITED KINGDOM
00-01-3E (hex)	Ascom Tateco AB
00013E (base 16)	Ascom Tateco AB Box 8783 40276 Goteborg SWEDEN
00-01-3F (hex)	Neighbor World Co., Ltd.
00013F (base 16)	Neighbor World Co., Ltd. 114A YERC, 134, Shinchon_dong Seodaemun_ku Seoul 120-749, KOREA
00-01-40 (hex)	Sendtek Corporation
000140 (base 16)	Sendtek Corporation 12F-3, 333, Sec.1 Kuang-Fu Road Hsinchu TAIWAN
00-01-41 (hex)	CABLE PRINT
000141 (base 16)	CABLE PRINT Jozef Cardynstraat 16 B - 9420 Erpe-Mere BELGIUM
00-01-42 (hex)	Cisco Systems, Inc.
000142 (base 16)	Cisco Systems, Inc. 170 West Tasman Drive - SJA-2 San Jose CA 95134
00-01-43 (hex)	Cisco Systems, Inc.

company_id	Organization Address
000143 (base 16)	Cisco Systems, Inc. 170 West Tasman Drive - SJA-2 San Jose CA 95134
00-01-44 (hex)	Cereva Networks, Inc.
000144 (base 16)	Cereva Networks, Inc. 100 Locke Drive Marlboro MA 01752
00-01-45 (hex)	WINSYSTEMS, INC.
000145 (base 16)	WINSYSTEMS, INC. 715 Stadium Drive Arlington TX 76011
00-01-46 (hex)	Tesco Controls, Inc.
000146 (base 16)	Tesco Controls, Inc. P.O. Box 239012 Sacramento CA 95823-9012
00-01-47 (hex)	Zhone Technologies
000147 (base 16)	Zhone Technologies 7677 Oakport Street - Ste. #1040 Oakland CA 94621
00-01-48 (hex)	X-traWeb Inc.
000148 (base 16)	X-traWeb Inc. 6750 West 93rd Street - Ste. #210 Overland Park KS 66212
00-01-49 (hex)	T.D.T. Transfer Data Test GmbH
000149 (base 16)	T.D.T. Transfer Data Test GmbH Siemensstrasse 18 84051 Essenbach GERMANY
00-01-4A (hex)	SONY COMPUTER SCIENCE LABS., I
00014A (base 16)	SONY COMPUTER SCIENCE LABS., I 3-14-13 Higashigotanda Shinagawa-Ku Tokyo 141 JAPAN
00-01-4B (hex)	Ennovate Networks, Inc.
00014B (base 16)	Ennovate Networks, Inc. 60 Codman Hill Road Boxborough MA 01719
00-01-4C (hex)	Berkeley Process Control
00014C (base 16)	Berkeley Process Control 1003 Canal Boulevard Richmond CA 94804
00-01-4D (hex)	Shin Kin Enterprises Co., Ltd
00014D (base 16)	Shin Kin Enterprises Co., Ltd 7, FU Hsing St. Tue Cheng Ind. Dist. Taipei TAIWAN, R.O.C.
00-01-4E (hex)	WIN Enterprises, Inc.
00014E (base 16)	WIN Enterprises, Inc. 300 Willow Street South North Andover MA 01845
00-01-4F (hex)	LUMINOUS Networks, Inc.
00014F (base 16)	LUMINOUS Networks, Inc. 6840 Via Del Oro #220 San Jose CA 95119
00-01-50 (hex)	GILAT COMMUNICATIONS, LTD.
000150 (base 16)	GILAT COMMUNICATIONS, LTD. 21/D Yegia Kapayim Street Petach-Tikva 49130 ISRAEL
00-01-51 (hex)	Ensemble Communications
000151 (base 16)	Ensemble Communications 6256 Greenman Drive - Ste. #400 San Diego CA 92122
00-01-52 (hex)	CHROMATEK INC.
000152 (base 16)	CHROMATEK INC. 6-10, Miyazaki 2-Chome Miyamae-Ku, Kawasaki-shi Kanagawa, 216-0033 JAPAN

company_id	Organization Address
00-01-53 (hex)	ARCHTEK TELECOM CORPORATION
000153 (base 16)	ARCHTEK TELECOM CORPORATION
	4F, No.9 Lane 130, Min-Chyuan Rd.
	Hsin-Tien
	Taipei
	231 TAIWAN
00-01-54 (hex)	G3M Corporation
000154 (base 16)	G3M Corporation
	4320 Stevens Creek Blvd. - Ste. #275
	San Jose CA 95129
00-01-55 (hex)	Promise Technology, Inc.
000155 (base 16)	Promise Technology, Inc.
	4F, 1, Prosperity 1st Road
	Science-Based Industrial Park
	Hsin-Chu
	TAIWAN
00-01-56 (hex)	FIREWIREDIRECT.COM, INC.
000156 (base 16)	FIREWIREDIRECT.COM, INC.
	4132 Spicewood Springs Rd - #I-4
	Austin TX 78759
00-01-57 (hex)	SYSWAVE CO., LTD
000157 (base 16)	SYSWAVE CO., LTD
	Dongho B/D 5F, 221-2
	Nonhyun-Dong, Kangnam-Gu
	Seoul
	KOREA 135-010
00-01-58 (hex)	Electro Industries/Gauge Tech
000158 (base 16)	Electro Industries/Gauge Tech
	1800 Shames Drive
	Westbury NY 11590
00-01-59 (hex)	S1 Corporation
000159 (base 16)	S1 Corporation
	R&D Center, S1 Bldg.
	59-8, Nonhyun-Dong
	Kangnam-Ku
	Seoul
	KOREA 135-010
00-01-5A (hex)	Digital Video Broadcasting
00015A (base 16)	Digital Video Broadcasting
	DVB, % European Broadcasting Union
	17A Ancienne Route
	CH-1218 Grand Saconnex
	SWITZERLAND
00-01-5B (hex)	ITALTEL S.p.A/RF-UP-I
00015B (base 16)	ITALTEL S.p.A/RF-UP-I
	20019 Cast.Settimo M.se (MI)
	ITALY
00-01-5C (hex)	CADANT INC.
00015C (base 16)	CADANT INC.
	4343 Commerce Court - Ste. #207
	Lisle IL 60532
00-01-5D (hex)	Pirus Networks
00015D (base 16)	Pirus Networks
	40 Nagog Park
	Acton MA 01720
00-01-5E (hex)	BEST TECHNOLOGY CO., LTD.
00015E (base 16)	BEST TECHNOLOGY CO., LTD.
	7F, Haesung B/D
	115-12 Nonhyun-dong
	Kangnam-Ku
	Seoul, 135-101
	KOREA
00-01-5F (hex)	DIGITAL DESIGN GmbH
00015F (base 16)	DIGITAL DESIGN GmbH
	Reginhardstrasse 34
	13409 Berlin
	GERMANY
00-01-60 (hex)	ELMEX Co., LTD.

company_id	Organization Address
000160 (base 16)	ELMEX Co., LTD.
	16-30 Kimachi
	Aobaku Sendai-Shi
	Miyagi-Ken
	JAPAN
00-01-61 (hex)	Meta Machine Technology
000161 (base 16)	Meta Machine Technology
	400 Silver Cedar Court - ste. #220
	Chapel Hill NC 27514
00-01-62 (hex)	Cygnet Technologies, Inc.
000162 (base 16)	Cygnet Technologies, Inc.
	1411 LeMay Drive #301
	Carrollton TX 75007
00-01-63 (hex)	Cisco Systems, Inc.
000163 (base 16)	Cisco Systems, Inc.
	170 West Tasman Drive - SJA-2
	San Jose CA 95134
00-01-64 (hex)	Cisco Systems, Inc.
000164 (base 16)	Cisco Systems, Inc.
	170 West Tasman Drive - SJA-2
	San Jose CA 95134
00-01-65 (hex)	AirSwitch Corporation
000165 (base 16)	AirSwitch Corporation
	37 East 200 South
	Springville UT 84663
00-01-66 (hex)	TC GROUP A/S
000166 (base 16)	TC GROUP A/S
	Sindalsvej 34
	DK-8240 Risskov
	DENMARK
00-01-67 (hex)	HIOKI E.E. CORPORATION
000167 (base 16)	HIOKI E.E. CORPORATION
	81 Koizumi, Ueda, Nagano
	386-1192, JAPAN
00-01-68 (hex)	VITANA CORPORATION
000168 (base 16)	VITANA CORPORATION
	2500 Don Reid Drive
	Ottawa, Ontario
	K1H 1E1, CANADA
00-01-69 (hex)	Celestix Networks Pte Ltd.
000169 (base 16)	Celestix Networks Pte Ltd.
	18 Tannery Lane #05-03
	Lian Tong Building
	SINGAPORE 347780
00-01-6A (hex)	ALITEC
00016A (base 16)	ALITEC
	Laval Technopole B.P. 102
	53001 LAVAL Cedex
	FRANCE
00-01-6B (hex)	LightChip, Inc.
00016B (base 16)	LightChip, Inc.
	5 Industrial Way
	Salem NH 03079
00-01-6C (hex)	FOXCONN
00016C (base 16)	FOXCONN
	6125 Phyllis Drive
	Cypress CA 90630
00-01-6D (hex)	Triton Network Systems
00016D (base 16)	Triton Network Systems
	8529 Southpark Circle
	Orlando FL 32819
00-01-6E (hex)	Conklin Corporation
00016E (base 16)	Conklin Corporation
	6141 Crooked Creek Road
	Norcross GA 30092-3193
00-01-6F (hex)	HAITAI ELECTRONICS CO., LTD.
00016F (base 16)	HAITAI ELECTRONICS CO., LTD.
	345-50 Gasan-dong, Geumcheon-gu
	Seoul
	SOUTH KOREA

company_id	Organization Address
00-01-70 (hex)	ESE Embedded System Engineer'g
000170 (base 16)	ESE Embedded System Engineer'g Muehlbachstr. 20 78351 Bodman-Ludwigshafen GERMANY
00-01-71 (hex)	Allied Data Technologies
000171 (base 16)	Allied Data Technologies Pascalweg 1, 3208 KL Spijkenisse THE NETHERLANDS
00-01-72 (hex)	TechnoLand Co., LTD.
000172 (base 16)	TechnoLand Co., LTD. 3-17-11 Akebono-cho Fukuyama-city Hiroshima 721-0925 JAPAN
00-01-73 (hex)	JNI Corporation
000173 (base 16)	JNI Corporation 9775 Towne Centre Drive San Diego CA 92128
00-01-74 (hex)	CyberOptics Corporation
000174 (base 16)	CyberOptics Corporation 5900 Golden Hills Drive Golden Valley MN 55416
00-01-75 (hex)	Radiant Communications Corp.
000175 (base 16)	Radiant Communications Corp. 5001 Hadley Road South Plainfield NJ 07080
00-01-76 (hex)	Orient Silver Enterprises
000176 (base 16)	Orient Silver Enterprises 8740 White Oak Avenue Rancho Cucamonga CA 91730
00-01-77 (hex)	EDSL
000177 (base 16)	EDSL Habarzel 1 st Ramat Ahayal Tel-Aviv ISRAEL 69710
00-01-78 (hex)	MARGI Systems, Inc.
000178 (base 16)	MARGI Systems, Inc. 3155 Kearney Street. - Ste.#200 Fremont CA 94538
00-01-79 (hex)	WIRELESS TECHNOLOGY, INC.
000179 (base 16)	WIRELESS TECHNOLOGY, INC. Anam Bldg. 2Fl, 154-17 Samsung-Dong, Kangnam-Ku Seoul, 135-090 KOREA
00-01-7A (hex)	Chengdu Maipu Electric Industrial Co., Ltd.
00017A (base 16)	Chengdu Maipu Electric Industrial Co., Ltd. NANYI BUILDING, CONSULATE RD., CHENGDU P.R. CHINA
00-01-7B (hex)	Heidelberger Druckmaschinen AG
00017B (base 16)	Heidelberger Druckmaschinen AG Kurfuerstenanlage 52-60 69115 Heidelberg GERMANY
00-01-7C (hex)	AG-E GmbH
00017C (base 16)	AG-E GmbH Dennewartstr. 27 52068 Aachen GERMANY
00-01-7D (hex)	ThermoQuest
00017D (base 16)	ThermoQuest 355 River Oaks Parkway San Jose CA 95134
00-01-7E (hex)	ADTEK System Science Co., Ltd.

company_id	Organization Address
00017E (base 16)	ADTEK System Science Co., Ltd. YBP HiTECH Center 134 Gohdo-cho, Hodogaya Yokohama JAPAN
00-01-7F (hex)	Experience Music Project
00017F (base 16)	Experience Music Project 110 -110th Avenue NE - Ste. #400 Bellevue WA 98004
00-01-80 (hex)	AOpen, Inc.
000180 (base 16)	AOpen, Inc. 6F, 88, Sec.1, Hsin Tai Wu Road, Hsichih Taipei Hsien 221 TAIWAN, R.O.C.
00-01-81 (hex)	Nortel Networks
000181 (base 16)	Nortel Networks 1100 Technology Park Drive Billerica MA 01821
00-01-82 (hex)	DICA TECHNOLOGIES AG
000182 (base 16)	DICA TECHNOLOGIES AG Rotherstr, 19 D-10245 Berlin GERMANY
00-01-83 (hex)	ANITE TELECOMS
000183 (base 16)	ANITE TELECOMS 127 Fleet Road, Fleet Hampshire, GUB 8PD UNITED KINGDOM
00-01-84 (hex)	SIEB & MEYER AG
000184 (base 16)	SIEB & MEYER AG Auf dem Schmaarkamp 21 D-21339 Luneburg GERMANY
00-01-85 (hex)	Aloka Co., Ltd.
000185 (base 16)	Aloka Co., Ltd. 3-7-19, Imai Ome-city Tokyo 198-8577 JAPAN
00-01-86 (hex)	DISCH GmbH
000186 (base 16)	DISCH GmbH Friedensplatz 3 91207 Lauf GERMANY
00-01-87 (hex)	i2SE GmbH
000187 (base 16)	i2SE GmbH Carl-Zeiss - Str. 46 47445 Moers GERMANY
00-01-88 (hex)	LXCO Technologies ag
000188 (base 16)	LXCO Technologies ag Gimmerstr. 69 D-10117 Berlin GERMANY
00-01-89 (hex)	Refraction Technology, Inc.
000189 (base 16)	Refraction Technology, Inc. 2626 Lombardy Lane - Ste. #105 Dallas TX 75220
00-01-8A (hex)	ROI COMPUTER AG
00018A (base 16)	ROI COMPUTER AG Werner-von-Siemens-Str. 1 93426 Roding GERMANY
00-01-8B (hex)	NetLinks Co., Ltd.
00018B (base 16)	NetLinks Co., Ltd. 3F Dscom Bldg., 238-3 Poi-dong, Kangnam-Ku Seoul KOREA
00-01-8C (hex)	Mega Vision

company_id	Organization Address
00018C (base 16)	Mega Vision 5765 Thornwood Drive Goleta CA 93117
00-01-8D (hex)	AudeSi Technologies
00018D (base 16)	AudeSi Technologies Suite 180, 6815 8th Street N.E. Calgary AB CANADA
00-01-8E (hex)	Logitec Corporation
00018E (base 16)	Logitec Corporation 8268 Rokudouhara, Misuzu Ina, Nagano JAPAN
00-01-8F (hex)	Kenetec, Inc.
00018F (base 16)	Kenetec, Inc. 115 Hurley Road Oxford CT 06748
00-01-90 (hex)	SMK-M
000190 (base 16)	SMK-M 1055 Tierra Del Rey Chula Vista CA 91910
00-01-91 (hex)	SYRED Data Systems
000191 (base 16)	SYRED Data Systems 272 Lanes Mill Road Howell NJ 07731
00-01-92 (hex)	Texas Digital Systems
000192 (base 16)	Texas Digital Systems 400 Technology Parkway College Station TX 77845
00-01-93 (hex)	Hanbyul Telecom Co., Ltd.
000193 (base 16)	Hanbyul Telecom Co., Ltd. 5th Fl. Oksan Bldg. 157-33 Samsung-Dong Kangnam-ku Seoul KOREA
00-01-94 (hex)	Capital Equipment Corporation
000194 (base 16)	Capital Equipment Corporation 900 Middlesex Turnpike - Bldg. 2 Billerica MA 01821
00-01-95 (hex)	Sena Technologies, Inc.
000195 (base 16)	Sena Technologies, Inc. 116-23 Shinlim-dong Onsung Bldg. 8th Floor Kwanak-ku Seoul KOREA
00-01-96 (hex)	Cisco Systems, Inc.
000196 (base 16)	Cisco Systems, Inc. 170 West Tasman Drive - SJA-2 San Jose CA 95134
00-01-97 (hex)	Cisco Systems, Inc.
000197 (base 16)	Cisco Systems, Inc. 170 West Tasman Drive - SJA-2 San Jose CA 95134
00-01-98 (hex)	Darim Vision
000198 (base 16)	Darim Vision Taejon Expo Venture Town 3-1 Doryong-dong, Yusung-gu Taejon KOREA
00-01-99 (hex)	HeiSei Electronics
000199 (base 16)	HeiSei Electronics 5/7 Alley 8, Lane 45 Poaltsin Road Hsintien City TAIWAN
00-01-9A (hex)	LEUNIG GmbH

company_id	Organization Address
00019A (base 16)	LEUNIG GmbH Wilhelm-Ostwald-Str. 17 53721 Siegburg GERMANY
00-01-9B (hex)	Kyoto Microcomputer Co., Ltd.
00019B (base 16)	Kyoto Microcomputer Co., Ltd. 2-27 Hachijogaoka Nagaokakyo-city Kyoto JAPAN
00-01-9C (hex)	JDS Uniphase Inc.
00019C (base 16)	JDS Uniphase Inc. 570 West Hunt Club Road Napeon, ON K1R 7T7 CANADA
00-01-9D (hex)	E-Control Systems, Inc.
00019D (base 16)	E-Control Systems, Inc. 9420 Lurline Ave., Unite "B" Chatsworth CA 91311
00-01-9E (hex)	ESS Technology, Inc.
00019E (base 16)	ESS Technology, Inc. 48401 Fremont Blvd. Fremont CA 94538
00-01-9F (hex)	Phonex Broadband
00019F (base 16)	Phonex Broadband 6952 High Tech Drive Midvale, UT 84047
00-01-A0 (hex)	Infinilink Corporation
0001A0 (base 16)	Infinilink Corporation 1740 E. Garry Ave. - Ste. #206 Santa Ana CA 92705
00-01-A1 (hex)	Mag-Tek, Inc.
0001A1 (base 16)	Mag-Tek, Inc. 20725 South Annalee Ave. Carson CA 90746
00-01-A2 (hex)	Logical Co., Ltd.
0001A2 (base 16)	Logical Co., Ltd. 4598 Murakushi-cho Hamamatsu-shi, Shizuoka-ken 431-1207 JAPAN
00-01-A3 (hex)	GENESYS LOGIC, INC.
0001A3 (base 16)	GENESYS LOGIC, INC. 10F, No. 11, Ln.3., Tsao Ti Wei, Shenkeng Taipei TAIWAN, R.O.C.
00-01-A4 (hex)	Microlink Corporation
0001A4 (base 16)	Microlink Corporation 11110 Ohio Ave., - Ste. #108 Los Angeles CA 90034
00-01-A5 (hex)	Nextcomm, Inc.
0001A5 (base 16)	Nextcomm, Inc. 12413 Willows Road NE - Ste. #210 Kirkland WA 98034
00-01-A6 (hex)	Scientific-Atlanta Arcodan A/S
0001A6 (base 16)	Scientific-Atlanta Arcodan A/S Avgustenborg Landevej 7 DK-6400 Sonderborg DENMARK
00-01-A7 (hex)	UNEX TECHNOLOGY CORPORATION
0001A7 (base 16)	UNEX TECHNOLOGY CORPORATION 8F-5, NO. 130 SZE WEI ROAD HSINCHU TAIWAN, R.O.C.
00-01-A8 (hex)	Welltech Computer Co., Ltd.
0001A8 (base 16)	Welltech Computer Co., Ltd. 13F-4, no. 150, Jian Yi Road Chung-Ho 235, Taipei TAIWAN, R.O.C.

company_id	Organization Address
00-01-A9 (hex)	BMW AG
0001A9 (base 16)	BMW AG EE-223 Knorrstr.147 80788 Munich, GERMANY
00-01-AA (hex)	Airspan Communications, Ltd.
0001AA (base 16)	Airspan Communications, Ltd. Cambridge House, Oxford Rd., Uxbridge, Middlesex UB1UN, UNITED KINGDOM
00-01-AB (hex)	Main Street Networks
0001AB (base 16)	Main Street Networks 4030 Moorpark Ave. Suite 200 San Jose, CA 95117-1849
00-01-AC (hex)	Sitara Networks, Inc.
0001AC (base 16)	Sitara Networks, Inc. 60 Hickory Drive Waltham, MA 02451
00-01-AD (hex)	Coach Master International d.b.a. CMI Worldwide, Inc.
0001AD (base 16)	Coach Master International d.b.a. CMI Worldwide, Inc. 600 Stewart Street Suite 700 Seattle, WA 98101
00-01-AE (hex)	Trex Enterprises
0001AE (base 16)	Trex Enterprises 590 Lipoa Parkway Suite 222 Kihei, HI 96753
00-01-AF (hex)	Motorola Computer Group
0001AF (base 16)	Motorola Computer Group 2900 S. Diablo Way Tempe, Arizona 85282-3214
00-01-B0 (hex)	Fulltek Technology Co., Ltd.
0001B0 (base 16)	Fulltek Technology Co., Ltd. 3F No. 8, Lane 130, Min Chuan Rd., Hsintien City, Taipei Hsein 231, TAIWAN R.O.C.
00-01-B1 (hex)	General Bandwidth
0001B1 (base 16)	General Bandwidth 12303-B Technology Blvd. Austin, TX 78727
00-01-B2 (hex)	Digital Processing Systems, Inc.
0001B2 (base 16)	Digital Processing Systems, Inc. 70 Valleywood Drive Markham, Ontario CANADA L3R 4T5
00-01-B3 (hex)	Precision Electronic Manufacturing
0001B3 (base 16)	Precision Electronic Manufacturing P0187, P.O. 527948 Miami, FL 33152-7948
00-01-B4 (hex)	Wayport, Inc.
0001B4 (base 16)	Wayport, Inc. 1609 Shoal Creek Blvd. Suite 301 Austin, TX 78701
00-01-B5 (hex)	Turin Networks, Inc.
0001B5 (base 16)	Turin Networks, Inc. 1415 North McDowell Blvd. Petaluma, CA 94954
00-01-B6 (hex)	SAEJIN T&M Co., Ltd.

company_id	Organization Address
0001B6 (base 16)	SAEJIN T&M Co., Ltd. 2nd Fl., Saejin Bldg., 689 Ilwon-Dong, Kangnam-Gu. Seoul, 135-230 KOREA
00-01-B7 (hex)	Centos, Inc.
0001B7 (base 16)	Centos, Inc. 6F-1, NO. 15, LANE 360 NEI-HU RD., SECT. 1, TAIPEI TAIWAN, R.O.C.
00-01-B8 (hex)	Netsensity, Inc.
0001B8 (base 16)	Netsensity, Inc. 15301 Dallas Parkway Suite 760 Addison, TX 75001
00-01-B9 (hex)	SKF Condition Monitoring
0001B9 (base 16)	SKF Condition Monitoring 4141 Ruffin Road San Diego, CA 92123
00-01-BA (hex)	IC-Net, Inc.
0001BA (base 16)	IC-Net, Inc. 5 Fl. Seasung Bldg., 311-27 Noryangjin-Dong Dongjak-Gu Seoul, KOREA
00-01-BB (hex)	Frequentis
0001BB (base 16)	Frequentis SPITTELBREITENGASSE 34 A-1120 VIENNA AUSTRIA
00-01-BC (hex)	Brains Corporation
0001BC (base 16)	Brains Corporation 2-27-8-4Fl TAMAGAWA SETAGAYA-KU, TOKYO 158-0094 JAPAN
00-01-BD (hex)	Peterson Electro-Musical Products, Inc.
0001BD (base 16)	Peterson Electro-Musical Products, Inc. 11601 S. Mayfield Avenue Alsip, IL 60803-2476
00-01-BE (hex)	Gigalink Co., Ltd.
0001BE (base 16)	Gigalink Co., Ltd. 6th F/L Diplomatic Center 1376-1 Seocho-dong Seocho-ku Seoul KOREA
00-01-BF (hex)	Teleforce Co., Ltd.
0001BF (base 16)	Teleforce Co., Ltd. 721 Yoshioka-Cho Kanonji-City Kagawa-prf. 768-0021 JAPAN
00-01-C0 (hex)	CompuLab, Ltd.
0001C0 (base 16)	CompuLab, Ltd. P.O. Box 66 Nesher 36770 ISRAEL
00-01-C1 (hex)	Exbit Technology
0001C1 (base 16)	Exbit Technology Hoerkaer 18 DK-2730 Herlev DENMARK
00-01-C2 (hex)	ARK Research Corp.
0001C2 (base 16)	ARK Research Corp. 1198 Saratoga Ave. #11D San Jose, CA 95129
00-01-C3 (hex)	Acromag, Inc.
0001C3 (base 16)	Acromag, Inc. 30765 S. Wixom Road P.O. Box 437 Wixom, MI 48393-7037

company_id	Organization Address	company_id	Organization Address
00-01-C4 (hex)	NeoWave, Inc.	0001D0 (base 16)	VitalPoint, Inc. 15770 Hopper Road Peyton, CO 80831
0001C4 (base 16)	NeoWave, Inc. 10th KRIHS Bldg. 1591-6 Kwan Yang-Dong, Dong An-Gu, Anyong-Si, KyoungGi-Do, 431-712 SOUTH KOREA	00-01-D1 (hex)	CoNet Communications, Inc.
		0001D1 (base 16)	CoNet Communications, Inc. 1616 E. Fourth Street Suite 240 Santa Ana, CA 92701
00-01-C5 (hex)	Simpler Networks	00-01-D2 (hex)	MacPower Peripherals, Ltd.
0001C5 (base 16)	Simpler Networks 555 Dr Frederick Philips Suite 210 St. Laurent, QUEBEC CANADA H4M 2X4	0001D2 (base 16)	MacPower Peripherals, Ltd. 3Fl, No.3, Alley 9, Lane 45, Baohsing Rd. Hsintien City, Taipei County, TAIWAN
00-01-C6 (hex)	Quarry Technologies	00-01-D3 (hex)	PAXCOMM, Inc.
0001C6 (base 16)	Quarry Technologies 8 New England Executive Park Burlington, MA 01803	0001D3 (base 16)	PAXCOMM, Inc. 7th F The Corp. Center Chungnam National University 220 Kung-Dong Yusong-Gu Taejeon, 305-764, KOREA
00-01-C7 (hex)	Cisco Systems, Inc.		
0001C7 (base 16)	Cisco Systems, Inc. 170 West Tasman Dr. San Jose, CA 95134	00-01-D4 (hex)	Leisure Time, Inc.
00-01-C8 (hex)	THOMAS CONRAD CORP.	0001D4 (base 16)	Leisure Time, Inc. 4258 Communications Drive Norcross, GA 30093
0001C8 (base 16)	THOMAS CONRAD CORP. 1908-R KRAMER LANE AUSTIN, TX 78758	00-01-D5 (hex)	HAEDONG INFO & COMM CO., LTD
00-01-C8 (hex)	CONRAD CORP.	0001D5 (base 16)	HAEDONG INFO & COMM CO., LTD #801 The Corporation Center for University, Reseach & Industry 220 Kung-Dong, Yuseong-Gu, Taejeon, Republic of Korea 305-764
0001C8 (base 16)	CONRAD CORP.		
00-01-C9 (hex)	Cisco Systems, Inc.	00-01-D6 (hex)	MAN Roland Druckmaschinen AG
0001C9 (base 16)	Cisco Systems, Inc. 170 West Tasman Drive San Jose, CA 95134	0001D6 (base 16)	MAN Roland Druckmaschinen AG Stadtbachstr. 1 86135 Augsburg GERMANY
00-01-CA (hex)	Geocast Network Systems, Inc.	00-01-D7 (hex)	F5 Networks, Inc.
0001CA (base 16)	Geocast Network Systems, Inc. 190 Independence Drive Menlo Park, CA 94025	0001D7 (base 16)	F5 Networks, Inc. 1227 N. Argonne Road Suite A Spokane, WA 99212
00-01-CB (hex)	NetGame, Ltd.	00-01-D8 (hex)	Teltronics, Inc.
0001CB (base 16)	NetGame, Ltd. 16 Hamelacha Street Rosh-Haain ISRAEL 48091	0001D8 (base 16)	Teltronics, Inc. 4125 Keller Springs Road Suite 166 Addison, TX 25001
00-01-CC (hex)	Japan Total Design Communication Co., Ltd.	00-01-D9 (hex)	Sigma, Inc.
0001CC (base 16)	Japan Total Design Communication Co., Ltd. Enesta Suginamihigashi Build., 3F, 3-7-1, Asagayaminami Suginami-ku, Tokyo 166-0004, JAPAN	0001D9 (base 16)	Sigma, Inc. 32-3 Seijyo 9 Chome Setagaya-ku Tokyo 157-0066 JAPAN
00-01-CD (hex)	ARtem	00-01-DA (hex)	WINCOMM Corporation
0001CD (base 16)	ARtem Olgastrasse 152 D-89073 ULM GERMANY	0001DA (base 16)	WINCOMM Corporation 2F, No. 3, Prosperity Road 1, Science-Based Industrial Park, Hsinchu, Taiwan, R.O.C. CHINA
00-01-CE (hex)	Custom Micro Products, Ltd.	00-01-DB (hex)	Freecom Technologies GmbH
0001CE (base 16)	Custom Micro Products, Ltd. 450 Blandford Road Hamworthy Poole Dorset BHIL 5BN UNITED KINGDOM	0001DB (base 16)	Freecom Technologies GmbH Obentrautstr. 72 D-10963, Berlin, GERMANY
00-01-CF (hex)	Alpha Data Parallel Systems, Ltd.	00-01-DC (hex)	Activetelco
0001CF (base 16)	Alpha Data Parallel Systems, Ltd. 58 Timber Bush Edinburgh EH6 6QH Scotland UNITED KINGDOM	0001DC (base 16)	Activetelco 43222 Christy Street Fremont, CA 94538
		00-01-DD (hex)	Avail Networks
00-01-D0 (hex)	VitalPoint, Inc.	0001DD (base 16)	Avail Networks 305 E. Eisenhower Parkway Ann Arbor, MI 48108

company_id	Organization Address
00-01-DE (hex)	Trango Systems, Inc.
0001DE (base 16)	Trango Systems, Inc. 9939 V/A Pasar San Diego, CA 92126
00-01-DF (hex)	ISDN Communications, Ltd.
0001DF (base 16)	ISDN Communications, Ltd. The Stable Block, Ronans Chavey Down Road, Winkfield Row Berkshire RG42 6Y ENGLAND
00-01-E0 (hex)	Fast Systems, Inc.
0001E0 (base 16)	Fast Systems, Inc. 87-9 Yang-Jae, Seo-Cho, Seoul, KOREA
00-01-E1 (hex)	Kinpo Electronics, Inc.
0001E1 (base 16)	Kinpo Electronics, Inc. TSAC TI WEI, WAN SHUN TSUN, SHEN KENG HSIANG, TAIPEI HSIEN TAIWAN (222) R.O.C. CHINA
00-01-E2 (hex)	Ando Electric Corporation
0001E2 (base 16)	Ando Electric Corporation 19-7, Kamata 4-Chrome, Ota-ku Tokyo, 144-0052 JAPAN
00-01-E3 (hex)	Siemens AG
0001E3 (base 16)	Siemens AG Schlavenhorst 88 46395 Bocholt GERMANY
00-01-E4 (hex)	Sitera, Inc.
0001E4 (base 16)	Sitera, Inc. 1820 Lefthand Circle Longmont, CO 80501
00-01-E5 (hex)	Supernet, Inc.
0001E5 (base 16)	Supernet, Inc. 135-080 Daemeong Bldg. 2nd Floor, 650-2, Yeoksam-dong Kangnam-ku, Seoul KOREA
00-01-E6 (hex)	Hewlett-Packard Company
0001E6 (base 16)	Hewlett-Packard Company 11000 Wolfe Road, Mailstop 42LE Cupertino, CA 95014
00-01-E7 (hex)	Hewlett-Packard Company
0001E7 (base 16)	Hewlett-Packard Company 11000 Wolfe Road, Mailstop 42LE Cupertino, CA 95014
00-01-E8 (hex)	Force10 Networks, Inc.
0001E8 (base 16)	Force10 Networks, Inc. 1440 McCarthy Blvd. Milpitas, CA 95035
00-01-E9 (hex)	Litton Marine Systems B.V.
0001E9 (base 16)	Litton Marine Systems B.V. 118 Burlington Road New Malden, Surrey ENGLAND, KT3 4NR
00-01-EA (hex)	Cirilium Corp.
0001EA (base 16)	Cirilium Corp. 1615 S. 52nd Street Tempe, AZ 85281
00-01-EB (hex)	C-COM Corporation
0001EB (base 16)	C-COM Corporation 3F, No. 48, Park Ave. II SBIP Hsinchu Taiwan, R.O.C.
00-01-EC (hex)	Ericsson Group

company_id	Organization Address
0001EC (base 16)	Ericsson Group Telefonaktiebolaget LM Ericsson Corp. 126 25 STOCKHOLM SWEDEN
00-01-ED (hex)	SETA Corp.
0001ED (base 16)	SETA Corp. Ariake Frontier Bldg. B Ariake, Koutou Ku Tokyo, JAPAN 135-0063
00-01-EE (hex)	Comtrol Europe, Ltd.
0001EE (base 16)	Comtrol Europe, Ltd. The Courtyard Studio Grange Farm, Station Road Launton Oxon Ocgoee U.K.
00-01-EF (hex)	Camtel Technology Corp.
0001EF (base 16)	Camtel Technology Corp. No. 2, Wu-Kung 5 Rd., Wu-Ku Ind. Park, Hsinchuang, Taipei Shien Taiwan, R.O.C.
00-01-F0 (hex)	Tridium, Inc.
0001F0 (base 16)	Tridium, Inc. 3951 Westerre Parkway Suite 350 Richmond, VA 23233
00-01-F1 (hex)	Innovative Concepts, Inc.
0001F1 (base 16)	Innovative Concepts, Inc. 8200 Greensboro Drive Suite 801 McLean, VA 22102
00-01-F3 (hex)	QPS, Inc.
0001F3 (base 16)	QPS, Inc. 23671 Via Del Rio Yorba Linda, CA 92887
00-01-F4 (hex)	Enterasys Networks
0001F4 (base 16)	Enterasys Networks 35 Industrial Way Rochester, NH 03867
00-01-F5 (hex)	ERIM S.A.
0001F5 (base 16)	ERIM S.A. 11 Av Republique 69692 Venissieux Cedex FRANCE
00-01-F6 (hex)	Association of Musical Electronics Industry
0001F6 (base 16)	Association of Musical Electronics Industry Ito Bldg. 4th Floor 2-16-9 Misaki-cho, Chiyoda-ku, Tokyo, 101-0061 JAPAN
00-01-F7 (hex)	Image Display Systems, Inc.
0001F7 (base 16)	Image Display Systems, Inc. 46560 Fremont Blvd. Suite #406 Fremont, CA 94538
00-01-F8 (hex)	Adherent Systems, Ltd.
0001F8 (base 16)	Adherent Systems, Ltd. Endeavour House, Vision Park Histon Cambridge CB4 4ZR UNITED KINGDOM
00-01-F9 (hex)	TeraGlobal Communications Corp.
0001F9 (base 16)	TeraGlobal Communications Corp. 9171 Towne Centre Drive Suite #600 San Diego, CA 92122
00-01-FA (hex)	HOROSCAS

company_id	Organization Address
0001FA (base 16)	HOROSCAS 26, LOUIS BLANC 69006 LYON FRANCE
00-01-FB (hex)	DoTop Technology, Inc.
0001FB (base 16)	DoTop Technology, Inc. 10F, No. 100, Min-Chyuan Road Hsin-Tien, Taipei TAIWAN
00-01-FC (hex)	Keyence Corporation
0001FC (base 16)	Keyence Corporation 1-3-14, Higashi-Nakajima, Higashi-Yodogawa-ku Osaka 533-8555 JAPAN
00-01-FD (hex)	Digital Voice Systems, Inc.
0001FD (base 16)	Digital Voice Systems, Inc. 1 Van De Graff Drive Burlington, MA 01803
00-01-FE (hex)	DIGITAL EQUIPMENT CORPORATION
0001FE (base 16)	DIGITAL EQUIPMENT CORPORATION M/S CX01-2/N26 301 ROCKRIMMON BLVD., S COLORADO SPRINGS CO 80919
00-01-FF (hex)	Data Direct Networks, Inc.
0001FF (base 16)	Data Direct Networks, Inc. 9320 Lurline Avenue Chatsworth, CA 91311
00-02-00 (hex)	Net & Sys Co., Ltd.
000200 (base 16)	Net & Sys Co., Ltd. Kuro Hitech Industrial Complex 304, 402-3, Shindorim-dong, Kuro-gu Seoul, KOREA
00-02-01 (hex)	IFM Electronic gmbh
000201 (base 16)	IFM Electronic gmbh Bechlingen 34 D-88069 Tettnang GERMANY
00-02-02 (hex)	Amino Communications, Ltd.
000202 (base 16)	Amino Communications, Ltd. Times House Fen End Willingham, Cambridge UK CB4 5LH
00-02-03 (hex)	Woonsang Telecom, Inc.
000203 (base 16)	Woonsang Telecom, Inc. 104-9, Munji-Dong, Yusong-Gu Taejon, 305-380, KOREA
00-02-04 (hex)	Bodmann Industries Elektronik GmbH
000204 (base 16)	Bodmann Industries Elektronik GmbH Messerschmittring 33 D-86343 Konigsbrunn GERMANY
00-02-05 (hex)	Hitachi Denshi, Ltd.
000205 (base 16)	Hitachi Denshi, Ltd. 32 Miyaki-cho Kodaira-shi Toyko, JAPAN 187-8511
00-02-06 (hex)	Telital R&D Denmark A/S
000206 (base 16)	Telital R&D Denmark A/S 9530 Stouring Denmark
00-02-08 (hex)	Unify Networks, Inc.
000208 (base 16)	Unify Networks, Inc. 3160 De La Cruz Blvd. #201 Santa Clara, CA 95054
00-02-09 (hex)	Shenzhen SED Information Technology Co., Ltd.

company_id	Organization Address
000209 (base 16)	Shenzhen SED Information Technology Co., Ltd. 4/F., West Block, Block 414, Zhenhua Rd. Futian Shenzhen, 518031 P.R. CHINA
00-02-0A (hex)	Gefran Spa
00020A (base 16)	Gefran Spa Via Sebina, 74 Provaglio D'Iseo 25050 Brescia ITALY
00-02-0B (hex)	Native Networks, Inc.
00020B (base 16)	Native Networks, Inc. P.O. Box 7165 Petah Tikva 49170 Israel
00-02-0C (hex)	Metro-Optix
00020C (base 16)	Metro-Optix 2201 Avenue K Plano, TX 75074
00-02-0D (hex)	Micronpc.com
00020D (base 16)	Micronpc.com 900 E. Karcher Rd. Nampa, IA 83687
00-02-0E (hex)	Laurel Networks, Inc.
00020E (base 16)	Laurel Networks, Inc. 2607 Nicholsen Road Building 2 Sawickley, PA 15143
00-02-0F (hex)	AATR
00020F (base 16)	AATR 306 Chemin des Miroirs 13330 Pelissanne FRANCE
00-02-10 (hex)	Fenecom
000210 (base 16)	Fenecom 7/F Kon-kuk University Alumni Association Building NO: 227-336 Jayang-dong KwangJin-ku Seoul, Korea
00-02-11 (hex)	Nature Worldwide Technology Corp.
000211 (base 16)	Nature Worldwide Technology Corp. No. 1, Min-Chuan Street Tu-Cheng Industrial Park Taipei Hsien, Taiwan, R.O.C.
00-02-12 (hex)	SierraCom
000212 (base 16)	SierraCom 99 South Street Hopkinton, Ma 01748
00-02-13 (hex)	S.D.E.L.
000213 (base 16)	S.D.E.L. Aeropole D2A Rue Nungerrer et Coli 44860 St Aignan de Grand Lieu FRANCE
00-02-14 (hex)	DTVRO
000214 (base 16)	DTVRO 813 Daegong Bldg., 823-21 Yeoksam-Dong, Kangnam-Gu, Seoul, KOREA, 135-080
00-02-15 (hex)	Cotas Computer Technology A/B
000215 (base 16)	Cotas Computer Technology A/B Paludan-Mullers Vej 82 DK-8200 Aarhus N DENMARK
00-02-16 (hex)	Cisco Systems, Inc.
000216 (base 16)	Cisco Systems, Inc. 170 West Tasman Drive San Jose, CA 95134

company_id	Organization Address
00-02-17 (hex)	Cisco Systems, Inc.
000217 (base 16)	Cisco Systems, Inc. 170 West Tasman Drive San Jose, CA 95134
00-02-18 (hex)	Advanced Scientific Corp
000218 (base 16)	Advanced Scientific Corp 1 Fl., No. 26, Industry East 9th Road Science-based Industrial Park Hsin-Chu TAIWAN
00-02-19 (hex)	Paralon Technologies
000219 (base 16)	Paralon Technologies 700 Fifth Ave, Suite 6101 Seattle, WA 98104
00-02-1A (hex)	Zuma Networks
00021A (base 16)	Zuma Networks 8928 Fullbright Ave. Chatsworth, CA 91311
00-02-1B (hex)	Kollmorgen-Servotronix
00021B (base 16)	Kollmorgen-Servotronix POB 3919, Petach Tikya 49130 ISRAEL
00-02-1C (hex)	Network Elements, Inc.
00021C (base 16)	Network Elements, Inc. 9782 SW Nimbus Avenue Beaverton, OR 97008
00-02-1D (hex)	Data General Communication Ltd.
00021D (base 16)	Data General Communication Ltd. Rm. 18C, Bldg. C, CEIEC Tower No. 2070, Rd. ShenNanZhong ShenZhen City, Guangdong, CHINA
00-02-1E (hex)	SIMTEL S.R.L.
00021E (base 16)	SIMTEL S.R.L. Via Bonifacio Lupi, 25 50129 Firenze ITALY
00-02-1F (hex)	Aculab PLC
00021F (base 16)	Aculab PLC Lakeside, Bramley Road Mount Farm Milton Keynes Bulks MK1 1PT UK
00-02-20 (hex)	Canon Aptex, Inc.
000220 (base 16)	Canon Aptex, Inc. 5-15, Shimomaruko 2-Chrome, Ota-ku Tokyo 156-0092 JAPAN
00-02-21 (hex)	DSP Application, Ltd.
000221 (base 16)	DSP Application, Ltd. 12F-12, No. 79, Sec. 1 Hsin Tai Wu Rd. HSICHI, Taipei County TAIWAN
00-02-22 (hex)	Chromisys, Inc.
000222 (base 16)	Chromisys, Inc. 1012 Stewart Drive Sunnyvale, CA 94086
00-02-23 (hex)	ClickTV
000223 (base 16)	ClickTV Kemong Bldg., 4th Fl., 772 Yoksam-Dong Kangnam-Ku Seoul, Korea 135-010
00-02-24 (hex)	Lantern Communications, Inc.
000224 (base 16)	Lantern Communications, Inc. 1248 Reamwood Ave. Sunnyvale, CA 94089
00-02-25 (hex)	Certus Technology, Inc.

company_id	Organization Address
000225 (base 16)	Certus Technology, Inc. 10225 Barnes Canyon Road Suite A-204 San Diego, CA 92121
00-02-26 (hex)	XESystems, Inc.
000226 (base 16)	XESystems, Inc. 317 Main Street East Rochester, NY 14445
00-02-27 (hex)	ESD GmbH
000227 (base 16)	ESD GmbH Vahrenwalder Str. 205 30 165 Hannover GERMANY
00-02-28 (hex)	Necsom, Ltd.
000228 (base 16)	Necsom, Ltd. Necsom Ltd. c/o Koirsto Saunamaentie 4 A 1 FIN-02770 ESP00 FINLAND
00-02-29 (hex)	Adtec Corporation
000229 (base 16)	Adtec Corporation 3F Megurohigashiyama Blg 1 4 4 Higashiyama, Meguro Ku Tokyo 153 0043 JAPAN
00-02-2A (hex)	Asound Electronic
00022A (base 16)	Asound Electronic Xianxi Industries Zone Changan Town Dong Guon City, Guong Dong Providence CHINA
00-02-2B (hex)	Tamura Electric Works, Ltd.
00022B (base 16)	Tamura Electric Works, Ltd. 2-3 Shimomeguro 2-Chrome, Meguro-ku Tokyo, JAPAN
00-02-2C (hex)	ABB-BOMEM
00022C (base 16)	ABB-BOMEM 450 St-Jean Baptist Ave, Quebec, CANADA, G2E 5S5
00-02-2D (hex)	Lucent Technologies WCND
00022D (base 16)	Lucent Technologies WCND P.O. Box 755 3430 At Nieuwegein The Netherlands
00-02-2E (hex)	TEAC Corp. R& D
00022E (base 16)	TEAC Corp. R& D 857 Koyata, Iruma Saitama JAPAN
00-02-2F (hex)	P-Cube, Ltd.
00022F (base 16)	P-Cube, Ltd. P.O. Box 12331 Herzlia 46766 ISRAEL
00-02-30 (hex)	Intersoft Electronics
000230 (base 16)	Intersoft Electronics Lammerdries 27 B2250 Olen BELGIUM
00-02-31 (hex)	Ingersoll-Rand
000231 (base 16)	Ingersoll-Rand 1467 Route 31 South P.O. Box 970 Annandale, NJ 08801
00-02-32 (hex)	Avision, Inc.
000232 (base 16)	Avision, Inc. No. 20, Creation Rd. 1, Science-Based Industrial Park, Hsinchu, Taiwan, R.O.C.
00-02-33 (hex)	Mantra Communications, Inc.

company_id	Organization Address	company_id	Organization Address
000233 (base 16)	Mantra Communications, Inc. 12850 Middlebrook Road Suite 1 Germantown, MD 20874	00-02-42 (hex)	Videoframe Systems
00-02-34 (hex)	Imperial Technology, Inc.	000242 (base 16)	Videoframe Systems 101 Providence Mine Road Suite 103 Nevada City, CA 95959
000234 (base 16)	Imperial Technology, Inc. 2305 Utah Avenue El Segundo, CA 90245	00-02-43 (hex)	Raysis Co., Ltd.
00-02-35 (hex)	Paragon Networks International	000243 (base 16)	Raysis Co., Ltd. 997-10, Daechi-Dong, Kangnam-Ku, Seoul, 135-280, South Korea
000235 (base 16)	Paragon Networks International 61 Commerce Drive Brookfield, CT 06804	00-02-44 (hex)	SURECOM Technology Co.
00-02-36 (hex)	INIT GmbH	000244 (base 16)	SURECOM Technology Co. 6F, No. 125, Sec. 2, Datung Rd. Shijr, Taipei County, 221 Taiwan, R.O.C.
000236 (base 16)	INIT GmbH Kaeppelestr. 6 D-76131 Karlsruhe GERMANY	00-02-45 (hex)	Lampus Co, Ltd.
00-02-37 (hex)	Cosmo Research Corp.	000245 (base 16)	Lampus Co, Ltd. 6th Bldg., Samgong, 58-7 Ranpo 4dong Scoch-go, Seoul, Korea, 137-044
000237 (base 16)	Cosmo Research Corp. Cosmo Bldg, 3-148-5 Miyaharacho, Omiya Saitama 330-0038 JAPAN	00-02-46 (hex)	All-Win Tech Co., Ltd.
00-02-38 (hex)	Serome Technology, Inc.	000246 (base 16)	All-Win Tech Co., Ltd. 11F, No. 111-7, Hsing De Rd., San Chung City, Taipei Hsien, Taiwan, R.O.C.
000238 (base 16)	Serome Technology, Inc. 555-14, Baekang B/D 7F Shinsa-dong, Kangnam-gu Seoul, Korea 135-120	00-02-47 (hex)	Great Dragon Information Technology (Group) Co., Ltd.
00-02-39 (hex)	Visicom	000247 (base 16)	Great Dragon Information Technology (Group) Co., Ltd. 169 Beiyuan Rd., Chaoyang District Beijing, 100101, CHINA
000239 (base 16)	Visicom 10052 Mesa Ridge Ct. San Diego, CA 92121	00-02-48 (hex)	Pila GmbH & Co.
00-02-3A (hex)	ZSK Stickmaschinen GmbH	000248 (base 16)	Pila GmbH & Co. Felix-Wankel-Strasse 2 D-73760 Ostfildern GERMANY
00023A (base 16)	ZSK Stickmaschinen GmbH Magdeburger Strasse 38-40 47800 Krefeld GERMANY	00-02-49 (hex)	Aviv Infocom Co, Ltd.
00-02-3B (hex)	Redback Networks	000249 (base 16)	Aviv Infocom Co, Ltd. 962-5, Kwanyang-Dong, Dongan-Gu, Anyang-City, Kyungki-Do, 431-060 Korea (ROK)
00023B (base 16)	Redback Networks 1195 Borregas Avenue Sunnyvale, CA 94089	00-02-4A (hex)	Cisco Systems, Inc.
00-02-3C (hex)	Creative Technology, Ltd.	00024A (base 16)	Cisco Systems, Inc. 170 West Tasman Dr. San Jose, CA 95134
00023C (base 16)	Creative Technology, Ltd. 31 International Business Park Singapore 609921 Republic of Singapore	00-02-4B (hex)	Cisco Systems, Inc.
00-02-3D (hex)	NuSpeed, Inc.	00024B (base 16)	Cisco Systems, Inc. 170 West Tasman Dr. San Jose, CA 95134
00023D (base 16)	NuSpeed, Inc. 7767 Elm Creek Blvd., Ste 300 Maple Grove, MN 55369	00-02-4C (hex)	SiByte, Inc.
00-02-3E (hex)	Selta Telematica S.p.a	00024C (base 16)	SiByte, Inc. 2805 Bowers Avenue Santa Clara, CA 95051-0917
00023E (base 16)	Selta Telematica S.p.a Via Nazionale km 404.5 64019 Tortoreto Lido TE ITALY	00-02-4D (hex)	Mannesman Dematic Colby Pty. Ltd.
00-02-3F (hex)	Compal Electronics, Inc.	00024D (base 16)	Mannesman Dematic Colby Pty. Ltd. 24 Narabang Way Belrose, NSW 2085 AUSTRALIA
00023F (base 16)	Compal Electronics, Inc. 581, Juikuang Rd., Neihu, Taipei, (114) TAIWAN, R.O.C.	00-02-4E (hex)	Datacard Group
00-02-40 (hex)	Seedek Co., Ltd.	00024E (base 16)	Datacard Group 11111 Bren Road West MS 210 Minnetonka, MN 55343
000240 (base 16)	Seedek Co., Ltd. #709, 1638-32, Sammo Shinrimbon-Dong, Kwanak-Gu, Seoul KOREA	00-02-4F (hex)	IPM Datacom S.R.L.
00-02-41 (hex)	Amer.com	00024F (base 16)	IPM Datacom S.R.L. Via Roma, 231 80027 Frattamaggiore Naples ITALY
000241 (base 16)	Amer.com 7259 Bryan Dairy Road Largo, FL 33777	00-02-50 (hex)	Geyser Networks, Inc.

company_id	Organization Address
000250 (base 16)	Geyser Networks, Inc. 535 Del Rey Avenue Sunnyvale, CA 94086
00-02-51 (hex)	Soma Networks
000251 (base 16)	Soma Networks 329 Bryant Street San Francisco, CA 94107
00-02-52 (hex)	Carrier Corporation
000252 (base 16)	Carrier Corporation One Carrier Place Farmington, CT 06034-4015
00-02-53 (hex)	Televideo, Inc.
000253 (base 16)	Televideo, Inc. 2345 Harris Way San Jose, CA 95131
00-02-54 (hex)	WorldGate
000254 (base 16)	WorldGate 3190 Tremont Avenue Trevose, PA 19053
00-02-55 (hex)	IBM Corporation
000255 (base 16)	IBM Corporation PO Box 12195 Dept. G85/Bldg 660-0210 Research Triangle Park, NC 27709-2195
00-02-56 (hex)	Alpha Processor, Inc.
000256 (base 16)	Alpha Processor, Inc. 130 C Baker Ave. Ext. Concord, MA 01742
00-02-57 (hex)	Microcom Corp.
000257 (base 16)	Microcom Corp. 8333A Green Meadows Dr. N. Westerville, OH 43081
00-02-58 (hex)	Flying Packets Communications
000258 (base 16)	Flying Packets Communications 388 Market Street Suite 380 San Francisco, CA 94111
00-02-59 (hex)	Tsann Kuen China (Shanghai) Enterprise Co., Ltd. IT Group
000259 (base 16)	Tsann Kuen China (Shanghai) Enterprise Co., Ltd. IT Group 8F, #99, Huaihai Rd, East, Shanghai, CHINA 200021
00-02-5A (hex)	Catena Networks
00025A (base 16)	Catena Networks 307 Legget Drive Kanata Ontario Canada K2K 3C8
00-02-5B (hex)	Cambridge Silicon Radio
00025B (base 16)	Cambridge Silicon Radio Unit 300, Science Park, Milton Road, Cambridge, CB4 OXL United Kingdom
00-02-5C (hex)	SCI Systems (Kunshan) Co., Ltd.
00025C (base 16)	SCI Systems (Kunshan) Co., Ltd. 312 QING YANG ROAD KUNSHAN, JIANGSU PROVICC CHINA, 215300
00-02-5E (hex)	High Technology Ltd
00025E (base 16)	High Technology Ltd Chongqing Jinghong A2-10-3 California Garden Yubei District, Chongqing 401147 People's Republic of China
00-02-5F (hex)	Nortel Networks

company_id	Organization Address
00025F (base 16)	Nortel Networks 9300 trans-CANADA Highway St. Laurenet, Quebec H4S 1KS CANADA
00-02-60 (hex)	Accordion Networks, Inc.
000260 (base 16)	Accordion Networks, Inc. 39899 Balentine Drive, #335 Newark, CA 94560
00-02-61 (hex)	i3 Micro Technology AB
000261 (base 16)	i3 Micro Technology AB Kanalvagen 10C SE-194 61 Upplands Vasby SWEDEN
00-02-62 (hex)	Soyo Group Soyo Com Tech Co., Ltd
000262 (base 16)	Soyo Group Soyo Com Tech Co., Ltd 5H. No. 21 Wu-gong 5 Rd, Hsing Chuang, Taipei Hsien, Taiwan R.O.C.
00-02-63 (hex)	UPS Manufacturing SRL
000263 (base 16)	UPS Manufacturing SRL Via Giordano, 54 37050 Vallese Di Oppeano Verona Italy
00-02-64 (hex)	AudioRamp.com
000264 (base 16)	AudioRamp.com 15941 Red Hill Suite 205 Tustin, CA 92780
00-02-65 (hex)	Virditech Co. Ltd.
000265 (base 16)	Virditech Co. Ltd. Hyundai Topics Blgd., 11th Fl 44-3 Pangi-dong, Songpa-Gu Seoul, KOREA
00-02-66 (hex)	Thermalogic Corporation
000266 (base 16)	Thermalogic Corporation 22 Kane Industrial Drive Hudson, MA 01749
00-02-67 (hex)	NODE RUNNER, INC.
000267 (base 16)	NODE RUNNER, INC. 2202 N. FORBES BLVD. TUCSON AZ 85745
00-02-68 (hex)	Harris Government Communications
000268 (base 16)	Harris Government Communications Systems Division P.O. Box 37 MS: 1-5856 Melbourne, FL 32902
00-02-69 (hex)	Nadatel Co., Ltd
000269 (base 16)	Nadatel Co., Ltd 9F CoWell Bldg, 66-1 Banpo-Dong Seocho-Gu, Seoul, KOREA 137-040
00-02-6A (hex)	Cocess Telecom Co., Ltd.
00026A (base 16)	Cocess Telecom Co., Ltd. Research & Development Dept. 43, Yoido-Dong, Youngdeungpo-Ku Seoul, KOREA
00-02-6B (hex)	BCM Computers Co., Ltd.
00026B (base 16)	BCM Computers Co., Ltd. 4F-1, No. 66, Sec 2, Nan Kan Rd., Lu-Chu Hsing, Tao Yuan TAIWAN, R.O.C.
00-02-6C (hex)	Philips CFT
00026C (base 16)	Philips CFT Building SAN 6 P.O. Box 218 5600 MD Eindhoven The Netherlands
00-02-6D (hex)	Adept Telecom

company_id	Organization Address
00026D (base 16)	Adept Telecom Avenue de l'Europe BP 161 F-71204 Le Creusot Cedex FRANCE
00-02-6E (hex)	NeGeN Access, Inc.
00026E (base 16)	NeGeN Access, Inc. 33 Boston Post Rd. West Suite 360 Marlborough, MA 01752
00-02-6F (hex)	Senao International Co., Ltd.
00026F (base 16)	Senao International Co., Ltd. 2F, No. 531, Chung-Cheng Rd., Hsin-Tien City, Taipei County, TAIWAN
00-02-70 (hex)	Crewave Co., Ltd.
000270 (base 16)	Crewave Co., Ltd. F7, Pureun Bldg., 28-1 Jamwon-dong, Seocho-gu Seoul, KOREA 137-030
00-02-71 (hex)	Vpacket Communications
000271 (base 16)	Vpacket Communications 1390 McCarthy Blvd. Milpitas, CA 95035
00-02-72 (hex)	CC&C Technologies, Inc.
000272 (base 16)	CC&C Technologies, Inc. 8F, 150, Chien I Rd., Chung Ho City, Taipei County 235, Taiwan R.O.C.
00-02-73 (hex)	Coriolis Networks
000273 (base 16)	Coriolis Networks 330 Codmanhill Road Boxborough, MA 01719
00-02-74 (hex)	Tommy Technologies Corp.
000274 (base 16)	Tommy Technologies Corp. #407 Heehoon Bld 110-1 Kuro-dong, Kuro-ku Seoul, KOREA
00-02-75 (hex)	SMART Technologies, Inc.
000275 (base 16)	SMART Technologies, Inc. #600, 1177 11 Ave. S.W. Calgary, Alberta Canada, T2R 1K9
00-02-76 (hex)	Primax Electronics Ltd.
000276 (base 16)	Primax Electronics Ltd. No. 669, Ruey Kuang Road, Neihu Taipei, Taiwan, R.O.C.
00-02-77 (hex)	Cash Systemes Industrie
000277 (base 16)	Cash Systemes Industrie 4 Rue Andre Citroen Ri La Pauld 83600 Frejus FRANCE
00-02-78 (hex)	Samsung Electro-Mechanics Co., Ltd.
000278 (base 16)	Samsung Electro-Mechanics Co., Ltd. 314, Mae-tan-dong, Pai-dal-gu, Kyoung-gi-do, Suwon, KOREA
00-02-79 (hex)	Control Applications, Ltd.
000279 (base 16)	Control Applications, Ltd. 3 Tevuot Haarets St. Tel-Aviv 69546 ISRAEL
00-02-7A (hex)	IOI Technology Corporation
00027A (base 16)	IOI Technology Corporation 4F-3 No. 125 Lane 235, Pao Chiao Road Hsin Tien City, Taipei, TAIWAN, R.O.C.
00-02-7B (hex)	Amplify Net, Inc.

company_id	Organization Address
00027B (base 16)	Amplify Net, Inc. 47381 Bayside Parkway Fremont, CA 94538
00-02-7C (hex)	Trilithic, Inc.
00027C (base 16)	Trilithic, Inc. 9202 E. 33rd Street Indianapolis, IN 46235
00-02-7D (hex)	Cisco Systems, Inc.
00027D (base 16)	Cisco Systems, Inc. 170 West Tasman Dr. San Jose, CA 95134
00-02-7E (hex)	Cisco Systems, Inc.
00027E (base 16)	Cisco Systems, Inc. 170 West Tasman Dr. San Jose, CA 95134
00-02-7F (hex)	ask-technologies.com
00027F (base 16)	ask-technologies.com 36 Wellington Business Park Dukes Ride, Crowthorne Berkshire RG45 6LS UNITED KINGDOM
00-02-80 (hex)	Mu Net, Inc.
000280 (base 16)	Mu Net, Inc. 442 Marrett Road Suite 9 Lexington, MA 02421
00-02-81 (hex)	Madge Networks, Ltd.
000281 (base 16)	Madge Networks, Ltd. Waxham Springs Framewood Road Wexham, Slough SL3 6PJ ENGLAND
00-02-82 (hex)	ViaClix, Inc.
000282 (base 16)	ViaClix, Inc. 1400 Dell Ave., Suite B Campbell, CA 95008
00-02-83 (hex)	Spectrum Controls, Inc.
000283 (base 16)	Spectrum Controls, Inc. PO Box 5533 Bellevue, WA 98006
00-02-84 (hex)	Alstom T&D P&C
000284 (base 16)	Alstom T&D P&C Avenue de Figuieres BP 75 34975 LATTES Cedex FRANCE
00-02-85 (hex)	Riverstone Networks
000285 (base 16)	Riverstone Networks 5200 Great America Parkway Santa Clara, CA 95054
00-02-86 (hex)	Occam Networks
000286 (base 16)	Occam Networks 4183 State Street Santa Barbara, CA 93110
00-02-87 (hex)	Adapcom
000287 (base 16)	Adapcom 172-A Component Drive San Jose, CA 95131
00-02-88 (hex)	GLOBAL VILLAGE COMMUNICATION
000288 (base 16)	GLOBAL VILLAGE COMMUNICATION 1144 EAST ARQUES AVE. SUNNYVALE CA 94086
00-02-89 (hex)	DNE Technologies
000289 (base 16)	DNE Technologies 50 Barnes Park N Wallingford, CT 06492
00-02-8A (hex)	Ambit Microsystems Corporation
00028A (base 16)	Ambit Microsystems Corporation 5F-1, 5 Hsin-An Road Hsinchu, Science Based Industrial Park, TAIWAN

company_id	Organization Address
00-02-8B (hex)	VDSL Systems OY
00028B (base 16)	VDSL Systems OY Tekniikantie 12 02 150 Espoo FINLAND
00-02-8C (hex)	Micrel-Synergy Semiconductor
00028C (base 16)	Micrel-Synergy Semiconductor 3250 Scott Boulevard Santa Clara, CA 95054
00-02-8D (hex)	Movita Technologies, Inc.
00028D (base 16)	Movita Technologies, Inc. No. 26 Wu-Chuan 7th Road, Wu-Ku Industrial Park Taipei, Taiwan, R.O.C.
00-02-8E (hex)	Rapid 5 Networks, Inc.
00028E (base 16)	Rapid 5 Networks, Inc. 180 Baytech Drive San Jose, CA 95134-2302
00-02-8F (hex)	Globetek, Inc.
00028F (base 16)	Globetek, Inc. 1607 Akron Peninsula Rd. Suite 103 Akron, OH 44313-5190
00-02-90 (hex)	Woorigisool, Inc.
000290 (base 16)	Woorigisool, Inc. Yoopoong Bldg. 1595-1, Bongchum-7dong, Seoul, KOREA
00-02-91 (hex)	Open Network Co., Ltd.
000291 (base 16)	Open Network Co., Ltd. Seishin Bldg., 2-5-10 Shinjuku Shinjuku-ku, Tokyo JAPAN 160-0022
00-02-92 (hex)	Logic Innovations, Inc.
000292 (base 16)	Logic Innovations, Inc. 6205 Lusk Blvd. San Diego, CA 92121-2731
00-02-93 (hex)	Solid Data Systems
000293 (base 16)	Solid Data Systems 2945 Oakmead Village Court Santa Clara, CA 95051
00-02-94 (hex)	Tokyo Sokushin Co., Ltd.
000294 (base 16)	Tokyo Sokushin Co., Ltd. 5-16-12 Nishi-Nippori Arakawa-ku, Tokyo 116-0013 JAPAN
00-02-95 (hex)	IP.Access Limited
000295 (base 16)	IP.Access Limited Melbourn Science Park Cambridge Road, Melbourn Royston, Hartfordshire, SG8 6EE, U.K.
00-02-96 (hex)	Lectron Co,. Ltd.
000296 (base 16)	Lectron Co,. Ltd. 9F, No.171, Sec. 2, Tatung Rd., Hsichih City, Taipei Hsien 221, Taiwan, R.O.C.
00-02-97 (hex)	C-COR.net
000297 (base 16)	C-COR.net 60 Decibel Road BMS Engineering State College, PA 16801
00-02-98 (hex)	Broadframe Corporation
000298 (base 16)	Broadframe Corporation 4029 Capital of Texas Highway S. Suite 220 Austin, TX 78704
00-02-99 (hex)	Apex, Inc.

company_id	Organization Address
000299 (base 16)	Apex, Inc. 9911 Willows Rd. N.E. Redmond, WA 95052
00-02-9A (hex)	Storage Apps
00029A (base 16)	Storage Apps 3 Princess Road Lawrenceville, NJ 08648
00-02-9B (hex)	Kreatel Communications AB
00029B (base 16)	Kreatel Communications AB Teknikringen 4C SE-58330 Linkoping SWEDEN
00-02-9D (hex)	Merix Corp.
00029D (base 16)	Merix Corp. Jin-Su Building, 49-16 Machum-Dong, Song-Pa-ku Seoul, KOREA
00-02-9E (hex)	Information Equipment Co., Ltd.
00029E (base 16)	Information Equipment Co., Ltd. 740-1 Eaho Bldg., Yeok Sam-Dong Kangnam-ku Seoul, Korea #135-080
00-02-9F (hex)	L-3 Communication Aviation Recorders
00029F (base 16)	L-3 Communication Aviation Recorders P.O. Box 3041 Sarasota, FL 34230
00-02-A0 (hex)	Flatstack Ltd.
0002A0 (base 16)	Flatstack Ltd. 1112 Budapest Peterhegyi UT 98 HUNGARY
00-02-A1 (hex)	World Wide Packets
0002A1 (base 16)	World Wide Packets PO Box 14645 Spokane, WA 99214
00-02-A2 (hex)	Hilscher GmbH
0002A2 (base 16)	Hilscher GmbH Rheinstraße 15 65795 Hattersheim GERMANY
00-02-A3 (hex)	ABB Power Automation
0002A3 (base 16)	ABB Power Automation Bahnhofstrasse CH-5300 Turgi SWITZERLAND
00-02-A4 (hex)	AddPac Technology Co., Ltd.
0002A4 (base 16)	AddPac Technology Co., Ltd. 3F Jeoung Am Bldg., 769-12 Yeoksam-dong, Kangnam-gu, Seoul, Korea
00-02-A5 (hex)	Compaq Computer Corporation
0002A5 (base 16)	Compaq Computer Corporation 20555 State Highway 249 Houston, TX 77070
00-02-A6 (hex)	Effinet Systems Co., Ltd.
0002A6 (base 16)	Effinet Systems Co., Ltd. Yugong Bldg. 502 1144-1, Sanbon-Dong Kunpo-shi, Kyonggi-Do Korea
00-02-A7 (hex)	Vivace Networks
0002A7 (base 16)	Vivace Networks 2730 Orchard Parkway San Jose, CA 95134
00-02-A8 (hex)	Air Link Technology
0002A8 (base 16)	Air Link Technology Bethel Bldg. 303 324-1 Yangjee-Dong, Seocho-Gu Seoul, KOREA 137-130
00-02-A9 (hex)	RACOM, s.r.o.

company_id	Organization Address
0002A9 (base 16)	RACOM, s.r.o. Mirova 1283, Nove Mesto na Morave 592 31, Czech Republic
00-02-AA (hex)	PLcom Co., Ltd.
0002AA (base 16)	PLcom Co., Ltd. Hosung B/D, #1083-1, Hogye-Dong Dongan-Ku, Anyang-City South Korea
00-02-AB (hex)	CTC Union Technologies Co., Ltd.
0002AB (base 16)	CTC Union Technologies Co., Ltd. 6F-3, Lane 360 Neihu Road, Section 1 Neihu, Taipei, Taiwan
00-02-AC (hex)	3PAR data
0002AC (base 16)	3PAR data 4215 Technology Dr. Fremont, CA 94538
00-02-AD (hex)	Asahi Optical Co., Ltd.
0002AD (base 16)	Asahi Optical Co., Ltd. 2-36-9, Maeno-cho, Itabashi-ku Tokyo 174-8639, Japan
00-02-AE (hex)	Scannex Electronics Ltd.
0002AE (base 16)	Scannex Electronics Ltd. Waterside House Basin Road North Hove, East Sussex BN41 1UY UK
00-02-AF (hex)	TeleCruz Technology, Inc.
0002AF (base 16)	TeleCruz Technology, Inc. 2391 Qume Dr. San Jose, CA 95131
00-02-B0 (hex)	Hokubu Communication & Industrial Co., Ltd.
0002B0 (base 16)	Hokubu Communication & Industrial Co., Ltd. Fukushima Technology Centre 1-12 Machiikedai Koriyama 963-0215 Japan
00-02-B1 (hex)	Anritsu, Ltd.
0002B1 (base 16)	Anritsu, Ltd. Rutherford Close Stevenage, Herts England, SG12EF UNITED KINGDOM
00-02-B2 (hex)	Cablevision
0002B2 (base 16)	Cablevision 420 Crossways Park Drive West Woodbury, NY 11787
00-02-B3 (hex)	Intel Corporation
0002B3 (base 16)	Intel Corporation M/S: JF3-420 2111 N.E. 25th Ave. Hillsboro, OR 97124
00-02-B4 (hex)	DAPHNE
0002B4 (base 16)	DAPHNE 101 Chaussee De Binche 7000 Hons BELGIUM
00-02-B5 (hex)	Avnet, Inc.
0002B5 (base 16)	Avnet, Inc. 2211 S. 47th Street Phoenix, AZ 85034
00-02-B6 (hex)	Acrosser Technology Co., Ltd.
0002B6 (base 16)	Acrosser Technology Co., Ltd. No. 116-2 Guang-Fu Rd. Sea 1, San Chung, Taipei, R.O.C.
00-02-B7 (hex)	Watanabe Electric Industry Co., Ltd.

company_id	Organization Address
0002B7 (base 16)	Watanabe Electric Industry Co., Ltd. 6-16-19, Jingumae, Shibuya-ku Tokyo 150-0001, JAPAN
00-02-B8 (hex)	WHI KONSULT AB
0002B8 (base 16)	WHI KONSULT AB Byangsgrand 6 12040 Arsta SWEDEN
00-02-B9 (hex)	Cisco Systems, Inc.
0002B9 (base 16)	Cisco Systems, Inc. 170 West Tasman Dr. San Jose, CA 95134
00-02-BA (hex)	Cisco Systems, Inc.
0002BA (base 16)	Cisco Systems, Inc. 170 West Tasman Dr. San Jose, CA 95134
00-02-BB (hex)	Continuous Computing
0002BB (base 16)	Continuous Computing 7966 Arjons Dr., Suite D San Diego, CA 92126
00-02-BC (hex)	LVL 7 Systems, Inc.
0002BC (base 16)	LVL 7 Systems, Inc. 13000 Weston Pkwy Suite 105 Cary, NC 27513
00-02-BD (hex)	Bionet Co., Ltd.
0002BD (base 16)	Bionet Co., Ltd. 3F, Medison Venture Tower, 997-4, Daechi-dong, Kangnam-gu, Seoul, KOREA
00-02-BE (hex)	Totsu Engineering, Inc.
0002BE (base 16)	Totsu Engineering, Inc. 5-13-13 Roppongi Minato-ku Zip: 106-0032 Tokyo, JAPAN
00-02-BF (hex)	dotRocket, Inc.
0002BF (base 16)	dotRocket, Inc. 1901 S. Bascom, Suite 300 Campbell, CA 95008
00-02-C0 (hex)	Bencent Tzeng Industry Co., Ltd.
0002C0 (base 16)	Bencent Tzeng Industry Co., Ltd. 4F-2, No. 2, Ruey Kuang Rd., Nei Hu Dist., Taipei 114 Taiwan, R.O.C.
00-02-C1 (hex)	Innovative Electronic Designs, Inc.
0002C1 (base 16)	Innovative Electronic Designs, Inc. 9701 Taylorsville Rd. Louisville, KY 40299
00-02-C2 (hex)	Net Vision Telecom
0002C2 (base 16)	Net Vision Telecom #206 Software Support Center 48 Jang-Dong Yusong-Gu, Taejon 305-343, Rep. of Korea
00-02-C3 (hex)	Arelnet Ltd.
0002C3 (base 16)	Arelnet Ltd. 3 Hayarden St. Yavne 70600 ISRAEL
00-02-C4 (hex)	Vector International BUBA
0002C4 (base 16)	Vector International BUBA Interleuvenlaan 46 - Research Park B-3001 Leuven BELGIUM
00-02-C5 (hex)	Evertz Microsystems Ltd.
0002C5 (base 16)	Evertz Microsystems Ltd. 3465 Mainway Dr. Burlington, ON, CANADA L7M 1A9

company_id	Organization Address
00-02-C6 (hex)	Data Track Technology PLC
0002C6 (base 16)	Data Track Technology PLC 153 Somerford Road Christchurch, Dorset BH23 3TY, UNITED KINGDOM
00-02-C7 (hex)	ALPS ELECTRIC Co., Ltd.
0002C7 (base 16)	ALPS ELECTRIC Co., Ltd. 1-2-1, Okinouchi, Sama-City, Fukushima-pref, 976-8501, JAPAN
00-02-C8 (hex)	Technocom Communications Technology (pte) Ltd
0002C8 (base 16)	Technocom Communications Technology (pte) Ltd 189 Kaki Buckit Avenue 1 #03-03 Shun Li Industrial Park Singapore 416029
00-02-C9 (hex)	Mellanox Technologies
0002C9 (base 16)	Mellanox Technologies 3333 Bowers Ave., Suite 145 Santa Clara, CA 95050
00-02-CA (hex)	EndPoints, Inc.
0002CA (base 16)	EndPoints, Inc. 4 Preston Court Bedford, MA 01730
00-02-CB (hex)	TriState Ltd.
0002CB (base 16)	TriState Ltd. Shinonaga Blg. 4-11-19 Hokko-cho Tomakomai-shi, Hokkaido 053-0852, Japan
00-02-CC (hex)	M.C.C.I
0002CC (base 16)	M.C.C.I 3520 Krums Corners Rd. Ithaca, NY 14850
00-02-CD (hex)	TeleDream, Inc.
0002CD (base 16)	TeleDream, Inc. Shinhwa Bldg., 940-10 Daechi-Dong Kangnam-ku, Seoul 135-280 S. Korea
00-02-CE (hex)	FoxJet, Inc.
0002CE (base 16)	FoxJet, Inc. 2016 E. Randal Mill Rd. #409 Arlington, TX 76011-8223
00-02-CF (hex)	ZyGate Communications, Inc.
0002CF (base 16)	ZyGate Communications, Inc. 2F, No.48, Lung-Chin Road Lung-Tan, Tanyuan, TAIWAN, R.O.C.
00-02-D0 (hex)	Comdial Corporation
0002D0 (base 16)	Comdial Corporation 1180 Seminole Trail Charlottesville, VA 22901
00-02-D1 (hex)	Vivotek, Inc.
0002D1 (base 16)	Vivotek, Inc. 5F-1, 168-1, Lien-Chen Rd, Chung-Ho, Taipei County, Taiwan, R.O.C.
00-02-D2 (hex)	Workstation AG
0002D2 (base 16)	Workstation AG Schaffhauserstr. 55 CH-8152 Glattbrugg Switzerland
00-02-D3 (hex)	NetBotz
0002D3 (base 16)	NetBotz 110044 Research Blvd. Suite B-200 Austin, TX 78759
00-02-D4 (hex)	PDA Peripherals, Inc.

company_id	Organization Address
0002D4 (base 16)	PDA Peripherals, Inc. 205 Orange St. Third Floor New Haven, CT 06510
00-02-D5 (hex)	ACR
0002D5 (base 16)	ACR Cardoulines B2 1360 rte Dolinis 06560 Valbonne FRANCE
00-02-D6 (hex)	NICE Systems
0002D6 (base 16)	NICE Systems 8 Hapnina St., POB 690 Ra'Anana 43107 ISRAEL
00-02-D7 (hex)	EMPEG Ltd
0002D7 (base 16)	EMPEG Ltd 1 Signet Court Swann's Road Cambridge, UK CB5 8LA
00-02-D8 (hex)	BRECIS Communications Corporation
0002D8 (base 16)	BRECIS Communications Corporation 2025 Gateway Place, Suite 380 San Jose, CA 95110
00-02-D9 (hex)	Reliable Controls
0002D9 (base 16)	Reliable Controls 203-3375 Whittier Ave. Victoria, B.C. Canada V82 3RI
00-02-DA (hex)	ExiO Communications, Inc.
0002DA (base 16)	ExiO Communications, Inc. 2362 Qume Drive Suite C San Jose, CA 95131
00-02-DB (hex)	NETSEC
0002DB (base 16)	NETSEC 13505 Dulles Technology Drive Suite 1 Hernandon, VA 20171
00-02-DC (hex)	Fujitsu General Limited
0002DC (base 16)	Fujitsu General Limited 1116, Suenaga, Takatsu-Ku, Kawasaki-City, Kanagawa-Pref., 213-8502 JAPAN
00-02-DD (hex)	Bromax Communications, Ltd.
0002DD (base 16)	Bromax Communications, Ltd. No. 20 Kuang Fu Road, Hsin Chu Industrial Park, Hu Kou, Hsin Chu 303, Taiwan, R.O.C.
00-02-DE (hex)	Astrodesign, Inc.
0002DE (base 16)	Astrodesign, Inc. 2-22-12 Kamikodana Ka Nakaharaku, Kawasai-City Kanagawa, JAPAN
00-02-DF (hex)	Net Com Systems, Inc.
0002DF (base 16)	Net Com Systems, Inc. 15-3, Yoido-Dong, Yeoungdongpo-ku, Seoul, Korea
00-02-E0 (hex)	ETAS GmbH
0002E0 (base 16)	ETAS GmbH Borsigstrasse 10 D70469 Stuttgart GERMANY
00-02-E1 (hex)	Integrated Network Corporation
0002E1 (base 16)	Integrated Network Corporation 757 Route 202/206 Bridgewater, NJ 08807
00-02-E2 (hex)	NDC Infared Engineering

company_id	Organization Address
0002E2 (base 16)	NDC Infared Engineering 5314 N. Irwindale Ave. Irwindale, CA 91706
00-02-E3 (hex)	LITE-ON Communications, Inc.
0002E3 (base 16)	LITE-ON Communications, Inc. 736 S. Hillview Drive Milpitas, CA 95035
00-02-E4 (hex)	JC HYUN Systems, Inc.
0002E4 (base 16)	JC HYUN Systems, Inc. Shinbong Bldg, 736-6, Yoksam-Dong, Kangnam-Ku, Seoul, KOREA (135-080)
00-02-E5 (hex)	Timeware Ltd.
0002E5 (base 16)	Timeware Ltd. Brookfield Grange 79 Falinge Rd, Rockdale Lancs, UK, 042 GLB
00-02-E6 (hex)	Gould Instrument Systems, Inc.
0002E6 (base 16)	Gould Instrument Systems, Inc. 8333 Rockside Road Valley View, OH 44125
00-02-E7 (hex)	CAB GmbH & Co KG
0002E7 (base 16)	CAB GmbH & Co KG Wilhelm-Schickard-Str 14 76131 Karlsruhe GERMANY
00-02-E8 (hex)	E.D.&A.
0002E8 (base 16)	E.D.&A. Energielaan 16 IZ Bosduin 2950 Kapellen BELGIUM
00-02-E9 (hex)	CS Systemes De Securite - C3S
0002E9 (base 16)	CS Systemes De Securite - C3S 23, rue de Schwobsheim 67600 Baldenheim FRANCE
00-02-EA (hex)	Videonics, Inc.
0002EA (base 16)	Videonics, Inc. 1370 Dell Ave. Campbell, CA 95008
00-02-EB (hex)	Easent Communications
0002EB (base 16)	Easent Communications 20085 Stevens Creek Blvd. Suite 100 Cupertino, CA 95014
00-02-EC (hex)	Maschoff Design Engineering
0002EC (base 16)	Maschoff Design Engineering 4454 Cedar Lake Rd. #8 St. Louis Park, MN 55416
00-02-ED (hex)	DXO Telecom Co., Ltd.
0002ED (base 16)	DXO Telecom Co., Ltd. 8F, 300-11, Yumgok-Dong, Seocho-Ku, Seoul 137-789 KOREA
00-02-EE (hex)	Nokia Danmark A/S
0002EE (base 16)	Nokia Danmark A/S Frederikskaj, Copenhagen V DK-1790 DENMARK
00-02-EF (hex)	CCC Network Systems Group Ltd.
0002EF (base 16)	CCC Network Systems Group Ltd. 13 Farnborough Business Centre Eelmoor Road, Farnborough, Hants, GU14 7XA ENGLAND
00-02-F0 (hex)	AME Optimedia Technology Co., Ltd.
0002F0 (base 16)	AME Optimedia Technology Co., Ltd. 17F-2, 79 Hsin Tai Wu Road, Sec. 1, Hsi-Chih, Taipei Hsien TAIWAN

company_id	Organization Address
00-02-F1 (hex)	Pinetron Co., Ltd.
0002F1 (base 16)	Pinetron Co., Ltd. Bldg. #1599-11, Seocho-Dong, Seocho-Ku, Seoul, KOREA 137-073
00-02-F2 (hex)	eDevice, Inc.
0002F2 (base 16)	eDevice, Inc. 420 Lexington Avenue Suite 2300 New York, NY 10170
00-02-F3 (hex)	Media Serve Co., Ltd.
0002F3 (base 16)	Media Serve Co., Ltd. Dongsung Bldg. #17-8, Youido-dong, Youngdeoungpo-ku, Seoul, Korea
00-02-F4 (hex)	PCTEL, Inc.
0002F4 (base 16)	PCTEL, Inc. 1331 California Circle Milpitas, CA 95035
00-02-F5 (hex)	VIVE Synergies, Inc.
0002F5 (base 16)	VIVE Synergies, Inc. 30 West Beaver Creek Road, Unit 101 Richmond Hill, Ontario L4B 3K1, Canada
00-02-F6 (hex)	Equipe Communications
0002F6 (base 16)	Equipe Communications 100 Nagog Park Acton, MA 01720
00-02-F7 (hex)	ARM
0002F7 (base 16)	ARM 110, Fulbourn Road Cherry Hinton Cambridge CB1 9NJ United Kingdom
00-02-F8 (hex)	SEAKR Engineering, Inc.
0002F8 (base 16)	SEAKR Engineering, Inc. 12847 E. Peakview Ave. Englewood, CO 80111
00-02-F9 (hex)	Mimos Semiconductor SDN BHD
0002F9 (base 16)	Mimos Semiconductor SDN BHD Taman Teknologi Malaysia Bukit Jalil 57000 Kuala Lumpur, Malaysia
00-02-FA (hex)	DX Antenna Co., Ltd.
0002FA (base 16)	DX Antenna Co., Ltd. 2-15 Hamazaki-Dori, Hyogo-ku, Kobe JAPAN
00-02-FB (hex)	Baumuller Aulugen-Systemtechnik GmbH
0002FB (base 16)	Baumuller Aulugen-Systemtechnik GmbH Ostendsts. 84 D-90482 Nuruberg GERMANY
00-02-FC (hex)	Cisco Systems, Inc.
0002FC (base 16)	Cisco Systems, Inc. 170 West Tasman Dr. San Jose, CA 95134
00-02-FD (hex)	Cisco Systems, Inc.
0002FD (base 16)	Cisco Systems, Inc. 170 West Tasman Dr. San Jose, CA 95134
00-02-FE (hex)	Viditec, Inc.
0002FE (base 16)	Viditec, Inc. 520 Central Parkway E. Suite 115 Plano, TX 75074
00-02-FF (hex)	Handan Broad InfoCom

company_id	Organization Address
0002FF (base 16)	Handan Broad InfoCom 5th Fl. Shinsung Plaza #697-11 Yeongsam-dong, Kangnam-gu, Seoul, Korea
00-03-00 (hex)	NetContinuum, Inc.
000300 (base 16)	NetContinuum, Inc. 1705 Wyatt Drive Santa Clara, CA 95054
00-03-01 (hex)	Avantas Networks Corporation
000301 (base 16)	Avantas Networks Corporation 9900 Cavendish Blvd., Suite #310 St-Laurent, Quebec Canada, H4M 2V2
00-03-02 (hex)	Oasys Telecom, Inc.
000302 (base 16)	Oasys Telecom, Inc. 7060 Koll Center Parkway Suite 340 Pleasanton, CA 94566
00-03-03 (hex)	JAMA Electronics Co., Ltd.
000303 (base 16)	JAMA Electronics Co., Ltd. 10F, No. 222-1, Sec. 3 Ta-Tung Rd., Hsi-Chih Taipei Hsien, Taiwan R.O.C.
00-03-04 (hex)	Pacific Broadband Communiations
000304 (base 16)	Pacific Broadband Communiations 3103 North First St. San Jose, CA 95134
00-03-05 (hex)	Smart Network Devices GmbH
000305 (base 16)	Smart Network Devices GmbH Karl Heinz Beckurts-Str. 13 52428 Julich GERMANY
00-03-06 (hex)	Fusion In Tech Co., Ltd.
000306 (base 16)	Fusion In Tech Co., Ltd. 6Fl, Daeyoon Bldg. 1688-5, Seocho-dong Seocho-ku, Seoul, KOREA
00-03-07 (hex)	Secure Works, Inc.
000307 (base 16)	Secure Works, Inc. 11 Executive Drive Suite 200 Atlanta, GA 30329
00-03-08 (hex)	AM Communications, Inc.
000308 (base 16)	AM Communications, Inc. 100 Commerce Blvd. Quakertown, PA 18951
00-03-09 (hex)	Texcel Technology PLC
000309 (base 16)	Texcel Technology PLC Thames Road Crayford Kent DA1 4SB ENGLAND
00-03-0A (hex)	Argus Technologies
00030A (base 16)	Argus Technologies 9F, 111, San Ho Rd., Sec. 4, San Chung City Taipei County, Taiwan, R.O.C.
00-03-0B (hex)	Hunter Technology, Inc.
00030B (base 16)	Hunter Technology, Inc. Hanbang Bldg., 3F. 418-4, Dokok-Dong, Kangnam-gu, Seoul, 135-270, KOREA
00-03-0C (hex)	Telesoft Technologies Ltd.
00030C (base 16)	Telesoft Technologies Ltd. Observatory House, Stour Park, Blandforum, Dorset, DT11 9LQ, UNITED KINGDOM
00-03-0D (hex)	Uniwill Computer Corp.

company_id	Organization Address
00030D (base 16)	Uniwill Computer Corp. No. 24, Pei Yuan Rd., Chung Li Industrial Park, Chung Li City, Taiwan, R.O.C.
00-03-0E (hex)	Core Communications Co., Ltd.
00030E (base 16)	Core Communications Co., Ltd. 3F Shopping Center Bd. of Sang Young Hwang-geum APT, #253 Mapo-Dong, Mapo Gu, Seoul (121-050), KOREA
00-03-0F (hex)	Legend Digital China Ltd.
00030F (base 16)	Legend Digital China Ltd. 2/F., Sigma Buildings, 49, Zhichunlu, Haidan 100080, Beijing PR CHINA
00-03-10 (hex)	Link Evolution Corp.
000310 (base 16)	Link Evolution Corp. 401 Pine Field Bldg., 3-40-7 Matsubura Seragaya-ku Tokyo, Japan 156-0043
00-03-11 (hex)	Micro Technology Co., Ltd.
000311 (base 16)	Micro Technology Co., Ltd. Suehiro Bldg. 1-2, Soto Kanda 5 Chome Chiyoda-ku, Tokyo 101-0021 JAPAN
00-03-12 (hex)	TR-Systemtechnik GmbH
000312 (base 16)	TR-Systemtechnik GmbH Eglishalde 6 D-78647 Trossingen GERMANY
00-03-13 (hex)	Access Media SPA
000313 (base 16)	Access Media SPA Via delle Industrie, 4/g 24035 LALLIO (BG) - Italy
00-03-14 (hex)	Teleware Network Systems
000314 (base 16)	Teleware Network Systems #7806 7th Dongil Technotown, Kinanyang Dong 823, Dongahn Gu, Anyang City, Kyungi Province, KOREA, 431-062
00-03-15 (hex)	Cidco Incorporated
000315 (base 16)	Cidco Incorporated 220 Cochrane Circle Morgan Hill, CA 95037
00-03-16 (hex)	Nobell Communications, Inc.
000316 (base 16)	Nobell Communications, Inc. 3410 Far West Blvd., Suite 240 Austin, TX 78731
00-03-17 (hex)	Merlin Systems, Inc.
000317 (base 16)	Merlin Systems, Inc. 3900 New Park Mall Rd. 3rd Floor Newark, CA 94560
00-03-18 (hex)	Cyras Systems, Inc.
000318 (base 16)	Cyras Systems, Inc. 47100 Bayside Parkway Fremont, CA 94538
00-03-19 (hex)	Infineon AG
000319 (base 16)	Infineon AG P.O. Box 800949 D-81609 Munich GERMANY
00-03-1A (hex)	Beijing Broad Telecom Ltd., China
00031A (base 16)	Beijing Broad Telecom Ltd., China P.O. Box #147 Beijing University of Posts and Telecommunications Beijing, P.R.CHINA 100876
00-03-1B (hex)	Cellvision Systems, Inc.

company_id	Organization Address
00031B (base 16)	Cellvision Systems, Inc. 3F-1, 75, Hsin Taiwu Road, Sec. 1 Hsichih, Taipei, Taiwan, R.O.C.
00-03-1C (hex)	Svenska Hardvarufabriken AB
00031C (base 16)	Svenska Hardvarufabriken AB Ole Romersvag 16, Ideon SE-223 70 Lund SWEDEN
00-03-1D (hex)	Taiwan Commate Computer, Inc.
00031D (base 16)	Taiwan Commate Computer, Inc. 8F, No. 94, Sec 1, Shin Tai Wu Rd. Hsi Chih, Taipei Hsien, Taiwan R.O.C.
00-03-1E (hex)	Optranet, Inc.
00031E (base 16)	Optranet, Inc. 7041 Koll Center Pkwy Suite 135 Pleasanton, CA 94566
00-03-1F (hex)	Condev Ltd.
00031F (base 16)	Condev Ltd. 200-1626 West 2nd Ave. Vancouver, B.C. V6J 1H4 CANADA
00-03-20 (hex)	Xpeed, Inc.
000320 (base 16)	Xpeed, Inc. 99 W. Tasman Drive Suite 110 San Jose, CA 95134
00-03-21 (hex)	Reco Research Co., Ltd.
000321 (base 16)	Reco Research Co., Ltd. No. 47-1, Sec. 2, Kuang Fu Rd.,San Chung City, Taipei, Taiwan, R.O.C.
00-03-22 (hex)	IDIS Co., Ltd.
000322 (base 16)	IDIS Co., Ltd. 7th Floor, 646-7 Yuksam-Dong, Kangnam-Gu, Seoul 135-280, KOREA
00-03-23 (hex)	Cornet Technology, Inc.
000323 (base 16)	Cornet Technology, Inc. 6800 Versar Center, Suite 216 Springfield, VA 22151-4147
00-03-24 (hex)	Tottori SANYO Electric Co., Ltd.
000324 (base 16)	Tottori SANYO Electric Co., Ltd. Information & Communicaiton Division Engineering Development Dept. 7-101, Tachikawa-cho, Tottori City 680-8634, Japan
00-03-25 (hex)	Arima Computer Corp.
000325 (base 16)	Arima Computer Corp. 6th Fl., No. 327, Sung-lung Rd., Taipei City, Taiwan R.O.C.
00-03-26 (hex)	Iwasaki Information Systems Co., Ltd.
000326 (base 16)	Iwasaki Information Systems Co., Ltd. 3361 Oshi Fukiage-machi, Saitama 369-0113 JAPAN
00-03-27 (hex)	ACT'L
000327 (base 16)	ACT'L Avenue de Artisanat 10A 1924 Braine l'Allard Belgium
00-03-28 (hex)	Mace Group, Inc.
000328 (base 16)	Mace Group, Inc. 5101 Commerce Dr. Baldwin Park, CA 91706
00-03-29 (hex)	F3, Inc.

company_id	Organization Address
000329 (base 16)	F3, Inc. 2F, No. 7, Industry E. Rd. 9, Science Based Industrial Park, Hsinchu, TAIWAN, R.O.C.
00-03-2A (hex)	UniData Communication Systems, Inc.
00032A (base 16)	UniData Communication Systems, Inc. 2F, OhSung-Bldg, 82-15, NonHyun-Dong, GangNam-Gu, Seoul,135-101 KOREA
00-03-2B (hex)	GAI Datenfunksysteme GmbH
00032B (base 16)	GAI Datenfunksysteme GmbH Riedleparkstrasse 28 D-88045 Friedrichshafen GERMANY
00-03-2C (hex)	ABB Industrie AG
00032C (base 16)	ABB Industrie AG Dept. ICT CH-5300 Turgi SWITZERLAND
00-03-2D (hex)	IBASE Technology, Inc.
00032D (base 16)	IBASE Technology, Inc. 5F, No. 221, Chung Yang Rd. Taipei, Taiwan, R.O.C.
00-03-2E (hex)	Scope Information Management, Ltd.
00032E (base 16)	Scope Information Management, Ltd. 2F Chanwoo b/o 736 Youksang-dong, Kangnam-gu, Seoul, KOREA 135-080
00-03-2F (hex)	Global Sun Technology, Inc.
00032F (base 16)	Global Sun Technology, Inc. No. 13, Tung Yuan Rd., Jung Li Industrial Park Jung Li City Taiwan, R.O.C.
00-03-30 (hex)	Imagenics, Co., Ltd.
000330 (base 16)	Imagenics, Co., Ltd. 1-31-5 Kokuryo-Cho Chofu-City Tokyo 182-0022 JAPAN
00-03-31 (hex)	Cisco Systems, Inc.
000331 (base 16)	Cisco Systems, Inc. 170 West Tasman Dr. San Jose, CA 95134
00-03-32 (hex)	Cisco Systems, Inc.
000332 (base 16)	Cisco Systems, Inc. 170 West Tasman Dr. San Jose, CA 95134
00-03-33 (hex)	Digitel Co., Ltd.
000333 (base 16)	Digitel Co., Ltd. 16F, Aju Bldg., 679-5, Yoksam-dong, Kangnam-gu, 135-080, Seoul, KOREA
00-03-34 (hex)	Newport Electronics
000334 (base 16)	Newport Electronics 2229 So. Yale St. Santa Ana, CA 92704
00-03-35 (hex)	Mirae Technology
000335 (base 16)	Mirae Technology 211-15, Hon Hyun-dong, Kangnam-ku 135-010 Seoul, Korea
00-03-36 (hex)	Zetes Technologies
000336 (base 16)	Zetes Technologies 3 Rue De Stras Bourg 1130 Brussels BELGIUM
00-03-37 (hex)	Vaone, Inc.

company_id	Organization Address	company_id	Organization Address
000337 (base 16)	Vaone, Inc. 6F Kyemong Art Center, 772 Yuksan2-Dong Kang HamGu, Seoul, KOREA 135-082	000344 (base 16)	Tietech.Co., Ltd. 2-13-1 Chikamatoori Minamiku Nagoya, JAPAN
00-03-38 (hex)	Oak Technology	00-03-45 (hex)	Routrek Networks Corporation
000338 (base 16)	Oak Technology 139 Kifer Court Sunnyvale, CA 94086-5160	000345 (base 16)	Routrek Networks Corporation Nilssei Shin Mizonokuchi Bldg. 1F 3-5-7 Hisamoto, Takatsu-Ku Kawasaki-shi, Kanagawa 23-0011 JAPAN
00-03-39 (hex)	Eurologic Systems, Ltd.	00-03-46 (hex)	Yagi Antenna Co., Ltd.
000339 (base 16)	Eurologic Systems, Ltd. Maple House South County Business Park Leopardstown Dublin 18 Ireland	000346 (base 16)	Yagi Antenna Co., Ltd. 1-6-10 Uchikanda Chiyoda-Ku Tokyo 1101 JAPAN
00-03-3A (hex)	Silicon Wave, Inc.	00-03-47 (hex)	Intel Corporation
00033A (base 16)	Silicon Wave, Inc. 6256 Greenwich Drive Suite 300 San Diego, CA 92122	000347 (base 16)	Intel Corporation MS: LF3-420 2111 N.E. 25th Avenue Hillsboro, OR 97124
00-03-3B (hex)	TAMI Tech Co., Ltd.	00-03-48 (hex)	Norscan Instruments, Ltd.
00033B (base 16)	TAMI Tech Co., Ltd. 4F, Chungdo Bencher Town 606 Tanbang-Dong, Seo-Gu Taejon, KOREA	000348 (base 16)	Norscan Instruments, Ltd. 7 Terracon Place Winnipeg, Manitoba, CANADA R2J 4B3
00-03-3C (hex)	Daiden Co., Ltd.	00-03-49 (hex)	Vidicode Datacommunicatie B.V.
00033C (base 16)	Daiden Co., Ltd. 2100-19 Tutumi, Kamimine-machi Miyaki-gun, Saga-ken JAPAN	000349 (base 16)	Vidicode Datacommunicatie B.V. Postbus 7164 2701 AD Zoetermeer THE NETHERLANDS
00-03-3D (hex)	ILSHin Lab	00-03-4A (hex)	RIAS Corporation
00033D (base 16)	ILSHin Lab KCS B/D 228-13 Young Dap-Dong SUNG DONG-GU, Seoul, KOREA	00034A (base 16)	RIAS Corporation 46600 Fremont Blvd. Fremont, CA 94538
00-03-3E (hex)	Tateyama System Laboratory Co., Ltd.	00-03-4B (hex)	Nortel Networks
00033E (base 16)	Tateyama System Laboratory Co., Ltd. 30 Shimonoban Oyama-cho Kaminikawa-gun Toyama Prof. Japan 930-1305	00034B (base 16)	Nortel Networks 8200 Dixie Road Suite 100 Dept. 6800 Brampton ON L6T 5 P6 Canada
00-03-3F (hex)	BigBand Networks, Ltd.	00-03-4C (hex)	Shanghai DigiVision Technology Co., Ltd.
00033F (base 16)	BigBand Networks, Ltd. 3 Azrieli Towers Tel-Aviv 67023 ISRAEL	00034C (base 16)	Shanghai DigiVision Technology Co., Ltd. 11F, Heng Tong International Building, 865 Chang Ning Rd., Shanghai 200050, P.R.C.
00-03-40 (hex)	Floware Wireless Systems, Ltd.	00-03-4D (hex)	Chiaro Networks, Ltd.
000340 (base 16)	Floware Wireless Systems, Ltd. 28 Hacharoshet Steet P.O.B. 812 Or-Yehuda 60250, ISRAEL	00034D (base 16)	Chiaro Networks, Ltd. P.O. Box 832427 Richardson, TX 75083-2427
00-03-41 (hex)	Axon Digital Design	00-03-4E (hex)	Pos Data Company, Ltd.
000341 (base 16)	Axon Digital Design P.O. Box 111 5070 AC Udenhout The NETHERLANDS	00034E (base 16)	Pos Data Company, Ltd. 276-2, Seo-Hyun Dong, Bun-Dang Gu, Sung-nam City, Kyoung-Gi Providence, SOUTH KOREA
00-03-42 (hex)	Nortel Networks	00-03-4F (hex)	Sur-Gard Security
000342 (base 16)	Nortel Networks 8200 Dixie Road - Ste #100 Dept. 6800 Brampton ON L6T 5P6 CANADA	00034F (base 16)	Sur-Gard Security 401 Magnetic Drive Units 24-28, Downsview Ontario, Canada M3J 3H9
00-03-43 (hex)	Martin Professional A/S	00-03-50 (hex)	BTICINO SPA
000343 (base 16)	Martin Professional A/S Olof Palmes Alle 18 DK-8200 Aarhusn DENMARK	000350 (base 16)	BTICINO SPA Via L. Manara, 4 22036 Erba (CO) ITALY
00-03-44 (hex)	Tietech.Co., Ltd.	00-03-51 (hex)	Diebold, Inc.
		000351 (base 16)	Diebold, Inc. 5995 Mayfair Road North Canton, OH 44720

company_id	Organization Address
00-03-52 (hex)	Colubris Networks
000352 (base 16)	Colubris Networks 440 Armand-Frappier Laval (Quebec) CANADA H7V 4B4
00-03-53 (hex)	Mitac, Inc.
000353 (base 16)	Mitac, Inc. No. 2, Chung-Hsiao Street Chitu, Keelung, TAIWAN, R.O.C.
00-03-54 (hex)	Fiber Logic Communications
000354 (base 16)	Fiber Logic Communications 5F-3, No. 9, Prosperity Road One, Science-Based Industrial Park, Hsinchu, TAIWAN, R.O.C.
00-03-55 (hex)	TeraBeam Internet Systems
000355 (base 16)	TeraBeam Internet Systems 14833 NE 87th St., Bldg. C Redmond, WA 98052
00-03-56 (hex)	Wincor Nixdorf GmbH & Co KG
000356 (base 16)	Wincor Nixdorf GmbH & Co KG Heinz-Nixdorf Ring 1 D-33094 Paderborn GERMANY
00-03-57 (hex)	Intervoice-Brite, Inc.
000357 (base 16)	Intervoice-Brite, Inc. 17811 Waterview Pkwy. Dallas, TX 75252
00-03-58 (hex)	iCable System Co., Ltd.
000358 (base 16)	iCable System Co., Ltd. 7th Fl., KMIT Bldg., 829-1 Yeoksam-Dong, Kangnam-ku, Seoul, KOREA
00-03-59 (hex)	DigitalSis
000359 (base 16)	DigitalSis B-1405 Samho Bldg. 275-6 Yangjae Seocho, Seoul, KOREA
00-03-5A (hex)	Phototron Limited
00035A (base 16)	Phototron Limited Shibuya 1-9-8 Shibuya-ku, Tokyo 150-0002, JAPAN
00-03-5B (hex)	Bridge Wave Communications
00035B (base 16)	Bridge Wave Communications 249 Humbolt Court Sunnyvale, CA 94059
00-03-5C (hex)	Saint Song Corp.
00035C (base 16)	Saint Song Corp. 4F, No. 12, Lane 94, Tsao Ti Wzi Shen Keng Hsiang, Taipei Hsien Taiwan, R.O.C. 222
00-03-5D (hex)	Bosung Hi-Net Co., Ltd.
00035D (base 16)	Bosung Hi-Net Co., Ltd. Youngil B/O 2F, YangJae-dong 12-7, Seocho-gu, Seoul KOREA Zip Code: 137-130
00-03-5E (hex)	Metropolitan Area Networks, Inc.
00035E (base 16)	Metropolitan Area Networks, Inc. 1299 Pennsylvania Avenue, NW Ninth Floor Washington, DC 20004
00-03-5F (hex)	Schuehle Mess - und. Kontrollsysteme
00035F (base 16)	Schuehle Mess - und. Kontrollsysteme Franz-Bayer-Str. 14 D-88213 Ravensburg GERMANY
00-03-60 (hex)	PAC Interactive Technology, Inc.

company_id	Organization Address
000360 (base 16)	PAC Interactive Technology, Inc. 6F, No. 30, Alley 18, Lane 478 Jai Guang Road, Nei-Hu Taipei, TAIWAN
00-03-61 (hex)	Widcomm, Inc.
000361 (base 16)	Widcomm, Inc. 9645 Scranton Road Suite 205 San Diego, CA 92121
00-03-62 (hex)	Vodtel Communications, Inc.
000362 (base 16)	Vodtel Communications, Inc. 12F, No 166 Chien-Yi Road Chung-Ho City, Taipei County Taiwan R.O.C. Zip Code: 235
00-09-63 (hex)	Miraesys Co., Ltd.
000363 (base 16)	Miraesys Co., Ltd. 650-2 4 Fl. Daemyung Bldg. Yuksam, Kangnam, Seoul, KOREA #135-080
00-03-64 (hex)	Scenix Semiconductor, Inc.
000364 (base 16)	Scenix Semiconductor, Inc. 1330 Charleston Rd. Mountainview, CA 94043
00-03-65 (hex)	Kira Information & Communications, Ltd.
000365 (base 16)	Kira Information & Communications, Ltd. 6th Fl. Anam Tower, 702-10 Yeoksam-dong, Kangnam-ku, Seoul KOREA
00-03-66 (hex)	ASM Pacific Technology
000366 (base 16)	ASM Pacific Technology 12/F Watson Centre 16 Kung Yip St. Kwai Chung, HONG KONG
00-03-67 (hex)	Jasmine Networks, Inc.
000367 (base 16)	Jasmine Networks, Inc. 1940 Zanker Road San Jose, CA 95112
00-03-68 (hex)	Embedone Co., Ltd.
000368 (base 16)	Embedone Co., Ltd. Fl. 9 Annex Samhwan B/D. 17-26 Yeoido-Dong, Youngdeungpo-ku, Seoul, KOREA (ROK) 150-010
00-03-69 (hex)	Nippon Antenna Co., Ltd.
000369 (base 16)	Nippon Antenna Co., Ltd. No. 49-8, Nishiogu, 7-Chome Arakawa-ku, Tokyo 116-8561, JAPAN
00-03-6A (hex)	Mainnet, Ltd.
00036A (base 16)	Mainnet, Ltd. P.O. Box 2324 Kfar Saba 44641 ISRAEL
00-03-6B (hex)	Cisco Systems, Inc.
00036B (base 16)	Cisco Systems, Inc. 170 West Tasman Dr. San Jose, CA 95134
00-03-6C (hex)	Cisco Systems, Inc.
00036C (base 16)	Cisco Systems, Inc. 170 West Tasman Dr. San Jose, C A95134
00-03-6D (hex)	Runtop, Inc.
00036D (base 16)	Runtop, Inc. 1, Lane 21, Hsin Hua Road, Kueishan Industrial Park, Taoyuan City, TAIWAN
00-03-6E (hex)	Nicon Systems (Pty) Limited

company_id	Organization Address
00036E (base 16)	Nicon Systems (Pty) Limited 11 Termo Street Technopark Stellenbosch, 7600 SOUTH AFRICA
00-03-6F (hex)	Telsey SPA
00036F (base 16)	Telsey SPA Viale Dell Industria, 1 31 055 Quinto Di Treviso- ITALY
00-03-70 (hex)	NXTV, Inc.
000370 (base 16)	NXTV, Inc. 5955 De Soto Ave, #160 Woodland Hills, CA 91367
00-03-71 (hex)	Acomz Networks Corp.
000371 (base 16)	Acomz Networks Corp. 7th Fl., Wooseok Bldg., 1007-37 Sadang1-dong, Dongjak-gu, Seoul, KOREA (ROK) 156-091
00-03-72 (hex)	ULAN
000372 (base 16)	ULAN 5F-3, No. 31-1, Lane 169, Kang Ning St., Hsi-Chin City, Taipei Hsien, TAIWAN, R.O.C.
00-03-73 (hex)	Aselsan A.S
000373 (base 16)	Aselsan A.S Mehmet Akif Ersoy Mah. 16 Cad. No. 16 Macunkoy/Ankara TURKEY
00-03-74 (hex)	Hunter Watertech
000374 (base 16)	Hunter Watertech 76 Munibung Rd. Cardiff NSW, 2285 AUSTRALIA
00-03-75 (hex)	NetMedia, Inc.
000375 (base 16)	NetMedia, Inc. 10940 N. Stallard Place Tuscon, AZ 85737
00-03-76 (hex)	Graphtec Technology, Inc.
000376 (base 16)	Graphtec Technology, Inc. 45 Parker, Suite A Irvine, CA 92618
00-03-77 (hex)	Gigabit Wireless
000377 (base 16)	Gigabit Wireless 3099 N. First Street San Jose, CA 95134
00-03-78 (hex)	HUMAX Co., Ltd.
000378 (base 16)	HUMAX Co., Ltd. 271-2, Suh-hyun-Dong, Bundang-Gu, Sungnam-City, Kyonggi-Do, 463-050 KOREA
00-03-79 (hex)	Proscend Communications, Inc.
000379 (base 16)	Proscend Communications, Inc. 17F-3, No. 295, Kwang Fu Rd., Sec. 2, Hsinchu, TAIWAN, R.O.C. 300
00-03-7A (hex)	Taiyo Yuden Co., Ltd.
00037A (base 16)	Taiyo Yuden Co., Ltd. 8-1 Sakae-Cho Takasaki-Shi Gunma 370-8522 JAPAN
00-03-7B (hex)	IDEC IZUMI Corporation
00037B (base 16)	IDEC IZUMI Corporation 7-31, Nishimiyahara 1-Chome Yodogawa-ku. Osaka 532-8550 JAPAN

company_id	Organization Address
00-03-7C (hex)	Coax Media
00037C (base 16)	Coax Media 1220 Oak Industrial Lane Suite B Cumming, GA 30041
00-03-7D (hex)	Stellcom
00037D (base 16)	Stellcom 10525 Vista Sorrento Parkway Suite 100 San Diego, CA 92121
00-03-7E (hex)	PORTech Communications, Inc.
00037E (base 16)	PORTech Communications, Inc. 150, Shiang-Shung N. Rd., Taichung, Taiwan 403, R.O.C.
00-03-7F (hex)	Atheros Communications, Inc.
00037F (base 16)	Atheros Communications, Inc. 529 Almanor Ave. Sunnyvale, CA 94085
00-03-81 (hex)	Ingenico International
000381 (base 16)	Ingenico International 1/9 Apollo Street Warriewood NSW 2102 AUSTRALIA
00-03-82 (hex)	A-One Co., Ltd.
000382 (base 16)	A-One Co., Ltd. 6-9-20, Shimoichiba-cho, Kasugai-shi, Aichi-ken, 486-0852 JAPAN
00-03-83 (hex)	Metera Networks, Inc.
000383 (base 16)	Metera Networks, Inc. 1202 Richardson Dr. Suite 100 Richardson, TX 75080
00-03-84 (hex)	AETA
000384 (base 16)	AETA 361 Avenue du General de Gaulle F92147 Clamart Cedex FRANCE
00-03-85 (hex)	Actelis Networks, Inc.
000385 (base 16)	Actelis Networks, Inc. 1 Bazel St., P.O.B. 10173 Petah - Tikva 49103 ISRAEL
00-03-86 (hex)	Ho Net, Inc.
000386 (base 16)	Ho Net, Inc. Venture Company Center San 94-6 Yiui-Dong, Paldal-Gu, Suwon-si, Kyonggi-Do, KOREA 442-760
00-03-87 (hex)	Blaze Network Products
000387 (base 16)	Blaze Network Products 5180 Hacienda Drive Dublin, CA 94568
00-03-88 (hex)	Fastfame Technology Co., Ltd.
000388 (base 16)	Fastfame Technology Co., Ltd. 7F, No. 111, Hsing De Rd., Sanchung, Taipei, TAIWAN, R.O.C.
00-03-89 (hex)	Plantronics
000389 (base 16)	Plantronics 345 Encinal St. Santa Cruz, CA 95060
00-03-8A (hex)	America Online, Inc.
00038A (base 16)	America Online, Inc. 44900 Prentice Drive Dulles, VA 20166
00-03-8B (hex)	PLUS-ONE I&T, Inc.

company_id	Organization Address	company_id	Organization Address
00038B (base 16)	PLUS-ONE I&T, Inc. 7F, A-San Venture Tower, YangJae-dong, Seocho-ku, Seoul, KOREA	00039A (base 16)	nSine, Ltd. Apex Plaza, Forbury Road, Reading, Berkshire, ENGLAND, RG11 1AX
00-03-8C (hex)	Total Impact	00-03-9B (hex)	NetChip Technology, Inc.
00038C (base 16)	Total Impact 295 Willis Ave. Suite E Camarillo, CA 93010	00039B (base 16)	NetChip Technology, Inc. 335 Pioneer Way Mountain View, CA 94041
		00-03-9C (hex)	OptiMight Communications, Inc.
00-03-8D (hex)	PCS Revenue Control Systems, Inc.	00039C (base 16)	OptiMight Communications, Inc. 980 Linda Vista Avenue Mountain View, CA 94043
00038D (base 16)	PCS Revenue Control Systems, Inc. 560 Sylvan Ave. Englewood Cliffs, NJ 07632	00-03-9D (hex)	Acer Communications & Multimedia, Inc.
00-03-8E (hex)	Atoga Systems, Inc.	00039D (base 16)	Acer Communications & Multimedia, Inc. 8 Jihu Road, Neihu, Taipei 114, TAIWAN R.O.C.
00038E (base 16)	Atoga Systems, Inc. 49026 Milmont Drive Fremont, CA 94538	00-03-9E (hex)	Tera System Co., Ltd.
00-03-8F (hex)	Weinschel Corporation	00039E (base 16)	Tera System Co., Ltd. Doosung B/F Rm 302 766-1 Shinchungdong Shihung City Kyungkido 429-020 Republic of Korea
00038F (base 16)	Weinschel Corporation 5305 Spectrum Drive Frederick, MD 21703		
00-03-90 (hex)	Digital Video Communications, Inc.	00-03-9F (hex)	Cisco Systems, Inc.
000390 (base 16)	Digital Video Communications, Inc. 500 W. Cummings Park Suite 2000 Woburn, MA 07801	00039F (base 16)	Cisco Systems, Inc. 170 West Tasman Dr. San Jose, CA 95134
		00-03-A0 (hex)	Cisco Systems, Inc.
00-03-92 (hex)	Hyundai Teletek Co., Ltd.	0003A0 (base 16)	Cisco Systems, Inc. 170 West Tasman Dr. San Jose, CA 95134
000392 (base 16)	Hyundai Teletek Co., Ltd. B-501, Techno Park, 148 Yatap-dong, Boondang-gu, Sungnam-si, Kyunggi-do, 463-070, KOREA Republic	00-03-A1 (hex)	HIPER Information & Communication, Inc.
		0003A1 (base 16)	HIPER Information & Communication, Inc. 1675-7, Sinil-dong, Taeduk-gu, Taejon, 306-230, South Korea
00-03-93 (hex)	Apple Computer, Inc.		
000393 (base 16)	Apple Computer, Inc. 20650 Valley Green Dr. Cupertino, CA 95014	00-03-A2 (hex)	Catapult Communications
		0003A2 (base 16)	Catapult Communications 160 S. Whisman Rd. Mountain View, CA 94041
00-03-94 (hex)	Connect One		
000394 (base 16)	Connect One 2 Hanagar Street Kfar Saba 44425 ISRAEL	00-03-A3 (hex)	MAVIX, Ltd.
		0003A3 (base 16)	MAVIX, Ltd. POB 217, Yokneam Illit, 20692 Israel
00-03-95 (hex)	California Amplifier	00-03-A4 (hex)	Data Storage and Information Management
000395 (base 16)	California Amplifier 460 Calle San Pablo Camarillo, CA 93012	0003A4 (base 16)	Data Storage and Information Management Discovery 2A30 Oakdale, MN 55128
00-03-96 (hex)	EZ Cast Co., Ltd.		
000396 (base 16)	EZ Cast Co., Ltd. 6th Floor, JungAng Building, 99-1, Nonhyun-Dong (135-010) Kangnam-ku, Seoul KOREA	00-03-A5 (hex)	Medea Corporation
		0003A5 (base 16)	Medea Corporation 5701 Lindero Canyon Rd. Bldg. 3-100 Wetlake Village, CA 91362
00-03-97 (hex)	Watchfront Electronics	00-03-A7 (hex)	Unixtar Technology, Inc.
000397 (base 16)	Watchfront Electronics 32 Ashbarn Crescent Winchester Hampshire SO22 4QJ UK	0003A7 (base 16)	Unixtar Technology, Inc. 13F No. 100 Ming Chuan Road Hsin Tien, Taipei, TAIWAN
		00-03-A8 (hex)	IDOT Computers, Inc.
00-03-98 (hex)	WISI	0003A8 (base 16)	IDOT Computers, Inc. 3F., No. 137, Lane 235 Pao-Chiao Road, Hsin-Tien Taipei Country, TAIWAN, R.O.C.
000398 (base 16)	WISI Pforzheimerstr. 26 D-75223 Niefern-Oeschelbronn GERMANY		
00-03-99 (hex)	Dong-Ju Information & Communication		
000399 (base 16)	Dong-Ju Information & Communication #305, Eunsuk Bldg. Samsung-dong Kangnam-gu Seoul Republic of KOREA	00-03-A9 (hex)	AXCENT Media AG
00-03-9A (hex)	nSine, Ltd.		

company_id	Organization Address
0003A9 (base 16)	AXCENT Media AG Technologiepark 13 33100 Paderborn GERMANY
00-03-AA (hex)	Watlow
0003AA (base 16)	Watlow 1241 Bundy Blvd. Winona, MN 55987
00-03-AB (hex)	Bridge Information Systems
0003AB (base 16)	Bridge Information Systems 717 Office Parkway St. Louis, MO 63141
00-03-AC (hex)	Fronius Schweissmaschinen
0003AC (base 16)	Fronius Schweissmaschinen Guenter Fronius Str. 1 A-4600 Weis-Thalheim AUSTRIA
00-03-AD (hex)	Emerson Energy Systems AB
0003AD (base 16)	Emerson Energy Systems AB SE-14182 Stockholm Sweden
00-03-AE (hex)	Allied Advanced Manufacturing Pte, Ltd.
0003AE (base 16)	Allied Advanced Manufacturing Pte, Ltd. 7 International Business Park #02-00 Singapore 609919
00-03-AF (hex)	Paragea Communications
0003AF (base 16)	Paragea Communications 207 Perry Parkway Gaithersburg, MD 20877
00-03-B0 (hex)	Xsense Technology Corp.
0003B0 (base 16)	Xsense Technology Corp. 11 F, 232, Sec. 3, ChengTeh Rd. Taipei, TAIWAN, 103
00-03-B1 (hex)	Abbott Laboratories HPD
0003B1 (base 16)	Abbott Laboratories HPD 755 Jarvis Drive Morgan Hill, CA 95037
00-03-B2 (hex)	Radware
0003B2 (base 16)	Radware 8 Hamrpe Harhozvim Jerusalem ISRAEL
00-03-B3 (hex)	IA Link Systems Co., Ltd.
0003B3 (base 16)	IA Link Systems Co., Ltd. 6F-4, No. 81 Hsin Tai Wu Rd., Sec. 1 Hsih-Chih, Taipei Hsien, TAIWAN, R.O.C.
00-03-B4 (hex)	Macrotek International Corp.
0003B4 (base 16)	Macrotek International Corp. 2F, No. 28, Lane 46 Kwang Fu 6 Road, Taipei, TAIWAN
00-03-B5 (hex)	Entra Technology Co.
0003B5 (base 16)	Entra Technology Co. Fl. 3, No. 5, Alley 2, Su-Wei Lane, Chung-Cheng Rd., Hsin-Dien, Taipei County, TAIWAN, R.O.C.
00-03-B6 (hex)	QSI Corporation
0003B6 (base 16)	QSI Corporation 2212 South West Temple #50 Salt Lake City, UT 84115
00-03-B7 (hex)	ZACCESS Systems
0003B7 (base 16)	ZACCESS Systems 275 Shoreline Drive, #110 Redwood City, CA 94065
00-03-B8 (hex)	NetKit Solutions, LLC

company_id	Organization Address
0003B8 (base 16)	NetKit Solutions, LLC 26630 Agoura Road Calabasas, CA 91302
00-03-B9 (hex)	Hualong Telecom Co., Ltd.
0003B9 (base 16)	Hualong Telecom Co., Ltd. 9 Guanghua St. Changzhou, Jiangsu, 213003 P.R. CHINA
00-03-BA (hex)	Sun Microsystems
0003BA (base 16)	Sun Microsystems 901 San Antonio Rd. MS: UNWK11-01 Palo Alto, CA 94303-4900
00-03-BB (hex)	Signal Communications Limited
0003BB (base 16)	Signal Communications Limited Unit 217, 2/F, HKITC, 72 Tat Chee Avenue, KLN., HONG KONG
00-03-BC (hex)	COT GmbH
0003BC (base 16)	COT GmbH Gueterstrasse 5 64807 Dieburg GERMANY
00-03-BD (hex)	OmniCluster Technologies, Inc.
0003BD (base 16)	OmniCluster Technologies, Inc. 4950 Blue Lake Drive Suite 900 Boca Raton, FL 33431
00-03-BE (hex)	Netility
0003BE (base 16)	Netility 298 South Sunnyvale Ave. Suite 102 Sunnyvale, CA 94086
00-03-BF (hex)	Centerpoint Broadband Technologies, Inc.
0003BF (base 16)	Centerpoint Broadband Technologies, Inc. 1741 Technology Drive, Suite 400 San Jose, CA 95110-1310
00-03-C0 (hex)	RFTNC Co., Ltd.
0003C0 (base 16)	RFTNC Co., Ltd. 3F, 1624-24, Bongchen-dong Kionak-gu, Seoul SOUTH KOREA
00-03-C1 (hex)	Packet Dynamics Ltd
0003C1 (base 16)	Packet Dynamics Ltd 2 Buckstane Park Edinburgh, Scotland UK, EH10 GPA
00-03-C2 (hex)	Solphone K.K.
0003C2 (base 16)	Solphone K.K. 2-11-1 Kandatsukasa-cho Chiyada, Tokyo 101-0048 Japan
00-03-C3 (hex)	Micronik Multimedia
0003C3 (base 16)	Micronik Multimedia Brueckenstr. 2 D-51379 Leverkusen GERMANY
00-03-C4 (hex)	Tomra Systems ASA
0003C4 (base 16)	Tomra Systems ASA Drengsrudhagen 2 Box 278 N-1371 Asker NORWAY
00-03-C5 (hex)	Mobotix AG
0003C5 (base 16)	Mobotix AG Wingertsweilerhof 6 D-67724 Horingen GERMANY
00-03-C6 (hex)	ICUE Systems, Inc.

company_id	Organization Address
0003C6 (base 16)	ICUE Systems, Inc. 17489 Gale Avenue City of Industry, CA 91748
00-03-C7 (hex)	hopf Elektronik GmbH
0003C7 (base 16)	hopf Elektronik GmbH P.O. Box 18 47 D-58468 Ludenscheid GERMANY
00-03-C8 (hex)	CML Emergency Services
0003C8 (base 16)	CML Emergency Services 75 Boulevard la Technologies Hull, Quebec JE23G4 CANADA
00-03-C9 (hex)	TECOM Co., Ltd.
0003C9 (base 16)	TECOM Co., Ltd. 23, R&D Road 2 Science-Based Industrial Park Hsin-Chu TAIWAN, R.O.C.
00-03-CA (hex)	MTS Systems Corp.
0003CA (base 16)	MTS Systems Corp. 16050 Stetson Road Los Gatos, CA 95033
00-03-CB (hex)	Nippon Systems Development Co., Ltd.
0003CB (base 16)	Nippon Systems Development Co., Ltd. 30-12, Komyo-cho, Takarabuka-city, Hyogo, 665-0045 JAPAN
00-03-CC (hex)	Momentum Computer, Inc.
0003CC (base 16)	Momentum Computer, Inc. 1815 Aston Avenue Suite 107 Carlsbad, CA 92008-7310
00-03-CD (hex)	Clovertech, Inc.
0003CD (base 16)	Clovertech, Inc. 3-1-5 Naka-cho Musashino-shi Tokyo 180-0006 JAPAN
00-03-CE (hex)	ETEN Technologies, Inc.
0003CE (base 16)	ETEN Technologies, Inc. 2F, No. 9, Lane 235, Pao-Chiao Rd., Hsien Tien City, Taipei Hsien 231 TAIWAN, R.O.C.
00-03-CF (hex)	Muxcom, Inc.
0003CF (base 16)	Muxcom, Inc. D 602, Bundang Technopark #151 Yatap Dong, Bundag Gu, Sungnam Si, Kyungki Do, KOREA 463-070
00-03-D0 (hex)	KOANKEISO Co., Ltd.
0003D0 (base 16)	KOANKEISO Co., Ltd. Zip Code 791-8042 2798 36 Minamiyoshida-Mati Matuyama-City Ehime-Prefecture JAPAN
00-03-D1 (hex)	Takaya Corporation
0003D1 (base 16)	Takaya Corporation Development Division 661-1, Ibara-cho Ibara-City Okayama, 715-8503 JAPAN
00-03-D2 (hex)	Crossbeam Systems, Inc.
0003D2 (base 16)	Crossbeam Systems, Inc. 200 Baker Ave. Concord, MA 01742
00-03-D3 (hex)	Internet Energy Systems, Inc.
0003D3 (base 16)	Internet Energy Systems, Inc. 4218 Trumbo Ct. Fairfax, VA 22033
00-03-D4 (hex)	Alloptic, Inc.

company_id	Organization Address
0003D4 (base 16)	Alloptic, Inc. 6960 Koll Center Parkway Suite 300 Pleasanton, CA 94566
00-03-D5 (hex)	Advanced Communications Co., Ltd.
0003D5 (base 16)	Advanced Communications Co., Ltd. 16-16 Takashima-honcho, Numazu Shizuoka, 4100055 JAPAN
00-03-D6 (hex)	RADVision, Ltd.
0003D6 (base 16)	RADVision, Ltd. 24 Raul Wallenberg St. Tel-Aviv 69719 ISRAEL
00-03-D7 (hex)	NextNet Wireless, Inc.
0003D7 (base 16)	NextNet Wireless, Inc. 9555 James Ave. So. Suite 270 Bloomington, MN 55431
00-03-D8 (hex)	iMPath Networks, Inc.
0003D8 (base 16)	iMPath Networks, Inc. 1431 Merivale Rd. Nepean, Ontario, CANADA K2E 1B9
00-03-D9 (hex)	Secheron SA
0003D9 (base 16)	Secheron SA Untermattweg 8 Ch-3027 Bern SWITZERLAND
00-03-DA (hex)	Takamisawa Cybernetics Co., Ltd.
0003DA (base 16)	Takamisawa Cybernetics Co., Ltd. Nakano Heiwa Bldg. 48 5-2-Chome Chuo, Nakano-ku Tokyo 164-0011, JAPAN
00-03-DB (hex)	Apogee Electronics Corp.
0003DB (base 16)	Apogee Electronics Corp. 3145 Donald Douglas Loop South Santa Monica, CA 90405-3210
00-03-DC (hex)	Lexar Media, Inc.
0003DC (base 16)	Lexar Media, Inc. 47421 Bayside Parkway Fremont, CA 94538
00-04-00 (hex)	LEXMARK INTERNATIONAL, INC.
000400 (base 16)	LEXMARK INTERNATIONAL, INC. 740 NEW CIRCLE RD - BLDG. #035 LEXINGTON KY 40550
00-04-AC (hex)	IBM CORP.
0004AC (base 16)	IBM CORP. P.O. BOX 12195 CE6A/664 3039 CORNWALLIS RTP, NC 27709-2195
00-05-02 (hex)	APPLE COMPUTER
000502 (base 16)	APPLE COMPUTER 20650 VALLEY GREEN DRIVE CUPERTINO' CA 95014
00-05-A8 (hex)	WYLE ELECTRONICS
0005A8 (base 16)	WYLE ELECTRONICS 3000 BOWERS AVENUE SANTA CLARA CA 95051-0919
00-06-29 (hex)	IBM CORPORATION
000629 (base 16)	IBM CORPORATION P.O. BOX 12195 CE6A/664 3039 CORNWALLIS RTP, NC 27709-2195
00-06-2B (hex)	INTRASERVER TECHNOLOGY
00062B (base 16)	INTRASERVER TECHNOLOGY SEVEN OCTOBER HILL RD. HOLLISTON MA 01746

company_id	Organization Address
00-06-7C (hex)	CISCO SYSTEMS, INC.
00067C (base 16)	CISCO SYSTEMS, INC. 170 W. TASMAN DRIVE SAN JOSE CA 95134-1706
00-06-C1 (hex)	CISCO SYSTEMS, INC.
0006C1 (base 16)	CISCO SYSTEMS, INC. 170 W. TASMAN DRIVE SAN JOSE CA 95134-1706
00-07-01 (hex)	RACAL-DATACOM
000701 (base 16)	RACAL-DATACOM LAN INTERNETWORKING DIVISION 155 SWANSON ROAD BOXBOROUGH MA 01719
00-08-00 (hex)	MULTITECH SYSTEMS, INC.
000800 (base 16)	MULTITECH SYSTEMS, INC. 2205 WOODALE DRIVE MOUNDS VIEW MN 55112
00-08-C7 (hex)	COMPAQ COMPUTER CORPORATION
0008C7 (base 16)	COMPAQ COMPUTER CORPORATION 20555 S.H. 249 HOUSTON TX 77070
00-0A-27 (hex)	Apple Computer, Inc.
000A27 (base 16)	Apple Computer, Inc. 20650 Valley Green Drive Cupertino CA 95014
00-10-00 (hex)	CABLE TELEVISION
001000 (base 16)	CABLE TELEVISION LABORATORIES, INC. 400 CENTENNIAL PARKWAY LOUISVILLE CO 80027
00-10-01 (hex)	MCK COMMUNICATIONS
001001 (base 16)	MCK COMMUNICATIONS 130 BOWNESS CENTRE N.W. CALGARY AB CANADA T3B 5M5
00-10-02 (hex)	ACTIA
001002 (base 16)	ACTIA 25 CHEMIN DE POUVOURVILLE 31432 TOULOUSE, CEDEX 04 FRANCE
00-10-03 (hex)	IMATRON, INC.
001003 (base 16)	IMATRON, INC. 389 OYSTER POINT BLVD. SO. SAN FRANCISCO CA 94080
00-10-04 (hex)	THE BRANTLEY COILE COMPANY,INC
001004 (base 16)	THE BRANTLEY COILE COMPANY,INC 545 RESEARCH DRIVE ATHENS GA 30605
00-10-05 (hex)	UEC COMMERCIAL
001005 (base 16)	UEC COMMERCIAL P.O. BOX 54, MT. EDGECOMBE 71 MARSHALL DRIVE 4300 DURBAN SOUTH AFRICA
00-10-06 (hex)	RACAL RECORDERS LTD.
001006 (base 16)	RACAL RECORDERS LTD. HARDLEY IND. EST HYTHE, SOUTHAMPTON ENGLAND SO45 3ZH
00-10-07 (hex)	CISCO SYSTEMS, INC.
001007 (base 16)	CISCO SYSTEMS, INC. 170 W. TASMAN DRIVE SJA-2 SAN JOSE CA 95134-1706
00-10-08 (hex)	VIENNA SYSTEMS CORPORATION
001008 (base 16)	VIENNA SYSTEMS CORPORATION 6651 FRASERWOOD PLACE SUITE #250 RICHMOND, B.C. CANADA V6W 1J3
00-10-09 (hex)	HORO QUARTZ
001009 (base 16)	HORO QUARTZ Z.I. ROUTE DE NIORT 85200 - FONTENAY LE COMTE FRANCE
00-10-0A (hex)	WILLIAMS COMMUNICATIONS GROUP
00100A (base 16)	WILLIAMS COMMUNICATIONS GROUP ADVANCED TECHNOLOGIES 111 EAST FIRST TULSA OK 74103
00-10-0B (hex)	CISCO SYSTEMS, INC.
00100B (base 16)	CISCO SYSTEMS, INC. 170 W. TASMAN DRIVE SJA-2 SAN JOSE CA 95134-1706
00-10-0C (hex)	ITO CO., LTD.
00100C (base 16)	ITO CO., LTD. 8-2 MIYANOSHITA-CHO HIRAKATA-CITY, OSAKA JAPAN
00-10-0D (hex)	CISCO SYSTEMS, INC.
00100D (base 16)	CISCO SYSTEMS, INC. . 170 W. TASMAN DR.-SJA-2 SAN JOSE CA 95134-1706
00-10-0E (hex)	MICRO LINEAR COPORATION
00100E (base 16)	MICRO LINEAR COPORATION 2092 CONCOURSE DRIVE SAN JOSE CA 95131
00-10-0F (hex)	INDUSTRIAL CPU SYSTEMS
00100F (base 16)	INDUSTRIAL CPU SYSTEMS 111-D W. DYER ROAD SANTA ANA CA 92707
00-10-10 (hex)	INITIO CORPORATION
001010 (base 16)	INITIO CORPORATION 2188 B DEL FRANCO STREET SAN JOSE CA 95118
00-10-11 (hex)	CISCO SYSTEMS, INC.
001011 (base 16)	CISCO SYSTEMS, INC. 170 W. TASMAN DRIVE SAN JOSE CA 95134-1706
00-10-12 (hex)	PROCESSOR SYSTEMS (I) PVT LTD
001012 (base 16)	PROCESSOR SYSTEMS (I) PVT LTD 24 RICHMOND ROAD BANGALORE 560 025 INDIA
00-10-13 (hex)	INDUSTRIAL COMPUTER SOURCE
001013 (base 16)	INDUSTRIAL COMPUTER SOURCE 6260 SEQUENCE DRIVE SAN DIEGO CA 92121
00-10-14 (hex)	CISCO SYSTEMS, INC.
001014 (base 16)	CISCO SYSTEMS, INC. 170 W. TASMAN DRIVE SAN JOSE CA 95134-1706
00-10-15 (hex)	OOMON INC.
001015 (base 16)	OOMON INC. PO BOX 8241 COBURG OR 97408
00-10-16 (hex)	T.SQWARE
001016 (base 16)	T.SQWARE 6, PARC ARIANE IMMEUBLE MERCURE 78284 GUYANCOURT CEDEX FRANCE
00-10-17 (hex)	MICOS GMBH
001017 (base 16)	MICOS GMBH ST.-JOBSER STR. 31 D-52146 WURSELEN GERMANY
00-10-18 (hex)	BROADCOM CORPORATION

company_id	Organization Address	company_id	Organization Address
001018 (base 16)	BROADCOM CORPORATION 16215 ALTON PARKWAY P.O. BOX 57013 IRVINE CA 92619-7013	00-10-27 (hex)	L-3 COMMUNICATIONS EAST
		001027 (base 16)	L-3 COMMUNICATIONS EAST ONE FEDERAL STREET - A&E-3ES CAMDEN NJ 08102
00-10-19 (hex)	SIRONA DENTAL SYSTEMS	00-10-28 (hex)	COMPUTER TECHNICA, INC.
001019 (base 16)	SIRONA DENTAL SYSTEMS GMBH & CO., KG FABRIKSTRASSE 31 64625 BENSHEIM GERMANY	001028 (base 16)	COMPUTER TECHNICA, INC. 3-5-19 HIGASHINAKA HAKATA-KU FUKUOKA-SI FUKUOKA 816 JAPAN
00-10-1A (hex)	PICTURETEL CORP.	00-10-29 (hex)	CISCO SYSTEMS, INC.
00101A (base 16)	PICTURETEL CORP. 100 MINUTEMAN ROAD, MS641 ANDOVER MA 01810	001029 (base 16)	CISCO SYSTEMS, INC. 170 W. TASMAN DRIVE SAN JOSE CA 95134-1706
00-10-1B (hex)	CORNET TECHNOLOGY, INC.	00-10-2A (hex)	ZF MICROSYSTEMS, INC.
00101B (base 16)	CORNET TECHNOLOGY, INC. 7F-4, NO. 46 CHUNG SHAN N.ROAD SEC. 2, TAIPEI TAIWAN, R.O.C.	00102A (base 16)	ZF MICROSYSTEMS, INC. 1052 ELWELL COURT PALO ALTO CA 94303-4307
00-10-1C (hex)	OHM TECHNOLOGIES INTL, LLC	00-10-2B (hex)	UMAX DATA SYSTEMS, INC.
00101C (base 16)	OHM TECHNOLOGIES INTL, LLC 4 EXECUTIVE CIRCLE ST. #185 IRVINE CA 92614	00102B (base 16)	UMAX DATA SYSTEMS, INC. NO. 1-1, R&D ROAD 2 SCIENCE-BASED INDUSTRIAL PARK HSINCHU TAIWAN
00-10-1D (hex)	WINBOND ELECTRONICS CORP.		
00101D (base 16)	WINBOND ELECTRONICS CORP. NO. 4 CREATION RD. III SCIENCE-BASED INDUSTRIAL PARK HSIN CHU TAIWAN, R.O.C.	00-10-2C (hex)	PNP TECHNOLOGY A/S
		00102C (base 16)	PNP TECHNOLOGY A/S AMALILEGADE 22 DK-1256 KOBENHAVNK DENMARK
00-10-1E (hex)	MATSUSHITA ELECTRONIC	00-10-2D (hex)	HITACHI SOFTWARE ENGINEERING
00101E (base 16)	MATSUSHITA ELECTRONIC INSTRUMENTS CORP. 23-9 KIYOHARA INDUSTRIAL PARK UTSUNOMIYA TOCHIGI 321-31 JAPAN	00102D (base 16)	HITACHI SOFTWARE ENGINEERING 5-79,ONOECHO, NAKA-KU YOKOHAMA 231 JAPAN
00-10-1F (hex)	CISCO SYSTEMS, INC.	00-10-2E (hex)	NETWORK SYSTEMS & TECHNOLOGIES
00101F (base 16)	CISCO SYSTEMS, INC. 170 W. TASMAN DR. SAN JOSE CA 95134-1706	00102E (base 16)	NETWORK SYSTEMS & TECHNOLOGIES PVT. LTD. PLOT NO. 2, COCHIN EXPORT PROCESSING ZONE, KAKKANAD, COCHIN 682 030, INDIA
00-10-20 (hex)	WELCH ALLYN, DATA COLLECTION		
001020 (base 16)	WELCH ALLYN, DATA COLLECTION 4619 JORDAN RD. P.O. BOX 187 SKANEATELES FALLS NY 13153	00-10-2F (hex)	CISCO SYSTEMS, INC.
		00102F (base 16)	CISCO SYSTEMS, INC. 170 W. TASMAN DR. SAN JOSE CA 95134-1706
00-10-21 (hex)	ENCANTO NETWORKS, INC.	00-10-30 (hex)	WI-LAN, INC.
001021 (base 16)	ENCANTO NETWORKS, INC. 2953 BUNKER HILL LANE SUITE #400 SANTA CLARA CA 95054	001030 (base 16)	WI-LAN, INC. 300-801 MANNING ROAD N.E. CALGARY, ALBERTA CANADA T2E 8J5
00-10-22 (hex)	SATCOM MEDIA CORPORATION	00-10-31 (hex)	OBJECTIVE COMMUNICATIONS, INC.
001022 (base 16)	SATCOM MEDIA CORPORATION 3255-7 SCOTT BLVD. SANTA CLARA CA 95054	001031 (base 16)	OBJECTIVE COMMUNICATIONS, INC. 75 ROCHESTER AVE. UNIT 1 PORTSMOUTH NH 03801
00-10-23 (hex)	FLOWWISE NETWORKS, INC.		
001023 (base 16)	FLOWWISE NETWORKS, INC. 2480 N. 1ST STREET SUITE #180 SAN JOSE CA 95131	00-10-32 (hex)	ALTA TECHNOLOGY
		001032 (base 16)	ALTA TECHNOLOGY 9500 SOUTH 500 WEST - STE #212 SANDY UT 84070
00-10-24 (hex)	NAGOYA ELECTRIC WORKS CO., LTD	00-10-33 (hex)	ACCESSLAN COMMUNICATIONS, INC.
001024 (base 16)	NAGOYA ELECTRIC WORKS CO., LTD 29-1 SHINODA, MIWA-CHO AMA-GUN, AICHI 490-12 JAPAN	001033 (base 16)	ACCESSLAN COMMUNICATIONS, INC. 44 AIRPORT PARKWAY SAN JOSE CA 95110
00-10-25 (hex)	GRAYHILL INC.	00-10-34 (hex)	GNP COMPUTERS
001025 (base 16)	GRAYHILL INC. 561 HILLGROVE AVE. LAGRANGE IL 60525	001034 (base 16)	GNP COMPUTERS 606 EAST HUNTINGTON DR. MONRORIA CA 91016
00-10-26 (hex)	ACCELERATED NETWORKS, INC.	00-10-35 (hex)	ELITEGROUP COMPUTER
001026 (base 16)	ACCELERATED NETWORKS, INC. 31238 VIA COLINAS, UNIT «E» WESTLAKE VILLAGE CA 91362		

company_id	Organization Address
001035 (base 16)	ELITEGROUP COMPUTER SYSTEMS CO., LTD 6F, NO. 88, SEC. 6 CHUNG SHAN N. RD, SHIH LIN TAIPEI, TAIWAN, R.O.C.
00-10-36 (hex)	INTER-TEL INTEGRATED SYSTEMS
001036 (base 16)	INTER-TEL INTEGRATED SYSTEMS 7300 W. BOSTON STREET CHANDLER AZ 85226
00-10-37 (hex)	CYQ'VE TECHNOLOGY CO., LTD.
001037 (base 16)	CYQ'VE TECHNOLOGY CO., LTD. COSMO BLDG. 10F, NO.1-7 SHINJUKU 1-CHOME SHINJUKU-KU, TOKYO 160, JAPAN
00-10-38 (hex)	MICRO RESEARCH INSTITUTE, INC.
001038 (base 16)	MICRO RESEARCH INSTITUTE, INC. 2F, 2L-2-5 MINAMI SHINAGAWA SHINAGAWA-KU TOKYO JAPAN
00-10-39 (hex)	VECTRON SYSTEMS GMBH
001039 (base 16)	VECTRON SYSTEMS GMBH AN DER KLEIMANNBRUECKE 13A 48157 MUENSTER GERMANY
00-10-3A (hex)	DIAMOND NETWORK TECH
00103A (base 16)	DIAMOND NETWORK TECH P.O. BOX 84525 GREENSIDE 2034 SOUTH AFRICA
00-10-3B (hex)	HIPPI NETWORKING FORUM
00103B (base 16)	HIPPI NETWORKING FORUM PO BOX 10173 ALBUQUERQUE NM 87184-0173
00-10-3C (hex)	IC ENSEMBLE, INC.
00103C (base 16)	IC ENSEMBLE, INC. 3255-2 SCOTT BLVD.–STE.#105 SANTA CLARA CA 95054
00-10-3D (hex)	PHASECOM, LTD.
00103D (base 16)	PHASECOM, LTD. P.O. BOX 45017 JERUSALEM 91450 ISRAEL
00-10-3E (hex)	NETSCHOOLS CORPORATION
00103E (base 16)	NETSCHOOLS CORPORATION 2003 LANDINGS DRIVE MOUNTAIN VIEW CA 94043
00-10-3F (hex)	TOLLGRADE COMMUNICATIONS, INC.
00103F (base 16)	TOLLGRADE COMMUNICATIONS, INC. 493 NIXON ROAD CHESWICK PA 15024
00-10-40 (hex)	INTERMEC CORPORATION
001040 (base 16)	INTERMEC CORPORATION 6001 36TH AVE WEST P.O. BOX 4280 EVERETT WA 98203-9280
00-10-41 (hex)	BRISTOL BABCOCK, INC.
001041 (base 16)	BRISTOL BABCOCK, INC. 1100 BUCKINGHAM STREET WATERTOWN CT 06795
00-10-42 (hex)	ALACRITECH
001042 (base 16)	ALACRITECH 888 NORTH FIRST ST. - STE.#302 SAN JOSE CA 95112
00-10-43 (hex)	A2 CORPORATION

company_id	Organization Address
001043 (base 16)	A2 CORPORATION 6-14-11 YUTAKA-CHO SHINAGAWA-KU TOKYO JAPAN
00-10-44 (hex)	INNOLABS CORPORATION
001044 (base 16)	INNOLABS CORPORATION 2F-4, NO. 16, LANE 609 CHUNG-HSIN RD. SEC. 5 SAN-CHUNG CITY, TAIPEI HSIEN TAIWAN, ROC
00-10-45 (hex)	Nortel Networks
001045 (base 16)	Nortel Networks OPTera Solutions Division 340 Terry Fox Drive Kanata, Ontario K2K 3A2
00-10-46 (hex)	ALCORN MCBRIDE INC.
001046 (base 16)	ALCORN MCBRIDE INC. 3300 S. HIAWASSEE #105 ORLANDO FL 32835
00-10-47 (hex)	ECHO ELETRIC CO. LTD.
001047 (base 16)	ECHO ELETRIC CO. LTD. NO.1800 ICHIGAO CHO MIDORI WARD YOKOHAMA CITY JAPAN 225
00-10-48 (hex)	HTRC AUTOMATION, INC.
001048 (base 16)	HTRC AUTOMATION, INC. 285 LAVAL STREET BROMPTONVILLE QUEBEC CANADA, J0B 1H0
00-10-49 (hex)	SHORELINE TELEWORKS, INC.
001049 (base 16)	SHORELINE TELEWORKS, INC. 900 N. SHORELINE BLVD. MOUNTAIN VIEW CA 94043-1931
00-10-4A (hex)	THE PARVUC CORPORATION
00104A (base 16)	THE PARVUC CORPORATION 396 W. IRONWOOD DRIVE SALT LAKE CITY UT 84115
00-10-4B (hex)	3COM CORPORATION
00104B (base 16)	3COM CORPORATION 5400 BAYFRONT PLAZA MAILSTOP: 4220 SANTA CLARA CA 95052
00-10-4C (hex)	COMPUTER ACCESS TECHNOLOGY
00104C (base 16)	COMPUTER ACCESS TECHNOLOGY 2403 WALSH AVE. SANTA CLARA CA 95051-1302
00-10-4D (hex)	SURTEC INDUSTRIES, INC.
00104D (base 16)	SURTEC INDUSTRIES, INC. NO.11, ALLEY 16, LANE 337 TA-TUNG ROAD SEC.1, SHI-CHIH TAIPEI TAIWAN, R.O.C.
00-10-4E (hex)	CEOLOGIC
00104E (base 16)	CEOLOGIC ZA DE PISSALOOP RUE EDOUARD BRANLY 78192 TRAPPES FRANCE
00-10-4F (hex)	STORAGE TECHNOLOGY CORPORATION
00104F (base 16)	STORAGE TECHNOLOGY CORPORATION 2270 SOUTH 88TH STREET LOUISVILLE CO 80028
00-10-50 (hex)	RION CO., LTD.
001050 (base 16)	RION CO., LTD. 3-20-41 HIGASHIMOTOMACHI KOKUBUNJI TOKYO 185 JAPAN

company_id	Organization Address
00-10-51 (hex)	CMICRO CORPORATION
001051 (base 16)	CMICRO CORPORATION 17-20-2 KAMINO-CHO TAKAMATSU-SHI KAGAWA JAPAN 761
00-10-52 (hex)	METTLER-TOLEDO (ALBSTADT) GMBH
001052 (base 16)	METTLER-TOLEDO (ALBSTADT) GMBH P.O. BOX 2 50 D-72423 ALBSTADT GERMANY
00-10-53 (hex)	COMPUTER TECHNOLOGY CORP.
001053 (base 16)	COMPUTER TECHNOLOGY CORP. 50 W. TECHNECENTER DRIVE MILFORD OH 45150
00-10-54 (hex)	CISCO SYSTEMS, INC.
001054 (base 16)	CISCO SYSTEMS, INC. 170 W. TASMAN DRIVE SAN JOSE CA 95134-1706
00-10-55 (hex)	FUJITSU MICROELECTRONICS, INC.
001055 (base 16)	FUJITSU MICROELECTRONICS, INC. 3545 NORTH FIRST STREET SAN JOSE CA 95134-1806
00-10-56 (hex)	SODICK CO., LTD.
001056 (base 16)	SODICK CO., LTD. 3-12-1 NAKAMACHIDAI TSUZUKI-KU, YOKOHAMA KANAGAWA 224 JAPAN
00-10-57 (hex)	Rebel.com, Inc.
001057 (base 16)	Rebel.com, Inc. 150 ISABELLA STREET–STE. 1000 OTTAWA, ONTARIO CANADA K1S 1V7
00-10-58 (hex)	ARROWPOINT COMMUNICATIONS,INC.
001058 (base 16)	ARROWPOINT COMMUNICATIONS,INC. 235 LITTLETON ROAD WESTFORD MA 01886
00-10-59 (hex)	DIABLO RESEARCH CO. LLC
001059 (base 16)	DIABLO RESEARCH CO. LLC 825 STEWART DRIVE SUNNYVALE CA 94086
00-10-5A (hex)	3COM CORPORATION
00105A (base 16)	3COM CORPORATION 5400 BAYFRONT PLAZA MAILSTOP: 4220 SANTA CLARA CA 95052
00-10-5B (hex)	NET INSIGHT AB
00105B (base 16)	NET INSIGHT AB INGENJORSVAGEN 3 SE-11743 STOCKHOLM SWEDEN
00-10-5C (hex)	QUANTUM DESIGNS (H.K.) LTD.
00105C (base 16)	QUANTUM DESIGNS (H.K.) LTD. 5/F., SOMERSET HOUSE TAIKOO PLACE 979 KING'S ROAD, QUARRY BAY HONG KONG
00-10-5D (hex)	DRAGER, BUSINESS UNIT
00105D (base 16)	DRAGER, BUSINESS UNIT MONITORING P.O. BOX 10.100 5680 GA BEST THE NETHERLANDS
00-10-5E (hex)	HEKIMIAN LABORATORIES, INC.
00105E (base 16)	HEKIMIAN LABORATORIES, INC. 15200 OMEGA DRIVE ROCKVILLE MD 20850-3240
00-10-5F (hex)	IN-SNEC

company_id	Organization Address
00105F (base 16)	IN-SNEC 2 RUE DE CAEN 14740 BRETTEVILLE L'ORGUEILLEUSE FRANCE
00-10-60 (hex)	BILLIONTON SYSTEMS, INC.
001060 (base 16)	BILLIONTON SYSTEMS, INC. 3F-1, NO. 8, LANE 99 PU-DING RD. HSIN-CHU TAIWAN, R.O.C.
00-10-61 (hex)	HOSTLINK CORP.
001061 (base 16)	HOSTLINK CORP. 10F-1, NO, 181 SEC.1, TA-TUNG RD. HSI-CHIH, TAIPEI TAIWAN, R.O.C.
00-10-62 (hex)	NX SERVER, ILNC.
001062 (base 16)	NX SERVER, ILNC. 5401 E. LA PALMA AVE. ANAHEIM CA 92807
00-10-63 (hex)	STARGUIDE DIGITAL NETWORKS
001063 (base 16)	STARGUIDE DIGITAL NETWORKS 5754 PACIFIC CENTER BLVD. SAN DIEGO CA 92121
00-10-64 (hex)	DIGITAL EQUIPMENT CORP.
001064 (base 16)	DIGITAL EQUIPMENT CORP. 550 KING ST., LKG1-3/D19 LITTLETON MA 01460-1289
00-10-65 (hex)	RADYNE CORPORATION
001065 (base 16)	RADYNE CORPORATION 5225 S. 37TH STREET PHOENIX AZ 85040
00-10-66 (hex)	ADVANCED CONTROL SYSTEMS, INC.
001066 (base 16)	ADVANCED CONTROL SYSTEMS, INC. 2755 NORTHWOODS PARKWAY NORCROSS GA 30071
00-10-67 (hex)	REDBACK NETWORKS, INC.
001067 (base 16)	REDBACK NETWORKS, INC. 2570 NORTH 1ST STREET SUITE #410 SAN JOSE CA 95131
00-10-68 (hex)	COMOS TELECOM
001068 (base 16)	COMOS TELECOM SAEHAN B/D/, 27-1 SUPYO-DONG CHUNG-GU SEOUL KOREA (100-230)
00-10-69 (hex)	HELIOSS COMMUNICATIONS, INC.
001069 (base 16)	HELIOSS COMMUNICATIONS, INC. 391 TOTTEM POND RD.- STE#303 WALTHAM MA 02154
00-10-6A (hex)	DIGITAL MICROWAVE CORPORATION
00106A (base 16)	DIGITAL MICROWAVE CORPORATION 170 ROSE ORCHARD WAY SAN JOSE CA 95134
00-10-6B (hex)	SONUS NETWORKS, INC.
00106B (base 16)	SONUS NETWORKS, INC. 5 CARLISLE ROAD WESTFORD MA 01886
00-10-6C (hex)	INFRATEC PLUS GMBH
00106C (base 16)	INFRATEC PLUS GMBH WERNER-VON-SIEMENS-STR. 7 64625 BENSHEIM GERMANY
00-10-6D (hex)	INTEGRITY COMMUNICATIONS, INC.
00106D (base 16)	INTEGRITY COMMUNICATIONS, INC. 5001 WEST BROAD ST., STE.#214 RICHMOND VA 23230
00-10-6E (hex)	TADIRAN COM. LTD.

company_id	Organization Address
00106E (base 16)	TADIRAN COM. LTD. 26 HASHOFTIM ST. HOLON 58102 ISRAEL
00-10-6F (hex)	TRENTON TECHNOLOGY INC.
00106F (base 16)	TRENTON TECHNOLOGY INC. 2350 CENTENNIAL DRIVE GAINESVILLE GA 30504
00-10-70 (hex)	CARADON TREND LTD.
001070 (base 16)	CARADON TREND LTD. P.O. BOX 34, HORSHAM WEST SUSSEX, RH12 2YF ENGLAND
00-10-71 (hex)	ADVANET INC.
001071 (base 16)	ADVANET INC. 3-20-8 NODA OKAYAMI 700 JAPAN
00-10-72 (hex)	GVN TECHNOLOGIES, INC.
001072 (base 16)	GVN TECHNOLOGIES, INC. 7421 114TH AVENUE NORTH SUITE #208 LARGO FL 33773
00-10-73 (hex)	TECHNOBOX, INC.
001073 (base 16)	TECHNOBOX, INC. 12-B THE ELLIPSE - STE. #300 MT. LAUREL NJ 08054
00-10-74 (hex)	ATEN INTERNATIONAL CO., LTD.
001074 (base 16)	ATEN INTERNATIONAL CO., LTD. 12F, NO.101, SUNG CHIANG RD. TAIPEI, 10428 TAIWAN, R.O.C.
00-10-75 (hex)	CREATIVE DESIGN SOLUTIONS,INC.
001075 (base 16)	CREATIVE DESIGN SOLUTIONS,INC. 3350 SCOTT BLVD.–BLDG. #9 SANTA CLARA CA 95054
00-10-76 (hex)	EUREM GMBH
001076 (base 16)	EUREM GMBH JULICHER STR. 338B D-52070 AACHEN GERMANY
00-10-77 (hex)	SAF DRIVE SYSTEMS, LTD.
001077 (base 16)	SAF DRIVE SYSTEMS, LTD. 88 ARDELT AVE. KITCHENER, ONTARIO CANADA N2C 2C9
00-10-78 (hex)	NUERA COMMUNICATIONS, INC.
001078 (base 16)	NUERA COMMUNICATIONS, INC. 10445 PACIFIC CENTER COURT SAN DIEGO CA 92121
00-10-79 (hex)	CISCO SYSTEMS, INC.
001079 (base 16)	CISCO SYSTEMS, INC. 170 W. TASMAN DR. SAN JOSE CA 95134-1706
00-10-7A (hex)	AMBICOM, INC.
00107A (base 16)	AMBICOM, INC. 2450 SCOTT BLVD., #305 SANTA CLARA CA 95050
00-10-7B (hex)	CISCO SYSTEMS, INC.
00107B (base 16)	CISCO SYSTEMS, INC. 170 W. TASMAN DR.-SJA-2 SAN JOSE CA 95134-1706
00-10-7C (hex)	P-COM, INC.
00107C (base 16)	P-COM, INC. 3175 S. WINCHESTER BLVD. CAMPBELL CA 95008
00-10-7D (hex)	AURORA COMMUNICATIONS, LTD.
00107D (base 16)	AURORA COMMUNICATIONS, LTD. P.O. BOX 1942 MACQUARIE CENTRE, NORTH RYDE NSW 2113 AUSTRALIA
00-10-7E (hex)	BACHMANN ELECTRONIC GMBH

company_id	Organization Address
00107E (base 16)	BACHMANN ELECTRONIC GMBH KREUZAECKERWEG 33 A 6806 FELDKIRCH AUSTRIA
00-10-7F (hex)	CRESTRON ELECTRONICS, INC.
00107F (base 16)	CRESTRON ELECTRONICS, INC. 101 BROADWAY CRESSKILL NJ 07626
00-10-80 (hex)	METAWAVE COMMUNICATIONS
001080 (base 16)	METAWAVE COMMUNICATIONS 8700 148TH AVENUE N.E. REDMOND WA 98052
00-10-81 (hex)	DPS, INC.
001081 (base 16)	DPS, INC. 4922 EAST YALE AVENUE FRESNO CA 93727
00-10-82 (hex)	JNA TELECOMMUNICATIONS LIMITED
001082 (base 16)	JNA TELECOMMUNICATIONS LIMITED 16 SMITH ST, CHATSWOOD NSW 2067 AUSTRALIA
00-10-83 (hex)	HEWLETT-PACKARD COMPANY
001083 (base 16)	HEWLETT-PACKARD COMPANY MAIL STOP 42LE 110000 WOLFE ROAD CUPERTINO CA 95014
00-10-84 (hex)	K-BOT COMMUNICATIONS
001084 (base 16)	K-BOT COMMUNICATIONS P.O. BOX 410 NORTON MA 02766
00-10-85 (hex)	POLARIS COMMUNICATIONS, INC.
001085 (base 16)	POLARIS COMMUNICATIONS, INC. 10200 SW ALLEN BLVD. BEAVERTON OR 97005
00-10-86 (hex)	ATTO TECHNOLOGY, INC.
001086 (base 16)	ATTO TECHNOLOGY, INC. 40 HAZELWOOD DRIVE AMHERST NY 14228
00-10-87 (hex)	Xstreamis PLC
001087 (base 16)	Xstreamis PLC OXFORD SCIENCE PARK G10. 2 MAGDALEN CENTRE ROBERT ROBINSON AVE OXFORD 0X4 4GA ENGLAND
00-10-88 (hex)	AMERICAN NETWORKS INC.
001088 (base 16)	AMERICAN NETWORKS INC. 6800 ORANGETHORPE AVE. #A BUENA PARK CA 90620
00-10-89 (hex)	WEBSONIC
001089 (base 16)	WEBSONIC 3466 EDWARD AVE. SANTA CLARA CA 95054
00-10-8A (hex)	TERALOGIC, INC.
00108A (base 16)	TERALOGIC, INC. 707 CALIFORNIA STREET MOUNTAIN VIEW CA 94041
00-10-8B (hex)	LASERANIMATION SOLLINGER GMBH
00108B (base 16)	LASERANIMATION SOLLINGER GMBH CRELLESTR. 19/20 D 10827 BERLIN GERMANY
00-10-8C (hex)	FUJITSU TELECOMMUNICATIONS
00108C (base 16)	FUJITSU TELECOMMUNICATIONS EUROPE, LTD. SOLIHULL PARKWAY BIRMINGHAM BUSINESS PARK BIRMINGHAM B37 7YU, ENGLAND
00-10-8D (hex)	JOHNSON CONTROLS, INC.

company_id	Organization Address
00108D (base 16)	JOHNSON CONTROLS, INC. 507 E. MICHIGAN ST. MILWAUKEE WI 53202
00-10-8E (hex)	HUGH SYMONS CONCEPT
00108E (base 16)	HUGH SYMONS CONCEPT TECHNOLOGIES, LTD. ALDER HILLS PARK 16 ALDER HILLS, POOLE, DORSET BH12 4AR UNITED KINGDOM
00-10-8F (hex)	RAPTOR SYSTEMS
00108F (base 16)	RAPTOR SYSTEMS 69 HICKORY AVE. WALTHAM MA 02154
00-10-90 (hex)	CIMETRICS, INC.
001090 (base 16)	CIMETRICS, INC. 55 TEMPLE PLACE BOSTON MA 02111
00-10-91 (hex)	NO WIRES NEEDED BV
001091 (base 16)	NO WIRES NEEDED BV P.O. BOX 343 3720 AH BILTHOVEN THE NETHERLANDS
00-10-92 (hex)	NETCORE INC.
001092 (base 16)	NETCORE INC. 12F-2, 537, SEC.2 KUANG-FU ROAD, HSINCHU TAIWAN
00-10-93 (hex)	CMS COMPUTERS, LTD.
001093 (base 16)	CMS COMPUTERS, LTD. 201 ARCADIA NARIMAN POINT MUMBAI 400 0021 INDIA
00-10-94 (hex)	ADTECH, INC.
001094 (base 16)	ADTECH, INC. 3465 WAIALAE AVENUE SUITE #200 HONOLULU HI 96816
00-10-95 (hex)	THOMSON CONSUMER ELECTRONICS
001095 (base 16)	THOMSON CONSUMER ELECTRONICS 101 W. 103RD STREET MAIL STOP INH 600 INDIANAPOLIS IN 46290-1102
00-10-96 (hex)	TRACEWELL SYSTEMS, INC.
001096 (base 16)	TRACEWELL SYSTEMS, INC. 567 ENTERPRISE DRIVE WESTERVILLE OH 43081
00-10-97 (hex)	WINNET METROPOLITAN
001097 (base 16)	WINNET METROPOLITAN COMMUNICATIONS SYSTEMS, INC. 661 EAST ARQUES AVE. SUNNYVALE CA 94086
00-10-98 (hex)	STARNET TECHNOLOGIES, INC.
001098 (base 16)	STARNET TECHNOLOGIES, INC. 2210 O'TOOLE AVE. SAN JOSE CA 95131
00-10-99 (hex)	INNOMEDIA, INC.
001099 (base 16)	INNOMEDIA, INC. 4800 GREAT AMERICA PARKWAY SUITE #400 SANTA CLARA CA 95054
00-10-9A (hex)	NETLINE
00109A (base 16)	NETLINE 7, RUE DE BIEVRES 92140 CLAMART FRANCE
00-10-9B (hex)	VIXEL CORPORATION
00109B (base 16)	VIXEL CORPORATION 11911 NORTHCREEK PKWY SO. SUITE #100 BOTHELL WA 98011

company_id	Organization Address
00-10-9C (hex)	M-SYSTEM CO., LTD.
00109C (base 16)	M-SYSTEM CO., LTD. 1-1-25 SHIN URASHIMA CHOU KANAGAWA-KU YOKOHAMA 221 JAPAN
00-10-9D (hex)	CLARINET SYSTEMS, INC.
00109D (base 16)	CLARINET SYSTEMS, INC. 1415 KOLL CIRCLE #101 SAN JOSE CA 95112
00-10-9E (hex)	AWARE, INC.
00109E (base 16)	AWARE, INC. ONE OAK PARK BEDFORD MA 01730
00-10-9F (hex)	PAVO, INC.
00109F (base 16)	PAVO, INC. 95 YESLER WAY SEATTLE WA 98104
00-10-A0 (hex)	INNOVEX TECHNOLOGIES, INC.
0010A0 (base 16)	INNOVEX TECHNOLOGIES, INC. KEYSTONE COMMONS 526 BRADDOCK AVE. TURTLE CREEK PA 15145
00-10-A1 (hex)	KENDIN SEMICONDUCTOR, INC.
0010A1 (base 16)	KENDIN SEMICONDUCTOR, INC. 1550 S. BASCOM AVE., STE. #250 CAMPBELL CA 95008
00-10-A2 (hex)	TNS
0010A2 (base 16)	TNS 800 Third Street, Suite B100 HERNDON VA 20170
00-10-A3 (hex)	OMNITRONIX, INC.
0010A3 (base 16)	OMNITRONIX, INC. 760 HARRISON STREET SEATTLE WA 98109
00-10-A4 (hex)	XIRCOM
0010A4 (base 16)	XIRCOM 2300 CORPORATE CENTER DR. THOUSAND OAKS CA 91320
00-10-A5 (hex)	OXFORD INSTRUMENTS
0010A5 (base 16)	OXFORD INSTRUMENTS INDUSTRIAL ANALYSIS GROUP 19/20 NUFFIELD WAY ABINGDON, OXON, OX14 1TX ENGLAND
00-10-A6 (hex)	CISCO SYSTEMS, INC.
0010A6 (base 16)	CISCO SYSTEMS, INC. 170 W. TASMAN DRIVE SAN JOSE CA 95134-1706
00-10-A7 (hex)	UNEX TECHNOLOGY CORPORATION
0010A7 (base 16)	UNEX TECHNOLOGY CORPORATION 8F-5, #130, SZE WEI RD., HSINCHU TAIWAN, R.O.C.
00-10-A8 (hex)	RELIANCE COMPUTER CORP.
0010A8 (base 16)	RELIANCE COMPUTER CORP. 3032 BUNKER HILL LANE SUITE 201 SANTA CLARA CA 95054
00-10-A9 (hex)	ADHOC TECHNOLOGIES
0010A9 (base 16)	ADHOC TECHNOLOGIES 1150 FIRST STREET SAN JOSE CA 95112
00-10-AA (hex)	MEDIA4, INC.
0010AA (base 16)	MEDIA4, INC. 250 14TH ST. NW - STE #4002 ATLANTA GA 30318
00-10-AB (hex)	KOITO INDUSTRIES, LTD.

company_id	Organization Address
0010AB (base 16)	KOITO INDUSTRIES, LTD. 100 MAEDA-CHO, TOTSUKA-KU YOKOHAMA 244 JAPAN
00-10-AC (hex)	IMCI TECHNOLOGIES
0010AC (base 16)	IMCI TECHNOLOGIES 8401 OLD COURT HOUSE RD SUITE #200 VIENNA VA 22182
00-10-AD (hex)	SOFTRONICS USB, INC.
0010AD (base 16)	SOFTRONICS USB, INC. 5085 LIST DRIVE COLORADO SPRINGS CO 80919
00-10-AE (hex)	SHINKO ELECTRIC INDUSTRIES CO.
0010AE (base 16)	SHINKO ELECTRIC INDUSTRIES CO. 80 OSHIMADA-MACHI NAGANO-SHI 381-22 JAPAN
00-10-AF (hex)	TAC SYSTEMS, INC.
0010AF (base 16)	TAC SYSTEMS, INC. 1035 PUTMAN DRIVE–STE. A HUNTSVILLE AL 35816-2271
00-10-B0 (hex)	MERIDIAN TECHNOLOGY CORP.
0010B0 (base 16)	MERIDIAN TECHNOLOGY CORP. 11 MCBRIDE CORP. CENTER DR. CHESTERFIELD MD 63005
00-10-B1 (hex)	FOR-A CO., LTD.
0010B1 (base 16)	FOR-A CO., LTD. 2-3-3 OOSAKU SAKURA CITY, CHIBA PREF. 285 JAPAN
00-10-B2 (hex)	COACTIVE AESTHETICS
0010B2 (base 16)	COACTIVE AESTHETICS 4000 BRIDGEWAY - STE. #303 SAUSALITA CA 94965
00-10-B3 (hex)	NOKIA MULTIMEDIA TERMINALS
0010B3 (base 16)	NOKIA MULTIMEDIA TERMINALS NOKIA HOME COMMUNICATIONS DISKETTGATAN 11 SE-583 35 LINKOPING SWEDEN
00-10-B4 (hex)	ATMOSPHERE NETWORKS
0010B4 (base 16)	ATMOSPHERE NETWORKS 10460 BANDLEY DRIVE CUPERTINO CA 95014
00-10-B5 (hex)	ACCTON TECHNOLOGY CORPORATION
0010B5 (base 16)	ACCTON TECHNOLOGY CORPORATION NO.1, CREATION RD. III SCIENCE-BASED INDUSTRIAL PARK HSINCHU 300 TAIWAN, R.O.C.
00-10-B6 (hex)	ENTRATA COMMUNICATIONS CORP.
0010B6 (base 16)	ENTRATA COMMUNICATIONS CORP. 574 HERITAGE RD. SOUTHBURY CT 06488
00-10-B7 (hex)	COYOTE TECHNOLOGIES, LLC
0010B7 (base 16)	COYOTE TECHNOLOGIES, LLC 4360 PARK TERRACE DRIVE WESTLAKE VILLAGE CA 91361
00-10-B8 (hex)	ISHIGAKI COMPUTER SYSTEM CO.
0010B8 (base 16)	ISHIGAKI COMPUTER SYSTEM CO. 1-1-1, KYOBASHI, CHUO-KU TOKYO JAPAN
00-10-B9 (hex)	MAXTOR CORP.
0010B9 (base 16)	MAXTOR CORP. 2190 MILLER DRIVE LONGMONT CO 80501-6744
00-10-BA (hex)	MARTINHO-DAVIS SYSTEMS, INC.

company_id	Organization Address
0010BA (base 16)	MARTINHO-DAVIS SYSTEMS, INC. 1260 OLD INNES ROAD OTTAWA, ONTARIO CANADA K1B 3V3
00-10-BB (hex)	DATA & INFORMATION TECHNOLOGY
0010BB (base 16)	DATA & INFORMATION TECHNOLOGY TECHNOLOGY HOUSE 1 NORMANTON LANE BOTTESFORD, NOTTINGHAM NG13 0EL UNITED KINGDOM
00-10-BC (hex)	APTIS COMMUNICATIONS, INC.
0010BC (base 16)	APTIS COMMUNICATIONS, INC. 11 ELIZABETH DRIVE CHELMSFORD MA 01824
00-10-BD (hex)	THE TELECOMMUNICATION
0010BD (base 16)	THE TELECOMMUNICATION TECHNOLOGY COMMITTEE 1-2-11, HAMAMATSU-CHO MINATO-KU, TOKYO 105 JAPAN
00-10-BE (hex)	TELEXIS CORP.
0010BE (base 16)	TELEXIS CORP. 2427 HOLLY LANE OTTAWA, ONTARIO CANADA K1V 7P2
00-10-BF (hex)	INTER AIR WIRELESS
0010BF (base 16)	INTER AIR WIRELESS 485 CAYUGA ROAD BUFFALO NY 14225-0222
00-10-C0 (hex)	ARMA, INC.
0010C0 (base 16)	ARMA, INC. 7887 DUNBROOK ROAD–STE. "A" SAN DIEGO CA 92126
00-10-C1 (hex)	OI ELECTRIC CO., LTD.
0010C1 (base 16)	OI ELECTRIC CO., LTD. 7-3-16 KIKUNA KOHOKU-KU YOKOHAMA 222 JAPAN
00-10-C2 (hex)	WILLNET, INC.
0010C2 (base 16)	WILLNET, INC. JOWA-TAKANAWA BLDG. 8F TAKANAWA 1-5-4 MINATO-KU, TOKYO JAPAN
00-10-C3 (hex)	CSI-CONTROL SYSTEMS
0010C3 (base 16)	CSI-CONTROL SYSTEMS INTERNATIONAL POB 59469 DALLAS TX 75229
00-10-C4 (hex)	MEDIA LINKS CO., LTD.
0010C4 (base 16)	MEDIA LINKS CO., LTD. KSP EAST BLDG. 604 SAKADO 3-2-1, TAKATSU-KU KAWASAKI-SHI, KANAGAWA-KEN 214 JAPAN
00-10-C5 (hex)	PROTOCOL TECHNOLOGIES, INC.
0010C5 (base 16)	PROTOCOL TECHNOLOGIES, INC. 4 FIRST STREET BRIDGEWATER MA 02324
00-10-C6 (hex)	USI
0010C6 (base 16)	USI 141, LANE 351, TAIPING RD. SEC.1, TSAO TUEN, NAN-TOU TAIWAN
00-10-C7 (hex)	DATA TRANSMISSION NETWORK
0010C7 (base 16)	DATA TRANSMISSION NETWORK 9110 W. DODGE RD. - STE.#200 OMAHA NE 68114
00-10-C8 (hex)	COMMUNICATIONS ELECTRONICS

company_id	Organization Address
0010C8 (base 16)	COMMUNICATIONS ELECTRONICS SECURITY GROUP 10/4W22 FIDDLERS GREEN LANE BENHALL, CHELTENHAM, GLOS. GL52 5AJ, ENGLAND
00-10-C9 (hex)	MITSUBISHI ELECTRONICS
0010C9 (base 16)	MITSUBISHI ELECTRONICS LOGISTIC SUPPORT CO. SHONAN WKS 730-11, KAMIMACHIYA KAMAKURA-CITY, KANAGAWA 247 JAPAN
00-10-CA (hex)	INTEGRAL ACCESS
0010CA (base 16)	INTEGRAL ACCESS 2021 MIDWEST ROAD, STE #203 OAKBROOK IL 60521
00-10-CB (hex)	FACIT K.K.
0010CB (base 16)	FACIT K.K. HIMEI NIHOMBASHI BLDG. 3F 12-3-NIHOMBASHI-KOBUNACHO CHUO-KU, TOKYO 103 JAPAN
00-10-CC (hex)	CLP COMPUTER LOGISTIK
0010CC (base 16)	CLP COMPUTER LOGISTIK PLANUNG GMBH BASSERMANNSTR. 21 D-81245 MUENCHEN GERMANY
00-10-CD (hex)	INTERFACE CONCEPT
0010CD (base 16)	INTERFACE CONCEPT 3 VENELLE DE KERGOS 29000 QUIMPER FRANCE
00-10-CE (hex)	VOLAMP, LTD.
0010CE (base 16)	VOLAMP, LTD. UNIT 3 RIVERSIDE BUSINESS PARK DOGFLUD WAY, FARNHAM, SURREY ENGLAND
00-10-CF (hex)	FIBERLANE COMMUNICATIONS
0010CF (base 16)	FIBERLANE COMMUNICATIONS 1318 REDWOOD WAY, #200 PETALUMA CA 94954
00-10-D0 (hex)	WITCOM, LTD.
0010D0 (base 16)	WITCOM, LTD. P.O.B. 2250 HAIFA 31021 ISRAEL
00-10-D1 (hex)	BLAZENET, INC.
0010D1 (base 16)	BLAZENET, INC. 4 MECHANIC ST.- STE#212 NATICK MA 01760
00-10-D2 (hex)	NITTO TSUSHINKI CO., LTD
0010D2 (base 16)	NITTO TSUSHINKI CO., LTD 7-27-11, TODOROKI, SETAGAYA-KU TOKYO 151 JAPAN
00-10-D3 (hex)	GRIPS ELECTRONIC GMBH
0010D3 (base 16)	GRIPS ELECTRONIC GMBH NIESENBERGERGASSE 37 A-8020 GRAZ AUSTRIA
00-10-D4 (hex)	STORAGE COMPUTER CORPORATION
0010D4 (base 16)	STORAGE COMPUTER CORPORATION 11 RIVERSIDE STREET NASHUA NH 03062
00-10-D5 (hex)	IMASDE CANARIAS, S.A.
0010D5 (base 16)	IMASDE CANARIAS, S.A. URB. EL CEBADAL C/DR. JUAN DGUEZ.PEREZ, 39-2 35008 LAS PALMAS G.C. SPAIN

company_id	Organization Address
00-10-D6 (hex)	ITT A/CD
0010D6 (base 16)	ITT A/CD DEPT. 8521 100 KINGSLAND ROAD CLIFTON NJ 07014
00-10-D7 (hex)	ARGOSY RESEARCH INC.
0010D7 (base 16)	ARGOSY RESEARCH INC. NO. 44, LANE 411, CHUNG HUA RD SEC.4, HSINCHU TAIWAN, R.O.C.
00-10-D8 (hex)	CALISTA
0010D8 (base 16)	CALISTA 98 HIGH STREET, THAME OXFORDSHIRE OX9 3EH ENGLAND
00-10-D9 (hex)	IBM JAPAN, FUJISAWA MT+D
0010D9 (base 16)	IBM JAPAN, FUJISAWA MT+D KIRIHARA-CHO 1, FUJISAWA CITY KANAGAWA 252 JAPAN
00-10-DA (hex)	MOTION ENGINEERING, INC.
0010DA (base 16)	MOTION ENGINEERING, INC. 33 S. LA PATERA LN SANTA BARBARA CA 93117
00-10-DB (hex)	NETSCREEN TECHNOLOGIES, INC.
0010DB (base 16)	NETSCREEN TECHNOLOGIES, INC. 4699 OLD IRONSIDES DRIVE-#300 SANTA CLARA CA 95054
00-10-DC (hex)	MICRO-STAR INTERNATIONAL
0010DC (base 16)	MICRO-STAR INTERNATIONAL CO., LTD. NO. 69, LI-DE ST., JUNG-HE CITY TAIPEI HSIEN TAIWAN, R.O.C.
00-10-DD (hex)	ENABLE SEMICONDUCTOR, INC.
0010DD (base 16)	ENABLE SEMICONDUCTOR, INC. 1740 TECHNOLOGY DRIVE SUITE #110 SAN JOSE CA 95110
00-10-DE (hex)	INTERNATIONAL DATACASTING
0010DE (base 16)	INTERNATIONAL DATACASTING CORPORATION 2680 QUEENSVIEW DRIVE OTTAWA, ONTARIO CANADA K2B 8H6
00-10-DF (hex)	RISE COMPUTER INC.
0010DF (base 16)	RISE COMPUTER INC. 9F, NO. 306-3, TATUNG RD. SEC. 1, HSI CHIH, TAIPEI HSIEN TAIWAN, R.O.C.
00-10-E0 (hex)	COBALT MICROSERVER, INC.
0010E0 (base 16)	COBALT MICROSERVER, INC. 411 CLYDE AVENUE MT. VIEW CA 94043
00-10-E1 (hex)	S.I. TECH, INC.
0010E1 (base 16)	S.I. TECH, INC. P.O. BOX 609 GENEVA IL 60134
00-10-E2 (hex)	ARRAYCOMM, INC.
0010E2 (base 16)	ARRAYCOMM, INC. 3141 ZANKER ROAD SAN JOSE CA 95134
00-10-E3 (hex)	COMPAQ COMPUTER CORPORATION
0010E3 (base 16)	COMPAQ COMPUTER CORPORATION 20555 S.H. 249 HOUSTON TX 77070
00-10-E4 (hex)	NSI CORPORATION
0010E4 (base 16)	NSI CORPORATION P.O. BOX 635 WILSONVILLE OR 97070

company_id	Organization Address
00-10-E5 (hex)	SOLECTRON TEXAS
0010E5 (base 16)	SOLECTRON TEXAS 12455 RESEARCH BLVD. M/S 2205 AUSTIN TX 78759
00-10-E6 (hex)	APPLIED INTELLIGENT
0010E6 (base 16)	APPLIED INTELLIGENT SYSTEMS, INC. 3923 RANCHERO DRIVE ANN ARBOR MI 48108
00-10-E7 (hex)	BREEZECOM
0010E7 (base 16)	BREEZECOM ATIDIM TECHNOLOGICAL PARK BLDG. 1, P.O. BOX 13139 TEL-AVIV ISRAEL
00-10-E8 (hex)	TELOCITY, INCORPORATED
0010E8 (base 16)	TELOCITY, INCORPORATED 992 SOUTH DE ANZA BLVD SAN JOSE CA 95129
00-10-E9 (hex)	RAIDTEC LTD.
0010E9 (base 16)	RAIDTEC LTD. CASTLE ROAD LITTLE ISLAND INDUST'L ESTATE LITTLE ISLAND CO. CORK IRELAND
00-10-EA (hex)	ADEPT TECHNOLOGY
0010EA (base 16)	ADEPT TECHNOLOGY 150 ROSE ORCHARD WAY SAN JOSE CA 95134
00-10-EB (hex)	SELSIUS SYSTEMS, ILNC.
0010EB (base 16)	SELSIUS SYSTEMS, ILNC. 5057 KELLER SPRINGS RD. DALLAS TX 75248
00-10-EC (hex)	RPCG, LLC
0010EC (base 16)	RPCG, LLC 749 MINDER ROAD HIGHLAND HTS OH 44143-2117
00-10-ED (hex)	SUNDANCE TECHNOLOGY, INC.
0010ED (base 16)	SUNDANCE TECHNOLOGY, INC. 20111 STEVENS CREEK BLVD. SUITE #138 CUPERTINO CA 95014
00-10-EE (hex)	CTI PRODUCTS, INC.
0010EE (base 16)	CTI PRODUCTS, INC. 1211 W. SHARON RD. CINCINNATI OH 45240
00-10-EF (hex)	DB NETWORKS, INC.
0010EF (base 16)	DB NETWORKS, INC. 2F., NO.29 TZU-CHIANG ST., TU-CHENG TAIPEI TAIWAN R.O.C.
00-10-F0 (hex)	RITTAL-WERK RUDOLF LOH
0010F0 (base 16)	RITTAL-WERK RUDOLF LOH GMBH & CO. KG AUF DEM STUTZELBERT D-35745 HERBORN GERMANY
00-10-F1 (hex)	I-O CORPORATION
0010F1 (base 16)	I-O CORPORATION 2256 SOUTH 3600 WEST SALT LAKE CITY UT 84119
00-10-F2 (hex)	ANTEC
0010F2 (base 16)	ANTEC 4920 AVALON RIDGE PKWY SUITE #600 NORCROSS GA 30071
00-10-F3 (hex)	NEXCOM INTERNATIONAL CO., LTD.
0010F3 (base 16)	NEXCOM INTERNATIONAL CO., LTD. 10F-13, NO.16, LANE 609 CHUNG-HSIN RD., SEC. 5 SAN-CHUNG CITY, TAIPEI HSIEN TAIWAN, R.O.C.
00-10-F4 (hex)	VERTICAL NETWORKS, INC.
0010F4 (base 16)	VERTICAL NETWORKS, INC. 1148 EAST ARQUES AVE. SUNNYVALE CA 94086
00-10-F5 (hex)	AMHERST SYSTEMS, INC.
0010F5 (base 16)	AMHERST SYSTEMS, INC. 30 WILSON ROAD BUFFALO NY 14221
00-10-F6 (hex)	CISCO SYSTEMS, INC.
0010F6 (base 16)	CISCO SYSTEMS, INC. 170 W. TASMAN DRIVE SAN JOSE CA 95134-1706
00-10-F7 (hex)	IRIICHI TECHNOLOGIES
0010F7 (base 16)	IRIICHI TECHNOLOGIES INCORPORATION 1-26-7 CHUO, NAKANA-KU TOKYO 164 JAPAN
00-10-F8 (hex)	KENWOOD TMI CORPORATION
0010F8 (base 16)	KENWOOD TMI CORPORATION 1-16-2, HAKUSAN, MIDORI-KU YOKOHAMA-SHI, KANAGAWA JAPAN
00-10-F9 (hex)	UNIQUE SYSTEMS, INC.
0010F9 (base 16)	UNIQUE SYSTEMS, INC. 181 DON PARK RD MARKHAM, ONTARIO CANADA L3R 1C2
00-10-FA (hex)	ZAYANTE, INC.
0010FA (base 16)	ZAYANTE, INC. 269 MT. HERMON RD. #111 SCOTTS VALLEY CA 95066
00-10-FB (hex)	ZIDA TECHNOLOGIES LIMITED
0010FB (base 16)	ZIDA TECHNOLOGIES LIMITED 8/F BLOCK A GOODVIEW INDUSTRIAL BUILDING KIN FAT STREET TMTL 213 TUEN MUN NT, HONG KONG
00-10-FC (hex)	BROADBAND NETWORKS, INC.
0010FC (base 16)	BROADBAND NETWORKS, INC. 37 STEVENSON ROAD WINNIPEG, MANITOBA CANADA R3H 0H9
00-10-FD (hex)	COCOM A/S
0010FD (base 16)	COCOM A/S TELETONVEJ 8 DK 2860 SOBORG DENMARK
00-10-FE (hex)	DIGITAL EQUIPMENT CORPORATION
0010FE (base 16)	DIGITAL EQUIPMENT CORPORATION 301 ROCKRIMMON BLVD, SOUTH M/S CXO1-2/N26 COLORADO SPRINGS CO 80919
00-10-FF (hex)	CISCO SYSTEMS, INC.
0010FF (base 16)	CISCO SYSTEMS, INC. 170 W. TASMAN DRIVE SAN JOSE CA 95134-1706
00-1C-7C (hex)	PERQ SYSTEMS CORPORATION
001C7C (base 16)	PERQ SYSTEMS CORPORATION 2600 LIBERTY AVENUE P.O. BOX 2600 PITTSBURGH PA 15230
00-20-00 (hex)	LEXMARK INTERNATIONAL, INC.

765

company_id	Organization Address
002000 (base 16)	LEXMARK INTERNATIONAL, INC. 740 NEW CIRCLE ROAD BLDG. 35 LEXINGTON KY 40550
00-20-01 (hex)	DSP SOLUTIONS, INC.
002001 (base 16)	DSP SOLUTIONS, INC. 2464 EMBARCADERO WAY PALO ALTO CA 94303
00-20-02 (hex)	SERITECH ENTERPRISE CO., LTD.
002002 (base 16)	SERITECH ENTERPRISE CO., LTD. FL. 182, NO. 531-1 CHUNG CHENG ROAD HSIN TIEN CITY TAIWAN, R.O.C.
00-20-03 (hex)	PIXEL POWER LTD.
002003 (base 16)	PIXEL POWER LTD. UNIT 1, TRINITY HALL FARM INDUSTRIAL ESTATE, NUFFIELD RD CAMBRIDGE, CB4 1TG UNITED KINGDOM
00-20-04 (hex)	YAMATAKE-HONEYWELL CO., LTD.
002004 (base 16)	YAMATAKE-HONEYWELL CO., LTD. 54 SUZUKAWA, ISEHARA KANAGAWA 259-11 JAPAN
00-20-05 (hex)	SIMPLE TECHNOLOGY
002005 (base 16)	SIMPLE TECHNOLOGY 3001 DAIMLER ROAD SANTA ANA CA 92705
00-20-06 (hex)	GARRETT COMMUNICATIONS, INC.
002006 (base 16)	GARRETT COMMUNICATIONS, INC. 48531 WARMSPRINGS BLVD. FREMONT CA 94539
00-20-07 (hex)	SFA, INC.
002007 (base 16)	SFA, INC. 1401 MCCORMICK DRIVE LANDOVER MD 20785
00-20-08 (hex)	CABLE & COMPUTER TECHNOLOGY
002008 (base 16)	CABLE & COMPUTER TECHNOLOGY 1555 SO. SINCLAIR STREET ANAHEIM CA 92806
00-20-09 (hex)	PACKARD BELL ELEC., INC.
002009 (base 16)	PACKARD BELL ELEC., INC. 9425 CANOGA AVENUE CHATSWORTH CA 913211
00-20-0A (hex)	SOURCE-COMM CORP.
00200A (base 16)	SOURCE-COMM CORP. 25020 W. AVENUE STANFORD UNIT 180 VALENCIA CA 91355
00-20-0B (hex)	OCTAGON SYSTEMS CORP.
00200B (base 16)	OCTAGON SYSTEMS CORP. 6510 W. 91ST AVENUE WESTMINSTER CO 80030
00-20-0C (hex)	ADASTRA SYSTEMS CORP.
00200C (base 16)	ADASTRA SYSTEMS CORP. 28310 INDUSTRIAL BLVD.-STE-K HAYWARD CA 94545
00-20-0D (hex)	CARL ZEISS
00200D (base 16)	CARL ZEISS POSTFACH 1380 ABT. 1-EL 73444 OBERKOCHEN GERMANY
00-20-0E (hex)	SATELLITE TECHNOLOGY MGMT, INC
00200E (base 16)	SATELLITE TECHNOLOGY MGMT, INC 3530 HYLAND AVENUE COSTA MESA CA 92626
00-20-0F (hex)	TANBAC CO., LTD.

company_id	Organization Address
00200F (base 16)	TANBAC CO., LTD. SAKURAI DAI 2 BG 27-4 IRIYA 1-CHOME TAITO-KU TOKYO 110 JAPAN
00-20-10 (hex)	JEOL SYSTEM TECHNOLOGY CO. LTD
002010 (base 16)	JEOL SYSTEM TECHNOLOGY CO. LTD 10TH-2 SHINJUKU-MITSUI BLDG. 3-2-11 NISHI SHINJUKU SINJUKU-KU, TOKYO 160 JAPAN
00-20-11 (hex)	CANOPUS CO., LTD.
002011 (base 16)	CANOPUS CO., LTD. KOBE HI-TECH PARK 1-2-2 MUROTANI NISHI-KU KOBE 651-22 JAPAN
00-20-12 (hex)	CAMTRONICS MEDICAL SYSTEMS
002012 (base 16)	CAMTRONICS MEDICAL SYSTEMS P.O. BOX 950 HARTLAND WI 53029
00-20-13 (hex)	DIVERSIFIED TECHNOLOGY, INC.
002013 (base 16)	DIVERSIFIED TECHNOLOGY, INC. 112 E. STATE STREET RIDGELAND MS 39157
00-20-14 (hex)	GLOBAL VIEW CO., LTD.
002014 (base 16)	GLOBAL VIEW CO., LTD. 4F, NO. 23, LANE 306 FU-TEH 1 RD. HSI-CHIH, TAIPEI, HSIEN TAIWAN R.O.C.
00-20-15 (hex)	ACTIS COMPUTER SA
002015 (base 16)	ACTIS COMPUTER SA 16 CHEMIN DES AULX 1228 PLAN LES OVATES SWITZERLAND
00-20-16 (hex)	SHOWA ELECTRIC WIRE & CABLE CO
002016 (base 16)	SHOWA ELECTRIC WIRE & CABLE CO NO. 20-25, SEISHIN 8-CHOME SAGAMIHARA, KANAGAWA 229 JAPAN
00-20-17 (hex)	ORBOTECH
002017 (base 16)	ORBOTECH INDUSTRIAL ZONE P.O. BOX 215 70651 YAVNE ISRAEL
00-20-18 (hex)	CIS TECHNOLOGY INC.
002018 (base 16)	CIS TECHNOLOGY INC. FL. 9-1, NO. 94, PAO CHUNG RD. HSIN TIEN CITY TAIPEI HSIEN TAIWAN, R.O.C.
00-20-19 (hex)	OHLER GMBH
002019 (base 16)	OHLER GMBH MAYBACHSTRASE 30 71332 WAIBLINGEN GERMANY
00-20-1A (hex)	N-BASE SWITCH COMMUNICATIONS
00201A (base 16)	N-BASE SWITCH COMMUNICATIONS 8943 FULLBRIGHT AVE. CHATSWORTH CA 91311
00-20-1B (hex)	NORTHERN TELECOM/NETWORK
00201B (base 16)	NORTHERN TELECOM/NETWORK SYSTEMS CORPORATION 250 SIDNEY STREET BELLEVILLE, ONTARIO CANADA, K8N 5B7
00-20-1C (hex)	EXCEL, INC.
00201C (base 16)	EXCEL, INC. 355 OLD PLYMOUTH ROAD SAGAMORE BEACH MA 02562

company_id	Organization / Address
00-20-1D (hex)	KATANA PRODUCTS
00201D (base 16)	KATANA PRODUCTS THE STUDIO, QUARRY HILL BOX, WILTSHIRE SN14 9HT GREAT BRITAIN
00-20-1E (hex)	NETQUEST CORPORATION
00201E (base 16)	NETQUEST CORPORATION 523 FELLOWSHIP ROAD-STE.#205 MT. LAUREL NJ 08054
00-20-1F (hex)	BEST POWER TECHNOLOGY, INC.
00201F (base 16)	BEST POWER TECHNOLOGY, INC. P.O. BOX 280 NECEDAH WI 54646
00-20-20 (hex)	MEGATRON COMPUTER INDUSTRIES
002020 (base 16)	MEGATRON COMPUTER INDUSTRIES PTY, LTD. UNIT 2, 62-64 CHARTER STREET RINGWOOD VICTORIA 3134 AUSTRALIA
00-20-21 (hex)	ALGORITHMS SOFTWARE PVT. LTD.
002021 (base 16)	ALGORITHMS SOFTWARE PVT. LTD. 83 JOLLY MAKER CHAMBERS II NARIMAN POINT BOMBAY 400021 INDIA
00-20-22 (hex)	TEKNIQUE, INC.
002022 (base 16)	TEKNIQUE, INC. 911 N. PLUM GROVE ROAD SCHAUMBURG IL 60173
00-20-23 (hex)	T.C. TECHNOLOGIES PTY. LTD
002023 (base 16)	T.C. TECHNOLOGIES PTY. LTD 6/60 FAIRFORD RD. PADSTOW NSW2211 AUSTRALIA
00-20-24 (hex)	PACIFIC COMMUNICATION SCIENCES
002024 (base 16)	PACIFIC COMMUNICATION SCIENCES 9645 SCRANTON ROAD SAN DIEGO CA 92121
00-20-25 (hex)	CONTROL TECHNOLOGY, INC.
002025 (base 16)	CONTROL TECHNOLOGY, INC. 5734 MIDDLEBROOK PIKE KNOXVILLE TN 37921
00-20-26 (hex)	AMKLY SYSTEMS, INC.
002026 (base 16)	AMKLY SYSTEMS, INC. 15801 ROCKFIELD BLVD., #P IRVINE CA 92718
00-20-27 (hex)	MING FORTUNE INDUSTRY CO., LTD
002027 (base 16)	MING FORTUNE INDUSTRY CO., LTD 4F, NO. 5, LANE 45 PAO HSIN RD, HSIN TIEN TAIPEI HSIEN TAIWAN, R.O.C.
00-20-28 (hex)	WEST EGG SYSTEMS, INC.
002028 (base 16)	WEST EGG SYSTEMS, INC. 65 HIGH RIDGE ROAD-STE.#286 STAMFORD CT 06905
00-20-29 (hex)	TELEPROCESSING PRODUCTS, INC.
002029 (base 16)	TELEPROCESSING PRODUCTS, INC. 4565 E. INDUSTRIAL STREET BUILDING #7K SIMI VALLEY CA 93063
00-20-2A (hex)	N.V. DZINE
00202A (base 16)	N.V. DZINE KONING LEOPOLD III LAAN 2 B - 8500 KORTRIJK BELGIUM
00-20-2B (hex)	ADVANCED TELECOMMUNICATIONS

company_id	Organization / Address
00202B (base 16)	ADVANCED TELECOMMUNICATIONS MODULES, LTD. MOUNT PLEASANT HOUSE HUNTINGDON ROAD, CAMBRIDGE UNITED KINGDOM CB3 OBL
00-20-2C (hex)	WELLTRONIX CO., LTD.
00202C (base 16)	WELLTRONIX CO., LTD. 3F, NO. 36-1, HWANG HSI STREET SHIN-LIN TAIPEI TAIWAN, R.O.C.
00-20-2D (hex)	TAIYO CORPORATION
00202D (base 16)	TAIYO CORPORATION 1-2-6 SANNOH, OHTA-KU TOKYO 143 JAPAN
00-20-2E (hex)	DAYSTAR DIGITAL
00202E (base 16)	DAYSTAR DIGITAL 5556 ATLANTA HIGHWAY FLOWERY BRANCH GA 30542
00-20-2F (hex)	ZETA COMMUNICATIONS, LTD.
00202F (base 16)	ZETA COMMUNICATIONS, LTD. ZENITH HOUSE GRESFORD INDUSTRIAL PARK WREXHAM, CLWYD, LL12 8LX UNITED KINGDOM
00-20-30 (hex)	ANALOG & DIGITAL SYSTEMS
002030 (base 16)	ANALOG & DIGITAL SYSTEMS 1/2 LAVELLE ROAD BANGALORE - 560001 INDIA
00-20-31 (hex)	ERTEC GMBH
002031 (base 16)	ERTEC GMBH AM PESTALOZZIRING 24 D-91058 ERLANGEN GERMANY
00-20-32 (hex)	ALCATEL TAISEL
002032 (base 16)	ALCATEL TAISEL 4, MING SHENG STREET TU-CHENG INDUSTRIAL DISTRICT TAIPEI HSIEH TAIWAN ROC
00-20-33 (hex)	SYNAPSE TECHNOLOGIES, INC.
002033 (base 16)	SYNAPSE TECHNOLOGIES, INC. 4822 ALBEMARLE ROAD, #104 CHARLOTTE NC 28205
00-20-34 (hex)	ROTEC INDUSTRIEAUTOMATION GMBH
002034 (base 16)	ROTEC INDUSTRIEAUTOMATION GMBH GUTENBERGSTR. 15 76437 RASTATT GERMANY
00-20-35 (hex)	IBM CORPORATION
002035 (base 16)	IBM CORPORATION P.O. BOX 12195 CE6A/664 3039 CORNWALLIS RTP, NC 27709-2195
00-20-36 (hex)	BMC SOFTWARE
002036 (base 16)	BMC SOFTWARE 1600 CITY WEST BLVD., #1600 HOUSTON TX 77042
00-20-37 (hex)	SEAGATE TECHNOLOGY
002037 (base 16)	SEAGATE TECHNOLOGY 8001 E. BLOOMINGTON FWY M/S - MPS043 BLOOMINGTON MN 55420
00-20-38 (hex)	VME MICROSYSTEMS INTERNATIONAL
002038 (base 16)	VME MICROSYSTEMS INTERNATIONAL CORPORATION 12090 S. MEMORIAL PARKWAY HUNTSVILLE AL 35803

company_id	Organization Address	company_id	Organization Address
00-20-39 (hex)	SCINETS	002047 (base 16)	STEINBRECHER CORP. 30 NORTH AVENUE BURLINGTON MA 01803
002039 (base 16)	SCINETS 1575 TENAKA - STE# N8 SUNNYVALE CA 94087	00-20-48 (hex)	FORE SYSTEMS, INC.
00-20-3A (hex)	DIGITAL BI0METRICS INC.	002048 (base 16)	FORE SYSTEMS, INC. 174 THORN HILL ROAD WARRENDALE PA 15086-7535
00203A (base 16)	DIGITAL BI0METRICS INC. 5600 ROWLAND ROAD- STE.#205 MINNETONKA MN 55364	00-20-49 (hex)	COMTRON, INC.
00-20-3B (hex)	WISDM LTD.	002049 (base 16)	COMTRON, INC. SANCATHERINA BLDG. 36-12 SHINJUKU 1-CHOME SHINJUKU-KU TOKYO 160 JAPAN
00203B (base 16)	WISDM LTD. ST. JOHNS INNOVATION CENTRE COWLEY ROAD CAMBRIDGE CB4 4WS ENGLAND	00-20-4A (hex)	PRONET GMBH
00-20-3C (hex)	EUROTIME AB	00204A (base 16)	PRONET GMBH KARLSTRASSE 49 D-7805 F VILLINGEN-SCHWENNINGEN GERMANY
00203C (base 16)	EUROTIME AB BOX 277 S-53224 SKARA SWEDEN	00-20-4B (hex)	AUTOCOMPUTER CO., LTD.
00-20-3D (hex)	NOVAR ELECTRONICS CORPORATION	00204B (base 16)	AUTOCOMPUTER CO., LTD. NO. 18, PEI YUAN ROAD CHUNG-LI CITY, TAO-YUAN HSIEN TAIWAN, R.O.C.
00203D (base 16)	NOVAR ELECTRONICS CORPORATION 24 BROWN STREET BARBERTON OH 44203	00-20-4C (hex)	MITRON COMPUTER PTE LTD.
00-20-3E (hex)	LOGICAN TECHNOLOGIES, INC.	00204C (base 16)	MITRON COMPUTER PTE LTD. 1020 HOUGANG AVENUE 1 #03-3504 SINGAPORE 1953
00203E (base 16)	LOGICAN TECHNOLOGIES, INC. 150 KARL CLARK ROAD EDMONTON, ALBERTA CANADA T6N 1E2	00-20-4D (hex)	INOVIS GMBH
00-20-3F (hex)	JUKI CORPORATION	00204D (base 16)	INOVIS GMBH HANNS-BRAUN STRASSE 50 85375 NEUFAHRN GERMANY
00203F (base 16)	JUKI CORPORATION 8-2-1 KOKURYO-CHO CHOFU-SHI TOKYO 182 JAPAN	00-20-4E (hex)	NETWORK SECURITY SYSTEMS, INC.
00-20-40 (hex)	GENERAL INSTRUMENT CORPORATION	00204E (base 16)	NETWORK SECURITY SYSTEMS, INC. 9401 WAPLES STREET, STE. #100 SAN DIEGO CA 92121
002040 (base 16)	GENERAL INSTRUMENT CORPORATION OF DELAWARE GI COMMUNICATIONS DIVISION 6262 LUSK BOULEVARD SAN DIEGO CA 92121	00-20-4F (hex)	DEUTSCHE AEROSPACE AG
00-20-41 (hex)	DATA NET	00204F (base 16)	DEUTSCHE AEROSPACE AG GESCHAEFTSFELD VERTEIDIGUNG UND ZIVILE SYSTEM 81663 MUENCHEN BUNDESREPUBLIK DEUTSCHLAND
002041 (base 16)	DATA NET SUWON P.O. BOX 106, SUWON KYUNGGI-DO KOREA 440-600	00-20-50 (hex)	KOREA COMPUTER INC.
00-20-42 (hex)	DATAMETRICS CORP.	002050 (base 16)	KOREA COMPUTER INC. 469, DAEHEUNG-DONG MAPO-GU, SEOUL KOREA
002042 (base 16)	DATAMETRICS CORP. 8966 COMANCHE AVE. CHATSWORTH CA 91311	00-20-51 (hex)	PHOENIX DATA COMMUNUNICATIONS
00-20-43 (hex)	NEURON COMPANY LIMITED	002051 (base 16)	PHOENIX DATA COMMUNUNICATIONS CORP. 55 ACCESS ROAD WARWICK RI 02886
002043 (base 16)	NEURON COMPANY LIMITED 15 KWAI YI ROAD, BLOCK 2, 21ST FLOOR, FLAT B KWAI CHUNG, N.T. HONG KONG	00-20-52 (hex)	RAGULA SYSTEMS
00-20-44 (hex)	GENITECH PTY LTD	002052 (base 16)	RAGULA SYSTEMS 4540 S. JUPITER DRIVE SALT LAKE CITY UT 84124
002044 (base 16)	GENITECH PTY LTD P.O. BOX 196 ASQUITH NSW 2077 AUSTRALIA	00-20-53 (hex)	HUNTSVILLE MICROSYSTEMS, INC.
00-20-45 (hex)	SOLCOM SYSTEMS, LTD.	002053 (base 16)	HUNTSVILLE MICROSYSTEMS, INC. P.O. BOX 12415 HUNTSVILLE AL 35815
002045 (base 16)	SOLCOM SYSTEMS, LTD. 1 DRUMMOND SQUARE BRUCEFIELD INDUSTRIAL ESTATE LIVINGSTON SCOTLAND, EH54 9DH	00-20-54 (hex)	EASTERN RESEARCH, INC.
00-20-46 (hex)	CIPRICO, INC.	002054 (base 16)	EASTERN RESEARCH, INC. 60 JAMES WAY SOUTHAMPTON PA 18966
002046 (base 16)	CIPRICO, INC. 2800 CAMPUS DRIVE—SUITE #60 PLYMOUTH MN 55441	00-20-55 (hex)	ALTECH CO., LTD.
00-20-47 (hex)	STEINBRECHER CORP.	002055 (base 16)	ALTECH CO., LTD. OHISHI BLDG., 2-23-11 NISHI-NIPPORI, ARAKAWA-KU TOKYO 116 JAPAN

company_id	Organization Address
00-20-56 (hex)	NEOPRODUCTS
002056 (base 16)	NEOPRODUCTS 25 CHAPMAN STREET BLACKBURN NORTH VICTORIA 3130 AUSTRALIA
00-20-57 (hex)	TITZE DATENTECHNIK GMBH
002057 (base 16)	TITZE DATENTECHNIK GMBH DIESELSTRASSE 10 D-71272 RENNINGEN-2 GERMANY
00-20-58 (hex)	ALLIED SIGNAL INC.
002058 (base 16)	ALLIED SIGNAL INC. ROUTE 46 TETERBORO NJ 07608
00-20-59 (hex)	MIRO COMPUTER PRODUCTS AG
002059 (base 16)	MIRO COMPUTER PRODUCTS AG CARL MIELE STR. 4 D-38112 BRAUNSCHWEIG GERMANY
00-20-5A (hex)	COMPUTER IDENTICS
00205A (base 16)	COMPUTER IDENTICS 5 SHAWMUT ROAD CANTON MA 02021
00-20-5B (hex)	SKYLINE TECHNOLOGY
00205B (base 16)	SKYLINE TECHNOLOGY 1590 CANADA LANE WOODSIDE CA 94062
00-20-5C (hex)	INTERNET SYSTEMS/ FLORIDA INC.
00205C (base 16)	INTERNET SYSTEMS/ FLORIDA INC. P.O. BOX 578 CRESTVIEW FL 32536
00-20-5D (hex)	NANOMATIC OY
00205D (base 16)	NANOMATIC OY PUISTOLAN RAITTI 4 00760 HELSINKI FINLAND
00-20-5E (hex)	CASTLE ROCK, INC.
00205E (base 16)	CASTLE ROCK, INC. 20 SOUTH SANTA CRUZ AVE. SUITE #310 LOS GATOS CA 95030
00-20-5F (hex)	GAMMADATA COMPUTER GMBH
00205F (base 16)	GAMMADATA COMPUTER GMBH GUTENBERGSTR. 13 82168 PUCHHEIM GERMANY
00-20-60 (hex)	ALCATEL ITALIA S.P.A.
002060 (base 16)	ALCATEL ITALIA S.P.A. VIA TRENTO, 30 20059 VIMERCATE (MI) ITALY
00-20-61 (hex)	DYNATECH COMMUNICATIONS, INC.
002061 (base 16)	DYNATECH COMMUNICATIONS, INC. 991 ANNAPOLIS WAY WOODBRIDGE VA 22191
00-20-62 (hex)	SCORPION LOGIC, LTD.
002062 (base 16)	SCORPION LOGIC, LTD. 19 BROOKSIDE ROAD OXHEY, WATFORD HERTS WD1 4BW UNITED KINGDOM
00-20-63 (hex)	WIPRO INFOTECH LTD.
002063 (base 16)	WIPRO INFOTECH LTD. UNITS 47-48, SDF BLOCK VII MEPZ, KADAPPERI MADRAS-600045 INDIA
00-20-64 (hex)	PROTEC MICROSYSTEMS, INC.
002064 (base 16)	PROTEC MICROSYSTEMS, INC. 297 LABROSSE POINTE-CLAIRE, QUEBEC CANADA H9R 1A3
00-20-65 (hex)	SUPERNET NETWORKING INC.
002065 (base 16)	SUPERNET NETWORKING INC. 16 TOZERET HA'ARETZ ST. TEL-AVIV 67891 ISRAEL
00-20-66 (hex)	GENERAL MAGIC, INC.
002066 (base 16)	GENERAL MAGIC, INC. 2465 LATHAM STREET MOUNTAIN VIEW CA 94040
00-20-68 (hex)	ISDYNE
002068 (base 16)	ISDYNE 11 ROXBURY AVENUE NATICK MA 01760
00-20-69 (hex)	ISDN SYSTEMS CORPORATION
002069 (base 16)	ISDN SYSTEMS CORPORATION 8320 OLD COURTHOUSE RD. SUITE #203 VIENNA VA 22182
00-20-6A (hex)	OSAKA COMPUTER CORP.
00206A (base 16)	OSAKA COMPUTER CORP. 2-8 KOYACHOU NEYAGAW-SHI OSAKA 572 JAPAN
00-20-6B (hex)	MINOLTA CO., LTD.
00206B (base 16)	MINOLTA CO., LTD. ADVANCED SYSTEMS CENTER SEIS'N 4-4-1, TAKATSUKADAI, NISHI-KU, KOBE, 651-22, JAPAN
00-20-6C (hex)	EVERGREEN TECHNOLOGY CORP.
00206C (base 16)	EVERGREEN TECHNOLOGY CORP. 231 EMERSON STREET PALO ALTO CA 94301
00-20-6D (hex)	DATA RACE, INC.
00206D (base 16)	DATA RACE, INC. 11550 IH-10 WEST STE #395 SAN ANTONIO TX 78230
00-20-6E (hex)	XACT, INC.
00206E (base 16)	XACT, INC. P.O. BOX 55 ARGYLE TX 76226
00-20-6F (hex)	FLOWPOINT CORPORATION
00206F (base 16)	FLOWPOINT CORPORATION 7291 CORONADO DRIVE, STE # 4 SAN JOSE CA 95129
00-20-70 (hex)	HYNET, LTD.
002070 (base 16)	HYNET, LTD. 102 JABOTINSKY ST. PO BOX 3638 PETACH TIKVA 49130 ISRAEL
00-20-71 (hex)	IBR GMBH
002071 (base 16)	IBR GMBH KOHLERSTR. 45 D-46286 DORSTEN GERMANY
00-20-72 (hex)	WORKLINK INNOVATIONS
002072 (base 16)	WORKLINK INNOVATIONS 2452 ARMSTRONG STREET LIVERMORE CA 94550
00-20-73 (hex)	FUSION SYSTEMS CORPORATION
002073 (base 16)	FUSION SYSTEMS CORPORATION 7600 STANDISH PLACE ROCKVILLE MD 20855
00-20-74 (hex)	SUNGWOON SYSTEMS

company_id	Organization Address
002074 (base 16)	SUNGWOON SYSTEMS YUSUN BLDG.44-4 SAMSUNG-DONG KANGNAM-KU, SEOUL 135-090 KOREA
00-20-75 (hex)	MOTOROLA COMMUNICATION ISRAEL
002075 (base 16)	MOTOROLA COMMUNICATION ISRAEL 3 KREMENETSKI STREET POB 25016 TEL-AVIV 61250 ISRAEL
00-20-76 (hex)	REUDO CORPORATION
002076 (base 16)	REUDO CORPORATION 4-1-10 SHINSAN NAGAOKA CITY, NIIGATA 940-21 JAPAN
00-20-77 (hex)	KARDIOS SYSTEMS CORP.
002077 (base 16)	KARDIOS SYSTEMS CORP. 26 N SUMMIT AVE. GAITHERSBURG MD 20877
00-20-78 (hex)	RUNTOP, INC.
002078 (base 16)	RUNTOP, INC. 5/F, NO. 10, ALLEY 8, LANE 45 PAO SHIN ROAD, HSINTIEN TAIPEI HSIEN TAIWAN R.O.C.
00-20-79 (hex)	MIKRON GMBH
002079 (base 16)	MIKRON GMBH BRESLAUERSTR. 1-3 85386 ECHING GERMANY
00-20-7A (hex)	WISE COMMUNICATIONS, INC.
00207A (base 16)	WISE COMMUNICATIONS, INC. 130 KNOWLES DRIVE LOS GATOS CA 95030
00-20-7B (hex)	LEVEL ONE COMMUNICATIONS
00207B (base 16)	LEVEL ONE COMMUNICATIONS 9750 GOETHE ROAD SACRAMENTO CA 95827
00-20-7C (hex)	AUTEC GMBH
00207C (base 16)	AUTEC GMBH BAHNHOFSTR. 57 55234 FRAMERSHEIM GERMANY
00-20-7D (hex)	ADVANCED COMPUTER APPLICATIONS
00207D (base 16)	ADVANCED COMPUTER APPLICATIONS 107 PENNS TRAIL NEWTOWN PA 18940
00-20-7E (hex)	FINECOM CO., LTD.
00207E (base 16)	FINECOM CO., LTD. 1108 HWAKOK-DONG, KANGSEO-KU SEOUL, SOUTH KOREA
00-20-7F (hex)	KYOEI SANGYO CO., LTD.
00207F (base 16)	KYOEI SANGYO CO., LTD. DIR. & GEN'L MGR.IND. SYSTEMS 20-4, SHOTO 2-CHOME SHIBUYA-KU TOKYO
00-20-80 (hex)	SYNERGY (UK) LTD.
002080 (base 16)	SYNERGY (UK) LTD. HARTCRAN HOUSE CARPENDERS PARK, WATFORD HERTS. WD1 5EZ UNITED KINGDOM
00-20-81 (hex)	TITAN ELECTRONICS
002081 (base 16)	TITAN ELECTRONICS 3033 SCIENCE PARK ROAD SAN DIEGO CA 92121
00-20-82 (hex)	ONEAC CORPORATION

company_id	Organization Address
002082 (base 16)	ONEAC CORPORATION 27944 N. BRADLEY RD. LIBERTYVILLE IL 60048
00-20-83 (hex)	PRESTICOM INCORPORATED
002083 (base 16)	PRESTICOM INCORPORATED 3275, 1ST STREET, STE. #1 ST-HUBERT (QUEBEC) CANADA J3Y 8Y6
00-20-84 (hex)	OCE PRINTING SYSTEMS, GMBH
002084 (base 16)	OCE PRINTING SYSTEMS, GMBH SIEMENSALLEE 2 D-85586 POING GERMANY
00-20-85 (hex)	EXIDE ELECTRONICS
002085 (base 16)	EXIDE ELECTRONICS P.O. BOX 58189 RALEIGH NC 27658
00-20-86 (hex)	MICROTECH ELECTRONICS LIMITED
002086 (base 16)	MICROTECH ELECTRONICS LIMITED LANCASTER ROAD CRESSEX INDUSTRIAL ESTATE HIGH WYCOMBE, BUCKS HP12 3QA UNITED KINGDOM
00-20-87 (hex)	MEMOTEC COMMUNICATIONS CORP.
002087 (base 16)	MEMOTEC COMMUNICATIONS CORP. ONE HIGH STREET NORTH ANDOVER MA 01845
00-20-88 (hex)	GLOBAL VILLAGE COMMUNICATION
002088 (base 16)	GLOBAL VILLAGE COMMUNICATION 1144 EAST ARQUES AVENUE SUNNYVALE CA 94086
00-20-89 (hex)	T3PLUS NETWORKING, INC.
002089 (base 16)	T3PLUS NETWORKING, INC. 2840 SAN TOMAS EXPRESSWAY SANTA CLARA CA 95051
00-20-8A (hex)	SONIX COMMUNICATIONS, LTD.
00208A (base 16)	SONIX COMMUNICATIONS, LTD. WILKINSON ROAD CIRENCESTER, GLOS. GL7 1YT ENGLAND
00-20-8B (hex)	LAPIS TECHNOLOGIES, INC.
00208B (base 16)	LAPIS TECHNOLOGIES, INC. 1100 MARINA VILLAGE PKWY SUITE #100 ALAMEDA CA 94501
00-20-8C (hex)	GALAXY NETWORKS, INC.
00208C (base 16)	GALAXY NETWORKS, INC. 9348 DE SOTO AVENUE CHATSWORTH CA 91311
00-20-8D (hex)	CMD TECHNOLOGY
00208D (base 16)	CMD TECHNOLOGY 1 VANDERBILT IRVINE CA 92718
00-20-8E (hex)	CHEVIN SOFTWARE ENG. LTD.
00208E (base 16)	CHEVIN SOFTWARE ENG. LTD. 2 BOROUGHGATE, OTLEY, LEEDS, WEST, YORKSHIRE LS21 3AL, UNITED KINGDOM
00-20-8F (hex)	ECI TELECOM LTD.
00208F (base 16)	ECI TELECOM LTD. HASIVIM ST. 30, PETACH-TIKVA ISRAEL, 49133
00-20-90 (hex)	ADVANCED COMPRESSION
002090 (base 16)	ADVANCED COMPRESSION TECHNOLOGY, INC. 820 FLYNN ROAD CAMARILLO CA 93012
00-20-91 (hex)	J125, NATIONAL SECURITY AGENCY

company_id	Organization Address
002091 (base 16)	J125, NATIONAL SECURITY AGENCY 9800 SAVAGE ROAD FT. MEADE MD 20755-6000
00-20-92 (hex)	CHESS ENGINEERING B.V.
002092 (base 16)	CHESS ENGINEERING B.V. NIEUWE GRACHT 74 2011 NJ HAARLEM NETHERLANDS
00-20-93 (hex)	LANDINGS TECHNOLOGY CORP.
002093 (base 16)	LANDINGS TECHNOLOGY CORP. 163 WATER STREET MERRILL BLOCK UNIT A2 EXETER NH 03833
00-20-94 (hex)	CUBIX CORPORATION
002094 (base 16)	CUBIX CORPORATION 2800 LOCKHEED WAY CARSON CITY NV 89706
00-20-95 (hex)	RIVA ELECTRONICS
002095 (base 16)	RIVA ELECTRONICS UNIT 17, BARRSFOLD RD. WINGATES INDUSTRIAL PARK WESTHOUGHTON, BOLTON, LANCASHIRE, ENGLAND BL5 3XW
00-20-96 (hex)	SIEBE ENVIRONMENTAL CONTROLS
002096 (base 16)	SIEBE ENVIRONMENTAL CONTROLS 1701 BYRD AVENUE RICHMOND VA 23230
00-20-97 (hex)	APPLIED SIGNAL TECHNOLOGY
002097 (base 16)	APPLIED SIGNAL TECHNOLOGY 160 SOBRANTE WAY SUNNYVALE CA 94086
00-20-98 (hex)	HECTRONIC AB
002098 (base 16)	HECTRONIC AB BOX 3002 S-75003 UPPSALA SWEDEN
00-20-99 (hex)	BON ELECTRIC CO., LTD.
002099 (base 16)	BON ELECTRIC CO., LTD. 4-4 28, MIZUDO-CHO AMAGASAKI, 661 HYOGO, JAPAN
00-20-9A (hex)	THE 3DO COMPANY
00209A (base 16)	THE 3DO COMPANY 600 GALVESTON DRIVE REDWOOD CITY CA 94063
00-20-9B (hex)	ERSAT ELECTRONIC GMBH
00209B (base 16)	ERSAT ELECTRONIC GMBH HAARBERGSTR. 61 D-99097 ERFURT GERMANY
00-20-9C (hex)	PRIMARY ACCESS CORP.
00209C (base 16)	PRIMARY ACCESS CORP. 10080 CARROLL CANYON RD SAN DIEGO CA 92131
00-20-9D (hex)	LIPPERT AUTOMATIONSTECHNIK
00209D (base 16)	LIPPERT AUTOMATIONSTECHNIK D-68165 MANNHEIM KRAPPMUEHLSTR. 34 GERMANY
00-20-9E (hex)	BROWN'S OPERATING SYSTEM
00209E (base 16)	BROWN'S OPERATING SYSTEM SERVICES, LTD. ST. AGNES HOUSE, CRESSWELL PK, BLACKHEATH, LONDON SE3 9RD UNITED KINGDOM
00-20-9F (hex)	MERCURY COMPUTER SYSTEMS, INC.
00209F (base 16)	MERCURY COMPUTER SYSTEMS, INC. 199 RIVERNECK ROAD CHELMSFORD MA 01824
00-20-A0 (hex)	OA LABORATORY CO., LTD.

company_id	Organization Address
0020A0 (base 16)	OA LABORATORY CO., LTD. 228 KAMIMACHIYA KAMAKURA KANAGAWA 247 JAPAN
00-20-A1 (hex)	DOVATRON
0020A1 (base 16)	DOVATRON PRODUCTS DIVISION 1198 BOSTON AVENUE LONGMONT CO 80501
00-20-A2 (hex)	GALCOM NETWORKING LTD.
0020A2 (base 16)	GALCOM NETWORKING LTD. P.O. BOX 1568 RAMAT HASHARON 47113 ISRAEL
00-20-A3 (hex)	DIVICOM INC.
0020A3 (base 16)	DIVICOM INC. 580 COTTONWOOD DRIVE MILPITAS CA 95035
00-20-A4 (hex)	MULTIPOINT NETWORKS
0020A4 (base 16)	MULTIPOINT NETWORKS 19 DAVIS DRIVE BELMONT CA 94002-3001
00-20-A5 (hex)	API ENGINEERING
0020A5 (base 16)	API ENGINEERING 2689 POPLARWOOD WAY SAN JOSE CA 95132
00-20-A6 (hex)	PROXIM, INC.
0020A6 (base 16)	PROXIM, INC. 295 NORTH BERNARDO AVENUE MOUNTAIN VIEW CA 94043
00-20-A7 (hex)	PAIRGAIN TECHNOLOGIES, INC.
0020A7 (base 16)	PAIRGAIN TECHNOLOGIES, INC. 14402 FRANKLIN AVENUE TUSTIN CA 92680-7013
00-20-A8 (hex)	SAST TECHNOLOGY CORP.
0020A8 (base 16)	SAST TECHNOLOGY CORP. 225 OLD NEW BRUNSWICK RD. SUITE #101 PISCATAWAY NJ 08854
00-20-A9 (hex)	WHITE HORSE INDUSTRIAL
0020A9 (base 16)	WHITE HORSE INDUSTRIAL 4F. NO.16, ALLEY 56, LANE 181 SEC.4, CHUNG HSIAO EAST ROAD TAIPEI TAIWAN, R.O.C.
00-20-AA (hex)	DIGIMEDIA VISION LTD.
0020AA (base 16)	DIGIMEDIA VISION LTD. CRAWLEY COURT WINCHESTER, HAMPSHIRE SO21 2QA, UNITED KINGDOM
00-20-AB (hex)	MICRO INDUSTRIES CORP.
0020AB (base 16)	MICRO INDUSTRIES CORP. 8399 GREEN MEADOWS DR. N. WESTERVILLE OH 43081
00-20-AC (hex)	INTERFLEX DATENSYSTEME GMBH
0020AC (base 16)	INTERFLEX DATENSYSTEME GMBH GROBWIESENSTRASE 24 W-7201 DURCHHAUSEN WESTGERMANY
00-20-AD (hex)	LINQ SYSTEMS
0020AD (base 16)	LINQ SYSTEMS P.O. BOX 11040 TUCSON AZ 85734
00-20-AE (hex)	ORNET DATA COMMUNICATION TECH.
0020AE (base 16)	ORNET DATA COMMUNICATION TECH. P.O. BOX 323 CARMIEL 20100 ISRAEL
00-20-AF (hex)	3COM CORPORATION

company_id	Organization Address
0020AF (base 16)	3COM CORPORATION 5400 BAYFRONT PLAZA SANTA CLARA CA 95052
00-20-B0 (hex)	GATEWAY DEVICES, INC.
0020B0 (base 16)	GATEWAY DEVICES, INC. 2440 STANWELL DRIVE CONCORD CA 94520
00-20-B1 (hex)	COMTECH RESEARCH INC.
0020B1 (base 16)	COMTECH RESEARCH INC. 24271 TAHOE LAGUNA NIGUEL CA 92656
00-20-B2 (hex)	GKD GESELLSCHAFT FUR
0020B2 (base 16)	GKD GESELLSCHAFT FUR KOMMUNIKATION UND DATENTECHNIK SAARBURGER RING 10-12 68229 MANNHEIM GERMANY
00-20-B3 (hex)	SCLTEC COMMUNICATIONS SYSTEMS
0020B3 (base 16)	SCLTEC COMMUNICATIONS SYSTEMS 3 APOLLO PLACE LANE COVE N.S.W. 2066 AUSTRALIA
00-20-B4 (hex)	TERMA ELEKTRONIK AS
0020B4 (base 16)	TERMA ELEKTRONIK AS HOVMARKEN 4, DK-8520 LYSTRUP DENMARK
00-20-B5 (hex)	YASKAWA ELECTRIC CORPORATION
0020B5 (base 16)	YASKAWA ELECTRIC CORPORATION 2-1 KUROSAKI-SHIROISHI YAHATANISHI-KU KITAKYUSHU-CITY JAPAN
00-20-B6 (hex)	AGILE NETWORKS, INC.
0020B6 (base 16)	AGILE NETWORKS, INC. 200 BAKER AVENUE CONCORD MA 01742
00-20-B7 (hex)	NAMAQUA COMPUTERWARE
0020B7 (base 16)	NAMAQUA COMPUTERWARE P.O. BOX 7155 STELLEN BOSCH 7599 REPUBLIC OF SOUTH AFRICA
00-20-B8 (hex)	PRIME OPTION, INC.
0020B8 (base 16)	PRIME OPTION, INC. 2341 W. 205TH STREET #116 TORRANCE CA 90501
00-20-B9 (hex)	METRICOM, INC.
0020B9 (base 16)	METRICOM, INC. 980 UNIVERSITY AVENUE LOS GATOS CA 95030
00-20-BA (hex)	CENTER FOR HIGH PERFORMANCE
0020BA (base 16)	CENTER FOR HIGH PERFORMANCE COMPUTING OF WPI SUITE #170 293 BOSTON POST ROAD W. MARLBORO MA 01752
00-20-BB (hex)	ZAX CORPORATION
0020BB (base 16)	ZAX CORPORATION 20-12 OGIKUBO 5-CHOME SUGINAMI-KU TOKYO 167 JAPAN
00-20-BC (hex)	JTEC PTY LTD.
0020BC (base 16)	JTEC PTY LTD. UNIT 3, 118-122 BOWDEN STREET MEADOWBANK NSW AUSTRALIA 2114
00-20-BD (hex)	NIOBRARA R & D CORPORATION

company_id	Organization Address
0020BD (base 16)	NIOBRARA R & D CORPORATION PO BOX 3418 JOPLIN MO 64803-3418
00-20-BE (hex)	LAN ACCESS CORP.
0020BE (base 16)	LAN ACCESS CORP. 2730 MONTEREY STREET, STE.#102 TORRANCE CA 90503
00-20-BF (hex)	AEHR TEST SYSTEMS
0020BF (base 16)	AEHR TEST SYSTEMS 1667 PLYMOUTH STREET MOUNTAIN VIEW CA 94043
00-20-C0 (hex)	PULSE ELECTRONICS, INC.
0020C0 (base 16)	PULSE ELECTRONICS, INC. 5706 FREDERICK AVENUE ROCKVILLE MD 20852
00-20-C1 (hex)	TAIKO ELECTRIC WORKS, LTD.
0020C1 (base 16)	TAIKO ELECTRIC WORKS, LTD. 10-13, 6-CHOME NAKANOBU SHINAGAWA-KU TOKYO JAPAN
00-20-C2 (hex)	TEXAS MEMORY SYSTEMS, INC.
0020C2 (base 16)	TEXAS MEMORY SYSTEMS, INC. 11200 WESTHEIMER RD-STE#1000 HOUSTON TX 77042
00-20-C3 (hex)	COUNTER SOLUTIONS LTD.
0020C3 (base 16)	COUNTER SOLUTIONS LTD. 263 HEAGE ROAD RIPLEY, DERBYS ENGLAND, DE5 3GH
00-20-C4 (hex)	INET,INC.
0020C4 (base 16)	INET,INC. 801 E. CAMPBELL-STE.#330 RICHARDSON TX 75081
00-20-C5 (hex)	EAGLE TECHNOLOGY
0020C5 (base 16)	EAGLE TECHNOLOGY 2865 ZANKER ROAD SAN JOSE CA 95134
00-20-C6 (hex)	NECTEC
0020C6 (base 16)	NECTEC RAMA VI ROAD RAJTHEVI BANGKOK 10400 THAILAND
00-20-C7 (hex)	AKAI Professional M.I. Corp.
0020C7 (base 16)	AKAI Professional M.I. Corp. 1-3, Hiranuma 1-Chome, Nishi-ku, Yokohama, 220-0023 JAPAN
00-20-C8 (hex)	LARSCOM INCORPORATED
0020C8 (base 16)	LARSCOM INCORPORATED 4600 PATRICK HENRY DRIVE SANTA CLARA CA 95054
00-20-C9 (hex)	VICTRON BV
0020C9 (base 16)	VICTRON BV POB 31 NL 9700 AA GRONINGEN THE NETHERLANDS
00-20-CA (hex)	DIGITAL OCEAN
0020CA (base 16)	DIGITAL OCEAN 11206 THOMPSON AVENUE LENEXA KS 66219-2303
00-20-CB (hex)	PRETEC ELECTRONICS CORP.
0020CB (base 16)	PRETEC ELECTRONICS CORP. 39899 BALENTINE DR. SUITE #305 NEWARK CA 94560
00-20-CC (hex)	DIGITAL SERVICES, LTD.

company_id	Organization Address
0020CC (base 16)	DIGITAL SERVICES, LTD. 9 WAYTE STREET COSHAM HAMPSHIRE ENGLAND PO6 3BS
00-20-CD (hex)	HYBRID NETWORKS, INC.
0020CD (base 16)	HYBRID NETWORKS, INC. 10201 BUBB ROAD CUPERTINO CA 95014-4167
00-20-CE (hex)	LOGICAL DESIGN GROUP, INC.
0020CE (base 16)	LOGICAL DESIGN GROUP, INC. 6301 CHAPEL HILL ROAD RALEIGH NC 27607
00-20-CF (hex)	TEST & MEASUREMENT SYSTEMS INC
0020CF (base 16)	TEST & MEASUREMENT SYSTEMS INC 2045 SITKA COURT LOVELAND CO 80538
00-20-D0 (hex)	VERSALYNX CORPORATION
0020D0 (base 16)	VERSALYNX CORPORATION 8950 CARLEY CIRCLE SAN DIEGO CA 92126
00-20-D1 (hex)	MICROCOMPUTER SYSTEMS (M) SDN.
0020D1 (base 16)	MICROCOMPUTER SYSTEMS (M) SDN. 23-25, JALAN JEJAKA TUJUH TAMAN MALURI, CHERAS 55100 KUALA LUMPUR MALAYSIA
00-20-D2 (hex)	RAD DATA COMMUNICATIONS, LTD.
0020D2 (base 16)	RAD DATA COMMUNICATIONS, LTD. 8 HANECHOSHET STREET TEL-AVIV 69710 ISRAEL
00-20-D3 (hex)	OST (OUEST STANDARD TELEMATIQU
0020D3 (base 16)	OST (OUEST STANDARD TELEMATIQU RUE DU BAS VILLAGE BP 158, Z.I. SUD-EST 35515 CESSON-SEVIGNE CEDEX FRANCE
00-20-D4 (hex)	CABLETRON - ZEITTNET INC.
0020D4 (base 16)	CABLETRON - ZEITTNET INC. 35 INDUSTRIAL WAY P.O. BOX 5005 ROHESTER NH 03866-5005
00-20-D5 (hex)	VIPA GMBH
0020D5 (base 16)	VIPA GMBH WETTERKREUZ 27 D-91058 ERLANGEN GERMANY
00-20-D6 (hex)	BREEZECOM
0020D6 (base 16)	BREEZECOM ATIDIM TECHNOLOGICAL PK-BLDG.3 TEL-AVIV 61131 ISRAEL
00-20-D7 (hex)	JAPAN MINICOMPUTER SYSTEMS CO.
0020D7 (base 16)	JAPAN MINICOMPUTER SYSTEMS CO. 3-33-18 TAKAIDOHIGASHI SUGINAMI-KU TOKYO 168 JAPAN
00-20-D8 (hex)	NETWAVE TECHNOLOGIES, INC.
0020D8 (base 16)	NETWAVE TECHNOLOGIES, INC. 6663 OWENS DRIVE PLEASANTON CA 94588
00-20-D9 (hex)	PANASONIC TECHNOLOGIES, INC./
0020D9 (base 16)	PANASONIC TECHNOLOGIES, INC./ MIECO-US 1703 N. RANDALL RD. ELGIN IL 60123
00-20-DA (hex)	XYLAN CORPORATION
0020DA (base 16)	XYLAN CORPORATION 26679 W. AGOURA ROAD CALABASAS CA 91302
00-20-DB (hex)	XNET TECHNOLOGY, INC.
0020DB (base 16)	XNET TECHNOLOGY, INC. 426 S. HILLVIEW DRIVE MILPITAS CA 95035
00-20-DC (hex)	DENSITRON TAIWAN LTD.
0020DC (base 16)	DENSITRON TAIWAN LTD. KYOWA NANABANKAN 5F 1-11-5 OMORI-KITA OTA-KU, TOKYO 143 JAPAN
00-20-DD (hex)	AWA LTD.
0020DD (base 16)	AWA LTD. 15 TALAVERA ROAD NORTH RYDE N.S.W. 2113 AUSTRALIA
00-20-DE (hex)	JAPAN DIGITAL LABORAT'Y CO.LTD
0020DE (base 16)	JAPAN DIGITAL LABORAT'Y CO.LTD JDL KAWASAKI R & D CENTER 10-1 MINAMI-KUROKAWA ASAO-KU, KAWASAKI-SHI KANAGAWA-KEN, JAPAN 215
00-20-DF (hex)	KYOSAN ELECTRIC MFG. CO., LTD.
0020DF (base 16)	KYOSAN ELECTRIC MFG. CO., LTD. 2-29, HEIAN-CHO, TSURUMI-KU YOKOHAMA, 230 JAPAN
00-20-E0 (hex)	PREMAX ELECTRONICS, INC.
0020E0 (base 16)	PREMAX ELECTRONICS, INC. 750 N. MARY AVENUE SUNNYVALE CA 94086
00-20-E1 (hex)	ALAMAR ELECTRONICS
0020E1 (base 16)	ALAMAR ELECTRONICS 489 DIVISION STREET CAMPBELL CA 95008
00-20-E2 (hex)	INFORMATION RESOURCE
0020E2 (base 16)	INFORMATION RESOURCE ENGINEERING 8029 CORPORATE DRIVE BALTIMORE MD 21236
00-20-E3 (hex)	MCD KENCOM CORPORATION
0020E3 (base 16)	MCD KENCOM CORPORATION 20950 CASTLE ROCK ROAD LAGUNA BEACH CA 92651-1115
00-20-E4 (hex)	HSING TECH ENTERPRISE CO., LTD
0020E4 (base 16)	HSING TECH ENTERPRISE CO., LTD NO. 2, LANE 128, SEC. 2 CHUNG SHAN N. RD. TEIPEI, TAIWAN, R.O.C.
00-20-E5 (hex)	APEX DATA, INC.
0020E5 (base 16)	APEX DATA, INC. 6624 OWENS DRIVE PLEASANTON CA 94588
00-20-E6 (hex)	LIDKOPING MACHINE TOOLS AB
0020E6 (base 16)	LIDKOPING MACHINE TOOLS AB BOX 910 531 19 LIDKOPING SWEDEN
00-20-E7 (hex)	B&W NUCLEAR SERVICE COMPANY
0020E7 (base 16)	B&W NUCLEAR SERVICE COMPANY SPECIAL PRODUCTS & INTEG.SVCS. 155 MILL RIDGE ROAD LYNCHBURG VA 24502
00-20-E8 (hex)	DATATREK CORPORATION
0020E8 (base 16)	DATATREK CORPORATION 4505 WYLAND DRIVE ELKHART IN 46516

company_id	Organization Address	company_id	Organization Address
00-20-E9 (hex)	DANTEL	0020F7 (base 16)	CYBERDATA 2700 GARDEN ROAD MONTEREY CA 93940
0020E9 (base 16)	DANTEL P.O. BOX 55013 2991 NORTH ARGYLE AVE. FRESNO CA 93727-1388	00-20-F8 (hex)	CARRERA COMPUTERS, INC.
		0020F8 (base 16)	CARRERA COMPUTERS, INC. 23181 VERDUGO DRIVE-STE.#105A LAGUNA HILLS CA 92653
00-20-EA (hex)	EFFICIENT NETWORKS, INC.		
0020EA (base 16)	EFFICIENT NETWORKS, INC. 4201 SPRING VALLEY ROAD SUITE #1200 DALLAS TX 75244-3666	00-20-F9 (hex)	PARALINK NETWORKS, INC.
		0020F9 (base 16)	PARALINK NETWORKS, INC. 4F, NO. 27, SEC.3, PATEH RD. TAIPEI TAIWAN, R.O.C.
00-20-EB (hex)	CINCINNATI MICROWAVE, INC.		
0020EB (base 16)	CINCINNATI MICROWAVE, INC. ONE MICROWAVE PLAZA CINCINNATI OII 45249	00-20-FA (hex)	GDE SYSTEMS, INC.
		0020FA (base 16)	GDE SYSTEMS, INC. P.O. BOX 85468 - BLDG.#61 SAN DIEGO CA 92186-5468
00-20-EC (hex)	TECHWARE SYSTEMS CORP.		
0020EC (base 16)	TECHWARE SYSTEMS CORP. #100 - 12051 HORSESHOE WAY RICHMOND, B.C. CANADA V7A 4V4	00-20-FB (hex)	OCTEL COMMUNICATIONS CORP.
		0020FB (base 16)	OCTEL COMMUNICATIONS CORP. 1001 MURPHY RANCH RD MILPITAS CA 95035
00-20-ED (hex)	GIGA-BYTE TECHNOLOGY CO., LTD.	00-20-FC (hex)	MATROX
0020ED (base 16)	GIGA-BYTE TECHNOLOGY CO., LTD. 365 CLOVERLEAF BALDWIN PARK CA 91706	0020FC (base 16)	MATROX 1055 ST. REGIS, DORVAL QUEBEC CANADA H9P-2T4
00-20-EE (hex)	GTECH CORPORATION		
0020EE (base 16)	GTECH CORPORATION 55 TECHNOLOGY WAY WEST GREENWICH RI 02817	00-20-FD (hex)	ITV TECHNOLOGIES, INC.
		0020FD (base 16)	ITV TECHNOLOGIES, INC. 6800 OWENSMOUTH AVE. #230 CANOGA PARK CA 91303
00-20-EF (hex)	USC CORPORATION		
0020EF (base 16)	USC CORPORATION 6-4, OSAKI 1-CHOME SHINAGAWA-KU TOKYO, 141 JAPAN	00-20-FE (hex)	TOPWARE INC. / GRAND COMPUTER
		0020FE (base 16)	TOPWARE INC. / GRAND COMPUTER CORPORATION B1, NO. 9, LANE 50 SECTION 3, NAN KANG ROAD TAIPEI, TAIWAN, R.O.C.
00-20-F0 (hex)	UNIVERSAL MICROELECTRONICS CO.		
0020F0 (base 16)	UNIVERSAL MICROELECTRONICS CO. 3, 27TH RD., TAICHUNG IND.PARK TAICHUN TAIWAN, R.O.C.	00-20-FF (hex)	SYMMETRICAL TECHNOLOGIES
		0020FF (base 16)	SYMMETRICAL TECHNOLOGIES 500 HUNTMAR PARK DRIVE HERNDON VA 22070
00-20-F1 (hex)	ALTOS INDIA LIMITED	00-30-00 (hex)	ALLWELL TECHNOLOGY CORP.
0020F1 (base 16)	ALTOS INDIA LIMITED D-60, OKLHLA INDUSTRIAL AREA, PHASE 1 NEW DELHI -110020 INDIA	003000 (base 16)	ALLWELL TECHNOLOGY CORP. 4F, #15, LANE 3, SEC.2 CHIEN KWO N. ROAD TAIPEI TAIWAN, R.O.C.
00-20-F2 (hex)	SUN MICROSYSTEMS, INC.	00-30-01 (hex)	SMP
0020F2 (base 16)	SUN MICROSYSTEMS, INC. 901 San Antonio Road MS UMPK02-106 Palo Alto, CA 94043-4900	003001 (base 16)	SMP 22, RUE DES COSMONAUTES 31400 TOULOUSE FRANCE
00-20-F3 (hex)	RAYNET CORPORATION	00-30-02 (hex)	Expand Networks
0020F3 (base 16)	RAYNET CORPORATION 155 CONSTITUTION DRIVE MENLO PARK CA 94025	003002 (base 16)	Expand Networks Atidim Tech Park, Bldg. 4 P.O. Box 58142 Tel-Aviv ISRAEL 61580
00-20-F4 (hex)	SPECTRIX CORPORATION		
0020F4 (base 16)	SPECTRIX CORPORATION 106 WILMOT ROAD, SUITE 250 DEERFIELD IL 60015-5150	00-30-03 (hex)	Phasys Ltd.
		003003 (base 16)	Phasys Ltd. #100-9404 41st Avenue Edmonton, Alberta CANADA T6X 1A2
00-20-F5 (hex)	PANDATEL AG		
0020F5 (base 16)	PANDATEL AG FASANENWEG 25 D-22145 HAMBURG GERMANY	00-30-04 (hex)	LEADTEK RESEARCH INC.
		003004 (base 16)	LEADTEK RESEARCH INC. 18F, No.166, Chien-Yi Road Chung-Ho Teipei, Hsien TAIWAN, (235) R.O.C.
00-20-F6 (hex)	NET TEK AND KARLNET, INC.		
0020F6 (base 16)	NET TEK AND KARLNET, INC. LITTLE STREAMS THE ABBOTSBROOK, BOURNE END BUCKS, SL8 5QY UNITED KINGDOM	00-30-05 (hex)	Fujitsu Siemens Computers
00-20-F7 (hex)	CYBERDATA		

company_id	Organization Address	company_id	Organization Address
003005 (base 16)	Fujitsu Siemens Computers Buergermeister ulrich 100 86199 Augsburg GERMANY	003013 (base 16)	NEC Corporation 1-10 Nisshincho, Fuchu Tokyo 183-8501 JAPAN
00-30-06 (hex)	SUPERPOWER COMPUTER	00-30-14 (hex)	DIVIO, INC.
003006 (base 16)	SUPERPOWER COMPUTER ELECTRONICS CO., LTD. NO. 20 WU-GONG 6TH ROAD WU-KU INDUSTR'L PK, TAIPEI 248 TAIWAN	003014 (base 16)	DIVIO, INC. 997 E. ARQUES AVENUE SUNNYVALE CA 94086
		00-30-15 (hex)	CP CLARE CORP.
00-30-07 (hex)	OPTI, INC.	003015 (base 16)	CP CLARE CORP. 78 CHERRY HILL DRIVE BEVERLY MA 01915
003007 (base 16)	OPTI, INC. 1440 MCCARTHY BLVD. MILPITAS CA 95035	00-30-16 (hex)	ISHIDA CO., LTD.
00-30-08 (hex)	AVIO DIGITAL, INC.	003016 (base 16)	ISHIDA CO., LTD. 959-1 SHIMOMAGARI RITTO-CHO KURITA-GUN SHIGA 520-3026 JAPAN
003008 (base 16)	AVIO DIGITAL, INC. 957 INDUSTRIAL ROAD SAN CARLOS CA 94070		
00-30-09 (hex)	Tachion Networks, Inc.	00-30-17 (hex)	TERASTACK LTD.
003009 (base 16)	Tachion Networks, Inc. 2 Meridian Road Eatontown NJ 07724	003017 (base 16)	TERASTACK LTD. UNIT 3, CUTBUSH COURT DANEHILL, LOWER GARLEY READING, RG6 4UW UNITED KINGDOM
00-30-0A (hex)	AZTECH SYSTEMS LTD.		
00300A (base 16)	AZTECH SYSTEMS LTD. 31 UBI ROAD 1, AZTECH BUILDING SINGAPORE 408694	00-30-18 (hex)	Jetway Information Co., Ltd.
		003018 (base 16)	Jetway Information Co., Ltd. 4F, No. 168, LI THE ST. Chung Ho City 235 Taipei TAIWAN, R.O.C.
00-30-0B (hex)	mPHASE Technologies, Inc.		
00300B (base 16)	mPHASE Technologies, Inc. 250 14th Street GCATT Bldg. - Room #248A Atlanta GA 30318	00-30-19 (hex)	CISCO SYSTEMS, INC.
		003019 (base 16)	CISCO SYSTEMS, INC. 170 WEST TASMAN DRIVE - SJA-2 SAN JOSE CA 95134
00-30-0C (hex)	CONGRUENCY, LTD.		
00300C (base 16)	CONGRUENCY, LTD. 23 HASIVIM STREET POB 7813 PETAH-TIKVA 49170 ISRAEL	00-30-1A (hex)	SMARTBRIDGES PTE. LTD.
		00301A (base 16)	SMARTBRIDGES PTE. LTD. 21 HENG MUI KENG TERRACE XRDL BLDG. SINGAPORE 119613 SINGAPORE
00-30-0D (hex)	MMC Technology, Inc.		
00300D (base 16)	MMC Technology, Inc. #1502, Seoul Venture Town, Aju Bldg 679-5, Yeoksam-Dong, Kangnam-Gu Seoul 135-080 SOUTH KOREA	00-30-1B (hex)	SHUTTLE, INC.
		00301B (base 16)	SHUTTLE, INC. 5F, No. 34, Lane 60 Wen-Hu St., Nei-Hu Dist., Taipei TAIWAN
00-30-0E (hex)	Klotz Digital AG		
00300E (base 16)	Klotz Digital AG Hans-Stiessbergerstr. 2A D-85540 Haar GERMANY	00-30-1C (hex)	ALTVATER AIRDATA SYSTEMS
		00301C (base 16)	ALTVATER AIRDATA SYSTEMS GMBH & CO. KG RIEMENSTRASSE 30 74906 BAD RAPPENAU GERMANY
00-30-0F (hex)	IMT - Information Management Technology AG		
00300F (base 16)	IMT - Information Management Technology AG Gewerbestrasse 8 CH-9470 Buchs SWITZERLAND	00-30-1D (hex)	SKYSTREAM, INC.
		00301D (base 16)	SKYSTREAM, INC. 555 CLYDE AVENUE MOUNTAIN VIEW CA 94043
00-30-10 (hex)	VISIONETICS INTERNATIONAL	00-30-1E (hex)	3COM Europe Ltd.
003010 (base 16)	VISIONETICS INTERNATIONAL 3F, NO. 3, PROSPERITY ROAD 1 SCIENCE-BASED INDUSTRIAL PARK HSINCHU TAIWAN R.O.C.	00301E (base 16)	3COM Europe Ltd. 3COM Centre Boundary Way Hemel Hempstead Herts. HP2 7YU UNITED KINGDOM
		00-30-1F (hex)	OPTICAL NETWORKS, INC.
00-30-11 (hex)	HMS FIELDBUS SYSTEMS AB	00301F (base 16)	OPTICAL NETWORKS, INC. 166 BAYPOINTE PARKWAY SAN JOSE CA 95134
003011 (base 16)	HMS FIELDBUS SYSTEMS AB PILEFELTSGATAN 93-95 30250 HALMSSTAD SWEDEN		
00-30-12 (hex)	DIGITAL ENGINEERING LTD.	00-30-20 (hex)	TSI, Inc.
003012 (base 16)	DIGITAL ENGINEERING LTD. 2 TRENCH ROAD, MALLUSK BELFAST BT36 4TY NORTHERN IRELAND	003020 (base 16)	TSI, Inc. 500 Cardigan Road Shoreview MN 55126
00-30-13 (hex)	NEC Corporation	00-30-21 (hex)	HSING TECH. ENTERPRISE CO.,LTD

company_id	Organization Address	company_id	Organization Address
003021 (base 16)	HSING TECH. ENTERPRISE CO.,LTD 2F, NO. 22, ALLLEY 38, LANE 91 SEC. 1, NEI HU ROAD TAIPEI TAIWAN, R.O.C.	00-30-2F (hex)	Smiths Industries
		00302F (base 16)	Smiths Industries 3290 Patterson Ave., S.E. Grand Rapids MI 49512
00-30-22 (hex)	Fong Kai Industrial Co., Ltd.	00-30-30 (hex)	HARMONIX CORPORATION
003022 (base 16)	Fong Kai Industrial Co., Ltd. 4F-3, No. 13, Wu Chuan 1st Road Hsin Chuang City Taipei Hsien TAIWAN, R.O.C.	003030 (base 16)	HARMONIX CORPORATION 1755 OSGOOD STREET NORTH ANDOVER MA 01845
00-30-23 (hex)	COGENT COMPUTER SYSTEMS, INC.	00-30-31 (hex)	LIGHTWAVE COMMUNICATIONS, INC.
003023 (base 16)	COGENT COMPUTER SYSTEMS, INC. 10 RIVER ROAD - STE. #205 UXBRIDGE MA 01569	003031 (base 16)	LIGHTWAVE COMMUNICATIONS, INC. 261 PEPE'S FARM ROAD MILFORD CT 06460
00-30-24 (hex)	CISCO SYSTEMS, INC.	00-30-32 (hex)	MAGICRAM, INC.
003024 (base 16)	CISCO SYSTEMS, INC. 170 WEST TASMAN DRIVE -SJA-2 SAN JOSE CA 95134	003032 (base 16)	MAGICRAM, INC. 1850 BEVERLY BLVD. LOS ANGELES CA 90057
00-30-25 (hex)	CHECKOUT COMPUTER SYSTEMS, LTD	00-30-33 (hex)	ORIENT TELECOM CO., LTD.
003025 (base 16)	CHECKOUT COMPUTER SYSTEMS, LTD TOWNSEND FARM ROAD HOUGHTON REGIS, DUNSTABLE BEDFORDSHIRE LU5 5BA UNITED KINGDOM	003033 (base 16)	ORIENT TELECOM CO., LTD. MISUNG BULDING 115-7 NONHYUN-DONG, KANGMAN-KU SEOUL KOREA
00-30-26 (hex)	HEITEL	00-30-36 (hex)	RMP ELEKTRONIKSYSTEME GMBH
003026 (base 16)	HEITEL KOMMUNIKATIONSELEKTRONIK GMBH SCHAUENBURGERSTR. 116 24118 KIEL GERMANY	003036 (base 16)	RMP ELEKTRONIKSYSTEME GMBH HANNS-MARTIN-SCHLE'R-STR.12-14 D-47877 WILLICH-MUNCHHEIDE GERMANY
00-30-27 (hex)	KERBANGO, INC.	00-30-37 (hex)	Packard Bell Nec Services
003027 (base 16)	KERBANGO, INC. 21771 STEVENS CREEK BLVD. #100 CUPERTINO CA 95014	003037 (base 16)	Packard Bell Nec Services 299 Avenue Patton, BP 645 49006 Angers Cedex 01 FRANCE
00-30-28 (hex)	FASE Saldatura srl	00-30-38 (hex)	XCP, INC.
003028 (base 16)	FASE Saldatura srl V.R. Bernardi 5 10042 Stupiniqi-Nichelino TORINO ITALY	003038 (base 16)	XCP, INC. 40 ELM STREET DRYDEN NY 13053
00-30-29 (hex)	OPICOM	00-30-39 (hex)	SOFTBOOK PRESS
003029 (base 16)	OPICOM ROOM #302, STYLE FACTORY 151 YATAB-DONG, BUNDANG-GU SUNGNAM-SI, KYUNGG:-DO 463-070 KOREA	003039 (base 16)	SOFTBOOK PRESS 7745 HERSCHEL AVENUE LA JOLLA CA 92037
00-30-2A (hex)	SOUTHERN INFORMATION	00-30-3A (hex)	MAATEL
00302A (base 16)	SOUTHERN INFORMATION SYSTEM, INC. NO.8, R&D RD. IV SCIENCE-BASED INDUSTRIAL PARK HSINCHU, TAIWAN, R.O.C.	00303A (base 16)	MAATEL 495 RUE DE POMMARIN 38360 VOREPPE FRANCE
00-30-2B (hex)	INALP NETWORKS, INC.	00-30-3B (hex)	PowerCom Technology
00302B (base 16)	INALP NETWORKS, INC. MERIEDWEG 7 CH-3172 NIEDERWANGEN SWITZERLAND	00303B (base 16)	PowerCom Technology 2F, No. 34, Industry E. Road IV Hsinchu Science-based Industrial Park Hsinchu TAIWAN, R.O.C.
00-30-2C (hex)	SYLANTRO SYSTEMS CORPORATION	00-30-3C (hex)	ONNTO CORP.
00302C (base 16)	SYLANTRO SYSTEMS CORPORATION 1686 DELL AVENUE CAMPBELL CA 95008	00303C (base 16)	ONNTO CORP. 12F-2, NO. 161 SUNG TEH RD., TAIPEI TAIWAN, R.O.C.
00-30-2D (hex)	QUANTUM BRIDGE COMMUNICATIONS	00-30-3D (hex)	IVA CORPORATION
00302D (base 16)	QUANTUM BRIDGE COMMUNICATIONS ONE HIGH STREET NORTH ANDOVER MA 01845	00303D (base 16)	IVA CORPORATION 29 HUDSON ROAD SUDBURY MA 01776
00-30-2E (hex)	Hoft & Wessel AG	00-30-3E (hex)	Radcom Ltd.
00302E (base 16)	Hoft & Wessel AG Rotenburger Strasse 20 30659 Hannover GERMANY	00303E (base 16)	Radcom Ltd. 12 Hanechoshet Street Tel-Aviv 69710 ISRAEL
		00-30-3F (hex)	TurboComm Tech Inc.
		00303F (base 16)	TurboComm Tech Inc. 4F-2, No 171, Sung-Tch Road Taipei TAIWAN, R.O.C.

company_id	Organization Address
00-30-40 (hex)	CISCO SYSTEMS, INC.
003040 (base 16)	CISCO SYSTEMS, INC. 170 WEST TASMAN DRIVE -SJA-2 SAN JOSE CA 95134
00-30-41 (hex)	SAEJIN T & M CO., LTD.
003041 (base 16)	SAEJIN T & M CO., LTD. 2ND FL., SAEJIN BLDG. 689 ILWON-DONG, KANGNAM-GU, SEOUL 135-230 KOREA
00-30-42 (hex)	DeTeWe-Deutsche Telephonwerke
003042 (base 16)	DeTeWe-Deutsche Telephonwerke Zeughofstrasse 1 D-10997 Berlin GERMANY
00-30-43 (hex)	IDREAM TECHNOLOGIES, PTE. LTD.
003043 (base 16)	IDREAM TECHNOLOGIES, PTE. LTD. 54 KALLANG BAHRU, #02-14 SINGAPORE 339336 SINGAPORE
00-30-44 (hex)	Portsmith LLC
003044 (base 16)	Portsmith LLC 1111 S. Orchard - Ste. #109 Boise ID 83705
00-30-45 (hex)	Village Networks, Inc. (VNI)
003045 (base 16)	Village Networks, Inc. (VNI) 100 Village Court - Ste. #301 Hazlet NJ 07730
00-30-46 (hex)	Controlled Electronic Management
003046 (base 16)	Controlled Electronic Management Unit 4 Ravenhill Business Park Ravenhill Road, Belfast BT6 8ANN N. IRELAND
00-30-47 (hex)	NISSEI ELECTRIC CO., LTD.
003047 (base 16)	NISSEI ELECTRIC CO., LTD. 32 MIYAWAKE, SHIMONOISHIKI-CHO NAKAGAWA-KU, NAGOYA 454-0945 JAPAN
00-30-48 (hex)	Supermicro Computer, Inc.
003048 (base 16)	Supermicro Computer, Inc. 2051 Junction Avenue San Jose CA 95131
00-30-49 (hex)	BRYANT TECHNOLOGY, LTD.
003049 (base 16)	BRYANT TECHNOLOGY, LTD. P.O. BOX 69557 BRYANSTON, 2021 SOUTH AFRICA
00-30-4A (hex)	FRAUNHOFER INSTITUTE IMS
00304A (base 16)	FRAUNHOFER INSTITUTE IMS GRENZSTRASSE 28 01109 DRESDEN GERMANY
00-30-4B (hex)	ORBACOM SYSTEMS, INC.
00304B (base 16)	ORBACOM SYSTEMS, INC. 1704 TAYLORS LANE CINNAMINSON NJ 08077
00-30-4C (hex)	APPIAN COMMUNICATIONS, INC.
00304C (base 16)	APPIAN COMMUNICATIONS, INC. 80 CENTRAL STREET BOXBOROUGH MA 01719
00-30-4D (hex)	ESI
00304D (base 16)	ESI 2601 Summit Avenue Plano TX 75074
00-30-4E (hex)	BUSTEC PRODUCTION LTD.
00304E (base 16)	BUSTEC PRODUCTION LTD. WORLD AVIATION PARK SHANNON, COUNTY CLARE IRELAND

company_id	Organization Address
00-30-4F (hex)	PLANET Technology Corporation
00304F (base 16)	PLANET Technology Corporation 11F, No. 96, Min-Chuan Road Hsin-Tien Taipei TAIWAN, R.O.C.
00-30-50 (hex)	Versa Technology
003050 (base 16)	Versa Technology 4430 E. Miraloma Ave., - Ste. "A" Anaheim CA 92807
00-30-51 (hex)	ORBIT AVIONIC & COMMUNICATION
003051 (base 16)	ORBIT AVIONIC & COMMUNICATION SYSTEMS, LTD. P.O. BOX 3171 INDUSTRIAL ZONE, NETANYA 42131 ISRAEL
00-30-52 (hex)	ELASTIC NETWORKS
003052 (base 16)	ELASTIC NETWORKS 6120 WINDWARD PARKWAY -STE#100 ALPHARETTA GA 30005
00-30-53 (hex)	Basler AG
003053 (base 16)	Basler AG An Der Strusbek 60-62 22926 Ahrensburg GERMANY
00-30-54 (hex)	CASTLENET TECHNOLOGY, INC.
003054 (base 16)	CASTLENET TECHNOLOGY, INC. NO. 130 WU-KUNG RD., WU-KU HSIANG TAIPEI HSIEN TAIWAN, R.O.C.
00-30-55 (hex)	Hitachi Semiconductor America
003055 (base 16)	Hitachi Semiconductor America 179 East Tasman Drive San Jose CA 95134
00-30-56 (hex)	Beck IPC GmbH
003056 (base 16)	Beck IPC GmbH Garbenheimer Str. 30-38 35578 Wetzlar GERMANY
00-30-57 (hex)	E-Tel Corporation
003057 (base 16)	E-Tel Corporation 297 Cowesett Avenue West Warwick RI 02893
00-30-58 (hex)	API MOTION
003058 (base 16)	API MOTION 45 HAZELWOOD DRIVE AMHERST NY 14228
00-30-59 (hex)	DIGITAL-LOGIC AG
003059 (base 16)	DIGITAL-LOGIC AG NORDSTR. 11/F CH-4542 LUTERBACH SWITZERLAND
00-30-5A (hex)	TELGEN CORPORATION
00305A (base 16)	TELGEN CORPORATION 3101 SOVEREIGN DR. - STE. "A" LANSING MI 48911
00-30-5B (hex)	MODULE DEPARTMENT
00305B (base 16)	MODULE DEPARTMENT 18 COMIGAYA, TSURUGASHIMA-SHI SAITAMA-KEN JAPAN 350-2281
00-30-5C (hex)	SMAR Laboratories Corp.
00305C (base 16)	SMAR Laboratories Corp. 10960 Millridge North - Ste. #107 Houston, TX 77070
00-30-5D (hex)	DIGITRA SYSTEMS, INC.

company_id	Organization Address
00305D (base 16)	DIGITRA SYSTEMS, INC. 8-61, GAWOL-DONG YONGSAN-KU SEOUL KOREA 140-150
00-30-5E (hex)	Abelko Innovation
00305E (base 16)	Abelko Innovation Box 808 S-97125 Lulea SWEDEN
00-30-5F (hex)	IMACON APS
00305F (base 16)	IMACON APS HEJREVEJ 26 DK-2400 COPENHAGEN NV DENMARK
00-30-60 (hex)	STARMATIX, INC.
003060 (base 16)	STARMATIX, INC. 718 UNIVERSITY AVENUE SUITE #100 LOS GATOS CA 95032-7608
00-30-61 (hex)	MobyTEL
003061 (base 16)	MobyTEL 4301 Connecticut Ave. NW Ste. #454 Washington, DC 20008
00-30-62 (hex)	PATH 1 NETWORK TECHNOL'S INC.
003062 (base 16)	PATH 1 NETWORK TECHNOL'S INC. 3636 NOBEL DRIVE - STE. #275 SAN DIEGO CA 92122
00-30-63 (hex)	SANTERA SYSTEMS, INC.
003063 (base 16)	SANTERA SYSTEMS, INC. 2901 SUMMIT AVENUE - STE. #100 PLANO TX 75074
00-30-64 (hex)	ADLINK TECHNOLOGY, INC.
003064 (base 16)	ADLINK TECHNOLOGY, INC. 9F, NO. 166, JIEN-YI R.D. CHUNG-HO CITY TAIPEI TAIWAN
00-30-65 (hex)	APPLE COMPUTER, INC.
003065 (base 16)	APPLE COMPUTER, INC. 20650 VALLEY GREEN DRIVE CUPERTINO CA 95014
00-30-66 (hex)	DIGITAL WIRELESS CORPORATION
003066 (base 16)	DIGITAL WIRELESS CORPORATION ONE MECA WAY NORCROSS GA 30093-2919
00-30-67 (hex)	BIOSTAR MICROTECH INT'L CORP.
003067 (base 16)	BIOSTAR MICROTECH INT'L CORP. 2FL. NO. 108-2 MIN CHUAN ROAD HSIN TIEN CITY, TAIPEI HSIEN TAIWAN R.O.C.
00-30-68 (hex)	CYBERNETICS TECH. CO., LTD.
003068 (base 16)	CYBERNETICS TECH. CO., LTD. DAITOH BLDG. 4F 3-32-1 TAKADA, TOSHIMA-KU, TOKYO JAPAN 171-0033
00-30-69 (hex)	IMPACCT TECHNOLOGY CORP.
003069 (base 16)	IMPACCT TECHNOLOGY CORP. 2F, NO. 12, R&D RD. II SCIENCE-BASED INDUSTRIAL PARK HSIN-CHU TAIWAN, R.O.C.
00-30-6A (hex)	PENTA MEDIA CO., LTD.
00306A (base 16)	PENTA MEDIA CO., LTD. 4TH FL. SDOAM BLDG. 66-1 YANG JAE DONG SEOCHO-KU SEOUL KOREA
00-30-6B (hex)	CMOS SYSTEMS, INC.

company_id	Organization Address
00306B (base 16)	CMOS SYSTEMS, INC. 23440 HAWTHORNE BLVD-STE #290 TORRANCE CA 90505
00-30-6C (hex)	Hitex Holding GmbH
00306C (base 16)	Hitex Holding GmbH Greschbachstr. 12 76229 Karlsruhe GERMANY
00-30-6D (hex)	LUCENT TECHNOLOGIES
00306D (base 16)	LUCENT TECHNOLOGIES 300 BAKER AVENUE - STE. #100 CONCORD MA 01742-2168
00-30-6E (hex)	HEWLETT-PACKARD COMPANY
00306E (base 16)	HEWLETT-PACKARD COMPANY 11000 WOLFE ROAD CUPERTINO CA 95014
00-30-6F (hex)	SEYEON TECH. CO., LTD.
00306F (base 16)	SEYEON TECH. CO., LTD. NAMCHEON BLDG. 6F, DAECHI-DONG, 957-013 KANGNAM-GU, SEOUL KOREA 135-280
00-30-70 (hex)	1Net Corporation
003070 (base 16)	1Net Corporation 347 Elizabeth Avenue - Ste. #100 Somerset NJ 08873
00-30-71 (hex)	Cisco Systems, Inc.
003071 (base 16)	Cisco Systems, Inc. 170 West Tasman Driv - SJA-2 San Jose CA 95134
00-30-72 (hex)	INTELLIBYTE INC.
003072 (base 16)	INTELLIBYTE INC. 397 DURIE STREET TORONTO, ONTARIO CANADA, M6S 365
00-30-73 (hex)	International Microsystems, In
003073 (base 16)	International Microsystems, In 521 Valley Way Milpitas CA 95035
00-30-74 (hex)	EQUIINET LTD.
003074 (base 16)	EQUIINET LTD. EDISON HOUSE EDISON ROAD SWINDON, SN3 5JA UNITED KINGDOM
00-30-75 (hex)	ADTECH
003075 (base 16)	ADTECH 10 rue Nicolas Fossoul 4100 Boncelles BELGIUM
00-30-76 (hex)	N-CUBED.NET
003076 (base 16)	N-CUBED.NET 1190 SARATOGA AVE. - STE. #150 SAN JOSE CA 95129
00-30-77 (hex)	ONPREM NETWORKS
003077 (base 16)	ONPREM NETWORKS 42501 ALBRAE STREET FREMONT CA 94538
00-30-78 (hex)	Cisco Systems, Inc.
003078 (base 16)	Cisco Systems, Inc. 170 West Tasman Drive - SJA-2 San Jose CA 95134
00-30-79 (hex)	CQOS, INC.
003079 (base 16)	CQOS, INC. 25 MAUCHLY - STE. #329 IRVINE CA 92618
00-30-7A (hex)	Advanced Technology & Systems

company_id	Organization Address
00307A (base 16)	Advanced Technology & Systems 1-2-7, Kugenumo Tachibana Fujisawa, Kanagawa JAPAN 251-0024
00-30-7B (hex)	Cisco Systems, Inc.
00307B (base 16)	Cisco Systems, Inc. 170 West Tasman Drive - SJA-2 San Jose CA 95134
00-30-7C (hex)	ADID SA
00307C (base 16)	ADID SA 70 RU ANATOLE FRANCE 92 300 LEVALLOIS-PERRET CEDEX FRANCE
00-30-7D (hex)	GRE AMERICA, INC.
00307D (base 16)	GRE AMERICA, INC. 425 HARBOR BLVD. BELMONT CA 94002
00-30-7E (hex)	Redflex Communication Systems
00307E (base 16)	Redflex Communication Systems 11-29 Eastern Road South Melbourne Victoria AUSTRALIA 3205
00-30-7F (hex)	IRLAN LTD.
00307F (base 16)	IRLAN LTD. 1 HATAMAR STREET P.O. BOX 288 YOKNEAM 20692 ISRAEL
00-30-80 (hex)	CISCO SYSTEMS, INC.
003080 (base 16)	CISCO SYSTEMS, INC. 170 WEST TASMAN DRIVE - SJA-2 SAN JOSE CA 95134
00-30-81 (hex)	ALTOS C&C
003081 (base 16)	ALTOS C&C 150-010 RM. 1012, 44-1 DAE YOUNG B/D, YOVIDO-DONG YOUNGCHUNGPO-GU, SEOUL KOREA
00-30-82 (hex)	TAIHAN ELECTRIC WIRE CO., LTD.
003082 (base 16)	TAIHAN ELECTRIC WIRE CO., LTD. Communication Engineering Team 996 Siheung-Dong Keym Cheon-ku Seoul KOREA
00-30-83 (hex)	Ivron Systems
003083 (base 16)	Ivron Systems 19-20 YORK ROAD DUN LAOGHAIRE COUNTY DUBLIN IRELAND
00-30-84 (hex)	ALLIED TELESYN INTERNAIONAL
003084 (base 16)	ALLIED TELESYN INTERNAIONAL CORPORATION 960 STEWART DRIVE, STE. "B" SUNNYVALE CA 94086
00-30-85 (hex)	CISCO SYSTEMS, INC.
003085 (base 16)	CISCO SYSTEMS, INC. 170 WEST TASMAN DRIVE SAN JOSE CA 95134
00-30-86 (hex)	Transistor Devices, Inc.
003086 (base 16)	Transistor Devices, Inc. 36A Newburgh Road Hackettstown NJ 07840
00-30-87 (hex)	VEGA GRIESHABER KG
003087 (base 16)	VEGA GRIESHABER KG AM HOHENSTEIN 113 77761 SCHULTACH GERMANY
00-30-88 (hex)	Siara Systems, Inc.

company_id	Organization Address
003088 (base 16)	Siara Systems, Inc. 300 Ferguson Drive - 2nd Floor Mountain View CA 94043
00-30-89 (hex)	Spectrapoint Wireless, LLC
003089 (base 16)	Spectrapoint Wireless, LLC 1125 E. Collins Blvd. Richardson TX 75081
00-30-8A (hex)	NICOTRA SISTEMI S.P.A
00308A (base 16)	NICOTRA SISTEMI S.P.A VIA V. MONTI, 23 20016 PERO (MI) ITALY
00-30-8B (hex)	Brix Networks
00308B (base 16)	Brix Networks 300 Concord Road Billerica MA 01821
00-30-8C (hex)	ADVANCED DIGITAL INFORMATION
00308C (base 16)	ADVANCED DIGITAL INFORMATION CORPORATION 10949 E. PEAKVIEW AVE. ENGLEWOOD CO 80111
00-30-8D (hex)	PINNACLE SYSTEMS, INC.
00308D (base 16)	PINNACLE SYSTEMS, INC. FRANKFURTER STR. 3C 38122 BRAUNSCHWEIG GERMANY
00-30-8E (hex)	CROSS MATCH TECHNOLOGIES, INC.
00308E (base 16)	CROSS MATCH TECHNOLOGIES, INC. 3960 RCA Blvd., Suite 6001 Palm Beach, FL 33410
00-30-8F (hex)	MICRILOR, Inc.
00308F (base 16)	MICRILOR, Inc. 17 Lakeside Office Park 607 North Avenue Wakefield MA 01880
00-30-90 (hex)	CYRA TECHNOLOGIES, INC.
003090 (base 16)	CYRA TECHNOLOGIES, INC. 8000 CAPWELL DRIVE OAKLAND CA 94621
00-30-91 (hex)	TAIWAN FIRST LINE ELEC. CORP.
003091 (base 16)	TAIWAN FIRST LINE ELEC. CORP. 4F, NO. 36-1, HUANG HSI STREET TAIPEI TAIWAN, R.O.C.
00-30-92 (hex)	ModuNORM GmbH
003092 (base 16)	ModuNORM GmbH Langrutistrasse 33 CH-8840 Einsiedeln SWITZERLAND
00-30-93 (hex)	SONNET TECHNOLOGIES, INC.
003093 (base 16)	SONNET TECHNOLOGIES, INC. 3390 BUFORD DRIVE - STE. #7 BUFORD GA 30519
00-30-94 (hex)	Cisco Systems, Inc.
003094 (base 16)	Cisco Systems, Inc. 170 West Tasman Drive - SJA-2 San Jose CA 95134
00-30-95 (hex)	Procomp Informatics, Ltd.
003095 (base 16)	Procomp Informatics, Ltd. 5F, 69-10, Sec. 2, Chung Cheng E. Road Tamshui, Taipei, Hsien TAIWAN, R.O.C.
00-30-96 (hex)	CISCO SYSTEMS, INC.
003096 (base 16)	CISCO SYSTEMS, INC. 170 WEST TASMAN DRIVE - SJA-2 SAN JOSE CA 95134
00-30-97 (hex)	EXOMATIC AB

company_id	Organization Address
003097 (base 16)	EXOMATIC AB INDUSTRI PARKEN BOX 64 S-260 20 TECKOMATORP SWEDEN
00-30-98 (hex)	Global Converging Technologies
003098 (base 16)	Global Converging Technologies 1800 Preston Park Blvd. Suite #250 Plano TX 75093
00-30-99 (hex)	BOENIG UND KALLENBACH OHG
003099 (base 16)	BOENIG UND KALLENBACH OHG AM SPOERKEL 100 44227 DORTMUND GERMANY
00-30-9A (hex)	ASTRO TERRA CORP.
00309A (base 16)	ASTRO TERRA CORP. 11526 SORRENTO VALLEY ROAD SAN DIEGO CA 92121
00-30-9B (hex)	Smartware
00309B (base 16)	Smartware 49 AV Aristide Briand 92160 Antony FRANCE
00-30-9C (hex)	Timing Applications, Inc.
00309C (base 16)	Timing Applications, Inc. 5335 Sterling Dr. - Ste. "B" Boulder CO 80301
00-30-9D (hex)	Nimble Microsystems, Inc.
00309D (base 16)	Nimble Microsystems, Inc. 50 Church Street - 5th Floor Cambridge MA 02138
00-30-9E (hex)	WORKBIT CORPORATION.
00309E (base 16)	WORKBIT CORPORATION. 1-2-2 Chuou, Yamato Kanagawa Zip: 242-0021 JAPAN
00-30-9F (hex)	AMBER NETWORKS
00309F (base 16)	AMBER NETWORKS 2475 AUGUSTINE DR. SANTA CLARA CA 95054
00-30-A0 (hex)	TYCO SUBMARINE SYSTEMS, LTD.
0030A0 (base 16)	TYCO SUBMARINE SYSTEMS, LTD. 250 INDUSTRIAL WAY WEST EATONTOWN NJ 07724
00-30-A1 (hex)	OPTI TECH CO., LTD.
0030A1 (base 16)	OPTI TECH CO., LTD. NAMKYUNG BD 2F 96-6 WOOMAN2-DONG, SUWAN-CITY KYUNGGI-DO KOREA
00-30-A2 (hex)	Lightner Engineering
0030A2 (base 16)	Lightner Engineering P.O. Box 8308 La Jolla CA 92038-8308
00-30-A3 (hex)	CISCO SYSTEMS, INC.
0030A3 (base 16)	CISCO SYSTEMS, INC. 170 WEST TASMAN DRIVE -SJA-2 SAN JOSE CA 95134
00-30-A4 (hex)	Woodwind Communications System
0030A4 (base 16)	Woodwind Communications System 16 E. Patrick Street - 3rd Floor Frederick MD 21701
00-30-A5 (hex)	ACTIVE POWER
0030A5 (base 16)	ACTIVE POWER 11525 STONEHOLLOW - STE.#255 AUSTIN TX 78758
00-30-A6 (hex)	VIANET TECHNOLOGIES, LTD.

company_id	Organization Address
0030A6 (base 16)	VIANET TECHNOLOGIES, LTD. 8 HACHARASH STREET RAMAT HASHARON 47262 ISRAEL
00-30-A7 (hex)	SCHWEITZER ENGINEERING
0030A7 (base 16)	SCHWEITZER ENGINEERING LABORATORIES, INC. 2350 NE HOPKINS COURT PULLMAN WA 99163
00-30-A8 (hex)	OL'E COMMUNICATIONS, INC.
0030A8 (base 16)	OL'E COMMUNICATIONS, INC. 1962 ZANKER ROAD SAN JOSE CA 95112
00-30-A9 (hex)	Netiverse, Inc.
0030A9 (base 16)	Netiverse, Inc. 100 Century Center Court Suite #600 San Jose CA 95112
00-30-AA (hex)	AXUS MICROSYSTEMS, INC.
0030AA (base 16)	AXUS MICROSYSTEMS, INC. 2F-4, NO.18/N. 609, SEC. 5 CHUN-HSIN ROAD, SAN CHUNG TAIPEI COUNTY TAIWAN, R.O.C.
00-30-AB (hex)	DELTA NETWORKS, INC.
0030AB (base 16)	DELTA NETWORKS, INC. 8, KON JAN WEST ROAD LIUTU INDUSTRIAL ZONE KEELUNG TAIWAN, R.O.C.
00-30-AC (hex)	Systeme Lauer GmbH & Co., Ltd.
0030AC (base 16)	Systeme Lauer GmbH & Co., Ltd. Kelterstrasse 59 72669 Unterensingen GERMANY
00-30-AD (hex)	SHANGHAI COMMUNICATION
0030AD (base 16)	SHANGHAI COMMUNICATION TECHNOLOGIES CENTER 15 GUI-QING ROAD SHANGHAI 200233 P.R. CHINA
00-30-AE (hex)	Times N System, Inc.
0030AE (base 16)	Times N System, Inc. 1826 Kramer Lane - Ste. "F" Austin TX 78758
00-30-AF (hex)	Honeywell Reqelsysteme GmbH
0030AF (base 16)	Honeywell Reqelsysteme GmbH Honeywellstr. 2-6 D-63477 Maintal GERMANY
00-30-B0 (hex)	Convergenet Technologies
0030B0 (base 16)	Convergenet Technologies 2222 Trade Zone Boulevard San Jose CA 95131
00-30-B1 (hex)	GOC GESELLSCHAFT FUR OPTISCHE
0030B1 (base 16)	GOC GESELLSCHAFT FUR OPTISCHE COMMUNICATION MBH SCHIEBGARTENSTR. 5 D-63303 DREIEICH GERMANY
00-30-B2 (hex)	WESCAM - HEALDSBURG
0030B2 (base 16)	WESCAM - HEALDSBURG 103 W. NORTH STREET HEALDSBURG CA 95448
00-30-B3 (hex)	San Valley Systems, Inc.
0030B3 (base 16)	San Valley Systems, Inc. 2105 S. Bascom Ave. - Ste. #390 Campbell CA 95008
00-30-B4 (hex)	INTERSIL CORP.

company_id	Organization Address
0030B4 (base 16)	INTERSIL CORP. P.O. BOX 883 2401 PALM BAY ROAD MELBOURNE FL 32902
00-30-B5 (hex)	Tadiran Microwave Networks
0030B5 (base 16)	Tadiran Microwave Networks 4000 Greenbriar Drive Stafford TX 77477
00-30-B6 (hex)	CISCO SYSTEMS, INC.
0030B6 (base 16)	CISCO SYSTEMS, INC. 170 WEST TASMAN DRIVE - SJA-2 SAN JOSE CA 95134
00-30-B7 (hex)	Teletrol Systems, Inc.
0030B7 (base 16)	Teletrol Systems, Inc. Technology Center 286 Commercial Street Manchester NH 03101
00-30-B8 (hex)	RiverDelta Networks
0030B8 (base 16)	RiverDelta Networks Three Highwood Drive East Tewksbury MA 01876
00-30-B9 (hex)	ECTEL
0030B9 (base 16)	ECTEL 22240 COMSAT DRIVE CLARKSBURG MD 20871
00-30-BA (hex)	AC&T SYSTEM CO., LTD.
0030BA (base 16)	AC&T SYSTEM CO., LTD. ROOM 702, KEUM-WHA PLAZA 1142-5, SANBON-DONG KOONPO-SHI, KYONGKI-DO 435-040, SOUTH KOREA
00-30-BB (hex)	CacheFlow, Inc.
0030BB (base 16)	CacheFlow, Inc. 650 Almanor Drive Sunnyvale CA 94086
00-30-BC (hex)	Optronic AG
0030BC (base 16)	Optronic AG Untereggerstrasse 53 9403 Goldach SWITZERLAND
00-30-BD (hex)	BELKIN COMPONENTS
0030BD (base 16)	BELKIN COMPONENTS 501 WEST WALNUT STREET COMPTON CA 90220
00-30-BE (hex)	City-Net Technology, Inc.
0030BE (base 16)	City-Net Technology, Inc. 135 E. Chesnut Ave., Ste. "5B" Monrovia CA 91016
00-30-BF (hex)	MULTIDATA GMBH
0030BF (base 16)	MULTIDATA GMBH ALSFELDER STR. 3 D-64289 DARMSTADT GERMANY
00-30-C0 (hex)	Lara Technology, Inc.
0030C0 (base 16)	Lara Technology, Inc. 2345 North First Street San Jose CA 95131
00-30-C1 (hex)	HEWLETT-PACKARD COMPANY
0030C1 (base 16)	HEWLETT-PACKARD COMPANY 11000 WOLFE ROAD CUPERTINO CA 95014
00-30-C2 (hex)	COMONE
0030C2 (base 16)	COMONE Parc De Marticot 33610 Cestas FRANCE
00-30-C3 (hex)	FLUECKIGER ELEKTRONIK AG

company_id	Organization Address
0030C3 (base 16)	FLUECKIGER ELEKTRONIK AG KIRCHBARGSTRASSE 201 CH-3400 BURGDORF SWITZERLAND
00-30-C4 (hex)	Niigata Canotec Co., Inc.
0030C4 (base 16)	Niigata Canotec Co., Inc. 1-24 Yoneyama, Niigota City Niigata JAPAN
00-30-C5 (hex)	CADENCE DESIGN SYSTEMS
0030C5 (base 16)	CADENCE DESIGN SYSTEMS CANADA, LTD. 240-1130 MORRISON DRIVE OTTAWA, ONTARIO K2H 9N6 CANADA
00-30-C6 (hex)	CONTROL SOLUTIONS, INC.
0030C6 (base 16)	CONTROL SOLUTIONS, INC. 201 85TH AVENUE NW MINNEAPOLIS MN 55433
00-30-C7 (hex)	MACROMATE CORP.
0030C7 (base 16)	MACROMATE CORP. 8F, UNIVERSAL CENTER, NO.179 SEC. 1, TA-TUNG RD., HSI-CHIH TAIPEI HSIEN TAIWAN, R.O.C.
00-30-C8 (hex)	GAD LINE, LTD.
0030C8 (base 16)	GAD LINE, LTD. BEIT ROKAR HAR HOTZVIM JERUSALEM ISRAEL
00-30-C9 (hex)	LuxN, N
0030C9 (base 16)	LuxN, N 570 Maude Court Sunnyvale CA 94086
00-30-CA (hex)	Discovery Com
0030CA (base 16)	Discovery Com 4935 Century Street Huntsville AL 35816
00-30-CB (hex)	OMNI FLOW COMPUTERS, INC.
0030CB (base 16)	OMNI FLOW COMPUTERS, INC. 10701 CORPORATE DRIVE-STE.#300 STAFFORD TX 77477
00-30-CC (hex)	Tenor Networks, Inc.
0030CC (base 16)	Tenor Networks, Inc. 50 Nagog Park Acton MA 01720
00-30-CD (hex)	CONEXANT SYSTEMS, INC.
0030CD (base 16)	CONEXANT SYSTEMS, INC. 4311 JAMBOREE ROAD NEWPORT BEACH CA 92660
00-30-CE (hex)	Zaffire
0030CE (base 16)	Zaffire 2630 Orchard Parkway San Jose, CA 95134-2020
00-30-CF (hex)	TWO TECHNOLOGIES, INC.
0030CF (base 16)	TWO TECHNOLOGIES, INC. 419 SARGON WAY HORSHAM PA 19044
00-30-D1 (hex)	INOVA CORPORATION
0030D1 (base 16)	INOVA CORPORATION 110 AVON STREET CHARLOTTESVILE VA 22902
00-30-D2 (hex)	WIN TECHNOLOGIES, CO., LTD.
0030D2 (base 16)	WIN TECHNOLOGIES, CO., LTD. 4F-6, No. 81, Sec. 1 Hsin Tai Wu Road, Hsi-Chi Taipei TAIWAN, R.O.C.
00-30-D3 (hex)	Agilent Technologies

company_id	Organization Address
0030D3 (base 16)	Agilent Technologies 1501 Page Mill Road Palo Alto CA 94304-1126
00-30-D4 (hex)	COMTIER
0030D4 (base 16)	COMTIER 2525 WALSH AVENUE SANTA CLARA CA 95051-1316
00-30-D5 (hex)	DResearch Digital Media Systems GmbH
0030D5 (base 16)	DResearch Digital Media Systems GmbH Otto-Schmirgal-Str. 3 10319 Berlin GERMANY
00-30-D6 (hex)	MSC VERTRIEBS GMBH
0030D6 (base 16)	MSC VERTRIEBS GMBH INDUSTRIESTR. 16 D-76297 STUTENSEE GERMANY
00-30-D7 (hex)	Innovative Systems, L.L.C.
0030D7 (base 16)	Innovative Systems, L.L.C. 209 E. 4th Avenue Mitchell SD 57301
00-30-D8 (hex)	SITEK
0030D8 (base 16)	SITEK VIA MONTE FIORINO 9 37057 - S. GIOVANNI LUP. VERONA ITALY
00-30-D9 (hex)	DATACORE SOFTWARE CORP.
0030D9 (base 16)	DATACORE SOFTWARE CORP. CORPORATE PARK 6261 NW 6TH WAY #110 FORT LAUDERDALE FL 33309
00-30-DA (hex)	COMTREND CO.
0030DA (base 16)	COMTREND CO. 3F-1 10 LANE 609 CHUNG HSIN ROAD, SEC 5, SAN CHUNG CITY, TAIPEI HSIEN TAIWAN 241
00-30-DB (hex)	SEDERTA INC.
0030DB (base 16)	SEDERTA INC. 5065 LEVY SAINT-LAURENT, QUEBEC CANADA H4R 2N9
00-30-DC (hex)	RIGHTECH CORPORATION
0030DC (base 16)	RIGHTECH CORPORATION 4F, NO. 351, CHUNG-SHUN RD. SEC. 2, CHUNG-HO CITY TAIPEI TAIWAN, R.O.C.
00-30-DD (hex)	INDIGITA CORPORATION
0030DD (base 16)	INDIGITA CORPORATION 1518 BROOKHOLLOW DRIVE SUITE #19 SANTA ANA CA 92705
00-30-DE (hex)	WAGO Kontakttechnik GmbH
0030DE (base 16)	WAGO Kontakttechnik GmbH Hansastrasse 27 32423 Minden GERMANY
00-30-DF (hex)	KB/TEL TELECOMUNICACIONES
0030DF (base 16)	KB/TEL TELECOMUNICACIONES S.A. DE C.V. TORRE TELMEX 4 PISO, PLAZA CUICUILCO, MEXICO CITY. 14060 MEXICO
00-30-E0 (hex)	OXFORD SEMICONDUCTOR LTD.
0030E0 (base 16)	OXFORD SEMICONDUCTOR LTD. 69 MILTON PARK ABINGDON, OXON, 0X14 4RX UNITED KINGDOM
00-30-E1 (hex)	ACROTRON SYSTEMS, INC.

company_id	Organization Address
0030E1 (base 16)	ACROTRON SYSTEMS, INC. 704 GINESI DRIVE - STE. #27 MORGANVILLE NJ 07751
00-30-E2 (hex)	GARNET SYSTEMS CO., LTD.
0030E2 (base 16)	GARNET SYSTEMS CO., LTD. Sungwon Bldg. 545-7 Dogok-Dong, Kangnam-Gu Seoul KOREA #135-270
00-30-E3 (hex)	SEDONA NETWORKS CORP.
0030E3 (base 16)	SEDONA NETWORKS CORP. 10A HEARST WAY KANATA, ONTARIO CANADA K2L 2P4
00 30 E4 (hex)	CHIYODA SYSTEM RIKEN
0030E4 (base 16)	CHIYODA SYSTEM RIKEN 2-7, KANDA-NISHIKI-CHO CHIYODA-KU TOKYO JAPAN
00-30-E5 (hex)	Amper Datos S.A.
0030E5 (base 16)	Amper Datos S.A. C/Marconi n*3 (PTM) Tres Cantos 28760 Madrid SPAIN
00-30-E6 (hex)	SIEMENS MEDICAL SYSTEMS
0030E6 (base 16)	SIEMENS MEDICAL SYSTEMS 16 ELECTRONICS AVENUE DANVERS MA 01923
00-30-E7 (hex)	CNF MOBILE SOLUTIONS, INC.
0030E7 (base 16)	CNF MOBILE SOLUTIONS, INC. 7722 E. GRAY ROAD SCOTTSDALE AZ 85260
00-30-E8 (hex)	ENSIM CORP.
0030E8 (base 16)	ENSIM CORP. 1215 Terra Bella Ave. Mountainview CA 94043
00-30-E9 (hex)	GMA COMMUNICATION MANUFACT'G
0030E9 (base 16)	GMA COMMUNICATION MANUFACT'G MARKETING, (1991) LTD. 102 JABUTINSKI STREET KIRYAT ARIE, PETACH-TIKVA ISRAEL, 49130
00-30-EA (hex)	INTELECT COMMUNICATIONS, INC.
0030EA (base 16)	INTELECT COMMUNICATIONS, INC. 1100 EXECUTIVE DRIVE RICHARDSON TX 75081
00-30-EB (hex)	TURBONET COMMUNICATIONS, INC.
0030EB (base 16)	TURBONET COMMUNICATIONS, INC. 19F-1, NO. 171, SUNG-TEH ROAD TAIPEI TAIWAN, R.O.C.
00-30-EC (hex)	BORGARDT
0030EC (base 16)	BORGARDT DIESELSTR. 15 D71665 VAIHINGEN/ENZ GERMANY
00-30-ED (hex)	Expert Magnetics Corp.
0030ED (base 16)	Expert Magnetics Corp. 12/f., unit d, mtg. bldg., 12-3, Nakase, Mihama-ku, Chiba-city 261-8501 JAPAN
00-30-EE (hex)	DSG Technology, Inc.
0030EE (base 16)	DSG Technology, Inc. 6F-4 No. 270, Chwig Hsiao East Road, Sec. 4 Taipei TAIWAN, ROC
00-30-EF (hex)	NEON TECHNOLOGY, INC.

company_id	Organization Address
0030EF (base 16)	NEON TECHNOLOGY, INC. 85 WEST MONTAGUE EXPRESSWAY MILPITAS CA 95035
00-30-F0 (hex)	Uniform Industrial Corp.
0030F0 (base 16)	Uniform Industrial Corp. 18F, 171, Shung Teh Road Taipei TAIWAN
00-30-F1 (hex)	Accton Technology Corp.
0030F1 (base 16)	Accton Technology Corp. No. 1, Creation Rd. IV S.G.Z.P Hsinchu TAIWAN, R.O.C.
00-30-F2 (hex)	CISCO SYSTEMS, INC.
0030F2 (base 16)	CISCO SYSTEMS, INC. 170 WEST TASMAN DRIVE - SJA-2 SAN JOSE CA 85134
00-30-F3 (hex)	At Work Computers
0030F3 (base 16)	At Work Computers P.O. Box 947 Corvallis OR 97339
00-30-F4 (hex)	STARDOT TECHNOLOGIES
0030F4 (base 16)	STARDOT TECHNOLOGIES 6820-H ORANGE THORPE AVE. BUENA PARK CA 90620
00-30-F5 (hex)	Wild Lab. Ltd.
0030F5 (base 16)	Wild Lab. Ltd. 1-33-17-604 Harayama Urawa City Saitama prif. 336-0931 JAPAN
00-30-F6 (hex)	SECURELOGIX CORPORATION
0030F6 (base 16)	SECURELOGIX CORPORATION 13750 SAN PEDRO SAN ANTONIO TX 78232
00-30-F7 (hex)	RAMIX INC.
0030F7 (base 16)	RAMIX INC. 1672 DONLON STREET VENTURA CA 93003
00-30-F8 (hex)	Dynapro Systems, Inc.
0030F8 (base 16)	Dynapro Systems, Inc. 800 Carleton Court Annacis Island New Westminster, BC CANADA V3M 6L3
00-30-F9 (hex)	Sollae Systems Co., Ltd.
0030F9 (base 16)	Sollae Systems Co., Ltd. Room #506 S/W Support Center 294 Songrim-dong Dong-gu Inchon-City South Korea (zip:401-070)
00-30-FA (hex)	TELICA, INC.
0030FA (base 16)	TELICA, INC. 734 FOREST STREET, BLDG. "G" SUITE #100 MARLBORO MA 01752
00-30-FB (hex)	AZS Technology AG
0030FB (base 16)	AZS Technology AG Steinbeisstrasse 2-4 72510 Stetten A.K.M. F.R. GERMANY
00-30-FC (hex)	Terawave Communications, Inc.
0030FC (base 16)	Terawave Communications, Inc. 30695 Huntwood Avenue Hayward CA 94544
00-30-FD (hex)	INTEGRATED SYSTEMS DESIGN
0030FD (base 16)	INTEGRATED SYSTEMS DESIGN 3650-G CENTRE CIRCLE DRIVE FORT MILL SC 29715
00-30-FE (hex)	DSA GmbH

company_id	Organization Address
0030FE (base 16)	DSA GmbH Pascalstr. 28 52076 Aachen GERMANY
00-30-FF (hex)	DATAFAB SYSTEMS, INC.
0030FF (base 16)	DATAFAB SYSTEMS, INC. ROOM #1910, 19F, NO. 333 KEELUNG ROAD SEC. 1, TAIPEI TAIWAN, R.O.C.
00-40-00 (hex)	PCI COMPONENTES DA AMZONIA LTD
004000 (base 16)	PCI COMPONENTES DA AMZONIA LTD RUA JOSEF KRYSS 129 - SAO PAULO - SP 01140 BRASIL
00-40-01 (hex)	ZYXEL COMMUNICATIONS, INC.
004001 (base 16)	ZYXEL COMMUNICATIONS, INC. 4F, 111, CHUNG SHAN N. ROAD SEC 2, TAIPEI TAIWAN R.O.C.
00-40-02 (hex)	PERLE SYSTEMS LIMITED
004002 (base 16)	PERLE SYSTEMS LIMITED 60 RENFREW DRIVE MARKHAM ONTARIO CANADA L3R 0E1
00-40-03 (hex)	WESTINGHOUSE PROCESS CONTROL
004003 (base 16)	WESTINGHOUSE PROCESS CONTROL DIVISION 200 BETA DRIVE PITTSBURGH PA 15238
00-40-04 (hex)	ICM CO. LTD.
004004 (base 16)	ICM CO. LTD. 4-2-9 NIHONBASHI NANIWA-KU OSAKA, (556) JAPAN
00-40-05 (hex)	ANI COMMUNICATIONS INC.
004005 (base 16)	ANI COMMUNICATIONS INC. 8 ANZIO IRVINE CA 92714
00-40-06 (hex)	SAMPO TECHNOLOGY CORPORATION
004006 (base 16)	SAMPO TECHNOLOGY CORPORATION 26-2 TING-HU, TA-KANG TSUN KUEI-SHAN HSIANG, TAOYUAN HIEN 33334 TAIWAN, R.O.C.
00-40-07 (hex)	TELMAT INFORMATIQUE
004007 (base 16)	TELMAT INFORMATIQUE 6 RUE DE L'INDUSTRIE BP 12 68360 SOULTZ FRANCE
00-40-08 (hex)	A PLUS INFO CORPORATION
004008 (base 16)	A PLUS INFO CORPORATION 5F, NO.2, LANE 235 BAO CHIAO ROAD HSIN TIEN, TAIPEI TAIWAN, R.O.C.
00-40-09 (hex)	TACHIBANA TECTRON CO., LTD.
004009 (base 16)	TACHIBANA TECTRON CO., LTD. SYSTEMATIC EQUIPMENT DIVISION 2-2-5 HIGASHIYAMA, MEGUROKU TOKYO, 153 JAPAN
00-40-0A (hex)	PIVOTAL TECHNOLOGIES, INC.
00400A (base 16)	PIVOTAL TECHNOLOGIES, INC. 100 W. RINCON AVENUE-STE #211 CAMPBELL CA 95008
00-40-0B (hex)	CISCO SYSTEMS, INC.
00400B (base 16)	CISCO SYSTEMS, INC. 170 WEST TASMAN DRIVE SAN JOSE CA 95134-1706

company_id	Organization Address
00-40-0C (hex)	GENERAL MICRO SYSTEMS, INC.
00400C (base 16)	GENERAL MICRO SYSTEMS, INC. P.O. BOX 3689 RANCHO CUCAMONGA CA 91729
00-40-0D (hex)	LANNET DATA COMMUNICATIONS,LTD
00400D (base 16)	LANNET DATA COMMUNICATIONS,LTD ATIDIM TECHNOLOG'L PARK, BG.#3 TEL AVIV 61131 ISRAEL
00-40-0E (hex)	MEMOTEC COMMUNICATIONS, INC.
00400E (base 16)	MEMOTEC COMMUNICATIONS, INC. 600 MCCAFFREY MONTREAL, QUEBEC H4T 1N1 CANADA
00-40-0F (hex)	DATACOM TECHNOLOGIES
00400F (base 16)	DATACOM TECHNOLOGIES 11001 31ST PLACE WEST EVERETT WA 98204
00-40-10 (hex)	SONIC SYSTEMS, INC.
004010 (base 16)	SONIC SYSTEMS, INC. 575 PASTORIA NORTH AVENUE SUNNYVALE CA 940867
00-40-11 (hex)	ANDOVER CONTROLS CORPORATION
004011 (base 16)	ANDOVER CONTROLS CORPORATION 300 BRICKSTONE SQUARE ANDOVER MA 01810
00-40-12 (hex)	WINDATA, INC.
004012 (base 16)	WINDATA, INC. 10 BEARFOOT ROAD NORTHBORO MA 01532
00-40-13 (hex)	NTT DATA COMM. SYSTEMS CORP.
004013 (base 16)	NTT DATA COMM. SYSTEMS CORP. DEVELOPMENT HEADQUARTERS TOYOSU CENTER BLDG., 3-3-3 TOYOSU, KOTO-KU TOKYO 135, JAPAN
00-40-14 (hex)	COMSOFT GMBH
004014 (base 16)	COMSOFT GMBH WACHHAUSSTR. 5A 7500 KARLSRUHE 41 GERMANY
00-40-15 (hex)	ASCOM INFRASYS AG
004015 (base 16)	ASCOM INFRASYS AG DPT. EASO 3726 GLUTZ-BLOTZHEIMSTR. 1 CH-4503 SOLOTHURN SWITZERLAND
00-40-16 (hex)	HADAX ELECTRONICS, INC.
004016 (base 16)	HADAX ELECTRONICS, INC. 11 TEANECK ROAD RICHFIELD PARK NJ 07660
00-40-17 (hex)	XCD INC.
004017 (base 16)	XCD INC. 2172 DUPONT #204 IRVINE CA 92715
00-40-18 (hex)	ADOBE SYSTEMS, INC.
004018 (base 16)	ADOBE SYSTEMS, INC. 1585 CHARLESTON ROAD MOUNTAIN VIEW, CA 94043
00-40-19 (hex)	AEON SYSTEMS, INC.
004019 (base 16)	AEON SYSTEMS, INC. 8401 WASHINGTON PLACE NE ALBUQUERQUE NM 87113
00-40-1A (hex)	FUJI ELECTRIC CO., LTD.
00401A (base 16)	FUJI ELECTRIC CO., LTD. NEW YURAKUCHO BLDG 12-1 YURAKUCHO 1-CHOME CHIYODA-KU, TOKYO 100 JAPAN
00-40-1B (hex)	PRINTER SYSTEMS CORP.

company_id	Organization Address
00401B (base 16)	PRINTER SYSTEMS CORP. 207 PERRY PARKWAY GAITHERSBURG MD 20877-2142
00-40-1C (hex)	AST RESEARCH, INC.
00401C (base 16)	AST RESEARCH, INC. MS 2-78 1615 ALTON PARKWAY IRVINE CA 92618
00-40-1D (hex)	INVISIBLE SOFTWARE, INC.
00401D (base 16)	INVISIBLE SOFTWARE, INC. 1142 CHESS DRIVE FOSTER CITY CA 94404
00-40-1E (hex)	ICC
00401E (base 16)	ICC 8230 MONTGOMERY ROAD CINCINNATI, OH 45236
00-40-1F (hex)	COLORGRAPH LTD
00401F (base 16)	COLORGRAPH LTD UNIT 2, MARS HOUSE CALLEVA PARK, ALDERMASTON NR. READING, BERKSHIRE RG7 4QW - UNITED KINGDOM
00-40-20 (hex)	PINACL COMMUNICATION
004020 (base 16)	PINACL COMMUNICATION SYSTEMS LIMITED UNIT 1, KINMEL PK, BODELWYDDAN RHYL, CLWYD, LL18 5TY UNITED KINGDOM
00-40-21 (hex)	RASTER GRAPHICS
004021 (base 16)	RASTER GRAPHICS 285 N. WOLFE ROAD SUNNYVALE CA 94086
00-40-22 (hex)	KLEVER COMPUTERS, INC.
004022 (base 16)	KLEVER COMPUTERS, INC. 1028 W. MAUDE AVENUE SUNNYVALE CA 94086
00-40-23 (hex)	LOGIC CORPORATION
004023 (base 16)	LOGIC CORPORATION 3-14-10 MEIJI-SEIMEI BUILDING MITA MINATO-KU TOKYO JAPAN
00-40-24 (hex)	COMPAC INC.
004024 (base 16)	COMPAC INC. 16-7 NIHONBASI HAMACHO 3-CHO CHUO-KU, TOKYO JAPAN
00-40-25 (hex)	MOLECULAR DYNAMICS
004025 (base 16)	MOLECULAR DYNAMICS 880 EAST ARQUES AVENUE SUNNYVALE CA 94086-4536
00-40-26 (hex)	MELCO, INC.
004026 (base 16)	MELCO, INC. MELCO HI-TECH CENTER0, SHIBATA HONDORI 4-15 MINAMI-KU, NAGOYA 457 JAPAN
00-40-27 (hex)	SMC MASSACHUSETTS, INC.
004027 (base 16)	SMC MASSACHUSETTS, INC. 25 WALKERS BROOK DRIVE READING MA 01867
00-40-28 (hex)	NETCOMM LIMITED
004028 (base 16)	NETCOMM LIMITED 3 OLYMPIC BUSINESS CENTRE PAYCOCKE ROAD BASILDON, ESSEX SS14 3EX UNITED KINGDOM
00-40-29 (hex)	COMPEX

company_id	Organization Address
004029 (base 16)	COMPEX B.P. 35 74371 PRINGY-FRANCE FRANCE
00-40-2A (hex)	CANOGA-PERKINS
00402A (base 16)	CANOGA-PERKINS 21012 LASSEN STREET CHATSWORTH CA 91311-4241
00-40-2B (hex)	TRIGEM COMPUTER, INC.
00402B (base 16)	TRIGEM COMPUTER, INC. KISUNG B/D 4F, 784-6 YEOKSAM-DONG, KANGNAM-GU SEOUL, KOREA 135-080
00-40-2C (hex)	ISIS DISTRIBUTED SYSTEMS, INC.
00402C (base 16)	ISIS DISTRIBUTED SYSTEMS, INC. 111 SOUTH CAYUGA STREET SUITE #200 ITHACA NY 14850
00-40-2D (hex)	HARRIS ADACOM CORPORATION
00402D (base 16)	HARRIS ADACOM CORPORATION 1100 VENTURE COURT CARROLLTON TX 75006-5412
00-40-2E (hex)	PRECISION SOFTWARE, INC.
00402E (base 16)	PRECISION SOFTWARE, INC. 600 S FEDERAL HWY STE DEERFIELD BEACH FL 33441-4193
00-40-2F (hex)	XLNT DESIGNS INC.
00402F (base 16)	XLNT DESIGNS INC. 15050 AVENUE OF SCIENCE SUITE 200 SAN DIEGO, CA 92128
00-40-30 (hex)	GK COMPUTER
004030 (base 16)	GK COMPUTER BASLER STRASSE 103 D-7800 FREIBURG GERMANY
00-40-31 (hex)	KOKUSAI ELECTRIC CO., LTD
004031 (base 16)	KOKUSAI ELECTRIC CO., LTD 2-1 YASUUCHI YATSUO-MACHI NEIGUN TOYAMA 939-23 JAPAN
00-40-32 (hex)	DIGITAL COMMUNICATIONS
004032 (base 16)	DIGITAL COMMUNICATIONS ASSOCIATES, INC. 2010 FORTUNE DRIVE, #101 SAN JOSE CA 95131
00-40-33 (hex)	ADDTRON TECHNOLOGY CO., LTD.
004033 (base 16)	ADDTRON TECHNOLOGY CO., LTD. 46560 FREMONT BLVD. #303 FREMONT CA 94538
00-40-34 (hex)	BUSTEK CORPORATION
004034 (base 16)	BUSTEK CORPORATION 4151 BURTON DRIVE SANTA CLARA CA 95054
00-40-35 (hex)	OPCOM
004035 (base 16)	OPCOM 1215 W. CROSBY RD. CARROLLTON, TX 75006
00-40-36 (hex)	TRIBE COMPUTER WORKS, INC.
004036 (base 16)	TRIBE COMPUTER WORKS, INC. 1195 PARK AVENUE-STE #211 EMERYVILLE CA 94608
00-40-37 (hex)	SEA-ILAN, INC.
004037 (base 16)	SEA-ILAN, INC. 14602 NORTH US HIGHWAY #31 CARMEL IN 46032
00-40-38 (hex)	TALENT ELECTRIC INCORPORATED

company_id	Organization Address
004038 (base 16)	TALENT ELECTRIC INCORPORATED 3RD FL., NO. 260, PA TEH ROAD SEC. 2 TAIPEI TAIWAN, R.O.C.
00-40-39 (hex)	OPTEC DAIICHI DENKO CO., LTD.
004039 (base 16)	OPTEC DAIICHI DENKO CO., LTD. FIBER OPTICS & TELECOM. DIV. 3-1-1 MARUNOUCHI CHIYODAKU TOKYO 100 JAPAN
00-40-3A (hex)	IMPACT TECHNOLOGIES
00403A (base 16)	IMPACT TECHNOLOGIES 6 RUE DE L'ACADIE Z.A. COURTABOEUF 91953 LES ULIS CEDEX FRANCE
00-40-3B (hex)	SYNERJET INTERNATIONAL CORP.
00403B (base 16)	SYNERJET INTERNATIONAL CORP. 5F, NO 35, KUANG FU S. ROAD TAIPEI, TAIWAN, R. O. C.
00-40-3C (hex)	FORKS, INC.
00403C (base 16)	FORKS, INC. 1-27-4 IRIYA, IRIYA 1-27-4 TAITO, 110 JAPAN
00-40-3D (hex)	TERADATA
00403D (base 16)	TERADATA 100 N. SEPULVEDA BLVD. EL SEGUNDO CA 90245
00-40-3E (hex)	RASTER OPS CORPORATION
00403E (base 16)	RASTER OPS CORPORATION 2500 WALSH AVENUE SANTA CLARA, CA 95051
00-40-3F (hex)	SSANGYONG COMPUTER SYSTEMS
00403F (base 16)	SSANGYONG COMPUTER SYSTEMS CORPORATION 60-1, 3GA, CHUNGMU-RO, JUNG-GU SEOUL KOREA 100-705
00-40-40 (hex)	RING ACCESS, INC.
004040 (base 16)	RING ACCESS, INC. 957-R INDUSTRIAL ROAD SAN CARLOS CA 94070
00-40-41 (hex)	FUJIKURA LTD.
004041 (base 16)	FUJIKURA LTD. 1-5-1, KIBA, KOTO-KU TOKYO 135 JAPAN
00-40-42 (hex)	N.A.T. GMBH
004042 (base 16)	N.A.T. GMBH GOETHESTR. 2 5210 TROISDORF-SIEGLAR GERMANY
00-40-43 (hex)	NOKIA TELECOMMUNICATIONS
004043 (base 16)	NOKIA TELECOMMUNICATIONS P.O. BOX 29 90831 HAUKIPUDAS FINLAND
00-40-44 (hex)	QNIX COMPUTER CO., LTD.
004044 (base 16)	QNIX COMPUTER CO., LTD. 8,9F KOREAN TEACHER'S MUT.BLDG 35-3, YEOUIDO_DONG, YEONGDEUNGPO_GU SEOUL, KOREA 150-010
00-40-45 (hex)	TWINHEAD CORPORATION
004045 (base 16)	TWINHEAD CORPORATION 1537 CENTRE POINTE DRIVE MILPITAS CA 95035
00-40-46 (hex)	UDC RESEARCH LIMITED

company_id	Organization Address
004046 (base 16)	UDC RESEARCH LIMITED 8A KING WAN INDUSTRIAL BLDG. 54 HUNG TO ROAD, KWUN TONG HONG KONG
00-40-47 (hex)	WIND RIVER SYSTEMS
004047 (base 16)	WIND RIVER SYSTEMS 1010 ATLANTIC AVENUE ALAMEDA, CA 94501
00-40-48 (hex)	SMD INFORMATICA S.A.
004048 (base 16)	SMD INFORMATICA S.A. LARGO MOVIMENTO DAS FORCAS ARMADAS, 4 ALFRAGIDE, 2700 AMADORA PORTUGAL
00-40-49 (hex)	TEGIMENTA AG
004049 (base 16)	TEGIMENTA AG FORRENSTRASSE CH-6343 ROTKREUZ SWITZERLAND
00-40-4A (hex)	WEST AUSTRALIAN DEPARTMENT
00404A (base 16)	WEST AUSTRALIAN DEPARTMENT OF EMPLOYMENT (DEVET) LEVER 2, 151 ROYAL ST. EAST PERTH 6001 WESTERN AUSTRALIA
00-40-4B (hex)	MAPLE COMPUTER SYSTEMS
00404B (base 16)	MAPLE COMPUTER SYSTEMS P.O. BOX 10050 ST. JOHN'S, NF CANADA ALA 4L5
00-40-4C (hex)	HYPERTEC PTY LTD.
00404C (base 16)	HYPERTEC PTY LTD. P.O. BOX 1782 MACQUARIE CENTRE NSW, 2113 AUSTRALIA
00-40-4D (hex)	TELECOMMUNICATIONS TECHNIQUES
00404D (base 16)	TELECOMMUNICATIONS TECHNIQUES M/S «O» 20400 OBSERVATION DRIVE GERMANTOWN MD 20876
00-40-4E (hex)	FLUENT, INC.
00404E (base 16)	FLUENT, INC. 594 WORCESTER ROAD-STE.#308 NATICK, MA 01760
00-40-4F (hex)	SPACE & NAVAL WARFARE SYSTEMS
00404F (base 16)	SPACE & NAVAL WARFARE SYSTEMS NUWC CODE 2222, BLDG 1171-3 NEWPORT RI 02841-5047
00-40-50 (hex)	IRONICS, INCORPORATED
004050 (base 16)	IRONICS, INCORPORATED 767 WARREN RD ITHACA, N.Y. 14850
00-40-51 (hex)	GRACILIS, INC.
004051 (base 16)	GRACILIS, INC. 623 PALACE STREET AURORA, IL 60506
00-40-52 (hex)	STAR TECHNOLOGIES, INC.
004052 (base 16)	STAR TECHNOLOGIES, INC. 515 SHAW ROAD STERLING, VA 22075
00-40-53 (hex)	AMPRO COMPUTERS
004053 (base 16)	AMPRO COMPUTERS 990 ALMONDOR AVENUE SUNNYVALE, CA 94086
00-40-54 (hex)	CONNECTION MACHINES SERVICES
004054 (base 16)	CONNECTION MACHINES SERVICES 12 HENSHAW STREET WOBURN MA 01801-466664

company_id	Organization Address
00-40-55 (hex)	METRONIX GMBH
004055 (base 16)	METRONIX GMBH NEUE KNOCHENHAUERSTRABE 5 D-3300 BRAUNSCHWEIG WEST GERMANY
00-40-56 (hex)	MCM JAPAN LTD.
004056 (base 16)	MCM JAPAN LTD. SYUUKAEN BLD. 2-11-1 KOMAZAWA SETAGAYA-KU TOKYO 154 JAPAN
00-40-57 (hex)	LOCKHEED - SANDERS
004057 (base 16)	LOCKHEED - SANDERS DANIEL WEBSTER HIGHWAY SOUTH P.O. BOX 868 NASHUA NH 03061-0868
00-40-58 (hex)	KRONOS, INC.
004058 (base 16)	KRONOS, INC. 400 FIFTH AVENUE WALTHAM MA 02154
00-40-59 (hex)	YOSHIDA KOGYO K. K.
004059 (base 16)	YOSHIDA KOGYO K. K. TECHNICAL RESEARCH DEPT. 200 YOSHIDA KUROBE CITY TOYAMA PREF. 939 JAPAN
00-40-5A (hex)	GOLDSTAR INFORMATION & COMM.
00405A (base 16)	GOLDSTAR INFORMATION & COMM. 533, HOGAE-DONG, ANYANG-SHI KYONGKI-DO 430-080 KOREA
00-40-5B (hex)	FUNASSET LIMITED
00405B (base 16)	FUNASSET LIMITED ORCHARDS, 14 TOWNSEND SOMERSET TA19 OAU ILMINSTER UNITED KINGDOM
00-40-5C (hex)	FUTURE SYSTEMS, INC.
00405C (base 16)	FUTURE SYSTEMS, INC. ROOM 102 DONG BANG B/D, YEOG SAM-DONG 740-5, KANG NAM-KU SEOUL 130-080, KOREA
00-40-5D (hex)	STAR-TEK, INC.
00405D (base 16)	STAR-TEK, INC. 71 LYMAN STREET NORTHBORO MA 01532
00-40-5E (hex)	NORTH HILLS ISRAEL
00405E (base 16)	NORTH HILLS ISRAEL P.O. BOX 1280 YOKNEAM 20692 ISRAEL
00-40-5F (hex)	AFE COMPUTERS LTD.
00405F (base 16)	AFE COMPUTERS LTD. 62 ANCHORAGE ROAD SUTTON COLDFIELD WEST MIDLANDS B74 2PG UNITED KINGDOM
00-40-60 (hex)	COMENDEC LTD
004060 (base 16)	COMENDEC LTD ENTERPRISE WAY, ASTON SCIENCE PARK, ASTON TRIANGLE BIRMINGHAM, ENGLAND
00-40-61 (hex)	DATATECH ENTERPRISES CO., LTD.
004061 (base 16)	DATATECH ENTERPRISES CO., LTD. (LIN KOU INDUSTRIAL ZONE SEC,4 27, HSI-SHIH LAKE ROAD KUEI-SHAN HSIANG TAOYUAN COUNTY, TAIWAN R.O.C.
00-40-62 (hex)	E-SYSTEMS, INC./GARLAND DIV.

company_id	Organization Address
004062 (base 16)	E-SYSTEMS, INC./GARLAND DIV. P.O. BOX 660023 MAIL STOP 63000 DALLAS TX 75266-0023
00-40-63 (hex)	VIA TECHNOLOGIES, INC.
004063 (base 16)	VIA TECHNOLOGIES, INC. 5020 BRANDIN COURT FREMONT CA 94538
00-40-64 (hex)	KLA INSTRUMENTS CORPORATION
004064 (base 16)	KLA INSTRUMENTS CORPORATION 160 RIO ROBLES SAN JOSE CA 95161-9055
00-40-65 (hex)	GTE SPACENET
004065 (base 16)	GTE SPACENET 1700 OLD MEADOW ROAD MCLEAN, VA 22102
00-40-66 (hex)	HITACHI CABLE, LTD.
004066 (base 16)	HITACHI CABLE, LTD. OPTO ELECTRONIC SYSTEM LAB 880 ISAGOZAW-CHO, HITACHI-SHI IBARAKI-KEN, 319-14 JAPAN
00-40-67 (hex)	OMNIBYTE CORPORATION
004067 (base 16)	OMNIBYTE CORPORATION 245 WEST ROOSEVELT ROAD WEST CHICAGO IL 60185
00-40-68 (hex)	EXTENDED SYSTEMS
004068 (base 16)	EXTENDED SYSTEMS 6123 NORTH MEEKER AVENUE BOISE, ID 83704
00-40-69 (hex)	LEMCOM SYSTEMS, INC.
004069 (base 16)	LEMCOM SYSTEMS, INC. 2104 WEST PEORIA AVENUE PHOENIX, AZ 85029
00-40-6A (hex)	KENTEK INFORMATION SYSTEMS,INC
00406A (base 16)	KENTEK INFORMATION SYSTEMS,INC 2945 WILDERNESS PLACE BOULDER CO 80301
00-40-6B (hex)	SYSGEN
00406B (base 16)	SYSGEN 556 GIBRALTAR DRIVE MILPITAS, CA 95035
00-40-6C (hex)	COPERNIQUE
00406C (base 16)	COPERNIQUE 6, MAIL DE L'EUROPE BP 25 78170 LA CELLE-SAINT-CLOUD FRANCE
00-40-6D (hex)	LANCO, INC.
00406D (base 16)	LANCO, INC. 800 WEST AIRPORT FREEWAY SUITE #1100 IRVING TX 75062
00-40-6E (hex)	COROLLARY, INC.
00406E (base 16)	COROLLARY, INC. 2802 KELVIN IRVINE CA 92714
00-40-6F (hex)	SYNC RESEARCH INC.
00406F (base 16)	SYNC RESEARCH INC. 7 STUDEBAKER IRVINE CA 92718
00-40-70 (hex)	INTERWARE CO., LTD.
004070 (base 16)	INTERWARE CO., LTD. 7F KUDAN NEW CENTRAL BLDG., 1-4-5 KUDAN-KITA, CHIYODA-KU TOKYO 102, JAPAN
00-40-71 (hex)	ATM COMPUTER GMBH
004071 (base 16)	ATM COMPUTER GMBH BUCKLESTR. 1-5,POSTFACH 101043 D7750 KONSTANZ GERMANY

company_id	Organization Address
00-40-72 (hex)	APPLIED INNOVATION, INC.
004072 (base 16)	APPLIED INNOVATION, INC. 651C LAKEVIEW PLAZA BLVD. COLUMBUS, OH 43085
00-40-73 (hex)	BASS ASSOCIATES
004073 (base 16)	BASS ASSOCIATES 435 TASSO STREET, STE. #325 PALO ALTO CA 94301
00-40-74 (hex)	CABLE AND WIRELESS
004074 (base 16)	CABLE AND WIRELESS COMMUNICATIONS, INC. 1919 GALLOWS ROAD VIENNA VA 22182-3964
00-40-75 (hex)	M-TRADE (UK) LTD
004075 (base 16)	M-TRADE (UK) LTD 11-12 NORTHFIELD PROSPECT PUTNEY BRIDGE ROAD LONDON SW18 1HR UNITED KINGDOM
00-40-76 (hex)	Sun Conversion Technologies
004076 (base 16)	Sun Conversion Technologies 100 Commerce Boulevard Quakertown, PA 78951-2237
00-40-77 (hex)	MAXTON TECHNOLOGY CORPORATION
004077 (base 16)	MAXTON TECHNOLOGY CORPORATION 4FK, 249, SEC. 3, CHUNG HSIAO E. RD., TAIPEI TAIWAN
00-40-78 (hex)	WEARNES AUTOMATION PTE LTD
004078 (base 16)	WEARNES AUTOMATION PTE LTD 801 LORONG 7, TOA PAYOH SINGAPORE 1231
00-40-79 (hex)	JUKO MANUFACTURE COMPANY, LTD.
004079 (base 16)	JUKO MANUFACTURE COMPANY, LTD. FLAT C, 3RD FLOOR, CDW BLDG. 388 CASTLE PEAK ROAD, TSUEN WAN, N.T. HONG KONG
00-40-7A (hex)	SOCIETE D'EXPLOITATION DU CNIT
00407A (base 16)	SOCIETE D'EXPLOITATION DU CNIT 2 GLACE DE LA DEFENSE 92053 PARIS-LA-DEFENSE FRANCE
00-40-7B (hex)	SCIENTIFIC ATLANTA
00407B (base 16)	SCIENTIFIC ATLANTA Information Technology 4311 Communications Drive Mail Code: 30-D, P.O. Box 6850 Norcross, GA 30091-6850
00-40-7C (hex)	QUME CORPORATION
00407C (base 16)	QUME CORPORATION 500 YOSEMITE DRIVE, M/S-29 MILPITAS CA 95035-5426
00-40-7D (hex)	EXTENSION TECHNOLOGY CORP.
00407D (base 16)	EXTENSION TECHNOLOGY CORP. 30 HOLLIS STREET FRAMINGHAM MA 01701
00-40-7E (hex)	EVERGREEN SYSTEMS, INC.
00407E (base 16)	EVERGREEN SYSTEMS, INC. 120 LANDING COURT-SUITE «A» NOVATO CA 94945
00-40-7F (hex)	AGEMA INFRARED SYSTEMS AB
00407F (base 16)	AGEMA INFRARED SYSTEMS AB BOX 3 182-11 DANDERYD SWEDEN
00-40-80 (hex)	ATHENIX CORPORATION
004080 (base 16)	ATHENIX CORPORATION 675 ALMANOR AVENUE SUNNYVALE, CA 94086

company_id	Organization Address
00-40-81 (hex)	MANNESMANN SCANGRAPHIC GMBH
004081 (base 16)	MANNESMANN SCANGRAPHIC GMBH RISSENER STRASSE 112-114 W-2000 WEDEL GERMANY
00-40-82 (hex)	LABORATORY EQUIPMENT CORP.
004082 (base 16)	LABORATORY EQUIPMENT CORP. 1-7-3 MINATOMACHI TUCHIURA-CITY IBARAGI-KEN, 300 JAPAN
00-40-83 (hex)	TDA INDUSTRIA DE PRODUTOS
004083 (base 16)	TDA INDUSTRIA DE PRODUTOS ELETRONICOS S.A. RUE AGOSTINO TOGNERI, 02 04690 - SAO PAULO -SP BRAZIL
00-40-84 (hex)	HONEYWELL INC.
004084 (base 16)	HONEYWELL INC. HONEYWELL SSDC - M.S. 2300 3660 TECHNOLOGY DRIVE MINNEAPOLIS MN 55418
00-40-85 (hex)	SAAB INSTRUMENTS AB
004085 (base 16)	SAAB INSTRUMENTS AB P.O. BOX 1017 S-551 11 JONKOPING SWEDEN
00-40-86 (hex)	MICHELS & KLEBERHOFF COMPUTER
004086 (base 16)	MICHELS & KLEBERHOFF COMPUTER GATHE 117 5600 WUPPERTAL 1 GERMANY
00-40-87 (hex)	UBITREX CORPORATION
004087 (base 16)	UBITREX CORPORATION 19TH FLOOR, 155 CARLTON STREET WINNIPEG, MANITOBA CANADA R3C 3H8
00-40-88 (hex)	MOBIUS TECHNOLOGIES, INC.
004088 (base 16)	MOBIUS TECHNOLOGIES, INC. 5835 DOYLE STREET EMERYVILLE CA 94608
00-40-89 (hex)	MEIDENSHA CORPORATION
004089 (base 16)	MEIDENSHA CORPORATION FACTORY NO.4, 515 KAMINAKAMIZO HIGASHI MAKADO NUMAZU-CITY SHIZUOKA-PREF. 410 JAPAN
00-40-8A (hex)	TPS TELEPROCESSING SYS. GMBH
00408A (base 16)	TPS TELEPROCESSING SYS. GMBH SCHWADERMUCHLSTRASSE 4-8 W-8501 CADOLZBURG GERMANY
00-40-8B (hex)	RAYLAN CORPORATION
00408B (base 16)	RAYLAN CORPORATION 120 INDEPENDENCE DRIVE MENLO PARK, CA 94025
00-40-8C (hex)	AXIS COMMUNICATIONS AB
00408C (base 16)	AXIS COMMUNICATIONS AB SCHEELEVAGEN 16 S-223 70 LUND SWEDEN
00-40-8D (hex)	THE GOODYEAR TIRE & RUBBER CO.
00408D (base 16)	THE GOODYEAR TIRE & RUBBER CO. 1144 EAST MARKET STREET AKRON OH 44316
00-40-8E (hex)	DIGILOG, INC.
00408E (base 16)	DIGILOG, INC. 2360 MARYLAND ROAD WILLOW GROVE PA 19090
00-40-8F (hex)	WM-DATA MINFO AB

company_id	Organization Address
00408F (base 16)	WM-DATA MINFO AB OLOF ASKLUNDS GATA 14 BOX 2065 421 02 GOTEBORG SWEDEN
00-40-90 (hex)	ANSEL COMMUNICATIONS
004090 (base 16)	ANSEL COMMUNICATIONS 1701 JUNCTION COURT SAN JOSE CA 95112
00-40-91 (hex)	PROCOMP INDUSTRIA ELETRONICA
004091 (base 16)	PROCOMP INDUSTRIA ELETRONICA AV. KENKITI SIMOMOTO, 767 05347 - SAO PAULO / SP BRAZIL
00-40-92 (hex)	ASP COMPUTER PRODUCTS, INC.
004092 (base 16)	ASP COMPUTER PRODUCTS, INC. 160 SAN GABRIEL DRIVE SUNNYVALE, CA 94086
00-40-93 (hex)	PAXDATA NETWORKS LTD.
004093 (base 16)	PAXDATA NETWORKS LTD. COMMUNICATIONS HOUSE, FROGMORE ROAD HEMEL HEMPSTEAD, HERTS HP3 9RW ENGLAND
00-40-94 (hex)	SHOGRAPHICS, INC.
004094 (base 16)	SHOGRAPHICS, INC. 1890 N. SHORELINE BLVD. MOUNTAIN VIEW CA 94043
00-40-95 (hex)	R.P.T. INTERGROUPS INT'L LTD.
004095 (base 16)	R.P.T. INTERGROUPS INT'L LTD. 9F, 50 MIN CHUAN RD HSIN TIEN, TAIPEI TAIWAN, R.O.C.
00-40-96 (hex)	Aironet Wireless Communication
004096 (base 16)	Aironet Wireless Communication 3875 Embassy Parkway Aksron OH 44334
00-40-97 (hex)	DATEX DIVISION OF
004097 (base 16)	DATEX DIVISION OF INSTRUMENTARIUM CORP. P.O. BOX 446, SF-00101 HELSINKI FINLAND
00-40-98 (hex)	DRESSLER GMBH & CO.
004098 (base 16)	DRESSLER GMBH & CO. KACKERTSTRASSE 10 D-52072 AACHEN GERMANY
00-40-99 (hex)	NEWGEN SYSTEMS CORP.
004099 (base 16)	NEWGEN SYSTEMS CORP. 17580 NEWHOPE STREET FOUNTAIN VALLEY CA 92708
00-40-9A (hex)	NETWORK EXPRESS, INC.
00409A (base 16)	NETWORK EXPRESS, INC. 2200 GREEN ROAD - STE «I» ANN ARBOR, MI 48170
00-40-9B (hex)	HAL COMPUTER SYSTEMS INC.
00409B (base 16)	HAL COMPUTER SYSTEMS INC. 1315 DELL AVENUE CAMPBELL CA 95008
00-40-9C (hex)	TRANSWARE
00409C (base 16)	TRANSWARE 21, RUE DU 8 MAI 1945 941107 ARCUEIL FRANCE
00-40-9D (hex)	DIGIBOARD, INC.
00409D (base 16)	DIGIBOARD, INC. 6400 FLYING CLOUD DRIVE EDEN PRAIRIE MN 55344
00-40-9E (hex)	CONCURRENT TECHNOLOGIES LTD.

company_id	Organization / Address
00409E (base 16)	CONCURRENT TECHNOLOGIES LTD. 654 THE CRESCENT COLCHESTER BUSINESS PARK COLCHESTER, ESSEX CO4 4YQ UNITED KINGDOM
00-40-9F (hex)	LANCAST/CASAT TECHNOLOGY, INC.
00409F (base 16)	LANCAST/CASAT TECHNOLOGY, INC. 10 NORTHERN BLVD.-UNIT 5 AMHERST NH 03031-2328
00-40-A0 (hex)	GOLDSTAR CO., LTD.
0040A0 (base 16)	GOLDSTAR CO., LTD. 6 GA 3B MUNLAE YEONGDEUNGPO SEOUL KOREA
00-40-A1 (hex)	ERGO COMPUTING
0040A1 (base 16)	ERGO COMPUTING ONE INTERCONTINENTAL WAY PEABODY, MA 01960
00-40-A2 (hex)	KINGSTAR TECHNOLOGY INC.
0040A2 (base 16)	KINGSTAR TECHNOLOGY INC. 1-3F, NO. 185, SEC. 3, CHENG TEH ROAD TAIPEI, TAIWAN, R.O.C.
00-40-A3 (hex)	MICROUNITY SYSTEMS ENGINEERING
0040A3 (base 16)	MICROUNITY SYSTEMS ENGINEERING 255 CASPIAN DRIVE SUNNYVALE, CA 94089-1015
00-40-A4 (hex)	ROSE ELECTRONICS
0040A4 (base 16)	ROSE ELECTRONICS P.O. BOX 742571 HOUSTON TX 77274-2571
00-40-A5 (hex)	CLINICOMP INTL.
0040A5 (base 16)	CLINICOMP INTL. 4510 EXECCUTIVE DRIVE-STE.#200 SAN DIEGO CA 92121
00-40-A6 (hex)	CRAY RESEARCH INC.
0040A6 (base 16)	CRAY RESEARCH INC. 655F LONE OAK DRIVE EAGAN MN 55121
00-40-A7 (hex)	ITAUTEC PHILCO S.A.
0040A7 (base 16)	ITAUTEC PHILCO S.A. GRUPO ITAUTEC PHILCO RUA SANTA CATARINA, 1 03086-020 SAO PAULO, SP BRAZIL
00-40-A8 (hex)	IMF INTERNATIONAL LTD.
0040A8 (base 16)	IMF INTERNATIONAL LTD. NO.5 2/F KINGSFORD IND. CENTRE 13 WANG HOI ROAD KOWLOON BAY, KOWLOON HONG KONG
00-40-A9 (hex)	DATACOM INC.
0040A9 (base 16)	DATACOM INC. 146 HIGHWAY ROUTE 34 - STE 250 HOLMDEL NJ 07733
00-40-AA (hex)	VALMET AUTOMATION INC.
0040AA (base 16)	VALMET AUTOMATION INC. P.O. BOX 237 SF-33101 TAMPERE FINLAND
00-40-AB (hex)	ROLAND DG CORPORATION
0040AB (base 16)	ROLAND DG CORPORATION 1227 OKUBO-CHO, HAMAMATSU-SHI SHIZUOKA-KEN 432 JAPAN
00-40-AC (hex)	SUPER WORKSTATION, INC.
0040AC (base 16)	SUPER WORKSTATION, INC. 2190 PARAGON DRIVE SAN JOSE CA 95131
00-40-AD (hex)	SMA REGELSYSTEME GMBH
0040AD (base 16)	SMA REGELSYSTEME GMBH HANNOVERSCHE STR. 1-5 D 3501 NIESTETAL GERMANY
00-40-AE (hex)	DELTA CONTROLS, INC.
0040AE (base 16)	DELTA CONTROLS, INC. 13520 78TH AVENUE SURREY, B.C. CANADA V3W 8J6
00-40-AF (hex)	DIGITAL PRODUCTS, INC.
0040AF (base 16)	DIGITAL PRODUCTS, INC. 411 WAVERLY OAKS ROAD WALTHAM MA 02154
00-40-B0 (hex)	BYTEX CORPORATION, ENGINEERING
0040B0 (base 16)	BYTEX CORPORATION, ENGINEERING 13873 PARK CENTER ROAD HERNDON, VA 22071
00-40-B1 (hex)	CODONICS INC.
0040B1 (base 16)	CODONICS INC. 17991 ENGLEWOOD DRIVE MIDDLEBURG HTS, OH 44130
00-40-B2 (hex)	SYSTEMFORSCHUNG
0040B2 (base 16)	SYSTEMFORSCHUNG KONIGSTRASSE 33A 5300 BONN 1 GERMANY
00-40-B3 (hex)	PAR MICROSYSTEMS CORPORATION
0040B3 (base 16)	PAR MICROSYSTEMS CORPORATION 220 SENECA TURNPIKE NEW HARTFORD NY 13413-1191
00-40-B4 (hex)	NEXTCOM K.K.
0040B4 (base 16)	NEXTCOM K.K. 1-12-1 SHIBUYA SHIBUYA-KU, TOKYO, 150 JAPAN
00-40-B5 (hex)	VIDEO TECHNOLOGY COMPUTERS LTD
0040B5 (base 16)	VIDEO TECHNOLOGY COMPUTERS LTD 33/F., BLOCK #1, TAI PING INDUSTRIAL CENTER 57 TING KOK ROAD, TAI PO N.T., HONG KONG
00-40-B6 (hex)	COMPUTERM CORPORATION
0040B6 (base 16)	COMPUTERM CORPORATION 111 WOOD STREET PITTSBURGH PA 15222
00-40-B7 (hex)	STEALTH COMPUTER SYSTEMS
0040B7 (base 16)	STEALTH COMPUTER SYSTEMS 2341 REGINA CT. SANTA CLARA CA 95054
00-40-B8 (hex)	IDEA ASSOCIATES
0040B8 (base 16)	IDEA ASSOCIATES 29 DUNHAM ROAD BILLERICA MA 01821
00-40-B9 (hex)	MACQ ELECTRONIQUE SA
0040B9 (base 16)	MACQ ELECTRONIQUE SA RUE DE L'AERONEF 2 B - 1140 BRUSSELS BELGIUM
00-40-BA (hex)	ALLIANT COMPUTER SYSTEMS CORP.
0040BA (base 16)	ALLIANT COMPUTER SYSTEMS CORP. ONE MONARCH DRIVE LITTLETON, MA 01460
00-40-BB (hex)	GOLDSTAR CABLE CO., LTD.
0040BB (base 16)	GOLDSTAR CABLE CO., LTD. 555, HOGYE-DONG, ANYANG-SHI KYUNGKI-DO, 430-080 KOREA
00-40-BC (hex)	ALGORITHMICS LTD.

company_id	Organization Address
0040BC (base 16)	ALGORITHMICS LTD. 3 DRAYTON PARK LONDON N5 1NU ENGLAND
00-40-BD (hex)	STARLIGHT NETWORKS, INC.
0040BD (base 16)	STARLIGHT NETWORKS, INC. 444 CASTRO STREET STE «301» MOUNTAIN VIEW CA 94041
00-40-BE (hex)	BOEING DEFENSE & SPACE
0040BE (base 16)	BOEING DEFENSE & SPACE P.O. BOX 3999 MAIL STOP 88-12 SEATTLE WA 98124-2499
00-40-BF (hex)	CHANNEL SYSTEMS INTERN'L INC.
0040BF (base 16)	CHANNEL SYSTEMS INTERN'L INC. 93 SO. LA PATERA LANE SANTA BARBARA, CA 93117
00-40-C0 (hex)	VISTA CONTROLS CORPORATION
0040C0 (base 16)	VISTA CONTROLS CORPORATION 27825 FREMONT COURT VALENCIA, CA 91355
00-40-C1 (hex)	BIZERBA-WERKE WILHELM KRAUT
0040C1 (base 16)	BIZERBA-WERKE WILHELM KRAUT GMBH & CO. KG, WILHELM-KRAUT-STR. 65 P.O. BOX 100164 D-7460 BALINGEN, GERMANY
00-40-C2 (hex)	APPLIED COMPUTING DEVICES
0040C2 (base 16)	APPLIED COMPUTING DEVICES ALEPH PARK 100 SOUTH CAMPUS DRIVE TERRE HAUTE, IN 47802
00-40-C3 (hex)	FISCHER AND PORTER CO.
0040C3 (base 16)	FISCHER AND PORTER CO. 125 E. COUNTY LINE ROAD WARMINSTER, PA 18974
00-40-C4 (hex)	KINKEI SYSTEM CORPORATION
0040C4 (base 16)	KINKEI SYSTEM CORPORATION 1-22-17, KAMIKITA, HIRANOKU OSAKA, 547 JAPAN
00-40-C5 (hex)	MICOM COMMUNICATIONS INC.
0040C5 (base 16)	MICOM COMMUNICATIONS INC. 4100 LOS ANGELES AVENUE SIMI VALLEY CA 93063
00-40-C6 (hex)	FIBERNET RESEARCH, INC.
0040C6 (base 16)	FIBERNET RESEARCH, INC. 1 TARA BOULEVARD-#405 NASHUA NH 03062
00-40-C7 (hex)	RUBY TECH CORPORATION
0040C7 (base 16)	RUBY TECH CORPORATION 6F-1, NO.3, LANE 250, SEC. 5 NANKING E.ROAD TAIPEI, TAIWAN, R.O.C.
00-40-C8 (hex)	MILAN TECHNOLOGY CORPORATION
0040C8 (base 16)	MILAN TECHNOLOGY CORPORATION 894 ROSS DRIVE—STE #105 SUNNYVALE CA 94089
00-40-C9 (hex)	NCUBE
0040C9 (base 16)	NCUBE 919 EAST HILLSDALE BLVD. SUITE 200 FOSTER CITY, CA 94404
00-40-CA (hex)	FIRST INTERNAT'L COMPUTER, INC
0040CA (base 16)	FIRST INTERNAT'L COMPUTER, INC 6F. FORMOSA PLASTICS REAR BLDG 201-24 TUNG HWA N. RD. TAIPEI TAIWAN
00-40-CB (hex)	LANWAN TECHNOLOGIES

company_id	Organization Address
0040CB (base 16)	LANWAN TECHNOLOGIES 1566 LA PRADERA DRIVE CAMPBELL, CA 95008
00-40-CC (hex)	SILCOM MANUF'G TECHNOLOGY INC.
0040CC (base 16)	SILCOM MANUF'G TECHNOLOGY INC. 5620 TIMBERLEA BOULEVARD MISSISSAUGA, ONTARIO CANADA L4W 4M6
00-40-CD (hex)	TERA MICROSYSTEMS, INC.
0040CD (base 16)	TERA MICROSYSTEMS, INC. 2500 GREAT AMERICA PARKWAY STE. #250 SANTA CLARA, CA 95054
00-40-CE (hex)	NET-SOURCE, INC.
0040CE (base 16)	NET-SOURCE, INC. 1265 EL CAMINO REAL SUITE 101 SANTA CLARA, CA 95050
00-40-CF (hex)	STRAWBERRY TREE, INC.
0040CF (base 16)	STRAWBERRY TREE, INC. 160 SOUTH WOLFE ROAD SUNNYVALE, CA 94086
00-40-D0 (hex)	MITAC INTERNATIONAL CORP.
0040D0 (base 16)	MITAC INTERNATIONAL CORP. 8TH FL. 585 MING SHENG E. RD. TAIPEI TAIWAN, R.O.C.
00-40-D1 (hex)	FUKUDA DENSHI CO., LTD.
0040D1 (base 16)	FUKUDA DENSHI CO., LTD. R & D DEPARTMENT NO. 1 35-8, HONGO 2-CHOME, BUNKYO-KU TOKYO 113 JAPAN
00-40-D2 (hex)	PAGINE CORPORATION
0040D2 (base 16)	PAGINE CORPORATION 1961-A CONCOURSE DRIVE SAN JOSE CA 95131
00-40-D3 (hex)	KIMPSION INTERNATIONAL CORP.
0040D3 (base 16)	KIMPSION INTERNATIONAL CORP. 4701 PATRICK HENRY DRIVE SUITE 401 SANTA CLARA, CA 95054
00-40-D4 (hex)	GAGE TALKER CORP.
0040D4 (base 16)	GAGE TALKER CORP. 13680 NE 16TH STREET BELLEVUE WA 98005
00-40-D5 (hex)	SARTORIUS AG
0040D5 (base 16)	SARTORIUS AG WEENDER LANDSTR: 94 - 108 3400 GOTTINGEN GERMANY
00-40-D6 (hex)	LOCAMATION B.V.
0040D6 (base 16)	LOCAMATION B.V. POSTBOX 360 7500 AJ ENSCHEDE HOLLAND
00-40-D7 (hex)	STUDIO GEN INC.
0040D7 (base 16)	STUDIO GEN INC. 3-12-8 TAKANAWA #202 MINATOKU, TOKYO 108 JAPAN
00-40-D8 (hex)	OCEAN OFFICE AUTOMATION LTD.
0040D8 (base 16)	OCEAN OFFICE AUTOMATION LTD. 4TH & 5TH FLOOR, KADER BLDG. 22 KAI CHEUNG ROAD KOWLOON BAY, KOWLOON HONG KONG
00-40-D9 (hex)	AMERICAN MEGATRENDS INC.
0040D9 (base 16)	AMERICAN MEGATRENDS INC. 6145F N BELT PARKWAY NORCROSS GA 30071

company_id	Organization Address
00-40-DA (hex)	TELSPEC LTD
0040DA (base 16)	TELSPEC LTD LANCASTER PARKER ROAD ROCHESTER AIRPORT, ROCHESTER KENT ME1 3QU ENGLAND
00-40-DB (hex)	ADVANCED TECHNICAL SOLUTIONS
0040DB (base 16)	ADVANCED TECHNICAL SOLUTIONS 8050 SEMINOLE OFFICE CENTER SUITE 210 SEMINOLE, FL 34642
00-40-DC (hex)	TRITEC ELECTRONIC GMBH
0040DC (base 16)	TRITEC ELECTRONIC GMBH ROBERT KOCH STR. 35 D6500 MAINZ 42 GERMANY
00-40-DD (hex)	HONG TECHNOLOGIES
0040DD (base 16)	HONG TECHNOLOGIES 532 WEDDELL DRIVE SUNNYVALE CA 94089
00-40-DE (hex)	ELETTRONICA SAN GIORGIO
0040DE (base 16)	ELETTRONICA SAN GIORGIO ELSAG S.P.A. VIA G. PUCCINI, 2 16154 GENOVA - ITALY
00-40-DF (hex)	DIGALOG SYSTEMS, INC.
0040DF (base 16)	DIGALOG SYSTEMS, INC. 3180 SOUTH 166TH STREET NEW BERLIN WI 53151
00-40-E0 (hex)	ATOMWIDE LTD.
0040E0 (base 16)	ATOMWIDE LTD. 23 THE GREENWAY ORPINGTON BR5 2AY UNITED KINGDOM
00-40-E1 (hex)	MARNER INTERNATIONAL, INC.
0040E1 (base 16)	MARNER INTERNATIONAL, INC. 1617 93RD LANE NE BLAINE MN 55449
00-40-E2 (hex)	MESA RIDGE TECHNOLOGIES, INC.
0040E2 (base 16)	MESA RIDGE TECHNOLOGIES, INC. 6725 MESA RIDGE ROAD-STE#100 SAN DIEGO CA 92121
00-40-E3 (hex)	QUIN SYSTEMS LTD
0040E3 (base 16)	QUIN SYSTEMS LTD OAKLANDS BUSINESS CENTRE OAKLANDS PARK, WOKINGHAM BERKS RG11 2FD UNITED KINGDOM
00-40-E4 (hex)	E-M TECHNOLOGY, INC.
0040E4 (base 16)	E-M TECHNOLOGY, INC. 9245 SOUTHWEST NIMBUS AVE. BEAVERTON OR 97005
00-40-E5 (hex)	SYBUS CORPORATION
0040E5 (base 16)	SYBUS CORPORATION 2300 TALL PINE DRIVE-STE. #100 LARGO FL 34641
00-40-E6 (hex)	C.A.E.N.
0040E6 (base 16)	C.A.E.N. 2, CHEMIN LATERAL F94290 VILLENEUVE LE ROI FRANCE
00-40-E7 (hex)	ARNOS INSTRUMENTS & COMPUTER
0040E7 (base 16)	ARNOS INSTRUMENTS & COMPUTER SYSTEMS (GROUP) CO., LTD. 4/F., EUREKA IND. BLDG., 1-17 SAI LAU KOK ROAD TSUEN WAN, N.T. HONG KONG
00-40-E8 (hex)	CHARLES RIVER DATA SYSTEMS,INC

company_id	Organization Address
0040E8 (base 16)	CHARLES RIVER DATA SYSTEMS,INC 983 CONCORD STREET FRAMINGHAM MA 01701
00-40-E9 (hex)	ACCORD SYSTEMS, INC.
0040E9 (base 16)	ACCORD SYSTEMS, INC. 572 VALLEY WAY MILPITAS CA 95035
00-40-EA (hex)	PLAIN TREE SYSTEMS INC
0040EA (base 16)	PLAIN TREE SYSTEMS INC CHIEF EXECUTVE OFFICER 59 IBER ROAD, STITTSVILLE ONTARIO K2S 1E7 CANADA
00-40-EB (hex)	MARTIN MARIETTA CORPORATION
0040EB (base 16)	MARTIN MARIETTA CORPORATION 12506 LAKE UNDERHILL ORLANDO FL 32825
00-40-EC (hex)	MIKASA SYSTEM ENGINEERING
0040EC (base 16)	MIKASA SYSTEM ENGINEERING CO., LTD. 1-3-10, MINAMI-SHINMACHI, CHUO-KU, OSAKA 540 JAPAN
00-40-ED (hex)	NETWORK CONTROLS INT'NATL INC.
0040ED (base 16)	NETWORK CONTROLS INT'NATL INC. 9 WOODLAWN GREEN CHARLOTTE NC 28217
00-40-EE (hex)	OPTIMEM
0040EE (base 16)	OPTIMEM 297 N. BERNARDO AVENUE MOUNTAIN VIEW, CA 94043-5205
00-40-EF (hex)	HYPERCOM, INC.
0040EF (base 16)	HYPERCOM, INC. 2851 WEST KATHLEEN ROAD PHOENIX, AZ 85023
00-40-F0 (hex)	MICRO SYSTEMS, INC.
0040F0 (base 16)	MICRO SYSTEMS, INC. 69-52 NAGAKUDE KANIHARA, NAGAKUT. CH. AICH-GUN AICHI-KEN 480-11 JAPAN
00-40-F1 (hex)	CHUO ELECTRONICS CO., LTD.
0040F1 (base 16)	CHUO ELECTRONICS CO., LTD. 1-9-9, MOTOHONGO-CHO HACHIOJI-SHI TOKYO 192 JAPAN
00-40-F2 (hex)	JANICH & KLASS COMPUTERTECHNIK
0040F2 (base 16)	JANICH & KLASS COMPUTERTECHNIK ZUM ALTEN ZOLLHAUS 20 W-5600 WUPPERTAL 2 GERMANY
00-40-F3 (hex)	NETCOR
0040F3 (base 16)	NETCOR 850 AUBURN COURT FREMONT, CA 94538
00-40-F4 (hex)	CAMEO COMMUNICATIONS, INC.
0040F4 (base 16)	CAMEO COMMUNICATIONS, INC. 71 SPITBROOK ROAD, STE #410 NASHUA NH 030603
00-40-F5 (hex)	OEM ENGINES
0040F5 (base 16)	OEM ENGINES 1190 DELL AVENUE, STE. D CAMPBELL CA 95008
00-40-F6 (hex)	KATRON COMPUTERS INC.
0040F6 (base 16)	KATRON COMPUTERS INC. 4 FL. NO. 2, ALLEY 23 LANE 91 SEC. 1 NEI HU ROAD TAIPEI, TAIWAN
00-40-F7 (hex)	POLAROID MEDICAL IMAGING SYS.

company_id	Organization Address
0040F7 (base 16)	POLAROID MEDICAL IMAGING SYS. 153 NEEDHAM STREET, NEW-3 NEWTON MA 02164
00-40-F8 (hex)	SYSTEMHAUS DISCOM
0040F8 (base 16)	SYSTEMHAUS DISCOM DISTRIBUTED COMPUTING GMBH ROERMONDERSTR. 615 D-5100 AACHEN GERMANY
00-40-F9 (hex)	COMBINET
0040F9 (base 16)	COMBINET 333 W. EL CAMINO REAL-STE#310 SUNNYVALE CA 94087
00-40-FA (hex)	MICROBOARDS, INC.
0040FA (base 16)	MICROBOARDS, INC. 31-8, TAKASECHO,FUNABASHI-CITY CHIBA 273, JAPAN
00-40-FB (hex)	CASCADE COMMUNICATIONS CORP.
0040FB (base 16)	CASCADE COMMUNICATIONS CORP. PRODUCTION QUALITY ENGINEER 239 LITTLETON ROAD-UNIT 4A WESTFORD MA 01886
00-40-FC (hex)	IBR COMPUTER TECHNIK GMBH
0040FC (base 16)	IBR COMPUTER TECHNIK GMBH FRANKFURTER STR. 114 D 6056 HEUSENSTAMM WEST GERMANY
00-40-FD (hex)	LXE
0040FD (base 16)	LXE 303 RESEARCH DRIVE NORCROSS GA 30092
00-40-FE (hex)	SYMPLEX COMMUNICATIONS
0040FE (base 16)	SYMPLEX COMMUNICATIONS 5 RESEARCH DRIVE ANN ARBOR MI 48103
00-40-FF (hex)	TELEBIT CORPORATION
0040FF (base 16)	TELEBIT CORPORATION 1315 CHESAPEAKE TERRACE SUNNYVALE CA 94089-1100
00-50-00 (hex)	NEXO COMMUNICATIONS, INC.
005000 (base 16)	NEXO COMMUNICATIONS, INC. 2ND FL., 160, MINGCHU ROAD HSINCHU CITY TAIWAN, R.O.C.
00-50-01 (hex)	YAMASHITA SYSTEMS CORP.
005001 (base 16)	YAMASHITA SYSTEMS CORP. 5-7-12 IKEGAMI OTA-KU TOKYO JAPAN
00-50-02 (hex)	OMNISEC AG
005002 (base 16)	OMNISEC AG RIETSTRASSE 14 CH-8108 DAELLIKON SWITZERLAND
00-50-03 (hex)	GRETAG MACBETH AG
005003 (base 16)	GRETAG MACBETH AG ALTHARDSTRASSE 70 CH-8105 REGENSDORF SWITZERLAND
00-50-04 (hex)	3COM CORPORATION
005004 (base 16)	3COM CORPORATION 5400 BAYFRONT PLAZA SANTA CLARA CA 95052
00-50-06 (hex)	TAC AB
005006 (base 16)	TAC AB JAGERSHILLGATON 18 21375 MALMO SWEDEN
00-50-07 (hex)	SIEMENS TELECOMMUNICATION

company_id	Organization Address
005007 (base 16)	SIEMENS TELECOMMUNICATION SYSTEMS LIMITED NO. 90, SEC. 1, CHIEN KUO NORTH ROAD TAIPEI, TAIWAN, R.O.C.
00-50-08 (hex)	TIVA MICROCOMPUTER CORP. (TMC)
005008 (base 16)	TIVA MICROCOMPUTER CORP. (TMC) 48550 FREMONT BLVD. FREMONT CA 94538
00-50-09 (hex)	PHILIPS BROADBAND NETWORKS
005009 (base 16)	PHILIPS BROADBAND NETWORKS 64 PERIMETER CENTRE EAST ATLANTA GA 30346
00-50-0A (hex)	IRIS TECHNOLOGIES, INC.
00500A (base 16)	IRIS TECHNOLOGIES, INC. WESTMORELAND INDUSRIAL PARK R.R. 12 BOX 36 GREENSBURG PA 15601
00-50-0B (hex)	CISCO SYSTEMS, INC.
00500B (base 16)	CISCO SYSTEMS, INC. 170 W. TASMAN DRIVE M/S SJA-2 SAN JOSE CA 95134-1706
00-50-0C (hex)	ETEK LABS, INC.
00500C (base 16)	ETEK LABS, INC. 1057 EAST HENRIETTA RD. ROCHESTER NY 14623
00-50-0D (hex)	SATORI ELECTORIC CO., LTD.
00500D (base 16)	SATORI ELECTORIC CO., LTD. TIGUSADAI 38-8 MIDORI-KU YOKOHAMA, KANAGAWA JAPAN
00-50-0E (hex)	CHROMATIS NETWORKS,INC.
00500E (base 16)	CHROMATIS NETWORKS,INC. 3 BETHESDA METRO CENTER BETHESDA MD 20814
00-50-0F (hex)	CISCO SYSTEMS, INC.
00500F (base 16)	CISCO SYSTEMS, INC. 170 W. TASMAN DRIVE - SJA-2 SAN JOSE CA 95134-1706
00-50-10 (hex)	NOVANET LEARNING, INC.
005010 (base 16)	NOVANET LEARNING, INC. 125 W. CHURCH STREET-STE. #300 CHAMPAIGN IL 61820
00-50-12 (hex)	CBL - GMBH
005012 (base 16)	CBL - GMBH DARMSTAEDTER STR. 81 D-64839 MUENSTER GERMANY
00-50-13 (hex)	Chaparral Technologies, Inc.
005013 (base 16)	Chaparral Technologies, Inc. 7420 E. Dry Creek Parkway Longmont, CO 80503
00-50-14 (hex)	CISCO SYSTEMS, INC.
005014 (base 16)	CISCO SYSTEMS, INC. M/S/ SJA-2 170 W. TASMAN DRIVE SAN JOSE CA 95134-1706
00-50-15 (hex)	BRIGHT STAR ENGINEERING
005015 (base 16)	BRIGHT STAR ENGINEERING 19 ENFIELD DRIVE ANDOVER MA 01810
00-50-16 (hex)	SST/WOODHEAD INDUSTRIES
005016 (base 16)	SST/WOODHEAD INDUSTRIES 50 NORTHLAND ROAD WATERLOO, ONTARIO N2V 1N3 CANADA
00-50-17 (hex)	RSR S.R.L.

company_id	Organization / Address	company_id	Organization / Address
005017 (base 16)	RSR S.R.L. VIA SINIGAGLIA, 38 LURATE CACCIVIO (CO) 22075 ITALY	00-50-28 (hex)	AVAL COMMUNICATIONS
00-50-18 (hex)	ADVANCED MULTIMEDIA INTERNET	005028 (base 16)	AVAL COMMUNICATIONS 1777 NORTH CALIFORNIA BLVD. WALNUT CREEK CA 94596
005018 (base 16)	ADVANCED MULTIMEDIA INTERNET TECHNOLOGY INC. 14F-4, NO.12, CHUNG HUA ROAD YUNG KANG CITY, TAINAN HSIEN TAIWAN, R.O.C. 710	00-50-29 (hex)	1394 PRINTER WORKING GROUP
		005029 (base 16)	1394 PRINTER WORKING GROUP P.O. BOX 23158 SAN JOSE CA 95153
00-50-19 (hex)	SPRING TIDE NETWORKS, INC.	00-50-2A (hex)	CISCO SYSTEMS, INC.
005019 (base 16)	SPRING TIDE NETWORKS, INC. 85 SWANSON ROAD BOXBOROUGH MA 01719	00502A (base 16)	CISCO SYSTEMS, INC. M/S SJA-2 170 W. TASMAN DRIVE SAN JOSE CA 95134-1706
00-50-1A (hex)	UISIQN	00-50-2B (hex)	GENRAD LTD.
00501A (base 16)	UISIQN 20361 IRVINE AVENUE SANTA ANA HEIGHTS CA 92707	00502B (base 16)	GENRAD LTD. ORION BUSINESS PARK BIRDHALL LANE STOCKPORT, CHESHIRE UNITED KINGDOM, SK3 0XG
00-50-1B (hex)	ABL CANADA, INC.		
00501B (base 16)	ABL CANADA, INC. 8550 COTE DE LIESSE ST-LAURENT (QUEBEC) CANADA H4T 1H2	00-50-2C (hex)	SOYO COMPUTER, INC.
		00502C (base 16)	SOYO COMPUTER, INC. NO. 21 WU-KUNG 5 RD. HSING CHUANG CITY TAIPEI HSIEN TAIWAN, R.O.C.
00-50-1C (hex)	JATOM SYSTEMS, INC.		
00501C (base 16)	JATOM SYSTEMS, INC. 99 MICHAEL COWPLAND DRIVE KANATA ONTARIO, K2M 1X3 CANADA	00-50-2D (hex)	ACCEL, INC.
		00502D (base 16)	ACCEL, INC. 1F, NO. 7, R&D 1ST ROAD SCIENCE-BASED INDUSTRIAL PARK HSINCHU TAIWAN
00-50-1E (hex)	MIRANDA TECHNOLOGIES, INC.		
00501E (base 16)	MIRANDA TECHNOLOGIES, INC. 2323 HALPERN ST. LAURENT, QUEBEC CANADA H4S 1S3	00-50-2E (hex)	CAMBEX CORPORATION
		00502E (base 16)	CAMBEX CORPORATION 360 SECOND AVENUE WALTHAM MA 02451
00-50-1F (hex)	MRG SYSTEMS, LTD.	00-50-2F (hex)	TOLLBRIDGE TECHNOLOGIES, INC.
00501F (base 16)	MRG SYSTEMS, LTD. WILLOW HOUSE, SLAD ROAD STROUD GLOS. GL5 1QG ENGLAND	00502F (base 16)	TOLLBRIDGE TECHNOLOGIES, INC. 872 HERMOSA DRIVE SUNNYVALE CA 94086
		00-50-30 (hex)	FUTURE PLUS SYSTEMS
00-50-20 (hex)	MEDIASTAR CO., LTD.	005030 (base 16)	FUTURE PLUS SYSTEMS 36 OLDE ENGLISH RD. BEDFORD NH 03110
005020 (base 16)	MEDIASTAR CO., LTD. 3FL, SOHUN BLDG. 951-33 DOGOK-DONG, KANGNAM-KU SEOUL KOREA	00-50-31 (hex)	AEROFLEX LABORATORIES, INC.
		005031 (base 16)	AEROFLEX LABORATORIES, INC. 35 SOUTH SERVICE ROAD PLAINVIEW, NY 11803
00-50-21 (hex)	EIS INTERNATIONAL, INC.	00-50-32 (hex)	PICAZO COMMUNICATIONS, INC.
005021 (base 16)	EIS INTERNATIONAL, INC. 1351 WASHINGTON BLVD. STAMFORD CT 06902	005032 (base 16)	PICAZO COMMUNICATIONS, INC. 61 DAGGETT DRIVE SAN JOSE CA 95134
00-50-22 (hex)	ZONET TECHNOLOGY, INC.	00-50-33 (hex)	MAYAN NETWORKS
005022 (base 16)	ZONET TECHNOLOGY, INC. 830 ROOM, BLDG. 53, 195, SEC.4 CHUNG HSIUNG RD, CHUTUNG HSINCHA, TAIWAN	005033 (base 16)	MAYAN NETWORKS 3350 SCOTT BLVD. - BLDG. #9 SANTA CLARA CA 95054
00-50-23 (hex)	PG DESIGN ELECTRONICS, INC.	00-50-36 (hex)	NETCAM, LTD.
005023 (base 16)	PG DESIGN ELECTRONICS, INC. 48700 STRUCTURAL DRIVE CHESTERFIELD MI 48051	005036 (base 16)	NETCAM, LTD. 6071 N. PASEO ZALDIVAR TUCSON AZ 85750
00-50-24 (hex)	NAVIC SYSTEMS, INC.	00-50-37 (hex)	KOGA ELECTRONICS CO.
005024 (base 16)	NAVIC SYSTEMS, INC. 74 CRESCENT STREET NEEDHAM MA	005037 (base 16)	KOGA ELECTRONICS CO. 5-8-10, TEHARA, RITTO-CHO KURITA GUN SHIGA, 420-3047 JAPAN
00-50-26 (hex)	COSYSTEMS, INC.		
005026 (base 16)	COSYSTEMS, INC. 1263 OAKMEAD PARKWAY SUNNYVALE CA 94086	00-50-38 (hex)	DAIN TELECOM CO., LTD.
00-50-27 (hex)	GENICOM CORPORATION		
005027 (base 16)	GENICOM CORPORATION 900 CLOPPER ROAD - STE. #110 GAITHERSBURG MD 20878		

company_id	Organization Address
005038 (base 16)	DAIN TELECOM CO., LTD. 2ND FR., OH-SUNG BLDG. #2-28 YANGJAE-DONG, SEOCHO-GU SEOUL KOREA
00-50-39 (hex)	MARINER NETWORKS
005039 (base 16)	MARINER NETWORKS 1585 S. MANCHESTER AVE. ANAHEIM CA 92802-2907
00-50-3A (hex)	DATONG ELECTRONICS LTD.
00503A (base 16)	DATONG ELECTRONICS LTD. CLAYTON WOOD CLOSE WEST PARK, LEEDS LS16 6QE, UNITED KINGDOM
00-50-3B (hex)	MEDIAFIRE CORPORATION
00503B (base 16)	MEDIAFIRE CORPORATION 11317 FREDERICK AVENUE BELTSVILLE MD 20705
00-50-3C (hex)	TSINGHUA NOVEL ELECTRONICS
00503C (base 16)	TSINGHUA NOVEL ELECTRONICS CO., LTD. ROOM 1205, HUAYE BUILDING TSINGHUA UNIVERSITY, BEIJING 100084, CHINA
00-50-3E (hex)	CISCO SYSTEMS, INC.
00503E (base 16)	CISCO SYSTEMS, INC. 170 W. TASMAN DRIVE M/S/ SJA-2 SAN JOSE CA 95134-1706
00-50-3F (hex)	ANCHOR GAMES
00503F (base 16)	ANCHOR GAMES 815 PILOT ROAD - STE «G» LAS VEGAS NV 89119
00-50-40 (hex)	EMWARE, INC.
005040 (base 16)	EMWARE, INC. 1225 FORT UNION BLVD.-STE.#200 SALT LAKE CITY UT 84047
00-50-41 (hex)	CTX OPTO ELECTRONIC CORP.
005041 (base 16)	CTX OPTO ELECTRONIC CORP. NO.11, LI HSIN RD. SCIENCE-BASED INDUSTRIAL PARK HISNCHU TAIWAN, R.O.C.
00-50-42 (hex)	SCI MANUFACTURING
005042 (base 16)	SCI MANUFACTURING SINGAPORE PTE, LTD. 3 DEPOT CLOSE SINGAPORE 109840
00-50-43 (hex)	MARVELL SEMICONDUCTOR, INC.
005043 (base 16)	MARVELL SEMICONDUCTOR, INC. 645 ALMANOR AVENUE SUNNYVALE CA 94086
00-50-44 (hex)	ASACA CORPORATION
005044 (base 16)	ASACA CORPORATION 420 CORPORATE CIRCLE UNITE «H» GOLDEN CO 80401
00-50-45 (hex)	RIOWORKS SOLUTIONS, INC.
005045 (base 16)	RIOWORKS SOLUTIONS, INC. 4F, NO.28, LANE 583 JUI-KWANG ROAD TAIPEI, 11457 TAIWAN, R.O.C.
00-50-46 (hex)	MENICX INTERNATIONAL CO., LTD.
005046 (base 16)	MENICX INTERNATIONAL CO., LTD. NO.9, MING TSUN ROAD CHUTUNG, HSINCHU TAIWAN 310, R.O.C.
00-50-48 (hex)	INFOLIBRIA

company_id	Organization Address
005048 (base 16)	INFOLIBRIA 411 WAVERLY OAKS RD-STE #323 WALTHAM MA 02154-8414
00-50-49 (hex)	ELLACOYA NETWORKS, INC.
005049 (base 16)	ELLACOYA NETWORKS, INC. 486 AMHERST STREET NASHUA NH 03063
00-50-4A (hex)	ELTECO A.S.
00504A (base 16)	ELTECO A.S. ROSINSKA CESTA P.O. BOX C-9 01001 ZILINA SLOVAKIA
00-50-4B (hex)	BARCO N.V. BCS
00504B (base 16)	BARCO N.V. BCS THEODOOR SEVENSLAAN 106 8500 KORTRIJK BELGIUM
00-50-4C (hex)	GALIL MOTION CONTROL, INC.
00504C (base 16)	GALIL MOTION CONTROL, INC. 203 RAVENDALE DRIVE MOUNTAIN VIEW CA 94043-5216
00-50-4D (hex)	TOKYO ELECTRON DEVICE LTD.
00504D (base 16)	TOKYO ELECTRON DEVICE LTD. 30-7, SUMIYOSHI-CHO 2-CHOME FUCHU-CITY, TOKYO 183-8705 JAPAN
00-50-4E (hex)	SIERRA MONITOR CORP.
00504E (base 16)	SIERRA MONITOR CORP. 1991 TAROB COURT MILPITAS CA 95035
00-50-4F (hex)	OLENCOM ELECTRONICS
00504F (base 16)	OLENCOM ELECTRONICS SOLTAM INDUSTRIAL PARK P.O. BOX 196 YOKNEAM ISRAEL 20692
00-50-50 (hex)	CISCO SYSTEMS, INC.
005050 (base 16)	CISCO SYSTEMS, INC. 170 W. TASMAN DRIVE- SJA-2 SAN JOSE CA 95134-1706
00-50-51 (hex)	IWATSU ELECTRIC CO., LTD.
005051 (base 16)	IWATSU ELECTRIC CO., LTD. 7-41, KUGAYAMA 1-CHOME SUGINAMI-KU, TOKYO 168-8501, JAPAN
00-50-52 (hex)	TIARA NETWORKS, INC.
005052 (base 16)	TIARA NETWORKS, INC. 113 FOORIER AVENUE FREMONT CA 94539
00-50-53 (hex)	CISCO SYSTEMS, INC.
005053 (base 16)	CISCO SYSTEMS, INC. 170 W. TASMAN DRIVE-SJA-2 SAN JOSE CA 95134-1706
00-50-54 (hex)	CISCO SYSTEMS, INC.
005054 (base 16)	CISCO SYSTEMS, INC. M/S SJA-2 170 W. TASMAN DRIVE SAN JOSE CA 95134-1706
00-50-55 (hex)	DOMS A/S
005055 (base 16)	DOMS A/S FORMERVANGEN 28 DK-2600 GLOSTRUP DENMARK
00-50-56 (hex)	VMWARE, INC.
005056 (base 16)	VMWARE, INC. 44 ENCINA AVENUE PALO ALTO CA 94301
00-50-57 (hex)	BROADBAND ACCESS SYSTEMS
005057 (base 16)	BROADBAND ACCESS SYSTEMS 201 FOREST STREET MARLBOROUGH MA 01752

company_id	Organization Address
00-50-58 (hex)	VEGASTREAM LIMITED
005058 (base 16)	VEGASTREAM LIMITED ROYAL ALBERT HOUSE SHEET ST., WINDSOR BERKS, SL4 1BE UNITED KINGDOM
00-50-59 (hex)	SUITE TECHNOLOGY SYSTEMS
005059 (base 16)	SUITE TECHNOLOGY SYSTEMS NETWORK 5983 REDWOOD ROAD SALT LAKE CITY UT 84123
00-50-5A (hex)	NETWORK ALCHEMY, INC.
00505A (base 16)	NETWORK ALCHEMY, INC. 1521.5 PACIFIC AVENUE SANTA CRUZ CA 95060
00-50-5B (hex)	KAWASAKI LSI U.S.A., INC.
00505B (base 16)	KAWASAKI LSI U.S.A., INC. 2570 NORTHFIRST STREET SUITE #301 SAN JOSE CA 95131
00-50-5C (hex)	TUNDO CORPORATION
00505C (base 16)	TUNDO CORPORATION 7 GIBOREI ISRAEL STREET NATANYA 42504 ISRAEL
00-50-5E (hex)	DIGITEK MICROLOGIC S.A.
00505E (base 16)	DIGITEK MICROLOGIC S.A. SANT JOAN DE LA SALLE 6 E08022 BARCELONA SPAIN
00-50-5F (hex)	BRAND INNOVATORS
00505F (base 16)	BRAND INNOVATORS DE PINCKART 54 5674 CC NUENEN NETHERLANDS
00-50-60 (hex)	TANDBERG TELECOM AS
005060 (base 16)	TANDBERG TELECOM AS P.O. BOX 92 N-1324 LYSAKER NORWAY
00-50-62 (hex)	KOUWELL ELECTRONICS CORP. **
005062 (base 16)	KOUWELL ELECTRONICS CORP. ** 7F, NO.99, NAN-KANG ROAD SEC. 3, TAIPEI TAIWAN R.O.C.
00-50-63 (hex)	OY COMSEL SYSTEM AB
005063 (base 16)	OY COMSEL SYSTEM AB STORALANGGATAN 28-30 FIN-65100 VASA FINLAND
00-50-64 (hex)	CAE ELECTRONICS
005064 (base 16)	CAE ELECTRONICS P.O. BOX 1800 ST. LAURENT, QUEBEC CANADA H4L 4X4
00-50-65 (hex)	DENSEI-LAMBAD Co., Ltd.
005065 (base 16)	DENSEI-LAMBAD Co., Ltd. 36-1 Kasuminosato Ami-Machi Inashiki-Gun Ibaraki, 300-0396 JAPAN
00-50-66 (hex)	ATECOM GMBH ADVANCED
005066 (base 16)	ATECOM GMBH ADVANCED TELECOMMUNICATION MODULES KAISERSTR. 100 D-52134 HERZOGENRATH GERMANY
00-50-67 (hex)	AEROCOMM, INC.

company_id	Organization Address
005067 (base 16)	AEROCOMM, INC. 13256 W. 98TH STREET LENEXA KS 66215
00-50-68 (hex)	ELECTRONIC INDUSTRIES
005068 (base 16)	ELECTRONIC INDUSTRIES ASSOCIATION 2500 WILSON BLVD. ARLINGTON VA 22201
00-50-69 (hex)	PIXSTREAM INCORPORATED
005069 (base 16)	PIXSTREAM INCORPORATED 180 COLUMBIA ST. W. WATERLOO, ONTARIO CANADA N2L-3L3
00-50-6A (hex)	EDEVA, INC.
00506A (base 16)	EDEVA, INC. 298 S. SUNNYVALE AVE. - #208 SUNNYVALE CA 94086
00-50-6B (hex)	SPX-ATEG
00506B (base 16)	SPX-ATEG 802 S. MAIN STREET WAYLAND MI 49348
00-50-6C (hex)	G & L BEIJER ELECTRONICS AB
00506C (base 16)	G & L BEIJER ELECTRONICS AB BOX 325, S-201 23 MALMO SWEDEN
00-50-6D (hex)	VIDEOJET SYSTEMS
00506D (base 16)	VIDEOJET SYSTEMS INTERNATIONAL INC. 1500 MITTEL BLVD. WOODDALE IL 60091-1073
00-50-6E (hex)	CORDER ENGINEERING CORPORATION
00506E (base 16)	CORDER ENGINEERING CORPORATION 151 KALMUS DRIVE - STE #A103 COSTA MESA CA 92626
00-50-6F (hex)	G-CONNECT
00506F (base 16)	G-CONNECT P.O. BOX 2200 HERZLIYA 46120 ISRAEL
00-50-70 (hex)	CHAINTECH COMPUTER CO., LTD.
005070 (base 16)	CHAINTECH COMPUTER CO., LTD. 5TH F, ALLEY 2, LANE 222 LIEN-CHENG RD., CHUNG-HO TAIPEI-HSIEN TAIWAN R.O.C.
00-50-71 (hex)	AIWA CO., LTD.
005071 (base 16)	AIWA CO., LTD. 1-11, KAMITOMATSURI 4-CHOME UTSUNOMIYA-SHI, TOCHIGI-KEN 320-8520 JAPAN
00-50-72 (hex)	CORVIS CORPORATION
005072 (base 16)	CORVIS CORPORATION 8320 GUILFORD ROAD COLUMBIA MD 21046
00-50-73 (hex)	CISCO SYSTEMS, INC.
005073 (base 16)	CISCO SYSTEMS, INC. 170 W. TASMAN DRIVE M/S SJA-2 SAN JOSE CA 95134-1706
00-50-74 (hex)	ADVANCED HI-TECH CORP.
005074 (base 16)	ADVANCED HI-TECH CORP. 1990 EAST GRAND AVE. EL SEGUNDO CA 90505
00-50-75 (hex)	KESTREL SOLUTIONS
005075 (base 16)	KESTREL SOLUTIONS 2370 CHARLESTON ROAD MT. VIEW CA 94043
00-50-76 (hex)	IBM

company_id	Organization Address
005076 (base 16)	IBM 3605 HIGHWAY 52 N. MS: 2B7 ROCHESTER MN 55901-7829
00-50-77 (hex)	PROLIFIC TECHNOLOGY, INC.
005077 (base 16)	PROLIFIC TECHNOLOGY, INC. 6F 1, LANE 51, SEC 1 NAN-CHAN ROAD TAIPEI TAIWAN 100, R.O.C.
00-50-78 (hex)	MEGATON HOUSE, LTD.
005078 (base 16)	MEGATON HOUSE, LTD. ZIP: 224 NO.1-3-5 NAKAMACHIBAI TSUDUKI WARD YOKOHAMA JAPAN
00-50-7A (hex)	XPEED, INC.
00507A (base 16)	XPEED, INC. 4699 OLD IRONSIDES DRIVE SUITE #300 SANTA CLARA CA 95054
00-50-7B (hex)	MERLOT COMMUNICATIONS
00507B (base 16)	MERLOT COMMUNICATIONS BERKSHIRE CORPORATE PARK 4 BERKSHIRE BLVD. BETHEL CT 06801
00-50-7C (hex)	VIDEOCON AG
00507C (base 16)	VIDEOCON AG ALBERT-SCHWEITZER-STR. 64 D-81735 MUNICH GERMANY
00-50-7D (hex)	IFP
00507D (base 16)	IFP LESSINGSTR. 4 D-78315 RADOLFZELL GERMANY
00-50-7E (hex)	NEWER TECHNOLOGY
00507E (base 16)	NEWER TECHNOLOGY 4848 WEST IRVING ST. WICHITA KS 67209-2621
00-50-7F (hex)	DRAYTEK CORP.
00507F (base 16)	DRAYTEK CORP. 1F, NO.29, ALLEY 6, LANE 485 SEC 1, KUANG FU ROAD HSIN-CHU TAIWAN R.O.C.
00-50-80 (hex)	CISCO SYSTEMS, INC.
005080 (base 16)	CISCO SYSTEMS, INC. M/S SJA-2 170 W. TASMAN DRIVE SAN JOSE CA 95134-1706
00-50-81 (hex)	MURATA MACHINERY, LTD.
005081 (base 16)	MURATA MACHINERY, LTD. 136, TAKEDA-MUKAISHIRO-CHO FUSHIMI-KU, KYOTO 612-8686 JAPAN
00-50-82 (hex)	FORESSON CORPORATION
005082 (base 16)	FORESSON CORPORATION 3F, NO.9 SEC.1 CHANG AN EAST ROAD TAIPEI 10404 TAIWAN, R.O.C.
00-50-83 (hex)	GILBARCO, INC.
005083 (base 16)	GILBARCO, INC. POB 22087 GREENSBORO NC 27420
00-50-84 (hex)	ATL PRODUCTS
005084 (base 16)	ATL PRODUCTS 2801 KELVIN AVENUE IRVINE CA 92614-5872
00-50-86 (hex)	TELKOM SA, LTD.

company_id	Organization Address
005086 (base 16)	TELKOM SA, LTD. TELKOM LABORATORY P. BAG X74 PRETORIA SOUTH AFRICA
00-50-87 (hex)	TERASAKI ELECTRIC CO., LTD.
005087 (base 16)	TERASAKI ELECTRIC CO., LTD. 7-2-10 HANNAN-CHO ABENO-KU OSAKA, 545-0021 JAPAN
00-50-88 (hex)	AMANO CORPORATION
005088 (base 16)	AMANO CORPORATION 275, MAMEDO-CHO KOUHOKU-KU, YOKOHAMA 222-8558, JAPAN
00-50-89 (hex)	SAFETY MANAGEMENT SYSTEMS
005089 (base 16)	SAFETY MANAGEMENT SYSTEMS BRANDERIJSTRAAT 6 5223 AS 'S-HERTOGENBOSCH THE NETHERLANDS
00-50-8B (hex)	COMPAQ COMPUTER CORPORATION
00508B (base 16)	COMPAQ COMPUTER CORPORATION 20555 S.H. 249 HOUSTON TX 77070
00-50-8C (hex)	RSI SYSTEMS
00508C (base 16)	RSI SYSTEMS 5555 W. 78TH STREET - STE. F EDINA MN 55439
00-50-8D (hex)	ABIT COMPUTER CORPORATION
00508D (base 16)	ABIT COMPUTER CORPORATION 3F-7, NO. 79, SEC.1 HSIN TAI WU ROAD, HSI CHIH TAIPEI HSIEN TAIWAN, R.O.C.
00-50-8E (hex)	OPTIMATION, INC.
00508E (base 16)	OPTIMATION, INC. P.O. BOX 14357 HUNTSVILLE AL 35815
00-50-8F (hex)	ASITA TECHNOLOGIES INT'L LTD.
00508F (base 16)	ASITA TECHNOLOGIES INT'L LTD. UNIT 2 BALLYBRIT BUSINESS PARK GALWAY IRELAND
00-50-90 (hex)	DCTRI
005090 (base 16)	DCTRI NO.40 XUE YUAN RD HAIDIAN DISTRICT BEIJING, 100083, P.R. CHINA
00-50-91 (hex)	NETACCESS, INC.
005091 (base 16)	NETACCESS, INC. 18 KEEWAYDIN DRIVE SALEM NH 03079
00-50-92 (hex)	RIGAKU INDUSTRIAL CORPORATION
005092 (base 16)	RIGAKU INDUSTRIAL CORPORATION 14-8 AKAOJI-CHO TAKATSUKI-SHI, OSAKA 569-1146, JAPAN
00-50-93 (hex)	BOEING
005093 (base 16)	BOEING 3370 MIRALOMA AVENUE ANAHEIM CA 92803-3105
00-50-94 (hex)	PACE MICRO TECHNOLOGY PLC
005094 (base 16)	PACE MICRO TECHNOLOGY PLC VICTORIA RD, SALTAIRE SHIPLEY, W. YORKSHIRE BRADFORD BD28 3LF ENGLAND
00-50-95 (hex)	PERACOM NETWORKS

company_id	Organization Address
005095 (base 16)	PERACOM NETWORKS 13000 WESTON PARKWAY SUITE #105 CARY NC 27513
00-50-96 (hex)	SALIX TECHNOLOGIES, INC.
005096 (base 16)	SALIX TECHNOLOGIES, INC. 904 WIND RIVER LANE- STE. #101 GAITHERSBURG MD 20878
00-50-97 (hex)	MMC-EMBEDDED
005097 (base 16)	MMC-EMBEDDED COMPUTERTECHNIK GMBH ULRICHSBERGERSTR. 17 D-94469 DEGGENDORF GERMANY
00-50-98 (hex)	GLOBALOOP, LTD.
005098 (base 16)	GLOBALOOP, LTD. 12 HASHARON ROAD KFAR SABA ISRAEL 44269
00-50-99 (hex)	3COM EUROPE, LTD.
005099 (base 16)	3COM EUROPE, LTD. BOUNDARY WAY HEMEL HEMPSTEAD HERTS. HP2 7YU UNITED KINGDOM
00-50-9A (hex)	TAG ELECTRONIC SYSTEMS
00509A (base 16)	TAG ELECTRONIC SYSTEMS GENESIS BUSINESS PARK WOKING, SURREY GU21, 5RW UNITED KINGDOM
00-50-9B (hex)	SWITCHCORE AB
00509B (base 16)	SWITCHCORE AB POSITIONEN 153 115 74 STOCKHOLM SWEDEN
00-50-9C (hex)	BETA RESEARCH
00509C (base 16)	BETA RESEARCH BETASTR. 1 85774 UNTERFOEHRING GERMANY
00-50-9D (hex)	THE INDUSTREE B.V.
00509D (base 16)	THE INDUSTREE B.V. P.O. BOX 462 5600 AL EINDHOVEN THE NETHERLANDS
00-50-9E (hex)	LES TECHNOLOGIES
00509E (base 16)	LES TECHNOLOGIES SOFTACOUSTIK, INC. 390,RUE SAINT-VALLIER EST. 4FL QUEBEC (QUEBEC) G1K 3P6 CANADA
00-50-9F (hex)	HORIZON COMPUTER
00509F (base 16)	HORIZON COMPUTER TRINITY BLDG. 4-22-7 NISHI-AZABU, MINATO-KU TOKYO 106 JAPAN
00-50-A0 (hex)	DELTA COMPUTER SYSTEMS, INC.
0050A0 (base 16)	DELTA COMPUTER SYSTEMS, INC. 11719 NE 95TH STREET - STE.»D» VANCOUVER WA 98682-2444
00-50-A1 (hex)	CARLO GAVAZZI, INC.
0050A1 (base 16)	CARLO GAVAZZI, INC. 222 PENNBRIGHT DR. - STE.#210 HOUSTON TX 77090
00-50-A2 (hex)	CISCO SYSTEMS, INC.
0050A2 (base 16)	CISCO SYSTEMS, INC. 170 W. TASMAN DRIVE - SJA-2 SAN JOSE CA 95134-1706
00-50-A3 (hex)	TRANSMEDIA COMMUNICATIONS, INC

company_id	Organization Address
0050A3 (base 16)	TRANSMEDIA COMMUNICATIONS, INC 20 GREAT OAKS BLVD., #210 SAN JOSE CA 95119
00-50-A4 (hex)	IO TECH, INC.
0050A4 (base 16)	IO TECH, INC. 25971 CANNON ROAD CLEVELAND OH 44146
00-50-A5 (hex)	CAPITOL BUSINESS SYSTEMS, LTD.
0050A5 (base 16)	CAPITOL BUSINESS SYSTEMS, LTD. 43/44 RIVERSIDE SIR THOMAS LONGLEY ROAD ROCHESTER, KENT ENGLAND ME2 4DP
00-50-A6 (hex)	OPTRONICS
0050A6 (base 16)	OPTRONICS 175 CREMONA DRIVE GOLETA CA 93117
00-50-A7 (hex)	CISCO SYSTEMS, INC.
0050A7 (base 16)	CISCO SYSTEMS, INC. 170 W. TASMAN DRIVE M/S SJA-2 SAN JOSE CA 95134-1706
00-50-A8 (hex)	OPENCON SYSTEMS, INC.
0050A8 (base 16)	OPENCON SYSTEMS, INC. 377 HOES LANE PISCATAWAY NJ 08854
00-50-A9 (hex)	MOLDAT WIRELESS TECHNOLGIES
0050A9 (base 16)	MOLDAT WIRELESS TECHNOLGIES 3 SHIMON ISRAELI STREET RISHON LE ZION 75654 ISRAEL
00-50-AA (hex)	KONICA CORPORATION
0050AA (base 16)	KONICA CORPORATION SHINJUKU NOMURA BLDG. NO. 26-2 NISHISHINJUKU 1-CHOME, SHINJUKU-KU, TOKYO 163-05, JAPAN
00-50-AB (hex)	NALTEC, INC.
0050AB (base 16)	NALTEC, INC. 2-10-1 ROMANKAN MINATOCHOU, SHIMIZU-SHI 424-0943 JAPAN
00-50-AC (hex)	MAPLE COMPUTER CORPORATION
0050AC (base 16)	MAPLE COMPUTER CORPORATION 2F, NO. 184, SEC. 2 CHANG-AN E. RD., TAIPEI TAIWAN, R.O.C.
00-50-AD (hex)	COMMUNIQUE WIRELESS CORP.
0050AD (base 16)	COMMUNIQUE WIRELESS CORP. 1070 MARINA VILLAGE PARKWAY SUITE #206 ALAMEDA CA 94501
00-50-AE (hex)	IWAKI ELECTRONICS CO., LTD.
0050AE (base 16)	IWAKI ELECTRONICS CO., LTD. 1, KAMANOMAE JOBAN-KAMIYUNAGAYA-MACHI IWAKI-CITY, FUKUSHIMA 972-8322, JAPAN
00-50-AF (hex)	INTERGON, INC.
0050AF (base 16)	INTERGON, INC. 5800 RANCHESTER DRIVE HOUSTON TX 77036
00-50-B0 (hex)	TECHNOLOGY ATLANTA CORPORATION
0050B0 (base 16)	TECHNOLOGY ATLANTA CORPORATION 141 W. WIEUCA RD, N.E. SUITE #200 ATLANTA GA 30342
00-50-B1 (hex)	GIDDINGS & LEWIS

company_id	Organization Address
0050B1 (base 16)	GIDDINGS & LEWIS 660 S. MILITARY RD. FOND DU LAC WI 54935
00-50-B2 (hex)	BRODEL AUTOMATION
0050B2 (base 16)	BRODEL AUTOMATION FRIEDRICH-EBERT-STRASSE 243 42549 VELBERT GERMANY
00-50-B3 (hex)	VOICEBOARD CORPORATION
0050B3 (base 16)	VOICEBOARD CORPORATION 3151 WEST FIFTH STREET OXNARD CA 93030
00-50-B4 (hex)	SATCHWELL CONTROL SYSTEMS, LTD
0050B4 (base 16)	SATCHWELL CONTROL SYSTEMS, LTD P.O. BOX 57, 94 FARNHAM ROAD SLOUGH, BERKSHIRE SL1 4UH UNITED KINGDOM
00-50-B5 (hex)	FICHET-BAUCHE
0050B5 (base 16)	FICHET-BAUCHE 15-17 AVE. MORANE-SAULNIER 78140 VELIZY FRANCE
00-50-B6 (hex)	GOOD WAY IND. CO., LTD.
0050B6 (base 16)	GOOD WAY IND. CO., LTD. 5F, NO.8, ALLEY 6, LANE 45 PAO-HSIN RD.-HSIN TIEN TAIPEI HSIEN TAIWAN R.O.C.
00-50-B7 (hex)	BOSER TECHNOLOGY CO., LTD.
0050B7 (base 16)	BOSER TECHNOLOGY CO., LTD. 15F-6, 77 HSIN TAI WU ROAD SEC. 1, HSI-CHI TAIPEI HSIEN TAIWAN R.O.C.
00-50-B8 (hex)	INOVA COMPUTERS GMBH & CO. KG
0050B8 (base 16)	INOVA COMPUTERS GMBH & CO. KG SUDETENSTRASSE 5 87600 KAUFBEUREN GERMANY
00-50-B9 (hex)	XITRON TECHNOLOGIES, INC.
0050B9 (base 16)	XITRON TECHNOLOGIES, INC. 6295-D FERRIS SQUARE SAN DIEGO CA 92121
00-50-BA (hex)	D-LINK
0050BA (base 16)	D-LINK 2F, NO. 233L-2, PAO-CHIAO RD. TAIPEI TAIWAN
00-50-BB (hex)	CMS TECHNOLOGIES
0050BB (base 16)	CMS TECHNOLOGIES 13955 FARMINGTON ROAD LIVONIA MI 48154
00-50-BC (hex)	HAMMER STORAGE SOLUTIONS
0050BC (base 16)	HAMMER STORAGE SOLUTIONS 8450 CENTRAL AVENUE NEWARK CA 94560
00-50-BD (hex)	CISCO SYSTEMS, INC.
0050BD (base 16)	CISCO SYSTEMS, INC. 170 W. TASMAN DRIVE - SJA-2 SAN JOSE CA 95134-1706
00-50-BE (hex)	FAST MULTIMEDIA AG
0050BE (base 16)	FAST MULTIMEDIA AG RUEDESHEIMERSTR. 11-13 80686 MUNICH GERMANY
00-50-BF (hex)	MOTOTECH INC.

company_id	Organization Address
0050BF (base 16)	MOTOTECH INC. NO.9, PARK AVENUE II SCIENCE-BASE INDUSTRIAL PARK HSIN-CHU TAIWAN, R.O.C.
00-50-C0 (hex)	GATAN, INC.
0050C0 (base 16)	GATAN, INC. 5933 CORONADO LANE PLEASANTON CA 94588
00-50-C1 (hex)	GEMFLEX NETWORKS, LTD.
0050C1 (base 16)	GEMFLEX NETWORKS, LTD. 230-6651 FRASERWOOD PL. RICHMOND, B.C. CANADA V6W 1J3
00-50-C2 (hex)	IEEE REGISTRATION AUTHORITY
0050C2 (base 16)	IEEE REGISTRATION AUTHORITY 445 HOES LANE PISCATAWAY NJ 08855
00-50-C4 (hex)	IMD
0050C4 (base 16)	IMD HERBSTRASSE 8 D-82178 PUCHHEIM GERMANY
00-50-C5 (hex)	ADS TECHNOLOGIES, INC.
0050C5 (base 16)	ADS TECHNOLOGIES, INC. 13909 BETTENCOURT ST. CERRITOS CA 90703
00-50-C6 (hex)	LOOP TELECOMMUNICATION
0050C6 (base 16)	LOOP TELECOMMUNICATION INTERNATIONAL, INC. 2F, NO. 22, PROSPERITY RD. 2 SCIENCE-BASED INDUSTRIAL PARK HSINCHU, TAIWAN, R.O.C.
00-50-C8 (hex)	ADDONICS COMMUNICATIONS, INC.
0050C8 (base 16)	ADDONICS COMMUNICATIONS, INC. 48434 MILMONT DRIVE FREMONT CA 94538
00-50-C9 (hex)	MASPRO DENKOH CORP.
0050C9 (base 16)	MASPRO DENKOH CORP. ASADA NISSHIN AICHI 470-0194 JAPAN
00-50-CA (hex)	NET TO NET TECHNOLOGIES
0050CA (base 16)	NET TO NET TECHNOLOGIES 680 CENTRAL AVENUE - STE. #301 DOVER NH 03820
00-50-CB (hex)	JETTER
0050CB (base 16)	JETTER GRAETERSTRASSE 2 D71642 LUDWIGSBURG GERMANY
00-50-CC (hex)	XYRATEX
0050CC (base 16)	XYRATEX MAIL POINT: 26/13 DEPT: STORAGE SYSTEMS (20459) LANGSTONE ROAD, HAVANT PO9 1SA, UNITED KINGDOM
00-50-CD (hex)	DIGIANSWER A/S
0050CD (base 16)	DIGIANSWER A/S SKALHUSE 5 9240 NIBE DENMARK
00-50-CE (hex)	LG INTERNATIONAL CORP.
0050CE (base 16)	LG INTERNATIONAL CORP. LG TWIN TOWERS 20 YOIDO-DONG, YOUNGDUNGPO-GU SEOUL, 150-606 KOREA
00-50-CF (hex)	VANLINK COMMUNICATION

company_id	Organization Address	company_id	Organization Address
0050CF (base 16)	VANLINK COMMUNICATION TECHNOLOGY RESEARCH INSTITUTE 210 YADI OFFICE BUILDING NO. 48 BEI SAN HUAN ZHONG LU BEIJING 100088, CHINA	00-50-DD (hex)	SERRA SOLDADURA, S.A.
00-50-D0 (hex)	MINERVA SYSTEMS	0050DD (base 16)	SERRA SOLDADURA, S.A. POL. IND. ZONA FRANCA, SECTOR C, CALLE D, N. 29 08040 BARCELONA SPAIN
0050D0 (base 16)	MINERVA SYSTEMS 1585 CHARLESTON ROAD MOUNTAIN VIEW CA 84943	00-50-DE (hex)	SIGNUM SYSTEMS CORP.
00-50-D1 (hex)	CISCO SYSTEMS, INC.	0050DE (base 16)	SIGNUM SYSTEMS CORP. 11992 CHALLENGER COURT MOORPARK CA 93021
0050D1 (base 16)	CISCO SYSTEMS, INC. 170 W. TASMAN DRIVE M/S SJA-2 SAN JOSE CA 95134-1706	00-50-DF (hex)	AIRFIBER, INC.
00-50-D2 (hex)	CANADIAN MARCONI COMPANY	0050DF (base 16)	AIRFIBER, INC. P.O. BOX 502148 SAN DIEGO CA 92150-2148
0050D2 (base 16)	CANADIAN MARCONI COMPANY 600 DR. FREDERIK-PHILIPS BLVD. ST-LAURENT, QUEBEC CANADA H4M 2S9	00-50-E1 (hex)	NS TECH ELECTRONICS SDN BHD
00-50-D3 (hex)	DIGITAL AUDIO	0050E1 (base 16)	NS TECH ELECTRONICS SDN BHD NO. 21 & 23 JALAN CANGGIH 10 TAMAN PERINDUSTRIAN CEMERLANG 81800 ULU TIRAM-JOHOR BAHRU MALAYSIA
0050D3 (base 16)	DIGITAL AUDIO PROCESSING PTY. LTD. PO BOX 40 CONCORD WEST NSW 2138 AUSTRALIA	00-50-E2 (hex)	CISCO SYSTEMS, INC.
00-50-D4 (hex)	JOOHONG INFORMATION & COMMUNICATIONS, LTD.	0050E2 (base 16)	CISCO SYSTEMS, INC. 170 W. TASMAN DRIVE - SJA-2 SAN JOSE CA 95134-1706
0050D4 (base 16)	JOOHONG INFORMATION & COMMUNICATIONS, LTD. JUNGNAM B/D, 721-39 YEOKSAM-DONG, KANGNAM-KU SEOUL, KOREA	00-50-E3 (hex)	TELEGATE
00-50-D5 (hex)	AD SYSTEMS CORP.	0050E3 (base 16)	TELEGATE 7 HAPLADA STREET OR YEHUDA 60218 ISRAEL
0050D5 (base 16)	AD SYSTEMS CORP. 1-4-1, NAKACHO, MUSASHINO CITY TOKYO 180-0006 JAPAN	00-50-E4 (hex)	APPLE COMPUTER, INC.
00-50-D6 (hex)	ATLAS COPCO TOOLS AB	0050E4 (base 16)	APPLE COMPUTER, INC. 20650 VALLEY GREEN DR. CUPERTINO CA 95014
0050D6 (base 16)	ATLAS COPCO TOOLS AB S-105 23 STOCKHOLM SWEDEN	00-50-E6 (hex)	HAKUSAN CORPORATION
00-50-D7 (hex)	TELSTRAT	0050E6 (base 16)	HAKUSAN CORPORATION J TOWER, 1-1, NIKKOU-CHO FUCHU-SHI TOKYO 183-0044 JAPAN
0050D7 (base 16)	TELSTRAT 3600 AVENUE «K» PLANO TX 75074	00-50-E7 (hex)	PARADISE INNOVATIONS (ASIA)
00-50-D8 (hex)	UNICORN COMPUTER CORP.	0050E7 (base 16)	PARADISE INNOVATIONS (ASIA) PTE. LTD. 25 SERANGOON NORTH AVE. 5 6TH FLOOR URACO BUILDING SINGAPORE 554914
0050D8 (base 16)	UNICORN COMPUTER CORP. 7 FL., NO. 96 KWANG FU NORTH ROAD TAIPEI TAIWAN, R.O.C.	00-50-E8 (hex)	NOMADIX INC.
00-50-D9 (hex)	ENGETRON-ENGENHARIA ELETRONICA	0050E8 (base 16)	NOMADIX INC. 2701 OCEAN PARK BLVD.-STE.#231 SANTA MONICA CA 90405
0050D9 (base 16)	ENGETRON-ENGENHARIA ELETRONICA IND. E COM. LTDA VIA SOCRATES M. BITTENCOURT #1099, 32010-010-CONTAGEM-MG- BRAZIL	00-50-EA (hex)	XEL COMMUNICATIONS, INC.
00-50-DA (hex)	3COM CORPORATION	0050EA (base 16)	XEL COMMUNICATIONS, INC. 17101 E. OHIO DRIVE AURORA CO 80017
0050DA (base 16)	3COM CORPORATION 5400 BAYFRONT PLAZA MS: 4220 SANTA CLARA CA 95052	00-50-EB (hex)	ALPHA-TOP CORPORATION
00-50-DB (hex)	CONTEMPORARY CONTROL	0050EB (base 16)	ALPHA-TOP CORPORATION 19F., NO. 2, LANE 150 SEC. 5, HSIN-YI ROAD TAIPEI TAIWAN, R.O.C.
0050DB (base 16)	CONTEMPORARY CONTROL SYSTEMS, INC. 2431 CURTISS STREET DOWNERS GROVE IL 60515	00-50-EC (hex)	OLICOM A/S
00-50-DC (hex)	TAS TELEFONBAU A. SCHWABE	0050EC (base 16)	OLICOM A/S NYBROVEJ 114, DK-2800 LYNGBY DENMARK
0050DC (base 16)	TAS TELEFONBAU A. SCHWABE GMBH & CO. KG LANGMAAR 25 D-41238 MOENCHENGLADBACH GERMANY	00-50-ED (hex)	ANDA NETWORKS
		0050ED (base 16)	ANDA NETWORKS 2921 COPPER ROAD SANTA CLARA CA 95051
		00-50-EE (hex)	TEK DIGITEL CORPORATION

company_id	Organization Address
0050EE (base 16)	TEK DIGITEL CORPORATION 20010 CENTURY BLVD. #300 GERMANTOWN MD 20874
00-50-EF (hex)	SPE SYSTEMHAUS GMBH
0050EF (base 16)	SPE SYSTEMHAUS GMBH WALDSTRASSE 7 63150 HEUSENSTAMM GERMANY
00-50-F0 (hex)	CISCO SYSTEMS, INC.
0050F0 (base 16)	CISCO SYSTEMS, INC. 170 W. TASMAN DRIVE M/S SJA-2 SAN JOSE CA 95134-1706
00-50-F1 (hex)	LIBIT SIGNAL PROCESSING, LTD.
0050F1 (base 16)	LIBIT SIGNAL PROCESSING, LTD. P.O. BOX 12670 2 SHANKER STREET HERZLIYA 46766 ISRAEL
00-50-F2 (hex)	MICROSOFT CORP.
0050F2 (base 16)	MICROSOFT CORP. ONE MICROSOFT WAY REDMOND WA 98052-6399
00-50-F3 (hex)	GLOBAL NET INFORMATION CO.,LTD
0050F3 (base 16)	GLOBAL NET INFORMATION CO.,LTD NORTH TOWER- RM 1305 WORLD TRADE CENTRE COMPLEX NO.371-375, HUAN SHI DONG RD GUANGZHOU 510095, CHINA
00-50-F4 (hex)	SIGMATEK GMBH & CO. KG
0050F4 (base 16)	SIGMATEK GMBH & CO. KG A-5112 LAMPRECHTSHAUSEN, BURMOOSER STRASSE 10 AUSTRIA
00-50-F6 (hex)	PAN-INTERNATIONAL
0050F6 (base 16)	PAN-INTERNATIONAL INDUSTRIAL CORP. 5F, NO. 176, CHANG CHUN RD. TAIPEI TAIWAN, R.O.C.
00-50-F7 (hex)	VENTURE MANUFACTURING
0050F7 (base 16)	VENTURE MANUFACTURING (SINGAPORE) LTD. 5006 ANG MO KIO AVENUE 5 #05-01 TECHPLACE II SINGAPORE 569873
00-50-F8 (hex)	ENTREGA TECHNOLOGIES, INC.
0050F8 (base 16)	ENTREGA TECHNOLOGIES, INC. 25691 ATLANTIC OCEAN DRIVE SUITE #18 LAKE FOREST CA 92630
00-50-FA (hex)	OXTEL, LTD.
0050FA (base 16)	OXTEL, LTD. THE MARKET PLACE DIDCOT 0X11 7LE, ENGLAND
00-50-FB (hex)	VSK ELECTRONICS
0050FB (base 16)	VSK ELECTRONICS VENETIELAAN 39 8530 HARELBEKE BELGIUM
00-50-FC (hex)	EDIMAX TECHNOLOGY CO., LTD.
0050FC (base 16)	EDIMAX TECHNOLOGY CO., LTD. 3F,50, WU-CHUN 7 ROAD, WU-KU TAIPEI COUNTY TAIWAN, R.O.C.
00-50-FD (hex)	ISIONCOMM CO., LTD.
0050FD (base 16)	ISIONCOMM CO., LTD. 4, 5F, DAEWON B/D 198-8, SEOBINGGO-DONG YONGSAN-GU, SEOUL KOREA

company_id	Organization Address
00-50-FE (hex)	PCTVNET ASA
0050FE (base 16)	PCTVNET ASA STRANDVEILEN 50 1324 LYSAKER NORWAY
00-50-FF (hex)	HAKKO ELECTRONICS CO., LTD.
0050FF (base 16)	HAKKO ELECTRONICS CO., LTD. 238, KAMIKASHIWANO-MACHI MATTO-SHI, ISHIKAWA 924-0035, JAPAN
00-60-00 (hex)	XYCOM INC.
006000 (base 16)	XYCOM INC. 750 N. MAPLE SALINE, MI 48176
00-60-01 (hex)	INNOSYS, INC.
006001 (base 16)	INNOSYS, INC. 3095 RICHMOND PKWY #207 RICHMOND CA 94806
00-60-02 (hex)	SCREEN SUBTITLING SYSTEMS, LTD
006002 (base 16)	SCREEN SUBTITLING SYSTEMS, LTD THE OLD RECTORY CHURCH LANE, CLAYDON IPSWICH IP6 OEQ UNITED KINGDOM
00-60-03 (hex)	TERAOKA WEIGH SYSTEM PTE, LTD.
006003 (base 16)	TERAOKA WEIGH SYSTEM PTE, LTD. 3A TUAS AVENUE 8 SINGAPORE 639128
00-60-04 (hex)	COMPUTADORES MODULARES SA
006004 (base 16)	COMPUTADORES MODULARES SA AVDA MONTESIERRA S/N EDIFICIO CONGRESOS 314 41020-SEVILLA SPAIN
00-60-05 (hex)	FEEDBACK DATA LTD.
006005 (base 16)	FEEDBACK DATA LTD. PARK ROAD CROWBOROUGH EAST SUSSEX, TN6 2QR UNITED KINGDOM
00-60-06 (hex)	SOTEC CO., LTD
006006 (base 16)	SOTEC CO., LTD YOKOHAMA BASHAMICHI BLDG., 4-55 OHTA-CHO NAKA-KU YOKOHAMA 231 JAPAN
00-60-07 (hex)	ACRES GAMING, INC.
006007 (base 16)	ACRES GAMING, INC. 815 NW 9TH STREET CORVALLIS OR 97330
00-60-08 (hex)	3COM CORPORATION
006008 (base 16)	3COM CORPORATION 5400 BAYFRONT PLAZA SANTA CLARA CA 95052
00-60-09 (hex)	CISCO SYSTEMS, INC.
006009 (base 16)	CISCO SYSTEMS, INC. 170 W. TASMAN DRIVE SAN JOSE CA 95134-1706
00-60-0A (hex)	SORD COMPUTER CORPORATION
00600A (base 16)	SORD COMPUTER CORPORATION 20-7, MASAGO 5-CHOME MIHAMA-KU, CHIBA-SHI CHIBA 261 JAPAN
00-60-0B (hex)	LOGWARE GMBH
00600B (base 16)	LOGWARE GMBH SCHWEDENSTR. 9 D-13359 BERLIN GERMANY
00-60-0C (hex)	APPLIED DATA SYSTEMS, INC.

company_id	Organization Address
00600C (base 16)	APPLIED DATA SYSTEMS, INC. 9140-A GUILFORD ROAD COLUMBIA MD 21046
00-60-0D (hex)	MICRODESIGN GMBH
00600D (base 16)	MICRODESIGN GMBH WERNER-VON SIEMENS-STRASSE 6 D-86159 AUGSBURG GERMANY
00-60-0E (hex)	WAVENET INTERNATIONAL, INC.
00600E (base 16)	WAVENET INTERNATIONAL, INC. 5825 KENNEDY ROAD MISSISSAUGA, ONTARIO CANADA L4Z 2G3
00-60-0F (hex)	WESTELL, INC.
00600F (base 16)	WESTELL, INC. 75 EXECUTIVE DRIVE AURORA IL 60504-4101
00-60-10 (hex)	NETWORK MACHINES, INC.
006010 (base 16)	NETWORK MACHINES, INC. 255 OLD NEW BRUNSWICK RD #N320 PISCATAWAY NJ 08854
00-60-11 (hex)	CRYSTAL SEMICONDUCTOR CORP.
006011 (base 16)	CRYSTAL SEMICONDUCTOR CORP. P.O. BOX 17847 AUSTIN TX 78760
00-60-12 (hex)	POWER COMPUTING CORPORATION
006012 (base 16)	POWER COMPUTING CORPORATION 10261 BUBB ROAD CUPERTINO CA 95014
00-60-13 (hex)	NETSTAL MASCHINEN AG
006013 (base 16)	NETSTAL MASCHINEN AG INDUSTRIESTRASSE CH-8752 NAEFELS SWITZERLAND
00-60-14 (hex)	EDEC CO., LTD.
006014 (base 16)	EDEC CO., LTD. 9F OF T.O.C. BUILDING 7-22-17 NISHIGOTANDA SHINAGAWAKU, TOKYO JAPAN
00-60-15 (hex)	NET2NET CORPORATION
006015 (base 16)	NET2NET CORPORATION 131 COOLIDGE STREET HUDSON MA 01749
00-60-16 (hex)	CLARIION
006016 (base 16)	CLARIION COSLIN DRIVE M/S C25 SOUTHBORO MA 01772
00-60-17 (hex)	TOKIMEC INC.
006017 (base 16)	TOKIMEC INC. 2-16, MINAMI-KAMATA, OHTA-KU TOKYO 144 JAPAN
00-60-18 (hex)	STELLAR ONE CORPORATION
006018 (base 16)	STELLAR ONE CORPORATION 500 108TH AVE. NE—STE. #2200 BELLEVUE WA 98004
00-60-19 (hex)	BOEHRINGER MANNHEIM CORP.
006019 (base 16)	BOEHRINGER MANNHEIM CORP. 9115 HAGUE ROAD PO BOX 50457 INDIANAPOLIS IN 46250-0457
00-60-1A (hex)	KEITHLEY INSTRUMENTS
00601A (base 16)	KEITHLEY INSTRUMENTS 30500 BAINBRIDGE RD. SOLON OH 44139
00-60-1B (hex)	MESA ELECTRONICS

company_id	Organization Address
00601B (base 16)	MESA ELECTRONICS 1323 61ST STREET EMERYVILLE CA 94608-2117
00-60-1C (hex)	TELXON CORPORATION
00601C (base 16)	TELXON CORPORATION 3330 W. MARKET STREET PO BOX 5582 AKRON OH 44334-0582
00-60-1D (hex)	LUCENT TECHNOLOGIES
00601D (base 16)	LUCENT TECHNOLOGIES 101 CRAWFORDS CORNER RD. ROOM 4K-321 HOLMDEL NJ 07733
00-60-1E (hex)	SOFTLAB, INC.
00601E (base 16)	SOFTLAB, INC. P.O. BOX 8 CHIMNEY ROCK CO 81127
00-60-1F (hex)	STALLION TECHNOLOGIES
00601F (base 16)	STALLION TECHNOLOGIES 33 WOODSTOCK ROAD TOOWONG Q-L-D- 4066 AUSTRALIA
00-60-20 (hex)	PIVOTAL NETWORKING, INC.
006020 (base 16)	PIVOTAL NETWORKING, INC. 7246 SHARON DR., STE «P» SAN JOSE CA 95129
00-60-21 (hex)	DSC CORPORATION
006021 (base 16)	DSC CORPORATION RECRUIT-SHINOHTSUKA BLDG., 2-25-15 MINAMIOHTSUKA TOSHIMA-KU, TOKYO 170 JAPAN
00-60-22 (hex)	VICOM SYSTEMS, INC.
006022 (base 16)	VICOM SYSTEMS, INC. 1961 LANDINGS DRIVE MOUNTAIN VIEW CA 94043
00-60-23 (hex)	PERICOM SEMICONDUCTOR CORP.
006023 (base 16)	PERICOM SEMICONDUCTOR CORP. 2380 BERING DRIVE SAN JOSE CA 95131
00-60-24 (hex)	GRADIENT TECHNOLOGIES, INC.
006024 (base 16)	GRADIENT TECHNOLOGIES, INC. 2 MOUNT ROYAL AVENUE MARLBORO MA 01752
00-60-25 (hex)	ACTIVE IMAGING PLC
006025 (base 16)	ACTIVE IMAGING PLC HATTORI HOUSE VANWALL BUSINESS PARK MAIDENHEAD, BERKSHIRE SL6 4UB UNITED KINGDOM
00-60-26 (hex)	VIKING COMPONENTS, INC.
006026 (base 16)	VIKING COMPONENTS, INC. 11 COLUMBIA LAGUNA HILLS CA 92656
00-60-27 (hex)	Superior Modular Products
006027 (base 16)	Superior Modular Products General Technology Division 415 PINEDA COURT MELBOURNE FL 32940
00-60-28 (hex)	MACROVISION CORPORATION
006028 (base 16)	MACROVISION CORPORATION 1341 ORLEANS DRIVE SUNNYVALE CA 94089
00-60-29 (hex)	CARY PERIPHERALS INC.
006029 (base 16)	CARY PERIPHERALS INC. 190 COLONNADE ROAD S, UNIT 9 NEPEAN, ONTARIO CANADA K2E 7J5
00-60-2A (hex)	SYMICRON COMPUTER

company_id	Organization Address
00602A (base 16)	SYMICRON COMPUTER COMMUNICATIONS, LTD. UNIT 4 GREEN LANE BUSINESS PRK 238 GREEN LANE, ELTHAM LONDON SE9 3TL ENGLAND
00-60-2B (hex)	PEAK AUDIO
00602B (base 16)	PEAK AUDIO 1790 30TH STREET STE #414 BOULDER CO 80301
00-60-2C (hex)	LINX DATA TERMINALS, INC.
00602C (base 16)	LINX DATA TERMINALS, INC. 625 DIGITAL DRIVE-STE #100 PLANO TX 75075
00-60-2D (hex)	ALERTON TECHNOLOGIES, INC.
00602D (base 16)	ALERTON TECHNOLOGIES, INC. 6670 185TH AVE. N.E. REDMOND WA 98052
00-60-2E (hex)	CYCLADES CORPORATION
00602E (base 16)	CYCLADES CORPORATION 41934 CHRISTY STREET FREMONT CA 94538
00-60-2F (hex)	CISCO SYSTEMS, INC.
00602F (base 16)	CISCO SYSTEMS, INC. 170 W. TASMAN DRIVE SAN JOSE CA 95134-1706
00-60-30 (hex)	VILLAGE TRONIC
006030 (base 16)	VILLAGE TRONIC WELLWEG 95 31157 SARSTEDT GERMANY
00-60-31 (hex)	HRK SYSTEMS
006031 (base 16)	HRK SYSTEMS P.O. BOX 514 WESTVILLE 3630 SOUTH AFRICA
00-60-32 (hex)	I-CUBE, INC.
006032 (base 16)	I-CUBE, INC. 2328-C WALSH AVENUE SANTA CLARA CA 95014
00-60-33 (hex)	ACUITY IMAGING, INC.
006033 (base 16)	ACUITY IMAGING, INC. 9 TOWNSEND WEST NASHUA NH 03063
00-60-34 (hex)	ROBERT BOSCH GMBH
006034 (base 16)	ROBERT BOSCH GMBH POSTBOX 11 62 D-64701 ERBACH GERMANY
00-60-35 (hex)	DALLAS SEMICONDUCTOR, INC.
006035 (base 16)	DALLAS SEMICONDUCTOR, INC. 4401 SOUTH BELTWOOD PARKWAY DALLAS TX 75244-3292
00-60-36 (hex)	AUSTRIAN RESEARCH CENTER
006036 (base 16)	AUSTRIAN RESEARCH CENTER SEIBERSDORF A-2444 SEIBERSDORF AUSTRIA
00-60-37 (hex)	PHILIPS SEMICONDUCTORS
006037 (base 16)	PHILIPS SEMICONDUCTORS 811 E. ARQUES AVE., M/S 38 SUNNYVALE CA 94088
00-60-38 (hex)	Nortel Networks
006038 (base 16)	Nortel Networks Global Operations Engineering Dep 6800 Program Manager 8200 Dixie Road, Suite 100 Brampton, ON 16T 5P6 Canada
00-60-39 (hex)	SANCOM TECHNOLOGY, INC.
006039 (base 16)	SANCOM TECHNOLOGY, INC. 7719 WOOD HOLLOW DRIVE SUITE #156 AUSTIN TX 78731
00-60-3A (hex)	QUICK CONTROLS LTD.
00603A (base 16)	QUICK CONTROLS LTD. DURHAM HOUSE, WARWICK COURT PARK ROAD, MIDDLETON MANCHESTER M24 1AE UNITED KINGDOM
00-60-3B (hex)	AMTEC SPA
00603B (base 16)	AMTEC SPA LOC. S. MARTINO 53025 PIANCASTAGNAIO (SIENA) ITALY
00-60-3C (hex)	HAGIWARA SYS-COM CO., LTD.
00603C (base 16)	HAGIWARA SYS-COM CO., LTD. 2-4-3 NISHIKI NAKA-KU NAGOYA AICHI 460 JAPAN
00-60-3D (hex)	3CX
00603D (base 16)	3CX 2085 HAMILTON AVE., -STE.#220 SAN JOSE CA 95125
00-60-3E (hex)	CISCO SYSTEMS, INC.
00603E (base 16)	CISCO SYSTEMS, INC. 170 W. TASMAN DRIVE SAN JOSE CA 95134-1706
00-60-3F (hex)	PATAPSCO DESIGNS
00603F (base 16)	PATAPSCO DESIGNS 5350 PARTNERS COURT FREDERICK MD 21703
00-60-40 (hex)	NETRO CORP.
006040 (base 16)	NETRO CORP. 3120 SCOTT BLVD. SANTA CLARA CA 95054
00-60-41 (hex)	3A INTERNATIONAL, INC.
006041 (base 16)	3A INTERNATIONAL, INC. 4014 E.BROADWAY RD. #402 PHOENIX AZ 85040
00-60-42 (hex)	TKS (USA), INC.
006042 (base 16)	TKS (USA), INC. 1201 COMMERCE RICHARDSON TX 75081
00-60-43 (hex)	COMSOFT SYSTEMS, INC.
006043 (base 16)	COMSOFT SYSTEMS, INC. 7405 COLSHIRE DRIVE- STE #240 MCLEAN VA 22101
00-60-44 (hex)	LITTON/POLY-SCIENTIFIC
006044 (base 16)	LITTON/POLY-SCIENTIFIC 2200 SOUTH MAIN STREET BLACKSBURG VA 24060
00-60-45 (hex)	PATHLIGHT TECHNOLOGIES
006045 (base 16)	PATHLIGHT TECHNOLOGIES 767 WARREN ROAD ITHACA, NY 14850
00-60-46 (hex)	VMETRO, INC.
006046 (base 16)	VMETRO, INC. 1880 DAIRY ASHFORD- STE #535 HOUSTON TX 77077
00-60-47 (hex)	CISCO SYSTEMS, INC.
006047 (base 16)	CISCO SYSTEMS, INC. 170 W. TASMAN DRIVE SAN JOSE CA 95134-1706
00-60-48 (hex)	EMC CORPORATION
006048 (base 16)	EMC CORPORATION 171 SOUTH ST., HOPKINTON MA 01748
00-60-49 (hex)	VINA TECHNOLOGIES

company_id	Organization Address
006049 (base 16)	VINA TECHNOLOGIES 6 UNION SQUARE - STE «F» UNION CITY CA 94587
00-60-4A (hex)	SAIC IDEAS GROUP
00604A (base 16)	SAIC IDEAS GROUP 7120 COLUMBIA GATEWAY DRIVE COLUMBIA, MD 21046
00-60-4B (hex)	BIODATA GMBH
00604B (base 16)	BIODATA GMBH 35104 LICHTENFELS GERMANY
00-60-4C (hex)	SAT
00604C (base 16)	SAT 58 B RUE DU DESSOUS DES BERGES B.P. 326 75625 PARIS CEDEX 13 FRANCE
00-60-4D (hex)	MMC NETWORKS, INC.
00604D (base 16)	MMC NETWORKS, INC. 1134 EAST ARQUES AVENUE SUNNYVALE CA 94086-4602
00-60-4E (hex)	CYCLE COMPUTER CORPORATION, INC.
00604E (base 16)	CYCLE COMPUTER CORPORATION, INC. 20245 STEVENS CREEK BLVD. CUPERTINO, CA 95014
00-60-4F (hex)	SUZUKI MFG. CO., LTD.
00604F (base 16)	SUZUKI MFG. CO., LTD. 552-51 AJIGAURA HITACHINAKA IBARAKI, 311-12 JAPAN
00-60-50 (hex)	INTERNIX INC.
006050 (base 16)	INTERNIX INC. 59-10 TAKAKURA-CHO HACHIOJI TOKYO 192
00-60-51 (hex)	QUALITY SEMICONDUCTOR
006051 (base 16)	QUALITY SEMICONDUCTOR 851 MARTIN AVENUE SANTA CLARA CA 95050
00-60-52 (hex)	PERIPHERALS ENTERPRISE CO., L.
006052 (base 16)	PERIPHERALS ENTERPRISE CO., L. 3F, NO.10, ALLEY 6, LANE 45 PAO SHIN ROAD, HSIN TIEN CITY TAIPEI TAIWAN, R.O.C.
00-60-53 (hex)	TOYODA MACHINE WORKS, LTD.
006053 (base 16)	TOYODA MACHINE WORKS, LTD. 1-7 KITAJIZOYAMA NODACHOU KARIYA CITY, AICHI JAPAN
00-60-54 (hex)	CONTROLWARE GMBH
006054 (base 16)	CONTROLWARE GMBH WALDSTRASSE 92 63128 DIETZENBACH GERMANY
00-60-55 (hex)	CORNELL UNIVERSITY
006055 (base 16)	CORNELL UNIVERSITY 110 MAPLE AVENUE ITHACA NY 14850-4902
00-60-56 (hex)	NETWORK TOOLS, INC.
006056 (base 16)	NETWORK TOOLS, INC. 2975 BOWERS AVENUE, #202 SANTA CLARA CA 95051-0955
00-60-57 (hex)	MURATA MANUFACTURING CO., LTD.
006057 (base 16)	MURATA MANUFACTURING CO., LTD. 1-18-1 HAKUSAN MIDORI-KU YOKOHAMA 226 JAPAN
00-60-58 (hex)	COPPER MOUNTAIN

company_id	Organization Address
006058 (base 16)	COPPER MOUNTAIN COMMUNICATIONS, INC. 6650 LUSK BLVD.-STE #B103 SAN DIEGO CA 92121
00-60-59 (hex)	TECHNICAL COMMUNICATIONS CORP.
006059 (base 16)	TECHNICAL COMMUNICATIONS CORP. 100 DOMINO DRIVE CONCORD MA 01742
00-60-5A (hex)	CELCORE, INC.
00605A (base 16)	CELCORE, INC. 8001 CENTERVIEW PARKWAY SUITE #201 MEMPHIS TN 38018
00-60-5B (hex)	INTRASERVER TECHNOLOGY INC.
00605B (base 16)	INTRASERVER TECHNOLOGY INC. 125 HOPPING BROOK PARK HOLLISTON MA 01746
00-60-5C (hex)	CISCO SYSTEMS, INC.
00605C (base 16)	CISCO SYSTEMS, INC. 170 W. TASMAN DRIVE SAN JOSE CA 95134-1706
00-60-5D (hex)	SCANIVALVE CORP.
00605D (base 16)	SCANIVALVE CORP. 1722 N. MADSON STREET LIBERTY LAKE WA 99019
00-60-5E (hex)	LIBERTY TECHNOLOGY NETWORKING
00605E (base 16)	LIBERTY TECHNOLOGY NETWORKING P.O. BOX 11566 HATFIELD, PRETORIA 0028 SOUTH AFRICA
00-60-5F (hex)	NIPPON UNISOFT CORPORATION
00605F (base 16)	NIPPON UNISOFT CORPORATION BR NINGYOCHO 1,2-13-9 NIHONBASHI-NINGYOCHO, CHUO-KU TOKYO 103 JAPAN
00-60-60 (hex)	DAWNING TECHNOLOGIES, INC.
006060 (base 16)	DAWNING TECHNOLOGIES, INC. 409 MASON ROAD FAIRPORT NY 14450
00-60-61 (hex)	WHISTLE COMMUNICATIONS CORP.
006061 (base 16)	WHISTLE COMMUNICATIONS CORP. 110 MARSH DRIVE-STE #100 FOSTER CITY CA 94404
00-60-62 (hex)	TELESYNC, INC.
006062 (base 16)	TELESYNC, INC. 5555 OAKBROOK PKWY-STE #110 NORCROSS GA 30093
00-60-63 (hex)	PSION DACOM PLC.
006063 (base 16)	PSION DACOM PLC. PSION DACOM HOUSE PRESLEY WAY, CROWNHILL MILTON KEYNES MK8 OEF UNITED KINGDOM
00-60-64 (hex)	NETCOMM LIMITED
006064 (base 16)	NETCOMM LIMITED PO BOX 379 NORTH RYDE, NSW, 2113 AUSTRALIA
00-60-65 (hex)	BERNECKER & RAINER
006065 (base 16)	BERNECKER & RAINER INDUSTRIE-ELEKTRONIC GMBH EGGELSBERG 120 5142 EGGELSBERG AUSTRIA
00-60-66 (hex)	LACROIX TECHNOLGIE
006066 (base 16)	LACROIX TECHNOLGIE 1 ERE AVENUE, 11 EME RUE 06516 CARROS FRANCE

company_id	Organization Address
00-60-67 (hex)	ACER NETXUS INC.
006067 (base 16)	ACER NETXUS INC. 5F-3, 5 HSIN ANN ROAD SBIP HSINCHU 300 TAIWAN, R.O.C.
00-60-68 (hex)	EICON TECHNOLOGY CORPORATION
006068 (base 16)	EICON TECHNOLOGY CORPORATION 2196 32ND AVENUE (LACHINE) MONTREAL, PQ, H8T3H7 CANADA
00-60-69 (hex)	BROCADE COMMUNICATIONS SYSTEMS
006069 (base 16)	BROCADE COMMUNICATIONS SYSTEMS 1901 GUADALUPE PKWY SAN JOSE CA 95131
00-60-6A (hex)	MITSUBISHI WIRELESS COMM. INC.
00606A (base 16)	MITSUBISHI WIRELESS COMM. INC. 2001 CHERRY DRIVE BRASELTON GA 30517
00-60-6B (hex)	AICHI ELECTRONICS CO.,LTD.
00606B (base 16)	AICHI ELECTRONICS CO.,LTD. 1-15 HIMEGAOKA SHIMOGIRI, KANI-CITY GIFU JAPAN 509-02
00-60-6C (hex)	ARESCOM
00606C (base 16)	ARESCOM 2833 JUNCTION AVE. - STE #206 SAN JOSE CA 95134
00-60-6D (hex)	DIGITAL EQUIPMENT CORP.
00606D (base 16)	DIGITAL EQUIPMENT CORP. 550 KING STREET M/S LKG1-3/A10 LITTLETON MA 01460
00-60-6E (hex)	DAVICOM SEMICONDUCTOR, INC.
00606E (base 16)	DAVICOM SEMICONDUCTOR, INC. 2457 AUGUSTINE DRIVE SANTA CLARA CA 95054
00-60-6F (hex)	CLARION CORPORATION OF AMERICA
00606F (base 16)	CLARION CORPORATION OF AMERICA 17 LAKESIDE OFFICE PARK 607 NORTH AVENUE WAKEFIELD MA 01880
00-60-70 (hex)	CISCO SYSTEMS, INC.
006070 (base 16)	CISCO SYSTEMS, INC. 170 W. TASMAN DRIVE SAN JOSE CA 95134-1706
00-60-71 (hex)	MIDAS LAB, INC.
006071 (base 16)	MIDAS LAB, INC. 4 KATAMACHI, SHINJUKU-KU TOKYO 160 JAPAN
00-60-72 (hex)	VXL INSTRUMENTS, LIMITED
006072 (base 16)	VXL INSTRUMENTS, LIMITED PLOT NO. 17,KONAPPANA AGRAHARA ELECTRONIC CITY BANGALORE - 561 229 INDIA
00-60-73 (hex)	REDCREEK COMMUNICATIONS, INC.
006073 (base 16)	REDCREEK COMMUNICATIONS, INC. 3900 NEWPARK MALL ROAD NEWARK CA 94560
00-60-74 (hex)	QSC AUDIO PRODUCTS
006074 (base 16)	QSC AUDIO PRODUCTS 1675 MACARTHUR BLVD. COSTA MESA CA 92626
00-60-75 (hex)	PENTEK, INC.
006075 (base 16)	PENTEK, INC. 1 PARK WAY UPPER SADDLE RIVER NJ 07458
00-60-76 (hex)	SCHLUMBERGER TECHNOLOGIES

company_id	Organization Address
006076 (base 16)	SCHLUMBERGER TECHNOLOGIES RETAIL PETROLEUM SYSTEMS 825-M GREENBRIER CIRCLE CHESAPEAKE VA 23320
00-60-77 (hex)	PRISA NETWORKS
006077 (base 16)	PRISA NETWORKS 5897 OBERLIN DRIVE-STE. #211 SAN DIEGO CA 92121
00-60-78 (hex)	POWER MEASUREMENT LTD.
006078 (base 16)	POWER MEASUREMENT LTD. 2195 KEATING CROSS ROAD VICTORIA, B.C. CANADA V8M 2A5
00-60-79 (hex)	WAVEPHORE NETWORKS, INC.
006079 (base 16)	WAVEPHORE NETWORKS, INC. 375 CHIPETA WAY-STE B SALT LAKE CITY UT 84108
00-60-7A (hex)	DVS GMBH
00607A (base 16)	DVS GMBH KREPENSTRASSE 8 D-30165 HANNOVER GERMANY
00-60-7B (hex)	FORE SYSTEMS, INC.
00607B (base 16)	FORE SYSTEMS, INC. 1000 FORE DRIVE WARRENDALE PA 15086
00-60-7C (hex)	WAVEACCESS, LTD.
00607C (base 16)	WAVEACCESS, LTD. P.O. BOX 2473 10 HAYEZIRA STREET RA'ANANA 43663 ISRAEL
00-60-7D (hex)	SENTIENT NETWORKS INC.
00607D (base 16)	SENTIENT NETWORKS INC. 2201 CANTU COURT-STE #205 SARASOTA FL 34232
00-60-7E (hex)	GIGALABS, INC.
00607E (base 16)	GIGALABS, INC. 290 SANTA ANA COURT SUNNYVALE CA 94086
00-60-7F (hex)	AURORA TECHNOLOGIES, INC.
00607F (base 16)	AURORA TECHNOLOGIES, INC. 176 SECOND AVENUE WALTHAM MA 02154
00-60-80 (hex)	MICROTRONIX DATACOM LTD.
006080 (base 16)	MICROTRONIX DATACOM LTD. 200 ABERDEEN DRIVE LONDON, ONTARIO CANADA N5V 4N2
00-60-81 (hex)	TV/COM INTERNATIONAL
006081 (base 16)	TV/COM INTERNATIONAL 16516 VIA ESPRILLO SAN DIEGO CA 92127
00-60-82 (hex)	NOVALINK TECHNOLOGIES, INC.
006082 (base 16)	NOVALINK TECHNOLOGIES, INC. 48511 WARM SPRINGS BLVD. #208 FREMONT CA 94539
00-60-83 (hex)	CISCO SYSTEMS, INC.
006083 (base 16)	CISCO SYSTEMS, INC. 170 W. TASMAN DRIVE SAN JOSE CA 95134-1706
00-60-84 (hex)	DIGITAL VIDEO
006084 (base 16)	DIGITAL VIDEO 4920 AVALON RIDGE PKWY SUITE #600 NORCROSS GA 30092
00-60-85 (hex)	STORAGE CONCEPTS
006085 (base 16)	STORAGE CONCEPTS 14352 Chamber Road Tustin CA 92780

company_id	Organization Address
00-60-86 (hex)	LOGIC REPLACEMENT TECH. LTD.
006086 (base 16)	LOGIC REPLACEMENT TECH. LTD. 14 ARKWRIGHT ROAD READING BERKS RG20LS UNITED KINGDOM
00-60-87 (hex)	KANSAI ELECTRIC CO., LTD.
006087 (base 16)	KANSAI ELECTRIC CO., LTD. 6-14-9 MIDORII, ASAMINAMI-KU HIROSHIMA 731-01 JAPAN
00-60-88 (hex)	WHITE MOUNTAIN DSP, INC.
006088 (base 16)	WHITE MOUNTAIN DSP, INC. 410 AMHERST STREET-STE #325 NASHUA NH 03063
00-60-89 (hex)	XATA
006089 (base 16)	XATA 151 EAST CLIFF ROAD-STE.#10 BURNSVILLE MN 55337
00-60-8A (hex)	CITADEL COMPUTER
00608A (base 16)	CITADEL COMPUTER 29 ARMORY RD MILFORD, MA 03055
00-60-8B (hex)	CONFERTECH INTERNATIONAL
00608B (base 16)	CONFERTECH INTERNATIONAL 12110 N. PECOS STREET WESTMINSTER CO 80234-2074
00-60-8C (hex)	3COM CORPORATION
00608C (base 16)	3COM CORPORATION 5400 BAYFRONT PLAZA SANTA CLARA, CA 95052-8145
00-60-8D (hex)	UNIPULSE CORP.
00608D (base 16)	UNIPULSE CORP. 2-7, SENGENDAI-NISHI KOSHIGAYA-CITY SAITAMA, 343 JAPAN
00-60-8E (hex)	HE ELECTRONICS, TECHNOLOGIE & SYSTEMTECHNIK GMBH
00608E (base 16)	HE ELECTRONICS, TECHNOLOGIE & SYSTEMTECHNIK GMBH AM GNEISENAUFLOT 8 D-66538 NEUNHIRCHEN GERMANY
00-60-8F (hex)	TEKRAM TECHNOLOGY CO., LTD.
00608F (base 16)	TEKRAM TECHNOLOGY CO., LTD. B1, NO. 17, LANE 159, SEC. 6 ROOSEVELT RD, TAIPEI TAIWAN, R.O.C.
00-60-90 (hex)	ABLE COMMUNICATIONS, INC.
006090 (base 16)	ABLE COMMUNICATIONS, INC. NAKAMURA LK BLDG. 3-6-6, NISHIKI-CHO TACHIKAWA-SHI, TOKYO 190 JAPAN
00-60-91 (hex)	FIRST PACIFIC NETWORKS, INC.
006091 (base 16)	FIRST PACIFIC NETWORKS, INC. 871 FOX LANE SAN JOSE CA 95131
00-60-92 (hex)	MICRO/SYS, INC.
006092 (base 16)	MICRO/SYS, INC. 3447 OCEAN VIEW BLVD. GLENDALE CA 91208
00-60-93 (hex)	VARIAN
006093 (base 16)	VARIAN 2700 MITCHELL DR. WALNUT GREEK, CA 94598
00-60-94 (hex)	IBM CORP.

company_id	Organization Address
006094 (base 16)	IBM CORP. PO BOX 12195 CE6A/664 3039 CORNWALLIS RTP, NC 27709-2195
00-60-95 (hex)	ACCU-TIME SYSTEMS, INC.
006095 (base 16)	ACCU-TIME SYSTEMS, INC. 420 SOMERS ROAD ELLINGTON CT 06029
00-60-96 (hex)	T.S. MICROTECH INC.
006096 (base 16)	T.S. MICROTECH INC. 20818 HIGGINS COURT TORRANCE CA 90501
00-60-97 (hex)	3COM CORPORATION
006097 (base 16)	3COM CORPORATION 5400 BAYFRONT PLAZA SANTA CLARA CA 95052
00-60-98 (hex)	HT COMMUNICATIONS
006098 (base 16)	HT COMMUNICATIONS 4480 SHOPPING LANE SIMI VALLEY CA 93063
00-60-99 (hex)	LAN MEDIA CORPORATION
006099 (base 16)	LAN MEDIA CORPORATION 686 WEST MAUDE AVE.,-STE #102 SUNNYVALE CA 94086
00-60-9A (hex)	NJK TECHNO CO.
00609A (base 16)	NJK TECHNO CO. N1-25 KAMIYASATO KOMATSU #923 JAPAN
00-60-9B (hex)	ASTRO-MED, INC.
00609B (base 16)	ASTRO-MED, INC. 600 EAST GREENWICH AVE. WEST WARWICK RI 02893
00-60-9C (hex)	PERKIN-ELMER CORPORATION
00609C (base 16)	PERKIN-ELMER CORPORATION 761 MAIN AVENUE M/S - 30 NORWALK CT 06859
00-60-9D (hex)	PMI FOOD EQUIPMENT GROUP
00609D (base 16)	PMI FOOD EQUIPMENT GROUP 701 RIDGE AVENUE TROY OH 45374
00-60-9E (hex)	X3 - INFORMATION TECHNOLOGY
00609E (base 16)	X3 - INFORMATION TECHNOLOGY STANDARDS SECRETARIATS 1250 EYE STREET NW - STE #200 WASHINGTON DC 20005
00-60-9F (hex)	PHAST CORPORATION
00609F (base 16)	PHAST CORPORATION 79 WEST 4500 SOUTH - BLDG.#14 SALT LAKE CITY UT 84107
00-60-A0 (hex)	SWITCHED NETWORK
0060A0 (base 16)	SWITCHED NETWORK TECHNOLOGIES, INC. 13805 1ST AVENUE NORTH PLYMOUTH MN 55441-5455
00-60-A1 (hex)	VPNET
0060A1 (base 16)	VPNET 555 N. MATHILDA AVE.,-STE #110 SUNNYVALE CA 94086
00-60-A2 (hex)	NIHON UNISYS LIMITED CO.
0060A2 (base 16)	NIHON UNISYS LIMITED CO. TOKYO-TO KOUTOU-KU SHINONOME 1-10-9 P.O. BOX 135 JAPAN
00-60-A3 (hex)	CONTINUUM TECHNOLOGY CORP.

company_id	Organization Address
0060A3 (base 16)	CONTINUUM TECHNOLOGY CORP. 220 CONTINUUM DRIVE FLETCHER NC 28732
00-60-A4 (hex)	GRINAKER SYSTEM TECHNOLOGIES
0060A4 (base 16)	GRINAKER SYSTEM TECHNOLOGIES BOX 912-561 SILVERTON 0127 SOUTH AFRICA
00-60-A5 (hex)	PERFORMANCE TELECOM CORP.
0060A5 (base 16)	PERFORMANCE TELECOM CORP. 10 CARLSON ROAD ROCHESTER NY 14610-1021
00-60-A6 (hex)	PARTICLE MEASURING SYSTEMS
0060A6 (base 16)	PARTICLE MEASURING SYSTEMS 5475 AIRPORT BLVD. BOULDER CO 80301
00-60-A7 (hex)	MICROSENS GMBH & CO. KG
0060A7 (base 16)	MICROSENS GMBH & CO. KG Kueferstrasse 16 D-59067 Hamm GERMANY
00-60-A8 (hex)	TIDOMAT AB
0060A8 (base 16)	TIDOMAT AB S-12089 STOCKHOLM SWEDEN
00-60-A9 (hex)	GESYTEC MBH
0060A9 (base 16)	GESYTEC MBH PASCALSTRASSE 6 D 52076 AACHEN GERMANY
00-60-AA (hex)	INTELLIGENT DEVICES INC. (IDI)
0060AA (base 16)	INTELLIGENT DEVICES INC. (IDI) 1718-L BELMONT AVENUE BALTIMORE MD 21244
00-60-AB (hex)	LARSCOM INCORPORATED
0060AB (base 16)	LARSCOM INCORPORATED 1845 MCCANDLESS DRIVE MILPITAS CA 95035
00-60-AC (hex)	RESILIENCE CORPORATION
0060AC (base 16)	RESILIENCE CORPORATION 1755 EMBARCADERO ROAD-STE #120 PALO ALTO CA 94303
00-60-AD (hex)	MEGACHIPS CORPORATION
0060AD (base 16)	MEGACHIPS CORPORATION 4-5-36 MIYAHARA, YODOGAWA-KU OSAKA, 532 JAPAN
00-60-AE (hex)	TRIO INFORMATION SYSTEMS AB
0060AE (base 16)	TRIO INFORMATION SYSTEMS AB FOGDEVAGEN 4B S-183 64 TABY SWEDEN
00-60-AF (hex)	PACIFIC MICRO DATA, INC.
0060AF (base 16)	PACIFIC MICRO DATA, INC. 16751 MILLIKAN AVENUE IRVINE CA 92714
00-60-B0 (hex)	HEWLETT-PACKARD CO.
0060B0 (base 16)	HEWLETT-PACKARD CO. MS 42LE 10000 WOLFE ROAD CUPERTINO CA 95014
00-60-B1 (hex)	INPUT/OUTPUT, INC.
0060B1 (base 16)	INPUT/OUTPUT, INC. 12300 PARC CREST DRIVE STAFFORD TX 77477-2416
00-60-B2 (hex)	PROCESS CONTROL CORP.
0060B2 (base 16)	PROCESS CONTROL CORP. 6875 MIMMS DRIVE ATLANTA GA 30340
00-60-B3 (hex)	Z-COM, INC.

company_id	Organization Address
0060B3 (base 16)	Z-COM, INC. 7F-2, NO.9, PROSPERITY 1ST RD. SCIENCE-BASED INDUSTRIAL PARK HSINCHU TAIWAN R.O.C.
00-60-B4 (hex)	GLENAYRE R&D INC.
0060B4 (base 16)	GLENAYRE R&D INC. 1570 KOOTENAY STREET VANCOUVER, BC CANADA V5K 5B8
00-60-B5 (hex)	KEBA GMBH
0060B5 (base 16)	KEBA GMBH GEWERBEPARK URFAHR A-4041 LINZ AUSTRIA
00-60-B6 (hex)	LAND COMPUTER CO., LTD.
0060B6 (base 16)	LAND COMPUTER CO., LTD. 7-4-17 NISHINAKAJIMA YODOGAWAKU JAPAN 532
00-60-B7 (hex)	CHANNELMATIC, INC.
0060B7 (base 16)	CHANNELMATIC, INC. 1700 GILLESPIE WAY EL CAJON CA 92020-0901
00-60-B8 (hex)	CORELIS INC.
0060B8 (base 16)	CORELIS INC. 12607 HIDDENCREEK WAY CERRITOS CA 90703
00-60-B9 (hex)	NITSUKO CORPORATION
0060B9 (base 16)	NITSUKO CORPORATION 2-6-1 KITAMIKATA, TAKATSU-KU KAWASAKI-SHI 213 JAPAN
00-60-BA (hex)	SAHARA NETWORKS, INC.
0060BA (base 16)	SAHARA NETWORKS, INC. 335 HIGHLAND AVE. CHESHIRE CT 06410
00-60-BB (hex)	CABLETRON - NETLINK, INC.
0060BB (base 16)	CABLETRON - NETLINK, INC. 35 INDUSTRIAL WAY P.O. BOX 5005 ROCHESTER NH 03866-5005
00-60-BC (hex)	KEUNYOUNG ELECTRONICS &
0060BC (base 16)	KEUNYOUNG ELECTRONICS & COMMUNICATION 325-76, DAEHEUNG-DONG, MAPO-GU, SEOUL KOREA
00-60-BD (hex)	HUBBELL-PULSECOM
0060BD (base 16)	HUBBELL-PULSECOM 2900 TOWERVIEW ROAD HERNDON VA 21071
00-60-BE (hex)	WEBTRONICS
0060BE (base 16)	WEBTRONICS 3B-1 8-2-12 NISHI-GOTANDA SHINAGAWA-KU TOKYO 141 JAPAN
00-60-BF (hex)	MACRAIGOR SYSTEMS, INC.
0060BF (base 16)	MACRAIGOR SYSTEMS, INC. PO BOX 1008 BROOKLINE VILLAGE MA 02147
00-60-C0 (hex)	NERA AS
0060C0 (base 16)	NERA AS B.O. BOX 10 N-5061 KOKSTAD NORWAY
00-60-C1 (hex)	WAVESPAN CORPORATION
0060C1 (base 16)	WAVESPAN CORPORATION 500 N. BERNARDO AVE. MOUNTAIN VIEW CA 94043

company_id	Organization Address
00-60-C2 (hex)	MPL AG
0060C2 (base 16)	MPL AG TAEFERNSTRASSE 20 CH-5405 BADEN-DAETTWIL SWITZERLAND
00-60-C3 (hex)	NETVISION CORPORATION
0060C3 (base 16)	NETVISION CORPORATION MS#1A ONE COMAC LOOP RONKONKOMA NY 11779
00-60-C4 (hex)	SOLITON SYSTEMS K.K.
0060C4 (base 16)	SOLITON SYSTEMS K.K. 2-4-3 SHINJUKU, SHINJUKU-KU TOKYO 160 JAPAN
00-60-C5 (hex)	ANCOT CORP.
0060C5 (base 16)	ANCOT CORP. 115 CONSTITUTION DR. MENLO PARK CA 94025
00-60-C6 (hex)	DCS AG
0060C6 (base 16)	DCS AG SALZACHSTRASS 31 D-14129 BERLIN GERMANY
00-60-C7 (hex)	AMATI COMMUNICATIONS CORP.
0060C7 (base 16)	AMATI COMMUNICATIONS CORP. 2043 SAMARITAN DRIVE SAN JOSE CA 95124
00-60-C8 (hex)	KUKA WELDING SYSTEMS & ROBOTS
0060C8 (base 16)	KUKA WELDING SYSTEMS & ROBOTS BLUECHERSTRASSE 144 DEPT. RE-SH D-86165 AUGSBURG GERMANY
00-60-C9 (hex)	CONTROLNET, INC.
0060C9 (base 16)	CONTROLNET, INC. 747 CAMDEN, STE. «A» CAMPBELL CA 95008
00-60-CA (hex)	HARMONIC SYSTEMS INCORPORATED
0060CA (base 16)	HARMONIC SYSTEMS INCORPORATED 199 1ST STREET - STE #302 LOS ALTOS CA 94022
00-60-CB (hex)	HITACHI ZOSEN CORPORATION
0060CB (base 16)	HITACHI ZOSEN CORPORATION 3-4, SAKURAJIMA 1-CHOME KONOHANA-KU, OSAKA 554 JAPAN
00-60-CC (hex)	EMTRAK, INCORPORATED
0060CC (base 16)	EMTRAK, INCORPORATED 7150 CAMPUS DRIVE, STE #180 COLORADO SPRINGS CO 80920
00-60-CD (hex)	VIDEOSERVER, INC.
0060CD (base 16)	VIDEOSERVER, INC. 5 FORBES ROAD LEXINGTON MA 02173
00-60-CE (hex)	ACCLAIM COMMUNICATIONS
0060CE (base 16)	ACCLAIM COMMUNICATIONS 5000 OLD IRONSIDES DRIVE SANTA CLARA CA 95054
00-60-CF (hex)	ALTEON NETWORKS, INC.
0060CF (base 16)	ALTEON NETWORKS, INC. 50 GREAT OAKS BLVD. SAN JOSE CA 95119
00-60-D0 (hex)	SNMP RESEARCH INCORPORATED
0060D0 (base 16)	SNMP RESEARCH INCORPORATED 3001 KIMBERLIN HEIGHTS ROAD KNOXVILLE TN 37920-9716
00-60-D1 (hex)	CASCADE COMMUNICATIONS
0060D1 (base 16)	CASCADE COMMUNICATIONS 6 TECHNOLOGY PARK DRIVE WESTFORD MA 01886

company_id	Organization Address
00-60-D2 (hex)	LUCENT TECHNOLOGIES TAIWAN
0060D2 (base 16)	LUCENT TECHNOLOGIES TAIWAN TELECOMMUNICATIONS CO., LTD. #2, INNOVATION ROAD II SCIENCE-BASED INDUSTRIAL PARK HSIN CHU, TAIWAN, R.O.C.
00-60-D3 (hex)	AT&T
0060D3 (base 16)	AT&T 101 CRAWFORDS CORNER ROAD ROOM #1J321 P.O. BOX 3030 HOLMDEL NJ 07733-3030
00-60-D4 (hex)	ELDAT COMMUNICATION LTD.
0060D4 (base 16)	ELDAT COMMUNICATION LTD. 10 HAKISHON STREET BNEI-BRAK 51203 ISRAEL
00-60-D5 (hex)	MIYACHI TECHNOS CORP.
0060D5 (base 16)	MIYACHI TECHNOS CORP. 95-3, FUTASUZUKA NODA CITY, CHIBA, 278 JAPAN
00-60-D6 (hex)	NOVATEL WIRELESS TECHNOLOGIES
0060D6 (base 16)	NOVATEL WIRELESS TECHNOLOGIES LTD. SUITE 200, 6715-8TH STREET NE CALGARY, ALBERTA T2E 7H7 CANADA
00-60-D7 (hex)	ECOLE POLYTECHNIQUE FEDERALE
0060D7 (base 16)	ECOLE POLYTECHNIQUE FEDERALE DE LAUSANNE (EPFL) ECUBLENS CH-1015 LAUSANNE SWITZERLAND
00-60-D8 (hex)	ELMIC SYSTEMS, INC.
0060D8 (base 16)	ELMIC SYSTEMS, INC. DAI-ICHI SEIMEI BLDG. 4-59 BENTEN-DORI, NAKA-KU YOKOHAMA 231 JAPAN
00-60-D9 (hex)	TRANSYS NETWORKS INC.
0060D9 (base 16)	TRANSYS NETWORKS INC. 3403 GRIFFITH ST. LAURENT, QUEBEC CANADA H4T 1W5
00-60-DA (hex)	JBM ELECTRONICS CO.
0060DA (base 16)	JBM ELECTRONICS CO. 4645 LAGUARDIA DRIVE ST. LOUIS MO 63134
00-60-DB (hex)	NTP ELEKTRONIK A/S
0060DB (base 16)	NTP ELEKTRONIK A/S KNAPHOLM 7 DK-2730 HERLEV DENMARK
00-60-DC (hex)	TOYO COMMUNICATION EQUIPMENT
0060DC (base 16)	TOYO COMMUNICATION EQUIPMENT 1-1, KOYHATO 2-CHOME, SAMUKAWA-MACHI, KOZA-GUN KANAGWAWA-PREFECTURE, 253-01 JAPAN
00-60-DD (hex)	MYRICOM, INC.
0060DD (base 16)	MYRICOM, INC. 325B N. SANTA ANITA AVE. ARCADIA CA 91006
00-60-DE (hex)	KAYSER-THREDE GMBH
0060DE (base 16)	KAYSER-THREDE GMBH D-81379 MUNCHEN PERCHTINGER - STR.3 GERMANY
00-60-DF (hex)	INRANGE TECHNOLOGIES CORP.

company_id	Organization Address
0060DF (base 16)	INRANGE TECHNOLOGIES CORP. 13000 MIDLANTIC DRIVE MT. LAUREL NJ 08054
00-60-E0 (hex)	AXIOM TECHNOLOGY CO., LTD.
0060E0 (base 16)	AXIOM TECHNOLOGY CO., LTD. 3F, 14, LANE 235 PAO CHIAO ROAD, HSIN TIEN TAIPEI HSIEN TAIWAN, R.O.C.
00-60-E1 (hex)	ORCKIT COMMUNICATIONS LTD.
0060E1 (base 16)	ORCKIT COMMUNICATIONS LTD. 38 NAHALAT YIZHAK STREET TEL-AVIV 67448 ISRAEL
00-60-E2 (hex)	QUEST ENGINEERING & DEV.
0060E2 (base 16)	QUEST ENGINEERING & DEV. 1345 EAST ROCK WREN ROAD PHOENIX, AZ 85048
00-60-E3 (hex)	ARBIN INSTRUMENTS
0060E3 (base 16)	ARBIN INSTRUMENTS 3206 LONGMIRE DRIVE COLLEGE STATION TX 77845
00-60-E4 (hex)	COMPUSERVE, INC.
0060E4 (base 16)	COMPUSERVE, INC. 5000 ARLINGTON CENTRE BLVD. P.O. BOX 20212 COLUMBUS OH 43220
00-60-E5 (hex)	FUJI AUTOMATION CO., LTD.
0060E5 (base 16)	FUJI AUTOMATION CO., LTD. 3-23-10, NEGISHI URAWA-SHI, 336 SAITOMA JAPAN
00-60-E6 (hex)	SHOMITI SYSTEMS INCORPORATED
0060E6 (base 16)	SHOMITI SYSTEMS INCORPORATED 2099 GATEWAY PLACE - STE.#220 SAN JOSE CA 95110
00-60-E7 (hex)	RANDATA
0060E7 (base 16)	RANDATA PO BOX 209 HAWTHORN VIC 3122 AUSTRALIA
00-60-E8 (hex)	HITACHI COMPUTER PRODUCTS
0060E8 (base 16)	HITACHI COMPUTER PRODUCTS (AMERICA), INC. 3101 TASMAN DRIVE SANTA CLARA CA 95054
00-60-E9 (hex)	ATOP TECHNOLOGIES, INC.
0060E9 (base 16)	ATOP TECHNOLOGIES, INC. SUITE 305, NO. 47, PARK AVENUE II, SCIENCE-BASED INDUSTRIAL PARK HSINCHU, TAIWAN 30047, R.O.C.
00-60-EA (hex)	STREAMLOGIC
0060EA (base 16)	STREAMLOGIC 21329 NORDHOFF STREET CHATSWORTH CA 91311
00-60-EB (hex)	FOURTHTRACK SYSTEMS
0060EB (base 16)	FOURTHTRACK SYSTEMS UNIT 3 THE SYCAMORES 27 MILL ROAD MARLOW - SL7 1QB UNITED KINGDOM
00-60-EC (hex)	HERMARY OPTO ELECTRONICS INC.
0060EC (base 16)	HERMARY OPTO ELECTRONICS INC. 201-4050 GRAVELEY ST BURNABY, BC V5C-3T6 CANADA
00-60-ED (hex)	RICARDO TEST AUTOMATION LTD.

company_id	Organization Address
0060ED (base 16)	RICARDO TEST AUTOMATION LTD. LOWESMOOR WHARF WORCESTER, WR12RS ENGLAND
00-60-EE (hex)	APOLLO
0060EE (base 16)	APOLLO 3610 BIRCH STREET–STE #100 NEWPORT BEACH CA 92660
00-60-EF (hex)	FLYTECH TECHNOLOGY CO., LTD.
0060EF (base 16)	FLYTECH TECHNOLOGY CO., LTD. 2FL. NO. 8, LANE 50, SEC.3 NAN KANG ROAD TAIPEI TAIWAN
00-60-F0 (hex)	JOHNSON & JOHNSON MEDICAL, INC
0060F0 (base 16)	JOHNSON & JOHNSON MEDICAL, INC 4110 GEORGE RD. TAMPA FL 33634
00-60-F1 (hex)	EXP COMPUTER, INC.
0060F1 (base 16)	EXP COMPUTER, INC. 141 EILEEN WAY SYOSSET NY 11791
00-60-F2 (hex)	LASERGRAPHICS, INC.
0060F2 (base 16)	LASERGRAPHICS, INC. 20 ADA IRVINE CA 92718
00-60-F3 (hex)	NETCOM SYSTEMS, INC.
0060F3 (base 16)	NETCOM SYSTEMS, INC. 20500 NORDHOFF STREET CHATSWORTH CA 91311
00-60-F4 (hex)	ADVANCED COMPUTER SOLUTIONS,
0060F4 (base 16)	ADVANCED COMPUTER SOLUTIONS, 12675 DANIELSON G. SUITE #407 POWAY CA 92064
00-60-F5 (hex)	ICON WEST, INC.
0060F5 (base 16)	ICON WEST, INC. 3342 SOUTH 300 EAST SALT LAKE CITY UT 84115
00-60-F6 (hex)	NEXTEST COMMUNICATION
0060F6 (base 16)	NEXTEST COMMUNICATION PRODUCTS, INC. TWO MID AMERICA PLAZA, STE.500 OAKBROOK TERRACE IL 60181
00-60-F7 (hex)	DATAFUSION SYSTEMS
0060F7 (base 16)	DATAFUSION SYSTEMS P.O. BOX 582 STELLENBOSCH, 7599 SOUTH AFRICA
00-60-F8 (hex)	LORAN INTERNATIONAL TECHN. INC
0060F8 (base 16)	LORAN INTERNATIONAL TECHN. INC 955 GREEN VALLEY CRESCENT SUITE #165 OTTAWA, ONTARIO CANADA K2C 3V4
00-60-F9 (hex)	DIAMOND LANE COMMUNICATIONS
0060F9 (base 16)	DIAMOND LANE COMMUNICATIONS 1310 REDWOOD WAY - STE. C PETALUMA CA 94954
00-60-FA (hex)	EDUCATIONAL TECHNOLOGY
0060FA (base 16)	EDUCATIONAL TECHNOLOGY RESOURCES, INC. 1742 CHURCH STREET HOLBROOK NY 11741
00-60-FB (hex)	PACKETEER, INC.
0060FB (base 16)	PACKETEER, INC. 273 E. HACIENDA AVENUE CAMPBELL CA 95008
00-60-FC (hex)	CONSERVATION THROUGH INNOVATION LTD.

company_id	Organization Address	company_id	Organization Address
0060FC (base 16)	CONSERVATION THROUGH INNOVATION LTD. 1040 WHIPPLE ST.- STE. #225 PRESCOTT AZ 86301	008008 (base 16)	DYNATECH COMPUTER SYSTEMS 280 BERNARDO AVENUE P.O. BOX 7400 MOUNTAIN VIEW, CA 94039-7400
00-60-FD (hex)	NETICS, INC.	00-80-09 (hex)	JUPITER SYSTEMS, INC.
0060FD (base 16)	NETICS, INC. 42 NAGOG PARK ACTON MA 01720	008009 (base 16)	JUPITER SYSTEMS, INC. 3073 TEAGARDEN STREET SAN LEANDRO CA 94577-5720
00-60-FE (hex)	LYNX SYSTEM DEVELOPERS, INC.	00-80-0A (hex)	JAPAN COMPUTER CORP.
0060FE (base 16)	LYNX SYSTEM DEVELOPERS, INC. 175N NEW BOSTON STREET WOBURN MA 01801	00800A (base 16)	JAPAN COMPUTER CORP. L. K. BLDG. HIGASHI KANDA 2-6-9 CHIYODA-KU TOKYO 101 JAPAN
00-60-FF (hex)	QUVIS, INC.	00-80-0B (hex)	CSK CORPORATION
0060FF (base 16)	QUVIS, INC. 2921 SW WANAMAKER DRIVE SUITE #107 TOPEKA KS 66614	00800B (base 16)	CSK CORPORATION 18F MATSUSHITA IMP BLDG, 1-3-7 SHIROMI CHUO-KU OSAKA JAPAN 540
00-70-B0 (hex)	M/A-COM INC. COMPANIES	00-80-0C (hex)	VIDECOM LIMITED
0070B0 (base 16)	M/A-COM INC. COMPANIES 11717 EXPLORATION LANE GERMANTOWN MD 20767	00800C (base 16)	VIDECOM LIMITED NEWTOWN ESTATE HENLEY-ON-THAMES OXON RG9 1HG ENGLAND
00-70-B3 (hex)	DATA RECALL LTD.	00-80-0D (hex)	VOSSWINKEL F.U.
0070B3 (base 16)	DATA RECALL LTD. SONDES PLACE DORKING SURREY RH4 3EF UNITED KINGDOM	00800D (base 16)	VOSSWINKEL F.U. AM JOSTENHOF 15 D-4130 MOERS GERMANY
00-80-00 (hex)	MULTITECH SYSTEMS, INC.	00-80-0E (hex)	ATLANTIX CORPORATION
008000 (base 16)	MULTITECH SYSTEMS, INC. 2205 WOODALE DRIVE MOUNDS VIEW MN 55112	00800E (base 16)	ATLANTIX CORPORATION 5401 NW BROKENSOUND BLVD. BOCA RATON, FL 33431
00-80-01 (hex)	PERIPHONICS CORPORATION	00-80-0F (hex)	STANDARD MICROSYSTEMS
008001 (base 16)	PERIPHONICS CORPORATION 4000 VETERANS MEMORIAL HIGHWAY BOHEMIA, NEW YORK 11716	00800F (base 16)	STANDARD MICROSYSTEMS 300 KENNEDY DRIVE HAUPPAUGE NY 11788
00-80-02 (hex)	SATELCOM (UK) LTD	00-80-10 (hex)	COMMODORE INTERNATIONAL
008002 (base 16)	SATELCOM (UK) LTD TECHNOLOGY TRANSFER CENTRE SILWOOD PARK, BUCKHURST ROAD ASCOT, BERKSHIRE, SL5 7PW ENGLAND	008010 (base 16)	COMMODORE INTERNATIONAL 1200 WILSON DRIVE WEST CHESTER, PA 19380
00-80-03 (hex)	HYTEC ELECTRONICS LTD.	00-80-11 (hex)	DIGITAL SYSTEMS INT'L. INC.
008003 (base 16)	HYTEC ELECTRONICS LTD. 5 CRADOCK ROAD READING BERKS RG5 4DX ENGLAND	008011 (base 16)	DIGITAL SYSTEMS INT'L. INC. 7659 178TH PL. NE P.O. BOX 908 REDMOND, WA 98073-0908
00-80-04 (hex)	ANTLOW COMMUNICATIONS, LTD.	00-80-12 (hex)	INTEGRATED MEASUREMENT SYSTEMS
008004 (base 16)	ANTLOW COMMUNICATIONS, LTD. 4 COLTHROP WAY THATCHAM RG19 4LW ENGLAND	008012 (base 16)	INTEGRATED MEASUREMENT SYSTEMS 9525 SW GEMINI DRIVE BEAVERTON, OR 97005
		00-80-13 (hex)	THOMAS-CONRAD CORPORATION
00-80-05 (hex)	CACTUS COMPUTER INC.	008013 (base 16)	THOMAS-CONRAD CORPORATION 1908-R KRAMER LANE AUSTIN, TX 78758
008005 (base 16)	CACTUS COMPUTER INC. 1120 METROCREST DRIVE SUITE 103 CARROLLTON, TX 75006	00-80-14 (hex)	ESPRIT SYSTEMS
00-80-06 (hex)	COMPUADD CORPORATION	008014 (base 16)	ESPRIT SYSTEMS 14F, NO. 1, SEC. 4 NAN KING EAST ROAD 10569 TAIPEI TAIWAN, R.O.C.
008006 (base 16)	COMPUADD CORPORATION ENGINEERING 12303 TECHNOLOGY BLVD. AUSTIN, TX 78727	00-80-15 (hex)	SEIKO SYSTEMS, INC.
00-80-07 (hex)	DLOG NC-SYSTEME	008015 (base 16)	SEIKO SYSTEMS, INC. SYSTEMS DEVELOPMENT DIVISION 5-4 HACCHOBORI 4-CHOUME CHUUOU-KU TOKOYO 104, JAPAN
008007 (base 16)	DLOG NC-SYSTEME WERNER-VON-SIEMENS STRASSE 13 D-8037, OLCHING GERMANY		
00-80-08 (hex)	DYNATECH COMPUTER SYSTEMS	00-80-16 (hex)	WANDEL AND GOLTERMANN

company_id	Organization Address
008016 (base 16)	WANDEL AND GOLTERMANN 1030 SWABIA COURT RESEARCH TRIANGLE PARK NC 27709
00-80-17 (hex)	PFU LIMITED
008017 (base 16)	PFU LIMITED NETWORK SEC. 658-1, TSURUMA MACHIDA-SHI, TOKYO 194-0004 JAPAN
00-80-18 (hex)	KOBE STEEL, LTD.
008018 (base 16)	KOBE STEEL, LTD. KOBE ISUZU RECRUIT BLDG. 7TH FLOOR 2-2, 4-CHOME, KUMOI-DORI, CHUO-KU, KOBE 651 JAPAN
00-80-19 (hex)	DAYNA COMMUNICATIONS, INC.
008019 (base 16)	DAYNA COMMUNICATIONS, INC. 50 SOUTH MAIN STREET-#530 SALT LAKE CITY UTAH 84144
00-80-1A (hex)	BELL ATLANTIC
00801A (base 16)	BELL ATLANTIC N92 W14612 ANTHONY AVENUE MENOMONEE FALLS, WI 53051
00-80-1B (hex)	KODIAK TECHNOLOGY
00801B (base 16)	KODIAK TECHNOLOGY 2340 HARRIS WAY SAN JOSE, CA 95131
00-80-1C (hex)	NEWPORT SYSTEMS SOLUTIONS
00801C (base 16)	NEWPORT SYSTEMS SOLUTIONS 4019 WESTERLY AVENUE SUITE 103 NEWPORT BEACH, CA 92660
00-80-1D (hex)	INTEGRATED INFERENCE MACHINES
00801D (base 16)	INTEGRATED INFERENCE MACHINES 1468 EAST KATELLA ANAHEIM, CA 92805
00-80-1E (hex)	XINETRON, INC.
00801E (base 16)	XINETRON, INC. 2330 B. WALSH AVE. SANTA CLARA, CA 95051
00-80-1F (hex)	KRUPP ATLAS ELECTRONIK GMBH
00801F (base 16)	KRUPP ATLAS ELECTRONIK GMBH P.O. BOX 448545 D-2800 BREMEN 44 WEST GERMANY
00-80-20 (hex)	NETWORK PRODUCTS
008020 (base 16)	NETWORK PRODUCTS DIVISION OF ANDREW CORPORATION 2771 PLAZA DEL AMO3 TORRANCE, CA 90503
00-80-21 (hex)	NEWBRIDGE RESEARCH CORP.
008021 (base 16)	NEWBRIDGE RESEARCH CORP. 600 MARCH ROAD P.O. BOX 13600 KANATA, ONTARIO K2K 2E6 CANADA
00-80-22 (hex)	SCAN-OPTICS
008022 (base 16)	SCAN-OPTICS 201 TECHNOLOGY DRIVE IRVINE, CA 92718
00-80-23 (hex)	INTEGRATED BUSINESS NETWORKS
008023 (base 16)	INTEGRATED BUSINESS NETWORKS 1BN THE SYSTEMS CENTRE 14, BRIDGEGATE BUSINESS PARK, GATEHOUSE WAY, AYLESBURY BUCKS HP19 3XN - ENGLAND
00-80-24 (hex)	KALPANA, INC.
008024 (base 16)	KALPANA, INC. 1154 EAST ARQUES AVENUE SUNNYVALE, CA 94086

company_id	Organization Address
00-80-25 (hex)	STOLLMANN GMBH
008025 (base 16)	STOLLMANN GMBH MAX-BRAUER-ALLEE 81 D-2000 HAMBURG 50 GERMANY
00-80-26 (hex)	NETWORK PRODUCTS CORPORATION
008026 (base 16)	NETWORK PRODUCTS CORPORATION 1440 WEST COLORADO BLVD. PASADENA, CA 91105
00-80-27 (hex)	ADAPTIVE SYSTEMS, INC.
008027 (base 16)	ADAPTIVE SYSTEMS, INC. 1400 N.W. COMPTON DRIVE SUITE 340 BEAVERTON, OR 97006
00-80-28 (hex)	TRADPOST (HK) LTD
008028 (base 16)	TRADPOST (HK) LTD 5/F, STAR CENTRE 443-451 CASTLE PEAK ROAD KWAI CHUNG, N.T. HONG KONG
00-80-29 (hex)	EAGLE TECHNOLOGY, INC.
008029 (base 16)	EAGLE TECHNOLOGY, INC. 6800 ORANGETHORPE AVE.UNIT «A» BUENA PARK CA 90620
00-80-2A (hex)	TEST SYSTEMS & SIMULATIONS INC
00802A (base 16)	TEST SYSTEMS & SIMULATIONS INC 32429 INDUSTRIAL DRIVE MADISON HEIGHTS, MI 48071-1528
00-80-2B (hex)	INTEGRATED MARKETING CO
00802B (base 16)	INTEGRATED MARKETING CO 1360 BORDEAUX DRIVE BLDG. #4 SUNNYVALE, CA 94089
00-80-2C (hex)	THE SAGE GROUP PLC
00802C (base 16)	THE SAGE GROUP PLC SAGE HOUSE, BENTON PARK ROAD NEWCASTLE UPON TYNE NE7 7LZ UNITED KINGDOM
00-80-2D (hex)	XYLOGICS INC
00802D (base 16)	XYLOGICS INC 53 THIRD AVENUE BURLINGTON, MA 01803
00-80-2E (hex)	CASTLE ROCK COMPUTING
00802E (base 16)	CASTLE ROCK COMPUTING 20837 BOYCE LANE SARATOGA CA 95070-4806
00-80-2F (hex)	NATIONAL INSTRUMENTS CORP.
00802F (base 16)	NATIONAL INSTRUMENTS CORP. 6504 BRIDGE POINT PARKWAY AUSTIN, TX 78730
00-80-30 (hex)	NEXUS ELECTRONICS
008030 (base 16)	NEXUS ELECTRONICS 39 SPRINGFIELD ROAD CAMBRIDGE CB4 1AD UNITED KINGDOM
00-80-31 (hex)	BASYS, CORP.
008031 (base 16)	BASYS, CORP. 501 MACARA AVENUE SUNNYVALE, CA 94086
00-80-32 (hex)	ACCESS CO., LTD.
008032 (base 16)	ACCESS CO., LTD. HIEI-KUDAN BLDG. B1 3-8-11 KUDAN-MINAMI, CHIYODA-KU, TOKYO 102 JAPAN
00-80-33 (hex)	FORMATION, INC.
008033 (base 16)	FORMATION, INC. 121 WHITTENDALE DRIVE MOORESTOWN, NJ 08057
00-80-34 (hex)	SMT GOUPIL

company_id	Organization Address
008034 (base 16)	SMT GOUPIL 3 RUE DES ARCHIVES 94000 CRETEIL FRANCE
00-80-35 (hex)	TECHNOLOGY WORKS, INC.
008035 (base 16)	TECHNOLOGY WORKS, INC. 4030 BRAKER LANE #350 AUSTIN, TX 78759
00-80-36 (hex)	REFLEX MANUFACTURING SYSTEMS
008036 (base 16)	REFLEX MANUFACTURING SYSTEMS UNIT D, THE FLEMING CENTRE, FLEMING WAY, CRAWLEY WEST SUSSEX RH10 2NN ENGLAND
00-80-37 (hex)	Ericsson Group
008037 (base 16)	Ericsson Group Telefonaktiebolaget LM Ericsson Corp. 126 25 STOCKHOLM SWEDEN
00-80-38 (hex)	DATA RESEARCH & APPLICATIONS
008038 (base 16)	DATA RESEARCH & APPLICATIONS 9041 EXECUTIVE PARK DR. SUITE 200 KNOXVILLE, TN 37923-4609
00-80-39 (hex)	ALCATEL STC AUSTRALIA
008039 (base 16)	ALCATEL STC AUSTRALIA 252-280 BOTANY ROAD ALEXANDRIA, NSW 2015 AUSTRALIA
00-80-3A (hex)	VARITYPER, INC.
00803A (base 16)	VARITYPER, INC. 900 MIDDLESEX TURNPIKE BILLERICA, MA 01821
00-80-3B (hex)	APT COMMUNICATIONS, INC.
00803B (base 16)	APT COMMUNICATIONS, INC. 9607 DR. PERRY ROAD IJAMSVILLE MD 21754
00-80-3C (hex)	TVS ELECTRONICS LTD
00803C (base 16)	TVS ELECTRONICS LTD 44, MILLER ROAD BANGALORE 560 052 INDIA
00-80-3D (hex)	SURIGIKEN CO., LTD.
00803D (base 16)	SURIGIKEN CO., LTD. YOUTH BLDG, 4-1-9 SHINJUKU SHINJUKU-KU, TOKYO JAPAN
00-80-3E (hex)	SYNERNETICS
00803E (base 16)	SYNERNETICS 85 RANGEWAY ROAD NORTH BILLERICA MA 01862
00-80-3F (hex)	TATUNG COMPANY
00803F (base 16)	TATUNG COMPANY 22 CHUNGSHANG N. RD. 3RD SEC. TAIPEI, TAIWAN R.O.C.
00-80-40 (hex)	JOHN FLUKE MANUFACTURING CO.
008040 (base 16)	JOHN FLUKE MANUFACTURING CO. P.O. BOX C9090-M/S 244F EVERETT WA 98206
00-80-41 (hex)	VEB KOMBINAT ROBOTRON
008041 (base 16)	VEB KOMBINAT ROBOTRON GRUNAER STRABE 2, DRESDEN 8010 GDR, EAST GERMANY
00-80-42 (hex)	FORCE COMPUTERS
008042 (base 16)	FORCE COMPUTERS PROF. MESSERSCHMITTSTR.-1 W - 8014 NEUBIBERG GERMANY
00-80-43 (hex)	NETWORLD, INC.

company_id	Organization Address
008043 (base 16)	NETWORLD, INC. KANDA 3 AMEREX BLDG. 3-10 KANDAJINBOCHO CHIYODA-KU TOKYO 101 JAPAN
00-80-44 (hex)	SYSTECH COMPUTER CORP.
008044 (base 16)	SYSTECH COMPUTER CORP. 6465 NANCY RIDGE DRIVE SAN DIEGO, CA 92121
00-80-45 (hex)	MATSUSHITA ELECTRIC IND. CO
008045 (base 16)	MATSUSHITA ELECTRIC IND. CO COMPUTER DIVISION 1006, KADOMA, OSAKA, 571 JAPAN
00-80-46 (hex)	UNIVERSITY OF TORONTO
008046 (base 16)	UNIVERSITY OF TORONTO DEPT. OF ELECTRICAL ENGIN'ING 10 KINGS COLLEGE RD. TORONTO, ONTARIO M5S 1A4 CANADA
00-80-47 (hex)	IN-NET CORP.
008047 (base 16)	IN-NET CORP. 16720 WEST BERNARDO DRIVE SAN DIEGO, CA 92127-1904
00-80-48 (hex)	COMPEX INCORPORATED
008048 (base 16)	COMPEX INCORPORATED 4055 EAST LA PALMA UNIT «C» ANAHEIM, CA 92807
00-80-49 (hex)	NISSIN ELECTRIC CO., LTD.
008049 (base 16)	NISSIN ELECTRIC CO., LTD. 47, UMEZU - TAKASE - CHO UKYO-KU, KYOTO, 615 JAPAN
00-80-4A (hex)	PRO-LOG
00804A (base 16)	PRO-LOG 12 UPPER RAGSDALE DRIVE MONTEREY, CA 93940
00-80-4B (hex)	EAGLE TECHNOLOGIES PTY.LTD.
00804B (base 16)	EAGLE TECHNOLOGIES PTY.LTD. 70 KEYS ROAD MOORABBIN VIC. 3189 AUSTRALIA
00-80-4C (hex)	CONTEC CO., LTD.
00804C (base 16)	CONTEC CO., LTD. 3-9-31, HIMESATO NISHIYODOGAWA-KU OSAKA, 555 JAPAN
00-80-4D (hex)	CYCLONE MICROSYSTEMS, INC.
00804D (base 16)	CYCLONE MICROSYSTEMS, INC. 25 SCIENCE PARK NEW HAVEN CT 06511
00-80-4E (hex)	APEX COMPUTER COMPANY
00804E (base 16)	APEX COMPUTER COMPANY 4500 150TH AVENUE, NE REDMOND, WA 98052
00-80-4F (hex)	DAIKIN INDUSTRIES, LTD.
00804F (base 16)	DAIKIN INDUSTRIES, LTD. ELECTRONICS DIVISION SHIGA PLANT 1000-2 OHTANI OKAMOTO-CHO, KUSATSU SHIGA JAPAN 525
00-80-50 (hex)	ZIATECH CORPORATION
008050 (base 16)	ZIATECH CORPORATION 3433 ROBERTO COURT SAN LUIS OBISPO, CA 93401
00-80-51 (hex)	FIBERMUX
008051 (base 16)	FIBERMUX 9310 TOPANGA CANYON BLVD. CHATSWORTH CA 91311

company_id	Organization Address
00-80-52 (hex)	TECHNICALLY ELITE CONCEPTS
008052 (base 16)	TECHNICALLY ELITE CONCEPTS 2615 PACIFIC COAST HIGHWAY HERMOSA BEACH, CA 90250
00-80-53 (hex)	INTELLICOM, INC.
008053 (base 16)	INTELLICOM, INC. 20415 NORDHOFF STREET CHATSWORTH, CA 91311
00-80-54 (hex)	FRONTIER TECHNOLOGIES CORP.
008054 (base 16)	FRONTIER TECHNOLOGIES CORP. 10201 NO. PT. WASHINGTON ROAD MEQUON, WI 53092
00-80-55 (hex)	FERMILAB
008055 (base 16)	FERMILAB P.O. BOX 500, MS-234 BATAVIA, IL 60510
00-80-56 (hex)	SPHINX ELEKTRONIK GMBH
008056 (base 16)	SPHINX ELEKTRONIK GMBH WALDMATTENSTR, 13 7808 WALDKIRCH 3 RAPPENECKSTRABE 1 WEST GERMANY
00-80-57 (hex)	ADSOFT, LTD.
008057 (base 16)	ADSOFT, LTD. LANDSTRASSE 27A CH-4313 MOHLIN SWITZERLAND
00-80-58 (hex)	PRINTER SYSTEMS CORPORATION
008058 (base 16)	PRINTER SYSTEMS CORPORATION 207 PARRY PARKWAY GAITHERSBURG, MD 20877
00-80-59 (hex)	STANLEY ELECTRIC CO., LTD
008059 (base 16)	STANLEY ELECTRIC CO., LTD R&D LABORATORY 1-3-1 EDA-NISHI, MIDORI-KU, YOKOHAMA-SHI KANAGAWA-KEN, 227 JAPAN
00-80-5A (hex)	TULIP COMPUTERS INTERNAT'L B.V
00805A (base 16)	TULIP COMPUTERS INTERNAT'L B.V P.O. BOX 3333 5203 DH 'S-HERTOGENBOSCH THE NETHERLANDS
00-80-5B (hex)	CONDOR SYSTEMS, INC.
00805B (base 16)	CONDOR SYSTEMS, INC. 2133 SAMARILTAN DRIVE SAN JOSE CA 95124
00-80-5C (hex)	AGILIS CORPORATION
00805C (base 16)	AGILIS CORPORATION 1101 SAN ANTONIO ROAD SUITE 101 MOUNTAIN VIEW, CA 94043-1008
00-80-5D (hex)	CANSTAR
00805D (base 16)	CANSTAR 3900 VICTORIA PARK AVENUE NORTH YORK ONTARIO, CANADA M2H 3H7
00-80-5E (hex)	LSI LOGIC CORPORATION
00805E (base 16)	LSI LOGIC CORPORATION 1551 MCCARTHY BOULEVARD MS G813 MILPITAS, CA 95035
00-80-5F (hex)	COMPAQ COMPUTER CORPORATION
00805F (base 16)	COMPAQ COMPUTER CORPORATION 20555 SH 249 HOUSTON, TEXAS 77070
00-80-60 (hex)	NETWORK INTERFACE CORPORATION

company_id	Organization Address
008060 (base 16)	NETWORK INTERFACE CORPORATION 15019 WEST 95 STREET LENEXA, KS 66215
00-80-61 (hex)	LITTON SYSTEMS, INC.
008061 (base 16)	LITTON SYSTEMS, INC. M/S 44-20 29851 AGOURA ROAD AGOURA HILLS CA 91301-0500
00-80-62 (hex)	INTERFACE CO.
008062 (base 16)	INTERFACE CO. 8-26 OZU 5-CHOME MINAMI-KU HIROSHIMA 732 JAPAN
00-80-63 (hex)	RICHARD HIRSCHMANN GMBH & CO.
008063 (base 16)	RICHARD HIRSCHMANN GMBH & CO. GESCHAFTSBEREICH OPTISCHE UBERTRAGUNGSTECHNIK OBERTURKHEIMER STRASS 78 7300 ESSLINGEN GERMANY
00-80-64 (hex)	WYSE TECHNOLOGY
008064 (base 16)	WYSE TECHNOLOGY 3471 NORTH FIRST STREET M/S SAN JOSE CA 95134
00-80-65 (hex)	CYBERGRAPHIC SYSTEMS PTY LTD.
008065 (base 16)	CYBERGRAPHIC SYSTEMS PTY LTD. 290 BURWOOD ROAD HAWTHORN, VICTORIA 3122 AUSTRALIA
00-80-66 (hex)	ARCOM CONTROL SYSTEMS, LTD.
008066 (base 16)	ARCOM CONTROL SYSTEMS, LTD. UNIT 8, CLIFTON ROAD CAMBRIDGE CBI 4WH UNITED KINGDOM
00-80-67 (hex)	SQUARE D COMPANY
008067 (base 16)	SQUARE D COMPANY 4041 NORTH RICHARD STREET P.O. BOX 472 MILWAUKEE, WI 53201
00-80-68 (hex)	YAMATECH SCIENTIFIC LTD.
008068 (base 16)	YAMATECH SCIENTIFIC LTD. 1255 LAIRD, SUITE 260 MONTREAL, QUEBEC H3P 2T1 CANADA
00-80-69 (hex)	COMPUTONE SYSTEMS
008069 (base 16)	COMPUTONE SYSTEMS 1100 NORTHMEADOW PARKWAY SUITE 150 ROSWELL, GA 30076
00-80-6A (hex)	ERI (EMPAC RESEARCH INC.)
00806A (base 16)	ERI (EMPAC RESEARCH INC.) 47560 SEABRIDGE DRIVE FREMONT CA 94538
00-80-6B (hex)	SCHMID TELECOMMUNICATION
00806B (base 16)	SCHMID TELECOMMUNICATION BINZSTRASSE 35, CH-8045 ZURICH SWITZERLAND
00-80-6C (hex)	CEGELEC PROJECTS LTD
00806C (base 16)	CEGELEC PROJECTS LTD DEPT. MDD, BOUGHTON RD, RUGBY WARKS, CO21 1BU ENGLAND
00-80-6D (hex)	CENTURY SYSTEMS CORP.
00806D (base 16)	CENTURY SYSTEMS CORP. 2-8-12 MINAMI-CHO KOKUBUNJI-SHI, TOKYO 185 JAPAN
00-80-6E (hex)	NIPPON STEEL CORPORATION

company_id	Organization Address
00806E (base 16)	NIPPON STEEL CORPORATION 31-1 SHINKAWA 2-CHOUME CHUO-KU TOKYO 104 JAPAN
00-80-6F (hex)	ONELAN LTD.
00806F (base 16)	ONELAN LTD. P.O. BOX 107 HENLEY ON THAMES OXFORDSHIRE RG9 3NOQ UNITED KINGDOM
00-80-70 (hex)	COMPUTADORAS MICRON
008070 (base 16)	COMPUTADORAS MICRON GUERRERO 2001 - 19 IRAPUATO GTO 36660 MEXICO
00-80-71 (hex)	SAI TECHNOLOGY
008071 (base 16)	SAI TECHNOLOGY 4224 CAMPUS POINT COURT SAN DIEGO, CA 92121-1513
00-80-72 (hex)	MICROPLEX SYSTEMS LTD.
008072 (base 16)	MICROPLEX SYSTEMS LTD. 8525 COMMERCE COURT BURNABY, BC V5A 4N3 CANADA
00-80-73 (hex)	DWB ASSOCIATES
008073 (base 16)	DWB ASSOCIATES 9360 SW GEMINI DRIVE BEAVERTON OR 97005-7151
00-80-74 (hex)	FISHER CONTROLS
008074 (base 16)	FISHER CONTROLS 1712 CENTRE CREEK DRIVE AUSTIN TX 78754
00-80-75 (hex)	PARSYTEC GMBH
008075 (base 16)	PARSYTEC GMBH JUELICHER STR. 338 D5100 AACHEN F.R. GERMANY
00-80-76 (hex)	MCNC
008076 (base 16)	MCNC P.O. BOX 12889 RTP, NC 27709
00-80-77 (hex)	BROTHER INDUSTRIES, LTD.
008077 (base 16)	BROTHER INDUSTRIES, LTD. RESEARCH LABORATORY 9-35 HORITA-DORI, MIZUHO-KU NAGOYA, 467 JAPAN
00-80-78 (hex)	PRACTICAL PERIPHERALS, INC.
008078 (base 16)	PRACTICAL PERIPHERALS, INC. 375 CONEJO RIDGE AVENUE THOUSAND OAKS CA 91361
00-80-79 (hex)	MICROBUS DESIGNS LTD.
008079 (base 16)	MICROBUS DESIGNS LTD. TREADAWAY HILL LOUDWATER HIGH WYCOMBE BUCKS HP10 9QL UNITED KINGDOM
00-80-7A (hex)	AITECH SYSTEMS LTD.
00807A (base 16)	AITECH SYSTEMS LTD. 3080 OLCOTT STREET SUITE 105A SANTA CLARA, CA 95054
00-80-7B (hex)	ARTEL COMMUNICATIONS CORP.
00807B (base 16)	ARTEL COMMUNICATIONS CORP. 22 KANE INDUSTRIAL DRIVE HUDSON MA 01749
00-80-7C (hex)	FIBERCOM, INC.

company_id	Organization Address
00807C (base 16)	FIBERCOM, INC. 3353 ORANGE AVENUE NE ROANOKE, VA 24012
00-80-7D (hex)	EQUINOX SYSTEMS INC.
00807D (base 16)	EQUINOX SYSTEMS INC. 14260 SW 119TH AVENUE MIAMI, FL 33186
00-80-7E (hex)	SOUTHERN PACIFIC LTD.
00807E (base 16)	SOUTHERN PACIFIC LTD. SANWA BLDG., 2-16-20 MINAMISAIWAI NISHI YOKOHAMA JAPAN, 220
00-80-7F (hex)	DY-4 INCORPORATED
00807F (base 16)	DY-4 INCORPORATED 333 PALLADIUM DRIVE, MS 312 KANATA, ONTARIO, K2V 1A6 CANADA
00-80-80 (hex)	DATAMEDIA CORPORATION
008080 (base 16)	DATAMEDIA CORPORATION 7401 CENTRAL HIGHWAY PENNSAUKEN, NJ 08109
00-80-81 (hex)	KENDALL SQUARE RESEARCH CORP.
008081 (base 16)	KENDALL SQUARE RESEARCH CORP. 170 TRACER LANE WALTHAM, MA 02154-1379
00-80-82 (hex)	PEP MODULAR COMPUTERS GMBH
008082 (base 16)	PEP MODULAR COMPUTERS GMBH APFELSTRANGER STR. 16 D - 8950 KAUFBEUREN WEST GERMANY
00-80-83 (hex)	AMDAHL
008083 (base 16)	AMDAHL 1250 EAST ARQUES AVENUE M/S 286 P.O. BOX 3470 SUNNYVALE CA 94088-3470
00-80-84 (hex)	THE CLOUD INC.
008084 (base 16)	THE CLOUD INC. CLOUD BLDG. 71-1, CHEONG-DAM DONG KANG-NAM KU, SEOUL KOREA
00-80-85 (hex)	H-THREE SYSTEMS CORPORATION
008085 (base 16)	H-THREE SYSTEMS CORPORATION 100 PARK DRIVE, SUITE 204 RESEARCH TRIANGLE PARK NC 27709
00-80-86 (hex)	COMPUTER GENERATION INC.
008086 (base 16)	COMPUTER GENERATION INC. 3855 PRESIDENTIAL PARKWAY ATLANTA GA 30340
00-80-87 (hex)	OKI ELECTRIC INDUSTRY CO., LTD
008087 (base 16)	OKI ELECTRIC INDUSTRY CO., LTD 10-3 SHIBAURA 4-CHOME MINATO-KU, TOKYO 108 JAPAN
00-80-88 (hex)	VICTOR COMPANY OF JAPAN, LTD.
008088 (base 16)	VICTOR COMPANY OF JAPAN, LTD. 58-7 SHINMEI-CHO, YOKOSUKA KANAGAWA 239 JAPAN
00-80-89 (hex)	TECNETICS (PTY) LTD.
008089 (base 16)	TECNETICS (PTY) LTD. P.O. BOX/POSBUS 56412 PINEGOWRIE, 2123 SOUTH AFRICA
00-80-8A (hex)	SUMMIT MICROSYSTEMS CORP.

company_id	Organization Address
00808A (base 16)	SUMMIT MICROSYSTEMS CORP. 710 LAKEWAY-STE.#150 SUNNYVALE CA 940867
00-80-8B (hex)	DACOLL LIMITED
00808B (base 16)	DACOLL LIMITED DACOLL HOUSE, GARDNERS LANE BATHGATE WEST LOTHIAN SCOTLAND EH48 1TP
00-80-8C (hex)	FRONTIER SOFTWARE DEVELOPMENT
00808C (base 16)	FRONTIER SOFTWARE DEVELOPMENT 1501 MAIN STREET SUITE #40 TEWKSBURY, MA 01876
00-80-8D (hex)	WESTCOAST TECHNOLOGY B.V.
00808D (base 16)	WESTCOAST TECHNOLOGY B.V. P.O. BOX 3317 2601 DH DELFT NETHERLANDS
00-80-8E (hex)	RADSTONE TECHNOLOGY
00808E (base 16)	RADSTONE TECHNOLOGY WATER LANE, TOWCESTER NORTHANTS NN12 7JN ENGLAND
00-80-8F (hex)	C. ITOH ELECTRONICS, INC.
00808F (base 16)	C. ITOH ELECTRONICS, INC. 2505 MCCABE WAY IRVINE, CA 92714
00-80-90 (hex)	MICROTEK INTERNATIONAL, INC.
008090 (base 16)	MICROTEK INTERNATIONAL, INC. 3300 NW 211TH TERRACE HILLSBOR OR 97124-7136
00-80-91 (hex)	TOKYO ELECTRIC CO.,LTD
008091 (base 16)	TOKYO ELECTRIC CO.,LTD 10-14 UCHIKANDA 1-CHOME CHIYODA-KU TOKYO JAPAN 101
00-80-92 (hex)	JAPAN COMPUTER INDUSTRY, INC.
008092 (base 16)	JAPAN COMPUTER INDUSTRY, INC. 1-6-20 KOSAKAHONMACHI HIGASHI-OSAKA 577 JAPAN
00-80-93 (hex)	XYRON CORPORATION
008093 (base 16)	XYRON CORPORATION 7864 LILY COURT CUPERTINO CA 95014
00-80-94 (hex)	ALFA LAVAL AUTOMATION AB
008094 (base 16)	ALFA LAVAL AUTOMATION AB ADN S-205 22 MALMO SWEDEN
00-80-95 (hex)	BASIC MERTON HANDELSGES.M.B.H.
008095 (base 16)	BASIC MERTON HANDELSGES.M.B.H. DURCHLASS-STRASSE 42 A - 9020 KLAGENFURT AUSTRIA
00-80-96 (hex)	HUMAN DESIGNED SYSTEMS, INC.
008096 (base 16)	HUMAN DESIGNED SYSTEMS, INC. 421 FEHELEY DRIVE KING OF PRUSSIA PA 19406
00-80-97 (hex)	CENTRALP AUTOMATISMES
008097 (base 16)	CENTRALP AUTOMATISMES 21, RUE MARCEL PAGNOL 69694 VENISSIEUX CEDEX FRANCE
00-80-98 (hex)	TDK CORPORATION

company_id	Organization Address
008098 (base 16)	TDK CORPORATION CORP. R&D DEPT. TECH. HDQTERS. 2-15-7, HIGASHI-OWADA, ICHIKAWA-SHI CHIBA-KEN, 272, JAPAN
00-80-99 (hex)	KLOCKNER MOELLER IPC
008099 (base 16)	KLOCKNER MOELLER IPC FRITZ-KOTZ-STR. 8 P.O. BOX 13 80 D-5276 WIEHL 1-BOMIG WEST GERMANY
00-80-9A (hex)	NOVUS NETWORKS LTD
00809A (base 16)	NOVUS NETWORKS LTD JOHN SCOTT HOUSE MARKET STREET BRACKNELL, BERKW RG12 1JB ENGLAND
00-80-9B (hex)	JUSTSYSTEM CORPORATION
00809B (base 16)	JUSTSYSTEM CORPORATION 3-46 OKINOHAMAHIGASHI TOKUSIMASHI 770 JAPAN
00-80-9C (hex)	LUXCOM, INC.
00809C (base 16)	LUXCOM, INC. 3249 LAURELVIEW COURT FREMONT, CA 94538
00-80-9D (hex)	Commscraft Ltd.
00809D (base 16)	Commscraft Ltd. PO BOX 160 BENTLEY, W.A. 6102 AUSTRALIA
00-80-9E (hex)	DATUS GMBH
00809E (base 16)	DATUS GMBH INDUSTRIESTR. 2 D-5102 WURSELEN/AACHEN WEST GERMANY
00-80-9F (hex)	ALCATEL BUSINESS SYSTEMS
00809F (base 16)	ALCATEL BUSINESS SYSTEMS 54, AVENUE JEAN JAURES 92707 COLOMBES CEDEX FRANCE
00-80-A0 (hex)	EDISA HEWLETT PACKARD S/A
0080A0 (base 16)	EDISA HEWLETT PACKARD S/A ALAMEDA RIO NEGRO, 750-ALPHAVILLE 06454-000 BARUERI SP BRAZIL
00-80-A1 (hex)	MICROTEST, INC.
0080A1 (base 16)	MICROTEST, INC. 4747 N. 22ND STREET PHOENIX AZ 85016-4708
00-80-A2 (hex)	CREATIVE ELECTRONIC SYSTEMS
0080A2 (base 16)	CREATIVE ELECTRONIC SYSTEMS 70 ROUTE DU PONT - BUTIN CH-1213 PETIT-LANCY GENEVA SWITZERLAND
00-80-A3 (hex)	LANTRONIX
0080A3 (base 16)	LANTRONIX 26072 MERIT CIRCLE SUITE 113 LAGUNA HILLS CA 92653
00-80-A4 (hex)	LIBERTY ELECTRONICS
0080A4 (base 16)	LIBERTY ELECTRONICS 332 HARBOR WAY SOUTH SAN FRANCISCO, CA 94080
00-80-A5 (hex)	SPEED INTERNATIONAL
0080A5 (base 16)	SPEED INTERNATIONAL 1320 ARBOLITA DR. LA HABRA, CA 90631
00-80-A6 (hex)	REPUBLIC TECHNOLOGY, INC.

company_id	Organization Address	company_id	Organization Address
0080A6 (base 16)	REPUBLIC TECHNOLOGY, INC. P.O. BOX 141006 AUSTIN, TX 78714	00-80-B6 (hex)	THEMIS COMPUTER
00-80-A7 (hex)	MEASUREX CORP.	0080B6 (base 16)	THEMIS COMPUTER 6681 OWENS DRIVE PLEASONTON, CA 94588
0080A7 (base 16)	MEASUREX CORP. 1 RESULTS WAY CUPERTINO, CA 95014-5991	00-80-B7 (hex)	STELLAR COMPUTER
00-80-A8 (hex)	VITACOM CORPORATION	0080B7 (base 16)	STELLAR COMPUTER 95 WELLS AVENUE NEWTON, MA 02159
0080A8 (base 16)	VITACOM CORPORATION 1330 CHARLESTON ROAD MOUNTAIN VIEW, CA 94043	00-80-B8 (hex)	BUG, INCORPORATED
00-80-A9 (hex)	CLEARPOINT RESEARCH	0080B8 (base 16)	BUG, INCORPORATED 1-14 TECHNO-PARK 1-CHOME SHIMONOPPORO, ATSUBETSU-KU SAPPORO 004, JAPAN
0080A9 (base 16)	CLEARPOINT RESEARCH 190 NORTH MAIN STREET NATICK MA	00-80-B9 (hex)	ARCHE TECHNOLIGIES INC.
00-80-AA (hex)	MAXPEED	0080B9 (base 16)	ARCHE TECHNOLIGIES INC. 48502 KATO ROAD FREMONT, CA 94538
0080AA (base 16)	MAXPEED 1120 CHESS DRIVE FOSTER CITY CA 94404	00-80-BA (hex)	SPECIALIX (ASIA) PTE, LTD
00-80-AB (hex)	DUKANE NETWORK INTEGRATION	0080BA (base 16)	SPECIALIX (ASIA) PTE, LTD 3 WINTERSELLS ROAD BYFLEET SURREY KT147LF UNITED KINGDOM
0080AB (base 16)	DUKANE NETWORK INTEGRATION 2900 DUKANE DRIVE ST. CHARLES, IL 60174	00-80-BB (hex)	HUGHES LAN SYSTEMS
00-80-AC (hex)	IMLOGIX, DIVISION OF GENESYS	0080BB (base 16)	HUGHES LAN SYSTEMS 1225 CHARLESTON ROAD MOUNTAIN VIEW CA 94043
0080AC (base 16)	IMLOGIX, DIVISION OF GENESYS 1900 SUMMIT TOWER BLVD.STE#770 ORLANDO FL 32810	00-80-BC (hex)	HITACHI ENGINEERING CO., LTD
00-80-AD (hex)	CNET TECHNOLOGY, INC.	0080BC (base 16)	HITACHI ENGINEERING CO., LTD 4-8-26, OMIKACHO HITACHI CITY IBARAKI PREFECTURE 319-12 JAPAN
0080AD (base 16)	CNET TECHNOLOGY, INC. 2199 ZANKER ROAD SAN JOSE CA 95131	00-80-BD (hex)	THE FURUKAWA ELECTRIC CO., LTD
00-80-AE (hex)	HUGHES NETWORK SYSTEMS	0080BD (base 16)	THE FURUKAWA ELECTRIC CO., LTD 6-1, MARUNOUCHI 2-CHOME CHIYODA-KU, TOKYO 100 JAPAN
0080AE (base 16)	HUGHES NETWORK SYSTEMS 11717 EXPLORATION LANE GERMANTOWN, MD 20876	00-80-BE (hex)	ARIES RESEARCH
00-80-AF (hex)	ALLUMER CO., LTD.	0080BE (base 16)	ARIES RESEARCH 46791 FREMOND BLVD. FREMONT, CA 94538
0080AF (base 16)	ALLUMER CO., LTD. 2-8-8 CHUO-CHO, MEGURO-KU TOKYO 152 JAPAN	00-80-BF (hex)	TAKAOKA ELECTRIC MFG. CO. LTD.
00-80-B0 (hex)	ADVANCED INFORMATION	0080BF (base 16)	TAKAOKA ELECTRIC MFG. CO. LTD. KANDA BRANCH OFFICE TONEN 2-1-11, SARUGAKU-CHO CHIYODA-KU, TOKYO, 101 JAPAN
0080B0 (base 16)	ADVANCED INFORMATION TECHNOLOGY, INC. 5F 1-2-6 NIHONBASHI-HONCHO CHUO-KU, TOKYO 103-0023 JAPAN	00-80-C0 (hex)	PENRIL DATACOMM
00-80-B1 (hex)	SOFTCOM A/S	0080C0 (base 16)	PENRIL DATACOMM 1300 QUINCE ORCHARD BLVD. GAITHERSBURG, MD 20878
0080B1 (base 16)	SOFTCOM A/S STUDIESTRAEDE 21 DK 1455 COPENNHAGEN K. DENMARK	00-80-C1 (hex)	LANEX CORPORATION
00-80-B2 (hex)	NETWORK EQUIPMENT TECHNOLOGIES	0080C1 (base 16)	LANEX CORPORATION 10727 TUCKER STREET BELTSVILLE, MD 20705
0080B2 (base 16)	NETWORK EQUIPMENT TECHNOLOGIES 800 SAGINAW DRIVE REDWOOD CITY CA 94063	00-80-C2 (hex)	IEEE 802 COMMITTEE
00-80-B3 (hex)	AVAL DATA CORPORATION	0080C2 (base 16)	IEEE 802 COMMITTEE FERMI NAT'L ACCELERATOR LAB M/S 368 P.O. BOX 500 BATAVIA IL 60510
0080B3 (base 16)	AVAL DATA CORPORATION MACHIDA ENGINEERING CENTER 1757-1 KANAI-CHO MACHIDA CITY TOKYO JAPAN JAPAN	00-80-C3 (hex)	BICC INFORMATION SYSTEMS & SVC
00-80-B4 (hex)	SOPHIA SYSTEMS	0080C3 (base 16)	BICC INFORMATION SYSTEMS & SVC 500 CAPABILITY GREEN, LUTON BEDFORDSHIRE ENGLAND LU1 3LT
0080B4 (base 16)	SOPHIA SYSTEMS 3337 KIFER ROAD SANTA CLARA, CA 95051	00-80-C4 (hex)	DOCUMENT TECHNOLOGIES, INC.
00-80-B5 (hex)	UNITED NETWORKS INC.		
0080B5 (base 16)	UNITED NETWORKS INC. 2178 PARAGON DRIVE SAN JOSE, CA 95131		

company_id	Organization Address	company_id	Organization Address
0080C4 (base 16)	DOCUMENT TECHNOLOGIES, INC. 1300 CHARLESTON ROAD MOUNTAIN VIEW, CA 94043	0080D4 (base 16)	CHASE RESEARCH LTD. 7 CHINEHAM BUSINESS PARK BASINGSTOKE, RG 24 OWD ENGLAND
00-80-C5 (hex)	NOVELLCO DE MEXICO	00-80-D5 (hex)	CADRE TECHNOLOGIES
0080C5 (base 16)	NOVELLCO DE MEXICO CONSTITUYENTES NO. 907 COL. LOMAS ALTAS 11950 MEXICO, D.F.	0080D5 (base 16)	CADRE TECHNOLOGIES 19545 NW VON NEUMANN DRIVE BEAVERTON, OR 97006
00-80-C6 (hex)	NATIONAL DATACOMM CORPORATION	00-80-D6 (hex)	NUVOTECH, INC.
0080C6 (base 16)	NATIONAL DATACOMM CORPORATION 2F, 28, INDUSTRY EAST 9TH RD. SCIENCE PARK, HSIN-CHU TAIWAN 30077, R.O.C.	0080D6 (base 16)	NUVOTECH, INC. 2015 BRIDGEWAY, SUITE 204 SAUSALITO, CA 94965
00-80-C7 (hex)	XIRCOM	00-80-D7 (hex)	FANTUM ENGINEERING, INC.
0080C7 (base 16)	XIRCOM 26025 MUREAU ROAD CALABASAS CA 91302	0080D7 (base 16)	FANTUM ENGINEERING, INC. 3706 BIG A ROAD ROWLETT TX 75088
00-80-C8 (hex)	D-LINK SYSTEMS, INC.	00-80-D8 (hex)	NETWORK PERIPHERALS INC.
0080C8 (base 16)	D-LINK SYSTEMS, INC. 5 MUSICK IRVINE, CA 92718	0080D8 (base 16)	NETWORK PERIPHERALS INC. 2890 ZONKER ROAD SUITE 209 SAN JOSE, CA 95134
00-80-C9 (hex)	ALBERTA MICROELECTRONIC CENTRE	00-80-D9 (hex)	EMK ELEKTRONIK
0080C9 (base 16)	ALBERTA MICROELECTRONIC CENTRE 318, 11315 - 87 AVENUE EDMONTON, AB T6G 2C2 CANADA	0080D9 (base 16)	EMK ELEKTRONIK KREUZSTR. 2 D-7518 BRETTEN 3 GERMANY
00-80-CA (hex)	NETCOM RESEARCH INCORPORATED	00-80-DA (hex)	BRUEL & KJAER
0080CA (base 16)	NETCOM RESEARCH INCORPORATED 201 TECHNOLOGY DRIVE IRVINE, CA 92718	0080DA (base 16)	BRUEL & KJAER 18, NAERUM HOVEDGADE DK-2850 NAERUM DENMARK
00-80-CB (hex)	FALCO DATA PRODUCTS	00-80-DB (hex)	GRAPHON CORPORATION
0080CB (base 16)	FALCO DATA PRODUCTS 440 POTRERO AVENUE SUNNYVALE, CA 94086-4196	0080DB (base 16)	GRAPHON CORPORATION 1506 DELL AVE - #«C» CAMPBELL CA 95008-6911
00-80-CC (hex)	MICROWAVE BYPASS SYSTEMS	00-80-DC (hex)	PICKER INTERNATIONAL
0080CC (base 16)	MICROWAVE BYPASS SYSTEMS 25 BRAINTREE HILL OFFICE PARK BRAINTREE, MA 02184	0080DC (base 16)	PICKER INTERNATIONAL 595 MINER ROAD CLEVELAND OH 44143
00-80-CD (hex)	MICRONICS COMPUTER, INC.	00-80-DD (hex)	GMX INC/GIMIX
0080CD (base 16)	MICRONICS COMPUTER, INC. 45365 NORTHPORT LOOP WEST FREMONT CA 94538	0080DD (base 16)	GMX INC/GIMIX 3223 ARNOLD LANE NORTHBROOK, IL 60062-2406
00-80-CE (hex)	BROADCAST TELEVISION SYSTEMS	00-80-DE (hex)	GIPSI S.A.
0080CE (base 16)	BROADCAST TELEVISION SYSTEMS P.O. BOX 30816 SALT LAKE CITY, UTAH 84130-0816	0080DE (base 16)	GIPSI S.A. 2,BD VAUBAN - B.P. 268 78053 ST. QUENTIN EN YVELINES CEDEX FRANCE
00-80-CF (hex)	EMBEDDED PERFORMANCE INC.	00-80-DF (hex)	ADC CODENOLL TECHNOLOGY CORP.
0080CF (base 16)	EMBEDDED PERFORMANCE INC. 3385 SCOTT BLVD. SANTA CLARA CA 95054-3115	0080DF (base 16)	ADC CODENOLL TECHNOLOGY CORP. 200 CORPORATE BLVD. SO. YONKERS NY 10701
00-80-D0 (hex)	COMPUTER PERIPHERALS, INC.	00-80-E0 (hex)	XTP SYSTEMS, INC.
0080D0 (base 16)	COMPUTER PERIPHERALS, INC. 667 RANCHO CONEJO BLVD. NEWBURY PARK, CA 91320	0080E0 (base 16)	XTP SYSTEMS, INC. 1900 STATE STREET , STE «D» SANTA BARBARA, CA 93101
00-80-D1 (hex)	KIMTRON CORPORATION	00-80-E1 (hex)	STMICROELECTRONICS
0080D1 (base 16)	KIMTRON CORPORATION 1709 JUNCTION COURT BUILDING 380 SAN JOSE, CA 95112	0080E1 (base 16)	STMICROELECTRONICS 1000, AZTECK WEST ALMONDSBURY BRISTOL BS32 4SQ UNITED KINGDOM
00-80-D2 (hex)	SHINNIHONDENKO CO., LTD.	00-80-E2 (hex)	T.D.I. CO., LTD.
0080D2 (base 16)	SHINNIHONDENKO CO., LTD. 6-8 NISHITENMA 2 CHOME KITA-KU, OSAKA 530 JAPAN	0080E2 (base 16)	T.D.I. CO., LTD. DEVELOPMENT DIV. #3 FUJI BLDG 1-3-13 ITACHIBORI NISHI-KU OSAKA 550 JAPAN
00-80-D3 (hex)	SHIVA CORP.		
0080D3 (base 16)	SHIVA CORP. 205 BURLINGTON ROAD BEDFORD MA 01730	00-80-E3 (hex)	CORAL NETWORK CORPORATION
00-80-D4 (hex)	CHASE RESEARCH LTD.		

company_id	Organization / Address
0080E3 (base 16)	CORAL NETWORK CORPORATION (NOW BAY NETWORKS) 4401 GREAT AMERICAN PKWY M/S: SC01-05 SANTA CLARA CA 95052-8185
00-80-E4 (hex)	NORTHWEST DIGITAL SYSTEMS, INC
0080E4 (base 16)	NORTHWEST DIGITAL SYSTEMS, INC P.O. BOX 15288 SEATTLE, WA 98115
00-80-E5 (hex)	MYLEX CORPORATION
0080E5 (base 16)	MYLEX CORPORATION 34551 ARDENWOOD BLVD. FREMONT, CA 94555-3607
00-80-E6 (hex)	PEER NETWORKS, INC.
0080E6 (base 16)	PEER NETWORKS, INC. 3350 SCOTT BLVD. BLDG. 14 SANTA CLARA, CA 95054
00-80-E7 (hex)	LYNWOOD SCIENTIFIC DEV. LTD.
0080E7 (base 16)	LYNWOOD SCIENTIFIC DEV. LTD. FARNHAM TRADING ESTATE FARNHAM, SURREY, GU9 9NN UNITED KINGDOM
00-80-E8 (hex)	CUMULUS CORPORATION
0080E8 (base 16)	CUMULUS CORPORATION 23500 MERCANTILE ROAD CLEVELAND, OH 44122
00-80-E9 (hex)	MADGE NETWORKS
0080E9 (base 16)	MADGE NETWORKS 625 INDUSTRIAL WAY EATONTOWN NJ 07724
00-80-EA (hex)	THE FIBER COMPANY
0080EA (base 16)	THE FIBER COMPANY CLIFTON TECHNOLOGY CENTRE CLIFTON MOOR GATE YORK YO3 8XF ENGLAND
00-80-EB (hex)	COMPCONTROL B.V.
0080EB (base 16)	COMPCONTROL B.V. STRATUMSED K31 5611 NB EINDHOVEN THE NETHERLANDS
00-80-EC (hex)	SUPERCOMPUTING SOLUTIONS, INC.
0080EC (base 16)	SUPERCOMPUTING SOLUTIONS, INC. 6175 NANCY RIDGE BLVD. SAN DIEGO, CA 92121
00-80-ED (hex)	IQ TECHNOLOGIES, INC.
0080ED (base 16)	IQ TECHNOLOGIES, INC. 11811 NE FIRST STREET SUITE 201 BELLEVUE, WA 98005
00-80-EE (hex)	THOMSON CSF
0080EE (base 16)	THOMSON CSF 51 ESPLANADE DU GENERAL DE GAULLE 92045 - PARIS LA DEFENSE - CEDEX 67 FRANCE
00-80-EF (hex)	RATIONAL
0080EF (base 16)	RATIONAL 3320 SCOTT BOULEVARD SANTA CLARA, CA 95054
00-80-F0 (hex)	KYUSHU MATSUSHITA ELECTRIC CO.
0080F0 (base 16)	KYUSHU MATSUSHITA ELECTRIC CO. BUSINESS EQUIPMENT DIVISION 1-62, 4-CHOME, MINOSHIMA HAKATA-KU, FUKUOKA 812 JAPAN
00-80-F1 (hex)	OPUS SYSTEMS
0080F1 (base 16)	OPUS SYSTEMS 3000 CORONADO DRIVE SANTA CLARA CA 95054

company_id	Organization / Address
00-80-F2 (hex)	RAYCOM SYSTEMS INC
0080F2 (base 16)	RAYCOM SYSTEMS INC 16525 SHERMAN WAY #C-8 VAN NUYS CA 91406
00-80-F3 (hex)	SUN ELECTRONICS CORP.
0080F3 (base 16)	SUN ELECTRONICS CORP. 250 ASAHI KOCHINO-CHO KONAN-CITY AICHI 483 JAPAN
00-80-F4 (hex)	TELEMECANIQUE ELECTRIQUE
0080F4 (base 16)	TELEMECANIQUE ELECTRIQUE 33 BIS AVENUE, DU MARECHAL JOFFRE 92002 NANTERRE CEDEX FRANCE
00-80-F5 (hex)	QUANTEL LTD
0080F5 (base 16)	QUANTEL LTD PEAR TREE LANE NEWBURY, BERKS. RG13 2LT ENGLAND
00-80-F6 (hex)	SYNERGY MICROSYSTEMS
0080F6 (base 16)	SYNERGY MICROSYSTEMS 9605 SCRANTON ROAD-STE #700 SAN DIEGO CA 92121-1773
00-80-F7 (hex)	ZENITH ELECTRONICS
0080F7 (base 16)	ZENITH ELECTRONICS 1000 MILWAUKEE AVENUE GLENVIEW, IL 60025
00-80-F8 (hex)	MIZAR, INC.
0080F8 (base 16)	MIZAR, INC. 1419 DUNN DRIVE CARROLLTON, TX 75006
00-80-F9 (hex)	HEURIKON CORPORATION
0080F9 (base 16)	HEURIKON CORPORATION 8310 EXCELSIOR DRIVE MADISON, WI 53717
00-80-FA (hex)	RWT GMBH
0080FA (base 16)	RWT GMBH TALANGERSTR. 5-7 D - 8033 KRAILLING WEST GERMANY
00-80-FB (hex)	BVM LIMITED
0080FB (base 16)	BVM LIMITED FLANDERS ROAD HEDGE END SOUTHAMPTON ENGLAND
00-80-FC (hex)	AVATAR CORPORATION
0080FC (base 16)	AVATAR CORPORATION 65 SOUTH STREET HOPKINTON, MA 01748
00-80-FD (hex)	EXSCEED CORPORATION
0080FD (base 16)	EXSCEED CORPORATION 1-15-12, KITAKASE, SAIWAI-KU KAWASAKI-CITY, 211 KANAGAWA JAPAN
00-80-FE (hex)	AZURE TECHNOLOGIES, INC.
0080FE (base 16)	AZURE TECHNOLOGIES, INC. 63 SOUTH STREET HOPKINTON MA 01748-2212
00-80-FF (hex)	SOC. DE TELEINFORMATIQUE RTC
0080FF (base 16)	SOC. DE TELEINFORMATIQUE RTC P.O. BOX 955 PLACE DU PARC 300 LEO-PARISTAU SUITE 725 MONTREAL (QUEBEC) CANADA H2W 2N1
00-90-00 (hex)	DIAMOND MULTIMEDIA

company_id	Organization Address
009000 (base 16)	DIAMOND MULTIMEDIA 312 SE STONEMILL DRIVE SUITE #150 VANCOUVER WA 98684
00-90-01 (hex)	NISHIMU ELCTRONICS INDUSTRIES
009001 (base 16)	NISHIMU ELCTRONICS INDUSTRIES CO., LTD. 700 TATENO MITAGAWA-CHO KANZAKI-GUN SAGA PREF. JAPAN
00-90-02 (hex)	ALLGON AB
009002 (base 16)	ALLGON AB GARDATORGET 1 412 50 GOTEBORG SWEDEN
00-90-03 (hex)	APLIO
009003 (base 16)	APLIO 18 AU. DU 8 MAI 1945 95200 SARCELLES FRANCE
00-90-04 (hex)	3COM EUROPE LTD.
009004 (base 16)	3COM EUROPE LTD. 3COM CENTRE, BOUNDRY WAY HEMEL HEMPSTEAD HERTS. HP27YU UNITED KINGDOM
00-90-05 (hex)	PROTECH SYSTEMS CO., LTD.
009005 (base 16)	PROTECH SYSTEMS CO., LTD. 5F, NO. 34, LANE 80, SEC. 3 NANKANG ROAD TAIPEI TAIWAN R.O.C.
00-90-06 (hex)	HAMAMATSU PHOTONICS K.K.
009006 (base 16)	HAMAMATSU PHOTONICS K.K. 812 JOKO-CHO HAMAMATSU CITY,431-3196 JAPAN
00-90-07 (hex)	DOMEX TECHNOLOGY CORP.
009007 (base 16)	DOMEX TECHNOLOGY CORP. NO. 2, TECHNOLOGY RD. 1 SCIENCE-BASED INDUSTRIAL PARK HSINCHU TAIWAN, R.O.C.
00-90-08 (hex)	HAN A SYSTEMS, INC.
009008 (base 16)	HAN A SYSTEMS, INC. EAHO B/D 740-1 YEOKSAM-DONG, KANGNAM-KU SEOUL, KOREA
00-90-09 (hex)	i Controls, Inc.
009009 (base 16)	i Controls, Inc. 12F Doosan Building, 105-7, Nonhyun-dong, Gangnam-gu Seoul KOREA 135-714
00-90-0A (hex)	PROTON ELECTRONIC INDUSTRIAL
00900A (base 16)	PROTON ELECTRONIC INDUSTRIAL CO., LTD. 4F, 45, SECTION 1, SAN-MIN RD PANCHIAO, TAIPEI COUNTY TAIWAN R.O.C.
00-90-0B (hex)	LANNER ELECTRONICS, INC.
00900B (base 16)	LANNER ELECTRONICS, INC. 8F-4, NO. 77, SEC. 1 HSIN TAI WU RD., HSICHIH TAIPEI HSIEN TAIWAN R.O.C.
00-90-0C (hex)	CISCO SYSTEMS, INC.
00900C (base 16)	CISCO SYSTEMS, INC. 170 W. TASMAN DRIVE - SJA-2 SAN JOSE CA 95134-1706
00-90-0D (hex)	OVERLAND DATA INC.

company_id	Organization Address
00900D (base 16)	OVERLAND DATA INC. 8975 BALBOA AVENUE SAN DIEGO CA 92123-1599
00-90-0E (hex)	HANDLINK TECHNOLOGIES, INC.
00900E (base 16)	HANDLINK TECHNOLOGIES, INC. BLDG.52, 195-29 SEC. 4 CHUNG HSING ROAD CHUTUNG, HSINCHU TAIWAN 310, R.O.C.
00-90-0F (hex)	KAWASAKI HEAVY INDUSTRIES, LTD
00900F (base 16)	KAWASAKI HEAVY INDUSTRIES, LTD ELEC. & CONTROL TECH CENTER 1-1 KAWASAKI-CHO AKASHI 673-8666 JAPAN
00-90-10 (hex)	SIMULATION LABORATORIES, INC.
009010 (base 16)	SIMULATION LABORATORIES, INC. 10078 TYLER PLACE #A IJAMSVILLE MD 21754
00-90-11 (hex)	WAVTRACE, INC.
009011 (base 16)	WAVTRACE, INC. 1555 132ND AVE. NE BELLEVUE WA 98005
00-90-12 (hex)	GLOBESPAN SEMICONDUCTOR, INC.
009012 (base 16)	GLOBESPAN SEMICONDUCTOR, INC. 100 SCHULZ DRIVE RED BANK NJ 07701
00-90-13 (hex)	SAMSAN CORP.
009013 (base 16)	SAMSAN CORP. ELECTRONICS & COMM DIVISION SAMSAN BLDG., 506-7, AMSA-DONG KANGDONG-GU, SEOUL, 134-050 KOREA
00-90-14 (hex)	ROTORK INSTRUMENTS, LTD.
009014 (base 16)	ROTORK INSTRUMENTS, LTD. CHAUL END LANE LUTON BEDFORDSHIRE LU4 8EZ ENGLAND
00-90-15 (hex)	CENTIGRAM COMMUNICATIONS CORP.
009015 (base 16)	CENTIGRAM COMMUNICATIONS CORP. 91 EAST TASMAN DRIVE SAN JOSE CA 95134
00-90-16 (hex)	ZAC
009016 (base 16)	ZAC TALSTRASSE 18 D-71272 RENNINGEN GERMANY
00-90-17 (hex)	ZYPCOM, INC.
009017 (base 16)	ZYPCOM, INC. 2301 INDUSTRIAL PARKWAY WEST BUILDING 7 HAYWARD CA 94545-5029
00-90-18 (hex)	ITO ELECTRIC INDUSTRY CO, LTD.
009018 (base 16)	ITO ELECTRIC INDUSTRY CO, LTD. 4-26-12 MEIEKI NAKAMURA-KU NAGOYA-CITY AICHI 450-0002 JAPAN
00-90-19 (hex)	HERMES ELECTRONICS CO., LTD.
009019 (base 16)	HERMES ELECTRONICS CO., LTD. 3-2-12 YUSHIMA, BUNKYO-KU TOKYO, 113-0034 JAPAN
00-90-1A (hex)	UNISPHERE SOLUTIONS
00901A (base 16)	UNISPHERE SOLUTIONS 5 CARLISLE ROAD WESTFORD MA 01886
00-90-1B (hex)	DIGITAL CONTROLS

company_id	Organization Address	company_id	Organization Address
00901B (base 16)	DIGITAL CONTROLS 305 PIONEER BLVD. SPRINGBORO OH 45066-1100	00902A (base 16)	COMMUNICATION DEVICES, INC. ONE FORSTMANN COURT CLIFTON NJ 07011
00-90-1C (hex)	MPS SOFTWARE GMBH	00-90-2B (hex)	CISCO SYSTEMS, INC.
00901C (base 16)	MPS SOFTWARE GMBH LUDWIGSTR 36 85551 KIRCHHEIM GERMANY	00902B (base 16)	CISCO SYSTEMS, INC. SJA-2 170 W. TASMAN DRIVE SAN JOSE CA 95134-1706
00-90-1D (hex)	PEC (NZ) LTD.	00-90-2C (hex)	DATA & CONTROL EQUIPMENT LTD.
00901D (base 16)	PEC (NZ) LTD. 2 STATION ROAD P.O. BOX 308 MARTON NEW ZEALAND	00902C (base 16)	DATA & CONTROL EQUIPMENT LTD. COUNTY FARM, WENDOVER RD. STOKE MANDEVILLE BUCKS. HP22 STA UNITED KINGDOM
00-90-1E (hex)	SELESTA INGEGNE RIA S.P.A.	00-90-2D (hex)	DATA ELECTRONICS
00901E (base 16)	SELESTA INGEGNE RIA S.P.A. VIA CANTORE, 8H GENOVA 16149 ITALY	00902D (base 16)	DATA ELECTRONICS (AUST.) PTY, LTD. 7 SEISMIC COURT ROWVILLE VICTORIA 3178 AUSTRALIA
00-90-1F (hex)	ADTEC PRODUCTIONS, INC.	00-90-2E (hex)	NAMCO LIMITED
00901F (base 16)	ADTEC PRODUCTIONS, INC. 408 RUSSELL STREET NASHVILLE TN 37206	00902E (base 16)	NAMCO LIMITED 1-1-32 SHIN-URASHIMA-CHO KANAGAWA-KU, YOKOHAMA KANAGAWA 221-0031 JAPAN
00-90-20 (hex)	PHILIPS ANALYTICAL X-RAY B.V.	00-90-2F (hex)	NETCORE SYSTEMS, INC.
009020 (base 16)	PHILIPS ANALYTICAL X-RAY B.V. LELYWEG 1 7602 EA ALMELO THE NETHERLANDS	00902F (base 16)	NETCORE SYSTEMS, INC. 187 BALLARDVALE STREET WILMINGTON MA 01887
00-90-21 (hex)	CISCO SYSTEMS, INC.	00-90-30 (hex)	HONEYWELL-DATING
009021 (base 16)	CISCO SYSTEMS, INC. 170 W. TASMAN DR. - SJA-2 SAN JOSE CA 95134-1706	009030 (base 16)	HONEYWELL-DATING VIA TINTORETTO, 15 21012 CASSANO MAGNAGO (VA) ITALY
00-90-22 (hex)	IVEX	00-90-31 (hex)	MYSTICOM, LTD.
009022 (base 16)	IVEX 4295 INTERNATIONAL BLVD. SUITE «F» NORCROSS GA 30093	009031 (base 16)	MYSTICOM, LTD. P.O. 8364 NATANIA ISRAEL ZIP CODE: 42504
00-90-23 (hex)	ZILOG INC.	00-90-32 (hex)	PELCOMBE GROUP LTD.
009023 (base 16)	ZILOG INC. 210 E. HACIENDA AVE. CAMPBELL CA 95008	009032 (base 16)	PELCOMBE GROUP LTD. MAIN ROAD DOVERCOURT, HARWICH ESSEX C012 4LP ENGLAND
00-90-24 (hex)	PIPELINKS, INC.	00-90-33 (hex)	INNOVAPHONE GMBH
009024 (base 16)	PIPELINKS, INC. 2710 WALSH AVE., STE #300 SANTA CLARA CA 95051	009033 (base 16)	INNOVAPHONE GMBH CARL-ORFF STR. 14 D-71069 SINDELFINGEN GERMANY
00-90-25 (hex)	VISION SYSTEMS LTD. PTY	00-90-34 (hex)	IMAGIC, INC.
009025 (base 16)	VISION SYSTEMS LTD. PTY SECOND AVE., TECHNOLOGY PARK MAWSON LAKES SA 5095 AUSTRALIA	009034 (base 16)	IMAGIC, INC. 111 MAIN STREET AMESBURY MA 01913
00-90-26 (hex)	ADVANCED SWITCHING	00-90-35 (hex)	ALPHA TELECOM, INC.
009026 (base 16)	ADVANCED SWITCHING COMMUNICATIONS, INC. 8330 BOONE BOULEVARD–5TH FL. VIENNA VA 22182	009035 (base 16)	ALPHA TELECOM, INC. 2F, NO.2, LIHSIN ROAD SCIENCE-BASED INDUSTRIAL PARK HSIN-CHU TAIWAN
00-90-27 (hex)	INTEL CORPORATION	00-90-36 (hex)	ENS, INC.
009027 (base 16)	INTEL CORPORATION HF1-06 5200 N.E. ELAM YOUNG PARKWAY HILLSBORO OR 97124	009036 (base 16)	ENS, INC. P.O. BOX 19207 RALEIGH NC 27619
00-90-28 (hex)	NIPPON SIGNAL CO., LTD.	00-90-37 (hex)	ACUCOMM, INC.
009028 (base 16)	NIPPON SIGNAL CO., LTD. 11 HIRAIDE-KOGIO-DANCHI UISUNOMIYA TOCHIGI 321-8651 JAPAN	009037 (base 16)	ACUCOMM, INC. 4633 OLD IRONSIDES - STE #310 SANTA CLARA CA 95054
00-90-29 (hex)	CRYPTO AG	00-90-38 (hex)	FOUNTAIN TECHNOLOGIES, INC.
009029 (base 16)	CRYPTO AG P.O. BOX CH-6301 ZUG SWITZERLAND		
00-90-2A (hex)	COMMUNICATION DEVICES, INC.		

company_id	Organization Address
009038 (base 16)	FOUNTAIN TECHNOLOGIES, INC. 50 RANDOLPH ROAD SOMERSET NJ 08873
00-90-39 (hex)	SHASTA NETWORKS
009039 (base 16)	SHASTA NETWORKS 249 HUMBOLDT COURT SUNNYVALE CA 94089-1300
00-90-3A (hex)	NIHON MEDIA TOOL INC.
00903A (base 16)	NIHON MEDIA TOOL INC. 1875 OYAMA-CHO YOKKAICHI-CITY MIE 512-1102 JAPAN
00-90-3B (hex)	TRIEMS RESEARCH LAB, INC.
00903B (base 16)	TRIEMS RESEARCH LAB, INC. 1275 N. TUSTIN AVENUE ANAHEIM CA 92807
00-90-3C (hex)	ATLANTIC NETWORK SYSTEMS
00903C (base 16)	ATLANTIC NETWORK SYSTEMS IMMEUBLE «KENNEDY» ZITER AVENUE JF KENNEDY 33700 MERIGNAC FRANCE
00-90-3D (hex)	BIOPAC SYSTEMS, INC.
00903D (base 16)	BIOPAC SYSTEMS, INC. 42 AERO CAMINO SANTA BARBARA CA 93117
00-90-3E (hex)	N.V. PHILIPS INDUSTRIAL
00903E (base 16)	N.V. PHILIPS INDUSTRIAL ACTIVITIES INTERLEUVENLAAN 74-76 B-3001 LEUVEN BELGIUM
00-90-3F (hex)	AZTEC RADIOMEDIA
00903F (base 16)	AZTEC RADIOMEDIA 31, RUE DU CHEMIN DE FER 67200 STRASBOURG FRANCE
00-90-40 (hex)	CASTLE NETWORKS, INC.
009040 (base 16)	CASTLE NETWORKS, INC. 235 LITTLETON RD - UNIT #2 WESTFORD MA 01886
00-90-41 (hex)	APPLIED DIGITAL ACCESS
009041 (base 16)	APPLIED DIGITAL ACCESS 9855 SCRANTON ROAD SAN DIEGO CA 92121
00-90-42 (hex)	ECCS
009042 (base 16)	ECCS ONE SHEILA DRIVE TINTON FALLS NJ 07724
00-90-43 (hex)	NICHIBEI DENSHI CO., LTD.
009043 (base 16)	NICHIBEI DENSHI CO., LTD. 1-13-10 SHIROGANE CHUO-KU FUKUOKA-CITY JAPAN
00-90-44 (hex)	ASSURED DIGITAL, INC.
009044 (base 16)	ASSURED DIGITAL, INC. 9-11 GOLDSMITH ST. LITTLETON MA 01460
00-90-45 (hex)	MARIPOSA TECHNOLOGY
009045 (base 16)	MARIPOSA TECHNOLOGY 1129 N. MC DOWELL BLVD. PETALUMA CA 94954
00-90-46 (hex)	DEXDYNE, LTD.
009046 (base 16)	DEXDYNE, LTD. 15 MARKET PL. CIRENCESTER GLOCESTERSHIRE UNITED KINGDOM GL7 2PB
00-90-47 (hex)	GIGA FAST E. LTD.

company_id	Organization Address
009047 (base 16)	GIGA FAST E. LTD. 14F, NO.112, SEC. 1 HSIN-TAI WU RD., HSICHIH TAIPEI HSIEN TAIWAN, R.O.C.
00-90-48 (hex)	ZEAL CORPORATION
009048 (base 16)	ZEAL CORPORATION 301, HIRAIKE NAGAKUTE-CHO, AICHI-PREF. 480-1155 JAPAN
00-90-49 (hex)	ENTRIDIA CORPORATION
009049 (base 16)	ENTRIDIA CORPORATION 101 PARK CENTER PLAZA SUITE #500 SAN JOSE CA 95113-2218
00-90-4A (hex)	CONCUR SYSTEM TECHNOLOGIES
00904A (base 16)	CONCUR SYSTEM TECHNOLOGIES 2525 WALLINGWOOD DR.-STE. #804 AUSTIN TX 78746
00-90-4B (hex)	GEMTEK TECHNOLOGY CO., LTD.
00904B (base 16)	GEMTEK TECHNOLOGY CO., LTD. 11 FL, NO.181,TATUNG RD, SEC 1 HSICHIH, TAIPEI HSIEN TAIWAN, R.O.C.
00-90-4C (hex)	EPIGRAM, INC.
00904C (base 16)	EPIGRAM, INC. 870 WEST MAUDE AVE. SUNNYVALE CA 94086
00-90-4D (hex)	SPEC S.A.
00904D (base 16)	SPEC S.A. CASP 172 3-B 08013 BARCELONA SPAIN
00-90-4E (hex)	DELEM BV
00904E (base 16)	DELEM BV LUCHTHAVEN WEG 42 5657 EB EINDHOVEN THE NETHERLANDS
00-90-4F (hex)	ABB POWER T&D COMPANY, INC.
00904F (base 16)	ABB POWER T&D COMPANY, INC. 7036 SNOWDRIFT ROAD ALLENTOWN PA 18106
00-90-50 (hex)	TELESTE OY
009050 (base 16)	TELESTE OY SEPONKATU 1 FIN-20660 LITTOINEN FINLAND
00-90-51 (hex)	ULTIMATE TECHNOLOGY CORP.
009051 (base 16)	ULTIMATE TECHNOLOGY CORP. 100 RAWSON ROAD VICTOR NY 14564
00-90-52 (hex)	SELCOM ELETTRONICA S.R.L.
009052 (base 16)	SELCOM ELETTRONICA S.R.L. VIA GRANDI, 5 40013 CASTELMAGGIORE BO ITALY
00-90-53 (hex)	DAEWOO ELECTRONICS CO., LTD.
009053 (base 16)	DAEWOO ELECTRONICS CO., LTD. DIT RESEARCH CENTER DAEWOO CENTER 541 NAMDAEMUNNO 5-GA CHUNG-GU, SEOUL, 100-714 KOREA
00-90-54 (hex)	INNOVATIVE SEMICONDUCTORS, INC
009054 (base 16)	INNOVATIVE SEMICONDUCTORS, INC 2570 W. EL CAMINO REAL SUITE #205 MOUNTAIN VIEW CA 94040
00-90-55 (hex)	PARKER HANNIFIN CORPORATION

company_id	Organization Address
009055 (base 16)	PARKER HANNIFIN CORPORATION COMPUMOTOR DIVISION 5500 BUSINESS PARK DRIVE ROHNERT PARK CA 94928
00-90-56 (hex)	TELESTREAM, INC.
009056 (base 16)	TELESTREAM, INC. 848 GOLD FLAT RD., SUITE 1 NEVADA CITY CA 95959
00-90-57 (hex)	AANETCOM, INC.
009057 (base 16)	AANETCOM, INC. 4949 LIBERTY LANE - STE. #200 ALLENTOWN PA 18106-9015
00-90-58 (hex)	ULTRA ELECTRONICS LTD.
009058 (base 16)	ULTRA ELECTRONICS LTD. KNAVES BEECH BUSINESS CENTRE LOUDWATER, HIGH WYCOMBE BUCKINGHAMSHIRE HP10 9UT ENGLAND
00-90-59 (hex)	TELECOM DEVICE K.K.
009059 (base 16)	TELECOM DEVICE K.K. SANMIYANAGA BLDG. 3F, 1-5-12 MOTOAKASAKA, MINATO-KU TOKYO 107 JAPAN
00-90-5A (hex)	DEARBORN GROUP, INC.
00905A (base 16)	DEARBORN GROUP, INC. 27007 HILLS TECH CT. FARMINGTON HILLS MI 48331
00-90-5B (hex)	RAYMOND AND LAE ENGINEERING
00905B (base 16)	RAYMOND AND LAE ENGINEERING 208 COMMERCE DR., UNIT #3C FORT COLLINS CO 80524
00-90-5C (hex)	EDMI
00905C (base 16)	EDMI 626 OLD GYMPIE ROAD NARANGBA QLD 4504 AUSTRALIA
00-90-5D (hex)	NETCOM SICHERHEITSTECHNIK GMBH
00905D (base 16)	NETCOM SICHERHEITSTECHNIK GMBH BOPPSTRASSE 38 55118 MAINZ GERMANY
00-90-5E (hex)	RAULAND-BORG CORPORATION
00905E (base 16)	RAULAND-BORG CORPORATION 3450 W. OAKTON ST. SKOKIE IL 60076
00-90-5F (hex)	CISCO SYSTEMS, INC.
00905F (base 16)	CISCO SYSTEMS, INC. SJA-2 170 W. TASMAN DRIVE SAN JOSE CA 95134-1706
00-90-60 (hex)	SYSTEM CREATE CORP.
009060 (base 16)	SYSTEM CREATE CORP. 3-13-6 YOSHIKAWA BLD. KINSHI SUMIDA KU TOKYO JAPAN
00-90-61 (hex)	PACIFIC RESEARCH & ENGINEERING
009061 (base 16)	PACIFIC RESEARCH & ENGINEERING CORPORATION 2070 LAS PALMAS DRIVE CARLSBAD CA 92009
00-90-62 (hex)	ICP VORTEX COMPUTERSYSTEME
009062 (base 16)	ICP VORTEX COMPUTERSYSTEME GMBH FALTERSTRASSE 51-53 D 74223 FLEIN GERMANY
00-90-63 (hex)	COHERENT COMMUNICATIONS

company_id	Organization Address
009063 (base 16)	COHERENT COMMUNICATIONS SYSTEMS CORPORATION 45085 UNIVERSITY DRIVE ASHBURN VA 20147
00-90-64 (hex)	THOMSON BROADCAST SYSTEMS
009064 (base 16)	THOMSON BROADCAST SYSTEMS RUE DU CLOS COURTEL 35517 CESSON SEVIGNE CEDEX FRANCE
00-90-65 (hex)	FINISAR CORPORATION
009065 (base 16)	FINISAR CORPORATION 274 FERGUSON DRIVE MOUNTAIN VIEW CA 94043
00-90-66 (hex)	TROIKA DESIGN, INC.
009066 (base 16)	TROIKA DESIGN, INC. 4510 E. THOUSAND OAKS BLVD. SUITE #201 WESTLAKE VILLAGE CA 91362
00-90-67 (hex)	WALKABOUT COMPUTERS, INC.
009067 (base 16)	WALKABOUT COMPUTERS, INC. 2655 N. OCEAN DRIVE—STE. #510 SINGER ISLAND FL 33404
00-90-68 (hex)	DVT CORP.
009068 (base 16)	DVT CORP. 1670 OAKBROOK DR. - STE. #330 NORCROSS GA 30093
00-90-69 (hex)	JUNIPER NETWORKS, INC.
009069 (base 16)	JUNIPER NETWORKS, INC. 1194 N. Mathilda Avenue Sunnyvale, CA 94089-1206
00-90-6A (hex)	TURNSTONE SYSTEMS, INC.
00906A (base 16)	TURNSTONE SYSTEMS, INC. 274 Ferguson Drive, MOUNTAIN VIEW CA 94043
00-90-6B (hex)	APPLIED RESOURCES, INC.
00906B (base 16)	APPLIED RESOURCES, INC. 9821 WIDMER ROAD LENEXA KS 66215-1239
00-90-6C (hex)	GWT GLOBAL WEIGHING
00906C (base 16)	GWT GLOBAL WEIGHING TECHNOLOGIES GMBH MEIENDORFER STR. 205 22145 HAMBURG GERMANY
00-90-6D (hex)	CISCO SYSTEMS, INC.
00906D (base 16)	CISCO SYSTEMS, INC. 170 W. TASMAN DR. - SJA-2 SAN JOSE CA 95134-1706
00-90-6E (hex)	PRAXON, INC.
00906E (base 16)	PRAXON, INC. 1700 DELL AVENUE CAMPBELL CA 95008
00-90-6F (hex)	CISCO SYSTEMS, INC.
00906F (base 16)	CISCO SYSTEMS, INC. 170 W. TASMAN DR. - SJA-2 SAN JOSE CA 95134-1706
00-90-70 (hex)	NEO NETWORKS, INC.
009070 (base 16)	NEO NETWORKS, INC. 10300 BREN ROAD EAST MINNETONKA MN 55343
00-90-71 (hex)	BADGER TECHNOLOGY, INC.
009071 (base 16)	BADGER TECHNOLOGY, INC. 1423 SOUTH MILPITAS BLVD. MILPITAS CA 95035-6828
00-90-72 (hex)	SIMRAD AS
009072 (base 16)	SIMRAD AS P.O. BOX 111 3191 HORTEN NORWAY
00-90-73 (hex)	GAIO TECHNOLOGY

company_id	Organization Address
009073 (base 16)	GAIO TECHNOLOGY OAK-YOKOHAMA BLDG. 2-15-10 KITA-SAIWAI, NISHI-KU YOKOHAMA-CITY, KANAGAWA JAPAN
00-90-74 (hex)	ARGON NETWORKS, INC.
009074 (base 16)	ARGON NETWORKS, INC. 25 PORTER ROAD LITTLETON MA 01460
00-90-75 (hex)	NEC DO BRASIL S.A.
009075 (base 16)	NEC DO BRASIL S.A. RODOVIA PRESIDENTE DUTRA,KM218 CUMBICA-GUARULHOS-SAO PAULO-SP CEP - 07210-902 BRAZIL
00-90-76 (hex)	FMT AIRCRAFT GATE SUPPORT
009076 (base 16)	FMT AIRCRAFT GATE SUPPORT SYSTEMS AB DALASLINGAN 8 SE-231 32 TRELLEBORG SWEDEN
00-90-77 (hex)	ADVANCED FIBRE COMMUNICATIONS
009077 (base 16)	ADVANCED FIBRE COMMUNICATIONS PO BOX #751239 1 WILLOWBROOK CT PETALUMA CA 94975
00-90-78 (hex)	MER TELEMANAGEMENT
009078 (base 16)	MER TELEMANAGEMENT SOLUTIONS, LTD. 5 HATSOREF STR. IND. AREA HOLON ISRAEL
00-90-79 (hex)	CLEARONE INC.
009079 (base 16)	CLEARONE INC. 299 WASHINGTON STREET WOBURN MA 01801
00-90-7A (hex)	SPECTRALINK CORP.
00907A (base 16)	SPECTRALINK CORP. 5755 CENTRAL AVENUE BOULDER CO 80301
00-90-7B (hex)	E-TECH, INC.
00907B (base 16)	E-TECH, INC. 30, R&D ROAD 2 SCIENCE PARK, HSINCHU TAIWAN, R.O.C.
00-90-7C (hex)	DIGITALCAST, INC.
00907C (base 16)	DIGITALCAST, INC. 503,ILKWANG BLDG., 1656-2 SEOCHO-DONG, SEOCHO-KU SEOUL KOREA
00-90-7D (hex)	HOME WIRELESS NETWORKS
00907D (base 16)	HOME WIRELESS NETWORKS 3145 AVALON RIDGE PL. NORCROSS GA 30071
00-90-7E (hex)	VETRONIX CORP.
00907E (base 16)	VETRONIX CORP. 2030 ALAMEDE PADRE SERRA SANTA BARBARA CA 93103
00-90-7F (hex)	WATCHGUARD TECHNOLOGIES, INC.
00907F (base 16)	WATCHGUARD TECHNOLOGIES, INC. 316 OCCIDENTAL AVE. S. SUITE #200 SEATTLE WA 98104
00-90-80 (hex)	NOT LIMITED, INC.
009080 (base 16)	NOT LIMITED, INC. 500 ALLERTON STREET, STE #102 REDWOOD CITY CA 94063
00-90-81 (hex)	ALOHA NETWORKS, INC.

company_id	Organization Address
009081 (base 16)	ALOHA NETWORKS, INC. 1001A O'REILLY AVENUE P.O. BOX 29472 SAN FRANCISCO CA 94129-0472
00-90-82 (hex)	FORCE INSTITUTE
009082 (base 16)	FORCE INSTITUTE PARK ALLE 345 DK-2605 BROENDBY DENMARK
00-90-83 (hex)	TURBO COMMUNICATION, INC.
009083 (base 16)	TURBO COMMUNICATION, INC. 4F-2, NO. 171, SUNG-TEH ROAD TAIPEI TAIWAN, R.O.C.
00-90-84 (hex)	ATECH SYSTEM
009084 (base 16)	ATECH SYSTEM 4F DAEBOONG BLDG. 1451-78 SEOCHO-DONG SEOCHO-KU SEOUL 137-070 KOREA
00-90-85 (hex)	GOLDEN ENTERPRISES, INC.
009085 (base 16)	GOLDEN ENTERPRISES, INC. 4450 WEST EAU GALLIE BLVD. 250 PERIMETER CENTER MELBOURNE FL 32934
00-90-86 (hex)	CISCO SYSTEMS, INC.
009086 (base 16)	CISCO SYSTEMS, INC. 170 W. TASMAN DR. - SJA-2 SAN JOSE CA 95134-1706
00-90-87 (hex)	ITIS
009087 (base 16)	ITIS CENTRE ESPACE PERFORMANCE ALPHASIS-BATIMENT C1 35769 SAINT-GREGOIRE CEDEX FRANCE
00-90-88 (hex)	BAXALL SECURITY LTD.
009088 (base 16)	BAXALL SECURITY LTD. UNIT 1 CASTLEHILL HORSEFIELD WAY BREDBURY PARK INDUST'L ESTATE STOCKPORT, SK6 2SU, G. BRITAIN
00-90-89 (hex)	SOFTCOM MICROSYSTEMS, INC.
009089 (base 16)	SOFTCOM MICROSYSTEMS, INC. 47509 SEABRIDGE DRIVE FREMONT CA 94538
00-90-8A (hex)	BAYLY COMMUNICATIONS, INC.
00908A (base 16)	BAYLY COMMUNICATIONS, INC. 105 GREEN COURT AJAX, ONTARIO CANADA, L1S 6W9
00-90-8B (hex)	CELL COMPUTING, INC.
00908B (base 16)	CELL COMPUTING, INC. 2099 GATEWAY PLACE - #750 SAN JOSE CA 95110
00-90-8C (hex)	ETREND ELECTRONICS, INC.
00908C (base 16)	ETREND ELECTRONICS, INC. 2F, 22 INDUSTRY E. 9TH ROAD HSINCHU SCIENCE PARK TAIWAN
00-90-8D (hex)	VICKERS ELECTRONICS SYSTEMS
00908D (base 16)	VICKERS ELECTRONICS SYSTEMS 1151 W. MASON-MORROW RD. LEBANON OH 45036
00-90-8E (hex)	Nortel Networks Broadband Access
00908E (base 16)	Nortel Networks Broadband Access 39660 Eureka Drive Newark, CA 94560
00-90-8F (hex)	AUDIOCODES LTD.

company_id	Organization Address	company_id	Organization Address
00908F (base 16)	AUDIOCODES LTD. 3A NETANYAHU STREET OR YEHUDA 60256 ISRAEL	00909E (base 16)	DELPHI ENGINEERING GROUP 485 EAST 17TH ST., STE #400 COSTA MESA CA 92627
00-90-90 (hex)	I-BUS	00-90-9F (hex)	DIGI-DATA CORPORATION
009090 (base 16)	I-BUS 9174 SKY PARK COURT SAN DIEGO CA 92123	00909F (base 16)	DIGI-DATA CORPORATION 8580 DORSEY RUN ROAD JESSUP MD 20794
00-90-91 (hex)	DIGITALSCAPE, INC.	00-90-A0 (hex)	8X8 INC.
009091 (base 16)	DIGITALSCAPE, INC. 6 MORGAN - STE.#100 IRVINE CA 92618	0090A0 (base 16)	8X8 INC. 2445 MISSION COLLEGE BLVD. SANTA CLARA CA 95054
00-90-92 (hex)	CISCO SYSTEMS, INC.	00-90-A1 (hex)	FLYING PIG SYSTEMS, LTD.
009092 (base 16)	CISCO SYSTEMS, INC. 170 W. TASMAN DRIVE M/S SJA-2 SAN JOSE CA 95134-1706	0090A1 (base 16)	FLYING PIG SYSTEMS, LTD. 53 NORTHFIELD ROAD LONDON W13 9SY ENGLAND
00-90-93 (hex)	NANAO CORPORATION	00-90-A2 (hex)	CYBERTAN TECHNOLOGY, INC.
009093 (base 16)	NANAO CORPORATION 153 SHIMOKASHIWANO, MATTO ISHIKAWA 924-8566 JAPAN	0090A2 (base 16)	CYBERTAN TECHNOLOGY, INC. BLDG.53, 195-56 SEC. 4, CHUNG HSING ROAD, CHUTUNG, HSINCHU TAIWAN, R.O.C.
00-90-94 (hex)	OSPREY TECHNOLOGIES, INC.	00-90-A3 (hex)	MEDIALINCS CO., LTD.
009094 (base 16)	OSPREY TECHNOLOGIES, INC. 600 AIRPORT BLVD. - STE. #900 MORRISVILLE NC 27560	0090A3 (base 16)	MEDIALINCS CO., LTD. 3F JOHUN BLDG., 834-46 YOKSAM-DONG, KANGNAM-GU SEOUL, 135-080 KOREA
00-90-95 (hex)	UNIVERSAL AVIONICS	00-90-A4 (hex)	ALTIGA NETWORKS
009095 (base 16)	UNIVERSAL AVIONICS 11351 WILLOWS ROAD NE REDMOND WA 98052-2552	0090A4 (base 16)	ALTIGA NETWORKS 124 GROVE STREET FRANKLIN MA 02038-3206
00-90-96 (hex)	ASKEY COMPUTER CORP.	00-90-A5 (hex)	SPECTRA LOGIC
009096 (base 16)	ASKEY COMPUTER CORP. 2F, NO. 2, LANE 497 CHUNG-CHENG RD., HSIN-TIEN TAIPEI 23136 TAIWAN	0090A5 (base 16)	SPECTRA LOGIC 1700 N. 55TH STREET BOULDER CO 80301
00-90-97 (hex)	SYCAMORE NETWORKS	00-90-A6 (hex)	CISCO SYSTEMS, INC.
009097 (base 16)	SYCAMORE NETWORKS 2 HIGHWOOD DRIVE TEWKSBURY MA 01876	0090A6 (base 16)	CISCO SYSTEMS, INC. 170 W. TASMAN DR. - SJA-2 SAN JOSE CA 95134-1706
00-90-98 (hex)	SBC DESIGNS, INC.	00-90-A7 (hex)	CLIENTEC CORPORATION
009098 (base 16)	SBC DESIGNS, INC. 3077-H LEEMAN FERRY ROAD HUNTSVILLE AL 35801	0090A7 (base 16)	CLIENTEC CORPORATION 8175 S. VIRGINIA ST. SUITE #850-249 RENO NV 89511
00-90-99 (hex)	ALLIED TELESIS,K.K.	00-90-A8 (hex)	NINETILES NETWORKS LTD.
009099 (base 16)	ALLIED TELESIS,K.K. NO. 2 TOC BUILDING, 7-21-11 MISHI-GOTANDA, SHINAGAWA-KU TOKYO 141 JAPAN	0090A8 (base 16)	NINETILES NETWORKS LTD. 25 GREENSIDE WATERBEACH, CAMBRIDGE CB5 9HW UNITED KINGDOM
00-90-9A (hex)	ONE WORLD SYSTEMS, INC.	00-90-A9 (hex)	WESTERN DIGITAL
00909A (base 16)	ONE WORLD SYSTEMS, INC. 1144 EAST ARQUES AVENUE SUNNYVALE CA 94086	0090A9 (base 16)	WESTERN DIGITAL 1599 NORTH BROADWAY ROCHESTER MN 55906
00-90-9B (hex)	MARKPOINT AB	00-90-AA (hex)	INDIGO ACTIVE VISION
00909B (base 16)	MARKPOINT AB SATERIGATAN 20 417 64 GOTEBORG SWEDEN	0090AA (base 16)	INDIGO ACTIVE VISION SYSTEMS LIMITED THE EDINBURGH TECHNOPOLE BUSH LOAN, EDINBURGH EH26 OPJ, UNITED KINGDOM
00-90-9C (hex)	COMBOX, LTD.	00-90-AB (hex)	CISCO SYSTEMS, INC.
00909C (base 16)	COMBOX, LTD. 16 BAZEL STREET P.O. BOX 10186 PETACH TIKVA 49001 ISRAEL	0090AB (base 16)	CISCO SYSTEMS, INC. 170 W. TASMAN DRIVE SJA-2 SAN JOSE CA 95134-1706
00-90-9D (hex)	GSE SYSTEMS, INC.	00-90-AC (hex)	OPTIVISION, INC.
00909D (base 16)	GSE SYSTEMS, INC. 7133 RUTHERFORD RD.–STE. #200 BALTIMORE MD 21244	0090AC (base 16)	OPTIVISION, INC. 3450 HILLVIEW AVENUE PALO ALTO CA 94304
00-90-9E (hex)	DELPHI ENGINEERING GROUP	00-90-AD (hex)	ASPECT ELECTRONICS, INC.

company_id	Organization Address
0090AD (base 16)	ASPECT ELECTRONICS, INC. 12740 EARHART AVE. AUBURN CA 95602
00-90-AE (hex)	ITALTEL SPA
0090AE (base 16)	ITALTEL SPA LOCALITA BOSCHETTO 67100 L'AQUILA ITALY
00-90-AF (hex)	J. MORITA MFG. CORP.
0090AF (base 16)	J. MORITA MFG. CORP. 680 HIGASHIHAMA MINAMI-CHO FUSHIMI-KU, KYOTO 612-8213 JAPAN
00-90-B0 (hex)	VADEM
0090B0 (base 16)	VADEM 1960 ZANKER RD SAN JOSE CA 95112
00-90-B1 (hex)	CISCO SYSTEMS, INC.
0090B1 (base 16)	CISCO SYSTEMS, INC. 170 W. TASMAN DR. - SJA-2 SAN JOSE CA 95134-1706
00-90-B2 (hex)	AVICI SYSTEMS INC.
0090B2 (base 16)	AVICI SYSTEMS INC. 12 ELIZABETH DRIVE CHELMSFORD MA 01824
00-90-B3 (hex)	AGRANAT SYSTEMS
0090B3 (base 16)	AGRANAT SYSTEMS 1345 MAIN STREET WALTHAM MA 02154
00-90-B4 (hex)	WILLOWBROOK TECHNOLOGIES
0090B4 (base 16)	WILLOWBROOK TECHNOLOGIES 7120 HAYVENHURST AVE.-STE.#401 VAN NUYS CA 91406
00-90-B5 (hex)	NIKON CORPORATION
0090B5 (base 16)	NIKON CORPORATION ELECTR. IMAGING DESIGN DEPT. 1-6-3, NISHI-OHI, SHINAGAWA-KU TOKYO 140-8601 JAPAN
00-90-B6 (hex)	FIBEX SYSTEMS
0090B6 (base 16)	FIBEX SYSTEMS 5350 OLD REDWOOD HIGHWAY PETALUMA CA 94954
00-90-B7 (hex)	DIGITAL LIGHTWAVE, INC.
0090B7 (base 16)	DIGITAL LIGHTWAVE, INC. 601 CLEVELAND STREET- 5TH FL. CLEARWATER FL 33755
00-90-B8 (hex)	ROHDE & SCHWARZ GMBH & CO. KG
0090B8 (base 16)	ROHDE & SCHWARZ GMBH & CO. KG POSTFACH: 80 14 69/ABT.: 3CK D-81614 MUNCHEN GERMANY
00-90-B9 (hex)	BERAN INSTRUMENTS LTD.
0090B9 (base 16)	BERAN INSTRUMENTS LTD. HATCHMOOR INDUSTRIAL ESTATE TORRINGTON N DEVON EX38 7HP UNITED KINGDOM
00-90-BA (hex)	VALID NETWORKS, INC.
0090BA (base 16)	VALID NETWORKS, INC. 6 CROMWELL #102 IRVINE CA 92618
00-90-BB (hex)	TAINET COMMUNICATION SYSTEM
0090BB (base 16)	TAINET COMMUNICATION SYSTEM CORPORATION 3 FL, NO. 6, ALLEY 23, LANE 91 SEC. 1, NEI-HU ROAD, TAIPEI TAIWAN
00-90-BC (hex)	TELEMANN CO., LTD.

company_id	Organization Address
0090BC (base 16)	TELEMANN CO., LTD. 6F DONGSIN BLDG. 543, DOGOK-DONG, KANGNAM-KU SEOUL, 135-270 KOREA
00-90-BD (hex)	OMNIA COMMUNICATIONS, INC.
0090BD (base 16)	OMNIA COMMUNICATIONS, INC. 100 NICKERSON ROAD MARLBOROUGH MA 01752
00-90-BE (hex)	IBC/INTEGRATED BUSINESS
0090BE (base 16)	IBC/INTEGRATED BUSINESS COMPUTERS 2685 C PARK CENTER DRIVE SIMI VALLEY CA 93065
00-90-BF (hex)	CISCO SYSTEMS, INC.
0090BF (base 16)	CISCO SYSTEMS, INC. 170 W. TASMAN DRIVE SJA-2 SAN JOSE CA 95134-1706
00-90-C0 (hex)	K.J. LAW ENGINEERS, INC.
0090C0 (base 16)	K.J. LAW ENGINEERS, INC. 42300 W. NINE MILE ROAD NOVI MI 48375
00-90-C1 (hex)	EDA INDUSTRIES
0090C1 (base 16)	EDA INDUSTRIES 7020A HUNTLEY ROAD COLUMBUS OH 43229
00-90-C2 (hex)	JK MICROSYSTEMS, INC.
0090C2 (base 16)	JK MICROSYSTEMS, INC. 1275 YUBA AVENUE SAN PABLO CA 94806
00-90-C3 (hex)	TOPIC SEMICONDUCTOR CORP.
0090C3 (base 16)	TOPIC SEMICONDUCTOR CORP. 11F-1, NO. 2, WU-LIN RD HSIN-CHU TAIWAN, R.O.C.
00-90-C4 (hex)	JAVELIN SYSTEMS, INC.
0090C4 (base 16)	JAVELIN SYSTEMS, INC. 1881 LANGLEY AVE. IRVINE CA 92614
00-90-C5 (hex)	INTERNET MAGIC, INC.
0090C5 (base 16)	INTERNET MAGIC, INC. 6450 LUSK BLVD.-STE. #E-201 SAN DIEGO CA 92121
00-90-C6 (hex)	OPTIM SYSTEMS, INC.
0090C6 (base 16)	OPTIM SYSTEMS, INC. 8201 GREENSBORO DR.-STE. #1000 MCLEAN VA 22102
00-90-C7 (hex)	ICOM INC.
0090C7 (base 16)	ICOM INC. 6-9-16 KAMIHIGASHI HIRANO-KU, OSAKA JAPAN
00-90-C8 (hex)	WAVERIDER COMMUNICATIONS
0090C8 (base 16)	WAVERIDER COMMUNICATIONS (CANADA) INC. 6120-1 A STREET SW CALGARY, AB T2H 0G3, CANADA
00-90-C9 (hex)	PRODUCTIVITY ENHANCEMENT
0090C9 (base 16)	PRODUCTIVITY ENHANCEMENT PRODUCTS., INC. 26072 MERIT CIRCLE - STE. #110 LAGUNA HILLS CA 92653
00-90-CA (hex)	ACCORD VIDEO
0090CA (base 16)	ACCORD VIDEO TELECOMMUNICATIONS, LTD. 10 MARTIN GEHL STR, P.O. BOX 3564, PETACH-TIKVA 49130 ISRAEL
00-90-CB (hex)	WIRELESS ONLINE, INC.

company_id	Organization Address
0090CB (base 16)	WIRELESS ONLINE, INC. 4410 EL CAMINO REAL, STE #101 LOS ALTOS CA 94022
00-90-CC (hex)	PLANEX COMMUNICATIONS, INC.
0090CC (base 16)	PLANEX COMMUNICATIONS, INC. 5F, KANDA-TAKAHASHI BLDG. 1-7, KANDA-SUDACHO CHIYODA-KU, TOKYO JAPAN 101-0041
00-90-CD (hex)	ENT-EMPRESA NACIONAL
0090CD (base 16)	ENT-EMPRESA NACIONAL DE TELECOMMUNICACOES, S.A. R. ENG FREDERICO ULRICH APARTADO 3081 - GUARDEIRAS 4470 MOREIRA MAIA PORTUGAL
00-90-CE (hex)	TETRA GMBH
0090CE (base 16)	TETRA GMBH GEWERBEPARK «AM WALD» 4 D-98693 ILMENAU GERMANY
00-90-CF (hex)	NORTEL
0090CF (base 16)	NORTEL 250 SIDNEY STREET BELLEVILLE, ONTARIO CANADA K8N 5B7
00-90-D0 (hex)	ALCATEL BELL
0090D0 (base 16)	ALCATEL BELL FRANCIS WELLESPLEIN 1 B-2018 ANTWERP BELGIUM
00-90-D1 (hex)	LEICHU ENTERPRISE CO., LTD.
0090D1 (base 16)	LEICHU ENTERPRISE CO., LTD. 8F, NO. 203, PA-TEH ROAD,SEC.2 TAIPEI CITY TAIWAN R.O.C.
00-90-D2 (hex)	ARTEL VIDEO SYSTEMS
0090D2 (base 16)	ARTEL VIDEO SYSTEMS 237 CEDAR HILL ST. MARLBORO MA 01752
00-90-D3 (hex)	GIESECKE & DEVRIENT GMBH
0090D3 (base 16)	GIESECKE & DEVRIENT GMBH PRINZREGENTENSTRASSE 159 D-81677 MUNCHEN GERMANY
00-90-D4 (hex)	BINDVIEW DEVELOPMENT CORP.
0090D4 (base 16)	BINDVIEW DEVELOPMENT CORP. 3355 WEST ALABAMA #1200 HOUSTON TX 77098
00-90-D5 (hex)	EUPHONIX, INC.
0090D5 (base 16)	EUPHONIX, INC. 220 PORTAGE AVE. PALO ALTO CA 94306
00-90-D6 (hex)	CRYSTAL GROUP
0090D6 (base 16)	CRYSTAL GROUP 850 KACENA RD. HIAWATHA IA 52233
00-90-D7 (hex)	NETBOOST CORP.
0090D7 (base 16)	NETBOOST CORP. 390 CAMBRIDGE AVENUE PALO ALTO CA 94306-1506
00-90-D8 (hex)	WHITECROSS SYSTEMS
0090D8 (base 16)	WHITECROSS SYSTEMS 3A WATERSIDE PARK, COOKHAM RD BRACKNELL, BERKSHIRE RG12 1RB UNITED KINGDOM
00-90-D9 (hex)	CISCO SYSTEMS, INC.
0090D9 (base 16)	CISCO SYSTEMS, INC. 170 W. TASMAN DRIVE M/S/ SJA-2 SAN JOSE CA 95134-1706

company_id	Organization Address
00-90-DA (hex)	DYNARC, INC.
0090DA (base 16)	DYNARC, INC. 1887 LANDINGS DRIVE MOUNTAIN VIEW CA 94043
00-90-DB (hex)	NEXT LEVEL COMMUNICATIONS
0090DB (base 16)	NEXT LEVEL COMMUNICATIONS 6085 STATE FARM DRIVE ROHNERT PARK CA 94928
00-90-DC (hex)	TECO INFORMATION SYSTEMS
0090DC (base 16)	TECO INFORMATION SYSTEMS CO., LTD. 2841 JUNCTION AVE., STE. #116 SAN JOSE CA 95134
00-90-DD (hex)	THE MIHARU COMMUNICATIONS
0090DD (base 16)	THE MIHARU COMMUNICATIONS CO., LTD. 1285, IWASE, KAMAKURA-CITY KANAGAWA JAPAN
00-90-DE (hex)	CARDKEY SYSTEMS, INC.
0090DE (base 16)	CARDKEY SYSTEMS, INC. 1757 TAPO CANYON ROAD SIMI VALLEY CA 93063
00-90-DF (hex)	MITSUBISHI CHEMICAL
0090DF (base 16)	MITSUBISHI CHEMICAL AMERICA, INC. 445 INDIO WAY SUNNYVALE CA 94086
00-90-E0 (hex)	SYSTRAN CORP.
0090E0 (base 16)	SYSTRAN CORP. 4126 LINDEN AVENUE DAYTON OH 45432
00-90-E1 (hex)	TELENA S.P.A.
0090E1 (base 16)	TELENA S.P.A. VIA SAVONA, 146 20144 MILANO ITALY
00-90-E2 (hex)	DISTRIBUTED PROCESSING
0090E2 (base 16)	DISTRIBUTED PROCESSING TECHNOLOGY 140 CANDACE DRIVE ORLANDO FL 32751
00-90-E3 (hex)	AVEX ELECTRONICS INC.
0090E3 (base 16)	AVEX ELECTRONICS INC. 4807 BRADFORD DRIVE HUNTSVILLE AL 35805
00-90-E4 (hex)	NEC AMERICA, INC.
0090E4 (base 16)	NEC AMERICA, INC. 3100 N.E. SHUTE ROAD HILLSBORO OR 97124
00-90-E5 (hex)	TEKNEMA, INC.
0090E5 (base 16)	TEKNEMA, INC. 2656 E. BAYSHORE ROAD PALO ALTO CA 94303
00-90-E6 (hex)	ACER LABORATORIES, INC.
0090E6 (base 16)	ACER LABORATORIES, INC. 11F, 45 TUNG HSING ROAD TAIPEI 110 TAIWAN, R.O.C.
00-90-E7 (hex)	HORSCH ELEKTRONIK AG
0090E7 (base 16)	HORSCH ELEKTRONIK AG HAAGERSTRASSE POSTFACH CH-9473 GAMS SWITZERLAND
00-90-E8 (hex)	MOXA TECHNOLOGIES CORP., LTD.

company_id	Organization Address
0090E8 (base 16)	MOXA TECHNOLOGIES CORP., LTD. 7F, NO. 2, ALY6, LN 235 PAO-CHIAO RD, SHIENG-TIEN CITY TAIPEI TAIWAN, R.O.C.
00-90-E9 (hex)	JANZ COMPUTER AG
0090E9 (base 16)	JANZ COMPUTER AG LM DOERENER FELD 8 D-33100 PADERBORN GERMANY
00-90-EA (hex)	ALPHA TECHNOLOGIES, INC.
0090EA (base 16)	ALPHA TECHNOLOGIES, INC. 3767 ALPHA WAY BELLINGHAM WA 98226
00-90-EB (hex)	SENTRY TELECOM SYSTEMS
0090EB (base 16)	SENTRY TELECOM SYSTEMS 8664 COMMERCE COURT BURNABY, BC V5A 4N7 CANADA
00-90-EC (hex)	PYRESCOM
0090EC (base 16)	PYRESCOM 3 ALLEE DU MOULIN 66680 CANOHES FRANCE
00-90-ED (hex)	CENTRAL SYSTEM RESEARCH
0090ED (base 16)	CENTRAL SYSTEM RESEARCH CO., LTD. 4-13-2 HIYOSHICHO KOKUBUNJI-CITY TOKYO JAPAN 185-0032
00-90-EE (hex)	PERSONAL COMMUNICATIONS
0090EE (base 16)	PERSONAL COMMUNICATIONS TECHNOLOGIES 50 STILES ROAD SALEM NH 03079
00-90-EF (hex)	INTEGRIX, INC.
0090EF (base 16)	INTEGRIX, INC. 2001 CORPORATE CENTER DRIVE NEWBURY PARK CA 91320
00-90-F0 (hex)	HARMONIC LIGHTWAVES, LTD.
0090F0 (base 16)	HARMONIC LIGHTWAVES, LTD. 19 ALON HATAVOR STREET CAESAREA 38900 ISRAEL
00-90-F1 (hex)	DOT HILL SYSTEMS CORPORATION
0090F1 (base 16)	DOT HILL SYSTEMS CORPORATION 6305 El Camino Real Carlsbad, CA 92009
00-90-F2 (hex)	CISCO SYSTEMS, INC.
0090F2 (base 16)	CISCO SYSTEMS, INC. 170 W. TASMAN DRIVE - SJA-2 SAN JOSE CA 95134-1706
00-90-F3 (hex)	ASPECT COMMUNICATIONS
0090F3 (base 16)	ASPECT COMMUNICATIONS 1310 Ridder Park Drive San Jose CA 95131-2313
00-90-F4 (hex)	LIGHTNING INSTRUMENTATION
0090F4 (base 16)	LIGHTNING INSTRUMENTATION BOVERESSES 50 1010 LAUSANNE SWITZERLAND
00-90-F5 (hex)	CLEVO CO.
0090F5 (base 16)	CLEVO CO. 35, WU-GON 6TH ROAD WU-KU INDUSTRIAL PARK TAIPEI HSIEN TAIWAN, R.O.C.
00-90-F6 (hex)	ESCALATE NETWORKS, INC.

company_id	Organization Address
0090F6 (base 16)	ESCALATE NETWORKS, INC. 6 HUGHES IRVINE CA 92617
00-90-F7 (hex)	NBASE COMMUNICATIONS LTD.
0090F7 (base 16)	NBASE COMMUNICATIONS LTD. INDUSTRIAL PARK YOQNEAM ILIT P.O. BOX 114 ISRAEL
00-90-F8 (hex)	MEDIATRIX TELECOM
0090F8 (base 16)	MEDIATRIX TELECOM 4229 GARLOCK SHERBROOKE, QUEBEC J1L 2C8 CANADA
00-90-F9 (hex)	LEITCH
0090F9 (base 16)	LEITCH 10 DYAS ROAD DON MILLS, ONTARIO M3B 1V5 CANADA
00-90-FA (hex)	GIGANET, INC.
0090FA (base 16)	GIGANET, INC. 2352 MAIN STREET STE #108 CONCORD MA 01742
00-90-FB (hex)	PORTWELL, INC.
0090FB (base 16)	PORTWELL, INC. 7F-4, NO. 160, SEC. 6 MING-CHUANG E. RD., TAIPEI TAIWAN
00-90-FC (hex)	NETWORK COMPUTING DEVICES
0090FC (base 16)	NETWORK COMPUTING DEVICES 301 RAVENDALE DRIVE MOUNTAIN VIEW CA 94043
00-90-FD (hex)	COPPERCOM, INC.
0090FD (base 16)	COPPERCOM, INC. 3255-1 SCOTT BLVD., STE. #103 SANTA CLARA CA 95054
00-90-FE (hex)	ELECOM CO., LTD. (LANEED DIV.)
0090FE (base 16)	ELECOM CO., LTD. (LANEED DIV.) SUMITOMO FUDOSAN HIGASHI IKEBUKURO BLDG. 6F, 3-13-2 HIGASHI IKEBUKURO TOSHIMA-KU, TOKYO, JAPAN
00-90-FF (hex)	TELLUS TECHNOLOGY INC.
0090FF (base 16)	TELLUS TECHNOLOGY INC. 40990 ENCYCLOPEDIA CIR. FREMONT CA 94538-2470
00-9D-8E (hex)	CARDIAC RECORDERS, INC.
009D8E (base 16)	CARDIAC RECORDERS, INC. 34 SCARBORO DRIVE LONDON N4 4L U UNITED KINGDOM
00-A0-00 (hex)	CENTILLION NETWORKS, INC.
00A000 (base 16)	CENTILLION NETWORKS, INC. 359 RAVENDALE DRIVE MOUNTAIN VIEW CA 94043
00-A0-01 (hex)	WATKINS-JOHNSON COMPANY
00A001 (base 16)	WATKINS-JOHNSON COMPANY 700 QUINCE ORCHARD RD. GAITHERSBURG MD 20878-1794
00-A0-02 (hex)	LEEDS & NORTHRUP AUSTRALIA
00A002 (base 16)	LEEDS & NORTHRUP AUSTRALIA PTY LTD PO BOX 4009 EIGHT MILE PLAINS QLD 4113 AUSTRALIA
00-A0-03 (hex)	STAEFA CONTROL SYSTEM

company_id	Organization Address
00A003 (base 16)	STAEFA CONTROL SYSTEM LAUBISRUTI 50 8712 STAEFA SWITZERLAND
00-A0-04 (hex)	NETPOWER, INC.
00A004 (base 16)	NETPOWER, INC. 545 OAKMEAD PARKWAY SUNNYVALE CA 94086
00-A0-05 (hex)	DANIEL INSTRUMENTS, LTD.
00A005 (base 16)	DANIEL INSTRUMENTS, LTD. TROLLSTRASSE 33 CH-8400 WINTERTHUR SWITZERLAND
00-A0-06 (hex)	IMAGE DATA PROCESSING
00A006 (base 16)	IMAGE DATA PROCESSING SYSTEM GROUP SHINTOYOFUTA 2-1 KASHIWA-CITY, CHIBA 277 JAPAN
00-A0-07 (hex)	APEXX TECHNOLOGY, INC.
00A007 (base 16)	APEXX TECHNOLOGY, INC. 506 S. 11TH PO BOX 9291 BOISE ID 83707
00-A0-08 (hex)	NETCORP
00A008 (base 16)	NETCORP 8 PLACE OF COMMERCE—STE #200 BROSSARD, QUEBEC CANADA J4W 3H2
00-A0-09 (hex)	WHITETREE NETWORK
00A009 (base 16)	WHITETREE NETWORK TECHNOLOGIES, INC. 3200 ASH STREET PALO ALTO CA 94306
00-A0-0A (hex)	R.D.C. COMMUNICATION
00A00A (base 16)	R.D.C. COMMUNICATION 11 BEIT HADFUS STREET JERUSALEM 95483 ISRAEL
00-A0-0B (hex)	COMPUTEX CO., LTD.
00A00B (base 16)	COMPUTEX CO., LTD. 432-13 GOJYOBASHI-HIGASHI 4-CHYOME HIGASHIYAMAKU, KYOTO-CITY 605 JAPAN
00-A0-0C (hex)	KINGMAX TECHNOLOGY, INC.
00A00C (base 16)	KINGMAX TECHNOLOGY, INC. 2FL., NO. 4, LANE 902, SEC.2 KUANG FU RD., HSIN-CHU CITY TAIWAN, R.O.C.
00-A0-0D (hex)	THE PANDA PROJECT
00A00D (base 16)	THE PANDA PROJECT 5201 CONGRESS AVE. - C-100 BOCA RATON FL 33487
00-A0-0E (hex)	VISUAL NETWORKS, INC.
00A00E (base 16)	VISUAL NETWORKS, INC. 2092 GAITHER ROAD- STE #220 ROCKVILLE MD 20850
00-A0-0F (hex)	Broadband Technologies
00A00F (base 16)	Broadband Technologies P.O. Box 13737 Research Triangle Park, North Carolina 27709-3737
00-A0-10 (hex)	SYSLOGIC DATENTECHNIK AG
00A010 (base 16)	SYSLOGIC DATENTECHNIK AG HEIMSTRASSE 46 CH-8953 DIETIKON SWITZERLAND
00-A0-11 (hex)	MUTOH INDUSTRIES LTD.

company_id	Organization Address
00A011 (base 16)	MUTOH INDUSTRIES LTD. 253 KANAGAWA-KEN, CHIGASAKI-SHI SHIMOMACHIYA 1-3-1 JAPAN
00-A0-12 (hex)	B.A.T.M. ADVANCED TECHNOLOGIES
00A012 (base 16)	B.A.T.M. ADVANCED TECHNOLOGIES P.O. BOX 203 YOKNEAM ELIT 20692 ISRAEL
00-A0-13 (hex)	TELTREND LTD.
00A013 (base 16)	TELTREND LTD. RINGWAY HOUSE,BELL ROAD DANESHILL, BASINGSTOKE HAMPSHIRE RG24 8FB UNITED KINGDOM
00-A0-14 (hex)	CSIR
00A014 (base 16)	CSIR P.O. BOX 395 PRETORIA 0001 SOUTH AFRICA
00-A0-15 (hex)	WYLE
00A015 (base 16)	WYLE 3000 BOWERS AVENUE SANTA CLARA CA 95051
00-A0-16 (hex)	MICROPOLIS CORP.
00A016 (base 16)	MICROPOLIS CORP. 21211 NORDHOFF STREET CHATSWORTH CA 91311
00-A0-17 (hex)	J B M CORPORATION
00A017 (base 16)	J B M CORPORATION 10-1, ARAMOTOSHIN MACHI HIGASHI OSAKA 577 JAPAN
00-A0-18 (hex)	CREATIVE CONTROLLERS, INC.
00A018 (base 16)	CREATIVE CONTROLLERS, INC. 128 KENDRICK LANE PICAYUNE MS 39466
00-A0-19 (hex)	NEBULA CONSULTANTS, INC.
00A019 (base 16)	NEBULA CONSULTANTS, INC. 1449 DUNCAN DRIVE DELTA, BC CANADA V4L 1R5
00-A0-1A (hex)	BINAR ELEKTRONIK AB
00A01A (base 16)	BINAR ELEKTRONIK AB MAGNETUAGEN 18 S-46138 TROLLHATTAN SWEDEN
00-A0-1B (hex)	PREMISYS COMMUNICATIONS, INC.
00A01B (base 16)	PREMISYS COMMUNICATIONS, INC. 48664 MILMONT DRIVE FREMONT CA 94538
00-A0-1C (hex)	NASCENT NETWORKS CORPORATION
00A01C (base 16)	NASCENT NETWORKS CORPORATION 277 MAIN STREET, 3RD FLR. MARLBORO MA 01752
00-A0-1D (hex)	SIXNET
00A01D (base 16)	SIXNET P.O. BOX 767 CLIFTON PARK NY 12065
00-A0-1E (hex)	EST CORPORATION
00A01E (base 16)	EST CORPORATION 120 ROYALL STREET CANTON MA 02021
00-A0-1F (hex)	TRICORD SYSTEMS, INC.
00A01F (base 16)	TRICORD SYSTEMS, INC. 2800 NORTHWEST BOULEVARD PLYMOUTH MN 55441-2625
00-A0-20 (hex)	CITICORP/TTI

827

company_id	Organization Address
00A020 (base 16)	CITICORP/TTI 3100 OCEAN PARK BLVD. SANTA MONICA CA 90405
00-A0-21 (hex)	GENERAL DYNAMICS-
00A021 (base 16)	GENERAL DYNAMICS- COMMUNICATION SYSTEMS 77 «A» STREET- BLDG. #8 NEEDHAM HEIGHTS MA 02494-2892
00-A0-22 (hex)	CENTRE FOR DEVELOPMENT OF
00A022 (base 16)	CENTRE FOR DEVELOPMENT OF ADVANCED COMPUTING UNIVERSITY OF POONA CAMPUS GANESH KHIND, PUNE - 411008 INDIA
00-A0-23 (hex)	APPLIED CREATIVE TECHNOLOGY,
00A023 (base 16)	APPLIED CREATIVE TECHNOLOGY, INC. 2626 LOMBARDY LANE–STE.#107 DALLAS TX 75220
00-A0-24 (hex)	3COM CORPORATION
00A024 (base 16)	3COM CORPORATION 5400 BAYFRONT PLAZA SANTA CLARA CA 95052
00-A0-25 (hex)	REDCOM LABS INC.
00A025 (base 16)	REDCOM LABS INC. ONE REDCOM CENTER VICTOR NY 14564-0995
00-A0-26 (hex)	TELDAT, S.A.
00A026 (base 16)	TELDAT, S.A. PARQUE TECNOLOGICO MADRID 28760 TACS CAN TOS (MADRID) SPAIN
00-A0-27 (hex)	FIREPOWER SYSTEMS, INC.
00A027 (base 16)	FIREPOWER SYSTEMS, INC. 190 INDEPENDENCE DRIVE MENLO PARK CA 94025
00-A0-28 (hex)	CONNER PERIPHERALS
00A028 (base 16)	CONNER PERIPHERALS 3061 ZANKER ROAD SAN JOSE CA 95134-2128
00-A0-29 (hex)	COULTER CORPORATION
00A029 (base 16)	COULTER CORPORATION 11800 S.W. 147TH AVE. MIAMI FL 33196
00-A0-2A (hex)	TRANCELL SYSTEMS
00A02A (base 16)	TRANCELL SYSTEMS 3180 DE LA CRUZ BLVD.-STE#200 SANTA CLARA CA 95054-2402
00-A0-2B (hex)	TRANSITIONS RESEARCH CORP.
00A02B (base 16)	TRANSITIONS RESEARCH CORP. SHELTER ROCK LANE DANBURY CT 06810
00-A0-2C (hex)	INTERWAVE COMMUNICATIONS
00A02C (base 16)	INTERWAVE COMMUNICATIONS 656 BAIR ISLAND BLVD.-STE.#108 REDWOOD CITY CA 94063-2704
00-A0-2D (hex)	SKIPSTONE, INC.
00A02D (base 16)	SKIPSTONE, INC. 3925 WEST BRAKER LANE AUSTIN TX 78759
00-A0-2E (hex)	BRAND COMMUNICATIONS, LTD.
00A02E (base 16)	BRAND COMMUNICATIONS, LTD. ENTERPRISE HOUSE, CHIVERS WAY, HISTON, CAMBRIDGE CB44ZR ENGLAND
00-A0-2F (hex)	PIRELLI CAVI
00A02F (base 16)	PIRELLI CAVI VIALE SARCA 222 20126 MILAN ITALY

company_id	Organization Address
00-A0-30 (hex)	CAPTOR NV/SA
00A030 (base 16)	CAPTOR NV/SA DE HENE 13 B-1780 WEMMEL BELGIUM
00-A0-31 (hex)	HAZELTINE CORPORATION, MS 1-17
00A031 (base 16)	HAZELTINE CORPORATION, MS 1-17 450 E. PULASKI ROAD GREENLAWN NY 11740
00-A0-32 (hex)	GES SINGAPORE PTE. LTD.
00A032 (base 16)	GES SINGAPORE PTE. LTD. 14 SUNGEI KADUT AVENUE SINGAPORE 2572
00 A0 33 (hex)	IMC MESS SYSTEME GMBH
00A033 (base 16)	IMC MESS-SYSTEME GMBH VOLTASTRASSE 5 D-13355 BERLIN GERMANY
00-A0-34 (hex)	AXEL
00A034 (base 16)	AXEL 16, AVENUE DU QUEBEC Z.A. COURTABOEUF 91962 LES ULIS FRANCE
00-A0-35 (hex)	CYLINK CORPORATION
00A035 (base 16)	CYLINK CORPORATION 910 HERMOSA COURT SUNNYVALE CA 94086
00-A0-36 (hex)	APPLIED NETWORK TECHNOLOGY
00A036 (base 16)	APPLIED NETWORK TECHNOLOGY 319 LITTLETON ROAD–STE #101 WESTFORD MA 01886-4133
00-A0-37 (hex)	DATASCOPE CORPORATION
00A037 (base 16)	DATASCOPE CORPORATION 580 WINTERS AVENUE PARAMUS NJ 07653-0005
00-A0-38 (hex)	EMAIL ELECTRONICS
00A038 (base 16)	EMAIL ELECTRONICS P.O. BOX 154 MOOROOLBARK, 3138 AUSTRALIA
00-A0-39 (hex)	ROSS TECHNOLOGY, INC.
00A039 (base 16)	ROSS TECHNOLOGY, INC. 5316 HWY 290 WEST - STE. #500 AUSTIN TX 78735
00-A0-3A (hex)	KUBOTEK CORPORATION
00A03A (base 16)	KUBOTEK CORPORATION 56 NISHIAKETA-CHO, HIGASHIKUJO MINAMI-KU, KYOTO 601 JAPAN
00-A0-3B (hex)	TOSHIN ELECTRIC CO., LTD.
00A03B (base 16)	TOSHIN ELECTRIC CO., LTD. 3FL. RIVER-STONE 3RD. BLG.234 MIZONOKUCHI, TAKATSU-KV, KAWASAKI-SHI, KANAGAWA 213 JAPAN
00-A0-3C (hex)	EG&G NUCLEAR INSTRUMENTS
00A03C (base 16)	EG&G NUCLEAR INSTRUMENTS 100 MIDLAND ROAD OAK RIDGE TN 37830
00-A0-3D (hex)	OPTO - 22
00A03D (base 16)	OPTO - 22 43044 BUSINESS PARK DR. TEMECULA CA 92590
00-A0-3E (hex)	ATM FORUM
00A03E (base 16)	ATM FORUM WORLDWIDE HEADQUARTERS 303 VINTAGE PARK DRIVE FOSTER CITY CA 94404-1138
00-A0-3F (hex)	COMPUTER SOCIETY MICROPROCES'R

company_id	Organization Address
00A03F (base 16)	COMPUTER SOCIETY MICROPROCES'R & MICROPRO'R STDS COMMITTEE APPLE COMPUTER, INC. 1 INFINITE LOOP, MS:301-4G CUPERTINO CA 95014
00-A0-40 (hex)	APPLE COMPUTER
00A040 (base 16)	APPLE COMPUTER 20650 VALLEY GREEN DRIVE CUPERTINO CA 95014
00-A0-41 (hex)	LEYBOLD-INFICON
00A041 (base 16)	LEYBOLD-INFICON 2 TECHNOLOGY PLACE EAST SYRACUSE NY 13057
00-A0-42 (hex)	SPUR PRODUCTS CORP.
00A042 (base 16)	SPUR PRODUCTS CORP. 9288 W. EMERALD STREET BOISE ID 83704
00-A0-43 (hex)	AMERICAN TECHNOLOGY LABS, INC.
00A043 (base 16)	AMERICAN TECHNOLOGY LABS, INC. 115 WEST 3RD STREET LOWER LEVEL STEVENSVILLE MT 59870
00-A0-44 (hex)	NTT INTELLIGENT TECHNOLOGY
00A044 (base 16)	NTT INTELLIGENT TECHNOLOGY CO., LTD. KANNAI-WISE BLDG., 2-9-1 FUROU-CHO, NAKA-KU, YOKOHAMA 231 JAPAN
00-A0-45 (hex)	PHOENIX CONTACT GMBH & CO.
00A045 (base 16)	PHOENIX CONTACT GMBH & CO. POSTFACH 1341 D-32819 BLOMBERG GERMANY
00-A0-46 (hex)	SCITEX CORP. LTD.
00A046 (base 16)	SCITEX CORP. LTD. P.O.BOX 330 HERZLIA B 46103 ISRAEL
00-A0-47 (hex)	INTEGRATED FITNESS CORP.
00A047 (base 16)	INTEGRATED FITNESS CORP. 26 6TH STREET STAMFORD CT 06905
00-A0-48 (hex)	QUESTECH, LTD.
00A048 (base 16)	QUESTECH, LTD. EASTHEATH AVENUE WOKINGHAM BERKS, RG11 2PP, UNITED KINGDOM
00-A0-49 (hex)	DIGITECH INDUSTRIES, INC.
00A049 (base 16)	DIGITECH INDUSTRIES, INC. PO BOX 2267 55 KENOSIA AVENUE DANBURY CT 06810
00-A0-4A (hex)	NISSHIN ELECTRIC CO., LTD.
00A04A (base 16)	NISSHIN ELECTRIC CO., LTD. 5, MEOTOGOSHI, MUTSUSHI, SHIKATSU-CYO, NISHIKASUGAI, AICHI 481 JAPAN
00-A0-4B (hex)	TFL LAN INC.
00A04B (base 16)	TFL LAN INC. 9F, NO. 499 CHUNG CHENG ROAD SHIH-LIN DISTRICT, TAIPEI TAIWAN, R.O.C.
00-A0-4C (hex)	INNOVATIVE SYSTEMS & TECH. INC
00A04C (base 16)	INNOVATIVE SYSTEMS & TECH. INC 48511 WARM SPRINGS BLVD. SUITE # 211C FREMONT CA 94539
00-A0-4D (hex)	EDA INSTRUMENTS, INC.

company_id	Organization Address
00A04D (base 16)	EDA INSTRUMENTS, INC. 4 THORNCLIFFE PARK DRIVE TORONTO, ONTARIO CANADA M4H 1H1
00-A0-4E (hex)	VOELKER TECHNOLOGIES, INC.
00A04E (base 16)	VOELKER TECHNOLOGIES, INC. 22 NEW BOSTON COURT DANVILLE CA 94526
00-A0-4F (hex)	AMERITEC CORP.
00A04F (base 16)	AMERITEC CORP. 760 ARROW GRAND CIRCLE COVINA CA 91722
00-A0-50 (hex)	CYPRESS SEMICONDUCTOR
00A050 (base 16)	CYPRESS SEMICONDUCTOR 3901 NORTH FIRST STREET SAN JOSE CA 95134
00-A0-51 (hex)	ANGIA COMMUNICATIONS. INC.
00A051 (base 16)	ANGIA COMMUNICATIONS. INC. 441 EAST BAY BLVD. PROVO UTAH 84606
00-A0-52 (hex)	STANILITE ELECTRONICS PTY. LTD
00A052 (base 16)	STANILITE ELECTRONICS PTY. LTD 424, LANE COVE ROAD NORTH RYDE NSW 2113 AUSTRALIA
00-A0-53 (hex)	COMPACT DEVICES, INC.
00A053 (base 16)	COMPACT DEVICES, INC. 16795 LARK AVENUE LOS GATOS CA 95030
00-A0-55 (hex)	LINKTECH, INC.
00A055 (base 16)	LINKTECH, INC. 30 ORVILLE DRIVE BOHEMIA NY 11716
00-A0-56 (hex)	MICROPROSS
00A056 (base 16)	MICROPROSS 33, RUE GANTOIS 59000 LILLE FRANCE
00-A0-57 (hex)	ELSA AG
00A057 (base 16)	ELSA AG SONNENWEG 11 D-52070 AACHEN GERMANY
00-A0-58 (hex)	GLORY, LTD.
00A058 (base 16)	GLORY, LTD. 1-3-1 SHIMOTENO, HIMEJI HYOGO PREF. JAPAN 670
00-A0-59 (hex)	HAMILTON HALLMARK
00A059 (base 16)	HAMILTON HALLMARK 2105 LUNDY AVENUE SAN JOSE CA 95131
00-A0-5A (hex)	KOFAX IMAGE PRODUCTS
00A05A (base 16)	KOFAX IMAGE PRODUCTS 3 JENNER STREET IRVINE CA 92718-3807
00-A0-5B (hex)	MARQUIP, INC.
00A05B (base 16)	MARQUIP, INC. 1245 E. WASHINGTON AVE. MADISON WI 53703
00-A0-5C (hex)	INVENTORY CONVERSION, INC.
00A05C (base 16)	INVENTORY CONVERSION, INC. NEKOTECH DIVISION 102 TIDE MILL ROAD -SUITE # 6 HAMPTON NH 03842
00-A0-5D (hex)	CS COMPUTER SYSTEME GMBH
00A05D (base 16)	CS COMPUTER SYSTEME GMBH ISARSTRASSE 3, 82065 BAIERBRUNN GERMANY

company_id	Organization Address
00-A0-5E (hex)	MYRIAD LOGIC INC.
00A05E (base 16)	MYRIAD LOGIC INC. 1109 SPRING STREET SILVER SPRING MD 20910
00-A0-5F (hex)	BTG ENGINEERING BV
00A05F (base 16)	BTG ENGINEERING BV P.O. BOX 5417 3299 ZG MAASDAM THE NETHERLANDS
00-A0-60 (hex)	ACER PERIPHERALS, INC.
00A060 (base 16)	ACER PERIPHERALS, INC. 9F, 135 CHIAN KUO N. RD. SEC 2 TAIPEI, 10479 TAIWAN, R.O.C.
00-A0-61 (hex)	PURITAN BENNETT
00A061 (base 16)	PURITAN BENNETT 2200 FARADAY AVENUE CARLSBAD CA 92008
00-A0-62 (hex)	AES PRODATA
00A062 (base 16)	AES PRODATA 249 BALCATTA ROAD BALCATTA WESTERN AUSTRALIA 6021
00-A0-63 (hex)	JRL SYSTEMS, INC.
00A063 (base 16)	JRL SYSTEMS, INC. 8305 HWY 71 WEST AUSTIN TX 78735
00-A0-64 (hex)	KVB/ANALECT
00A064 (base 16)	KVB/ANALECT 9420 JERONIMO ROAD IRVINE CA 92718
00-A0-65 (hex)	NEXLAND, INC.
00A065 (base 16)	NEXLAND, INC. P.O. BOX 9096 DAYTONA BEACH FL 32120
00-A0-66 (hex)	ISA CO., LTD.
00A066 (base 16)	ISA CO., LTD. SHINJUKU LAMBDAX BLDG. 5F., 2-4-12 OKUBO, SHINJUKU-KU TOKYO JAPAN
00-A0-67 (hex)	NETWORK SERVICES GROUP
00A067 (base 16)	NETWORK SERVICES GROUP 3421 COMMISSION COURT-STE #202 WOODBRIDGE VA 22192
00-A0-68 (hex)	BHP LIMITED
00A068 (base 16)	BHP LIMITED GPO BOX 86A MELBOURNE 3001 VICTORIA AUSTRALIA
00-A0-69 (hex)	TRUETIME
00A069 (base 16)	TRUETIME 2835 DUKE COURT SANTA ROSA CA 95407
00-A0-6A (hex)	VERILINK CORP.
00A06A (base 16)	VERILINK CORP. 145 BAYTECH DRIVE SAN JOSE CA 95134
00-A0-6B (hex)	DMS DORSCH MIKROSYSTEM GMBH
00A06B (base 16)	DMS DORSCH MIKROSYSTEM GMBH HOLMLUECK 13-15 D-24972 STEINBERQKIRCHE GERMANY
00-A0-6C (hex)	SHINDENGEN ELECTRIC MFG.
00A06C (base 16)	SHINDENGEN ELECTRIC MFG. CO., LTD. 10-13, MINAMI-CHO, HANNOU-CITY SAITAMA 357 JAPAN

company_id	Organization Address
00-A0-6D (hex)	MANNESMANN TALLY CORPORATION
00A06D (base 16)	MANNESMANN TALLY CORPORATION P.O. BOX 97018 KENT WA 98064-9718
00-A0-6E (hex)	AUSTRON, INC.
00A06E (base 16)	AUSTRON, INC. P.O. BOX 14766 AUSTIN TX 78761-4766
00-A0-6F (hex)	THE APPCON GROUP, INC.
00A06F (base 16)	THE APPCON GROUP, INC. 23 RICHMOND STREET ROCHESTER NY 14607
00-A0-70 (hex)	COASTCOM
00A070 (base 16)	COASTCOM 1151 HARBOR BAY PARKWAY ALAMEDA CA 94502-6511
00-A0-71 (hex)	VIDEO LOTTERY TECHNOLOGIES,INC
00A071 (base 16)	VIDEO LOTTERY TECHNOLOGIES,INC 2311 SOUTH 7TH AVENUE BOZEMAN MT 59715
00-A0-72 (hex)	OVATION SYSTEMS LTD.
00A072 (base 16)	OVATION SYSTEMS LTD. GREAT HASELEY TRAD. EST. GREAT HASELEY, OXFORDSHIRE OX9 7PF ENGLAND
00-A0-73 (hex)	COM21, INC.
00A073 (base 16)	COM21, INC. 2113 LANDINGS DRIVE MOUNTAIN VIEW CA 94043
00-A0-74 (hex)	PERCEPTION TECHNOLOGY
00A074 (base 16)	PERCEPTION TECHNOLOGY 40 SHAWMUT ROAD CANTON MA 02021-1409
00-A0-75 (hex)	MICRON TECHNOLOGY, INC.
00A075 (base 16)	MICRON TECHNOLOGY, INC. 2359 WALNUT STREET ROSEVILLE MN 55113
00-A0-76 (hex)	CARDWARE LAB, INC.
00A076 (base 16)	CARDWARE LAB, INC. 285 SOBRANTE WAY, STE. «K» SUNNYVALE CA 94086
00-A0-77 (hex)	FUJITSU NEXION, INC.
00A077 (base 16)	FUJITSU NEXION, INC. 289 GREAT ROAD ACTON MA 01720-4739
00-A0-78 (hex)	CELLACCESS TECHNOLOGY, INC.
00A078 (base 16)	CELLACCESS TECHNOLOGY, INC. 761 UNIVERSITY AVE., STE.»B» LOS GATOS CA 95030
00-A0-79 (hex)	ALPS ELECTRIC (USA), INC.
00A079 (base 16)	ALPS ELECTRIC (USA), INC. 3553 NORTH 1ST STREET SAN JOSE CA 95134
00-A0-7A (hex)	ADVANCED PERIPHERALS
00A07A (base 16)	ADVANCED PERIPHERALS TECHNOLOGIES, INC. KOJIMA BUILDING, 1031 FUJISAWA FUJISAWA-SHI, KANAGAWA-KEN 251, JAPAN
00-A0-7B (hex)	DAWN COMPUTER INCORPORATION
00A07B (base 16)	DAWN COMPUTER INCORPORATION 6 KEXUEYUAN SOUTH ROAD ZHONG GUAN CUN BEIJING 100080 PEOPLE'S REPUBLIC OF CHINA
00-A0-7C (hex)	TONYANG NYLON CO., LTD.

company_id	Organization Address
00A07C (base 16)	TONYANG NYLON CO., LTD. ELECTRONIC RESEARCH LAB 183, HOGE-DONG, DONGAN-GU ANYANG-CITY, KYUNGKI-DO 430-080, KOREA
00-A0-7D (hex)	SEEQ TECHNOLOGY, INC.
00A07D (base 16)	SEEQ TECHNOLOGY, INC. 47131 BAYSIDE PARKWAY FREMONT CA 94538
00-A0-7E (hex)	AVID TECHNOLOGY, INC.
00A07E (base 16)	AVID TECHNOLOGY, INC. METROPOLITAN TECHNOLOGY PARK ONE PARK WEST TEWKSBURY MA 01876
00-A0-7F (hex)	GSM-SYNTEL, LTD.
00A07F (base 16)	GSM-SYNTEL, LTD. VICTORIA WORKS, QUEENS MILL RD HUDDERSFIELD WEST YORKSHIRE HD1 3PG ENGLAND
00-A0-80 (hex)	ANTARES MICROSYSTEMS
00A080 (base 16)	ANTARES MICROSYSTEMS 160B ALBRIGHT WAY LOS GATOS CA 95030
00-A0-81 (hex)	ALCATEL DATA NETWORKS
00A081 (base 16)	ALCATEL DATA NETWORKS 12502 SUNRISE VALLEY DRIVE RESTON VA 22096
00-A0-82 (hex)	NKT ELEKTRONIK A/S
00A082 (base 16)	NKT ELEKTRONIK A/S NKT ALLE 85 DK-2605 BRONDBY DENMARK
00-A0-83 (hex)	ASIMMPHONY TURKEY
00A083 (base 16)	ASIMMPHONY TURKEY ELECTRONICS, LTD. #160.260 - 6651 ELMBRIDGE WAY RICHMOND B.C. CANADA V7C 4N1
00-A0-84 (hex)	DATAPLEX PTY. LTD.
00A084 (base 16)	DATAPLEX PTY. LTD. 234 WHITEHORSE ROAD BLACKBURN, VICTORIA 3130 AUSTRALIA
00-A0-86 (hex)	AMBER WAVE SYSTEMS, INC.
00A086 (base 16)	AMBER WAVE SYSTEMS, INC. 403 MASSACHUSETTS AVENUE SUITE #202 ACTON MA 01720
00-A0-87 (hex)	MITEL SEMICONDUCTOR, LTD.
00A087 (base 16)	MITEL SEMICONDUCTOR, LTD. DODDINGTON ROAD LINCOLN LN6 3LF UNITED KINGDOM
00-A0-88 (hex)	ESSENTIAL COMMUNICATIONS
00A088 (base 16)	ESSENTIAL COMMUNICATIONS 4374 ALEXANDER BLVD. NE-STE»T» ALBUQUERQUE NM 87107
00-A0-89 (hex)	XPOINT TECHNOLOGIES, INC.
00A089 (base 16)	XPOINT TECHNOLOGIES, INC. 902 CLINT MOORE RD.-STE#132 BOCA RATON FL 33487
00-A0-8A (hex)	BROOKTROUT TECHNOLOGY, INC.
00A08A (base 16)	BROOKTROUT TECHNOLOGY, INC. 144 GOULD STREET- SUITE #200 NEEDHAM MA 02194
00-A0-8B (hex)	ASTON ELECTRONIC DESIGNS LTD.

company_id	Organization Address
00A08B (base 16)	ASTON ELECTRONIC DESIGNS LTD. 123/127 DEEPCUT BRIDGE ROAD DEEPCUT, CAMBERLEY SURREY, GU16 6SD ENGLAND
00-A0-8C (hex)	MULTIMEDIA LANS, INC.
00A08C (base 16)	MULTIMEDIA LANS, INC. 5600 EXECUTIVE CENTER DRIVE SUITE #312 CHARLOTTE NC 28212
00-A0-8D (hex)	JACOMO CORPORATION
00A08D (base 16)	JACOMO CORPORATION 26900 E. PINK HILL ROAD INDEPENDENCE MO 64057
00-A0-8E (hex)	Nokia Internet Communications
00A08E (base 16)	Nokia Internet Communications 313 Fairchild Drive Mountain View, CA 94043
00-A0-8F (hex)	DESKNET SYSTEMS, INC.
00A08F (base 16)	DESKNET SYSTEMS, INC. 80 BUSINESS PARK DRIVE ARMONK NY 10504
00-A0-90 (hex)	TIMESTEP CORPORATION
00A090 (base 16)	TIMESTEP CORPORATION 359 TERRY FOX DRIVE KANATA, ONTARIO CANADA K2K 2E7
00-A0-91 (hex)	APPLICOM INTERNATIONAL
00A091 (base 16)	APPLICOM INTERNATIONAL 43, RUE MAZAGRAN 76320 CAUDEBEC-LES-ELBEUF FRANCE
00-A0-92 (hex)	H. BOLLMANN MANUFACTURERS, LTD
00A092 (base 16)	H. BOLLMANN MANUFACTURERS, LTD 26 VICTORIA WAY BURGESS HILL W. SUSSEX RH 15 9NF ENGLAND
00-A0-93 (hex)	B/E AEROSPACE
00A093 (base 16)	B/E AEROSPACE 17481 RED HILL IRVINE CA 92714-5630
00-A0-94 (hex)	COMSAT CORPORATION
00A094 (base 16)	COMSAT CORPORATION 22300 COMSAT DRIVE CLARKSBURG MD 20871-9475
00-A0-95 (hex)	ACACIA NETWORKS, INC.
00A095 (base 16)	ACACIA NETWORKS, INC. 831 WOBURN STREET WILMINGTON MA 01887
00-A0-96 (hex)	MITSUMI ELECTRIC CO., LTD.
00A096 (base 16)	MITSUMI ELECTRIC CO., LTD. 8-8-2, KOKURYO-CHO CHOFU-SHI TOKYO 182 JAPAN
00-A0-97 (hex)	JC INFORMATION SYSTEMS
00A097 (base 16)	JC INFORMATION SYSTEMS 4487 TECHNOLOGY DRIVE FREMONT CA 94538-6343
00-A0-98 (hex)	NETWORK APPLIANCE CORP.
00A098 (base 16)	NETWORK APPLIANCE CORP. 2770 SAN TOMAS EXPRESSWAY SANTA CLARA CA 95051
00-A0-99 (hex)	K-NET LTD.
00A099 (base 16)	K-NET LTD. SADDLERS HOUSE-100 READING RD. YATELEY, SURREY GU17 7RX ENGLAND

company_id	Organization Address
00-A0-9A (hex)	NIHON KOHDEN AMERICA
00A09A (base 16)	NIHON KOHDEN AMERICA 2446 DUPONT DRIVE IRVINE CA 92715
00-A0-9B (hex)	QPSX COMMUNICATIONS, LTD.
00A09B (base 16)	QPSX COMMUNICATIONS, LTD. 33 RICHARDSON STREET WEST PERTH 6005 WESTERN AUSTRALIA
00-A0-9C (hex)	XYPLEX, INC.
00A09C (base 16)	XYPLEX, INC. 25 FOSTER STREET LITTLETON MA 01460
00-A0-9D (hex)	JOHNATHON FREEMAN TECHNOLOGIES
00A09D (base 16)	JOHNATHON FREEMAN TECHNOLOGIES P.O. BOX 880114 SAN FRANCISCO CA 94188
00-A0-9E (hex)	ICTV
00A09E (base 16)	ICTV 14600 WINCHESTER BLVD. LOS GATOS CA 95030
00-A0-9F (hex)	COMMVISION CORP.
00A09F (base 16)	COMMVISION CORP. 510 LOGUE AVE. MOUNTAIN VIEW CA 94043
00-A0-A0 (hex)	COMPACT DATA, LTD.
00A0A0 (base 16)	COMPACT DATA, LTD. 58 DITTON WALK CAMBRIDGE CB5 8QE UNITED KINGDOM
00-A0-A1 (hex)	EPIC DATA INC.
00A0A1 (base 16)	EPIC DATA INC. 7280 RIVER ROAD RICHMOND, B.C. CANADA V6X 1X5
00-A0-A2 (hex)	DIGICOM S.P.A.
00A0A2 (base 16)	DIGICOM S.P.A. VIA VOLTA 39 21010 CARDANO AL CAMPO (VA) ITALY
00-A0-A3 (hex)	RELIABLE POWER METERS
00A0A3 (base 16)	RELIABLE POWER METERS 400 BLOSSOM HILL ROAD LOS GATOS CA 95032-4511
00-A0-A4 (hex)	MICROS SYSTEMS, INC.
00A0A4 (base 16)	MICROS SYSTEMS, INC. 12000 BALTIMORE AVENUE BELTSVILLE MD 20705
00-A0-A5 (hex)	TEKNOR MICROSYSTEME, INC.
00A0A5 (base 16)	TEKNOR MICROSYSTEME, INC. 616 CURE BOIVIN BOISBRIAND QUEBEC CANADA J7G 2A7
00-A0-A6 (hex)	M.I. SYSTEMS, K.K.
00A0A6 (base 16)	M.I. SYSTEMS, K.K. 1-20-9, HATA, IKEDA-SHI OSAKA JAPAN 563
00-A0-A7 (hex)	VORAX CORPORATION
00A0A7 (base 16)	VORAX CORPORATION 1031 EAST DUANE AVENUE, STE»H» SUNNYVLAE CA 94086
00-A0-A8 (hex)	RENEX CORPORATION
00A0A8 (base 16)	RENEX CORPORATION 2750 KILLARNEY DRIVE WOODBRIDGE VA 22192
00-A0-A9 (hex)	GN NETTEST (CANADA) INC.

company_id	Organization Address
00A0A9 (base 16)	GN NETTEST (CANADA) INC. NAVTEL DIVISION 55 RENFREW DRIVE MARKHAM, ONTARIO CANADA L3R 8H3
00-A0-AA (hex)	SPACELABS MEDICAL
00A0AA (base 16)	SPACELABS MEDICAL 15220 N.E. 40TH STREET—MS 14 REDMOND WA 98053
00-A0-AB (hex)	NETCS INFORMATIONSTECHNIK GMBH
00A0AB (base 16)	NETCS INFORMATIONSTECHNIK GMBH KATHARINENSTRASSE 17-18 D-10711 BERLIN, GERMANY
00-A0-AC (hex)	GILAT SATELLITE NETWORKS, LTD.
00A0AC (base 16)	GILAT SATELLITE NETWORKS, LTD. 24A HABARZEL STREET TEL AVIV 69710 ISRAEL
00-A0-AD (hex)	MARCONI SPA
00A0AD (base 16)	MARCONI SPA VIA NEGRONE, 1A 16153 GENOVA CORNIGLIANO ITALY
00-A0-AE (hex)	NUCOM SYSTEMS, INC.
00A0AE (base 16)	NUCOM SYSTEMS, INC. 9F-6, NO 4, LANE 609 CHUNG HSIN ROAD, SEC. 5, SAN CHUNG CITY, TAIPEI TAIWAN, R.O.C.
00-A0-AF (hex)	WMS INDUSTRIES
00A0AF (base 16)	WMS INDUSTRIES 3401 N. CALIFORNIA CHICAGO IL 60618
00-A0-B0 (hex)	I-O DATA DEVICE, INC.
00A0B0 (base 16)	I-O DATA DEVICE, INC. 24-1, SAKURADA-MACHI KANAZAWA, ISHIKAWA 920 JAPAN
00-A0-B1 (hex)	FIRST VIRTUAL CORPORATION
00A0B1 (base 16)	FIRST VIRTUAL CORPORATION 3393 OCTAVIUS DR.-STE.# 102 SANTA CLARA CA 95054
00-A0-B2 (hex)	SHIMA SEIKI
00A0B2 (base 16)	SHIMA SEIKI 85, SAKATA WAKAYAMA-CITY WAKAYAMA 641 JAPAN
00-A0-B3 (hex)	ZYKRONIX
00A0B3 (base 16)	ZYKRONIX 7248 SOUTH TUCSON WAY ENGLEWOOD CO 80112
00-A0-B4 (hex)	TEXAS MICROSYSTEMS, INC.
00A0B4 (base 16)	TEXAS MICROSYSTEMS, INC. 5959 CORPORATE DRIVE HOUSTON TX 77036
00-A0-B5 (hex)	3H TECHNOLOGY
00A0B5 (base 16)	3H TECHNOLOGY 3375 SCOTT BLVD. #336 SANTA CLARA CA 95054
00-A0-B6 (hex)	SANRITZ AUTOMATION CO., LTD.
00A0B6 (base 16)	SANRITZ AUTOMATION CO., LTD. 4-21 MINAMI NARUSE MACHIDA CITY TOKYO 194 JAPAN
00-A0-B7 (hex)	CORDANT, INC.
00A0B7 (base 16)	CORDANT, INC. 11400 COMMERCE PARK DR. RESTON VA 22091-1506

company_id	Organization Address
00-A0-B8 (hex)	SYMBIOS LOGIC INC.
00A0B8 (base 16)	SYMBIOS LOGIC INC. 3718 N. ROCK ROAD WICHITA KS 67226-1397
00-A0-B9 (hex)	EAGLE TECHNOLOGY, INC.
00A0B9 (base 16)	EAGLE TECHNOLOGY, INC. 6800 ORANGETHORPE AVE., UNIT A BUENA PARK CA 90620
00-A0-BA (hex)	PATTON ELECTRONICS CO.
00A0BA (base 16)	PATTON ELECTRONICS CO. 7622 RICKENBACKER DRIVE GAITHERSBURG MD 20879
00-A0-BB (hex)	HILAN GMBH
00A0BB (base 16)	HILAN GMBH HAID-UND-NEU-STRASSE 7 D-76131 KARLSRUHE GERMANY
00-A0-BC (hex)	VIASAT, INCORPORATED
00A0BC (base 16)	VIASAT, INCORPORATED 2290 COSMOS COURT CARLSBAD CA 92009
00-A0-BD (hex)	I-TECH CORP.
00A0BD (base 16)	I-TECH CORP. 10200 VALLEY VIEW ROAD EDEN PRAIRIE MN 55344
00-A0-BE (hex)	INTEGRATED CIRCUIT SYSTEMS,INC
00A0BE (base 16)	INTEGRATED CIRCUIT SYSTEMS,INC COMMUNICATIONS GROUP 1271 PARKMOOR AVENUE SAN JOSE CA 95126-3448
00-A0-BF (hex)	WIRELESS DATA GROUP MOTOROLA
00A0BF (base 16)	WIRELESS DATA GROUP MOTOROLA 1201 E. WILEY ROAD SCHAUMBURG IL 60173
00-A0-C0 (hex)	DIGITAL LINK CORP.
00A0C0 (base 16)	DIGITAL LINK CORP. 217 HUMBOLDT COURT SUNNYVALE CA 94089
00-A0-C1 (hex)	ORTIVUS MEDICAL AB
00A0C1 (base 16)	ORTIVUS MEDICAL AB BOX 513 S-18325 TABY SWEDEN
00-A0-C2 (hex)	R.A. SYSTEMS CO., LTD.
00A0C2 (base 16)	R.A. SYSTEMS CO., LTD. 1850-3 HIROOKANOMURA SHIOJIRI-SHI, NAGAMO 399-07 JAPAN
00-A0-C3 (hex)	UNICOMPUTER GMBH
00A0C3 (base 16)	UNICOMPUTER GMBH LIMBURGER STRASSE 48 D-61476 KRONBERG I.T.S. GERMANY
00-A0-C4 (hex)	CRISTIE ELECTRONICS LTD.
00A0C4 (base 16)	CRISTIE ELECTRONICS LTD. BOND'S MILL STONEHOUSE GLOUCESTERSHIRE GL10 3RG UNITED KINGDOM
00-A0-C5 (hex)	ZYXEL COMMUNICATION
00A0C5 (base 16)	ZYXEL COMMUNICATION 2ND FLR. 58 PARK AVENUE II SCIENCE BASED INDUSTRIAL PARK HSINCHU TAIWAN 30077
00-A0-C6 (hex)	QUALCOMM INCORPORATED
00A0C6 (base 16)	QUALCOMM INCORPORATED 6455 LUSK BLVD SAN DIEGO CA 92121
00-A0-C7 (hex)	TADIRAN TELECOMMUNICATIONS

company_id	Organization Address
00A0C7 (base 16)	TADIRAN TELECOMMUNICATIONS P.O. BOX 500 PETAH-TIKVA 49104 ISRAEL
00-A0-C8 (hex)	ADTRAN INC.
00A0C8 (base 16)	ADTRAN INC. 901 EXPLORER BLVD. HUNTSVILLE AL 35806-2807
00-A0-C9 (hex)	INTEL CORPORATION - HF1-06
00A0C9 (base 16)	INTEL CORPORATION - HF1-06 5200 NE ELAM YOUNG PARKWAY HILLSBORO OR 97124
00-A0-CA (hex)	FUJITSU DENSO LTD.
00A0CA (base 16)	FUJITSU DENSO LTD. 3055 ORCHARD DRIVE SAN JOSE CA 95134
00-A0-CB (hex)	ARK TELECOMMUNICATIONS, INC.
00A0CB (base 16)	ARK TELECOMMUNICATIONS, INC. 124 CARMEN LANE—SUITE «K» SANTA MARIA CA 93454
00-A0-CC (hex)	LITE-ON COMMUNICATIONS, INC.
00A0CC (base 16)	LITE-ON COMMUNICATIONS, INC. 720 S. HILLVIEW DRIVE MILPITAS CA 95035
00-A0-CD (hex)	DR. JOHANNES HEIDENHAIN GMBH
00A0CD (base 16)	DR. JOHANNES HEIDENHAIN GMBH DR.-JOHANNES-HEIDENHAIN STR. 83301 TRAUNREUT GERMANY
00-A0-CE (hex)	ASTROCOM CORPORATION
00A0CE (base 16)	ASTROCOM CORPORATION 2700 SUMMER ST. N.E. MINNEAPOLIS MN 55413
00-A0-CF (hex)	SOTAS, INC.
00A0CF (base 16)	SOTAS, INC. 2 RESEARCH PLACE, STE. «101» ROCKVILLE MD 20850
00-A0-D0 (hex)	TEN X TECHNOLOGY, INC.
00A0D0 (base 16)	TEN X TECHNOLOGY, INC. 13091 POND SPRINGS ROAD AUSTIN TX 78729
00-A0-D1 (hex)	INVENTEC CORPORATION
00A0D1 (base 16)	INVENTEC CORPORATION INVENTEC BUILDING 66 HOU-KANG STREET SHI-LIN DISTRICT, TAIPEI TAIWAN, R.O.C.
00-A0-D2 (hex)	ALLIED TELESIS INTERNATIONAL
00A0D2 (base 16)	ALLIED TELESIS INTERNATIONAL CORPORATION 950 KIFER ROAD SUNNYVALE CA 94086
00-A0-D3 (hex)	INSTEM COMPUTER SYSTEMS, LTD.
00A0D3 (base 16)	INSTEM COMPUTER SYSTEMS, LTD. WALTON INDUSTRIAL ESTATE STONE, STAFFORDSHIRE ST15 OLT UNITED KINGDOM
00-A0-D4 (hex)	RADIOLAN, INC.
00A0D4 (base 16)	RADIOLAN, INC. 454 DEGUIGNE DRIVE - STE «D» SUNNYVALE CA 94086
00-A0-D5 (hex)	SIERRA WIRELESS INC.
00A0D5 (base 16)	SIERRA WIRELESS INC. #260 - 13151 VANIER PLACE RICHMOND B.C. CANADA V6V 2J2
00-A0-D6 (hex)	SBE, INC.

company_id	Organization Address
00A0D6 (base 16)	SBE, INC. 4550 NORRIS CANYON ROAD SAN RAMON CA 94583-1369
00-A0-D7 (hex)	KASTEN CHASE APPLIED RESEARCH
00A0D7 (base 16)	KASTEN CHASE APPLIED RESEARCH 5100 ORBITOR DRIVE MISSISSAUGA, ONTARIO L4W 4Z4 CANADA
00-A0-D8 (hex)	SPECTRA - TEK
00A0D8 (base 16)	SPECTRA - TEK OUTGANG LANE PICKERING NORTH YORKSHIRE ENGLAND Y018 FJA
00-A0-D9 (hex)	CONVEX COMPUTER CORPORATION
00A0D9 (base 16)	CONVEX COMPUTER CORPORATION 3000 WATERVIEW PARKWAY P.O. BOX 833851 RICHARDSON TX 75083-3851
00-A0-DA (hex)	INTEGRATED SYSTEMS
00A0DA (base 16)	INTEGRATED SYSTEMS 4601 PRESIDENTS DRIVE SUITE #210 LANHAM MD 20706
00-A0-DB (hex)	FISHER & PAYKEL PRODUCTION
00A0DB (base 16)	FISHER & PAYKEL PRODUCTION MACHINERY LIMITED P.O. BOX 58-223, GREENMOUNT AUCKLAND NEW ZEALAND
00-A0-DC (hex)	O.N. ELECTRONIC CO., LTD.
00A0DC (base 16)	O.N. ELECTRONIC CO., LTD. 3-20-27, TARUMI SUITA, OSAKA 564 JAPAN
00-A0-DD (hex)	AZONIX CORPORATION
00A0DD (base 16)	AZONIX CORPORATION 900 MIDDLESEX TURNPIKE BLDG. «6» BILLERICA MA 01821
00-A0-DE (hex)	YAMAHA CORPORATION
00A0DE (base 16)	YAMAHA CORPORATION ELECTRONIC DEVICES DIVISION 203 MATSUNOKIJIMA TOYOOKA-MURA IWATA-GUN SHIZUOKA-KEN JAPAN, 438-01
00-A0-DF (hex)	STS TECHNOLOGIES, INC.
00A0DF (base 16)	STS TECHNOLOGIES, INC. 13765 ST. CHARLES ROCK RD. SUITE #108 BRIDGETON MO 63044
00-A0-E0 (hex)	TENNYSON TECHNOLOGIES PTY LTD
00A0E0 (base 16)	TENNYSON TECHNOLOGIES PTY LTD 14 BUSINESS PARK DRIVE NOTTING HILL VICTORIA - 3168 AUSTRALIA
00-A0-E1 (hex)	WESTPORT RESEARCH
00A0E1 (base 16)	WESTPORT RESEARCH ASSOCIATES, INC. 6102 ARLINGTON RAYTOWN MO 64133
00-A0-E2 (hex)	KEISOKU GIKEN CORP.
00A0E2 (base 16)	KEISOKU GIKEN CORP. 503-1 TAKEBAYASHI-MACHI UTSUNOMIYA, TOCHIGI-KEN 321 JAPAN
00-A0-E3 (hex)	XKL SYSTEMS CORP.
00A0E3 (base 16)	XKL SYSTEMS CORP. 8420 154TH AVE. NE REDMOND WA 98052

company_id	Organization Address
00-A0-E4 (hex)	OPTIQUEST
00A0E4 (base 16)	OPTIQUEST 20490 BUSINESS PARKWAY WALNUT CA 91789
00-A0-E5 (hex)	NHC COMMUNICATIONS
00A0E5 (base 16)	NHC COMMUNICATIONS 5450 COTE DE LIESSE MONTREAL, QUEBEC CANADA H4P 1A5
00-A0-E6 (hex)	DIALOGIC CORPORATION
00A0E6 (base 16)	DIALOGIC CORPORATION 1515 ROUTE 10 PARSIPPANY NJ 07054
00-A0-E7 (hex)	CENTRAL DATA CORPORATION
00A0E7 (base 16)	CENTRAL DATA CORPORATION 1602 NEWTON DRIVE CHAMPAIGN IL 61821
00-A0-E8 (hex)	REUTERS HOLDINGS PLC
00A0E8 (base 16)	REUTERS HOLDINGS PLC 85, FLEET STREET LONDON EC4P 4AJ ENGLAND
00-A0-E9 (hex)	ELECTRONIC RETAILING SYSTEMS
00A0E9 (base 16)	ELECTRONIC RETAILING SYSTEMS INTERNATIONAL 372 DANBURY ROAD WILTON CT 06897-2523
00-A0-EA (hex)	ETHERCOM CORP.
00A0EA (base 16)	ETHERCOM CORP. 45990 HOTCHKISS ST. FREEMONT CA 94539
00-A0-EB (hex)	FASTCOMM COMMUNICATIONS CORP.
00A0EB (base 16)	FASTCOMM COMMUNICATIONS CORP. 45472 HOLIDAY DRIVE—STE#3 STERLING VA 20166
00-A0-EC (hex)	TRANSMITTON LTD.
00A0EC (base 16)	TRANSMITTON LTD. SMISBY ROAD ASHBY DE LA ZOUCH LEICESTERSHIRE LE65 2UG UNITED KINGDOM
00-A0-ED (hex)	PRI AUTOMATION
00A0ED (base 16)	PRI AUTOMATION 805 MIDDLESEX TURNPIKE BILLERICA MA 01821-3986
00-A0-EE (hex)	NASHOBA NETWORKS
00A0EE (base 16)	NASHOBA NETWORKS 9-11 GOLDSMITH ST. LITTLETON MA 01460
00-A0-EF (hex)	LUCIDATA LTD.
00A0EF (base 16)	LUCIDATA LTD. LUCIDATA HOUSE SELWYN CLOSE, GREAT SHELFORD CAMBS. CB2 5HA UNITED KINGDOM
00-A0-F0 (hex)	TORONTO MICROELECTRONICS INC.
00A0F0 (base 16)	TORONTO MICROELECTRONICS INC. 5149 BRADCO BOULEVARD MISSISSAUGA, ONTARIO CANADA, L4W 2A6
00-A0-F1 (hex)	MTI
00A0F1 (base 16)	MTI 4905 E. LA PALMA AVENUE ANAHEIM CA 92807
00-A0-F2 (hex)	INFOTEK COMMUNICATIONS, INC.
00A0F2 (base 16)	INFOTEK COMMUNICATIONS, INC. 111 ANZA BLVD., #203 BURLINGAME CA 94010
00-A0-F3 (hex)	STAUBLI

company_id	Organization Address
00A0F3 (base 16)	STAUBLI ⬧183 RUE DES USINES BP 70 F74210 FAVERGES FRANCE
00-A0-F4 (hex)	GE
00A0F4 (base 16)	GE W-657 3000 N. GRANDVIEW BLVD. WAUKESHA WI 53188
00-A0-F5 (hex)	RADGUARD LTD.
00A0F5 (base 16)	RADGUARD LTD. 8 HANECHOSHET STREET TEL-AVIV 69710 ISRAEL
00-A0-F6 (hex)	AUTOGAS SYSTEMS, INC.
00A0F6 (base 16)	AUTOGAS SYSTEMS, INC. P.O. BOX 6957 ABIOLENE TX 79608
00-A0-F7 (hex)	V.I COMPUTER CORP.
00A0F7 (base 16)	V.I COMPUTER CORP. 531 ENCINITAS BLVD–#114 ENCINITAS CA 92024
00-A0-F8 (hex)	SYMBOL TECHNOLOGIES, INC.
00A0F8 (base 16)	SYMBOL TECHNOLOGIES, INC. 1101 SOUTH WINCHESTER BLVD. SUITE # B-110 SAN JOSE CA 95128
00-A0-F9 (hex)	BINTEC COMMUNICATIONS GMBH
00A0F9 (base 16)	BINTEC COMMUNICATIONS GMBH SUEDWESTPARK 94 90449 NUERNBERG GERMANY
00-A0-FA (hex)	Marconi Communication GmbH
00A0FA (base 16)	Marconi Communication GmbH Gerberstrasse 33 D-71522 Bacnknang GERMANY
00-A0-FB (hex)	TORAY ENGINEERING CO., LTD.
00A0FB (base 16)	TORAY ENGINEERING CO., LTD. 1-45, OE 1-CHOME, OTSU CITY SHIGA, 520-21 JAPAN
00-A0-FC (hex)	IMAGE SCIENCES, INC.
00A0FC (base 16)	IMAGE SCIENCES, INC. 7500 INNOVATION WAY MASON OH 45040
00-A0-FD (hex)	SCITEX DIGITAL PRINTING, INC.
00A0FD (base 16)	SCITEX DIGITAL PRINTING, INC. 3100 RESEARCH BLVD. DAYTON OH 45420
00-A0-FE (hex)	BOSTON TECHNOLOGY, INC.
00A0FE (base 16)	BOSTON TECHNOLOGY, INC. 100 QUANNAPOWITT PARKWAY WAKEFIELD MA 01880
00-A0-FF (hex)	TELLABS OPERATIONS, INC.
00A0FF (base 16)	TELLABS OPERATIONS, INC. 1000 REMINGTON BLVD. BOLINGBROOK IL 60440 708-378-6151
00-AA-00 (hex)	INTEL CORPORATION
00AA00 (base 16)	INTEL CORPORATION 5200 NE ELAM YOUNG PARKWAY HILLSBORO OR 97124
00-AA-01 (hex)	INTEL CORPORATION
00AA01 (base 16)	INTEL CORPORATION SANTA CLARA CA
00-AA-02 (hex)	INTEL CORPORATION
00AA02 (base 16)	INTEL CORPORATION SANTA CLARA CA

company_id	Organization Address
00-AA-3C (hex)	OLIVETTI TELECOM SPA (OLTECO)
00AA3C (base 16)	OLIVETTI TELECOM SPA (OLTECO) 10062 MILLER AVE.-STE.#204 CUPERTINO CA 95014
00-B0-09 (hex)	Grass Valley Group
00B009 (base 16)	Grass Valley Group P.O. Box 599000 Nevada City CA 95959-7900
00-B0-17 (hex)	InfoGear Technology Corp.
00B017 (base 16)	InfoGear Technology Corp. 2055 Woodside Road Redwood City CA 94061
00-B0-19 (hex)	Casi-Rusco
00B019 (base 16)	Casi-Rusco 1155 Broken Sound Pkwy Boca Raton FL 33498
00-B0-1C (hex)	Westport Technologies
00B01C (base 16)	Westport Technologies
00-B0-1E (hex)	Rantic Labs, Inc.
00B01E (base 16)	Rantic Labs, Inc. 702 Brazos, Suite #500 Austin TX 78701
00-B0-2A (hex)	ORSYS GmbH
00B02A (base 16)	ORSYS GmbH Am Stadtgraben 1 D-88677 Markdorf GERMANY
00-B0-2D (hex)	ViaGate Technologies, Inc.
00B02D (base 16)	ViaGate Technologies, Inc. 757 Route 202/206 Bridgewater NJ 08807
00-B0-3B (hex)	HiQ Networks
00B03B (base 16)	HiQ Networks 2475 Augustine Drive Santa Clara CA 95054
00-B0-48 (hex)	Marconi Communications Inc.
00B048 (base 16)	Marconi Communications Inc. 8616 Freeport Parkway MS A2 Irving TX 75063
00-B0-4A (hex)	Cisco Systems, Inc.
00B04A (base 16)	Cisco Systems, Inc. 170 West Tasman Drive - SJA-2 San Jose CA 95134
00-B0-52 (hex)	Intellon Corporation
00B052 (base 16)	Intellon Corporation 5100 West Silver Springs Blvd. Ocala FL 34482
00-B0-64 (hex)	Cisco Systems, Inc.
00B064 (base 16)	Cisco Systems, Inc. 170 West Tasman Drive - SJA-2 San Jose CA 95134
00-B0-69 (hex)	Honewell Oy
00B069 (base 16)	Honewell Oy P.O. Box 168, FIN-78201 Varkaus FINLAND
00-B0-6D (hex)	Jones Futurex Inc.
00B06D (base 16)	Jones Futurex Inc. 3715 Atherton Road Rocklin CA 95765
00-B0-80 (hex)	Mannesmann Ipulsys B.V.
00B080 (base 16)	Mannesmann Ipulsys B.V. Bordewijklaan 18 2591 XR Den Haag THE NETHERLANDS
00-B0-86 (hex)	LocSoft Limited

company_id	Organization Address
00B086 (base 16)	LocSoft Limited 4 Charnwood Court Newport Street Swindon, Wiltshire ENGLAND, SN1 3DX
00-B0-8E (hex)	Cisco Systems, Inc.
00B08E (base 16)	Cisco Systems, Inc. 170 West Tasman Drive -SJA-2 San Jose CA 95134
00-B0-91 (hex)	Transmeta Corp.
00B091 (base 16)	Transmeta Corp. 3940 Freedom Circle Santa Clara CA 95054
00-B0-94 (hex)	Alaris, Inc.
00B094 (base 16)	Alaris, Inc. 47338 Fremont Boulevard Fremont CA 94538
00-B0-9A (hex)	Morrow Technologies Corp.
00B09A (base 16)	Morrow Technologies Corp. 2300 Tall Pines Drive Largo FL 33771-5342
00-B0-9D (hex)	Point Grey Research Inc.
00B09D (base 16)	Point Grey Research Inc. 305-1847 West Broadway Vancouver, BC V6J -1Y6 CANADA
00-B0-AC (hex)	SIAE-Microelettronica S.p.A.
00B0AC (base 16)	SIAE-Microelettronica S.p.A. Via Michelangelo Buonarroti, 21 20093 Cologno M. (MI) ITALY
00-B0-AE (hex)	Symmetricom
00B0AE (base 16)	Symmetricom 2300 Orchard Parkway San Jose CA 95131
00-B0-B3 (hex)	Xstreamis PLC
00B0B3 (base 16)	Xstreamis PLC Magdalen Centre Oxford Science Park Oxford 0X4 4GA UNITED KINGDOM
00-B0-C2 (hex)	Cisco Systems, Inc.
00B0C2 (base 16)	Cisco Systems, Inc. 170 West Tasman Drive - SJA-2 San Jose CA 95134
00-B0-C7 (hex)	Tellabs Operations, Inc.
00B0C7 (base 16)	Tellabs Operations, Inc. 1000 Remington Blvd. Bolingbrook Il 60440
00-B0-D0 (hex)	Dell Computer Corp.
00B0D0 (base 16)	Dell Computer Corp. One Dell Way Round Rock TX 78682
00-B0-DB (hex)	Nextcell, Inc.
00B0DB (base 16)	Nextcell, Inc. 651 East 18th Street Plano TX 75074
00-B0-DF (hex)	Reliable Data Technology, Inc.
00B0DF (base 16)	Reliable Data Technology, Inc. 1719 Route 10 - Suite #209 Parsippany NJ 07054
00-B0-E7 (hex)	British Federal Ltd.
00B0E7 (base 16)	British Federal Ltd. Castle Mill Works Dudley, Dy1 4DA ENGLAND
00-B0-EC (hex)	EACEM

company_id	Organization Address
00B0EC (base 16)	EACEM Avenue Louise 140, Bte 6 B-1050 BRUSSELS BELGIUM
00-B0-EE (hex)	Ajile Systems, Inc.
00B0EE (base 16)	Ajile Systems, Inc. M105 Oakdale Hall Oakdale IA 52319
00-B0-F0 (hex)	CALY NETWORKS
00B0F0 (base 16)	CALY NETWORKS 295 Santa Anna Court Sunnyvale CA 94086
00-B0-F5 (hex)	NetWorth Technologies, Inc.
00B0F5 (base 16)	NetWorth Technologies, Inc. 1000 Germantown Pike ldg. J-1 Plymouth Metting PA 19462
00-BB-01 (hex)	OCTOTHORPE CORP.
00BB01 (base 16)	OCTOTHORPE CORP. 285 WEST GREEN STREET PASADENA CA 91105
00-BB-F0 (hex)	UNGERMANN-BASS INC.
00BBF0 (base 16)	UNGERMANN-BASS INC. 3900 FREEDOM CIRCLE SANTA CLARA, CA 95054
00-C0-00 (hex)	LANOPTICS, LTD.
00C000 (base 16)	LANOPTICS, LTD. P.O. BOX 184 MIGDAL HA-EMEK ISRAEL, 10551
00-C0-01 (hex)	DIATEK PATIENT MANAGMENT
00C001 (base 16)	DIATEK PATIENT MANAGMENT SYSTEMS, INC. 5720 OBERLIN DRIVE SAN DIEGO CA 92121-1723
00-C0-02 (hex)	SERCOMM CORPORATION
00C002 (base 16)	SERCOMM CORPORATION 5TH FL,420 FU HSIN NORTH ROAD TAIPEI TAIWAN, R.O.C.
00-C0-03 (hex)	GLOBALNET COMMUNICATIONS
00C003 (base 16)	GLOBALNET COMMUNICATIONS 912, PLACE TRANS CANADA LONGUEUIL, QC CANADA J4G 2M1
00-C0-04 (hex)	JAPAN BUSINESS COMPUTER CO.LTD
00C004 (base 16)	JAPAN BUSINESS COMPUTER CO.LTD 1368 FUTOO-CHO, KOHOKU-KU YOKOHAMA-CITY 222 JAPAN
00-C0-05 (hex)	LIVINGSTON ENTERPRISES, INC.
00C005 (base 16)	LIVINGSTON ENTERPRISES, INC. 6920 KOLL CENTER PARKWAY #220 PLEASANTON CA 94566
00-C0-06 (hex)	NIPPON AVIONICS CO., LTD.
00C006 (base 16)	NIPPON AVIONICS CO., LTD. INDUSTRIAL SYSTEM DIVISION 28-2, HONGOH 2-CHOME, SEYA-KU YOKOHAMA JAPAN
00-C0-07 (hex)	PINNACLE DATA SYSTEMS, INC.
00C007 (base 16)	PINNACLE DATA SYSTEMS, INC. 1350 WEST FIFTH AVENUE COLUMBUS OH 43212
00-C0-08 (hex)	SECO SRL
00C008 (base 16)	SECO SRL VIA CALAMANDREI 91 52100 AREZZO ITALY
00-C0-09 (hex)	KT TECHNOLOGY (S) PTE LTD

company_id	Organization Address
00C009 (base 16)	KT TECHNOLOGY (S) PTE LTD KT BUILDING 100E PASIR PANJANG ROAD SINGAPORE 0511
00-C0-0A (hex)	MICRO CRAFT
00C00A (base 16)	MICRO CRAFT 2-4-3 NISHIFURUMATSU OKAYAMA CITY OKAYAMA PREF. 700 JAPAN
00-C0-0B (hex)	NORCONTROL A.S.
00C00B (base 16)	NORCONTROL A.S. P.O. BOX 1024 N-3194 HORTEN NORWAY
00-C0-0C (hex)	RELIA TECHNOLGIES
00C00C (base 16)	RELIA TECHNOLGIES 1F., NO. 24, INDUSTRY E. 9TH RD., SCIENCE-BASED INDUSTRIAL PARK HSIN-CHU TAIWAN, R.O.C.
00-C0-0D (hex)	ADVANCED LOGIC RESEARCH, INC.
00C00D (base 16)	ADVANCED LOGIC RESEARCH, INC. 9401 JERONIMO IRVINE CA 92618
00-C0-0E (hex)	PSITECH, INC.
00C00E (base 16)	PSITECH, INC. 18368 BANDILIER CIRCLE FOUNTAIN VALLEY CA 92708
00-C0-0F (hex)	QUANTUM SOFTWARE SYSTEMS LTD.
00C00F (base 16)	QUANTUM SOFTWARE SYSTEMS LTD. 175 TERRENCE MATTHEWS CRESCENT KANATA, ONTARIO CANADA K2L 3T5
00-C0-10 (hex)	HIRAKAWA HEWTECH CORP.
00C010 (base 16)	HIRAKAWA HEWTECH CORP. 7F, BLDG.B, OMORI BELLPORT 6-26-2, MINAMI-OI,SHINAGAWA-KU TOKYO 140, JAPAN
00-C0-11 (hex)	INTERACTIVE COMPUTING DEVICES
00C011 (base 16)	INTERACTIVE COMPUTING DEVICES 1735 TECHNOLOGY DRIVE-STE #720 SAN JOSE CA 95110
00-C0-12 (hex)	NETSPAN CORPORATION
00C012 (base 16)	NETSPAN CORPORATION 1411 E. CAMPBELL RD SUITE #1000 RICHARDSON TX 75081
00-C0-13 (hex)	NETRIX
00C013 (base 16)	NETRIX 13595 DULLES TECHNOLOGY DRIVE HERNDON VA 22071
00-C0-14 (hex)	TELEMATICS CALABASAS INT'L,INC
00C014 (base 16)	TELEMATICS CALABASAS INT'L,INC 26630 AGOURA ROAD CALABASAS CA 91302-1988
00-C0-15 (hex)	NEW MEDIA CORPORATION
00C015 (base 16)	NEW MEDIA CORPORATION 15375 BARRANCA PARKWAY BUILDING «B-101» IRVINE CA 92718
00-C0-16 (hex)	ELECTRONIC THEATRE CONTROLS
00C016 (base 16)	ELECTRONIC THEATRE CONTROLS 3030 LAURA LANE MIDDLETON WI 53562
00-C0-17 (hex)	FORTE NETWORKS
00C017 (base 16)	FORTE NETWORKS P.O. BOX 62296 COLORADO SPRINGS CO 80962

company_id	Organization Address
00-C0-18 (hex)	LANART CORPORATION
00C018 (base 16)	LANART CORPORATION 145 ROSEMARY STREET NEEDHAM MA 02194
00-C0-19 (hex)	LEAP TECHNOLOGY, INC.
00C019 (base 16)	LEAP TECHNOLOGY, INC. 20 «B» STREET BURLINGTON MA 01803
00-C0-1A (hex)	COROMETRICS MEDICAL SYSTEMS
00C01A (base 16)	COROMETRICS MEDICAL SYSTEMS 61 BARNES PARK ROAD NORTH WALLINGFORD CT 06492-0333
00-C0-1B (hex)	SOCKET COMMUNICATIONS, INC.
00C01B (base 16)	SOCKET COMMUNICATIONS, INC. 2823 WHIPPLE RD. UNION CITY CA 94587
00-C0-1C (hex)	INTERLINK COMMUNICATIONS LTD.
00C01C (base 16)	INTERLINK COMMUNICATIONS LTD. BRUNEL ROAD, GORSE LANE INDUSTRIAL ESTATE CLACTON-ON-SEA, ESSEX CO15 4LU ENGLAND
00-C0-1D (hex)	GRAND JUNCTION NETWORKS, INC.
00C01D (base 16)	GRAND JUNCTION NETWORKS, INC. 3101 WHIPPLE RD., #27 UNION CITY CA 94587
00-C0-1E (hex)	LA FRANCAISE DES JEUX
00C01E (base 16)	LA FRANCAISE DES JEUX CENTRE DE ROUSSY/DTI 77230 ROUSSY-LE-VIEUX FRANCE
00-C0-1F (hex)	S.E.R.C.E.L.
00C01F (base 16)	S.E.R.C.E.L. B.P. 439 44474 CARQUEFOU CEDEX FRANCE
00-C0-20 (hex)	ARCO ELECTRONIC, CONTROL LTD.
00C020 (base 16)	ARCO ELECTRONIC, CONTROL LTD. 2750 NORTH 29TH AVE.-STE.#316 HOLLYWOOD FL 33020
00-C0-21 (hex)	NETEXPRESS
00C021 (base 16)	NETEXPRESS 989 EAST HILLSDALE BLVD. SUITE #290 FOSTER CITY CA 94404-2113
00-C0-22 (hex)	LASERMASTER TECHNOLOGIES, INC.
00C022 (base 16)	LASERMASTER TECHNOLOGIES, INC. 7156 SHADY OAK ROAD EDEN PRAIRIE MN 55344
00-C0-23 (hex)	TUTANKHAMON ELECTRONICS
00C023 (base 16)	TUTANKHAMON ELECTRONICS 2446 ESTAND WAY PLEASANT HILL CA 94523
00-C0-24 (hex)	EDEN SISTEMAS DE COMPUTACAO SA
00C024 (base 16)	EDEN SISTEMAS DE COMPUTACAO SA RUA DO OUVIDOR 121 5 ANDAR RIO DE JANEIRO BRAZIL
00-C0-25 (hex)	DATAPRODUCTS CORPORATION
00C025 (base 16)	DATAPRODUCTS CORPORATION 6219 DESOTO AVENUE WOODLAND HILLS CA 91365-0746
00-C0-26 (hex)	LANS TECHNOLOGY CO., LTD.
00C026 (base 16)	LANS TECHNOLOGY CO., LTD. 153 MINTSU RD. 2F, TAOYUAN, TAIWAN, R. O. C.
00-C0-27 (hex)	CIPHER SYSTEMS, INC.
00C027 (base 16)	CIPHER SYSTEMS, INC. P.O. BOX 329 NORTH PLAINS OR 97133

company_id	Organization Address	company_id	Organization Address
00-C0-28 (hex)	JASCO CORPORATION	00C035 (base 16)	QUINTAR COMPANY
00C028 (base 16)	JASCO CORPORATION 2967-5 ISHIKAWA-CHO, HACHIOJI-SHI TOKYO 192 JAPAN		370 AMAPOLA AVE., STE.#106 TORRANCE CA 90501
		00-C0-36 (hex)	RAYTECH ELECTRONIC CORP.
00-C0-29 (hex)	KABEL RHEYDT AG	00C036 (base 16)	RAYTECH ELECTRONIC CORP. 2F, NO.6, LANE 497 CHUNG CHENG RD, HSIN TIEN CITY TAIPEI HSIEN TAIWAN R.O.C.
00C029 (base 16)	KABEL RHEYDT AG ABT. N52, HR. THEISSEN BONNENBROICHER STR. 2-14 4050 MOENCHENGLADBACH 2 GERMANY		
		00-C0-37 (hex)	DYNATEM
00-C0-2A (hex)	OHKURA ELECTRIC CO., LTD.	00C037 (base 16)	DYNATEM 15795 ROCKFIELD BLVD. SUITE «G» IRVINE, CA 92718
00C02A (base 16)	OHKURA ELECTRIC CO., LTD. 2-90-20 SHIRAKO WAKO CITY SAITAMA PREF. 351-01 JAPAN		
		00-C0-38 (hex)	RASTER IMAGE PROCESSING SYSTEM
00-C0-2B (hex)	GERLOFF GESELLSCHAFT FUR	00C038 (base 16)	RASTER IMAGE PROCESSING SYSTEM 4665 NAUTILUS COURT SOUTH BOULDER CO 80301
00C02B (base 16)	GERLOFF GESELLSCHAFT FUR ELEKRONISCHE SYSTEMENTWICKLUNG FASANENWEG 25 W-2000 HAMBURG 73 GERMANY		
		00-C0-39 (hex)	TDK SEMICONDUCTOR CORPORATION
		00C039 (base 16)	TDK SEMICONDUCTOR CORPORATION 2642 MICHELLE DRIVE TUSTIN CA 92780
00-C0-2C (hex)	CENTRUM COMMUNICATIONS, INC.	00-C0-3A (hex)	MEN-MIKRO ELEKTRONIK GMBH
00C02C (base 16)	CENTRUM COMMUNICATIONS, INC. 2880 ZANKER ROAD-STE #108 SAN JOSE CA 95134	00C03A (base 16)	MEN-MIKRO ELEKTRONIK GMBH WIESENTALSTRASSE 40 W-8500 NUERNBERG 90 GERMANY
00-C0-2D (hex)	FUJI PHOTO FILM CO., LTD.	00-C0-3B (hex)	MULTIACCESS COMPUTING CORP.
00C02D (base 16)	FUJI PHOTO FILM CO., LTD. 798 MIYANODAI KAISEI-MACHI ASHIGARA-KAMI-GUN KANAGAWA JAPAN	00C03B (base 16)	MULTIACCESS COMPUTING CORP. 5350 HOLLISTER AVE., STE. «C» SANTA BARBARA CA 93111
		00-C0-3C (hex)	TOWER TECH S.R.L.
00-C0-2E (hex)	NETWIZ	00C03C (base 16)	TOWER TECH S.R.L. VIA RIDOLFI 6,8 56124 PISA ITALY
00C02E (base 16)	NETWIZ 26 GOLOMB STREET HAIFA 33391 ISRAEL		
		00-C0-3D (hex)	WIESEMANN & THEIS GMBH
00-C0-2F (hex)	OKUMA CORPORATION	00C03D (base 16)	WIESEMANN & THEIS GMBH WITTENER STR. 312 5600 WUPPERTAL 2 GERMANY
00C02F (base 16)	OKUMA CORPORATION OGUCHI-CHO, NIWA-GUN AICHI 480-01 JAPAN		
		00-C0-3E (hex)	FA. GEBR. HELLER GMBH
00-C0-30 (hex)	INTEGRATED ENGINEERING B. V.	00C03E (base 16)	FA. GEBR. HELLER GMBH P.O. BOX 1428, DEP. EE7 7440 NURTINGEN GERMANY
00C030 (base 16)	INTEGRATED ENGINEERING B. V. ELLERMANSTRAAT 15 1099 BW AMSTERDAM THE NETHERLANDS		
		00-C0-3F (hex)	STORES AUTOMATED SYSTEMS, INC.
00-C0-31 (hex)	DESIGN RESEARCH SYSTEMS, INC.	00C03F (base 16)	STORES AUTOMATED SYSTEMS, INC. 1360 ADAMS ROAD BENSALEM PA 19020
00C031 (base 16)	DESIGN RESEARCH SYSTEMS, INC. 925 E. EXECUTIVE PARK DR. SUITE «A» SALT LAKE CITY UT 84117		
		00-C0-40 (hex)	ECCI
00-C0-32 (hex)	I-CUBED LIMITED	00C040 (base 16)	ECCI 15070-B AVENUE OF SCIENCE SAN DIEGO CA 92128
00C032 (base 16)	I-CUBED LIMITED UNIT J1, THE POADDOCKS 347 CHERRY HINTON ROAD CAMBRIDGE CB1 4DH, ENGLAND		
		00-C0-41 (hex)	DIGITAL TRANSMISSION SYSTEMS
		00C041 (base 16)	DIGITAL TRANSMISSION SYSTEMS 4830 RIVER GREEN PARKWAY DULUTH GA 30136
00-C0-33 (hex)	TELEBIT COMMUNICATIONS APS	00-C0-42 (hex)	DATALUX CORP.
00C033 (base 16)	TELEBIT COMMUNICATIONS APS SKANDERBORGVEJ 234 DK-8260 VIBY DENMARK	00C042 (base 16)	DATALUX CORP. 2836 CESSNA DRIVE WINCHESTER VA 22601
		00-C0-43 (hex)	STRATACOM
00-C0-34 (hex)	TRANSACTION NETWORK	00C043 (base 16)	STRATACOM 1400 PARKMOOR AVENUE SAN JOSE CA 95126
00C034 (base 16)	TRANSACTION NETWORK SERVICES, INC. OMNILINK COMMUNICATIONS DIV. 3101 TECHNOLOGY BLVD. STE «C» LANSING MI 48910-8356		
		00-C0-44 (hex)	EMCOM CORPORATION
00-C0-35 (hex)	QUINTAR COMPANY	00C044 (base 16)	EMCOM CORPORATION 840 AVENUE «F» PLANO TX 75074

company_id	Organization Address	company_id	Organization Address
00-C0-45 (hex)	ISOLATION SYSTEMS, LTD.	00C053 (base 16)	DAVOX CORPORATION 6 TECHNOLOGY PARK DRIVE WESTFORD MA 01886
00C045 (base 16)	ISOLATION SYSTEMS, LTD. 26 SIX POINT ROAD TORONTO, ONTARIO CANADA M8Z 2W9	00-C0-54 (hex)	NETWORK PERIPHERALS, LTD.
00-C0-46 (hex)	KEMITRON LTD.	00C054 (base 16)	NETWORK PERIPHERALS, LTD. 4TH FLOOR, 17 BOWATER RD. WESTMINSTER INDUSTRIAL ESTATE LONDON SE 18 STF ENGLAND
00C046 (base 16)	KEMITRON LTD. HAWARDEN INDUSTRIAL ESTATE MANOR LANE DEESIDE, CLWYD UNITED KINGDOM CH5 3PP	00-C0-55 (hex)	MODULAR COMPUTING TECHNOLOGIES
00-C0-47 (hex)	UNIMICRO SYSTEMS, INC.	00C055 (base 16)	MODULAR COMPUTING TECHNOLOGIES 2352 MAIN STREET CONCORD MA 01742
00C047 (base 16)	UNIMICRO SYSTEMS, INC. 44382 S. GRIMMER BLVD. FREMONT CA 94538	00-C0-56 (hex)	SOMELEC
00-C0-48 (hex)	BAY TECHNICAL ASSOCIATES	00C056 (base 16)	SOMELEC BP 7010 - 95050 CERGY PONTOISE CEDEX FRANCE
00C048 (base 16)	BAY TECHNICAL ASSOCIATES 200 N. SECOND STREET P.O. BOX 387 BAY ST. LOUIS MS 39520	00-C0-57 (hex)	MYCO ELECTRONICS
00-C0-49 (hex)	U.S. ROBOTICS, INC.	00C057 (base 16)	MYCO ELECTRONICS MUSSERONGRAND 1G S-756 UPPSALA SWEDEN
00C049 (base 16)	U.S. ROBOTICS, INC. 8100 NORTH MCCORMICK BLVD. SKOKIE IL 60076-2999	00-C0-58 (hex)	DATAEXPERT CORP.
00-C0-4A (hex)	GROUP 2000 AG	00C058 (base 16)	DATAEXPERT CORP. 1156 SONOPRA COURTN-KANG RD. SUNNYVALE CA 94086
00C04A (base 16)	GROUP 2000 AG P.O. BOX 331 TANNAGERTENSTR. 9 CH-8635 DURNTEN SWITZERLAND	00-C0-59 (hex)	NIPPON DENSO CO., LTD.
00-C0-4B (hex)	CREATIVE MICROSYSTEMS	00C059 (base 16)	NIPPON DENSO CO., LTD. 1-1 SHOWA-CHO KARIYA CITY AICHI 448 JAPAN
00C04B (base 16)	CREATIVE MICROSYSTEMS 9, AVENUE DU CANADA PARC HIGHTEC 6 Z.A. DE COURTABOEUF 91966 LES ULIS–FRANCE	00-C0-5A (hex)	SEMAPHORE COMMUNICATIONS CORP.
00-C0-4C (hex)	DEPARTMENT OF FOREIGN AFFAIRS	00C05A (base 16)	SEMAPHORE COMMUNICATIONS CORP. 217 HUMBOLDT COURT SUNNYVALE CA 94089-1300
00C04C (base 16)	DEPARTMENT OF FOREIGN AFFAIRS & TRADE ADMINISTRATIVE BUILDING PARKES PLACE, PARKES ACT 2600 AUSTRALIA	00-C0-5B (hex)	NETWORKS NORTHWEST, INC.
		00C05B (base 16)	NETWORKS NORTHWEST, INC. P.O. BOX 1188 ISSAQUAH WA 98027
00-C0-4D (hex)	MITEC, INC.	00-C0-5C (hex)	ELONEX PLC
00C04D (base 16)	MITEC, INC. BR-KAMEIDO 1 BUILDING Z-33-1, KAMEIDO, KOUTOU-KU TOKYO, 136 JAPAN	00C05C (base 16)	ELONEX PLC 2 APSLEY WAY LONDON, NW2 7HF UNITED KINGDOM
00-C0-4E (hex)	COMTROL CORPORATION	00-C0-5D (hex)	L&N TECHNOLOGIES
00C04E (base 16)	COMTROL CORPORATION 2675 PATTON ROAD ST. PAUL MN 55113	00C05D (base 16)	L&N TECHNOLOGIES 2899 AGOURA ROAD #196 WESTLAKE VILLAGE CA 91361-3200
00-C0-4F (hex)	DELL COMPUTER CORPORATION	00-C0-5E (hex)	VARI-LITE, INC.
00C04F (base 16)	DELL COMPUTER CORPORATION 1807 WEST BRAKER LANE-BLDG."C" AUSTIN TX 78758-3610	00C05E (base 16)	VARI-LITE, INC. 201 REGAL ROW DALLAS TX 75247
00-C0-50 (hex)	TOYO DENKI SEIZO K.K.	00-C0-5F (hex)	FINE-PAL COMPANY LIMITED
00C050 (base 16)	TOYO DENKI SEIZO K.K. 4-6-32 HIGASHIKASHIWAGAYA EBINASHI KANAGAWA, JAPAN 243-04	00C05F (base 16)	FINE-PAL COMPANY LIMITED RM. 9, 11F, KINGSFORD IND. CTR 13, WANG HOI ROAD KOWLOON BAY, KLN HONG KONG
00-C0-51 (hex)	ADVANCED INTEGRATION RESEARCH	00-C0-60 (hex)	ID SCANDINAVIA AS
00C051 (base 16)	ADVANCED INTEGRATION RESEARCH 2188 DEL FRANCO STREET SAN JOSE CA 95131	00C060 (base 16)	ID SCANDINAVIA AS P.O. BOX 4227 N-5028 BERGEN NORWAY
00-C0-52 (hex)	BURR-BROWN	00-C0-61 (hex)	SOLECTEK CORPORATION
00C052 (base 16)	BURR-BROWN P.O. BOX 11400 TUCSON AZ 85734-1400	00C061 (base 16)	SOLECTEK CORPORATION 6370 NANCY RIDGE DR.-STE.#109 SAN DIEGO CA 92121
00-C0-53 (hex)	DAVOX CORPORATION	00-C0-62 (hex)	IMPULSE TECHNOLOGY

company_id	Organization Address
00C062 (base 16)	IMPULSE TECHNOLOGY 210 DAHLONEGA ST.#204 CUMMING GA 30130
00-C0-63 (hex)	MORNING STAR TECHNOLOGIES, INC
00C063 (base 16)	MORNING STAR TECHNOLOGIES, INC 1760 ZOLLINGER ROAD COLUMBUS, OH 43221
00-C0-64 (hex)	GENERAL DATACOMM IND. INC.
00C064 (base 16)	GENERAL DATACOMM IND. INC. PARK ROAD EXTENSION P.O. BOX 1299 MIDDLEBURY CT 06762
00-C0-65 (hex)	SCOPE COMMUNICATIONS, INC.
00C065 (base 16)	SCOPE COMMUNICATIONS, INC. 100 OTIS STREET NORTHBORO MA 01532
00-C0-66 (hex)	DOCUPOINT, INC.
00C066 (base 16)	DOCUPOINT, INC. 2701 BAYVIEW DRIVE FREMONT CA 94538
00-C0-67 (hex)	UNITED BARCODE INDUSTRIES
00C067 (base 16)	UNITED BARCODE INDUSTRIES 12240 INDIAN CREEK COURT BELTSVILLE MD 20705
00-C0-68 (hex)	PHILIP DRAKE ELECTRONICS LTD.
00C068 (base 16)	PHILIP DRAKE ELECTRONICS LTD. THE HYDEWAY WELWYN GARDEN CITY HERTS. AL7 3UQ, UNITED KINGDOM
00-C0-69 (hex)	ADAPTIVE BROADBAND CORPORATION
00C069 (base 16)	ADAPTIVE BROADBAND CORPORATION 175 SCIENCE PARKWAY ROCHESTER NY 14620-4261
00-C0-6A (hex)	ZAHNER-ELEKTRIK GMBH & CO. KG
00C06A (base 16)	ZAHNER-ELEKTRIK GMBH & CO. KG P.O. BOX 1846 THUERINGER STRASSE 12 DW-8640 KRONACH-GUNDELSDORF GERMANY
00-C0-6B (hex)	OSI PLUS CORPORATION
00C06B (base 16)	OSI PLUS CORPORATION 2-1-23 NAKAMEGURO MEGURO-KU, TOKYO 153 JAPAN
00-C0-6C (hex)	SVEC COMPUTER CORP.
00C06C (base 16)	SVEC COMPUTER CORP. 3F, 531-1 CHUNG CHENG RD. HSIN-TIEN CITY, TAIPEI TAIWAN, R.O.C.
00-C0-6D (hex)	BOCA RESEARCH, INC.
00C06D (base 16)	BOCA RESEARCH, INC. 6401 CONGRESS AVENUE BOCA RATON FL 33487
00-C0-6E (hex)	HAFT TECHNOLOGY, INC.
00C06E (base 16)	HAFT TECHNOLOGY, INC. DAINI-DOHO BLDG. 3-CHOME 24-7 NINOMIYA TSUKUBA IBARAGI 305 JAPAN
00-C0-6F (hex)	KOMATSU LTD.
00C06F (base 16)	KOMATSU LTD. 2597 SHINOMIYA HIRATSUKA-SHI KANAGAWA 254 JAPAN
00-C0-70 (hex)	SECTRA SECURE-TRANSMISSION AB
00C070 (base 16)	SECTRA SECURE-TRANSMISSION AB TEKNIKRINGEN 2 S-583 30 LINKOPING SWEDEN

company_id	Organization Address
00-C0-71 (hex)	AREANEX COMMUNICATIONS, INC.
00C071 (base 16)	AREANEX COMMUNICATIONS, INC. 3333 OCTAVIUS DRIVE UNIT C SANTA CLARA CA 95051
00-C0-72 (hex)	KNX LTD.
00C072 (base 16)	KNX LTD. HOLLINGWOOD HOUSE WEST CHEVIN ROAD OTLEY, W. YORKSHIRE LS21 3HA UNITED KINGDOM
00-C0-73 (hex)	XEDIA CORPORATION
00C073 (base 16)	XEDIA CORPORATION 301 BALLARDVALE STREET WILMINGTON MA 01887
00-C0-74 (hex)	TOYODA AUTOMATIC LOOM
00C074 (base 16)	TOYODA AUTOMATIC LOOM WORKS, LTD. 2-1, TOYODA-CHO, KARIYA-SHI AICHI-KEN 448 JAPAN
00-C0-75 (hex)	XANTE CORPORATION
00C075 (base 16)	XANTE CORPORATION 2559 EMOGENE STREET MOBILE AL 36606
00-C0-76 (hex)	I-DATA INTERNATIONAL A-S
00C076 (base 16)	I-DATA INTERNATIONAL A-S 35-43 VADSTRUPVEJ DK-2880 BAGSVAERD DENMARK
00-C0-77 (hex)	DAEWOO TELECOM LTD.
00C077 (base 16)	DAEWOO TELECOM LTD. PRODUCTS DESIGN DEPT. 1 PRODUCTS DESIGN CENTER SOCHO. P.O. BOX 187 SEOUL, KOREA
00-C0-78 (hex)	COMPUTER SYSTEMS ENGINEERING
00C078 (base 16)	COMPUTER SYSTEMS ENGINEERING 46791 FREMONT BLVD. FREMONT CA 94538
00-C0-79 (hex)	FONSYS CO.,LTD.
00C079 (base 16)	FONSYS CO.,LTD. 209-5, YANGJAE, SEOCHO SEOUL A37130 KOREA
00-C0-7A (hex)	PRIVA B.V.
00C07A (base 16)	PRIVA B.V. P.O. BOX 18 2678 ZG DE LIER (Z-H) THE NETHERLANDS
00-C0-7B (hex)	ASCEND COMMUNICATIONS, INC.
00C07B (base 16)	ASCEND COMMUNICATIONS, INC. 1701 HARBOR BAY PARKWAY ALAMEDA CA 94502
00-C0-7C (hex)	HIGHTECH INFORMATION
00C07C (base 16)	HIGHTECH INFORMATION SYSTEM LTD. UNIT 7, 2/F, PO LUNG CENTRE 11 WANG CHIU ROAD–KOWLOON BAY HONG KONG
00-C0-7D (hex)	RISC DEVELOPMENTS LTD.
00C07D (base 16)	RISC DEVELOPMENTS LTD. 117 HATFIELD ROAD ST. ALBANS, HERTS AL14J5 ENGLAND
00-C0-7E (hex)	KUBOTA CORPORATION ELECTRONIC

company_id	Organization / Address
00C07E (base 16)	KUBOTA CORPORATION ELECTRONIC DEVICE DEPT. 2-35, JINMU-CHO, YAO-CITY OSAKA PREF. JAPAN #581
00-C0-7F (hex)	NUPON COMPUTING CORP.
00C07F (base 16)	NUPON COMPUTING CORP. 1391 WARNER AVE., -SUITE «A» TUSTIN CA 92680
00-C0-80 (hex)	NETSTAR, INC.
00C080 (base 16)	NETSTAR, INC. CEDAR BUSINESS CENTER 1801 E. 79TH STREET MINNEAPOLIS MN 55425-1235
00-C0-81 (hex)	METRODATA LTD.
00C081 (base 16)	METRODATA LTD. BLENHEIM HOUSE CRABTREE OFFICE VILLAGE EVERSLEY WAY, EGHAM, SURREY TW20 8RY, ENGLAND
00-C0-82 (hex)	MOORE PRODUCTS CO.
00C082 (base 16)	MOORE PRODUCTS CO. SUMNEYTOWN PIKE SPRING HOUSE PA 19477
00-C0-83 (hex)	TRACE MOUNTAIN PRODUCTS, INC.
00C083 (base 16)	TRACE MOUNTAIN PRODUCTS, INC. 1040 EAST BROKAW ROAD SAN JOSE CA 95131
00-C0-84 (hex)	DATA LINK CORP. LTD.
00C084 (base 16)	DATA LINK CORP. LTD. 3-15-3 MIDORICHO TOKOROZAWA-CITY SAITAMA 359 JAPAN
00-C0-85 (hex)	ELECTRONICS FOR IMAGING, INC.
00C085 (base 16)	ELECTRONICS FOR IMAGING, INC. 2855 CAMPUS DRIVE SAN MATEO CA 94403
00-C0-86 (hex)	THE LYNK CORPORATION
00C086 (base 16)	THE LYNK CORPORATION 101 QUEENS DRIVE KING OF PRUSSIA PA 19406
00-C0-87 (hex)	UUNET TECHNOLOGIES, INC.
00C087 (base 16)	UUNET TECHNOLOGIES, INC. 3110 FAIRVIEW PARK DR. #570 FALLS CHURCH VA 22042
00-C0-88 (hex)	EKF ELEKTRONIK GMBH
00C088 (base 16)	EKF ELEKTRONIK GMBH PHILIPP-REIS-STR. 4 4700 HAMM GERMANY
00-C0-89 (hex)	TELINDUS DISTRIBUTION
00C089 (base 16)	TELINDUS DISTRIBUTION GELDENAAKSEBAAN 335 3001 HEVERLEE BELGIUM
00-C0-8A (hex)	LAUTERBACH DATENTECHNIK GMBH
00C08A (base 16)	LAUTERBACH DATENTECHNIK GMBH FICHENSTR. 27 D-85649 HOFOLDING GERMANY
00-C0-8B (hex)	RISQ MODULAR SYSTEMS, INC.
00C08B (base 16)	RISQ MODULAR SYSTEMS, INC. 39899 BALENTINE DRIVE-STE #375 NEWARK CA 94560
00-C0-8C (hex)	PERFORMANCE TECHNOLOGIES, INC.
00C08C (base 16)	PERFORMANCE TECHNOLOGIES, INC. 315 SCIENCE PARKWAY ROCHESTER, NY 14620
00-C0-8D (hex)	TRONIX PRODUCT DEVELOPMENT

company_id	Organization / Address
00C08D (base 16)	TRONIX PRODUCT DEVELOPMENT 4908 E. MCDOWELL RD. STE.#100 PHOENIX AZ 85008
00-C0-8E (hex)	NETWORK INFORMATION TECHNOLOGY
00C08E (base 16)	NETWORK INFORMATION TECHNOLOGY 10430 S. DE ANZA BLVD. CUPERTINO, CA 95014
00-C0-8F (hex)	MATSUSHITA ELECTRIC WORKS, LTD
00C08F (base 16)	MATSUSHITA ELECTRIC WORKS, LTD 1048 KADOMA, KADOMA-SI OSAKA 571, JAPAN
00-C0-90 (hex)	PRAIM S.R.L.
00C090 (base 16)	PRAIM S.R.L. VIA MACCANI, 169 38100 TRENTO (TN) ITALY
00-C0-91 (hex)	JABIL CIRCUIT, INC.
00C091 (base 16)	JABIL CIRCUIT, INC. 32275 MALLY ROAD MADISON HEIGHTS MI 48071
00-C0-92 (hex)	MENNEN MEDICAL INC.
00C092 (base 16)	MENNEN MEDICAL INC. 10123 MAIN STREET CLARENCE NY 14031-2095
00-C0-93 (hex)	ALTA RESEARCH CORP.
00C093 (base 16)	ALTA RESEARCH CORP. 614 SOUTH FEDERAL HIGHWAY DEERFIELD BEACH FL 33441
00-C0-94 (hex)	VMX INC.
00C094 (base 16)	VMX INC. 2115 O'NEL DRIVE SAN JOSE CA 95131
00-C0-95 (hex)	ZNYX
00C095 (base 16)	ZNYX 48501 WARMSPRINGS BLVD-STE.107 FREMONT CA 94539
00-C0-96 (hex)	TAMURA CORPORATION
00C096 (base 16)	TAMURA CORPORATION COMMUNICATION SYSTEMS DIV. 19-43 HIGASHI OIZUMI 1 CHOME NERIMA-KU, TOKYO 178 JAPAN
00-C0-97 (hex)	ARCHIPEL SA
00C097 (base 16)	ARCHIPEL SA 1 RUE DU BULLOZ F 74940 ANNECY-LE-VIEUX FRANCE
00-C0-98 (hex)	CHUNTEX ELECTRONIC CO., LTD.
00C098 (base 16)	CHUNTEX ELECTRONIC CO., LTD. 6F., NO.2, ALLEY 6, LANE 235 PAO CHIAO RD., HSIN TIEN, TAIPEI HSIEN TAIWAN, R.O.C.
00-C0-99 (hex)	YOSHIKI INDUSTRIAL CO.,LTD.
00C099 (base 16)	YOSHIKI INDUSTRIAL CO.,LTD. 1-38 MATSUGASAKI 2-CHOME YONEZAWA YAMAGATA 992 JAPAN
00-C0-9A (hex)	PHOTONICS CORPORATION
00C09A (base 16)	PHOTONICS CORPORATION 2940 NORTH FIRST STREET SAN JOSE CA 95123-2021
00-C0-9B (hex)	RELIANCE COMM/TEC, R-TEC
00C09B (base 16)	RELIANCE COMM/TEC, R-TEC SYSTEMS INC. 2100 RELIANCE PARKWAY, MS 22 BEDFORD TX 76021
00-C0-9C (hex)	TOA ELECTRONIC LTD.

841

company_id	Organization Address
00C09C (base 16)	TOA ELECTRONIC LTD. 613 KITAIRISO SAYAMA SAITAMA, PREF 350-13 JAPAN
00-C0-9D (hex)	DISTRIBUTED SYSTEMS INT'L, INC
00C09D (base 16)	DISTRIBUTED SYSTEMS INT'L, INC 531 WEST ROOSEVELT RD., STE #2 WHEATON IL 60187
00-C0-9E (hex)	CACHE COMPUTERS, INC.
00C09E (base 16)	CACHE COMPUTERS, INC. 46600 LANDING PARKWAY FREMONT CA 94538
00-C0-9F (hex)	QUANTA COMPUTER, INC.
00C09F (base 16)	QUANTA COMPUTER, INC. 7F., 116, HOU-KANG ST., SHIH-LIN DIST. TAIPEI TAIWAN, R.O.C.
00-C0-A0 (hex)	ADVANCE MICRO RESEARCH, INC.
00C0A0 (base 16)	ADVANCE MICRO RESEARCH, INC. 2045 CORPORATE COURT SAN JOSE CA 95131
00-C0-A1 (hex)	TOKYO DENSHI SEKEI CO.
00C0A1 (base 16)	TOKYO DENSHI SEKEI CO. 255-1 RENKOJI, TAMA-SHI TOKYO JAPAN 206
00-C0-A2 (hex)	INTERMEDIUM A/S
00C0A2 (base 16)	INTERMEDIUM A/S ODINSVEJ 19 DK-2600 GLOSTRUP DENMARK
00-C0-A3 (hex)	DUAL ENTERPRISES CORPORATION
00C0A3 (base 16)	DUAL ENTERPRISES CORPORATION 9TH FLOOR 48 NAN-KANG ROAD SEC.3, TAIPEI TAIWAN, R.O.C.
00-C0-A4 (hex)	UNIGRAF OY
00C0A4 (base 16)	UNIGRAF OY RUUKINTIE 18 02320 ESP00 FINLAND
00-C0-A5 (hex)	DICKENS DATA SYSTEMS
00C0A5 (base 16)	DICKENS DATA SYSTEMS 1175 NORTHMEADOW PKWY-STE #150 ROSWELL GA 30076
00-C0-A6 (hex)	EXICOM AUSTRALIA PTY. LTD
00C0A6 (base 16)	EXICOM AUSTRALIA PTY. LTD 44-46 MANDARIN STREET VILLAWOOD NSW 2163 AUSTRALIA
00-C0-A7 (hex)	SEEL LTD.
00C0A7 (base 16)	SEEL LTD. 3 YOUNG SQUARE LIVINGSTON EH54 9BJ SCOTLAND
00-C0-A8 (hex)	GVC CORPORATION
00C0A8 (base 16)	GVC CORPORATION 1961 CONCOURSE DRIVE-STE B SAN JOSE CA 95131
00-C0-A9 (hex)	BARRON MCCANN LTD.
00C0A9 (base 16)	BARRON MCCANN LTD. BEMAC HOUSE FIFTH AVENUE, LETCHWORTH HERTS., SG6 2HF UNITED KINGDOM
00-C0-AA (hex)	SILICON VALLEY COMPUTER
00C0AA (base 16)	SILICON VALLEY COMPUTER 441 N. WHISMAN RD., BLDG.#13 MT. VIEW CA 94043

company_id	Organization Address
00-C0-AB (hex)	Telco Systems, Inc.
00C0AB (base 16)	Telco Systems, Inc. 63 Nathan Street Norwood, MA 02072
00-C0-AC (hex)	GAMBIT COMPUTER COMMUNICATIONS
00C0AC (base 16)	GAMBIT COMPUTER COMMUNICATIONS SOLTAM INDUSTRIAL PARK P.O. BOX 107 YOKNEAM 20692 ISRAEL
00-C0-AD (hex)	MARBEN COMMUNICATION SYSTEMS
00C0AD (base 16)	MARBEN COMMUNICATION SYSTEMS 1 RUE DU BOIS CHALAND LISSES 91029 EVRY CEDEX FRANCE
00-C0-AE (hex)	TOWERCOM CO. INC. DBA PC HOUSE
00C0AE (base 16)	TOWERCOM CO. INC. DBA PC HOUSE 841 E. ARTESIA BLVD. CARSON CA 90746
00-C0-AF (hex)	TEKLOGIX INC.
00C0AF (base 16)	TEKLOGIX INC. 2100 MEADOWVALE BOULEVARD MISSISSAUGA, ONTARIO, CANADA L5N 7J9
00-C0-B0 (hex)	GCC TECHNOLOGIES,INC.
00C0B0 (base 16)	GCC TECHNOLOGIES,INC. 580 WINTER STREET WALTHAM MA 02154
00-C0-B1 (hex)	GENIUS NET CO.
00C0B1 (base 16)	GENIUS NET CO. 4F, HANSOO B/D 210-5 YANGJAE-DONG, SEOCHO-GU SEOUL SOUTH KOREA
00-C0-B2 (hex)	NORAND CORPORATION
00C0B2 (base 16)	NORAND CORPORATION 550 2ND STREET SE CEDAR RAPIDS IA 52401
00-C0-B3 (hex)	COMSTAT DATACOMM CORPORATION
00C0B3 (base 16)	COMSTAT DATACOMM CORPORATION 1720 SPECTRUM DRIVE LAWRENCEVILLE GA 30243
00-C0-B4 (hex)	MYSON TECHNOLOGY, INC.
00C0B4 (base 16)	MYSON TECHNOLOGY, INC. 2F, NO. 3, INDUSTRY E. RD.IV SCIENCE-BASED INDUSTRIAL PARK HSINCHU, (R.O.C.) TAIWAN
00-C0-B5 (hex)	CORPORATE NETWORK SYSTEMS,INC.
00C0B5 (base 16)	CORPORATE NETWORK SYSTEMS,INC. 5711 SIX FORKS ROAD–STE #306 RALEIGH NC 27609
00-C0-B6 (hex)	MERIDIAN DATA, INC.
00C0B6 (base 16)	MERIDIAN DATA, INC. 5615 SCOTTS VALLEY DRIVE SCOTTS VALLEY CA 95066
00-C0-B7 (hex)	AMERICAN POWER CONVERSION CORP
00C0B7 (base 16)	AMERICAN POWER CONVERSION CORP 267 BOSTON ROAD #2 NORTH BILLERICA MA 01862
00-C0-B8 (hex)	FRASER'S HILL LTD.
00C0B8 (base 16)	FRASER'S HILL LTD. 27502 W. GILL ROAD P.O. BOX 189 MORRISTOWN AZ 85342
00-C0-B9 (hex)	FUNK SOFTWARE, INC.
00C0B9 (base 16)	FUNK SOFTWARE, INC. 222 THIRD STREET CAMBRIDGE MA 02142
00-C0-BA (hex)	NETVANTAGE

company_id	Organization Address
00C0BA (base 16)	NETVANTAGE 201 CONTINENTAL BLVD.-STE.#201 EL SECUNDO CA 90245
00-C0-BB (hex)	FORVAL CREATIVE, INC.
00C0BB (base 16)	FORVAL CREATIVE, INC. 3-27-12 HONGO BUNKYO-KU TOKYO 113 JAPAN
00-C0-BC (hex)	TELECOM AUSTRALIA/CSSC
00C0BC (base 16)	TELECOM AUSTRALIA/CSSC LOCKED BAG 8812 SOUTHCOAST MAIL CENTRE 2521 N.S.W. AUSTRALIA
00-C0-BD (hex)	INEX TECHNOLOGIES, INC.
00C0BD (base 16)	INEX TECHNOLOGIES, INC. 3350 SCOTT BLVD. BLDG.#29 SANTA CLARA CA 95054
00-C0-BE (hex)	ALCATEL - SEL
00C0BE (base 16)	ALCATEL - SEL LORENZ STR. 7000 STUTTGART 40 GERMANY
00-C0-BF (hex)	TECHNOLOGY CONCEPTS, LTD.
00C0BF (base 16)	TECHNOLOGY CONCEPTS, LTD. GRANGE ESTATE CWMBRAN, GWENT, NP44 3XR UNITED KINGDOM
00-C0-C0 (hex)	SHORE MICROSYSTEMS, INC.
00C0C0 (base 16)	SHORE MICROSYSTEMS, INC. 23 POCAHONTAS AVENUE OCEANPORT NJ 07757
00-C0-C1 (hex)	QUAD/GRAPHICS, INC.
00C0C1 (base 16)	QUAD/GRAPHICS, INC. N63 W23075 HWY 74 SUSSEX WI 53089
00-C0-C2 (hex)	INFINITE NETWORKS LTD.
00C0C2 (base 16)	INFINITE NETWORKS LTD. 19 BROOKSIDE ROAD, OXHEY WATFORD, HERTS WD1 4BW ENGLAND UNITED KINGDOM
00-C0-C3 (hex)	ACUSON COMPUTED SONOGRAPHY
00C0C3 (base 16)	ACUSON COMPUTED SONOGRAPHY 1220 CHARLESTON ROAD P.O. BOX 7393 MOUNTAIN VIEW CA 94039-7393
00-C0-C4 (hex)	COMPUTER OPERATIONAL
00C0C4 (base 16)	COMPUTER OPERATIONAL REQUIREMENT ANALYSTS LTD CORAL HOUSE, 274A HIGH STREET ALDERSHOT, HAMPSHIRE GU12 4LZ, ENGLAND
00-C0-C5 (hex)	SID INFORMATICA
00C0C5 (base 16)	SID INFORMATICA RUA DR. GERALDO CAMPOS MOREIRA 240 - 5 ANDAR CEP 04571-020 SAO PAULO - SP BRAZIL
00-C0-C6 (hex)	PERSONAL MEDIA CORP.
00C0C6 (base 16)	PERSONAL MEDIA CORP. 1-7-7 MY BLDG. HIRATSUKA SHINAGAWA, TOKYO 142 JAPAN
00-C0-C7 (hex)	SPARKTRUM MICROSYSTEMS, INC.
00C0C7 (base 16)	SPARKTRUM MICROSYSTEMS, INC. 2860 ZANKER ROAD, STE.#210 SAN JOSE CA 95134
00-C0-C8 (hex)	MICRO BYTE PTY. LTD.

company_id	Organization Address
00C0C8 (base 16)	MICRO BYTE PTY. LTD. 197 SHERBOURNE RD. MONTMORENCY MELBOURNE VIC AUSTRALIA 3094
00-C0-C9 (hex)	ELSAG BAILEY PROCESS
00C0C9 (base 16)	ELSAG BAILEY PROCESS AUTOMATION 29801 EUCLID AVENUE MS-3S1 WICKLIFFE OH 44092
00-C0-CA (hex)	ALFA, INC.
00C0CA (base 16)	ALFA, INC. 11-1, INDUSTRY EAST ROAD IV SCIENCE BASED INDUSTRIAL PARK HSINCHU TAIWAN
00-C0-CB (hex)	CONTROL TECHNOLOGY CORPORATION
00C0CB (base 16)	CONTROL TECHNOLOGY CORPORATION 25 SOUTH STREET HOPKINTON MA 01748
00-C0-CC (hex)	TELESCIENCES CO SYSTEMS, INC.
00C0CC (base 16)	TELESCIENCES CO SYSTEMS, INC. 351 NEW ALBANY RD. MOORESTOWN NJ 08057-1177
00-C0-CD (hex)	COMELTA, S.A.
00C0CD (base 16)	COMELTA, S.A. AVDA. PARC TECNOLOGIC, 4 08290 CERDANYOLA DEL VALLES BARCELONA SPAIN
00-C0-CE (hex)	CEI SYSTEMS & ENGINEERING PTE
00C0CE (base 16)	CEI SYSTEMS & ENGINEERING PTE BLK 73 #02-18 AYER RAJAH CRESC AYER RAJAH INDUSTRIAL ESTATE SINGAPORE 0513
00-C0-CF (hex)	IMATRAN VOIMA OY
00C0CF (base 16)	IMATRAN VOIMA OY IVO P.O. BOX 340 02151 ESPOO FINLAND
00-C0-D0 (hex)	RATOC SYSTEM INC.
00C0D0 (base 16)	RATOC SYSTEM INC. ASAHI NAMBA BLDG. 1-6-14 SHIKITSU HIGASHI NANIWAKU OSAKA CITY 556 JAPAN
00-C0-D1 (hex)	COMTREE TECHNOLOGY CORPORATION
00C0D1 (base 16)	COMTREE TECHNOLOGY CORPORATION 5F-7, NO. 1, FU-HSING NORTH RD TAIPEI TAIWAN R.O.C.
00-C0-D2 (hex)	SYNTELLECT, INC.
00C0D2 (base 16)	SYNTELLECT, INC. 15810 N. 28TH AVENUE PHOENIX AZ 85023
00-C0-D3 (hex)	OLYMPUS IMAGE SYSTEMS, INC.
00C0D3 (base 16)	OLYMPUS IMAGE SYSTEMS, INC. 15271 BARRANCA PARKWAY IRVINE CA 92718-2201
00-C0-D4 (hex)	AXON NETWORKS, INC.
00C0D4 (base 16)	AXON NETWORKS, INC. 104 SPRUCE STREET WATERTOWN MA 02172
00-C0-D5 (hex)	QUANCOM ELECTRONIC GMBH
00C0D5 (base 16)	QUANCOM ELECTRONIC GMBH HEINRICH-ESSER-STRASSE 27 W-5040 BRUHL GERMANY
00-C0-D6 (hex)	J1 SYSTEMS, INC.

company_id	Organization Address
00C0D6 (base 16)	J1 SYSTEMS, INC. 3 DUNWOODY PARK-STE.#103 ATLANTA GA 30338
00-C0-D7 (hex)	TAIWAN TRADING CENTER DBA
00C0D7 (base 16)	TAIWAN TRADING CENTER DBA TTC COMPUTER PRODUCTS 3244 N. SKYWAY CIRCLE #102 IRVING TX 75038
00-C0-D8 (hex)	UNIVERSAL DATA SYSTEMS
00C0D8 (base 16)	UNIVERSAL DATA SYSTEMS 5000 BRADFORD DRIVE HUNTSVILLE AL 35805-1993
00-C0-D9 (hex)	QUINTE NETWORK CONFIDENTIALITY
00C0D9 (base 16)	QUINTE NETWORK CONFIDENTIALITY EQUIPMENT INC. 207 - 121 DIMDAS STREET EAST BELLEVILLE, ONTARIO CANADA, K8N 1C3
00-C0-DA (hex)	NICE SYSTEMS LTD.
00C0DA (base 16)	NICE SYSTEMS LTD. 3 TEVUOT HA'ARETZ ST TEL AVIV 69546 ISRAEL
00-C0-DB (hex)	IPC CORPORATION (PTE) LTD.
00C0DB (base 16)	IPC CORPORATION (PTE) LTD. 122 EUNOS AVE., 7 #05-10 SINGAPORE 1440
00-C0-DC (hex)	EOS TECHNOLOGIES, INC.
00C0DC (base 16)	EOS TECHNOLOGIES, INC. 3945 FREEDOM CIRCLE, STE.#770 SANTA CLARA CA 95054
00-C0-DD (hex)	ANCOR COMMUNICATIONS
00C0DD (base 16)	ANCOR COMMUNICATIONS 6130 BLUE CIRCLE DRIVE MINNETONKA MN 55343
00-C0-DE (hex)	ZCOMM, INC.
00C0DE (base 16)	ZCOMM, INC. 1050 C EAST DUANE AVENUE SUNNYVALE CA 94086
00-C0-DF (hex)	KYE SYSTEMS CORP.
00C0DF (base 16)	KYE SYSTEMS CORP. 11F, NO. 116, SEC. 2, NANKING E. RD. TAIPEI TAIWAN, R.O.C.
00-C0-E0 (hex)	DSC COMMUNICATION CORP.
00C0E0 (base 16)	DSC COMMUNICATION CORP. 1000 COIT ROAD, MS#ADVP 3 PLANO TX 75075
00-C0-E1 (hex)	SONIC SOLUTIONS
00C0E1 (base 16)	SONIC SOLUTIONS 1891 E. FRANCISCO BLVD. SAN RAFAEL CA 94901
00-C0-E2 (hex)	CALCOMP, INC.
00C0E2 (base 16)	CALCOMP, INC. 2411 W. LAPALMA AVENUE P.O. BOX 3250, MS22 ANAHEIM CA 92803-3250
00-C0-E3 (hex)	OSITECH COMMUNICATIONS, INC.
00C0E3 (base 16)	OSITECH COMMUNICATIONS, INC. 679 SOUTHGATE DRIVE GUELPH, ONTARIO CANADA N1G 4S2
00-C0-E4 (hex)	SIEMENS BUILDING
00C0E4 (base 16)	SIEMENS BUILDING TECHNOLOGIES, INC. 1000 DEERFIELD PARKWAY BUFFALO GROVE IL 60089
00-C0-E5 (hex)	GESPAC, S.A.

company_id	Organization Address
00C0E5 (base 16)	GESPAC, S.A. CHEMIN DES AULX 18 CH-1228 GENEVA SWITZERLAND
00-C0-E6 (hex)	TXPORT
00C0E6 (base 16)	TXPORT 125 WEST PARK LOOP HUNTSVILLE AL 35806
00-C0-E7 (hex)	FIBERDATA AB
00C0E7 (base 16)	FIBERDATA AB P.O. BOX 20095 S-16102 BROMMA SWEDEN
00-C0-E8 (hex)	PLEXCOM, INC.
00C0E8 (base 16)	PLEXCOM, INC. 65 MORELAND ROAD SIMI VALLEY CA 93065
00-C0-E9 (hex)	OAK SOLUTIONS, LTD.
00C0E9 (base 16)	OAK SOLUTIONS, LTD. BROADWAY HOUSE 149-151 ST NEOTS RD, HARDWICK CAMBRIDGE CB3 7QJ ENGLAND
00-C0-EA (hex)	ARRAY TECHNOLOGY LTD.
00C0EA (base 16)	ARRAY TECHNOLOGY LTD. 145 FRIMLEY ROAD CAMBERLEY, SURREY ENGLAND GU15 2PS
00-C0-EB (hex)	SEH COMPUTERTECHNIK GMBH
00C0EB (base 16)	SEH COMPUTERTECHNIK GMBH SUNDERWEG 4 P.O. BOX 140829 D-33628 BIELEFELD GERMANY
00-C0-EC (hex)	DAUPHIN TECHNOLOGY
00C0EC (base 16)	DAUPHIN TECHNOLOGY 450 EISENHOWER LANE NORTH LOMBARD IL 60148
00-C0-ED (hex)	US ARMY ELECTRONIC
00C0ED (base 16)	US ARMY ELECTRONIC PROVING GROUND 1838 PASEO SAN LUIS SIERRA VISTA AZ 85635
00-C0-EE (hex)	KYOCERA CORPORATION
00C0EE (base 16)	KYOCERA CORPORATION 2-14-9 TAMAGAWADAI SETAGAYA-KU, TOKYO 158 JAPAN
00-C0-EF (hex)	ABIT CORPORATION
00C0EF (base 16)	ABIT CORPORATION 29-11 HIRAOKA-CHO HACHIOUJI-SHI TOKYO 192 JAPAN
00-C0-F0 (hex)	KINGSTON TECHNOLOGY CORP.
00C0F0 (base 16)	KINGSTON TECHNOLOGY CORP. 17600 NEWHOPE STREET FOUNTAIN VALLEY CA 92708
00-C0-F1 (hex)	SHINKO ELECTRIC CO., LTD.
00C0F1 (base 16)	SHINKO ELECTRIC CO., LTD. COMPUTER SYSTEM DIVISION 150 MOTOYASHIKI, SANYA-CHO TOYOHASHI-SHI, AICHI PREF. JAPAN 441-31
00-C0-F2 (hex)	TRANSITION NETWORKS
00C0F2 (base 16)	TRANSITION NETWORKS 6475 CITY WEST PARKWAY MINNEAPOLIS MN 55344
00-C0-F3 (hex)	NETWORK COMMUNICATIONS CORP.
00C0F3 (base 16)	NETWORK COMMUNICATIONS CORP. 5501 GREEN VALLEY DRIVE BLOOMINGTON MN 55437-1085

company_id	Organization Address
00-C0-F4 (hex)	INTERLINK SYSTEM CO., LTD.
00C0F4 (base 16)	INTERLINK SYSTEM CO., LTD. INTERLINK B/D, 476-20 SEOGYO-DONG, MAPO-KU SEOUL KOREA
00-C0-F5 (hex)	METACOMP, INC.
00C0F5 (base 16)	METACOMP, INC. 10989 VIA FRONTERA SAN DIEGO CA 92127
00-C0-F6 (hex)	CELAN TECHNOLOGY INC.
00C0F6 (base 16)	CELAN TECHNOLOGY INC. NO. 101, MIN-HSIANG ST. HSIN-CHU CITY TAIWAN, R.O.C.
00-C0-F7 (hex)	ENGAGE COMMUNICATION, INC.
00C0F7 (base 16)	ENGAGE COMMUNICATION, INC. 9053 SOQUEL DRIVE APTOS CA 95003-4034
00-C0-F8 (hex)	ABOUT COMPUTING INC.
00C0F8 (base 16)	ABOUT COMPUTING INC. P.O. BOX 172 BELMONT MA 02178
00-C0-F9 (hex)	HARRIS AND JEFFRIES, INC.
00C0F9 (base 16)	HARRIS AND JEFFRIES, INC. 888 WASHINGTON ST.– STE. #130 DEDHAM MA 02026
00-C0-FA (hex)	CANARY COMMUNICATIONS, INC.
00C0FA (base 16)	CANARY COMMUNICATIONS, INC. 1851 ZANKER ROAD SAN JOSE CA 95112-4213
00-C0-FB (hex)	ADVANCED TECHNOLOGY LABS
00C0FB (base 16)	ADVANCED TECHNOLOGY LABS 22100 BOTHELL HIGHWAY S.E. P.O. BOX 3003 BOTHELL WA 98041-3003
00-C0-FC (hex)	ELASTIC REALITY, INC.
00C0FC (base 16)	ELASTIC REALITY, INC. 925 STEWART STREET MADISON WI 53713
00-C0-FD (hex)	PROSUM
00C0FD (base 16)	PROSUM 12 RUE SADI-CARNOT 94370 NOISEAU FRANCE
00-C0-FE (hex)	APTEC COMPUTER SYSTEMS, INC.
00C0FE (base 16)	APTEC COMPUTER SYSTEMS, INC. P.O. BOX 6750 PORTLAND OR 97228-6750
00-C0-FF (hex)	DOT HILL SYSTEMS CORPORATION
00C0FF (base 16)	DOT HILL SYSTEMS CORPORATION 6305 El Camino Real Carlsbad, CA 92009
00-CF-1C (hex)	COMMUNICATION MACHINERY CORP.
00CF1C (base 16)	COMMUNICATION MACHINERY CORP. 1226 ANACAPA SANTA BARBARA CA 93101
00-D0-00 (hex)	FERRAN SCIENTIFIC, INC.
00D000 (base 16)	FERRAN SCIENTIFIC, INC. 11558 SORRENTO VALLEY ROAD SUITE #1 SAN DIEGO CA 92121
00-D0-01 (hex)	VST TECHNOLOGIES, INC.
00D001 (base 16)	VST TECHNOLOGIES, INC. 125 NAGOG PARK ACTON MA 01720
00-D0-02 (hex)	DITECH CORPORATION
00D002 (base 16)	DITECH CORPORATION 825 EAST MIDDLEFIELD RD MOUNTAIN VIEW CA 94043

company_id	Organization Address
00-D0-03 (hex)	COMDA ENTERPRISES CORP.
00D003 (base 16)	COMDA ENTERPRISES CORP. 2F, NO. 501-18, CHUNGCHEN ROAD HSINTIEN, TAIPEI TAIWAN, ROC
00-D0-04 (hex)	PENTACOM LTD.
00D004 (base 16)	PENTACOM LTD. 8 HASADNAOT STREET P.O. BOX 12109 HERZLIA 46733 ISRAEL
00-D0-05 (hex)	ZHS ZEITMANAGEMENTSYSTEME
00D005 (base 16)	ZHS ZEITMANAGEMENTSYSTEME HARD-UND SOFTWARE GMBH KREUZBERGER RING 56 65205 WIESBADEN GERMANY
00-D0-06 (hex)	CISCO SYSTEMS, INC.
00D006 (base 16)	CISCO SYSTEMS, INC. 170 WEST TASMAN DRIVE SAN JOSE CA 95134
00-D0-07 (hex)	MIC ASSOCIATES, INC.
00D007 (base 16)	MIC ASSOCIATES, INC. 1510-1, KAIDOKI TAMA, TOKYO JAPAN, 206-0012
00-D0-08 (hex)	MACTELL CORPORATION
00D008 (base 16)	MACTELL CORPORATION 7000 CAMERON ROAD AUSTIN TX 78752
00-D0-09 (hex)	HSING TECH. ENTERPRISE CO. LTD
00D009 (base 16)	HSING TECH. ENTERPRISE CO. LTD NO.2, LANE 128, SEC. 2 CHUNG SHAN N. RD. TAIPEI TAIWAN, R.O.C.
00-D0-0A (hex)	LANACCESS TELECOM S.A.
00D00A (base 16)	LANACCESS TELECOM S.A. GRAN VIA 8-10 4 1 08902 L'HOSPITALET DE LLOBREGAT SPAIN
00-D0-0B (hex)	RHK TECHNOLOGY, INC.
00D00B (base 16)	RHK TECHNOLOGY, INC. 1050 EAST MAPLE ROAD TROY MI 48083
00-D0-0C (hex)	SNIJDER MICRO SYSTEMS
00D00C (base 16)	SNIJDER MICRO SYSTEMS P.O. BOX 300 NL-5750 AH DEURNE THE NETHERLANDS
00-D0-0D (hex)	MICROMERITICS INSTRUMENT
00D00D (base 16)	MICROMERITICS INSTRUMENT CORPORATION ONE MICROMERITICS DRIVE NORCROSS GA 30093-1877
00-D0-0E (hex)	PLURIS, INC.
00D00E (base 16)	PLURIS, INC. 10455 BANDLEY DRIVE CUPERTINO CA 95014
00-D0-0F (hex)	SPEECH DESIGN GMBH
00D00F (base 16)	SPEECH DESIGN GMBH INDUSTRIESTR. 1 D-82110 GERMERING GERMANY
00-D0-10 (hex)	CONVERGENT NETWORKS, INC.
00D010 (base 16)	CONVERGENT NETWORKS, INC. 2 HIGHWOOD DRIVE TEWKSBURY MA 01876
00-D0-11 (hex)	PRISM VIDEO, INC.

845

company_id	Organization Address
00D011 (base 16)	PRISM VIDEO, INC. 15851 DALLAS PARKWAY-STE.#1060 ADDISON TX 75001
00-D0-12 (hex)	GATEWORKS CORP.
00D012 (base 16)	GATEWORKS CORP. 7631 MORRO ROAD ATASCADERO CA 93422
00-D0-13 (hex)	PRIMEX AEROSPACE COMPANY
00D013 (base 16)	PRIMEX AEROSPACE COMPANY P.O. BOX 97009 11441 WILLOWS ROAD NE REDMOND WA 98073-9709
00-D0-14 (hex)	ROOT, INC.
00D014 (base 16)	ROOT, INC. 3-23-2 MINAMI OHTSUKA TOSHIMA-KU TOKYO JAPAN 170-0005
00-D0-15 (hex)	UNIVEX MICROTECHNOLOGY CORP.
00D015 (base 16)	UNIVEX MICROTECHNOLOGY CORP. 2, TZE-CHIANG 3RD ROAD CHUNG-LI INDUSTRIAL PARK, CHUNG-LI TAIWAN
00-D0-16 (hex)	SCM MICROSYSTEMS, INC.
00D016 (base 16)	SCM MICROSYSTEMS, INC. 160 KNOWLES DRIVE LOS GATOS CA 95032
00-D0-17 (hex)	SYNTECH INFORMATION CO., LTD.
00D017 (base 16)	SYNTECH INFORMATION CO., LTD. 8F, 210, TA-TUNG RD., SEC. 3 HSI-CHIH, TAIPEI HSIEN TAIWAN, ROC
00-D0-18 (hex)	QWES. COM, INC.
00D018 (base 16)	QWES. COM, INC. 14742 NEWPORT AVE. - STE. #203 TUSTIN CA 92780
00-D0-19 (hex)	DAINIPPON SCREEN CORPORATE
00D019 (base 16)	DAINIPPON SCREEN CORPORATE REPRESENTATIVES OF AMERICA,INC 17942 COWAN AVENUE IRVINE CA 92614
00-D0-1A (hex)	URMET SUD S.P.A.
00D01A (base 16)	URMET SUD S.P.A. VIA DI CASTEL ROMANO 167 00128 - ROMA ITALY
00-D0-1B (hex)	MIMAKI ENGINEERING CO., LTD.
00D01B (base 16)	MIMAKI ENGINEERING CO., LTD. 5-9-41 KITA SHINAGAWA SHINAGAWA-KU TOKYO 141-0001 JAPAN
00-D0-1C (hex)	SBS TECHNOLOGIES,
00D01C (base 16)	SBS TECHNOLOGIES, CONNECTIVITY PRODUCTS 1284 CORPORATE CENTER DRIVE ST. PAUL MN 55121-1245
00-D0-1D (hex)	FURUNO ELECTRIC CO., LTD.
00D01D (base 16)	FURUNO ELECTRIC CO., LTD. NO. 9-52, ASHIHARA-CHO NISHINOMIYA-CITY 662-8580 JAPAN
00-D0-1E (hex)	PINGTEL CORP.
00D01E (base 16)	PINGTEL CORP. 773 WINTER STREET N. ANDOVER MA 01845
00-D0-1F (hex)	CTAM PTY. LTD.

company_id	Organization Address
00D01F (base 16)	CTAM PTY. LTD. 399 HIGH STREET ASHBURTON 3147 VICTORIA AUSTRALIA
00-D0-20 (hex)	AIM SYSTEM, INC.
00D020 (base 16)	AIM SYSTEM, INC. 4TH FLOOR CHUNGWOO B/D 219-1 POYEE-DONG, GANGNAM-KU SEOUL, 135-200 KOREA
00-D0-21 (hex)	REGENT ELECTRONICS CORP.
00D021 (base 16)	REGENT ELECTRONICS CORP. 200 CENTENNIAL AVE.-STE. #201 PISCATAWAY NJ 08854
00-D0-22 (hex)	INCREDIBLE TECHNOLOGIES, INC.
00D022 (base 16)	INCREDIBLE TECHNOLOGIES, INC. 1600 HICKS ROAD ROLLING MEADOWS IL 60008
00-D0-23 (hex)	INFORTREND TECHNOLOGY, INC.
00D023 (base 16)	INFORTREND TECHNOLOGY, INC. 10F, NO. 33 SAN-MIN RD. SEC. 2 PANCHIAO CITY TAIPEI HSIEN TAIWAN
00-D0-24 (hex)	Cognex Corporation
00D024 (base 16)	Cognex Corporation Modular Vision Systems Division In-Sight Products Group 15865 SW 74th Avenue, Suite 105 Portland, OR 97224
00-D0-25 (hex)	XROSSTECH, INC.
00D025 (base 16)	XROSSTECH, INC. HABDONG B/D 5F 210-2 YANGJAE-DONG, SEOCHO-KU SEOUL KOREA
00-D0-26 (hex)	HIRSCHMANN AUSTRIA GMBH
00D026 (base 16)	HIRSCHMANN AUSTRIA GMBH OBERER PASPELSWEG 6 - 8 6830 RANKWEIL-BREDERIS AUSTRIA
00-D0-27 (hex)	APPLIED AUTOMATION, INC.
00D027 (base 16)	APPLIED AUTOMATION, INC. P.O. BOX 9999 BARTLESVILLE OK 74005-9999
00-D0-28 (hex)	OMNEON VIDEO NETWORKS
00D028 (base 16)	OMNEON VIDEO NETWORKS 965 Stewart Drive Sunnyvale, CA 94086-3913
00-D0-29 (hex)	WAKEFERN FOOD CORPORATION
00D029 (base 16)	WAKEFERN FOOD CORPORATION 230 RARITAN CENTER PARKWAY EDISON NJ 08837
00-D0-2A (hex)	FLEXION SYSTEMS
00D02A (base 16)	FLEXION SYSTEMS HARTHAM PARK CORSHAM WILTS. SN13 0RP UNITED KINGDOM
00-D0-2B (hex)	JETCELL, INC.
00D02B (base 16)	JETCELL, INC. 173 CONSTITUTION DRIVE MENLO PARK CA 94025-1106
00-D0-2C (hex)	CAMPBELL SCIENTIFIC, INC.
00D02C (base 16)	CAMPBELL SCIENTIFIC, INC. 815 W. 1800 N. LOGAN UT 84321-1784
00-D0-2D (hex)	ADEMCO

company_id	Organization Address
00D02D (base 16)	ADEMCO 165 EILEEN WAY SYOSSET NY 11791
00-D0-2E (hex)	COMMUNICATION AUTOMATION CORP.
00D02E (base 16)	COMMUNICATION AUTOMATION CORP. 1180 MCDERMOTT DRIVE WEST CHESTER PA 19380
00-D0-2F (hex)	VLSI TECHNOLOGY INC.
00D02F (base 16)	VLSI TECHNOLOGY INC. 8375 S. RIVER PARKWAY TEMPE AZ 85284
00-D0-30 (hex)	SAFETRAN SYSTEMS CORP.
00D030 (base 16)	SAFETRAN SYSTEMS CORP. 10655 7TH STREET RANCHO CUCAMONGA CA 91730
00-D0-31 (hex)	INDUSTRIAL LOGIC CORPORATION
00D031 (base 16)	INDUSTRIAL LOGIC CORPORATION 15 PIEDMONT CENTER-STE #700 ATLANTA GA 30305
00-D0-32 (hex)	YANO ELECTRIC CO., LTD.
00D032 (base 16)	YANO ELECTRIC CO., LTD. 7-3-1 IBUKIDAIHIGASHIMACHI NISHI-KU, KOBE, 651-2242 JAPAN
00-D0-33 (hex)	DALIAN DAXIAN NETWORK
00D033 (base 16)	DALIAN DAXIAN NETWORK SYSTEM CO., LTD. 98 SHENGLI RD XIGANG DISTRICT DALIAN, P.R. CHINA
00-D0-34 (hex)	ORMEC SYSTEMS CORP.
00D034 (base 16)	ORMEC SYSTEMS CORP. 19 LINDEN PARK ROCHESTER NY 14625
00-D0-35 (hex)	BEHAVIOR TECH. COMPUTER CORP.
00D035 (base 16)	BEHAVIOR TECH. COMPUTER CORP. 2F, 51, TUNG HSING ROAD TAIPEI TAIWAN R.O.C.
00-D0-36 (hex)	TECHNOLOGY ATLANTA CORP.
00D036 (base 16)	TECHNOLOGY ATLANTA CORP. 141 W. WIEUCA RD. N.E. SUITE #300 ATLANTA GA 30342
00-D0-37 (hex)	PHILIPS-DVS-LO BDR
00D037 (base 16)	PHILIPS-DVS-LO BDR 51, RUE CARNOT 92156 SURESNES FRANCE
00-D0-38 (hex)	FIVEMERE, LTD.
00D038 (base 16)	FIVEMERE, LTD. UNIT 1-HERON INDUSTRIAL ESTATE BASINGSTOKE ROAD SPENCERS WOOD, READING, BERK RG7 1PJ ENGLAND
00-D0-39 (hex)	UTILICOM, INC.
00D039 (base 16)	UTILICOM, INC. 323 LOVE PLACE SANTA BARBARA CA 93112-3289
00-D0-3A (hex)	ZONEWORX, INC.
00D03A (base 16)	ZONEWORX, INC. 40925 COUNTY CENTER DRIVE SUITE #200 TEMECULA CA 92592
00-D0-3B (hex)	VISION PRODUCTS PTY. LTD.
00D03B (base 16)	VISION PRODUCTS PTY. LTD. SECOND AVENUE, TECHNOLOGY PARK MAWSON LAKES AUSTRALIA 5095
00-D0-3C (hex)	POWER MICRO RESEARCH

company_id	Organization Address
00D03C (base 16)	POWER MICRO RESEARCH 1411 EAST CAMPBELL ROAD SUITE #1100 RICHARDSON TX 75081
00-D0-3E (hex)	ROCKETCHIPS, INC.
00D03E (base 16)	ROCKETCHIPS, INC. 7901 XERXES AVE. S. MINNEAPOLIS MN 55431
00-D0-3F (hex)	AMERICAN COMMUNICATION
00D03F (base 16)	AMERICAN COMMUNICATION TECHNOLOGIES INTERNATIONAL INC. 320 PROFESSIONAL CENTER DR. SUITE #100 ROHNERT PARK CA 94928
00-D0-40 (hex)	SYSMATE CO., LTD.
00D040 (base 16)	SYSMATE CO., LTD. 1091 WOLPYONG-DONG SEO-GU, DEAJCON 302-280 SOUTH KOREA
00-D0-41 (hex)	AMIGO TECHNOLOGY CO., LTD.
00D041 (base 16)	AMIGO TECHNOLOGY CO., LTD. 4F-1B, NO.12, LANE 609, SEC.5, CHUNG HSIN ROAD, SAN CHUNG TAIPEI HSIEN TAIWAN, R.O.C.
00-D0-42 (hex)	MAHLO GMBH & CO. UG
00D042 (base 16)	MAHLO GMBH & CO. UG DONAUSTRASSE 12 D-93342 SAAL/DONAU GERMANY
00-D0-43 (hex)	ZONAL RETAIL DATA SYSTEMS
00D043 (base 16)	ZONAL RETAIL DATA SYSTEMS 24 FORTH STREET EDINBURGH SCOTLAND
00-D0-44 (hex)	ALIDIAN NETWORKS, INC.
00D044 (base 16)	ALIDIAN NETWORKS, INC. 1330 W. MIDDLEFIELD ROAD MOUNTAIN VIEW CA 94043
00-D0-45 (hex)	KVASER AB
00D045 (base 16)	KVASER AB BOX 4076 511 04 KINNAHULT SWEDEN
00-D0-46 (hex)	DOLBY LABORATORIES, INC.
00D046 (base 16)	DOLBY LABORATORIES, INC. 999 BRANNAN STREET SAN FRANCISCO CA 94103-4938
00-D0-47 (hex)	XN TECHNOLOGIES
00D047 (base 16)	XN TECHNOLOGIES P.O. BOX 350 CHENEY WA 99004
00-D0-48 (hex)	ECTON, INC.
00D048 (base 16)	ECTON, INC. 5168 CAMPUS DRIVE PLYMOUTH MEETING PA 19462
00-D0-49 (hex)	IMPRESSTEK CO., LTD.
00D049 (base 16)	IMPRESSTEK CO., LTD. 6F, SPECIALTY CONSTRUCTION CTR 1290, SUNSAN-DONG,SO-GU 302-120, KOREA (REP.)
00-D0-4A (hex)	PRESENCE TECHNOLOGY GMBH
00D04A (base 16)	PRESENCE TECHNOLOGY GMBH + CO. KG SENDENHORSTER STR. 32 D-48317 DRENSTEINFURT GERMANY
00-D0-4B (hex)	LA CIE GROUP S.A.

company_id	Organization Address
00D04B (base 16)	LA CIE GROUP S.A. 17 RUE AMPERE 91349 MASSY CEDEX FRANCE
00-D0-4C (hex)	EUROTEL TELECOM LTD.
00D04C (base 16)	EUROTEL TELECOM LTD. CANISTER HOUSE JEWRY STREET WINCHESTER B023 8SA UNITED KINGDOM
00-D0-4D (hex)	DIV OF RESEARCH & STATISTICS
00D04D (base 16)	DIV OF RESEARCH & STATISTICS BOG OF THE FEDERAL RESERVE SYS MAIL STOP 96 20TH & «C» STREETS, NW WASHINGTON DC 20551
00-D0-4E (hex)	LOGIBAG
00D04E (base 16)	LOGIBAG 2, RUE DE LA MANDINIERE 72300 SABLE/SARTHE FRANCE
00-D0-4F (hex)	BITRONICS, INC.
00D04F (base 16)	BITRONICS, INC. P.O. BOX 22290 LEHIGH VALLEY PA 18002-2290
00-D0-50 (hex)	ISKRATEL
00D050 (base 16)	ISKRATEL LJUBLJANSKA C. 24A 4000 KRANJ SLOVENIA
00-D0-51 (hex)	O2 MICRO, INC.
00D051 (base 16)	O2 MICRO, INC. 2901 TASMAN DRIVE, STE.#205 SANTA CLARA CA 95054
00-D0-52 (hex)	ASCEND COMMUNICATIONS, INC.
00D052 (base 16)	ASCEND COMMUNICATIONS, INC. ONE ASCEND PLAZA 1701 HARBOR BAY PARKWAY ALAMEDA CA 94502-3002
00-D0-53 (hex)	CONNECTED SYSTEMS
00D053 (base 16)	CONNECTED SYSTEMS 126 W. FIGUEROA STREET SANTA BARBARA CA 93101
00-D0-54 (hex)	SAS INSTITUTE INC.
00D054 (base 16)	SAS INSTITUTE INC. SAS CAMPUS DRIVE, R4 CARY NC 27511
00-D0-55 (hex)	KATHREIN-WERKE KG
00D055 (base 16)	KATHREIN-WERKE KG ANTON-KATHREIN-STRASS 1-3 D-83004 ROSENHEIM GERMANY
00-D0-56 (hex)	SOMAT CORPORATION
00D056 (base 16)	SOMAT CORPORATION 702 KILLARNEY STREET URBANA IL 61801
00-D0-57 (hex)	ULTRAK, INC.
00D057 (base 16)	ULTRAK, INC. 1301 WATERS RIDGE DRIVE LEWISVILLE TX 75057
00-D0-58 (hex)	CISCO SYSTEMS, INC.
00D058 (base 16)	CISCO SYSTEMS, INC. 170 WEST TASMAN DRIVE SAN JOSE CA 95134
00-D0-59 (hex)	AMBIT MICROSYSTEMS CORP.
00D059 (base 16)	AMBIT MICROSYSTEMS CORP. 5F-1, 5 HSIN-AN ROAD SCIENCE-BASED INDUSTRIAL PARK HSINCHU TAIWAN, R.O.C.

company_id	Organization Address
00-D0-5A (hex)	SYMBIONICS, LTD.
00D05A (base 16)	SYMBIONICS, LTD. ST. JOHN'S INNOVATION PARK CAMBRIDGE CB4 0WS ENGLAND
00-D0-5B (hex)	ACROLOOP MOTION CONTROL
00D05B (base 16)	ACROLOOP MOTION CONTROL SYSTEMS 3650 CHESTNUT ST. N. CHASKA MN 55318
00-D0-5C (hex)	TECHNOTREND SYSTEMTECHNIK GMBH
00D05C (base 16)	TECHNOTREND SYSTEMTECHNIK GMBH WILHELM-WOLFF-STRASSE 6 GER-99099 ERFURT GERMANY
00-D0-5D (hex)	INTELLIWORXX, INC.
00D05D (base 16)	INTELLIWORXX, INC. 1819 MAIN STREET, STE #1101 SARASOTA FL 34236
00-D0-5E (hex)	STRATABEAM TECHNOLOGY, INC.
00D05E (base 16)	STRATABEAM TECHNOLOGY, INC. 1943 LANDINGS DRIVE MOUNTAIN VIEW CA 94043
00-D0-5F (hex)	VALCOM, INC.
00D05F (base 16)	VALCOM, INC. 1111 INDUSTRY AVENUE ROANOKE VA 24013
00-D0-60 (hex)	PANASONIC EUROPEAN
00D060 (base 16)	PANASONIC EUROPEAN LABORATORIES GMBH MONZASTR. 4C D-63225 LANGEN GERMANY
00-D0-61 (hex)	TREMON ENTERPRISES CO., LTD.
00D061 (base 16)	TREMON ENTERPRISES CO., LTD. 15F, NO. 116, SEC. 1 HSIN-TAI 5TH ROAD HSICHIH, TAIPEI COUNTY TAIWAN, ROC
00-D0-62 (hex)	DIGIGRAM
00D062 (base 16)	DIGIGRAM PARC DE PRE MILLIET 38330 MONTBONNOT FRANCE
00-D0-63 (hex)	CISCO SYSTEMS, INC.
00D063 (base 16)	CISCO SYSTEMS, INC. 170 WEST TASMAN DRIVE SAN JOSE CA 95134
00-D0-64 (hex)	MULTITEL
00D064 (base 16)	MULTITEL 2905 RUE DE CELLES QUEBEC CITY, QUEBEC PROVINCE CANADA, G2C-1W7
00-D0-65 (hex)	TOKO ELECTRIC
00D065 (base 16)	TOKO ELECTRIC 4008 KUROHAMA, HASUDA-SHI SAITAMA 349-0192 JAPAN
00-D0-66 (hex)	WINTRISS ENGINEERING CORP.
00D066 (base 16)	WINTRISS ENGINEERING CORP. 6344 FERRIS SQUARE SAN DIEGO CA 92121
00-D0-67 (hex)	CAMPIO COMMUNICATIONS
00D067 (base 16)	CAMPIO COMMUNICATIONS 2033 GATEWAY PL, SUITE #600 SAN JOSE CA 95110
00-D0-68 (hex)	IWILL CORPORATION

company_id	Organization Address
00D068 (base 16)	IWILL CORPORATION NO.10, WU-CHUAN 3 RD, HSIN-CHUAN CITY TAIPEI TAIWAN
00-D0-69 (hex)	TECHNOLOGIC SYSTEMS
00D069 (base 16)	TECHNOLOGIC SYSTEMS 16610 E. LASER DRIVE-STE. #10 FOUNTAIN HILLS AZ 85268
00-D0-6A (hex)	LINKUP SYSTEMS CORPORATION
00D06A (base 16)	LINKUP SYSTEMS CORPORATION 1190 COLEMAN AVE.- STE #2C SAN JOSE CA 95110
00-D0-6B (hex)	SR TELECOM INC.
00D06B (base 16)	SR TELECOM INC. 425 LEGGET DRIVE KANATA, ONTARIO CANADA K2K 2W2
00-D0-6C (hex)	SHAREWAVE, INC.
00D06C (base 16)	SHAREWAVE, INC. 5175 HILLSDALE CIRCLE EL DORADO HILLS CA 95762
00-D0-6D (hex)	ACRISON, INC.
00D06D (base 16)	ACRISON, INC. 20 EMPIRE BLVD. MOONACHIE NJ 07074
00-D0-6E (hex)	TRENDVIEW RECORDERS LTD.
00D06E (base 16)	TRENDVIEW RECORDERS LTD. 4 AIRFIELD WAY CHRISTCHURCH DORSET BH23 3TS UNITED KINGDOM
00-D0-6F (hex)	KMC CONTROLS
00D06F (base 16)	KMC CONTROLS P.O. BOX 497 19476 NEW PARIS INDUSTRIAL DR. NEW PARIS IN 46553
00-D0-70 (hex)	LONG WELL ELECTRONICS CORP.
00D070 (base 16)	LONG WELL ELECTRONICS CORP. 4F, NO. 59-1, TSAO DI WEI SHENGKENG HSIANG, TAIPEI HSIEN TAIWAN 222, R.O.C.
00-D0-71 (hex)	ECHELON CORP.
00D071 (base 16)	ECHELON CORP. 4015 MIRANDA AVENUE PALO ALTO CA 94304
00-D0-72 (hex)	BROADLOGIC
00D072 (base 16)	BROADLOGIC 463 S. MILPITAS BLVD. MILPITAS CA 95035
00-D0-73 (hex)	ACN ADVANCED COMMUNICATIONS
00D073 (base 16)	ACN ADVANCED COMMUNICATIONS NETWORKS SA RUE DU PUITS-GODET BA CH-2000 NEUCHATEL SWITZERLAND
00-D0-74 (hex)	TAQUA SYSTEMS, INC.
00D074 (base 16)	TAQUA SYSTEMS, INC. 1600 FALMOUTH RD. - STE «3» CENTERVILLE MA 02632
00-D0-75 (hex)	ALARIS MEDICAL SYSTEMS, INC.
00D075 (base 16)	ALARIS MEDICAL SYSTEMS, INC. P.O. BOX 85335 10221 WATERIDGE CIRCLE SAN DIEGO CA 92121-2733
00-D0-76 (hex)	MERRILL LYNCH & CO., INC.
00D076 (base 16)	MERRILL LYNCH & CO., INC. 103 MORGAN LANE PLAINSBORO NJ 08536
00-D0-77 (hex)	LUCENT TECHNOLOGIES
00D077 (base 16)	LUCENT TECHNOLOGIES CLIENT ACCESS BUSINESS UNIT 101 CRAWFORDS CORNER ROAD ROOM #1E-437AL HOLMDEL NJ 07733
00-D0-78 (hex)	ELTEX OF SWEDEN AB
00D078 (base 16)	ELTEX OF SWEDEN AB BOX 608 34324 ELMHULT SWEDEN
00-D0-79 (hex)	CISCO SYSTEMS, INC.
00D079 (base 16)	CISCO SYSTEMS, INC. 170 WEST TASMAN DRIVE SAN JOSE CA 95134
00-D0-7A (hex)	AMAQUEST COMPUTER CORP.
00D07A (base 16)	AMAQUEST COMPUTER CORP. 8/F, 79 HSIN-TAI 5TH ROAD, SEC. 1 HS1-CHIH, TAIPEI TAIWAN R.O.C.
00-D0-7B (hex)	COMCAM INTERNATIONAL LTD.
00D07B (base 16)	COMCAM INTERNATIONAL LTD. PARK VALLEY CORPORATE CNTR#107 1157 PHOENIXVILLE PIKE WEST CHESTER PA 19380
00-D0-7C (hex)	KOYO ELECTRONICS INC. CO.,LTD.
00D07C (base 16)	KOYO ELECTRONICS INC. CO.,LTD. 1-171 TENJIN-CHO KODAIRA TOKYO 187-0004 JAPAN
00-D0-7D (hex)	COSINE COMMUNICATIONS
00D07D (base 16)	COSINE COMMUNICATIONS 1200 BRIDGE PARKWAY REDWOOD CITY CA 94065
00-D0-7E (hex)	KEYCORP LTD.
00D07E (base 16)	KEYCORP LTD. P.O. BOX 199 CHATSWOOD NSW 2057 AUSTRALIA
00-D0-7F (hex)	STRATEGY & TECHNOLOGY, LIMITED
00D07F (base 16)	STRATEGY & TECHNOLOGY, LIMITED 6 HILL VIEW HENLEAZE BRISTOL, BS9 4PZ UNITED KINGDOM
00-D0-80 (hex)	EXABYTE CORPORATION
00D080 (base 16)	EXABYTE CORPORATION 1685 38TH STREET BOULDER CO 80301
00-D0-81 (hex)	REAL TIME DEVICES USA, INC.
00D081 (base 16)	REAL TIME DEVICES USA, INC. P.O. BOX 906 STATE COLLEGE PA 16804
00-D0-82 (hex)	IOWAVE INC.
00D082 (base 16)	IOWAVE INC. 1010 WISCONSIN AVENUE WASHINGTON DC 20007
00-D0-83 (hex)	INVERTEX, INC.
00D083 (base 16)	INVERTEX, INC. 1012 MORSE AVENUE- STE.#9 SUNNYVALE CA 94089
00-D0-84 (hex)	NEXCOMM SYSTEMS, INC.
00D084 (base 16)	NEXCOMM SYSTEMS, INC. SUIT #NAL-903, SUNGNAM TECHNO-PARK 148 YATAP-DONG, BUNDANG-KU SUNGNAM-CITY, KYUNGGI-DO,KOREA
00-D0-85 (hex)	OTIS ELEVATOR COMPANY

company_id	Organization Address
00D085 (base 16)	OTIS ELEVATOR COMPANY 5 FARM SPRINGS RD. FARMINGTON CT 06032
00-D0-86 (hex)	FOVEON, INC.
00D086 (base 16)	FOVEON, INC. 3565 MONROE STREET SANTA CLARA CA 95051
00-D0-87 (hex)	MICROFIRST INC.
00D087 (base 16)	MICROFIRST INC. 11 EAST OAK STREET OAKLAND NJ 07436
00-D0-88 (hex)	MAINSAIL NETWORKS, INC.
00D088 (base 16)	MAINSAIL NETWORKS, INC. 4655 OLD IRONSIDES DR. STE.400 SANTA CLARA CA 95054
00-D0-89 (hex)	DYNACOLOR, INC.
00D089 (base 16)	DYNACOLOR, INC. 18F-1, NO. 97, SECTION 4 CHUNG HSIN RD, SAN-CHUNG CITY TAIPEI HSIEN TAIWAN, R.O.C.
00-D0-8A (hex)	PHOTRON USA
00D08A (base 16)	PHOTRON USA 1101 S. WINCHESTER BLVD. SUITE #D-144 SAN JOSE CA 95128
00-D0-8B (hex)	STORAGE AREA NETWORKS, LTD.
00D08B (base 16)	STORAGE AREA NETWORKS, LTD. RUSTAT HOUSE, 62 CLIFTON ROAD CAMBRIDGE UNITED KINGDOM CB1 7EG
00-D0-8C (hex)	GENOA TECHNOLOGY, INC.
00D08C (base 16)	GENOA TECHNOLOGY, INC. 5401 TECH CIRCLE MOORPARK CA 93021
00-D0-8D (hex)	PHOENIX GROUP, INC.
00D08D (base 16)	PHOENIX GROUP, INC. 123 MARCUS BLVD. HAUPPAUGE NY 11788
00-D0-8E (hex)	NVISION INC.
00D08E (base 16)	NVISION INC. 125 CROWN POINT COURT GRASS VALLEY CA 95945
00-D0-8F (hex)	ARDENT TECHNOLOGIES, INC.
00D08F (base 16)	ARDENT TECHNOLOGIES, INC. 250 N. WOLFE ROAD SUNNYVALE CA 94086
00-D0-90 (hex)	CISCO SYSTEMS, INC.
00D090 (base 16)	CISCO SYSTEMS, INC. 170 WEST TASMAN DRIVE SAN JOSE CA 95134
00-D0-91 (hex)	SMARTSAN SYSTEMS, INC.
00D091 (base 16)	SMARTSAN SYSTEMS, INC. 4655 OLD IRONSIDES DR. #480 SANTA CLARA CA 95054
00-D0-92 (hex)	GLENAYRE WESTERN MULTIPLEX
00D092 (base 16)	GLENAYRE WESTERN MULTIPLEX 1196 BORREGAS AVENUE SUNNYVALE CA 94089
00-D0-93 (hex)	TQ - COMPONENTS GMBH
00D093 (base 16)	TQ - COMPONENTS GMBH GUT DELLING - MUHLSTR 2 D-82229 SEEFELD GERMANY
00-D0-94 (hex)	TIMELINE VISTA, INC.
00D094 (base 16)	TIMELINE VISTA, INC. 1755-B LA COSTA MEADOWS DRIVE SAN MARCOS CA 92069
00-D0-95 (hex)	XYLAN CORPORATION

company_id	Organization Address
00D095 (base 16)	XYLAN CORPORATION 26801 W. AGOUTA ROAD CALABASAS CA 91302
00-D0-96 (hex)	3COM EUROPE LTD.
00D096 (base 16)	3COM EUROPE LTD. BOUNDARY WAY HEMEL HEMPSTEAD HERTS. HP2 7YU UNITED KINGDOM
00-D0-97 (hex)	CISCO SYSTEMS, INC.
00D097 (base 16)	CISCO SYSTEMS, INC. 170 WEST TASMAN DRIVE M/S SJA-2 SAN JOSE CA 95134
00-D0-98 (hex)	IPS AUTOMATION
00D098 (base 16)	IPS AUTOMATION 221 WHITEHALL DRIVE MARKHAM, ONTARIO CANADA, L3R 9T1
00-D0-99 (hex)	ELCARD OY
00D099 (base 16)	ELCARD OY P.O. BOX 120/BECKERINTIC 38 51201 KANGASNIEMI FINLAND
00-D0-9A (hex)	FILANET CORPORATION
00D09A (base 16)	FILANET CORPORATION 931 Benecia Avenue Sunnyvale CA 94085
00-D0-9B (hex)	SPECTEL LTD.
00D09B (base 16)	SPECTEL LTD. 21 STILLORGAN INDUSTRIAL PARK STILLORGAN, CO. DUBLIN IRELAND
00-D0-9C (hex)	KAPADIA COMMUNICATIONS
00D09C (base 16)	KAPADIA COMMUNICATIONS 3925 WEST BROKER LANE AUSTIN TX 78759
00-D0-9D (hex)	VERIS INDUSTRIES
00D09D (base 16)	VERIS INDUSTRIES 10831 SW CASCADE PORTLAND OR 97223
00-D0-9E (hex)	2WIRE, INC.
00D09E (base 16)	2WIRE, INC. 694 TASMAN DRIVE MILPITAS CA 95035
00-D0-9F (hex)	NOVTEK TEST SYSTEMS
00D09F (base 16)	NOVTEK TEST SYSTEMS 2170 PARAGON DRIVE SAN JOSE CA 95131
00-D0-A0 (hex)	MIPS DENMARK
00D0A0 (base 16)	MIPS DENMARK LAUTRUPVANG 2B 2750 BALLERUP DK - DENMARK
00-D0-A1 (hex)	OSKAR VIERLING GMBH + CO. KG
00D0A1 (base 16)	OSKAR VIERLING GMBH + CO. KG PRETZFELDER STR. 21 91320 EBERMANNSTADT GERMANY
00-D0-A2 (hex)	INTEGRATED DEVICE
00D0A2 (base 16)	INTEGRATED DEVICE TECHNOLOGY, INC. 2975 STENDER WAY M/S 0-318 SANTA CLARA CA 95054
00-D0-A3 (hex)	VOCAL DATA, INC.
00D0A3 (base 16)	VOCAL DATA, INC. 1701 N GREENVILLE #304 RICHARDSON TX 75081
00-D0-A4 (hex)	ALANTRO COMMUNICATIONS

company_id	Organization Address
00D0A4 (base 16)	ALANTRO COMMUNICATIONS 141 STONY CIRCLE, STE. #210 SANTAROSA CA 95401
00-D0-A5 (hex)	AMERICAN ARIUM
00D0A5 (base 16)	AMERICAN ARIUM 14281 CHAMBERS ROAD TUSTIN CA 92780
00-D0-A6 (hex)	LANBIRD TECHNOLOGY CO., LTD.
00D0A6 (base 16)	LANBIRD TECHNOLOGY CO., LTD. ROOM A-211, S.B.I. 647-26, DEUNGCHON-DONG, KANGSEO-GU, SEOUL KOREA 157-030
00-D0-A7 (hex)	TOKYO SOKKI KENKYUJO CO., LTD.
00D0A7 (base 16)	TOKYO SOKKI KENKYUJO CO., LTD. 8-2, MINAMI-OHI 6-CHOME SHINAGAWA-KU TOKYO JAPAN 140-8560
00-D0-A8 (hex)	NETWORK ENGINES, INC.
00D0A8 (base 16)	NETWORK ENGINES, INC. 61 PLEASANT STREET RANDOLPH MA 02368
00-D0-A9 (hex)	SHINANO KENSHI CO., LTD.
00D0A9 (base 16)	SHINANO KENSHI CO., LTD. ELECTRONIC EQUIPMENT DIVISION 6-15-26, CHUO, UEDA-SHI NAGANO-KEN, 386-0012 JAPAN
00-D0-AA (hex)	CHASE COMMUNICATIONS
00D0AA (base 16)	CHASE COMMUNICATIONS ST. LEONARDS ROAD EAST SHEEN LONDON SW16 7LY UNITED KINGDOM
00-D0-AB (hex)	DELTAKABEL TELECOM CV
00D0AB (base 16)	DELTAKABEL TELECOM CV HANZEWEG 14 2803 MC GOUDA THE NETHERLANDS
00-D0-AC (hex)	GRAYSON WIRELESS
00D0AC (base 16)	GRAYSON WIRELESS 140 VISTA CENTRE DRIVE FOREST VA 24551
00-D0-AD (hex)	TL INDUSTRIES
00D0AD (base 16)	TL INDUSTRIES 2541 TRACY ROAD NORTHWOOD OH 43619
00-D0-AE (hex)	ORESIS COMMUNICATIONS, INC.
00D0AE (base 16)	ORESIS COMMUNICATIONS, INC. 14670 NW GREENBRIER PKWY BEAVERTON OR 97006
00-D0-AF (hex)	CUTLER-HAMMER, INC.
00D0AF (base 16)	CUTLER-HAMMER, INC. PMP CENTER 240 VISTA PARK DRIVE PITTSBURGH PA 15205
00-D0-B0 (hex)	BITSWITCH LTD.
00D0B0 (base 16)	BITSWITCH LTD. 3 MEADOW COURT, AMOS ROAD MEADOWHALL, SHEFFIELD S9 1BX UNITED KINGDOM
00-D0-B1 (hex)	OMEGA ELECTRONICS SA
00D0B1 (base 16)	OMEGA ELECTRONICS SA ROUTE DE SOLEURE 68 CH-2500 BIENNE 4 SWITZERLAND
00-D0-B2 (hex)	XIOTECH CORPORATION

company_id	Organization Address
00D0B2 (base 16)	XIOTECH CORPORATION 6509 FLYING CLOUD DRIVE SUITE #200 EDEN PRAIRIE MN 55344
00-D0-B3 (hex)	DRS FLIGHT SAFETY AND
00D0B3 (base 16)	DRS FLIGHT SAFETY AND COMMUNICATIONS 40 CONCOURSE GATE NEPEAN CANADA K2E 8A6
00-D0-B4 (hex)	KATSUJIMA CO., LTD.
00D0B4 (base 16)	KATSUJIMA CO., LTD. 1-6-1-, SHIRATORI KATSUSHIKA-KU TOKYO 125-0063 JAPAN
00-D0-B5 (hex)	DOTCOM
00D0B5 (base 16)	DOTCOM 16, RUE MOULIN DES BRUYERES F-92400 COURBEVOIE FRANCE
00-D0-B6 (hex)	CRESCENT NETWORKS, INC.
00D0B6 (base 16)	CRESCENT NETWORKS, INC. 201 RIVERNECK ROAD CHELMSFORD MA 01842
00-D0-B7 (hex)	INTEL CORPORATION
00D0B7 (base 16)	INTEL CORPORATION 5200 NE ELAM YOUNG PARKWAY HF1-08 HILLSBORO OR 97124
00-D0-B8 (hex)	IOMEGA CORP.
00D0B8 (base 16)	IOMEGA CORP. 1821 WEST IOMEGA WAY ROY UT 84067
00-D0-B9 (hex)	MICROTEK INTERNATIONAL, INC.
00D0B9 (base 16)	MICROTEK INTERNATIONAL, INC. NO. 6 INDUSTRY EAST ROAD 3 SCIENCE-BASED INDUSTRIAL PARK HSINCHU TAIWAN 30077, R.O.C.
00-D0-BA (hex)	CISCO SYSTEMS, INC.
00D0BA (base 16)	CISCO SYSTEMS, INC. 170 WEST TASMAN DRIVE- SJA-2 SAN JOSE CA 95134
00-D0-BB (hex)	CISCO SYSTEMS, INC.
00D0BB (base 16)	CISCO SYSTEMS, INC. 170 WEST TASMAN DRIVE SJA-2 SAN JOSE CA 95134
00-D0-BC (hex)	CISCO SYSTEMS, INC.
00D0BC (base 16)	CISCO SYSTEMS, INC. 170 WEST TASMAN DRIVE-SJA-2 SAN JOSE CA 95134
00-D0-BD (hex)	SICAN GMBH
00D0BD (base 16)	SICAN GMBH GARBSENER LANDSTR. 10 D-30419 HANNOVER GERMANY
00-D0-BE (hex)	EMUTEC INC.
00D0BE (base 16)	EMUTEC INC. P.O. BOX 3035 EVERETT WA 98203
00-D0-BF (hex)	PIVOTAL TECHNOLOGIES
00D0BF (base 16)	PIVOTAL TECHNOLOGIES 70 S. LAKE AVENUE - STE. #900 PASADENA CA 91101
00-D0-C0 (hex)	CISCO SYSTEMS, INC.
00D0C0 (base 16)	CISCO SYSTEMS, INC. 170 WEST TASMAN DR. SJA-2 SAN JOSE CA 95134
00-D0-C1 (hex)	HARMONIC DATA SYSTEMS, LTD.

company_id	Organization Address
00D0C1 (base 16)	HARMONIC DATA SYSTEMS, LTD. 10 BEIT SHAMAI STREET TEL-AVIV ISRAEL 67018
00-D0-C2 (hex)	BALTHAZAR TECHNOLOGY AB
00D0C2 (base 16)	BALTHAZAR TECHNOLOGY AB ANKDAMMSGATAN 24 S-17143 SOLNA SWEDEN
00-D0-C3 (hex)	VIVID TECHNOLOGY PTE, LTD.
00D0C3 (base 16)	VIVID TECHNOLOGY PTE, LTD. 1003 BUKIT MERAH CENTRAL #03-09, S159836 SINGAPORE
00-D0-C4 (hex)	TERATECH CORPORATION
00D0C4 (base 16)	TERATECH CORPORATION 223 MIDDLESEX TRPK. BURLINGTON MA 01803-3308
00-D0-C5 (hex)	COMPUTATIONAL SYSTEMS, INC.
00D0C5 (base 16)	COMPUTATIONAL SYSTEMS, INC. 835 INNOVATION DRIVE KNOXVILLE TN 37932
00-D0-C6 (hex)	THOMAS & BETTS CORP.
00D0C6 (base 16)	THOMAS & BETTS CORP. 76 FAIRBANKS IRVINE CA 92618
00-D0-C7 (hex)	PATHWAY, INC.
00D0C7 (base 16)	PATHWAY, INC. 777 BETA DRIVE MAYFIELD VILLAGE OH 44143
00-D0-C8 (hex)	I/O CONSULTING A/S
00D0C8 (base 16)	I/O CONSULTING A/S LAUTRUPVANG 1B DK-2750 BALLERUP DENMARK
00-D0-C9 (hex)	ADVANTECH CO., LTD.
00D0C9 (base 16)	ADVANTECH CO., LTD. FL. 4, NO. 108-3 MING-CHUAN ROAD SHING-TIEN CITY TAIPEI, TAIWAN
00-D0-CA (hex)	INTRINSYC SOFTWARE INC.
00D0CA (base 16)	INTRINSYC SOFTWARE INC. 1075 WEST GEORGIA ST. SUITE #1050 VANCOUVER, BC, V6E 3C9 CANADA
00-D0-CB (hex)	DASAN CO., LTD.
00D0CB (base 16)	DASAN CO., LTD. 6F, KOSMO TOWER 1002, DAECHI-DONG, KANGNAM-KU SEOUL KOREA (ZIP 135-280)
00-D0-CC (hex)	TECHNOLOGIES LYRE INC.
00D0CC (base 16)	TECHNOLOGIES LYRE INC. 1200 ST-JEAN-BAPTISTE, SUITE #120 QUEBEC, QUEBEC CANADA G2E 5E8
00-D0-CD (hex)	ATAN TECHNOLOGY INC.
00D0CD (base 16)	ATAN TECHNOLOGY INC. #5, ALLEY 18, LANE 81, CHIEN KANG, 2ND ROAD HINCHU TAIWAN, R.O.C.
00-D0-CE (hex)	ASYST ELECTRONIC
00D0CE (base 16)	ASYST ELECTRONIC BRODISCE 7, 10C TRZIN 1236 TRZIN SLOVENIA
00-D0-CF (hex)	MORETON BAY

company_id	Organization Address
00D0CF (base 16)	MORETON BAY 12/97 JIJAWS STREET SUMNER PARK. 4074 QLD. AUSTRALIA
00-D0-D0 (hex)	ZHONGXING TELECOM LTD.
00D0D0 (base 16)	ZHONGXING TELECOM LTD. 8-9F BUILDING 54,301# ZHONG SHAN DONGLU, NANJING PRC, PC=210002 CHINA
00-D0-D1 (hex)	SIROCCO SYSTEMS, INC.
00D0D1 (base 16)	SIROCCO SYSTEMS, INC. 4 FAIRFIELD BLVD. WALLINGFORD CT 06492
00-D0-D2 (hex)	EPILOG CORPORATION
00D0D2 (base 16)	EPILOG CORPORATION 500 CORPORATE CIRCLE - STE. L GOLDEN CO 80401
00-D0-D3 (hex)	CISCO SYSTEMS, INC.
00D0D3 (base 16)	CISCO SYSTEMS, INC. 170 WEST TASMAN DRIVE M/S SJA-2 SAN JOSE CA 95134
00-D0-D4 (hex)	V-BITS, INC.
00D0D4 (base 16)	V-BITS, INC. 2150 TRADE ZONE BLVD. SUITE #105 SAN JOSE CA 95131
00-D0-D5 (hex)	GRUNDIG AG
00D0D5 (base 16)	GRUNDIG AG KURGARTENSGTREET 37 D-90762 FUERTH/BAYERN GERMANY
00-D0-D6 (hex)	AETHRA TELECOMUNICAZIONI
00D0D6 (base 16)	AETHRA TELECOMUNICAZIONI VIA MATTEO RICCI, 10 60020 ANCONA ITALY
00-D0-D7 (hex)	B2C2, INC.
00D0D7 (base 16)	B2C2, INC. 2020 CHALLENGER DRIVE- SUITE #101 ALAMEDA CA 94501
00-D0-D8 (hex)	NOMADIC TECHNOLOGIES
00D0D8 (base 16)	NOMADIC TECHNOLOGIES 2133 LEGHORN STREET MOUNTAIN VIEW CA 94043
00-D0-D9 (hex)	DEDICATED MICROCOMPUTERS
00D0D9 (base 16)	DEDICATED MICROCOMPUTERS GROUP, LTD. 11 OAK STREET, PENDLEBURY SWINTON, MANCHESTER M274FL UNITED KINGDOM
00-D0-DA (hex)	TAICOM DATA SYSTEMS CO., LTD.
00D0DA (base 16)	TAICOM DATA SYSTEMS CO., LTD. 45, WU-KUNG 5 ROAD WU-KU IND. PARK TAIPEI-HSIEN TAIWAN
00-D0-DB (hex)	MCQUAY INTERNATIONAL
00D0DB (base 16)	MCQUAY INTERNATIONAL 13600 INDUSTRIAL PARK BLVD. MINNEAPOLIS MN 55441
00-D0-DC (hex)	MODULAR MINING SYSTEMS, INC.
00D0DC (base 16)	MODULAR MINING SYSTEMS, INC. 3289 E. HEMISPHERE LOOP TUCSON AZ 85706
00-D0-DD (hex)	SUNRISE TELECOM, INC.

company_id	Organization Address
00-D0-DD (hex)	SUNRISE TELECOM, INC.
00D0DD (base 16)	SUNRISE TELECOM, INC. 22 GREAT OAKS BLVD. SAN JOSE CA 95119
00-D0-DE (hex)	PHILIPS MULTIMEDIA NETWORK
00D0DE (base 16)	PHILIPS MULTIMEDIA NETWORK SYSTEMS GMBH FICHTESTRASSE 1A D-02601 BAUTZEN GERMANY
00-D0-DF (hex)	KUZUMI ELECTRONICS, INC.
00D0DF (base 16)	KUZUMI ELECTRONICS, INC. 28-6 IIJIMA-CHYO, SAKAE-KU YOKOHAMA-SHI KANAGAWA, 244-0842 JAPAN
00-D0-E0 (hex)	DOOIN ELECTRONICS CO.
00D0E0 (base 16)	DOOIN ELECTRONICS CO. DOOIN BLDG. 16-6, SOONAE-DONG BUNDANG-GU, SUNGNAM-SI KYUNGGI-DO KOREA 463-020
00-D0-E1 (hex)	AVIONITEK ISRAEL INC.
00D0E1 (base 16)	AVIONITEK ISRAEL INC. 1 ETGAR STREET TIRAT CARMEL 39120 ISRAEL
00-D0-E2 (hex)	MRT MICRO, INC.
00D0E2 (base 16)	MRT MICRO, INC. 14000 S. MILITARY TRAIL DELRAY BEACH FL 33484
00-D0-E3 (hex)	ELE-CHEM ENGINEERING CO., LTD.
00D0E3 (base 16)	ELE-CHEM ENGINEERING CO., LTD. WINDSTONE OFFICE 1-803, 275-2 YANGJUE-DONG, SEOCHO-KU SEOUL 137-130, KOREA
00-D0-E4 (hex)	CISCO SYSTEMS, INC.
00D0E4 (base 16)	CISCO SYSTEMS, INC. 170 WEST TASMAN DRIVE SAN JOSE CA 95134
00-D0-E5 (hex)	SOLIDUM SYSTEMS CORP.
00D0E5 (base 16)	SOLIDUM SYSTEMS CORP. 940 BELFAST ROAD 1S.217 OTTAWA, ONTARIO K1G 4A2 CANADA
00-D0-E6 (hex)	IBOND INC.
00D0E6 (base 16)	IBOND INC. 3160, DE LA CRUZ BLVD. SUITE #101 SANTA CLARA CA 95054
00-D0-E7 (hex)	VCON TELECOMMUNICATION LTD.
00D0E7 (base 16)	VCON TELECOMMUNICATION LTD. 22 MASKIT STREET HERZLIYA 46733 ISRAEL
00-D0-E8 (hex)	MAC SYSTEM CO., LTD.
00D0E8 (base 16)	MAC SYSTEM CO., LTD. R&D INSTITUTE MAC SYSTEM CO., LTD. 219-2 ANANG7-DONG, MANAN-GU,ANANG-SS KYUNGKI-DO, KOREA, 430-017
00-D0-E9 (hex)	ADVANTAGE CENTURY
00D0E9 (base 16)	ADVANTAGE CENTURY TELECOMMUNICATION CORP. (ACT) 8F-806, NO. 129, MIN SENG E. ROAD, SEC. 3 TAIPEI, TAIWAN
00-D0-EA (hex)	NEXTONE COMMUNICATIONS, INC.
00D0EA (base 16)	NEXTONE COMMUNICATIONS, INC. 9700 GREAT SENECA HGHWY ROCKVILLE MD 20850

company_id	Organization Address
00-D0-EB (hex)	LIGHTERA NETWORKS, INC.
00D0EB (base 16)	LIGHTERA NETWORKS, INC. 10201 BUBB ROAD CUPERTINO CA 95014
00-D0-EC (hex)	NAKAYO TELECOMMUNICATIONS, INC
00D0EC (base 16)	NAKAYO TELECOMMUNICATIONS, INC 1-3-2 SOUJYA-MACHI MAEBASHI-SHI GUNMA, 371-0853 JAPAN
00-D0-ED (hex)	XIOX
00D0ED (base 16)	XIOX 150 DOW STREET MANCHESTER NH 03101
00-D0-EE (hex)	DICTAPHONE CORPORATION
00D0EE (base 16)	DICTAPHONE CORPORATION 3191 BROADBRIDGE AVE. STRATFORD CT 06614-2559
00-D0-EF (hex)	IGT
00D0EF (base 16)	IGT 9295 PROTOTYPE DRIVE RENO NV 89511
00-D0-F0 (hex)	CONVISION TECHNOLOGY GMBH
00D0F0 (base 16)	CONVISION TECHNOLOGY GMBH REBENRING 33 D-38106 BRAUNSCHWEIG GERMANY
00-D0-F1 (hex)	SEGA ENTERPRISES, LTD.
00D0F1 (base 16)	SEGA ENTERPRISES, LTD. 12-14 HIGASHIKOUJIYA 2-CHOME OHTA-KU TOKYO 144-8532 JAPAN
00-D0-F2 (hex)	MONTEREY NETWORKS
00D0F2 (base 16)	MONTEREY NETWORKS 1909 N. GLENVILLE DRIVE RICHARDSON TX 75081
00-D0-F3 (hex)	SOLARI DI UDINE SPA
00D0F3 (base 16)	SOLARI DI UDINE SPA VIA GINO PIERI 29 33100 UDINE ITALY
00-D0-F4 (hex)	CARINTHIAN TECH INSTITUTE
00D0F4 (base 16)	CARINTHIAN TECH INSTITUTE RICHARD-WAGNER STR. 19 9500 VILLACH AUSTRIA
00-D0-F5 (hex)	ORANGE MICRO, INC.
00D0F5 (base 16)	ORANGE MICRO, INC. 1400 N. LAKEVIEW AVE. ANAHEIM CA 92807
00-D0-F6 (hex)	NORTHCHURCH COMMUNICATIONS INC
00D0F6 (base 16)	NORTHCHURCH COMMUNICATIONS INC 5 CORPORATE DRIVE ANDOVER MA 01810
00-D0-F7 (hex)	NEXT NETS CORPORATION
00D0F7 (base 16)	NEXT NETS CORPORATION MITA KOKUSAI BLDG. 17F 1-4-28 MITA MINATO-KU TOKYO 108-0073 JAPAN
00-D0-F8 (hex)	FUJIAN STAR TERMINAL
00D0F8 (base 16)	FUJIAN STAR TERMINAL DEVICE CO., LTD. FUER INDUSTRIAL ZONE STAR SCIENCE & TECHNOLOGY CITY FUZHOU, FUJIAN, CHINA 350002
00-D0-F9 (hex)	ACUTE COMMUNICATIONS CORP.

company_id	Organization Address
00D0F9 (base 16)	ACUTE COMMUNICATIONS CORP. NO. 1, CREATION ROAD III SCIENCE BASED INDUSTRIAL PARK HSINCHU 300 TAIWAN
00-D0-FA (hex)	RACAL GUARDATA
00D0FA (base 16)	RACAL GUARDATA 1601 N. HARRISON PKWY BUILDING "A" -SUITE #100 SUNRISE FL 33323
00-D0-FB (hex)	TEK MICROSYSTEMS, INCORPORATED
00D0FB (base 16)	TEK MICROSYSTEMS, INCORPORATED ONE NORTH AVENUE BURLINGTON MA 01803
00-D0-FC (hex)	GRANITE MICROSYSTEMS
00D0FC (base 16)	GRANITE MICROSYSTEMS 10202 N. ENTERPRISE DRIVE MEQUON WI 53092
00-D0-FD (hex)	OPTIMA TELE.COM, INC.
00D0FD (base 16)	OPTIMA TELE.COM, INC. 112 TEA ROSE STREET MARKHAM ONTARIO L6C 1X3 CANADA
00-D0-FE (hex)	ASTRAL POINT
00D0FE (base 16)	ASTRAL POINT COMMUNICATIONS, INC. 27 INDUSTRIAL AVE.,-STE. #3 CHELMSFORD MA 01824
00-D0-FF (hex)	CISCO SYSTEMS, INC.
00D0FF (base 16)	CISCO SYSTEMS, INC. 170 WEST TASMAN DRIVE SAN JOSE CA 95134
00-DD-00 (hex)	UNGERMANN-BASS INC.
00DD00 (base 16)	UNGERMANN-BASS INC. 3900 FREEDOM CIRCLE SANTA CLARA, CA 95054
00-DD-01 (hex)	UNGERMANN-BASS INC.
00DD01 (base 16)	UNGERMANN-BASS INC. 3900 FREEDOM CIRCLE SANTA CLARA CA 95054
00-DD-02 (hex)	UNGERMANN-BASS INC.
00DD02 (base 16)	UNGERMANN-BASS INC. 3900 FREEDOM CIRCLE SANTA CLARA CA 95054
00-DD-03 (hex)	UNGERMANN-BASS INC.
00DD03 (base 16)	UNGERMANN-BASS INC. 3900 FREEDOM CIRCLE SANTA CLARA CA 95054
00-DD-04 (hex)	UNGERMANN-BASS INC.
00DD04 (base 16)	UNGERMANN-BASS INC. 3900 FREEDOM CIRCLE SANTA CLARA CA 95054
00-DD-05 (hex)	UNGERMANN-BASS INC.
00DD05 (base 16)	UNGERMANN-BASS INC. 3900 FREEDOM CIRCLE SANTA CLARA CA 95054
00-DD-06 (hex)	UNGERMANN-BASS INC.
00DD06 (base 16)	UNGERMANN-BASS INC. 3900 FREEDOM CIRCLE SANTA CLARA CA 95054
00-DD-07 (hex)	UNGERMANN-BASS INC.
00DD07 (base 16)	UNGERMANN-BASS INC. 3900 FREEDOM CIRCLE SANTA CLARA CA 95054
00-DD-08 (hex)	UNGERMANN-BASS INC.
00DD08 (base 16)	UNGERMANN-BASS INC. 3900 FREEDOM CIRCLE SANTA CLARA CA 95054
00-DD-09 (hex)	UNGERMANN-BASS INC.

company_id	Organization Address
00DD09 (base 16)	UNGERMANN-BASS INC. 3900 FREEDOM CIRCLE SANTA CLARA CA 95054
00-DD-0A (hex)	UNGERMANN-BASS INC.
00DD0A (base 16)	UNGERMANN-BASS INC. 3900 FREEDOM CIRCLE SANTA CLARA CA 95054
00-DD-0B (hex)	UNGERMANN-BASS INC.
00DD0B (base 16)	UNGERMANN-BASS INC. 3900 FREEDOM CIRCLE SANTA CLARA CA 95054
00-DD-0C (hex)	UNGERMANN-BASS INC.
00DD0C (base 16)	UNGERMANN-BASS INC. 3900 FREEDOM CIRCLE SANTA CLARA CA 95054
00-DD-0D (hex)	UNGERMANN-BASS INC.
00DD0D (base 16)	UNGERMANN-BASS INC. 3900 FREEDOM CIRCLE SANTA CLARA CA 95054
00-DD-0E (hex)	UNGERMANN-BASS INC.
00DD0E (base 16)	UNGERMANN-BASS INC. 3900 FREEDOM CIRCLE SANTA CLARA CA 95054
00-DD-0F (hex)	UNGERMANN-BASS INC.
00DD0F (base 16)	UNGERMANN-BASS INC. 3900 FREEDOM CIRCLE SANTA CLARA CA 95054
00-E0-00 (hex)	FUJITSU, LTD
00E000 (base 16)	FUJITSU, LTD CO-MAIL NO. HON 180 1-1 KAMIKODANAKA 4-CHOME NAKAHARA-KU, KAWASAKI 211-88 JAPAN
00-E0-01 (hex)	STRAND LIGHTING LIMITED
00E001 (base 16)	STRAND LIGHTING LIMITED GRAND WAY ISLEWORTH, MIDDLESEX ENGLAND TW7 5QD
00-E0-02 (hex)	CROSSROADS SYSTEMS, INC.
00E002 (base 16)	CROSSROADS SYSTEMS, INC. 9390 RESEARCH BLVD. SUITE 2-300 AUSTIN TX 78759
00-E0-03 (hex)	NOKIA WIRELESS BUSINESS COMMUN
00E003 (base 16)	NOKIA WIRELESS BUSINESS COMMUN ACCESS POINT PRODUCTS GROUP UNIT 6, CAMBRIDGE BUS PARK MILTON RD, CAMBRIDGE CB4 0WS UNITED KINGDOM
00-E0-04 (hex)	PMC-SIERRA, INC.
00E004 (base 16)	PMC-SIERRA, INC. 105-8555 BAXTER PLACE BURNABY, BC CANADA V5A-4V7
00-E0-05 (hex)	TECHNICAL CORP.
00E005 (base 16)	TECHNICAL CORP. 22-6 MINAMI SENGENCHO NISHIKU YOKOHAMA CITY KANAGAWA JAPAN
00-E0-06 (hex)	SILICON INTEGRATED SYS. CORP.
00E006 (base 16)	SILICON INTEGRATED SYS. CORP. 16, CREATION RD. I SCIENCE-BASED INDUSTRIAL PARK HSIN CHU TAIWAN, R.O.C.
00-E0-07 (hex)	NETWORK ALCHEMY LTD.

company_id	Organization Address
00E007 (base 16)	NETWORK ALCHEMY LTD. 6 THE ORCHARD ON THE GREEN CROXLEY GREEN, RICKMANSWORTH HERTFORDSHIRE WD3 3GS UNITED KINGDOM
00-E0-08 (hex)	AMAZING CONTROLS! INC.
00E008 (base 16)	AMAZING CONTROLS! INC. 1615 WYATT DRIVE SANTA CLARA CA 95054
00-E0-09 (hex)	MARATHON TECHNOLOGIES CORP.
00E009 (base 16)	MARATHON TECHNOLOGIES CORP. 1300 MASSACHUSETTS AVENUE BOXBOROUGH MA 01719
00-E0-0A (hex)	DIBA, INC.
00E00A (base 16)	DIBA, INC. 3355 EDISON WAY MENLO PARK CA 94025
00-E0-0B (hex)	ROOFTOP COMMUNICATIONS CORP.
00E00B (base 16)	ROOFTOP COMMUNICATIONS CORP. 468 PACO DRIVE LOS ALTOS CA 94024
00-E0-0C (hex)	MOTOROLA
00E00C (base 16)	MOTOROLA 5401 N. BEACH ST. S243 FT. WORTH TX 76137
00-E0-0D (hex)	RADIANT SYSTEMS
00E00D (base 16)	RADIANT SYSTEMS 1000 ALDERMAN DR. ALPHARETTA GA 30202
00-E0-0E (hex)	AVALON IMAGING SYSTEMS, INC.
00E00E (base 16)	AVALON IMAGING SYSTEMS, INC. 3133 INDIAN ROAD BOULDER CO 80301
00-E0-0F (hex)	SHANGHAI BAUD DATA
00E00F (base 16)	SHANGHAI BAUD DATA COMMUNICATION DEVELOPMENT CORP 3F, GOLD LUCK BUILDING 2507 PUDONG ROAD SHANGHAI, CHINA
00-E0-10 (hex)	HESS SB-AUTOMATENBAU GMBH
00E010 (base 16)	HESS SB-AUTOMATENBAU GMBH HINDENBURGSTRASSE 27-29 D-71106 MAGSTADT GERMANY
00-E0-11 (hex)	UNIDEN SAN DIEGO
00E011 (base 16)	UNIDEN SAN DIEGO R&D CENTER, INC. 5808 PACIFIC CENTER BLVD. SAN DIEGO CA 92121
00-E0-12 (hex)	PLUTO TECHNOLOGIES
00E012 (base 16)	PLUTO TECHNOLOGIES 2511 55TH STREET BOULDER CO 80301
00-E0-13 (hex)	EASTERN ELECTRONIC CO., LTD.
00E013 (base 16)	EASTERN ELECTRONIC CO., LTD. NO. 4, SHIN-LONG ROAD, KWEI-SHAN INDUSTRIAL AREA TAO-YUAN TAIWAN, R.O.C.
00-E0-14 (hex)	CISCO SYSTEMS, INC.
00E014 (base 16)	CISCO SYSTEMS, INC. 170 W. TASMAN DRIVE SAN JOSE CA 95134-1706
00-E0-15 (hex)	HEIWA CORPORATION
00E015 (base 16)	HEIWA CORPORATION 2-3014-8, HIROSAWA-CHO KIRYU-SHI GUNMA PREF. 376 JAPAN
00-E0-16 (hex)	RAPID CITY COMMUNICATIONS

company_id	Organization Address
00E016 (base 16)	RAPID CITY COMMUNICATIONS 555 CLYDE AVE. MOUNTAIN VIEW CA 94043
00-E0-17 (hex)	EXXACT GMBH
00E017 (base 16)	EXXACT GMBH RHEINSTRASE 7 D-41836 HUCKELHOVEN GERMANY
00-E0-18 (hex)	ASUSTEK COMPUTER INC.
00E018 (base 16)	ASUSTEK COMPUTER INC. 150 LI-TE RD. PEITOU TAIPEI TAIWAN
00-E0-19 (hex)	ING. GIORDANO ELETTRONICA
00E019 (base 16)	ING. GIORDANO ELETTRONICA VIA PIETRO COSSA 115/12 10146-TORINO ITALY
00-E0-1A (hex)	COMTEC SYSTEMS. CO., LTD.
00E01A (base 16)	COMTEC SYSTEMS. CO., LTD. 404-9 CHOUNGCHEN-DONG BUPYOUNG-KU, INCHON KOREA
00-E0-1B (hex)	SPHERE COMMUNICATIONS, INC.
00E01B (base 16)	SPHERE COMMUNICATIONS, INC. 2 ENERGY DRIVE LAKE BLUFF IL 60044
00-E0-1C (hex)	MOBILITY ELECTRONICSY
00E01C (base 16)	MOBILITY ELECTRONICSY 7955 E. REDFIELD RD. SCOTTSDALE AZ 85260
00-E0-1D (hex)	WEBTV NETWORKS, INC.
00E01D (base 16)	WEBTV NETWORKS, INC. 305 LYTTON AVE. PALO ALTO CA 94301
00-E0-1E (hex)	CISCO SYSTEMS, INC.
00E01E (base 16)	CISCO SYSTEMS, INC. 170 W. TASMAN DRIVE SAN JOSE CA 95134-1706
00-E0-1F (hex)	AVIDIA SYSTEMS, INC.
00E01F (base 16)	AVIDIA SYSTEMS, INC. 135 NORTH PLAINS INDUSTRIAL RD WALLINGFORD CT 06492
00-E0-20 (hex)	TECNOMEN OY
00E020 (base 16)	TECNOMEN OY P.O. BOX 93 FIN-02271 ESPOO FINLAND
00-E0-21 (hex)	FREEGATE CORP.
00E021 (base 16)	FREEGATE CORP. 710 LAKEWAY STE.#230 SUNNYVALE CA 94086
00-E0-22 (hex)	MEDIALIGHT INC.
00E022 (base 16)	MEDIALIGHT INC. 20 QUEEN ST. WEST, STE#208 TORONTO, ONTARIO M5H 3R3 CANADA
00-E0-23 (hex)	TELRAD
00E023 (base 16)	TELRAD P.O. BOX 50 LOD 71100 ISRAEL
00-E0-24 (hex)	GADZOOX NETWORKS
00E024 (base 16)	GADZOOX NETWORKS 5850 HELLYER AVENUE SAN JOSE CA 95138
00-E0-25 (hex)	DIT CO., LTD.

company_id	Organization Address
00E025 (base 16)	DIT CO., LTD. 1-6-35 SHINSUNA KOTO-KU TOKYO 136 JAPAN
00-E0-26 (hex)	EASTMAN KODAK CO.
00E026 (base 16)	EASTMAN KODAK CO. 11633 SORRENTO VALLEY RD SAN DIEGO CA 92121
00-E0-27 (hex)	DUX, INC.
00E027 (base 16)	DUX, INC. 5-18-19, NISHIKAMATA, OTA-KU TOKYO-TO 144 JAPAN
00-E0-28 (hex)	APTIX CORPORATION
00E028 (base 16)	APTIX CORPORATION 2880 N. FIRST STREET SAN JOSE CA 95134
00-E0-29 (hex)	STANDARD MICROSYSTEMS CORP.
00E029 (base 16)	STANDARD MICROSYSTEMS CORP. 6 HUGHES IRVINE CA 92718
00-E0-2A (hex)	TANDBERG TELEVISION AS
00E02A (base 16)	TANDBERG TELEVISION AS PHILIP PEDERSENS V 20 N-1324 LYSAKER NORWAY
00-E0-2B (hex)	EXTREME NETWORKS
00E02B (base 16)	EXTREME NETWORKS 10460 BANDLEY DRIVE CUPERINT0 CA 95014
00-E0-2C (hex)	AST COMPUTER
00E02C (base 16)	AST COMPUTER 16215 ALTON PARKWAY IRVINE CA 92718
00-E0-2D (hex)	INNOMEDIALOGIC, INC.
00E02D (base 16)	INNOMEDIALOGIC, INC. 3653 CHEMIN CHAMBLY LONGUEUIL, QUEBEC CANADA J4L IN9
00-E0-2E (hex)	SPC ELECTRONICS CORPORATION
00E02E (base 16)	SPC ELECTRONICS CORPORATION 2-1-3 SHIBASAKI, CHOFU-SHI TOKYO, 182 JAPAN
00-E0-2F (hex)	MCNS HOLDINGS, L.P.
00E02F (base 16)	MCNS HOLDINGS, L.P. TCI, INC.-TECHNOLOGY VENTURES P.O. BOX 5630 DENVER CO 80217-5630
00-E0-30 (hex)	MELITA INTERNATIONAL CORP.
00E030 (base 16)	MELITA INTERNATIONAL CORP. 5051 PEACHTREE CORNERS CIRCLE NORCROSS GA 30092
00-E0-31 (hex)	HAGIWARA ELECTRIC CO., LTD.
00E031 (base 16)	HAGIWARA ELECTRIC CO., LTD. 7, SHIMOKOFUKADA, ASADA-CHO NISSHIN-SHI, AICHI JAPAN 470-01
00-E0-32 (hex)	MISYS FINANCIAL SYSTEMS, LTD.
00E032 (base 16)	MISYS FINANCIAL SYSTEMS, LTD. BUCKHOLT DRIVE, WARNDON, WORCESTER WR49SR UNITED KINGDOM
00-E0-33 (hex)	E.E.P.D. GMBH
00E033 (base 16)	E.E.P.D. GMBH ROEMER-STRASSE 4 85229 MARKT INDERSDORF GERMANY
00-E0-34 (hex)	CISCO SYSTEMS, INC.

company_id	Organization Address
00E034 (base 16)	CISCO SYSTEMS, INC. 170 W. TASMAN DRIVE SAN JOSE CA 95134-1706
00-E0-35 (hex)	LOUGHBOROUGH SOUND IMAGES, PLC
00E035 (base 16)	LOUGHBOROUGH SOUND IMAGES, PLC LOUGHBOROUGH PARK, ASHBY ROAD LOUGHBOROUGH, LESCESTERSHIRE LE11 3NE ENGLAND
00-E0-36 (hex)	PIONEER CORPORATION
00E036 (base 16)	PIONEER CORPORATION 2610 Hanazono 4-Chome Tokorozawa-Shi Saitama Prefecture, 359-8522 JAPAN
00-E0-37 (hex)	CENTURY CORPORATION
00E037 (base 16)	CENTURY CORPORATION WIZEM BLDG., 3F, 3-3-8-, UENO TAITO-KU, TOKYO 101 JAPAN
00-E0-38 (hex)	PROXIMA CORPORATION
00E038 (base 16)	PROXIMA CORPORATION 9440 CARROLL PARK DRIVE SAN DIEGO CA 92121-2298
00-E0-39 (hex)	PARADYNE CORP.
00E039 (base 16)	PARADYNE CORP. 8545 126TH AVENUE NORTH LARGO FL 33773
00-E0-3A (hex)	CABLETRON SYSTEMS, INC.
00E03A (base 16)	CABLETRON SYSTEMS, INC. 35 INDUSTRIAL WAY - BLDG. #36 ROCHESTER NH 03867
00-E0-3B (hex)	PROMINET CORPORATION
00E03B (base 16)	PROMINET CORPORATION 110 TURNPIKE RD. - STE. #208 WESTBOROUGH MA 01581
00-E0-3C (hex)	ADVANSYS
00E03C (base 16)	ADVANSYS 1150 RINGWOOD COURT SAN JOSE CA 95131
00-E0-3D (hex)	FOCON ELECTRONIC SYSTEMS A/S
00E03D (base 16)	FOCON ELECTRONIC SYSTEMS A/S DAMVANG PO BOX 269 DK-6400 SONDERBORG DENMARK
00-E0-3E (hex)	ALFATECH, INC.
00E03E (base 16)	ALFATECH, INC. SHIN-OSAKA EITO BLDG. 4-15-18 NISHINAKAJIMA, YODOGAWA-KU, OSAKA, JAPAN
00-E0-3F (hex)	JATON CORPORATION
00E03F (base 16)	JATON CORPORATION 556 SOUTH MILPITAS BLVD. MILPITAS CA 95035
00-E0-40 (hex)	DESKSTATION TECHNOLOGY, INC.
00E040 (base 16)	DESKSTATION TECHNOLOGY, INC. 15729 COLLEGE BLVD. LENEXA KS 66219
00-E0-41 (hex)	CSPI
00E041 (base 16)	CSPI 40 LINNELL CIRCLE BILLERICA MA 01821
00-E0-42 (hex)	PACOM DATA LTD.
00E042 (base 16)	PACOM DATA LTD. UNIT 25 38/46 SOUTH ST. RYDALMERE 2116 NSW, AUSTRALIA
00-E0-43 (hex)	VITALCOM

company_id	Organization Address	company_id	Organization Address
00E043 (base 16)	VITALCOM 15222 DEL AMO AVE. TUSTIN CA 92780	00E052 (base 16)	FOUNDRY NETWORKS, INC. 680 W. MAUDE AVE. - STE. #3 SUNNYVALE CA 94086
00-E0-44 (hex)	LSICS CORPORATION	00-E0-53 (hex)	CELLPORT LABS, INC.
00E044 (base 16)	LSICS CORPORATION 3-8-3 NINOMIYA, TSKUKUBA SHI IBARAGI-KEN, 305 JAPAN	00E053 (base 16)	CELLPORT LABS, INC. 885 ARAPAHOE AVE., BOULDER CO 80302
00-E0-45 (hex)	TOUCHWAVE, INC.	00-E0-54 (hex)	KODAI HITEC CO., LTD.
00E045 (base 16)	TOUCHWAVE, INC. 994 SAN ANTONIA RD. PALO ALTO CA 94303	00E054 (base 16)	KODAI HITEC CO., LTD. 2-45 ONUMA HANYU CITY SAITAMA.348 JAPAN
00-E0-46 (hex)	BENTLY NEVADA CORP.	00-E0-55 (hex)	INGENIERIA ELECTRONICA
00E046 (base 16)	BENTLY NEVADA CORP. PO BOX 157 MINDEN NV 89423	00E055 (base 16)	INGENIERIA ELECTRONICA COMERCIAL INELCOM S.A. CL. PIQUER NO.3 28033 MADRID SPAIN
00-E0-47 (hex)	INFOCUS SYSTEMS	00-E0-56 (hex)	HOLONTECH CORPORATION
00E047 (base 16)	INFOCUS SYSTEMS 27700B SW PARKWAY AVE. WILLSONVILLE OR 97070	00E056 (base 16)	HOLONTECH CORPORATION 2039 SAMARITAN DRIVE SAN JOSE CA 95124
00-E0-48 (hex)	SDL COMMUNICATIONS, INC.	00-E0-57 (hex)	HAN MICROTELECOM. CO., LTD.
00E048 (base 16)	SDL COMMUNICATIONS, INC. P.O. BOX 1303 EASTON MA 02334	00E057 (base 16)	HAN MICROTELECOM. CO., LTD. FASHION BD., 3RD FR, 1194, DOONSAN 2 DONG SEO-GU, TAEJON KOREA, 302-173
00-E0-49 (hex)	MICROWI ELECTRONIC GMBH	00-E0-58 (hex)	PHASE ONE DENMARK A/S
00E049 (base 16)	MICROWI ELECTRONIC GMBH ZUSAMSTRASSE 8 D 86165 AUGSBURG GERMANY	00E058 (base 16)	PHASE ONE DENMARK A/S ROSKILDEVEJ 39 DK-2000 FREDERIKSBERG DENMARK
00-E0-4A (hex)	ENHANCED MESSAGING SYSTEMS,INC	00-E0-59 (hex)	CONTROLLED ENVIRONMENTS, LTD.
00E04A (base 16)	ENHANCED MESSAGING SYSTEMS,INC 250 WEST SOUTHLAKE BLVD. SOUTHLAKE TX 76092	00E059 (base 16)	CONTROLLED ENVIRONMENTS, LTD. 590 BERRY STREET WINNEPEG CANADA 43H OR9
00-E0-4B (hex)	JUMP INDUSTRIELLE	00-E0-5A (hex)	GALEA NETWORK SECURITY
00E04B (base 16)	JUMP INDUSTRIELLE COMPUTERTECHNIK GMBH VEILCHENGASSE 7 D94469 DEGGENDORF GERMANY	00E05A (base 16)	GALEA NETWORK SECURITY 2 PLACE DU COMMERCE - STE #320 BROSSARD, QUEBEC CANADA J4W 2T8
00-E0-4C (hex)	REALTEK SEMICONDUCTOR CORP.	00-E0-5B (hex)	WEST END SYSTEMS CORP.
00E04C (base 16)	REALTEK SEMICONDUCTOR CORP. 1F, NO. 11, INDUSTRY E. RD. IX SCIENCE-BASED INDUSTRIAL PARK HSINCHU, 300 TAIWAN, R.O.C.	00E05B (base 16)	WEST END SYSTEMS CORP. 39 WINNER'S CIRCLE DR., ARNPRIOR, ONTARIO K7S 3G9 CANADA
00-E0-4D (hex)	INTERNET INITIATIVE JAPAN, INC	00-E0-5C (hex)	MATSUSHITA KOTOBUKI
00E04D (base 16)	INTERNET INITIATIVE JAPAN, INC 1-4, SANBAN-CHO, CHIYODA-KU TOKYO 102 JAPAN	00E05C (base 16)	MATSUSHITA KOTOBUKI ELECTRONICS INDUSTRIES, LTD. 247, FUKUTAKE SAIJO EHIME, 793 JAPAN
00-E0-4E (hex)	SANYO DENKI CO., LTD.	00-E0-5D (hex)	UNITEC CO., LTD.
00E04E (base 16)	SANYO DENKI CO., LTD. 1-15-1, KITAOTSUKA, TOSHIMA TOKYO JAPAN 170	00E05D (base 16)	UNITEC CO., LTD. KISOGAWA-CHO ICHINOTORI 24 HAGURI-GUN AICHI 493 JAPAN
00-E0-4F (hex)	CISCO SYSTEMS, INC.	00-E0-5E (hex)	JAPAN AVIATION ELECTRONICS
00E04F (base 16)	CISCO SYSTEMS, INC. 170 W. TASMAN DRIVE SAN JOSE CA 95134-1706	00E05E (base 16)	JAPAN AVIATION ELECTRONICS INDUSTRY, LTD. 3-1-1 MUSASHINO AKISHIMA-SHI TOKYO JAPAN 196
00-E0-50 (hex)	EXECUTONE INFORMATION	00-E0-5F (hex)	E-NET, INC.
00E050 (base 16)	EXECUTONE INFORMATION SYSTEMS, INC. 478 WHEELERS FARMS ROAD MILFORD CT 06460	00E05F (base 16)	E-NET, INC. 12325 HYMEADOW DRIVE SUITE #2-200 AUSTIN TX 78750
00-E0-51 (hex)	TALX CORPORATION		
00E051 (base 16)	TALX CORPORATION 1850 BORMAN COURT ST. LOUIS MO 63146		
00-E0-52 (hex)	FOUNDRY NETWORKS, INC.		

company_id	Organization Address
00-E0-60 (hex)	SHERWOOD
00E060 (base 16)	SHERWOOD 21056 FORBES STREET HAYWARD CA 94545
00-E0-61 (hex)	EDGEPOINT NETWORKS, INC.
00E061 (base 16)	EDGEPOINT NETWORKS, INC. 2238 MARTIN AVENUE SANTA CLARA CA 95050
00-E0-62 (hex)	HOST ENGINEERING
00E062 (base 16)	HOST ENGINEERING 200 EAST MAIN STREET -STE.#700 JOHNSON CITY TN 37604
00-E0-63 (hex)	CABLETRON - YAGO SYSTEMS, INC.
00E063 (base 16)	CABLETRON - YAGO SYSTEMS, INC. 35 INDUSTRIAL WAY P.O. BOX 5005 ROCHESTER NH 03866-5005
00-E0-64 (hex)	SAMSUNG ELECTRONICS
00E064 (base 16)	SAMSUNG ELECTRONICS 99 W. TASMAN DRIVE SAN JOSE CA 95134
00-E0-65 (hex)	OPTICAL ACCESS INTERNATIONAL
00E065 (base 16)	OPTICAL ACCESS INTERNATIONAL 500 WEST CUMMINGS PL. #3400 WOBURN MA 01801
00-E0-66 (hex)	PROMAX SYSTEMS, INC.
00E066 (base 16)	PROMAX SYSTEMS, INC. 16 TECHNOLOGY DRIVE—BLDG.#106 IRVINE CA 92656
00-E0-67 (hex)	EAC AUTOMATION-CONSULTING GMBH
00E067 (base 16)	EAC AUTOMATION-CONSULTING GMBH HERMSDORFER DAMM 222 73467 BERLIN GERMANY
00-E0-68 (hex)	MERRIMAC SYSTEMS INC.
00E068 (base 16)	MERRIMAC SYSTEMS INC. 2144 MC COY ROAD CARROLLTON TX 75006
00-E0-69 (hex)	JAYCOR NETWORKS, INC.
00E069 (base 16)	JAYCOR NETWORKS, INC. 9775 TOWNE CENTRE DRIVE SAN DIEGO CA 92121
00-E0-6A (hex)	KAPSCH AG
00E06A (base 16)	KAPSCH AG WAGENSEILGASSE 1 1120-VIENNA AUSTRIA
00-E0-6B (hex)	W&G SPECIAL PRODUCTS
00E06B (base 16)	W&G SPECIAL PRODUCTS SCIENCE PARK EINDHOVIN 5049 5692 EB SON THE NETHERLANDS
00-E0-6C (hex)	BALTIMORE TECHNOLOGIES, LTD.
00E06C (base 16)	BALTIMORE TECHNOLOGIES, LTD. INNOVATION HOUSE MARK ROAD, HEMEL HEMSTEAD, HERTFORDSHIRE, HP2 7DN UNITED KINGDOM
00-E0-6D (hex)	COMPUWARE CORPORATION
00E06D (base 16)	COMPUWARE CORPORATION 1901 SOUTH BASCOM AVE. STE#105 CAMPBELL CA 95008
00-E0-6E (hex)	FAR SYSTEMS SPA
00E06E (base 16)	FAR SYSTEMS SPA VIA F. ZENI 8 3868 ROVERETO (TN) ITALY
00-E0-6F (hex)	TERAYON CORP.

company_id	Organization Address
00E06F (base 16)	TERAYON CORP. 2952 BUNKER HILL LANE SANTA CLARA CA 95054
00-E0-70 (hex)	DH TECHNOLOGY
00E070 (base 16)	DH TECHNOLOGY 3003 ROLLIE GATES DRIVE PASO ROBLES CA 93446
00-E0-71 (hex)	EPIS MICROCOMPUTER
00E071 (base 16)	EPIS MICROCOMPUTER 72458 ALBSTADT LAUTLINGER STRASSE 147 GERMANY
00-E0-72 (hex)	LYNK
00E072 (base 16)	LYNK RABIN BUILDING TERADION INDUSTRIAL PARK D.N. MISGAV 20179 ISRAEL
00-E0-73 (hex)	NATIONAL AMUSEMENT
00E073 (base 16)	NATIONAL AMUSEMENT NETWORK, INC. 401 N. MICHIGAN AVENUE CHICAGO IL 60611
00-E0-74 (hex)	TIERNAN COMMUNICATIONS, INC.
00E074 (base 16)	TIERNAN COMMUNICATIONS, INC. 11025 ROSELLE ST. SAN DIEGO CA 92121
00-E0-75 (hex)	ATLAS COMPUTER EQUIPMENT, INC.
00E075 (base 16)	ATLAS COMPUTER EQUIPMENT, INC. 3700 STATE ST., STE#200 SANTA BARBARA CA 93105
00-E0-76 (hex)	DEVELOPMENT CONCEPTS, INC.
00E076 (base 16)	DEVELOPMENT CONCEPTS, INC. 1000 N. BROAD STREET LANSDALE PA 19446
00-E0-77 (hex)	WEBGEAR, INC.
00E077 (base 16)	WEBGEAR, INC. 1263 OAKMEAD PKWY SUNNYVALE CA 94080
00-E0-78 (hex)	BERKELEY NETWORKS
00E078 (base 16)	BERKELEY NETWORKS 683 RIVER OAKS PARKWAY SAN JOSE CA 95134
00-E0-79 (hex)	A.T.N.R.
00E079 (base 16)	A.T.N.R. BP 966 91976 COURTABOEUF FRANCE
00-E0-7A (hex)	MIKRODIDAKT AB
00E07A (base 16)	MIKRODIDAKT AB GASVERKSGATAN 3A S222 29 LUND SWEDEN
00-E0-7B (hex)	BAY NETWORKS
00E07B (base 16)	BAY NETWORKS 125 NAGOG PARK ACTON MA 01720
00-E0-7C (hex)	METTLER-TOLEDO, INC.
00E07C (base 16)	METTLER-TOLEDO, INC. 1150 DEARBORN DRIVE WORTHINGTON OH 43085
00-E0-7D (hex)	NETRONIX, INC.
00E07D (base 16)	NETRONIX, INC. 340 THOR PLACE BREA CA 92821
00-E0-7E (hex)	WALT DISNEY IMAGINEERING
00E07E (base 16)	WALT DISNEY IMAGINEERING 1401 FLOWER ST. GLENDALE CA 91221
00-E0-7F (hex)	LOGISTISTEM SRL

company_id	Organization Address
00E07F (base 16)	LOGISTISTEM SRL VIA PANCIATICHI 94/18 ZIP 50127 FIRENZE ITALY
00-E0-80 (hex)	CONTROL RESOURCES CORPORATION
00E080 (base 16)	CONTROL RESOURCES CORPORATION 16-00 POLLITT DRIVE FAIR LAWN NJ 07410
00-E0-81 (hex)	TYAN COMPUTER CORP.
00E081 (base 16)	TYAN COMPUTER CORP. 1753 S. MAIN STREET MILPITAS CA 95035
00-E0-82 (hex)	ANERMA
00E082 (base 16)	ANERMA SCHAAPSDRIES 25 2260 WESTERLO BELGIUM
00-E0-83 (hex)	JATO TECHNOLOGIES, INC.
00E083 (base 16)	JATO TECHNOLOGIES, INC. 505 EAST HUNTLAND DR. STE #550 AUSTIN TX 78752
00-E0-84 (hex)	COMPULITE R&D
00E084 (base 16)	COMPULITE R&D 3 HAROSHET STR. NEW IND. ZONE RAMAT-HASHARON 47279 ISRAEL
00-E0-85 (hex)	GLOBAL MAINTECH, INC.
00E085 (base 16)	GLOBAL MAINTECH, INC. 6468 CITY WEST PARKWAY EDEN PRAIRIE MN 55344
00-E0-86 (hex)	CYBEX COMPUTER PRODUCTS
00E086 (base 16)	CYBEX COMPUTER PRODUCTS 4912 RESEARCH DRIVE HUNTSVILLE AL 35805
00-E0-87 (hex)	LECROY
00E087 (base 16)	LECROY NETWORKING PRODUCTS DIVISION 25 BURLINGTON MALL ROAD BURLINGTON MA 01803
00-E0-88 (hex)	LTX CORPORATION
00E088 (base 16)	LTX CORPORATION 145 UNIVERSITY AVENUE WESTWOOD MA 02090-2306
00-E0-89 (hex)	MICROFRAME INC.
00E089 (base 16)	MICROFRAME INC. 21 MERIDIAN ROAD EDISON NJ 08820
00-E0-8A (hex)	GEC AVERY, LTD.
00E08A (base 16)	GEC AVERY, LTD. FOUNDRY LANE SMETHWICK, WARLEY WEST MIDLANDS, ENGLAND B66 2LP
00-E0-8B (hex)	QLOGIC CORP.
00E08B (base 16)	QLOGIC CORP. 3545 HARBOR BLVD. COSTA MESA CA 92626
00-E0-8C (hex)	NEOPARADIGM LABS, INC.
00E08C (base 16)	NEOPARADIGM LABS, INC. 1735 N. FIRST ST., STE #108 SAN JOSE CA 95112
00-E0-8D (hex)	PRESSURE SYSTEMS, INC.
00E08D (base 16)	PRESSURE SYSTEMS, INC. 34 RESEARCH DRIVE HAMPTON VA 23666
00-E0-8E (hex)	UTSTARCOM
00E08E (base 16)	UTSTARCOM 33 WOOD AVE. SOUTH ISELIN NJ 08830
00-E0-8F (hex)	CISCO SYSTEMS, INC.

company_id	Organization Address
00E08F (base 16)	CISCO SYSTEMS, INC. 170 W. TASMAN DRIVE SAN JOSE CA 95134-1706
00-E0-90 (hex)	BECKMAN LAB. AUTOMATION DIV.
00E090 (base 16)	BECKMAN LAB. AUTOMATION DIV. 90 BOROLINE ROAD ALLENDALE NJ 07401
00-E0-91 (hex)	LG ELECTRONICS, INC.
00E091 (base 16)	LG ELECTRONICS, INC. 16, WOOMYEON-DONG, SEOCHO-GU, SEOUL, 137-140, KOREA
00-E0-92 (hex)	ADMTEK INCORPORATED
00E092 (base 16)	ADMTEK INCORPORATED 1962 ZANKER ROAD SAN JOSE CA 95112
00-E0-93 (hex)	ACKFIN NETWORKS
00E093 (base 16)	ACKFIN NETWORKS 575 N. PASTORIA AVE. SUNNYVALE CA 94086
00-E0-94 (hex)	OSAI SRL
00E094 (base 16)	OSAI SRL VIA TORINO 603-IVREA(TO) ITALY
00-E0-95 (hex)	ADVANCED-VISION TECHNOLGIES
00E095 (base 16)	ADVANCED-VISION TECHNOLGIES CORP. 8F-1, 87 SECTION 3, CHUNG YANG RD, TU CHENG TAIPEI, TAIWAN, R.O.C.
00-E0-96 (hex)	SHIMADZU CORPORATION
00E096 (base 16)	SHIMADZU CORPORATION NISHINOKYO-KUWABARACHO NAKAGYO-KU, KYOTO 604 JAPAN
00-E0-97 (hex)	CARRIER ACCESS CORPORATION
00E097 (base 16)	CARRIER ACCESS CORPORATION 5395 PEARL PARKWAY BOULDER CO 80301
00-E0-98 (hex)	ABOCOM SYSTEMS, INC.
00E098 (base 16)	ABOCOM SYSTEMS, INC. 12F-3, NO. 333, SEC. 1 GUAN-FU ROAD HSIN-CHU TAIWAN, R.O.C.
00-E0-99 (hex)	SAMSON AG
00E099 (base 16)	SAMSON AG D-60314 FRANKFURT WEISMULLERSTR. 3 GERMANY
00-E0-9A (hex)	POSITRON INDUSTRIES, INC.
00E09A (base 16)	POSITRON INDUSTRIES, INC. 5101 BUCHAN STREET MONTREAL, QUEBEC CANADA H4P-2R9
00-E0-9B (hex)	ENGAGE NETWORKS, INC.
00E09B (base 16)	ENGAGE NETWORKS, INC. 316 N. MILWAUKEE ST., STE.#214 MILWAUKEE WI 53202
00-E0-9C (hex)	MII
00E09C (base 16)	MII LE PARC DU MOULIN 2 GRANDE RUE PROLONGEE F95650 PUISEUX-PONTOISE FRANCE
00-E0-9D (hex)	SARNOFF CORPORATION
00E09D (base 16)	SARNOFF CORPORATION CN 5300 PRINCETON NJ 08543-5300
00-E0-9E (hex)	QUANTUM CORPORATION

company_id	Organization Address
00E09E (base 16)	QUANTUM CORPORATION 500 McCarthy Boulevard Milpitas CA 95035
00-E0-9F (hex)	PIXEL VISION
00E09F (base 16)	PIXEL VISION 43 NAGOG PARK ACTON MA 01720
00-E0-A0 (hex)	WILTRON CO.
00E0A0 (base 16)	WILTRON CO. 490 JARVIS DRIVE MORGAN HILL, CA 95037
00-E0-A1 (hex)	HIMA PAUL HILDEBRANDT
00E0A1 (base 16)	HIMA PAUL HILDEBRANDT GMBH CO KG POSTBOX 1261 D-68777 BRUEHL NEAR MANNHEIM GERMANY
00-E0-A2 (hex)	MICROSLATE INC.
00E0A2 (base 16)	MICROSLATE INC. 9625 IGNACE - STE. "D" BROSSARD QC J4Y 2P3 CANADA
00-E0-A3 (hex)	CISCO SYSTEMS, INC.
00E0A3 (base 16)	CISCO SYSTEMS, INC. 170 W. TASMAN DRIVE SAN JOSE CA 95134-1706
00-E0-A4 (hex)	ESAOTE S.P.A.
00E0A4 (base 16)	ESAOTE S.P.A. VIA DI CACIOLLE, 15 50127 FLORENCE ITALY
00-E0-A5 (hex)	COMCORE SEMICONDUCTOR, INC.
00E0A5 (base 16)	COMCORE SEMICONDUCTOR, INC. 4505 LAS VIRGENES #202 CALABASAS CA 91302
00-E0-A6 (hex)	TELOGY NETWORKS, INC.
00E0A6 (base 16)	TELOGY NETWORKS, INC. 20250 CENTURY BLVD. GERMANTOWN MD 20874
00-E0-A7 (hex)	IPC INFORMATION SYSTEMS, INC.
00E0A7 (base 16)	IPC INFORMATION SYSTEMS, INC. METRO CENTER ONE STATION PLACE STAMFORD CT 06907
00-E0-A8 (hex)	SAT GMBH&CO
00E0A8 (base 16)	SAT GMBH&CO RUTHNERGASSE 1 VIENNA AUSTRIA A-1210
00-E0-A9 (hex)	FUNAI ELECTRIC CO., LTD.
00E0A9 (base 16)	FUNAI ELECTRIC CO., LTD. 7-1, NAKAGAITO 7-CHOME, DAITO OSAKA 574 JAPAN
00-E0-AA (hex)	ELECTROSONIC LTD.
00E0AA (base 16)	ELECTROSONIC LTD. HAWLEY MILL, HAWLEY RD. DARTFORD, KENT ENGLAND DA2 7SY
00-E0-AB (hex)	DIMAT S.A.
00E0AB (base 16)	DIMAT S.A. C/BISCAIA 383 3 08023 BARCELONA SPAIN
00-E0-AC (hex)	MIDSCO, INC.
00E0AC (base 16)	MIDSCO, INC. 710 ROUTE 46 EAST FAIRFIELD NJ 07004
00-E0-AD (hex)	EES TECHNOLOGY, LTD.

company_id	Organization Address
00E0AD (base 16)	EES TECHNOLOGY, LTD. 25 EASTWAYS WITHAM, ESSEX, CM8 3AL UNITED KINGDOM
00-E0-AE (hex)	XAQTI CORPORATION
00E0AE (base 16)	XAQTI CORPORATION 1630 OAKLAND RD. #A-214 SAN JOSE CA 95131
00-E0-AF (hex)	GENERAL DYNAMICS INFORMATION
00E0AF (base 16)	GENERAL DYNAMICS INFORMATION SYSTEMS COMPUTING DEVICES, LTD. 3190 FAIRVIEW PARK DRIVE FALLS CHURCH VA 22042-4523
00-E0-B0 (hex)	CISCO SYSTEMS, INC.
00E0B0 (base 16)	CISCO SYSTEMS, INC. 170 W. TASMAN DRIVE SAN JOSE CA 95134-1706
00-E0-B1 (hex)	PACKET ENGINES, INC.
00E0B1 (base 16)	PACKET ENGINES, INC. PO BOX 14497 SPOKANE WA 99214-0497
00-E0-B2 (hex)	TELMAX COMMUNICATIONS CORP.
00E0B2 (base 16)	TELMAX COMMUNICATIONS CORP. 46515 LANDING PARKWAY FREMONT CA 94538
00-E0-B3 (hex)	ETHERWAN SYSTEMS, INC.
00E0B3 (base 16)	ETHERWAN SYSTEMS, INC. 14 HUGHES, STE.B-105 IRVINE CA 92618
00-E0-B4 (hex)	TECHNO SCOPE CO., LTD.
00E0B4 (base 16)	TECHNO SCOPE CO., LTD. 13-6-7 KISHIMATI URAWASI SAITAMA 336 JAPAN
00-E0-B5 (hex)	ARDENT COMMUNICATIONS CORP.
00E0B5 (base 16)	ARDENT COMMUNICATIONS CORP. 3801 ZANKER ROAD, STE. A SAN JOSE CA 95134
00-E0-B6 (hex)	OSICOM TECHNOLOGIES
00E0B6 (base 16)	OSICOM TECHNOLOGIES 9020 JUNCTION DRIVE ANNAPOLIS JUNCTION MD 20701
00-E0-B7 (hex)	PI GROUP, LTD.
00E0B7 (base 16)	PI GROUP, LTD. MILTON HALL, CHURCH LANE MILTON, CAMBRIDGE CBA 6AB UNITED KINGDOM
00-E0-B8 (hex)	GATEWAY 2000
00E0B8 (base 16)	GATEWAY 2000 610 GATEWAY DRIVE N. SIOUX CITY SD 57049
00-E0-B9 (hex)	BYAS SYSTEMS
00E0B9 (base 16)	BYAS SYSTEMS 2250 MONROE STREET, #371 SANTA CLARA CA 95050
00-E0-BA (hex)	BERGHOF AUTOMATIONSTECHNIK
00E0BA (base 16)	BERGHOF AUTOMATIONSTECHNIK GMBH HARRET STRASSE 1 D 72800 ENINGEN GERMANY
00-E0-BB (hex)	NBX CORPORATION
00E0BB (base 16)	NBX CORPORATION 100 BRICKSTONE SQUARE ANDOVER MA 01810
00-E0-BC (hex)	SYMON COMMUNICATIONS, INC.

company_id	Organization Address
00E0BC (base 16)	SYMON COMMUNICATIONS, INC. 10701 CORPORATE DR.-STE. #290 STAFFORD TX 77477
00-E0-BD (hex)	INTERFACE SYSTEMS, INC.
00E0BD (base 16)	INTERFACE SYSTEMS, INC. 5855 INTERFACE DRIVE ANN ARBOR MI 48103-9515
00-E0-BE (hex)	GENROCO INTERNATIONAL, INC.
00E0BE (base 16)	GENROCO INTERNATIONAL, INC. 255 ENDERS COURT SLINGER WI 53086
00-E0-BF (hex)	TORRENT NETWORKING
00E0BF (base 16)	TORRENT NETWORKING 8181 PROFESSIONAL PLACE SUITE #160 LANDOVER MD 20785
00-E0-C0 (hex)	SEIWA ELECTRIC MFG. CO., LTD.
00E0C0 (base 16)	SEIWA ELECTRIC MFG. CO., LTD. 86 TARADA SHIN-IKE, JOYO, KYOTO PREFECTURE JAPAN
00-E0-C1 (hex)	MEMOREX TELEX JAPAN, LTD.
00E0C1 (base 16)	MEMOREX TELEX JAPAN, LTD. YAESUGUCHI KAIKAN, 1-7-20 YAESU, CHUO-KU TOKYO 103 JAPAN
00-E0-C2 (hex)	NECSY SPA
00E0C2 (base 16)	NECSY SPA VIA LISBONA 28 35020 PADOVA ITALY
00-E0-C3 (hex)	SAKAI SYSTEM DEVELOPMENT CORP.
00E0C3 (base 16)	SAKAI SYSTEM DEVELOPMENT CORP. PORTUS CENTER BLD., 4-45-1 EBISUJIMA-CHO, SAKAI-CITY OSAKA-FU, 590 JAPAN
00-E0-C4 (hex)	HORNER ELECTRIC, INC.
00E0C4 (base 16)	HORNER ELECTRIC, INC. 1521 E. WASHINGTON ST. INDIANAPOLIS IN 46201
00-E0-C5 (hex)	BCOM ELECTRONICS INC.
00E0C5 (base 16)	BCOM ELECTRONICS INC. 8 FL, NO. 64, AN HO ROAD, SEC. 2 TAIPEI TAIWAN, R.O.C.
00-E0-C6 (hex)	LINK2IT, L.L.C.
00E0C6 (base 16)	LINK2IT, L.L.C. 4256 BECK AVENUE STUDIO CITY CA 91604
00-E0-C7 (hex)	EUROTECH SRL
00E0C7 (base 16)	EUROTECH SRL VIA JACOPO LINUSSIO 1 33030 AMAROO (UD) ITALY
00-E0-C8 (hex)	VIRTUAL ACCESS, LTD.
00E0C8 (base 16)	VIRTUAL ACCESS, LTD. WOODSIDE HOUSE, WINKFIELD, WINDSOR, BERKSHIRE SL4 2DX ENGLAND
00-E0-C9 (hex)	AUTOMATEDLOGIC CORPORATION
00E0C9 (base 16)	AUTOMATEDLOGIC CORPORATION 1150 ROBERTS BOULEVARD KENNESAW GA 30144-3618
00-E0-CA (hex)	BEST DATA PRODUCTS

company_id	Organization Address
00E0CA (base 16)	BEST DATA PRODUCTS 21800 NORDHOFF STREET CHATSWORTH CA 91311
00-E0-CB (hex)	RESON, INC.
00E0CB (base 16)	RESON, INC. 300 LOPEZ ROAD GOLETA CA 93117
00-E0-CC (hex)	HERO SYSTEMS, LTD.
00E0CC (base 16)	HERO SYSTEMS, LTD. THE BARNES, COOMBELANDS LANE, ADDLESTONE, WEYBRIDGE SURREY KT15 1HY ENGLAND
00-E0-CD (hex)	SENSIS CORPORATION
00E0CD (base 16)	SENSIS CORPORATION 5793 WIDEWATERS PARKWAY DEWITT NY 13214
00-E0-CE (hex)	ARN
00E0CE (base 16)	ARN 51, RUE GASTON LAURIAU F-93512 MONTREUIL CEDEX FRANCE
00-E0-CF (hex)	INTEGRATED DEVICE
00E0CF (base 16)	INTEGRATED DEVICE TECHNOLOGY, INC. 2975 STENDER WAY, M/S J-019 SANTA CLARA CA 95054
00-E0-D0 (hex)	NETSPEED, INC.
00E0D0 (base 16)	NETSPEED, INC. 12303 TECHNOLOGY BLVD. AUSTIN TX 78727
00-E0-D1 (hex)	TELSIS LIMITED
00E0D1 (base 16)	TELSIS LIMITED 16 BARNES WALLACE ROAD FAREHAM, HAMPSHIRE PO15 5TT ENGLAND
00-E0-D2 (hex)	VERSANET COMMUNICATIONS, INC.
00E0D2 (base 16)	VERSANET COMMUNICATIONS, INC. 628 N. DIAMOND BAR BLVD. DIAMOND BAR CA 91765
00-E0-D3 (hex)	DATENTECHNIK GMBH
00E0D3 (base 16)	DATENTECHNIK GMBH A-1040 WIEN THERESIANUMGASSE 11 AUSTRIA
00-E0-D4 (hex)	EXCELLENT COMPUTER
00E0D4 (base 16)	EXCELLENT COMPUTER 551, M.K.N. ROAD ALANDUR, CHENNAI 600016 INDIA
00-E0-D5 (hex)	ARCXEL TECHNOLOGIES, INC.
00E0D5 (base 16)	ARCXEL TECHNOLOGIES, INC. 2691 RICHTER AVE.- STE.#106 IRVINE CA 92606
00-E0-D6 (hex)	COMPUTER & COMMUNICATION
00E0D6 (base 16)	COMPUTER & COMMUNICATION RESEARCH LAB. 195 SEC.4, CHUNG HSING RD CHUTUNG, HSINCHU TAIWAN, R.O.C.
00-E0-D7 (hex)	SUNSHINE ELECTRONICS, INC.
00E0D7 (base 16)	SUNSHINE ELECTRONICS, INC. 46560 FREMONT BLVD. -STE. #113 FREMONT CA 94538
00-E0-D8 (hex)	LANBIT COMPUTER, INC.
00E0D8 (base 16)	LANBIT COMPUTER, INC. 12F, 552 CHUNG HSIAO E., RD. SEC. 5, TAIPEI 110 TAIWAN, R.O.C.

company_id	Organization Address
00-E0-D9 (hex)	TAZMO CO., LTD.
00E0D9 (base 16)	TAZMO CO., LTD. 6186 KINOKO, IBARA-SHI OKAYAMA 715 JAPAN
00-E0-DA (hex)	ASSURED ACCESS
00E0DA (base 16)	ASSURED ACCESS TECHNOLOGY, INC. 720 S. MILPITAS BLVD. MILPITAS CA 95035
00-E0-DB (hex)	VIAVIDEO COMMUNICATIONS
00E0DB (base 16)	VIAVIDEO COMMUNICATIONS 8900 SHOAL CREEK BLVD. BLDG. #300 AUSTIN TX 78757
00-E0-DC (hex)	NEXWARE CORP.
00E0DC (base 16)	NEXWARE CORP. 825 STEWART DR., STE #4 SUNNYVALE CA 94086
00-E0-DD (hex)	ZENITH ELECTRONICS CORPORATION
00E0DD (base 16)	ZENITH ELECTRONICS CORPORATION 1000 MILWAUKEE AVENUE GLENVIEW IL 60025
00-E0-DE (hex)	DATAX NV
00E0DE (base 16)	DATAX NV RINGLAAN 51 B-2600 BERCHEM BELGIUM
00-E0-DF (hex)	KE KOMMUNIKATIONS-ELECTRONIK
00E0DF (base 16)	KE KOMMUNIKATIONS-ELECTRONIK GMBH 30179 HANNOVER KABELKAMP 20 GERMANY
00-E0-E0 (hex)	SI ELECTRONICS, LTD.
00E0E0 (base 16)	SI ELECTRONICS, LTD. 28-16, SHIMOMARUKO 2-CHOME, TOKYO 146 JAPAN
00-E0-E1 (hex)	G2 NETWORKS, ILNC.
00E0E1 (base 16)	G2 NETWORKS, ILNC. 142 SO. SANTA CRUZ AVE. LOS GATOS CA 95030-6702
00-E0-E2 (hex)	INNOVA CORP.
00E0E2 (base 16)	INNOVA CORP. 3325 SOUTH 116TH STREET SEATTLE WA 98168
00-E0-E3 (hex)	SK-ELEKTRONIK GMBH
00E0E3 (base 16)	SK-ELEKTRONIK GMBH HEMMELRATHERWEG 201 51377 LEVERKUSEN GERMANY
00-E0-E4 (hex)	FANUC ROBOTICS NORTH AMERICA,
00E0E4 (base 16)	FANUC ROBOTICS NORTH AMERICA, INC. 3900 W. HAMLIN RD. ROCHESTER HILLS MI 48309-3253
00-E0-E5 (hex)	CINCO NETWORKS, INC.
00E0E5 (base 16)	CINCO NETWORKS, INC. 6601 KOLL CENTER PARK WAY SUITE #140 PLEASANTON CA 94566
00-E0-E6 (hex)	INCAA DATACOM B.V.
00E0E6 (base 16)	INCAA DATACOM B.V. P.O. BOX 211 7300 AE APELDOORN NETHERLANDS
00-E0-E7 (hex)	RAYTHEON E-SYSTEMS, INC.

company_id	Organization Address
00E0E7 (base 16)	RAYTHEON E-SYSTEMS, INC. 1301 E. COLLINS RICHARDSON TX 75081
00-E0-E8 (hex)	GRETACODER DATA SYSTEMS AG
00E0E8 (base 16)	GRETACODER DATA SYSTEMS AG ALTHARDSTRASSE 150 CH-8105 REGENSDORF SWITZERLAND
00-E0-E9 (hex)	DATA LABS, INC.
00E0E9 (base 16)	DATA LABS, INC. 444 NORTH FREDERICK AVE. SUITE #240 GAITHERSBURG MD 20877
00-E0-EA (hex)	INNOVAT COMMUNICATIONS, INC.
00E0EA (base 16)	INNOVAT COMMUNICATIONS, INC. 1257 N. PLANO ROAD RICHARDSON TX 75081
00-E0-EB (hex)	DIGICOM SYSTEMS, INCORPORATED
00E0EB (base 16)	DIGICOM SYSTEMS, INCORPORATED 188 TOPAZ STREET MILPITAS CA 95035
00-E0-EC (hex)	CELESTICA INC.
00E0EC (base 16)	CELESTICA INC. 844 DON MILLS ROAD NORTH YORK ONTARIO M3C 1V7 CANADA
00-E0-ED (hex)	SILICOM, LTD.
00E0ED (base 16)	SILICOM, LTD. 8 HANAGER ST. P.O. BOX 2164 KFAR-SAVA 44000 ISRAEL
00-E0-EE (hex)	MAREL HF
00E0EE (base 16)	MAREL HF HOFOABAKKI 9 112 REYKJAVIK ICELAND
00-E0-EF (hex)	DIONEX
00E0EF (base 16)	DIONEX PO BOX 3603 SUNNYVALE CA 94088-3603
00-E0-F0 (hex)	ABLER TECHNOLOGY, INC.
00E0F0 (base 16)	ABLER TECHNOLOGY, INC. 4F, NO. 54 SEC. 4 MIN-SHENG E. RD., TAIPEI TAIWAN R.O.C.
00-E0-F1 (hex)	THAT CORPORATION
00E0F1 (base 16)	THAT CORPORATION 734 FOREST STREET MARLBOROUGH MA 01752
00-E0-F2 (hex)	ARLOTTO COMNET, INC.
00E0F2 (base 16)	ARLOTTO COMNET, INC. 7F-4,55,TUNG-KUANG ROAD HSIN-CHU, 300 TAIWAN, R.O.C.
00-E0-F3 (hex)	WEBSPRINT COMMUNICATIONS, INC.
00E0F3 (base 16)	WEBSPRINT COMMUNICATIONS, INC. 3026 SCOTT BLVD. SANTA CLARA CA 95054
00-E0-F4 (hex)	INSIDE TECHNOLOGY A/S
00E0F4 (base 16)	INSIDE TECHNOLOGY A/S VENLIGHEDSVEJ 6 DK-2970 HOERSHOLM DENMARK
00-E0-F5 (hex)	TELES AG
00E0F5 (base 16)	TELES AG DOVESTR. 2-4 10587 BERLIN GERMANY

company_id	Organization Address
00-E0-F6 (hex)	DECISION EUROPE
00E0F6 (base 16)	DECISION EUROPE 3, RUE DE LATTRE DE TASSIGNY 85170 SAINT DENIS LA CHEVASSE FRANCE
00-E0-F7 (hex)	CISCO SYSTEMS, INC.
00E0F7 (base 16)	CISCO SYSTEMS, INC. 170 W. TASMAN DRIVE SAN JOSE CA 95134-1706
00-E0-F8 (hex)	DIANA CONTROL AB
00E0F8 (base 16)	DIANA CONTROL AB STENYXEGATAN 21 C 213 76 MALMOE SWEDEN
00-E0-F9 (hex)	CISCO SYSTEMS, INC.
00E0F9 (base 16)	CISCO SYSTEMS, INC. 170 W. TASMAN DRIVE SAN JOSE CA 95134-1706
00-E0-FA (hex)	TRL TECHNOLOGY, LTD.
00E0FA (base 16)	TRL TECHNOLOGY, LTD. SHANNON WAY, ASHCHURCH, TEWKESBURY, GLOS. GL20 8ND UNITED KINGDOM
00-E0-FB (hex)	LEIGHTRONIX, INC.
00E0FB (base 16)	LEIGHTRONIX, INC. 2330 JARCO DR. HOLT MI 48842
00-E0-FC (hex)	HUAWEI TECHNOLOGIES CO., LTD.
00E0FC (base 16)	HUAWEI TECHNOLOGIES CO., LTD. KEFA ROAD, SCIENCE-BASED IND. PARK, NANSHAN DISTRICT, SHENZHEN, P.R.C. ZIP: 518057 CHINA
00-E0-FD (hex)	A-TREND TECHNOLOGY CO., LTD.
00E0FD (base 16)	A-TREND TECHNOLOGY CO., LTD. 10F, NO. 75, HSIN TAI WU RD., SEC. 1, HSI CHIH, TAIPEI HSIEN TAIWAN 221, R.O.C.
00-E0-FE (hex)	CISCO SYSTEMS, INC.
00E0FE (base 16)	CISCO SYSTEMS, INC. 170 W. TASMAN DRIVE SAN JOSE CA 95134-1706
00-E0-FF (hex)	SECURITY DYNAMICS TECHNOLOGIES
00E0FF (base 16)	SECURITY DYNAMICS TECHNOLOGIES 20 CROSBY DRIVE BEDFORD MA 01730
00-E6-D3 (hex)	NIXDORF COMPUTER CORP.
00E6D3 (base 16)	NIXDORF COMPUTER CORP. 2520 MISSION COLLEGE ROAD SANTA CLARA CA 95054
02-07-01 (hex)	RACAL-DATACOM
020701 (base 16)	RACAL-DATACOM LAN INTERNETWORKING DIVISION 155 SWANSON ROAD BOXBOROUGH MA 01719
02-1C-7C (hex)	PERQ SYSTEMS CORPORATION
021C7C (base 16)	PERQ SYSTEMS CORPORATION 2600 LIBERTY AVENUE P.O. BOX 2600 PITTSBURGH PA 15230
02-60-86 (hex)	LOGIC REPLACEMENT TECH. LTD.
026086 (base 16)	LOGIC REPLACEMENT TECH. LTD. 14 ARKWRIGHT ROAD READING BERKS RG2OLS UNITED KINGDOM
02-60-8C (hex)	3COM CORPORATION
02608C (base 16)	3COM CORPORATION 2081 N. SHORLINE BLVD. MOUNTAIN VIEW, CA 94043
02-70-01 (hex)	RACAL-DATACOM

company_id	Organization Address
027001 (base 16)	RACAL-DATACOM LAN INTERNETWORKING DIVISION 155 SWANSON ROAD BOXBOROUGH MA 01719
02-70-B0 (hex)	M/A-COM INC. COMPANIES
0270B0 (base 16)	M/A-COM INC. COMPANIES 11717 EXPLORATION LANE GERMANTOWN MD 20767
02-70-B3 (hex)	DATA RECALL LTD
0270B3 (base 16)	DATA RECALL LTD SONDES PLACE DORKING SURREY RH4 3EF UNITED KINGDOM
02-9D-8E (hex)	CARDIAC RECORDERS INC.
029D8E (base 16)	CARDIAC RECORDERS INC. 34 SCARBORO RD LONDON N4 4L U UNITED KINGDOM
02-AA-3C (hex)	OLIVETTI TELECOMM SPA (OLTECO)
02AA3C (base 16)	OLIVETTI TELECOMM SPA (OLTECO) 20300 STEVENS CREEK BLVD. CUPERTINO CA 95014
02-BB-01 (hex)	OCTOTHORPE CORP.
02BB01 (base 16)	OCTOTHORPE CORP. 285 WEST GREEN STREET PASADENA CA 91105
02-C0-8C (hex)	3COM CORPORATION
02C08C (base 16)	3COM CORPORATION 5400 BAYFRONT PLAZA P.O. BOX 58145 SANTA CLARA, CA 95052
02-CF-1C (hex)	COMMUNICATION MACHINERY CORP.
02CF1C (base 16)	COMMUNICATION MACHINERY CORP. 1226 ANACAPA SANTA BARBARA CA 93101
02-E6-D3 (hex)	NIXDORF COMPUTER CORPORATION
02E6D3 (base 16)	NIXDORF COMPUTER CORPORATION NIXDORF TECHNOLOGY CENTER 2520 MISSION COLLEGE BLVD SANTA CLARA, CA 95054
04-0A-E0 (hex)	XMIT AG COMPUTER NETWORKS
040AE0 (base 16)	XMIT AG COMPUTER NETWORKS 11 AVENUE DE BAUMETTES 1020 RENANS SWITZERLAND
04-E0-C4 (hex)	TRIUMPH-ADLER AG
04E0C4 (base 16)	TRIUMPH-ADLER AG HUNDINGSTRABE 11B 8500 NURNBURG 80 GERMANY
08-00-01 (hex)	COMPUTERVISION CORPORATION
080001 (base 16)	COMPUTERVISION CORPORATION 14 CROSBY DRIVE MS 5-1 BEDFORD MA 01730
08-00-02 (hex)	BRIDGE COMMUNICATIONS INC.
080002 (base 16)	BRIDGE COMMUNICATIONS INC. 2081 STIERLING ROAD MOUNTAIN VIEW, CA 94043
08-00-03 (hex)	ADVANCED COMPUTER COMM.
080003 (base 16)	ADVANCED COMPUTER COMM. 720 SANTA BARBARA ST. SANTA BARBARA, CA 93101
08-00-04 (hex)	CROMEMCO INCORPORATED
080004 (base 16)	CROMEMCO INCORPORATED 280 BERNARDO AVENUE MOUNTAIN VIEW CA 94043
08-00-05 (hex)	SYMBOLICS INC.

company_id	Organization Address
080005 (base 16)	SYMBOLICS INC. 257 VASSAR STREET CAMBRIDGE MA 02139
08-00-06 (hex)	SIEMENS AG
080006 (base 16)	SIEMENS AG HOFMANNSTRASSE 51 POSTFACH 70 00 73 D-81359 MUNCHEN GERMANY
08-00-07 (hex)	APPLE COMPUTER INC.
080007 (base 16)	APPLE COMPUTER INC. 20650 VALLEY GREEN DRIVE CUPERTINO CA 95014
08-00-08 (hex)	BOLT BERANEK AND NEWMAN INC.
080008 (base 16)	BOLT BERANEK AND NEWMAN INC. 70 FAWCETT STREET CAMBRIDGE MA 02138
08-00-09 (hex)	HEWLETT-PACKARD COMPANY
080009 (base 16)	HEWLETT-PACKARD COMPANY ENTERPRISE SYSTEMS TECH.CENTER 11000 WOLFE ROAD CUPERTINO CA 95014
08-00-0A (hex)	NESTAR SYSTEMS INCORPORATED
08000A (base 16)	NESTAR SYSTEMS INCORPORATED 2585 EAST BAYSHORE ROAD PALO ALTO CA 94303
08-00-0B (hex)	UNISYS CORPORATION
08000B (base 16)	UNISYS CORPORATION TOWNSHIP LINE ROAD BLUE BELL PA 19424
08-00-0C (hex)	MIKLYN DEVELOPMENT CO.
08000C (base 16)	MIKLYN DEVELOPMENT CO. 3613 ANDOVER DIVE BEDFORD TX 76021
08-00-0D (hex)	INTERNATIONAL COMPUTERS LTD.
08000D (base 16)	INTERNATIONAL COMPUTERS LTD. WENLOCK WAY WEST GORTON MANCHESTER, M12 5DR UNITED KINGDOM
08-00-0E (hex)	NCR CORPORATION
08000E (base 16)	NCR CORPORATION WORLD HEADQUARTERS DAYTON OH 45479
08-00-0F (hex)	MITEL CORPORATION
08000F (base 16)	MITEL CORPORATION 350 LEGGET DRIVE P.O. BOX 13089 KANATA ONTARIO CANADA K2K 1X3
08-00-11 (hex)	TEKTRONIX INC.
080011 (base 16)	TEKTRONIX INC. TECHNICAL STANDARDS 13975 SW KARL BRAUN DRIVE PO BOX 500, MS 46-530 BEAVERTON OR 97077
08-00-12 (hex)	BELL ATLANTIC INTEGRATED SYST.
080012 (base 16)	BELL ATLANTIC INTEGRATED SYST. 40 TALL PINE DRIVE SUDBURY MA 01776
08-00-13 (hex)	EXXON
080013 (base 16)	EXXON
08-00-14 (hex)	EXCELAN
080014 (base 16)	EXCELAN 1599 FLICKINGER AVENUE SAN JOSE CA 95131
08-00-15 (hex)	STC BUSINESS SYSTEMS
080015 (base 16)	STC BUSINESS SYSTEMS HOLBROOK HOUSE COCKFOSTERS ROAD COCKFOSTERS HERTS EN4 0BU UNITED KINGDOM
08-00-16 (hex)	BARRISTER INFO SYS CORP
080016 (base 16)	BARRISTER INFO SYS CORP ONE TECHNOLOGY CENTER 45 OAK STREET BUFFALO NY 14203
08-00-17 (hex)	NATIONAL SEMICONDUCTOR
080017 (base 16)	NATIONAL SEMICONDUCTOR 2900 SEMICONDUCTOR DRIVE SANTA CLARA CA 95051
00-00-18 (hex)	PIRELLI FOCOM NETWORKS
080018 (base 16)	PIRELLI FOCOM NETWORKS DENTON DRIVE NORTHWICH CHESHIRE CW9 7LU ENGLAND
08-00-19 (hex)	GENERAL ELECTRIC CORPORATION
080019 (base 16)	GENERAL ELECTRIC CORPORATION 1285 BOSTON AVENUE BRIDGEPORT CT 06602
08-00-1A (hex)	TIARA/ 10NET
08001A (base 16)	TIARA/ 10NET 7777 WASHINGTON VILLAGE DRIVE SUITE 200 DAYTON, OHIO 45459-3957
08-00-1B (hex)	DATA GENERAL
08001B (base 16)	DATA GENERAL 4400 COMPUTER DRIVE WESTBORO MA 01580
08-00-1C (hex)	KDD-KOKUSAI DEBNSIN DENWA CO.
08001C (base 16)	KDD-KOKUSAI DEBNSIN DENWA CO. FUJI XEROX CO., LTD. TELEGRAPH NO. 3-5, AKASAKA 3-CHOME MINATO-KU, TOKYO 107 JAPAN
08-00-1D (hex)	ABLE COMMUNICATIONS INC.
08001D (base 16)	ABLE COMMUNICATIONS INC. 17891 CARTWRIGHT ROAD IRVINE CA 92714-6216
08-00-1E (hex)	APOLLO COMPUTER INC.
08001E (base 16)	APOLLO COMPUTER INC. 15 ELIZABETH DRIVE CHELMSFORD MA 01824
08-00-1F (hex)	SHARP CORPORATION
08001F (base 16)	SHARP CORPORATION ENGINEERING DEPARTMENT 6 492 MINOSHO-CHO YAMATOKOORIYMA-SHI, NARA, 639-11 JAPAN
08-00-20 (hex)	SUN MICROSYSTEMS INC.
080020 (base 16)	SUN MICROSYSTEMS INC. 901 SAN ANTONIO ROAD MS UMPK02-106 PALO ALTO CA 94303-4900
08-00-21 (hex)	3M COMPANY
080021 (base 16)	3M COMPANY 3M VISUAL SYSTEMS DIVISION BLDG. A148-5N-01 6801 RIVER PLACE BLVD. AUSTIN TX 78726-9000
08-00-22 (hex)	NBI INC.
080022 (base 16)	NBI INC. 3450 MITCHELL LANE P.O. BOX 9001 BOULDER CO 80301
08-00-23 (hex)	MATSUHITA GRAPHIC COMM SYS INC

company_id	Organization Address
080023 (base 16)	MATSUHITA GRAPHIC COMM SYS INC
08-00-24 (hex)	10NET COMMUNICATIONS/DCA
080024 (base 16)	10NET COMMUNICATIONS/DCA 7777 WASHINGTON VILLAGE DR. SUITE 200 DAYTON, OH 45459-3957
08-00-25 (hex)	CONTROL DATA
080025 (base 16)	CONTROL DATA 4201 LEXINGTON AVE NORTH ARDEN HILLS MN 55112
08-00-26 (hex)	NORSK DATA A.S.
080026 (base 16)	NORSK DATA A.S. P.O. BOX 25 BOGERUD OSLO 6 NORWAY
08-00-27 (hex)	CADMUS COMPUTER SYSTEMS
080027 (base 16)	CADMUS COMPUTER SYSTEMS 600 SUFFOLK ST LOWELL MA 08154
08-00-28 (hex)	TEXAS INSTRUMENTS
080028 (base 16)	TEXAS INSTRUMENTS 8505 FOREST LANE, MS 8650 DALLAS TX 75243
08-00-29 (hex)	MEGATEK CORPORATION
080029 (base 16)	MEGATEK CORPORATION 9645 SCRANTON ROAD SAN DIEGO CA 92121
08-00-2A (hex)	MOSAIC TECHNOLOGIES INC.
08002A (base 16)	MOSAIC TECHNOLOGIES INC. 47 MANNING ROAD BILLERICA MA 01821-3970
08-00-2B (hex)	DIGITAL EQUIPMENT CORPORATION
08002B (base 16)	DIGITAL EQUIPMENT CORPORATION LKG 1-2/A19 550 KING STREET LITTLETON MA 01460-1289
08-00-2C (hex)	BRITTON LEE INC.
08002C (base 16)	BRITTON LEE INC. 14600 WINCHESTER BLVD LOS GATOS CA 95030
08-00-2D (hex)	LAN-TEC INC.
08002D (base 16)	LAN-TEC INC. 2131 UNIVERSITY AVENUE BERKELEY CA 94704
08-00-2E (hex)	METAPHOR COMPUTER SYSTEMS
08002E (base 16)	METAPHOR COMPUTER SYSTEMS 2500 GARCIA AVENUE MOUNTAIN VIEW CA 94043
08-00-2F (hex)	PRIME COMPUTER INC.
08002F (base 16)	PRIME COMPUTER INC. 100 CROSBY DRIVE BEDFORD MA 01730-1402
08-00-30 (hex)	NETWORK RESEARCH CORPORATION
080030 (base 16)	NETWORK RESEARCH CORPORATION 2380 N. ROSE AVENUE OXNARD CA 93010
08-00-30 (hex)	CERN
080030 (base 16)	CERN CH-1211 GENEVE 23 SUISSE/SWITZERLAND
08-00-30 (hex)	ROYAL MELBOURNE INST OF TECH
080030 (base 16)	ROYAL MELBOURNE INST OF TECH GPO BOX 2476V MELBOURNE VIC 3001
08-00-31 (hex)	LITTLE MACHINES INC.
080031 (base 16)	LITTLE MACHINES INC. 4141 JUTLAND DRIVE SAN DIEGO CA 92117

company_id	Organization Address
08-00-32 (hex)	TIGAN INCORPORATED
080032 (base 16)	TIGAN INCORPORATED 4020 FABIAN WAY SUITE D PALO ALTO CA 94303
08-00-33 (hex)	BAUSCH & LOMB
080033 (base 16)	BAUSCH & LOMB INTERACTIVE GRAPHICS DIVISION P.O. BOX 14547 AUSITN TX 78671
08-00-34 (hex)	FILENET CORPORATION
080034 (base 16)	FILENET CORPORATION 1575 CORPORATE DRIVE COSTA MESA CA 92626
08-00-35 (hex)	MICROFIVE CORPORATION
080035 (base 16)	MICROFIVE CORPORATION 3560 HYLAND AVENUE P.O. BOX 5011 COSTA MESA CA 92626
08-00-36 (hex)	INTERGRAPH CORPORATION
080036 (base 16)	INTERGRAPH CORPORATION ONE MADISON INDUSTRIAL PARK HUNTSVILLE AL 35807
08-00-37 (hex)	FUJI-XEROX CO. LTD.
080037 (base 16)	FUJI-XEROX CO. LTD. ADVANCED TECH & ENG'G CENTER 9-50 CHUO 2-CHOME, EBINA-SHI KANAGAWA 243-0432 JAPAN
08-00-38 (hex)	CII HONEYWELL BULL
080038 (base 16)	CII HONEYWELL BULL 68 ROUTE DE VERSAILLES 78430 LOUVECIENNES FRANCE
08-00-39 (hex)	SPIDER SYSTEMS LIMITED
080039 (base 16)	SPIDER SYSTEMS LIMITED SPIDER PARK STANWELL STREET EDINBURGH EH6 5NG SCOTLAND
08-00-3A (hex)	ORCATECH INC.
08003A (base 16)	ORCATECH INC. 2680 QUEENSVIEW DRIVE OTTAWA ONTARIO CANADA K2B 8H6
08-00-3B (hex)	TORUS SYSTEMS LIMITED
08003B (base 16)	TORUS SYSTEMS LIMITED SCIENCE PARK MILTON ROAD CAMBRIDGE CB4 4BH UNITED KINGDOM
08-00-3C (hex)	SCHLUMBERGER WELL SERVICES
08003C (base 16)	SCHLUMBERGER WELL SERVICES AUSTIN ENGINEERING SERVICES P.O. BOX 200015 AUSTIN, TX 78720-0015
08-00-3D (hex)	CADNETIX CORPORATIONS
08003D (base 16)	CADNETIX CORPORATIONS 5797 CENTRAL AVENUE BOULDER CO 80301
08-00-3E (hex)	CODEX CORPORATION
08003E (base 16)	CODEX CORPORATION 50 EAST COMMERCE DRIVE SUITE M1 SCHAUMBURG IL 60173
08-00-3F (hex)	FRED KOSCHARA ENTERPRISES
08003F (base 16)	FRED KOSCHARA ENTERPRISES
08-00-40 (hex)	FERRANTI COMPUTER SYS. LIMITED

company_id	Organization Address
080040 (base 16)	FERRANTI COMPUTER SYS. LIMITED WYTHENSHAWE DIVISION WESTERN ROAD BRACKNELL RG12 1RA UNITED KINGDOM
08-00-41 (hex)	RACAL-MILGO INFORMATION SYS..
080041 (base 16)	RACAL-MILGO INFORMATION SYS.. 400 EMBASSY ROW SUITE 300 ATLANTA, GA 30328
08-00-42 (hex)	JAPAN MACNICS CORP.
080042 (base 16)	JAPAN MACNICS CORP.
08-00-43 (hex)	PIXEL COMPUTER INC.
080043 (base 16)	PIXEL COMPUTER INC. 260 FORDHAM ROAD WILMINGTON MA 01887
08-00-44 (hex)	DAVID SYSTEMS INC.
080044 (base 16)	DAVID SYSTEMS INC. 615 TASMAN DRIVE SUNNYVALE CA 94088
08-00-45 (hex)	CONCURRENT COMPUTER CORP.
080045 (base 16)	CONCURRENT COMPUTER CORP. 2 CRESCENT PLACE OCEANPORT NJ 07757
08-00-46 (hex)	SONY CORPORATION LTD.
080046 (base 16)	SONY CORPORATION LTD. 4-14-1 ASAHIMACHI ATSUGI CITY KANAGAWA PREFECTURE 243 JAPAN
08-00-47 (hex)	SEQUENT COMPUTER SYSTEMS INC.
080047 (base 16)	SEQUENT COMPUTER SYSTEMS INC. 15450 S.W. KOLL PARKWAY MAILSTOP COL2-831 BEAVERTON, OR 97006
08-00-48 (hex)	EUROTHERM GAUGING SYSTEMS
080048 (base 16)	EUROTHERM GAUGING SYSTEMS 900 MIDDLESEX TURNPIKE, BDG. 6 BILLERICA MA 01821
08-00-49 (hex)	UNIVATION
080049 (base 16)	UNIVATION 1037 NORTH FAIR OAKS AVE. SUNNYVALE CA 94089
08-00-4A (hex)	BANYAN SYSTEMS INC.
08004A (base 16)	BANYAN SYSTEMS INC. 135 FLANDERS ROAD WESTBORO MA 01581
08-00-4B (hex)	PLANNING RESEARCH CORP.
08004B (base 16)	PLANNING RESEARCH CORP. 1DHS SYSTEMS 1508 KENNEDY DRIVE-STE#215 BELLEVUE NE 68–5
08-00-4C (hex)	HYDRA COMPUTER SYSTEMS INC.
08004C (base 16)	HYDRA COMPUTER SYSTEMS INC. 12 MERCER ROAD NATICK MA 01760
08-00-4D (hex)	CORVUS SYSTEMS INC.
08004D (base 16)	CORVUS SYSTEMS INC. 2100 CORVUS DRIVE SAN JOSE CA 95124
08-00-4E (hex)	3COM EUROPE LTD.
08004E (base 16)	3COM EUROPE LTD. 3COM CENTRE BOUNDARY WAY, HEMEL HEMPSTEAD HERTFORSHIRE, HP2 7YU UNITED KINGDOM
08-00-4F (hex)	CYGNET SYSTEMS
08004F (base 16)	CYGNET SYSTEMS 2560 JUNCTION AVENUE SAN JOSE, CA 95134

company_id	Organization Address
08-00-50 (hex)	DAISY SYSTEMS CORP.
080050 (base 16)	DAISY SYSTEMS CORP. 139 KIFER COURT SUNNYVALE CA 94086
08-00-51 (hex)	EXPERDATA
080051 (base 16)	EXPERDATA 88, RUE BRILLAT SAVARIN 75013 PARIS FRANCE
08-00-52 (hex)	INSYSTEC
080052 (base 16)	INSYSTEC 450 LAKEMONT AVENUE WINTER PARK FL 32792
08-00-53 (hex)	MIDDLE EAST TECH. UNIVERSITY
080053 (base 16)	MIDDLE EAST TECH. UNIVERSITY DEPARTMENT OF COMPUTER ENGINEERING ANKARA TURKEY
08-00-55 (hex)	STANFORD TELECOMM. INC.
080055 (base 16)	STANFORD TELECOMM. INC. 1221 CROSSMAN SUNNYVALE, CA 94089
08-00-56 (hex)	STANFORD LINEAR ACCEL. CENTER
080056 (base 16)	STANFORD LINEAR ACCEL. CENTER 2575 SANDHILL ROAD MENLO PARK CA 94025
08-00-57 (hex)	EVANS & SUTHERLAND
080057 (base 16)	EVANS & SUTHERLAND P.O. BOX 8700 580 ARAPEEN DRIVE SALT LAKE CITY UT 84108
08-00-58 (hex)	SYSTEMS CONCEPTS
080058 (base 16)	SYSTEMS CONCEPTS 520 THIRD STREET SAN FRANCISCO CA 94107
08-00-59 (hex)	A/S MYCRON
080059 (base 16)	A/S MYCRON PO BOX 6199 N-0602 OSLO 6 NORWAY
08-00-5A (hex)	IBM CORPORATION
08005A (base 16)	IBM CORPORATION P.O. BOX 12195 CE6A/664 3039 CORNWALLIS RTP, NC 27709-2195
08-00-5B (hex)	VTA TECHNOLOGIES INC.
08005B (base 16)	VTA TECHNOLOGIES INC. 2040 SHERMAN STREET HOLLYWOOD FL 33020
08-00-5C (hex)	FOUR PHASE SYSTEMS
08005C (base 16)	FOUR PHASE SYSTEMS 2001 LOGIC DRIVE SAN JOSE CA 95124-3452
08-00-5D (hex)	GOULD INC.
08005D (base 16)	GOULD INC. 6901 WEST SUNRISE BLVD. P.O. BOX 9148 FT. LAUDERDALE FL 33310-9148
08-00-5E (hex)	COUNTERPOINT COMPUTER INC.
08005E (base 16)	COUNTERPOINT COMPUTER INC. 2127 RINGWOOD AVENUE SAN JOSE CA 95131
08-00-5F (hex)	SABER TECHNOLOGY CORP.
08005F (base 16)	SABER TECHNOLOGY CORP. 2381 BERING DRIVE SAN JOSE CA 95131-1125
08-00-60 (hex)	INDUSTRIAL NETWORKING INC.

company_id	Organization Address
080060 (base 16)	INDUSTRIAL NETWORKING INC. 3990 FREEDOM CIRCLE SANTA CLARA CA 95050
08-00-61 (hex)	JAROGATE LTD.
080061 (base 16)	JAROGATE LTD. 197-213 LYHAM ROAD BRISTON LONDON SW2 5PY UNITED KINGDOM
08-00-62 (hex)	GENERAL DYNAMICS
080062 (base 16)	GENERAL DYNAMICS FORT WORTH DIVISION P.O. BOX 748 FT. WORTH TX 76101
08-00-63 (hex)	PLESSEY
080063 (base 16)	PLESSEY PLESSEY - UK LIMITED 167-55 148TH AVENUE JAMAICA NY 11434
08-00-64 (hex)	AUTOPHON AG
080064 (base 16)	AUTOPHON AG ABT. TZM 307 ZIEGELMATTSTRASSE 1-15 4503 SOLOTHURN SWITZERLAND
08-00-65 (hex)	GENRAD INC.
080065 (base 16)	GENRAD INC: 300 BAKER AVENUE MAIL STOP 26 CONCORD, MA 01742
08-00-66 (hex)	AGFA CORPORATION
080066 (base 16)	AGFA CORPORATION 200 BALLARDVALE STREET WILMINGTON MA 01887
08-00-67 (hex)	COMDESIGN
080067 (base 16)	COMDESIGN 751 SOUTH KELLOG AVENUE GOLETA CA 93117-3880
08-00-68 (hex)	RIDGE COMPUTERS
080068 (base 16)	RIDGE COMPUTERS 2451 MISSION COLLEGE BLVD. SANTA CLARA CA 95054
08-00-69 (hex)	SILICON GRAPHICS INC.
080069 (base 16)	SILICON GRAPHICS INC. 2011 N. SHORELINE BLVD. P.O. BOX 7311 CA 94043 MOUNTAIN VIEW CA 94039-7311
08-00-6A (hex)	ATT BELL LABORATORIES
08006A (base 16)	ATT BELL LABORATORIES 1100 EAST WARRENVILLE ROAD NAPERVILLE IL 60566
08-00-6B (hex)	ACCEL TECHNOLOGIES INC.
08006B (base 16)	ACCEL TECHNOLOGIES INC. 7358 TRADE STREET SAN DIEGO CA 92121
08-00-6C (hex)	SUNTEK TECHNOLOGY INT'L
08006C (base 16)	SUNTEK TECHNOLOGY INT'L 586 NO. FIRST STREET SAN JOSE, CA 95112
08-00-6D (hex)	WHITECHAPEL COMPUTER WORKS
08006D (base 16)	WHITECHAPEL COMPUTER WORKS 75 WHITECHAPEL ROAD LONDON E1 1DU
08-00-6E (hex)	MASSCOMP
08006E (base 16)	MASSCOMP ONE TECHNOLOGY PARK WESTFORD MA 01886
08-00-6F (hex)	PHILIPS APELDOORN B.V.

company_id	Organization Address
08006F (base 16)	PHILIPS APELDOORN B.V. P.O. BOX 105 7300 AC APELDOORN THE NETHERLANDS
08-00-70 (hex)	MITSUBISHI ELECTRIC CORP.
080070 (base 16)	MITSUBISHI ELECTRIC CORP. 325 KAMIMACHIYA KAMAKURA CITY KANAGWA PREFECTURE 247 JAPAN
08-00-71 (hex)	MATRA (DSIE)
080071 (base 16)	MATRA (DSIE) PARC D'AFFAIRES - B.P. 262 27100 VAL DE REUIL FRANCE
08-00-72 (hex)	XEROX CORP UNIV GRANT PROGRAM
080072 (base 16)	XEROX CORP UNIV GRANT PROGRAM ZEROX SYSTEMS INSTITUTE M/S 105 50C 800 PHILLIPS ROAD WEBSTER NY 14580
08-00-73 (hex)	TECMAR INC.
080073 (base 16)	TECMAR INC. 6225 COCHRAN ROAD SOLON OH 44139
08-00-74 (hex)	CASIO COMPUTER CO. LTD.
080074 (base 16)	CASIO COMPUTER CO. LTD. 3-2-1 SAKAE-CHO HAMURAMACHI, NISHITMAGUN TOKYO 190-11 JAPAN
08-00-75 (hex)	DANSK DATA ELECTRONIK
080075 (base 16)	DANSK DATA ELECTRONIK HERLEV HOVEDGADE 199 DK 2730 HERLEV DENMARK
08-00-76 (hex)	PC LAN TECHNOLOGIES
080076 (base 16)	PC LAN TECHNOLOGIES 5780 LINCOLN DRIVE SUITE 106 MINNEAPOLIS MN 55436
08-00-77 (hex)	TSL COMMUNICATIONS LTD.
080077 (base 16)	TSL COMMUNICATIONS LTD. THE LANDSBURY ESTATE LOWER GUILDFORD ROAD KNAPHIL WOKING SURREY GU21 2EP ENGLAND
08-00-78 (hex)	ACCELL CORPORATION
080078 (base 16)	ACCELL CORPORATION 50 SAGINAW DRIVE ROCHESTER NY 14623
08-00-79 (hex)	THE DROID WORKS
080079 (base 16)	THE DROID WORKS P.O. BOX CS 8180 SAN RAFAEL CA 94912
08-00-7A (hex)	INDATA
08007A (base 16)	INDATA GJERDRUMS VEI 12 C N-0486 OSLO 4 NORWAY
08-00-7B (hex)	SANYO ELECTRIC CO. LTD.
08007B (base 16)	SANYO ELECTRIC CO. LTD. 1-18-13 HASHIRIDANI HIRAKATA-SHI OSAKA 573 JAPAN
08-00-7C (hex)	VITALINK COMMUNICATIONS CORP.
08007C (base 16)	VITALINK COMMUNICATIONS CORP. 48761 KATO ROAD FREMONT CA 94538
08-00-7E (hex)	AMALGAMATED WIRELESS(AUS) LTD

company_id	Organization Address
08007E (base 16)	AMALGAMATED WIRELESS(AUS) LTD NORTH RYDE DIVISION P.O. BOX 96 NORTH RYDE NSW AUSTRALIA 2113
08-00-7F (hex)	CARNEGIE-MELLON UNIVERSITY
08007F (base 16)	CARNEGIE-MELLON UNIVERSITY INFORMATION TECHNOLOGY SCHENLEY PARK PITTSBURGE PA 15213
08-00-80 (hex)	AES DATA INC.
080080 (base 16)	AES DATA INC. 1900 MINNESOTA COURT MISSISAUGA ONTARIO CANADA L5N 3C9
08-00-81 (hex)	ASTECH, INC.
080081 (base 16)	ASTECH, INC. 670 NORTH COMMERCIAL STREET MANCHESTER NH 03101
08-00-82 (hex)	VERITAS SOFTWARE
080082 (base 16)	VERITAS SOFTWARE 4800 GREAT AMERICA PARKWAY SANTA CLARA, CA 95054
08-00-83 (hex)	SEIKO INSTRUM. AND ELECTRONICS
080083 (base 16)	SEIKO INSTRUM. AND ELECTRONICS 1-1-1 AKANEHAMA NARASHINO-SHI CHIBA 275 JAPAN
08-00-84 (hex)	TOMEN ELECTRONICS CORP.
080084 (base 16)	TOMEN ELECTRONICS CORP. 1-1 UCHISAIWAI-CHO 2CHOME CHIYODA-KU TOKYO 100 JAPAN
08-00-85 (hex)	ELXSI
080085 (base 16)	ELXSI 2334 LUNDY PLACE SAN JOSE CA 95131
08-00-86 (hex)	IMAGEN CORPORATION
080086 (base 16)	IMAGEN CORPORATION 2650 SAN TOMAS EXPRESSWAY P.O. BOX 58101 SANTA CLARA, CA 95052
08-00-87 (hex)	XYPLEX
080087 (base 16)	XYPLEX 295 FOSTER STREET LITTLETON MA 01460
08-00-88 (hex)	MCDATA CORPORATION
080088 (base 16)	MCDATA CORPORATION 310 INTERLOCKEN PARKWAY BROOMFIELD CO 80021-3464
08-00-89 (hex)	KINETICS
080089 (base 16)	KINETICS 3182 OLD TUNNEL ROAD SUITE H LAFAYETTE CA 94549
08-00-8A (hex)	PERFORMANCE TECHNOLOGY
08008A (base 16)	PERFORMANCE TECHNOLOGY 801 LINCOLN CENTER 7800 1H10 WEST SAN ANTONIO TX 78230
08-00-8B (hex)	PYRAMID TECHNOLOGY CORP.
08008B (base 16)	PYRAMID TECHNOLOGY CORP. 1295 CHARLESTON ROAD MOUNTAIN VIEW CA 94043
08-00-8C (hex)	NETWORK RESEARCH CORPORATION

company_id	Organization Address
08008C (base 16)	NETWORK RESEARCH CORPORATION 2380 N. ROSE AVENUE OXNARD CA 93010
08-00-8D (hex)	XYVISION INC.
08008D (base 16)	XYVISION INC. 101 EDGEWATER DRIVE WAKEFIELD, MA 01880
08-00-8E (hex)	TANDEM COMPUTERS
08008E (base 16)	TANDEM COMPUTERS 14321 TANDEM BLVD. AUSTIN TX 78728-6610
08-00-8F (hex)	CHIPCOM CORPORATION
08008F (base 16)	CHIPCOM CORPORATION SOUTHBOROUGH OFFICE 118 TURNPIKE ROAD SOUTHBOROUGH MA 01772-1886
08-00-90 (hex)	SONOMA SYSTEMS
080090 (base 16)	SONOMA SYSTEMS 4640 ADMIRALTY WAY, STE. #600 MARINA DEL REY CA 90292-6695
08-BB-CC (hex)	AK-NORD EDV VERTRIEBSGES. MBH
08BBCC (base 16)	AK-NORD EDV VERTRIEBSGES. MBH FRIEDRICHSTRASSE 10 25436 TORNESCH GERMANY
10-00-5A (hex)	IBM CORPORATION
10005A (base 16)	IBM CORPORATION P.O. BOX 12195 CE6A/664 3039 CORNWALLIS RTP, NC 27709-2195
10-00-E8 (hex)	NATIONAL SEMICONDUCTOR
1000E8 (base 16)	NATIONAL SEMICONDUCTOR 2900 SEMICONDUCTOR DRIVE SANTA CLARA CA 95051
80-00-10 (hex)	ATT BELL LABORATORIES
800010 (base 16)	ATT BELL LABORATORIES 1100 EAST WARRENVILLE ROAD NAPERVILLE IL 60566
AA-00-00 (hex)	DIGITAL EQUIPMENT CORPORATION
AA0000 (base 16)	DIGITAL EQUIPMENT CORPORATION LKG 1-2/A19 550 KING STREET LITTLETON MA 01460-1289
AA-00-01 (hex)	DIGITAL EQUIPMENT CORPORATION
AA0001 (base 16)	DIGITAL EQUIPMENT CORPORATION LKG 1-2/A19 550 KING STREET LITTLETON MA 01460-1289
AA-00-02 (hex)	DIGITAL EQUIPMENT CORPORATION
AA0002 (base 16)	DIGITAL EQUIPMENT CORPORATION LKG 1-2/A19 550 KING STREET LITTLETON MA 01460-1289
AA-00-03 (hex)	DIGITAL EQUIPMENT CORPORATION
AA0003 (base 16)	DIGITAL EQUIPMENT CORPORATION LKG 1-2/A19 550 KING STREET LITTLETON MA 01460-1289
AA-00-04 (hex)	DIGITAL EQUIPMENT CORPORATION
AA0004 (base 16)	DIGITAL EQUIPMENT CORPORATION LKG 1-2/A19 550 KING STREET LITTLETON MA 01460-1289

Novell Tables

Novell IPX Private Socket Numbers

The IPX protocol addresses packets in a Network:Node:Socket format. The Network field of an IPX address contains a value that represents a logical IPX network segment. This value is assigned to the IPX network segment by the network administrator and must be unique throughout the entire IPX internetwork. The Node field of an IPX address contains a value that represents a logical node on an IPX network segment. This value is generally a number that is 'burned' into the Network Interface Adaptor (NIC) at the factory. The Socket field of an IPX address contains a value that represents a logical process within the node. This value is generally obtained by an IPX application dynamically using the IPXOpenSocket() function. Novell also administers a list of IPX sockets that are "well-known" in all IPX network environments. "Well-known" or "Static" IPX sockets are virtual resources that are assigned to qualified applications by Novell. An IPX Static Socket is a 2-byte value that is uniquely assigned to an IPX application. The list of public IPX Static Sockets is published quarterly by Novell;

http://developer.novell.com/support/sample/tids/dsoc1b/dsoc1b.htm

Socket#	Description
8000	Company: NATIONAL ADVANCED SYSTEMS
8001	Company: NATIONAL ADVANCED SYSTEMS
8002	Company: NATIONAL ADVANCED SYSTEMS
8003	COMM DRIVER Company: SPERRY CORP. COMPUTER SYSTEMS Contact: GARY L EMPEY Ph#: 8015394374
8004	Company: KTA
8005	Company: KTA
8006	Company: KTA
8007	Company: KTA
8008	Company: NOVELL - PROVO Contact: JACK C HARRIS Ph#: 8014293135
8009	SPERRY TERM EMULATOR Company: TURNBULL AUTOMATIONS Contact: CHG INFO Ph#: 2036880689
800A	PRINT SERVER Company: COMMUNICATION HORIZONS Contact: NEIL WEICHER Ph#: 2033242323
800B	Company: DATA LANGUAGE CORP Contact: Ph#: 6176635000
800F	BATRAM Company: SANTA CLARA SYSTEMS
8010	OFFICE WARE Company: CENTURY ANALYSIS Contact: STEVE DINNING Ph#: 4156807800

Socket#	Description
8011	UPS Company: ELGAR CORP Contact: CHG INFO Ph#: 8008542213
8012	UPS
8013	Company: CHI CORP Contact: Ph#: 5124741511
8014	Company: INTEL - AMERICAN FORK Contact: DANA DOGGETT
8015	Company: COMPASS COMPUTING
8016	Company: COMPASS COMPUTING
8017	Company: COMPASS COMPUTING
8018	Company: COMPASS COMPUTING
8019	Company: COMPASS COMPUTING
801A	Company: COMPASS COMPUTING
801B	Company: COMPASS COMPUTING
801C	Company: COMPASS COMPUTING
801D	Company: COMPASS COMPUTING
801E	Company: COMPASS COMPUTING
801F	Company: NOVELL - SUNNYVALE LATIN AMERI Contact: CHG INFO Ph#: 4087474162
8020	Company: NOVELL - SUNNYVALE LATIN AMERICA
8021	Company: NOVELL - SUNNYVALE LATIN AMERICA
8022	Company: NOVELL - SUNNYVALE LATIN AMERICA

Socket#	Description
8023	Company: MCAFEE ASSOCIATES Contact: CAROL GERAGHTY Ph#: 9085300440
8024	Company: BLUE LANCE NETWORK INFO SYS Contact: DAVID L HEATH Ph#: 7136801187
8027	Company: GATEWAY COMMUNICATIONS INC Contact: CHG INFO Ph#: 7145531555
8028	Company: GATEWAY COMMUNICATIONS INC
8029	Company: GATEWAY COMMUNICATIONS INC
802A	FILE SHARING Company: NETLINE INC Contact: CHG INFO
802B	FILE SHARING
802C	Company: INTEL - AMERICAN FORK Contact: DANA DOGGETT
802D	Company: INTEL - AMERICAN FORK
802E	Company: ICM Contact: Ph#: 7146300964
802F	C-TREE VAP Company: FAIR COM Contact: WILLIAM FAIRMAN Ph#: 3144456833
8030	Company: MICROMIND Contact: Ph#: 2122222849
8031	Company: MICROMIND
8032	Company: NORTH STAR COMPUTERS Contact: Ph#: 4153578500
8033	Company: NORTH STAR COMPUTERS
8034	X.25 GATEWAY Company: RSJ SOFTWARE Contact: CHG INFO
8035	Company: SANYO ICON INC Contact: STEVE HANKA Ph#: 8012256888
8036	Company: DATA ACCESS CORP Contact: CRAIG P JORGENSEN Ph#: 3052380012
8039	NET MANAGEMENT Company: NOVELL - AUSTIN Contact: CHG INFO Ph#: 5123468380
803A	Company: BETA SOFT Contact: CHG INFO
803B	Company: PHASER SYSTEMS Contact: CHG INFO Ph#: 4159566300
803C	Company: PHASER SYSTEMS
803D	Company: PHASER SYSTEMS
803E	Company: PERFORMANCE GROUP Contact: Ph#: 4084798100
803F	Company: PERFORMANCE GROUP
8040	Mvd frm #12638-1, 1-9-92 Company: HORIZON TECHNOLOGY INC Contact: GREG MCCARTY Ph#: 7036845850
8041	CD-ROM SERVER Company: MERIDIAN DATA CORP Contact: JEROME N HARRIS Ph#: 4084383100
8042	Company: NATIONWIDE COMPUTER SERVICES Contact: KEVIN RUSSELL Ph#: 3057487700
8043	COMM SERVER Company: COMPUTER LANGUAGE RESEARCH INC Contact: NANCY KEMP Ph#: 2149607035
8047	3274 CONTROLLER EMULATORS Company: SOFTWARE DYNAMICS Contact: TED HAMLIN Ph#: 8137338784
8048	3274 CONTROLLER EMULATORS
8049	3274 CONTROLLER EMULATORS
804A	3274 CONTROLLER EMULATORS
804B	MIC SNA DFV SERVER Company: COMPUTERLAND - BONN Contact: JURGEN HAAKERT
804C	MIC SNA DFV SERVER
804D	DATABASE SERVER Company: MIGENT SOFTWARE INC Contact: CHG INFO Ph#: 7028323700

Socket#	Description
804E	Company: SWITCH LINK SYSTEMS Contact: STEVE GINN Ph#: 5032452400
804F	Company: INTERACTIVE FINANCIAL SOL INC Contact: JIM MAHAN Ph#: 4049524721
8050	Company: INTERACTIVE FINANCIAL SOL INC
8051	Company: INTERACTIVE FINANCIAL SOL INC
8052	Company: INTERACTIVE FINANCIAL SOL INC
8053	CUSTOMER UNKNOWN
8054	CUSTOMER UNKNOWN
8055	E-MAIL CHAT Company: NICHE CO Contact: CHG INFO
8056	MONEY TRANSFER Company: IPI INC Contact: ERIC KAGAN Ph#. 2016962086
8057	E-MAIL CHAT Company: NICHE CO Contact: CHG INFO
805E	Company: TELEBASE SYSTEMS Contact: DAVID FLASCHEN Ph#: 2152934724
805F	Company: TELEBASE SYSTEMS
8060	PRINT SERVER Company: NOVELL - PROVO Contact: DALE BETHERS Ph#: 8014297000
8061	T-NET, LAN BRIDGES Company: BRITISH TELECOM Contact: ANDY MERCER Ph#: 4416312741
8062	Company: WOLLONGONG GROUP Contact: LEO MCLAUGHLIN Ph#: 4159627100
8064	Company: MICRO DATA BASE SYSTEMS Contact: J B WOLSIEFFER Ph#: 3174471122
8065	Company: MICRO DATA BASE SYSTEMS
8066	Company: NORTON LAMBERT CORP Contact: RICHARD DEMORNAY Ph#: 80596467675210
8067	Company: NORTON LAMBERT CORP
8068	Company: NORTON LAMBERT CORP
8069	NETWARE TO HP LAN GATEWAY Company: HEWLETT PACKARD - SUNNYVALE Contact: STEVE ROTH Ph#: 4087465639
806A	REMOTE PC SOFTWARE Company: ALM Contact: CHG INFO
806C	CHAT PROGRAM Company: DIGITAL AV INC Contact: GREG L WEINSTEIN Ph#: 6156936822
806D	PC DEX Company: MERGENT INTERNATIONAL Contact: KAREN GAGNON Ph#: 2032574223
806E	DART Company: COLLEGE HILL SYSTEMS Contact: CHARLES ELIOT Ph#: 714075955
8070	NETWORK COURIER Company: MICROSOFT WORKGROUP CANADA Contact: STEPHEN LOUIE Ph#: 6046884548
8071	PIPES Company: PEER LOGIC Contact: DAVID FARRELL Ph#: 4156264545
8072	Company: WORDPERFECT CORP Contact: JIM JOHNSON Ph#: 8012225000
8073	DATABASE & 4GL Company: PROGRESS SOFTWARE CORP Contact: KATHY BAGDONAS Ph#: 6172754500
8074	RIGHT HAND MAN Company: FUTURESOFT Contact: CHG INFO Ph#: 5048371554
8075	RIGHT HAND MAN
8076	LASER DISK PROGRAM Company: U OF WISCONSIN - SUPERIOR Contact: PAT MCGILLAN Ph#: 7153948191

Socket#	Description
8077	FAX LINK & VAX MANAGER Company: OPTUS INFORMATION SYSTEMS Contact: ROBERT CICHIELO Ph#: 9082719568
8078	FAX LINK & VAX MANAGER
8079	TELECOMMUNICATIONS Company: VAN AUTO PARTS Contact: DAN EDINGTON Ph#: 2198790062
807A	TELECOMMUNICATIONS
807B	TELECOMMUNICATIONS
807C	TELECOMMUNICATIONS
807D	TELECOMMUNICATIONS
807E	R21PX Company: CROSSTALK Contact: ROB WATERSON Ph#: 4049983998
807F	Company: ORACLE CORP Contact: STANLEY YAU Ph#: 4155983610
8080	Company: ORACLE CORP
8081	Company: ORACLE CORP
8082	Company: ORACLE CORP
8083	Company: ORACLE CORP
8084	Company: ORACLE CORP
8085	Company: ORACLE CORP
8086	Company: ORACLE CORP
8087	Company: ORACLE CORP
8088	Company: ORACLE CORP
8089	REMOTE PC SOFTWARE Company: ALM Contact: CHG INFO
808A	CUSTOMER UNKNOWN
808B	CUSTOMER UNKNOWN
808C	CUSTOMER UNKNOWN
808D	CUSTOMER UNKNOWN
808E	CUSTOMER UNKNOWN
808F	CUSTOMER UNKNOWN
8090	VAP Company: PILLSBURY CO Contact: CHG INFO Ph#: 6123307143
8091	VAP
8092	VAP
8093	VAP
8094	VAP
8095	VAP
8096	VAP
8097	VAP
8098	VAP
8099	VAP
809A	Company: MARSHFIELD CLINIC Contact: CARL CHRISTENSON Ph#: 7153879333
809B	Company: MARSHFIELD CLINIC
809C	Company: MARSHFIELD CLINIC
809D	Company: MARSHFIELD CLINIC
809E	Company: MARSHFIELD CLINIC
809F	Company: MARSHFIELD CLINIC
80AF	Company: DSI DYNAPRO SYSTEMS INC Contact: DAVID MAURO Ph#: 6045213962
80B0	Company: DSI DYNAPRO SYSTEMS INC
80B1	Company: DSI DYNAPRO SYSTEMS INC
80B2	Company: DSI DYNAPRO SYSTEMS INC
80B3	Company: DSI DYNAPRO SYSTEMS INC
80B4	Company: CHICAGO RESEARCH & TRADING Contact: BOB STEINBERG Ph#: 3124312641
80B5	Company: STREETWISE SYSTEMS INC Contact: JEFF ICE Ph#: 4073914442
80B6	Company: STREETWISE SYSTEMS INC

Socket#	Description
80B7	FAX SERVER Company: DIGITAL VISIONS CORP Contact: RAY JOHNSTON Ph#: 4073910979
80B8	VOICE SERVER Company: DIGITAL VISIONS CORP Contact: RAY JOHNSTON Ph#: 4073910979
80B9	VOICE SERVER
80BA	NETWARE MANAGEMENT APPLICATION Company: FRYE COMPUTER SYSTEMS Contact: BILL DORTCH Ph#: 6172472300
80BB	MAJOR BBS SOFTWARE Company: GALACTICOMM INC Contact: TIM STRYKER Ph#: 3055835990
80BC	MAJOR BBS SOFTWARE
80BD	MAJOR BBS SOFTWARE
80BE	MAJOR BBS SOFTWARE
80BF	MAJOR BBS SOFTWARE
80C0	MAJOR BBS SOFTWARE
80C1	MAJOR BBS SOFTWARE
80C2	MAJOR BBS SOFTWARE
80C3	CHAT PROGRAM/IPX TALK Company: FELSINA SOFTWARE Contact: MARCO PAPA Ph#: 2136691497
80C4	IPX/SPX COMM PROTOCOL APPLICATIONS Company: MAGEE ENTERPRISES INC Contact: DON BRYANT Ph#: 4044466611
80C5	Company: WATCOM Contact: DAVE NEUDOERFFER Ph#: 8002654555
80C6	Company: NEWPORT SYSTEMS SOLUTIONS INC Contact: CHG INFO Ph#: 7147521511
80C7	Company: NEWPORT SYSTEMS SOLUTIONS INC
80C8	Company: NEWPORT SYSTEMS SOLUTIONS INC
80C9	Company: NEWPORT SYSTEMS SOLUTIONS INC
80CA	Company: NEWPORT SYSTEMS SOLUTIONS INC
80CB	Company: NEWPORT SYSTEMS SOLUTIONS INC
80CC	Company: NEWPORT SYSTEMS SOLUTIONS INC
80CD	Company: NEWPORT SYSTEMS SOLUTIONS INC
80CE	SPX DRIVER/NOVA FOCUS REMOTE PC ACCESS Company: DRIGGS CORPORATION Contact: RAYMOND E JOHNSON Ph#: 3014991950x327
80CF	APPL IPX/SPX COMMUNICATIONS Company: MAGEE ENTERPRISES INC Contact: DON BRYANT Ph#: 4044466611
80D0	APPL IPX/SPX COMMUNICATIONS
80D1	APPL IPX/SPX COMMUNICATIONS
80D2	APPL IPX/SPX COMMUNICATIONS
80D3	APPL 1PX/SPX COMMUNICATIONS
80D5	DATABASE SERVER Company: GUPTA TECHNOLOGIES Contact: MIKE GEIGER Ph#: 4153219500
80D6	DATABASE SERVER
80D7	LAN/FILE TRANSFER, COMM SERVERS, REMOTES Company: US ROBOTICS SOFTWARE Contact: JOHN MAGYARI
80D8	POWERCHUTE–VAP/NLM SERVER POWER SUPPLY Company: AMERICAN POWER CONVERSION Contact: MATT BLAIS Ph#: 6178946332
80D9	COREL DRIVER PRODUCT UNDER NOVELL 386 Company: COREL SYSTEMS, OPTICAL DIV Contact: YIU MING LEUNG Ph#: 6137288200
80DA	ARCHIVE SERVER Company: GIGATREND INC Contact: JOSEPH WIDMAN Ph#: 6199319122
80DB	GATEWAY PRODUCT Company: ATLANTA TECHNOLOGIES Contact: STEVE LONG Ph#: 4046427425x135
80DC	GATEWAY PRODUCT

Socket#	Description
80DD	OFFICE ORGANIZER NLM Company: UNISYS - CAMARILLO Contact: CHG INFO Ph#: 80598734412479
80DE	Company: UNIVERSAL NETWORK SYSTEMS Contact: DAVID MONHEIT Ph#: 3014848722
80DF	APPLICATION SERVER Company: NATIONSBANK APPL SYSTEMS SUPP Contact: PHILIP R REZNEK Ph#: 7043868125
80E1	Company: MODULAR SOFTWARE CORPORATION Contact: DON DUMITRU Ph#: 7148410444
80E2	CLIENT SERVER APPLICATION Company: SOFTWARE AG Contact: GALEN AOKI Ph#: 7038605050
80E4	LANPORT VIRTUAL EXTENSION OF PORTS Company: MICROTEST INC Contact: KELLY KINNARD Ph#: 6029716464
80E5	WORK STATION PEER-TO-PEER Company: CONVEYANT SYSTEMS INC Contact: SAM LIANG Ph#: 7147567142
80E6	DESKVIEW X - IPX SOCKET INTERFACE Company: QUARTERDECK OFFICE SYSTEMS Contact: STEVE SPRIGG Ph#: 3103143210
80E7	DESKVIEW X - IPX SOCKET INTERFACE
80E8	DESKVIEW X - IPX SOCKET INTERFACE
80E9	DESKVIEW X - IPX SOCKET INTERFACE
80EA	DESKVIEW X - IPX SOCKET INTERFACE
80EB	DESKVIEW X - IPX SOCKET INTERFACE
80EC	Company: MERIDIAN DATA INC Contact: JOE MARTORANO Ph#: 4084386401x265
80ED	Company: BIZTECH Contact: CHG INFO Ph#: 5167354006
80EE	Company: RATIONAL DATA SYSTEMS Contact: DOUG KAYE Ph#: 4154993354
80EF	Company: RATIONAL DATA SYSTEMS
80F0	Company: RATIONAL DATA SYSTEMS
80F1	Company: RATIONAL DATA SYSTEMS
80F4	GARP SERVER COMMUNICATION Company: NET RESEARCH PTY LTD Contact: JOHN BRADNAM Ph#: 61 2 238 7696
80F5	NETWORK MANAGEMENT PRODUCT Company: NCR - COLUMBIA Contact: CHRIS W MATRAS Ph#: 8037969740
80F6	NETWORK MANAGEMENT PRODUCT
80F7	NETWORK MANAGEMENT PRODUCT
80F8	NETWORK MANAGEMENT PRODUCT
80F9	NETWORK MANAGEMENT PRODUCT
80FA	NETWORK MANAGEMENT PRODUCT
80FB	Company: PROFESSIONAL PROGRAMMING SVCS Contact: JON B BUSHEY Ph#: 8013596200
80FC	Company: PROFESSIONAL PROGRAMMING SVCS Contact: JON B BUSHEY Ph#: 8013596200
80FD	Company: PEER LOGIC Contact: MOHAMED SHAFIQ Ph#: 4156264545
80FE	Company: WALL DATA Contact: ALAN LI Ph#: 2068834777
80FF	DISTRIBUTED APPLICATION Company: FOLIO CORPORATION Contact: PAUL MECHAM Ph#: 8013753700
8100	Company: MARSHFIELD CLINIC Contact: CARL CHRISTENSON Ph#: 7153879333
8101	Company: MARSHFIELD CLINIC
8102	Company: MARSHFIELD CLINIC
8103	Company: MARSHFIELD CLINIC
8105	Company: VIA Contact: Ph#: 4156512796
8106	
8107	
8108	

Socket#	Description
8109	
810A	
810B	
810C	
810D	
810E	
810F	NET 3270 Company: MCGILL UNIVERSITY COMPUTING CT Contact: ROBERT CRAIG Ph#: 5143983710
8110	Company: PROFESSIONAL PRODUCTIVITY CORP Contact: CHG INFO
8111	TODS Company: TELETRAK Contact: AVI SCHACHAF Ph#: 2122234470
8112	LUFTHANSA BS Company: LUFTHANSA GERMAN AIRLINES Contact: GEORG RENSONET Ph#: 49696963765
8113	LANPORT Company: MICROTEST Contact: JACK GUSKIN Ph#: 6029716464
8114	LANPORT
8115	LANPORT
8116	LANPORT
8117	LANPORT
8118	LANPORT
8119	LANPORT
811A	LANPORT
811B	LANPORT
811C	LANPORT
811D	IMAGE SERVER Company: FILE NET CORPORATION Contact: ANDY GUTMAN Ph#: 7149663596
811F	RTK OPERATING SYSTEM Company: OWL MICRO SYSTEMS
8120	TXD Company: THOMAS CONRAD CORP Contact: WALTER THIRION Ph#: 5128361935
8121	SPECIAL REQUEST Company: SPECTRAFAX Contact: Ph#: 4044797562
8122	NET MONITOR Company: ARTEFACT NETWORK SUPPORT Contact: HENK VANDOORN Ph#: 3115617532
8123	NET MONITOR
8124	NET MONITOR
8125	NET MONITOR
8126	NET MONITOR
8127	NET MONITOR
8128	NET MONITOR
8129	NET MONITOR
812A	NET MONITOR
812B	NET MONITOR
812C	NET MONITOR
812D	NET MONITOR
8138	LANSIGHT Company: LAN SYSTEMS Contact: CHG INFO
8139	PC CHALKBOARD Company: INTEL - AMERICAN FORK Contact: DANA DOGGETT
813B	REAL TIME BACK-UP Company: EMERALD SYSTEMS Contact: RICK WINTER Ph#: 3034499684
813C	NETWORK MANAGEMENT Company: PURE DATA INC Contact: REGGIE GARRETT Ph#: 2142422040

872

Socket#	Description
813E	FILE TRANSFER Company: AAC SYSTEMS Contact: KENNETH CHEN Ph#: 7034488666
813F	IMAGE SERVER Company: WANG LABORATORIES Contact: CHG INFO
8140	IMAGE SERVER
8141	IMAGE SERVER
8142	IMAGE SERVER
8143	Company: NETWORK DESIGNERS LTD Contact: GARY PANTON Ph#: 937580101
8144	MAYNESTREAM Company: ARCADA SOFTWARE Contact: PAT HANAVAN Ph#: 4072628016
8145	MAYNESTREAM
8146	NETWORK MANAGEMENT SYSTEM Company: ACCUNETICS Contact: STEPHEN BRANDER Ph#: 8004467769
8147	NETWORK MANAGEMENT SYSTEM
8148	NETWORK MANAGEMENT SYSTEM
8149	NETWORK MANAGEMENT SYSTEM
814A	Company: BR COMPUTING Contact: CHG INFO
814B	NLM Company: AUTOMATED DESIGN SYSTEMS Contact: MARGARET CLEARY Ph#: 4043942552
814C	Company: BR COMPUTING Contact: CHG INFO
814D	Company: BR COMPUTING
814E	Company: BR COMPUTING
814F	Company: BR COMPUTING
8150	Company: BR COMPUTING
8151	Company: BR COMPUTING
8152	Company: BR COMPUTING
8153	Company: BR COMPUTING
8154	Company: BR COMPUTING
8155	Company: BR COMPUTING
8156	Company: BR COMPUTING
8157	Company: BR COMPUTING
8158	Company: BR COMPUTING
8159	Company: BR COMPUTING
815A	Company: BR COMPUTING
815B	Company: BR COMPUTING
815C	Company: BR COMPUTING
815D	Company: BR COMPUTING
815E	Company: BR COMPUTING
815F	Company: BR COMPUTING
8160	PRINTQLAN Company: SOFTWARE DIRECTIONS INC Contact: GEOFF WIENER Ph#: 2015848466
8161	PRINTQLAN
8162	PRINTQLAN
8163	PRINTQLAN
8164	PRINTQLAN
8165	PRINTQLAN
8166	PRINTQLAN
8167	PRINTQLAN
8168	PRINTQLAN
8169	PRINTQLAN
816A	PRINTQLAN
816B	PRINTQLAN
816C	PRINTQLAN
816D	PRINTQLAN
816E	PRINTQLAN

Socket#	Description
816F	PRINTQLAN
8170	CDROM Company: ONLINE COMPUTER SYSTEMS Contact: IVAN LIN Ph#: 3014283700
8171	CDROM
8172	Company: BENTLEY SYSTEMS Contact: DAVID LANGDON Ph#: 2154585000
8173	Company: AVALAN Contact: ANTHONY AMUNDSON Ph#: 5084296482
8174	Company: AVALAN
8175	Company: AVALAN
8176	Company: AVALAN
8177	Company: AVALAN
8178	Company: AVALAN
8179	Company: AVALAN
817A	Company: AVALAN
817B	ACCOUNTING APD Company: SUPERNET Contact: CHG INFO Ph#: 34293111
817C	ACS
817D	SERVER DB Company: XDB SYSTEMS Contact: CHG INFO
817E	PIPES Company: PEER LOGIC Contact: MOHAMED SHAFIQ Ph#: 4156264545
817F	PIPES
8180	Company: NETWARE SOFTWARE ASSOCIATES Contact: STEVE HIGGINS
8181	PEER-TO-PEER Company: LODGISTIX INC Contact: CHARLES CARTER Ph#: 3166852216
8182	PEER-TO-PEER
8183	PEER-TO-PEER
8184	PEER-TO-PEER
8185	PEER-TO-PEER
8186	Company: DANWARE Contact: CHG INFO
8187	Company: DANWARE
8188	Company: DANWARE
8189	Company: DANWARE
818A	Company: DANWARE
818B	NETFRAME NW 386 Company: NETFRAME Contact: CHG INFO Ph#: 4084344070
818C	NETFRAME NW 386
818D	NETFRAME NW 386
818E	NETFRAME NW 386
818F	MAXIBACK Company: SYSGEN INC Contact: BOB WHEELER Ph#: 4082634411
8190	MAXIBACK
8191	MAXIBACK
8192	MAXIBACK
8193	DCA IPX COMM PRODUCT Company: DIGITAL COMMUNICATIONS ASSOC Contact: SCOTT P HERTZOG Ph#: 5122443871
8194	DCA IPX COMM PRODUCT
8195	DCA IPX COMM PRODUCT
8196	QUICKCHART Company: HEALTHWARE Contact: RAYMOND KUBISCHTA Ph#: 2063298379
8197	QUICKCHART
8198	QUICKCHART
8199	QUICKCHART
819A	Company: U OF OTAGO Contact: DAVID HARRIS Ph#: 6424798598

Socket#	Description		Socket#	Description
819B	Company: U OF OTAGO		81D8	DEALING ROOM SYSTEMS
819C	MINI SQL		81D9	DEALING ROOM SYSTEMS
	Company: ISICAD		81DA	DEALING ROOM SYSTEMS
	Contact: DICK PEDERSON Ph#: 7145338910		81DB	DEALING ROOM SYSTEMS
81A0	DEALING ROOM SYSTEMS		81DC	DEALING ROOM SYSTEMS
81A1	DEALING ROOM SYSTEMS		81DD	DEALING ROOM SYSTEMS
81A2	DEALING ROOM SYSTEMS		81DE	DEALING ROOM SYSTEMS
81A3	DEALING ROOM SYSTEMS		81DF	DEALING ROOM SYSTEMS
81A4	DEALING ROOM SYSTEMS		81E0	DEALING ROOM SYSTEMS
81A5	DEALING ROOM SYSTEMS		81E1	DEALING ROOM SYSTEMS
81A6	DEALING ROOM SYSTEMS		81E2	DEALING ROOM SYSTEMS
81A7	DEALING ROOM SYSTEMS		81E3	DEALING ROOM SYSTEMS
81A8	DEALING ROOM SYSTEMS		81E4	DEALING ROOM SYSTEMS
81A9	DEALING ROOM SYSTEMS		81E5	DEALING ROOM SYSTEMS
81AA	DEALING ROOM SYSTEMS		81E6	DEALING ROOM SYSTEMS
81AB	DEALING ROOM SYSTEMS		81E7	DEALING ROOM SYSTEMS
81AC	DEALING ROOM SYSTEMS		81E8	DEALING ROOM SYSTEMS
81AD	DEALING ROOM SYSTEMS		81E9	DEALING ROOM SYSTEMS
81AE	DEALING ROOM SYSTEMS		81EA	DEALING ROOM SYSTEMS
81AF	DEALING ROOM SYSTEMS		81EB	DEALING ROOM SYSTEMS
81B0	DEALING ROOM SYSTEMS		81EC	DEALING ROOM SYSTEMS
81B1	DEALING ROOM SYSTEMS		81ED	DEALING ROOM SYSTEMS
81B2	DEALING ROOM SYSTEMS		81EE	DEALING ROOM SYSTEMS
81B3	DEALING ROOM SYSTEMS		81EF	DEALING ROOM SYSTEMS
81B4	DEALING ROOM SYSTEMS		81F0	DEALING ROOM SYSTEMS
81B5	DEALING ROOM SYSTEMS		81F1	DEALING ROOM SYSTEMS
81B6	DEALING ROOM SYSTEMS		81F2	DEALING ROOM SYSTEMS
81B7	DEALING ROOM SYSTEMS		81F3	DEALING ROOM SYSTEMS
81B8	DEALING ROOM SYSTEMS		81F4	DEALING ROOM SYSTEMS
81B9	DEALING ROOM SYSTEMS		81F5	DEALING ROOM SYSTEMS
81BA	DEALING ROOM SYSTEMS		81F6	DEALING ROOM SYSTEMS
81BB	DEALING ROOM SYSTEMS		81F7	DEALING ROOM SYSTEMS
81BC	DEALING ROOM SYSTEMS		81F8	DEALING ROOM SYSTEMS
81BD	DEALING ROOM SYSTEMS		81F9	DEALING ROOM SYSTEMS
81BE	DEALING ROOM SYSTEMS		81FA	DEALING ROOM SYSTEMS
81BF	DEALING ROOM SYSTEMS		81FB	DEALING ROOM SYSTEMS
81C0	DEALING ROOM SYSTEMS		81FC	NETWORK SUPPORT MGR/PC REMOTE CNTRL PRGM
81C1	DEALING ROOM SYSTEMS			Company: PCI LTD
81C2	DEALING ROOM SYSTEMS			Contact: PAUL SANDERS
81C3	DEALING ROOM SYSTEMS		81FD	NETWORK SUPPORT MGR/PC REMOTE CNTRL PRGM
81C4	DEALING ROOM SYSTEMS		81FE	Company: IWI
81C5	DEALING ROOM SYSTEMS			Contact: MEHRDAD AMIR Ph#: 4089230301 32
81C6	DEALING ROOM SYSTEMS		81FF	Company: MARTELLO & ASSOCIATES
81C7	DEALING ROOM SYSTEMS			Contact: HERBERT H MARTELLO Ph#: 4108360439
81C8	DEALING ROOM SYSTEMS		8203	Company: NETWORK COMPUTING INC - NCI
81C9	DEALING ROOM SYSTEMS			Contact: JOHN FERRICK
81CA	DEALING ROOM SYSTEMS		8204	Company: NETWORK COMPUTING INC - NCI
81CB	DEALING ROOM SYSTEMS		8205	Company: NETWORK COMPUTING INC - NCI
81CC	DEALING ROOM SYSTEMS		8206	Company: NETWORK COMPUTING INC - NCI
81CD	DEALING ROOM SYSTEMS		8207	Company: NETWORK COMPUTING INC - NCI
81CE	DEALING ROOM SYSTEMS		8208	Company: NETWORK COMPUTING INC - NCI
81CF	DEALING ROOM SYSTEMS		8209	Company: NETWORK COMPUTING INC - NCI
81D0	DEALING ROOM SYSTEMS		820A	Company: NETWORK COMPUTING INC - NCI
81D1	DEALING ROOM SYSTEMS		820B	Company: NETWORK COMPUTING INC - NCI
81D2	DEALING ROOM SYSTEMS		820C	Company: NETWORK COMPUTING INC - NCI
81D3	DEALING ROOM SYSTEMS		820D	Company: DATA VOICE SOLUTIONS CORP
81D4	DEALING ROOM SYSTEMS			Contact: ROB CULVER Ph#: 7144740330bad#
81D5	DEALING ROOM SYSTEMS		820E	ID 5001 WEATHER STATION
81D6	DEALING ROOM SYSTEMS			Company: ZENITH DATA SYSTEMS
81D7	DEALING ROOM SYSTEMS			Contact: FRANK ONEAL Ph#: 6169823869
			820F	WRITE SERVER
				Company: ARC CALCULON
				Contact: BRETT PLATKO Ph#: 3012585359

Socket#	Description
8210	WRITE SERVER Company: QUANTUM CONSULTING Contact: BRET PLATKO Ph#: 3019268884
8211	SYSTEM 9 Company: HBF GROUP Contact: KEVIN ESPENSHADE Ph#: 7139957000
8212	SYSTEM 9
8213	SYSTEM 9
8214	SYSTEM 9
8215	SYSTEM 9
8216	SYSTEM 9
8217	SYSTEM 9
8218	SYSTEM 9
8219	ARGUS Company: TRITICOM Contact: LOREN MORIEARTY Ph#: 6129370772
821A	ARGUS
821B	TCP/IP GATEWAY Company: COMPUTERVISION SERVICES Contact: JOHN FENEY Ph#: 5086202800
821C	PICKIT (COMM SERVER) Company: INTEL Contact: KEVIN BROSS Ph#: 5036297515
821D	Company: PEER LOGIC Contact: MOHAMED SHAFIQ Ph#: 4156264545
821E	Company: PEER LOGIC
821F	DATA FACE NET BATCH
8220	DATA FACE NET BATCH
8221	LUMINAR OPTICAL SERVER Company: COREL SYSTEMS CORP Contact: RICHARD WOODEND Ph#: 6137288200
8222	CUSTOMER UNKNOWN
8223	CUSTOMER UNKNOWN
8224	CUSTOMER UNKNOWN
8225	CUSTOMER UNKNOWN
8226	CUSTOMER UNKNOWN
8227	X-BRIDGE Company: ADVANCED POLICY COMMUNICATIONS Contact: JOHN PHARES Ph#: 5033459178
8228	X-BRIDGE
8229	FLEXCOM Company: EVERGREEN SYSTEMS Contact: BILL GRACE Ph#: 4158978888
822A	FLEXCOM
822B	FLEXCOM
822C	FLEXCOM
822D	FLEXCOM
822E	GATEWAYS & WKST PROCESSOR Company: TEKNOS SYSTEMS Contact: TOM WHITTAKER Ph#: 44-825764-224
822F	GATEWAYS & WKST PROCESSOR
8230	GATEWAYS & WKST PROCESSOR
8231	GATEWAYS & WKST PROCESSOR
8232	GATEWAYS & WKST PROCESSOR
8233	GATEWAYS & WKST PROCESSOR
8234	GATEWAYS & WKST PROCESSOR
8235	GATEWAYS & WKST PROCESSOR
8236	GATEWAYS & WKST PROCESSOR
8237	GATEWAYS & WKST PROCESSOR
8238	LANWARE Mvd frm #12638-7, 1-9-92 Company: HORIZON TECHNOLOGY INC Contact: GREG MCCARTY Ph#: 7036845850
8239	LANWARE Mvd frm #12638-7, 1-9-92
823A	LANWARE Mvd frm #12638-7, 1-9-92
823B	LANWARE Mvd frm #12638-7, 1-9-92
823C	LANWARE Mvd frm #12638-7, 1-9-92

Socket#	Description
823D	CUSTOMER UNKNOWN
823E	TEAM 286 Company: IWI Contact: MAJID SOLEIMANI Ph#: 4089230301
823F	DBMS LOCK MANAGER Company: RAIMA CORP Contact: STAN GAZAWAY Ph#: 2065570200
8240	DBMS LOCK MANAGER
8241	REMOTE COMPUTING Company: CENTRAL POINT SOFTWARE Contact: JOHN BABB Ph#: 5036908088
8242	REMOTE COMPUTING
8243	REMOTE COMPUTING
8244	REMOTE COMPUTING
8245	REMOTE COMPUTING
8246	REMOTE COMPUTING
8247	REMOTE COMPUTING
8248	REMOTE COMPUTING
8249	TOKEN RING RPL Company: NCR - DAYTON Contact: JOE HENDRICKS Ph#: 5134456631
824A	TOKEN RING RPL
824B	DEALING ROOM SYSTEMS
824C	DEALING ROOM SYSTEMS
824D	DEALING ROOM SYSTEMS
824E	DEALING ROOM SYSTEMS
824F	DEALING ROOM SYSTEMS
8250	DEALING ROOM SYSTEMS
8251	DEALING ROOM SYSTEMS
8252	DEALING ROOM SYSTEMS
8253	TOTAL AUTOMATION SYSTEMS Company: DYNATECH UTAH SCIENTIFIC Contact: CHG INFO Ph#: 8015755210
8254	TOTAL AUTOMATION SYSTEMS
8255	VANTAGE POINT Company: CONNECT COMPUTER Contact: JAMES MOONEY Ph#: 6129440181
8256	NETARC SCHEDULER Company: EMERALD SYSTEMS Contact: RICK WINTER Ph#: 3034499684
8257	DISTRIBUTED PROCESSING Company: BRIGHAM YOUNG UNIVERSITY Contact: WILLIAM BARRETT
8258	XTREE NET - MVD FRM 23539-001 11-12-93 Company: CENTRAL POINT SOFTWARE Contact: DALE CABELL Ph#: 7142623224
8259	XTREE NET - MVD FRM 23539-001 11-12-93
825A	SYSM/LAN2 Company: H&W COMPUTER SYSTEMS Contact: ROBERT M WHITE Ph#: 2083850336
825B	VANTAGE POINT Company: CONNECT COMPUTER Contact: CHG INFO Ph#: 6129440181
825C	VANTAGE POINT
825D	VANTAGE POINT
825E	TIME OUT Company: NORDRA INC Contact: NORM HUGHES Ph#: 2017866878
825F	MULTI-PROCESSOR CONTROLLER Company: MBAC Contact: JAMES LEONARD Ph#: 2135317259
8260	MULTI-PROCESSOR CONTROLLER
8261	MULTI-PROCESSOR CONTROLLER
8262	MULTI-PROCESSOR CONTROLLER
8263	MULTI-PROCESSOR CONTROLLER
8264	TIME OUT Company: NORDRA INC Contact: NORM HUGHES Ph#: 2017866878

Socket#	Description
8265	INGRES DATABASE Company: INGRES CORPORATION Contact: VALERIE RIVEIRO Ph#: 5107472875
8266	EASY STREET PREM FINANCE Company: STREETWISE SYSTEMS INC Contact: JEFF ICE Ph#: 4073914442
8267	EASY STREET PREM FINANCE
8269	APT NET Company: AUTOMATED PROGRAMMING TECH Contact: BILL WELCH Ph#: 8105409877
826A	APT NET
826B	APT NET
826C	APT NET
826D	TOTAL AUTOMATION SYS ED Company: LUTHERAN SOCIAL SERVICES Contact: DON MUELLER Ph#: 4143427175
826E	TOTAL AUTOMATION SYS MC Company: LUTHERAN SOCIAL SERVICES Contact: DON MUELLER Ph#: 4143427175
826F	TOTAL AUTOMATION SYS ML Company: DYNATECH UTAH SCIENTIFIC Contact: CHG INFO Ph#: 8015755210
8270	TOTAL AUTOMATION SYS - ADI Company: DYNATECH UTAH SCIENTIFIC Contact: CHG INFO Ph#: 8015755210
8271	TOTAL AUTOMATION SYS - FAX Company: DYNATECH UTAH SCIENTIFIC Contact: CHG INFO Ph#: 8015755210
8272	SERVICE POINT Company: INTERPOINT SOFTWARE Contact: ALLEN HALES Ph#: 8014232524
8273	SERVICE POINT
8274	PRODIGY GATEWAY Company: COMPUTEREASE SOFTWARE Contact: CHG INFO Ph#: 4012451523
8275	PRODIGY GATEWAY
8276	NEWSMANAGER Company: VSS INC Contact: MARK DARBAGALLO Ph#: 7033691531
8277	NEWSMANAGER
8278	NEWSMANAGER
827F	Company: MARTELLO & ASSOCIATES Contact: HERBERT H MARTELLO Ph#: 4108360439
8280	Company: MARK HURST Contact: CHG INFO
8281	Company: MARK HURST
8282	Company: MARK HURST
8283	Company: MARK HURST
8284	BARR GATE/PC-TO-MAINFRAME COMMUNICATION Company: BARR SYSTEMS INC Contact: ROB VAN HORN Ph#: 9043713050
8285	BARR GATE/PC-TO-MAINFRAME COMMUNICATION
8286	Company: PURE DATA RESEARCH LTD Contact: MICHAEL BANKOVITCH Ph#: 4167316444x144
8287	VOICE MAIL Company: PLAN COMMUNICATIONS Contact: CHING-YUN CHAO Ph#: 4074873847
8288	Company: CENTERS FOR DISEASE CONTROL Contact: PETER PAGES Ph#: 4046393266
8289	RPC CALLS Company: INTEGRATED DATA SYSTEMS Contact: DAVID BENNING Ph#: 8182233344
828A	Company: INTEGRATED DATA SYSTEMS
828B	Company: FOLIO CORPORATION Contact: PAUL MECHAM Ph#: 8013753700
828C	Company: MULTITECH Contact: HUNG NGO Ph#: 6127853504
828D	Company: MULTITECH
828E	Company: MULTITECH

Socket#	Description
828F	Company: MULTITECH
8290	Company: MULTITECH
8291	Company: BUS TECH Contact: LARRY MCCLOSKEY Ph#: 3107914633
8292	Company: AMERICAN AIRLINES DECISION TEC Contact: STEVE FORRESTER Ph#: 8179638264
8293	REQ BY DORELOWITZ - CONSULTING Company: MICROCOM INC Contact: LASZLO CASABA Ph#: 6175511905
8294	Company: GATEWAY USA Contact: J P STALSWORTH Ph#: 8055460129
8295	Company: GATEWAY USA
8296	Company: GATEWAY USA
8297	Company: GATEWAY USA
8298	Company: GATEWAY USA
8299	Company: GATEWAY USA
829A	Company: COMPUTERVISION SERVICES Contact: ROBERT SIKKEMA Ph#: 50862028007349
829B	Company: COMPUTERVISION SERVICES
829C	Company: COMPUTERVISION SERVICES
829D	Company: SHIVA CORP Contact: BERT VINCENT Ph#: 6172708300
829E	Company: SHIVA CORP
829F	Company: TODD WEISS Contact: TODD WEISS Ph#: 7183492934
82A0	Company: TODD WEISS
82A1	Company: TODD WEISS
82A2	TAPE NLM Company: ARCADA SOFTWARE Contact: JOHN - CONSULTING MATZE
82A3	LANLORD PRODUCT Company: MICROCOM CLIENT SERVER TECHNOL Contact: DAVID ORELOWITZ Ph#: 9143772700
82A4	LANLORD PRODUCT
82A5	X25 AUTOMATED BRIDGE MONITOR & CONTROL
82A6	REQ BY DORELOWITZ - CONSULTING Company: MICROCOM INC Contact: LASZLO CASABA Ph#: 6175511905
82A7	PEER-TO-PEER COMMUNICATIONS Company: WITNESS SYSTEMS Contact: MICHAEL DRISCOLL Ph#: 7033276569
82A8	Company: MICRO INTEGRATION Contact: JOHN OROURKE Ph#: 3017773313
82A9	Company: MICRO INTEGRATION
82AA	Company: IBM - POUGHKEEPSIE Contact: CHUCK BERGHORN
82AB	Company: IBM - POUGHKEEPSIE
82AC	Company: IBM - POUGHKEEPSIE
82AD	Company: IBM - POUGHKEEPSIE
82AE	Company: IBM - POUGHKEEPSIE
82AF	Company: IBM - POUGHKEEPSIE
82B0	Company: J&L INFORMATION SYSTEMS Contact: REX JACKSON Ph#: 8187091778
82B1	Company: J&L INFORMATION SYSTEMS
82B2	Company: J&L INFORMATION SYSTEMS
82B3	Company: J&L INFORMATION SYSTEMS
82B4	Company: J&L INFORMATION SYSTEMS
82B5	Company: J&L INFORMATION SYSTEMS
82B6	Company: J&L INFORMATION SYSTEMS
82B7	Company: J&L INFORMATION SYSTEMS
82B8	Company: J&L INFORMATION SYSTEMS
82B9	Company: J&L INFORMATION SYSTEMS
82BA	Company: J&L INFORMATION SYSTEMS
82BB	Company: J&L INFORMATION SYSTEMS
82BC	Company: J&L INFORMATION SYSTEMS

Socket#	Description
82BD	Company: J&L INFORMATION SYSTEMS
82BE	Company: J&L INFORMATION SYSTEMS
82BF	Company: J&L INFORMATION SYSTEMS
82C0	Company: J&L INFORMATION SYSTEMS
82C1	Company: J&L INFORMATION SYSTEMS
82C2	Company: J&L INFORMATION SYSTEMS
82C3	Company: J&L INFORMATION SYSTEMS
82C4	Company: J&L INFORMATION SYSTEMS
82C5	Company: J&L INFORMATION SYSTEMS
82C6	Company: J&L INFORMATION SYSTEMS
82C7	Company: J&L INFORMATION SYSTEMS
82C8	Company: J&L INFORMATION SYSTEMS
82C9	Company: J&L INFORMATION SYSTEMS
82CA	Company: J&L INFORMATION SYSTEMS
82CB	Company: J&L INFORMATION SYSTEMS
82CC	Company: J&L INFORMATION SYSTEMS
82CD	Company: J&L INFORMATION SYSTEMS
82CE	Company: J&L INFORMATION SYSTEMS
82CF	Company: J&L INFORMATION SYSTEMS
82D0	Company: J&L INFORMATION SYSTEMS
82D1	Company: J&L INFORMATION SYSTEMS
82D2	Company: J&L INFORMATION SYSTEMS
82D3	Company: J&L INFORMATION SYSTEMS
82D4	Company: J&L INFORMATION SYSTEMS
82D5	Company: J&L INFORMATION SYSTEMS
82D6	Company: J&L INFORMATION SYSTEMS
82D7	Company: J&L INFORMATION SYSTEMS
82D8	Company: LEGATO SYSTEMS Contact: JOHN KEPECS Ph#: 4153297880
82D9	Company: LEGATO SYSTEMS
82DA	Company: LEGATO SYSTEMS
82DB	Company: LEGATO SYSTEMS
82DC	Company: LEGATO SYSTEMS
82DD	Company: LEGATO SYSTEMS
82DE	VALUE ADDED SERVER Company: SKYLINE TECHNOLOGY Contact: PAUL MARTIN - CONSULTING Ph#: 4158515195
82DF	VALUE ADDED SERVER
82E0	FCP FOR OS/2 SUPPORT (FOUNDTN COOP PROC) Company: ANDERSEN CONSULTING - CHICAGO Contact: MATTHEW BARNES Ph#: 3125075330
82E1	FCP FOR OS/2 SUPPORT (FOUNDTN COOP PROC)
82E3	Company: SYTRON CORP Contact: BILL SEROVY Ph#: 50889801008520
82E4	Company: AMERICAN AIRLINES DECISION TEC Contact: STEVE FORRESTER Ph#: 8179638264
82E5	Company: IMAGE RETRIEVAL INC Contact: GREG ENGLISH Ph#: 2144922855
82E6	Company: CONNECT COMPUTER Contact: CHG INFO Ph#: 6129440181
82E7	Company: CONNECT COMPUTER
82E8	Company: CONNECT COMPUTER
82E9	Company: CONNECT COMPUTER
82EA	Company: CONNECT COMPUTER
82EB	Company: CONNECT COMPUTER
82EC	Company: CONNECT COMPUTER
82ED	Company: CONNECT COMPUTER
82EE	Company: CONNECT COMPUTER
82EF	Company: CONNECT COMPUTER
82F0	Company: CONNECT COMPUTER
82F1	Company: CONNECT COMPUTER

Socket#	Description
82F2	Company: CONNECT COMPUTER
82F3	Company: CONNECT COMPUTER
82F4	Company: CONNECT COMPUTER
82F5	Company: CONNECT COMPUTER
82F6	HELLO-1 Company: JOSHIN DENKI CO LTD J&P DIV Contact: MASAHIRO NAKAJIMA Ph#: 66352108
82F7	HELLO-1
82F8	HELLO-1
82F9	HELLO-1
82FA	HELLO-1
82FD	NETWARE JUKEBOX Company: COREL SYSTEMS, OPTICAL DIV Contact: YIU MING LEUNG Ph#: 6137288200
82FE	FCP FOR WINDOWS SUPPORT (FNDTN COOP PROC) Company: ANDERSEN CONSULTING - CHICAGO Contact: MATTHEW BARNES Ph#: 3125075330
82FF	FCP FOR WINDOWS SUPPORT (FNDTN COOP PROC)
8300	Company: SMITH MICRO SOFTWARE INC Contact: DAVE SPERLING Ph#: 7143625800
8301	Company: SMITH MICRO SOFTWARE INC
8302	Company: SMITH MICRO SOFTWARE INC
8303	Company: SMITH MICRO SOFTWARE INC
8304	Company: SMITH MICRO SOFTWARE INC
8305	Company: SMITH MICRO SOFTWARE INC
8306	Company: SMITH MICRO SOFTWARE INC
8307	Company: SMITH MICRO SOFTWARE INC
8308	Company: SMITH MICRO SOFTWARE INC
8309	Company: SMITH MICRO SOFTWARE INC
830A	Company: SMITH MICRO SOFTWARE INC
830B	Company: SMITH MICRO SOFTWARE INC
830C	Company: SMITH MICRO SOFTWARE INC
830D	Company: SMITH MICRO SOFTWARE INC
830E	Company: SMITH MICRO SOFTWARE INC
830F	Company: SMITH MICRO SOFTWARE INC
8310	Company: SMITH MICRO SOFTWARE INC
8311	Company: SMITH MICRO SOFTWARE INC
8312	Company: SMITH MICRO SOFTWARE INC
8313	Company: SMITH MICRO SOFTWARE INC
8314	Company: SMITH MICRO SOFTWARE INC
8315	Company: SMITH MICRO SOFTWARE INC
8316	Company: SMITH MICRO SOFTWARE INC
8317	Company: SMITH MICRO SOFTWARE INC
8318	Company: SMITH MICRO SOFTWARE INC
8319	Company: SMITH MICRO SOFTWARE INC
831A	Company: SMITH MICRO SOFTWARE INC
831B	Company: SMITH MICRO SOFTWARE INC
831C	Company: SMITH MICRO SOFTWARE INC
831D	Company: SMITH MICRO SOFTWARE INC
831E	Company: SMITH MICRO SOFTWARE INC
831F	Company: SMITH MICRO SOFTWARE INC
8320	Company: SMITH MICRO SOFTWARE INC
8321	Company: SMITH MICRO SOFTWARE INC
8322	Company: SMITH MICRO SOFTWARE INC
8323	Company: SMITH MICRO SOFTWARE INC
8324	Company: SMITH MICRO SOFTWARE INC
8325	Company: SMITH MICRO SOFTWARE INC
8326	Company: SMITH MICRO SOFTWARE INC
8327	Company: SMITH MICRO SOFTWARE INC
8328	Company: SMITH MICRO SOFTWARE INC
8329	Company: SMITH MICRO SOFTWARE INC

Socket#	Description
832A	Company: SMITH MICRO SOFTWARE INC
832B	Company: SMITH MICRO SOFTWARE INC
832C	Company: SMITH MICRO SOFTWARE INC
832D	Company: SMITH MICRO SOFTWARE INC
832E	Company: SMITH MICRO SOFTWARE INC
832F	Company: SMITH MICRO SOFTWARE INC
8330	Company: SMITH MICRO SOFTWARE INC
8331	Company: SMITH MICRO SOFTWARE INC
8332	Company: SMITH MICRO SOFTWARE INC
8333	Company: SMITH MICRO SOFTWARE INC
8334	Company: SMITH MICRO SOFTWARE INC
8335	Company: SMITH MICRO SOFTWARE INC
8336	Company: SMITH MICRO SOFTWARE INC
8337	Company: SMITH MICRO SOFTWARE INC
8338	Company: SMITH MICRO SOFTWARE INC
8339	Company: SMITH MICRO SOFTWARE INC
833A	Company: SMITH MICRO SOFTWARE INC
833B	Company: SMITH MICRO SOFTWARE INC
833C	Company: SMITH MICRO SOFTWARE INC
833D	Company: SMITH MICRO SOFTWARE INC
833E	Company: SMITH MICRO SOFTWARE INC
833F	Company: SMITH MICRO SOFTWARE INC
8340	Company: SMITH MICRO SOFTWARE INC
8341	Company: SMITH MICRO SOFTWARE INC
8342	Company: SMITH MICRO SOFTWARE INC
8343	Company: SMITH MICRO SOFTWARE INC
8344	Company: SMITH MICRO SOFTWARE INC
8345	Company: SMITH MICRO SOFTWARE INC
8346	Company: SMITH MICRO SOFTWARE INC
8347	Company: SMITH MICRO SOFTWARE INC
8348	Company: SMITH MICRO SOFTWARE INC
8349	Company: SMITH MICRO SOFTWARE INC
834A	Company: SMITH MICRO SOFTWARE INC
834B	Company: SMITH MICRO SOFTWARE INC
834C	Company: SMITH MICRO SOFTWARE INC
834D	Company: SMITH MICRO SOFTWARE INC
834E	Company: SMITH MICRO SOFTWARE INC
834F	Company: SMITH MICRO SOFTWARE INC
8350	POWER GRID SERVER Company: COGNOS INC Contact: CHG INFO Ph#: 6137381440
8351	DATA SERVICE TO WORKSTATION/SCHOOL ADMIN Company: CHANCERY SOFTWARE Contact: ALEX NICOL Ph#: 6042941233
8352	TRANSMITTING Company: UNISYNC Contact: THANG NGO Ph#: 7149855088
8353	RECEIVING Company: UNISYNC Contact: THANG NGO Ph#: 7149855088
8354	MULTICOM NET - MODEM SHARING SOFTWARE
8355	MULTICOM NET - MODEM SHARING SOFTWARE
8356	MULTICOM NET - MODEM SHARING SOFTWARE
8357	CD CONNECTIONS Company: CBIS INC Contact: JEFF WEYRICH Ph#: 4044461332
8359	Company: RIVERVIEW SYSTEMS Contact: JACK BONGE
835A	TOTAL AUTOMATION SYSTEMS Company: DYNATECH UTAH SCIENTIFIC Contact: CHG INFO Ph#: 8015755210
835B	TOTAL AUTOMATION SYSTEMS
835C	Company: ITAC INC Contact: PAUL MIHALIC Ph#: 6194563738

Socket#	Description
835D	Company: ASP COMPUTER PRODUCTS INC Contact: RUTH ANN HANSON Ph#: 4087462965x446
835E	Company: ASP COMPUTER PRODUCTS INC
835F	Company: ASP COMPUTER PRODUCTS INC
8361	FAX SERVER Company: TRANSFAX CORPORATION Contact: STEVE MORGAN Ph#: 2136410439
8362	FAX PRINT SERVER Company: TRANSFAX CORPORATION Contact: STEVE MORGAN Ph#: 2136410439
8363	FAX MERGE SERVER Company: TRANSFAX CORPORATION Contact: STEVE MORGAN Ph#: 2136410439
8364	NETWORK MANAGEMENT SERVER Company: TRANSFAX CORPORATION Contact: STEVE MORGAN Ph#: 2136410439
8365	Company: FUNK SOFTWARE Contact: RALPH DAVIS
8366	Company: MICRO INTEGRATION Contact: JOHN OROURKE Ph#: 3017773313
8367	Company: MICRO INTEGRATION
8368	Company: MICRO INTEGRATION
8369	Company: MICRO INTEGRATION
836A	Company: MICRO INTEGRATION
836B	Company: TRIPLE A MOTOR CLUB Contact: MARK SNYDER Ph#: 7083909000x513
836C	SOCKET # FOR LAN TIMES JAPAN ARTICLE Company: LAN TIMES JAPAN, SOFTBANK CORP Contact: MASAKATSU SAKAI Ph#: 81356428250
836D	WATCHTOWER Contact: FRANZ SCHREDL Ph#: 7186253600
836E	CLIENT SERVER COMM SYSTEMS, SPX PROTOCOL Company: MICRORIM Contact: JIM WILHELM
836F	Company: NORTON LAMBERT CORP Contact: RICHARD DEMORNAY Ph#: 80596467675210
8370	Company: NORTON LAMBERT CORP
8371	Company: NORTON LAMBERT CORP
8372	Company: NORTON LAMBERT CORP
8373	Company: NORTON LAMBERT CORP
8374	MVD FRM 23539-001 11-12-93 Company: CENTRAL POINT SOFTWARE Contact: DALE CABELL Ph#: 7142623224
8375	DRIVERS Company: PRESOFT ARCHITECTS Contact: STEVE KOHLENBERGER Ph#: 7145386002
8376	NLM FOR REMOTE VOLUME MOUNT Company: INTECK CORPORATION Contact: JOHN BOEHM Ph#: 4025932080
8377	NLM FOR REMOTE VOLUME MOUNT
8378	Company: SYMANTEC PETER NORTON GROUP Contact: TORSTEN HOFF Ph#: 31045346004261
8379	Company: SYMANTEC PETER NORTON GROUP
837A	Company: DIGITAL EQUIPMENT - MERRIMACK Contact: SHAILA GOLIKERI Ph#: 6038848571
837B	CBS FACILITIES ASSIGNMENT - REQUEST Company: DYNATECH UTAH SCIENTIFIC Contact: CHG INFO Ph#: 8015755210
837C	CBS FACILITIES ASSIGNMENT - REPLY
837D	MULTI-PROTOCOL ROUTER INSIDE IPX Company: RESEARCH MACHINES PLC Contact: DUNCAN MOFFAT Ph#: 44 865 796362
837E	SHAREWARE Company: CHERRY TREE SOFTWARE Contact: RICK CHERRY Ph#: 8048622479 hm
837F	ENTERPRISE ECS Company: INTEL CORP Contact: DAN DEXTER Ph#: 5036296402
8380	ENTERPRISE MMT

Socket#	Description
8381	STOCK TICKER BROADCAST SERVER Company: NCOMPASS DEVELOPMENT INTL Contact: DOUGLAS P ERB Ph#: 2129250020
8382	QUERY UNIQUE USERS Company: US ROBOTICS SOFTWARE Contact: JOHN MAGYARI
8383	CBS ADA SERVER Company: DYNATECH UTAH SCIENTIFIC Contact: CHG INFO Ph#: 8015755210
8384	Company: PACE SOFTWARE SYSTEMS INC Contact: ROBERT DYE Ph#: 8014120126
8385	Company: ANDERSEN CONSULTING - CHICAGO Contact: MATTHEW BARNES Ph#: 3125075330
8386	GATEWAY MANAGEMENT Company: WALL DATA Contact: ALAN LI Ph#: 2068834777
8387	GATEWAY MANAGEMENT
838B	POWERCHUTE ALERT - UPS MONITORING Company: AMERICAN POWER CONVERSION Contact: BOB THURSTON Ph#: 4017895735
838D	Company: AVAIL SYSTEMS CORP Contact: RICK WINTER Ph#: 3034444018
838E	QA+ FOR WINDOWS/REMOTE DIAGNOSTICS Company: DIAGSOFT INC Contact: EARL RUSSELL Ph#: 4084388247
838F	POWERCHUTE ADMINSTRATIVE SOCKET Company: AMERICAN POWER CONVERSION Contact: BOB THURSTON Ph#: 4017895735
8390	Company: DATAMEDIC Contact: DAVID LEVITT Ph#: 5164358880
8391	COREL DRIVER Company: COREL SYSTEMS, OPTICAL DIV Contact: YIU MING LEUNG Ph#: 6137288200
8392	ID FOR LASERMASTER PRINTER PRODUCTS Company: LASER MASTER CORP Contact: NATE DICKERSON Ph#: 6129446069
8393	TFTP TRIVIAL FILE TRANSFER PROTOCOL Company: HEWLETT PACKARD - ROSEVILLE Contact: KIM BANKER Ph#: 9167855380
8394	FTP FILE TRANSFER PROTOCOL Company: HEWLETT PACKARD - ROSEVILLE
8395	Company: HEWLETT PACKARD - ROSEVILLE
8396	Company: HEWLETT PACKARD - ROSEVILLE
8397	Company: SITA Contact: LALITHA PARAMESWARAN Ph#: 51656731114345
8398	Company: SITA Contact: LALITHA PARAMESWARAN Ph#: 51656731114345
8399	Company: TECHGNOSIS INC Contact: JAY HOROWITZ Ph#: 4079976687
839A	QA+ FOR WINDOWS/REMOTE DIAGNOSTICS Company: DIAGSOFT INC Contact: EARL RUSSELL Ph#: 4084388247
839B	MAIL SYSTEMS Company: SYNECTIC SYSTEMS LTD Contact: JEFF CHAPPELL Ph#: 8023487101
839C	MAIL SYSTEMS
839D	NLM/VIDEO FILES ON NOVELL SERVICE Company: PROTOCOMM CORPORATION Contact: DICK ROTH Ph#: 2152452040
839E	TURNAX EMULATION GATEWAY Company: IDE CORPORATION Contact: CHG INFO Ph#: 5086636878
839F	CNF 16000 CONNECTION STATION Company: COROLLARY INC Contact: DOUG C MASON Ph#: 7142504040
83A0	CNF 16000 CONNECTION STATION
83A1	CNF 16000 CONNECTION STATION
83A2	CNF 16000 CONNECTION STATION
83A3	CNF 16000 CONNECTION STATION

Socket#	Description
83A4	CNF 16000 CONNECTION STATION
83A5	WORKSTATION PEER-TO-PEER COMMUNICATIONS Company: IBM - RESEARCH TRIANGLE PARK Contact: STEVE SCHMIDT Ph#: 9195439304
83A6	WORKSTATION PEER-TO-PEER COMMUNICATIONS
83A7	WORKSTATION PEER-TO-PEER COMMUNICATIONS
83A8	WORKSTATION PEER-TO-PEER COMMUNICATIONS
83A9	WORKSTATION PEER-TO-PEER COMMUNICATIONS
83AA	WORKSTATION PEER-TO-PEER COMMUNICATIONS
83AB	Company: DATANEX CORPORATION Contact: ROB PARSONS Ph#: 9198517292
83AC	HP OPEN MAIL & PORTABLE NETWARE HEWLETT PACKARD - BERKSHIRE Contact: DAVE MORRIS Ph#: 44 344 763758
83AD	COMMUNICATION/MAIL SERVER SOFTWARE Company: DATOR 3 SPOL SRO Contact: PAVEL KORENSKY Ph#: 02/7822053
83AE	COMMUNICATION/MAIL SERVER SOFTWARE
83AF	COMMUNICATION/MAIL SERVER SOFTWARE
83B0	COMMUNICATION/MAIL SERVER SOFTWARE
83B1	POWER MANAGEMENT SERVER Company: ELGAR CORP Contact: CHG INFO Ph#: 6194580244
83B2	POWER MANAGEMENT CLIENT
83B3	NETWORK PERIPHERALS - PRINT SERVER Company: CANON INFORMATION SYSTEMS Contact: GEORGE KALWITZ Ph#: 7144387178
83B4	NETWORK PERIPHERALS
83B5	NETWORK PERIPHERALS
83B6	NETWORK PERIPHERALS
83B7	NETWORK PERIPHERALS
83B8	NETWORK PERIPHERALS
83B9	FAX SERVER Company: FERRARI ELECTRONIC GMBH Contact: JOHANN DEUTINGER Ph#: 49332845590
83BA	FAX SERVER
83BB	FAX SERVER
83BC	FAX SERVER
83BD	CLIENT SERVER DATABASE ENGINE/SQL FOR NW Company: SYBASE INC Contact: JOHN WONG Ph#: 5105963904
83BE	PRINTER CONTROLLER BOARD/VAP OR NLM Company: DP TEK Contact: BOB MROSS Ph#: 3166873000
83BF	PRINTER CONTROLLER BOARD/VAP OR NLM
83C0	Company: IWI Contact: MEHRDAD AMIR Ph#: 4089230301 32
83C1	Company: LEXMARK INTERNATIONAL Contact: KEVIN GOFFINETT Ph#: 6022326253
83C2	Company: LEXMARK INTERNATIONAL
83C3	Company: LEXMARK INTERNATIONAL
83C4	Company: LEXMARK INTERNATIONAL
83C5	Company: LEXMARK INTERNATIONAL
83C6	Company: LEXMARK INTERNATIONAL
83C7	Company: OKNA CORP Contact: KONSTANTIN MONASTYRSKY Ph#: 2014600677
83C8	Company: OKNA CORP
83C9	Company: OKNA CORP
83CA	Company: OKNA CORP
83CB	Company: OKNA CORP
83CC	Company: OKNA CORP
83CD	DEVELOPMENT/COMMUNICATIONS TOOLKIT Company: MICHAEL RICH Contact: MICHAEL RICH Ph#: 8012217551

Socket#	Description
83CE	RESET PRINT SERVERS Company: MOTOROLA Contact: RUSS VAN ZANDT Ph#: 7084805006
83CF	Company: NETWORK DESIGNERS Contact: J M ROBSON Ph#: 0937580101
83D0	REMOTE PRINTER SOCKET Company: INDUSTRIAL EXOTICA Contact: KEN HILLIARD Ph#: 8184073900
83D1	FILE MANAGEMENT SERVICES Company: SYSTEMS AXIS PLC Contact: NICK TUCKER Ph#: 0278-421020
83D2	QUEUE MANAGEMENT SERVICES
83D4	Company: LANTECH SERVICES Contact: ALEX GRIFFITHS Ph#: 01027217902979
83D5	CC MAIL GATEWAY 3.30/SPX TRANSPORT Company: CC MAIL Contact: HUBERT LIPINSKI
83D6	REMOTE CONTROL - NODE-TO-NODE Company: DST - DISTRIBUTED SYSTEMS TECH Contact: MURLI ADVANI Ph#: 7146397115
83D7	REMOTE CONTROL - BANK OF MODEMS
83D9	GENERAL COMMUNICATION FORUM ON NOVELL NW Company: CREDIT LYONNAIS Contact: DAVID CHAMBERLAIN Ph#: 7364308000
83DA	DATABASE ENGINES Company: SYBASE INC Contact: JOHN WONG Ph#: 5105963904
83DB	DATABASE ENGINES
83DC	DATABASE ENGINES
83DD	DATABASE ENGINES
83DE	DATABASE ENGINES
83DF	DATABASE ENGINES
83E0	DATABASE ENGINES
83E1	DATABASE ENGINES
83E2	GATEWAY SERVER PRODUCT TO SPERRY HOST Company: ICC Contact: HARRY MEYER Ph#: 5137450500
83E3	WAN CONNECTION SERVER Company: IDEASSOCIATION Contact: JOAN O'NEIL Ph#: 5086636878x152
83E4	LAN SPOOL 3.5 Company: INTEL - AMERICAN FORK Contact: DANA DOGGETT
83E6	REMOTE INTERNAL HUB DRIVER Company: INTEL PCED Contact: RAVI VEDANAYAGAM Ph#: 5036965044
83E7	SOFTWARE ACCESS CONTROL SERVER Company: U OF PLYMOUTH Contact: GEOFF BOUCH Ph#: 441752233917
83E9	COMMUNICATIONS SYSTEM Company: UNICABLES SA Contact: NICOLAS LOPEZ Ph#: 3448265350
83EA	COMMUNICATIONS SYSTEM
83EB	COMMUNICATIONS SYSTEM
83EC	COMMUNICATIONS SYSTEM
83ED	COMMUNICATIONS SYSTEM
83EE	COMMUNICATIONS SYSTEM
83EF	COMMUNICATIONS SYSTEM
83F0	COMMUNICATIONS SYSTEM
83F1	COMMUNICATIONS SYSTEM
83F2	COMMUNICATIONS SYSTEM
83F3	COMMUNICATIONS SYSTEM
83F4	COMMUNICATIONS SYSTEM
83F5	COMMUNICATIONS SYSTEM
83F6	COMMUNICATIONS SYSTEM
83F7	COMMUNICATIONS SYSTEM
83F8	COMMUNICATIONS SYSTEM

Socket#	Description
83F9	COMMUNICATIONS SYSTEM
83FA	COMMUNICATIONS SYSTEM
83FB	COMMUNICATIONS SYSTEM
83FC	COMMUNICATIONS SYSTEM
83FD	COMMUNICATIONS SYSTEM
83FE	COMMUNICATIONS SYSTEM
83FF	COMMUNICATIONS SYSTEM
8400	COMMUNICATIONS SYSTEM
8401	COMMUNICATIONS SYSTEM
8402	GENERIC SERVER Company: GREENBAUM ASSOCIATES Contact: PAUL GREENBAUM Ph#: 2034547300
8403	OBJECT-STORE, DATABASE ACCESS PROTOCOL Company: OBJECT DESIGN Contact: BENSON MARGULIES Ph#: 6172709797
8404	OBJECT-STORE, DATABASE ACCESS PROTOCOL
8405	OBJECT-STORE, DIRECTORY PROTOCOL
8406	OBJECT-STORE, DIRECTORY PROTOCOL
8407	OBJECT-STORE, CACHE COHERENCE PROTOCOL
8408	OBJECT-STORE, CACHE COHERENCE PROTOCOL
8409	VISINET NLM ID# Company: TECHNOLOGY DYNAMICS INC Contact: DAVID CATER Ph#: 4043200077
840A	WDAGR - VAP Company: JOSTENS LEARNING CORP Contact: WARREN STRINGHAM Ph#: 8012246400
840B	WKILL Company: JOSTENS LEARNING CORP Contact: WARREN STRINGHAM Ph#: 8012246400
840C	INTERNET LAN CONTROLLER FOR NETWARE SAA Company: BUS TECH Contact: LARRY MCCLOSKEY Ph#: 3107914633
840D	PEER-TO-PEER COMMUNICATIONS Company: M&M MARS INC Contact: BRENT INGRAHAM Ph#: 6153396283
840E	PEER-TO-PEER COMMUNICATIONS
840F	CONNECTION MANAGER (SOFTWARE HOUSE PROD) Company: TBR INTERNATIONAL CORP Contact: RICHARD B TALMADGE
8410	CONNECTION MANAGER (SOFTWARE HOUSE PROD)
8411	CONNECTION MANAGER (SOFTWARE HOUSE PROD)
8412	CONNECTION MANAGER (SOFTWARE HOUSE PROD)
8413	CONNECTION MANAGER (SOFTWARE HOUSE PROD)
8414	CONNECTION MANAGER (SOFTWARE HOUSE PROD)
8415	FOR PROXY HOST Company: FUNK SOFTWARE Contact: PAUL FUNK Ph#: 6174976339
8416	WORKSTATION 3-LAN Company: ADVANCED TECHNICAL SOLUTIONS Contact: MARK MOFFITT Ph#: 8133914091
8417	DEVELOPING SERVER PERFORMANCE ANALIZER Company: BANYAN SYSTEMS INC Contact: JAY SEATON Ph#: 5088361841
8418	DEVELOPING SERVER PERFORMANCE ANALYZER
8419	DEVELOPING SERVER PERFORMANCE ANALYZER
841A	DEVELOPING SERVER PERFORMANCE ANALYZER
841B	DEVELOPING SERVER PERFORMANCE ANALYZER
841C	DEVELOPING SERVER PERFORMANCE ANALYZER
841D	REMOTE DATABASE SERVICES Company: INTERACTIVE DATA Contact: MICHAEL BENVENISTE Ph#: 6178608485
841E	REMOTE DATABASE SERVICES
841F	ENVELOPE PRINTER FOR NETWORK Company: THURIDION SOFTWARE ENGINEERING Contact: GREG BRYANT Ph#: 4084396981
8420	DACS OFFICE II Company: DOCUNET GMBH Contact: JURGEN BIFFAR Ph#: 0/89 841 4

Socket#	Description
8421	TERMINAL EMULATOR FOR MDOS - TRANSMIT Company: INTELLIGENT MICRO SOFTWARE LTD Contact: TONY SPRAGUE
8422	TERMINAL EMULATOR FOR MDOS - RECEIVE
8423	Company: PRAXIS Contact: JONATHAN LEVINSON Ph#: 6174928860x778
8424	REFLEX COMPLIANCE Company: PRODIGY SERVICES Contact: MICHAEL WHITING Ph#: 9149938311
8425	REFLEX COMPLIANCE
8426	REFLEX COMPLIANCE
8427	REFLEX COMPLIANCE
8428	REFLEX COMPLIANCE
8429	REFLEX COMPLIANCE
842A	IPX REMOTE CONTROL FUNCTION Company: NETWORTH INC Contact: JOE CALHOUN Ph#: 2149296864
842B	IPX REMOTE CONTROL FUNCTION
842C	SERVER-CLIENT COMMUNICATION VIA SPX Company: AT&T JENS CORP Contact: TORU YOSHIMATSU Ph#: 81-3-5561-5732
842D	TSR BROADCASTING VIA IPX
842E	Company: SITA Contact: LALITHA PARAMESWARAN Ph#: 51656731114345
842F	Company: SITA
8430	INSTANT RECALL I(MVD FRM 27203 6/16/94) Company: DAYTIMER TECHNOLOGIES Contact: ROB HUMPHREY Ph#: 41557227003305
8431	APPLICATION SERVER FC1 Company: THOMSON FINANCIAL Contact: LARRY STILLWELL Ph#: 6173452535
8432	APPLICATION SERVER FC2
8433	APPLICATION SERVER FC3
8434	APPLICATION SERVER FC3
8435	ENVELOPE MANAGER SOFTWARE Company: PSI ASSOCIATES Contact: HARRY T WHITEHOUSE Ph#: 4153212640
8436	ENVELOPE MANAGER SOFTWARE
8437	ENVELOPE MANAGER SOFTWARE
8438	ENVELOPE MANAGER SOFTWARE
8439	LAA SERVER BINDARY SOCKET Company: SABER SOFTWARE Contact: SCOTT HUTCHINSON Ph#: 2143618086
843A	440 IPX COMMUNICATIONS Company: INFORMATION BUILDERS Contact: BUD KOPMAN Ph#: 21273662503197
843B	VITAL SIGNS/LAN SERVER Company: BLUELINE SOFTWARE INC Contact: PETE PEDERSEN Ph#: 6125421072
843C	VITAL SIGNS/LAN SERVER
843D	ENVELOPE PRINTER FOR NETWORK Company: THURIDION SOFTWARE ENGINEERING Contact: GREG BRYANT Ph#: 4084396981
843E	OS2 SEQUEL SERVER IPX/SPX SUPPORT Company: MICROSOFT Contact: DAN TYACK Ph#: 2069364111
843F	ASYNCHRONOUS SERIAL COMMUNICATIONS Company: BLACK CREEK INTEGRATED SYSTEMS Contact: BILL MENNINGER
8440	ASYNCHRONOUS SERIAL COMMUNICATIONS
8441	ASYNCHRONOUS SERIAL COMMUNICATIONS
8442	ASYNCHRONOUS SERIAL COMMUNICATIONS
8443	COMMUNICATION BETWEEN SAGES Company: AMERICAN AUTO MATRIX INC Contact: PATTY BRANDSTETTER Ph#: 4127332000
8444	TV BROADCAST AUTOMATION STATUS Company: UTAH SCIENTIFIC Contact: TONY ROMANO Ph#: 8015753279
8445	TV BROADCAST AUTOMATION STATUS
8446	TV BROADCAST AUTOMATION STATUS
8447	CLIENT-SERVER VERSION OF CC MAIL Company: CC MAIL Contact: HUBERT LIPINSKI
8448	TV BROADCAST AUTOMATION STATUS Company: UTAH SCIENTIFIC Contact: TONY ROMANO Ph#: 8015753279
8449	NETSPRINT Company: DIGITAL PRODUCTS INC Contact: CHUNG SHIEH Ph#: 6176471234x274
844A	WORKSTATION REMOTE CONTROL Company: CALIFORNIA FEDERAL Contact: MICHAEL MULLER
844B	FULL TEXT RETRIEVAL CLIENT/SERVER DB ENG Company: IMPACT ITALIANA SRL Contact: MR SALLAHE HASSAN Ph#: 44-81-858-4815
844C	GATEWAY IPX Company: ICOT Contact: ELLIOTT HOWARD Ph#: 9168780595 x30
844D	GATEWAY SPX
844E	WORKSTATION IPX
844F	WORKSTATION SPX
8450	NETWORK SERVICES IPX
8451	NETWORK SERVICES SPX
8452	NETWORK LOGGER IPX
8453	NETWORK LOGGER SPX
8454	GATEWAY SOFTWARE Company: DATEV EG Contact: MANFRED WELLMEIER
8455	GATEWAY SOFTWARE Company: DATEV EG Contact: MANFRED WELLMEIER
8456	Company: NOVELL - PROVO Contact: LORI GAUTHIER Ph#: 8014293328
8457	RE:ACTION Company: CONCENTRIC TECHNOLOGIES Contact: PAUL MCDONALD Ph#: 7032648900
8458	RE:ACTION
8459	CAD SERVER Company: ISICAD Contact: JOHN MILIUS Ph#: 7142392758
845A	CAD SERVER
845B	ICL PORTABLE NETWARE Company: ICL Contact: IAN HARDWICK Ph#: 4406122313
845C	LOCATE Company: ZENITH DATA SYSTEMS Contact: MARK HAMMER Ph#: 6169823946
845D	BOML Company: ZENITH DATA SYSTEMS Contact: WILLIAM JUSELA Ph#: 6169823992
845E	RHOTHEOS
845F	CHAT PROGRAM Company: INTEL - AMERICAN FORK Contact: DANA DOGGETT
8460	MAILSLOTS (Chgd from 08840-134 10-21-91) Company: IBM - FRANKLIN LAKES Contact: WILLIAM KLINE
8461	MAILSLOTS (Chgd from 08840-134 10-21-91) IBM - FRANKLIN LAKES Contact: WILLIAM KLINE
8462	FILE TALK Company: MOUNTAIN NETWORK SOLUTIONS INC Contact: CHG INFO Ph#: 6194509091
8463	FILE TALK
8464	FILE TALK
8465	FILE TALK
8466	FILE TALK
8467	FILE TALK

Socket#	Description
8468	Company: MICROCOM Contact: CHG INFO
8469	Company: MICROCOM
846A	Company: MICROCOM
846B	Company: MICROCOM
846C	Company: MICROCOM
846D	Company: MICROCOM
846E	Company: MICROCOM
846F	Company: MICROCOM
8470	Company: MICROCOM
8471	Company: MICROCOM
8472	Company: MICROCOM
8473	Company: MICROCOM
8474	Company: MICROCOM
8475	Company: MICROCOM
8476	Company: MICROCOM
8478	DOCUMENT MANAGEMENT PACKAGE Company: PERFECT SOLUTIONS CORPORATION Contact: ALVIN TEDJAMULIA Ph#: 8012266000
8479	LITIGATION SUPPORT Company: GIBSON OCHSNER & ADKINS Contact: VINCENT LARSEN Ph#: 8063789754
847A	MONOTREX Company: PRIME COMPUTER Contact: CHG INFO Ph#: 50887929604000
847B	MONOTREX
847C	MONOTREX
847D	MONOTREX
847E	MONOTREX
847F	MONOTREX
8480	MONOTREX
8481	MONOTREX
8482	MONOTREX
8483	MONOTREX
8484	LITIGATION SUPPORT Company: GIBSON OCHSNER & ADKINS Contact: VINCENT LARSEN Ph#: 8063789754
8485	LITIGATION SUPPORT
8486	LITIGATION SUPPORT
8487	ARGUS/N Company: TRITICOM Contact: LOREN MORIEARTY Ph#: 6129370772
8488	ARGUS/N
8489	ARGUS/N
848A	CHANNEL SWITCHER APPLICATION Company: DYNATECH UTAH SCIENTIFIC Contact: CHG INFO Ph#: 8015755210
848B	CHANNEL SWITCHER APPLICATION
848C	CHANNEL SWITCHER APPLICATION
848D	CHANNEL SWITCHER APPLICATION
848E	CHANNEL SWITCHER APPLICATION
848F	CHANNEL SWITCHER APPLICATION
8490	CHANNEL SWITCHER APPLICATION
8491	CHANNEL SWITCHER APPLICATION
8492	Company: OXFORD INFORMATION TECHNOLOGY Contact: DAVID MICHAEL Ph#: 44865721321
8493	GATEWAY INTEGRATION ARCHITECT Company: MORRISEY ASSOCIATES Contact: DAVID FRANKEL Ph#: 7088694000
8494	BOOTWARE/MSD Company: LANWORKS Contact: GEORGE KOSTIUK Ph#: 4162385528
8495	WORKGROUP COMPUTING TOOL Company: MEMOREX TELEX Contact: CHRIS PATTERSON Ph#: 9182540446

Socket#	Description
8496	WORKGROUP COMPUTING TOOL
8497	WORKGROUP COMPUTING TOOL
8498	WORKGROUP COMPUTING TOOL
8499	WORKGROUP COMPUTING TOOL
849A	WORKGROUP COMPUTING TOOL
849B	WORKGROUP COMPUTING TOOL
84A0	IPX/SPX SOCKETS Company: ARTEFACT NETWORK SUPPORT Contact: PATRICK ROSENDAAL Ph#: 3115617532
84A1	IPX/SPX SOCKETS
84A2	IPX/SPX SOCKETS
84A3	IPX/SPX SOCKETS
84A4	IPX/SPX SOCKETS
84A5	IPX/SPX SOCKETS
84A6	IPX/SPX SOCKETS
84A7	IPX/SPX SOCKETS
84A8	IPX/SPX SOCKETS
84A9	IPX/SPX SOCKETS
84AA	CLIENT-SERVER DRIVER FOR IPX/SPX Company: REFERENCE POINT SOFTWARE Contact: DAVID BENNION Ph#: 8012247400
84AB	Company: INTRAK INC Contact: FRANK FULLEN Ph#: 6196951900
84AC	Company: INTRAK INC
84AD	Company: INTRAK INC
84AE	Company: INTRAK INC
84AF	Company: INTRAK INC
84B0	Company: INTRAK INC
84B1	DATABASE APPLICATIONS Company: DIGITAL EQUIPMENT - NASHUA Contact: JEFF MANNING Ph#: 6038841650
84B2	DATABASE APPLICATIONS
84B3	LOADER SOCKET Company: NETWORK TECHNICAL SOLUTIONS Contact: ROBERT WYMAN
84B4	FINDER SOCKET Company: NETWORK TECHNICAL SOLUTIONS Contact: ROBERT WYMAN
84B5	AUTOMATED CONTROL SYSTEM Company: AIR PRODUCTS & CHEMICALS Contact: TERRY OHM Ph#: 2154812859
84B6	AUTOMATED CONTROL SYSTEM
84B7	AUDIT TRAIL PACKAGE Company: BLUE LANCE INC Contact: ARULMANI PERIASAMY Ph#: 7136801187x237
84B8	SBACKUP ENHANCEMENT PRODUCT Company: SYTRON CORP Contact: STEPHEN GENTILE
84B9	TAPE BACKUP SYSTEMS Company: COLORADO MEMORY SYSTEMS Contact: HARRY WANG Ph#: 3036356823
84BA	QA+ ATTENTION SOCKET Company: DIAGSOFT INC Contact: RICK FARRINGTON Ph#: 4084388247
84BB	ADMINISTRATION SERVER Company: MCGILL UNIVERSITY FAC OF ENGIN Contact: DAVID DEDIC Ph#: 5143984784
84BC	ADMINISTRATION SERVER
84BD	WORKSTATION COMMUNICATIONS Company: SYMANTEC PETER NORTON GROUP Contact: TORSTEN HOFF Ph#: 31045346004261
84BE	WORKSTATION COMMUNICATIONS
84BF	NETWORK DYNAMIC DATA EXCHANGE Company: NETLOGIC INC Contact: BRET SCHLUSSMAN Ph#: 2125339090
84C0	ASYNCHRONOUS COMMUNICATIONS SERVER Company: US ROBOTICS SOFTWARE Contact: JOHN MAGYARI

Socket#	Description
84C1	MISCELLANEOUS SOFTWARE COMMUNICATIONS Company: TENTERA COMPUTER SERVICES Contact: ILES WADE Ph#: 4035325829
84C2	FORUM SEND Company: TEXAS A&M UNIVERSITY Contact: DONALD DYLLA Ph#: 4098453517
84C3	FORUM RECEIVE Company: TEXAS A&M UNIVERSITY Contact: DONALD DYLLA Ph#: 4098453517
84C4	FORUM CONTROL Company: TEXAS A&M UNIVERSITY Contact: DONALD DYLLA Ph#: 4098453517
84C5	REMOTE PRINTER CONFIGURATION Company: NEWGEN SYSTEMS CORP Contact: LINDA JIANG Ph#: 7146418600
84C6	AUDIT TRAIL PACKAGE Company: BLUE LANCE INC Contact: ARULMANI PERIASAMY Ph#: 7136801187x237
84C7	PEER-TO-PEER COMMUNICATIONS Company: FUJITSU SYSTEMS BUSINESS Contact: CHARLES HIGGINS Ph#: 3157324640
84C8	SNA GATEWAY Company: MICROSOFT Contact: GORDON MANGIONE
84C9	SNA GATEWAY
84CA	WORKSTATION TERMINAL ACCESS Company: HSD HARDWARE SOFTWARE DEVELOPMENT Contact: ANDRAS POGANY
84CB	Company: SERCOMM Contact: BEN LIN Ph#: 88625775400
84CC	Company: DE INTERNATIONAL LTD Contact: RICHARD TRINDER Ph#: 44943817985
84CD	APPLICATION TRACKING SYSTEM Company: HOLTEN WHITE & ASSOCIATES Contact: JEREMY WHITE Ph#: 6125456711
84CE	IBM HOST GATEWAY Company: IDEA COURIER Contact: JACK HILDWINE
84CF	CREDIT AUTHORIZATION GATEWAY Company: MERCHANTEC INTERNATIONAL Contact: STEPHEN CHARSKY Ph#: 4087377700
84D0	GRAPHICAL HOTEL MANAGEMENT APPLICATION Company: INSURE INC Contact: GREG VANOSS Ph#: 6126882170
84D1	GRAPHICAL HOTEL MANAGEMENT APPLICATION
84D2	NETWORK BACK-UP Company: DIGITAL EQUIPMENT - SHREWSBURY Contact: HUGO CURBELO Ph#: 5088413052
84D3	CLIENT SERVER APPLICATION Company: ALCON SYSTEMS Contact: KUI SENG SOON Ph#: 3142891792
84D4	CLIENT SERVER APPLICATION Company: ALCON SYSTEMS Contact: KUI SENG SOON Ph#: 3142891792
84D5	COMMUNICATIONS SERVER SDD SYNTHESIZER Company: SCANDINAVIAN AIRLINES DATA Contact: NILS HENDRIKSEN Ph#: 4532324125
84D6	INFORMATION SYSTEMS PRODUCT Company: PROSOFTIA AB Contact: JOHAN PERSSON
84D7	INFORMATION SYSTEMS PRODUCT
84D8	INFORMATION SYSTEMS PRODUCT
84D9	INFORMATION SYSTEMS PRODUCT
84DA	INFORMATION SYSTEMS PRODUCT Company: PROSOFTIA AB Contact: JOHAN PERSSON
84DB	INFORMATION SYSTEMS PRODUCT
84DC	INFORMATION SYSTEMS PRODUCT
84DD	INFORMATION SYSTEMS PRODUCT
84DE	INFORMATION SYSTEMS PRODUCT

Socket#	Description
84DF	INFORMATION SYSTEMS PRODUCT
84E0	OBJECT ORIENTED DATABASE SYSTEM Company: ONTOS INC Contact: JERRY THOMAS Ph#: 6172727110
84E1	OBJECT ORIENTED DATABASE SYSTEM
84E2	TAPE BACK-UP FOR NLM APPLICATION Company: MOUNTAIN NETWORK SOLUTIONS INC Contact: YOUNG-AN HSIEH Ph#: 4084386650x334
84E3	TAPE BACK-UP FOR NLM APPLICATION
84E4	TAPE BACK-UP FOR NLM APPLICATION
84E5	TAPE BACK-UP FOR NLM APPLICATION
84E6	Company: ATTACHMATE CORPORATION Contact: SCOTT WOOD Ph#: 2066444010x377
84E7	TAPE BACK-UP FOR NLM APPLICATION Company: MOUNTAIN NETWORK SOLUTIONS INC Contact: YOUNG-AN HSIEH Ph#: 4084386650x334
84E8	TAPE BACK-UP FOR NLM APPLICATION
84E9	BRMSG NETWORK MAIL SERVER Company: SOFTBRIDGE INC Contact: STEVE SQUIRES
84EA	CLIENT SERVER MONITORING UTILITY Company: DELL COMPUTER Contact: TONY PATTERSON Ph#: 5123433517
84EB	SYNECTICS FOR OS/2 VERSION 2.0 Company: PARALLEL PCS INC Contact: STEVE ROSENBERRY Ph#: 2156701710
84EC	SYNECTICS FOR OS/2 VERSION 2.0
84ED	INFORMATION SYSTEMS PRODUCT Company: PROSOFTIA AB Contact: JOHAN PERSSON
84EE	INFORMATION SYSTEMS PRODUCT
84EF	INFORMATION SYSTEMS PRODUCT
84F0	INFORMATION SYSTEMS PRODUCT
84F1	INFORMATION SYSTEMS PRODUCT
84F2	INFORMATION SYSTEMS PRODUCT
84F3	INFORMATION SYSTEMS PRODUCT
84F4	INFORMATION SYSTEMS PRODUCT
84F5	INFORMATION SYSTEMS PRODUCT
84F6	INFORMATION SYSTEMS PRODUCT
84F7	INFORMATION SYSTEMS PRODUCT
84F8	INFORMATION SYSTEMS PRODUCT
84F9	INFORMATION SYSTEMS PRODUCT
84FA	INFORMATION SYSTEMS PRODUCT
84FB	NETSCRIBE Company: MERIDIAN DATA CORP Contact: MIKE PRICE Ph#: 4084383100
84FC	NETSCRIBE
84FD	NETSCRIBE
84FE	NETSCRIBE
84FF	FAX SERVER Company: FERRARI ELECTRONIC GMBH Contact: JOHANN DEUTINGER Ph#: 49332845590
8502	FOURTH SHIFT MFG ADD-ON PACKAGE
8503	
8504	
8505	
8506	
8507	
8508	
8509	
850A	MODEM-SHARING SOFTWARE - DOS Company: LANSOURCE TECHNOLOGIES Contact: CHRIS WELLS Ph#: 4168668575
850B	MODEM-SHARING SOFTWARE - WINDOWS
850C	TELEPHONE ANSWERING SYSTEM Company: A&M COMMUNICATIONS Contact: DANIEL G AMBROSE Ph#: 3149466222 WK

Socket#	Description
850D	FILE/IPX-BASED RPC SYSTEM
850E	NETWORK DISC BACK-UP SOFTWARE Company: FORTUNET INC Contact: FRANK THROCKMORTON Ph#: 8014676887
850F	ARCHIVES & MUSEUM MANAGEMENT Company: CACTUS SOFTWARE Contact: GEOFF MOTTRAM Ph#: 2015400980
8510	FAX SERVER Company: EXTENDED SYSTEMS Contact: JERRY MAJDIC Ph#: 4065877575
8511	TELETEXT SERVICE Company: U OF PLYMOUTH Contact: GEOFF BOUCH Ph#: 441752233917
8512	NETWORK ERROR LOG Company: U OF PLYMOUTH Contact: GEOFF BOUCH Ph#: 441752233917
8513	MEASURE SERVERS AND MEASURE CLIENTS Company: ADVANTECH BENELUX BV Contact: AD VANDENBROEK Ph#: 31165050505
8514	3270 NETWARE FOR SAA EMULATOR Company: FORVUS RESEARCH INC Contact: KEVIN D JONES Ph#: 9199540063
8515	3270 NETWARE FOR SAA EMULATOR
8516	WORKSTATION UTILIZATION DATA COLLECTION Company: NETWORK SECURITY SYSTEMS Contact: CARLTON H SMITH Ph#: 6196228716
8517	WORKSTATION UTILIZATION DATABASE MGMT
8518	DATABASE GATEWAY Company: INFORMATION BUILDERS Contact: GARY GOLDBERG Ph#: 2127364433
8519	FAX SERVER EXTENDED SYSTEMS Contact: JERRY MAJDIC Ph#: 4065877575
851A	REMOTE PRINTER CONSOLE Company: PEERLESS GROUP Contact: PAUL REINER Ph#: 3105484488
851B	BATCHFILER IPX SOCKET Company: JOVANDI INTERNATIONAL INC Contact: FRANK R OPPEDIJK Ph#: 4045231772
851C	TIME SYNCHRONIZATION IPX SOCKET
851D	FAX SERVER LOGIN SOCKET Company: ASCOM TELECOMMUNICATION LTD Contact: PRAKASH SOLANKI
851E	FAX SERVER - CAS REQUEST SOCKET Company: ASCOM TELECOMMUNICATION LTD Contact: PRAKASH SOLANKI
851F	FAX SERVER - WORKSTATION UTILITY REQUEST Company: ASCOM TELECOMMUNICATION LTD Contact: PRAKASH SOLANKI
8520	FAX SERVER - FAXBIOS REQUEST SOCKET Company: ASCOM TELECOMMUNICATION LTD Contact: PRAKASH SOLANKI
8521	FAX SERVER - NETWORKED ATTACHED FAX UNIT Company: ASCOM TELECOMMUNICATION LTD Contact: PRAKASH SOLANKI
8522	DFDSM DATA FACILITIES DATA STORAGE MGMT Company: IBM - SAN JOSE Contact: AMY LIM Ph#: 4082846453
8523	RELATIONAL DATABASE Company: GUPTA TECHNOLOGIES Contact: MARK THOMAS Ph#: 4156174729
8524	REPORT SERVER STATS/FRM 23539-1 11-12-93 Company: CENTRAL POINT SOFTWARE Contact: DALE CABELL Ph#: 7142623224
8525	REPORT SERVER STATS/FRM 23539-1 11-12-93
8526	COMMUNICATION BETWEEN CLIENT AND SERVER Company: CDC - OFFICE OF PROGRAM SUPPRT Contact: STAN VANSANT Ph#: 4046392275
8529	DOCUMENT PROCESSING SERVER NLM Company: BOSS LOGIC INC Contact: PAUL KWAN Ph#: 4159037036
852A	DOCUMENT PROCESSING SERVER NLM
852B	DOCUMENT PROCESSING SERVER NLM

Socket#	Description
852C	DOCUMENT PROCESSING SERVER NLM
852D	DOCUMENT PROCESSING SERVER NLM
852E	DOCUMENT PROCESSING SERVER NLM
852F	FINANCIAL MARKETS INFORMATION SERVER Company: AT FINANCIAL Contact: KEN LEA Ph#: 7087171930
8530	EMAIL NOTIFICATION Company: ON TECHNOLOGY Contact: CHRISTOPHER RISLEY Ph#: 6177344317
8531	NETVIEW SUPPORT Company: MEMOREX TELEX Contact: DAVID SCOTT Ph#: 9192506614
8532	LANLORD PRODUCT Company: MICROCOM CLIENT SERVER TECHNOL Contact: DAVID ORELOWITZ Ph#: 9143772700
8533	RTS TERMINAL EMULATION Company: DATA RESEARCH & APPLICATIONS Contact: GEORGE PHELPS Ph#: 6156901345
8534	RSCF CLIENT-SERVER API
8535	CD NETWORKER IPX VERSION
8536	SQL SERVER IPX/SPX HIDDEN SERVER Company: MICROSOFT Contact: PETER HUSSEY Ph#: 2068828080
853D	DATABASE LOCK SERVER Company: HIGH ASPECT DEVELOPMENT Contact: DAN REYNOLDS Ph#: 2197624725
853E	MESSAGE MANAGER Company: LANCORP PTY LTD Contact: ESMOND PITT Ph#: 6136467100
853F	OBJECT MANAGER
8540	OBJECT AGENT
8541	REQUEST MANAGER
8544	WORKSTATION 4-LAN Company: ADVANCED TECHNICAL SOLUTIONS Contact: MARK MOFFITT Ph#: 8133914091
8545	GENESYS NETWORK PRODUCT DOS Company: GENESYS DATA TECHNOLOGY Contact: CHG INFO Ph#: 4107850000
8546	GENESYS NETWORK PRODUCT OS/2 Company: GENESYS DATA TECHNOLOGY Contact: CHG INFO Ph#: 4107850000
8548	INTERNET GATEWAY Company: METASCYBE SYSTEMS LTD Contact: MARK HELAS
8549	INTELLIGENT HOST GATEWAY Company: AMERICAN AIRLINES DECISION TEC Contact: STEVE FORRESTER Ph#: 8179638264
854C	INTERNAL PROTOCOL/WIRELESS LAN PRODUCT Company: IBM - LA GAUDE Contact: JOSE-LOUIS MARTINEZ Ph#: 33-92-11-50-53
854D	MULTI-SYSTEM MGR - ACCESS TO SERVER INFO Company: IBM - RESEARCH TRIANGLE PARK Contact: RICH NEWPOL Ph#: 9195431171
854E	NETPRINT CALLING CHANNEL Company: INTERLINK COMMUNICATIONS LTD Contact: NEIL HORTON Ph#: 255426147
854F	NETPRINT WORKING CHANNEL
8550	REMOTE SESSION Company: DST - DISTRIBUTED SYSTEMS TECH Contact: MURLI ADVANI Ph#: 7146397115
8551	REMOTE SESSION
8552	REMOTE SESSION
8553	REMOTE SESSION
8554	PEER-TO-PEER COMMUNICATIONS - DESKTOP Company: FUJITSU SYSTEMS BUSINESS Contact: CHARLES HIGGINS Ph#: 3157324640
8555	DIAGNOSTIC UTILITY Company: FUJITSU SYSTEMS BUSINESS Contact: CHARLES HIGGINS Ph#: 3157324640
8556	NLM HEALTH MONITOR Company: PRESOFT ARCHITECTS Contact: STEVE KOHLENBERGER Ph#: 7145386002

Socket#	Description
8557	CRISLER MCGEE Company: CRISLER MCKEE SOFTWARE DEVELOP Contact: CHARLES CRISLER Ph#: 6038986252
8558	CRISLER MCGEE
8559	INFORMATION SHARING BETWEEN WORKSTATIONS Company: INTEL Contact: KEN REESE
855A	POLICY ENGINE Company: EMERALD SYSTEMS Contact: RYN CORBEIL Ph#: 6196732161
855B	POLICY ENGINE Company: EMERALD SYSTEMS Contact: RYN CORBEIL Ph#: 6196732161
855C	POLICY ENGINE
855D	POLICY ENGINE
855E	POLICY ENGINE
855F	POLICY ENGINE
8560	STAND-ALONE PRINT SERVER Company: BAY TECHNICAL ASSOCIATES Contact: MARC LOSH Ph#: 6014678231
8561	SERVICE DISTRIBUTION US WEST ADVANCED TECHNOLOGIES Contact: JAMES SHELBY Ph#: 3035416329
8562	SERVICE DISTRIBUTION
8563	SERVICE DISTRIBUTION
8564	SERVICE DISTRIBUTION
8565	SERVICE DISTRIBUTION
8566	SERVICE DISTRIBUTION
8568	MPRST PEER-TO-PEER Company: US SPRINT Contact: JEFF FRENCH Ph#: 7036896462
8569	MPRST BROADCAST
856A	LAN ASSIST PLUS REMOTE CONTROL Company: MICROTEST Contact: JAYESH PATEL
856B	LAN ASSIST PLUS REMOTE CONTROL
856C	LAN ASSIST PLUS REMOTE CONTROL
856D	LAN ASSIST PLUS REMOTE CONTROL
856E	MAP ASSIST PEER-TO-PEER Company: MICROTEST Contact: JAYESH PATEL
856F	MAP ASSIST PEER-TO-PEER
8570	MAP ASSIST PEER-TO-PEER
8571	MAP ASSIST PEER-TO-PEER
8572	ASYNCHRONOUS COMMUNICATIONS SERVERS Company: US ROBOTICS SOFTWARE Contact: JOHN MAGYARI
8573	DATABASE SERVER Company: FAIR COM Contact: JIM SLATTERY Ph#: 7166472005
8574	NLM-BASED DATABASE ENGINE Company: AUTO GRAPHICS INC Contact: GARY GILLIAM Ph#: 7145957204
8575	TIGER QUOTE INCOMING SERVER REQUESTS Company: JOSHUA GROUP LTD Contact: JOSHUA LEVINE Ph#: 2123939273
8576	TIGER QUOTE BROADCAST
8577	USER SOCKET Company: NETWORK TECHNICAL SOLUTIONS Contact: ROBERT WYMAN
8578	GHOST SOCKET Company: NETWORK TECHNICAL SOLUTIONS Contact: ROBERT WYMAN
8579	REMOTE PROCEDURE PROTOCOL Company: FORTUNET INC Contact: BORIS ITKIS Ph#: 7027969090
857A	EICON INTERCONNECT SERVER Company: EICON TECHNOLOGY Contact: PAT CALHOUN Ph#: 5146312592
857B	EICON SECURITY AGENT

Socket#	Description
857C	COST RECOVERY SERVER Company: VINCENT LARSEN Contact: VINCENT LARSEN Ph#: 8063583635
857D	COST RECOVERY SERVER
857E	PC-BASED SNA GATEWAY Company: UNGERMANN BASS Contact: SHIGETO MORI Ph#: 81337988508
857F	COMMUNICATION BETWEEN PRINT SERVER & W/S Company: NISSIN ELECTRIC CO LTD Contact: YOSHIO KASHIWAGI Ph#: 8175864840
8580	PEER-TO-PEER MESSAGING Company: HANS SPATZIER Contact: DIPL-ING HANS SPATZIER Ph#: +49-6173-79047
8581	BANKING DEALING ROOMS Company: ART & SCIENCE LTD Contact: KEN BALDRY Ph#: +44 71 3576294
8582	BANKING DEALING ROOMS
8583	BANKING DEALING ROOMS
8584	BANKING DEALING ROOMS
858E	CLIENT UTILITY - WS TO PRINTER COMMUNICATION Company: TOKYO DENSHI SEKKEI KK Contact: YUICH NAGATA Ph#: 81-423-71-1121
8590	NETWORK WORKSTATION CONTROL Company: WESTERN PACIFIC TECHNOLOGIES Contact: TOM KLEIN Ph#: 3125596234
8591	TELETEXT SERVER Company: TEVESCOM Contact: BERNARDO ALTAMIRANO Ph#: 525/520-4274
8592	PRINT SERVER Company: FORESYTE TECHNOLOGIES Contact: LARRY HSIAO Ph#: 6195302881
8599	WAN NETWORKS
859A	WAN NETWORKS
859B	WAN NETWORKS
859C	WAN NETWORKS
859D	WAN NETWORKS
859E	WAN NETWORKS
859F	WAN NETWORKS
85A0	WAN NETWORKS
85A1	WAN NETWORKS
85A2	WAN NETWORKS
85A7	DATABASE SERVER Company: SOFTWRIGHT SYSTEMS Contact: BOB JONES Ph#: 44-753-811833
85A8	CHANGE CONTROL PRODUCT Company: OCCIDENTAL PETROLEUM SVCS INC Contact: DAVID CALVIN Ph#: 9185611442
85A9	CHANGE CONTROL PRODUCT
85AA	STATISTIC MANAGEMENT Company: MULTITECH Contact: HUNG NGO Ph#: 6127853504
85AB	STATISTIC MANAGEMENT
85AC	REMOTE CONTROL SOFTWARE Company: MULTITECH Contact: HUNG NGO Ph#: 6127853504
85AD	REMOTE CONTROL SOFTWARE
85AE	REMOTE CONTROL SOFTWARE
85AF	REMOTE ACCESS SERVER Company: DCA Contact: BRIAN KEAN Ph#: 5137450500x244
85B0	WINDOWS-BASED FAX SYSTEM Company: ICONOGRAPHIC SYSTEMS Contact: NICK RIORDAN Ph#: 44908222255
85B1	PRINT SERVER ADD-ON INTEL - AMERICAN FORK Contact: ALAN COLLINS Ph#: 8017632222

Socket#	Description
85B2	AGV CONTROLLER COMMUNICATIONS Company: CONTROL ENGINEERING Contact: GARRETT HARTWIG
85B3	INDEX SEQUENTIAL ACCESS NLM Company: INFOPOINT SYSTEMS Contact: JOHN COLE Ph#: 2146694700
85B4	ASSOCIATIVE INDEX SERVER Company: INFOPOINT SYSTEMS Contact: JOHN COLE Ph#: 2146694700
85B5	STRESSMAGIC SERVER UTILITY Company: NETMAGIC SYSTEMS INC Contact: RICHARD C LUNA Ph#: 9147394579
85B6	NETWORK POWER TOOLS Company: NETMAGIC SYSTEMS INC Contact: RICHARD C LUNA Ph#: 9147394579
85B7	DOCUMENT MANAGEMENT SVC MVD FRM 35943-7 Company: IMAGERY SOFTWARE INC Contact: DAVE HABERMEHL Ph#: 6172809693
85B8	IMAGE MANAGEMENT SVC MVD FRM 35943-7 Company: IMAGERY SOFTWARE INC Contact: DAVE HABERMEHL Ph#: 6172809693
85B9	MASS STORAGE SVC MVD FRM 35943-7 Company: IMAGERY SOFTWARE INC Contact: DAVE HABERMEHL Ph#: 6172809693
85BA	CITRIX APPLICATION SERVER Company: CITRIX SYSTEMS Contact: TERRY TREDER
85BB	CITRIX APPLICATION SERVER
85BC	Company: KLOS TECHNOLOGIES INC Contact: PATRICK KLOS Ph#: 6034248300
85BD	HOSPITAL MANAGEMENT PACKAGE Company: SOFTWORK GMBH Contact: PETER HOLZLEITNER Ph#: 4317130980
85BE	ROUTER MANAGEMENT APPLICATION Company: CISCO SYSTEMS Contact: GLENN WENIG
85BF	NETWORK MODEM Company: NANAGRAM Contact: MARK HUNTZINGER
85C0	NETWORK MODEM
85C4	5250 GATEWAY COMMUNICATIONS Company: MICRO INTEGRATION Contact: JOHN OROURKE Ph#: 3017773313
85C5	SOFTWARE DISTRIBUTION SUITE Company: CENTERA PTY LTD Contact: GUY VENTER Ph#: 27113292000
85C6	SOFTWARE DISTRIBUTION SUITE
85C7	SOFTWARE DISTRIBUTION SUITE
85C8	SOFTWARE DISTRIBUTION SUITE
85CC	AVL NLM DATABASE Company: AETNA LIFE & CASUALTY Contact: KEVIN VIETEN Ph#: 2036835977
85D0	REMOTE DOWNLOAD SOFTWARE Company: ASANTE TECHNOLOGIES Contact: ALEX LIN Ph#: 4084358401x367
85D5	LAN EXPANDERS MANAGEMENT & DATA TRANSFER Company: GATEWAY COMMUNICATIONS INC Contact: CHRIS HAWKES Ph#: 7145531555
85D6	CALENDAR SERVER Company: CAMPBELL SERVICES Contact: KEITH RHODES Ph#: 3135595955x619
85D7	CA UNICENTER Company: COMPUTER ASSOCIATES Contact: DAVE GELTNER Ph#: 7085056441
85D8	CA UNICENTER
85D9	CA UNICENTER
85DA	CA UNICENTER
85DB	CA UNICENTER
85DC	CA UNICENTER
85DD	NET MODEM SPX SOCKET Company: PRACTICAL PERIPHERALS INC Contact: DAN WILSON Ph#: 8054974742704

Socket#	Description
85DE	NET MODEM IPX SOCKET
85DF	ALERT SERVER NLM Company: CENTRAL POINT SOFTWARE Contact: JIM HILL Ph#: 5036908088
85E0	MESSAGE ROUTER Company: CENTRAL POINT SOFTWARE Contact: JIM HILL Ph#: 5036908088
85E1	OPTICAL FILE SERVER COMMUNICATIONS Company: PEGASUS DISK TECHNOLOGIES INC Contact: BRAD BAKER Ph#: 5109385340
85E2	OPTICAL FILE SERVER LOGIN/LOGOUT
85E5	PRINT SERVER Company: RASTEROPS PRINTER TECH DIV Contact: BOB STUERCKE Ph#: 3034448704
85E6	QUARK EXPRESS Company: QUARK INC Contact: LEE HUNT Ph#: 3038948888
85E7	SECURITY NLM Company: NOVELL - OREM Contact: KEITH CLARKE Ph#: 226-6000
85E8	ENDPOINT MAPPER FOR RPC Company: MICROSOFT Contact: ALEX MITCHELL
85E9	PC ANYWHERE/NETWARE LITE Company: SYMANTEC CORP Contact: JON ROSARKY Ph#: 5164932072
85EA	INTERSERVER FILE COPYING Company: BANKERS TRUST CO Contact: MARC SIMKIN Ph#: 2122507120
85EB	CONNECTION SERVICES Company: RABBIT SOFTWARE CORP Contact: CHG INFO
85EC	DISCOVERY SERVICES Company: RABBIT SOFTWARE CORP Contact: CHG INFO
85ED	NETWORK MONITOR SERVICES Company: RABBIT SOFTWARE CORP Contact: CHG INFO
85EE	CA-DATACOM/PC Company: COMPUTER ASSOCIATES Contact: MICHAEL J COHEN
85EF	CA-IDMS/PC Company: COMPUTER ASSOCIATES Contact: MICHAEL J COHEN
85F1	INDUSTRIAL CONTROL AUTOMATION NETWORK Company: TELE DENKEN Contact: OGUZ MURTEAZAOGLU Ph#: 7138525366
85F2	PRINT SERVER Company: RINGDALE UK LTD Contact: PAUL GOWER Ph#: 44444871349
85F3	COMMUNICATIONS SERVER Company: CSB SYSTEMS GMBH Contact: W MOLLERS Ph#: 024-51-6250
85F6	DATABASE DATAGRAM SOCKET Company: LYNC INC Contact: FRED WOODS Ph#: 3139811628
85F7	NETPORT EXPRESS STATUS RESPONDER Company: INTEL - AMERICAN FORK Contact: DANA DOGGETT
85F8	CADENCE TIME SYNCHRONIZATION PRODUCT Company: POLYGON INC Contact: BRUCE BAEBLER Ph#: 3149979689
85F9	CADENCE TIME SYNCHRONIZATION PRODUCT
85FA	REMOTE VIRUS SCANNING Company: MCAFEE ASSOCIATES Contact: DEREK BROWN Ph#: 4089883832
85FB	REMOTE MEMORY CONTROL
85FC	NORTON BACK-UP DEVICE SHARING PROTOCOL Company: ASTORA SOFTWARE INC Contact: GREG MCCAIN Ph#: 8055441496
85FD	SAMS:EXPERT Company: STERLING TEFEN LAB Contact: RAZI INBAR Ph#: 972-4-977782

Socket#	Description
85FE	SAMS:CONTROL STERLING TEFEN LAB Contact: RAZI INBAR Ph#: 972-4-977782
85FF	SAMS:VANTAGE Company: STERLING TEFEN LAB Contact: RAZI INBAR Ph#: 972-4-977782
8600	SAMS:SAVE Company: STERLING TEFEN LAB Contact: RAZI INBAR Ph#: 972-4-977782
8601	SAMS:DISPATCHER Company: STERLING TEFEN LAB Contact: RAZI INBAR Ph#: 972-4-977782
8602	RENDEZVOUS IPX Company: GREYHOUSE TECHNOLOGIES Contact: CHRISTOPHER STONE Ph#: 0453-544770
8603	RENDEZVOUS IPX
8604	RENDEZVOUS SPX Company: GREYHOUSE TECHNOLOGIES Contact: CHRISTOPHER STONE Ph#: 0453-544770
8605	RENDEZVOUS SPX
8606	VOICE/FAX RESPONDING MACHINE Company: SYSTEM SOPHIA Contact: MASAO OHBAYASHI Ph#: 81878314400
8608	SHARE MODE BROADCAST
8609	IPX ENCAPSULATED RM3 PACKETS Company: CAYMAN SYSTEMS INC Contact: TOM PINCINCE Ph#: 6174941999
860A	DATABASE SERVICE Company: TRIFOX INC Contact: NIKLAS BACK Ph#: 4155135900
860B	IMAGESOLVE_OFS Company: IMAGESOLVE INTERNATIONAL Contact: STEVE CLARKE Ph#: 44-81-343-8181
860C	TECHRA: CLIENT\SERVER RDBMS Company: KVATRO AS Contact: ROY TINGSTAD Ph#: 477520090
860D	DOCRA: CLIENT\SERVER DOC MGMT SYSTEM Company: KVATRO AS Contact: ROY TINGSTAD Ph#: 477520090
860E	NETWORK MANAGEMENT APPLICATION Company: WANDEL & GOLTERMANN Contact: DAVID WALTERS Ph#: 9199415730
860F	NETWORK MANAGEMENT APPLICATION
8610	NETWORK MANAGEMENT APPLICATION
8611	NETWORK MANAGEMENT APPLICATION
8612	NETWORK MANAGEMENT APPLICATION
8613	NETWORK MANAGEMENT APPLICATION
8614	CONNECTION ACCEPTANCE SOCKET Company: CHANCERY SOFTWARE LTD Contact: DAVID MACK Ph#: 6042941233
8615	OPTIDRIVER-NET Company: OPTISYS Contact: MIKE WEBB Ph#: 6029979699
8616	EDM CLIENT/PC Company: COMPUTER VISION Contact: DAVID ROBINSON Ph#: 61727518002774
8617	VIDEO CONFERENCING Company: LLOYD ALLAN CORPORATION Contact: BARTON ANDERSON Ph#: 7033694153
8618	PRINTER GATEWAY/ PEER-TO-PEER COMMUNICATION Company: ADACOM GROUP Contact: ITAY KARIV Ph#: 9724899899
861C	COMMUNICATIONS UTILITY Company: LEXMARK INTERNATIONAL INC Contact: DAVID WHITEHEAD Ph#: 6062324914
861D	COMMUNICATIONS UTILITY
861E	PRINT SERVER Company: LEXMARK INTERNATIONAL INC Contact: DAVID WHITEHEAD Ph#: 6062324914
861F	PRINT SERVER

Socket#	Description
8620	PHONE SYSTEM CONTROL Company: DASH OPEN PHONE SYSTEMS Contact: CHARLES YAHN Ph#: 9138887936
8621	PHONE SYSTEM CONTROL
8622	PHONE SYSTEM CONTROL
8623	PHONE SYSTEM CONTROL
8624	OVERSIGHT AGENT Company: NETWORK UTILITIES SOFTWARE LTD Contact: IAN GORDON Ph#: 44813919200
8625	OVERSIGHT MASTER
8626	ERL DATABASE SERVER Company: SILVER PLATTER INFORMATION LTD Contact: PAUL SANDERS Ph#: 44819958242
8627	ERL DIRECTORY SERVER
8628	IPX BROADCAST Company: INTERTECH IMAGING CORPORATION Contact: DAVID BAHR Ph#: 4046711125 204
8629	SPX CONNECT Company: INTERTECH IMAGING CORPORATION Contact: DAVID BAHR Ph#: 4046711125 204
862A	ZIFF PROPRIETARY SERVICES Company: ZIFF INFORMATION SERVICES Contact: JAMES PETERSON Ph#: 6173933255
862B	GAMES Company: LOOKING GLASS Contact: ERIC MCCALL Ph#: 6178635810
862C	LPT PORTS Company: LEXMARK INTERNATIONAL INC Contact: DAVID WHITEHEAD Ph#: 6062324914
862D	LPT PORTS
862E	LPT PORTS
862F	LPT PORTS
8630	LPT PORTS
8631	LPT PORTS
8632	LPT PORTS
8633	LPT PORTS
8634	TIME SERVER BROADCAST SOCKET Company: MEINBERG FUNKUHREN Contact: MR MARTIN BURNICKI Ph#: 49-5281-2018
8635	ACCELERATION DATA Company: SABLE TECHNOLOGY CORP Contact: RODNEY THAYER Ph#: 6173327292
8636	CALLPATH Company: IBM - RESEARCH TRIANGLE PARK Contact: STEVE SCHMIDT Ph#: 9195439304
8637	CALLPATH
8638	COMMUNICATION INTEGRATOR - SPX Company: COVIA CORP Contact: CHING MING KUNG Ph#: 3033976134
8639	COMMUNICATION INTEGRATOR - IPX
863B	NETWARE AWARE INFORMATION MGMT SYSTEM Company: INTUITIVE SOLUTIONS Contact: WAYNE GRAY Ph#: 4082551620
863C	NETWARE AWARE INFORMATION MGMT SYSTEM
863D	NETWARE AWARE INFORMATION MGMT SYSTEM
863E	NETWARE AWARE INFORMATION MGMT SYSTEM
863F	ARTS RLOGIN APPLICATION Company: AMERICAN REAL TIME, REUTERS CO Contact: MARK J DEFILIPPIS Ph#: 2127421100
8640	ARTS GENERIC SERVER
8641	NETOP PROGRAM Company: DANWARE DATA AS Contact: PETER ENGELBRECHT Ph#: 4544532525
8642	NETOP PROGRAM
8643	NETOP PROGRAM
8644	NETOP PROGRAM
8645	NETOP PROGRAM

Socket#	Description		Socket#	Description

Socket#   Description

8646 DOCUMENT MANAGEMENT SYSTEM
Company: SR ASSOCIATES/CYBERMEDIA
Contact: RAVI KANNAN

8647 SECURITY CHECK
Company: MCAFEE ASSOCIATES
Contact: PERRY SMITH Ph#: 9085300440

8648 NEWSWIRE NOTIFICATION
Company: GENERATION TECHNOLOGIES CORP
Contact: BILL PARROTT Ph#: 9133451012

8649 P-NET GATEWAY
Company: PROCES DATA SILKEBORG APS
Contact: CARSTEN NOKLEBY, PHD Ph#: 4586814033

864A VIRTUAL MANUFACTURING DEVICE
Company: PROCES DATA SILKEBORG APS
Contact: CARSTEN NOKLEBY, PHD Ph#: 4586814033

864B SALES APPLICATION
Company: PROXIM INC
Contact: ARTHUR COLEMAN Ph#: 4159601630

864C BROADCASTS
Company: NETWORK XCELLENCE
Contact: CLIFF LAPENSKIE Ph#: 6132352321

864D COMMUNICATIONS
Company: NETWORK XCELLENCE
Contact: CLIFF LAPENSKIE Ph#: 6132352321

864E LAN/CD ROM SERVER
Company: LOGICRAFT
Contact: MICHAEL LYNCH Ph#: 6038800300

8650 SERVER SOCKET
Company: KNIGHT RIDDER FINANCIAL INC
Contact: JOHN SCHNEIDER Ph#: 9139676178

8651 PING SOCKET
Company: KNIGHT RIDDER FINANCIAL INC
Contact: JOHN SCHNEIDER Ph#: 9139676178

8652 BROADCAST DATAGRAM SOCKET
Company: KNIGHT RIDDER FINANCIAL INC
Contact: JOHN SCHNEIDER Ph#: 9139676178

8653 EMPOWER LINK APPLICATION LOADER
Company: NETWORK SECURITY SYSTEMS
Contact: RON PITT Ph#: 6195877950

8654 NAME RESOLUTION
Company: INTELEC SYSTEMS CORPORATION
Contact: BRAD GREENWAY Ph#: 5012213600

8655 MESSAGE LINE
Company: NORMAN DATA DEFENSE SYSTEMS
Contact: CARL BRETTEVILLE Ph#: 473813490

8656 CLIENT MESSAGE LINE
Company: NORMAN DATA DEFENSE SYSTEMS
Contact: CARL BRETTEVILLE Ph#: 473813490

8657 CD SHARING ON NOVELL WORKSTATION
Company: CROSS INTERNATIONAL CORP
Contact: THOMAS B CROSS Ph#: 3034407313

8658 NETTALK LAN COMMUNICATIONS SOFTWARE
Company: CROSS INTERNATIONAL CORP
Contact: THOMAS B CROSS Ph#: 3034407313

8659 TELEPHONE COMMUNICATIONS SOFTWARE
Company: CROSS INTERNATIONAL CORP
Contact: THOMAS B CROSS Ph#: 3034407313

865A LAN CHATTING
Company: CROSS INTERNATIONAL CORP
Contact: THOMAS B CROSS Ph#: 3034407313

865B NETWORK MANAGEMENT SERVER
Company: POLE POSITION SOFTWARE GMBH
Contact: MARTIN BESTMANN Ph#: 4991347447

865C REMOTE ACCESS SOCKET #1
Company: TRAVELING SOFTWARE
Contact: TODD L PAUL Ph#: 2064875428

865D REMOTE ACCESS SOCKET #2
Company: TRAVELING SOFTWARE
Contact: TODD L PAUL Ph#: 2064875428

865E NET TRAX ADMINISTRATION
Company: NET X CORP
Contact: DAVE MCGOVERN Ph#: 2146442599

865F NET TRAX AGENT
Company: NET X CORP
Contact: DAVE MCGOVERN Ph#: 2146442599

Socket#   Description

8660 NET TRAX ALARM MONITOR
Company: NET X CORP
Contact: DAVE MCGOVERN Ph#: 2146442599

8661 AO CLIENT
Company: ICL PERSONAL SYSTEMS OY
Contact: JARI WESTERHOLM Ph#: 35805675293

8662 AO SERVER FOR CLIENT
Company: ICL PERSONAL SYSTEMS OY
Contact: JARI WESTERHOLM Ph#: 35805675293

8663 AO DIRECTORY SERVER
Company: ICL PERSONAL SYSTEMS OY
Contact: JARI WESTERHOLM Ph#: 35805675293

8664 AO SERVER ALARMER
Company: ICL PERSONAL SYSTEMS OY
Contact: JARI WESTERHOLM Ph#: 35805675293

8665 AO CLIENT ALARMER

8666 AO LAN RTS
Company: ICL PERSONAL SYSTEMS OY
Contact: JARI WESTERHOLM Ph#: 35805675293

8667 AO REMOTE CMD SERVER
Company: ICL PERSONAL SYSTEMS OY
Contact: JARI WESTERHOLM Ph#: 35805675293

8668 AO REMOTE CMD CLIENT
Company: ICL PERSONAL SYSTEMS OY
Contact: JARI WESTERHOLM Ph#: 35805675293

8669 AO DIR JOIN SERVER
Company: ICL PERSONAL SYSTEMS OY
Contact: JARI WESTERHOLM Ph#: 35805675293

866A AO STORAGE SERVER FOR CLIENT
Company: ICL PERSONAL SYSTEMS OY
Contact: JARI WESTERHOLM Ph#: 35805675293

866B SAVE UTILTIY/2
Company: IBM - CARY
Contact: PETER JERKEWITZ Ph#: 9193013250

866C SAVE UTILTIY/LIBRARIAN
Company: IBM - CARY
Contact: PETER JERKEWITZ Ph#: 9193013250

866D SAVE UTILTIY/CURATOR
Company: IBM - CARY
Contact: PETER JERKEWITZ Ph#: 9193013250

866E SAVE UTILTIY/JANITOR
Company: IBM - CARY
Contact: PETER JERKEWITZ Ph#: 9193013250

866F SAVE UTILTIY/ARCHIVES I
Company: IBM - CARY
Contact: PETER JERKEWITZ Ph#: 9193013250

8670 SAVE UTILTIY/ARCHIVES II
Company: IBM - CARY
Contact: PETER JERKEWITZ Ph#: 9193013250

8671 SAVE UTILTIY/ARCHIVES III
Company: IBM - CARY
Contact: PETER JERKEWITZ Ph#: 9193013250

8672 SAVE UTILTIY/ARCHIVES IV
Company: IBM - CARY
Contact: PETER JERKEWITZ Ph#: 9193013250

8673 SAVE UTILTIY/ARCHIVES V
Company: IBM - CARY
Contact: PETER JERKEWITZ Ph#: 9193013250

8674 SAVE UTILTIY/ARCHIVES VI
Company: IBM - CARY
Contact: PETER JERKEWITZ Ph#: 9193013250

8675 SAVE UTILTIY/ARCHIVES VII
Company: IBM - CARY
Contact: PETER JERKEWITZ Ph#: 9193013250

8676 SAVE UTILTIY/ARCHIVES VIII
Company: IBM - CARY
Contact: PETER JERKEWITZ Ph#: 9193013250

8677 SAFE SERVER REQUEST SOCKET
Company: OMNITECH CORPORATE SOLUTIONS
Contact: DAVID ONEILL Ph#: 2018370900

8678 CLIENT NLM COMMUNICATIONS
Company: SOFTWARE SECURITY INC
Contact: ELEANOR BOOKMAN Ph#: 2033298870

Socket#	Description
8679	NLM SERVER TO SERVER Company: SOFTWARE SECURITY INC Contact: ELEANOR BOOKMAN Ph#: 2033298870
867A	FILE TRANSFER APPLICATION URS ZURBUCHEN Contact: URS ZURBUCHEN Ph#: 41-55-31-4244
867B	SD ROM JUKEBOX COMMAND SERVER Company: TODD ENTERPRISES INC Contact: BRUCE MCKAY Ph#: 7183431040
867C	COURSEWARE SERVER Company: FIRST CLASS SYSTEMS Contact: BOB MCDONALD Ph#: 6045387246
867D	UDP OVER IPX TRANSMIT Company: SYNOPTICS Contact: TOM DYAL Ph#: 4156914069
867E	UDP OVER IPX RECEIVE Company: SYNOPTICS Contact: TOM DYAL Ph#: 4156914069
867F	REALTIME VOICE COMMUNICATION SOFTWARE Company: VOCALTEC INC Contact: ALON COHEN Ph#: 2017689400
8681	PERSON TO PERSON PRODUCT
8682	NET TUNE Company: HAWKNET INC Contact: MIKE PRICE Ph#: 6199299966
8683	NET TUNE
8684	NET TUNE
8685	NET TUNE
868A	ACCESS CONTROL & LICENSE MANAGEMENT Company: DALLAS SEMICONDUCTOR Contact: JOHN DICKINSON Ph#: 2144503850
868B	STAND-ALONE PRINT SERVER Company: SERCOMM Contact: BEN LIN Ph#: 88625775400
868C	CD-VINE PEER-TO-PEER COMMUNICATIONS Company: INFO LINE Contact: KYUNG SOO YI Ph#: 82-2-875-0181
868D	FTP Company: CENTRAL POINT SOFTWARE Contact: DALE CABELL Ph#: 7142623224
868E	TFTP Company: CENTRAL POINT SOFTWARE Contact: DALE CABELL Ph#: 7142623224
868F	BOOT PS Company: CENTRAL POINT SOFTWARE Contact: DALE CABELL Ph#: 7142623224
8690	BOOT PC Company: CENTRAL POINT SOFTWARE Contact: DALE CABELL Ph#: 7142623224
8692	CLIENT TO SERVER COMMUNICATION Company: NBS SYSTEMS INC Contact: MARK LU Ph#: 2037412244
8693	SERVER TO SERVER COMMUNICATION Company: NBS SYSTEMS INC Contact: MARK LU Ph#: 2037412244
8694	NOTIFICATION PURPOSES Company: NBS SYSTEMS INC Contact: MARK LU Ph#: 2037412244
8695	FUTURE EXPANSION Company: NBS SYSTEMS INC Contact: MARK LU Ph#: 2037412244
8696	FUTURE EXPANSION Company: NBS SYSTEMS INC Contact: MARK LU Ph#: 2037412244
8697	SNA SERVICES Company: NETWORK CONTROLS INTERNATIONAL Contact: PETER NORTH Ph#: 7045274357
8698	SNA SERVICES Company: NETWORK CONTROLS INTERNATIONAL Contact: PETER NORTH Ph#: 7045274357
869A	PROTOCOL IPX Company: OST-OUEST STANDARD TELEMATIQUE Contact: ROBERT CHANTAL Ph#: 33-99-415859

Socket#	Description
869B	PROTOCOL IPX
869C	MULTI-PLAYER GAME - DOOM Company: ID SOFTWARE Contact: JAY WILBUR Ph#: 2146133589
869D	NETWORK MANAGEMENT Company: HEWLETT PACKARD - GRENOBLE Contact: FABRIZIO DANTE Ph#: 3376625527
869E	NETWORK MANAGEMENT
869F	DISTRIBUTION SERVICES DISCOVERY Company: IBM - ROME Contact: STEVEN POGUE Ph#: 39651872614
86A0	DOCUMENT MANAGEMENT PACKAGE Company: NOVELL - OREM Contact: KEITH CLARKE Ph#: 226-6000
86A1	DOCUMENT MANAGEMENT PACKAGE
86A2	DOCUMENT MANAGEMENT PACKAGE
86A3	DOCUMENT MANAGEMENT PACKAGE
86A8	CENTRAL MONITORING SYSTEM Company: TALX CORP Contact: GARTH DAVIS Ph#: 3144340046
86A9	CENTRAL MONITORING SYSTEM
86AA	CENTRAL MONITORING SYSTEM
86AB	CENTRAL MONITORING SYSTEM
86AC	CENTRAL MONITORING SYSTEM
86AD	END POINT MAPPER ID'S Company: MICROSOFT Contact: ALEX MITCHELL
86AE	END POINT MAPPER ID'S
86AF	END POINT MAPPER ID'S
86B0	CALENDAR SERVER Company: CAMPBELL SERVICES INC Contact: RAY PEABODY Ph#: 3135595955
86BA	NETWORK MANAGEMENT APPLICATION Company: XIRCOM Contact: GLORIA LEONARD Ph#: 4156912500
86BB	NETWORK MANAGEMENT APPLICATION Company: XIRCOM Contact: GLORIA LEONARD Ph#: 4156912500
86BC	NETWORK MANAGEMENT APPLICATION
86BD	NETWORK MANAGEMENT APPLICATION
86BE	NETWORK MANAGEMENT APPLICATION
86BF	NETWORK MANAGEMENT APPLICATION
86CE	SERVICE LOCATION PROTOCOL Company: EICON TECHNOLOGY Contact: PAT CALHOUN Ph#: 5146312592
86CF	TWINSCOPE FOR IPX Company: NIPPON SYSTEM KAIHUTSU Contact: MASAYUKI KURIBAYASHI Ph#: 81333673761
86D0	MAJOR BBS SOFTWARE Company: GALACTICOMM INC Contact: BERT LOVE Ph#: 3055835990
86D1	MAJOR BBS SOFTWARE
86D2	MAJOR BBS SOFTWARE
86D3	MAJOR BBS SOFTWARE
86D4	MAJOR BBS SOFTWARE
86D5	MAJOR BBS SOFTWARE
86D6	MAJOR BBS SOFTWARE
86D7	MAJOR BBS SOFTWARE
86D8	MAJOR BBS SOFTWARE
86D9	MAJOR BBS SOFTWARE
86DC	FAXWARE 3.0 (C-REQ) Company: TOBIT SOFTWARE GMBH Contact: TOBIAS GROTEN Ph#: 49-2561-40001
86DD	FAXWARE 3.0 (HS-COMM) Company: TOBIT SOFTWARE GMBH Contact: TOBIAS GROTEN Ph#: 49-2561-40001

Socket#	Description
86DE	FAXWARE 3.0 (TLD) Company: TOBIT SOFTWARE GMBH Contact: TOBIAS GROTEN Ph#: 49-2561-40001
86DF	HIGH PERFORMANCE COMMUNICATION SERVER Company: TOBIT SOFTWARE GMBH Contact: TOBIAS GROTEN Ph#: 49-2561-40001
86E0	HIGH PERFORMANCE COMMUNICATION SERVER
86E1	HIGH PERFORMANCE COMMUNICATION SERVER
86E2	HIGH PERFORMANCE COMMUNICATION SERVER
86E3	HIGH PERFORMANCE COMMUNICATION SERVER
86E4	HIGH PERFORMANCE COMMUNICATION SERVER
86E5	ELECTRONIC SPELLING BOOK (SPOOK!) Company: TOBIT SOFTWARE GMBH Contact: TOBIAS GROTEN Ph#: 49 2561-40001
86E6	ELECTRONIC SPELLING BOOK (SPOOK!)
86E7	ELECTRONIC SPELLING BOOK (SPOOK!)
86E8	ELECTRONIC SPELLING BOOK (SPOOK!)
86F1	OFFICE EXTEND SERVER Company: FRANSEN KING Contact: CRAIG FRANSEN Ph#: 2065644000
86F2	WINDOWS NT FACSYS SERVER Company: OPTUS INFORMATION SYSTEMS Contact: ROBERT CICHIELO Ph#: 9082719568
86F3	WINDOWS NT FACSYS SERVER
86F4	WINDOWS NT FACSYS SERVER
86F7	KEYFILE NAME SERVICE Company: KEYFILE CORP Contact: PATRICK MURPHY
86F8	EVERGREEN MANAGEMENT AGENT Company: GOODALL SOFTWARE Contact: DOUG GOODALL Ph#: 7077952335
86F9	EVERGREEN MANAGEMENT AGENT
86FA	EVERGREEN MANAGEMENT AGENT
86FB	EVERGREEN MANAGEMENT AGENT
86FC	EVERGREEN MANAGEMENT AGENT
86FD	EVERGREEN MANAGEMENT AGENT
86FE	FILE SYNCHRONIZATION (MVD TO -003 041294) Company: NOMADIC SYSTEMS Contact: KEN HENRY Ph#: 4159031228
86FF	WINDOWS BULLETIN BOARD SYSTEM Company: PACER SOFTWARE Contact: DAVE HORNBAKER Ph#: 5088983300
8702	LAN NETVIEW MANAGEMENT UTILITIES Company: IBM - RESEARCH TRIANGLE PARK Contact: MIKE COLEMAN Ph#: 9192547920
8703	LAN NETVIEW MANAGEMENT UTILITIES
8704	LAN NETVIEW MANAGEMENT UTILITIES
8705	LAN NETVIEW MANAGEMENT UTILITIES
8706	LAN NETVIEW MANAGEMENT UTILITIES
8707	ETHERNET-MANAGED STACKABLE HUB Company: IBM - RESEARCH TRIANGLE PARK Contact: DALE COMPLIMENT Ph#: 9192544927
8708	DOCUMENT MANAGEMENT PACKAGE Company: NOVELL - OREM Contact: TONY CARAS Ph#: 228-5218
8709	DOCUMENT MANAGEMENT PACKAGE
870A	DOCUMENT MANAGEMENT PACKAGE
870B	DOCUMENT MANAGEMENT PACKAGE
870C	DOCUMENT MANAGEMENT PACKAGE
870D	GOODALL VIRTUAL PROTOCOL ADAPTOR Company: GOODALL SOFTWARE Contact: DOUG GOODALL Ph#: 7077952335
870E	GOODALL VIRTUAL PROTOCOL ADAPTOR
870F	GOODALL VIRTUAL PROTOCOL ADAPTOR
8710	GOODALL VIRTUAL PROTOCOL ADAPTOR
8712	ENTERPRISE WAN BVNCS Company: LAN SUPPORT GROUP Contact: DAVID LANGROCK Ph#: 7137890882 527

Socket#	Description
871D	PINNACLE RELATIONAL ENGINE Company: VERMONT DATABASE CORP Contact: JOHN ELKINS Ph#: 8022534437
871E	FAULT TOLERANCE Company: CLONE STAR SOFTWARE Contact: DON CHEESEMAN Ph#: 7132562886
8724	UNIX MAIL SERVER Company: FELPAUSCH Contact: MICHAEL FABER Ph#: 6169453485
8727	INDUSTRIAL TEST & HANDLING EQUIPMENT Company: Q CORP Contact: ALAN SIEGMAN Ph#: 3167883746
8728	INDUSTRIAL TEST & HANDLING EQUIPMENT
8729	INDUSTRIAL TEST & HANDLING EQUIPMENT
872A	TELI-LINK VOICE SERVER Company: COMPUTER & COMMUNICATIONS CO Contact: DAVID CONNELL Ph#: 0223423562
872B	SECURE FAX CLIENT SOCKET Company: RUSSELL CONSULTING Contact: RAJINDER BASI Ph#: 44602242030
8733	BRIDGE ROUTER MENU CONNECTION Company: NETWORKS NORTHWEST INC Contact: DAVE EITELBACH Ph#: 2066418779
8734	BRIDGE ROUTER ERROR LOG
8735	IMAGE SERVER CONNECTION Company: WATERMARK SOFTWARE Contact: HERB ERICKSON Ph#: 6172292600x230
8737	EXSEKEY INTERFACE FOR PROTECTED PROGRAMS Company: CLOVER INFORMATICA SNC Contact: PATRIZIO COLOMBO Ph#: 39-363-65828
8738	METERING PROGRAM Company: SECURE DESIGN Contact: STEPHEN HERZOG Ph#: 5037580955
873C	COMET TERMINAL SERVER Company: GOODALL SOFTWARE Contact: DOUG GOODALL Ph#: 7077952335
873D	COMET TERMINAL SERVER
873E	COMET TERMINAL SERVER
873F	COMET TERMINAL SERVER
8740	COMET TERMINAL SERVER
8741	COMET TERMINAL SERVER
8742	COMET FILE SERVER Company: GOODALL SOFTWARE Contact: DOUG GOODALL Ph#: 7077952335
8743	COMET FILE SERVER
8744	COMET FILE SERVER
8745	COMET FILE SERVER
8746	COMET FILE SERVER
8747	COMET FILE SERVER
874A	MAXSERV COMMUNICATIONS Company: MAXSERV Contact: STEVE SHANAFELT Ph#: 5129084859
874B	MAXSERV COMMUNICATIONS
874C	NCP COMMUNICATION - JOB SCHEDULER & NLM Company: LEGENT Contact: LYNN JOHNSTON Ph#: 61322851004064
874E	TRACE ROUTE Company: 3COM Contact: EUGENE KIM
874F	CLIENT COLLABORATIVE DATA SHARE PRODUCT Company: AT&T Contact: CHRIS MCCANN Ph#: 7089797478
875B	TVI DESKTOP SERVER Company: TARGET VISION Contact: LARRY HELBER Ph#: 7162480550
875C	MASTERSHOW Company: TARGET VISION Contact: LARRY HELBER Ph#: 7162480550
875D	USER-ACCESS SERVER Company: TMD CONSULTING Contact: JOHN FLANAGAN Ph#: 6128960047

Socket#	Description
875E	TCP GATEWAY Company: TMD CONSULTING Contact: JOHN FLANAGAN Ph#: 6128960047
875F	CAM SERVER Company: TMD CONSULTING Contact: JOHN FLANAGAN Ph#: 6128960047
8760	CAM SECURE DATABASE Company: TMD CONSULTING Contact: JOHN FLANAGAN Ph#: 6128960047
8761	CAM RESOURCE MANAGER Company: TMD CONSULTING Contact: JOHN FLANAGAN Ph#: 6128960047
8762	CAM BACK-UP Company: TMD CONSULTING Contact: JOHN FLANAGAN Ph#: 6128960047
8763	FIREFOX NLMS AND CLIENT SOFTWARE Company: FIREFOX COMMUNICATIONS LTD Contact: PETER SIMKIN Ph#: 44 21 609 6090
8764	FIREFOX NLMS AND CLIENT SOFTWARE
8765	FIREFOX NLMS AND CLIENT SOFTWARE
8766	FIREFOX NLMS AND CLIENT SOFTWARE
8767	FIREFOX NLMS AND CLIENT SOFTWARE
8768	FIREFOX NLMS AND CLIENT SOFTWARE
8769	FIREFOX NLMS AND CLIENT SOFTWARE
876A	FIREFOX NLMS AND CLIENT SOFTWARE
876B	FIREFOX NLMS AND CLIENT SOFTWARE
876C	FIREFOX NLMS AND CLIENT SOFTWARE
876D	DATA TRANSACTIONS Company: TENFORE RESEARCH & DEVELOPMENT Contact: KIM NYHOLM Ph#: 45-38-347070
876E	FLOW CONTROL Company: TENFORE RESEARCH & DEVELOPMENT Contact: KIM NYHOLM Ph#: 45-38-347070
8770	REMOTE CONTROL PRODUCT Company: IBM - RALEIGH Contact: GARY LARSON Ph#: 9193015541
8771	REMOTE CONTROL PRODUCT
8772	REMOTE CONTROL PRODUCT
8773	REMOTE CONTROL PRODUCT
877C	HITECSOFT SEND SOCKET Company: HITECSOFT CORP Contact: SIA MOSHIR Ph#: 6029701025x244
877D	HITECSOFT RECEIVE SOCKET Company: HITECSOFT CORP Contact: SIA MOSHIR Ph#: 6029701025x244
877E	LAN SCHOOL FOR WINDOWS Company: LAN FAN TECHNOLOGIES Contact: DANA DOGGETT Ph#: 8012257975
877F	REMOTE ACCESS PROTOCOL FOR DESKTOP MGMT Company: INTEL - AMERICAN FORK Contact: DANA DOGGETT
8787	VIDEO SERVER Company: COREL SYSTEMS CORP Contact: MING POON
8788	LAN PERFORMANCE MNGMT TOOL IPX/SPX Company: DIGITAL EQUIPMENT CORP Contact: FRANK CACCAVALE Ph#: 5084866053
8789	LAN PERFORMANCE MNGMT TOOL TCP Company: DIGITAL EQUIPMENT CORP Contact: FRANK CACCAVALE Ph#: 5084866053
878B	STATUS SOCKET Company: NATIONAL SOFTWARE DEVELOPMENT Contact: DR. TOMMY HUFF Ph#: 7139373890
878C	PRODUCTION SOCKET Company: NATIONAL SOFTWARE DEVELOPMENT Contact: DR. TOMMY HUFF Ph#: 7139373890
878E	U OF WISCONSIN UTILITIES Company: U OF WISCONSIN - MADISON, CAE Contact: JAMES DREWS Ph#: 6082653312
878F	U OF WISCONSIN UTILITIES Company: U OF WISCONSIN - MADISON, CAE Contact: JAMES DREWS Ph#: 6082653312

Socket#	Description
8790	MARC SOFTWARE SYSTEMS Company: QDATA Contact: IAN CLARK Ph#: 44349830950
8791	TIMBUKTU APPLICATION Company: FARALLON COMPUTING Contact: JIM HOLDEN Ph#: 5108145254
8792	LED DISPLAY SERVER Company: INOVA CORPORATION Contact: JIM PISANO Ph#: 8049732227
8794	BORLAND INTERFACE SERVER FOR NW Company: BORLAND INTERNATIONAL Contact: JERRY WALDEN Ph#: 4084315433
8795	NPTN SPX Company: IBM - RTP Contact: JOHN FETVEDT Ph#: 9192544366
8796	NPTN IPX Company: IBM - RTP Contact: JOHN FETVEDT Ph#: 9192544366
8797	REMOTE ACCESS SOCKET 3 Company: TRAVELING SOFTWARE Contact: TODD L PAUL Ph#: 2064875428
8798	SERVER BENCH
8799	INITIAL CONNECTION TO NLM FLAGSTAR Contact: RICH ROTH Ph#: 8035978470
879B	SITE METER SECURITY Company: MCAFEE ASSOCIATES Contact: JEFF DREW Ph#: 9085300440
879C	SITE METER COMMAND
879D	PROXY AGENT SITE METER Company: MCAFEE ASSOCIATES Contact: JEFF DREW Ph#: 9085300440
879E	DATABASE SERVER/DB2 INSTANCES Company: IBM - CANADA LTD. Contact: JULIANA HSU Ph#: 4164482830
879F	DATABASE SERVER/DB2 INSTANCES
87A0	DATABASE SERVER/DB2 INSTANCES
87A1	DATABASE SERVER/DB2 INSTANCES
87A9	FILE TRANSFER BETWEEN LAN/MAINFRAME Company: PROGINET CORP Contact: KEVIN BOHAN Ph#: 5162286613
87AA	CONNECTION SERVICE AND SECURITY Company: PROGINET CORP Contact: KEVIN BOHAN Ph#: 5162286613
87AD	ENTERTAINMENT PRODUCT-BILLIARD POOL Company: CELERIS INC. Contact: STEVE CHAPMAN Ph#: 8187092181
87AE	GAME DEVELOPMENT Company: GOLDSTEIN GOLLUB KESSLER & CO Contact: MARK GREENBERG Ph#: 2125231356
87B2	NOVELL SERVER MNGMT BY MAESTROVISION Company: CALYPSO SOFTWARE Contact: JOHN JANIGIAN Ph#: 6036693377
87BA	HEALTHCARE VALIDATIONS APP FOR DOS Company: OPEN VISION Contact: BRENT VERNON Ph#: 4167677086
87BB	HEALTHCARE VALIDATIONS APP FOR UNIX Company: OPEN VISION Contact: BRENT VERNON Ph#: 4167677086
87BD	ASYNCHRONOUS COMMUNICATION Company: LAN ACCESS Contact: DAVID IACOVELLI Ph#: 3103289700
87BE	NETHOPPER SOCKETS Company: ROCKWELL NETWORK SYSTEMS Contact: TIM HAYES Ph#: 805-562-3181
87BF	NETHOPPER SOCKETS
87C0	NETHOPPER SOCKETS
87C1	BACNET TUNNELING OVER IPX Company: ASHRAE Contact: DAVID FISHER Ph#: 4046468400
87C7	MULTIMEDIA DISTRIBUTION SERVER Company: EMOTION INC Contact: JESUS ORTIZ Ph#: 4158129016

Socket#	Description		Socket#	Description
87C8	MULTIMEDIA CONTENT CATALOG SERVER Company: EMOTION INC Contact: JESUS ORTIZ Ph#: 4158129016		87FC	OFF LINE COPYING Company: ON TECHNOLOGIES Contact: MATT HOOVER
87C9	VOICE PROCESSING SERVER Company: INTERNATIONAL VOICE EXCHANGE Contact: JOE SMITH Ph#: 8014818974		87FD	INTEREGISTER COMMUNICATIONS Company: ARNEL LTD Contact: RICHARD COOK Ph#: 441992714080
87CC	MULTIPOINT CONFERENCING PRODUCT BROWSE Company: DATABEAM CORPORATION Contact: CINDY MARTIN Ph#: 6062453633		87FE	EFT SERVER Company: ARNEL LTD Contact: RICHARD COOK Ph#: 441992714080
87CD	X1180 POINT OF SELL TICKETING SYSTEM Company: GATEWAY TICKETING SYSTEMS INC Contact: MICHAEL M. ANDRE Ph#: 6109874000		87FF	SCI MULTIPLAYER GAMES SOCKET Company: SALES CURVE INTERACTIVE LTD Contact: WARREN HUMPHREYS Ph#: 441703330930
87D9	T-MEK VIDEO GAME FOR TIME-WARNER Company: BITS CORP Contact: GARY SHEINWALD Ph#: 441814507733		8802	PIN64-AUTOMATED DATA TRANSMITTING Company: ASAHI ELECTRONICS CO LTD Contact: MASAHIRO KITAJIMA Ph#: 81935116471
87DA	THRASH-RACE VIDEO GAME Company: BITS CORP Contact: GARY SHEINWALD Ph#: 441814507733		8805	INTELLECT USER AUTHENTICATION SYSTEM Company: INTELLECT AUSTRALIA P/L Contact: STEVEN TEE Ph#: 6193334378
87DB	ARCUS NETWORK COMMANDER & EXECUTOR Company: ARCUS COMPUTER Contact: MASANOBU SAKAGUCHI Ph#: 81797620581		8807	TO BE ASSURED NO ONE WILL PROCESS PACKET Company: IBM - RESEARCH TRIANGLE PARK Contact: JEFF CRIPS
87DC	ARCUS CLIPBOARD SYNCHRONIZER Company: ARCUS COMPUTER Contact: MASANOBU SAKAGUCHI Ph#: 81797620581		880B	DINA GATEWAY Company: DENSAN SYSTEM CO LTD Contact: YASUNORI TANAKA Ph#: 81582793462
87DD	ARCUS MENU FOR NW USERS & ADMINISTRATORS Company: ARCUS COMPUTER Contact: MASANOBU SAKAGUCHI Ph#: 81797620581		8813	INTERACTIVE MULTI-PLAYER GAMES Company: VIRGIN INTRACTIVE ENTERTAINMET Contact: STEVE CLARK Ph#: 441819602255
87DF	MULTIPOINT DATA CONFERENCING APP ON SPX Company: INTEL - HILLSBORO Contact: GREGORY KISOR Ph#: 5032649324		8814	LAN UTILITY PROGRAMS Company: LAN UTILITIES, L.L.C. Contact: ROBERT K. ROSS Ph#: 8017851784
87E0	LAN COMMUNICATIONS Company: CROSS INTERNATIONAL CORP Contact: THOMAS B CROSS Ph#: 3034407313		8815	ATLANTA/3 DIAGNOSTIC SOCKET Company: KELLY COMPUTER SYSTEMS Contact: PHILIP RONZONE Ph#: 4159601010
87E1	ZIP CODE SERVER Company: THIRD PLANET SOFTWARE Contact: DANNY SCHULMAN Ph#: 3105532808		881D	DOS AUDITING AGENT Company: LAN SUPPORT GROUP Contact: MIKE KRETZER Ph#: 7137890882 607
87E2	WING COMMANDER VERMADA PROVING GROUNDS Company: ORIGIN SYSTEMS INC Contact: JEFF GRILLS Ph#: 5123355200		881E	OS2 AUDITING AGENT Company: LAN SUPPORT GROUP Contact: MIKE KRETZER Ph#: 7137890882 607
87E5	SOFTWARE ENTERTAINMENT Company: ORIGIN SYSTEMS Contact: AARON MARTIN Ph#: 5123355200X668		881F	MAC AUDITING AGENT LAN SUPPORT GROUP Contact: MIKE KRETZER Ph#: 7137890882 607
87E8	OINET-120 Company: OI ELECTRIC CO LTD Contact: YASUAKI NAKANISHI Ph#: 81454331361		8820	WINDOWS NT AUDITING AGENT Company: LAN SUPPORT GROUP Contact: MIKE KRETZER Ph#: 7137890882 607
87E9	HELP DESK TSR Company: HILLARD CO Contact: DAVID HILLARD Ph#: 5026952410		8821	WINDOWS 95 AUDITING AGENT Company: LAN SUPPORT GROUP Contact: MIKE KRETZER Ph#: 7137890882 607
87EA	HELP DESK APPLICATION Company: HILLARD CO Contact: DAVID HILLARD Ph#: 5026952410		8822	WINDOWS 3X AUDITING AGENT Company: LAN SUPPORT GROUP Contact: MIKE KRETZER Ph#: 7137890882 607
87EC	MULTI-PLAYER PLATE SIMULATION Company: ELECTRONIC ARTS Contact: NICHOLAS FULLAGAN Ph#: 4155137131		8828	CUBIX COMMUNICATION Company: CUBIX Contact: MIKE SCHUMACHER Ph#: 8106811780
87EE	CCTV CONTROL SYSTEM Company: DIMEX LTD Contact: TEDDY GILAAD Ph#: 9723498357		882F	IP TO IPX GATEWAY Company: INTERNET JUNCTION Contact: RATINDER AHUJA Ph#: 4159343600
87F0	PRINT SERVER FOR NW3.X Company: ISHIGAKI COMPUTER SYSTEM CORP Contact: RYUJI MANABE Ph#: 81332745550		8830	IP TO IPX GATEWAY
			8844	ASHWIN SOCKET Company: CI TECHNOLOGIES Contact: ANIL PERES-DA-SILVA Ph#: 919-419-1694
87F1	DISTRIBUTED FILE SYSTEM FOR TALXWARE Company: TALX CORP Contact: GARTH DAVIS Ph#: 3144340046		8848	NETWARE DIAGNOSTIC & PERFORMANCE TOOL Company: NAUDUS TECHNOLOGIES Contact: STANLEY NAUOUS Ph#: 7033238496
87F2	DISTRIBUTED FILE SYSTEM FOR TALXWARE Company: TALX CORP Contact: GARTH DAVIS Ph#: 3144340046		8849	DUKE NUKEM 3D Company: 3D REALMS Contact: MARK DOCHTERMANN Ph#: 2142711365
87F4	ALERT MANAGEMENT SYSTEM Company: INTEL Contact: CHRISTY HOLLIS Ph#: 8017632430		884A	SHADOW WARRIORS Company: 3D REALMS Contact: MARK DOCHTERMANN Ph#: 2142711365
87F5	SERVER COMMANDS ON UXP/DS Company: FUJITSU LTD Contact: YUTAKA AOYAMA Ph#: 81454741925		884B	RUINS Company: 3D REALMS Contact: MARK DOCHTERMANN Ph#: 2142711365
87FB	PREVAIL/XP Company: LEGENT Contact: LYNN JOHNSTON Ph#: 61322851004064			

Socket#	Description
884C	BLOOD Company: 3D REALMS Contact: MARK DOCHTERMANN Ph#: 2142711365
8856	MANUAL CONFIG OF CLIENT TO REACH SERVER Company: IBM - ROCHESTER Contact: KEITH CRAMER Ph#: 507-253-5712
8859	RAS Company: US ROBOTICS Contact: CRAIG BOYLE Ph#: 508-8982600220
885A	MEDIA PATH Company: BRM TECHNOLOGIES LTD Contact: TAL NEVO Ph#: 972-2-870444
885B	AIRONET Company: VIRTUAL MOTION INC Contact: KEN HILLIARD Ph#: 415-778-0101
885C	GOLF SCORING SYSTEM Company: INFORMATION AND DISPLAY SYST Contact: FRANK MITCHELL Ph#: 904-642-1755
885D	VIRATA SWITCH Company: ADVANCED TELECOM MODULES LTD Contact: DAVID BRAY Ph#: 441223566919
9000	NP/SQL SERVER Company: NOVELL - PROVO Contact: JIM NICOLET Ph#: 8014293136
9001	WIDE AREA ROUTER Company: NOVELL - SUNNYVALE (CPD) Contact: RECEIVING DEPT Ph#: 4087474000
9002	WIDE AREA ROUTER
9003	WIDE AREA ROUTER
9004	WIDE AREA ROUTER
9005	WIDE AREA ROUTER
9006	WIDE AREA ROUTER
9007	WIDE AREA ROUTER
9008	WIDE AREA ROUTER
9009	WIDE AREA ROUTER
900A	WIDE AREA ROUTER
900B	WIDE AREA ROUTER
900C	WIDE AREA ROUTER
900F	SMNP OVER IPX Company: NOVELL - SAN JOSE Contact: CHG INFO Ph#: 4084342300
9010	SMNP OVER IPX
9012	SOFTWARE DISTRIBUTION Company: PHASER SYSTEMS Contact: CHG INFO Ph#: 4159566300
9013	SOFTWARE DISTRIBUTION
9014	SOFTWARE DISTRIBUTION
9015	SOFTWARE DISTRIBUTION
9016	SOFTWARE DISTRIBUTION
9017	CHAT - WINDOWS Company: NOVELL - PROVO CORP HQ Contact: MORGAN ADAIR
9019	RPC BIND Company: NOVELL - AUSTIN Contact: CHG INFO Ph#: 5123468380
901A	RPC BIND
901E	Company: NOVELL - PROVO Contact: J D BRISK
901F	NETWARE 'SLURPY' Company: NOVELL - PROVO Contact: TIM BIRD Ph#: 8012239093
9021	SPX CONNECTION Company: NOVELL - PROVO Contact: ALAN JEX Ph#: 8014293378
9022	JOB SERVER Company: NOVELL - PROVO Contact: ALAN JEX Ph#: 8014293378
9023	NETWARE 'SLURPY' Company: NOVELL - PROVO Contact: TIM BIRD Ph#: 8012239093

Socket#	Description
9024	NETWARE 'SLURPY'
9025	NETWARE 'SLURPY'
9026	NETWARE 'SLURPY'
9027	Company: NOVELL - PROVO Contact: DAVE LIND, NLM TESTING GROUP Ph#: 8014295713
9028	NETWORK MANAGEMENT Company: NOVELL - PROVO Contact: STEVE BUNCH Ph#: 8014293093
9029	Company: NOVELL - SALT LAKE CITY Contact: LINDA SHELTON Ph#: 8013507300
902A	Company: NOVELL - SALT LAKE CITY
902B	Company: NOVELL - SALT LAKE CITY
902C	NETWORK MANAGEMENT CLIENT INFO Company: NOVELL - PROVO Contact: KURT VOUTAZ Ph#: 1-800-LANSWER
902D	Company: NOVELL - PROVO Contact: STEVE BUNCH Ph#: 8014293093
902E	DOS TARGET SERVICE AGENT Company: NOVELL - PROVO Contact: TOM BOGART Ph#: 8014293010
902F	Company: NOVELL - PROVO Contact: STEVE BUNCH Ph#: 8014293093
9030	SUPERLAB AUTOMATION SERVER NOVELL - PROVO Contact: CHAD ADAMS Ph#: 8014293370
9031	RPC BIND Company: NOVELL - AUSTIN Contact: CHG INFO Ph#: 5123468380
9032	IPX BIFF Company: UNIVEL Contact: SCOTT HARRISON Ph#: 8015688666
9033	IPX BOOTPC Company: UNIVEL Contact: SCOTT HARRISON Ph#: 8015688666
9034	IPX BOOTPS Company: UNIVEL Contact: SCOTT HARRISON Ph#: 8015688666
9035	IPX CHARGEN Company: UNIVEL Contact: SCOTT HARRISON Ph#: 8015688666
9036	IPX DAYTIME Company: UNIVEL Contact: SCOTT HARRISON Ph#: 8015688666
9037	IPX DISCARD Company: UNIVEL Contact: SCOTT HARRISON Ph#: 8015688666
9038	IPX ECHO Company: UNIVEL Contact: SCOTT HARRISON Ph#: 8015688666
9039	IPX EPRC Company: UNIVEL Contact: SCOTT HARRISON Ph#: 8015688666
903A	IPX MONITOR Company: UNIVEL Contact: SCOTT HARRISON Ph#: 8015688666
903B	IPX NAME Company: UNIVEL Contact: SCOTT HARRISON Ph#: 8015688666
903C	IPX NAMESERVER Company: UNIVEL Contact: SCOTT HARRISON Ph#: 8015688666
903D	IPX NETSTAT Company: UNIVEL Contact: SCOTT HARRISON Ph#: 8015688666
903E	IPX NEW-RWHO Company: UNIVEL Contact: SCOTT HARRISON Ph#: 8015688666
903F	IPX NFSD Company: UNIVEL Contact: SCOTT HARRISON Ph#: 8015688666

Socket#	Description		Socket#	Description
9040	IPX NTP Company: UNIVEL Contact: SCOTT HARRISON Ph#: 8015688666		9059	SPX FTP-DATA Company: UNIVEL Contact: SCOTT HARRISON Ph#: 8015688666
9041	IPX QOTD Company: UNIVEL Contact: SCOTT HARRISON Ph#: 8015688666		905A	SPX HOSTNAMES Company: UNIVEL Contact: SCOTT HARRISON Ph#: 8015688666
9042	IPX RMONITOR Company: UNIVEL Contact: SCOTT HARRISON Ph#: 8015688666		905B	SPX INGRESLOCK Company: UNIVEL Contact: SCOTT HARRISON Ph#: 8015688666
9043	IPX ROUTE Company: UNIVEL Contact: SCOTT HARRISON Ph#: 8015688666		905C	SPX ISO-IP Company: UNIVEL Contact: SCOTT HARRISON Ph#: 8015688666
9044	IPX SYSLOG Company: UNIVEL Contact: SCOTT HARRISON Ph#: 8015688666		905D	SPX ISO-TP0 Company: UNIVEL Contact: SCOTT HARRISON Ph#: 8015688666
9045	IPX SYSTAT Company: UNIVEL Contact: SCOTT HARRISON Ph#: 8015688666		905E	SPX ISO-TSAP Company: UNIVEL Contact: SCOTT HARRISON Ph#: 8015688666
9046	IPX TALK Company: UNIVEL Contact: SCOTT HARRISON Ph#: 8015688666		905F	SPX LINK Company: UNIVEL Contact: SCOTT HARRISON Ph#: 8015688666
9047	IPX TIME Company: UNIVEL Contact: SCOTT HARRISON Ph#: 8015688666		9060	SPX LISTEN Company: UNIVEL Contact: SCOTT HARRISON Ph#: 8015688666
9048	IPX WHO Company: UNIVEL Contact: SCOTT HARRISON Ph#: 8015688666		9061	SPX LOGIN Company: UNIVEL Contact: SCOTT HARRISON Ph#: 8015688666
9049	IPX WHOIS Company: UNIVEL Contact: SCOTT HARRISON Ph#: 8015688666		9062	SPX NAME Company: UNIVEL Contact: SCOTT HARRISON Ph#: 8015688666
904A	SPX APFS Company: UNIVEL Contact: SCOTT HARRISON Ph#: 8015688666		9063	SPX NAMESERVER Company: UNIVEL Contact: SCOTT HARRISON Ph#: 8015688666
904B	SPX APTS Company: UNIVEL Contact: SCOTT HARRISON Ph#: 8015688666		9064	SPX NETSTAT Company: UNIVEL Contact: SCOTT HARRISON Ph#: 8015688666
904C	SPX AUTH Company: UNIVEL Contact: SCOTT HARRISON Ph#: 8015688666		9065	SPX NNTP Company: UNIVEL Contact: SCOTT HARRISON Ph#: 8015688666
904D	SPX BFTP Company: UNIVEL Contact: SCOTT HARRISON Ph#: 8015688666		9066	SPX NTP Company: UNIVEL Contact: SCOTT HARRISON Ph#: 8015688666
904E	SPX CHARGEN Company: UNIVEL Contact: SCOTT HARRISON Ph#: 8015688666		9067	SPX PCSERVER Company: UNIVEL Contact: SCOTT HARRISON Ph#: 8015688666
904F	SPX CMIP-AGENT Company: UNIVEL Contact: SCOTT HARRISON Ph#: 8015688666		9068	SPX POP-2 Company: UNIVEL Contact: SCOTT HARRISON Ph#: 8015688666
9050	SPX CMIP-MANAGE Company: UNIVEL Contact: SCOTT HARRISON Ph#: 8015688666		9069	SPX PRINT-SRV Company: UNIVEL Contact: SCOTT HARRISON Ph#: 8015688666
9051	SPX COURIER Company: UNIVEL Contact: SCOTT HARRISON Ph#: 8015688666		906A	SPX PRINTER Company: UNIVEL Contact: SCOTT HARRISON Ph#: 8015688666
9052	SPX CSNET-NS Company: UNIVEL Contact: SCOTT HARRISON Ph#: 8015688666		906B	SPX QOTD UNIVEL Contact: SCOTT HARRISON Ph#: 8015688666
9053	SPX DAYTIME Company: UNIVEL Contact: SCOTT HARRISON Ph#: 8015688666		906C	SPX RJE Company: UNIVEL Contact: SCOTT HARRISON Ph#: 8015688666
9054	SPX DISCARD Company: UNIVEL Contact: SCOTT HARRISON Ph#: 8015688666		906D	SPX SFTP Company: UNIVEL Contact: SCOTT HARRISON Ph#: 8015688666
9055	SPX ECHO Company: UNIVEL Contact: SCOTT HARRISON Ph#: 8015688666		906E	SPX SHELL Company: UNIVEL Contact: SCOTT HARRISON Ph#: 8015688666
9056	SPX EXEC Company: UNIVEL Contact: SCOTT HARRISON Ph#: 8015688666		906F	SPX SMTP Company: UNIVEL Contact: SCOTT HARRISON Ph#: 8015688666
9057	SPX FINGER Company: UNIVEL Contact: SCOTT HARRISON Ph#: 8015688666		9070	SPX SUPDUP Company: UNIVEL Contact: SCOTT HARRISON Ph#: 8015688666
9058	SPX FTP Company: UNIVEL Contact: SCOTT HARRISON Ph#: 8015688666		9071	SPX SYSTAT Company: UNIVEL Contact: SCOTT HARRISON Ph#: 8015688666

Socket#	Description
9072	SPX TELNET Company: UNIVEL Contact: SCOTT HARRISON Ph#: 8015688666
9073	SPX TIME Company: UNIVEL Contact: SCOTT HARRISON Ph#: 8015688666
9074	SPX TTYMON Company: UNIVEL Contact: SCOTT HARRISON Ph#: 8015688666
9075	SPX UUCP Company: UNIVEL Contact: SCOTT HARRISON Ph#: 8015688666
9076	SPX UUCP-PATH Company: UNIVEL Contact: SCOTT HARRISON Ph#: 8015688666
9077	SPX WHOIS Company: UNIVEL Contact: SCOTT HARRISON Ph#: 8015688666
9078	SPX X400 Company: UNIVEL Contact: SCOTT HARRISON Ph#: 8015688666
9079	SPX X400-SND Company: UNIVEL Contact: SCOTT HARRISON Ph#: 8015688666
907A	SPX XSERVER0 Company: UNIVEL Contact: SCOTT HARRISON Ph#: 8015688666
907B	SMS Company: NOVELL - PROVO Contact: MARK ELLSWORTH Ph#: 8014293117
907C	SMS Company: NOVELL - PROVO Contact: MARK ELLSWORTH Ph#: 8014293117
907D	QUEUE SERVER FOR IBM PSF/2 Company: NOVELL - PROVO CORP HQ Contact: CARL SEAVER Ph#: 8014297552
907E	IPX SOCKET FOR BTRIEVE REQUESTER Company: NOVELL - AUSTIN Contact: CHG INFO Ph#: 51234683801540
907F	NETWARE FOR SAA Company: NOVELL - SUNNYVALE Contact: REYNOLD WONG
9080	ADDRESS SERVER Company: NOVELL - PROVO Contact: DOUG SMITH
9081	NOVELL MHS DS GATEWAY FOR OCE Company: NOVELL - WALNUT CREEK Contact: ED CHANG Ph#: 5109474516
9082	NDS GATEWAY FOR OCE Company: NOVELL - WALNUT CREEK Contact: ED CHANG Ph#: 5109474516
9083	X.400 PROTOCOL ACCESS MODULE Company: NOVELL - RICHMOND HILL Contact: STEVE BOND Ph#: 4168865700

Socket#	Description
9084	SNADS PROTOCOL ACCESS MODULE Company: NOVELL - RICHMOND HILL Contact: STEVE BOND Ph#: 4168865700
9085	REMOTE PROGRAM SPAWNING Company: NOVELL - SAN JOSE Contact: BILL HUNT Ph#: 4084342300
9086	IPX PING Company: NOVELL - SAN JOSE Contact: JOHN MCCLENNON Ph#: 4085778767
9087	ENHANCED NCP COMMUNICATIONS Company: NOVELL - PROVO Contact: GRANT ECHOLS Ph#: 8014293149
9088	MPR - NETWARE MOBILE IPX Company: NOVELL - SAN JOSE Contact: MICHAEL ALLEN Ph#: 408-577-8412
9089	NETWARE FOR SAA - LOAD BALANCING Company: NOVELL - SUNNYVALE Contact: REYNOLD WONG
9094	DATALINK SWITCHING (DLSW) Company: NOVELL - SAN JOSE Contact: ANDY SUBRAMANIAM Ph#: 4084342300
9095	REMOTE CONTROL SOFTWARE PROGRAM Company: NOVELL - PROVO CORP HQ Contact: LEE WILTBANK Ph#: 8004531267
9097	NETWORK INSTALL OF UNIXWARE #2 Company: NOVELL Contact: JANET FRAZER Ph#: 9085225163
9098	NEST DEVICE Company: NOVELL - PROVO Contact: KAY GAMEIRO Ph#: 801-429-5357
9099	DATABASE SERVER DOC. MNGMT. PKG. Company: NOVELL - OREM Contact: TONY CARAS Ph#: 228-5218
909A	DATABASE SERVER DOC. MNGMT. PKG.
909B	DATABASE SERVER DOC. MNGMT. PKG.
909C	DATABASE SERVER DOC. MNGMT. PKG.
909D	DATABASE SERVER DOC. MNGMT. PKG.
909E	DATABASE SERVER DOC. MNGMT. PKG.
909F	DATABASE SERVER DOC. MNGMT. PKG.
90A0	DATABASE SERVER DOC. MNGMT. PKG.
90A1	DATABASE SERVER DOC. MNGMT. PKG.
90A2	DATABASE SERVER DOC. MNGMT. PKG.
90B0	MPR-IPX ADDRESS MAPPING GATEWAY Company: NOVELL - SAN JOSE Contact: MICHAEL ALLEN Ph#: 408-577-8412
90B2	NDPS PRINTER AGENT Company: NOVELL - PROVO Contact: KEN ISLE Ph#: 8014293154

IP/TCP Tables

G.1   IP Protocol Assignments

Code	Protocol	Description
0		Reserved
1	ICMP	Internet Control Message
2	IGMP	Internet Group Management
3	GGP	Gateway-to-Gateway
4	IP	IP in IP (encapsulation)
5	ST	Stream
6	TCP	Transmission Control
7	UCL	UCL
8	EGP	Exterior Gateway Protocol
9	IGP	any Private Interior Gateway
10	BBN-RCC-MON	BBN RCC Monitoring
11	NVP-II	Network Voice Protocol
12	PUP	PUP
13	ARGUS	ARGUS
14	EMCON	EMCON
15	XNET	Cross Net Debugger
16	CHAOS	Chaos
17	UDP	User Datagram
18	MUX	Multiplexing
19	DCN-MEAS	DCN Measurement Subsystems
20	HMP	Host Monitoring
21	PRM	Packet Radio Measurement
22	XNS-IDP	XEROX NS IDP
23	TRUNK-1	Trunk-1
24	TRUNK-2	Trunk-2
25	LEAF-1	Leaf-1
26	LEAF-2	Leaf-2
27	RDP	Reliable Data Protocol
28	IRTP	Internet Reliable Transaction
29	ISO-TP4	ISO Transport Protocol Class 4
30	NETBLT	Bulk Data Transfer Protocol
31	MFE-NSP	MFE Network Services Protocol
32	MERIT-INP	MERIT Internodal Protocol
33	SEP	Sequential Exchange Protocol
34	3PC	Third Party Connect Protocol
35	IDPR	Inter Domain Policy Routing Protocol
36	XTP	XTP
37	DDP	Datagram Delivery Protocol
38	IDPR-CMTP	IDPR Control Message Transport Protocol
39	TP++	TP++ Transport Protocol
40	IL	IL Transport Protocol
41	SIP	Simple Internet Protocol
42	SDRP	Source Demand Routing Protocol
43	SIP-SR	SIP Source Route
44	SIP-FRAG	SIP Fragment
45	IDRP	Inter Domain Routing Protocol
46	RSVP	Reservation Protocol
47	GRE	General Routing Encapsulation
48	MHRP	Mobile Host Routing Protocol
49	BNA	BNA
50	SIPP-ESP	SIPP Encap Security Payload
51	SIPP-AH	SIPP Authentication Header
52	I-NLSP	Integrated Net Layer Security
53	SWIPE	IP with Encryption
54	NHRP	NBMA Next Hop Resolution Protocol

Code	Protocol	Description
55-60		Unassigned
61		any host internal protocol
62	CFTP	CFTP
63		any local network
64	SAT-EXPAK	SATNET and Backroom EXPAK
65	KRYPTOLAN	Kryptolan
66	RVD	MIT Remote Virtual Disk Protocol
67	IPPC	Internet Pluribus Packet Core
68		any distributed file system
69	SAT-MON	SATNET Monitoring
70	VISA	VISA Protocol
71	IPCV	Internet Packet Core Utility
72	CPNX	Computer Protocol Network Executive
73	CPHB	Computer Protocol Heart Beat
74	WSN	Wang Span Network
75	PVP	Packet Video Protocol
76	BR-SAT-MON	Backroom SATNET Monitoring
77	SUN-ND	SUN ND PROTOCOL-Temporary
78	WB-MON	WIDEBAND Monitoring
79	WB-EXPAK	WIDEBAND EXPAK
80	ISO-IP	ISO Internet Protocol
81	VMTP	VMTP
82	SECURE-VMTP	SECURE-VMTP
83	VINES	VINES
84	TTP	TTP
85	NSFNET-IGP	NSFNET-IGP
86	DGP	Dissimilar Gateway Protocol
87	TCF	TCF
88	IGRP	IGRP
89	OSPFIGP	OSPFIGP
90	Sprite-RPC	Sprite RPC Protocol
91	LARP	Locus Address Resolution Protocol
92	MTP	Multicast Transport Protocol
93	AX.25	AX.25 Frames
94	IPIP	IP-within-IP Encapsulation Protocol
95	MICP	Mobile Internetworking Control Protocol
96	SCC-SP	Semaphore Communications Sec. Protocol
97	ETHERIP	Ethernet-within-IP Encapsulation
98	ENCAP	Encapsulation Header
99		any private encryption scheme
100	GMTP	GMTP
101	IFMP	Ipsilon Flow Management Protocol
102	PNNI	PNNI
103	PIM	Protocol Independent Multicast
104	ARIS	ARIS
105	SCPS	SCPS
106	QNX	QNX
107	A/N	Active Networks
108	IPPCP	IP Payload Compression Protocol
109	SNP	Sitara Networks Protocol
110	Compaq-Peer	Compaq Peer Protocol
111	IPX-in-IP	IPX in IP
112	VRRP	Virtual Router Redundancy Protocol
113-254		Unassigned
255		Reserved

G.2   Selected ICMP Port Assignments

Code	Description	Code	Description
0	Echo Reply	14	Timestamp Reply
1	Unassigned	15	Information Request
2	Unassigned	16	Information Reply
3	Destination Unreachable	17	Address Mask Request
4	Source Quench	18	Address Mask Reply
5	Redirect	19	Reserved (for Security)
6	Alternate Host Address	20 -29	Reserved (for Robustness Experiment)
7	Unassigned	30	Traceroute
8	Echo	31	Datagram Conversion Error
9	Router Advertisement	32	Mobile Host Redirect
10	Router Selection	33	IPv6 Where-Are-You
11	Time Exceeded	34	IPv6 I-Am-Here
12	Parameter Problem	35	Mobile Registration Request
13	Timestamp	37-255	Reserved

G.3   TCP/UDP Port Assignments

Three types of TCP/UDP port numbers can be distinguished: Well Known Ports (0 – 1024, controlled by IANA), Registered Ports (1024 – 65535, not controlled by IANA) and Dynamic (Private) Ports (49152 – 65535, subset of Registered Ports). The most recent list of the IANA port assignements is available from:

ftp://ftp.isi.edu/in-notes/iana/assignments/port-numbers

G.3.1   Well Known Port Numbers

Keyword	Decimal	Description	Keyword	Decimal	Description
	0/tcp	Reserved	#	15/tcp	Unassigned [was netstat]
	0/udp	Reserved	#	15/udp	Unassigned
tcpmux	1/tcp	TCP Port Service Multiplexer	#	16/tcp	Unassigned
tcpmux	1/udp	TCP Port Service Multiplexer	#	16/udp	Unassigned
compressnet	2/tcp	Management Utility	qotd	17/tcp	Quote of the Day
compressnet	2/udp	Management Utility	qotd	17/udp	Quote of the Day
compressnet	3/tcp	Compression Process	msp	18/tcp	Message Send Protocol
compressnet	3/udp	Compression Process	msp	18/udp	Message Send Protocol
#	4/tcp	Unassigned	chargen	19/tcp	Character Generator
#	4/udp	Unassigned	chargen	19/udp	Character Generator
rje	5/tcp	Remote Job Entry	ftp-data	20/tcp	File Transfer [Default Data]
rje	5/udp	Remote Job Entry	ftp-data	20/udp	File Transfer [Default Data]
#	6/tcp	Unassigned	ftp	21/tcp	File Transfer [Control]
#	6/udp	Unassigned	ftp	21/udp	File Transfer [Control]
echo	7/tcp	Echo	ssh	22/tcp	SSH Remote Login Protocol
echo	7/udp	Echo	ssh	22/udp	SSH Remote Login Protocol
#	8/tcp	Unassigned	telnet	23/tcp	Telnet
#	8/udp	Unassigned	telnet	23/udp	Telnet
discard	9/tcp	Discard		24/tcp	any private mail system
discard	9/udp	Discard		24/udp	any private mail system
#	10/tcp	Unassigned	smtp	25/tcp	Simple Mail Transfer
#	10/udp	Unassigned	smtp	25/udp	Simple Mail Transfer
systat	11/tcp	Active Users	#	26/tcp	Unassigned
systat	11/udp	Active Users	#	26/udp	Unassigned
#	12/tcp	Unassigned	nsw-fe	27/tcp	NSW User System FE
#	12/udp	Unassigned	nsw-fe	27/udp	NSW User System FE
daytime	13/tcp	Daytime (RFC 867)	#	28/tcp	Unassigned
daytime	13/udp	Daytime (RFC 867)	#	28/udp	Unassigned
#	14/tcp	Unassigned	msg-icp	29/tcp	MSG ICP
#	14/udp	Unassigned	msg-icp	29/udp	MSG ICP

Keyword	Decimal	Description	Keyword	Decimal	Description
#	30/tcp	Unassigned	sql*net	66/tcp	Oracle SQL*NET
#	30/udp	Unassigned	sql*net	66/udp	Oracle SQL*NET
msg-auth	31/tcp	MSG Authentication	bootps	67/tcp	Bootstrap Protocol Server
msg-auth	31/udp	MSG Authentication	bootps	67/udp	Bootstrap Protocol Server
#	32/tcp	Unassigned	bootpc	68/tcp	Bootstrap Protocol Client
#	32/udp	Unassigned	bootpc	68/udp	Bootstrap Protocol Client
dsp	33/tcp	Display Support Protocol	tftp	69/tcp	Trivial File Transfer
dsp	33/udp	Display Support Protocol	tftp	69/udp	Trivial File Transfer
#	34/tcp	Unassigned	gopher	70/tcp	Gopher
#	34/udp	Unassigned	gopher	70/udp	Gopher
	35/tcp	any private printer server	netrjs-1	71/tcp	Remote Job Service
	35/udp	any private printer server	netrjs-1	71/udp	Remote Job Service
#	36/tcp	Unassigned	netrjs-2	72/tcp	Remote Job Service
#	36/udp	Unassigned	netrjs-2	72/udp	Remote Job Service
time	37/tcp	Time	netrjs-3	73/tcp	Remote Job Service
time	37/udp	Time	netrjs-3	73/udp	Remote Job Service
rap	38/tcp	Route Access Protocol	netrjs-4	74/tcp	Remote Job Service
rap	38/udp	Route Access Protocol	netrjs-4	74/udp	Remote Job Service
rlp	39/tcp	Resource Location Protocol		75/tcp	any private dial out service
rlp	39/udp	Resource Location Protocol		75/udp	any private dial out service
#	40/tcp	Unassigned	deos	76/tcp	Distributed External Object
#	40/udp	Unassigned			Store
graphics	41/tcp	Graphics	deos	76/udp	Distributed External Object
graphics	41/udp	Graphics			Store
name	42/tcp	Host Name Server		77/tcp	any private RJE service
name	42/udp	Host Name Server		77/udp	any private RJE service
nameserver	42/tcp	Host Name Server	vettcp	78/tcp	vettcp
nameserver	42/udp	Host Name Server	vettcp	78/udp	vettcp
nicname	43/tcp	whois	finger	79/tcp	Finger
nicname	43/udp	whois	finger	79/udp	Finger
mpm-flags	44/tcp	MPM FLAGS Protocol	http	80/tcp	World Wide Web HTTP
mpm-flags	44/udp	MPM FLAGS Protocol	http	80/udp	World Wide Web HTTP
mpm	45/tcp	Message Processing Module	www	80/tcp	World Wide Web HTTP
		[recv]	www	80/udp	World Wide Web HTTP
mpm	45/udp	Message Processing Module	www-http	80/tcp	World Wide Web HTTP
		[recv]	www-http	80/udp	World Wide Web HTTP
mpm-snd	46/tcp	MPM [default send]	hosts2-ns	81/tcp	HOSTS2 Name Server
mpm-snd	46/udp	MPM [default send]	hosts2-ns	81/udp	HOSTS2 Name Server
ni-ftp	47/tcp	NI FTP	xfer	82/tcp	XFER Utility
ni-ftp	47/udp	NI FTP	xfer	82/udp	XFER Utility
auditd	48/tcp	Digital Audit Daemon	mit-ml-dev	83/tcp	MIT ML Device
auditd	48/udp	Digital Audit Daemon	mit-ml-dev	83/udp	MIT ML Device
tacacs	49/tcp	Login Host Protocol	ctf	84/tcp	Common Trace Facility
		(TACACS)	ctf	84/udp	Common Trace Facility
tacacs	49/udp	Login Host Protocol	mit-ml-dev	85/tcp	MIT ML Device
		(TACACS)	mit-ml-dev	85/udp	MIT ML Device
re-mail-ck	50/tcp	Remote Mail Checking	mfcobol	86/tcp	Micro Focus Cobol
		Protocol	mfcobol	86/udp	Micro Focus Cobol
re-mail-ck	50/udp	Remote Mail Checking		87/tcp	any private terminal link
		Protocol		87/udp	any private terminal link
la-maint	51/tcp	IMP Logical Address	kerberos	88/tcp	Kerberos
		Maintenance	kerberos	88/udp	Kerberos
la-maint	51/udp	IMP Logical Address	su-mit-tg	89/tcp	SU/MIT Telnet Gateway
		Maintenance	su-mit-tg	89/udp	SU/MIT Telnet Gateway
xns-time	52/tcp	XNS Time Protocol		90	also being used unofficially by
xns-time	52/udp	XNS Time Protocol			Pointcast
domain	53/tcp	Domain Name Server	dnsix	90/tcp	DNSIX Security Attribute
domain	53/udp	Domain Name Server			Token Map
xns-ch	54/tcp	XNS Clearinghouse	dnsix	90/udp	DNSIX Security Attribute
xns-ch	54/udp	XNS Clearinghouse			Token Map
isi-gl	55/tcp	ISI Graphics Language	mit-dov	91/tcp	MIT Dover Spooler
isi-gl	55/udp	ISI Graphics Language	mit-dov	91/udp	MIT Dover Spooler
xns-auth	56/tcp	XNS Authentication	npp	92/tcp	Network Printing Protocol
xns-auth	56/udp	XNS Authentication	npp	92/udp	Network Printing Protocol
	57/tcp	any private terminal access	dcp	93/tcp	Device Control Protocol
	57/udp	any private terminal access	dcp	93/udp	Device Control Protocol
xns-mail	58/tcp	XNS Mail	objcall	94/tcp	Tivoli Object Dispatcher
xns-mail	58/udp	XNS Mail	objcall	94/udp	Tivoli Object Dispatcher
	59/tcp	any private file service	supdup	95/tcp	SUPDUP
	59/udp	any private file service	supdup	95/udp	SUPDUP
	60/tcp	Unassigned	dixie	96/tcp	DIXIE Protocol Specification
	60/udp	Unassigned	dixie	96/udp	DIXIE Protocol Specification
ni-mail	61/tcp	NI MAIL	swift-rvf	97/tcp	Swift Remote Virtual File
ni-mail	61/udp	NI MAIL			Protocol
acas	62/tcp	ACA Services	swift-rvf	97/udp	Swift Remote Virtual File
acas	62/udp	ACA Services			Protocol
whois++	63/tcp	whois	tacnews	98/tcp	TAC News
whois++	63/udp	whois	tacnews	98/udp	TAC News
covia	64/tcp	Communications Integrator	metagram	99/tcp	Metagram Relay
		(CI)	metagram	99/udp	Metagram Relay
covia	64/udp	Communications Integrator	newacct	100/tcp	[unauthorized use]
		(CI)	hostname	101/tcp	NIC Host Name Server
tacacs-ds	65/tcp	TACACS-Database Service	hostname	101/udp	NIC Host Name Server
tacacs-ds	65/udp	TACACS-Database Service	iso-tsap	102/tcp	ISO-TSAP Class 0

Keyword	Decimal	Description	Keyword	Decimal	Description
iso-tsap	102/udp	ISO-TSAP Class 0	ingres-net	134/tcp	INGRES-NET Service
gppitnp	103/tcp	Genesis Point-to-Point Trans Net	ingres-net	134/udp	INGRES-NET Service
			epmap	135/tcp	DCE endpoint resolution
gppitnp	103/udp	Genesis Point-to-Point Trans Net	epmap	135/udp	DCE endpoint resolution
			profile	136/tcp	PROFILE Naming System
acr-nema	104/tcp	ACR-NEMA Digital Imag. & Comm. 300	profile	136/udp	PROFILE Naming System
			netbios-ns	137/tcp	NETBIOS Name Service
acr-nema	104/udp	ACR-NEMA Digital Imag. & Comm. 300	netbios-ns	137/udp	NETBIOS Name Service
			netbios-dgm	138/tcp	NETBIOS Datagram Service
cso	105/tcp	CCSO name server protocol	netbios-dgm	138/udp	NETBIOS Datagram Service
cso	105/udp	CCSO name server protocol	netbios-ssn	139/tcp	NETBIOS Session Service
csnet-ns	105/tcp	Mailbox Nameserver	netbios-ssn	139/udp	NETBIOS Session Service
csnet-ns	105/udp	Mailbox Nameserver	emfis-data	140/tcp	EMFIS Data Service
3com-tsmux	106/tcp	3COM-TSMUX	emfis-data	140/udp	EMFIS Data Service
3com-tsmux	106/udp	3COM-TSMUX	emfis-cntl	141/tcp	EMFIS Control Service
rtelnet	107/tcp	Remote Telnet Service	emfis-cntl	141/udp	EMFIS Control Service
rtelnet	107/udp	Remote Telnet Service	bl-idm	142/tcp	Britton-Lee IDM
snagas	108/tcp	SNA Gateway Access Server	bl-idm	142/udp	Britton-Lee IDM
snagas	108/udp	SNA Gateway Access Server	imap	143/tcp	Internet Message Access Protocol
pop2	109/tcp	Post Office Protocol - Version 2	imap	143/udp	Internet Message Access Protocol
pop2	109/udp	Post Office Protocol - Version 2	uma	144/tcp	Universal Management Architecture
pop3	110/tcp	Post Office Protocol - Version 3	uma	144/udp	Universal Management Architecture
pop3	110/udp	Post Office Protocol - Version 3	uaac	145/tcp	UAAC Protocol
sunrpc	111/tcp	SUN Remote Procedure Call	uaac	145/udp	UAAC Protocol
sunrpc	111/udp	SUN Remote Procedure Call	iso-tp0	146/tcp	ISO-IP0
mcidas	112/tcp	McIDAS Data Transmission Protocol	iso-tp0	146/udp	ISO-IP0
			iso-ip	147/tcp	ISO-IP
mcidas	112/udp	McIDAS Data Transmission Protocol	iso-ip	147/udp	ISO-IP
			jargon	148/tcp	Jargon
ident	113/tcp		jargon	148/udp	Jargon
auth	113/tcp	Authentication Service	aed-512	149/tcp	AED 512 Emulation Service
auth	113/udp	Authentication Service	aed-512	149/udp	AED 512 Emulation Service
audionews	114/tcp	Audio News Multicast	sql-net	150/tcp	SQL-NET
audionews	114/udp	Audio News Multicast	sql-net	150/udp	SQL-NET
sftp	115/tcp	Simple File Transfer Protocol	hems	151/tcp	HEMS
sftp	115/udp	Simple File Transfer Protocol	hems	151/udp	HEMS
ansanotify	116/tcp	ANSA REX Notify	bftp	152/tcp	Background File Transfer Program
ansanotify	116/udp	ANSA REX Notify			
uucp-path	117/tcp	UUCP Path Service	bftp	152/udp	Background File Transfer Program
uucp-path	117/udp	UUCP Path Service			
sqlserv	118/tcp	SQL Services	sgmp	153/tcp	SGMP
sqlserv	118/udp	SQL Services	sgmp	153/udp	SGMP
nntp	119/tcp	Network News Transfer Protocol	netsc-prod	154/tcp	NETSC
			netsc-prod	154/udp	NETSC
nntp	119/udp	Network News Transfer Protocol	netsc-dev	155/tcp	NETSC
			netsc-dev	155/udp	NETSC
cfdptkt	120/tcp	CFDPTKT	sqlsrv	156/tcp	SQL Service
cfdptkt	120/udp	CFDPTKT	sqlsrv	156/udp	SQL Service
erpc	121/tcp	Encore Expedited Remote Pro Call	knet-cmp	157/tcp	KNET/VM Command/Message Protocol
erpc	121/udp	Encore Expedited Remote Pro Call	knet-cmp	157/udp	KNET/VM Command/Message Protocol
smakynet	122/tcp	SMAKYNET	pcmail-srv	158/tcp	PCMail Server
smakynet	122/udp	SMAKYNET	pcmail-srv	158/udp	PCMail Server
ntp	123/tcp	Network Time Protocol	nss-routing	159/tcp	NSS-Routing
ntp	123/udp	Network Time Protocol	nss-routing	159/udp	NSS-Routing
ansatrader	124/tcp	ANSA REX Trader	sgmp-traps	160/tcp	SGMP-TRAPS
ansatrader	124/udp	ANSA REX Trader	sgmp-traps	160/udp	SGMP-TRAPS
locus-map	125/tcp	Locus PC-Interface Net Map Server	snmp	161/tcp	SNMP
			snmp	161/udp	SNMP
locus-map	125/udp	Locus PC-Interface Net Map Server	snmptrap	162/tcp	SNMPTRAP
			snmptrap	162/udp	SNMPTRAP
nxedit	126/tcp	NXEdit	cmip-man	163/tcp	CMIP/TCP Manager
nxedit	126/udp	NXEdit	cmip-man	163/udp	CMIP/TCP Manager
locus-con	127/tcp	Locus PC-Interface Conn Server	cmip-agent	164/tcp	CMIP/TCP Agent
			smip-agent	164/udp	CMIP/TCP Agent
locus-con	127/udp	Locus PC-Interface Conn Server	xns-courier	165/tcp	Xerox
			xns-courier	165/udp	Xerox
gss-xlicen	128/tcp	GSS X License Verification	s-net	166/tcp	Sirius Systems
gss-xlicen	128/udp	GSS X License Verification	s-net	166/udp	Sirius Systems
pwdgen	129/tcp	Password Generator Protocol	namp	167/tcp	NAMP
pwdgen	129/udp	Password Generator Protocol	namp	167/udp	NAMP
cisco-fna	130/tcp	Cisco FNATIVE	rsvd	168/tcp	RSVD
cisco-fna	130/udp	Cisco FNATIVE	rsvd	168/udp	RSVD
cisco-tna	131/tcp	Cisco TNATIVE	send	169/tcp	SEND
cisco-tna	131/udp	Cisco TNATIVE	send	169/udp	SEND
cisco-sys	132/tcp	Cisco SYSMAINT	print-srv	170/tcp	Network PostScript
cisco-sys	132/udp	Cisco SYSMAINT	print-srv	170/udp	Network PostScript
statsrv	133/tcp	Statistics Service	multiplex	171/tcp	Network Innovations Multiplex
statsrv	133/udp	Statistics Service			

Keyword	Decimal	Description	Keyword	Decimal	Description
multiplex	171/udp	Network Innovations Multiplex	at-3	203/tcp	AppleTalk Unused
			at-3	203/udp	AppleTalk Unused
cl/1	172/tcp	Network Innovations CL/1	at-echo	204/tcp	AppleTalk Echo
cl/1	172/udp	Network Innovations CL/1	at-echo	204/udp	AppleTalk Echo
xyplex-mux	173/tcp	Xyplex	at-5	205/tcp	AppleTalk Unused
xyplex-mux	173/udp	Xyplex	at-5	205/udp	AppleTalk Unused
mailq	174/tcp	MAILQ	at-zis	206/tcp	AppleTalk Zone Information
mailq	174/udp	MAILQ	at-zis	206/udp	AppleTalk Zone Information
vmnet	175/tcp	VMNET	at-7	207/tcp	AppleTalk Unused
vmnet	175/udp	VMNET	at-7	207/udp	AppleTalk Unused
genrad-mux	176/tcp	GENRAD-MUX	at-8	208/tcp	AppleTalk Unused
genrad-mux	176/udp	GENRAD-MUX	at-8	208/udp	AppleTalk Unused
xdmcp	177/tcp	X Display Manager Control Protocol	qmtp	209/tcp	The Quick Mail Transfer Protocol
xdmcp	177/udp	X Display Manager Control Protocol	qmtp	209/udp	The Quick Mail Transfer Protocol
nextstep	178/tcp	NextStep Window Server	z39.50	210/tcp	ANSI Z39.50
nextstep	178/udp	NextStep Window Server	z39.50	210/udp	ANSI Z39.50
bgp	179/tcp	Border Gateway Protocol	914c/g	211/tcp	Texas Instruments 914C/G Terminal
bgp	179/udp	Border Gateway Protocol	914c/g	211/udp	Texas Instruments 914C/G Terminal
ris	180/tcp	Intergraph			
ris	180/udp	Intergraph	anet	212/tcp	ATEXSSTR
unify	181/tcp	Unify	anet	212/udp	ATEXSSTR
unify	181/udp	Unify	ipx	213/tcp	IPX
audit	182/tcp	Unisys Audit SITP	ipx	213/udp	IPX
audit	182/udp	Unisys Audit SITP	vmpwscs	214/tcp	VM PWSCS
ocbinder	183/tcp	OCBinder	vmpwscs	214/udp	VM PWSCS
ocbinder	183/udp	OCBinder	softpc	215/tcp	Insignia Solutions
ocserver	184/tcp	OCServer	softpc	215/udp	Insignia Solutions
ocserver	184/udp	OCServer	CAllic	216/tcp	Computer Associates Int'l License Server
remote-kis	185/tcp	Remote-KIS			
remote-kis	185/udp	Remote-KIS	CAllic	216/udp	Computer Associates Int'l License Server
kis	186/tcp	KIS Protocol			
kis	186/udp	KIS Protocol	dbase	217/tcp	dBASE Unix
aci	187/tcp	Application Communication Interface	dbase	217/udp	dBASE Unix
			mpp	218/tcp	Netix Message Posting Protocol
aci	187/udp	Application Communication Interface	mpp	218/udp	Netix Message Posting Protocol
mumps	188/tcp	Plus Five's MUMPS	uarps	219/tcp	Unisys ARPs
mumps	188/udp	Plus Five's MUMPS	uarps	219/udp	Unisys ARPs
qft	189/tcp	Queued File Transport	imap3	220/tcp	Interactive Mail Access Protocol v3
qft	189/udp	Queued File Transport	imap3	220/udp	Interactive Mail Access Protocol v3
gacp	190/tcp	Gateway Access Control Protocol	fln-spx	221/tcp	Berkeley rlogind with SPX authentication
gacp	190/udp	Gateway Access Control Protocol	fln-spx	221/udp	Berkeley rlogind with SPX authentication
prospero	191/tcp	Prospero Directory Service	rsh-spx	222/tcp	Berkeley rshd with SPX auth
prospero	191/udp	Prospero Directory Service	rsh-spx	222/udp	Berkeley rshd with SPX auth
osu-nms	192/tcp	OSU Network Monitoring System	cdc	223/tcp	Certificate Distribution Center
osu-nms	192/udp	OSU Network Monitoring System	cdc	223/udp	Certificate Distribution Center
srmp	193/tcp	Spider Remote Monitoring Protocol	#### Possible Conflict of Port 222 with "Masqdialer"####		
srmp	193/udp	Spider Remote Monitoring Protocol	masqdialer	224/tcp	masqdialer
irc	194/tcp	Internet Relay Chat Protocol	masqdialer	224/udp	masqdialer
irc	194/udp	Internet Relay Chat Protocol	#	225-241	Reserved
dn6-nlm-aud	195/tcp	DNSIX Network Level Module Audit	direct	242/tcp	Direct
			direct	242/udp	Direct
dn6-nlm-aud	195/udp	DNSIX Network Level Module Audit	sur-meas	243/tcp	Survey Measurement
			sur-meas	243/udp	Survey Measurement
dn6-smm-red	196/tcp	DNSIX Session Mgt Module Audit Redir	inbusiness	244/tcp	inbusiness
			inbusiness	244/udp	inbusiness
dn6-smm-red	196/udp	DNSIX Session Mgt Module Audit Redir	link	245/tcp	LINK
			link	245/udp	LINK
dls	197/tcp	Directory Location Service	dsp3270	246/tcp	Display Systems Protocol
dls	197/udp	Directory Location Service	dsp3270	246/udp	Display Systems Protocol
dls-mon	198/tcp	Directory Location Service Monitor	subntbcst_tftp	247/tcp	SUBNTBCST_TFTP
			subntbcst_tftp	247/udp	SUBNTBCST_TFTP
dls-mon	198/udp	Directory Location Service Monitor	bhfhs	248/tcp	bhfhs
			bhfhs	248/udp	bhfhs
smux	199/tcp	SMUX	#	249-255	Reserved
smux	199/udp	SMUX	rap	256/tcp	RAP
src	200/tcp	IBM System Resource Controller	rap	256/udp	RAP
			set	257/tcp	Secure Electronic Transaction
src	200/udp	IBM System Resource Controller	set	257/udp	Secure Electronic Transaction
at-rtmp	201/tcp	AppleTalk Routing Maintenance	yak-chat	258/tcp	Yak Winsock Personal Chat
at-rtmp	201/udp	AppleTalk Routing Maintenance	yak-chat	258/udp	Yak Winsock Personal Chat
at-nbp	202/tcp	AppleTalk Name Binding			
at-nbp	202/udp	AppleTalk Name Binding			

Keyword	Decimal	Description	Keyword	Decimal	Description
esro-gen	259/tcp	Efficient Short Remote Operations	fatserv	347/udp	Fatmen Server
esro-gen	259/udp	Efficient Short Remote Operations	csi-sgwp	348/tcp	Cabletron Management Protocol
openport	260/tcp	Openport	csi-sgwp	348/udp	Cabletron Management Protocol
openport	260/udp	Openport	mftp	349/tcp	mftp
nsiiops	261/tcp	IIOP Name Service over TLS/SSL	mftp	349/udp	mftp
nsiiops	261/udp	IIOP Name Service over TLS/SSL	matip-type-a	350/tcp	MATIP Type A
arcisdms	262/tcp	Arcisdms	matip-type-a	350/udp	MATIP Type A
arcisdms	262/udp	Arcisdms	matip-type-b	351/tcp	MATIP Type B
hdap	263/tcp	HDAP	matip-type-b	351/udp	MATIP Type B
hdap	263/udp	HDAP			The following entry records an unassigned but widespread use
bgmp	264/tcp	BGMP	bhoetty	351/tcp	bhoetty (added 5/21/97)
bgmp	264/udp	BGMP	bhoetty	351/udp	bhoetty
x-bone-ctl	265/tcp	X-Bone CTL	dtag-ste-sb	352/tcp	DTAG (assigned long ago)
x-bone-ctl	265/udp	X-Bone CTL	dtag-ste-sb	352/udp	DTAG
sst	266/tcp	SCSI on ST			The following entry records an unassigned but widespread use
sst	266/udp	SCSI on ST	bhoedap4	352/tcp	bhoedap4 (added 5/21/97)
td-service	267/tcp	Tobit David Service Layer	bhoedap4	352/udp	bhoedap4
td-service	267/udp	Tobit David Service Layer	ndsauth	353/tcp	NDSAUTH
td-replica	268/tcp	Tobit David Replica	ndsauth	353/udp	NDSAUTH
td-replica	268/udp	Tobit David Replica	bh611	354/tcp	bh611
#	269-279	Unassigned	bh611	354/udp	bh611
http-mgmt	280/tcp	http-mgmt	datex-asn	355/tcp	DATEX-ASN
http-mgmt	280/udp	http-mgmt	datex-asn	355/udp	DATEX-ASN
personal-link	281/tcp	Personal Link	cloanto-net-1	356/tcp	Cloanto Net 1
personal-link	281/udp	Personal Link	cloanto-net-1	356/udp	Cloanto Net 1
cableport-ax	282/tcp	Cable Port A/X	bhevent	357/tcp	bhevent
cableport-ax	282/udp	Cable Port A/X	bhevent	357/udp	bhevent
rescap	283/tcp	rescap	shrinkwrap	358/tcp	Shrinkwrap
rescap	283/udp	rescap	shrinkwrap	358/udp	Shrinkwrap
corerjd	284/tcp	corerjd	tenebris_nts	359/tcp	Tenebris Network Trace Service
corerjd	284/udp	corerjd	tenebris_nts	359/udp	Tenebris Network Trace Service
#	285	Unassigned			
fxp-1	286/tcp	FXP-1	scoi2odialog	360/tcp	scoi2odialog
fxp-1	286/udp	FXP-1	scoi2odialog	360/udp	scoi2odialog
k-block	287/tcp	K-BLOCK	semantix	361/tcp	Semantix
k-block	287/udp	K-BLOCK	semantix	361/udp	Semantix
#	288-307	Unassigned	srssend	362/tcp	SRS Send
novastorbakcup	308/tcp	Novastor Backup	srssend	362/udp	SRS Send
novastorbakcup	308/udp	Novastor Backup	rsvp_tunnel	363/tcp	RSVP Tunnel
entrusttime	309/tcp	EntrustTime	rsvp_tunnel	363/udp	RSVP Tunnel
entrusttime	309/udp	EntrustTime	aurora-cmgr	364/tcp	Aurora CMGR
bhmds	310/tcp	bhmds	aurora-cmgr	364/udp	Aurora CMGR
bhmds	310/udp	bhmds	dtk	365/tcp	DTK
asip-webadmin	311/tcp	AppleShare IP WebAdmin	dtk	365/udp	DTK
asip-webadmin	311/udp	AppleShare IP WebAdmin	odmr	366/tcp	ODMR
vslmp	312/tcp	VSLMP	odmr	366/udp	ODMR
vslmp	312/udp	VSLMP	mortgageware	367/tcp	MortgageWare
magenta-logic	313/tcp	Magenta Logic	mortgageware	367/udp	MortgageWare
magenta-logic	313/udp	Magenta Logic	qbikgdp	368/tcp	QbikGDP
opalis-robot	314/tcp	Opalis Robot	qbikgdp	368/udp	QbikGDP
opalis-robot	314/udp	Opalis Robot	rpc2portmap	369/tcp	rpc2portmap
dpsi	315/tcp	DPSI	rpc2portmap	369/udp	rpc2portmap
dpsi	315/udp	DPSI	codaauth2	370/tcp	codaauth2
decauth	316/tcp	decAuth	codaauth2	370/udp	codaauth2
decauth	316/udp	decAuth	clearcase	371/tcp	Clearcase
zannet	317/tcp	Zannet	clearcase	371/udp	Clearcase
zannet	317/udp	Zannet	ulistproc	372/tcp	ListProcessor
pkix-timestamp	318/tcp	PKIX TimeStamp	ulistproc	372/udp	ListProcessor
pkix-timestamp	318/udp	PKIX TimeStamp	legent-1	373/tcp	Legent Corporation
ptp-event	319/tcp	PTP Event	legent-1	373/udp	Legent Corporation
ptp-event	319/udp	PTP Event	legent-2	374/tcp	Legent Corporation
ptp-general	320/tcp	PTP General	legent-2	374/udp	Legent Corporation
ptp-general	320/udp	PTP General	hassle	375/tcp	Hassle
pip	321/tcp	PIP	hassle	375/udp	Hassle
pip	321/udp	PIP	nip	376/tcp	Amiga Envoy Network Inquiry Proto
rtsps	322/tcp	RTSPS			
rtsps	322/udp	RTSPS	nip	376/udp	Amiga Envoy Network Inquiry Proto
#	323-332	Unassigned			
texar	333/tcp	Texar Security Port	tnETOS	377/tcp	NEC Corporation
texar	333/udp	Texar Security Port	tnETOS	377/udp	NEC Corporation
#	334-343	Unassigned	dsETOS	378/tcp	NEC Corporation
pdap	344/tcp	Prospero Data Access Protocol	dsETOS	378/udp	NEC Corporation
pdap	344/udp	Prospero Data Access Protocol	is99c	379/tcp	TIA/EIA/IS-99 modem client
			is99c	379/udp	TIA/EIA/IS-99 modem client
pawserv	345/tcp	Perf Analysis Workbench	is99s	380/tcp	TIA/EIA/IS-99 modem server
pawserv	345/udp	Perf Analysis Workbench	is99s	380/udp	TIA/EIA/IS-99 modem server
zserv	346/tcp	Zebra server	hp-collector	381/tcp	hp performance data collector
zserv	346/udp	Zebra server			
fatserv	347/tcp	Fatmen Server			

Keyword	Decimal	Description	Keyword	Decimal	Description
hp-collector	381/udp	hp performance data collector	synoptics-trap	412/tcp	Trap Convention Port
			synoptics-trap	412/udp	Trap Convention Port
hp-managed-node	382/tcp	hp performance data managed node	smsp	413/tcp	Storage Management Services Protocol
hp-managed-node	382/udp	hp performance data managed node	smsp	413/udp	Storage Management Services Protocol
hp-alarm-mgr	383/tcp	hp performance data alarm manager	infoseek	414/tcp	InfoSeek
			infoseek	414/udp	InfoSeek
hp-alarm-mgr	383/udp	hp performance data alarm manager	bnet	415/tcp	BNet
			bnet	415/udp	BNet
arns	384/tcp	A Remote Network Server System	silverplatter	416/tcp	Silverplatter
			silverplatter	416/udp	Silverplatter
arns	384/udp	A Remote Network Server System	onmux	417/tcp	Onmux
			onmux	417/udp	Onmux
ibm-app	385/tcp	IBM Application	hyper-g	418/tcp	Hyper-G
ibm-app	385/udp	IBM Application	hyper-g	418/udp	Hyper-G
asa	386/tcp	ASA Message Router Object Def.	ariel1	419/tcp	Ariel
			ariel1	419/udp	Ariel
asa	386/udp	ASA Message Router Object Def.	smpte	420/tcp	SMPTE
			smpte	420/udp	SMPTE
aurp	387/tcp	Appletalk Update-Based Routing Pro.	ariel2	421/tcp	Ariel
			ariel2	421/udp	Ariel
aurp	387/udp	Appletalk Update-Based Routing Pro.	ariel3	422/tcp	Ariel
			ariel3	422/udp	Ariel
unidata-ldm	388/tcp	Unidata LDM	opc-job-start	423/tcp	IBM Operations Planning and Control Start
unidata-ldm	388/udp	Unidata LDM			
#	389/tcp	Lightweight Directory Access Protocol	opc-job-start	423/udp	IBM Operations Planning and Control Start
ldap	389/udp	Lightweight Directory Access Protocol	opc-job-track	424/tcp	IBM Operations Planning and Control Track
uis	390/tcp	UIS	opc-job-track	424/udp	IBM Operations Planning and Control Track
uis	390/udp	UIS			
synotics-relay	391/tcp	SynOptics SNMP Relay Port	icad-el	425/tcp	ICAD
synotics-relay	391/udp	SynOptics SNMP Relay Port	icad-el	425/udp	ICAD
synotics-broker	392/tcp	SynOptics Port Broker Port	smartsdp	426/tcp	smartsdp
synotics-broker	392/udp	SynOptics Port Broker Port	smartsdp	426/udp	smartsdp
meta5	393/tcp	Meta5	svrloc	427/tcp	Server Location
meta5	393/udp	Meta5	svrloc	427/udp	Server Location
embl-ndt	394/tcp	EMBL Nucleic Data Transfer	ocs_cmu	428/tcp	OCS_CMU
embl-ndt	394/udp	EMBL Nucleic Data Transfer	ocs_cmu	428/udp	OCS_CMU
netcp	395/tcp	NETScout Control Protocol	ocs_amu	429/tcp	OCS_AMU
netcp	395/udp	NETScout Control Protocol	ocs_amu	429/udp	OCS_AMU
netware-ip	396/tcp	Novell Netware over IP	utmpsd	430/tcp	UTMPSD
netware-ip	396/udp	Novell Netware over IP	utmpsd	430/udp	UTMPSD
mptn	397/tcp	Multi Protocol Trans. Net.	utmpcd	431/tcp	UTMPCD
mptn	397/udp	Multi Protocol Trans. Net.	utmpcd	431/udp	UTMPCD
kryptolan	398/tcp	Kryptolan	iasd	432/tcp	IASD
kryptolan	398/udp	Kryptolan	iasd	432/udp	IASD
iso-tsap-c2	399/tcp	ISO Transport Class 2 Non-Control over TCP	nnsp	433/tcp	NNSP
			nnsp	433/udp	NNSP
iso-tsap-c2	399/udp	ISO Transport Class 2 Non-Control over TCP	mobileip-agent	434/tcp	MobileIP-Agent
			mobileip-agent	434/udp	MobileIP-Agent
work-sol	400/tcp	Workstation Solutions	mobilip-mn	435/tcp	MobilIP-MN
work-sol	400/udp	Workstation Solutions	mobilip-mn	435/udp	MobilIP-MN
ups	401/tcp	Uninterruptible Power Supply	dna-cml	436/tcp	DNA-CML
ups	401/udp	Uninterruptible Power Supply	dna-cml	436/udp	DNA-CML
genie	402/tcp	Genie Protocol	comscm	437/tcp	comscm
genie	402/udp	Genie Protocol	comscm	437/udp	comscm
decap	403/tcp	decap	dsfgw	438/tcp	dsfgw
decap	403/udp	decap	dsfgw	438/udp	dsfgw
nced	404/tcp	nced	dasp	439/tcp	dasp
nced	404/udp	nced	sgcp	440/tcp	sgcp
ncld	405/tcp	ncld	sgcp	440/udp	sgcp
ncld	405/udp	ncld	decvms-sysmgt	441/tcp	decvms-sysmgt
imsp	406/tcp	Interactive Mail Support Protocol	decvms-sysmgt	441/udp	decvms-sysmgt
			cvc_hostd	442/tcp	cvc_hostd
imsp	406/udp	Interactive Mail Support Protocol	cvc_hostd	442/udp	cvc_hostd
			https	443/tcp	http protocol over TLS/SSL
timbuktu	407/tcp	Timbuktu	https	443/udp	http protocol over TLS/SSL
timbuktu	407/udp	Timbuktu	snpp	444/tcp	Simple Network Paging Protocol
prm-sm	408/tcp	Prospero Resource Manager Sys. Man.	snpp	444/udp	Simple Network Paging Protocol [RFC1568]
prm-sm	408/udp	Prospero Resource Manager Sys. Man.			
prm-nm	409/tcp	Prospero Resource Manager Node Man.	microsoft-ds	445/tcp	Microsoft-DS
			microsoft-ds	445/udp	Microsoft-DS
prm-nm	409/udp	Prospero Resource Manager Node Man.	ddm-rdb	446/tcp	DDM-RDB
			ddm-rdb	446/udp	DDM-RDB
decladebug	410/tcp	DECLadebug Remote Debug Protocol	ddm-dfm	447/tcp	DDM-RFM
			ddm-dfm	447/udp	DDM-RFM
decladebug	410/udp	DECLadebug Remote Debug Protocol	ddm-ssl	448/tcp	DDM-SSL
			ddm-ssl	448/udp	DDM-SSL
rmt	411/tcp	Remote MT Protocol	as-servermap	449/tcp	AS Server Mapper
rmt	411/udp	Remote MT Protocol	as-servermap	449/udp	AS Server Mapper

Keyword	Decimal	Description	Keyword	Decimal	Description
tserver	450/tcp	TServer	nest-protocol	489/udp	nest-protocol
tserver	450/udp	TServer	micom-pfs	490/tcp	micom-pfs
sfs-smp-net	451/tcp	Cray Network Semaphore server	micom-pfs	490/udp	micom-pfs
			go-login	491/tcp	go-login
sfs-smp-net	451/udp	Cray Network Semaphore server	go-login	491/udp	go-login
			ticf-1	492/tcp	Transport Independent Convergence for FNA
sfs-config	452/tcp	Cray SFS config server			
sfs-config	452/udp	Cray SFS config server	ticf-1	492/udp	Transport Independent Convergence for FNA
creativeserver	453/tcp	CreativeServer			
creativeserver	453/udp	CreativeServer	ticf-2	493/tcp	Transport Independent Convergence for FNA
contentserver	454/tcp	ContentServer			
contentserver	454/udp	ContentServer	ticf-2	493/udp	Transport Independent Convergence for FNA
creativepartnr	455/tcp	CreativePartnr			
creativepartnr	455/udp	CreativePartnr	pov-ray	494/tcp	POV-Ray
macon-tcp	456/tcp	macon-tcp	pov-ray	494/udp	POV-Ray
macon-udp	456/udp	macon-udp	intecourier	495/tcp	intecourier
scohelp	457/tcp	scohelp	intecourier	495/udp	intecourier
scohelp	457/udp	scohelp	pim-rp-disc	496/tcp	PIM-RP-DISC
appleqtc	458/tcp	apple quick time	pim-rp-disc	496/udp	PIM-RP-DISC
appleqtc	458/udp	apple quick time	dantz	497/tcp	dantz
ampr-rcmd	459/tcp	ampr-rcmd	dantz	497/udp	dantz
ampr-rcmd	459/udp	ampr-rcmd	siam	498/tcp	siam
skronk	460/tcp	skronk	siam	498/udp	siam
skronk	460/udp	skronk	iso-ill	499/tcp	ISO ILL Protocol
datasurfsrv	461/tcp	DataRampSrv	iso-ill	499/udp	ISO ILL Protocol
datasurfsrv	461/udp	DataRampSrv	isakmp	500/tcp	isakmp
datasurfsrvsec	462/tcp	DataRampSrvSec	isakmp	500/udp	isakmp
datasurfsrvsec	462/udp	DataRampSrvSec	stmf	501/tcp	STMF
alpes	463/tcp	alpes	stmf	501/udp	STMF
alpes	463/udp	alpes	asa-appl-proto	502/tcp	asa-appl-proto
kpasswd	464/tcp	kpasswd	asa-appl-proto	502/udp	asa-appl-proto
kpasswd	464/udp	kpasswd	intrinsa	503/tcp	Intrinsa
#	465	Unassigned	intrinsa	503/udp	Intrinsa
digital-vrc	466/tcp	digital-vrc	citadel	504/tcp	citadel
digital-vrc	466/udp	digital-vrc	citadel	504/udp	citadel
mylex-mapd	467/tcp	mylex-mapd	mailbox-lm	505/tcp	mailbox-lm
mylex-mapd	467/udp	mylex-mapd	mailbox-lm	505/udp	mailbox-lm
photuris	468/tcp	proturis	ohimsrv	506/tcp	ohimsrv
photuris	468/udp	proturis	ohimsrv	506/udp	ohimsrv
rcp	469/tcp	Radio Control Protocol	crs	507/tcp	crs
rcp	469/udp	Radio Control Protocol	crs	507/udp	crs
scx-proxy	470/tcp	scx-proxy	xvttp	508/tcp	xvttp
scx-proxy	470/udp	scx-proxy	xvttp	508/udp	xvttp
mondex	471/tcp	Mondex	snare	509/tcp	snare
mondex	471/udp	Mondex	snare	509/udp	snare
ljk-login	472/tcp	ljk-login	fcp	510/tcp	FirstClass Protocol
ljk-login	472/udp	ljk-login	fcp	510/udp	FirstClass Protocol
hybrid-pop	473/tcp	hybrid-pop	passgo	511/tcp	PassGo
hybrid-pop	473/udp	hybrid-pop	passgo	511/udp	PassGo
tn-tl-w1	474/tcp	tn-tl-w1	exec	512/tcp	remote process execution; authentication performed using passwords and UNIX login names
tn-tl-w2	474/udp	tn-tl-w2			
tcpnethaspsrv	475/tcp	tcpnethaspsrv			
tcpnethaspsrv	475/udp	tcpnethaspsrv			
tn-tl-fd1	476/tcp	tn-tl-fd1	comsat	512/udp	
tn-tl-fd1	476/udp	tn-tl-fd1	biff	512/udp	used by mail system to notify users of new mail received; currently receives messages only from processes on the same machine
ss7ns	477/tcp	ss7ns			
ss7ns	477/udp	ss7ns			
spsc	478/tcp	spsc			
spsc	478/udp	spsc			
iafserver	479/tcp	iafserver	login	513/tcp	remote login a la telnet; automatic authentication performed based on privileged port numbers and distributed data bases which identify "authentication domains"
iafserver	479/udp	iafserver			
iafdbase	480/tcp	iafdbase			
iafdbase	480/udp	iafdbase			
ph	481/tcp	Ph service			
ph	481/udp	Ph service			
bgs-nsi	482/tcp	bgs-nsi			
bgs-nsi	482/udp	bgs-nsi	who	513/udp	maintains data bases showing who's logged into machines on a local net and the load average of the machine
ulpnet	483/tcp	ulpnet			
ulpnet	483/udp	ulpnet			
integra-sme	484/tcp	Integra Software Management Environment	shell	514/tcp	cmd like exec, but automatic authentication is performed as for login server
integra-sme	484/udp	Integra Software Management Environment			
powerburst	485/tcp	Air Soft Power Burst	syslog	514/udp	syslog
powerburst	485/udp	Air Soft Power Burst	printer	515/tcp	spooler
avian	486/tcp	avian	printer	515/udp	spooler
avian	486/udp	avian	videotex	516/tcp	videotex
saft	487/tcp	saft Simple Asynchronous File Transfer	videotex	516/udp	videotex
			talk	517/tcp	like tenex link, but across machine - unfortunately, doesn't use link protocol (this is actually just a rendezvous port from which a tcp connection is established)
saft	487/udp	saft Simple Asynchronous File Transfer			
gss-http	488/tcp	gss-http			
gss-http	488/udp	gss-http			
nest-protocol	489/tcp	nest-protocol			

Keyword	Decimal	Description	Keyword	Decimal	Description
talk	517/udp	like tenex link, but across machine - unfortunately, doesn't use link protocol (this is actually just a rendezvous port from which a tcp connection is established)	pirp	553/udp	pirp
			rtsp	554/tcp	Real Time Stream Control Protocol
			rtsp	554/udp	Real Time Stream Control Protocol
			dsf	555/tcp	dsf
ntalk	518/tcp	ntalk	dsf	555/udp	dsf
ntalk	518/udp	ntalk	remotefs	556/tcp	rfs server
utime	519/tcp	unixtime	remotefs	556/udp	rfs server
utime	519/udp	unixtime	openvms-sysipc	557/tcp	openvms-sysipc
efs	520/tcp	extended file name server	openvms-sysipc	557/udp	openvms-sysipc
router	520/udp	local routing process (on site); uses variant of Xerox NS routing information protocol - RIP	sdnskmp	558/tcp	SDNSKMP
			sdnskmp	558/udp	SDNSKMP
			teedtap	559/tcp	TEEDTAP
			teedtap	559/udp	TEEDTAP
ripng	521/tcp	ripng	rmonitor	560/tcp	rmonitord
ripng	521/udp	ripng	rmonitor	560/udp	rmonitord
ulp	522/tcp	ULP	monitor	561/tcp	monitor
ulp	522/udp	ULP	monitor	561/udp	monitor
ibm-db2	523/tcp	IBM-DB2	chshell	562/tcp	chcmd
ibm-db2	523/udp	IBM-DB2	chshell	562/udp	chcmd
ncp	524/tcp	NCP	nntps	563/tcp	nntp protocol over TLS/SSL (was snntp)
ncp	524/udp	NCP			
timed	525/tcp	timeserver	nntps	563/udp	nntp protocol over TLS/SSL (was snntp)
timed	525/udp	timeserver			
tempo	526/tcp	newdate	9pfs	564/tcp	plan 9 file service
tempo	526/udp	newdate	9pfs	564/udp	plan 9 file service
stx	527/tcp	Stock IXChange	whoami	565/tcp	whoami
stx	527/udp	Stock IXChange	whoami	565/udp	whoami
custix	528/tcp	Customer IXChange	streettalk	566/tcp	streettalk
custix	528/udp	Customer IXChange	streettalk	566/udp	streettalk
irc-serv	529/tcp	IRC-SERV	banyan-rpc	567/tcp	banyan-rpc
irc-serv	529/udp	IRC-SERV	banyan-rpc	567/udp	banyan-rpc
courier	530/tcp	rpc	ms-shuttle	568/tcp	Microsoft shuttle
courier	530/udp	rpc	ms-shuttle	568/udp	Microsoft shuttle
conference	531/tcp	chat	ms-rome	569/tcp	Microsoft rome
conference	531/udp	chat	ms-rome	569/udp	Microsoft rome
netnews	532/tcp	readnews	meter	570/tcp	demon
netnews	532/udp	readnews	meter	570/udp	demon
netwall	533/tcp	for emergency broadcasts	meter	571/tcp	udemon
netwall	533/udp	for emergency broadcasts	meter	571/udp	udemon
mm-admin	534/tcp	MegaMedia Admin	sonar	572/tcp	sonar
mm-admin	534/udp	MegaMedia Admin	sonar	572/udp	sonar
iiop	535/tcp	iiop	banyan-vip	573/tcp	banyan-vip
iiop	535/udp	iiop	banyan-vip	573/udp	banyan-vip
opalis-rdv	536/tcp	opalis-rdv	ftp-agent	574/tcp	FTP Software Agent System
opalis-rdv	536/udp	opalis-rdv	ftp-agent	574/udp	FTP Software Agent System
nmsp	537/tcp	Networked Media Streaming Protocol	vemmi	575/tcp	VEMMI
			vemmi	575/udp	VEMMI
nmsp	537/udp	Networked Media Streaming Protocol	ipcd	576/tcp	ipcd
			ipcd	576/udp	ipcd
gdomap	538/tcp	gdomap	vnas	577/tcp	vnas
gdomap	538/udp	gdomap	vnas	577/udp	vnas
apertus-ldp	539/tcp	Apertus Technologies Load Determination	ipdd	578/tcp	ipdd
			ipdd	578/udp	ipdd
apertus-ldp	539/udp	Apertus Technologies Load Determination	decbsrv	579/tcp	decbsrv
			decbsrv	579/udp	decbsrv
uucp	540/tcp	uucpd	sntp-heartbeat	580/tcp	SNTP HEARTBEAT
uucp	540/udp	uucpd	sntp-heartbeat	580/udp	SNTP HEARTBEAT
uucp-rlogin	541/tcp	uucp-rlogin	bdp	581/tcp	Bundle Discovery Protocol
uucp-rlogin	541/udp	uucp-rlogin	bdp	581/udp	Bundle Discovery Protocol
commerce	542/tcp	commerce	scc-security	582/tcp	SCC Security
commerce	542/udp	commerce	scc-security	582/udp	SCC Security
klogin	543/tcp	klogin	philips-vc	583/tcp	Philips Video-Conferencing
klogin	543/udp	klogin	philips-vc	583/udp	Philips Video-Conferencing
kshell	544/tcp	krcmd	keyserver	584/tcp	Key Server
kshell	544/udp	krcmd	keyserver	584/udp	Key Server
appleqtcsrvr	545/tcp	appleqtcsrvr	imap4-ssl	585/tcp	IMAP4+SSL (use 993 instead)
appleqtcsrvr	545/udp	appleqtcsrvr			
dhcpv6-client	546/tcp	DHCPv6 Client	imap4-ssl	585/udp	IMAP4+SSL Use of 585 is not recommended, use 993 instead
dhcpv6-client	546/udp	DHCPv6 Client			
dhcpv6-server	547/tcp	DHCPv6 Server			
dhcpv6-server	547/udp	DHCPv6 Server			
afpovertcp	548/tcp	AFP over TCP	password-chg	586/tcp.	Password Change
afpovertcp	548/udp	AFP over TCP	password-chg	586/udp	Password Change
idfp	549/tcp	IDFP	submission	587/tcp	Submission
idfp	549/udp	IDFP	submission	587/udp	Submission
new-rwho	550/tcp	new-who	cal	588/tcp	CAL
new-rwho	550/udp	new-who	cal	588/udp	CAL
cybercash	551/tcp	cybercash	eyelink	589/tcp	EyeLink
cybercash	551/udp	cybercash	eyelink	589/udp	EyeLink
deviceshare	552/tcp	deviceshare	tns-cml	590/tcp	TNS CML
deviceshare	552/udp	deviceshare	tns-cml	590/udp	TNS CML
pirp	553/tcp	pirp	http-alt	591/tcp	FileMaker, Inc. - HTTP Alternate (see Port 80)

Keyword	Decimal	Description	Keyword	Decimal	Description
http-alt	591/udp	FileMaker, Inc. - HTTP Alternate (see Port 80)	bmpp	632/tcp	bmpp
			bmpp	632/udp	bmpp
eudora-set	592/tcp	Eudora Set	servstat	633/tcp	Service Status update (Sterling Software)
eudora-set	592/udp	Eudora Set			
http-rpc-epmap	593/tcp	HTTP RPC Ep Map	servstat	633/udp	Service Status update (Sterling Software)
http-rpc-epmap	593/udp	HTTP RPC Ep Map			
tpip	594/tcp	TPIP	ginad	634/tcp	ginad
tpip	594/udp	TPIP	ginad	634/udp	ginad
cab-protocol	595/tcp	CAB Protocol	rlzdbase	635/tcp	RLZ DBase
cab-protocol	595/udp	CAB Protocol	rlzdbase	635/udp	RLZ DBase
smsd	596/tcp	SMSD	ldaps	636/tcp	ldap protocol over TLS/SSL (was sldap)
smsd	596/udp	SMSD			
ptcnameservice	597/tcp	PTC Name Service	ldaps	636/udp	ldap protocol over TLS/SSL (was sldap)
ptcnameservice	597/udp	PTC Name Service			
sco-websrvrmg3	598/tcp	SCO Web Server Manager 3	lanserver	637/tcp	lanserver
sco-websrvrmg3	598/udp	SCO Web Server Manager 3	lanserver	637/udp	lanserver
acp	599/tcp	Aeolon Core Protocol	mcns-sec	638/tcp	mcns-sec
acp	599/udp	Aeolon Core Protocol	mcns-sec	638/udp	mcns-sec
ipcserver	600/tcp	Sun IPC server	msdp	639/tcp	MSDP
ipcserver	600/udp	Sun IPC server	msdp	639/udp	MSDP
#	601-605	Unassigned	entrust-sps	640/tcp	entrust-sps
urm	606/tcp	Cray Unified Resource Manager	entrust-sps	640/udp	entrust-sps
			repcmd	641/tcp	repcmd
urm	606/udp	Cray Unified Resource Manager	repcmd	641/udp	repcmd
			esro-emsdp	642/tcp	ESRO-EMSDP V1.3
nqs	607/tcp	nqs	esro-emsdp	642/udp	ESRO-EMSDP V1.3
nqs	607/udp	nqs	sanity	643/tcp	SANity
sift-uft	608/tcp	Sender-Initiated/Unsolicited File Transfer	sanity	643/udp	SANity
			dwr	644/tcp	dwr
sift-uft	608/udp	Sender-Initiated/Unsolicited File Transfer	dwr	644/udp	dwr
			pssc	645/tcp	PSSC
npmp-trap	609/tcp	npmp-trap	pssc	645/udp	PSSC
npmp-trap	609/udp	npmp-trap	ldp	646/tcp	LDP
npmp-local	610/tcp	npmp-local	ldp	646/udp	LDP
npmp-local	610/udp	npmp-local	dhcp-failover	647/tcp	DHCP Failover
npmp-gui	611/tcp	npmp-gui	dhcp-failover	647/udp	DHCP Failover
npmp-gui	611/udp	npmp-gui	rrp	648/tcp	Registry Registrar Protocol (RRP)
hmmp-ind	612/tcp	HMMP Indication			
hmmp-ind	612/udp	HMMP Indication	rrp	648/udp	Registry Registrar Protocol (RRP)
hmmp-op	613/tcp	HMMP Operation			
hmmp-op	613/udp	HMMP Operation	aminet	649/tcp	Aminet
sshell	614/tcp	SSLshell	aminet	649/udp	Aminet
sshell	614/udp	SSLshell	obex	650/tcp	OBEX
sco-inetmgr	615/tcp	Internet Configuration Manager	obex	650/udp	OBEX
			ieee-mms	651/tcp	IEEE MMS
sco-inetmgr	615/udp	Internet Configuration Manager	ieee-mms	651/udp	IEEE MMS
			udlr-dtcp	652/tcp	UDLR_DTCP
sco-sysmgr	616/tcp	SCO System Administration Server	udlr-dtcp	652/udp	UDLR_DTCP
			repscmd	653/tcp	RepCmd
sco-sysmgr	616/udp	SCO System Administration Server	repscmd	653/udp	RepCmd
			aodv	654/tcp	AODV
sco-dtmgr	617/tcp	SCO Desktop Administration Server	aodv	654/udp	AODV
			tinc	655/tcp	TINC
sco-dtmgr	617/udp	SCO Desktop Administration Server	tinc	655/udp	TINC
			spmp	656/tcp	SPMP
dei-icda	618/tcp	DEI-ICDA	spmp	656/udp	SPMP
dei-icda	618/udp	DEI-ICDA	rmc	657/tcp	RMC
digital-evm	619/tcp	Digital EVM	rmc	657/udp	RMC
digital-evm	619/udp	Digital EVM	tenfold	658/tcp	TenFold
sco-websrvrmgr	620/tcp	SCO WebServer Manager	tenfold	658/udp	TenFold
sco-websrvrmgr	620/udp	SCO WebServer Manager	url-rendezvous	659/tcp	URL Rendezvous
escp-ip	621/tcp	ESCP	url-rendezvous	659/udp	URL Rendezvous
escp-ip	621/udp	ESCP	mac-srvr-admin	660/tcp	MacOS Server Admin
collaborator	622/tcp	Collaborator	mac-srvr-admin	660/udp	MacOS Server Admin
collaborator	622/udp	Collaborator	hap	661/tcp	HAP
aux_bus_shunt	623/tcp	Aux Bus Shunt	hap	661/udp	HAP
aux_bus_shunt	623/udp	Aux Bus Shunt	pftp	662/tcp	PFTP
cryptoadmin	624/tcp	Crypto Admin	pftp	662/udp	PFTP
cryptoadmin	624/udp	Crypto Admin	purenoise	663/tcp	PureNoise
dec_dlm	625/tcp	DEC DLM	purenoise	663/udp	PureNoise
dec_dlm	625/udp	DEC DLM	secure-aux-bus	664/tcp	Secure Aux Bus
asia	626/tcp	ASIA	secure-aux-bus	664/udp	Secure Aux Bus
asia	626/udp	ASIA	sun-dr	665/tcp	Sun DR
passgo-tivoli	627/tcp	PassGo Tivoli	sun-dr	665/udp	Sun DR
passgo-tivoli	627/udp	PassGo Tivoli	mdqs	666/tcp	mdqs
qmqp	628/tcp	QMQP	mdqs	666/udp	mdqs
qmqp	628/udp	QMQP	doom	666/tcp	doom Id Software
3com-amp3	629/tcp	3Com AMP3	doom	666/udp	doom Id Software
3com-amp3	629/udp	3Com AMP3	disclose	667/tcp	campaign contribution disclosures - SDR Technologies
rda	630/tcp	RDA			
rda	630/udp	RDA			
ipp	631/tcp	IPP (Internet Printing Protocol)	disclose	667/udp	campaign contribution disclosures - SDR Technologies
ipp	631/udp	IPP (Internet Printing Protocol)			

Keyword	Decimal	Description	Keyword	Decimal	Description
mecomm	668/tcp	MeComm	entrust-ash	710/udp	Entrust Administration Service Handler
mecomm	668/udp	MeComm			
meregister	669/tcp	MeRegister	cisco-tdp	711/tcp	Cisco TDP
meregister	669/udp	MeRegister	cisco-tdp	711/udp	Cisco TDP
vacdsm-sws	670/tcp	VACDSM-SWS	#	712-728	Unassigned
vacdsm-sws	670/udp	VACDSM-SWS	netviewdm1	729/tcp	IBM NetView DM/6000 Server/Client
vacdsm-app	671/tcp	VACDSM-APP			
vacdsm-app	671/udp	VACDSM-APP	netviewdm1	729/udp	IBM NetView DM/6000 Server/Client
vpps-qua	672/tcp	VPPS-QUA			
vpps-qua	672/udp	VPPS-QUA	netviewdm2	730/tcp	IBM NetView DM/6000 send/tcp
cimplex	673/tcp	CIMPLEX			
cimplex	673/udp	CIMPLEX	netviewdm2	730/udp	IBM NetView DM/6000 send/tcp
acap	674/tcp	ACAP			
acap	674/udp	ACAP	netviewdm3	731/tcp	IBM NetView DM/6000 receive/tcp
dctp	675/tcp	DCTP			
dctp	675/udp	DCTP	netviewdm3	731/udp	IBM NetView DM/6000 receive/tcp
vpps-via	676/tcp	VPPS Via			
vpps-via	676/udp	VPPS Via	#	732-740	Unassigned
vpp	677/tcp	Virtual Presence Protocol	netgw	741/tcp	netGW
vpp	677/udp	Virtual Presence Protocol	netgw	741/udp	netGW
ggf-ncp	678/tcp	GNU Gereration Foundation NCP	netrcs	742/tcp	Network based Rev. Cont. Sys.
			netrcs	742/udp	Network based Rev. Cont. Sys.
ggf-ncp	678/udp	GNU Generation Foundation NCP	#	743	Unassigned
			flexlm	744/tcp	Flexible License Manager
mrm	679/tcp	MRM	flexlm	744/udp	Flexible License Manager
mrm	679/udp	MRM	#	745-746	Unassigned
entrust-aaas	680/tcp	entrust-aaas	fujitsu-dev	747/tcp	Fujitsu Device Control
entrust-aaas	680/udp	entrust-aaas	fujitsu-dev	747/udp	Fujitsu Device Control
entrust-aams	681/tcp	entrust-aams	ris-cm	748/tcp	Russell Info Sci Calendar Manager
entrust-aams	681/udp	entrust-aams			
xfr	682/tcp	XFR	ris-cm	748/udp	Russell Info Sci Calendar Manager
xfr	682/udp	XFR			
corba-iiop	683/tcp	CORBA IIOP	kerberos-adm	749/tcp	kerberos administration
corba-iiop	683/udp	CORBA IIOP	kerberos-adm	749/udp	kerberos administration
corba-iiop-ssl	684/tcp	CORBA IIOP SSL	rfile	750/tcp	
corba-iiop-ssl	684/udp	CORBA IIOP SSL	loadav	750/udp	
mdc-portmapper	685/tcp	MDC Port Mapper	kerberos-iv	750/udp	kerberos version iv
mdc-portmapper	685/udp	MDC Port Mapper	pump	751/tcp	
hcp-wismar	686/tcp	Hardware Control Protocol Wismar	pump	751/udp	
			qrh	752/tcp	
hcp-wismar	686/udp	Hardware Control Protocol Wismar	qrh	752/udp	
			rrh	753/tcp	
asipregistry	687/tcp	asipregistry	rrh	753/udp	
asipregistry	687/udp	asipregistry	tell	754/tcp	send
realm-rusd	688/tcp	REALM-RUSD	tell	754/udp	send
realm-rusd	688/udp	REALM-RUSD	#	755-756	Unassigned
nmap	689/tcp	NMAP	nlogin	758/tcp	
nmap	689/udp	NMAP	nlogin	758/udp	
vatp	690/tcp	VATP	con	759/tcp	
vatp	690/udp	VATP	con	759/udp	
msexch-routing	691/tcp	MS Exchange Routing	ns	760/tcp	
msexch-routing	691/udp	MS Exchange Routing	ns	760/udp	
hyperwave-isp	692/tcp	Hyperwave-ISP	rxe	761/tcp	
hyperwave-isp	692/udp	Hyperwave-ISP	rxe	761/udp	
connendp	693/tcp	connendp	quotad	762/tcp	
connendp	693/udp	connendp	quotad	762/udp	
ha-cluster	694/tcp	ha-cluster	cycleserv	763/tcp	
ha-cluster	694/udp	ha-cluster	cycleserv	763/udp	
ieee-mms-ssl	695/tcp	IEEE-MMS-SSL	omserv	764/tcp	
ieee-mms-ssl	695/udp	IEEE-MMS-SSL	omserv	764/udp	
rushd	696/tcp	RUSHD	webster	765/tcp	
rushd	696/udp	RUSHD	webster	765/udp	
uuidgen	697/tcp	UUIDGEN	#	766	Unassigned
uuidgen	697/udp	UUIDGEN	phonebook	767/tcp	phone
olsr	698/tcp	OLSR	phonebook	767/udp	phone
olsr	698/udp	OLSR	#	768	Unassigned
accessnetwork	699/tcp	Access Network	vid	769/tcp	
accessnetwork	699/udp	Access Network	vid	769/udp	
#	700-703	Unassigned	cadlock	770/tcp	
elcsd	704/tcp	errlog copy/server daemon	cadlock	770/udp	
elcsd	704/udp	errlog copy/server daemon	rtip	771/tcp	
agentx	705/tcp	AgentX	rtip	771/udp	
agentx	705/udp	AgentX	cycleserv2	772/tcp	
silc	706/tcp	SILC	cycleserv2	772/udp	
silc	706/udp	SILC	submit	773/tcp	
borland-dsj	707/tcp	Borland DSJ	notify	773/udp	
borland-dsj	707/udp	Borland DSJ	rpasswd	774/tcp	
#	708	Unassigned	acmaint_dbd	774/udp	
entrust-kmsh	709/tcp	Entrust Key Management Service Handler	entomb	775/tcp	
			acmaint_transd	775/udp	
entrust-kmsh	709/udp	Entrust Key Management Service Handler	wpages	776/tcp	
			wpages	776/udp	
entrust-ash	710/tcp	Entrust Administration Service Handler	multiling-http	777/tcp	Multiling HTTP
			multiling-http	777/udp	Multiling HTTP

Keyword	Decimal	Description	Keyword	Decimal	Description
#	778-779	Unassigned	#	904-910	Unassigned
wpgs	780/tcp		xact-backup	911/tcp	xact-backup
wpgs	780/udp		xact-backup	911/udp	xact-backup
#	781-785	Unassigned	#	912-988	Unassigned
concert	786/tcp	Concert	ftps-data	989/tcp	ftp protocol, data, over TLS/SSL
concert	786/udp	Concert	ftps-data	989/udp	ftp protocol, data, over TLS/SSL
qsc	787/tcp	QSC	ftps	990/tcp	ftp protocol, control, over TLS/SSL
qsc	787/udp	QSC	ftps	990/udp	ftp protocol, control, over TLS/SSL
#	788-799	Unassigned			
mdbs_daemon	800/tcp		nas	991/tcp	Netnews Administration System
mdbs_daemon	800/udp				
device	801/tcp		nas	991/udp	Netnews Administration System
device	801/udp				
#	802-809	Unassigned	telnets	992/tcp	telnet protocol over TLS/SSL
fcp-udp	810/tcp	FCP	telnets	992/udp	telnet protocol over TLS/SSL
fcp-udp	810/udp	FCP Datagram	imaps	993/tcp	imap4 protocol over TLS/SSL
#	811-827	Unassigned	imaps	993/udp	imap4 protocol over TLS/SSL
itm-mcell-s	828/tcp	itm-mcell-s	ircs	994/tcp	irc protocol over TLS/SSL
itm-mcell-s	828/udp	itm-mcell-s	ircs	994/udp	irc protocol over TLS/SSL
pkix-3-ca-ra	829/tcp	PKIX-3 CA/RA	pop3s	995/tcp	pop3 protocol over TLS/SSL (was spop3)
pkix-3-ca-ra	829/udp	PKIX-3 CA/RA			
#	830-846	Unassigned	pop3s	995/udp	pop3 protocol over TLS/SSL (was spop3)
dhcp-failover2	847/tcp	dhcp-failover 2			
dhcp-failover2	847/udp	dhcp-failover 2	vsinet	996/tcp	vsinet
#	848-872	Unassigned	vsinet	996/udp	vsinet
rsync	873/tcp	rsync	maitrd	997/tcp	
rsync	873/udp	rsync	maitrd	997/udp	
#	874-885	Unassigned	busboy	998/tcp	
iclcnet-locate	886/tcp	ICL coNETion locate server	puparp	998/udp	
iclcnet-locate	886/udp	ICL coNETion locate server	garcon	999/tcp	
iclcnet_svinfo	887/tcp	ICL coNETion server info	applix	999/udp	Applix ac
iclcnet_svinfo	887/udp	ICL coNETion server info	puprouter	999/tcp	
accessbuilder	888/tcp	AccessBuilder	puprouter	999/udp	
accessbuilder	888/udp	AccessBuilder	cadlock2	1000/tcp	
		The following entry records an unassigned but widespread use	cadlock2	1000/udp	
			#	1001-1009	Unassigned
cddbp	888/tcp	CD Database Protocol	#	1008/udp	Possibly used by Sun Solaris
#	889-899	Unassigned	surf	1010/tcp	surf
omginitialrefs	900/tcp	OMG Initial Refs	surf	1010/udp	surf
omginitialrefs	900/udp	OMG Initial Refs	#	1011-1022	Reserved
smpnameres	901/tcp	SMPNAMERES		1023/tcp	Reserved
smpnameres	901/udp	SMPNAMERES		1023/udp	Reserved
ideafarm-chat	902/tcp	IDEAFARM-CHAT			
ideafarm-chat	902/udp	IDEAFARM-CHAT			
ideafarm-catch	903/tcp	IDEAFARM-CATCH			
ideafarm-catch	903/udp	IDEAFARM-CATCH			

G.3.2   Registered Port Numbers

The Registered Ports are listed by the IANA and on most systems can be used by ordinary user processes or programs.

Ports are used in the TCP [RFC793] to name the ends of logical connections that carry long term conversations. For the purpose of providing services to un-known callers, a service contact port is defined. This list specifies the port used by the server process as its contact port.

The IANA registers uses of these ports as a convienence to the community.

To the extent possible, these same port assignments are used with the UDP [RFC 768].

The Registered Ports are in the range 1024-49151.

Keyword	Decimal	Description	Keyword	Decimal	Description
	1024/tcp	Reserved	emanagecstp	1078/tcp	eManageCstp
	1024/udp	Reserved	emanagecstp	1078/udp	eManageCstp
blackjack	1025/tcp	network blackjack	asprovatalk	1079/tcp	ASPROVATalk
blackjack	1025/udp	network blackjack	asprovatalk	1079/udp	ASPROVATalk
#	1026-1029	Unassigned	socks	1080/tcp	Socks
iad1	1030/tcp	BBN IAD	socks	1080/udp	Socks
iad1	1030/udp	BBN IAD	pvuniwien	1081/tcp	PVUNIWIEN
iad2	1031/tcp	BBN IAD	pvuniwien	1081/udp	PVUNIWIEN
iad2	1031/udp	BBN IAD	amt-esd-prot	1082/tcp	AMT-ESD-PROT
iad3	1032/tcp	BBN IAD	amt-esd-prot	1082/udp	AMT-ESD-PROT
iad3	1032/udp	BBN IAD	ansoft-lm-1	1083/tcp	Anasoft License Manager
#	1033-1046	Unassigned	ansoft-lm-1	1083/udp	Anasoft License Manager
neod1	1047/tcp	Sun's NEO Object Request Broker	ansoft-lm-2	1084/tcp	Anasoft License Manager
			ansoft-lm-2	1084/udp	Anasoft License Manager
neod1	1047/udp	Sun's NEO Object Request Broker	webobjects	1085/tcp	Web Objects
			webobjects	1085/udp	Web Objects
neod2	1048/tcp	Sun's NEO Object Request Broker	cplscrambler-lg	1086/tcp	CPL Scrambler Logging
			cplscrambler-lg	1086/udp	CPL Scrambler Logging
neod2	1048/udp	Sun's NEO Object Request Broker	cplscrambler-in	1087/tcp	CPL Scrambler Internal
			cplscrambler-in	1087/udp	CPL Scrambler Internal
d-postman	1049/tcp	Tobit David Postman VPMN	cplscrambler-al	1088/tcp	CPL Scrambler Alarm Log
td-postman	1049/udp	Tobit David Postman VPMN	cplscrambler-al	1088/udp	CPL Scrambler Alarm Log
cma	1050/tcp	CORBA Management Agent	ff-annunc	1089/tcp	FF Annunciation
cma	1050/udp	CORBA Management Agent	ff-annunc	1089/udp	FF Annunciation
optima-vnet	1051/tcp	Optima VNET	ff-fms	1090/tcp	FF Fieldbus Message Specification
optima-vnet	1051/udp	Optima VNET			
ddt	1052/tcp	Dynamic DNS Tools	ff-fms	1090/udp	FF Fieldbus Message Specification
ddt	1052/udp	Dynamic DNS Tools			
remote-as	1053/tcp	Remote Assistant (RA)	ff-sm	1091/tcp	FF System Management
remote-as	1053/udp	Remote Assistant (RA)	ff-sm	1091/udp	FF System Management
brvread	1054/tcp	BRVREAD	obrpd	1092/tcp	OBRPD
brvread	1054/udp	BRVREAD	obrpd	1092/udp	OBRPD
ansyslmd	1055/tcp	ANSYS - License Manager	proofd	1093/tcp	PROOFD
ansyslmd	1055/udp	ANSYS - License Manager	proofd	1093/udp	PROOFD
vfo	1056/tcp	VFO	rootd	1094/tcp	ROOTD
vfo	1056/udp	VFO	rootd	1094/udp	ROOTD
startron	1057/tcp	STARTRON	nicelink	1095/tcp	NICELink
startron	1057/udp	STARTRON	nicelink	1095/udp	NICELink
nim	1058/tcp	nim	cnrprotocol	1096/tcp	Common Name Resolution Protocol
nim	1058/udp	nim			
nimreg	1059/tcp	nimreg	cnrprotocol	1096/udp	Common Name Resolution Protocol
nimreg	1059/udp	nimreg			
polestar	1060/tcp	POLESTAR	sunclustermgr	1097/tcp	Sun Cluster Manager
polestar	1060/udp	POLESTAR	sunclustermgr	1097/udp	Sun Cluster Manager
kiosk	1061/tcp	KIOSK	rmiactivation	1098/tcp	RMI Activation
kiosk	1061/udp	KIOSK	rmiactivation	1098/udp	RMI Activation
veracity	1062/tcp	Veracity	rmiregistry	1099/tcp	RMI Registry
veracity	1062/udp	Veracity	rmiregistry	1099/udp	RMI Registry
kyoceranetdev	1063/tcp	KyoceraNetDev	mctp	1100/tcp	MCTP
kyoceranetdev	1063/udp	KyoceraNetDev	mctp	1100/udp	MCTP
jstel	1064/tcp	JSTEL	pt2-discover	1101/tcp	PT2-DISCOVER
jstel	1064/udp	JSTEL	pt2-discover	1101/udp	PT2-DISCOVER
syscomlan	1065/tcp	SYSCOMLAN	adobeserver-1	1102/tcp	ADOBE SERVER 1
syscomlan	1065/udp	SYSCOMLAN	adobeserver-1	1102/udp	ADOBE SERVER 1
fpo-fns	1066/tcp	FPO-FNS	adobeserver-2	1103/tcp	ADOBE SERVER 2
fpo-fns	1066/udp	FPO-FNS	adobeserver-2	1103/udp	ADOBE SERVER 2
instl_boots	1067/tcp	Installation Bootstrap Proto. Server	xrl	1104/tcp	XRL
			xrl	1104/udp	XRL
instl_boots	1067/udp	Installation Bootstrap Proto. Server	ftranhc	1105/tcp	FTRANHC
			ftranhc	1105/udp	FTRANHC
instl_bootc	1068/tcp	Installation Bootstrap Proto. Client	isoipsigport-1	1106/tcp	ISOIPSIGPORT-1
			isoipsigport-1	1106/udp	ISOIPSIGPORT-1
instl_bootc	1068/udp	Installation Bootstrap Proto. Client	isoipsigport-2	1107/tcp	ISOIPSIGPORT-2
			isoipsigport-2	1107/udp	ISOIPSIGPORT-2
cognex-insight	1069/tcp	COGNEX-INSIGHT	ratio-adp	1108/tcp	ratio-adp
cognex-insight	1069/udp	COGNEX-INSIGHT	ratio-adp	1108/udp	ratio-adp
gmrupdateserv	1070/tcp	GMRUpdateSERV	#	1109	Unassigned
gmrupdateserv	1070/udp	GMRUpdateSERV	nfsd-status	1110/tcp	Cluster status info
bsquare-voip	1071/tcp	BSQUARE-VOIP	nfsd-keepalive	1110/udp	Client status info
bsquare-voip	1071/udp	BSQUARE-VOIP	lmsocialserver	1111/tcp	LM Social Server
cardax	1072/tcp	CARDAX	lmsocialserver	1111/udp	LM Social Server
cardax	1072/udp	CARDAX	icp	1112/tcp	Intelligent Communication Protocol
bridgecontrol	1073/tcp	BridgeControl			
bridgecontrol	1073/udp	BridgeControl	icp	1112/udp	Intelligent Communication Protocol
fastechnologlm	1074/tcp	FASTechnologies License Manager			
			#	1113	Unassigned
fastechnologlm	1074/udp	FASTechnologies License Manager	mini-sql	1114/tcp	Mini SQL
			mini-sql	1114/udp	Mini SQL
rdrmshc	1075/tcp	RDRMSHC	ardus-trns	1115/tcp	ARDUS Transfer
rdrmshc	1075/udp	RDRMSHC	ardus-trns	1115/udp	ARDUS Transfer
dab-sti-c	1076/tcp	DAB STI-C	ardus-cntl	1116/tcp	ARDUS Control
dab-sti-c	1076/udp	DAB STI-C	ardus-cntl	1116/udp	ARDUS Control
imgames	1077/tcp	IMGames	ardus-mtrns	1117/tcp	ARDUS Multicast Transfer
imgames	1077/udp	IMGames	ardus-mtrns	1117/udp	ARDUS Multicast Transfer

Keyword	Decimal	Description	Keyword	Decimal	Description
#	1118-1122	Unassigned	menandmice-lpm	1231/udp	menandmice-lpm
murray	1123/tcp	Murray	mtrgtrans	1232/tcp	mtrgtrans
murray	1123/udp	Murray	mtrgtrans	1232/udp	mtrgtrans
#	1124-1154	Unassigned	univ-appserver	1233/tcp	Universal App Server
nfa	1155/tcp	Network File Access	univ-appserver	1233/udp	Universal App Server
nfa	1155/udp	Network File Access	search-agent	1234/tcp	Infoseek Search Agent
#	1156-1160	Unassigned	search-agent	1234/udp	Infoseek Search Agent
health-polling	1161/tcp	Health Polling	mosaicsyssvc1	1235/tcp	mosaicsyssvc1
health-polling	1161/udp	Health Polling	mosaicsyssvc1	1235/udp	mosaicsyssvc1
health-trap	1162/tcp	Health Trap	bvcontrol	1236/tcp	bvcontrol
health-trap	1162/udp	Health Trap	bvcontrol	1236/udp	bvcontrol
#	1163-1168	Unassigned	tsdos390	1237/tcp	tsdos390
tripwire	1169/tcp	TRIPWIRE	tsdos390	1237/udp	tsdos390
tripwire	1169/udp	TRIPWIRE	hacl-qs	1238/tcp	hacl-qs
#	1170-1179	Unassigned	hacl-qs	1238/udp	hacl-qs
mc-client	1180/tcp	Millicent Client Proxy	nmsd	1239/tcp	NMSD
mc-client	1180/udp	Millicent Client Proxy	nmsd	1239/udp	NMSD
#	1181-1187	Unassigned	instantia	1240/tcp	Instantia
hp-webadmin	1188/tcp	HP Web Admin	instantia	1240/udp	Instantia
hp-webadmin	1188/udp	HP Web Admin	nessus	1241/tcp	nessus
#	1189-1199	Unassigned	nessus	1241/udp	nessus
scol	1200/tcp	SCOL	nmasoverip	1242/tcp	NMAS over IP
scol	1200/udp	SCOL	nmasoverip	1242/udp	NMAS over IP
nucleus-sand	1201/tcp	Nucleus Sand	serialgateway	1243/tcp	SerialGateway
nucleus-sand	1201/udp	Nucleus Sand	serialgateway	1243/udp	SerialGateway
caiccipc	1202/tcp	caiccipc	isbconference1	1244/tcp	isbconference1
caiccipc	1202/udp	caiccipc	isbconference1	1244/udp	isbconference1
ssslic-mgr	1203/tcp	License Validation	isbconference2	1245/tcp	isbconference2
ssslic-mgr	1203/udp	License Validation	isbconference2	1245/udp	isbconference2
ssslog-mgr	1204/tcp	Log Request Listener	payrouter	1246/tcp	payrouter
ssslog-mgr	1204/udp	Log Request Listener	payrouter	1246/udp	payrouter
accord-mgc	1205/tcp	Accord-MGC	visionpyramid	1247/tcp	VisionPyramid
accord-mgc	1205/udp	Accord-MGC	visionpyramid	1247/udp	VisionPyramid
anthony-data	1206/tcp	Anthony Data	hermes	1248/tcp	hermes
anthony-data	1206/udp	Anthony Data	hermes	1248/udp	hermes
metasage	1207/tcp	MetaSage	mesavistaco	1249/tcp	Mesa Vista Co
metasage	1207/udp	MetaSage	mesavistaco	1249/udp	Mesa Vista Co
seagull-ais	1208/tcp	SEAGULL AIS	swldy-sias	1250/tcp	swldy-sias
seagull-ais	1208/udp	SEAGULL AIS	swldy-sias	1250/udp	swldy-sias
ipcd3	1209/tcp	IPCD3	servergraph	1251/tcp	servergraph
ipcd3	1209/udp	IPCD3	servergraph	1251/udp	servergraph
eoss	1210/tcp	EOSS	bspne-pcc	1252/tcp	bspne-pcc
eoss	1210/udp	EOSS	bspne-pcc	1252/udp	bspne-pcc
groove-dpp	1211/tcp	Groove DPP	q55-pcc	1253/tcp	q55-pcc
groove-dpp	1211/udp	Groove DPP	q55-pcc	1253/udp	q55-pcc
lupa	1212/tcp	lupa	de-noc	1254/tcp	de-noc
lupa	1212/udp	lupa	de-noc	1254/udp	de-noc
mpc-lifenet	1213/tcp	MPC LIFENET	de-cache-query	1255/tcp	de-cache-query
mpc-lifenet	1213/udp	MPC LIFENET	de-cache-query	1255/udp	de-cache-query
kazaa	1214/tcp	KAZAA	de-server	1256/tcp	de-server
kazaa	1214/udp	KAZAA	de-server	1256/udp	de-server
scanstat-1	1215/tcp	scanSTAT 1.0	shockwave2	1257/tcp	Shockwave 2
scanstat-1	1215/udp	scanSTAT 1.0	shockwave2	1257/udp	Shockwave 2
etebac5	1216/tcp	ETEBAC 5	opennl	1258/tcp	Open Network Library
etebac5	1216/udp	ETEBAC 5	opennl	1258/udp	Open Network Library
hpss-ndapi	1217/tcp	HPSS-NDAPI	opennl-voice	1259/tcp	Open Network Library Voice
hpss-ndapi	1217/udp	HPSS-NDAPI	opennl-voice	1259/udp	Open Network Library Voice
aeroflight-ads	1218/tcp	AeroFlight-ADs	ibm-ssd	1260/tcp	ibm-ssd
aeroflight-ads	1218/udp	AeroFlight-ADs	ibm-ssd	1260/udp	ibm-ssd
aeroflight-ret	1219/tcp	AeroFlight-Ret	mpshrsv	1261/tcp	mpshrsv
aeroflight-ret	1219/udp	AeroFlight-Ret	mpshrsv	1261/udp	mpshrsv
qt-serveradmin	1220/tcp	QT SERVER ADMIN	qnts-orb	1262/tcp	QNTS-ORB
qt-serveradmin	1220/udp	QT SERVER ADMIN	qnts-orb	1262/udp	QNTS-ORB
sweetware-apps	1221/tcp	SweetWARE Apps	dka	1263/tcp	dka
sweetware-apps	1221/udp	SweetWARE Apps	dka	1263/udp	dka
nerv	1222/tcp	SNI R&D network	prat	1264/tcp	PRAT
nerv	1222/udp	SNI R&D network	prat	1264/udp	PRAT
tgp	1223/tcp	TGP	dssiapi	1265/tcp	DSSIAPI
tgp	1223/udp	TGP	dssiapi	1265/udp	DSSIAPI
vpnz	1224/tcp	VPNz	dellpwrappks	1266/tcp	DELLPWRAPPKS
vpnz	1224/udp	VPNz	dellpwrappks	1266/udp	DELLPWRAPPKS
slinkysearch	1225/tcp	SLINKYSEARCH	pcmlinux	1267/tcp	pcmlinux
slinkysearch	1225/udp	SLINKYSEARCH	pcmlinux	1267/udp	pcmlinux
stgxfws	1226/tcp	STGXFWS	propel-msgsys	1268/tcp	PROPEL-MSGSYS
stgxfws	1226/udp	STGXFWS	propel-msgsys	1268/udp	PROPEL-MSGSYS
dns2go	1227/tcp	DNS2Go	watilapp	1269/tcp	WATiLaPP
dns2go	1227/udp	DNS2Go	watilapp	1269/udp	WATiLaPP
florence	1228/tcp	FLORENCE	opsman	1270/tcp	opsman
florence	1228/udp	FLORENCE	opsman	1270/udp	opsman
novell-zfs	1229/tcp	Novell ZFS	dabew	1271/tcp	Dabew
novell-zfs	1229/udp	Novell ZFS	dabew	1271/udp	Dabew
periscope	1230/tcp	Periscope	cspmlockmgr	1272/tcp	CSPMLockMgr
periscope	1230/udp	Periscope	cspmlockmgr	1272/udp	CSPMLockMgr
menandmice-lpm	1231/tcp	menandmice-lpm	emc-gateway	1273/tcp	EMC-Gateway

Keyword	Decimal	Description	Keyword	Decimal	Description
emc-gateway	1273/udp	EMC-Gateway	#	1336-1344	Unassigned
t1distproc	1274/tcp	t1distproc	vpjp	1345/tcp	VPJP
t1distproc	1274/udp	t1distproc	vpjp	1345/udp	VPJP
ivcollector	1275/tcp	ivcollector	alta-ana-lm	1346/tcp	Alta Analytics License Manager
ivcollector	1275/udp	ivcollector			
ivmanager	1276/tcp	ivmanager	alta-ana-lm	1346/udp	Alta Analytics License Manager
ivmanager	1276/udp	ivmanager			
miva-mqs	1277/tcp	mqs	bbn-mmc	1347/tcp	multi media conferencing
miva-mqs	1277/udp	mqs	bbn-mmc	1347/udp	multi media conferencing
dellwebadmin-1	1278/tcp	Dell Web Admin 1	bbn-mmx	1348/tcp	multi media conferencing
dellwebadmin-1	1278/udp	Dell Web Admin 1	bbn-mmx	1348/udp	multi media conferencing
dellwebadmin-2	1279/tcp	Dell Web Admin 2	sbook	1349/tcp	Registration Network Protocol
dellwebadmin-2	1279/udp	Dell Web Admin 2			
pictrography	1280/tcp	Pictrography	sbook	1349/udp	Registration Network Protocol
pictrography	1280/udp	Pictrography			
healthd	1281/tcp	healthd	editbench	1350/tcp	Registration Network Protocol
healthd	1281/udp	healthd			
emperion	1282/tcp	Emperion	editbench	1350/udp	Registration Network Protocol
emperion	1282/udp	Emperion			
productinfo	1283/tcp	ProductInfo	equationbuilder	1351/tcp	Digital Tool Works (MIT)
productinfo	1283/udp	ProductInfo	equationbuilder	1351/udp	Digital Tool Works (MIT)
iee-qfx	1284/tcp	IEE-QFX	lotusnote	1352/tcp	Lotus Note
iee-qfx	1284/udp	IEE-QFX	lotusnote	1352/udp	Lotus Note
neoiface	1285/tcp	neoiface	relief	1353/tcp	Relief Consulting
neoiface	1285/udp	neoiface	relief	1353/udp	Relief Consulting
netuitive	1286/tcp	netuitive	rightbrain	1354/tcp	RightBrain Software
netuitive	1286/udp	netuitive	rightbrain	1354/udp	RightBrain Software
#	1287	Unassigned	intuitive-edge	1355/tcp	Intuitive Edge
navbuddy	1288/tcp	NavBuddy	intuitive-edge	1355/udp	Intuitive Edge
navbuddy	1288/udp	NavBuddy	cuillamartin	1356/tcp	CuillaMartin Company
jwalkserver	1289/tcp	JWalkServer	cuillamartin	1356/udp	CuillaMartin Company
jwalkserver	1289/udp	JWalkServer	pegboard	1357/tcp	Electronic PegBoard
winjaserver	1290/tcp	WinJaServer	pegboard	1357/udp	Electronic PegBoard
winjaserver	1290/udp	WinJaServer	connlcli	1358/tcp	CONNLCLI
seagulllms	1291/tcp	SEAGULLLMS	connlcli	1358/udp	CONNLCLI
seagulllms	1291/udp	SEAGULLLMS	ftsrv	1359/tcp	FTSRV
dsdn	1292/tcp	dsdn	ftsrv	1359/udp	FTSRV
dsdn	1292/udp	dsdn	mimer	1360/tcp	MIMER
#	1293	Unassigned	mimer	1360/udp	MIMER
cmmdriver	1294/tcp	CMMdriver	linx	1361/tcp	LinX
cmmdriver	1294/udp	CMMdriver	linx	1361/udp	LinX
eetp	1295/tcp	EETP	timeflies	1362/tcp	TimeFlies
eetp	1295/udp	EETP	timeflies	1362/udp	TimeFlies
dproxy	1296/tcp	dproxy	ndm-requester	1363/tcp	Network DataMover Requester
dproxy	1296/udp	dproxy			
sdproxy	1297/tcp	sdproxy	ndm-requester	1363/udp	Network DataMover Requester
sdproxy	1297/udp	sdproxy			
lpcp	1298/tcp	lpcp	ndm-server	1364/tcp	Network DataMover Server
lpcp	1298/udp	lpcp	ndm-server	1364/udp	Network DataMover Server
hp-sci	1299/tcp	hp-sci	adapt-sna	1365/tcp	Network Software Associates
hp-sci	1299/udp	hp-sci	adapt-sna	1365/udp	Network Software Associates
h323hostcallsc	1300/tcp	H323 Host Call Secure	netware-csp	1366/tcp	Novell NetWare Comm Service Platform
h323hostcallsc	1300/udp	H323 Host Call Secure			
ci3-software-1	1301/tcp	CI3-Software-1	netware-csp	1366/udp	Novell NetWare Comm Service Platform
ci3-software-1	1301/udp	CI3-Software-1			
ci3-software-2	1302/tcp	CI3-Software-2	dcs	1367/tcp	DCS
ci3-software-2	1302/udp	CI3-Software-2	dcs	1367/udp	DCS
sftsrv	1303/tcp	sftsrv	screencast	1368/tcp	ScreenCast
sftsrv	1303/udp	sftsrv	screencast	1368/udp	ScreenCast
#	1304-1309	Unassigned	gv-us	1369/tcp	GlobalView to Unix Shell
husky	1310/tcp	Husky	gv-us	1369/udp	GlobalView to Unix Shell
husky	1310/udp	Husky	us-gv	1370/tcp	Unix Shell to GlobalView
rxmon	1311/tcp	RxMon	us-gv	1370/udp	Unix Shell to GlobalView
rxmon	1311/udp	RxMon	fc-cli	1371/tcp	Fujitsu Config Protocol
sti-envision	1312/tcp	STI Envision	fc-cli	1371/udp	Fujitsu Config Protocol
sti-envision	1312/udp	STI Envision	fc-ser	1372/tcp	Fujitsu Config Protocol
bmc_patroldb	1313/tcp	BMC_PATROLDB	fc-ser	1372/udp	Fujitsu Config Protocol
bmc_patroldb	1313/udp	BMC_PATROLDB	chromagrafx	1373/tcp	Chromagrafx
pdps	1314/tcp	Photoscript Distributed Printing System	chromagrafx	1373/udp	Chromagrafx
			molly	1374/tcp	EPI Software Systems
pdps	1314/udp	Photoscript Distributed Printing System	molly	1374/udp	EPI Software Systems
			bytex	1375/tcp	Bytex
els	1315/tcp	els	bytex	1375/udp	Bytex
els	1315/udp	els	ibm-pps	1376/tcp	IBM Person to Person Software
#	1316-1318	Unassigned			
panja-icsp	1319/tcp	Panja-ICSP	ibm-pps	1376/udp	IBM Person to Person Software
panja-icsp	1319/udp	Panja-ICSP			
panja-axbnet	1320/tcp	Panja-AXBNET	cichlid	1377/tcp	Cichlid License Manager
panja-axbnet	1320/udp	Panja-AXBNET	cichlid	1377/udp	Cichlid License Manager
pip	1321/tcp	PIP	elan	1378/tcp	Elan License Manager
pip	1321/udp	PIP	elan	1378/udp	Elan License Manager
#	1322-1334	Unassigned	dbreporter	1379/tcp	Integrity Solutions
digital-notary	1335/tcp	Digital Notary Protocol	dbreporter	1379/udp	Integrity Solutions
digital-notary	1335/udp	Digital Notary Protocol			

911

Keyword	Decimal	Description	Keyword	Decimal	Description
telesis-licman	1380/tcp	Telesis Network License Manager	innosys	1412/tcp	InnoSys
telesis-licman	1380/udp	Telesis Network License Manager	innosys	1412/udp	InnoSys
apple-licman	1381/tcp	Apple Network License Manager	innosys-acl	1413/tcp	Innosys-ACL
apple-licman	1381/udp	Apple Network License Manager	innosys-acl	1413/udp	Innosys-ACL
udt_os	1382/tcp		ibm-mqseries	1414/tcp	IBM MQSeries
udt_os	1382/udp		ibm-mqseries	1414/udp	IBM MQSeries
gwha	1383/tcp	GW Hannaway Network License Manager	dbstar	1415/tcp	DBStar
gwha	1383/udp	GW Hannaway Network License Manager	dbstar	1415/udp	DBStar
os-licman	1384/tcp	Objective Solutions License Manager	novell-lu6.2	1416/tcp	Novell LU6.2
os-licman	1384/udp	Objective Solutions License Manager	novell-lu6.2	1416/udp	Novell LU6.2
atex_elmd	1385/tcp	Atex Publishing License Manager	timbuktu-srv1	1417/tcp	Timbuktu Service 1 Port
atex_elmd	1385/udp	Atex Publishing License Manager	timbuktu-srv1	1417/udp	Timbuktu Service 1 Port
checksum	1386/tcp	CheckSum License Manager	timbuktu-srv2	1418/tcp	Timbuktu Service 2 Port
checksum	1386/udp	CheckSum License Manager	timbuktu-srv2	1418/udp	Timbuktu Service 2 Port
cadsi-lm	1387/tcp	Computer Aided Design Software Inc LM	timbuktu-srv3	1419/tcp	Timbuktu Service 3 Port
cadsi-lm	1387/udp	Computer Aided Design Software Inc LM	timbuktu-srv3	1419/udp	Timbuktu Service 3 Port
			timbuktu-srv4	1420/tcp	Timbuktu Service 4 Port
objective-dbc	1388/tcp	Objective Solutions DataBase Cache	timbuktu-srv4	1420/udp	Timbuktu Service 4 Port
objective-dbc	1388/udp	Objective Solutions DataBase Cache	gandalf-lm	1421/tcp	Gandalf License Manager
			gandalf-lm	1421/udp	Gandalf License Manager
iclpv-dm	1389/tcp	Document Manager	autodesk-lm	1422/tcp	Autodesk License Manager
iclpv-dm	1389/udp	Document Manager	autodesk-lm	1422/udp	Autodesk License Manager
iclpv-sc	1390/tcp	Storage Controller	essbase	1423/tcp	Essbase Arbor Software
iclpv-sc	1390/udp	Storage Controller	essbase	1423/udp	Essbase Arbor Software
iclpv-sas	1391/tcp	Storage Access Server	hybrid	1424/tcp	Hybrid Encryption Protocol
iclpv-sas	1391/udp	Storage Access Server	hybrid	1424/udp	Hybrid Encryption Protocol
iclpv-pm	1392/tcp	Print Manager	zion-lm	1425/tcp	Zion Software License Manager
iclpv-pm	1392/udp	Print Manager			
iclpv-nls	1393/tcp	Network Log Server	zion-lm	1425/udp	Zion Software License Manager
iclpv-nls	1393/udp	Network Log Server			
iclpv-nlc	1394/tcp	Network Log Client	sais	1426/tcp	Satellite-data Acquisition System 1
iclpv-nlc	1394/udp	Network Log Client	sais	1426/udp	Satellite-data Acquisition System 1
iclpv-wsm	1395/tcp	PC Workstation Manager software	mloadd	1427/tcp	mloadd monitoring tool
			mloadd	1427/udp	mloadd monitoring tool
iclpv-wsm	1395/udp	PC Workstation Manager software	informatik-lm	1428/tcp	Informatik License Manager
			informatik-lm	1428/udp	Informatik License Manager
dvl-activemail	1396/tcp	DVL Active Mail	nms	1429/tcp	Hypercom NMS
dvl-activemail	1396/udp	DVL Active Mail	nms	1429/udp	Hypercom NMS
audio-activmail	1397/tcp	Audio Active Mail	tpdu	1430/tcp	Hypercom TPDU
audio-activmail	1397/udp	Audio Active Mail	tpdu	1430/udp	Hypercom TPDU
video-activmail	1398/tcp	Video Active Mail	rgtp	1431/tcp	Reverse Gossip Transport
video-activmail	1398/udp	Video Active Mail	rgtp	1431/udp	Reverse Gossip Transport
cadkey-licman	1399/tcp	Cadkey License Manager	blueberry-lm	1432/tcp	Blueberry Software License Manager
cadkey-licman	1399/udp	Cadkey License Manager			
cadkey-tablet	1400/tcp	Cadkey Tablet Daemon	blueberry-lm	1432/udp	Blueberry Software License Manager
cadkey-tablet	1400/udp	Cadkey Tablet Daemon			
goldleaf-licman	1401/tcp	Goldleaf License Manager	ms-sql-s	1433/tcp	Microsoft-SQL-Server
goldleaf-licman	1401/udp	Goldleaf License Manager	ms-sql-s	1433/udp	Microsoft-SQL-Server
prm-sm-np	1402/tcp	Prospero Resource Manager	ms-sql-m	1434/tcp	Microsoft-SQL-Monitor
prm-sm-np	1402/udp	Prospero Resource Manager	ms-sql-m	1434/udp	Microsoft-SQL-Monitor
prm-nm-np	1403/tcp	Prospero Resource Manager	ibm-cics	1435/tcp	IBM CICS
prm-nm-np	1403/udp	Prospero Resource Manager	ibm-cics	1435/udp	IBM CICS
igi-lm	1404/tcp	Infinite Graphics License Manager	saism	1436/tcp	Satellite-data Acquisition System 2
igi-lm	1404/udp	Infinite Graphics License Manager	saism	1436/udp	Satellite-data Acquisition System 2
ibm-res	1405/tcp	IBM Remote Execution Starter	tabula	1437/tcp	Tabula
			tabula	1437/udp	Tabula
ibm-res	1405/udp	IBM Remote Execution Starter	eicon-server	1438/tcp	Eicon Security Agent/Server
			eicon-server	1438/udp	Eicon Security Agent/Server
netlabs-lm	1406/tcp	NetLabs License Manager	eicon-x25	1439/tcp	Eicon X25/SNA Gateway
netlabs-lm	1406/udp	NetLabs License Manager	eicon-x25	1439/udp	Eicon X25/SNA Gateway
dbsa-lm	1407/tcp	DBSA License Manager	eicon-slp	1440/tcp	Eicon Service Location Protocol
dbsa-lm	1407/udp	DBSA License Manager	eicon-slp	1440/udp	Eicon Service Location Protocol
sophia-lm	1408/tcp	Sophia License Manager			
sophia-lm	1408/udp	Sophia License Manager	cadis-1	1441/tcp	Cadis License Management
here-lm	1409/tcp	Here License Manager	cadis-1	1441/udp	Cadis License Management
here-lm	1409/udp	Here License Manager	cadis-2	1442/tcp	Cadis License Management
hiq	1410/tcp	HiQ License Manager	cadis-2	1442/udp	Cadis License Management
hiq	1410/udp	HiQ License Manager	ies-lm	1443/tcp	Integrated Engineering Software
af	1411/tcp	AudioFile			
af	1411/udp	AudioFile	ies-lm	1443/udp	Integrated Engineering Software
			marcam-lm	1444/tcp	Marcam License Management
			marcam-lm	1444/udp	Marcam License Management
			proxima-lm	1445/tcp	Proxima License Manager
			proxima-lm	1445/udp	Proxima License Manager
			ora-lm	1446/tcp	Optical Research Associates License Manager

Keyword	Decimal	Description	Keyword	Decimal	Description
ora-lm	1446/udp	Optical Research Associates License Manager	airs	1481/udp	AIRS
apri-lm	1447/tcp	Applied Parallel Research LM	miteksys-lm	1482/tcp	Miteksys License Manager
apri-lm	1447/udp	Applied Parallel Research LM	miteksys-lm	1482/udp	Miteksys License Manager
oc-lm	1448/tcp	OpenConnect License Manager	afs	1483/tcp	AFS License Manager
oc-lm	1448/udp	OpenConnect License Manager	afs	1483/udp	AFS License Manager
peport	1449/tcp	PEport	confluent	1484/tcp	Confluent License Manager
peport	1449/udp	PEport	confluent	1484/udp	Confluent License Manager
dwf	1450/tcp	Tandem Distributed Workbench Facility	lansource	1485/tcp	LANSource
dwf	1450/udp	Tandem Distributed Workbench Facility	lansource	1485/udp	LANSource
infoman	1451/tcp	IBM Information Management	nms_topo_serv	1486/tcp	nms_topo_serv
infoman	1451/udp	IBM Information Management	nms_topo_serv	1486/udp	nms_topo_serv
gtegsc-lm	1452/tcp	GTE Government Systems License Man	localinfosrvr	1487/tcp	LocalInfoSrvr
gtegsc-lm	1452/udp	GTE Government Systems License Man	localinfosrvr	1487/udp	LocalInfoSrvr
genie-lm	1453/tcp	Genie License Manager	docstor	1488/tcp	DocStor
genie-lm	1453/udp	Genie License Manager	docstor	1488/udp	DocStor
interhdl_elmd	1454/tcp	interHDL License Manager	dmdocbroker	1489/tcp	dmdocbroker
interhdl_elmd	1454/udp	interHDL License Manager	dmdocbroker	1489/udp	dmdocbroker
esl-lm	1455/tcp	ESL License Manager	insitu-conf	1490/tcp	insitu-conf
esl-lm	1455/udp	ESL License Manager	insitu-conf	1490/udp	insitu-conf
dca	1456/tcp	DCA	anynetgateway	1491/tcp	anynetgateway
dca	1456/udp	DCA	anynetgateway	1491/udp	anynetgateway
valisys-lm	1457/tcp	Valisys License Manager	stone-design-1	1492/tcp	stone-design-1
valisys-lm	1457/udp	Valisys License Manager	stone-design-1	1492/udp	stone-design-1
nrcabq-lm	1458/tcp	Nichols Research Corp.	netmap_lm	1493/tcp	netmap_lm
nrcabq-lm	1458/udp	Nichols Research Corp.	netmap_lm	1493/udp	netmap_lm
proshare1	1459/tcp	Proshare Notebook Application	ica	1494/tcp	ica
proshare1	1459/udp	Proshare Notebook Application	ica	1494/udp	ica
proshare2	1460/tcp	Proshare Notebook Application	cvc	1495/tcp	cvc
proshare2	1460/udp	Proshare Notebook Application	cvc	1495/udp	cvc
ibm_wrless_lan	1461/tcp	IBM Wireless LAN	liberty-lm	1496/tcp	liberty-lm
ibm_wrless_lan	1461/udp	IBM Wireless LAN	liberty-lm	1496/udp	liberty-lm
world-lm	1462/tcp	World License Manager	rfx-lm	1497/tcp	rfx-lm
world-lm	1462/udp	World License Manager	rfx-lm	1497/udp	rfx-lm
nucleus	1463/tcp	Nucleus	sybase-sqlany	1498/tcp	Sybase SQL Any
nucleus	1463/udp	Nucleus	sybase-sqlany	1498/udp	Sybase SQL Any
msl_lmd	1464/tcp	MSL License Manager	fhc	1499/tcp	Federico Heinz Consultora
msl_lmd	1464/udp	MSL License Manager	fhc	1499/udp	Federico Heinz Consultora
pipes	1465/tcp	Pipes Platform	vlsi-lm	1500/tcp	VLSI License Manager
oceansoft-lm	1466/tcp	Ocean Software License Manager	vlsi-lm	1500/udp	VLSI License Manager
oceansoft-lm	1466/udp	Ocean Software License Manager	saiscm	1501/tcp	Satellite-data Acquisition System 3
csdmbase	1467/tcp	CSDMBASE	saiscm	1501/udp	Satellite-data Acquisition System 3
csdmbase	1467/udp	CSDMBASE			
csdm	1468/tcp	CSDM	shivadiscovery	1502/tcp	Shiva
csdm	1468/udp	CSDM	shivadiscovery	1502/udp	Shiva
aal-lm	1469/tcp	Active Analysis Limited License Manager	imtc-mcs	1503/tcp	Databeam
aal-lm	1469/udp	Active Analysis Limited License Manager	imtc-mcs	1503/udp	Databeam
uaiact	1470/tcp	Universal Analytics	evb-elm	1504/tcp	EVB Software Engineering License Manager
uaiact	1470/udp	Universal Analytics	evb-elm	1504/udp	EVB Software Engineering License Manager
csdmbase	1471/tcp	csdmbase	funkproxy	1505/tcp	Funk Software, Inc.
csdmbase	1471/udp	csdmbase	funkproxy	1505/udp	Funk Software, Inc.
csdm	1472/tcp	csdm	utcd	1506/tcp	Universal Time daemon (utcd)
csdm	1472/udp	csdm	utcd	1506/udp	Universal Time daemon (utcd)
openmath	1473/tcp	OpenMath	symplex	1507/tcp	symplex
openmath	1473/udp	OpenMath	symplex	1507/udp	symplex
telefinder	1474/tcp	Telefinder	diagmond	1508/tcp	diagmond
telefinder	1474/udp	Telefinder	diagmond	1508/udp	diagmond
taligent-lm	1475/tcp	Taligent License Manager	robcad-lm	1509/tcp	Robcad, Ltd. License Manager
taligent-lm	1475/udp	Taligent License Manager	robcad-lm	1509/udp	Robcad, Ltd. License Manager
clvm-cfg	1476/tcp	clvm-cfg	mvx-lm	1510/tcp	Midland Valley Exploration Ltd. Lic. Man.
clvm-cfg	1476/udp	clvm-cfg	mvx-lm	1510/udp	Midland Valley Exploration Ltd. Lic. Man.
ms-sna-server	1477/tcp	ms-sna-server	3l-l1	1511/tcp	3l-l1
ms-sna-server	1477/udp	ms-sna-server	3l-l1	1511/udp	3l-l1
ms-sna-base	1478/tcp	ms-sna-base	wins	1512/tcp	Microsoft's Windows Internet Name Service
ms-sna-base	1478/udp	ms-sna-base	wins	1512/udp	Microsoft's Windows Internet Name Service
dberegister	1479/tcp	dberegister	fujitsu-dtc	1513/tcp	Fujitsu Systems Business of America, Inc
dberegister	1479/udp	dberegister	fujitsu-dtc	1513/udp	Fujitsu Systems Business of America, Inc
pacerforum	1480/tcp	PacerForum	fujitsu-dtcns	1514/tcp	Fujitsu Systems Business of America, Inc
pacerforum	1480/udp	PacerForum	fujitsu-dtcns	1514/udp	Fujitsu Systems Business of America, Inc
airs	1481/tcp	AIRS	ifor-protocol	1515/tcp	ifor-protocol
			ifor-protocol	1515/udp	ifor-protocol
			vpad	1516/tcp	Virtual Places Audio data

Keyword	Decimal	Description
vpad	1516/udp	Virtual Places Audio data
vpac	1517/tcp	Virtual Places Audio control
vpac	1517/udp	Virtual Places Audio control
vpvd	1518/tcp	Virtual Places Video data
vpvd	1518/udp	Virtual Places Video data
vpvc	1519/tcp	Virtual Places Video control
vpvc	1519/udp	Virtual Places Video control
atm-zip-office	1520/tcp	atm zip office
atm-zip-office	1520/udp	atm zip office
ncube-lm	1521/tcp	nCube License Manager
ncube-lm	1521/udp	nCube License Manager
ricardo-lm	1522/tcp	Ricardo North America License Manager
ricardo-lm	1522/udp	Ricardo North America License Manager
cichild-lm	1523/tcp	cichild
cichild-lm	1523/udp	cichild
ingreslock	1524/tcp	ingres
ingreslock	1524/udp	ingres
orasrv	1525/tcp	oracle
orasrv	1525/udp	oracle
prospero-np	1525/tcp	Prospero Directory Service non-priv
prospero-np	1525/udp	Prospero Directory Service non-priv
pdap-np	1526/tcp	Prospero Data Access Prot non-priv
pdap-np	1526/udp	Prospero Data Access Prot non-priv
tlisrv	1527/tcp	oracle
tlisrv	1527/udp	oracle
mciautoreg	1528/tcp	micautoreg
mciautoreg	1528/udp	micautoreg
coauthor	1529/tcp	oracle
coauthor	1529/udp	oracle
rap-service	1530/tcp	rap-service
rap-service	1530/udp	rap-service
rap-listen	1531/tcp	rap-listen
rap-listen	1531/udp	rap-listen
miroconnect	1532/tcp	miroconnect
miroconnect	1532/udp	miroconnect
virtual-places	1533/tcp	Virtual Places Software
virtual-places	1533/udp	Virtual Places Software
micromuse-lm	1534/tcp	micromuse-lm
micromuse-lm	1534/udp	micromuse-lm
ampr-info	1535/tcp	ampr-info
ampr-info	1535/udp	ampr-info
ampr-inter	1536/tcp	ampr-inter
ampr-inter	1536/udp	ampr-inter
sdsc-lm	1537/tcp	isi-lm
sdsc-lm	1537/udp	isi-lm
3ds-lm	1538/tcp	3ds-lm
3ds-lm	1538/udp	3ds-lm
intellistor-lm	1539/tcp	Intellistor License Manager
intellistor-lm	1539/udp	Intellistor License Manager
rds	1540/tcp	rds
rds	1540/udp	rds
rds2	1541/tcp	rds2
rds2	1541/udp	rds2
gridgen-elmd	1542/tcp	gridgen-elmd
gridgen-elmd	1542/udp	gridgen-elmd
simba-cs	1543/tcp	simba-cs
simba-cs	1543/udp	simba-cs
aspeclmd	1544/tcp	aspeclmd
aspeclmd	1544/udp	aspeclmd
vistium-share	1545/tcp	vistium-share
vistium-share	1545/udp	vistium-share
abbaccuray	1546/tcp	abbaccuray
abbaccuray	1546/udp	abbaccuray
laplink	1547/tcp	laplink
laplink	1547/udp	laplink
axon-lm	1548/tcp	Axon License Manager
axon-lm	1548/udp	Axon License Manager
shivahose	1549/tcp	Shiva Hose
shivasound	1549/udp	Shiva Sound
3m-image-lm	1550/tcp	Image Storage license manager 3M Company
3m-image-lm	1550/udp	Image Storage license manager 3M Company
hecmtl-db	1551/tcp	HECMTL-DB
hecmtl-db	1551/udp	HECMTL-DB
pciarray	1552/tcp	pciarray
pciarray	1552/udp	pciarray
sna-cs	1553/tcp	sna-cs

Keyword	Decimal	Description
sna-cs	1553/udp	sna-cs
caci-lm	1554/tcp	CACI Products Company License Manager
caci-lm	1554/udp	CACI Products Company License Manager
livelan	1555/tcp	livelan
livelan	1555/udp	livelan
ashwin	1556/tcp	AshWin CI Tecnologies
ashwin	1556/udp	AshWin CI Tecnologies
arbortext-lm	1557/tcp	ArborText License Manager
arbortext-lm	1557/udp	ArborText License Manager
xingmpeg	1558/tcp	xingmpeg
xingmpeg	1558/udp	xingmpeg
web2host	1559/tcp	web2host
web2host	1559/udp	web2host
asci-val	1560/tcp	asci-val
asci-val	1560/udp	asci-val
facilityview	1561/tcp	facilityview
facilityview	1561/udp	facilityview
pconnectmgr	1562/tcp	pconnectmgr
pconnectmgr	1562/udp	pconnectmgr
cadabra-lm	1563/tcp	Cadabra License Manager
cadabra-lm	1563/udp	Cadabra License Manager
pay-per-view	1564/tcp	Pay-Per-View
pay-per-view	1564/udp	Pay-Per-View
winddlb	1565/tcp	WinDD
winddlb	1565/udp	WinDD
corelvideo	1566/tcp	CORELVIDEO
corelvideo	1566/udp	CORELVIDEO
jlicelmd	1567/tcp	jlicelmd
jlicelmd	1567/udp	jlicelmd
tsspmap	1568/tcp	tsspmap
tsspmap	1568/udp	tsspmap
ets	1569/tcp	ets
ets	1569/udp	ets
orbixd	1570/tcp	orbixd
orbixd	1570/udp	orbixd
rdb-dbs-disp	1571/tcp	Oracle Remote Data Base
rdb-dbs-disp	1571/udp	Oracle Remote Data Base
chip-lm	1572/tcp	Chipcom License Manager
chip-lm	1572/udp	Chipcom License Manager
itscomm-ns	1573/tcp	itscomm-ns
itscomm-ns	1573/udp	itscomm-ns
mvel-lm	1574/tcp	mvel-lm
mvel-lm	1574/udp	mvel-lm
oraclenames	1575/tcp	oraclenames
oraclenames	1575/udp	oraclenames
moldflow-lm	1576/tcp	moldflow-lm
moldflow-lm	1576/udp	moldflow-lm
hypercube-lm	1577/tcp	hypercube-lm
hypercube-lm	1577/udp	hypercube-lm
jacobus-lm	1578/tcp	Jacobus License Manager
jacobus-lm	1578/udp	Jacobus License Manager
ioc-sea-lm	1579/tcp	ioc-sea-lm
ioc-sea-lm	1579/udp	ioc-sea-lm
tn-tl-r1	1580/tcp	tn-tl-r1
tn-tl-r2	1580/udp	tn-tl-r2
mil-2045-47001	1581/tcp	MIL-2045-47001
mil-2045-47001	1581/udp	MIL-2045-47001
msims	1582/tcp	MSIMS
msims	1582/udp	MSIMS
simbaexpress	1583/tcp	simbaexpress
simbaexpress	1583/udp	simbaexpress
tn-tl-fd2	1584/tcp	tn-tl-fd2
tn-tl-fd2	1584/udp	tn-tl-fd2
intv	1585/tcp	intv
intv	1585/udp	intv
ibm-abtact	1586/tcp	ibm-abtact
ibm-abtact	1586/udp	ibm-abtact
pra_elmd	1587/tcp	pra_elmd
pra_elmd	1587/udp	pra_elmd
triquest-lm	1588/tcp	triquest-lm
triquest-lm	1588/udp	triquest-lm
vqp	1589/tcp	VQP
vqp	1589/udp	VQP
gemini-lm	1590/tcp	gemini-lm
gemini-lm	1590/udp	gemini-lm
ncpm-pm	1591/tcp	ncpm-pm
ncpm-pm	1591/udp	ncpm-pm
commonspace	1592/tcp	commonspace
commonspace	1592/udp	commonspace
mainsoft-lm	1593/tcp	mainsoft-lm
mainsoft-lm	1593/udp	mainsoft-lm
sixtrak	1594/tcp	sixtrak

Keyword	Decimal	Description
sixtrak	1594/udp	sixtrak
radio	1595/tcp	radio
radio	1595/udp	radio
radio-sm	1596/tcp	radio-sm
radio-bc	1596/udp	radio-bc
orbplus-iiop	1597/tcp	orbplus-iiop
orbplus-iiop	1597/udp	orbplus-iiop
picknfs	1598/tcp	picknfs
picknfs	1598/udp	picknfs
simbaservices	1599/tcp	simbaservices
simbaservices	1599/udp	simbaservices
issd	1600/tcp	issd
issd	1600/udp	issd
aas	1601/tcp	aas
aas	1601/udp	aas
inspect	1602/tcp	inspect
inspect	1602/udp	inspect
picodbc	1603/tcp	pickodbc
picodbc	1603/udp	pickodbc
icabrowser	1604/tcp	icabrowser
icabrowser	1604/udp	icabrowser
slp	1605/tcp	Salutation Manager (Salutation Protocol)
slp	1605/udp	Salutation Manager (Salutation Protocol)
slm-api	1606/tcp	Salutation Manager (SLM-API)
slm-api	1606/udp	Salutation Manager (SLM-API)
stt	1607/tcp	stt
stt	1607/udp	stt
smart-lm	1608/tcp	Smart Corp. License Manager
smart-lm	1608/udp	Smart Corp. License Manager
isysg-lm	1609/tcp	isysg-lm
isysg-lm	1609/udp	isysg-lm
taurus-wh	1610/tcp	taurus-wh
taurus-wh	1610/udp	taurus-wh
ill	1611/tcp	Inter Library Loan
ill	1611/udp	Inter Library Loan
netbill-trans	1612/tcp	NetBill Transaction Server
netbill-trans	1612/udp	NetBill Transaction Server
netbill-keyrep	1613/tcp	NetBill Key Repository
netbill-keyrep	1613/udp	NetBill Key Repository
netbill-cred	1614/tcp	NetBill Credential Server
netbill-cred	1614/udp	NetBill Credential Server
netbill-auth	1615/tcp	NetBill Authorization Server
netbill-auth	1615/udp	NetBill Authorization Server
netbill-prod	1616/tcp	NetBill Product Server
netbill-prod	1616/udp	NetBill Product Server
nimrod-agent	1617/tcp	Nimrod Inter-Agent Communication
nimrod-agent	1617/udp	Nimrod Inter-Agent Communication
skytelnet	1618/tcp	skytelnet
skytelnet	1618/udp	skytelnet
xs-openstorage	1619/tcp	xs-openstorage
xs-openstorage	1619/udp	xs-openstorage
faxportwinport	1620/tcp	faxportwinport
faxportwinport	1620/udp	faxportwinport
softdataphone	1621/tcp	softdataphone
softdataphone	1621/udp	softdataphone
ontime	1622/tcp	ontime
ontime	1622/udp	ontime
jaleosnd	1623/tcp	jaleosnd
jaleosnd	1623/udp	jaleosnd
udp-sr-port	1624/tcp	udp-sr-port
udp-sr-port	1624/udp	udp-sr-port
svs-omagent	1625/tcp	svs-omagent
svs-omagent	1625/udp	svs-omagent
shockwave	1626/tcp	Shockwave
shockwave	1626/udp	Shockwave
t128-gateway	1627/tcp	T.128 Gateway
t128-gateway	1627/udp	T.128 Gateway
lontalk-norm	1628/tcp	LonTalk normal
lontalk-norm	1628/udp	LonTalk normal
lontalk-urgnt	1629/tcp	LonTalk urgent
lontalk-urgnt	1629/udp	LonTalk urgent
oraclenet8cman	1630/tcp	Oracle Net8 Cman
oraclenet8cman	1630/udp	Oracle Net8 Cman
visitview	1631/tcp	Visit view
visitview	1631/udp	Visit view
pammratc	1632/tcp	PAMMRATC
pammrtc	1632/udp	PAMMRATC
pammrpc	1633/tcp	PAMMRPC

Keyword	Decimal	Description
pammrpc	1633/udp	PAMMRPC
loaprobe	1634/tcp	Log On America Probe
loaprobe	1634/udp	Log On America Probe
edb-server1	1635/tcp	EDB Server 1
edb-server1	1635/udp	EDB Server 1
cncp	1636/tcp	CableNet Control Protocol
cncp	1636/udp	CableNet Control Protocol
cnap	1637/tcp	CableNet Admin Protocol
cnap	1637/udp	CableNet Admin Protocol
cnip	1638/tcp	CableNet Info Protocol
cnip	1638/udp	CableNet Info Protocol
cert-initiator	1639/tcp	cert-initiator
cert-initiator	1639/udp	cert-initiator
cert-responder	1640/tcp	cert-responder
cert-responder	1640/udp	cert-responder
invision	1641/tcp	InVision
invision	1641/udp	InVision
isis-am	1642/tcp	isis-am
isis-am	1642/udp	isis-am
isis-ambc	1643/tcp	isis-ambc
isis-ambc	1643/udp	isis-ambc
saiseh	1644/tcp	Satellite-data Acquisition System 4
datametrics	1645/tcp	datametrics
datametrics	1645/udp	datametrics
sa-msg-port	1646/tcp	sa-msg-port
sa-msg-port	1646/udp	sa-msg-port
rsap	1647/tcp	rsap
rsap	1647/udp	rsap
concurrent-lm	1648/tcp	concurrent-lm
concurrent-lm	1648/udp	concurrent-lm
kermit	1649/tcp	kermit
kermit	1649/udp	kermit
nkd	1650/tcp	nkd
nkd	1650/udp	nkd
shiva_confsrvr	1651/tcp	shiva_confsrvr
shiva_confsrvr	1651/udp	shiva_confsrvr
xnmp	1652/tcp	xnmp
xnmp	1652/udp	xnmp
alphatech-lm	1653/tcp	alphatech-lm
alphatech-lm	1653/udp	alphatech-lm
stargatealerts	1654/tcp	stargatealerts
stargatealerts	1654/udp	stargatealerts
dec-mbadmin	1655/tcp	dec-mbadmin
dec-mbadmin	1655/udp	dec-mbadmin
dec-mbadmin-h	1656/tcp	dec-mbadmin-h
dec-mbadmin-h	1656/udp	dec-mbadmin-h
fujitsu-mmpdc	1657/tcp	fujitsu-mmpdc
fujitsu-mmpdc	1657/udp	fujitsu-mmpdc
sixnetudr	1658/tcp	sixnetudr
sixnetudr	1658/udp	sixnetudr
sg-lm	1659/tcp	Silicon Grail License Manager
sg-lm	1659/udp	Silicon Grail License Manager
skip-mc-gikreq	1660/tcp	skip-mc-gikreq
skip-mc-gikreq	1660/udp	skip-mc-gikreq
netview-aix-1	1661/tcp	netview-aix-1
netview-aix-1	1661/udp	netview-aix-1
netview-aix-2	1662/tcp	netview-aix-2
netview-aix-2	1662/udp	netview-aix-2
netview-aix-3	1663/tcp	netview-aix-3
netview-aix-3	1663/udp	netview-aix-3
netview-aix-4	1664/tcp	netview-aix-4
netview-aix-4	1664/udp	netview-aix-4
netview-aix-5	1665/tcp	netview-aix-5
netview-aix-5	1665/udp	netview-aix-5
netview-aix-6	1666/tcp	netview-aix-6
netview-aix-6	1666/udp	netview-aix-6
netview-aix-7	1667/tcp	netview-aix-7
netview-aix-7	1667/udp	netview-aix-7
netview-aix-8	1668/tcp	netview-aix-8
netview-aix-8	1668/udp	netview-aix-8
netview-aix-9	1669/tcp	netview-aix-9
netview-aix-9	1669/udp	netview-aix-9
netview-aix-10	1670/tcp	netview-aix-10
netview-aix-10	1670/udp	netview-aix-10
netview-aix-11	1671/tcp	netview-aix-11
netview-aix-11	1671/udp	netview-aix-11
netview-aix-12	1672/tcp	netview-aix-12
netview-aix-12	1672/udp	netview-aix-12
proshare-mc-1	1673/tcp	Intel Proshare Multicast
proshare-mc-1	1673/udp	Intel Proshare Multicast
proshare-mc-2	1674/tcp	Intel Proshare Multicast
proshare-mc-2	1674/udp	Intel Proshare Multicast
pdp	1675/tcp	Pacific Data Products

Keyword	Decimal	Description
pdp	1675/udp	Pacific Data Products
netcomm1	1676/tcp	netcomm1
netcomm2	1676/udp	netcomm2
groupwise	1677/tcp	groupwise
groupwise	1677/udp	groupwise
prolink	1678/tcp	prolink
prolink	1678/udp	prolink
darcorp-lm	1679/tcp	darcorp-lm
darcorp-lm	1679/udp	darcorp-lm
microcom-sbp	1680/tcp	microcom-sbp
microcom-sbp	1680/udp	microcom-sbp
sd-elmd	1681/tcp	sd-elmd
sd-elmd	1681/udp	sd-elmd
lanyon-lantern	1682/tcp	lanyon-lantern
lanyon-lantern	1682/udp	lanyon-lantern
ncpm-hip	1683/tcp	ncpm-hip
ncpm-hip	1683/udp	ncpm-hip
snaresecure	1684/tcp	SnareSecure
snaresecure	1684/udp	SnareSecure
n2nremote	1685/tcp	n2nremote
n2nremote	1685/udp	n2nremote
cvmon	1686/tcp	cvmon
cvmon	1686/udp	cvmon
nsjtp-ctrl	1687/tcp	nsjtp-ctrl
nsjtp-ctrl	1687/udp	nsjtp-ctrl
nsjtp-data	1688/tcp	nsjtp-data
nsjtp-data	1688/udp	nsjtp-data
firefox	1689/tcp	firefox
firefox	1689/udp	firefox
ng-umds	1690/tcp	ng-umds
ng-umds	1690/udp	ng-umds
empire-empuma	1691/tcp	empire-empuma
empire-empuma	1691/udp	empire-empuma
sstsys-lm	1692/tcp	sstsys-lm
sstsys-lm	1692/udp	sstsys-lm
rrirtr	1693/tcp	rrirtr
rrirtr	1693/udp	rrirtr
rrimwm	1694/tcp	rrimwm
rrimwm	1694/udp	rrimwm
rrilwm	1695/tcp	rrilwm
rrilwm	1695/udp	rrilwm
rrifmm	1696/tcp	rrifmm
rrifmm	1696/udp	rrifmm
rrisat	1697/tcp	rrisat
rrisat	1697/udp	rrisat
rsvp-encap-1	1698/tcp	RSVP-ENCAPSULATION-1
rsvp-encap-1	1698/udp	RSVP-ENCAPSULATION-1
rsvp-encap-2	1699/tcp	RSVP-ENCAPSULATION-2
rsvp-encap-2	1699/udp	RSVP-ENCAPSULATION-2
mps-raft	1700/tcp	mps-raft
mps-raft	1700/udp	mps-raft
l2f	1701/tcp	l2f
l2f	1701/udp	l2f
l2tp	1701/tcp	l2tp
l2tp	1701/udp	l2tp
deskshare	1702/tcp	deskshare
deskshare	1702/udp	deskshare
hb-engine	1703/tcp	hb-engine
hb-engine	1703/udp	hb-engine
bcs-broker	1704/tcp	bcs-broker
bcs-broker	1704/udp	bcs-broker
slingshot	1705/tcp	slingshot
slingshot	1705/udp	slingshot
jetform	1706/tcp	jetform
jetform	1706/udp	jetform
vdmplay	1707/tcp	vdmplay
vdmplay	1707/udp	vdmplay
gat-lmd	1708/tcp	gat-lmd
gat-lmd	1708/udp	gat-lmd
centra	1709/tcp	centra
centra	1709/udp	centra
impera	1710/tcp	impera
impera	1710/udp	impera
pptconference	1711/tcp	pptconference
pptconference	1711/udp	pptconference
registrar	1712/tcp	resource monitoring service
registrar	1712/udp	resource monitoring service
conferencetalk	1713/tcp	ConferenceTalk
conferencetalk	1713/udp	ConferenceTalk
sesi-lm	1714/tcp	sesi-lm
sesi-lm	1714/udp	sesi-lm
houdini-lm	1715/tcp	houdini-lm
houdini-lm	1715/udp	houdini-lm
xmsg	1716/tcp	xmsg

Keyword	Decimal	Description
xmsg	1716/udp	xmsg
fj-hdnet	1717/tcp	fj-hdnet
fj-hdnet	1717/udp	fj-hdnet
h323gatedisc	1718/tcp	h323gatedisc
h323gatedisc	1718/udp	h323gatedisc
h323gatestat	1719/tcp	h323gatestat
h323gatestat	1719/udp	h323gatestat
h323hostcall	1720/tcp	h323hostcall
h323hostcall	1720/udp	h323hostcall
caicci	1721/tcp	caicci
caicci	1721/udp	caicci
hks-lm	1722/tcp	HKS License Manager
hks-lm	1722/udp	HKS License Manager
pptp	1723/tcp	pptp
pptp	1723/udp	pptp
csbphonemaster	1724/tcp	csbphonemaster
csbphonemaster	1724/udp	csbphonemaster
idcn-ralp	1725/tcp	idcn-ralp
iden-ralp	1725/udp	iden-ralp
iberiagames	1726/tcp	IBERIAGAMES
iberiagames	1726/udp	IBERIAGAMES
winddx	1727/tcp	winddx
winddx	1727/udp	winddx
telindus	1728/tcp	TELINDUS
telindus	1728/udp	TELINDUS
citynl	1729/tcp	CityNL License Management
citynl	1729/udp	CityNL License Management
roketz	1730/tcp	roketz
roketz	1730/udp	roketz
msiccp	1731/tcp	MSICCP
msiccp	1731/udp	MSICCP
proxim	1732/tcp	proxim
proxim	1732/udp	proxim
siipat	1733/tcp	SIMS - SIIPAT Protocol for Alarm Transmission
siipat	1733/udp	SIMS - SIIPAT Protocol for Alarm Transmission
cambertx-lm	1734/tcp	Camber Corporation License Management
cambertx-lm	1734/udp	Camber Corporation License Management
privatechat	1735/tcp	PrivateChat
privatechat	1735/udp	PrivateChat
street-stream	1736/tcp	street-stream
street-stream	1736/udp	street-stream
ultimad	1737/tcp	ultimad
ultimad	1737/udp	ultimad
gamegen1	1738/tcp	GameGen1
gamegen1	1738/udp	GameGen1
webaccess	1739/tcp	webaccess
webaccess	1739/udp	webaccess
encore	1740/tcp	encore
encore	1740/udp	encore
cisco-net-mgmt	1741/tcp	cisco-net-mgmt
cisco-net-mgmt	1741/udp	cisco-net-mgmt
3Com-nsd	1742/tcp	3Com-nsd
3Com-nsd	1742/udp	3Com-nsd
cinegrfx-lm	1743/tcp	Cinema Graphics License Manager
cinegrfx-lm	1743/udp	Cinema Graphics License Manager
ncpm-ft	1744/tcp	ncpm-ft
ncpm-ft	1744/udp	ncpm-ft
remote-winsock	1745/tcp	remote-winsock
remote-winsock	1745/udp	remote-winsock
ftrapid-1	1746/tcp	ftrapid-1
ftrapid-1	1746/udp	ftrapid-1
ftrapid-2	1747/tcp	ftrapid-2
ftrapid-2	1747/udp	ftrapid-2
oracle-em1	1748/tcp	oracle-em1
oracle-em1	1748/udp	oracle-em1
aspen-services	1749/tcp	aspen-services
aspen-services	1749/udp	aspen-services
sslp	1750/tcp	Simple Socket Library's PortMaster
sslp	1750/udp	Simple Socket Library's PortMaster
swiftnet	1751/tcp	SwiftNet
swiftnet	1751/udp	SwiftNet
lofr-lm	1752/tcp	Leap of Faith Research License Manager
lofr-lm	1752/udp	Leap of Faith Research License Manager
translogic-lm	1753/tcp	Translogic License Manager

Keyword	Decimal	Description	Keyword	Decimal	Description
translogic-lm	1753/udp	Translogic License Manager	rsc-robot	1793/udp	rsc-robot
oracle-em2	1754/tcp	oracle-em2	cera-bcm	1794/tcp	cera-bcm
oracle-em2	1754/udp	oracle-em2	cera-bcm	1794/udp	cera-bcm
ms-streaming	1755/tcp	ms-streaming	dpi-proxy	1795/tcp	dpi-proxy
ms-streaming	1755/udp	ms-streaming	dpi-proxy	1795/udp	dpi-proxy
capfast-lmd	1756/tcp	capfast-lmd	vocaltec-admin	1796/tcp	Vocaltec Server Administration
capfast-lmd	1756/udp	capfast-lmd			
cnhrp	1757/tcp	cnhrp	vocaltec-admin	1796/udp	Vocaltec Server Administration
cnhrp	1757/udp	cnhrp			
tftp-mcast	1758/tcp	tftp-mcast	uma	1797/tcp	UMA
tftp-mcast	1758/udp	tftp-mcast	uma	1797/udp	UMA
spss-lm	1759/tcp	SPSS License Manager	etp	1798/tcp	Event Transfer Protocol
spss-lm	1759/udp	SPSS License Manager	etp	1798/udp	Event Transfer Protocol
www-ldap-gw	1760/tcp	www-ldap-gw	netrisk	1799/tcp	NETRISK
www-ldap-gw	1760/udp	www-ldap-gw	netrisk	1799/udp	NETRISK
cft-0	1761/tcp	cft-0	ansys-lm	1800/tcp	ANSYS-License manager
cft-0	1761/udp	cft-0	ansys-lm	1800/udp	ANSYS-License manager
cft-1	1762/tcp	cft-1	msmq	1801/tcp	Microsoft Message Que
cft-1	1762/udp	cft-1	msmq	1801/udp	Microsoft Message Que
cft-2	1763/tcp	cft-2	concomp1	1802/tcp	ConComp1
cft-2	1763/udp	cft-2	concomp1	1802/udp	ConComp1
cft-3	1764/tcp	cft-3	hp-hcip-gwy	1803/tcp	HP-HCIP-GWY
cft-3	1764/udp	cft-3	hp-hcip-gwy	1803/udp	HP-HCIP-GWY
cft-4	1765/tcp	cft-4	enl	1804/tcp	ENL
cft-4	1765/udp	cft-4	enl	1804/udp	ENL
cft-5	1766/tcp	cft-5	enl-name	1805/tcp	ENL-Name
cft-5	1766/udp	cft-5	enl-name	1805/udp	ENL-Name
cft-6	1767/tcp	cft-6	musiconline	1806/tcp	Musiconline
cft-6	1767/udp	cft-6	musiconline	1806/udp	Musiconline
cft-7	1768/tcp	cft-7	fhsp	1807/tcp	Fujitsu Hot Standby Protocol
cft-7	1768/udp	cft-7	fhsp	1807/udp	Fujitsu Hot Standby Protocol
bmc-net-adm	1769/tcp	bmc-net-adm	oracle-vp2	1808/tcp	Oracle-VP2
bmc-net-adm	1769/udp	bmc-net-adm	oracle-vp2	1808/udp	Oracle-VP2
bmc-net-svc	1770/tcp	bmc-net-svc	oracle-vp1	1809/tcp	Oracle-VP1
bmc-net-svc	1770/udp	bmc-net-svc	oracle-vp1	1809/udp	Oracle-VP1
vaultbase	1771/tcp	vaultbase	jerand-lm	1810/tcp	Jerand License Manager
vaultbase	1771/udp	vaultbase	jerand-lm	1810/udp	Jerand License Manager
essweb-gw	1772/tcp	EssWeb Gateway	scientia-sdb	1811/tcp	Scientia-SDB
essweb-gw	1772/udp	EssWeb Gateway	scientia-sdb	1811/udp	Scientia-SDB
kmscontrol	1773/tcp	KMSControl	radius	1812/tcp	RADIUS
kmscontrol	1773/udp	KMSControl	radius	1812/udp	RADIUS
global-dtserv	1774/tcp	global-dtserv	radius-acct	1813/tcp	RADIUS Accounting
global-dtserv	1774/udp	global-dtserv	radius-acct	1813/udp	RADIUS Accounting
femis	1776/tcp	Federal Emergency Management Information System	tdp-suite	1814/tcp	TDP Suite
			tdp-suite	1814/udp	TDP Suite
femis	1776/udp	Federal Emergency Management Information System	mmpft	1815/tcp	MMPFT
			mmpft	1815/udp	MMPFT
powerguardian	1777/tcp	powerguardian	harp	1816/tcp	HARP
powerguardian	1777/udp	powerguardian	harp	1816/udp	HARP
prodigy-intrnet	1778/tcp	prodigy-internet	rkb-oscs	1817/tcp	RKB-OSCS
prodigy-intrnet	1778/udp	prodigy-internet	rkb-oscs	1817/udp	RKB-OSCS
pharmasoft	1779/tcp	pharmasoft	etftp	1818/tcp	Enhanced Trivial File Transfer Protocol
pharmasoft	1779/udp	pharmasoft			
dpkeyserv	1780/tcp	dpkeyserv	etftp	1818/udp	Enhanced Trivial File Transfer Protocol
dpkeyserv	1780/udp	dpkeyserv			
answersoft-lm	1781/tcp	answersoft-lm	plato-lm	1819/tcp	Plato License Manager
answersoft-lm	1781/udp	answersoft-lm	plato-lm	1819/udp	Plato License Manager
hp-hcip	1782/tcp	hp-hcip	mcagent	1820/tcp	mcagent
hp-hcip	1782/udp	hp-hcip	mcagent	1820/udp	mcagent
#	1783	Decommissioned Port 04/14/00, ms	donnyworld	1821/tcp	donnyworld
			donnyworld	1821/udp	donnyworld
finle-lm	1784/tcp	Finle License Manager	es-elmd	1822/tcp	es-elmd
finle-lm	1784/udp	Finle License Manager	es-elmd	1822/udp	es-elmd
windlm	1785/tcp	Wind River Systems License Manager	unisys-lm	1823/tcp	Unisys Natural Language License Manager
windlm	1785/udp	Wind River Systems License Manager	unisys-lm	1823/udp	Unisys Natural Language License Manager
funk-logger	1786/tcp	funk-logger	metrics-pas	1824/tcp	metrics-pas
funk-logger	1786/udp	funk-logger	metrics-pas	1824/udp	metrics-pas
funk-license	1787/tcp	funk-license	direcpc-video	1825/tcp	DirecPC Video
funk-license	1787/udp	funk-license	direcpc-video	1825/udp	DirecPC Video
psmond	1788/tcp	psmond	ardt	1826/tcp	ARDT
psmond	1788/udp	psmond	ardt	1826/udp	ARDT
hello	1789/tcp	hello	asi	1827/tcp	ASI
hello	1789/udp	hello	asi	1827/udp	ASI
nmsp	1790/tcp	Narrative Media Streaming Protocol	itm-mcell-u	1828/tcp	itm-mcell-u
			itm-mcell-u	1828/udp	itm-mcell-u
nmsp	1790/udp	Narrative Media Streaming Protocol	optika-emedia	1829/tcp	Optika eMedia
			optika-emedia	1829/udp	Optika eMedia
ea1	1791/tcp	EA1	net8-cman	1830/tcp	Oracle Net8 CMan Admin
ea1	1791/udp	EA1	net8-cman	1830/udp	Oracle Net8 CMan Admin
ibm-dt-2	1792/tcp	ibm-dt-2	myrtle	1831/tcp	Myrtle
ibm-dt-2	1792/udp	ibm-dt-2	myrtle	1831/udp	Myrtle
rsc-robot	1793/tcp	rsc-robot	tht-treasure	1832/tcp	ThoughtTreasure

Keyword	Decimal	Description	Keyword	Decimal	Description
tht-treasure	1832/udp	ThoughtTreasure	tpmd	1906/udp	TPortMapperReq
udpradio	1833/tcp	udpradio	intrastar	1907/tcp	IntraSTAR
udpradio	1833/udp	udpradio	intrastar	1907/udp	IntraSTAR
ardusuni	1834/tcp	ARDUS Unicast	dawn	1908/tcp	Dawn
ardusuni	1834/udp	ARDUS Unicast	dawn	1908/udp	Dawn
ardusmul	1835/tcp	ARDUS Multicast	global-wlink	1909/tcp	Global World Link
ardusmul	1835/udp	ARDUS Multicast	global-wlink	1909/udp	Global World Link
ste-smsc	1836/tcp	ste-smsc	ultrabac	1910/tcp	ultrabac
ste-smsc	1836/udp	ste-smsc	ultrabac	1910/udp	ultrabac
csoft1	1837/tcp	csoft1	mtp	1911/tcp	Starlight Networks Multimedia Transport Protocol
csoft1	1837/udp	csoft1			
talnet	1838/tcp	TALNET			
talnet	1838/udp	TALNET	mtp	1911/udp	Starlight Networks Multimedia Transport Protocol
netopia-vo1	1839/tcp	netopia-vo1			
netopia-vo1	1839/udp	netopia-vo1			
netopia-vo2	1840/tcp	netopia-vo2	rhp-iibp	1912/tcp	rhp-iibp
netopia-vo2	1840/udp	netopia-vo2	rhp-iibp	1912/udp	rhp-iibp
netopia-vo3	1841/tcp	netopia-vo3	armadp	1913/tcp	armadp
netopia-vo3	1841/udp	netopia-vo3	armadp	1913/udp	armadp
netopia-vo4	1842/tcp	netopia-vo4	elm-momentum	1914/tcp	Elm-Momentum
netopia-vo4	1842/udp	netopia-vo4	elm-momentum	1914/udp	Elm-Momentum
netopia-vo5	1843/tcp	netopia-vo5	facelink	1915/tcp	FACELINK
netopia-vo5	1843/udp	netopia-vo5	facelink	1915/udp	FACELINK
direcpc-dll	1844/tcp	DirecPC-DLL	persona	1916/tcp	Persoft Persona
direcpc-dll	1844/udp	DirecPC-DLL	persona	1916/udp	Persoft Persona
#	1845-1849	Unassigned	noagent	1917/tcp	nOAgent
gsi	1850/tcp	GSI	noagent	1917/udp	nOAgent
gsi	1850/udp	GSI	can-nds	1918/tcp	Candle Directory Service - NDS
ctcd	1851/tcp	ctcd			
ctcd	1851/udp	ctcd	can-nds	1918/udp	Candle Directory Service - NDS
#	1852-1859	Unassigned			
sunscalar-svc	1860/tcp	SunSCALAR Services	can-dch	1919/tcp	Candle Directory Service - DCH
sunscalar-svc	1860/udp	SunSCALAR Services			
lecroy-vicp	1861/tcp	LeCroy VICP	can-dch	1919/udp	Candle Directory Service - DCH
lecroy-vicp	1861/udp	LeCroy VICP			
techra-server	1862/tcp	techra-server	can-ferret	1920/tcp	Candle Directory Service - FERRET
techra-server	1862/udp	techra-server			
msnp	1863/tcp	MSNP	can-ferret	1920/udp	Candle Directory Service - FERRET
msnp	1863/udp	MSNP			
paradym-31port	1864/tcp	Paradym 31 Port	noadmin	1921/tcp	NoAdmin
paradym-31port	1864/udp	Paradym 31 Port	noadmin	1921/udp	NoAdmin
entp	1865/tcp	ENTP	tapestry	1922/tcp	Tapestry
entp	1865/udp	ENTP	tapestry	1922/udp	Tapestry
#	1866-1869	Unassigned	spice	1923/tcp	SPICE
sunscalar-dns	1870/tcp	SunSCALAR DNS Service	spice	1923/udp	SPICE
sunscalar-dns	1870/udp	SunSCALAR DNS Service	xiip	1924/tcp	XIIP
canocentral0	1871/tcp	Cano Central 0	xiip	1924/udp	XIIP
canocentral0	1871/udp	Cano Central 0	#	1925-1929	Unassigned
canocentral1	1872/tcp	Cano Central 1	driveappserver	1930/tcp	Drive AppServer
canocentral1	1872/udp	Cano Central 1	driveappserver	1930/udp	Drive AppServer
fjmpjps	1873/tcp	Fjmpjps	amdsched	1931/tcp	AMD SCHED
fjmpjps	1873/udp	Fjmpjps	amdsched	1931/udp	AMD SCHED
fjswapsnp	1874/tcp	Fjswapsnp	#	1932-1940	Unassigned
fjswapsnp	1874/udp	Fjswapsnp	dic-aida	1941/tcp	DIC-Aida
#	1875-1880	Unassigned	dic-aida	1941/udp	DIC-Aida
ibm-mqseries2	1881/tcp	IBM MQSeries	#	1942-1943	Unassigned
ibm-mqseries2	1881/udp	IBM MQSeries	close-combat	1944/tcp	close-combat
#	1882-1894	Unassigned	close-combat	1944/udp	close-combat
vista-4gl	1895/tcp	Vista 4GL	dialogic-elmd	1945/tcp	dialogic-elmd
vista-4gl	1895/udp	Vista 4GL	dialogic-elmd	1945/udp	dialogic-elmd
#	1896-1898	Unassigned	tekpls	1946/tcp	tekpls
mc2studios	1899/tcp	MC2Studios	tekpls	1946/udp	tekpls
mc2studios	1899/udp	MC2Studios	hlserver	1947/tcp	hlserver
ssdp	1900/tcp	SSDP	hlserver	1947/udp	hlserver
ssdp	1900/udp	SSDP	eye2eye	1948/tcp	eye2eye
fjicl-tep-a	1901/tcp	Fujitsu ICL Terminal Emulator Program A	eye2eye	1948/udp	eye2eye
			ismaeasdaqlive	1949/tcp	ISMA Easdaq Live
fjicl-tep-a	1901/udp	Fujitsu ICL Terminal Emulator Program A	ismaeasdaqlive	1949/udp	ISMA Easdaq Live
			ismaeasdaqtest	1950/tcp	ISMA Easdaq Test
fjicl-tep-b	1902/tcp	Fujitsu ICL Terminal Emulator Program B	ismaeasdaqtest	1950/udp	ISMA Easdaq Test
			bcs-lmserver	1951/tcp	bcs-lmserver
fjicl-tep-b	1902/udp	Fujitsu ICL Terminal Emulator Program B	bcs-lmserver	1951/udp	bcs-lmserver
			mpnjsc	1952/tcp	mpnjsc
linkname	1903/tcp	Local Link Name Resolution	mpnjsc	1952/udp	mpnjsc
linkname	1903/udp	Local Link Name Resolution	rapidbase	1953/tcp	Rapid Base
fjicl-tep-c	1904/tcp	Fujitsu ICL Terminal Emulator Program C	rapidbase	1953/udp	Rapid Base
			#	1954-1956	Unassigned
fjicl-tep-c	1904/udp	Fujitsu ICL Terminal Emulator Program C	unix-status	1957/tcp	unix-status
			unix-status	1957/udp	unix-status
sugp	1905/tcp	Secure UP.Link Gateway Protocol	#	1958-1960	Unassigned
			bts-appserver	1961/tcp	BTS APPSERVER
sugp	1905/udp	Secure UP.Link Gateway Protocol	bts-appserver	1961/udp	BTS APPSERVER
			biap-mp	1962/tcp	BIAP-MP
tpmd	1906/tcp	TPortMapperReq	biap-mp	1962/udp	BIAP-MP

Keyword	Decimal	Description
webmachine	1963/tcp	WebMachine
webmachine	1963/udp	WebMachine
solid-e-engine	1964/tcp	SOLID E ENGINE
solid-e-engine	1964/udp	SOLID E ENGINE
tivoli-npm	1965/tcp	Tivoli NPM
tivoli-npm	1965/udp	Tivoli NPM
slush	1966/tcp	Slush
slush	1966/udp	Slush
sns-quote	1967/tcp	SNS Quote
sns-quote	1967/udp	SNS Quote
#	1968-1971	Unassigned
intersys-cache	1972/tcp	Cache
intersys-cache	1972/udp	Cache
dlsrap	1973/tcp	Data Link Switching Remote Access Protocol
dlsrap	1973/udp	Data Link Switching Remote Access Protocol
drp	1974/tcp	DRP
drp	1974/udp	DRP
tcoflashagent	1975/tcp	TCO Flash Agent
tcoflashagent	1975/udp	TCO Flash Agent
tcoregagent	1976/tcp	TCO Reg Agent
tcoregagent	1976/udp	TCO Reg Agent
tcoaddressbook	1977/tcp	TCO Address Book
tcoaddressbook	1977/udp	TCO Address Book
unisql	1978/tcp	UniSQL
unisql	1978/udp	UniSQL
unisql-java	1979/tcp	UniSQL Java
unisql-java	1979/udp	UniSQL Java
#	1980-1983	Unassigned
bb	1984/tcp	BB
bb	1984/udp	BB
hsrp	1985/tcp	Hot Standby Router Protocol
hsrp	1985/udp	Hot Standby Router Protocol
licensedaemon	1986/tcp	cisco license management
licensedaemon	1986/udp	cisco license management
tr-rsrb-p1	1987/tcp	cisco RSRB Priority 1 port
tr-rsrb-p1	1987/udp	cisco RSRB Priority 1 port
tr-rsrb-p2	1988/tcp	cisco RSRB Priority 2 port
tr-rsrb-p2	1988/udp	cisco RSRB Priority 2 port
tr-rsrb-p3	1989/tcp	cisco RSRB Priority 3 port
tr-rsrb-p3	1989/udp	cisco RSRB Priority 3 port
		The following entry records an unassigned but widespread use
mshnet	1989/tcp	MHSnet system
mshnet	1989/udp	MHSnet system
stun-p1	1990/tcp	cisco STUN Priority 1 port
stun-p1	1990/udp	cisco STUN Priority 1 port
stun-p2	1991/tcp	cisco STUN Priority 2 port
stun-p2	1991/udp	cisco STUN Priority 2 port
stun-p3	1992/tcp	cisco STUN Priority 3 port
stun-p3	1992/udp	cisco STUN Priority 3 port
		The following entry records an unassigned but widespread use
ipsendmsg	1992/tcp	IPsendmsg
ipsendmsg	1992/udp	IPsendmsg
snmp-tcp-port	1993/tcp	cisco SNMP TCP port
snmp-tcp-port	1993/udp	cisco SNMP TCP port
stun-port	1994/tcp	cisco serial tunnel port
stun-port	1994/udp	cisco serial tunnel port
perf-port	1995/tcp	cisco perf port
perf-port	1995/udp	cisco perf port
tr-rsrb-port	1996/tcp	cisco Remote SRB port
tr-rsrb-port	1996/udp	cisco Remote SRB port
gdp-port	1997/tcp	cisco Gateway Discovery Protocol
gdp-port	1997/udp	cisco Gateway Discovery Protocol
x25-svc-port	1998/tcp	cisco X.25 service (XOT)
x25-svc-port	1998/udp	cisco X.25 service (XOT)
tcp-id-port	1999/tcp	cisco identification port
tcp-id-port	1999/udp	cisco identification port
callbook	2000/tcp	
callbook	2000/udp	
dc	2001/tcp	
wizard	2001/udp	curry
globe	2002/tcp	
globe	2002/udp	
mailbox	2004/tcp	
emce	2004/udp	CCWS mm conf
berknet	2005/tcp	
oracle	2005/udp	
invokator	2006/tcp	
raid-cc	2006/udp	raid

Keyword	Decimal	Description
dectalk	2007/tcp	
raid-am	2007/udp	
conf	2008/tcp	
terminaldb	2008/udp	
news	2009/tcp	
whosockami	2009/udp	
search	2010/tcp	
pipe_server	2010/udp	
raid-cc	2011/tcp	raid
servserv	2011/udp	
ttyinfo	2012/tcp	
raid-ac	2012/udp	
raid-am	2013/tcp	
raid-cd	2013/udp	
troff	2014/tcp	
raid-sf	2014/udp	
cypress	2015/tcp	
raid-cs	2015/udp	
bootserver	2016/tcp	
bootserver	2016/udp	
cypress-stat	2017/tcp	
bootclient	2017/udp	
terminaldb	2018/tcp	
rellpack	2018/udp	
whosockami	2019/tcp	
about	2019/udp	
xinupageserver	2020/tcp	
xinupageserver	2020/udp	
servexec	2021/tcp	
xinuexpansion1	2021/udp	
down	2022/tcp	
xinuexpansion2	2022/udp	
xinuexpansion3	2023/tcp	
xinuexpansion3	2023/udp	
xinuexpansion4	2024/tcp	
xinuexpansion4	2024/udp	
ellpack	2025/tcp	
xribs	2025/udp	
scrabble	2026/tcp	
scrabble	2026/udp	
shadowserver	2027/tcp	
shadowserver	2027/udp	
submitserver	2028/tcp	
submitserver	2028/udp	
device2	2030/tcp	
device2	2030/udp	
blackboard	2032/tcp	
blackboard	2032/udp	
glogger	2033/tcp	
glogger	2033/udp	
scoremgr	2034/tcp	
scoremgr	2034/udp	
imsldoc	2035/tcp	
imsldoc	2035/udp	
objectmanager	2038/tcp	
objectmanager	2038/udp	
lam	2040/tcp	
lam	2040/udp	
interbase	2041/tcp	
interbase	2041/udp	
isis	2042/tcp	isis
isis	2042/udp	isis
isis-bcast	2043/tcp	isis-bcast
isis-bcast	2043/udp	isis-bcast
rimsl	2044/tcp	
rimsl	2044/udp	
cdfunc	2045/tcp	
cdfunc	2045/udp	
sdfunc	2046/tcp	
sdfunc	2046/udp	
dls	2047/tcp	
dls	2047/udp	
dls-monitor	2048/tcp	
dls-monitor	2048/udp	
#		NOTE Conflict on 2049 !
shilp	2049/tcp	
shilp	2049/udp	
nfs	2049/tcp	Network File System - Sun Microsystems
nfs	2049/udp	Network File System - Sun Microsystems
#	2050-2064	Unassigned
dlsrpn	2065/tcp	Data Link Switch Read Port Number

Keyword	Decimal	Description	Keyword	Decimal	Description
dlsrpn	2065/udp	Data Link Switch Read Port Number	pktcable-cops	2126/udp	PktCable-COPS
			index-pc-wb	2127/tcp	INDEX-PC-WB
dlswpn	2067/tcp	Data Link Switch Write Port Number	index-pc-wb	2127/udp	INDEX-PC-WB
			net-steward	2128/tcp	Net Steward Control
dlswpn	2067/udp	Data Link Switch Write Port Number	net-steward	2128/udp	Net Steward Control
			cs-live	2129/tcp	cs-live.com
#	2068-2088	Unassigned	cs-live	2129/udp	cs-live.com
sep	2089/tcp	Security Encapsulation Protocol - SEP	swc-xds	2130/tcp	SWC-XDS
			swc-xds	2130/udp	SWC-XDS
sep	2089/udp	Security Encapsulation Protocol - SEP	avantageb2b	2131/tcp	Avantageb2b
			avantageb2b	2131/udp	Avantageb2b
lrp	2090/tcp	Load Report Protocol	avail-epmap	2132/tcp	AVAIL-EPMAP
lrp	2090/udp	Load Report Protocol	avail-epmap	2132/udp	AVAIL-EPMAP
prp	2091/tcp	PRP	zymed-zpp	2133/tcp	ZYMED-ZPP
prp	2091/udp	PRP	zymed-zpp	2133/udp	ZYMED-ZPP
descent3	2092/tcp	Descent 3	avenue	2134/tcp	AVENUE
descent3	2092/udp	Descent 3	avenue	2134/udp	AVENUE
nbx-cc	2093/tcp	NBX CC	gris	2135/tcp	Grid Resource Information Server
nbx-cc	2093/udp	NBX CC			
nbx-au	2094/tcp	NBX AU	gris	2135/udp	Grid Resource Information Server
nbx-au	2094/udp	NBX AU			
nbx-ser	2095/tcp	NBX SER	appworxsrv	2136/tcp	APPWORXSRV
nbx-ser	2095/udp	NBX SER	appworxsrv	2136/udp	APPWORXSRV
nbx-dir	2096/tcp	NBX DIR	connect	2137/tcp	CONNECT
nbx-dir	2096/udp	NBX DIR	connect	2137/udp	CONNECT
jetformpreview	2097/tcp	Jet Form Preview	unbind-cluster	2138/tcp	UNBIND-CLUSTER
jetformpreview	2097/udp	Jet Form Preview	unbind-cluster	2138/udp	UNBIND-CLUSTER
dialog-port	2098/tcp	Dialog Port	ias-auth	2139/tcp	IAS-AUTH
dialog-port	2098/udp	Dialog Port	ias-auth	2139/udp	IAS-AUTH
h2250-annex-g	2099/tcp	H.225.0 Annex G	ias-reg	2140/tcp	IAS-REG
h2250-annex-g	2099/udp	H.225.0 Annex G	ias-reg	2140/udp	IAS-REG
amiganetfs	2100/tcp	amiganetfs	ias-admind	2141/tcp	IAS-ADMIND
amiganetfs	2100/udp	amiganetfs	ias-admind	2141/udp	IAS-ADMIND
rtcm-sc104	2101/tcp	rtcm-sc104	tdm-over-ip	2142/tcp	TDM-OVER-IP
rtcm-sc104	2101/udp	rtcm-sc104	tdm-over-ip	2142/udp	TDM-OVER-IP
zephyr-srv	2102/tcp	Zephyr server	lv-jc	2143/tcp	Live Vault Job Control
zephyr-srv	2102/udp	Zephyr server	lv-jc	2143/udp	Live Vault Job Control
zephyr-clt	2103/tcp	Zephyr serv-hm connection	lv-ffx	2144/tcp	Live Vault Fast Object Transfer
zephyr-clt	2103/udp	Zephyr serv-hm connection			
zephyr-hm	2104/tcp	Zephyr hostmanager	lv-ffx	2144/udp	Live Vault Fast Object Transfer
zephyr-hm	2104/udp	Zephyr hostmanager			
minipay	2105/tcp	MiniPay	lv-pici	2145/tcp	Live Vault Remote Diagnostic Console Support
minipay	2105/udp	MiniPay			
mzap	2106/tcp	MZAP	lv-pici	2145/udp	Live Vault Remote Diagnostic Console Support
mzap	2106/udp	MZAP			
bintec-admin	2107/tcp	BinTec Admin	lv-not	2146/tcp	Live Vault Admin Event Notification
bintec-admin	2107/udp	BinTec Admin			
comcam	2108/tcp	Comcam	lv-not	2146/udp	Live Vault Admin Event Notification
comcam	2108/udp	Comcam			
ergolight	2109/tcp	Ergolight	lv-auth	2147/tcp	Live Vault Authentication
ergolight	2109/udp	Ergolight	lv-auth	2147/udp	Live Vault Authentication
umsp	2110/tcp	UMSP	veritas-ucl	2148/tcp	VERITAS UNIVERSAL COMMUNICATION LAYER
umsp	2110/udp	UMSP			
dsatp	2111/tcp	DSATP	veritas-ucl	2148/udp	VERITAS UNIVERSAL COMMUNICATION LAYER
dsatp	2111/udp	DSATP			
idonix-metanet	2112/tcp	Idonix MetaNet	acptsys	2149/tcp	ACPTSYS
idonix-metanet	2112/udp	Idonix MetaNet	acptsys	2149/udp	ACPTSYS
hsl-storm	2113/tcp	HSL StoRM	dynamic3d	2150/tcp	DYNAMIC3D
hsl-storm	2113/udp	HSL StoRM	dynamic3d	2150/udp	DYNAMIC3D
newheights	2114/tcp	NEWHEIGHTS	docent	2151/tcp	DOCENT
newheights	2114/udp	NEWHEIGHTS	docent	2151/udp	DOCENT
kdm	2115/tcp	KDM	gtp-user	2152/tcp	GTP-User Plane (3GPP)
kdm	2115/udp	KDM	gtp-user	2152/udp	GTP-User Plane (3GPP)
ccowcmr	2116/tcp	CCOWCMR	#	2153-2164	Unassigned
ccowcmr	2116/udp	CCOWCMR	x-bone-api	2165/tcp	X-Bone API
mentaclient	2117/tcp	MENTACLIENT	x-bone-api	2165/udp	X-Bone API
mentaclient	2117/udp	MENTACLIENT	iwserver	2166/tcp	IWSERVER
mentaserver	2118/tcp	MENTASERVER	iwserver	2166/udp	IWSERVER
mentaserver	2118/udp	MENTASERVER	#	2167-2179	Unassigned
gsigatekeeper	2119/tcp	GSIGATEKEEPER	mc-gt-srv	2180/tcp	Millicent Vendor Gateway Server
gsigatekeeper	2119/udp	GSIGATEKEEPER			
qencp	2120/tcp	Quick Eagle Networks CP	mc-gt-srv	2180/udp	Millicent Vendor Gateway Server
qencp	2120/udp	Quick Eagle Networks CP			
scientia-ssdb	2121/tcp	SCIENTIA-SSDB	eforward	2181/tcp	eforward
scientia-ssdb	2121/udp	SCIENTIA-SSDB	eforward	2181/udp	eforward
caupc-remote	2122/tcp	CauPC Remote Control	ici	2200/tcp	ICI
caupc-remote	2122/udp	CauPC Remote Control	ici	2200/udp	ICI
gtp-control	2123/tcp	GTP-Control Plane (3GPP)	ats	2201/tcp	Advanced Training System Program
gtp-control	2123/udp	GTP-Control Plane (3GPP)			
elatelink	2124/tcp	ELATELINK	ats	2201/udp	Advanced Training System Program
elatelink	2124/udp	ELATELINK			
lockstep	2125/tcp	LOCKSTEP	imtc-map	2202/tcp	Int. Multimedia Teleconferencing Cosortium
lockstep	2125/udp	LOCKSTEP			
pktcable-cops	2126/tcp	PktCable-COPS			

Keyword	Decimal	Description	Keyword	Decimal	Description
imtc-map	2202/udp	Int. Multimedia Teleconferencing Cosortium	binderysupport	2302/tcp	Bindery Support
			binderysupport	2302/udp	Bindery Support
kali	2213/tcp	Kali	proxy-gateway	2303/tcp	Proxy Gateway
kali	2213/udp	Kali	proxy-gateway	2303/udp	Proxy Gateway
netiq	2220/tcp	NetIQ Pegasus	attachmate-uts	2304/tcp	Attachmate UTS
netiq	2220/udp	NetIQ Pegasus	attachmate-uts	2304/udp	Attachmate UTS
rockwell-csp1	2221/tcp	Rockwell CSP1	mt-scaleserver	2305/tcp	MT ScaleServer
rockwell-csp1	2221/udp	Rockwell CSP1	mt-scaleserver	2305/udp	MT ScaleServer
rockwell-csp2	2222/tcp	Rockwell CSP2	tappi-boxnet	2306/tcp	TAPPI BoxNet
rockwell-csp2	2222/udp	Rockwell CSP2	tappi-boxnet	2306/udp	TAPPI BoxNet
rockwell-csp3	2223/tcp	Rockwell CSP3	pehelp	2307/tcp	pehelp
rockwell-csp3	2223/udp	Rockwell CSP3	pehelp	2307/udp	pehelp
ivs-video	2232/tcp	IVS Video default	sdhelp	2308/tcp	sdhelp
ivs-video	2232/udp	IVS Video default	sdhelp	2308/udp	sdhelp
infocrypt	2233/tcp	INFOCRYPT	sdserver	2309/tcp	SD Server
infocrypt	2233/udp	INFOCRYPT	sdserver	2309/udp	SD Server
directplay	2234/tcp	DirectPlay	sdclient	2310/tcp	SD Client
directplay	2234/udp	DirectPlay	sdclient	2310/udp	SD Client
sercomm-wlink	2235/tcp	Sercomm-WLink	messageservice	2311/tcp	Message Service
sercomm-wlink	2235/udp	Sercomm-WLink	messageservice	2311/udp	Message Service
nani	2236/tcp	Nani	iapp	2313/tcp	IAPP (Inter Access Point Protocol)
nani	2236/udp	Nani			
optech-port1-lm	2237/tcp	Optech Port1 License Manager	iapp	2313/udp	IAPP (Inter Access Point Protocol)
optech-port1-lm	2237/udp	Optech Port1 License Manager	cr-websystems	2314/tcp	CR WebSystems
			cr-websystems	2314/udp	CR WebSystems
aviva-sna	2238/tcp	AVIVA SNA SERVER	precise-sft	2315/tcp	Precise Sft.
aviva-sna	2238/udp	AVIVA SNA SERVER	precise-sft	2315/udp	Precise Sft.
imagequery	2239/tcp	Image Query	sent-lm	2316/tcp	SENT License Manager
imagequery	2239/udp	Image Query	sent-lm	2316/udp	SENT License Manager
recipe	2240/tcp	RECIPe	attachmate-g32	2317/tcp	Attachmate G32
recipe	2240/udp	RECIPe	attachmate-g32	2317/udp	Attachmate G32
ivsd	2241/tcp	IVS Daemon	cadencecontrol	2318/tcp	Cadence Control
ivsd	2241/udp	IVS Daemon	cadencecontrol	2318/udp	Cadence Control
foliocorp	2242/tcp	Folio Remote Server	infolibria	2319/tcp	InfoLibria
foliocorp	2242/udp	Folio Remote Server	infolibria	2319/udp	InfoLibria
magicom	2243/tcp	Magicom Protocol	siebel-ns	2320/tcp	Siebel NS
magicom	2243/udp	Magicom Protocol	siebel-ns	2320/udp	Siebel NS
nmsserver	2244/tcp	NMS Server	rdlap	2321/tcp	RDLAP over UDP
nmsserver	2244/udp	NMS Server	rdlap	2321/udp	RDLAP
hao	2245/tcp	HaO	ofsd	2322/tcp	ofsd
hao	2245/udp	HaO	ofsd	2322/udp	ofsd
#	2245-2278	Unassigned	3d-nfsd	2323/tcp	3d-nfsd
xmquery	2279/tcp	xmquery	3d-nfsd	2323/udp	3d-nfsd
xmquery	2279/udp	xmquery	cosmocall	2324/tcp	Cosmocall
lnvpoller	2280/tcp	LNVPOLLER	cosmocall	2324/udp	Cosmocall
lnvpoller	2280/udp	LNVPOLLER	designspace-lm	2325/tcp	Design Space License Management
lnvconsole	2281/tcp	LNVCONSOLE	designspace-lm	2325/udp	Design Space License Management
lnvconsole	2281/udp	LNVCONSOLE			
lnvalarm	2282/tcp	LNVALARM	idcp	2326/tcp	IDCP
lnvalarm	2282/udp	LNVALARM	idcp	2326/udp	IDCP
lnvstatus	2283/tcp	LNVSTATUS	xingcsm	2327/tcp	xingcsm
lnvstatus	2283/udp	LNVSTATUS	xingcsm	2327/udp	xingcsm
lnvmaps	2284/tcp	LNVMAPS	netrix-sftm	2328/tcp	Netrix SFTM
lnvmaps	2284/udp	LNVMAPS	netrix-sftm	2328/udp	Netrix SFTM
lnvmailmon	2285/tcp	LNVMAILMON	nvd	2329/tcp	NVD
lnvmailmon	2285/udp	LNVMAILMON	nvd	2329/udp	NVD
nas-metering	2286/tcp	NAS-Metering	tscchat	2330/tcp	TSCCHAT
nas-metering	2286/udp	NAS-Metering	tscchat	2330/udp	TSCCHAT
dna	2287/tcp	DNA	agentview	2331/tcp	AGENTVIEW
dna	2287/udp	DNA	agentview	2331/udp	AGENTVIEW
netml	2288/tcp	NETML	rcc-host	2332/tcp	RCC Host
netml	2288/udp	NETML	rcc-host	2332/udp	RCC Host
#	2289-2293	Unassigned	snapp	2333/tcp	SNAPP
konshus-lm	2294/tcp	Konshus License Manager (FLEX)	snapp	2333/udp	SNAPP
			ace-client	2334/tcp	ACE Client Auth
konshus-lm	2294/udp	Konshus License Manager (FLEX)	ace-client	2334/udp	ACE Client Auth
advant-lm	2295/tcp	Advant License Manager	ace-proxy	2335/tcp	ACE Proxy
advant-lm	2295/udp	Advant License Manager	ace-proxy	2335/udp	ACE Proxy
theta-lm	2296/tcp	Theta License Manager (Rainbow)	appleugcontrol	2336/tcp	Apple UG Control
			appleugcontrol	2336/udp	Apple UG Control
theta-lm	2296/udp	Theta License Manager (Rainbow)	ideesrv	2337/tcp	ideesrv
			ideesrv	2337/udp	ideesrv
d2k-datamover1	2297/tcp	D2K DataMover 1	norton-lambert	2338/tcp	Norton Lambert
d2k-datamover1	2297/udp	D2K DataMover 1	norton-lambert	2338/udp	Norton Lambert
d2k-datamover2	2298/tcp	D2K DataMover 2	3com-webview	2339/tcp	3Com WebView
d2k-datamover2	2298/udp	D2K DataMover 2	3com-webview	2339/udp	3Com WebView
pc-telecommute	2299/tcp	PC Telecommute	wrs_registry	2340/tcp	WRS Registry
pc-telecommute	2299/udp	PC Telecommute	wrs_registry	2340/udp	WRS Registry
cvmmon	2300/tcp	CVMMON	xiostatus	2341/tcp	XIO Status
cvmmon	2300/udp	CVMMON	xiostatus	2341/udp	XIO Status
cpq-wbem	2301/tcp	Compaq HTTP	manage-exec	2342/tcp	Seagate Manage Exec
cpq-wbem	2301/udp	Compaq HTTP	manage-exec	2342/udp	Seagate Manage Exec

Keyword	Decimal	Description	Keyword	Decimal	Description
nati-logos	2343/tcp	nati logos	wusage	2396/tcp	Wusage
nati-logos	2343/udp	nati logos	wusage	2396/udp	Wusage
fcmsys	2344/tcp	fcmsys	ncl	2397/tcp	NCL
fcmsys	2344/udp	fcmsys	ncl	2397/udp	NCL
dbm	2345/tcp	dbm	orbiter	2398/tcp	Orbiter
dbm	2345/udp	dbm	orbiter	2398/udp	Orbiter
redstorm_join	2346/tcp	Game Connection Port	fmpro-fdal	2399/tcp	FileMaker, Inc. - Data Access Layer
redstorm_join	2346/udp	Game Connection Port			
redstorm_find	2347/tcp	Game Announcement and Location	fmpro-fdal	2399/udp	FileMaker, Inc. - Data Access Layer
redstorm_find	2347/udp	Game Announcement and Location	opequus-server	2400/tcp	OpEquus Server
			opequus-server	2400/udp	OpEquus Server
redstorm_info	2348/tcp	Information to query for game status	cvspserver	2401/tcp	cvspserver
			cvspserver	2401/udp	cvspserver
redstorm_info	2348/udp	Information to query for game status	taskmaster2000	2402/tcp	TaskMaster 2000 Server
			taskmaster2000	2402/udp	TaskMaster 2000 Server
redstorm_diag	2349/tcp	Diagnostics Port	taskmaster2000	2403/tcp	TaskMaster 2000 Web
redstorm_diag	2349/udp	Disgnostics Port	taskmaster2000	2403/udp	TaskMaster 2000 Web
psbserver	2350/tcp	psbserver	iec870-5-104	2404/tcp	IEC870-5-104
psbserver	2350/udp	psbserver	iec870-5-104	2404/udp	IEC870-5-104
psrserver	2351/tcp	psrserver	trc-netpoll	2405/tcp	TRC Netpoll
psrserver	2351/udp	psrserver	trc-netpoll	2405/udp	TRC Netpoll
pslserver	2352/tcp	pslserver	jediserver	2406/tcp	JediServer
pslserver	2352/udp	pslserver	jediserver	2406/udp	JediServer
pspserver	2353/tcp	pspserver	orion	2407/tcp	Orion
pspserver	2353/udp	pspserver	orion	2407/udp	Orion
psprserver	2354/tcp	psprserver	optimanet	2408/tcp	OptimaNet
psprserver	2354/udp	psprserver	optimanet	2408/udp	OptimaNet
psdbserver	2355/tcp	psdbserver	sns-protocol	2409/tcp	SNS Protocol
psdbserver	2355/udp	psdbserver	sns-protocol	2409/udp	SNS Protocol
gxtelmd	2356/tcp	GXT License Managemant	vrts-registry	2410/tcp	VRTS Registry
gxtelmd	2356/udp	GXT License Managemant	vrts-registry	2410/udp	VRTS Registry
unihub-server	2357/tcp	UniHub Server	netwave-ap-mgmt	2411/tcp	Netwave AP Management
unihub-server	2357/udp	UniHub Server	netwave-ap-mgmt	2411/udp	Netwave AP Management
futrix	2358/tcp	Futrix	cdn	2412/tcp	CDN
futrix	2358/udp	Futrix	cdn	2412/udp	CDN
flukeserver	2359/tcp	FlukeServer	orion-rmi-reg	2413/tcp	orion-rmi-reg
flukeserver	2359/udp	FlukeServer	orion-rmi-reg	2413/udp	orion-rmi-reg
nexstorindltd	2360/tcp	NexstorIndLtd	interlingua	2414/tcp	Interlingua
nexstorindltd	2360/udp	NexstorIndLtd	interlingua	2414/udp	Interlingua
tl1	2361/tcp	TL1	comtest	2415/tcp	COMTEST
tl1	2361/udp	TL1	comtest	2415/udp	COMTEST
digiman	2362/tcp	digiman	rmtserver	2416/tcp	RMT Server
digiman	2362/udp	digiman	rmtserver	2416/udp	RMT Server
mediacntrlnfsd	2363/tcp	Media Central NFSD	composit-server	2417/tcp	Composit Server
mediacntrlnfsd	2363/udp	Media Central NFSD	composit-server	2417/udp	Composit Server
oi-2000	2364/tcp	OI-2000	cas	2418/tcp	cas
oi-2000	2364/udp	OI-2000	cas	2418/udp	cas
dbref	2365/tcp	dbref	attachmate-s2s	2419/tcp	Attachmate S2S
dbref	2365/udp	dbref	attachmate-s2s	2419/udp	Attachmate S2S
qip-login	2366/tcp	qip-login	dslremote-mgmt	2420/tcp	DSL Remote Management
qip-login	2366/udp	qip-login	dslremote-mgmt	2420/udp	DSL Remote Management
service-ctrl	2367/tcp	Service Control	g-talk	2421/tcp	G-Talk
service-ctrl	2367/udp	Service Control	g-talk	2421/udp	G-Talk
opentable	2368/tcp	OpenTable	crmsbits	2422/tcp	CRMSBITS
opentable	2368/udp	OpenTable	crmsbits	2422/udp	CRMSBITS
acs2000-dsp	2369/tcp	ACS2000 DSP	rnrp	2423/tcp	RNRP
acs2000-dsp	2369/udp	ACS2000 DSP	rnrp	2423/udp	RNRP
l3-hbmon	2370/tcp	L3-HBMon	kofax-svr	2424/tcp	KOFAX-SVR
l3-hbmon	2370/udp	L3-HBMon	kofax-svr	2424/udp	KOFAX-SVR
#	2371-2380	Unassigned	fjitsuappmgr	2425/tcp	Fujitsu App Manager
compaq-https	2381/tcp	Compaq HTTPS	fjitsuappmgr	2425/udp	Fujitsu App Manager
compaq-https	2381/udp	Compaq HTTPS	applianttcp	2426/tcp	Appliant TCP
ms-olap3	2382/tcp	Microsoft OLAP	appliantudp	2426/udp	Appliant UDP
ms-olap3	2382/udp	Microsoft OLAP	mgcp-gateway	2427/tcp	Media Gateway Control Protocol Gateway
ms-olap4	2383/tcp	Microsoft OLAP			
ms-olap4	2383/udp	Microsoft OLAP	mgcp-gateway	2427/udp	Media Gateway Control Protocol Gateway
sd-request	2384/tcp	SD-REQUEST			
sd-request	2384/udp	SD-REQUEST	ott	2428/tcp	One Way Trip Time
#	2384-2388	Unassigned	ott	2428/udp	One Way Trip Time
ovsessionmgr	2389/tcp	OpenView Session Mgr	ft-role	2429/tcp	FT-ROLE
ovsessionmgr	2389/udp	OpenView Session Mgr	ft-role	2429/udp	FT-ROLE
rsmtp	2390/tcp	RSMTP	venus	2430/tcp	venus
rsmtp	2390/udp	RSMTP	venus	2430/udp	venus
3com-net-mgmt	2391/tcp	3COM Net Management	venus-se	2431/tcp	venus-se
3com-net-mgmt	2391/udp	3COM Net Management	venus-se	2431/udp	venus-se
tacticalauth	2392/tcp	Tactical Auth	codasrv	2432/tcp	codasrv
tacticalauth	2392/udp	Tactical Auth	codasrv	2432/udp	codasrv
ms-olap1	2393/tcp	MS OLAP 1	codasrv-se	2433/tcp	codasrv-se
ms-olap1	2393/udp	MS OLAP 1	codasrv-se	2433/udp	codasrv-se
ms-olap2	2394/tcp	MS OLAP 2	pxc-epmap	2434/tcp	pxc-epmap
ms-olap2	2394/udp	MA OLAP 2	pxc-epmap	2434/udp	pxc-epmap
lan900_remote	2395/tcp	LAN900 Remote	optilogic	2435/tcp	OptiLogic
lan900_remote	2395/udp	LAN900 Remote	optilogic	2435/udp	OptiLogic

Keyword	Decimal	Description	Keyword	Decimal	Description
topx	2436/tcp	TOP/X	ssm-cvs	2477/tcp	SecurSight Certificate Verification Service
topx	2436/udp	TOP/X	ssm-cvs	2477/udp	SecurSight Certificate Verification Service
unicontrol	2437/tcp	UniControl	ssm-cssps	2478/tcp	SecurSight Authentication Server (SLL)
unicontrol	2437/udp	UniControl	ssm-cssps	2478/udp	SecurSight Authentication Server (SSL)
msp	2438/tcp	MSP	ssm-els	2479/tcp	SecurSight Event Logging Server (SSL)
msp	2438/udp	MSP	ssm-els	2479/udp	SecurSight Event Logging Server (SSL)
sybasedbsynch	2439/tcp	SybaseDBSynch	lingwood	2480/tcp	Lingwood's Detail
sybasedbsynch	2439/udp	SybaseDBSynch	lingwood	2480/udp	Lingwood's Detail
spearway	2440/tcp	Spearway	giop	2481/tcp	Oracle GIOP
spearway	2440/udp	Spearway	giop	2481/udp	Oracle GIOP
pvsw-inet	2441/tcp	pvsw-inet	giop-ssl	2482/tcp	Oracle GIOP SSL
pvsw-inet	2441/udp	pvsw-inet	giop-ssl	2482/udp	Oracle GIOP SSL
netangel	2442/tcp	Netangel	ttc	2483/tcp	Oracle TTC
netangel	2442/udp	Netangel	ttc	2483/udp	Oracel TTC
powerclientcsf	2443/tcp	PowerClient Central Storage Facility	ttc-ssl	2484/tcp	Oracle TTC SSL
powerclientcsf	2443/udp	PowerClient Central Storage Facility	ttc-ssl	2484/udp	Oracle TTC SSL
btpp2sectrans	2444/tcp	BT PP2 Sectrans	netobjects1	2485/tcp	Net Objects1
btpp2sectrans	2444/udp	BT PP2 Sectrans	netobjects1	2485/udp	Net Objects1
dtn1	2445/tcp	DTN1	netobjects2	2486/tcp	Net Objects2
dtn1	2445/udp	DTN1	netobjects2	2486/udp	Net Objects2
bues_service	2446/tcp	bues_service	pns	2487/tcp	Policy Notice Service
bues_service	2446/udp	bues_service	pns	2487/udp	Policy Notice Service
ovwdb	2447/tcp	OpenView NNM daemon	moy-corp	2488/tcp	Moy Corporation
ovwdb	2447/udp	OpenView NNM daemon	moy-corp	2488/udp	Moy Corporation
hpppssvr	2448/tcp	hpppsvr	tsilb	2489/tcp	TSILB
hpppssvr	2448/udp	hpppsvr	tsilb	2489/udp	TSILB
ratl	2449/tcp	RATL	qip-qdhcp	2490/tcp	qip_qdhcp
ratl	2449/udp	RATL	qip-qdhcp	2490/udp	qip_qdhcp
netadmin	2450/tcp	netadmin	conclave-cpp	2491/tcp	Conclave CPP
netadmin	2450/udp	netadmin	conclave-cpp	2491/udp	Conclave CPP
netchat	2451/tcp	netchat	groove	2492/tcp	GROOVE
netchat	2451/udp	netchat	groove	2492/udp	GROOVE
snifferclient	2452/tcp	SnifferClient	talarian-mqs	2493/tcp	Talarian MQS
snifferclient	2452/udp	SnifferClient	talarian-mqs	2493/udp	Talarian MQS
madge-om	2453/tcp	madge-om	bmc-ar	2494/tcp	BMC AR
madge-om	2453/udp	madge-om	bmc-ar	2494/udp	BMC AR
indx-dds	2454/tcp	IndX-DDS	fast-rem-serv	2495/tcp	Fast Remote Services
indx-dds	2454/udp	IndX-DDS	fast-rem-serv	2495/udp	Fast Remote Services
wago-io-system	2455/tcp	WAGO-IO-SYSTEM	dirgis	2496/tcp	DIRGIS
wago-io-system	2455/udp	WAGO-IO-SYSTEM	dirgis	2496/udp	DIRGIS
altav-remmgt	2456/tcp	altav-remmgt	quaddb	2497/tcp	Quad DB
altav-remmgt	2456/udp	altav-remmgt	quaddb	2497/udp	Quad DB
rapido-ip	2457/tcp	Rapido_IP	odn-castraq	2498/tcp	ODN-CasTraq
rapido-ip	2457/udp	Rapido_IP	odn-castraq	2498/udp	ODN-CasTraq
griffin	2458/tcp	griffin	unicontrol	2499/tcp	UniControl
griffin	2458/udp	griffin	unicontrol	2499/udp	UniControl
community	2459/tcp	Community	rtsserv	2500/tcp	Resource Tracking system server
community	2459/udp	Community	rtsserv	2500/udp	Resource Tracking system server
ms-theater	2460/tcp	ms-theater	rtsclient	2501/tcp	Resource Tracking system client
ms-theater	2460/udp	ms-theater	rtsclient	2501/udp	Resource Tracking system client
qadmifoper	2461/tcp	qadmifoper	kentrox-prot	2502/tcp	Kentrox Protocol
qadmifoper	2461/udp	qadmifoper	kentrox-prot	2502/udp	Kentrox Protocol
qadmifevent	2462/tcp	qadmifevent	nms-dpnss	2503/tcp	NMS-DPNSS
qadmifevent	2462/udp	qadmifevent	nms-dpnss	2503/udp	NMS-DPNSS
symbios-raid	2463/tcp	Symbios Raid	wlbs	2504/tcp	WLBS
symbios-raid	2463/udp	Symbios Raid	wlbs	2504/udp	WLBS
direcpc-si	2464/tcp	DirecPC SI	torque-traffic	2505/tcp	torque-traffic
direcpc-si	2464/udp	DirecPC SI	torque-traffic	2505/udp	torque-traffic
lbm	2465/tcp	Load Balance Management	jbroker	2506/tcp	jbroker
lbm	2465/udp	Load Balance Management	jbroker	2506/udp	jbroker
lbf	2466/tcp	Load Balance Forwarding	spock	2507/tcp	spock
lbf	2466/udp	Load Balance Forwarding	spock	2507/udp	spock
high-criteria	2467/tcp	High Criteria	jdatastore	2508/tcp	JDataStore
high-criteria	2467/udp	High Criteria	jdatastore	2508/udp	JDataStore
qip-msgd	2468/tcp	qip_msgd	fjmpss	2509/tcp	fjmpss
qip-msgd	2468/udp	qip_msgd	fjmpss	2509/udp	fjmpss
mti-tcs-comm	2469/tcp	MTI-TCS-COMM	fjappmgrbulk	2510/tcp	fjappmgrbulk
mti-tcs-comm	2469/udp	MTI-TCS-COMM	fjappmgrbulk	2510/udp	fjappmgrbulk
taskman-port	2470/tcp	taskman-port	metastorm	2511/tcp	Metastorm
taskman-port	2470/udp	taskman port	metastorm	2511/udp	Metastorm
seaodbc	2471/tcp	SeaODBC	citrixima	2512/tcp	Citrix IMA
seaodbc	2471/udp	SeaODBC	citrixima	2512/udp	Citrix IMA
c3	2472/tcp	C3	citrixadmin	2513/tcp	Citrix ADMIN
c3	2472/udp	C3	citrixadmin	2513/udp	Citrix ADMIN
aker-cdp	2473/tcp	Aker-cdp			
aker-cdp	2473/udp	Aker-cdp			
vitalanalysis	2474/tcp	Vital Analysis			
vitalanalysis	2474/udp	Vital Analysis			
ace-server	2475/tcp	ACE Server			
ace-server	2475/udp	ACE Server			
ace-svr-prop	2476/tcp	ACE Server Propagation			
ace-svr-prop	2476/udp	ACE Server Propagation			

Keyword	Decimal Description		Keyword	Decimal Description
facsys-ntp	2514/tcp	Facsys NTP	vcnet-link-v10	2554/tcp	VCnet-Link v10
facsys-ntp	2514/udp	Facsys NTP	vcnet-link-v10	2554/udp	VCnet-Link v10
facsys-router	2515/tcp	Facsys Router	compaq-wcp	2555/tcp	Compaq WCP
facsys-router	2515/udp	Facsys Router	compaq-wcp	2555/udp	Compaq WCP
maincontrol	2516/tcp	Main Control	nicetec-nmsvc	2556/tcp	nicetec-nmsvc
maincontrol	2516/udp	Main Control	nicetec-nmsvc	2556/udp	nicetec-nmsvc
call-sig-trans	2517/tcp	H.323 Annex E call signaling transport	nicetec-mgmt	2557/tcp	nicetec-mgmt
call-sig-trans	2517/udp	H.323 Annex E call signaling transport	nicetec-mgmt	2557/udp	nicetec-mgmt
			pclemultimedia	2558/tcp	PCLE Multi Media
			pclemultimedia	2558/udp	PCLE Multi Media
willy	2518/tcp	Willy	lstp	2559/tcp	LSTP
willy	2518/udp	Willy	lstp	2559/udp	LSTP
globmsgsvc	2519/tcp	globmsgsvc	labrat	2560/tcp	labrat
globmsgsvc	2519/udp	globmsgsvc	labrat	2560/udp	labrat
pvsw	2520/tcp	pvsw	mosaixcc	2561/tcp	MosaixCC
pvsw	2520/udp	pvsw	mosaixcc	2561/udp	MosaixCC
adaptecmgr	2521/tcp	Adaptec Manager	delibo	2562/tcp	Delibo
adaptecmgr	2521/udp	Adaptec Manager	delibo	2562/udp	Delibo
windb	2522/tcp	WinDb	cti-redwood	2563/tcp	CTI Redwood
windb	2522/udp	WinDb	cti-redwood	2563/udp	CTI Redwood
qke-llc-v3	2523/tcp	Qke LLC V.3	hp-3000-telnet	2564/tcp	HP 3000 NS/VT block mode telnet
qke-llc-v3	2523/udp	Qke LLC V.3			
optiwave-lm	2524/tcp	Optiwave License Management	coord-svr	2565/tcp	Coordinator Server
			coord-svr	2565/udp	Coordinator Server
optiwave-lm	2524/udp	Optiwave License Management	pcs-pcw	2566/tcp	pcs-pcw
			pcs-pcw	2566/udp	pcs-pcw
ms-v-worlds	2525/tcp	MS V-Worlds	clp	2567/tcp	Cisco Line Protocol
ms-v-worlds	2525/udp	MS V-Worlds	clp	2567/udp	Cisco Line Protocol
ema-sent-lm	2526/tcp	EMA License Manager	spamtrap	2568/tcp	SPAM TRAP
ema-sent-lm	2526/udp	EMA License Manager	spamtrap	2568/udp	SPAM TRAP
iqserver	2527/tcp	IQ Server	sonuscallsig	2569/tcp	Sonus Call Signal
iqserver	2527/udp	IQ Server	sonuscallsig	2569/udp	Sonus Call Signal
ncr_ccl	2528/tcp	NCR CCL	hs-port	2570/tcp	HS Port
ncr_ccl	2528/udp	NCR CCL	hs-port	2570/udp	HS Port
utsftp	2529/tcp	UTS FTP	cecsvc	2571/tcp	CECSVC
utsftp	2529/udp	UTS FTP	cecsvc	2571/udp	CECSVC
vrcommerce	2530/tcp	VR Commerce	ibp	2572/tcp	IBP
vrcommerce	2530/udp	VR Commerce	ibp	2572/udp	IBP
ito-e-gui	2531/tcp	ITO-E GUI	trustestablish	2573/tcp	Trust Establish
ito-e-gui	2531/udp	ITO-E GUI	trustestablish	2573/udp	Trust Establish
ovtopmd	2532/tcp	OVTOPMD	blockade-bpsp	2574/tcp	Blockade BPSP
ovtopmd	2532/udp	OVTOPMD	blockade-bpsp	2574/udp	Blockade BPSP
snifferserver	2533/tcp	SnifferServer	hl7	2575/tcp	HL7
snifferserver	2533/udp	SnifferServer	hl7	2575/udp	HL7
combox-web-acc	2534/tcp	Combox Web Access	tclprodebugger	2576/tcp	TCL Pro Debugger
combox-web-acc	2534/udp	Combox Web Access	tclprodebugger	2576/udp	TCL Pro Debugger
madcap	2535/tcp	MADCAP	scipticslsrvr	2577/tcp	Scriptics Lsrvr
madcap	2535/udp	MADCAP	scipticslsrvr	2577/udp	Scriptics Lsrvr
btpp2audctr1	2536/tcp	btpp2audctr1	rvs-isdn-dcp	2578/tcp	RVS ISDN DCP
btpp2audctr1	2536/udp	btpp2audctr1	rvs-isdn-dcp	2578/udp	RVS ISDN DCP
upgrade	2537/tcp	Upgrade Protocol	mpfoncl	2579/tcp	mpfoncl
upgrade	2537/udp	Upgrade Protocol	mpfoncl	2579/udp	mpfoncl
vnwk-prapi	2538/tcp	vnwk-prapi	tributary	2580/tcp	Tributary
vnwk-prapi	2538/udp	vnwk-prapi	tributary	2580/udp	Tributary
vsiadmin	2539/tcp	VSI Admin	argis-te	2581/tcp	ARGIS TE
vsiadmin	2539/udp	VSI Admin	argis-te	2581/udp	ARGIS TE
lonworks	2540/tcp	LonWorks	argis-ds	2582/tcp	ARGIS DS
lonworks	2540/udp	LonWorks	argis-ds	2582/udp	ARGIS DS
lonworks2	2541/tcp	LonWorks2	mon	2583/tcp	MON
lonworks2	2541/udp	LonWorks2	mon	2583/udp	MON
davinci	2542/tcp	daVinci	cyaserv	2584/tcp	cyaserv
davinci	2542/udp	daVinci	cyaserv	2584/udp	cyaserv
reftek	2543/tcp	REFTEK	netx-server	2585/tcp	NETX Server
reftek	2543/udp	REFTEK	netx-server	2585/udp	NETX Server
novell-zen	2544/tcp	Novell ZEN	netx-agent	2586/tcp	NETX Agent
novell-zen	2544/udp	Novell ZEN	netx-agent	2586/udp	NETX Agent
sis-emt	2545/tcp	sis-emt	masc	2587/tcp	MASC
sis-emt	2545/udp	sis-emt	masc	2587/udp	MASC
vytalvaultbrtp	2546/tcp	vytalvaultbrtp	privilege	2588/tcp	Privilege
vytalvaultbrtp	2546/udp	vytalvaultbrtp	privilege	2588/udp	Privilege
vytalvaultvsmp	2547/tcp	vytalvaultvsmp	quartus-tcl	2589/tcp	quartus tcl
vytalvaultvsmp	2547/udp	vytalvaultvsmp	quartus-tcl	2589/udp	quartus tcl
vytalvaultpipe	2548/tcp	vytalvaultpipe	idotdist	2590/tcp	idotdist
vytalvaultpipe	2548/udp	vytalvaultpipe	idotdist	2590/udp	idotdist
ipass	2549/tcp	IPASS	maytagshuffle	2591/tcp	Maytag Shuffle
ipass	2549/udp	IPASS	maytagshuffle	2591/udp	Maytag Shuffle
ads	2550/tcp	ADS	netrek	2592/tcp	netrek
ads	2550/udp	ADS	netrek	2592/udp	netrek
isg-uda-server	2551/tcp	ISG UDA Server	mns-mail	2593/tcp	MNS Mail Notice Service
isg-uda-server	2551/udp	ISG UDA Server	mns-mail	2593/udp	MNS Mail Notice Service
call-logging	2552/tcp	Call Logging	dts	2594/tcp	Data Base Server
call-logging	2552/udp	Call Logging	dts	2594/udp	Data Base Server
efidiningport	2553/tcp	efidiningport	worldfusion1	2595/tcp	World Fusion 1
efidiningport	2553/udp	efidiningport	worldfusion1	2595/udp	World Fusion 1

Keyword	Decimal	Description	Keyword	Decimal	Description
worldfusion2	2596/tcp	World Fusion 2	sybaseanywhere	2638/tcp	Sybase Anywhere
worldfusion2	2596/udp	World Fusion 2	sybaseanywhere	2638/udp	Sybase Anywhere
homesteadglory	2597/tcp	Homestead Glory	aminet	2639/tcp	AMInet
homesteadglory	2597/udp	Homestead Glory	aminet	2639/udp	AMInet
citriximaclient	2598/tcp	Citrix MA Client	sai_sentlm	2640/tcp	Sabbagh Associates Licence Manager
citriximaclient	2598/udp	Citrix MA Client	sai_sentlm	2640/udp	Sabbagh Associates Licence Manager
meridiandata	2599/tcp	Meridian Data			
meridiandata	2599/udp	Meridian Data	hdl-srv	2641/tcp	HDL Server
hpstgmgr	2600/tcp	HPSTGMGR	hdl-srv	2641/udp	HDL Server
hpstgmgr	2600/udp	HPSTGMGR	tragic	2642/tcp	Tragic
discp-client	2601/tcp	discp client	tragic	2642/udp	Tragic
discp-client	2601/udp	discp client	gte-samp	2643/tcp	GTE-SAMP
discp-server	2602/tcp	discp server	gte-samp	2643/udp	GTE-SAMP
discp-server	2602/udp	discp server	travsoft-ipx-t	2644/tcp	Travsoft IPX Tunnel
servicemeter	2603/tcp	Service Meter	travsoft-ipx-t	2644/udp	Travsoft IPX Tunnel
servicemeter	2603/udp	Service Meter	novell-ipx-cmd	2645/tcp	Novell IPX CMD
nsc-ccs	2604/tcp	NSC CCS	novell-ipx-cmd	2645/udp	Novell IPX CMD
nsc-ccs	2604/udp	NSC CCS	and-lm	2646/tcp	AND Licence Manager
nsc-posa	2605/tcp	NSC POSA	and-lm	2646/udp	AND License Manager
nsc-posa	2605/udp	NSC POSA	syncserver	2647/tcp	SyncServer
netmon	2606/tcp	Dell Netmon	syncserver	2647/udp	SyncServer
netmon	2606/udp	Dell Netmon	upsnotifyprot	2648/tcp	Upsnotifyprot
connection	2607/tcp	Dell Connection	upsnotifyprot	2648/udp	Upsnotifyprot
connection	2607/udp	Dell Connection	vpsipport	2649/tcp	VPSIPPORT
wag-service	2608/tcp	Wag Service	vpsipport	2649/udp	VPSIPPORT
wag-service	2608/udp	Wag Service	eristwoguns	2650/tcp	eristwoguns
system-monitor	2609/tcp	System Monitor	eristwoguns	2650/udp	eristwoguns
system-monitor	2609/udp	System Monitor	ebinsite	2651/tcp	EBInSite
versa-tek	2610/tcp	VersaTek	ebinsite	2651/udp	EBInSite
versa-tek	2610/udp	VersaTek	interpathpanel	2652/tcp	InterPathPanel
lionhead	2611/tcp	LIONHEAD	interpathpanel	2652/udp	InterPathPanel
lionhead	2611/udp	LIONHEAD	sonus	2653/tcp	Sonus
qpasa-agent	2612/tcp	Qpasa Agent	sonus	2653/udp	Sonus
qpasa-agent	2612/udp	Qpasa Agent	corel_vncadmin	2654/tcp	Corel VNC Admin
smntubootstrap	2613/tcp	SMNTUBootstrap	corel_vncadmin	2654/udp	Corel VNC Admin
smntubootstrap	2613/udp	SMNTUBootstrap	unglue	2655/tcp	UNIX Nt Glue
neveroffline	2614/tcp	Never Offline	unglue	2655/udp	UNIX Nt Glue
neveroffline	2614/udp	Never Offline	kana	2656/tcp	Kana
firepower	2615/tcp	firepower	kana	2656/udp	Kana
firepower	2615/udp	firepower	sns-dispatcher	2657/tcp	SNS Dispatcher
appswitch-emp	2616/tcp	appswitch-emp	sns-dispatcher	2657/udp	SNS Dispatcher
appswitch-emp	2616/udp	appswitch-emp	sns-admin	2658/tcp	SNS Admin
cmadmin	2617/tcp	Clinical Context Managers	sns-admin	2658/udp	SNS Admin
cmadmin	2617/udp	Clinical Context Managers	sns-query	2659/tcp	SNS Query
priority-e-com	2618/tcp	Priority E-Com	sns-query	2659/udp	SNS Query
priority-e-com	2618/udp	Priority E-Com	gcmonitor	2660/tcp	GC Monitor
bruce	2619/tcp	bruce	gcmonitor	2660/udp	GC Monitor
bruce	2619/udp	bruce	olhost	2661/tcp	OLHOST
lpsrecommender	2620/tcp	LPSRecommender	olhost	2661/udp	OLHOST
lpsrecommender	2620/udp	LPSRecommender	bintec-capi	2662/tcp	BinTec-CAPI
miles-apart	2621/tcp	Miles Apart Jukebox Server	bintec-capi	2662/udp	BinTec-CAPI
miles-apart	2621/udp	Miles Apart Jukebox Server	bintec-tapi	2663/tcp	BinTec-TAPI
metricadbc	2622/tcp	MetricaDBC	bintec-tapi	2663/udp	BinTec-TAPI
metricadbc	2622/udp	MetricaDBC	command-mq-gm	2664/tcp	Command MQ GM
lmdp	2623/tcp	LMDP	command-mq-gm	2664/udp	Command MQ GM
lmdp	2623/udp	LMDP	command-mq-pm	2665/tcp	Command MQ PM
aria	2624/tcp	Aria	command-mq-pm	2665/udp	Command MQ PM
aria	2624/udp	Aria	extensis	2666/tcp	extensis
blwnkl-port	2625/tcp	Blwnkl Port	extensis	2666/udp	extensis
blwnkl-port	2625/udp	Blwnkl Port	alarm-clock-s	2667/tcp	Alarm Clock Server
gbjd816	2626/tcp	gbjd816	alarm-clock-s	2667/udp	Alarm Clock Server
gbjd816	2626/udp	gbjd816	alarm-clock-c	2668/tcp	Alarm Clock Client
moshebeeri	2627/tcp	Moshe Beeri	alarm-clock-c	2668/udp	Alarm Clock Client
moshebeeri	2627/udp	Moshe Beeri	toad	2669/tcp	TOAD
dict	2628/tcp	DICT	toad	2669/udp	TOAD
dict	2628/udp	DICT	tve-announce	2670/tcp	TVE Announce
sitaraserver	2629/tcp	Sitara Server	tve-announce	2670/udp	TVE Announce
sitaraserver	2629/udp	Sitara Server	newlixreg	2671/tcp	newlixreg
sitaramgmt	2630/tcp	Sitara Management	newlixreg	2671/udp	newlixreg
sitaramgmt	2630/udp	Sitara Management	nhserver	2672/tcp	nhserver
sitaradir	2631/tcp	Sitara Dir	nhserver	2672/udp	nhserver
sitaradir	2631/udp	Sitara Dir	firstcall42	2673/tcp	First Call 42
irdg-post	2632/tcp	IRdg Post	firstcall42	2673/udp	First Call 42
irdg-post	2632/udp	IRdg Post	ewnn	2674/tcp	ewnn
interintelli	2633/tcp	InterIntelli	ewnn	2674/udp	ewnn
interintelli	2633/udp	InterIntelli	ttc-etap	2675/tcp	TTC ETAP
pk-electronics	2634/tcp	PK Electronics	ttc-etap	2675/udp	TTC ETAP
pk-electronics	2634/udp	PK Electronics	simslink	2676/tcp	SIMSLink
backburner	2635/tcp	Back Burner	simslink	2676/udp	SIMSLink
backburner	2635/udp	Back Burner	gadgetgate1way	2677/tcp	Gadget Gate 1 Way
solve	2636/tcp	Solve	gadgetgate1way	2677/udp	Gadget Gate 1 Way
solve	2636/udp	Solve	gadgetgate2way	2678/tcp	Gadget Gate 2 Way
imdocsvc	2637/tcp	Import Document Service	gadgetgate2way	2678/udp	Gadget Gate 2 Way
imdocsvc	2637/udp	Import Document Service			

Keyword	Decimal	Description	Keyword	Decimal	Description
syncserverssl	2679/tcp	Sync Server SSL	wkars	2720/tcp	wkars
syncserverssl	2679/udp	Sync Server SSL	wkars	2720/udp	wkars
pxc-sapxom	2680/tcp	pxc-sapxom	smart-diagnose	2721/tcp	Smart Diagnose
pxc-sapxom	2680/udp	pxc-sapxom	smart-diagnose	2721/udp	Smart Diagnose
mpnjsomb	2681/tcp	mpnjsomb	proactivesrvr	2722/tcp	Proactive Server
mpnjsomb	2681/udp	mpnjsomb	proactivesrvr	2722/udp	Proactive Server
srsp	2682/tcp	SRSP	watchdognt	2723/tcp	WatchDog NT
srsp	2682/udp	SRSP	watchdognt	2723/udp	WatchDog NT
ncdloadbalance	2683/tcp	NCDLoadBalance	qotps	2724/tcp	qotps
ncdloadbalance	2683/udp	NCDLoadBalance	qotps	2724/udp	qotps
mpnjsosv	2684/tcp	mpnjsosv	msolap-ptp2	2725/tcp	MSOLAP PTP2
mpnjsosv	2684/udp	mpnjsosv	msolap-ptp2	2725/udp	MSOLAP PTP2
mpnjsocl	2685/tcp	mpnjsocl	tams	2726/tcp	TAMS
mpnjsocl	2685/udp	mpnjsocl	tams	2726/udp	TAMS
mpnjsomg	2686/tcp	mpnjsomg	mgcp-callagent	2727/tcp	Media Gateway Control Protocol Call Agent
mpnjsomg	2686/udp	mpnjsomg			
pq-lic-mgmt	2687/tcp	pq-lic-mgmt	mgcp-callagent	2727/udp	Media Gateway Control Protocol Call Agent
pq-lic-mgmt	2087/udp	pq-lic-mgmt			
md-cg-http	2688/tcp	md-cf-http	sqdr	2728/tcp	SQDR
md-cg-http	2688/udp	md-cf-http	sqdr	2728/udp	SQDR
fastlynx	2689/tcp	FastLynx	tcim-control	2729/tcp	TCIM Control
fastlynx	2689/udp	FastLynx	tcim-control	2729/udp	TCIM Control
hp-nnm-data	2690/tcp	HP NNM Embedded Database	nec-raidplus	2730/tcp	NEC RaidPlus
hp-nnm-data	2690/udp	HP NNM Embedded Database	nec-raidplus	2730/udp	NEC RaidPlus
itinternet	2691/tcp	IT Internet	netdragon-msngr	2731/tcp	NetDragon Messenger
itinternet	2691/udp	IT Internet	netdragon-msngr	2731/udp	NetDragon Messenger
admins-lms	2692/tcp	Admins LMS	g5m	2732/tcp	G5M
admins-lms	2692/udp	Admins LMS	g5m	2732/udp	G5M
belarc-http	2693/tcp	belarc-http	signet-ctf	2733/tcp	Signet CTF
belarc-http	2693/udp	belarc-http	signet-ctf	2733/udp	Signet CTF
pwrsevent	2694/tcp	pwrsevent	ccs-software	2734/tcp	CCS Software
pwrsevent	2694/udp	pwrsevent	ccs-software	2734/udp	CCS Software
vspread	2695/tcp	VSPREAD	netiq-mc	2735/tcp	NetIQ Monitor Console
vspread	2695/udp	VSPREAD	netiq-mc	2735/udp	NetIQ Monitor Console
unifyadmin	2696/tcp	Unify Admin	radwiz-nms-srv	2736/tcp	RADWIZ NMS SRV
unifyadmin	2696/udp	Unify Admin	radwiz-nms-srv	2736/udp	RADWIZ NMS SRV
oce-snmp-trap	2697/tcp	Oce SNMP Trap Port	srp-feedback	2737/tcp	SRP Feedback
oce-snmp-trap	2697/udp	Oce SNMP Trap Port	srp-feedback	2737/udp	SRP Feedback
mck-ivpip	2698/tcp	MCK-IVPIP	ndl-tcp-ois-gw	2738/tcp	NDL TCP-OSI Gateway
mck-ivpip	2698/udp	MCK-IVPIP	ndl-tcp-ois-gw	2738/udp	NDL TCP-OSI Gateway
csoft-plusclnt	2699/tcp	Csoft Plus Client	tn-timing	2739/tcp	TN Timing
csoft-plusclnt	2699/udp	Csoft Plus Client	tn-timing	2739/udp	TN Timing
tqdata	2700/tcp	tqdata	alarm	2740/tcp	Alarm
tqdata	2700/udp	tqdata	alarm	2740/udp	Alarm
sms-rcinfo	2701/tcp	SMS RCINFO	tsb	2741/tcp	TSB
sms-rcinfo	2701/udp	SMS RCINFO	tsb	2741/udp	TSB
sms-xfer	2702/tcp	SMS XFER	tsb2	2742/tcp	TSB2
sms-xfer	2702/udp	SMS XFER	tsb2	2742/udp	TSB2
sms-chat	2703/tcp	SMS CHAT	murx	2743/tcp	murx
sms-chat	2703/udp	SMS CHAT	murx	2743/udp	murx
sms-remctrl	2704/tcp	SMS REMCTRL	honyaku	2744/tcp	honyaku
sms-remctrl	2704/udp	SMS REMCTRL	honyaku	2744/udp	honyaku
sds-admin	2705/tcp	SDS Admin	urbisnet	2745/tcp	URBISNET
sds-admin	2705/udp	SDS Admin	urbisnet	2745/udp	URBISNET
ncdmirroring	2706/tcp	NCD Mirroring	cpudpencap	2746/tcp	CPUDPENCAP
ncdmirroring	2706/udp	NCD Mirroring	cpudpencap	2746/udp	CPUDPENCAP
emcsymapiport	2707/tcp	EMCSYMAPIPORT	fjippol-swrly	2747/tcp	
emcsymapiport	2707/udp	EMCSYMAPIPORT	fjippol-swrly	2747/udp	
banyan-net	2708/tcp	Banyan-Net	fjippol-polsvr	2748/tcp	
banyan-net	2708/udp	Banyan-Net	fjippol-polsvr	2748/udp	
supermon	2709/tcp	Supermon	fjippol-cnsl	2749/tcp	
supermon	2709/udp	Supermon	fjippol-cnsl	2749/udp	
sso-service	2710/tcp	SSO Service	fjippol-port1	2750/tcp	
sso-service	2710/udp	SSO Service	fjippol-port1	2750/udp	
sso-control	2711/tcp	SSO Control	fjippol-port2	2751/tcp	
sso-control	2711/udp	SSO Control	fjippol-port2	2751/udp	
aocp	2712/tcp	Axapta Object Communication Protocol	rsisysaccess	2752/tcp	RSISYS ACCESS
			rsisysaccess	2752/udp	RSISYS ACCESS
aocp	2712/udp	Axapta Object Communication Protocol	de-spot	2753/tcp	de-spot
			de-spot	2753/udp	de-spot
raven1	2713/tcp	Raven1	apollo-cc	2754/tcp	APOLLO CC
raven1	2713/udp	Raven1	apollo-cc	2754/udp	APOLLO CC
raven2	2714/tcp	Raven2	expresspay	2755/tcp	Express Pay
raven2	2714/tcp	Raven2	expresspay	2755/udp	Express Pay
hpstgmgr2	2715/tcp	HPSTGMGR2	simplement-tie	2756/tcp	simplement-tie
hpstgmgr2	2715/udp	HPSTGMGR2	simplement-tie	2756/udp	simplement-tie
inova-ip-disco	2716/tcp	Inova IP Disco	cnrp	2757/tcp	CNRP
inova-ip-disco	2716/udp	Inova IP Disco	cnrp	2757/udp	CNRP
pn-requester	2717/tcp	PN REQUESTER	apollo-status	2758/tcp	APOLLO Status
pn-requester	2717/udp	PN REQUESTER	apollo-status	2758/udp	APOLLO Status
pn-requester2	2718/tcp	PN REQUESTER 2	apollo-gms	2759/tcp	APOLLO GMS
pn-requester2	2718/udp	PN REQUESTER 2	apollo-gms	2759/udp	APOLLO GMS
scan-change	2719/tcp	Scan & Change	sabams	2760/tcp	Saba MS
scan-change	2719/udp	Scan & Change	sabams	2760/udp	Saba MS

Keyword	Decimal	Description	Keyword	Decimal	Description
dicom-iscl	2761/tcp	DICOM ISCL	esp-encap	2797/tcp	esp-encap
dicom-iscl	2761/udp	DICOM ISCL	esp-encap	2797/udp	esp-encap
dicom-tls	2762/tcp	DICOM TLS	tmesis-upshot	2798/tcp	TMESIS-UPShot
dicom-tls	2762/udp	DICOM TLS	tmesis-upshot	2798/udp	TMESIS-UPShot
desktop-dna	2763/tcp	Desktop DNA	icon-discover	2799/tcp	ICON Discover
desktop-dna	2763/udp	Desktop DNA	icon-discover	2799/udp	ICON Discover
data-insurance	2764/tcp	Data Insurance	acc-raid	2800/tcp	ACC RAID
data-insurance	2764/udp	Data Insurance	acc-raid	2800/udp	ACC RAID
qip-audup	2765/tcp	qip-audup	igcp	2801/tcp	IGCP
qip-audup	2765/udp	qip-audup	igcp	2801/udp	IGCP
compaq-scp	2766/tcp	Compaq SCP	veritas-tcp1	2802/tcp	Veritas TCP1
compaq-scp	2766/udp	Compaq SCP	veritas-udp1	2802/udp	Veritas UDP1
uadtc	2767/tcp	UADTC	btprjctrl	2803/tcp	btprjctrl
uadtc	2767/udp	UADTC	btprjctrl	2803/udp	btprjctrl
uacs	2768/tcp	UACS	telexis-vtu	2804/tcp	Telexis VTU
uacs	2768/udp	UACS	telexis-vtu	2804/udp	Telexis VTU
singlept-mvs	2769/tcp	Single Point MVS	wta-wsp-s	2805/tcp	WTA WSP-S
singlept-mvs	2769/udp	Single Point MVS	wta-wsp-s	2805/udp	WTA WSP-S
veronica	2770/tcp	Veronica	cspuni	2806/tcp	cspuni
veronica	2770/udp	Veronica	cspuni	2806/udp	cspuni
vergencecm	2771/tcp	Vergence CM	cspmulti	2807/tcp	cspmulti
vergencecm	2771/udp	Vergence CM	cspmulti	2807/udp	cspmulti
auris	2772/tcp	auris	j-lan-p	2808/tcp	J-LAN-P
auris	2772/udp	auris	j-lan-p	2808/udp	J-LAN-P
pcbakcup1	2773/tcp	PC Backup	corbaloc	2809/tcp	CORBA LOC
pcbakcup1	2773/udp	PC Backup	corbaloc	2809/udp	CORBA LOC
pcbakcup2	2774/tcp	PC Backup	netsteward	2810/tcp	Active Net Steward
pcbakcup2	2774/udp	PC Backup	netsteward	2810/udp	Active Net Steward
smpp	2775/tcp	smpp	gsiftp	2811/tcp	GSI FTP
smpp	2775/udp	smpp	gsiftp	2811/udp	GSI FTP
ridgeway1	2776/tcp	Ridgeway Systems & Software	atmtcp	2812/tcp	atmtcp
			atmtcp	2812/udp	atmtcp
ridgeway1	2776/udp	Ridgeway Systems & Software	llm-pass	2813/tcp	llm-pass
			llm-pass	2813/udp	llm-pass
ridgeway2	2777/tcp	Ridgeway Systems & Software	llm-csv	2814/tcp	llm-csv
			llm-csv	2814/udp	llm-csv
ridgeway2	2777/udp	Ridgeway Systems & Software	lbc-measure	2815/tcp	LBC Measurement
			lbc-measure	2815/udp	LBC Measurement
gwen-sonya	2778/tcp	Gwen-Sonya	lbc-watchdog	2816/tcp	LBC Watchdog
gwen-sonya	2778/udp	Gwen-Sonya	lbc-watchdog	2816/udp	LBC Watchdog
lbc-sync	2779/tcp	LBC Sync	nmsigport	2817/tcp	NMSig Port
lbc-sync	2779/udp	LBC Sync	nmsigport	2817/udp	NMSig Port
lbc-control	2780/tcp	LBC Control	rmlnk	2818/tcp	rmlnk
lbc-control	2780/udp	LBC Control	rmlnk	2818/udp	rmlnk
whosells	2781/tcp	whosells	fc-faultnotify	2819/tcp	FC Fault Notification
whosells	2781/udp	whosells	fc-faultnotify	2819/udp	FC Fault Notification
everydayrc	2782/tcp	everydayrc	univision	2820/tcp	UniVision
everydayrc	2782/udp	everydayrc	univision	2820/udp	UniVision
aises	2783/tcp	AISES	vml-dms	2821/tcp	vml_dms
aises	2783/udp	AISES	vml-dms	2821/udp	vml_dms
www-dev	2784/tcp	world wide web - development	ka0wuc	2822/tcp	ka0wuc
			ka0wuc	2822/udp	ka0wuc
www-dev	2784/udp	world wide web - development	cqg-netlan	2823/tcp	CQG Net/LAN
			cqg-netlan	2823/udp	CQG Net/LAN
aic-np	2785/tcp	aic-np	slc-systemlog	2826/tcp	slc systemlog
aic-np	2785/udp	aic-np	slc-systemlog	2826/udp	slc systemlog
aic-oncrpc	2786/tcp	aic-oncrpc - Destiny MCD database	slc-ctrlrloops	2827/tcp	slc ctrlrloops
			slc-ctrlrloops	2827/udp	slc ctrlrloops
aic-oncrpc	2786/udp	aic-oncrpc - Destiny MCD database	itm-lm	2828/tcp	ITM License Manager
			itm-lm	2828/udp	ITM License Manager
piccolo	2787/tcp	piccolo - Cornerstone Software	silkp1	2829/tcp	silkp1
			silkp1	2829/udp	silkp1
piccolo	2787/udp	piccolo - Cornerstone Software	silkp2	2830/tcp	silkp2
			silkp2	2830/udp	silkp2
fryeserv	2788/tcp	NetWare Loadable Module - Seagate Software	silkp3	2831/tcp	silkp3
			silkp3	2831/udp	silkp3
fryeserv	2788/udp	NetWare Loadable Module - Seagate Software	silkp4	2832/tcp	silkp4
			silkp4	2832/udp	silkp4
media-agent	2789/tcp	Media Agent	glishd	2833/tcp	glishd
media-agent	2789/udp	Media Agent	glishd	2833/udp	glishd
plgproxy	2790/tcp	PLG Proxy	evtp	2834/tcp	EVTP
plgproxy	2790/udp	PLG Proxy	evtp	2834/udp	EVTP
mtport-regist	2791/tcp	MT Port Registrator	evtp-data	2835/tcp	EVTP-DATA
mtport-regist	2791/udp	MT Port Registrator	evtp-data	2835/udp	EVTP-DATA
f5-globalsite	2792/tcp	f5-globalsite	catalyst	2836/tcp	catalyst
f5-globalsite	2792/udp	f5-globalsite	catalyst	2836/udp	catalyst
initlsmsad	2793/tcp	initlsmsad	repliweb	2837/tcp	Repliweb
initlsmsad	2793/udp	initlsmsad	repliweb	2837/udp	Repliweb
aaftp	2794/tcp	aaftp	starbot	2838/tcp	Starbot
aaftp	2794/udp	aaftp	starbot	2838/udp	Starbot
livestats	2795/tcp	LiveStats	nmsigport	2839/tcp	NMSigPort
livestats	2795/udp	LiveStats	nmsigport	2839/udp	NMSigPort
ac-tech	2796/tcp	ac-tech	l3-exprt	2840/tcp	l3-exprt
ac-tech	2796/udp	ac-tech	l3-exprt	2840/udp	l3-exprt

Keyword	Decimal	Description	Keyword	Decimal	Description
l3-ranger	2841/tcp	l3-ranger	flashmsg	2884/tcp	Flash Msg
l3-ranger	2841/udp	l3-ranger	flashmsg	2884/udp	Flash Msg
l3-hawk	2842/tcp	l3-hawk	topflow	2885/tcp	TopFlow
l3-hawk	2842/udp	l3-hawk	topflow	2885/udp	TopFlow
pdnet	2843/tcp	PDnet	responselogic	2886/tcp	RESPONSELOGIC
pdnet	2843/udp	PDnet	responselogic	2886/udp	RESPONSELOGIC
bpcp-poll	2844/tcp	BPCP POLL	aironetddp	2887/tcp	aironet
bpcp-poll	2844/udp	BPCP POLL	aironetddp	2887/udp	aironet
bpcp-trap	2845/tcp	BPCP TRAP	spcsdlobby	2888/tcp	SPCSDLOBBY
bpcp-trap	2845/udp	BPCP TRAP	spcsdlobby	2888/udp	SPCSDLOBBY
aimpp-hello	2846/tcp	AIMPP Hello	rsom	2889/tcp	RSOM
aimpp-hello	2846/udp	AIMPP Hello	rsom	2889/udp	RSOM
aimpp-port-req	2847/tcp	AIMPP Port Req	cspclmulti	2890/tcp	CSPCLMULTI
aimpp-port-req	2847/udp	AIMPP Port Req	cspclmulti	2890/udp	CSPCLMULTI
amt-blc-port	2848/tcp	AMT-BLC-PORT	cinegrfx-elmd	2891/tcp	CINEGRFX-ELMD License Manager
amt-blc-port	2848/udp	AMT-BLC-PORT			
fxp	2849/tcp	FXP	cinegrfx-elmd	2891/udp	CINEGRFX-ELMD License Manager
fxp	2849/udp	FXP			
metaconsole	2850/tcp	MetaConsole	snifferdata	2892/tcp	SNIFFERDATA
metaconsole	2850/udp	MetaConsole	snifferdata	2892/udp	SNIFFERDATA
webemshttp	2851/tcp	webemshttp	vseconnector	2893/tcp	VSECONNECTOR
webemshttp	2851/udp	webemshttp	vseconnector	2893/udp	VSECONNECTOR
bears-01	2852/tcp	bears-01	abacus-remote	2894/tcp	ABACUS-REMOTE
bears-01	2852/udp	bears-01	abacus-remote	2894/udp	ABACUS-REMOTE
ispipes	2853/tcp	ISPipes	natuslink	2895/tcp	NATUS LINK
ispipes	2853/udp	ISPipes	natuslink	2895/udp	NATUS LINK
infomover	2854/tcp	InfoMover	ecovisiong6-1	2896/tcp	ECOVISIONG6-1
infomover	2854/udp	InfoMover	ecovisiong6-1	2896/udp	ECOVISIONG6-1
cesdinv	2856/tcp	cesdinv	citrix-rtmp	2897/tcp	Citrix RTMP
cesdinv	2856/udp	cesdinv	citrix-rtmp	2897/udp	Citrix RTMP
simctlp	2857/tcp	SimCtlP	appliance-cfg	2898/tcp	APPLIANCE-CFG
simctlp	2857/udp	SimCtlP	appliance-cfg	2898/udp	APPLIANCE-CFG
ecnp	2858/tcp	ECNP	powergemplus	2899/tcp	POWERGEMPLUS
ecnp	2858/udp	ECNP	powergemplus	2899/udp	POWERGEMPLUS
activememory	2859/tcp	Active Memory	quicksuite	2900/tcp	QUICKSUITE
activememory	2859/udp	Active Memory	quicksuite	2900/udp	QUICKSUITE
dialpad-voice1	2860/tcp	Dialpad Voice 1	allstorcns	2901/tcp	ALLSTORCNS
dialpad-voice1	2860/udp	Dialpad Voice 1	allstorcns	2901/udp	ALLSTORCNS
dialpad-voice2	2861/tcp	Dialpad Voice 2	netaspi	2902/tcp	NET ASPI
dialpad-voice2	2861/udp	Dialpad Voice 2	netaspi	2902/udp	NET ASPI
ttg-protocol	2862/tcp	TTG Protocol	suitcase	2903/tcp	SUITCASE
ttg-protocol	2862/udp	TTG Protocol	suitcase	2903/udp	SUITCASE
sonardata	2863/tcp	Sonar Data	m2ua	2904/tcp	M2UA
sonardata	2863/udp	Sonar Data	m2ua	2904/udp	M2UA
astromed-main	2864/tcp	main 5001 cmd	m3ua	2905/tcp	M3UA
astromed-main	2864/udp	main 5001 cmd	m3ua	2905/udp	M3UA
pit-vpn	2865/tcp	pit-vpn	caller9	2906/tcp	CALLER9
pit-vpn	2865/udp	pit-vpn	caller9	2906/udp	CALLER9
lwlistener	2866/tcp	lwlistener	webmethods-b2b	2907/tcp	WEBMETHODS B2B
lwlistener	2866/udp	lwlistener	webmethods-b2b	2907/udp	WEBMETHODS B2B
esps-portal	2867/tcp	esps-portal	mao	2908/tcp	mao
esps-portal	2867/udp	esps-portal	mao	2908/udp	mao
npep-messaging	2868/tcp	NPEP Messaging	funk-dialout	2909/tcp	Funk Dialout
npep-messaging	2868/udp	NPEP Messaging	funk-dialout	2909/udp	Funk Dialout
icslap	2869/tcp	ICSLAP	tdaccess	2910/tcp	TDAccess
icslap	2869/udp	ICSLAP	tdaccess	2910/udp	TDAccess
daishi	2870/tcp	daishi	blockade	2911/tcp	Blockade
daishi	2870/udp	daishi	blockade	2911/udp	Blockade
msi-selectplay	2871/tcp	MSI Select Play	epicon	2912/tcp	Epicon
msi-selectplay	2871/udp	MSI Select Play	epicon	2912/udp	Epicon
contract	2872/tcp	CONTRACT	boosterware	2913/tcp	Booster Ware
contract	2872/udp	CONTRACT	boosterware	2913/udp	Booster Ware
paspar2-zoomin	2873/tcp	PASPAR2 ZoomIn	gamelobby	2914/tcp	Game Lobby
paspar2-zoomin	2873/udp	PASPAR2 ZoomIn	gamelobby	2914/udp	Game Lobby
dxmessagebase1	2874/tcp	dxmessagebase1	tksocket	2915/tcp	TK Socket
dxmessagebase1	2874/udp	dxmessagebase1	tksocket	2915/udp	TK Socket
dxmessagebase2	2875/tcp	dxmessagebase2	elvin_server	2916/tcp	Elvin Server
dxmessagebase2	2875/udp	dxmessagebase2	elvin_server	2916/udp	Elvin Server
sps-tunnel	2876/tcp	SPS Tunnel	elvin_client	2917/tcp	Elvin Client
sps-tunnel	2876/udp	SPS Tunnel	elvin_client	2917/udp	Elvin Client
bluelance	2877/tcp	BLUELANCE	kastenchasepad	2918/tcp	Kasten Chase Pad
bluelance	2877/udp	BLUELANCE	kastenchasepad	2918/udp	Kasten Chase Pad
aap	2878/tcp	AAP	roboer	2919/tcp	ROBOER
aap	2878/udp	AAP	roboer	2919/udp	ROBOER
ucentric-ds	2879/tcp	ucentric-ds	roboeda	2920/tcp	ROBOEDA
ucentric-ds	2879/udp	ucentric-ds	roboeda	2920/udp	ROBOEDA
synapse	2880/tcp	synapse	cesdcdman	2921/tcp	CESD Contents Delivery Management
synapse	2880/udp	synapse			
ndsp	2881/tcp	NDSP	cesdcdman	2921/udp	CESD Contents Delivery Management
ndsp	2881/udp	NDSP			
ndtp	2882/tcp	NDTP	cesdcdtrn	2922/tcp	CESD Contents Delivery Data Transfer
ndtp	2882/udp	NDTP			
ndnp	2883/tcp	NDNP	cesdcdtrn	2922/udp	CESD Contents Delivery Data Transfer
ndnp	2883/udp	NDNP			

Keyword	Decimal	Description
wta-wsp-wtp-s	2923/tcp	WTA-WSP-WTP-S
wta-wsp-wtp-s	2923/udp	WTA-WSP-WTP-S
precise-vip	2924/tcp	PRECISE-VIP
precise-vip	2924/udp	PRECISE-VIP
frp	2925/tcp	Firewall Redundancy Protocol
frp	2925/udp	Firewall Redundancy Protocol
mobile-file-dl	2926/tcp	MOBILE-FILE-DL
mobile-file-dl	2926/udp	MOBILE-FILE-DL
unimobilectrl	2927/tcp	UNIMOBILECTRL
unimobilectrl	2927/udp	UNIMOBILECTRL
redstone-cpss	2928/tcp	REDSTONE-CPSS
redstone-cpss	2928/udp	REDSONTE-CPSS
panja-webadmin	2929/tcp	PANJA-WEBADMIN
panja-webadmin	2929/udp	PANJA-WEBADMIN
panja-weblinx	2930/tcp	PANJA-WEBLINX
panja-weblinx	2930/udp	PANJA-WEBLINX
circle-x	2931/tcp	Circle-X
circle-x	2931/udp	Circle-X
incp	2932/tcp	INCP
incp	2932/udp	INCP
4-tieropmgw	2933/tcp	4-TIER OPM GW
4-tieropmgw	2933/udp	4-TIER OPM GW
4-tieropmcli	2934/tcp	4-TIER OPM CLI
4-tieropmcli	2934/udp	4-TIER OPM CLI
qtp	2935/tcp	QTP
qtp	2935/udp	QTP
otpatch	2936/tcp	OTPatch
otpatch	2936/udp	OTPatch
pnaconsult-lm	2937/tcp	PNACONSULT-LM
pnaconsult-lm	2937/udp	PNACONSULT-LM
sm-pas-1	2938/tcp	SM-PAS-1
sm-pas-1	2938/udp	SM-PAS-1
sm-pas-2	2939/tcp	SM-PAS-2
sm-pas-2	2939/udp	SM-PAS-2
sm-pas-3	2940/tcp	SM-PAS-3
sm-pas-3	2940/udp	SM-PAS-3
sm-pas-4	2941/tcp	SM-PAS-4
sm-pas-4	2941/udp	SM-PAS-4
sm-pas-5	2942/tcp	SM-PAS-5
sm-pas-5	2942/udp	SM-PAS-5
ttnrepository	2943/tcp	TTNRepository
ttnrepository	2943/udp	TTNRepository
megaco-h248	2944/tcp	Megaco H-248
megaco-h248	2944/udp	Megaco H-248
h248-binary	2945/tcp	H248 Binary
h248-binary	2945/udp	H248 Binary
fjsvmpor	2946/tcp	FJSVmpor
fjsvmpor	2946/udp	FJSVmpor
gpsd	2947/tcp	GPSD
gpsd	2947/udp	GPSD
wap-push	2948/tcp	WAP PUSH
wap-push	2948/udp	WAP PUSH
wap-pushsecure	2949/tcp	WAP PUSH SECURE
wap-pushsecure	2949/udp	WAP PUSH SECURE
esip	2950/tcp	ESIP
esip	2950/udp	ESIP
ottp	2951/tcp	OTTP
ottp	2951/udp	OTTP
mpfwsas	2952/tcp	MPFWSAS
mpfwsas	2952/udp	MPFWSAS
ovalarmsrv	2953/tcp	OVALARMSRV
ovalarmsrv	2953/udp	OVALARMSRV
ovalarmsrv-cmd	2954/tcp	OVALARMSRV-CMD
ovalarmsrv-cmd	2954/udp	OVALARMSRV-CMD
csnotify	2955/tcp	CSNOTIFY
csnotify	2955/udp	CSNOTIFY
ovrimosdbman	2956/tcp	OVRIMOSDBMAN
ovrimosdbman	2956/udp	OVRIMOSDBMAN
jmact5	2957/tcp	JAMCT5
jmact5	2957/udp	JAMCT5
jmact6	2958/tcp	JAMCT6
jmact6	2958/udp	JAMCT6
rmopagt	2959/tcp	RMOPAGT
rmopagt	2959/udp	RMOPAGT
dfoxserver	2960/tcp	DFOXSERVER
dfoxserver	2960/udp	DFOXSERVER
boldsoft-lm	2961/tcp	BOLDSOFT-LM
boldsoft-lm	2961/udp	BOLDSOFT-LM
iph-policy-cli	2962/tcp	IPH-POLICY-CLI
iph-policy-cli	2962/udp	IPH-POLICY-CLI
iph-policy-adm	2963/tcp	IPH-POLICY-ADM
iph-policy-adm	2963/udp	IPH-POLICY-ADM

Keyword	Decimal	Description
bullant-srap	2964/tcp	BULLANT SRAP
bullant-srap	2964/udp	BULLANT SRAP
bullant-rap	2965/tcp	BULLANT RAP
bullant-rap	2965/udp	BULLANT RAP
idp-infotrieve	2966/tcp	IDP-INFOTRIEVE
idp-infotrieve	2966/udp	IDP-INFOTRIEVE
ssc-agent	2967/tcp	SSC-AGENT
ssc-agent	2967/udp	SSC-AGENT
enpp	2968/tcp	ENPP
enpp	2968/udp	ENPP
essp	2969/tcp	ESSP
essp	2969/udp	ESSP
index-net	2970/tcp	INDEX-NET
index-net	2970/udp	INDEX-NET
netclip	2971/tcp	Net Clip
netclip	2971/udp	Net Clip
pmsm-webrctl	2972/tcp	PMSM Webrctl
pmsm-webrctl	2972/udp	PMSM Webrctl
svnetworks	2973/tcp	SV Networks
svnetworks	2973/udp	SV Networks
signal	2974/tcp	Signal
signal	2974/udp	Signal
fjmpcm	2975/tcp	Fujitsu Configuration Management Service
fjmpcm	2975/udp	Fujitsu Configuration Management Service
cns-srv-port	2976/tcp	CNS Server Port
cns-srv-port	2976/udp	CNS Server Port
ttc-etap-ns	2977/tcp	TTCs Enterprise Test Access Protocol - NS
ttc-etap-ns	2977/udp	TTCs Enterprise Test Access Protocol - NS
ttc-etap-ds	2978/tcp	TTCs Enterprise Test Access Protocol - DS
ttc-etap-ds	2978/udp	TTCs Enterprise Test Access Protocol - DS
h263-video	2979/tcp	H.263 Video Streaming
h263-video	2979/udp	H.263 Video Streaming
wimd	2980/tcp	Instant Messaging Service
wimd	2980/udp	Instant Messaging Service
mylxamport	2981/tcp	MYLXAMPORT
mylxamport	2981/udp	MYLXAMPORT
iwb-whiteboard	2982/tcp	IWB-WHITEBOARD
iwb-whiteboard	2982/udp	IWB-WHITEBOARD
netplan	2983/tcp	NETPLAN
netplan	2983/udp	NETPLAN
hpidsadmin	2984/tcp	HPIDSADMIN
hpidsadmin	2984/udp	HPIDSADMIN
hpidsagent	2985/tcp	HPIDSAGENT
hpidsagnet	2985/udp	HPIDSAGENT
stonefalls	2986/tcp	STONEFALLS
stonefalls	2986/udp	STONEFALLS
identify	2987/tcp	IDENTIFY
identify	2987/udp	IDENTIFY
classify	2988/tcp	CLASSIFY
classify	2988/udp	CLASSIFY
zarkov	2989/tcp	ZARKOV
zarkov	2989/udp	ZARKOV
boscap	2990/tcp	BOSCAP
boscap	2990/udp	BOSCAP
wkstn-mon	2991/tcp	WKSTN-MON
wkstn-mon	2991/udp	WKSTN-MON
itb301	2992/tcp	ITB301
itb301	2992/udp	ITB301
veritas-vis1	2993/tcp	VERITAS VIS1
veritas-vis1	2993/udp	VERITAS VIS1
veritas-vis2	2994/tcp	VERITAS VIS2
veritas-vis2	2994/udp	VERITAS VIS2
idrs	2995/tcp	IDRS
idrs	2995/udp	IDRS
vsixml	2996/tcp	vsixml
vsixml	2996/udp	vsixml
rebol	2997/tcp	REBOL
rebol	2997/udp	REBOL
realsecure	2998/tcp	Real Secure
realsecure	2998/udp	Real Secure
remoteware-un	2999/tcp	RemoteWare Unassigned
remoteware-un	2999/udp	RemoteWare Unassigned
hbci	3000/tcp	HBCI
hbci	3000/udp	HBCI
		The following entry records an unassigned but widespread use
remoteware-cl	3000/tcp	RemoteWare Client
remoteware-cl	3000/udp	RemoteWare Client

Keyword	Decimal	Description	Keyword	Decimal	Description
redwood-broker	3001/tcp	Redwood Broker	tomato-springs	3040/tcp	Tomato Springs
redwood-broker	3001/udp	Redwood Broker	tomato-springs	3040/udp	Tomato Springs
exlm-agent	3002/tcp	EXLM Agent	di-traceware	3041/tcp	di-traceware
exlm-agent	3002/udp	EXLM Agent	di-traceware	3041/udp	di-traceware
		The following entry records an unassigned	journee	3042/tcp	journee
		but widespread use	journee	3042/udp	journee
remoteware-srv	3002/tcp	RemoteWare Server	brp	3043/tcp	BRP
remoteware-srv	3002/udp	RemoteWare Server	brp	3043/udp	BRP
cgms	3003/tcp	CGMS	responsenet	3045/tcp	ResponseNet
cgms	3003/udp	CGMS	responsenet	3045/udp	ResponseNet
csoftragent	3004/tcp	Csoft Agent	di-ase	3046/tcp	di-ase
csoftragent	3004/udp	Csoft Agent	di-ase	3046/udp	di-ase
geniuslm	3005/tcp	Genius License Manager	hlserver	3047/tcp	Fast Security HL Server
geniuslm	3005/udp	Genius License Manager	hlserver	3047/udp	Fast Security HL Server
ii-admin	3006/tcp	Instant Internet Admin	pctrader	3048/tcp	Sierra Net PC Trader
ii-admin	3006/udp	Instant Internet Admin	pctrader	3048/udp	Sierra Net PC Trader
lotusmtap	3007/tcp	Lotus Mail Tracking Agent	nsws	3049/tcp	NSWS
		Protocol	nsws	3049/udp	NSWS
lotusmtap	3007/udp	Lotus Mail Tracking Agent	gds_db	3050/tcp	gds_db
		Protocol	gds_db	3050/udp	gds_db
midnight-tech	3008/tcp	Midnight Technologies	galaxy-server	3051/tcp	Galaxy Server
midnight-tech	3008/udp	Midnight Technologies	galaxy-server	3051/udp	Galaxy Server
pxc-ntfy	3009/tcp	PXC-NTFY	apcpcns	3052/tcp	APCPCNS
pxc-ntfy	3009/udp	PXC-NTFY	apcpcns	3052/udp	APCPCNS
gw	3010/tcp	Telerate Workstation	dsom-server	3053/tcp	dsom-server
ping-pong	3010/udp	Telerate Workstation	dsom-server	3053/udp	dsom-server
trusted-web	3011/tcp	Trusted Web	amt-cnf-prot	3054/tcp	AMT CNF PROT
trusted-web	3011/udp	Trusted Web	amt-cnf-prot	3054/udp	AMT CNF PROT
twsdss	3012/tcp	Trusted Web Client	policyserver	3055/tcp	Policy Server
twsdss	3012/udp	Trusted Web Client	policyserver	3055/udp	Policy Server
gilatskysurfer	3013/tcp	Gilat Sky Surfer	cdl-server	3056/tcp	CDL Server
gilatskysurfer	3013/udp	Gilat Sky Surfer	cdl-server	3056/udp	CDL Server
broker_service	3014/tcp	Broker Service	goahead-fldup	3057/tcp	GoAhead FldUp
broker_service	3014/udp	Broker Service	goahead-fldup	3057/udp	GoAhead FldUp
nati-dstp	3015/tcp	NATI DSTP	videobeans	3058/tcp	videobeans
nati-dstp	3015/udp	NATI DSTP	videobeans	3058/udp	videobeans
notify_srvr	3016/tcp	Notify Server	qsoft	3059/tcp	qsoft
notify_srvr	3016/udp	Notify Server	qsoft	3059/udp	qsoft
event_listener	3017/tcp	Event Listener	interserver	3060/tcp	interserver
event_listener	3017/udp	Event Listener	interserver	3060/udp	interserver
srvc_registry	3018/tcp	Service Registry	cautcpd	3061/tcp	cautcpd
srvc_registry	3018/udp	Service Registry	cautcpd	3061/udp	cautcpd
resource_mgr	3019/tcp	Resource Manager	ncacn-ip-tcp	3062/tcp	ncacn-ip-tcp
resource_mgr	3019/udp	Resource Manager	ncacn-ip-tcp	3062/udp	ncacn-ip-tcp
cifs	3020/tcp	CIFS	ncadg-ip-udp	3063/tcp	ncadg-ip-udp
cifs	3020/udp	CIFS	ncadg-ip-udp	3063/udp	ncadg-ip-udp
agriserver	3021/tcp	AGRI Server	slinterbase	3065/tcp	slinterbase
agriserver	3021/udp	AGRI Server	slinterbase	3065/udp	slinterbase
csregagent	3022/tcp	CSREGAGENT	netattachsdmp	3066/tcp	NETATTACHSDMP
csregagent	3022/udp	CSREGAGENT	netattachsdmp	3066/udp	NETATTACHSDMP
magicnotes	3023/tcp	magicnotes	fjhpjp	3067/tcp	FJHPJP
magicnotes	3023/udp	magicnotes	fjhpjp	3067/udp	FJHPJP
nds_sso	3024/tcp	NDS_SSO	ls3bcast	3068/tcp	ls3 Broadcast
nds_sso	3024/udp	NDS_SSO	ls3bcast	3068/udp	ls3 Broadcast
arepa-raft	3025/tcp	Arepa Raft	ls3	3069/tcp	ls3
arepa-raft	3025/udp	Arepa Raft	ls3	3069/udp	ls3
agri-gateway	3026/tcp	AGRI Gateway	mgxswitch	3070/tcp	MGXSWITCH
agri-gateway	3026/udp	AGRI Gateway	mgxswitch	3070/udp	MGXSWITCH
LiebDevMgmt_C	3027/tcp	LiebDevMgmt_C	#	3071-3074	Unassigned
LiebDevMgmt_C	3027/udp	LiebDevMgmt_C	orbix-locator	3075/tcp	Orbix 2000 Locator
LiebDevMgmt_DM	3028/tcp	LiebDevMgmt_DM	orbix-locator	3075/udp	Orbix 2000 Locator
LiebDevMgmt_DM	3028/udp	LiebDevMgmt_DM	orbix-config	3076/tcp	Orbix 2000 Config
LiebDevMgmt_A	3029/tcp	LiebDevMgmt_A	orbix-config	3076/udp	Orbix 2000 Config
LiebDevMgmt_A	3029/udp	LiebDevMgmt_A	orbix-loc-ssl	3077/tcp	Orbix 2000 Locator SSL
arepa-cas	3030/tcp	Arepa Cas	orbix-loc-ssl	3077/udp	Orbix 2000 Locator SSL
arepa-cas	3030/udp	Arepa Cas	orbix-cfg-ssl	3078/tcp	Orbix 2000 Locator SSL
agentvu	3031/tcp	AgentVU	orbix-cfg-ssl	3078/udp	Orbix 2000 Locator SSL
agentvu	3031/udp	AgentVU	lv-frontpanel	3079/tcp	LV Front Panel
redwood-chat	3032/tcp	Redwood Chat	lv-frontpanel	3079/udp	LV Front Panel
redwood-chat	3032/udp	Redwood Chat	stm_pproc	3080/tcp	stm_pproc
pdb	3033/tcp	PDB	stm_pproc	3080/udp	stm_pproc
pdb	3033/udp	PDB	tl1-lv	3081/tcp	TL1-LV
osmosis-aeea	3034/tcp	Osmosis AEEA	tl1-lv	3081/udp	TL1-LV
osmosis-aeea	3034/udp	Osmosis AEEA	tl1-raw	3082/tcp	TL1-RAW
fjsv-gssagt	3035/tcp	FJSV gssagt	tl1-raw	3082/udp	TL1-RAW
fjsv-gssagt	3035/udp	FJSV gssagt	tl1-telnet	3083/tcp	TL1-TELNET
hagel-dump	3036/tcp	Hagel DUMP	tl1-telnet	3083/udp	TL1-TELNET
hagel-dump	3036/udp	Hagel DUMP	itm-mccs	3084/tcp	ITM-MCCS
hp-san-mgmt	3037/tcp	HP SAN Mgmt	itm-mccs	3084/udp	ITM-MCCS
hp-san-mgmt	3037/udp	HP SAN Mgmt	pcihreq	3085/tcp	PCIHReq
santak-ups	3038/tcp	Santak UPS	pcihreq	3085/udp	PCIHReq
santak-ups	3038/udp	Santak UPS	jdl-dbkitchen	3086/tcp	JDL-DBKitchen
cogitate	3039/tcp	Cogitate, Inc.	jdl-dbkitchen	3086/udp	JDL-DBKitchen
cogitate	3039/udp	Cogitate, Inc.	#	3087-3104	Unassigned

Keyword	Decimal	Description	Keyword	Decimal	Description
cardbox	3105/tcp	Cardbox	datusorb	3282/tcp	Datusorb
cardbox	3105/udp	Cardbox	datusorb	3282/udp	Datusorb
cardbox-http	3106/tcp	Cardbox HTTP	net-assistant	3283/tcp	Net Assistant
cardbox-http	3106/udp	Cardbox HTTP	net-assistant	3283/udp	Net Assistant
#	3107-3129	Unassigned	4talk	3284/tcp	4Talk
icpv2	3130/tcp	ICPv2	4talk	3284/udp	4Talk
icpv2	3130/udp	ICPv2	plato	3285/tcp	Plato
netbookmark	3131/tcp	Net Book Mark	plato	3285/udp	Plato
netbookmark	3131/udp	Net Book Mark	e-net	3286/tcp	E-Net
#	3132-3140	Unassigned	e-net	3286/udp	E-Net
vmodem	3141/tcp	VMODEM	directvdata	3287/tcp	DIRECTVDATA
vmodem	3141/udp	VMODEM	directvdata	3287/udp	DIRECTVDATA
rdc-wh-eos	3142/tcp	RDC WH EOS	cops	3288/tcp	COPS
rdc-wh-eos	3142/udp	RDC WH EOS	cops	3288/udp	COPS
seaview	3143/tcp	Sea View	enpc	3289/tcp	ENPC
seaview	3143/udp	Sea View	enpc	3289/udp	ENPC
tarantella	3144/tcp	Tarantella	caps-lm	3290/tcp	CAPS LOGISTICS TOOLKIT - LM
tarantella	3144/udp	Tarantella			
csi-lfap	3145/tcp	CSI-LFAP	caps-lm	3290/udp	CAPS LOGISTICS TOOLKIT - LM
csi-lfap	3145/udp	CSI-LFAP			
#	3146	Unassigned	sah-lm	3291/tcp	S A Holditch & Associates-LM
rfio	3147/tcp	RFIO	sah-lm	3291/udp	S A Holditch & Associates-LM
rfio	3147/udp	RFIO	cart-o-rama	3292/tcp	Cart O Rama
nm-game-admin	3148/tcp	NetMike Game Administrator	cart-o-rama	3292/udp	Cart O Rama
nm-game-admin	3148/udp	NetMike Game Administrator	fg-fps	3293/tcp	fg-fps
nm-game-server	3149/tcp	NetMike Game Server	fg-fps	3293/udp	fg-fps
nm-game-server	3149/udp	NetMike Game Server	fg-gip	3294/tcp	fg-gip
nm-asses-admin	3150/tcp	NetMike Assessor Administrator	fg-gip	3294/udp	fg-gip
			dyniplookup	3295/tcp	Dynamic IP Lookup
nm-asses-admin	3150/udp	NetMike Assessor Administrator	dyniplookup	3295/udp	Dynamic IP Lookup
			rib-slm	3296/tcp	Rib License Manager
nm-assessor	3151/tcp	NetMike Assessor	rib-slm	3296/udp	Rib License Manager
nm-assessor	3151/udp	NetMike Assessor	cytel-lm	3297/tcp	Cytel License Manager
#	3152-3179	Unassigned	cytel-lm	3297/udp	Cytel License Manager
mc-brk-srv	3180/tcp	Millicent Broker Server	transview	3298/tcp	Transview
mc-brk-srv	3180/udp	Millicent Broker Server	transview	3298/udp	Transview
bmcpatrolagent	3181/tcp	BMC Patrol Agent	pdrncs	3299/tcp	pdrncs
bmcpatrolagent	3181/udp	BMC Patrol Agent	pdrncs	3299/udp	pdrncs
bmcpatrolrnvu	3182/tcp	BMC Patrol Rendezvous	#####	3300-3301	Unauthorized Use by SAP R/3
bmcpatrolrnvu	3182/udp	BMC Patrol Rendezvous	mcs-fastmail	3302/tcp	MCS Fastmail
#	3183-3261	Unassigned	mcs-fastmail	3302/udp	MCS Fastmail
necp	3262/tcp	NECP	opsession-clnt	3303/tcp	OP Session Client
necp	3262/udp	NECP	opsession-clnt	3303/udp	OP Session Client
#	3263	Unassigned	opsession-srvr	3304/tcp	OP Session Server
ccmail	3264/tcp	cc:mail/lotus	opsession-srvr	3304/udp	OP Session Server
ccmail	3264/udp	cc:mail/lotus	odette-ftp	3305/tcp	ODETTE-FTP
altav-tunnel	3265/tcp	Altav Tunnel	odette-ftp	3305/udp	ODETTE-FTP
altav-tunnel	3265/udp	Altav Tunnel	mysql	3306/tcp	MySQL
ns-cfg-server	3266/tcp	NS CFG Server	mysql	3306/udp	MySQL
ns-cfg-server	3266/udp	NS CFG Server	opsession-prxy	3307/tcp	OP Session Proxy
ibm-dial-out	3267/tcp	IBM Dial Out	opsession-prxy	3307/udp	OP Session Proxy
ibm-dial-out	3267/udp	IBM Dial Out	tns-server	3308/tcp	TNS Server
msft-gc	3268/tcp	Microsoft Global Catalog	tns-server	3308/udp	TNS Server
msft-gc	3268/udp	Microsoft Global Catalog	tns-adv	3309/tcp	TNS ADV
msft-gc-ssl	3269/tcp	Microsoft Global Catalog with LDAP/SSL	tns-adv	3309/udp	TND ADV
			dyna-access	3310/tcp	Dyna Access
msft-gc-ssl	3269/udp	Microsoft Global Catalog with LDAP/SSL	dyna-access	3310/udp	Dyna Access
			mcns-tel-ret	3311/tcp	MCNS Tel Ret
verismart	3270/tcp	Verismart	mcns-tel-ret	3311/udp	MCNS Tel Ret
verismart	3270/udp	Verismart	appman-server	3312/tcp	Application Management Server
csoft-prev	3271/tcp	CSoft Prev Port			
csoft-prev	3271/udp	CSoft Prev Port	appman-server	3312/udp	Application Management Server
user-manager	3272/tcp	Fujitsu User Manager			
user-manager	3272/udp	Fujitsu User Manager	uorb	3313/tcp	Unify Object Broker
sxmp	3273/tcp	Simple Extensible Multiplexed Protocol	uorb	3313/udp	Unify Object Broker
			uohost	3314/tcp	Unify Object Host
sxmp	3273/udp	Simple Extensible Multiplexed Protocol	uohost	3314/udp	Unify Object Host
			cdid	3315/tcp	CDID
ordinox-server	3274/tcp	Ordinox Server	cdid	3315/udp	CDID
ordinox-server	3274/udp	Ordinox Server	aicc-cmi	3316/tcp	AICC/CMI
samd	3275/tcp	SAMD	aicc-cmi	3316/udp	AICC/CMI
samd	3275/udp	SAMD	vsaiport	3317/tcp	VSAI PORT
maxim-asics	3276/tcp	Maxim ASICs	vsaiport	3317/udp	VSAI PORT
maxim-asics	3276/udp	Maxim ASICs	ssrip	3318/tcp	Swith to Swith Routing Information Protocol
awg-proxy	3277/tcp	AWG Proxy			
awg-proxy	3277/udp	AWG Proxy	ssrip	3318/udp	Swith to Swith Routing Information Protocol
lkcmserver	3278/tcp	LKCM Server			
lkcmserver	3278/udp	LKCM Server	sdt-lmd	3319/tcp	SDT License Manager
admind	3279/tcp	admind	sdt-lmd	3319/udp	SDT License Manager
admind	3279/udp	admind	officelink2000	3320/tcp	Office Link 2000
vs-server	3280/tcp	VS Server	officelink2000	3320/udp	Office Link 2000
vs-server	3280/udp	VS Server	vnsstr	3321/tcp	VNSSTR
sysopt	3281/tcp	SYSOPT	vnsstr	3321/udp	VNSSTR
sysopt	3281/udp	SYSOPT	active-net	3322-3325	Active Networks

931

Keyword	Decimal	Description	Keyword	Decimal	Description
sftu	3326/tcp	SFTU	tip2	3372/udp	TIP 2
sftu	3326/udp	SFTU	lavenir-lm	3373/tcp	Lavenir License Manager
bbars	3327/tcp	BBARS	lavenir-lm	3373/udp	Lavenir License Manager
bbars	3327/udp	BBARS	cluster-disc	3374/tcp	Cluster Disc
egptlm	3328/tcp	Eaglepoint License Manager	cluster-disc	3374/udp	Cluster Disc
egptlm	3328/udp	Eaglepoint License Manager	vsnm-agent	3375/tcp	VSNM Agent
hp-device-disc	3329/tcp	HP Device Disc	vsnm-agent	3375/udp	VSNM Agent
hp-device-disc	3329/udp	HP Device Disc	cdborker	3376/tcp	CD Broker
mcs-calypsoicf	3330/tcp	MCS Calypso ICF	cdbroker	3376/udp	CD Broker
mcs-calypsoicf	3330/udp	MCS Calypso ICF	cogsys-lm	3377/tcp	Cogsys Network License Manager
mcs-messaging	3331/tcp	MCS Messaging			
mcs-messaging	3331/udp	MCS Messaging	cogsys-lm	3377/udp	Cogsys Network License Manager
mcs-mailsvr	3332/tcp	MCS Mail Server			
mcs-mailsvr	3332/udp	MCS Mail Server	wsicopy	3378/tcp	WSICOPY
dec-notes	3333/tcp	DEC Notes	wsicopy	3378/udp	WSICOPY
dec-notes	3333/udp	DEC Notes	socorfs	3379/tcp	SOCORFS
directv-web	3334/tcp	Direct TV Webcasting	socorfs	3379/udp	SOCORFS
directv-web	3904/udp	Direct TV Webcasting	sns-channels	3380/tcp	SNS Channels
directv-soft	3335/tcp	Direct TV Software Updates	sns-channels	3380/udp	SNS Channels
directv-soft	3335/udp	Direct TV Software Updates	geneous	3381/tcp	Geneous
directv-tick	3336/tcp	Direct TV Tickers	geneous	3381/udp	Geneous
directv-tick	3336/udp	Direct TV Tickers	fujitsu-neat	3382/tcp	Fujitsu Network Enhanced Antitheft function
directv-catlg	3337/tcp	Direct TV Data Catalog			
directv-catlg	3337/udp	Direct TV Data Catalog	fujitsu-neat	3382/udp	Fujitsu Network Enhanced Antitheft function
anet-b	3338/tcp	OMF data b			
anet-b	3338/udp	OMF data b	esp-lm	3383/tcp	Enterprise Software Products License Manager
anet-l	3339/tcp	OMF data l			
anet-l	3339/udp	OMF data l	esp-lm	3383/udp	Enterprise Software Products License Manager
anet-m	3340/tcp	OMF data m			
anet-m	3340/udp	OMF data m	hp-clic	3384/tcp	Cluster Management Services
anet-h	3341/tcp	OMF data h	hp-clic	3384/udp	Hardware Management
anet-h	3341/udp	OMF data h	qnxnetman	3385/tcp	qnxnetman
webtie	3342/tcp	WebTIE	qnxnetman	3385/udp	qnxnetman
webtie	3342/udp	WebTIE	gprs-data	3386/tcp	GPRS Data
ms-cluster-net	3343/tcp	MS Cluster Net	gprs-sig	3386/udp	GPRS SIG
ms-cluster-net	3343/udp	MS Cluster Net	backroomnet	3387/tcp	Back Room Net
bnt-manager	3344/tcp	BNT Manager	backroomnet	3387/udp	Back Room Net
bnt-manager	3344/udp	BNT Manager	cbserver	3388/tcp	CB Server
influence	3345/tcp	Influence	cbserver	3388/udp	CB Server
influence	3345/udp	Influence	ms-wbt-server	3389/tcp	MS WBT Server
trnsprntproxy	3346/tcp	Trnsprnt Proxy	ms-wbt-server	3389/udp	MS WBT Server
trnsprntproxy	3346/udp	Trnsprnt Proxy	dsc	3390/tcp	Distributed Service Coordinator
phoenix-rpc	3347/tcp	Phoenix RPC			
phoenix-rpc	3347/udp	Phoenix RPC	dsc	3390/udp	Distributed Service Coordinator
pangolin-laser	3348/tcp	Pangolin Laser			
pangolin-laser	3348/udp	Pangolin Laser	savant	3391/tcp	SAVANT
chevinservices	3349/tcp	Chevin Services	savant	3391/udp	SAVANT
chevinservices	3349/udp	Chevin Services	efi-lm	3392/tcp	EFI License Management
findviatv	3350/tcp	FINDVIATV	efi-lm	3392/udp	EFI License Management
findviatv	3350/udp	FINDVIATV	d2k-tapestry1	3393/tcp	D2K Tapestry Client to Server
btrieve	3351/tcp	BTRIEVE	d2k-tapestry1	3393/udp	D2K Tapestry Client to Server
btrieve	3351/udp	BTRIEVE	d2k-tapestry2	3394/tcp	D2K Tapestry Server to Server
ssql	3352/tcp	SSQL			
ssql	3352/udp	SSQL	d2k-tapestry2	3394/udp	D2K Tapestry Server to Server
fatpipe	3353/tcp	FATPIPE			
fatpipe	3353/udp	FATPIPE	dyna-lm	3395/tcp	Dyna License Manager (Elam)
suitjd	3354/tcp	SUITJD	dyna-lm	3395/udp	Dyna License Manager (Elam)
suitjd	3354/udp	SUITJD	printer_agent	3396/tcp	Printer Agent
ordinox-dbase	3355/tcp	Ordinox Dbase	printer_agent	3396/udp	Printer Agent
ordinox-dbase	3355/udp	Ordinox Dbase	cloanto-lm	3397/tcp	Cloanto License Manager
upnotifyps	3356/tcp	UPNOTIFYPS	cloanto-lm	3397/udp	Cloanto License Manager
upnotifyps	3356/udp	UPNOTIFYPS	mercantile	3398/tcp	Mercantile
adtech-test	3357/tcp	Adtech Test IP	mercantile	3398/udp	Mercantile
adtech-test	3357/udp	Adtech Test IP	csms	3399/tcp	CSMS
mpsysrmsvr	3358/tcp	Mp Sys Rmsvr	csms	3399/udp	CSMS
mpsysrmsvr	3358/udp	Mp Sys Rmsvr	csms2	3400/tcp	CSMS2
wg-netforce	3359/tcp	WG NetForce	csms2	3400/udp	CSMS2
wg-netforce	3359/udp	WG NetForce	filecast	3401/tcp	filecast
kv-server	3360/tcp	KV Server	filecast	3401/udp	filecast
kv-server	3360/udp	KV Server	#	3402-3420	Unassigned
kv-agent	3361/tcp	KV Agent	bmap	3421/tcp	Bull Apprise portmapper
kv-agent	3361/udp	KV Agent	bmap	3421/udp	Bull Apprise portmapper
dj-ilm	3362/tcp	DJ ILM	#	3422-3453	Unassigned
dj-ilm	3362/udp	DJ ILM	mira	3454/tcp	Apple Remote Access Protocol
nati-vi-server	3363/tcp	NATI Vi Server			
nati-vi-server	3363/udp	NATI Vi Server	prsvp	3455/tcp	RSVP Port
creativeserver	3364/tcp	Creative Server	prsvp	3455/udp	RSVP Port
creativeserver	3364/udp	Creative Server	vat	3456/tcp	VAT default data
contentserver	3365/tcp	Content Server	vat	3456/udp	VAT default data
contentserver	3365/udp	Content Server	vat-control	3457/tcp	VAT default control
creativepartnr	3366/tcp	Creative Partner	vat-control	3457/udp	VAT default control
creativepartnr	3366/udp	Creative Partner	d3winosfi	3458/tcp	D3WinOsfi
satvid-datalnk	3367-3371	Satellite Video Data Link	d3winosfi	3458/udp	DsWinOSFI
tip2	3372/tcp	TIP 2	integral	3459/tcp	TIP Integral

Keyword	Decimal	Description
integral	3459/udp	TIP Integral
edm-manager	3460/tcp	EDM Manager
edm-manager	3460/udp	EDM Manager
edm-stager	3461/tcp	EDM Stager
edm-stager	3461/udp	EDM Stager
edm-std-notify	3462/tcp	EDM STD Notify
edm-std-notify	3462/udp	EDM STD Notify
edm-adm-notify	3463/tcp	EDM ADM Notify
edm-adm-notify	3463/udp	EDM ADM Notify
edm-mgr-sync	3464/tcp	EDM MGR Sync
edm-mgr-sync	3464/udp	EDM MGR Sync
edm-mgr-cntrl	3465/tcp	EDM MGR Cntrl
edm-mgr-cntrl	3465/udp	EDM MGR Cntrl
workflow	3466/tcp	WORKFLOW
workflow	3466/udp	WORKFLOW
rcst	3467/tcp	RCST
rcst	3467/udp	RCST
ttcmremotectrl	3468/tcp	TTCM Remote Control
ttcmremotectrl	3468/udp	TTCM Remote Control
pluribus	3469/tcp	Pluribus
pluribus	3469/udp	Pluribus
jt400	3470/tcp	jt400
jt400	3470/udp	jt400
jt400-ssl	3471/tcp	jt400-ssl
jt400-ssl	3471/udp	jt400-ssl
#	3472-3534	Unassigned
ms-la	3535/tcp	MS-LA
ms-la	3535/udp	MS-LA
#	3536-3562	Unassigned
watcomdebug	3563/tcp	Watcom Debug
watcomdebug	3563/udp	Watcom Debug
#	3564-3671	Unassigned
harlequinorb	3672/tcp	harlequinorb
harlequinorb	3672/udp	harlequinorb
#	3673-3801	Unassigned
vhd	3802/tcp	VHD
vhd	3802/udp	VHD
#	3803-3844	Unassigned
v-one-spp	3845/tcp	V-ONE Single Port Proxy
v-one-spp	3845/udp	V-ONE Single Port Proxy
#	3846-3861	Unassigned
giga-pocket	3862/tcp	GIGA-POCKET
giga-pocket	3862/udp	GIGA-POCKET
#	3863-3874	Unassigned
pnbscada	3875/tcp	PNBSCADA
pnbscada	3875/udp	PNBSCADA
#	3876-3899	Unassigned
udt_os	3900/tcp	Unidata UDT OS
udt_os	3900/udp	Unidata UDT OS
#	3901-3983	Unassigned
mapper-nodemgr	3984/tcp	MAPPER network node manager
mapper-nodemgr	3984/udp	MAPPER network node manager
mapper-mapethd	3985/tcp	MAPPER TCP/IP server
mapper-mapethd	3985/udp	MAPPER TCP/IP server
mapper-ws_ethd	3986/tcp	MAPPER workstation server
mapper-ws_ethd	3986/udp	MAPPER workstation server
centerline	3987/tcp	Centerline
centerline	3987/udp	Centerline
#	3988-3999	Unassigned
terabase	4000/tcp	Terabase
terabase	4000/udp	Terabase
###### PORT 4000 also used by ICQ <www.icq.com> ######		
############## Potential Conflict of ports ############		
newoak	4001/tcp	NewOak
newoak	4001/udp	NewOak
pxc-spvr-ft	4002/tcp	pxc-spvr-ft
pxc-spvr-ft	4002/udp	pxc-spvr-ft
pxc-splr-ft	4003/tcp	pxc-splr-ft
pxc-splr-ft	4003/udp	pxc-splr-ft
pxc-roid	4004/tcp	pxc-roid
pxc-roid	4004/udp	pxc-roid
pxc-pin	4005/tcp	pxc-pin
pxc-pin	4005/udp	pxc-pin
pxc-spvr	4006/tcp	pxc-spvr
pxc-spvr	4006/udp	pxc-spvr
pxc-splr	4007/tcp	pxc-splr
pxc-splr	4007/udp	pxc-splr
netcheque	4008/tcp	NetCheque accounting
netcheque	4008/udp	NetCheque accounting
chimera-hwm	4009/tcp	Chimera HWM
chimera-hwm	4009/udp	Chimera HWM
samsung-unidex	4010/tcp	Samsung Unidex

Keyword	Decimal	Description
samsung-unidex	4010/udp	Samsung Unidex
altserviceboot	4011/tcp	Alternate Service Boot
altserviceboot	4011/udp	Alternate Service Boot
pda-gate	4012/tcp	PDA Gate
pda-gate	4012/udp	PDA Gate
acl-manager	4013/tcp	ACL Manager
acl-manager	4013/udp	ACL Manager
taiclock	4014/tcp	TAICLOCK
taiclock	4014/udp	TAICLOCK
talarian-mcast1	4015/tcp	Talarian Mcast
talarian-mcast1	4015/udp	Talarian Mcast
talarian-mcast2	4016/tcp	Talarian Mcast
talarian-mcast2	4016/udp	Talarian Mcast
talarian-mcast3	4017/tcp	Talarian Mcast
talarian-mcast3	4017/udp	Talarian Mcast
talarian-mcast4	4018/tcp	Talarian Mcast
talarian-mcast4	4018/udp	Talarian Mcast
talarian-mcast5	4019/tcp	Talarian Mcast
talarian-mcast5	4019/udp	Talarian Mcast
#	4020-4095	Unassigned
bre	4096/tcp	BRE (Bridge Relay Element)
bre	4096/udp	BRE (Bridge Relay Element)
patrolview	4097/tcp	Patrol View
patrolview	4097/udp	Patrol View
drmsfsd	4098/tcp	drmsfsd
drmsfsd	4098/udp	drmsfsd
dpcp	4099/tcp	DPCP
dpcp	4099/udp	DPCP
#	4100-4131	Unassigned
nuts_dem	4132/tcp	NUTS Daemon
nuts_dem	4132/udp	NUTS Daemon
nuts_bootp	4133/tcp	NUTS Bootp Server
nuts_bootp	4133/udp	NUTS Bootp Server
nifty-hmi	4134/tcp	NIFTY-Serve HMI protocol
nifty-hmi	4134/udp	NIFTY-Serve HMI protocol
oirtgsvc	4141/tcp	Workflow Server
oirtgsvc	4141/udp	Workflow Server
oidocsvc	4142/tcp	Document Server
oidocsvc	4142/udp	Document Server
oidsr	4143/tcp	Document Replication
oidsr	4143/udp	Document Replication
###### Compuserve (unoffically) is using port 4144 ######		
#	4144-4159	Unassigned
jini-discovery	4160/tcp	Jini Discovery
jini-discovery	4160/udp	Jini Discovery
#	4161-4198	Unassigned
eims-admin	4199/tcp	EIMS ADMIN
eims-admin	4199/udp	EIMS ADMIN
vrml-multi-use	4200-4299	VRML Multi User Systems
corelccam	4300/tcp	Corel CCam
corelccam	4300/udp	Corel CCam
#	4301-4320	Unassigned
rwhois	4321/tcp	Remote Who Is
rwhois	4321/udp	Remote Who Is
unicall	4343/tcp	UNICALL
unicall	4343/udp	UNICALL
vinainstall	4344/tcp	VinaInstall
vinainstall	4344/udp	VinaInstall
m4-network-as	4345/tcp	Macro 4 Network AS
m4-network-as	4345/udp	Macro 4 Network AS
elanlm	4346/tcp	ELAN LM
elanlm	4346/udp	ELAN LM
lansurveyor	4347/tcp	LAN Surveyor
lansurveyor	4347/udp	LAN Surveyor
itose	4348/tcp	ITOSE
itose	4348/udp	ITOSE
fsportmap	4349/tcp	File System Port Map
fsportmap	4349/udp	File System Port Map
net-device	4350/tcp	Net Device
net-device	4350/udp	Net Device
plcy-net-svcs	4351/tcp	PLCY Net Services
plcy-net-svcs	4351/udp	PLCY Net Services
#	4352	Unassigned
f5-iquery	4353/tcp	F5 iQuery
f5-iquery	4353/udp	F5 iQuery
#	4354-4441	Unassigned
saris	4442/tcp	Saris
saris	4442/udp	Saris
pharos	4443/tcp	Pharos
pharos	4443/udp	Pharos
krb524	4444/tcp	KRB524
krb524	4444/udp	KRB524
###### PROBLEM krb524 assigned the port ############		
###### PROBLEM nv used it without an assignment ######		

Keyword	Decimal	Description	Keyword	Decimal	Description
nv-video	4444/tcp	NV Video default	#	4984-4999	Unassigned
nv-video	4444/udp	NV Video default	commplex-main	5000/tcp	
upnotifyp	4445/tcp	UPNOTIFYP	commplex-main	5000/udp	
upnotifyp	4445/udp	UPNOTIFYP	commplex-link	5001/tcp	
n1-fwp	4446/tcp	N1-FWP	commplex-link	5001/udp	
n1-fwp	4446/udp	N1-FWP	rfe	5002/tcp	radio free ethernet
n1-rmgmt	4447/tcp	N1-RMGMT	rfe	5002/udp	radio free ethernet
n1-rmgmt	4447/udp	N1-RMGMT	fmpro-internal	5003/tcp	FileMaker, Inc. - Proprietary
asc-slmd	4448/tcp	ASC Licence Manager			transport
asc-slmd	4448/udp	ASC Licence Manager	fmpro-internal	5003/udp	FileMaker, Inc. - Proprietary
privatewire	4449/tcp	PrivateWire			name binding
privatewire	4449/udp	PrivateWire	avt-profile-1	5004/tcp	avt-profile-1
camp	4450/tcp	Camp	avt-profile-1	5004/udp	avt-profile-1
camp	4450/udp	Camp	avt-profile-2	5005/tcp	avt-profile-2
ctisystemmsg	4451/tcp	CTI System Msg	avt-profile-2	5005/udp	avt-profile-2
ctisystemmsg	4451/udp	CTI System Msg	wsm-server	5006/tcp	wsm server
ctiprogramload	4452/tcp	CTI Program Load	wsm-server	5006/udp	wsm server
ctiprogramload	4452/udp	CTI Program Load	wsm-server-ssl	5007/tcp	wsm server ssl
nssalertmgr	4453/tcp	NSS Alert Manager	wsm-server-ssl	5007/udp	wsm server ssl
nssalertmgr	4453/udp	NSS Alert Manager	#	5008-5009	Unassigned
nssagentmgr	4454/tcp	NSS Agent Manager	telelpathstart	5010/tcp	TelepathStart
nssagentmgr	4454/udp	NSS Agent Manager	telelpathstart	5010/udp	TelepathStart
prchat-user	4455/tcp	PR Chat User	telelpathattack	5011/tcp	TelepathAttack
prchat-user	4455/udp	PR Chat User	telelpathattack	5011/udp	TelepathAttack
prchat-server	4456/tcp	PR Chat Server	#	5012-5019	Unassigned
prchat-server	4456/udp	PR Chat Server	zenginkyo-1	5020/tcp	zenginkyo-1
prRegister	4457/tcp	PR Register	zenginkyo-1	5020/udp	zenginkyo-1
prRegister	4457/udp	PR Register	zenginkyo-2	5021/tcp	zenginkyo-2
#	4458-4499	Unassigned	zenginkyo-2	5021/udp	zenginkyo-2
sae-urn	4500/tcp	sae-urn	#	5022-5041	Unassigned
sae-urn	4500/udp	sae-urn	asnaacceler8db	5042/tcp	asnaacceler8db
urn-x-cdchoice	4501/tcp	urn-x-cdchoice	asnaacceler8db	5042/udp	asnaacceler8db
urn-x-cdchoice	4501/udp	urn-x-cdchoice	#	5043-5049	Unassigned
worldscores	4545/tcp	WorldScores	mmcc	5050/tcp	multimedia conference
worldscores	4545/udp	WorldScores			control tool
sf-lm	4546/tcp	SF License Manager	mmcc	5050/udp	multimedia conference
		(Sentinel)			control tool
sf-lm	4546/udp	SF License Manager	ita-agent	5051/tcp	ITA Agent
		(Sentinel)	ita-agent	5051/udp	ITA Agent
lanner-lm	4547/tcp	Lanner License Manager	ita-manager	5052/tcp	ITA Manager
lanner-lm	4547/udp	Lanner License Manager	ita-manager	5052/udp	ITA Manager
#	4548-4566	Unassigned	#	5053-5054	Unassigned
tram	4567/tcp	TRAM	unot	5055/tcp	UNOT
tram	4567/udp	TRAM	unot	5055/udp	UNOT
bmc-reporting	4568/tcp	BMC Reporting	intecom-ps1	5056/tcp	Intecom PS 1
bmc-reporting	4568/udp	BMC Reporting	intecom-ps1	5056/udp	Intecom PS 1
#	4569-4599	Unassigned	intecom-ps2	5057/tcp	Intecom PS 2
piranha1	4600/tcp	Piranha1	intecom-ps2	5057/udp	Intecom PS 2
piranha1	4600/udp	Piranha1	#	5058-5059	Unassigned
piranha2	4601/tcp	Piranha2	sip	5060/tcp	SIP
piranha2	4601/udp	Piranha2	sip	5060/udp	SIP
#	4602-4671	Unassigned	#	5061-5068	Unassigned
rfa	4672/tcp	remote file access server	i-net-2000-npr	5069/tcp	I/Net 2000-NPR
rfa	4672/udp	remote file access server	i-net-2000-npr	5069/udp	I/Net 2000-NPR
#	4673-4799	Unassigned	#	5070	Unassigned
iims	4800/tcp	Icona Instant Messenging	powerschool	5071/tcp	PowerSchool
		System	powerschool	5071/udp	PowerSchool
iims	4800/udp	Icona Instant Messenging	#	5072-5092	Unassigned
		System	sentinel-lm	5093/tcp	Sentinel LM
iwec	4801/tcp	Icona Web Embedded Chat	sentinel-lm	5093/udp	Sentinel LM
iwec	4801/udp	Icona Web Embedded Chat	#	5094-5098	Unassigned
ilss	4802/tcp	Icona License System Server	sentlm-srv2srv	5099/tcp	SentLM Srv2Srv
ilss	4802/udp	Icona License System Server	sentlm-srv2srv	5099/udp	SentLM Srv2Srv
#	4803-4826	Unassigned	#	5100-5144	Unassigned
htcp	4827/tcp	HTCP	rmonitor_secure	5145/tcp	RMONITOR SECURE
htcp	4827/udp	HTCP	rmonitor_secure	5145/udp	RMONITOR SECURE
#	4828-4836	Unassigned	#	5146-5149	Unassigned
varadero-0	4837/tcp	Varadero-0	atmp	5150/tcp	Ascend Tunnel Management
varadero-0	4837/udp	Varadero-0			Protocol
varadero-1	4838/tcp	Varadero-1	atmp	5150/udp	Ascend Tunnel Management
varadero-1	4838/udp	Varadero-1			Protocol
varadero-2	4839/tcp	Varadero-2	esri_sde	5151/tcp	ESRI SDE Instance
varadero-2	4839/udp	Varadero-2	esri_sde	5151/udp	ESRI SDE Remote Start
#	4840-4867	Unassigned	sde-discovery	5152/tcp	ESRI SDE Instance Discovery
phrelay	4868/tcp	Photon Relay	sde-discovery	5152/udp	ESRI SDE Instance Discovery
phrelay	4868/udp	Photon Relay	#	5153-5164	Unassigned
phrelaydbg	4869/tcp	Photon Relay Debug	ife_icorp	5165/tcp	ife_1corp
phrelaydbg	4869/udp	Photon Relay Debug	ife_icorp	5165/udp	ife_1corp
#	4870-4884	Unassigned	#	5166-5189	Unassigned
abbs	4885/tcp	ABBS	aol	5190/tcp	American-Online
abbs	4885/udp	ABBS	aol	5190/udp	American-Online
#	4886-4982	Unassigned	aol-1	5191/tcp	American-Online1
att-intercom	4983/tcp	AT&T Intercom	aol-1	5191/udp	American-Online1
att-intercom	4983/udp	AT&T Intercom	aol-2	5192/tcp	American-Online2

Keyword	Decimal	Description	Keyword	Decimal	Description
aol-2	5192/udp	American-Online2	cylink-c	5420/tcp	Cylink-C
aol-3	5193/tcp	American-Online3	cylink-c	5420/udp	Cylink-C
aol-3	5193/udp	American-Online3	netsupport2	5421/tcp	Net Support 2
#	5194-5199	Unassigned	netsupport2	5421/udp	Net Support 2
targus-getdata	5200/tcp	TARGUS GetData	salient-mux	5422/tcp	Salient MUX
targus-getdata	5200/udp	TARGUS GetData	salient-mux	5422/udp	Salient MUX
targus-getdata1	5201/tcp	TARGUS GetData 1	virtualuser	5423/tcp	VIRTUALUSER
targus-getdata1	5201/udp	TARGUS GetData 1	virtualuser	5423/udp	VIRTUALUSER
targus-getdata2	5202/tcp	TARGUS GetData 2	#	5424-5425	Unassigned
targus-getdata2	5202/udp	TARGUS GetData 2	devbasic	5426/tcp	DEVBASIC
targus-getdata3	5203/tcp	TARGUS GetData 3	devbasic	5426/udp	DEVBASIC
targus-getdata3	5203/udp	TARGUS GetData 3	sco-peer-tta	5427/tcp	SCO-PEER-TTA
#	5204-5235	Unassigned	sco-peer-tta	5427/udp	SCO-PEER-TTA
padl2sim	5236/tcp		telaconsole	5428/tcp	TELACONSOLE
padl2sim	5236/udp		telaconsole	5428/udp	TELACONSOLE
#	5237-5271	Unassigned	base	5429/tcp	Billing and Accounting System Exchange
pk	5272/tcp	PK			
pk	5272/udp	PK	base	5429/udp	Billing and Accounting System Exchange
#	5273-5299	Unassigned			
hacl-hb	5300/tcp	# HA cluster heartbeat	radec-corp	5430/tcp	RADEC CORP
hacl-hb	5300/udp	# HA cluster heartbeat	radec-corp	5430/udp	RADEC CORP
hacl-gs	5301/tcp	# HA cluster general services	park-agent	5431/tcp	PARK AGENT
hacl-gs	5301/udp	# HA cluster general services	park-agnet	5431/udp	PARK AGENT
hacl-cfg	5302/tcp	# HA cluster configuration	#	5432-5434	Unassigned
hacl-cfg	5302/udp	# HA cluster configuration	dttl	5435/tcp	Data Tunneling Transceiver Linking (DTTL)
hacl-probe	5303/tcp	# HA cluster probing			
hacl-probe	5303/udp	# HA cluster probing	dttl	5435/udp	Data Tunneling Transceiver Linking (DTTL)
hacl-local	5304/tcp	# HA Cluster Commands			
hacl-local	5304/udp		#	5436-5453	Unassigned
hacl-test	5305/tcp	# HA Cluster Test	apc-tcp-udp-4	5454/tcp	apc-tcp-udp-4
hacl-test	5305/udp		apc-tcp-udp-4	5454/udp	apc-tcp-udp-4
sun-mc-grp	5306/tcp	Sun MC Group	apc-tcp-udp-5	5455/tcp	apc-tcp-udp-5
sun-mc-grp	5306/udp	Sun MC Group	apc-tcp-udp-5	5455/udp	apc-tcp-udp-5
sco-aip	5307/tcp	SCO AIP	apc-tcp-udp-6	5456/tcp	apc-tcp-udp-6
sco-aip	5307/udp	SCO AIP	apc-tcp-udp-6	5456/udp	apc-tcp-udp-6
cfengine	5308/tcp	CFengine	#	5457-5460	Unassigned
cfengine	5308/udp	CFengine	silkmeter	5461/tcp	SILKMETER
jprinter	5309/tcp	J Printer	silkmeter	5461/udp	SILKMETER
jprinter	5309/udp	J Printer	ttl-publisher	5462/tcp	TTL Publisher
outlaws	5310/tcp	Outlaws	ttl-publisher	5462/udp	TTL Publisher
outlaws	5310/udp	Outlaws	#	5463-5464	Unassigned
tmlogin	5311/tcp	TM Login	netops-broker	5465/tcp	NETOPS-BROKER
tmlogin	5311/udp	TM Login	netops-broker	5465/udp	NETOPS-BROKER
#	5312-5399	Unassigned	#	5466-5499	Unassigned
excerpt	5400/tcp	Excerpt Search	fcp-addr-srvr1	5500/tcp	fcp-addr-srvr1
excerpt	5400/udp	Excerpt Search	fcp-addr-srvr1	5500/udp	fcp-addr-srvr1
excerpts	5401/tcp	Excerpt Search Secure	fcp-addr-srvr2	5501/tcp	fcp-addr-srvr2
excerpts	5401/udp	Excerpt Search Secure	fcp-addr-srvr2	5501/udp	fcp-addr-srvr2
mftp	5402/tcp	MFTP	fcp-srvr-inst1	5502/tcp	fcp-srvr-inst1
mftp	5402/udp	MFTP	fcp-srvr-inst1	5502/udp	fcp-srvr-inst1
hpoms-ci-lstn	5403/tcp	HPOMS-CI-LSTN	fcp-srvr-inst2	5503/tcp	fcp-srvr-inst2
hpoms-ci-lstn	5403/udp	HPOMS-CI-LSTN	fcp-srvr-inst2	5503/udp	fcp-srvr-inst2
hpoms-dps-lstn	5404/tcp	HPOMS-DPS-LSTN	fcp-cics-gw1	5504/tcp	fcp-cics-gw1
hpoms-dps-lstn	5404/udp	HPOMS-DPS-LSTN	fcp-cics-gw1	5504/udp	fcp-cics-gw1
netsupport	5405/tcp	NetSupport	#	5505-5553	Unassigned
netsupport	5405/udp	NetSupport	sgi-esphttp	5554/tcp	SGI ESP HTTP
systemics-sox	5406/tcp	Systemics Sox	sgi-esphttp	5554/udp	SGI ESP HTTP
systemics-sox	5406/udp	Systemics Sox	########## Port 5555 also used by HP Omniback########		
foresyte-clear	5407/tcp	Foresyte-Clear	personal-agent	5555/tcp	Personal Agent
foresyte-clear	5407/udp	Foresyte-Clear	personal-agent	5555/udp	Personal Agent
foresyte-sec	5408/tcp	Foresyte-Sec	#	5556-5565	Unassigned
foresyte-sec	5408/udp	Foresyte-Sec	udpplus	5566/tcp	UDPPlus
salient-dtasrv	5409/tcp	Salient Data Server	udpplus	5566/udp	UDPPlus
salient-dtasrv	5409/udp	Salient Data Server	#	5567-5598	Unassigned
salient-usrmgr	5410/tcp	Salient User Manager	esinstall	5599/tcp	Enterprise Security Remote Install
salient-usrmgr	5410/udp	Salient User Manager			
actnet	5411/tcp	ActNet	esinstall	5599/udp	Enterprise Security Remote Install
actnet	5411/udp	ActNet			
continuus	5412/tcp	Continuus	esmmanager	5600/tcp	Enterprise Security Manager
continuus	5412/udp	Continuus	esmmanager	5600/udp	Enterprise Security Manager
wwiotalk	5413/tcp	WWIOTALK	esmagent	5601/tcp	Enterprise Security Agent
wwiotalk	5413/udp	WWIOTALK	esmagent	5601/udp	Enterprise Security Agent
statusd	5414/tcp	StatusD	a1-msc	5602/tcp	A1-MSC
statusd	5414/udp	StatusD	a1-msc	5602/udp	A1-MSC
ns-server	5415/tcp	NS Server	a1-bs	5603/tcp	A1-BS
ns-server	5415/udp	NS Server	a1-bs	5603/udp	A1-BS
sns-gateway	5416/tcp	SNS Gateway	a3-sdunode	5604/tcp	A3-SDUNode
sns-gateway	5416/udp	SNS Gateway	a3-sdunode	5604/udp	A3-SDUNode
sns-agent	5417/tcp	SNS Agent	a4-sdunode	5605/tcp	A4-SDUNode
sns-agent	5417/udp	SNS Agent	a4-sdunode	5605/udp	A4-SDUNode
mcntp	5418/tcp	MCNTP	#	5606-5630	Unassigned
mcntp	5418/udp	MCNTP	pcanywheredata	5631/tcp	pcANYWHEREdata
dj-ice	5419/tcp	DJ-ICE	pcanywheredata	5631/udp	pcANYWHEREdata
dj-ice	5419/udp	DJ-ICE	pcanywherestat	5632/tcp	pcANYWHEREstat

Keyword	Decimal	Description	Keyword	Decimal	Description
pcanywherestat	5632/udp	pcANYWHEREstat	diagnose-proc	6072/tcp	DIAGNOSE-PROC
#	5633-5677	Unassigned	diagmose-proc	6072/udp	DIAGNOSE-PROC
rrac	5678/tcp	Remote Replication Agent Connection	directplay8	6073/tcp	DirectPlay8
			directplay8	6073/udp	DirectPlay8
rrac	5678/udp	Remote Replication Agent Connection	#	6074-6099	Unassigned
			synchronet-db	6100/tcp	SynchroNet-db
dccm	5679/tcp	Direct Cable Connect Manager	synchronet-db	6100/udp	SynchroNet-db
			synchronet-rtc	6101/tcp	SynchroNet-rtc
dccm	5679/udp	Direct Cable Connect Manager	synchronet-rtc	6101/udp	SynchroNet-rtc
			synchronet-upd	6102/tcp	SynchroNet-upd
proshareaudio	5713/tcp	proshare conf audio	synchronet-upd	6102/udp	SynchroNet-upd
proshareaudio	5713/udp	proshare conf audio	rets	6103/tcp	RETS
prosharevideo	5714/tcp	proshare conf video	rets	6103/udp	RETS
prosharevideo	5714/udp	proshare conf video	dbdb	6104/tcp	DBDB
prosharedata	5715/tcp	proshare conf data	dbdb	6104/udp	DBDB
prosharedata	5715/udp	proshare conf data	primaserver	6105/tcp	Prima Server
prosharerequest	5716/tcp	proshare conf request	primaserver	6105/udp	Prima Server
prosharerequest	5716/udp	proshare conf request	mp3server	6106/tcp	MP3 Server
prosharenotify	5717/tcp	proshare conf notify	mpsserver	6106/udp	MPS Server
prosharenotify	5717/udp	proshare conf notify	etc-control	6107/tcp	ETC Control
#	5718-5728	Unassigned	etc-control	6107/udp	ETC Control
openmail	5729/tcp	Openmail User Agent Layer	sercomm-scadmin	6108/tcp	Sercomm-SCAdmin
openmail	5729/udp	Openmail User Agent Layer	sercomm-scadmin	6108/udp	Sercomm-SCAdmin
#	5730-5740	Unassigned	globecast-id	6109/tcp	GLOBECAST-ID
ida-discover1	5741/tcp	IDA Discover Port 1	globecast-id	6109/udp	GLOBECAST-ID
ida-discover1	5741/udp	IDA Discover Port 1	softcm	6110/tcp	HP SoftBench CM
ida-discover2	5742/tcp	IDA Discover Port 2	softcm	6110/udp	HP SoftBench CM
ida-discover2	5742/udp	IDA Discover Port 2	spc	6111/tcp	HP SoftBench Sub-Process Control
#	5743-5744	Unassigned			
fcopy-server	5745/tcp	fcopy-server	spc	6111/udp	HP SoftBench Sub-Process Control
fcopy-server	5745/udp	fcopy-server			
fcopys-server	5746/tcp	fcopys-server	dtspcd	6112/tcp	dtspcd
fcopys-server	5746/udp	fcopys-server	dtspcd	6112/udp	dtspcd
#	5747-5754	Unassigned	#	6113-6122	Unassigned
openmailg	5755/tcp	OpenMail Desk Gateway server	backup-express	6123/tcp	Backup Express
			backup-express	6123/udp	Backup Express
openmailg	5755/udp	OpenMail Desk Gateway server	#	6124-6140	Unassigned
			meta-corp	6141/tcp	Meta Corporation License Manager
x500ms	5757/tcp	OpenMail X.500 Directory Server	meta-corp	6141/udp	Meta Corporation License Manager
x500ms	5757/udp	OpenMail X.500 Directory Server	aspentec-lm	6142/tcp	Aspen Technology License Manager
openmailns	5766/tcp	OpenMail NewMail Server	aspentec-lm	6142/udp	Aspen Technology License Manager
openmailns	5766/udp	OpenMail NewMail Server	watershed-lm	6143/tcp	Watershed License Manager
s-openmail	5767/tcp	OpenMail Agent (Secure)	watershed-lm	6143/udp	Watershed License Manager
s-openmail	5767/udp	OpenMail Agent (Secure)	statsci1-lm	6144/tcp	StatSci License Manager - 1
openmailpxy	5768/tcp	OpenMail CMTS Server	statsci1-lm	6144/udp	StatSci License Manager - 1
openmailpxy	5768/udp	OpenMail CMTS Server	statsci2-lm	6145/tcp	StatSci License Manager - 2
#	5769-5770	Unassigned	statsci2-lm	6145/udp	StatSci License Manager - 2
netagent	5771/tcp	NetAgent	lonewolf-lm	6146/tcp	Lone Wolf Systems License Manager
netagent	5771/udp	NetAgent			
#	5772-5812	Unassigned	lonewolf-lm	6146/udp	Lone Wolf Systems License Manager
icmpd	5813/tcp	ICMPD			
icmpd	5813/udp	ICMPD	montage-lm	6147/tcp	Montage License Manager
#	5814-5858	Unassigned	montage-lm	6147/udp	Montage License Manager
wherehoo	5859/tcp	WHEREHOO	ricardo-lm	6148/tcp	Ricardo North America License Manager
wherehoo	5859/udp	WHEREHOO			
#	5860-5967	Unassigned	ricardo-lm	6148/udp	Ricardo North America License Manager
mppolicy-v5	5968/tcp	mppolicy-v5			
mppolicy-v5	5968/udp	mppolicy-v5	tal-pod	6149/tcp	tal-pod
mppolicy-mgr	5969/tcp	mppolicy-mgr	tal-pod	6149/udp	tal-pod
mppolicy-mgr	5969/udp	mppolicy-mgr	#	6150-6252	Unassigned
#	5970-5998	Unassigned	crip	6253/tcp	CRIP
cvsup	5999/tcp	CVSup	crip	6253/udp	CRIP
cvsup	5999/udp	CVSup	#	6254-6320	Unassigned
x11	6000-6063/tcp	X Window System	emp-server1	6321/tcp	Empress Software Connectivity Server 1
x11	6000-6063/udp	X Window System			
ndl-ahp-svc	6064/tcp	NDL-AHP-SVC	emp-server1	6321/udp	Empress Software Connectivity Server 1
ndl-ahp-svc	6064/udp	NDL-AHP-SVC			
winpharaoh	6065/tcp	WinPharaoh	emp-server2	6322/tcp	Empress Software Connectivity Server 2
winpharaoh	6065/udp	WinPharaoh			
ewctsp	6066/tcp	EWCTSP	emp-server2	6322/udp	Empress Software Connectivity Server 2
ewctsp	6066/udp	EWCTSP			
srb	6067/tcp	SRB	#	6323-6388	Unassigned
srb	6067/udp	SRB	clariion-evr01	6389/tcp	clariion-evr01
gsmp	6068/tcp	GSMP	clariion-evr01	6389/udp	clariion-evr01
gsmp	6068/udp	GSMP	#	6390-6399	Unassigned
trip	6069/tcp	TRIP	#		The following blocks are in use by Seagate Software 6400-6410 #
trip	6069/udp	TRIP			
messageasap	6070/tcp	Messageasap	info-aps	6400	
messageasap	6070/udp	Messageasap	info-was	6401	
ssdtp	6071/tcp	SSDTP	info-eventsvr	6402	
ssdtp	6071/udp	SSDTP			

936

Keyword	Decimal	Description
info-cachesvr	6403	
info-filesvr	6404	
info-pagesvr	6405	
info-processvr	6406	
reserved1	6407	
reserved2	6408	
reserved3	6409	
reserved4	6410	
#		The previous ports are in use by Seagate Software 6400-6410 #
#	6411-6454	Unassigned
skip-cert-recv	6455/tcp	SKIP Certificate Receive
skip-cert-send	6456/tcp	SKIP Certificate Send
#	6457-6470	Unassigned
lvision-lm	6471/tcp	LVision License Manager
lvision-lm	6471/udp	LVision License Manager
#	6472-6499	Unassigned
boks	6500/tcp	BoKS Master
boks	6500/udp	BoKS Master
boks_servc	6501/tcp	BoKS Servc
boks_servc	6501/udp	BoKS Servc
boks_servm	6502/tcp	BoKS Servm
boks_servm	6502/udp	BoKS Servm
boks_clntd	6503/tcp	BoKS Clntd
boks_clntd	6503/udp	BoKS Clntd
#	6504	Unassigned
badm_priv	6505/tcp	BoKS Admin Private Port
badm_priv	6505/udp	BoKS Admin Private Port
badm_pub	6506/tcp	BoKS Admin Public Port
badm_pub	6506/udp	BoKS Admin Public Port
bdir_priv	6507/tcp	BoKS Dir Server, Private Port
bdir_priv	6507/udp	BoKS Dir Server, Private Port
bdir_pub	6508/tcp	BoKS Dir Server, Public Port
bdir_pub	6508/udp	BoKS Dir Server, Public Port
#	6509-6546	Unassigned
apc-tcp-udp-1	6547/tcp	apc-tcp-udp-1
apc-tcp-udp-1	6547/udp	apc-tcp-udp-1
apc-tcp-udp-2	6548/tcp	apc-tcp-udp-2
apc-tcp-udp-2	6548/udp	apc-tcp-udp-2
apc-tcp-udp-3	6549/tcp	apc-tcp-udp-3
apc-tcp-udp-3	6549/udp	apc-tcp-udp-3
fg-sysupdate	6550/tcp	fg-sysupdate
fg-sysupdate	6550/udp	fg-sysupdate
#	6551-6557	Unassigned
xdsxdm	6558/tcp	
xdsxdm	6558/udp	
ircu	6665-6669/tcp	IRCU
ircu	6665-6669/udp	IRCU
vocaltec-gold	6670/tcp	Vocaltec Global Online Directory
vocaltec-gold	6670/udp	Vocaltec Global Online Directory
vision_server	6672/tcp	vision_server
vision_server	6672/udp	vision_server
vision_elmd	6673/tcp	vision_elmd
vision_elmd	6673/udp	vision_elmd
kti-icad-srvr	6701/tcp	KTI/ICAD Nameserver
kti-icad-srvr	6701/udp	KTI/ICAD Nameserver
#	6702-6766	Unassigned
bmc-perf-agent	6767/tcp	BMC PERFORM AGENT
bmc-perf-agent	6767/udp	BMC PERFORM AGENT
bmc-perf-mgrd	6768/tcp	BMC PERFORM MGRD
bmc-perf-mgrd	6768/udp	BMC PERFORM MGRD
#	6769-6789	Unassigned
hnmp	6790/tcp	HNMP
hnmp	6790/udp	HNMP
ambit-lm	6831/tcp	ambit-lm
ambit-lm	6831/udp	ambit-lm
netmo-default	6841/tcp	Netmo Default
netmo-default	6841/udp	Netmo Default
netmo-http	6842/tcp	Netmo HTTP
netmo-http	6842/udp	Netmo HTTP
#	6843-6849	Unassigned
iccrushmore	6850/tcp	ICCRUSHMORE
iccrushmore	6850/udp	ICCRUSHMORE
#	6851-6887	Unassigned
muse	6888/tcp	MUSE
muse	6888/udp	MUSE
#	6889-6960	Unassigned
jmact3	6961/tcp	JMACT3
jmact3	6961/udp	JMACT3
jmevt2	6962/tcp	jmevt2
jmevt2	6962/udp	jmevt2
swismgr1	6963/tcp	swismgr1
swismgr1	6963/udp	swismgr1
swismgr2	6964/tcp	swismgr2
swismgr2	6964/udp	swismgr2
swistrap	6965/tcp	swistrap
swistrap	6965/udp	swistrap
swispol	6966/tcp	swispol
swispol	6966/udp	swispol
acmsoda	6969/tcp	acmsoda
acmsoda	6969/udp	acmsoda
iatp-highpri	6998/tcp	IATP-highPri
iatp-highpri	6998/udp	IATP-highPri
iatp-normalpri	6999/tcp	IATP-normalPri
iatp-normalpri	6999/udp	IATP-normalPri
afs3-fileserver	7000/tcp	file server itself
afs3-fileserver	7000/udp	file server itself
afs3-callback	7001/tcp	callbacks to cache managers
afs3-callback	7001/udp	callbacks to cache managers
afs3-prserver	7002/tcp	users & groups database
afs3-prserver	7002/udp	users & groups database
afs3-vlserver	7003/tcp	volume location database
afs3-vlserver	7003/udp	volume location database
afs3-kaserver	7004/tcp	AFS/Kerberos authentication service
afs3-kaserver	7004/udp	AFS/Kerberos authentication service
afs3-volser	7005/tcp	volume managment server
afs3-volser	7005/udp	volume managment server
afs3-errors	7006/tcp	error interpretation service
afs3-errors	7006/udp	error interpretation service
afs3-bos	7007/tcp	basic overseer process
afs3-bos	7007/udp	basic overseer process
afs3-update	7008/tcp	server-to-server updater
afs3-update	7008/udp	server-to-server updater
afs3-rmtsys	7009/tcp	remote cache manager service
afs3-rmtsys	7009/udp	remote cache manager service
ups-onlinet	7010/tcp	onlinet uninterruptable power supplies
ups-onlinet	7010/udp	onlinet uninterruptable power supplies
talon-disc	7011/tcp	Talon Discovery Port
talon-disc	7011/udp	Talon Discovery Port
talon-engine	7012/tcp	Talon Engine
talon-engine	7012/udp	Talon Engine
microtalon-dis	7013/tcp	Microtalon Discovery
microtalon-dis	7013/udp	Microtalon Discovery
microtalon-com	7014/tcp	Microtalon Communications
microtalon-com	7014/udp	Microtalon Communications
talon-webserver	7015/tcp	Talon Webserver
talon-webserver	7015/udp	Talon Webserver
#	7016-7019	Unassigned
dpserve	7020/tcp	DP Serve
dpserve	7020/udp	DP Serve
dpserveadmin	7021/tcp	DP Serve Admin
dpserveadmin	7021/udp	DP Serve Admin
#	7022-7069	Unassigned
arcp	7070/tcp	ARCP
arcp	7070/udp	ARCP
#	7071-7098	Unassigned
lazy-ptop	7099/tcp	lazy-ptop
lazy-ptop	7099/udp	lazy-ptop
font-service	7100/tcp	X Font Service
font-service	7100/udp	X Font Service
#	7101-7120	Unassigned
virprot-lm	7121/tcp	Virtual Prototypes License Manager
virprot-lm	7121/udp	Virtual Prototypes License Manager
#	7122-7173	Unassigned
clutild	7174/tcp	Clutild
clutild	7174/udp	Clutild
#	7175-7199	Unassigned
fodms	7200/tcp	FODMS FLIP
fodms	7200/udp	FODMS FLIP
dlip	7201/tcp	DLIP
dlip	7201/udp	DLIP
#	7202-7279	Unassigned
itactionserver1	7280/tcp	ITACTIONSERVER 1
itactionserver1	7280/udp	ITACTIONSERVER 1
itactionserver2	7281/tcp	ITACTIONSERVER 2
itactionserver2	7281/udp	ITACTIONSERVER 2
#	7282-7299	Unassigned
swx	7300-7390	The Swiss Exchange

Keyword	Decimal	Description	Keyword	Decimal	Description
#	7391-7394	Unassigned	http-alt	8008/tcp	HTTP Alternate
winqedit	7395/tcp	winqedit	http-alt	8008/udp	HTTP Alternate
winqedit	7395/udp	winqedit	#	8009-8031	Unassigned
#	7396-7425	Unassigned	pro-ed	8032/tcp	ProEd
pmdmgr	7426/tcp	OpenView DM Postmaster Manager	pro-ed	8032/udp	ProEd
			mindprint	8033/tcp	MindPrint
pmdmgr	7426/udp	OpenView DM Postmaster Manager	mindprint	8033/udp	MindPrint
			#	8034-8079	Unassigned
oveadmgr	7427/tcp	OpenView DM Event Agent Manager	http-alt	8080/tcp	HTTP Alternate (see port 80)
			http-alt	8080/udp	HTTP Alternate (see port 80)
oveadmgr	7427/udp	OpenView DM Event Agent Manager	#	8081-8129	Unassigned
			indigo-vrmi	8130/tcp	INDIGO-VRMI
ovladmgr	7428/tcp	OpenView DM Log Agent Manager	indigo-vrmi	8130/udp	INDIGO-VRMI
			indigo-vbcp	8131/tcp	INDIGO-VBCP
ovladmgr	7428/udp	OpenView DM Log Agent Manager	indigo-vbcp	8131/udp	INDIGO-VBCP
			dbabble	8132/tcp	dbabble
opi-sock	7429/tcp	OpenView DM rqt communication	dbabble	8132/udp	dbabble
			#	8133-8159	Unassigned
opi-sock	7429/udp	OpenView DM rqt communication	patrol	8160/tcp	Patrol
			patrol	8160/udp	Patrol
xmpv7	7430/tcp	OpenView DM xmpv7 api pipe	patrol-snmp	8161/tcp	Patrol SNMP
xmpv7	7430/udp	OpenView DM xmpv7 api pipe	patrol-snmp	8161/udp	Patrol SNMP
pmd	7431/tcp	OpenView DM ovc/xmpv3 api pipe	#	8162-8199	Unassigned
			trivnet1	8200/tcp	TRIVNET
pmd	7431/udp	OpenView DM ovc/xmpv3 api pipe	trivnet1	8200/udp	TRIVNET
			trivnet2	8201/tcp	TRIVNET
faximum	7437/tcp	Faximum	trivnet2	8201/udp	TRIVNET
faximum	7437/udp	Faximum	#	8202-8203	Unassigned
telops-lmd	7491/tcp	telops-lmd	lm-perfworks	8204/tcp	LM Perfworks
telops-lmd	7491/udp	telops-lmd	lm-perfworks	8204/udp	LM Perfworks
pafec-lm	7511/tcp	pafec-lm	lm-instmgr	8205/tcp	LM Instmgr
pafec-lm	7511/udp	pafec-lm	lm-instmgr	8205/udp	LM Instmgr
nta-ds	7544/tcp	FlowAnalyzer DisplayServer	lm-dta	8206/tcp	LM Dta
nta-ds	7544/udp	FlowAnalyzer DisplayServer	lm-dta	8206/udp	LM Dta
nta-us	7545/tcp	FlowAnalyzer UtilityServer	lm-sserver	8207/tcp	LM SServer
nta-us	7545/udp	FlowAnalyzer UtilityServer	lm-sserver	8207/udp	LM SServer
vsi-omega	7566/tcp	VSI Omega	lm-webwatcher	8208/tcp	LM Webwatcher
vsi-omega	7566/udp	VSI Omega	lm-webwatcher	8208/udp	LM Webwatcher
#	7567-7569	Unassigned	#	8209-8350	Unassigned
aries-kfinder	7570/tcp	Aries Kfinder	server-find	8351/tcp	Server Find
aries-kfinder	7570/udp	Aries Kfinder	server-find	8351/udp	Server Find
#	7571-7587	Unassigned	#	8352-8375	Unassigned
sun-lm	7588/tcp	Sun License Manager	cruise-enum	8376/tcp	Cruise ENUM
sun-lm	7588/udp	Sun License Manager	cruise-enum	8376/udp	Cruise ENUM
#	7589-7632	Unassigned	cruise-swroute	8377/tcp	Cruise SWROUTE
pmdfmgt	7633/tcp	PMDF Management	cruise-swroute	8377/udp	Cruise SWROUTE
pmdfmgt	7633/udp	PMDF Management	cruise-config	8378/tcp	Cruise CONFIG
#	7634-7776	Unassigned	cruise-config	8378/udp	Cruise CONFIG
cbt	7777/tcp	cbt	cruise-diags	8379/tcp	Cruise DIAGS
cbt	7777/udp	cbt	cruise-diags	8379/udp	Cruise DIAGS
interwise	7778/tcp	Interwise	cruise-update	8380/tcp	Cruise UPDATE
interwise	7778/udp	Interwise	cruise-update	8380/udp	Cruise UPDATE
vstat	7779/tcp	VSTAT	#	8381-8399	Unassigned
vstat	7779/udp	VSTAT	cvd	8400/tcp	cvd
#	7780	Unassigned	cvd	8400/udp	cvd
accu-lmgr	7781/tcp	accu-lmgr	sabarsd	8401/tcp	sabarsd
accu-lmgr	7781/udp	accu-lmgr	sabarsd	8401/udp	sabarsd
#	7782-7785	Unassigned	abarsd	8402/tcp	abarsd
minivend	7786/tcp	MINIVEND	abarsd	8402/udp	abarsd
minivend	7786/udp	MINIVEND	admind	8403/tcp	admind
#	7787-7931	Unassigned	admind	8403/udp	admind
t2-drm	7932/tcp	Tier 2 Data Resource Manager	#	8404-8449	Unassigned
t2-drm	7932/udp	Tier 2 Data Resource Manager	npmp	8450/tcp	npmp
t2-brm	7933/tcp	Tier 2 Business Rules Manager	npmp	8450/udp	npmp
			#	8451-8472	Unassigned
t2-brm	7933/udp	Tier 2 Business Rules Manager	vp2p	8473/tcp	Virtual Point to Point
			vp2p	8473/udp	Virtual Point to Point
supercell	7967/tcp	Supercell	#	8474-8553	Unassigned
supercell	7967/udp	Supercell	rtsp-alt	8554/tcp	RTSP Alternate (see port 554)
#	7968-7978	Unassigned			
micromuse-ncps	7979/tcp	Micromuse-ncps	rtsp-alt	8554/udp	RTSP Alternate (see port 554)
micromuse-ncps	7979/udp	Micromuse-ncps			
quest-vista	7980/tcp	Quest Vista	#	8555-8732	Unassigned
quest-vista	7980/udp	Quest Vista	ibus	8733/tcp	iBus
#	7981-7998	Unassigned	ibus	8733/udp	iBus
irdmi2	7999/tcp	iRDMI2	#	8734-8762	Unassigned
irdmi2	7999/udp	iRDMI2	mc-appserver	8763/tcp	MC-APPSERVER
irdmi	8000/tcp	iRDMI	mc-appserver	8763/udp	MC-APPSERVER
irdmi	8000/udp	iRDMI	openqueue	8764/tcp	OPENQUEUE
vcom-tunnel	8001/tcp	VCOM Tunnel	openqueue	8764/udp	OPENQUEUE
vcom-tunnel	8001/udp	VCOM Tunnel	ultraseek-http	8765/tcp	Ultraseek HTTP
teradataordbms	8002/tcp	Teradata ORDBMS	ultraseek-http	8765/udp	Ultraseek HTTP
teradataordbms	8002/udp	Teradata ORDBMS	#	8766-8803	Unassigned
#	8003-8007	Unassigned	truecm	8804/tcp	truecm

938

Keyword	Decimal	Description	Keyword	Decimal	Description
truecm	8804/udp	truecm	#	9322-9342	Unassigned
#	8805-8879		mpidcmgr	9343/tcp	MpIdcMgr
cddbp-alt	8880/tcp	CDDBP	mpidcmgr	9343/udp	MpIdcMgr
cddbp-alt	8880/udp	CDDBP	mphlpdmc	9344/tcp	Mphlpdmc
#	8881-8887	Unassigned	mphlpdmc	9344/udp	Mphlpdmc
ddi-tcp-1	8888/tcp	NewsEDGE server TCP (TCP 1)	#	9345-9373	Unassigned
			fjdmimgr	9374/tcp	fjdmimgr
ddi-udp-1	8888/udp	NewsEDGE server UDP (UDP 1)	fjdmimgr	9374/udp	fjdmimgr
			#	9375-9395	Unassigned
ddi-tcp-2	8889/tcp	Desktop Data TCP 1	fjinvmgr	9396/tcp	fjinvmgr
ddi-udp-2	8889/udp	NewsEDGE server broadcast	fjinvmgr	9396/udp	fjinvmgr
ddi-tcp-3	8890/tcp	Desktop Data TCP 2	mpidcagt	9397/tcp	MpIdcAgt
ddi-udp-3	8890/udp	NewsEDGE client broadcast	mpidcagt	9397/udp	MpIdcAgt
ddi-tcp-4	8891/tcp	Desktop Data TCP 3: NESS application	#	9398-9499	Unassigned
			ismserver	9500/tcp	ismserver
ddi-udp-4	8891/udp	Desktop Data UDP 3: NESS application	ismserver	9500/udp	ismserver
			#	9501-9534	Unassigned
ddi-tcp-5	8892/tcp	Desktop Data TCP 4: FARM product	mngsuite	9535/tcp	
			mngsuite	9535/udp	
ddi-udp-5	8892/udp	Desktop Data UDP 4: FARM product	#	9536-9593	Unassigned
			msgsys	9594/tcp	Message System
ddi-tcp-6	8893/tcp	Desktop Data TCP 5: NewsEDGE/Web application	msgsys	9594/udp	Message System
			pds	9595/tcp	Ping Discovery Service
ddi-udp-6	8893/udp	Desktop Data UDP 5: NewsEDGE/Web application	pds	9595/udp	Ping Discovery Service
			#	9596-9599	Unassigned
ddi-tcp-7	8894/tcp	Desktop Data TCP 6: COAL application	micromuse-ncpw	9600/tcp	MICROMUSE-NCPW
			micromuse-ncpw	9600/udp	MICROMUSE-NCPW
ddi-udp-7	8894/udp	Desktop Data UDP 6: COAL application	#	9601-9752	Unassigned
			rasadv	9753/tcp	rasadv
#	8895-8899	Unassigned	rasadv	9753/udp	rasadv
jmb-cds1	8900/tcp	JMB-CDS 1	#	9754-9875	Unassigned
jmb-cds1	8900/udp	JMB-CDS 1	sd	9876/tcp	Session Director
jmb-cds2	8901/tcp	JMB-CDS 2	sd	9876/udp	Session Director
jmb-cds2	8901/udp	JMB-CDS 2	cyborg-systems	9888/tcp	CYBORG Systems
#	8902-8999	Unassigned	cyborg-systems	9888/udp	CYBORG Systems
cslistener	9000/tcp	CSlistener	monkeycom	9898/tcp	MonkeyCom
cslistener	9000/udp	CSlistener	monkeycom	9898/udp	MonkeyCom
#	9001-9005	Unassigned	sctp-tunneling	9899/tcp	SCTP TUNNELING
#	9006	De-Commissioned Port 02/24/00, ms	sctp-tunneling	9899/udp	SCTP TUNNELING
			iua	9900/tcp	IUA
#	9007-9089	Unassigned	iua	9900/udp	IUA
websm	9090/tcp	WebSM	#	9901-9908	Unassigned
websm	9090/udp	WebSM	domaintime	9909/tcp	domaintime
#	9091-9159	Unassigned	domaintime	9909/udp	domaintime
netlock1	9160/tcp	NetLOCK1	#	9910-9949	Unassigned
netlock1	9160/udp	NetLOCK1	apcpcpluswin1	9950/tcp	APCPCPLUSWIN1
netlock2	9161/tcp	NetLOCK2	apcpcpluswin1	9950/udp	APCPCPLUSWIN1
netlock2	9161/udp	NetLOCK2	apcpcpluswin2	9951/tcp	APCPCPLUSWIN2
netlock3	9162/tcp	NetLOCK3	apcpcpluswin2	9951/udp	APCPCPLUSWIN2
netlock3	9162/udp	NetLOCK3	apcpcpluswin3	9952/tcp	APCPCPLUSWIN3
netlock4	9163/tcp	NetLOCK4	apcpcpluswin3	9952/udp	APCPCPLUSWIN3
netlock4	9163/udp	NetLOCK4	#	9953-9991	Unassigned
netlock5	9164/tcp	NetLOCK5	palace-1	9992/tcp	OnLive-1
netlock5	9164/udp	NetLOCK5	palace-1	9992/udp	OnLive-1
#	9165-9199	Unassigned	palace-2	9993/tcp	OnLive-2
wap-wsp	9200/tcp	WAP connectionless session service	palace-2	9993/udp	OnLive-2
			palace-3	9994/tcp	OnLive-3
wap-wsp	9200/udp	WAP connectionless session service	palace-3	9994/udp	OnLive-3
			palace-4	9995/tcp	Palace-4
wap-wsp-wtp	9201/tcp	WAP session service	palace-4	9995/udp	Palace-4
wap-wsp-wtp	9201/udp	WAP session service	palace-5	9996/tcp	Palace-5
wap-wsp-s	9202/tcp	WAP secure connectionless session service	palace-5	9996/udp	Palace-5
			palace-6	9997/tcp	Palace-6
wap-wsp-s	9202/udp	WAP secure connectionless session service	palace-6	9997/udp	Palace-6
			distinct32	9998/tcp	Distinct32
wap-wsp-wtp-s	9203/tcp	WAP secure session service	distinct32	9998/udp	Distinct32
wap-wsp-wtp-s	9203/udp	WAP secure session service	distinct	9999/tcp	distinct
wap-vcard	9204/tcp	WAP vCard	distinct	9999/udp	distinct
wap-vcard	9204/udp	WAP vCard	ndmp	10000/tcp	Network Data Management Protocol
wap-vcal	9205/tcp	WAP vCal			
wap-vcal	9205/udp	WAP vCal	ndmp	10000/udp	Network Data Management Protocol
wap-vcard-s	9206/tcp	WAP vCard Secure			
wap-vcard-s	9206/udp	WAP vCard Secure	#	10001-10006	Unassigned
wap-vcal-s	9207/tcp	WAP vCal Secure	mvs-capacity	10007/tcp	MVS Capacity
wap-vcal-s	9207/udp	WAP vCal Secure	mvs-capacity	10007/udp	MVS Capacity
#	9208-9282	Unassigned	#	10008-10079	Unassigned
callwaveiam	9283/tcp	CallWaveIAM	amanda	10080/tcp	Amanda
callwaveiam	9283/udp	CallWaveIAM	amanda	10080/udp	Amanda
#	9284-9291	Unassigned	#	10081-10112	Unassigned
armtechdaemon	9292/tcp	ArmTech Daemon	netiq-endpoint	10113/tcp	NetIQ Endpoint
armtechdaemon	9292/udp	ArmTech Daemon	netiq-endpoint	10113/udp	NetIQ Endpoint
#	9293-9320	Unassigned	netiq-qcheck	10114/tcp	NetIQ Qcheck
guibase	9321/tcp	guibase	netiq-qcheck	10114/udp	NetIQ Qcheck
guibase	9321/udp	guibase	netiq-endpt	10115/tcp	NetIQ Endpoint

Keyword	Decimal	Description	Keyword	Decimal	Description
netiq-endpt	10115/udp	NetIQ Endpoint	dsmcc-passthru	13820/tcp	DSMCC Pass-Thru Messages
#	10116-10127	Unassigned	dsmcc-passthru	13820/udp	DSMCC Pass-Thru Messages
bmc-perf-sd	10128/tcp	BMC-PERFORM-SERVICE DAEMON	dsmcc-download	13821/tcp	DSMCC Download Protocol
bmc-perf-sd	10128/udp	BMC-PERFORM-SERVICE DAEMON	dsmcc-download	13821/udp	DSMCC Download Protocol
#	10129-10287	Unassigned	dsmcc-ccp	13822/tcp	DSMCC Channel Change Protocol
blocks	10288/tcp	Blocks	dsmcc-ccp	13822/udp	DSMCC Channel Change Protocol
blocks	10288/udp	Blocks			ISO/IEC 13818-6 MPEG-2 DSM-CC
#	10289-10999	Unassigned	#	13823-14000	Unassigned
irisa	11000/tcp	IRISA	itu-sccp-ss7	14001/tcp	ITU SCCP (SS7)
irisa	11000/udp	IRISA	itu-sccp-ss7	14001/udp	ITU SCCP (SS7)
metasys	11001/tcp	Metasys	#	14002-16359	Unassigned
metasys	11001/udp	Metasys	netserialext1	16360/tcp	netserialext1
#	11002-11110	Unassigned	netserialext1	16360/udp	netserialext1
vce	11111/tcp	Viral Computing Environment (VCE)	netserialext2	16361/tcp	netserialext2
vce	11111/udp	Viral Computing Environment (VCE)	netserialext2	16361/udp	netserialext2
#	11112-11200	Unassigned	#	16362-16366	Unassigned
smsqp	11201/tcp	smsqp	netserialext3	16367/tcp	netserialext3
smsqp	11201/udp	smsqp	netserialext3	16367/udp	netserialext3
#	11202-11366	Unassigned	netserialext4	16368/tcp	netserialext4
atm-uhas	11367/tcp	ATM UHAS	netserialext4	16368/udp	netserialext4
atm-uhas	11367/udp	ATM UHAS	#	16369-16990	Unassigned
#	11368-11719	Unassigned	intel-rci-mp	16991/tcp	INTEL-RCI-MP
h323callsigalt	11720/tcp	h323 Call Signal Alternate	intel-rci-mp	16991/udp	INTEL-RCI-MP
h323callsigalt	11720/udp	h323 Call Signal Alternate	#	16992-17006	Unassigned
#	11721-11999	Unassigned	isode-dua	17007/tcp	
entextxid	12000/tcp	IBM Enterprise Extender SNA XID Exchange	isode-dua	17007/udp	
entextxid	12000/udp	IBM Enterprise Extender SNA XID Exchange	#	17008-17218	Unassigned
entextnetwk	12001/tcp	IBM Enterprise Extender SNA COS Network Priority	chipper	17219/tcp	Chipper
entextnetwk	12001/udp	IBM Enterprise Extender SNA COS Network Priority	chipper	17219/udp	Chipper
entexthigh	12002/tcp	IBM Enterprise Extender SNA COS High Priority	#	17220-17999	Unassigned
entexthigh	12002/udp	IBM Enterprise Extender SNA COS High Priority	biimenu	18000/tcp	Beckman Instruments, Inc.
entextmed	12003/tcp	IBM Enterprise Extender SNA COS Medium Priority	biimenu	18000/udp	Beckman Instruments, Inc.
entextmed	12003/udp	IBM Enterprise Extender SNA COS Medium Priority	#	18001-18180	Unassigned
entextlow	12004/tcp	IBM Enterprise Extender SNA COS Low Priority	opsec-cvp	18181/tcp	OPSEC CVP
entextlow	12004/udp	IBM Enterprise Extender SNA COS Low Priority	opsec-cvp	18181/udp	OPSEC CVP
#	12005-12171	Unassigned	opsec-ufp	18182/tcp	OPSEC UFP
hivep	12172/tcp	HiveP	opsec-ufp	18182/udp	OPSEC UFP
hivep	12172/udp	HiveP	opsec-sam	18183/tcp	OPSEC SAM
#	12173-12752	Unassigned	opsec-sam	18183/udp	OPSEC SAM
tsaf	12753/tcp	tsaf port	opsec-lea	18184/tcp	OPSEC LEA
tsaf	12753/udp	tsaf port	opsec-lea	18184/udp	OPSEC LEA
#	12754-13159	Unassigned	opsec-omi	18185/tcp	OPSEC OMI
i-zipqd	13160/tcp	I-ZIPQD	opsec-omi	18185/udp	OPSEC OMI
i-zipqd	13160/udp	I-ZIPQD	#	18186	Unassigned
#	13161-13222	Unassigned	opsec-ela	18187/tcp	OPSEC ELA
powwow-client	13223/tcp	PowWow Client	opsec-ela	18187/udp	OPSEC ELA
powwow-client	13223/udp	PowWow Client	ac-cluster	18463/tcp	AC Cluster
powwow-server	13224/tcp	PowWow Server	ac-cluster	18463/udp	AC Cluster
powwow-server	13224/udp	PowWow Server	#	18464-18887	Unassigned
#	13225-13719	Unassigned	apc-necmp	18888/tcp	APCNECMP
bprd	13720/tcp	BPRD Protocol (VERITAS NetBackup)	apc-necmp	18888/udp	APCNECMP
bprd	13720/udp	BPRD Protocol (VERITAS NetBackup)	#	18889-19190	Unassigned
bpbrm	13721/tcp	BPBRM Protocol (VERITAS NetBackup)	opsec-uaa	19191/tcp	opsec-uaa
bpbrm	13721/udp	BPBRM Protocol (VERITAS NetBackup)	opsec-uaa	19191/udp	opsec-uaa
bpjava-msvc	13722/tcp	BP Java MSVC Protocol	#	19192-19282	Unassigned
bpjava-msvc	13722/udp	BP Java MSVC Protocol	keysrvr	19283/tcp	Key Server for SASSAFRAS
#	13723-13781	Unassigned	keysrvr	19283/udp	Key Server for SASSAFRAS
bpcd	13782/tcp	VERITAS NetBackup	#	19284-19314	Unassigned
bpcd	13782/udp	VERITAS NetBackup	keyshadow	19315/tcp	Key Shadow for SASSAFRAS
vopied	13783/tcp	VOPIED Protnocol	keyshadow	19315/udp	Key Shadow for SASSAFRAS
vopied	13783/udp	VOPIED Protocol	#	19316-19409	Unassigned
#	13784-13817	Unassigned	hp-sco	19410/tcp	hp-sco
dsmcc-config	13818/tcp	DSMCC Config	hp-sco	19410/udp	hp-sco
dsmcc-config	13818/udp	DSMCC Config	hp-sca	19411/tcp	hp-sca
dsmcc-session	13819/tcp	DSMCC Session Messages	hp-sca	19411/udp	hp-sca
dsmcc-session	13819/udp	DSMCC Session Messages	hp-sessmon	19412/tcp	HP-SESSMON
			hp-sessmon	19412/udp	HP-SESSMON
			#	19413-19540	Unassigned
			jcp	19541/tcp	JCP Client
			jcp	19541/udp	JCP Client
			#	19542-19999	Unassigned
			dnp	20000/tcp	DNP
			dnp	20000/udp	DNP
			#	20001-20669	Unassigned
			track	20670/tcp	Track
			track	20670/udp	Track
			#	20671-20998	Unassigned
			athand-mmp	20999/tcp	At Hand MMP
			athand-mmp	20999/udp	At Hand MMP
			#	20300-21589	Unassigned
			vofr-gateway	21590/tcp	VoFR Gateway

Keyword	Decimal	Description	Keyword	Decimal	Description
vofr-gateway	21590/udp	VoFR Gateway	icl-twobase10	25009/tcp	icl-twobase10
#	21591-21844	Unassigned	icl-twobase10	25009/udp	icl-twobase10
webphone	21845/tcp	webphone	#	25010-25792	Unassigned
webphone	21845/udp	webphone	vocaltec-hos	25793/tcp	Vocaltec Address Server
netspeak-is	21846/tcp	NetSpeak Corp. Directory Services	vocaltec-hos	25793/udp	Vocaltec Address Server
netspeak-is	21846/udp	NetSpeak Corp. Directory Services	#	25794-25999	Unassigned
			quake	26000/tcp	quake
netspeak-cs	21847/tcp	NetSpeak Corp. Connection Services	quake	26000/udp	quake
netspeak-cs	21847/udp	NetSpeak Corp. Connection Services	#	26001-26207	Unassigned
			wnn6-ds	26208/tcp	wnn6-ds
netspeak-acd	21848/tcp	NetSpeak Corp. Automatic Call Distribution	wnn6-ds	26208/udp	wnn6-ds
netspeak-acd	21848/udp	NetSpeak Corp. Automatic Call Distribution	#	26209-26261	Unassigned
			k3software-svr	26262/tcp	K3 Software-Server
netspeak-cps	21849/tcp	NetSpeak Corp. Credit Processing System	k3software-svr	26262/tcp	K3 Software-Server
netspeak-cps	21849/udp	NetSpeak Corp. Credit Processing System	k3software-cli	26263/udp	K3 Software-Client
			k3software-cli	26263/udp	K3 Software-Client
#	21850-21999	Unassigned	#	26263-26999	Unassigned
snapenetio	22000/tcp	SNAPenetIO	flex-lm	27000-27009	FLEX LM (1-10)
snapenetio	22000/udp	SNAPenetIO	#	27010-27344	Unassigned
optocontrol	22001/tcp	OptoControl	imagepump	27345/tcp	ImagePump
optocontrol	22001/udp	OptoControl	imagepump	27345/udp	ImagePump
#	22002-22272	Unassigned	#	27346-27998	Unassigned
wnn6	22273/tcp	wnn6	tw-auth-key	27999/tcp	TW Authentication/ Key Distribution and
wnn6	22273/udp	wnn6	tw-auth-key	27999/udp	Attribute Certificate Services
#	22274-22554	Unassigned	#	28000-32767	Unassigned
vocaltec-wconf	22555/tcp	Vocaltec Web Conference	filenet-tms	32768/tcp	Filenet TMS
vocaltec-phone	22555/udp	Vocaltec Internet Phone	filenet-tms	32768/udp	Filenet TMS
#	22556-22799	Unassigned	filenet-rpc	32769/tcp	Filenet RPC
aws-brf	22800/tcp	Telerate Information Platform LAN	filenet-rpc	32769/udp	Filenet RPC
			filenet-nch	32770/tcp	Filenet NCH
aws-brf	22800/udp	Telerate Information Platform LAN	filenet-nch	32770/udp	Filenet NCH
			#	32771-33433	Unassigned
#	22801-22950	Unassigned	traceroute	33434/tcp	traceroute use
brf-gw	22951/tcp	Telerate Information Platform WAN	traceroute	33434/udp	traceroute use
			#	33435-36864	Unassigned
brf-gw	22951/udp	Telerate Information Platform WAN	kastenxpipe	36865/tcp	KastenX Pipe
			kastenxpipe	36865/udp	KastenX Pipe
#	22952-23999	Unassigned	#	36866-40840	Unassigned
med-ltp	24000/tcp	med-ltp	cscp	40841/tcp	CSCP
med-ltp	24000/udp	med-ltp	cscp	40841/udp	CSCP
med-fsp-rx	24001/tcp	med-fsp-rx	#	40842-43187	Unassigned
med-fsp-rx	24001/udp	med-fsp-rx	reachout	43188/tcp	REACHOUT
med-fsp-tx	24002/tcp	med-fsp-tx	reachout	43188/udp	REACHOUT
med-fsp-tx	24002/udp	med-fsp-tx	ndm-agent-port	43189/tcp	NDM-AGENT-PORT
med-supp	24003/tcp	med-supp	ndm-agent-port	43189/udp	NDM-AGENT-PORT
med-supp	24003/udp	med-supp	ip-provision	43190/tcp	IP-PROVISION
med-ovw	24004/tcp	med-ovw	ip-provision	43190/udp	IP-PROVISION
med-ovw	24004/udp	med-ovw	#	43191-44817	Unassigned
med-ci	24005/tcp	med-ci	rockwell-encap	44818/tcp	Rockwell Encapsulation
med-ci	24005/udp	med-ci	rockwell-encap	44818/udp	Rockwell Encapsulation
med-net-svc	24006/tcp	med-net-svc	#	44819-45677	Unassigned
med-net-svc	24006/udp	med-net-svc	eba	45678/tcp	EBA PRISE
#	24007-24385	Unassigned	eba	45678/udp	EBA PRISE
intel_rci	24386/tcp	Intel RCI	#	45679-45965	Unassigned
intel_rci	24386/udp	Intel RCI	ssr-servermgr	45966/tcp	SSRServerMgr
#	24387-24553	Unassigned	ssr-servermgr	45966/udp	SSRServerMgr
binkp	24554/tcp	BINKP	#	45967-47556	Unassigned
binkp	24554/udp	BINKP	dbbrowse	47557/tcp	Databeam Corporation
#	24554-34676	Unassigned	dbbrowse	47557/udp	Databeam Corporation
flashfiler	24677/tcp	FlashFiler	#	47558-47623	Unassigned
flashfiler	24677/udp	FlashFiler	directplaysrvr	47624/tcp	Direct Play Server
#	24678-24999	Unassigned	directplaysrvr	47624/udp	Direct Play Server
icl-twobase1	25000/tcp	icl-twobase1	#	47625-47805	Unassigned
icl-twobase1	25000/udp	icl-twobase1	ap	47806/tcp	ALC Protocol
icl-twobase2	25001/tcp	icl-twobase2	ap	47806/udp	ALC Protocol
icl-twobase2	25001/udp	icl-twobase2	#	47807	Unassigned
icl-twobase3	25002/tcp	icl-twobase3	bacnet	47808/tcp	Building Automation and Control Networks
icl-twobase3	25002/udp	icl-twobase3	bacnet	47808/udp	Building Automation and Control Networks
icl-twobase4	25003/tcp	icl-twobase4			
icl-twobase4	25003/udp	icl-twobase4	#	47809-47999	Unassigned
icl-twobase5	25004/tcp	icl-twobase5	nimcontroller	48000/tcp	Nimbus Controller
icl-twobase5	25004/udp	icl-twobase5	nimcontroller	48000/udp	Nimbus Controller
icl-twobase6	25005/tcp	icl-twobase6	nimspooler	48001/tcp	Nimbus Spooler
icl-twobase6	25005/udp	icl-twobase6	nimspooler	48001/udp	Nimbus Spooler
icl-twobase7	25006/tcp	icl-twobase7	nimhub	48002/tcp	Nimbus Hub
icl-twobase7	25006/udp	icl-twobase7	nimhub	48002/udp	Nimbus Hub
icl-twobase8	25007/tcp	icl-twobase8	nimgtw	48003/tcp	Nimbus Gateway
icl-twobase8	25007/udp	icl-twobase8	nimgtw	48003/udp	Nimbus Gateway
icl-twobase9	25008/tcp	icl-twobase9	#	48004-49151	Unassigned
icl-twobase9	25008/udp	icl-twobase9			

Dec/Hex/ASCII/EBCDIC-
Conversion Table

ASCII = American National Standard Code for Information Interchange
EBCDIC = Extended Binary Coded Decimal Interchange Code
Dec = Decimal
Hex = Hexadecimal

Dec	Hex	ASCII		EBCDIC	
0	00	NUL	Null	NUL	Null
1	01	SOH	Start of Heading (CC)	SOH	Start of Heading
2	02	STX	Start of Text (CC)	STX	Start of Text
3	03	ETX	End of Text (CC)	ETX	End of Text
4	04	EOT	End of Transmission (CC)	PF	Punch Off
5	05	ENQ	Enquiry (CC)	HT	Horizontal Tab
6	06	ACK	Acknowledge (CC)	LC	Lower Case
7	07	BEL	Bell	DEL	Delete
8	08	BS	Backspace (FE)		
9	09	HT	Horizontal Tabulation (FE)		
10	0A	LF	Line Feed (FE)	SMM	Start of Manual Message
11	0B	VT	Vertical Tabulation (FE)	VT	Vertical Tab
12	0C	FF	Form Feed (FE)	FF	Form Feed
13	0D	CR	Carriage Return (FE)	CR	Carriage Return
14	0E	SO	Shift Out	SO	Shift Out
15	0F	SI	Shift In	SI	Shift In
16	10	DLE	Data Link Escape (CC)	DLE	Data Link Escape
17	11	DC1	Device Control 1	DC1	Device Control 1
18	12	DC2	Device Control 2	DC2	Device Control 2
19	13	DC3	Device Control 3	TM	Tape Mark

Dec	Hex	ASCII		EBCDIC	
20	14	DC4	Device Control 4	RES	Restore
21	15	NAK	Negative Acknowledge (CC)	NL	New Line
22	16	SYN	Synchronous Idle (CC)	BS	Backspace
23	17	ETB	End of Transmission Block (CC)	IL	Idle
24	18	CAN	Cancel	CAN	Cancel
25	19	EM	End of Medium	EM	End of Medium
26	1A	SUB	Substitute	CC	Cursor Control
27	1B	ESC	Escape	CU1	Customer Use 1
28	1C	FS	File Separator (IS)	IFS	Interchange File Separator
29	1D	GS	Group Separator (IS)	IGS	Interchange Group Separator
30	1E	RS	Record Separator (IS)	IRS	Interchange Record Separator
31	1F	US	Unit Separator (IS)	IUS	Interchange Unit Separator
32	20	SP	Space	DS	Digit Select
33	21	!	Exclamation Point	SOS	Start of Significance
34	22	"	Quotation Mark	FS	Field Separator
35	23	#	Number Sign, Octothorp, "pound"		
36	24	$	Dollar Sign	BYP	Bypass
37	25	%	Percent	LF	Line Feed
38	26	&	Ampersand	ETB	End of Transmission Block
39	27	'	Apostrophe, Prime	ESC	Escape
40	28	(	Left Parenthesis		
41	29	)	Right Parenthesis		
42	2A	*	Asterisk, "star"	SM	Set Mode
43	2B	+	Plus Sign	CU2	Customer Use 2

Dec	Hex	ASCII		EBCDIC	
44	2C	,	Comma		
45	2D	-	Hyphen, Minus Sign	ENQ	Enquiry
46	2E	.	Period, Decimal Point, "dot"	ACK	Acknowledge
47	2F	/	Slash, Virgule	BEL	Bell
48	30	0	0		
49	31	1	1		
50	32	2	2	SYN	Synchronous Idle
51	33	3	3		
52	34	4	4	PN	Punch On
53	35	5	5	RS	Reader Stop
54	36	6	6	UC	Upper Case
55	37	7	7	EOT	End of Transmission
56	38	8	8		
57	39	9	9		
58	3A	:	Colon		
59	3B	;	Semicolon	CU3	Customer Use 3
60	3C	<	Less-than Sign	DC4	Device Control 4
61	3D	=	Equal Sign	NAK	Negative Acknowledge
62	3E	>	Greater-than Sign		
63	3F	?	Question Mark	SUB	Substitute
64	40	@	At Sign	SP	Space
65	41	A	A		
66	42	B	B		
67	43	C	C		
68	44	D	D		
69	45	E	E		
70	46	F	F		

Dec	Hex	ASCII			EBCDIC	
71	47	G	G			
72	48	H	H			
73	49	I	I			
74	4A	J	J		¢	Cent Sign
75	4B	K	K		.	Period, Decimal Point, "dot"
76	4C	L	L		<	Less-than Sign
77	4D	M	M		(	Left Parenthesis
78	4E	N	N		+	Plus Sign
79	4F	O	O		|	Logical OR
80	50	P	P		&	Ampersand
81	51	Q	Q			
82	52	R	R			
83	53	S	S			
84	54	T	T			
85	55	U	U			
86	56	V	V			
87	57	W	W			
88	58	X	X			
89	59	Y	Y			
90	5A	Z	Z		!	Exclamation Point
91	5B	[	Opening Bracket		$	Dollar Sign
92	5C	\	Reverse Slant		*	Asterisk, "star"
93	5D	]	Closing Bracket		)	Right Parenthesis
94	5E	^	Circumflex, Caret		;	Semicolon
95	5F	_	Underline, Underscore		¬	Logical NOT
96	60	`	Grave Accent		-	Hyphen, Minus Sign
97	61	a	a			

Dec	Hex	ASCII		EBCDIC	
98	62	b	b		
99	63	c	c		
100	64	d	d		
101	65	e	e		
102	66	f	f		
103	67	g	g		
104	68	h	h		
105	69	i	i		
106	6A	j	j		
107	6B	k	k	,	Comma
108	6C	l	l	%	Percent
109	6D	m	m	_	Underline, Under-score
110	6E	n	n	>	Greater-than Sign
111	6F	o	o	?	Question Mark
112	70	p	p		
113	71	q	q		
114	72	r	r		
115	73	s	s		
116	74	t	t		
117	75	u	u		
118	76	v	v		
119	77	w	w		
120	78	x	x		
121	79	y	y		
122	7A	z	z	:	Colon
123	7B	{	Opening Brace	#	Number Sign, Octothorp, «pound»

Dec	Hex	ASCII		EBCDIC	
124	7C	|	Vertical Line	@	At Sign
125	7D	}	Closing Brace	'	Apostrophe, Prime
126	7E	~	Tilde	=	Equal Sign
127	7F	DEL	Delete	"	Quotation Mark
128	80		Reserved		
129	81		Reserved	a	a
130	82		Reserved	b	b
131	83		Reserved	c	c
132	84	IND	Index (FE)	d	d
133	85	NEL	Next Line (FE)	e	e
134	86	SSA	Start of Selected Area	f	f
135	87	ESA	End of Selected Area	g	g
136	88	HTS	Horizontal Tabulation Set (FE)	h	h
137	89	HTJ	Horizontal Tabulation with Justification (FE)	i	i
138	8A	VTS	Vertical Tabulation Set (FE)		
139	8B	PLD	Partial Line Down (FE)		
140	8C	PLU	Partial Line Up (FE)		
141	8D	RI	Reverse Index (FE)		
142	8E	SS2	Single Shift Two (1)		
143	8F	SS3	Single Shift Three (1)		
144	90	DCS	Device Control String (2)		
145	91	PU1	Private Use One	j	j
146	92	PU2	Private Use Two	k	k
147	93	STS	Set Transmit State	l	l
148	94	CCH	Cancel Character	m	m
149	95	MW	Message Waiting	n	n
150	96	SPA	Start of Protected Area	o	o

Dec	Hex	ASCII		EBCDIC	
151	97	EPA	End of Protected Area	p	p
152	98		Reserved	q	q
153	99		Reserved	r	r
154	9A		Reserved		
155	9B	CSI	Control Sequence Introducer (1)		
156	9C	ST	String Terminator (2)		
157	9D	OSC	Operating System Command (2)		
158	9E	PM	Privacy Message (2)		
159	9F	APC	Application Program Command (2)		
160	A0				
161	A1				
162	A2			s	s
163	A3			t	t
164	A4			u	u
165	A5			v	v
166	A6			w	w
167	A7			x	x
168	A8			y	y
169	A9			z	z
170	AA				
171	AB				
172	AC				
173	AD				
174	AE				
175	AF				
176	B0				
177	B1				
178	B2				

Dec	Hex	ASCII	EBCDIC	
179	B3			
180	B4			
181	B5			
182	B6			
183	B7			
184	B8			
185	B9		'	Grave Accent
186	BA			
187	BB			
188	BC			
189	BD			
190	BE			
191	BF			
192	C0			
193	C1		A	A
194	C2		B	B
195	C3		C	C
196	C4		D	D
197	C5		E	E
198	C6		F	F
199	C7		G	G
200	C8		H	H
201	C9		I	I
202	CA			
203	CB			
204	CC			
205	CD			
206	CE			

Dec	Hex	ASCII	EBCDIC	
207	CF			
208	D0			
209	D1		J	J
210	D2		K	K
211	D3		L	L
212	D4		M	M
213	D5		N	N
214	D6		O	O
215	D7		P	P
216	D8		Q	Q
217	D9		R	R
218	DA			
219	DB			
220	DC			
221	DD			
222	DE			
223	DF			
224	E0			
225	E1			
226	E2		S	S
227	E3		T	T
228	E4		U	U
229	E5		V	V
230	E6		W	W
231	E7		X	X
232	E8		Y	Y
233	E9		Z	Z
234	EA			

Dec	Hex	ASCII	EBCDIC	
235	EB			
236	EC			
237	ED			
238	EE			
239	EF			
240	F0		0	0
241	F1		1	1
242	F2		2	2
243	F3		3	3
244	F4		4	4
245	F5		5	5
246	F6		6	6
247	F7		7	7
248	F8		8	8
249	F9		9	9
250	FA			
251	FB			
252	FC			
253	FD			
254	FE			
255	FF			

Standards

I.1 10/100/1,000 MBit/s Ethernet:

http://grouper.ieee.org/groups/802/3/index.html

IEEE Std 802.3,	Carrier Sense Multiple Access with Collision Detection (CSMA/CD) Access Method and Physical Layer
IEEE Std 802.3a-1988,	10 Mb/s MAU 10BASE2 (Clause 10).
IEEE Std 802.3b-1985,	Broadband Medium Attachment Unit and Broadband Medium Specifications, Type 10BROAD36 (Clause 11).
IEEE Std 802.3c-1985,	Repeater Unit for 10 Mb/s Baseband Networks (Subclauses 9.1-9.8)
IEEE Std 802.3d-1987,	Medium Attachment Unit and Baseband Medium Specification for a Vendor Independent Fiber Optic Inter Repeater Link (Section 9.9).
IEEE Std 802.3e-1987,	Physical Signaling, Medium Attachment, and Baseband Medium Specifications, Type 1BASE5 (Clause 12).
IEEE Std 802.3h-1990,	Layer Management (Clause 5).
IEEE Std 802.3i-1990,	System Considerations for Multisegment 10 Mb/s Baseband Networks (Clause 13) AND Twisted-Pair Medium Attachment Unit (MAU) and Baseband Medium, Type 10BASE-T (Section 14).
IEEE Std 802.3j-1993,	Fiber Optic Active and Passive Star-Based Segments, Type 10BASE-F (Clauses 15-18).
IEEE Std 802.3k-1992,	Layer Management for 10 Mb/s Baseband Repeaters (Clause 19).
IEEE Std 802.3l-1992,	Type 10BASE-T Medium Attachment Unit (MAU) Protocol Implementation Conformance Statement (PICS) Proforma (Subclause 14.10).
IEEE Std 802.3m-1995,	Second Maintenance Ballot.
IEEE Std 802.3n-1995,	Third Maintenance Ballot. IEEE Std 802.3p-1993, Layer Management for 10 Mb/s Baseband Medium Attachment Units (MAUs) (Clause 20).
IEEE Std 802.3q-1993,	Guidelines for the Development of Managed Objects (GDMO) (ISO 10165-4) Format for Layer-Managed Objects (Clause 5)
IEEE Std 802.3r-1997,	Type 10BASE5 Medium Attachment Unit PICS Proforma.
IEEE Std 802.3s-1995,	Fourth Maintenance Ballot.
IEEE Std 802.3t-1995,	Informative Annex for Support of 120 Ohm Cables in 10BASE-T Simplex Link Segment (Annex D.5).
IEEE Std 802.3u-1995,	Type 100BASE-T MAC Parameters, Physical Layer, MAUs, and Repeater for 100 Mb/s Operation.
IEEE Std 802.3v-1995,	Informative Annex for Support of 150 Ohm Cables in 10 BASE-T Link Segment (Annex D.6).
IEEE Std 802.3x&y-1997,	Specification for 802.3 Full Duplex Operation and Physical Layer Specification for 100 Mb/s Operation on Two Pairs of Category 3 or Better Balanced Twisted Pair Cable (100BASE-T2).
IEEE Std 802.3z-1998,	Physical Layers, Repeater, and Management Parameters for 1000 Mb/s Operation.
IEEE Std 802.3aa-1998,	Maintenance Revision #5 (Revisions to 100BASE-T)
IEEE 802.3.ab,	Physical Layer Parameters and Specifications for 1000 Mb/s Operation Over 4-Pair Category 5 Balanced Copper Cabling, Type 1000BASE 07/99
IEEE Std 802.3ac-1998,	Supplement to IEEE Std 802.3, 1998 Edition, Carrier Sense Multiple Access with Collision Detection (CSMA/CD)–Frame Extensions for Virtual Bridged Local Area Network (VLAN) Tagging on 802.3 Networks.
IEEE802.3w,	Standard for Enhanced Media Access Control Algorithm
IEEE 1802.3 d-1993,	Supplement to IEEE Std 1802.3-1991, Local and Metropolitan Area Networks: Conformance Test Methodology: Carrier Sense Multiple Access with Collision Detection (CSMA/CD) Access Method and Physical Layer Specifications
IEEE 802.3ae,	10 Gbit/s Ethernet PAR approved 01/00
RFC 1271	Remote Network Monitoring Management Information Base
RFC 2074	Remote Network Monitoring MIB Protocol Identifiers

I.2   Token Ring

http://www.8025.org

IEEE Std 802.5c-19 91, ... Supplement to IEEE Std 802.5-1989, Local and metropolitan area networks: Recommended practice for dual ring operation with wrapback reconfiguration.

IEEE 802.5e, ... Token ring station management entity specifications

IEEE Std 802.5j-1997, ... Supplement to information technology–Telecommunications and information exchange between systems - Local and metropolitan area networks–Specific requirements –Part 5: Token Ring access method and physical layer specifications Fibre Optic Media requirements.

IEEE Std 802.5r-1997, ... Standard for Information technology - Telecommunications and information exchange between systems - Local and metropolitan area networks - Specific requirements - Part 5: Token Ring access method and physical layer specifications–Dedicated Token Ring Operation.

IEEE 802.5t, ... Supplement to ISO/IEC 8802-5: 1995 Specific requirements–Part 5: Token Ring access method and physical layer specifications - 100 Mbit/s dedicated Token Ring operation over 2-pair cabling.

IEEE 802.5u, ... Supplement to ISO/IEC 8802-5: 1995 Specific requirements - Part 5: Token Ring access method and physical layer specifications - 100 Mbit/s dedicated Token Ring operation over multi-mode fibre.

IEEE 802.5v, ... Supplement to ISO/IEC 8802-5: 1995, Specific requirements - Part 5: Token Ring access method and physical layer specifications. Media access control parameters, physical layers, and management parameters for 1,000 Mbit/s operation or above.

RFC 1231 IEEE 802.5 ...... Token Ring MIB

I.3   FDDI

http://www.ansi.org

ANSI X3.139-1987, ISO 9314-2:1989, Media Access Control (MAC)

ANSI X3.148-1988, ISO 9314-1:1989, Physical Layer Protocol (PHY)

ANSI X3.166-1990, ISO 9314-3:1990, Physical Layer, Medium Dependent (PMD)

ANSI X3.229-1994, ISO 9314-6, Station Management (SMT)

ANSI X3.184-1993, ISO 9314-4, Single Mode Fiber PMD (SMF-PMD)

ANSI X3.237-1995, ISO 9314-9, Low Cost Fiber PMD (LCF-PMD)

ANSI X3.263.1995, ISO 9314-10, Twisted Pair PMD (TP-PMD)

ANSI X3.278, Physical Layer Repeater (PHY-REP)

ANSI X3.262 ISO 9314-13, Conformance Test PICS Proforma for FDDI (CT-PICS)

ANSI X3.245-199x, ISO 9314-26, Abstract Test Suite for MAC (MAC-ATS)

ANSI X3.248-199x, ISO 9314-21, Abstract Test Suite for PHY (PHY-ATS)

ANSI X3.255-199x, ISO 9314-20, Abstract Test Suite for PMD (PMD-ATS)

ANSI X3T9.5/92-102, Rev 1.4, Abstract Test Suite for SMT (SMT-ATS)

RFC 1285, FDDI-MIB

I.4 ATM

I.4.1 ITU-T Series I: Integrated Services Digital Network

http://www.itu.ch

Overview

Terminology (I.112 - I.114)
Description of ISDNs (I.120 - I.122)
General modeling methods (I.130 - I.130)
Telecommunication network and service attributes (I.140 - I.141)
General description of asynchronous transfer mode (I.150 - I.150)
Scope (I.200 - I.200)
General aspects of services in ISDN (I.210 - I.211)
Common aspects of services in the ISDN (I.220 - I.221)
Bearer services supported by an ISDN (I.230 - I.233.2)
Teleservices supported by an ISDN (I.240 - I.241.8)
Supplementary services in ISDN (I.250 - I.259.1)
Network functional principles (I.310 - I.312)
Reference models (I.320 - I.329)
Numbering, addressing and routing (I.330 - I.334)
Connection types (I.340 - I.340)
Performance objectives (I.350 - I.357)
Protocol layer requirements (I.361 - I.365.4)
General network requirements and functions (I.370 - I.376)
ISDN user-network interfaces (I.410 - I.414)
Application of I-series Recommendations to ISDN user-network interfaces (I.420 - I.421)
Layer 1 Recommendations (I.430 - I.432.5)
Layer 2 Recommendations (I.440 - I.441)
Layer 3 Recommendations (I.450 - I.452)
Multiplexing, rate adaption and support of existing interfaces (I.460 - I.465)
Aspects of ISDN affecting terminal requirements (I.470 - I.470)
Internetwork interfaces (I.500 - I.580)
Maintenance principles (I.601 - I.620)
ATM equipment (I.731 - I.732)
Management of ATM equipment (I.751 - I.751)

ITU-T I-Series Recommendations

[I.112] .... Recommendation I.112 (03/93) - Vocabulary of terms for ISDNs
[I.113] .... Recommendation I.113 (06/97) - Vocabulary of terms for broadband aspects of ISDN
[I.114] .... Recommendation I.114 (03/93) - Vocabulary of terms for universal personal telecommunication
[I.120] .... Recommendation I.120 (03/93) - Integrated services digital networks (ISDNs)
[I.121] .... Recommendation I.121 (04/91) - Broadband aspects of ISDN
[I.122] .... Recommendation I.122 (03/93) - Framework for frame mode bearer services
[I.130] .... Recommendation I.130 (11/88) - Method for the characterization of telecommunication services supported by an ISDN and network capabilities of an ISDN
[I.140] .... Recommendation I.140 (03/93) - Attribute technique for the characterization of telecommunication services supported by an ISDN and network capabilities of an ISDN
[I.141] .... Recommendation I.141 (11/88) - ISDN network charging capabilities attributes
[I.150] .... Recommendation I.150 (02/99) - B-ISDN asynchronous transfer mode functional characteristics
[I.200] .... Recommendation I.200 (11/88) - Guidance to the I.200-Series of Recommendations
[I.210] .... Recommendation I.210 (03/93) - Principles of telecommunication services supported by an ISDN and the means to describe them
[I.211] .... Recommendation I.211 (03/93) - B-ISDN service aspects
[I.220] .... Recommendation I.220 (11/88) - Common dynamic description of basic telecommunication services

ITU-T I-Series Recommendations

ITU-T I-Series Recommendations

ITU-T I-Series Recommendations

ITU-T I-Series Recommendations

I.4.2   ITU-T Series Q: Switching and signaling

Overview

Signaling in the international manual service (Q.1 - Q.2)

Basic Recommendations (Q.4 - Q.9)

Numbering plan and dialing procedures in the international service (Q.11 ter - Q.11)

Routing plan for international service (Q.12 - Q.14)

General recommendations relative to signaling and switching systems (national or international) (Q.20 - Q.33)

Tones for use in national signaling systems (Q.35 - Q.35)

General characteristics for international telephone connections and circuits (Q.44 - Q.45)

Signaling for satellite systems (Q.48 - Q.48)

Signaling for circuit multiplication equipment (Q.50 - Q.50)

Methodology (Q.65 - Q.65)

Basic services (Q.68 - Q.76)

Supplementary services (Q.80 - Q.87.2)

General clauses (Q.101 - Q.109)

Transmission clauses for signaling (Q.110 - Q.114)

Control of echo suppressors (Q.115 - Q.115)

Abnormal conditions (Q.116 - Q.118)

Specifications of signaling system No. 4 (Q.120 - Q.139)

Specifications of signaling system No. 5 (Q.140 - Q.164)

Interworking of signaling systems No. 4 and No. 5 (Q.180 - Q.180)

Functional description of the signaling system (Q.251 - Q.253)

Definition and function of signals (Q.254 - Q.256)

Signal unit formats and codes (Q.257 - Q.260)

Signaling procedures (Q.261 - Q.268)

Continuity check of the speech path (Q.271 - Q.271)

Signaling link (Q.272 - Q.279)

Signal traffic characteristics (Q.285 - Q.287)

Security arrangements (Q.291 - Q.293)

Testing and maintenance (Q.295 - Q.296)

Network management (Q.297 - Q.297)

Interworking between ITU-T signaling system No. 6 and national common channel signaling systems (Q.300 - Q.300)

Definition and function of signals (Q.310 - Q.310)

Line signaling (Q.311 - Q.319)

Register signaling (Q.320 - Q.326)

Testing arrangements (Q.327 - Q.331)

Interworking of signaling system R1 with other standardized systems (Q.332 - Q.332)

Definition and function of signals (Q.400 - Q.400)

Line signaling, analog version (Q.411 - Q.416)

Line signaling, digital version (Q.421 - Q.430)

Interregister signaling (Q.440 - Q.458)

Signaling procedures (Q.460 - Q.480)

Testing and maintenance (Q.490 - Q.490)

Introduction and field of application (Q.500 - Q.500)

Exchange interfaces, functions and connections (Q.511 - Q.522)

Design objectives and measurement (Q.541 - Q.544)

Transmission characteristics (Q.551 - Q.554)

General considerations (Q.601 - Q.608)

Logic procedures (Q.611 - Q.696)

Interworking of signaling systems No. 7 and No. 6 (Q.698 - Q.698)

Interworking between Digital subscriber signaling system No. 1 and signaling system No. 7 (Q.699 - Q.699)

General (Q.700 - Q.700)

Message transfer part (MTP) (Q.701 - Q.709)

Specifications of signaling system No. 7 (Q.710 - Q.710)

Signaling connection control part (SCCP) (Q.711 - Q.716)

Telephone user part (TUP) (Q.721 - Q.725)

ISDN supplementary services (Q.730 - Q.737.1)

Data user part (Q.741 - Q.741)

signaling system No. 7 management (Q.750 - Q.756)

ISDN user part (Q.761 - Q.768)

Transaction capabilities application part (Q.771 - Q.775)

Test specification (Q.780 - Q.788)

Q3 interface (Q.811 - Q.824.4)

General (Q.850 - Q.850)

Data link layer (Q.920 - Q.923)

Network layer (Q.930 - Q.939)

User-network management (Q.940 - Q.941)

Stage 3 description for supplementary services using DSS 1 (Q.950 - Q.957.1)

General (Q.1000 - Q.1005)

Interworking with ISDN and PSTN (Q.1031 - Q.1032)

Digital PLMN user-network interfaces (Q.1061 - Q.1063)

Interworking with Standard-A INMARSAT system (Q.1100 - Q.1103)

Interworking with Standard-B INMARSAT system (Q.1111 - Q.1112)

Interworking with the INMARSAT aeronautical mobile-satellite system (Q.1151 - Q.1152)

Intelligent Network (Q.1200 - Q.1551)

General aspects (Q.2010 - Q.2010)

Signaling ATM adaptation layer (SAAL) (Q.2100 - Q.2144)

Signaling network protocols (Q.2210 - Q.2210)

Common aspects of B-ISDN application protocols for access signaling and network signaling and interworking (Q.2610 - Q.2660)

B-ISDN application protocols of the network (Q.2721.1 - Q.2764)

B-ISDN application protocols for access signaling (Q.2931 - Q.2971)

Supplements to the Series Q.300 and Q.400 Recommendations (Q.Sup1 - Q.Sup7)

Supplements to the Series Q.500 Recommendations (Q.Sup1 - Q.Sup2)

Test specification (Q.Sup1 - Q.Sup1)

Supplements to the Series Q.100 Recommendations (Q.Sup1 - Q.Sup8)

ITU-T Q-Series Recommendations

ITU-T Q-Series Recommendations

ITU-T Q-Series Recommendations

ITU-T Q-Series Recommendations

ITU-T Q-Series Recommendations

ITU-T Q-Series Recommendations

ITU-T Q-Series Recommendations

ITU-T Q-Series Recommendations

ITU-T Q-Series Recommendations

ITU-T Q-Series Recommendations

ITU-T Q-Series Recommendations

ITU-T Q-Series Recommendations

ITU-T Q-Series Recommendations

[Q.2961.2] .... Recommendation Q.2961.2 (06/97) - Digital subscriber signaling system No. 2 - Additional traffic parameters: Support of ATM transfer capability in the broadband bearer capability information element

[Q.2961.2 Cor.1] .. Corrigendum 1 (03/99) to Recommendation Q.2961.2 - Digital subscriber signaling system No. 2 - Additional traffic parameters: Support of ATM transfer capability in the broadband bearer capability information element

[Q.2961.3] .... Recommendation Q.2961.3 (09/97) - Digital subscriber signaling system No. 2 - Additional traffic parameters: Signaling capabilities to support traffic parameters for the available bit rate (ABR) ATM transfer capability

[Q.2961.4] .... Recommendation Q.2961.4 (09/97) - Digital subscriber signaling system No. 2 - Additional traffic parameters: Signaling capabilities to support traffic parameters for the ATM Block Transfer (ABT) ATM transfer capability

[Q.2961.5] .... Recommendation Q.2961.5 (03/99) - Digital subscriber signaling system No. 2 - Additional traffic parameters: Additional traffic parameters for cell delay variation tolerance indication

[Q.2961.6] .... Recommendation Q.2961.6 (05/98) - Digital subscriber signaling system No. 2 - Additional traffic parameters: Additional signaling procedures for the support of the SBR2 and SBR3 ATM transfer capabilities

[Q.2962] .... Recommendation Q.2962 (05/98) - Digital subscriber signaling system No. 2 - Connection characteristics negotiation during call/connection establishment phase

[Q.2963.2] .... Recommendation Q.2963.2 (09/97) - Digital subscriber signaling systems No. 2 - Connection modification: Modification procedures for sustainable cell rate parameters

[Q.2963.3] .... Recommendation Q.2963.3 (05/98) - Digital subscriber signaling system No. 2 - Connection modification: ATM traffic descriptor modification with negotiation by the connection owner

[Q.2964.1] .... Recommendation Q.2964.1 (07/96) - Digital subscriber signaling system No. 2: Basic look-ahead

[Q.2965.1] .... Recommendation Q.2965.1 (03/99) - Digital subscriber signaling system No. 2 - Support of quality of service classes

[Q.2965.1 Am.1] .. Amendment 1 (06/00) to Recommendation Q.2965.1

[Q.2971] .... Recommendation Q.2971 (10/95) - Broadband integrated services digital network B-ISDN - DSS 2 - Digital subscriber signaling system N.o 2 - User-network interface layer 3 specification for point-to-multipoint call/connection control

[Q.2971 Corr.1] .... Corrigendum 1 (12/99) to Recommendation Q.2971 - Digital subscriber signaling system No. 2 (DSS2) - User-Network interface layer 3 specification for point-to-multipoint call/connection control

[Q.2982] .... Recommendation Q.2982 (12/99) - Broadband integrated services digital network (B-ISDN) Digital subscriber signaling system No. 2 (DSS 2) Q.2931-based separated call control protocol

[Q.2983] .... Recommendation Q.2983 (12/99) - Broadband integrated services digital network (B-ISDN) Digital subscriber signaling No. 2 (DSS 2): Bearer control protocol

I.4.3   ATM-Forum-Standards

http://www.atmforum.com

Technical Working Group	Approved Specifications	Technical Working Group	Approved Specifications
	Specification Approved Date		Specification Approved Date
B-ICI			PNNI Transported Address Stack, Version 1.0 af-cs-0115.000 May, 1999
	B-ICI 1.0 af-bici-0013.000 Sep, 1993		PNNI Version 1.0 Security Signaling Addendum af-cs-0116.000 May, 1999
	B-ICI 1.1 af-bici-0013.001		UNI Signaling 4.0 Security Addendum af-cs-0117.000 May, 1999
	B-ICI 2.0 (delta spec to B-ICI 1.1) af-bici-0013.002 Dec, 1995		ATM Inter-Network Interface (AINI) Specification af-cs-0125.000 July, 1999
	B-ICI 2.0 (integrated specification) af-bici-0013.003 Dec, 1995		PNNI Addendum for Generic Application Transport Version 1.0 af-cs-0126.000 July, 1999
	B-ICI 2.0 Addendum or 2.1 af-bici-0068.000 Nov, 1996		PNNI SPVC Addendum Version 1.0 af-cs-0127.000 July, 1999
Control Signaling	PNNI Addendum on PNNI/B-QSIG Interworking and Generic Functional Protocol for the Support of Supplementary Services af-cs-0102.000 Oct, 1998		PHY/MAC Identifier Addendum to UNI Signaling 4.0 af-cs-0135.000 Nov, 1999
	Addressing Addendum for UNI Signaling 4.0 af-cs-0107.000 Feb, 1999		

Technical Working Group	Approved Specifications
	Specification / **Approved Date**

Network Call Correlation Identifier
v1.0
af-cs-0140.000
March, 2000

PNNI Addendum for Path and
Connection Trace, Version 1.0
af-cs-0141.000
March, 2000

Operation of the Bearer Independent
Call Control (BICC) Protocol with SIG
4.0/PNNI 1.0-AINI
af-cs-vmoa-0146.000
July, 2000

UBR with MDCR Addendum to UNI
4.0/PNNI 1.0 AINI
af-cs-0147.000
July, 2000

Modification of Traffic Descriptor for
an Active Connection
af-cs-0148.000
July, 2000

Data Exchange Interface ....
Data Exchange Interface version 1.0
af-dxi-0014.000
Aug, 1993

Directory and Naming Services ....
ATM Named System v2.0
af-dans-0152.000
July, 2000

Frame-based ATM ....
Frame-based ATM Transport over
Ethernet (FATE)
af-fbatm-0139.000
Mar, 2000

Frame based ATM over Sonet/SDH
af-fbatm-0151.000
July, 2000

ILMI (Integrated Local Mgmt. Interface) ....
ILMI 4.0
af-ilmi-0065.000
Sep, 1996

Lan Emulation/MPOA ....
LAN Emulation over ATM 1.0
af-lane-0021.000
Jan, 1995

LAN Emulation Client Management
Specification
af-lane-0038.000
Sep, 1995

LANE 1.0 Addendum
af-lane-0050.000
Dec, 1995

LANE Servers Management Spec v1.0
af-lane-0057.000
Mar, 1996

LANE v2.0 LUNI Interface
af-lane-0084.000
July, 1997

LAN Emulation Client Management
Specification Version 2.0
af-lane-0093.000
Oct, 1998

LAN Emulation over ATM Version 2 -
LNNI Specification
af-lane-0112.000
Feb. 1999

Multi-Protocol over ATM Specification
v1.0
af-mpoa-0087.000
July, 1997

Technical Working Group	Approved Specifications
	Specification / **Approved Date**

Multi-Protocol over ATM Version 1.0
MIB
af-mpoa-0092.000
July, 1998

Multi-protocol over ATM Specification,
Version 1.1
af-mpoa-0114.000
May, 1999

MPOA v1.1 Addendum on VPN Support
af-mpoa-0129.000
Oct, 1999

Network Management ....
Customer Network Management (CNM)
for ATM Public Network Service
af-nm-0019.000
Oct, 1994

M4 Interface Requirements and Logical
MIB
af-nm-0020.000
Oct, 1994

M4 Interface Requirements and Logical
MIB: ATM Network Element View
af-nm-0020.001
Oct, 1998

CMIP Specification for the
M4 Interface
af-nm-0027.000
Sep, 1995

CMIP Specification for the M4
Interface: ATM Network Element View,
Version 2
af-nm-0027.001
July, 1999

M4 Public Network View
af-nm-0058.000
Mar, 1996

M4 Interface Requirements and Logical
MIB: ATM Network View, Version 2
af-nm-0058.001
May, 1999

M4 "NE View"
af-nm-0071.000
Jan, 1997

Circuit Emulation Service
Interworking Requirements, Logical
and CMIP MIB
af-nm-0072.000
Jan, 1997

M4 Network View CMIP MIB Spec v1.0
af-nm-0073.000
Jan, 1997

M4 Network View Requirements &
Logical MIB Addendum
af-nm-0074.000
Jan, 1997

ATM Remote Monitoring SNMP MIB
af-nm-test-0080.000
July, 1997

SNMP M4 Network Element View MIB
af-nm-0095.001
July, 1998

Network Management M4 Security
Requirements and Logical MIB
af-nm-0103.000
Jan, 1999

Auto-configuration of PVCs
af-nm-0122.000
May, 1999

Technical Working Group	Approved Specifications
	Specification **Approved Date**
Physical Layer	Issued as part of UNI 3.1:44.736 DS3 Mbps Physical Layer100 Mbps Multimode Fiber Interface Physical Layer155.52 Mbps SONET STS-3c Physical Layer155.52 Mbps Physical Layer af-uni-0010.002
ATM Physical Medium Dependent Interface Specification for 155 Mb/s over Twisted Pair Cable af-phy-0015.000 Sep, 1994	
	DS1 Physical Layer Specification af-phy-0016.000 Sep, 1994
	Utopia af-phy-0017.000 Mar, 1994
	Mid-range Physical Layer Specification for Category 3 UTP af-phy-0018.000 Sep, 1994
	6,312 Kbps UNI Specification af-phy-0029.000 June, 1995
	E3 UNI af-phy-0034.000 Aug, 1995
	Utopia Level 2 af-phy-0039.000 June, 1995
	Physical Interface Specification for 25.6 Mb/s over Twisted Pair af-phy-0040.000 Nov, 1995
	A Cell-based Transmission Convergence Sublayer for Clear Channel Interfaces af-phy-0043.000 Jan, 1996
	622.08 Mbps Physical Layer af-phy-0046.000 Jan, 1996
	155.52 Mbps Physical Layer Specification for Category 3 UTP (See also UNI 3.1, af-uni-0010.002) af-phy-0047.000 Nov, 1995
	120 Ohm Addendum to ATM PMD Interface Spec for 155 Mbps over TP af-phy-0053.000 Jan, 1996
	DS3 Physical Layer Interface Spec af-phy-0054.000 Mar, 1996
	155 Mbps over MMF Short Wave Length Lasers, Addendum to UNI 3.1 af-phy-0062.000 July, 1996
	WIRE (PMD to TC layers) af-phy-0063.000 July, 1996
	E-1 Physical Layer Interface Specification af-phy-0064.000 Sep, 1996
	155 Mbps over Plastic Optical Fiber (POF) Version 1.0 af-phy-0079.000 May, 1997

Technical Working Group	Approved Specifications
	Specification **Approved Date**
	155 Mb/s Plastic Optical Fiber and Hard Polymer Clad Fiber PMD Specification Version 1.1 af-phy-0079.001 Jan, 1999
	Inverse ATM Mux Version 1.0 af-phy-0086.000 July, 1997
	Inverse Multiplexing for ATM (IMA) Specification Version 1.1 af-phy-0086.001 March, 1999
	Physical Layer High Density Glass Optical Fiber Annex af-phy-0110.000 Feb, 1999
	622 and 2488 Mbit/s Cell-Based Physical Layer af-phy-0128.000 July, 1999
	ATM on Fractional E1/T1 af-phy-0130.000 Oct, 1999
	2.4 Gbps Physical Layer Specification af-phy-0133.000 Oct, 1999
	Physical Layer Control af-phy-0134.000 Oct, 1999
	Utopia 3 Physical Layer Interface af-phy-0136.000 Nov, 1999
	Specification of the Device Control Protocol (DCP) Version 1.0 af-phy-0138.000 Mar, 2000
	Multiplexed Status Mode (MSM3) af-phy-0142.000 March, 2000
	Frame-based ATM Interface (Level 3) af-phy-0143.000 March, 2000
	UTOPIA Level 4 af-phy-0144.001 March, 2000
PNNI	Interim Inter-Switch Signaling Protocol af-pnni-0026.000 Dec, 1994
	PNNI V1.0 af-pnni-0055.000 Mar, 1996
	PNNI 1.0 Addendum (soft PVC MIB) af-pnni-0066.000 Sep, 1996
	PNNI ABR Addendum af-pnni-0075.000 Jan, 1997
	PNNI v1.0 Errata and PICs af-pnni-0081.000 July, 1997
Routing and Addressing	PNNI Augmented Routing (PAR) Version 1.0 af-ra-0104.000 Jan, 1999
	ATM Forum Addressing: User Guide Version 1.0 af-ra-0105.000 Jan, 1999

975

Technical Working Group	Approved Specifications
	Specification **Approved Date**

ATM Forum Addressing: Reference
Guide
af-ra-0106.000
Feb, 1999

PNNI Addendum for Mobility
Extensions Version 1.0
af-ra-0123.000
May, 1999

Residential Broadband ....

Residential Broadband Architectural
Framework
af-rbb-0099.000
July, 1998

RBB Physical Interfaces Specification
af-rbb-phy-0101.000
Jan, 1999

Service Aspects and Applications ....

Frame UNI
af-saa-0031.000
Sep, 1995

Circuit Emulation
af-saa-0032.000
Sep, 1995

Native ATM Services: Semantic
Description
af-saa-0048.000
Feb, 1996

Audio/Visual Multimedia Services:
Video on Demand v1.0
af-saa-0049.000
Jan, 1996

Audio/Visual Multimedia Services:
Video on Demand v1.1
af-saa-0049.001
Mar, 1997

ATM Names Service
af-saa-0069.000
Nov, 1996

FUNI 2.0
af-saa-0088.000
July, 1997

Native ATM Services DLPI Addendum
Version 1.0
af-saa-api-dlpi-0091.000
Feb, 1998

API Semantics for Native ATM Services
af-saa-0108.000
Feb, 1999

FUNI Extensions for Multimedia
af-saa-0109.000
Feb, 1999

H.323 Media Transport over ATM
af-saa-0124.000
July, 1999

Security ....

ATM Security Framework Version 1.0
af-sec-0096.000
February, 1998

ATM Security Specification Version 1.0
af-sec-0100.001
Feb, 1999

Signaling ....

(See UNI 3.1, af-uni-0010.002)

UNI Signaling 4.0
af-sig-0061.000
July, 1996

Signaling ABR Addendum
af-sig-0076.000
Jan, 1997

Technical Working Group	Approved Specifications
	Specification **Approved Date**

Testing ....

Introduction to ATM Forum Test
Specifications
af-test-0022.000
Dec, 1994

PICS Proforma for the DS3 Physical
Layer Interface
af-test-0023.000
Sep, 1994

PICS Proforma for the SONET STS-3c
Physical Layer Interface
af-test-0024.000
Sep, 1994

PICS Proforma for the 100 Mbps
Multimode Fibre Physical Layer
Interface
af-test-0025.000
Sep, 1994

PICS Proforma for the ATM Layer
(UNI 3.0)
af-test-0028.000
Apr, 1995

Conformance Abstract Test Suite for
the ATM Layer for Intermediate
Systems (UNI 3.0)
af-test-0030.000
Sep, 1995

Interoperability Test Suite
for the ATM Layer (UNI 3.0)
af-test-0035.000
Apr, 1995

Interoperability Test Suites
for the Physical Layer:
DS-3, STS-3c, 100 Mbps MMF (TAXI)
af-test-0036.000
Apr, 1995

PICS Proforma
for the DS1 Physical Layer
af-test-0037.000
Apr, 1995

Conformance Abstract Test Suite for
the ATM Layer (End Systems) UNI 3.0
af-test-0041.000
Jan, 1996

PICS for AAL5 (ITU spec)
af-test-0042.000
Jan, 1996

PICS Proforma for the 51.84 Mbps
Mid-Range PHY Layer Interface
af-test-0044.000
Jan, 1996

Conformance Abstract Test Suite for
the ATM Layer of Intermediate
Systems (UNI 3.1)
af-test-0045.000
Jan, 1996

PICS for the 25.6 Mbps over Twisted
Pair Cable (UTP-3) Physical Layer
af-test-0051.000
Mar, 1996

Conformance Abstract Test Suite for
the ATM Adaptation Layer (AAL) Type
5 Common Part (Part 1)
af-test-0052.000
Mar, 1996

PICS for ATM Layer (UNI 3.1)
af-test-0059.000
July, 1996

Conformance Abstract Test Suite for
the UNI 3.1 ATM Layer of End Systems
af-test-0060.000
June, 1996

Technical Working Group	Approved Specifications
	Specification **Approved Date**

Conformance Abstract Test Suite for the SSCOP Sublayer (UNI 3.1)
af-test-0067.000
Sep, 1996

SSCOP Conformance Abstract Test Suite, Version 1.1
af-test-0067.001
May, 1999

PICS for the 155 Mbps over Twisted Pair Cable (UTP-5/STP-5) Physical Layer
af-test-0070.000
Nov, 1996

PICS for Direct Mapped DS3
af-test-0082.000
July, 1997

Conformance Abstract Test Suite for Signaling (UNI 3.1) for the Network Side
af-test-0090.000
September, 1997

Abstract Test Suite for UNI 3.1 ATM Signaling for the Network Side v2.0
af-test-0090.001
March, 2000

ATM Test Access Function (ATAF) Specification Version 1.0
af-test-nm-0094.000
February, 1998

PICS for Signaling (UNI v3.1) - User Side
af-test-0097.000
April, 1998

Interoperability Test for PNNI Version 1.0
af-test-csra-0111.000
Feb, 1999

PICS Proforma for UNI 3.1 Signaling (Network Side)
af-test-csra-0118.000
May, 1999

ATM Forum Performance Testing Specification
af-test-tm-0131.000
Oct, 1999

Implementation Conformance Statement (ICS) Proforma Style Guide
af-test-0137.000
Mar, 2000

Traffic Management ....
(See UNI 3.1, af-uni-0010.002)

Traffic Management 4.0
af-tm-0056.000
Apr, 1996

Traffic Management ABR Addendum
af-tm-0077.000
Jan, 1997

Traffic Management 4.1
af-tm-0121.000
March, 1999

Addendum to TM 4.1: Differentiated UBR
af-tm-0149.000
July, 2000

Addendum to Traffic Management v4.1 Optional Minimum Desired Cell Rate Indication for UBR
af-tm-0150.000
July, 2000

Technical Working Group	Approved Specifications
	Specification **Approved Date**

Voice & Telephony over ATM ....
Circuit Emulation Service 2.0
af-vtoa-0078.000
Jan, 1997

Voice and Telephony Over ATM to the Desktop
af-vtoa-0083.000
May, 1997

Voice and Telephony over ATM to the Desktop
af-vtoa-0083.001
Feb, 1999

(DBCES) Dynamic Bandwith Utilization in 64 KBPS Time Slot Trunking over ATM - Using CES
af-vtoa-0085.000
July, 1997

ATM Trunking Using AAL1 for Narrow Band Services v1.0
af-vtoa-0089.000
July, 1997

ATM Trunking Using AAL2 for Narrowband Services
af-vtoa-0113.000
Feb, 1999

Low Speed Circuit Emulation Service
af-vtoa-0119.000
May, 1999

ICS for ATM Trunking Using AAL2 for Narrowband Services
af-vtoa-0120.000
May, 1999

Low Speed Circuit Emulation Service (LSCES) Implementation Conformance Statement Performance
af-vtoa-0132.000
Oct, 1999

Loop Emulation Service Using AAL2
af-vmoa-0145.000
July, 2000

User-Network Interface (UNI) ....
ATM User-Network Interface Specification V2.0
af-uni-0010.000
June, 1992

ATM User-Network Interface Specification V3.0
af-uni-0010.001
Sep, 1993

ATM User-Network Interface Specification V3.1
af-uni-0010.002
1994

I.5   Frame Relay

I.5.1   ITU

http://www.itu.ch

I.122 .... Framework for Providing Additional Packet Mode Bearer Services
I.233 .... Frame Relay Bearer Service Description
Q.921 .... ISDN User-Network Interface (D-Channel) Layer 2 Specification
Q.922 .... ISDN Data Link Layer Specification for Frame Mode Bearer Services
Q.933 .... DSS1 - Signaling Specification for Frame Mode Bearer Services

I.5.2   ANSI

http://www.ansi.org

T1S1 .... Architectural Framework and Service Description
T1.602 .... Telecommunications ISDN Data Link Layer Signaling Specification
T1.606 .... Frame Relay Bearer Service Description
T1.617 .... Signaling Specification for Frame Relay Bearer Service
T1.618 .... Core Aspects of Frame Protocol for Use with Frame Relay Bearer Service

I.5.3   Frame Relay Forum

http://www.frforum.com/

FRF.1 ...... User-to-Network Implementation Agreement (UNI)
FRF.2 ...... Network-to-Network Implementation Agreement (NNI)
FRF.3 ...... Multiprotocol Encapsulation Implementation Agreement
FRF.4 ...... User-to-Network SVC Implementation Agreement
FRF.5 ...... Frame Relay ATM PVC Network Interworking Implementation Agreement
FRF.6 ...... Frame Relay Service Customer Network Manager Implementation Agreement (MIB)
FRF.7 ...... Frame Relay PVC Multicast Service and Protocol Description Implementation Agreement
FRF.8 ...... Frame Relay/ATM PVC Service Interworking Implementation Agreement
FRF.9 ...... Data Compression Over Frame Relay Implementation Agreement
FRF.10 .... Frame Relay Network-to-Network SVC Implementation Agreement
FRF.11 .... Voice Over Frame Relay Implementation Agreement
FRF.12 .... Frame Relay Fragmentation Implementation Agreement
FRF.13 .... Service Level Definitions I.A
FRF.14 .... Physical Layer Interface I.A
FRF.15 .... End-to-End Multilink Frame Relay I.A
FRF.16 .... Multilink Frame Relay UNI/NNI I.A
FRF.17 .... Frame Relay Privacy I.A
FRF.18 .... Network-to-Network FR/ATM SVC Service Interworking I.A

I.6   SDH/SONET/PDH

I.6.1   ITU

http://www.itu.ch

G.702 ...... Digital hierarchy bit rates

G.703 ...... Physical/electrical characteristics of hierarchical digital interfaces

G.704 ...... Synchronous frame structures used at 1544, 6312, 2048, 8488 and 44,736 Kbit/s hierarchical levels

G.706 ...... Frame alignment and cyclic redundancy check (CRC) procedures relating to basic frame structures defined in Recommendation G.704

G.707 ...... Network node interface for the synchronous digital hierarchy (SDH)

G.772 ...... Protected monitoring points provided on digital transmission systems

G.810 ...... Definitions and terminology for synchronization networks

G.811 ...... Timing characteristics of primary reference clocks

G.812 ...... Timing requirements of slave clocks suitable for use as node clocks in synchronization networks

G.813 ...... Timing characteristics of SDH equipment slave clocks (SEC)

G.821 ...... Error performance of an international digital connection operating at a bit rate below the primary rate and forming part of an integrated services digital network

G.822 ...... Controlled slip rate objectives on an international digital connection

G.823 ...... The control of jitter and wander within digital networks which are based on the 2048 Kbit/s hierarchy

G.824 ...... The control of jitter and wander within digital networks which are based on the 1544 Kbit/s hierarchy

G.825 ...... The control of jitter and wander within digital networks which are based on the synchronous digital hierarchy (SDH)

G.826 ...... Error performance parameters and objectives for international, constant bit rate digital paths at or above the primary rate

G.827 ...... Availability parameters and objectives for path elements of international constant bit-rate digital paths at or above the primary rate

G.832 ...... Transport of SDH elements on PDH networks – Frame and multiplexing structures

G.841 ...... Types and characteristics of SDH network protection architectures

G.957 ...... Optical interfaces for equipments and systems relating to the synchronous digital hierarchy

G.958 ...... Digital line systems based on the synchronous digital hierarchy for use on optical fibre cables

M.2100 ... Performance limits for bringing-into-service and maintenance of international PDH paths, sections and transmission systems

M.2101.1 Performance limits for bringing-into-service and maintenance of international SDH paths and multiplex sections

M.2110 ... Bringing-into-service of international PDH paths, sections and transmission systems and SDH paths and multiplex sections

M.2120 ... PDH path, section and transmission system and SDH path and multiplex section fault detection and localization procedures

M.2130 ... Operational procedures in locating and clearing transmission faults

O.150 ...... General requirements for instrumentation for performance measurements on digital transmission equipment

O.151 ...... Error performance measuring equipment operating at the primary rate and above

O.152 ...... Error performance measuring equipment for bit rates of 64 Kbit/s and N x 64 Kbit/s

O.162 ...... Equipment to perform in-service monitoring on 2048, 8448, 34 368 and 139 264 Kbit/s signals

O.163 ...... Equipment to perform in-service monitoring on 1544 Kbit/s signals

O.171 ...... Timing jitter and wander measuring equipment for digital systems which are based on the plesiochronous digital hierarchy (PDH)

O.181 ...... Equipment to assess error performance on STM-N interfaces

I.6.2   ANSI

http://www.ansi.org

ANSI T1.105-1995 .... Telecommunications - Synchronous Optical Network (SONET) - Basic Description Including Multiplex Structures, Rates, and Formats

ANSI T1.105.01-1995 .... Telecommunications - Synchronous Optical Network (SONET) - Automatic Protection Switching

ANSI T1.105.02-1995 .... Telecommunications - Synchronous Optical Network (SONET) - Payload Mappings

ANSI T1.105.03-1994 .... Telecommunications - Synchronous Optical Network (SONET) - Jitter at Network Interfaces

ANSI T1.105.03a-1995 ..... Telecommunications - Synchronous Optical Network (SONET) - Jitter at Network Interfaces - DS1 Supplement

ANSI T1.105.03b-1997 ..... Telecommunications - Synchronous Optical Network (SONET) - Jitter at Network Interfaces - DS3 Wander Supplement

ANSI T1.105.04-1995 .... Telecommunications - Synchronous Optical Network (SONET) - Data Communication Channel Protocols and Architectures

ANSI T1.105.05-1994 .... Telecommunications - Synchronous Optical Network (SONET) - Tandem Connection Maintenance

ANSI T1.105.06-1996 .... Telecommunications - Synchronous Optical Network (SONET) - Physical Layer Specifications

ANSI T1.105.07-1996 .... Telecommunications - Synchronous Optical Network (SONET) - Sub STS-1 Interface Rates and Formats Specification

ANSI T1.105.07a-1997 ..... Telecommunications - Synchronous Optical Network (SONET) - Sub STS-1 Interface Rates and Formats Specification (Inclusion of N X VT Group Interfaces)

ANSI T1.105.09-1996 .... Telecommunications - Synchronous Optical Network (SONET) - Network Element Timing and Synchronization

ANSI T1.119-1994 .... Telecommunications - Synchronous Optical Network (SONET) - Operations, Administration, Maintenance, and Provisioning (OAM&P) Communications

ANSI T1.119.01-1995 .... Telecommunications - Synchronous Optical Network (SONET) - Operations, Administration, Maintenance, and Provisioning (OAM&P) Communications - Protection Switching Fragment

ANSI T1.245-1997 .... Telecommunications - Directory Service for Telecommunications Management Network (TMN) and Synchronous Optical Network (SONET)

ANSI T1.514-1995 .... Telecommunications - Network Performance Parameters and Objectives for Dedicated Digital Services - SONET Bit Rates

I.7   Internet Protocols

http://www.ieft.org/rfc.html

The current document containing all official Internet protocols is RFC 2700: Internet Official Protocol Standards.

Mnemonic	Title	RFC#	STD#
	Internet Official Protocol Standards	2700	1
	Assigned Numbers	1700	2
	Requirements for Internet hosts – Communication Layers	1122	3
	Requirements for Internet hosts – Application and Support	1123	3
IP	Internet Protocol	791	5
ICMP	Internet Control Message Protocol	792	5
	Broadcasting Internet Datagrams	919	5
	Broadcasting Internet Datagrams in the Presence of Subnets	922	5
	Internet Standard Subnetting Procedure	950	5
IGMP	Host Extensions for IP Multicasting	1112	5
UDP	User Datagram Protocol	768	6
TCP	Transmission Control Protocol	793	7
TELNET	Telnet Protocol Specification	854	8
TELNET	Telnet Option Specifications	855	8

Mnemonic	Title	RFC#	STD#
FTP	File Transfer Protocol	959	9
SMTP	Simple Mail Transfer Protocol	821	10
SMTP-EXT	SMTP Service Extensions	1869	10
SMTP-SIZE	SMTP Service Extension for Message Size Declaration	1870	10
MAIL	Standard for the Format of ARPA Internet Text Messages	822	11
DOMAIN	Domain Names - Concepts and Facilities	1034	13
DOMAIN	Domain Names - Implementation and Specification	1035	13
DNS-MX	Mail Routing and the Domain System	974	14
SNMP	Simple Network Management Protocol (SNMP)	1157	15
SMI	Structure and Identification of Management Information for TCP/IP-based Internets	1155	16
Concise-MI	Concise MIB Definitions	1212	16
MIB-II	Management Information Base for Network Management of TCP/IP-based Internets: MIB-II	1213	17
NETBIOS	Protocol Standard for a NetBIOS Service on a TCP/UDP Transport	1001	19
NETBIOS	Protocol Standard for a NetBIOS Service on a TCP/UDP Transport	1002	19
ECHO	Echo Protocol	862	20
DISCARD	Discard Protocol	863	21
CHARGEN	Character Generator Protocol	864	22
QUOTE	Quote of the Day Protocol	865	23
USERS	Active Users	866	24
DAYTIME	Daytime Protocol	867	25
TIME	Time Protocol	868	26
TOPT-BIN	Telnet Binary Transmission	856	27
TOPT-ECHO	Telnet Echo Option	857	28
TOPT-SUPP	Telnet Suppress Go Ahead Option	858	29
TOPT-STAT	Telnet Status Option	859	30
TOPT-TIM	Telnet Timing Mark Option	860	31
TOPT-EXTOP	Telnet Extended Options	861	32
TFTP	The TFTP Protocol (Revision 2)	1350	33
TP-TCP	ISO Transport Services on Top of the TCP	1006	35

Mnemonic	Title	RFC#	STD#
IP-FDDI	Transmission of IP and ARP over FDDI Networks	1390	36
ARP	Ethernet Address Resolution Protocol	826	37
RARP	Reverse Address Resolution Protocol	903	38
IP-WB	Host Access Protocol specification	907	40
IP-E	Standard for the Transmission of IP Datagrams over Ethernet Networks	894	41
IP-EE	Standard for the Transmission of IP Datagrams over Experimental Ethernet Networks	895	42
IP-IEEE	Standard for the transmission of IP Datagrams over IEEE 802 Networks	1042	43
IP-DC	DCN Local-Network Protocols	891	44
IP-HC	Internet Protocol on Network System's HYPERchannel	1044	45
IP-ARC	Transmitting IP Traffic over ARCNET Networks	1201	46
IP-SLIP	Nonstandard for Transmission of IP Datagrams over Serial Lines	1055	47
IP-NETBIOS	Standard for the Transmission of IP Datagrams over NetBIOS Networks	1088	48
IP-IPX	Standard for the Transmission of 802.2 Packets over IPX Networks	1132	49
ETHER-MIB	Definitions of Managed Objects for the Ethernet-like Interface Types	1643	50
PPP	The Point-to-Point Protocol (PPP)	1661	51
PPP-HDLC	PPP in HDLC-like Framing	1662	51
IP-SMDS	Transmission of IP Datagrams over the SMDS Service	1209	52
POP3	Post Office Protocol - Version 3	1939	53
OSPF2	OSPF Version 2	2328	54
IP-FR	Multiprotocol Interconnect over Frame Relay	2427	55
RIP2	RIP Version 2	2453	56
RIP2-APP	RIP Version 2 Protocol Applicability Statement	1722	57
SMIv2	Structure of Management Information Version 2 (SMIv2)	2578	58
CONV-MIB	Textual Conventions for SMIv2	2579	58
CONF-MIB	Conformance Statements for SMIv2	2580	58
RMON-MIB	Remote Network Monitoring Management Information Base	2819	59

Internet Addresses and Newsgroups

J

J.1   Troubleshooting

The ultimative troubleshooting site
http://www.networktroubleshooting.com

Human Errors Page
http://www.wcinet.net/~aspect/he_links.htm

Troubleshooting tips from Cisco
http://www.cisco.com/public/technotes/serv_tips.shtml.

Troubleshooting tutorials from Agilent
http://www.onenetworks.com/

IBM Networking technical support page
http://www.networking.ibm.com/netsupt.html

Compaq Maintenance and Service Guides
*http://www.compaq.com/support/techpubs/maintenance_guides/
index.html*

SUN Microsystems Sunsolve Knowledge Database
http://sunsolve.sun.com/

HP Customer Care Site (drivers, software, troubleshooting for printers and computers)
http://www.hp.com/cposupport/eschome.html

Dell support site
http://support.dell.com

Microsoft support site
http://support.microsoft.com

Novell support site
http://support.novell.com

3COM support site
http://support.3com.com

3COM Knowledge Database
http://knowledgebase.3com.com/

J.2   Standards and Usergroups

ITU
http://www.itu.ch

ANSI
http://www.ansi.org

IEEE working group 802.3
http://grouper.ieee.org/groups/802/3/index.html

IEEE working group 802.5
http://www.8025.org

ATM-Forum
http://www.atmforum.com

North American ISDN Users Forum
http://www.niuf.nist.gov/

National ISDN Council
http://www.bellcore.com/NIC/

Frame-Relay-Forum
http://www.frforum.com

InterNIC document archive
http://www.internic.net/

Global Engineering Documents – distributor for US and international standards
(e.g. TIA/TSB-67 Standard)
http://www.global.ihs.com

J.3   Newsgroups

comp.dcom.cabling

comp.dcom.lans.ethernet

comp.dcom.lans.fddi.

comp.dcom.lans.misc

comp.dcom.lans.token-ring

comp.dcom.modems

comp.dcom.modems.cable

comp.dcom.sys.cisco

comp.dcom.xdsl

comp.os.linux.networking

comp.os.linux.setup

comp.os.ms-windows.networking.misc

comp.os.ms-windows.networking.tcp-ip

comp.os.ms-windows.networking.win95

comp.os.ms-windows.nt.admin.misc

comp.os.ms-windows.nt.admin.networking

comp.os.ms-windows.nt.misc

comp.protocols.tcp-ip

comp.sys.mac.misc

comp.unix.solaris

han.comp.os.linux

han.comp.os.winnt

microsoft.public.win95.networking

microsoft.public.win98.networking

microsoft.public.win98.performance

microsoft.public.win98.setup

microsoft.public.windowsnt.protocol.tcpip

comp.dcom.cabling

Easy web based access to newsgroups is available via

http://www.deja.com/usenet

Index

About the Author

Othmar Kyas is the Product Marketing Section Manager for the Network Systems Test Division of Agilent Technologies. With over 11 years at Agilent (formerly Hewlett-Packard), Othmar has led the way in developing Agilent's telecommunications products. Othmar holds an M.S. degree in Electrical Engineering from the University of Technology, Vienna, which has enabled him to contribute significantly to Agilent's product offerings in WAN, LAN, and ATM technologies.

In addition to speaking at seminars and trade shows, Othmar is recognized internationally as a renowned author of several books in data communications and telecommunications. Many of these have been translated into Japanese, Danish, Russian, English, and German. Books authored by Othmar include the following:

- ATM Networks
- Internet Security
- Corporate Intranets
- Fast Ethernet

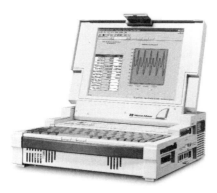

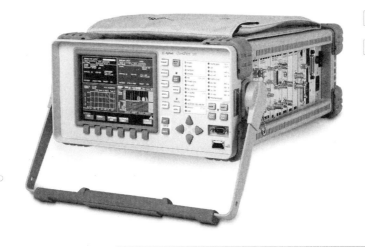

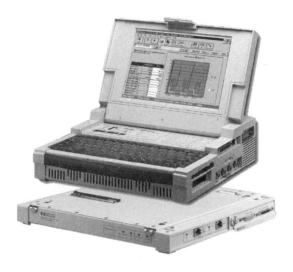

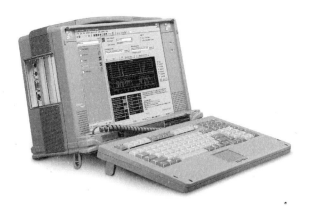

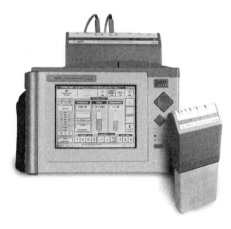

❏ *YES, Please send me Agilent's newly updated Network Communications Protocol Poster. FREE !*

 **Agilent Technologies**

Name ——————————————————————— Title ———————————————————
Company ——
Street Address ——
City ——————————————————————— State ——————————— Zip ————————
Country ———
Email ——
Daytime Telephone (   ) ——————————————————————————————————————
Fax (   ) ———

(check box) **Yes, please contact me to discuss Agilent's solutions for:**
❏ **LAN/WAN/ATM and VoIP Network Troubleshooting (hardware)**
❏ **LAN/VoIP NetworkTroubleshooting (software)**
❏ **Voice Quality Testing**
❏ **Transmission Testing**
❏ **Troubleshooting Signaling Networks**
❏ **LAN and Cable Certification Testing**
❏ **Telco, Residential Access and Line Qualification Application Testing**
❏ **Optical Network Installation and Maintenance Testing**

BUSINESS REPLY MAIL

FIRST CLASS MAIL PERMIT No 1303 Colorado Springs, CO

POSTAGE WILL BE PAID BY ADDRESSEE

CHRIS WOLFE
AGILENT TECHNOLOGIES
5070 CENTENNIAL BLVD.
COLORADO SPRINGS, CO 80919-2497

IIııIıIIıııIıIıııııIIIıIıııIıIıIııIIIıIıIııIIıııIIIıııIıII